Australia
and
the
Australians

It is the virtue of the average Australian, when faced with a particular human problem, to consider it as just that and to respond to human need wherever he meets it. So it is, I am convinced, we can do even greater things in the future than we have done in the past.

Ian Clunies Ross
Memoirs and Papers (1957)

Australia and the Australians

A NEW CONCISE HISTORY

R.M. YOUNGER

RIGBY

ACKNOWLEDGEMENTS

Sources of a wide variety of quotations are identified in the text. Permission to quote substantial extracts from copyright material has been granted generously by the publishers concerned.

Special acknowledgement is given to the following for use of copyright material: *Time* (1960), *Fortune* (1950 and 1960), and *Newsweek* (1965), of New York; *The Times, Manchester Guardian* and *New Statesman,* of London. Other copyright holders who have graciously permitted use of extracts (numerous, in some cases) are: The *Herald* and the *Age* (Melbourne), the *Sydney Morning Herald, The Bulletin,* and the *Australian.*

Acknowledgement is also made for use of extracts from books and other publications from Australia and abroad; these are identified in the text. Books from which quotations are given are listed in the general bibliography.

RIGBY LIMITED, ADELAIDE
Sydney, Melbourne, Brisbane, Perth

First published 1970
Reprinted 1974
Copyright © 1969 by R. M. Younger
Library of Congress Catalog Card Number 66–10438
National Library of Australia Registry Card Number
and ISBN 0 85179 755 5

This edition printed in Hong Kong

CONTENTS

Contents

PREFACE

In writing this book I have concerned myself with the ideas, events, and people shaping Australia's destiny down the years, and particularly with the central experience of the Australian people: the continuing process of settling a continent. Finding ways to develop the country has been an unending theme; no less important today is the quite recent national effort directed towards defining an appropriate international role for Australia, having in mind its political complexion, its responsibilities, and its geographical location.

Conversion of a wayward continent into a thriving modern nation has been made possible by the efforts of capable, enterprising, hard-working, and courageous men and women, but it has been far from a succession of unalloyed successes. Along with victories have gone setbacks, disappointments, and failures. The tragic elements are as much part of the Australian fabric as the determination to win out against great odds. The trials the Australian people have gone through have sometimes come from the community's excessive optimism about immediate prospects, sometimes from the actions of people far from Australia's shores, and even more frequently they have been the trials imposed by an unpredictable climate; the triumphs the country has enjoyed have arisen to a great extent from the successes of those whose work has been directed to reshaping their environment and to those at home and abroad who have shown confidence in the country's future.

In all countries that are the creation of eighteenth and nineteenth century settlement from Western Europe, the dynamics of expansion, with waves of settlers seeking land opportunity, produced somewhat parallel conditions and generally rather similar attitudes. Nevertheless, the Australian experience has been different from that of other "new" countries—such as Argentina, Canada, the United States, and New Zealand—which shared a comparable experience of opening up a new land. The unique Australian matrix has been provided by the peculiar nature of the continental environment with its special climatic factors and its extreme remoteness from the North Atlantic communities to which its people are joined by language, cultural, and economic ties. The challenge of settling and developing such a capricious and distant land has thus been largely responsible for Australians' distinctive outlook and approach to affairs at home and abroad.

Central to the theme is the interplay of forces, economic, cultural, and political, tying Australians to their British heritage, and the contrary forces striving to emphasize local factors and create a nation in its own right. The experience of sailing from the northern latitudes to Australia, from a cool and populated island-nation to a dry and empty wilderness, brought new objectives to light. Men and women began to dream, to believe the impossible could be brought about—and sometimes, partly through the boundlessness of their ambition and the intensity of their hope, sometimes by sheer good fortune, it was. Individual achievement was the touchstone of success; the intuitive, the bold, and the self-reliant had exceptional opportunities to succeed. Such men, their outlooks coloured by the practical problems of opening up a new land, were impatient at slow and legalistic aspects of the political-legal system they had inherited. Often they came into sharp conflict with those who could not see beyond the traditional British culture-pattern which some strove to maintain intact in the new land. Even in the second half of the twentieth century, the battle between the two elements has scarcely been resolved.

Side by side with the political tussles went the slow and difficult struggle to understand and master agricultural techniques suited to an environment so different from that of the homeland.

What impelled men of action, and how they earned their livelihood, and the ways in which they expressed themselves, are important aspects of the common experience, and it has been my objective to trace the evolution of political, economic, and social institutions, the changes in basic ideas and aspirations, and the impact of events and demand abroad, without losing sight of the mass of citizens. Inevitably there is an emphasis on relatively few men and even fewer women—the exceptional people, sometimes —but I have tried to sketch in behind the main characters not only the circumstances but the other people around them, both their supporters and those whose lives were cast in the same pattern, and others whose economic circumstances or political objectives or general ideas were quite different.

In setting down—and interpreting anew—the history of this land and its people, my objective has been to write a book that anyone who wishes may read and understand. Of necessity my story is a synthesis, and I freely acknowledge my debt to those who have pioneered the way.

Eight or nine years ago, when I began to think seriously about tackling the task of writing the Australian story—a story of successes, failures, hopes, fears, fantasies, and achievements—and began the research for it, I was scarcely aware of the immensity of the task that lay ahead. In 1962 I completed a shorter documentary, *The Changing World of Australia*, giving the broad sweep of the nation's story, which was published in New York; but this new and more comprehensive history was to take me another four years to complete.

The book is divided into seven sections, each covering a distinct phase and period of the story. Each section has an introduction which is intended to function as a bridge to the ensuing chapters and to help set the background. Because of differing circumstances in the various phases of the story, section introductions are not all treated in quite the same way; instead, each is developed in the form that seems best suited to the purpose of clarifying the unfolding story. And whereas each chapter is largely self-contained, the introductory material is intended to draw together and expound the dominant theme for the period covered in the entire section.

Throughout, I have been helped and encouraged by discussions and correspondence with many people—mainly experts within Australia, but some residing abroad—who have a special understanding of Australia's past or present. Many have been kind enough to read and comment upon early drafts of the text. My understanding of special aspects was greatly assisted by the resulting exchange of ideas. It would be difficult to give acknowledgement individually to everyone who has helped in the project.

Among those whose assistance has been invaluable is C. P. Puzey, whose knowledge of Australian industry is encyclopaedic; he not only tracked down obscure facts but he was able to throw new light on many facets, and his comments often led me to a wider appreciation of various issues. On aspects related to the expansion of banking in Victoria following the gold rushes, I have to thank the research staff of the National Bank of Australasia, and particularly G. R. Mountain, the bank's Chief Inspector, while executives of the Reserve Bank of Australia checked references to central banking in recent times.

For data and clarification of many issues, I am also indebted to several experts who wish to remain anonymous. Officials of the Commonwealth Scientific and Industrial Research Organization, and state and federal officials who were consulted on various aspects, were all most helpful. The staffs of the Public Library of Victoria, the Mitchell Library, Sydney, the National Library, Canberra, and the British Museum, all deserve thanks. For assistance in authenticating the special tables related to the stages of representative and responsible government in the colonies and the Commonwealth, I am indebted to Dr H. L. White and the National Library's research staff, and to the staffs of the parliamentary libraries in the various states. Miss Betty Thorpe, B. Com., research officer, Australian Industries Development Association, supplied valuable material on economic aspects, and Professor Findlay MacKenzie, of New York, generously made available clippings of the 1920s–1930s period from which quotations have been extracted. Statistical and factual information has been drawn from scores of publications, official and unofficial, while newspapers and journals published in Australia and abroad have provided background information and contemporary comment.

Among the many other individuals whose encouragement and help I acknowledge with gratitude are Miss Dulcie Penfold and her staff at the Australian Reference Library, New York; S. W. Ivory, of the Queensland Government Tourist Bureau, Brisbane; Alan Underwood of the *Courier-Mail*; E. K. Sinclair, editor of the *Age*, and Sir John Williams, managing editor of the Melbourne *Herald*. The Rural Bank of New South Wales and J. B. Were and Son (Melbourne) supplied information.

For unstinted and invaluable assistance throughout the entire work, I owe a special debt to Miss Margaret Lawrence, M. A., Dip. Ed., Dip. J., of Melbourne, without whose consistent and untiring help eight thousand miles away in digging out facts, checking material, and suggesting alternative approaches on many difficult sections, the project might not have been completed.

To all these individuals I am deeply grateful; they must share credit for whatever merit the book is deemed to possess.

Finally, I should like to thank my publishers, and particularly Ian Mudie, former editor-in-chief of Rigby Limited, for helpful guidance, as well as for patience and forbearance, during the preparation of the manuscript.

R. M. Younger

San Mateo, California.
January, 1969.

Part
One

Part
One

Discovery

AUSTRALIA AND OTHER PACIFIC LANDS remained unknown to the Western world until comparatively recent times. Legends and grotesque tales about remote sectors of the globe had long been in existence, but there was nothing to substantiate the stories. It was the emergence in fifteenth century Europe of new ideas and a new spirit of inquiry and enterprise that suddenly pushed back the horizons of the known world; yet even after Africa, Asia, and the Americas had been reached by European navigators in increasingly sturdy vessels with improved navigational aids, Australia was isolated for a remarkably long time. The movement of people along Pacific island chains had skirted the great land mass, and left it untouched, just as it had remained remote from Asian influences.

The great voyages of discovery that resulted in the redrawing of the map of the world began at the close of the fifteenth century, when the sovereigns of Portugal and Spain backed mariners who were prepared to face the unknown in search of fame and riches. Navigators found both a south-east passage and a south-west passage out of the Atlantic Ocean, sailing east round the Cape of Good Hope and west round South America. The Portuguese sailed round the southernmost point of Africa on their way to India and the East Indies; the Spaniards crossed the Atlantic to the Americas, then sailed down the coast of South America, with an expedition under the spices-seeking Ferdinand Magellan breaking through the strait named after him and going on to circumnavigate the world from east to west. For the first time, the seemingly boundless realm of water stretching from Africa in the west to the Americas in the east, and from the frozen Antarctica northward to Asia and the Bering Strait, was entered—more than 80,000,000 square miles of oceans and seas, with only about 5 per cent of the area taken up by land.

Pope Alexander VI's decision in 1493 to divide all newly discovered lands between the kingdoms of Spain and Portugal according to longitude caused the Portuguese and the Spaniards to come upon the rich, coveted, spice-bearing islands off south east Asia from almost opposite directions. This circumstance might soon have led to contact with Australia had it not been for the ocean currents and prevailing winds that imposed precise sailing patterns upon the masters of the little caravels.

Mariners had reason to fear the southern latitudes, with their tempestuous winds and wild seas. When the Portuguese rounded Africa and picked up favourable currents to sail north-east across the western rim of the Indian Ocean, they kept clear of the winds streaming eastward in the Roaring Forties. In the Pacific the Spanish ships that emerged from the Strait of Magellan (or rounded Cape Horn) were immediately confronted with the still more tempestuous seas and the ferocious contrary west winds of the high southern latitudes, and so the Spaniards turned north to take advantage of winds and currents that would carry them to warmer and calmer waters where they could pick up the westbound equatorial drift. Later, the Spaniards made contact with the area through Mexico and across the northern Pacific.

Because of these sailing patterns, both Portuguese and Spaniards converged upon South-East Asia and the rich spice lands of the East Indies without breaking into the vast unknown area to the south. The voyages of the English and Dutch adventurers who first dared challenge the Spanish did not vary from the known routes.

The cockleshells that crossed the Pacific were mere specks in the immensity of ocean. Even the charts of their predecessors were of only limited use to their bold captains for, although they could measure latitude with reasonable accuracy, they had no way of accurately determining longitude. Once out of sight of known landmarks, a captain could only estimate his speed, and from that make a further estimate of how far he had sailed. Sustained errors of calculation might mean that, at the end of several months' sailing in the Pacific, a captain would miscalculate his position by many hundreds of miles. So, although the islands discovered by the early Spanish explorers were marked on the maps, later captains could not necessarily steer a straight course for them; thus some of the early discoveries were not rediscovered for another two hundred years.

The Pacific mariners of the sixteenth and seventeenth centuries never knew what new lands they might find, or what strange adventures might befall them as they probed deeper into this great and mysterious sector of the earth's surface that had been thrown open to the daring and the avaricious. Ancient geographers had conjured up a great continent in the southern hemisphere to balance the land masses in the northern half of the world. They called it variously *Terra Australis Incognita* and the Great South Land. Speculation invested this chimerical realm with varied and extraordinary qualities. As voyage followed voyage, discoveries multiplied, fables were revived, and mariners, nagged by the challenge, convinced themselves that somewhere, far away in the southern seas, the world's strangest, richest, and most wondrous continent awaited discovery.

From the time of the first voyages of oceanic exploration by the Portuguese and the Spaniards it was more than three hundred years before the greatest and most persistent enigma of geography—the nature of southern land masses—was finally resolved. During those years other maritime powers—Holland, France, and England—had developed along Europe's western seaboard, and each in turn had some part in the continuing process of discovery. But it was not until late in the eighteenth century that French and English navigators penetrated the last remaining voids and found that the surface of the southern hemisphere was mainly ocean.

During the centuries of exploration, the map of the Pacific gradually took shape—island by island, strait by strait, sea by sea. One of the land masses was Australia—not the Great South Land of vision and speculation, but the island continent of reality. Slowly the shape of Australia emerged on the map of the world, but before the final details of Australia's outline were known, the first settlements had been made upon its coasts.

From myth 1
to mystery

Belief in a great southern land had persisted among European scholars from the days of the Greek-Egyptian mathematician and geographer, Claudius Ptolemy, who, in the middle of the second century, speculated upon the existence of a continent set somewhere south of Asia and east of Africa. Nothing was known of this area, however, and there was no way to investigate it, even if anyone had thought of doing so. The Mediterranean area, and the land masses adjacent to it, could be charted, but the great world beyond was still a long way from being mapped. Until late in the fifteenth century, maps contained vast blanks, the unknown areas in the southern hemisphere bearing such picturesque names as Sea of Darkness and *Terra Incognita* (Unknown Land).

The golden age of exploration, during which many new lands were discovered and charted, opened in 1415 with the setting up, at Sagres in Portugal, of a maritime academy from which Prince Henry the Navigator dispatched his expeditions. As a boy, Prince Henry had often heard of great caravans arriving along Africa's northern coast carrying gold-dust from across the Sahara, and as a young man the information he had gathered from the Moors and from merchants in Africa had led him to the idea of seeking the golden land of Guinea by way of the sea. He encouraged explorers to move boldly along the forbidding west coast of Africa, where no seaman knew when he might reach the land's end or meet with the terrifying monsters thought to guard those distant latitudes.

In 1434 Henry's ships rounded desolate Cape Bojador, a point more than a hundred miles beyond the Canary Islands, the southernmost limit of Christian knowledge and European navigation, beyond which, mariners believed, the tides were so strong that ships caught in them would never return. Seven years later, the first cargo of gold and slaves—more than 230 in all—was brought back from near Rio d'Ouro (Rio de Oro), and a slave market was opened at Lagos, in Portugal. In 1443 slaves for another shipload were seized from an island off the Guinea coast.

The academy at Sagres was staffed by scholars who worked as a team on mathematics, astronomy, navigation, and sailing ship design. Among these men skilled in the arts of the sea, Henry led the life of a student and directed the work of exploration. Captains and navigators were trained there, and Henry, as his ships sailed greater distances, saw that improvements were needed. He therefore had new and better vessels designed and built—caravels of more than 500 tons that were a great advance on older types of sailing craft. Bell-bottomed, with hinged rudders, and with sides that sloped inwards as they rose towards the decks, these ships had fore-and-aft rigging for sails that could be swung to either side of the vessel, and for carrying small sheets to supplement the main spread of canvas.

Steadily the Portuguese caravels nosed their way down the African coast, always hoping to find the mysterious River of Gold in whose gravel, ran the legend, gold grew like carrots! In his quest, Henry had a Christian missionary purpose as well, and he believed it might be possible somehow to reach Prester John, legendary priest-king of fabulous wealth and power believed to be head of a kingdom somewhere in Asia or Africa.

Even with the sturdier ships carrying cannon and adjustable sails, the Portuguese had to hug the coast, since they still did not have knowledge of the art of ocean navigation. By 1461, a year after Prince Henry's death, his ships had charted Madeira and the Azores, discovered the Cape Verde Islands, and explored the coast of Africa as far as Sierra Leone. By 1445 they reached the fabled Bilad Ghana or Land of Riches, and soon they began a small-scale trade in pepper, gold, ivory, sealskins, and slaves. They used the profits accruing from this trade to finance extended explorations.

Now a sea route had been found to the mysterious lands, almost on the equator, where the caravan traders of the Sahara, it seemed, gained the gold and other treasure that they carried across northern Africa and into the Mediterranean countries. Returning seamen told of fearsome, black, forest-dwelling people who used poisoned arrows and wore great headdresses, and of savage animals and bright birds that lived in dense jungles—stories that were awesome and amazing to Europeans who had not realized before that such a strange and different world lay hidden south of the equator. There, in the hot and steamy regions, endless wonders were certain to unfold as the adventurers travelled further, although slaves were proving so profitable that many vessels preferred returning with a human cargo instead of extending exploration. Yet another and richer prize must lie ahead, argued Prince Henry's successors: sail far enough south and this long land of Africa would surely come to an end; sail around the continent and a new, all-sea route would be found to India, gateway to the spice islands, to China, and to all the riches of the East.

Then in 1488, Bartolomeo Diaz reached the southern tip of Africa, calling it Cape of Storms, a name soon changed to Cape of Good Hope. Meanwhile, Pero da Covilham, travelling in disguise with Arabs, had reached Calicut on the west coast of India, by a completely different route, through the Mediterranean and the Red Sea. He later returned by way of the eastern coast of Africa and the great island of Madagascar, eventually reaching Cairo, where he arranged for word to be taken back to Lisbon regarding this ocean route to India.

The news reached Sagres in 1493. With it arrived the report that the Arabs had conquered the shores all the way from Arabia to India, and—even more important—that Arab sailors knew how to sail vessels in the path of monsoons, travelling along the arc of the Indian Ocean without landfalls. Four years later, in 1497, Vasco da Gama by-passed the entire west coast of Africa in a three-month voyage from the Cape Verde Islands to the Cape of Good Hope, then sailed northward past Madagascar to Malindi, a port in Kenya. Here he enlisted an Arab pilot to guide his ships directly to his Indian landfall at Calicut, where the spice trade was centred.

The Portuguese did not immediately challenge the Arab traders who controlled Calicut. Instead, they set about building rival strongholds. First, Arab towns along the east coast of Africa were stormed, and Portuguese forts established; then Hindu rulers on the west coast of the Indian peninsula were forced to accept Portuguese trading-posts and garrisons. But not until 1510 was Calicut taken. Then Goa, to the north, was seized from its Moslem ruler by Alfonso de Albuquerque and became the splendid Portuguese capital in the East. Steadily the Arab trading dominance around the rim of the Indian Ocean was destroyed and replaced by Portuguese overlordship.

The most significant conquest came in 1511 when Albuquerque, who had been granted the title of governor of India, captured the small but influential kingdom of Malacca, in the south-western part of the Malay peninsula. Malacca was used as a trading post by Chinese merchants (who sailed in ungainly but seaworthy junks), and the Portuguese made it a centre from which to launch further explorations. Envoys were sent to Canton, to Siam, to China, and to Sumatra, and in 1512 an expedition, sent to explore the spice islands, reached Java, Bali, Ternate, and other islands in the area.

Accidentally, the Portuguese were also moving into new areas along the equatorial zone. Jorge de Meneses, sent from Malacca in 1526 to take charge in the Moluccas, followed a new route that took him by way of Borneo and Gildo; then, by a miscalculation, he sailed on south across the equator. He arrived eventually at a land with a densely forested shore, and anchored near the northernmost point of land. The inhabitants, curly-haired and black-skinned, were unlike others in the island chain. The Moluccans called these people Papuas, because of their woolly hair, and the island was said to be known as Versija. Meneses waited for the change of monsoon wind, then picked up his course to the Moluccas. He had touched either the great island now known as New Guinea, or one of its offshore islands.

While the Portuguese were spreading their power around the Indian Ocean, the Spaniards had embarked on a series of voyages that added the new world of the Americas to European knowledge. Following the marriage of Ferdinand of Aragon and Isabella of Castille in 1469 and their defeat of the Moors, a strong and stable central Spanish government had replaced the former conglomerate of petty kingdoms, princedoms, and sovereign city states; wealth was available to finance exploration as an investment to new riches in the spice trade.

The Spanish ships that sailed west across the Atlantic under Columbus in 1492 were seeking the same goal as Diaz and da Gama—the spice islands and China—even though their route was quite different from that followed by the Portuguese. The conquests in the Americas that followed Columbus's voyages gave the Spaniards the world's first transoceanic empire. It also gave them vast wealth. Whereas Portuguese hopes of finding the legendary River of Gold in Africa proved futile, the Spaniards soon found in their conquests a great store of the yellow metal. The new territories of Mexico and Peru proved to be a huge mine of gold and silver, and back in Seville the Spanish coin-makers were soon busily melting down the golden idols and the breast-plates found in the conquered lands.

But the Spaniards were not content. Their objective remained the riches of the spice islands. In 1519 Ferdinand Magellan, a Portuguese who had served with his country's forces in India and Malacca, persuaded the Spanish king to let him lead an expedition in search of a westward route to the spice islands. It was hoped that this voyage would settle the question of the limits of Spanish and Portuguese spheres of influence under the papal decrees of 1493 and 1494. Pope Alexander VI had divided the undiscovered world into two parts according to longitude, granting the Portuguese all new dis-coveries to the east of the meridian of longitude 370 leagues to the west of the Cape Verde Islands, and to the Spanish those to the west. The line of demarcation would apply similarly at a point exactly half-way round the world from this; with only dead reckoning as a guide, however, longitude could be only guessed at, and the question of rights to new lands on the other side of the world was thus an open one. Portugal and Spain each hoped the spice islands would fall within their sphere. Magellan argued that he would be able to prove that the most important of these islands—the Moluccas—lay within the Spanish dominions.

He set off with five ships on September 20, 1519. After crossing the Atlantic he coasted southward, always searching for a passage that would carry him towards the west. In October 1520 he finally began the tedious and hazardous passage through the strait that now bears his name. With three of his vessels, he moved into the Pacific—which he named—running north and then striking west-nor'west, sailing for ninety-eight days across unknown waters in a prodigious voyage. Sickness and starvation came near to creating disaster for the expedition, but by eating rats and even leather from the rig-ging, the voyagers managed to survive. They reached Guam, in the Mari-anas, early in March 1521, and the Philippines ten days later. Magellan persuaded the ruler of Cebu to swear allegiance to Spain; a month later the great captain was killed by natives during an attempt to capture a near-by island. One of the remaining ships, the *Victoria*, made the voyage back to

Spain by way of the Timor Sea and the Indian Ocean, rounding the Cape of Good Hope and completing the first voyage right round the world. Although the expedition had been away almost three years, and only eighteen men returned, the cargo of spices more than paid the material cost of the expedition.

Until the Spaniards could find some new route to their newly discovered treasure-house, they could not readily acquire the tropical islands reached by the expedition or hope to colonize them, for the Portuguese held the Indian Ocean route, and the way round South America seemed too hazardous. The first move towards developing a new and better route came even as Magellan's expedition was nearing home. The ever-spreading conquests of Hernan Cortes in Mexico were overwhelming the last resistance of the Aztecs, and soon the colonizers were pushing forward to the Pacific shore. Henceforth, just as Vera Cruz was authorized to handle shipping and commerce on the Gulf of Mexico, so Acapulco, established on the Pacific, would become a way-station, with mules carrying goods overland between the two ports.

A cousin of Cortes, Alvaro de Saavedra, was the first to venture into the Spice Islands using the northern Pacific route from Acapulco. Late in 1527 he left for the Philippines with three ships. After sailing along the coast of Mindanao he moved on from island to island in the Moluccas. From Tidore, where he stayed two months, he set sail for the south and, after being becalmed for weeks, reached an island where he anchored. "This is a large island," a member of his expedition wrote, "well-peopled by a black race with woolly hair who go naked. They supplied us with fowls, pigs, rice, and beans."

By a coincidence, Saavedra had reached the land that Meneses had visited only two before. He named the large island Isla del Oro, in the belief that because the setting was so like that of Africa's Gold Coast, and the people much the same, this must surely be a treasure-house of gold! There was, however, no evidence of such wealth and nothing to suggest that trade could be undertaken. In fact, only unfavourable weather delayed Saavedra's departure; after thirty-two days he sailed on, coming to more islands, where the inhabitants rowed out and either shot arrows at the intruders or attempted to attack them with slings and stones. Eventually the ship went north, back to Mindanao.

The Spaniards were steadily developing links with the scattered islands of the Philippines. Prevailing winds made their voyage back to Mexico slow and difficult, and the captains were constantly seeking a better sailing route. It was thought that more favourable winds might be encountered on a more southerly course. In 1537 a ship that had sailed west the year before ran aground on Isla del Oro after a mutinous crew had murdered Fernando de Grijalba, their commander. The shipwrecked crew were rescued many years later by a passing Portuguese vessel. In 1545 a vessel under the command of Ynigo Ortiz de Retes sailed from Tidore for Mexico and fell in with the northern coast of the same great island, which he then followed. Retes

named the land Nova Guinea (New Guinea) because the inhabitants reminded him of the Negroes he had seen on a similar shore of Africa's Guinea
coast.

The quest by the Spaniards for a practical sailing route across the northern
Pacific from west to east was solved in 1565 when Andres de Urdaneta, who was
chief pilot of an expedition sent in 1564 to found a colony in the Philippines,
discovered that it was possible to follow a great circle route along the coast
of Japan and just south of the Aleutians, picking up land again at Cape
Mendocino, California, and coasting to Acapulco. It was an easy route, for
the wind was fair all the way. After sailing due west on the outward voyage,
the Spaniards could follow Urdaneta's passage, as it came to be called, on
the way back. Before long the village of Manila, on the south-west coast of
Luzon, had been established as the seat of Spanish government. The new
sailing route meant that there was no longer any great inclination to probe
south from the Philippines, especially as New Guinea was obviously inhospit-
able and unpromising.

There were, however, other prospects. The Spaniards in Peru became
heirs to Peruvian Indian stories about islands or continents lost in the awesome immensity of the southern hemisphere, stories that reinforced the old
European legends about a Great South Land. They determined to probe
the unknown area from a southerly starting point in the hope of substantiating the persistent stories of a wondrous continent in southern latitudes.

In 1567 Alvaro Mendaña de Neira sailed with two ships from Callao,
Peru, using the prevailing current and the south-east trade winds to follow
a westerly course about 8° south of the equator. After some weeks he saw his
first islands—some of the Ellice group—and in February 1568 he arrived off
the coast of a mountainous land mass. At first he thought this must be part
of the continent that he was seeking, but later he found it to be an island,
which he named Ysabel. He went on to discover Guadalcanal and San
Christobal, both of which he named. The cluster of large and rugged islands
led Mendaña to believe that he had reached the outposts of the long sought
southern continent. Hopefully the described his discovery as "an extent of
land that seemed to have no limit."

When Mendaña returned to Peru in June 1569, he spoke in extravagant
terms of the lands he had discovered, declaring that they must surely contain
untold wealth in gold and other precious things that would profit Spain.
Nothing of actual value had been discovered, but back in Callao the seamen's
tales were soon embellished, and there was everlasting talk of incalculable
riches surely to be unearthed in the far-off land. Speculation built the reputation of the islands—for such they were—until their wealth became fabulous,
and, in the belief that King Solomon's gold had been mined there, they came
to be named the Islands of Solomon.

The grandiose Spanish and Portuguese claims to ownership of all new-
discovered lands, based on the papal decrees, were not accepted by other
nations. First to stake a counter-claim was England.

England's entry into world exploration came in the reign of Henry VII,
founder of the stable Tudor dynasty that emerged from the dynastic-feudal

struggles of the mid-fifteenth century. The new contender's first world explorer was John Cabot, a Genoa-born merchant who, like Columbus, believed that a way to the riches of the East could be found by sailing westward. He proposed to find this route in more northerly latitudes than those in which Columbus had sailed. In 1496 he obtained letters patent from King Henry for a voyage of discovery, and next year his small ship sailed from Bristol with a crew of only eighteen and reached what is now Canada—probably at Cape Breton Island. Cabot believed he had reached the mainland of Asia, but neither on this voyage nor on a much larger expedition the following year did he find any prospects for trade in this land of cold, fog, and snow. When, in 1553, a company was formed to equip an expedition to seek a trade route around the north of Asia, Cabot's son, Sebastian, drew up the plans; but again English traders failed to reach the lands of spice and pepper.

The first half of the sixteenth century marked the strengthening of the English navy—with fighting services and mercantile marine closely interlocked—that was to make possible England's maritime successes in the reign of Elizabeth. By mid-century, English joint-stock companies were carrying on trade with Russia, Morocco, and the Guinea coast; in the 1560s trade began with the Caribbean. And in 1578, for the first time, an English ship sailed on the broad waters of the Pacific.

Francis Drake set out from Plymouth in 1577, crossed the Atlantic to Brazil, rounded Cape Horn, and sailed north "along the back side of America," plundering the unprepared Spaniards at sea and on the Isthmus of Panama. Searching from the Pacific, Drake hoped to find the so-called Strait of Anian, a passage believed to cut through North America, and to sail through it on his way home to England. But, although he worked his way along the coast to a point north of San Francisco, he failed to find any strait, and he had to content himself with crossing the Pacific to the Moluccas, where he picked up a cargo of spices. He then sailed on across the Indian Ocean, round the Cape of Good Hope, and—the first commander to circumnavigate the world—arrived in Plymouth in 1580.

The excitement caused by the great treasure he brought back overcame any disappointment at his failure to discover the north-west passage, and the dividends paid to his backers, who included Queen Elizabeth, provided a tremendous stimulus to business enterprises and trade.

Less than a decade after his triumphant return, Drake and his fellow captains shattered the Spanish Armada, making it possible for both England and Holland to use the established trade routes. In 1580 Portugal was absorbed by the Spanish monarchy, and so the strength of both the first great trading power and the first great colonizer was sapped by the defeat of the Armada. Henceforth English ships and Dutch ships could sail round Africa or South America with impunity.

Like England, Holland was well situated to take advantage of the new-found Atlantic trade routes, but until Portugal ceased to be independent of Spain the Dutch had no motive to seek overseas possessions, for the Portuguese were so heavily involved in the East that they were willing to work with the Dutch by allowing them the European coasting trade. Thus the Dutch had been able to develop a lucrative carrying trade, picking up Oriental goods brought by the Portuguese to Lisbon and distributing them in northern Europe. When, Philip II closed the port of Lisbon to the Dutch in 1595, this trade came to an end. The Dutch at once determined to accept the challenge, and to send their ships to the East Indies to open up direct trade.

In 1595 the first fleet of four armed Dutch ships sailed round the Cape of Good Hope and reached Java without interference from Portuguese or Spanish. This was the forerunner of numerous well-armed, well-rigged, and well-handled flotillas that before very long were to upset the balance of European power in the East.

The initiative in Pacific exploration still lay with Spain — yet, in spite of the fact that the first Spaniard to make a definite search for the Great South Land, Alvaro Mendaña, longed to revisit the islands he had discovered, not until twenty-seven years after his return to Peru was he able to set out on another expedition. Wars had intervened, and many changes had taken place in Spanish fortunes; but Mendaña had never wavered in his efforts to induce his countrymen to colonize the new lands, which, as his memories became embellished by imagination, took on ever-richer aspects.

The Spaniards had long been lured by tales of a Great South Land with a shoreline which some thought might run more or less directly from Tierra del Fuego to somewhere near New Guinea. After the first attempt to reach the mythical continent in 1567–68 the Spanish had become preoccupied with other problems, and, although Mendaña secured a colonizing licence in 1541, he was not able to sail from Peru on his second voyage until 1595.

The expedition was large and well equipped. Mendaña's wife went with him, and her three brothers, and many colonists and their wives. With high hopes they sailed west; but the Solomon Islands could not be found. Instead, the expedition came to the Santa Cruz Islands, slightly to the east of the Solomons, and there, in September 1595, Mendaña's party set about establishing the long-dreamt-of colony.

They did not succeed. Within a few weeks, Mendaña died. Disputes had already arisen, and the high hopes of founding a Christian colony in this sector of the globe vanished with him. The chief navigating officer for the expedition, Fernandes Quiros, took charge of the enterprise, and, gathering the remnants of the colonizing group, departed for the Philippines, hoping to regain the isles of Solomon on the way. The islands, however, eluded him —in fact they were not to be sighted again for two hundred years. Quiros, nevertheless, rediscovered the Carolines, and reached Manila in February 1596.

Quiros took over Mendaña's dreams as well as his command. He was positive that wondrous riches would be revealed if only the Great South Land could be reached. He urged the authorities to send him on another expedition, which would rediscover those lands, acquire them for Spain, christianize their peoples, and set up a Spanish colony.

In 1605 all was ready, and he set off to put an end to doubts and speculation about the Great South Land, and to establish a settlement. His expedition of three ships sailed from Callao on a course that, if persisted in, would eventually have taken him to New Zealand or Australia—yet he too was to be frustrated in his purpose of solving the age-old riddle of the southern continent.

Quiros had planned his trip so that he could sail in summer; this would have made it possible for him to take advantage of favourable winds across the Pacific. Delays occurred, and by the time he reached the south Pacific it was already winter. Week after week, gales and heavy seas were encountered; seamen became restive and even mutinous: sailing in these latitudes against contrary winds and currents was dangerous and unpleasant. There was neither sight nor sign of land in this vast immensity, and eventually Quiros was persuaded to veer north west in the hope of picking up Mendaña's course of 1567 and coming once again upon the "golden" Solomons.

Soon the ships were in more favourable latitudes. On January 22, 1606, land came in view; it was followed by other sightings. On May 1 the expedition was in a large bay. Quiros was convinced he had at last found the great and elusive South Land, which he now believed stretched to the pole. In honour of his patron, Philip II, a prince of the royal house of Austria, he conferred the name Austrialia del Espiritu Santo (South Land of the Holy Spirit) on his landfall.

He anchored in a large bay, which he named St Philip and St James, and at the point where a stream flowed into the bay he established the settlement of New Jerusalem. His enthusiasm was boundless. Kneeling to kiss the soil on which he intended to found his city, he said: "Oh land, sought for so long, intended to be found by many, and so desired by me!" Piously he conferred the name Vera Cruz upon the proposed port. But his venture was doomed to failure. Quiros himself was ill; disaffection simmered among the seamen; and there was serious dissension among the would-be colonizers.

Suddenly the flagship, the *Capitana*, with Quiros aboard, slipped out of the harbour in the dead of night, leaving the two other ships with the second-in-command, Luis Vaez de Torres, a stern and dedicated man. Torres was not inclined to drop the venture so quickly, and, after trying vainly to catch up with the *Capitana*, determined to continue the expedition instead of setting sail for Callao, as most of his men wanted him to do.

He did not accept Quiros's view that they had reached the Great South Land. He decided to investigate, and he found that Espiritu Santo was no more than an island. He then sailed north west, crossing the expanse of water now known as the Coral Sea, reaching the Louisiade Islands, and going on until he fell in with the easternmost part of New Guinea. Here he met with winds of such strength that the only thing he could do was to sail westward along the south coast of the island.

For months he threaded his way through a treacherous sea dotted with "islands without number," sand banks, and hidden coral reefs, and succeeded in negotiating the strait which now bears his name, separating New Guinea and Australia. The hills he saw to the south were, he thought, more islands, so he did not investigate them. The savage nature of the islanders he encountered did not encourage him to associate the area with the South Land of mariners' dreams. Pushing westward, he eventually emerged into the open sea and, following round New Guinea, struck north to the Philippines.

One member of Torres's expedition, Diego de Prado y Tovar, recorded his interest in the uncommon birds that came into view at San Millan Bay, on the southern coast of New Guinea, close to the shoals of Torres Strait:

> Here we saw numbers of parrots, some were very white with a crest of yellow feathers and the beak and the feet black; there are other larger ones of purple colour with yellow and red patches on the body and green, yellow, and red wings, the beak and feet red; there are others entirely bright red, wonderfully beautiful. We saw some magpies with red feet and bill; they are very black and larger than those of Castille, and their chattering is like the human voice. After we had anchored for three days in the harbour, one day at dawn they persisted in chattering thus ay ay ay aya yaya yaya ay, so that I thought they were Indians in ambush who were waiting for us. I caused the men to be roused so as to be on the watch, and in a few minutes magpies came out of the wood flying and chattering in the same way, which amused us for some time.

The report Torres gave the King of Spain was not publicized—and in any case he could not realize that he had passed close to the northernmost tip of Australia. In the area of the strait he recorded only "very large islands," noting that there appeared to be more to the southward. He wrote:

> They were inhabited by black people, very corpulent and naked; their arms were lances, arrows, and clubs of stone, ill-fashioned. We could not get any of their weapons. We captured in all lands twenty persons. They have given much information of other people although as yet they do not make themselves well understood.

Torres was inclined to be somewhat matter-of-fact about the whole enterprise, whereas Quiros, who at Espiritu Santo had been no nearer than 500 miles to the continent of his dreams, stoutly professed that he had in fact reached the Great South Land. On his return to Spain he set about pushing his claims to leadership of another colonizing expedition, bombarding the indifferent Court officials with long memorials and with maps and charts of his last voyage. In his eighth and last memorial he wrote regarding Austrialia del Espiritu Santo:

> The greatness of the land newly discovered, judged from what I saw and from what the Captain, Don Luis Vaez de Torres, the admiral under my command, reported to Your Majesty, is well established. Its length is as much as all Europe and Asia Minor. . . . The lands I saw in 15° are better than Spain . . . and others, which were on the heights in front, should be an earthly Paradise.

Quiros went on to tell of native people who were clean, cheerful, amiable, and grateful—people who would be easy to pacify and indoctrinate. The land contained abundant flesh food and fish, numerous fine fruits, silver, pearls, and gold. He said that there were vast quantities of spice, nuts, mace, pepper, and ginger, which he had seen, and, according to reports, cinnamon. There were aloes, sugar, and indigo, good ebony, and many sorts of wood for ship-building. There might be cloves and other spices. He saw a bright future for Spain in the new land:

> The industry of the Spaniards in raising the native products as well as our own products (which I propose to introduce presently) will make the products of this country better and more profitable than those raised in Peru and New Spain.

The Spanish authorities were not impressed by Quiros's optimism. Torres's unembellished narration did not say anything exciting about the products or prospects of the countries visited. The Council of State recommended to Philip III against further support for Quiros. They had come to the conclusion that Quiros had deluded himself with the thought of being a second Columbus, and he was put to work on marine charts and globes. His persistent advocacy of colonization of the southern land eventually became so annoying that he was sent to the New World with instructions that he should be given a ship for exploration; but counter-instructions were sent telling the authorities to do nothing about it, just to keep him quiet. He died soon after he reached Panama.

By this time, Spanish initiative had already been sapped and the Spanish treasury exhausted. The fear that other nations would reap the benefit of any discoveries tended to dampen Spanish enthusiasm for new ventures. Perhaps England might have been expected to send ships to follow Drake's path across the Pacific, for his report of the slow, ill-armed Spanish treasure galleons that crossed the Pacific each year from the Philippines to Mexico created much interest.

Some English ships did follow Drake, but the booty they brought back from the Pacific could not compare with his treasure—and in any case there were richer pickings nearer home, in the Caribbean, where the slow Spanish galleons threaded the West Indies on their voyage from Panama to Spain.

England had now spread her trading interests to many parts of the world. Her joint-stock companies were trading profitably with Morocco, the Levant, Russia, India, the coast of Guinea, and the Caribbean. Englishmen still hoped to find a route to the East in northerly latitudes, for such a course, besides being exclusively English, would provide opportunities for selling woollen cloth to inhabitants of the cold lands along the route.

So England's urge for exploration spent itself amid ice and snow in the hopeless search for a north-west passage. Later, by the 1620s, England's colonizing energies were fully occupied by her settlements in North America, where climate and vegetation could remind transplanted English people of their homeland.

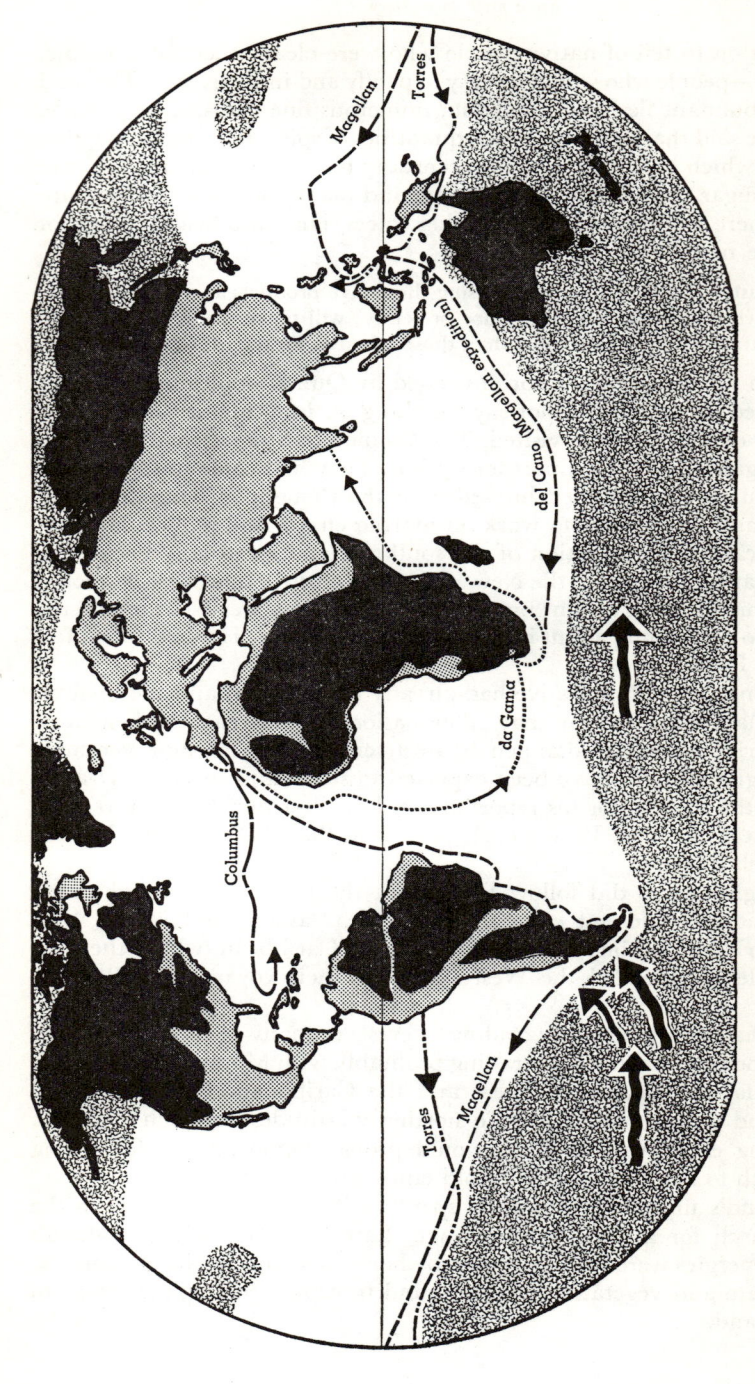

General sketch map indicating the known (light) and unknown (shaded) areas of the world in 1620, and some key voyages to that time. Columbus' voyages to the West Indies (1492 and later) had been followed by da Gama's expedition to India (1497–98) and the Magellan expedition's circumnavigation (1519–22). Prevailing winds and currents in southern latitudes (arrows) forced navigators to cling to the African or South American coast once they rounded their southernmost land. In 1605 Torres sailed west from Callao, finally passing through Torres Strait, and after 1606 contact was made (by Dutch navigators) with the northern shores of New Holland.

The Dutch were the immediate successors to Spain's dreams of exploration, as they were to Portugal's empire in the East. Their first tentative expeditions to the Indies having been successful, they sent flotilla after flotilla against the Portuguese garrisons and trading posts. In a few years the sturdy Dutch ships had captured the main strongholds in the East Indies. Soon they had mopped up practically all the strongposts the Portuguese had established around the Indian Ocean during a century of conquest. By the middle of the seventeenth century they had taken over all but a few remnants—which could be by-passed or ignored—of what had once been Portugal's great and far-flung empire.

In 1602 the various companies trading with the East Indies amalgamated as the United Dutch East Indies Company. Like its English counterpart, which had been incorporated a little more than a year earlier, the Dutch company's aim was profitable trading. An administrative system was created, trading posts were set up, and political arrangements made with local rulers, all with the aim of furthering the company's trade. Soon the Dutch were reaching out from their newly won strongholds in the East Indies in search of new lands where trade might be developed.

Among the spoils seized by the Dutch from the Portuguese and Spaniards were maps and geographical records containing new information about lands to the south. Although the records were vague, there were indications that the Portuguese had some idea that a great land mass lay somewhere south east from the Indonesian chain; such knowledge had probably come from occasional voyages by native fishermen from Timor or Macassar.

The Portuguese had first reached New Guinea's northern shores in the 1520s; now, nearly eighty years later, the Dutch leaders in the East Indies decided to explore the southern shores of "the vast country of New Guinea" in the hope of finding opportunities for trade. An experienced navigator, Captain Willem Jansz, who had first come to the Indies in 1598 as mate of the second Dutch fleet, was given command of the pinnace *Duyfken*. Early in 1606 the *Duyfken* coasted along the southern shores of New Guinea to the point where the island comes relatively close to the Australian mainland— the Torres Strait. Pushing cautiously among the scattered islands and reefs in the shallow sea, Jansz, missing the strait, veered southward and picked up the western shore of what we now know as Cape York Peninsula. He coasted southwards for two hundred miles, until in March he turned back at a point which he called Cap Keerweer, meaning Cape Turnagain.

Jansz is thus the first European known to have visited the coast of Australia —but he did not realize that he had discovered a new continent. Accepting his belief that the land he had sailed along was joined to New Guinea, for many years after him the Dutch map-makers charted his discovery as one continuous coastline, or else left blank the undiscovered part, including the strait that separates New Guinea from Australia. Meanwhile, Torres's discovery of the strait, made just a few months after Jansz's voyage past this point, remained a secret, hidden in the Spanish archives in Manila.

The hope had been to find a new land of spice and gold, but nothing that Jansz saw on his voyage suggested any prospect for the development of commerce. Men were sent ashore "to entreat the inhabitants to trade"—but the inhabitants were found to be "wild, cruel, black savages," and nine members of the crew were killed by them. It was found that in the vast regions there was little or no cultivation.

In moving east across the narrow Lombok Strait separating the islands of Bali and Lombok, Jansz had passed out of the Asiatic zoogeographic region that runs down through the Indies and into the Australian region—or, in the term of the day, into the Realm of Parrots. Clearly the vegetation was distinctive and the savage inhabitants in this realm were primitive—and the financial promise in this area was not great. Jansz noted that no information could be gained on the commodities available or in demand among the savages, and the expedition turned back. More than a decade passed before any new Dutch enterprise penetrated the area.

Meanwhile, Dutch contact with the west coast of the continent had begun as a result of a change in the course followed by the Dutch captains on their way to the Indies. When the Dutch first sailed into these seas they kept to the route pioneered by the Portuguese: after clearing the Cape of Good Hope they stayed close to the coast of Africa as far as Madagascar before striking out for Java. Seamen found this route a trying one—painfully long, with uncertain winds and unpleasant weather conditions. The Dutch ships were sturdier than their predecessors, being better rigged and easier to handle; and their commanders did not shrink from high winds or wild seas. In 1611, Henrik Brouwer made the discovery that by holding to an easterly course from the Cape of Good Hope it was possible to take advantage of the strong westerlies for a thousand leagues or so; from this point a run directly north to Java could be made, again with favourable winds. In 1613 the directors of the Dutch East India Company instructed sailing-masters to follow Brouwer's route. This made it inevitable that some captains, running before a free wind and anxious to make the most of it, would hold to the easterly course beyond the appointed distance, and so would touch the western shores of Australia.

In 1616 the *Eendracht*, commanded by Dirk Hartog, overran the suggested turning point, and as a result reached Shark's Bay, landing on the island that to this day bears the commander's name. The name of his vessel came to be used to identify the landfall (as Eendrachtsland), and subsequently Dutch sailing instructions were modified to take cognisance of the discovery. Mariners were told that they should sail from the Cape between latitudes 30° and 40° for about 4,000 miles until the New Southland of Eendracht was sighted. Because of contrary winds or other difficulties or errors, different points on the coast were touched by navigators whose landfalls—like Edelsland (1618) and Leeuwinsland (1623) to the south of it—soon became shown on the excellent Dutch maps. One of these navigators was Willem Jansz, by then supercargo (or commercial manager) on board the *Mauritius*. In 1618 he discovered the stretch of coast from Port Cloates to North West Cape.

About this time the first English ship to make its appearance in Australian waters met with disaster off the north-west coast. This was the *Tryal*, carrying a company of 133, which had left Plymouth in September 1621 bound for

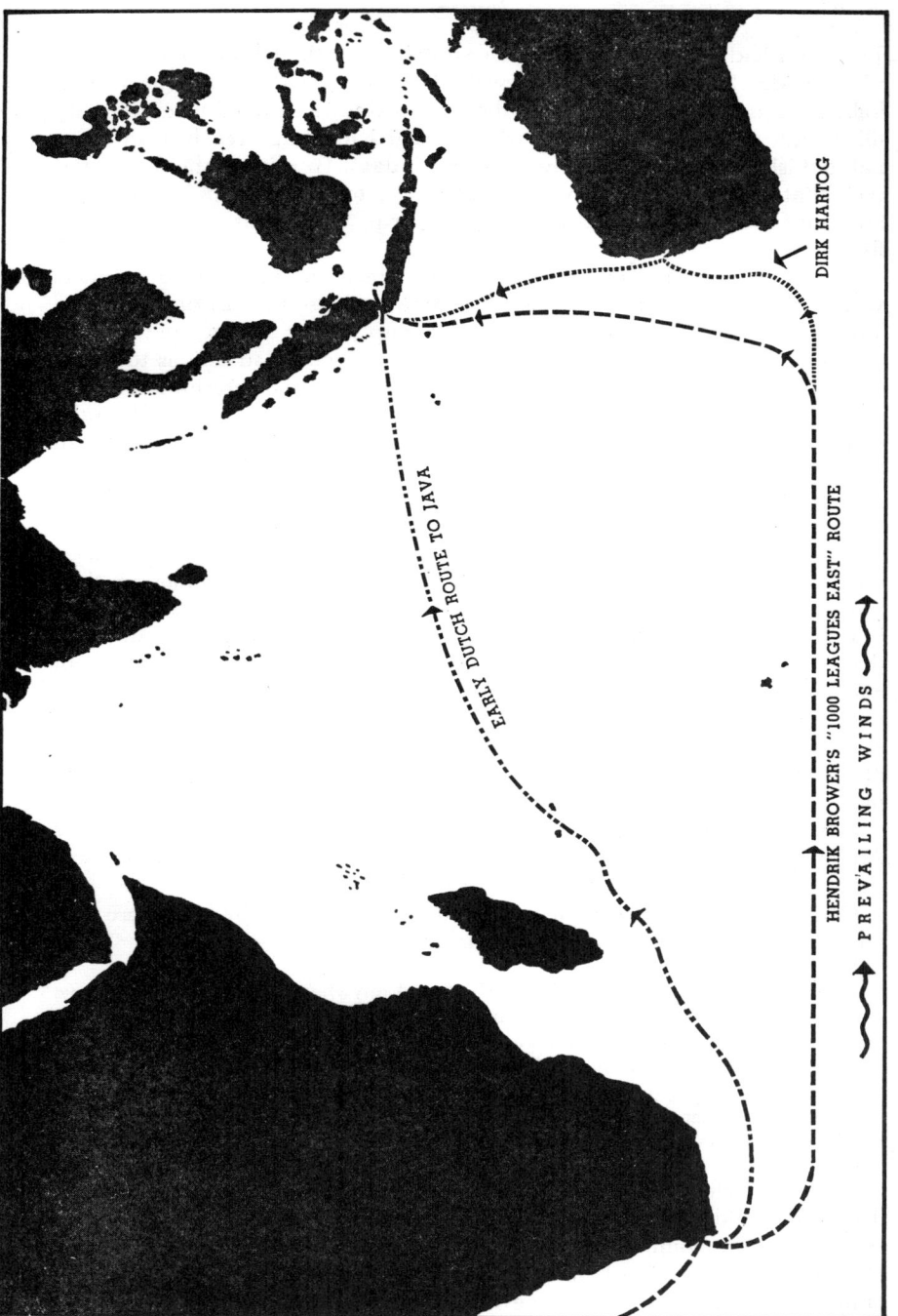

From 1613 Dutch captains sailed directly east after rounding the Cape of Good Hope, before turing north to Java, taking them clossr to Australia's shores.

Java, and had crossed the Indian Ocean following the Dutch route. On the night of May 25, 1622, in a heavy swell, the vessel struck a reef in the Montebello Islands, and ninety-seven of those aboard were trapped when the ship filled with water. The forty-six who managed to escape reached an uninhabited island, where they stayed for seven days. In spite of the shoals and reefs that dotted the sea they decided to take to the boat and pinnace in an effort to reach Batavia. The gruelling trip, which was successful, took five weeks.

At the time, optimism expressed in the prevailing talk among mariners was helping to keep interest alive in the area to the south east of the Indies. The governor of Amboina decided to follow up Jansz's voyage, and in 1623 two small vessels, *Arnhem* and *Pera*, were sent out with instructions to follow the course of *Duyfken* in 1606 and extend it. They were to determine whether a strait existed south of New Guinea, as was now suspected; and to find the extent of the great waterway in which Jansz had sailed to 13°45' south latitude.

The leader of the expedition, Jan Carstenz, put in on New Guinea's southwestern shore, where he lost ten of his men in native attacks. He found the inhabitants to be "tall black men with curly heads of hair and two large holes through their noses; in appearance they are more like monsters than human beings." The land was covered with trees. Carstenz sailed south, found himself among treacherous reefs, shoals, and shallows, and was deceived by the form of the islands into believing that Torres Strait did not exist—just as Jansz had been deceived seventeen years before. The *Arnhem* and *Pera* sailed south along the gulf coast for 450 miles—more than twice as far as Jansz—when Carstenz convinced himself that he was near the head of the gulf. He assumed that the shore along which he was sailing was still part of New Guinea.

When a storm blew up, the vessels were separated. The *Pera* struck out for Amboina; the *Arnhem* crossed the gulf and touched land to the west—now Arnhem Land—before returning home.

Carstenz dampened hopes with his report. The natives, he said, were lean and fearsome. The land was, he declared, the

> ... most arid and barren that could be found anywhere on the earth. We have not seen one fruit bearing tree nor anything that man could make use of; there are no mountains or even hills, so it can be safely concluded that the land contains no metals and does not yield any precious woods such as sandalwood, aloes or columba. In our judgment this is the most arid and barren region that could be found anywhere on the earth. The inhabitants too are the most wretched and poorest creatures that I have ever seen.

Carstenz was clearly disturbed to find that nothing growing in this pitilessly dry land could be turned to trade. Similar conclusions to his had been reached by the commanders who touched the north-western shores. Dirk Hartog, who had gone ashore at Shark's Bay, was unenthusiastic. Like other Dutch captains who sailed along the shore, he found the coastline to be dangerous, with heavy surf, many reefs and rocks, and violent storms and gales, all contributing to the possibility of shipwreck.

On June 4, 1619, the *Batavia*, under Commander Franz Pelsart, was wrecked on the Houtman's Abrolhos when the ship's rudder struck rock with a violent shock, two hours before daylight. The survivors sighted the mainland—a barren rocky coast without trees. Pelsart wrote of this uninviting coast:

> We ran close along the land with a south-east wind but could find no means of getting near the land with the pinnace owing to the violent surf; we found the coast falling off very steeply without any foreland or inlets such as other lands are found to have; in short it seemed to us a barren accursed earth without leafage or grass.

Some of the men swam ashore, seeking water. They saw four black men but could not find any water; further up the coast they landed again, and collected some water from rock-cavities. Pelsart complained there were swarms of flies "that got about our mouths and in our eyes so that we could not get away from them." Eventually he reached Batavia, and on his return picked up the men he had left ashore—those who had not been murdered by their fellows—on this "very barren and unpromising land."

Further south the coast seemed a little better, but there was no sign of inhabitants. In 1627, when the *Gulden Zeepaard* sailed along the southern coast from Leeuwin's Land to the head of the Great Australian Bight, it seemed to Pieter Nuyts, a high Dutch official aboard the vessel, that the new land slowly taking shape on the maps was indeed a disappointment. Surely this was not the golden South Land on which so many high hopes had been centred! This western section could profit no one. Was it, men asked, merely a barren and isolated promontory, or was it a land quite separate from Quiros's golden continent?

These questions were still unanswered when, in 1629, Admiral Willem Jansz retired from the service of the Dutch East India Company. He could look back on many achievements in thirty years of distinguished service to Holland and the company: successful battles against the ships of Portugal and England; governorship of Solar, and of Banda, one of the most important islands in the Dutch Indonesian chain; membership of the influential Council of the Indies; numerous voyages, in every capacity from steersman to admiral of the fleet. Which of these voyages would the old navigator have thought of, if he could have been told that one of them would give him a place in history? We cannot tell; but it is unlikely to have been that voyage in the little *Duyfken*, in 1606, during which he had discovered Australia!

The Dutch had still not quite given up hope of profitable discoveries in the northern area which, following Jansz and Carstenz, was still associated with New Guinea. In 1636 Gerrit Thomaszoon Pool was commissioned to search for a "saltwater inlet" that might lead through from the southernmost point reached by Carstenz to the remote south coast; but Pool was killed by natives on the New Guinea coast before the expedition had gone very far, and after some desultory sailing about Arnhem Land the expedition returned to Amboina.

The Dutch now knew that a vast land existed. Yet after more than a century of penetration of the main oceans of the southern hemisphere by mariners—Portuguese, Spanish, and Dutch—the configuration of land masses was still subject to speculation. At this point the Dutch Governor-General of the Indies, Anthony van Diemen, felt it was time to send a capable navigator on a voyage deep into the southern seas to seek definite knowledge of the area, and to determine whether a southern route could be found to South America so that the Spaniards could be challenged there. He chose for the task Abel Tasman, a young captain whose rise as seaman and navigator had been rapid. Tasman's great reconnaissance would determine where the elusive continent might be.

With two ships, the *Heemskerk* and the *Zeehan*, Tasman set out in August 1642. He sailed to Mauritius and continued south until he reached the Roaring Forties, where he encountered tempestuous gales. The ships reached as far south as 40° before Tasman decided to return to slightly warmer seas, and in latitude 42° they had fast but fair sailing before the stiff westerlies. Three months and ten days out from Batavia, they sighted a coastline. "This," Tasman recorded in his journal, "being the first land we have met within the South Sea and not known to any European nation, we have conferred on it the name of Anthony van Diemensland." Tasman's landfall was the rugged and forbidding south-west coast of Tasmania. From the direction of the coastline he sensed he could continue his course by skirting southward. Finally, at South West Cape, he considered he "had already passed the south land at present known."

The eastern coast of the island proved to be less awesome. Columns of smoke from several fires were sighted. When inquisitiveness could be held in check no longer, Tasman sent men ashore. On a high shingle beach with a single group of trees, they found abundant vegetation, some excellent timber, and a "gently sloping" watercourse. No natives were to be seen, but the seamen who moved in from the beach heard voices and noticed that notches had been cut about five feet apart in the tall trees. The Dutchmen were sure that the purpose of these notches was to provide footholds for the natives climbing the trees in search of birds' nests, and they convinced themselves that only giants could have them. The natives obviously were of "extraordinary stature," Tasman noted; but it was considered unwise to investigate too closely. There were other signs of inhabitants: the earth had been dug out in places, by hand, to form fire places. Round about on the ground there were the footprints of animals, some not unlike the claw marks of a tiger, but no animal was seen.

Before the expedition departed, the ship's carpenter was sent ashore to raise the flag of the Stadholder of the Netherlands, Prince Frederick Henry. Tasman then set sail again, keeping nor'-north east for a short distance and then turning due east "for the purpose of making further discoveries." He noted happily, "the wind from the west, a brisk steady breeze and good clear weather." After sailing for about 400 leagues he came, nine days later, to another landfall. On the first day, two boats came out from the shore at dusk and the men in them called out in a "rough, hollow voice" and blew several times on a trumpet-like instrument before paddling off. Next morning a boat manned with thirteen natives appeared; Tasman recorded that so far as could be observed "these people were of ordinary height." Later seven more boats put out from the shore (with from seven to thirteen men in each) and attacked one of the small boats put out by the *Zeehan*. Four of Tasman's men were killed in the skirmish, and he called the place Murderers' Bay.

Tasman considered his new discovery to be "a very fine land." He named it Staten Land, in honour of the States-General of the Netherlands. To the sea that he had crossed between Van Diemen's Land and his new landfall he gave the name Abel Tasman's Passage. He believed—erroneously—that he had finally reached "the mainland coast of the unknown South Land." He could not know that he had reached the islands of New Zealand, and that he had already passed by the southern continent.

Tasman believed that his Staten Land barred the way and made it impossible to achieve his mission of seeking a direct southern route to South America. Deciding to sail northward, he made a broad sweep to the reputed area of the Solomons, discovered the Friendly Islands, reached the eastern tip of New Guinea, and then made his way well north of New Guinea to Java.

His trip had yielded no treasures and, if anything, his discoveries had added to the uncertainty surrounding the southern lands. He had revealed little about the land south of Java and New Guinea, except to show that its southern extremity was weird and forbidding; the other land, which was supposed to stretch all the way from Murderers' Bay to Tierra del Fuego and to the South Pole itself, had produced nothing but formidable natives who clearly would not welcome any intrusion.

Van Diemen and his advisers were very disappointed with all this, but Tasman buoyed their spirits—and his own—with boundless zeal. Though less enthusiastic, Governor van Diemen felt it worth-while to support further exploration, and in reports sent home from Java he hinted that the "vast and hitherto unknown South Land might yield wealth."

To the practical men directing Dutch affairs, the search for riches in this far-off land seemed at once a challenge and a waste of effort. The sporadic contact that Dutch ships had made with barren coasts had resulted in only disappointing reports, and Tasman's latest voyage had produced nothing tangible. They persisted, nonetheless, in the hope that the east coast of the land whose western shores Dutch ships had sighted so regularly might be more promising, and other voyages were approved. Tasman was to attempt to trace the eastern coastline of the land around which he had sailed completely in 1642 and 1643; on the way he was to test the truth of the maps that showed a strait between it and New Guinea.

He set out in 1644, sailing along the south coast of New Guinea. Like the others who had searched for a strait from the west, he failed to find a way through the reefs and islands. Instead he was tricked into following the tracks of Jansz and Carstenz down the western shore of Cape York Peninsula, which he named Carpentaria Land after Pieter Carpentaria, a former Governor-General of the Indies. Caught in the great gulf, Tasman followed the coastline westward and finally returned to Batavia, again empty-handed.

This time there was no enthusiasm for further ventures. A general missive from the Governor-General and council of the company on December 23, 1644, summarized the situation by saying that the explorers had found "nothing that could be turned to profit, but had only come across naked beach-roving wretches, destitute even of rice, and not possessed of any fruits worth mentioning." And so Dutch exploration faded out after its achievement of setting down in fairly precise form ten thousand miles or so of coastline from the Gulf of Carpentaria to the Bight, and part of Van Diemen's Land. To the northern section they had given the name New Holland.

After Tasman, no important voyages were made into the South Seas for more than a century; but at least the mists had been partly cleared, even if many mysteries remained.

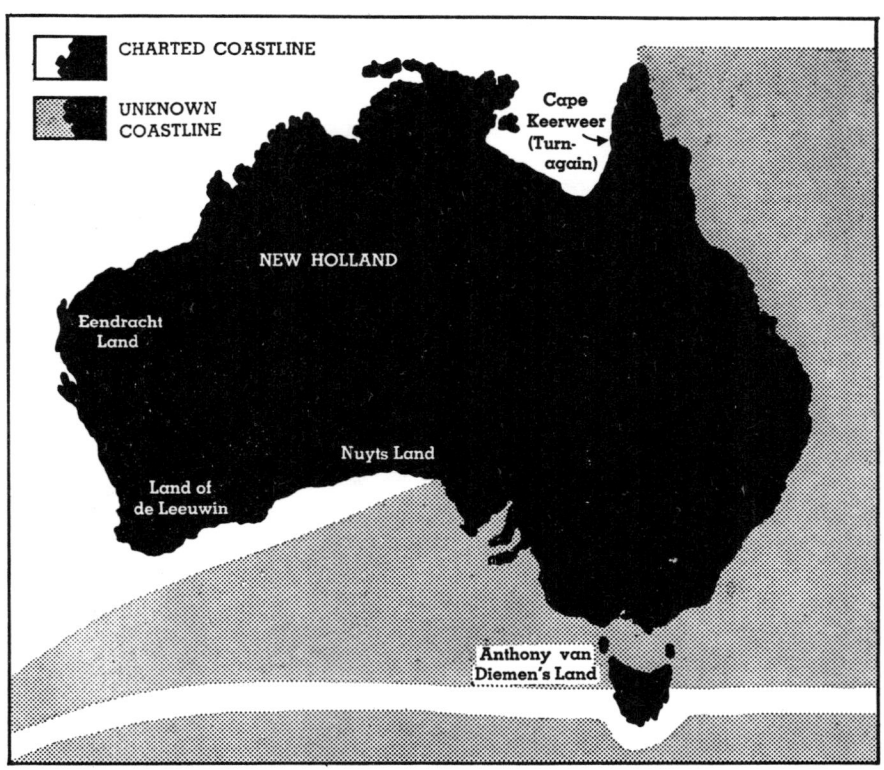

CHARTED COASTLINE

UNKNOWN COASTLINE

Cape
Keerweer
(Turn-
again)

NEW HOLLAND

Eendracht
Land

Nuyts Land

Land of
de Leeuwin

Anthony van
Diemen's Land

Discovery to 1769.—Contact with Australia was made first in the North, where Dutch
navigators touched its shores in the early years of the 17th century; then Dutch and English
ships sailed along parts of the west coast, and finally the Dutch pushed part-way along the
southern shore. In 1642 van Diemen, sailing farther south, reached Tasmania, coasting this
island to the south.

A continent defined 2

Tasman's second voyage had produced results as disappointing as those of the first, and the Dutch had no more enthusiasm for exploration in the South Seas. Events near home had been changing relationships and destroying old associations. Now a new maritime-commercial power, England, was to challenge the Dutch, as the Dutch had challenged the Portuguese.

Since the massacre of English traders in Amboina in 1623, the Dutch East India Company had been left alone in the spice islands by its English counterpart, while the Dutch merchants had tended to leave India to the ever-expanding interests of the English company. Elsewhere, however, the division was not so clear-cut. By the time Tasman's voyage was over, the Civil War in England, which had begun in 1642, had disrupted industry and destroyed much of the nation's foreign commerce, and this had enabled the Dutch to take over most of the trade with the colonies that Englishmen, from 1607 on, had set up on the North American continent.

Then came a prolonged struggle between the two maritime powers. In 1651, two years after the end of the Civil War, Cromwell's Government passed a Navigation Act designed to deprive the Dutch of their trade with English America. This sparked off the first of the three Anglo-Dutch wars that took place over the next twenty years; by the end of this period the Dutch had lost their colonies in North America as well as their trade with the English colonies there. Even had Holland's energies not been engrossed by the long struggle with France, the business-like Dutch in the East Indies would have had no further interest in the barren and remote lands, inhabited by wild and cruel savages, mapped by Jansz, Tasman, and their fellow navigators. The vision of a great and rich South Land faded into oblivion.

For their part the English were beginning to realize the wealth and the wonders of India, and as yet there seemed no reason to seek a new continent in the remote southern latitudes. The prospect of riches in the tropical lands, however, attracted many adventurers. Some were pirates, some were privateersmen. Among those who became interested in the southern area was William Dampier, an English buccaneer who sailed the Pacific in 1686. Dampier and his companions reached the Philippines where the captain was put ashore. From Mindanao, the adventurers sailed through eastern seas and on to New Holland—"to see," Dampier said, "what the country would afford us."

On January 4, 1688 they reached the same barren north-west coast that had repelled the Dutch mariners who had visited it. The *Cygnet* dropped anchor below Cape L'Evêque, on a major promontory in north-western Australia, and remained there for some weeks while repairs were completed. Dampier found the scene depressing. It was a land with "dry and dusty soil" and savage people of "very unpleasant aspect"—the worst he had ever encountered.

When Dampier reported his experience it was clear that this new land, and its native people, outdid any other for weirdness. Earlier tales of the strange people and places of Africa, of the Indies, and of India itself, of China, and the Americas, all seemed to fade into banality by comparison with Dampier's descriptions of this outlandish new realm. His first-hand report, *A New Voyage Round the World*, published in 1697, strengthened the aura of grotesqueness that had long hung over the mysterious South Land.

His descriptions made it abundantly clear that New Holland was indeed a fantastic place. Perhaps its inhabitants did not walk upside down, as some had imagined they might; but Dampier reported that they went without clothes—wearing only "the rind of a tree"—and that they had no villages, dwelling instead in the open and carrying their few possessions with them wherever they went, that they spoke an incomprehensible language in guttural tones, and that they possessed great heads and massive brows and every one of them had two front teeth missing. Dampier drew an equally harsh picture of the land:

> There is neither herb, root, pulse nor any sort of Grain for them to eat. We saw no trees that bore fruit or berries. We saw no sort of animal nor any track of beast but once, and that seemed to be the tread of a beast as big as a great mastiff.

The people were obviously not interested in trade, and the land had nothing to offer for commerce.

It was hard for Englishmen to take such an outlandish place seriously. Nevertheless Dampier, who combined the roles of practical observer and enterprising adventurer, opened new horizons by bringing vividly to life the nature of the strange places he visited. His curiosity aroused, he was intrigued with the prospect in New Holland, and he thought that eventually better areas might be found. He pointed to the large area of land that was believed to exist, and said one might hope "to meet with some fruitful lands, continents, or islands, productive of fruits, drugs or spices (perhaps minerals also)."

Such speculation was new in London, and before long there was great interest in Dampier's proposal to undertake a thorough exploration. Leading men of affairs became convinced that his speculation about areas of New Holland as yet unknown should be investigated. The Admiralty agreed to support Dampier, and in 1699 he sailed in command of the 300-ton *Roebuck* on a voyage of discovery to New Holland.

Dampier's intention was to explore the "eastern and less well-known side of the Southern Lands." He was to round Cape Horn and strike westward across the Pacific—but like others before him he was thwarted in this purpose by the prevailing climatic and sailing conditions. Because of the severe cold, he chose the alternative route round the Cape of Good Hope, and soon he was following the path of so many Dutch mariners before him. Instead of being the first to reach the fertile eastern areas, as he well might have been, he fell in with the north-west coast, which he carefully charted. He had hoped to find some hidden way to the east; but the charts he had did not show the strait Torres had discovered nearly a century before, and he turned north to skirt New Guinea. He discovered the passage separating New Guinea from New Britain—an island which, he thought, might become a valuable "spice island" for Britain.

Now it was his intention to sail south and so continue his search; but "many difficulties" connected with the state of the *Roebuck* and its crew prevented him from continuing. The ship was old and in poor condition, and Dampier realized it was likely to founder. Even though he was so close to his real objective he was forced to turn back, his mission unfulfilled. The *Roebuck* sailed no farther than the South Atlantic, foundering near Ascension Island. Dampier and the crew were rescued, and the peregrinating navigator somehow saved his precious notes, the basis of a book later published for all to read. He told of sweet-scented trees and shrubs, most of them with flowers or berries on them, on the coast of New Holland. There were brilliant scarlet-and-black peaflowers on ground creepers; and:

> The blossoms of the different sort of trees were of several colours, as red, white, yellow, etc., but mostly blue; and these generally smelt very sweet and fragrant, as did some of the rest. There were also, beside some plants, herbs, and tall flowers, some very small flowers, growing on the ground, that were sweet and beautiful, and for the most part unlike I had seen elsewhere.

Dampier also noted "a sort of raccoon" with very short forelegs—a kangaroo or wallaby—and the little stumpy-tail lizard, which he considered offensive in appearance.

Dampier's reports helped to bring the unknown south vividly to notice in a Britain that was already expanding its horizons. The stories still pictured it as an incredible region—enigmatic, a perfect setting for fantasy as well as for fiction. To outdo the adventures of Robinson Crusoe, Jonathon Swift put Gulliver ashore in two of his four voyages on imaginary islands located south of the coastline Dampier had explored.

With the founding, in 1711, of the South Sea Company, one of London's joint-stock ventures to seize public imagination, the distant Pacific became a region for more than literary fantasy. The South Sea Company was to trade with Spanish America, and concessions were gained for it for that purpose, but its great appeal to the speculator lay in its hoped-for trade with the rich lands thought to await discovery in the Pacific. Expectations of dazzling wealth were conjured up, although operations never became profitable. The fraudulent booming of the company's shares was followed by a collapse of the so-called South Sea Bubble in 1720, causing disillusionment as well as a great scandal. The collapse brought to a sudden and calamitous end all speculative interest in nebulous plans for trade in the Pacific. Nevertheless, the English period of Pacific discovery had begun. It was an era of scientific exploration, undertaken against a background of great expansion in scientific thought. Significant advance in the theoretical sciences of mathematics and astronomy had been made in the seventeenth century; now these new principles were being applied to navigation. The invention of the sextant in England in 1730, and the subsequent development of the chronometer, made it possible to take exact celestial measurements, and so to chart a ship's position with accuracy. These inventions, with modifications in ship-design resulting in greatly strengthened vessels, opened the way for new geographical discoveries.

Perhaps it was the aura of unreality associated with the southern lands as much as the British preoccupation with European wars, that held back further exploration for so long. Dampier had returned to London, hinting at prospects in lands still untouched, in 1701. Yet, apart from the wartime expedition of Captain George Anson in 1739, it was not until 1764 that the British government sent another ship into the area.

By that time many changes had taken place elsewhere. As the Anglo-Dutch rivalry declined, an intense rivalry had developed between England and France. Between 1689 and 1763 these two great maritime-commercial-colonial powers fought a series of wars for which the prize was world leadership. The combat areas in this first series of world wars were Europe, North America, India, and the high seas. The wars did not follow any uniform pattern. They did not even carry the same names in the different combat areas; thus Americans spoke of "King William's War" (1689–97) and "Queen Anne's War" (1702–13), meaning the wars that in their European aspect were called the War of the League of Augsburg and the War of the Spanish Succession. Sometimes English and American backwoodsmen were fighting Frenchmen in the Ohio Valley and on the banks of the Mississippi while England and France were at peace. Less often, there was peace in the Ohio valley, and Anglo-French battles in Europe. The battles between the European-trained sepoys of the English East India Company and the French East India Company (the latter founded in 1664) did not always occur during the periods of officially declared war between the mother-countries. Sometimes Britain's European ally of one war was her opponent in the next struggle. But always, in spite of inconsistencies and incongruities, the main struggle was between France and England, and always naval warfare was a feature.

For much of the eighteenth century there was a distinct possibility that this naval warfare would be extended into the Pacific. Both French and English were doing their share of voyaging in these waters, sometimes no more than a few months, or a few leagues, apart. England's victory in the Seven Years war, acknowledged at the Treaty of Paris in 1763, resulted in England's supremacy over the French in India, and the loss of France's North American colonies to England. (France, however, retained some possessions in India and the best of her sugar-islands.) In the long run the English victory also decided the future of the Pacific.

During the years of struggle, increasing attention was given to scientific inquiry and geographical speculation, both in England and France. Now that practically all the remainder of the world was charted, the Great South Land—Terra Australis or Terra Incognita—had become a matter of immediate concern. Books about voyages in the Pacific and southern seas, proposing further exploration or the founding of settlements, and speculating about unknown parts, contributed to the growing interest.

Between 1744 and 1748, a handsome new edition was published in London of the *Complete Collection of Voyages and Travels* (which had originally appeared in 1705, edited by John Harris) urging further discoveries. As well as narratives of navigators, the book contained prefaces and notations by John Campbell, who sought to draw attention to opportunities for new enterprise believed to exist for enterprising Englishmen. Pointing to the value of commerce, Campbell explained the narratives of travel in the South Sea in terms of the new challenge that awaited those with foresight and courage to act:

> It is most evident from Tasman's voyages that New Guinea, Carpentaria [i.e., Cape York Peninsula], New Holland, Van Diemen's Land and the country discovered by Quiros make all one continent, from which New Zealand seems to be separated by a strait, and perhaps is part of another continent.

Campbell went on to suggest that there were great prospects for Britain if settlements (or, as he termed them, plantations) were established there. Convinced of the immense value of the southern continent, which he termed Terra Australis, he was opposed to a monopoly being granted to the East India Company to trade there. He made a strong plea that the South Sea Company should have rights there "as a point of high importance," and wrote that if Britain wished to make the greatest gain "it may, indeed, be requisite to remove ill judged prohibitions, and to break down illegal exclusions."

He urged that New Guinea should be settled at once, "and with competent force, since without doubt the Spaniards would leave no means unattempted to dispossess them." In the space of a very few years, he believed, settlement of New Guinea (and a trade in slaves from there) would prove of great consequence to the South Sea Company. He also recommended the formation of a settlement on the southern coast of Terra Australis. This, he believed, would lead the way to the opening of a new trade route "which must carry a great quantity of our goods and manufactures." Such a settlement would also be attended by other advantages. "There is in all probability," he wrote, "another Southern continent which is still to be discovered."

In France in 1756 Charles de Brosses published his *Histoire de Navigations aux Terres Australes (History of Navigation to Southern Lands)* in which he argued that there must be a great south land in the Pacific, and urged France to continue her explorations, contending that the early French voyages had made France the logical power to colonize the area. His favoured sites were New Britain and Austrialia del Espiritu Santo, and he considered that the expedition should start from Pondicherry, in India.

The Seven Years War began in the year that de Brosses's book was published. The future of the Pacific was decided in the waters of Quiberon Bay in 1759. This naval victory began a long period of English naval supremacy, not to be reversed except during the War of American Independence. England's maritime supremacy made it certain that in the long run the visions of John Campbell should prevail over those of Charles de Brosses. In ironical commentary on this, three years after the end of the Seven Years War there appeared in London the first three volumes of John Callender's *Terra Australis Cognita*. In this book the whole of the arguments put forward by de Brosses, including the details of his idea for settlement, were appropriated by Callender. The only difference was that these arguments were now advanced to urge Britain's discovery and settlement of the Great South Land!

Callender's book was timely. The British Admiralty had no intention of allowing the French to forestall them in the race to new lands, and after 1763 a number of expeditions to the far South Pacific were organized.

Commodore John Byron sailed from Plymouth in 1764 with orders that, in order to avoid arousing Spanish jealousies and retaliation, were kept secret. After passing through the Straits of Magellan he sailed on the familiar north-westerly course over the Pacific, making few discoveries; he sighted only outlying islands of minor groups, and after visiting Tinian he went on to Batavia and returned home, completing the circumnavigation in the record time of twenty-two months. On his return to England in 1766 his ship, the frigate *Dolphin*, was placed under Captain Samuel Wallis who, with Captain Philip Carteret in the *Swallow*, set off on another circumnavigation. The two ships were separated soon after passing through the Straits of Magellan. Wallis reached Tahiti (naming it King George Island), the Society Islands, and the Wallis Archipelago, sailing home by way of Batavia. Carteret discovered Pitcairn Island and sailed through St George's Channel, so proving that New Ireland and New Britain were separated.

These voyages were all undertaken by Britain to advance "the honour of this nation as a maritime power—and the trade and navigation thereof." The English ships each followed a course through the Straits of Magellan and then struck north west, finally coasting New Guinea. Close behind them were the French, who had the same objectives and who directed their efforts to the same area. Captain Louis Antoine de Bougainville reached the Society Islands and Tahiti a year after Wallis, and continued westward, making some new discoveries in the Samoa group. His next landfall was an archipelago which he decided—correctly—was Quiros's long-lost, long-sought Austrialia del Espiritu Santo. Here, he told himself, was the opportunity to solve the old riddle of the Southern Continent:

> Was it by guess that the geographers made this Tierra del Espiritu Santo the same continent of New Guinea? To resolve this problem it was necessary to keep in the same latitude for the space of three hundred and fifty leagues further. I resolved to do it.

Accordingly he continued westward along the parallel of 15°, helped by fresh easterly winds. A week after losing sight of land, he saw breakers and a very low sandy coast about half a league to the south. All next day pieces of wood and some unknown kind of fruit drifted past the ships; the sea was very low, in spite of a strong wind from the south, all of which made Bougainville believe "that we had land pretty near us to the south-west." Next day, early in the afternoon of June 6, 1768:

> A sandbank appeared about three-quarters of a league distant ahead and convinced me that it was time to alter the course that I had always continued to the westward. This land extended at least half a league from west by south-west to west-north-west; some of our people even were of opinion that they saw a low-lying land to the south-west of the breakers. We set to the northward till four o'clock and then again to the westward. This however did not last long; for at half past five o'clock the men at the mastheads saw fresh breakers to the north-west and north-west by west about a league and a half from us. We approached nearer in order to view them better. They were seen to extend above two miles from north-north-west to south-south-west, and we could not see an end of them. In all probability they joined those that we had discovered three hours before. The sea broke with great violence on these shoals and some summits of rocks appeared above water from space to space. This last discovery was the voice of God and we were obedient to it . . . and on the 7th in the morning I gave orders to steer north-east by north, abandoning the scheme of proceeding further westwards in the latitude of 15°.

And so Bougainville sailed away from the Great Barrier Reef. He still believed he had been close to land, but consoled himself with the reflection that it could easily have been "a cluster of islands," not the east coast of New Holland. His subsequent course took him through the hazardous waters of the Louisiade Archipelago, through the Solomons and New Britain, and north of New Ireland to the Moluccas and eventually to Europe.

Meanwhile, an English geographer, Alexander Dalrymple, had written a book in which he explained how easy it would be to move into what he imagined to be the great, rich, populous continent of the south—a land "sufficient to maintain the power, dominion, and sovereignty of Britain by employing all its manufacturers and ships." Dalrymple, who had spent many years in the employ of the East India Company, returned to London in 1765 and set about a study of material available on the South Seas. He secured a copy of a memorial printed in 1640—discovered by the English expedition that captured Manila in 1762—and from this long-hidden document he deduced the existence of a strait to the south of New Guinea. In a little book, *Discoveries in the South Pacific to 1764*, which was written in 1767 but not published until 1769, Dalrymple included a map in which the strait was marked, as well as the routes of Tasman and Torres. In this booklet he recapitulated all the discoveries that had been made in the South Pacific, including Juan Fernandez Islands off the coast of Chile, the discoveries of Quiros and Tasman, and those of Le Maire to the north of New Guinea. He drew the conclusion that all these widely separated fragments were probably parts of the same great continent—a continent possibly extending over a hundred degrees of longitude in latitude 40° S., so that it was larger than the whole of Asia from Turkey to the extremity of China!

Dalrymple hoped that he would be appointed to command the next British expedition into the area—but he was to be disappointed. In 1767 the Admiralty appointed James Cook, a lieutenant who, through his charts of the St Lawrence River, Newfoundland, and Labrador, had already gained for himself the name of the ablest navigator in the Royal Navy. The immediate objective of Cook's voyage was to take astronomers to the South Pacific to observe from the newly discovered island of Tahiti the transit of the planet Venus across the face of the sun.

With Cook went Joseph Banks, a member of the Royal Society, taking with him a leading botanist, four artists, and four servants, to help with the collection of material for a study of the natural history of the new land. Banks's outlay was said to be about £10,000—three times the cost of the *Endeavour bark* (as the ship was officially designated by the Admiralty, to avoid confusion with the other *Endeavour* in service at the time). On August 26, 1768, the 320-ton vessel, with Cook in command of a crew of eighty-four men, sailed from Plymouth. In addition to normal stores, the *Endeavour* was laden with astronomical instruments and other scientific equipment and botanists' collecting vessels.

After rounding Cape Horn, Cook struck north-west for Tahiti. He anchored there in April 1769, and on June 3 the transit of the planet across the face of the sun was observed. Cook was now free to open the sealed orders he carried from the Admiralty. They instructed him to sail south and west in search of the land about which Dalrymple had speculated.

By August, Cook and his men were heading south in search of the elusive continent whose coast was thought to be quite close to Tahiti. At 40° S. latitude there were still "not the least visible signs of land," and, as the *Endeavour* was being lashed by tempestuous gales, Cook struck westward, seeking Tasman's landfall of 127 years before—which had been called Staten Land and, later, New Zealand. On October 7 the ship's boy, Nick Young, at the masthead lookout, shouted "Land ahead!" The *Endeavour* had reached the north island of New Zealand. For almost six months Cook was busy charting the 2,400-mile coastline of New Zealand, demolishing the theory— "much," noted Banks, "to the regret of the continent-mongers"—that the land was a promontory of some great continent stretching away to the South Pole.

Cook had only a limited opportunity to examine the land, but he concluded that it would be suitable for settlement.

> It was the opinion of everybody on board that all sorts of European grain, fruit, plants, etc., would thrive here. In short, was this country settled by an industrious people they would very soon be supplied not only with the necessities but many of the luxuries, of life. . . . It does not appear to me to be at all difficult for strangers to form a settlement in this country.

The inhabitants struck Cook as "strong, rawboned, well made and active, rather above than under common size." He described them as being very dark brown in colour, with black hair, and having black beards and white teeth. Those who did not disfigure their faces by tattooing had very good features.

> Their common clothing are very much like square thumbed matts, that are made of rope yarns, to lay at the doors or passages into houses to clean one's shoes upon. These tie round their necks, the thumbed side out, and are generally large enough to cover the body as low as the knee. . . . They have other much finer clothing, made of the same plant after it is bleached and prepared in such a manner that it is as white and almost as soft as flax, but much stronger. . . . Both men and women wear ornaments at their ears and about their necks; these are made of stone, bone, shells, etc., and are variously shaped. The men, when they are dressed, generally wear 2 or 3 long white feathers stuck upright in their hair.
>
> The people show great ingenuity and good workmanship in the building and framing of their boats or canoes. . . . Their large canoes are, I believe, built wholly for war, and will carry from 40 to 80 or 100 men, with their arms, etc. . . . The houses of their people . . . are built low, and in the form of an oblong square. The framing is of wood or small sticks, and the sides and covering of thatch made of long grass.

On March 31 Cook left New Zealand, resolved to continue westward until he reached "the east coast of New Holland, and then to follow the directions of that coast to the northward and what other direction it might take until we arrive at its northern extremity." Aboard the *Endeavour* were various publications in which all the earlier voyages were recorded—the discoveries of Tasman, Dutch discoveries on the western and adjoining northern and southern coasts, and the indication of a strait separating New Guinea from New Holland in Dalrymple's book, of which Banks carried a pre-publication presentation copy.

Cook intended first to retrace Tasman's course back to the point on the east coast of Van Diemen's Land at which Tasman had landed, but he encountered hard southerly gales and a great sea that carried the *Endeavour* somewhat off the intended course, and when, at six o'clock on the morning of April 20, 1770, land came into sight it was the extreme south-east point of the continent that had been reached. Lieutenant Zachary Hicks had sighted what is now Cape Hicks Hill, near Cape Everard.

Cook could not be sure whether a strait separated the land from Tasman's discovery to the south, but instead of investigating this detail he turned north. He conducted a running survey of the coast, naming and describing various landmarks. When he made an attempt to land, near what is now Wollongong, the surf was found to be too great. From the ship's yawl, however, Cook and Banks caught a glimpse of four or five natives "who took to the woods."

After nine days' sailing along the coast, Cook put into a bay and anchored there at three o'clock on the afternoon of April 29. His landfall was Kurnell (named from the Aboriginal, Kundel) in Botany Bay, which Cook at first called Stingrays Bay. Some Aborigines were seen ashore, but most of them made off. Only two remained to challenge Cook and his men, and after throwing their spears they made off quickly when Cook fired three shots. Cook then advanced cautiously from the beach. The party was relieved to find that the natives' "darts" were not poisoned, as they had at first feared.

In the wooded area behind the shore, the explorers came on a few small bark shelters. In one of these they found some children, for whom they left strings of beads. There were canoes on the beach, 12 feet or more in length. Each was made from "one piece of the bark of a tree drawn or tied up at each end and the middle kept open by means of pieces of sticks."

The countryside appealed to Cook, apparently reminding him of the pleasant scenes of his native Yorkshire. It was in a temperate zone, and in the late autumn the land was green and well grassed. He was impressed and gratified with its fertile aspect. It was country

> ... diversified with woods, lawns, and marshes. The woods are free from under-wood of every kind, and the trees are at such a distance from one another that the whole country, or at least a great part of it, might be cultivated without [one's] being obliged to cut down a single tree. We found the soil every where, except in the marshes, to be a light white sand, and it produceth a quantity of good grass, which grows in little tufts. [Cook noted two sorts of gum] ... one sort of which is like Gum Dragon, and is the same, I suppose, Tasman took for Gum lac; it is extracted from the largest tree in the woods.

Cook made a trip to the head of the inlet, where he found the country much the same as around the shore, but "much richer," with a deep black soil capable, he believed, of producing any kind of grain. The land formed as fine a meadow "as ever was seen." Banks noted that the climate was like that of the south of France. He considered that although the proportion of rich soil was small in comparison to the barren, there was sufficient of the good to support "a very large number" of people. There were no beasts of prey, and sheep and cattle would thrive. There was plenty of timber for fuel and for building.

Cook was anxious to meet the inhabitants, but whenever he or his party approached they fled. This seemed to be the result of shyness rather than of fear. Once, seeing smoke and some canoes on a beach, Cook went directly there, but the group made off.

> There were six canoes and six small fires on the shore, and mussels roasting upon them, and a few oysters laying near. From this we conjectured that there had been just six people, who had been out each in his canoe picking up the shell fish, and come ashore to eat them. We tasted of their cheer, and left them in return strings of beads, etc.

Cook noted that the natives did not appear to be numerous and that they did not live in large groups. Those whom he saw were about as tall as Europeans,

> . . . of very dark brown colour, but not black, nor had they woolly, frizzled hair, but black and lank like ours. No sort of cloathing or ornaments were ever seen by any of us upon any of them, or in or about their huts; from this I conclude they never wear any. Some that we saw had their faces and bodies painted with a sort of white paint or pigment. . . . However, we could know but very little of their customs as we never were able to form any connections with them; they had not so much as touched the things we had left in their huts on purpose for them to take away.

Early on May 7 Cook weighed anchor and set off to resume the northward voyage. Soon the ship was abreast of an open bay that could be seen between bold headlands: this was Port Jackson, which Cook was aware might be a good anchorage—but he did not investigate it. He pushed on northward, and after two weeks he observed the Glasshouse Mountains, and gave the name Glasshouse Bay to the present Moreton Bay. At various points he noted "smokes in the day and fires in the night," and some Aborigines gathered to gaze at his strange craft. He sailed on, and on May 23 he reached a large, open bay where he decided to land in order to replenish the water-supplies. With Banks and some others he went ashore, and in the bush they saw most of the species of birds they had seen at Botany Bay, "besides bustards such as we have in England, which occasioned my giving the place the name of Bustard Bay." There was a wealth of new plants, true mangroves, cockle-shells, a group of native-built fires protected by windbreaks of bark, green ants building nests among the leaves of trees, and swarms of hairy green caterpillars.

Soon the *Endeavour* was at sea again, still moving northward, charting the features of the coast as it unfolded before the explorers, league after league. On May 31 there was another landing, this time at the northern extremity of Shoalwater Bay. Once again the Aborigines made off almost as soon as they were sighted, and once again Joseph Banks was absorbed with the new species and the variety of plants and animals that came to his notice. Among the mangroves the members of the party saw the little mud-skipper (lung fish) which seemed to be as much at home hopping among the roots and rocks as in the water.

Unknown to Cook, the ramparts of the Great Barrier Reef lay to the east, for he was sailing in the channel running between the mainland and the chain of outer reefs. The water was often shallow, and it was necessary to take constant soundings. Reefs and shoals were on every hand, and, in spite of gentle breezes and fair weather, Cook had to pick his passage cautiously. To the beautiful mile long strip of water between the mainland and the Cumberland Islands he gave the name Whit Sunday's Passage to mark the day in the church calendar; a small island he called Pentecost Island. Here among the offshore islands Cook saw a canoe fitted with an outrigger. This he recorded as being "large, and differently built to any we have seen upon the coast." There were many islands, and on some of them he noted that groups of natives "looked attentively" at his ship. Another brief landing was made on June 10, near Cape Grafton. Cook was now in the most intricate parts of what he named The Labyrinth—the countless coral outcropping where only his magnificent seamanship made it possible for the ship to proceed.

Deciding that the conditions made it unwise to attempt to take water aboard at Cape Grafton, Cook continued the voyage; but toward midnight the following night, in clear moonlight, the *Endeavour* drove heavily on to a reef nearly 20 miles offshore.

The vessel stuck fast, and as the hours passed the position became more and more perilous. Stores, water-casks, and guns, as well as ballast, were jettisoned, but it was not until the height of the tide that came in late on June 13 that the *Endeavour* was refloated. A new peril was immediately apparent: the vessel began to fill more rapidly, even though a great spear of coral had snapped off and partially plugged the hole in the hull. It was now suggested that the ship might be "fothered" by having a mixture of oakum and wool, chopped small, passed under the hull in a sheet of sailcloth and dragged over the leak. Cook ordered this to be done, and the measure succeeded. The vessel remained afloat, and during the next five days was taken to the south bank of a river, the Endeavour, where repairs could be undertaken. Lightened by the removal of everything possible, the vessel was hauled well up the bank at high tide, with the bow among the mangroves. When the tide ebbed, and the hull was exposed, they found that the coral had cut through three planks near the bow, and had damaged others. Partial repairs were made, and on July 5 the *Endeavour* was refloated. As the leak still persisted, repairs had to be continued, this time with the aid of a staging alongside which the vessel was moored.

Whereas previously shore excursions had been wholly incidental to the main purpose of coastal discovery and charting, the enforced stay on Endeavour River gave Cook and his party an opportunity to undertake extended shore observations. On June 24 a kangaroo was seen by one of the men for the first time. Cook recorded it as very slender, swift of foot, and mousecolour. When more were seen and one or two killed, Banks described this as the typical animal of the country, noting that these creatures bounded on their hind legs, escaping by leaping nimbly over the thickets of long dense grass that stopped his dog. "To compare it to any European animal would be impossible," Cook wrote. He described "the animal" as "hare-lipt" and possessing forelegs eight inches long and hind legs of twenty-two inches. The name kangaroo (or *kanguru*, or *kangaru*) was recorded by Cook because he believed this to be the name by which the Aborigines knew the animal; actually this was merely their general response to a question asked by Cook; they had no such name for the creature that so intrigued the explorers.

On July 11, the Aborigines came under close scrutiny for the first time when four men arrived in a small canoe with an outrigger—the first group to make contact with the visitors. They were prevailed upon to lay down their weapons, and they were given presents. None was above 5 feet 6 inches in height, and all, Cook noted, had small limbs.

They were naked, their skins the colour of wood soot; their hair black, lank and cropt short, and neither woolly nor frizzled; nor did they want any of their fore teeth, as Dampier has mentioned those did [whom] he saw on the western side of the country. Some part of their bodies had been painted over with red and one of them had his upper lip and breast painted with streaks of white. . . . Their features were far from being disagreeable, their voices were soft and tunable, and they could easily repeat any word after us. But no one could understand a word they said.

Cook and his party saw more Aborigines, and on July 20 nearly a score of them—men and women—came close to the *Endeavour*. Ten clambered aboard to ask for turtle meat, and on being refused they tried to drag two large turtles overboard. When Cook's men repulsed them, they angrily went ashore and set fire to dry grass beside the shore camp, destroying valuable goods and property. A round of small shot then scared them away , and from then until Cook put to sea again, early on August 6, they were not seen again.

From high land ashore Cook had observed a tangled series of reefs and shoals barring the way seaward. Back on ship, he worked his way northward through reef-strewn waters, then anchored at Lizard Island where, on climbing to its peak, he was relieved to find that a passage led to the open sea. As he sailed out through it he found this passage free of all reefs and very deep. Obviously relieved to be clear of The Labyrinth, Cook noted in his journal that this was the first open sailing since May 26, "in which time we have sailed above 360 leagues by the lead, without ever having a leadman out of the chains when the ship was under sail—a circumstance that perhaps never happened to any ship before."

His satisfaction was shortlived. After a few days, a change of wind drove the *Endeavour* back toward the reefs, and the dangerous currents, and a flat calm brought them close to disaster on August 17. The boats were used to tow the vessel clear of the breakers, relieving what Cook later described as a "truly terrible situation." The *Endeavour* had come close to being smashed upon "the great wall of coral rock rising almost perpendicularly out of the unfathomable ocean," where, as Banks said, "the very large waves of the vast ocean meeting with so sudden a resistance make a most terrible surf, breaking mountains high."

Fortunately a light breeze sprang up and, at full speed upon the flood tide, the *Endeavour*, which was still leaking, was steered toward an opening that had been sighted in the reef—Providential Passage, as Cook named it— and soon was once more at anchor in the calm waters behind the barrier. "It is but a few days ago," Cook wrote, "that I rejoiced at having got without the Reef; but that joy was nothing compared to what I now felt at being safe at an Anchor within it."

Cook was still following his instructions. The final point to be cleared up was whether or not New Guinea "joins to or makes a part of this land." He determined to keep close to the mainland—no matter how difficult the sailing conditions. Picking his way northward, with the boats ahead almost all the time, Cook found himself three or four miles north of the mainland at noon on August 22. "The northern promontory of this country," he noted,

"I have named York Cape." He entered Endeavour Strait, and as he passed beyond Cape York and an island near by, he wrote: "Between these two points we could see no land so we were in great hopes we had found out a passage into the Indian Seas."

Cook realized that he had reached the northern point of the eastern coast of New Holland, and that to the west of him the coastline had already been explored and charted by the Dutch. At several points on his northward journey he had taken possession of sections of the coast, but now he decided to make a formal annexation. Landing on August 23 on a small island off Cape York (he named it Possession Island), he hoisted the English flag and in the name of George III took possession of the whole eastern coast from latitude 38° S., together with all the bays, harbours, rivers, and islands situated along it. Three volleys of small arms fired from the shore were answered by a like number from the *Endeavour*.

As Cook sailed on from Possession Island he narrowly escaped running on a reef. He next made his way to the New Guinea coast, and had no great difficulty in reaching Savu, near Timor, where he made a brief stay. On October 11 he reached Batavia and again came near to disaster; a bolt of lightning struck a Dutch vessel moored alongside the *Endeavour* and carried away its main mast. Fortunately, a lightning-conductor had been raised on the *Endeavour*. "This," as Cook said, "carried the lightning or electrical matter over the side clear of the ship"; without it the vessel might have shared the fate of the Dutch merchantman.

Supplies were obtained for the voyage home from the Governor-General, and Cook dispatched copy of his journal to London. In that journal he gave the name New Wales to the land he had annexed. He sailed from Batavia on October 14, and reached England almost nine months later. By that time he had decided to adopt the name New South Wales for his discovery, and he used that name in the two copies of his journal that he wrote on the final stage of his voyage.

The London *Evening Post* of July 15, 1771 was one of several newspapers that reported "the agreeable news of the arrival in the Downs of the *Endeavour*, Captain Cooke, from the East Indies." Nine days later, the same paper carried a news story that the *Endeavour* had "discovered a Southern Continent on the latitude of the Dutch Spice Islands." The reporter had some of his details confused, but he ended his story prophetically: "In consequence of this discovery, more ships will be destined in search of this new territorial acquisition."

Cook's great and perilous voyage had finally settled the mystery of the continent's eastern coastline, and had demonstrated its separation from New Guinea, a matter in dispute for so long. Not only had his discoveries unravelled the greatest of the mysteries of the South Seas; his explorations had resulted in the greatest extent of geograhical discovery ever made at one time by any navigator.

Cook was a painstaking man, and he and Banks had recorded with exactitude the nature of the land they had visited. In his youth Cook, like his father before him, had worked on a farm, and he was keenly interested in the agricultural possibilities of the places he visited. His unhurried observations led him to sound conclusions:

> In this extensive country it can never be doubted but that most sorts of grain, fruit, roots, etc. of every kind, would flourish were they once brought hither, planted, and cultivated by the hands of industry; and here is provender for more cattle, at all seasons of the year, than ever can be brought into the country.

Such heartening descriptions of the newly discovered eastern seaboard attracted less interest in England than the bizarre nature of the animals, birds, and plants that the expedition had collected or recorded. The scientific collections were considered "the greatest treasure of natural history that ever was brought into any country at one time."

For his capable work, Cook was highly commended by the Admiralty, and was presented to the King. Joseph Banks and the botanist David Solander were also hailed as heroes and lionized by society. To a very large extent the interest of influential and learned society centred on Banks rather than on the leader of the expedition or on the great geographical discoveries that had been made. The celebrated botanist Linnaeus even wrote that the new-found country ought to be named Banksia, from its discoverer.

Almost at once Cook had to begin preparing for a second great expedition, its purpose being to circumnavigate the world in high southern latitudes.

At the time, another gifted navigator was already on his way to the southern oceans—Marion du Fresne, a Frenchman whose expedition left Cape Town in December 1771 and sailed on an easterly course at high latitudes. Du Fresne discovered Prince Edward Islands, then the Crozets (both groups far south in the Indian Ocean), and on March 3, 1772 sighted the west coast of Van Diemen's Land a little north of Port Davey. Exploring the coast that Tasman had reached 130 years before, he anchored in Frederick Henry Bay, where he found the aspect of the land "most pleasing, judging by the beauty of the countryside before us."

His party made the first contact with the island's Aborigines when officers, soldiers, and sailors landed without opposition. The savages, a member of the party recorded, had flat noses and woolly hair gathered in knotted rolls and powdered with red chalk. The tribesmen scornfully refused everything offered to them—iron, mirrors, handkerchiefs, and pieces of cloth. When du Fresne, taking a bundle of burning sticks proffered by a native, set fire to a stand made of timber, the action was misconstrued by the tribe as a sign of hostility; they attacked, and du Fresne and one of his officers were wounded. The whites embarked quickly, and moved to a new landing. Here, in a further engagement, several Aborigines were wounded and one was killed.

The expedition then left for New Zealand, where the commander and sixteen companions were killed when they landed. Others from the ships, ignorant of what had happened, then went ashore and were clubbed to death. Finally the remainder took reprisals, and numbers of Maoris were killed in encounters during which two villages were razed. After repair-work had been completed to one of the ships, the survivors sailed north, reaching Mauritius in 1773 by way of the Marianas and the Philippines. The report of the voyage was a great disappointment to the French; no trade, it seemed, would be possible with the southern lands, and no products suitable for cultivation had been found.

Meanwhile, Cook's second expedition had begun. The Admiralty considered that a systematic survey in high latitudes should be undertaken. Cook's ship, the *Resolution*, was of 452 tons; the other, the *Adventure*, 336 tons, was under the command of Captain Tobias Furneaux. After months of preparation the two vessels sailed from Plymouth in July 1772, touched Cape Town, and ran down to the Antarctic icefields, crossing the Antarctic Circle on January 17, 1773—the first in history to do so. Cook then worked north, intending to fall in with Tasman's eastward route of 1642 (about latitude 42° South) and clear up the unresolved issue of whether the land he sighted first in April 1770 was joined to Tasman's Van Diemen's Land. As he was faced with contrary winds, however, and could not pursue this course, he proceeded to New Zealand, passing south of Van Diemen's Land.

The commander of the *Adventure*, Captain Furneaux, who had parted from Cook, decided to direct his course to the land charted by Tasman. He picked up the southern extremity of Van Diemen's Land on March 9. The crew of a cutter sent ashore at Adventure Bay saw no one, even though there were signs of the inhabitants.

> The soil seems to be very rich; the country well clothed with wood. We never found more than three or four huts in a place, capable of containing three or four persons each only; and what is remarkable, we never saw the least marks either of canoe or boat, and it is generally thought they have none; being altogether, from what we could judge, a very ignorant and wretched set of people.

Nonetheless, Furneaux went on to say that the country seemed "capable of producing every necessity of life," and its climate was "the finest in the world."

He coasted north along the eastern shore in bad weather. The coast finally fell away, but he did not investigate; from his observations he was convinced that only a deep bay existed, and so he sailed off to New Zealand without discovering the strait between the island and the mainland.

The *Adventure* was at anchor in Queen Charlotte Sound when Cook arrived. Furneaux reported his opinions of the Van Diemen's Land shoreline, and although these did not convince Cook—who thought of revisiting the area to resolve the issue—the matter was left in abeyance. More than eighteen months were spent in criss-crossing the southern Pacific, one sweep taking Cook as far south as latitude 71° 10'. Most of the known islands of the entire area were visited, and some new discoveries—including New Caledonia and Norfolk Island—were made. There could be no further doubt that no enormous southern continent (apart from Australia) existed north of the Antarctic Circle.

Cook was back in New Zealand in October 1774; on November 10 he left to sail eastward along latitude 54° South; he finally rounded Cape Horn at the end of the year and reached Portsmouth on July 30, 1775. By the time he arrived Furneaux who had lost two officers and eight seamen in New Zealand, had already been home a year.

Cook's three-year voyage was recognized as one of the greatest ever undertaken. It had been carried out with the loss of only four men—three by accident and one by "a complication of disorders"—but scurvy, that great scourge of mariners, had been allayed by Cook's preventive measures.

In Cook's absence, Hawkesworth's edition of Cook's journal on the *Endeavour* voyage had been published, and Cook returned to find himself a celebrated man. He was elected to the Royal Society, and he personally prepared an account of his second voyage before setting off in July 1776 on his third and final voyage of discovery in the Pacific, in search of a north-west passage—which was still hopefully believed to exist—from the Pacific side. Sailing in the *Resolution*, in January 1777 he followed his 1772–1774 course by way of Cape Town. The following month he put into Adventure Bay, in southern Tasmania. He recorded that eight men and a boy emerged from the woods, most of them with their hair and beards smeared with "red ointment"; some also had their faces painted. "They received every present we made to them," Cook noted, "without the least appearance of satisfaction." He had grass cut to feed the animals they had aboard; he released a few pigs; and after meeting some more groups of tribesmen he put to sea, striking east to New Zealand. He then crossed to Tahiti, and in January 1778 discovered the Hawaiian Islands on his way to the frozen shores of North America. On his return to Hawaii he was killed, on February 14, 1778, in a struggle with the islanders.

With Cook's death the story of Pacific exploration and discovery came to a close. He had filled in the great blank spaces on the map, and had solved all the mysteries which had persisted for so long. Only minor details remained to be added to the map of the Pacific.

There remained the challenge of the temperate lands that Cook had visited and charted.

Part
Two

Settlement

COOK'S FIRST GREAT VOYAGE through the South Seas led to some talk in London about the value of establishing naval bases and trade centres in the Pacific, but no action was taken to follow up the expedition's discoveries by forming settlements. Commercial interests were not attracted, for it was clear that the wealth of tropic lands was missing from the area. The temperate lands Cook had discovered would involve hard pioneering, and the establishment of towns, not merely the setting-up of trading posts; and there was no compelling reason why, with the North American colonies and the West Indies open for expansion, free men should think of going to the farthest ends of the earth to open up a raw continent or islands peopled with warlike tribes. The only possibility was that the government itself might sponsor colonization.

The fact was that no British government in the past had been directly responsible for initiating the permanent settlement of any territory. The American colonial enterprises, dating back to the early seventeenth century, had been the work of individuals seeking a better life, or of companies acting with the general support of the government or under Royal charter, but none had been directly fostered by the government.

With no private or commercial interests likely to set up a pioneering enterprise in the newly charted territories, emigration from the British Isles to various American colonies went on free from any thought of the more distant places as alternatives. Not only remoteness but the very nature of the lands observed by members of Cook's expedition inhibited serious interest. New Zealand's ferocious tribesmen inspired fear, and Sir Joseph Banks wrote of New South Wales that "a soil so barren and at the same time entirely void of the helps derived from cultivation could not be supposed to yield much towards the support of man."

Thus, settlement of the remote and unproductive places did not appeal to any private group, and the British government saw no reason for action. A readiness to take possession (as Cook had done in the name of King George III, both in New Zealand and along the coast of New South Wales) did not imply a readiness to follow such action with occupation; nor did the mere declaration of possession in itself confer any substantial right.

England's acquisition of the French territories in North America at the close of the Seven Years' War had created new problems, which became ever more urgent, for the British government. With the French menace removed and with North America from the Atlantic to the Mississippi in British hands, American frontiersmen began to push westward into new terriroty, clearing the forest and driving off game, and fomenting trouble with the Indians as they did so. Soon bitter clashes developed into a general uprising of tribes along the whole frontier from the Great Lakes to Florida.

To pay for the local defence of the new empire, London decided in 1765 to raise funds by direct taxes, and by enforcing control of the colonists' trade and reintroducing a monopoly that had long been relaxed. The thirteen colonies had in fact gained a considerable measure of self-government over the preceding years as a result of the strengthening of their representative assemblies; and as almost every British law regulating the colonies interfered with some activity which was profitable to colonial groups, the issue of London's control over the colonies and their revenues became steadily more pressing in the early 1770s.

A break was inevitable. It came in the wake of a series of restrictive Acts passed by Lord North's government in 1774, and the War of Independence began in 1775 with the battle of Bunker's Hill. Within a year the Declaration of Independence had been drafted at Philadelphia. As the war dragged on, the intervention of the French—whose navy had been rebuilt—was a decisive influence in the colonies' success. It was that success which resulted in London's developing ideas for settlement in New South Wales.

Immediate pressures arose from the changes that had been taking place in England itself. There had been a marked increase in the birth-rate from the middle of the century, while improved medical knowledge and success in the battle against many dread diseases had helped to lower the deathrate of young and old alike, so that whereas there had been a population of about 6,000,000 in England and Wales in 1750, annual increases of over 300,000 were now occurring. In the rural districts, the enclosure of open fields had been gathering pace, reducing the amount of labour needed and adding greatly to the number of the dispossessed, who soon found themselves seeking work in towns and cities. Meanwhile industrial growth had accelerated with the introduction of mechanized power for mill wheels and new steam-engines. The people of European countries that had no colonial trade were drawing increasingly upon England for articles made from colonial raw materials. London and the other centres were growing rapidly; a change away from the older rural England in which four out of five people lived outside the cities and large towns was already taking place.

As more people were uprooted or found themselves struggling for an existence in London or in other cities ill-equipped to absorb them, so crime increased. The penal code was severe; but there was no effective means of coping with the problem of convicted persons except by transportation, and with the American colonies no longer available as a dumping ground, the question arose of what to do with the swelling numbers in the prisons. Previously, a thousand or more felons a year had been sent to the American colonies; with this outlet blocked at a time when the number of offenders was growing, jails were soon overflowing. In 1776 the government decided to alleviate the situation by commissioning unseaworthy ships as prisons. Hulks were moored in the Thames and in some naval harbours for the purpose. Soon stories were circulating of dangers that could arise from this innovation in the penal system. There was fear of wholesale escapes and concern at the menace of health should an epidemic of fever break out aboard overcrowded hulks.

The need to deal with the prison problem led to the development of interest in the possibility of founding a settlement in the lands that Cook had claimed. It was suggested that two objectives might be achieved with the one move: a way might be opened to ease the pressure on English prisons, and at the same time a new home might be provided for those who had been dispossessed of their fortunes in the United States because of support for the British cause during the War of Independence.

Prison congestion eventually became so acute that the British government decided to relieve it by founding a penal settlement at Botany Bay. Hopefully the government believed that at the end of three years the penal colony would be self-sufficient. There was, however, no thought of founding any great colonial enterprise.

Those who sailed with the First Fleet in 1787 were nearly all convicts or their guards. They had none of the fervour that in the seventeenth century had driven groups of English people to establish footholds on the shores of North America and go on to penetrate the wilderness there. Instead, the Botany Bay assignees were people who made the long, hazardous, and dreary trip by direction. To some it was a release from the pestilence-ridden hulks of the Thames, but it was a journey almost without hope, for it was to finish on the wild shore of what to them was the remotest of lands.

At Port Jackson, which was soon chosen as the site for settlement instead of the disapppointing Botany Bay, a tedious, heartbreaking job began as the convicts and their overseers struggled to make life bearable. The wilderness seemed absolute. It was a land that grew timber almost too tough to cut; there were no edible plants; the soil was hard, and the summer heat was trying. It was a strange world, with new conditions and unexpected situations. Not only was life different because of the emptiness of the land, but the landscape seemed alien and pallid.

To Governor Arthur Phillip, the establishment of the penal colony was an undertaking of duty; he graced it with his personal dedication and a benevolence unusual in his day. To those under Phillip, the assignment was an obligation to be accepted dutifully—but it was not an undertaking to anyone's particular liking. Most of those who accompanied Phillip were men whose training had done little to qualify them to deal with the practical problems and challenge of taming the wilderness. The care of the few surviving livestock and plants, and the sowing of crops, were in the hands of men who had little experience in such matters.

Rocky or unfertile soil seemed to predominate along the shores of Port Jackson. Instead of the little settlement rapidly becoming a self-supporting enterprise, crops were poor, supplies were often short, and rations had to be cut severely. Phillip was a man of vision, as well as a tolerant and capable leader; faced with the barrenness of the prospect about him, he urged London to send him farmers and other free men who might set about the practical tasks. He believed that only by the addition of such people could the penal settlement become self-supporting. The Colonial Office, however, was content to keep to the original purpose of maintaining a penal colony, and it was not quickly impressed by Phillip's pleas. Once launched, the Port Jackson venture was almost forgotten in London.

The first harbourside attempts to grow grain failed, but Phillip persevered, and when better land was found to the west, near the Parramatta river, crops of wheat and maize were grown. The first attempts at farming were all run by the administration. From the beginning it had been intended, however, that the governor should make grants of land to convicts who had served their sentences, as well as to marines and seamen who wished to take their discharge in the colony, and to "others who may resort thither on their private occupations . . . hereafter." Accordingly, after the first experimental land grant to an ex-convict had proved successful, Phillip made grants to a number of ex-convicts and ex-servicemen. At the end of 1792 when he left the colony, 67 of these farmer-settlers were cultivating land on the mainland, and 102 at Norfolk Island. Almost twice as much land was still being farmed by the government as by private farmers, however.

The first real advance in the settlement's economy came when more private farms were set up, during the period when the colony was administered by the commanding officer of the New South Wales Corps, the military garrison which succeeded the marines. Grants of land were made to the first free immigrants, who arrived early in 1793, and to the very few other free men who followed them. More importantly, a change of policy allowed the lieutenant-governor to grant land to military and civil officers still serving in the colony. Major Francis Grose appointed as Inspector of Public Works one of his officers, John Macarthur, who thus became virtual dictator of the colony's labour supply. The officer-farmers were allowed the services of convict-labourers, who were fed and clothed by the commissary, in numbers greatly exceeding those that had been allowed to settlers in Phillip's time. Progress was rapid under the new form of estate agriculture. Almost 3,000 acres were put into cultivation during the first seventeen months of the military administration (as against 1,703 acres in Phillip's time) and two years later the total crop of wheat and maize had expanded to a point where it represented a full year's supply for the little colony. Mills were set up and New South Wales, with just over 4,000 people, was producing sufficient grain to be self-supporting for the time being.

This was not solely because of the efficiency of the private-enterprise farmers. During the two years and nine months of the military administration, only 400 convicts were landed in the colony, compared with the 4,000, many of them too sick to work, who arrived during Phillip's administration. So the farming community had to feed a population whose numbers remained practically unchanged, instead of one subject to sudden enormous increases, which had been Phillip's problem in 1790 and 1791. Even so, shortages occurred and grain still had to be imported.

The sharp decrease in convict-immigration was due to the commencement of Britain's war with Revolutionary France, a war which continued when the young General Bonaparte took over the government of the country. The war took very different patterns at land and at sea. France won victory after victory on land, while at sea the English navy captured most of the overseas possessions of France (notably in the West Indies) and of her ally Holland (Cape Colony, Ceylon, Guiana). When a compromise peace was signed at Amiens in 1802, Britain returned most of the colonies she had captured; Cape Colony was returned to the Dutch, but Ceylon remained British. It was an uneasy peace, and no one really expected it to last. So when, towards the end of the year, a French scientific expedition appeared in Australian waters, the authorities promptly ordered settlements to be made in the north and south of Van Diemen's Land, as a deterrent to possible French annexation. These were the first settlements beyond New South Wales (apart from Norfolk Island) and they were planned, carried out, and controlled by the administration; a limited number of convicts accompanied the expeditions, to provide the labour necessary for their maintenance.

The peace of Amiens lasted only a year. When hostilities began again, a French squadron was operating in the Indian Ocean, based on the strong and heavily fortified Île de France (Mauritius), now the only French possession in the area. In sending out this squadron Bonaparte had hoped to persuade the Indian rulers into an alliance that would drive the British out of India; he had no thought whatsoever of attacking the lightly held British colony in Sydney, nor of acquiring any territory in Australia. The safety of British India, and the control of the routes to India, were fundamentals of British policy. There was a saying that "Whichever Power has the Cape [of Good Hope] may govern India." No one at this time would have dreamed of adding that this power might also govern New South Wales; yet in making safe the route to great, rich, and valuable India, the British navy also ensured the safety of the new and despised little penal settlement at Port Jackson.

Nelson's victory at Trafalgar gave Britain the control of the seas, of which the first fruit was the recapture of the Cape of Good Hope in 1806. In the years that followed, the British navy patrolled the seas of the world, recapturing the French and Dutch colonies she had given up at Amiens. While Napoleon was reshaping the map of Europe, the British navy was redrawing the map of the world.

Only once in those years did the Emperor Napoleon's thoughts turn to New South Wales; in 1810, when he started to fit out a naval squadron for the Indian Ocean, he sent the Governor of Île de France instructions to "take the English colony of Jackson." Britain's control of the sea mocked his plans: the squadron never left France. Île de France, under heavy blockade, surrendered, and was followed by the Dutch colonies in the East Indies.

By the end of the war the British navy had swept all opponents out of the Indian Ocean, and the congress of Vienna in 1815 confirmed this dominance, even though the East Indies were returned to the Dutch, and Bourbon and Madagascar to the French. A few years later Britain purchased Singapore from the Sultan of Johore, and established the island as the guardian of the north-east gateway of the Indian Ocean, providing another link in the chain of bases all the way from the English Channel to Sydney and Hobart. Although the Australian settlements were militarily indefensible, the British mastery of the sea provided a curtain of security behind which they would be able to shelter without serious fear of attack from the sea for nearly a century to come.

Before long, the military outposts in Van Diemen's Land had hardened into penal compounds, where the harshest of punishments were meted out, especially to the worst and most vicious criminals. Rural activities spread nevertheless, and freebooters offshore won wealth from whaling and sealing, their vessels coming in for repair or refitting. Once a great area of the island's massive forests had been cleared, the better soil and heavier rainfall than that near Sydney made farming more productive, and from 1815 onwards Van Diemen's Land was able to export grain to New South Wales.

Largely because of the character of the penal establishments, the lieutenant-governor's control in Van Diemen's Land was still more autocratic than that of the governor in New South Wales, where governors who followed the two commandants of the New South Wales Corps found their authority challenged whenever their actions threatened the interests of determined and assertive men.

In the final analysis the colonies were each subject to British law, yet the governor possessed extraordinary powers and the individual who opposed him, no matter how wealthy or powerful, had no legal way of securing redress within the colony. At the same time, during the three years in which New South Wales had been administered by the military commandant, the military and civil officers had acquired a practical monopoly of trade and land that virtually gave them economic control of the colony. This division of power led to extreme tension, with successive naval governors attempting to check abuses, and men of wealth and influence countering with intrigues and appeals to politicians and administrators in London. In the power-struggle that developed, the governors felt their authority was being undermined; and while a counter-force remained among officers of the New South Wales Corps the governor's ability to enforce his authority was indeed in jeopardy—as Governor William Bligh found to his anguish when the issue came to its climactic point in his clash with John Macarthur.

It was clear that proper control could not be exercised while the Corps remained, and in 1810 it was replaced by the 73rd Regiment of Highlanders whose colonel, Lachlan Macquarie, became the new governor. Macquarie concentrated his attention on immediate issues, and in the early years of his rule his firm control, practical administration, and commercial reforms brought the colony out of the confusion that had beset it.

It was still mainly a convict colony. As yet New South Wales—much the farthest from England of any colony—could have little attraction for the free immigrant, even if it had not carried the old stigma of the "thief colony." For twenty of the colony's first twenty-seven years England was at war; all available shipping was needed to police the seas; men were needed for the armies and navies; and the authorities frowned on the emigration of men with skill or capital. Very few free settlers made the long and often harrowing voyage to the colony. And it was just as hard for convicts to get back as it was for free settlers to arrive. In theory the men and women convicts who had served their sentences were free to return to England; but ships were few, fares were expensive, and so it was inevitable that the great majority of ex-convicts should remain in the colony.

When Macquarie arrived in New South Wales at least five out of every six inhabitants of the colony were convicts or ex-convicts; and the convict preponderance was even greater when he left the colony twelve years later. The close of the war in 1815 brought an increase in the numbers of free immigrants; but this was completely outweighed by the postwar resumption of transportation on a much larger scale than ever before.

More than 18,500 convicts were sent to Australia from 1814 to 1821. Macquarie's first consideration had to be the accommodation, the employment, and the welfare of these newcomers and of their predecessors who by now had gained their freedom "by servitude" or were conditionally free, mainly on tickets of leave. Dour, stubborn, and unswayed by any consideration but that of operating the colony as a vast reformatory, the governor made the rehabilitation of convicted persons his overrriding objective. He did not look beyond immediate issues. Because of this restrictive outlook, to which he held more and more rigidly as time passed, he tended to favour the emancipists at the expense of the free settlers, to oppose any increase of free immigration, and to ignore the expansive constructive forces that were already beginning to shape the next phase of the colony's economy.

The man who represented these forces was the officer-farmer John Macarthur, who as early as 1802 had written that the colony's future depended on "raising as an export some raw material which would be produced with little labour, but in considerable amount, and be capable of bearing the expenses of a long sea voyage." He found this product in fine wool. When he first showed his Spanish wool fleeces to wool-spinners in England in 1804, their enthusiasm for the quality of the fleeces induced the Secretary of State to grant Macarthur 5,000 acres of land, the largest grant made up to that time. Back in Australia in 1806, Macarthur estimated that in twenty years New South Wales could produce almost twice as much wool as England was then purchasing from Spain. In a report for the Secretary of State he wrote:

What [ever] the demands of Great Britain may be for that commodity [fine wool] we certainly may supply it. The universal use of machinery might then be safely sanctioned. and the British manufacturers would be enabled so to reduce the price of woollen cloths as would secure throughout the world the most complete monopoly that any people ever possessed.

Macarthur returned to England again in 1809, this time in contention because of his part in the rebellion against Governor Bligh. He was still there in 1813, when the hitherto impenetrable Blue Mountains were crossed, opening the way to vast new grasslands in the interior. He was still in England when the long war ended in 1815. Business revived with the coming of peace, and the Yorkshire wool-spinners began to demand ever-increasing quantities of fine wool, a demand that could be only partly met by the war-ravished traditional European sources. Macarthur was convinced that New South Wales could fulfil this demand, and his return to the colony in 1817 gave a stimulus to the development of wool-growing. Thus, thirty years after the establishment of the settlement, wool was already revealing its significance, though Governor Macquarie still failed to perceive its value.

By this time the governor's rigid concept of the colony as a large-scale reformatory was beginning to be outmoded in London. The fact was that new prospects were opening, and ambitious and assertive men were persuading Westminster that, after more than thirty years of authoritarian control, New South Wales should be seen in a new light, and a way opened for private capital to develop the land. Van Diemen's Land, although still cramped and constrained, was nevertheless able to share in the progressive measures introduced in the early 1820s to bring broader influences into the administration of affairs. The political aspect was changed with the establishment in New South Wales and Van Diemen's Land of nominated councils—in each case consisting of a few leading citizens—to advise the Governor. On the economic side, a new system of large land grants opened the way for private capital to develop the land.

By the end of Macquarie's term of office, the economy of New South Wales had reached a point where developments were increasingly under the influence of private enterprise rather than that of Government. Macquarie was the last governor able to impose a personal stamp on the colony. The expansionist phase that followed his departure was shaped primarily by private investment. Occupation spread over the hinterland behind Sydney, for sheep were found to flourish on the sweet grasses that grew there, and money was freely available to support the expansion. Wealthy private individuals and jointstock companies, with their greater resources, both with lavish government encouragement, were the entrepreneurs of new colonial enterprises that were to sweep New South Wales forward into the opening stage of independent colonial development, before more than a small fraction of the continent had even been explored, much less occupied.

As New South Wales moved forward to a burgeoning future based on wool, new footholds were being established at scattered points around the periphery of the continent. The first of these, like those in Van Diemen's Land, were established for political reasons to satisfy military fears and were direct offshoots of the Sydney administration; some of them were abandoned when the military situation eased. Then, in the far west at the end of the 1820s, and in South Australia a few years later, experimental colonizing enterprises were set up, direct from London, with funds provided by private investors in England and with governmental approval and some governmental backing. In each case, overriding control soon had to be assumed by the British government, and the machinery of colonial administration provided as part of a carefully planned settlement programme.

Although in New South Wales the sheep-owners were establishing themselves as the true masters of the colony's destinies by the mid-1820s, the initial processes of development still had to be undertaken in each of the new and isolated settlements. The various phases, from the process of establishment to that of individual enterprise, were not simultaneous in the different colonies. Each new settlement in turn brought to light the basic problems that had to be faced in the struggle to establish any outpost in the raw land of Australia. Theorizing in the security of London was one thing; carrying the ideas into effect thousands of miles away in the wilderness another. In spite of good intentions and excellent paperwork, the enterprises went through difficult and almost calamitous times as each in turn faced the same fundamental problem of trying to begin economic development so that a viable economy might be created.

Thus by circumstances, official enterprise, as opposed to private enterprise, was an important factor in the early formative years in each of the colonies planted from London or under official auspices from Sydney. Government support, either in the form of actual control of affairs or as an intervention in the final crisis, was the crucial factor in maintaining activity. The significance of this official involvement was not quickly forgotten, and the part played by the government was to leave a deep impression on each community.

Botany Bay 3
and Sydney Town

Accounts of Captain Cook's voyage which began appearing in London soon after the *Endeavour's* return to England in July 1771 created widespread interest and brought to notice an area that had remained almost a void in men's minds. The expedition had not only defined thousands of miles of coastline previously unrecorded but it had made the most astonishing discoveries in natural history. It was inevitable that such an event should touch off intense speculation and discussion about the remote lands revealed in the antipodes, and throughout the 1770s London society found the subject one for reflection and discourse.

The first short, 130-page, journal of the voyage was published only two months or so after Cook's return. The author was, according to his publisher, "a gentleman and a scholar who made the voyage." This was followed two years later by the illustrated record of Sydney Parkinson, the expedition's draughtsman, and then by the official version, based on Cook's journal and Banks's papers, and prepared at the request of the Admiralty by John Hawkesworth with wordy embellishments. A second edition of the Hawkesworth version was soon on the market, and French, American, and German editions followed. Cook had left on his second great voyage before the first edition appeared; on his return in 1775 he found himself an important public figure.

Hawkesworth's volumes covered earlier British voyages in the south Pacific besides Cook's—those of Commodore Byron, Captain Wallis, and Captain Carteret—but naturally it was the section dealing with the recent voyage of the *Endeavour* that attracted most attention. Since it dealt with such outlandish places, many readers were incredulous, and John Wesley, who began to read it with "huge expectation," was one who refused to accept its veracity, saying, "I cannot but rank this narrative with that of *Robinson*

Crusoe." Cook, who was not happy with the liberties Hawkesworth had taken with the material given him, prepared the text of his report on his second voyage. With its publication Cook moved to the centre of the spotlight; and after his death in 1778 he became a legend.

By this time, speculation about the south Pacific area was taking new forms. Increasingly, attention was being given to the thought that something should be done about occupying the newly charted lands, and in conversation and discussion in coffee houses, and in pamphlets, the prospect was canvassed of sending prisoners to them. There appeared to be reasonable prospects for settlement. Cook's view had been that in both New Zealand and New South Wales every kind of grain, fruit, and plants would thrive, and he saw no serious impediment to settlement.

When a committee of the House of Commons was appointed in 1779 to consider the problem of dealing with convicts who could no longer be sent to the American colonies, Banks was one of the people who gave evidence. Asked which distant part of the globe would be most suitable if it was decided to found a "colony of convicted persons," Banks said that he thought that Botany Bay would be the best. He now believed a colony there could be self-supporting even though he had noted in his journal, written during the voyage of the *Endeavour*, that New South Wales was the most barren country he had seen. He had also noted that water was scarce, and that the timber of the trees was so hard that carpenters who cut down the trees complained that they damaged their tools. Distance had lent enchantment to his memories of Botany Bay, however, and he no longer tended to dwell on such drawbacks to settlement.

Nothing came of the committee's inquiry; the government was still preoccupied with the American War of Independence—and still hoping that convicts might one day again be sent to the recalcitrant colonies. Interest in the southern lands faded as that war dragged on.

Throughout the war, loyalists—those who were devoted to the royal cause—endured sufferings and losses at the hands of the militant colonists, and they hastened to seek shelter, either in Canada or by crossing the Atlantic. The authorities in London spent large sums on resettling them and supporting them. Their numbers continued to grow, and their plight attracted increasing attention. In 1783, James Mario Matra, an American-born midshipman who had sailed with Cook, suggested to Lord Sydney, the Home Secretary, that New South Wales would "afford asylum" for the thousands who, following the victory of the secessionists, were deprived of their possessions and were seeking a new home. There, under British protection, Matra declared, these people who had lost everything in the British cause might build up new estates and new fortunes.

Lord Sydney decided that Matra's suggestion for a settlement in New Holland had little value so far as it might affect the loyalists, but it appealed to him as a possible solution to the even more troublesome problem of what to do about the convicts crowding jails and prison-hulks as they awaited transportation. Lord Sydney discussed the matter with Matra, who then added a postscript to his proposal, drawing attention to the abundant possibilities for setting up a penal colony in New Holland.

The concept was supported in a detailed plan submitted a year or two later by Admiral Sir George Young, who considered that a government-sponsored settlement could solve the convict issue and at the same time assist in the development of British trade. He declared that "a territory so happily situated must be superior to all others for establishing a very extensive commerce, and of consequence must greatly increase our shipping and number of seamen." The admiral considered it no disadvantage that New Holland was so far from England; its very distance meant that by sending convicts there the homeland would be rid of them "for ever."

The need for a solution to the prison problem became ever more pressing. It was a time of upheaval in British society when the beginnings of the economic revolution were being felt, and insecurity arising from long years of war and high prices, with famine and crowding, was creating special problems. Crime had increased, and there were by now tens of thousands of prisoners in England under sentence of transportation; a way had to be found to relieve the situation.

Sites on the west African coast were considered for penal settlements, and some groups of convicts were landed there—only to be overwhelmed by pestilence, plague, or famine. The government, under sharp criticism for sending convicted people and their jailers to almost certain death in such places, decided to turn instead to Botany Bay. Isolation would make it possible to set up a prison without bars where the convicted person could be set free and might become self-supporting. Because of an absence of commercial prospects, there would be no mercantile speculators to interfere. The government woud be responsible for everything.

In 1786 Lord Sydney, with some guidance from Banks, had legislation passed to authorize the establishment of the settlement. The expectation was that the whole enterprise would be self-supporting, so that there would be little cost involved to the government in the long run. The claims of displaced loyalists did not appear in the enactment, and in the royal speech to Parliament the proposed undertaking was described simply as a means of removing "the inconvenience which arose from the crowded state of the gaols in different parts of the Kingdom."

The only strong opposition to the foundation of such a settlement came from the East India Company. The company's monopoly of trading rights—extending across the Indian and Pacific Oceans from the Cape of Good Hope to the Straits of Magellan—was zealously guarded, and when proposals for the Botany Bay settlement were first put forward the company made its opposition known in high places. After it became clear that the foundation of the settlement was imminent, the company's concern became greater. An anonymous pamphlet, obviously inspired by the company, was published in London in 1786 as "a serious admonition to the public." It bitterly condemned the government for not consulting the company's court of directors.

before deciding to plant a "thief colony" in New South Wales.

The government was, however, ready to proceed. The settlement was to be a penal colony, nothing more. To lead the expedition and to set up and administer the settlement, Lord Sydney chose Captain Arthur Phillip, aged forty-eight, a naval officer of wide experience and some knowledge of farming. In October 1786 Phillip began organizing the expedition. He worked with meticulous care and great foresight on the preparations for the undertaking. He saw the venture as one of higher purpose than merely ridding England of unwanted subjects: he hoped to found a colony that would endure. In his instructions, flax was mentioned as a plant that should be grown as an article for export, and the expectation was that the land would grow sufficient food to supply the garrison and the convicts—without much cost to the government.

Phillip's appointment was as "governor and commander-in-chief of the territory of New South Wales and of his Majesty's ships and vessels on the coast." His domain extended from Cape York in the north to the southern extremity of Van Diemen's Land—still thought to be part of the continent—and westward as far as longitude 135° (200 miles west of the present boundary of Queensland and the Northern Territory) together with islands, including New Zealand, adjacent in the Pacific Ocean. The force of marines accompanying the expedition was to provide against attack by the Aborigines, and to guard the settlement from other danger.

Two naval vessels were provided, and the Admiralty commissioned transports to convey about 750 convicts to Botany Bay. Provisions sufficient to feed the settlement for two years were placed on board. It was imagined that after the first year, half the settlement's requirements would be produced locally, so that in the second and third year, only one complete year's rations would be needed. Then, so it was hopefully estimated, "local industry would be fully sufficient" to sustain the settlement.

On May 13, 1787, the founding expedition of eleven vessels —the First Fleet—sailed from the Mother Bank, off the Isle of Wight. Phillip sailed as commodore in H.M.S. *Sirius* (formerly the *Berwick*), in which Captain John Hunter was commander. The tender H.M.S. *Supply* was under Lieutenant Ball, and there were three store ships and six transports carrying the prisoners. On each ship, officers of the Marine Corps were responsible for convict health and discipline. At Rio de Janeiro, plants and seeds—including seeds of coffee, cotton, guava, banana, orange, lemon, tamarind, and prickly pear—were acquired; at the Cape of Good Hope more seeds and a wide variety of fruit trees and plants were added, and some 500 domestic animals—mainly cattle and horses—were taken on board.

On November 25, when well clear of the Cape, Phillip transferred to the *Supply* and, with engineers and artificers, moved ahead in order to choose a place for the reception of the fleet. Three transports followed, and the other vessels remained with Hunter. The route lay south of Van Diemen's Land, then northward to Botany Bay.

The *Supply* reached Botany Bay on January 18, 1788, and on this midsummer morning the first impressions were disappointing. The "green meadows" of 1770 had become sterile lands or barren swamps, and Phillip felt that the bay itself, though extensive, was dangerously open to the full sweep of easterly winds and the heavy seas that ran before them. The vessel anchored a little distance from land. Forty or so Aborigines were near the south shore, catching fish. On seeing the ship, the men moved to the beach and dragged their canoes ashore, while the women gathered the children and ran off into the bush. Only a handful of men remained, challenging the intruders and calling to them to be gone, and brandishing spears and clubs. Very few Aborigines appeared on the northern shore of the bay, and it was here that Captain Phillip prepared to land. The small band showed such unrelieved hostility, however, that the party decided to row along the shore to a spot where Phillip hoped he might get water, and when this quest proved unsuccessful the party rowed back to the ship. By this time more men armed with spears and clubs had gathered, gazing in amazement at the ship, and restive at the white men's intrusion. By signs Phillip indicated that he was seeking water; but it was not until he left the boat, handed his musket to a seaman, and fearlessly walked toward the group offering presents as he went, that his friendly intentions were understood. A leader stepped forward from the group and, putting his spear aside, led Phillip and his men to a stream near by.

Next day, the three transports arrived. Supplies of hay were almost exhausted, and at once a party of men set to work to cut grass and take it aboard to feed the cattle. Phillip moved to the southern shore, and when some Aborigines came into sight he went forward alone to meet them. Bunches of leaves were carried by the Aborigines as a sign of friendship, and when this gesture was reciprocated they put aside their spears. When the sailors gave them pieces of gaily coloured cloth and paper, beads, and other small objects, they showed themselves to be skilled mimics. Some sounds delighted them, others frightened them; they were happy to listen to the fife, but drums caused them to retreat hastily.

Phillip coasted along the shore for many miles, noting two streams which entered the bay. He went six miles up one that came in from the northeast. He saw many native fishermen on the banks and some bark shelters on the land back from the river. For the first time he noticed that the Aborigines had dogs, which were covered with long shaggy hair.

The following day, January 20, the *Sirius* reached Botany Bay with the remainder of the fleet. Phillip was already convinced that a search should be undertaken for a more suitable spot for settlement; there were difficulties or drawbacks at each point along the shores of Botany Bay. He decided to examine the coast to the north in the hope of finding a better site, and next day he set out with Collins and Hunter. The three open boats sailed close to the land in heavy swell as they edged along the Pacific shore, with the intention of exploring the opening, 16 miles to the north, that Cook had marked on his chart and named Port Jackson.

At the rocky headlands marking the entrance, groups of Aborigines gathered and excitedly shouted and gesticulated as they moved along abreast of the boats. The boats passed from rolling swells into quieter water

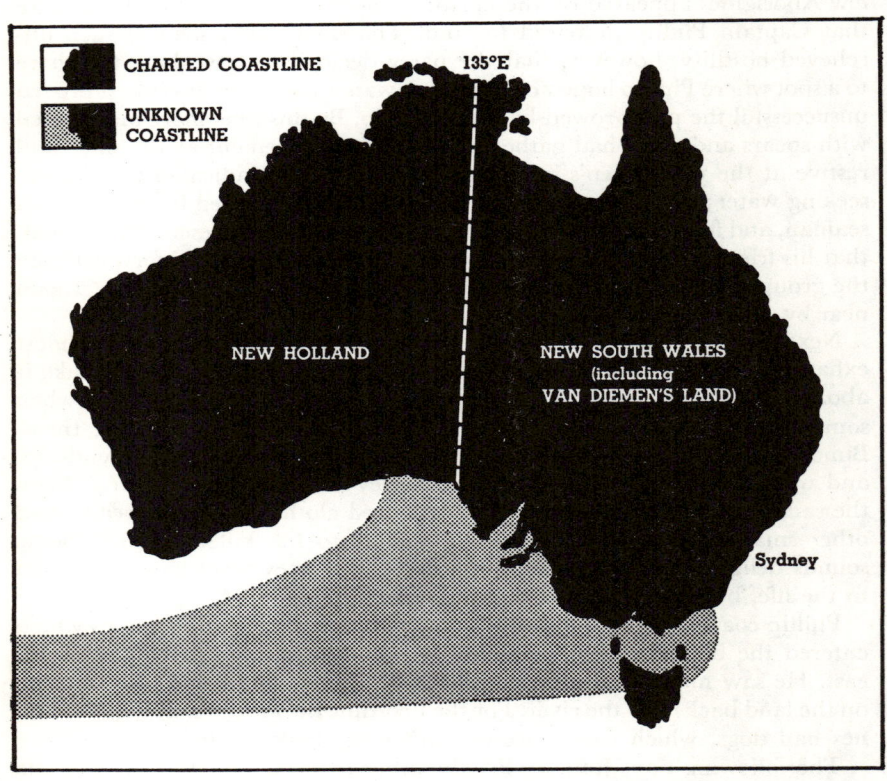

CHARTED COASTLINE

UNKNOWN COASTLINE

135°E

NEW HOLLAND

NEW SOUTH WALES
(including
VAN DIEMEN'S LAND)

Sydney

Discovery to 1788.—Cook in the *Endeavour* sailed along and charted the entire east coast in 1770, taking possession of all land east of 135°E. longitude; and in 1788 settlement began at Sydney. The sailing route was south of Van Diemen's Land; the existence of a water route north of the island was not known.

as they entered the great harbour early in the afternoon—a harbour with many bays and coves, some marked by yellow sands and some by rocky points, many of them clothed to the water's edge with soft green foliage. Back from the water the ridges were covered with tall trees.

Phillip realized at once that somewhere along the shores of this splendid, safe harbour would be the place for the new settlement—the first ever to be made by Englishmen in the southern hemisphere. The deeply indented inlet was, he wrote in his first dispatch, "the finest harbour in the world, in which a thousand sail of the line may ride in the most perfect security." The governor and his party examined several coves until they found one where the water close to the shore was deep and there was running stream. He named this Sydney Cove, in honour of the Home Secretary, and called the stream of fresh water the Tanks, a name later changed to the Tank Stream.

The survey of Port Jackson went on for three days. Phillip was pleased to find that there was no hostility on the part of the Aborigines. A tribal "chief," who accompanied Phillip as he inspected the camp where the seamen were preparing food, appeared to the commander as courageous and intelligent. At another point a group waded into the water to accept gifts from Phillip, and their bearing so impressed him that he named the spot Manly Cove. On January 23 the party returned to Botany Bay, arriving toward evening. Directions were given for a transfer of the expedition to Port Jackson. As preparations were being made the following morning, much to the surprise of Phillip's party, two strange vessels appeared offshore.

The vessels were *La Boussole* and *L'Astrolabe*, under the Comte de La Pérouse. The expedition had left France in 1785. La Pérouse knew of the intended settlement at Botany Bay, and after visiting rocky Norfolk Island (which one of his officers described as "a place fit only for angels and eagles to reside in") he had decided to proceed there. After the French vessels' first arrival off the coast of Botany Bay, variable winds and contrary currents forced them southward of their reckoning. La Pérouse wrote:

> We did not get in to Botany Bay till the 26th, at nine in the morning. I let go the anchor at a mile from the north coast in 7 fathoms of water. At the moment I was at the mouth of the channel, an English lieutenant and a midshipman were sent on board my ship by Captain Hunter. They offered me in his name all the services in his power, adding, however, that as he was on the point of getting under way to run to the northward, circumstances did not permit him to furnish us either with provisions, ammunition, or sails; so that his services were confined to wishes for the further success of our voyage. I sent an officer to return my thanks to Captain Hunter, who was already apeak, with his top sails hoisted. I intimated to him that my wants did not go beyond wood and water, of which we should find plenty in the bay; and that I realized that ships destined to establish a colony at so great a distance from Europe could not afford to succour navigators.

Phillip wasted no time in getting to Port Jackson with the *Supply*, arriving on Friday, January 25. Early the following day a party landed at Sydney Cove; and during the afternoon Hunter entered the harbour and anchored close by the shore. Towards sundown a formal ceremony took place ashore; the flag was raised, toasts to the King were drunk, and volleys fired.

Ground had to be cleared so that tents could be raised. The great adventure of setting up a settlement in a new continent—and, indeed, in a sector of the globe that had remained unchanged for ages—was in fact a somewhat dreary and unexciting undertaking for those who set about the task. For the voyagers, after eight months at sea in cramped quarters, and with their clothes ragged and stiff with salt and grime, the early days were full of difficulty and confusion. Only under strict supervision could the convicts be induced to work.

The task of setting up a planned, orderly little town began. As provisions were taken ashore, timber was cut for building purposes and for firewood, a forge was set up, and officers paraded their men.

On March 9 the surgeon, John White, recorded that the principal business then in progress was the erection of cabbage-tree huts for officers, soldiers, and convicts, some store-houses, and a "very good" hospital. The foundation stone of a house for the governor had been laid. A few weeks later Dr White commented on the difficulty of securing timber for building purposes. "It will scarcely be credited," he wrote, "when I declare that I have known twelve men employed for five days in grubbing one tree; and when this has been effected the timber has been fit only for firewood." By July, huts had been completed for some of the convicts, although the governor as well as the civilian and military officers and the marines were still under canvas.

The countryside was open and interspersed with trees, "resembling the woody parts of a deer park in England." But the sun was hot and the ground was hard. The familiar English trees and shrubs were absent; in their place were plants of a different nature—trees of harsher timber, with sparse, dull-toned foliage, and grass that had been seared by a long dry summer. Cook's description of Botany Bay seemed incongruous, and Dr White felt constrained to write, after a party had made an extensive survey of the shores of the bay, that "that great navigator, notwithstanding his usual accuracy and candour, was certainly too lavish in his praises of Botany Bay." Another member of the group wrote:

> Had not the nautical part of Mr Cook's description, in which we include the latitude and longitude of the bay, been so accurately laid down, there would exist the utmost reason to believe that those who have described the contiguous country had never seen it.

Little about the setting appeared attractive, and few could appreciate the scene. Most of the newcomers were there not by choice but by direction. The convicts numbered 520 men and 197 women; the rest were soldiers and officials sent to watch over them. The staff of officers, marines, and extra hands, with their families, numbered 290.

On the first Sunday ashore, divine service was conducted in the shade of a spreading gum tree by Reverend Richard Johnson, the chaplain of the settlement, who preached a sermon from the 116th psalm, verse 12, "What shall I render unto the Lord for all his benefits towards us?" Johnson celebrated the first baptism on the same day. It was on February 7 that David Collins, the Judge-Advocate, read before an assemblage of all ashore—

except the deserters who had escaped at Botany Bay and had disappeared—the Captain-General's commission and the Letters Patent setting up the courts. Captain Phillip took the oaths as Governor-in-Chief, and Major Robert Ross, commanding officer of the Marines, as Lieutenant-Governor.

The letters patent contained provisions for setting up courts of civil and criminal justice, both of which were to be conducted by the Judge-Advocate asisted by a panel of officers. The colony thus became subject to British jurisdiction, though not as yet heir to British judicial procedures. Phillip had the confidence of the authorities in London, and the powers entrusted to him were exceptionally wide. He could sentence, reprieve, or pardon those under his charge, he could regulate trade, make grants of land, make appointments, erect buildings and fortifications, direct the labour of the convicts, and distribute supplies and equipment as he saw fit.

Phillip looked upon the people of the outpost in his charge as though they were a ship's company. The Commissary, who kept the accounts and was responsible for distributing the rations of food and clothing, was like the purser on board ship; the chaplain and governor's secretary had their equivalents in a ship of the line. The governor struggled to instil a sense of orderliness in a setting where none existed; but the tasks he assigned to all and sundry were not always discharged satisfactorily. His own staff gave him loyal support, but Major Ross and the marines were completely uncooperative. After ten months in the colony, the major let off steam in a letter for the "private perusal" of the Under Secretary of State; he began with a sneer at the governor—"he has, I daresay, described this country as capable of being made the Empire of the East"—and continued with a long tirade:

> I do not scruple to pronounce that in the whole world there is not a worse country than that we have yet seen of this. All that is contiguous to us is so very barren and forbidding that it may with truth be said that here nature is reversed; if not so, she is nearly worn out, for almost all the seed we have put into the ground has rotted and I have no doubt but will, like the wood of this vile country when burned or rotten, turn to sand. This latter is a fact that has been proved and will, I much fear, be fatally felt by some of its present inhabitants. I say the present because if the Minister has a true and just description given him of it, he will not surely think of sending any more people here. If he does, I shall not scruple to say that he will entail more misery on all that are sent and an expense on the mother country that in the days of her greatest prosperity she was not equal to, for there is not one article that can ever be necessary for use by men but which must be imported into this country.

Following the lead of their commanding officer, the marines refused to help in the work of getting the settlement on its feet. Contending they had been sent to New South Wales merely to perform garrison duties, the officers even declined to serve on the judicial courts; in fact, at one time, out of a mainland staff of sixteen marine officers, two were under suspension and five under arrest by their commandant. Their principal garrison duty was to protect the colony against the spears and clubs of the Aborigines.

Phillip, who saw to it that the Aborigines were not molested, realized that there was always some danger that the little settlement might come under surprise attack from them, particularly as the tribesmen had quarrelled frequently with the French during La Perouse's sojourn. Once, in the dead of night, sentries were aroused when the voices of Aborigines were heard near their post, but when the bells of the ships in the harbour were struck and sentries exchanged assurances, the tribesmen fell silent and soon afterward moved off into the night. The settlement's preparedness had thwarted any plans they might have entertained for an attack, and no further incident took place.

When the Aborigines realized that the white intruders were not mere visitors but were there to stay, most of them withdrew from the settlement area. Although they had been curious about the turn of events when the settlers first came ashore, their established ways gave them no role in the white man's ventures. They now gave themselves up once again to their fishing and their quest for game, for, without cultivating the land, they managed to secure all the food they needed from fruits, roots, animals, honey, and fish. Phillip must have wished that his charges could do as well. From the onset, the food problem was acute. The poor soil in the area immediately about Sydney Cove and inefficient labour thwarted Phillip's efforts to make the enterprise self-supporting. Acting on orders given him before he left England to settle Norfolk Island as soon as practicable, "to prevent it being occupied by the subjects of any other European power," in February Phillip sent Lieutenant Philip Gidley King in the *Supply*, with a party of two naval men, six other free men, and fifteen convicts, to form a settlement there. They carried livestock and seed, and provisions for six months. On arrival at Norfolk Island, the group at once set about clearing a site, and building began. A few months later a second party of convicts was sent to the island.

The transfers to Norfolk Island meant that Phillip was left with fewer people in Sydney. His problem of feeding the settlement was scarcely diminished, however; he found little land around the shores of Port Jackson suitable for cultivation. His searches farther afield proved no more helpful; in March he had rowed north along the coast to Broken Bay seeking cultivable land, but heavy rains had forced him to return, and he had failed to find the great river flowing into the estuary. In June the small herd of cattle in the settlement strayed and were lost. Other livestock had dwindled in numbers. The danger of famine was already present. Many of the animals and poultry birds shipped to the colony had died on the voyage, and those that survived were a pitiful collection. The pasture was so sparse and poor that only ten of the forty-four sheep survived the first few weeks.

Meanwhile the wheat, rice, and barley which had been sown at Farm Cove under Phillip's orders failed to thrive. The hard rocky soil was very different from England's well-tilled fields, and the harsh, almost rainless Australian summer contrasted with the mild English season. Most of Phillip's charges were disinclined to work; many were old and infirm. The convicts hid or destroyed tools issued to them, robbed the commissary stores, and tried to plan ways of escape. Since the officers and men of the marine corps considered they were "not sent out to do more than the duty as soldiers," the duties of supervising the convict labourers and seeing supplies issued had to be entrusted to selected convicts; and, Phillip commented ruefully, "The convicts who are proper for this are those who have had some little education, and they are the greatest villians we have."

For his part, Phillip was confident, even though he recognized the dangers that arose from the lack of capable farmers and artisans, the poor quality of tools, and the shortage of supplies. Phillip realized that if the new settlement were to become a self-supporting colony, the people sent to it would have to be chosen with greater care. "I hope few convicts will be sent out for a year at least, except carpenters, masons, and bricklayers, or farmers who can support themselves and assist in supporting others," he wrote in a dispatch. "If fifty farmers were sent out with their families, they would do more in one year in rendering this country independent of the mother-country as to provisions, than a thousand convicts." But such reiterated requests met with little response from Whitehall.

Meat and vegetables were always in short supply. Vegetables were grown on some of the small islands in the harbour, close to Farm Cove, on which soil was good. Scanty supplies of salted meat could be supplemented with fish, birds, or kangaroo-meat, but the colony was still dependent on overseas shipping for its survival.

The departure of the convict transports and supply ships left the colony with only two ocean-going ships, *Sirius* and the armed tender, *Supply*. By October 1788 food was so short that Phillip sent Captain Hunter in *Sirius* to the Cape of Good Hope to purchase it and general supplies; but Hunter did not return until May 1789, and by then the situation was desperate. Nor did the supplies from the Cape last very long. In March 1790 Phillip sent both *Supply* and *Sirius* (which had needed extensive repairs) to Norfolk Island with supplies and a detachment of marines and convicts; next month *Supply* returned to Port Jackson with the news that *Sirius* had been wrecked off the island; all on board had been saved, but the supplies had been lost. The food position was now so bad that Phillip had to send *Supply*, his only link with the outside world, to Batavia for provisions. Rations had to be reduced repeatedly—a reduction from which the governor did not exempt himself; indeed, he added his own private stores to the common stock. It seemed as if the British government had completely forgotten the men and women it had sent to the ends of the earth.

Not until the arrival of the *Lady Juliana* and the storeship *Justinian* in June 1790, followed by the three·convict transports of the Second Fleet, was threat of starvation averted and the long silence explained. The ships brought the news that H.M.S. *Guardian* had sailed from England, with two years' provisions on board as well as some of the superintendents and artificers Phillip had asked for, in July 1789; she should have reached Port Jackson early in 1790, but instead she had struck an iceberg soon after leaving Cape Town, and only just managed to limp back to port before sinking. The wrecks of *Sirius* and *Guardian*, Phillip believed, set the colony back a full twelve months.

Meanwhile, a district that Phillip had discovered during an exploratory journey quite soon after his arrival was proving a cultivable and fertile district. It was in the area near the western extremity of Port Jackson, 15 miles or so west of Sydney. On its discovery in April 1788, Phillip named it Rose Hill, and three years later it was to be renamed Parramatta. Here land was cleared and put under crops. In November 1789, more than 700 bushels of wheat and small supplies of barley and maize were harvested.

In June 1790, Phillip decided to lay out a regular town at Rose Hill. A residence was built for him, construction of grain stores and a military barracks was begun, a blacksmith's shop was built, and huts were put up for convicts. The first land grant had already been made, as an experiment to see how long it would take a farmer to become self-supporting. In November 1789, James Ruse, a "very industrious" time-expired convict with some farming experience, was given an acre of cleared land, a hut and tools, seeds, and rations from the commissary, with the promise that if he made a success of his efforts, the area would be increased to thirty acres. Early in 1791, when Ruse was able to support himself, he was granted the larger area.

By the end of the year, 147 men had been granted land, forty-five of them around Parramatta, the rest at Norfolk Island. Seventy-three of the grantees were convicts whose sentences had expired, the rest were ex-marines and ex-sailors who had elected to stay in the colony after completion of their terms of service. The normal land grant (after mid-1790, when Phillip received detailed instructions on the matter) was 130 acres for a non-commissioned officer, with 30 acres more for a wife and 10 acres extra for each child; 80 acres was the scale for privates and 30 for ex-convicts, with the same bonus acreage for wives and children in each case. Free settlers—if and when any arrived—were to get the same size grants as non-commissioned officers. The type of practical assistance given to the settlers can be seen from a typical entry in Phillip's records:

> Robert Webb and William Reid: to be supported and cloathed from the public stores for eighteen months; to have huts built for them and to receive the necessary quantity of seed, grain and implements of husbandry requisite for sowing the ground the first year; two sow pigs, one cock, six hens; the above two settlers likewise were assisted in clearing two acres of ground.

Sydney had come to be regarded only as a depot for stores, with cultivation practically abandoned and its huts surrounded by derelict gardens. By late 1792, Parramatta had 1,970 inhabitants to Sydney's 1,170. Several smaller farming settlements had sprung up in the district, and a regular ferry service was inaugurated to link Parramatta with Sydney. Before long, fertile land areas in the Hawkesbury River district, well to the north, were discovered, and Sydney, as it remained the only port, grew more rapidly. Parramatta's farmlands had helped the settlement through its food crisis however, and for some years it remained the home of the colony's leading citizens.

It was two and a half years after the arrival of the First Fleet before the next batch of convicts, 221 women, reached Sydney on board the *Lady Juliana*. Soon afterwards, 757 convicts were landed from the three transports of the

Second Fleet. Conditions on board the ships of the Second Fleet were extremely bad, and treatment of the convicts was brutal; the private contractors responsible for the transportation of the convicts gained by over-crowding the ships and reducing rations, for this made room for more freight. Scurvy, dysentery, and fever raged among the convicts; the sick and dying were kept below decks for most of the time, so that atrocities were added to the hazards of the voyage.

A sensitive officer on the *Surprize* wrote that he had seen convicts wearing the same shackles as had been used in the Guinea slave trade, but "the slave trade is merciful compared to what I have seen in this fleet." Of 1,017 convicts embarked, 280 died during the voyage, one in three dying aboard the hell-ship *Neptune*. On arrival in Sydney, many of the convicts faced apalling conditions; the hospitals could not accommodate all the sick and dying, and scores of sick were left to lie on damp ground without adequate clothing; eighty-nine more deaths occurred in the two months following the arrival of the fleet.

The convict transports brought foodstuffs and other supplies, but so many of the convicts were sick, and incapable of hard work even when off the sick list, that the colony could not possibly make much progress towards self-sufficiency. It was almost the same story the following year, when the Third Fleet, made up of ten transports and H.M.S. *Gorgon*, landed only 1,861 convicts of the 2,041 embarked in England and Ireland. In March 1792 Phillip had to write:

> I am very sorry to say that most of the convicts who were received by the last ships still continue in the same debilitated state in which they landed; of them, in less than seven months, two hundred and eighty-eight men have died.

He added grimly, "In the seven months prior to the arrival of these ships the deaths were nineteen."

Despite these handicaps, and despite a drought that lasted from the beginning of July 1790 to August 1791, the colony was making progress. In October 1792, Phillip reported that "our last crop of maize, notwithstanding the long drought, was four thousand eight hundred and forty-four and a half bushels, of which two thousand six hundred and forty-nine and a half bushels have been issued as food for the colony, six hundred and ninety-five bushels reserved for seed and other purposes." Unfortunately Phillip's charges were more expert at thieving than at farming, and 1,500 bushels were stolen from the stores.

A return of land under cultivation on the mainland at this time showed just over 1,700 acres under cultivation, including 100 acres cleared and ready for planting. Besides the government farms at Parramatta and Toongabbie (1,017 acres), this included 517 being cultivated by farmer-settlers, all ex-convicts or ex-servicemen, on farms in the neighbourhood of Parramatta. There were 1,186 acres under maize, and 200 under wheat, with a little under barley. Cultivation was also well under way at Norfolk Island. The first private shipping had arrived; and some whalers and sealers were working out of Sydney Harbour.

After nearly five years, the colony's population was made up of just over 3,500 people. Nearly 4,000 convicts had been landed during this period, besides civil and military staff, but the mortality had been heavy following the arrivals of the Second and Third Fleets. After early troubles that had brought the whole venture near to total collapse, the settlement appeared to have every chance of survival, even though it was still no more than a tiny outpost on a raw continent; it had come through its years of crisis.

For some time Phillip, whose health had been causing him concern, had been pressing to return to England. His request for permission to do so brought a vague reply and, believing the permission had been granted, he sailed on December 11, 1792, in the *Atlantic*. He took with him a collection of kangaroos and other native animals, many beautiful birds, and several examples of Aboriginal weapons and artifacts. He hoped that two Aborigines, Bennelong and Yemmerrawannie, who accompanied him, would acquire knowledge that would assist them in helping to civilize their own people. They were well received in London; Yemmerrawannie died there, but Bennelong, who wore the clothes of polite society and became a great favourite, remained until 1795, when he returned to Sydney.

Phillip planned originally to return, for he hoped to resume his task at a later date. Soon after his arrival in London, however, his resignation was accepted, and later he took on other assignments.

He had established a settlement different in character from any that preceded or followed it—a settlement in a new continent founded under the auspices and direct control of the British government itself. His strong sense of duty, his selflessness and his unshakable determination, had made it possible for him to set the enterprise on its feet in spite of the unpromising human material, and in spite of the many practical difficulties he faced. The purpose behind the settlement and the nature of the undertaking made it inevitable that the administration would be wholly authoritarian; yet Phillip had tempered his power with kindliness and a common-sense approach, and his constructive measures had achieved success even when most of those around him feared disaster.

His assignment had been to run a penal colony and make it self-supporting. He had set about establishing government farms, as the situation demanded, but exigencies had made it necessary for him to go beyond this, and he had wisely opened the way for private farming. His instructions empowered him to make land grants, and to help aspiring farmers in certain stated ways for a limited time. In stipulating these conditions of aid, the British government made insufficient allowance for the heart-breaking difficulties of clearing timbered land by hand and growing satisfactory crops in the hard and poorly watered soil of coastal New South Wales.

Reading his precise and confident instructions, which so blithely ignored local conditions, Phillip must sometimes have wondered whether the clerks in Whitehall expected crops to grow, and people to be fed, by the stroke of a pen. Accordingly he stretched his instructions to the limit, especially by allowing farmers to be supported from the government stores for longer than the one year permitted in his instructions. He wrote that had he limited support to one year, he "must have given up all thought of procuring settlers from the detachment." In the same spirit he made a grant of land to one of the colony's civil officers, an assistant surgeon who wanted to retire and become a farmer, in advance of official permission for grants to such officers.

By his willingness to adapt the system he administered to circumstances and local conditions, he set the enterprise on a course that would ensure its survival in spite of immediate shortages and shortcomings. At the same time he began the process of change that would free the colony from the confining framework of a purely penal settlement cut off from all activities that might draw it into trade or commerce, such as had apparently been envisaged in the earliest parliamentary statement about the prospective settlement. Whitehall still looked on the colony primarily as a dumping-ground for England's unwanted criminal population. So, probably, did most of the officers of the colony. Not so Phillip. Despite constant frustrations, he was sustained by the conviction that he was the founder of a colony, not merely the governor of a jail. While still in England, he had thought that convicts and ex-convicts should not be allowed to mix with the garrison and the expected free settlers. This was a strange and impossible notion, but his motive was noble, even though austere: "I would not wish convicts," he said, "to lay the foundations of an Empire."

In his dispatches to London, Phillip stressed the inadequacies of convict labour, and the advantages that would accrue if experienced practical hard-working free settlers could be sent to the colony. His administrative policies provided a framework within which free settlers could be fitted. No immigrants (apart from discharged sailors and marines) had arrived in the colony up to the time when, in December 1792, Phillip sailed through Sydney Heads for the last time; but he did not doubt that they would come. Nor did he waver in the prophecy that he had once made, "that this colony will prove the most valuable acquisition Great Britain ever made."

Growing pains 4

It was partly because of the Sydney settlement's special character that Phillip had faced the danger of being left without provisions. The powerful East India Company's charter gave it a complete monopoly of trade in the whole area—yet the company could not have any commercial interest in what was intended to be no more than a jail. The government's instructions to Phillip had made it clear that the company's monopoly rights were not to be jeopardized. Stringent clauses had been included which forbade the building of any vessel which might be used for trade, and Phillip was instructed to prevent any vessels that might arrive at the settlement "from having communication with any of the inhabitants residing within your government without receiving special permission from you for that purpose." Thus when government-chartered ships were shipwrecked or delayed, there was no likelihood of private shipping filling the gap.

The tiny settlement in the remotest sector of the globe might have faced even greater hardships in its early years if it had not been for a new circumstance, coupled with the ingenuity of American sea traders—who, unlike the chartered British traders, were unfettered in their commercial ties. By a coincidence, Sydney was close to the course that American captains began to follow after 1788 on their voyages from Philadelphia or Salem or Boston to the China seas. Working on the information contained in Captain Cook's reports, the Americans realized that a course could be followed round the Cape of Good Hope, across the Indian Ocean, and round southern Van Diemen's Land, then northward through the Tasman Sea and on to Canton. This was an all-season route, superior to the former Sunda Strait route which could be used only in spring and summer. The new course took American captains practically past Sydney's door. As time went on, they came to realize that some useful trading could be carried on there.

American vessels were beyond the East India Company's control, and they were able to take goods to the colony without running the risk of seizure.

As Phillip was preparing to leave for England, the first American trading ship to reach Sydney arrived on November 1, 1792, with a mixed cargo. Captain Thomas Patrickson, of the *Philadelphia*, had learnt in Cape Town of the severe shortage of provisions and he decided to put into Sydney and offer his cargo of "assorted notions." The governor's office gladly bought the main items—meat, pitch, and tar—as official stores. Included in the ship's hold were rum and other spirits which Patrickson was anxious to sell. Buyers were found—army officers and officials, principally—their objective being to resell the liquor at a high profit.

The Americans' trade with China, prompted by economic expansion in the United States after the close of the Revolution, was branching out into many sectors of the Pacific; and although the port of Sydney was not yet a significant trading point, enough American ships appeared there—one or two a year—to contribute significantly to colonial affairs.

Shortly after Phillip's departure aboard the *Atlantic*, a second American trading ship, the *Hope*, from Rhode Island, arrived. A condition of the sale of the *Hope's* cargo was that the liquor would be included and, although the new lieutenant-governor saw the danger of such a traffic developing and declared himself against this stipulation, the spirits were purchased. Rum was already becoming a means of hiring labour and a medium of exchange. Successive administrators were to lament the rum and liquor trade ever more deeply as time went on.

No governor was appointed for some time after Phillip's retirement, and the administration was left in the hands of the Lieutenant-Governor, Major Francis Grose, commanding officer of the New South Wales Corps. This corps had been specially recruited for service in the colony, in succession to the marines. The first detachment, a hundred strong, had arrived with the ships of the Second Fleet in June 1790, and a second unit, under Grose himself, in February 1792.

As trade with the outside world began to expand, it was inevitable that it should create opportunities for the small group of military officers and civil officials—the only people able to make the necessary payment for goods by drafts on London. There was no price control, and so the fortunate few were able to charge prices that gave them huge profits on their outlay.

First came the captains of the early transports, who had augmented their human cargoes with additional cargoes of merchandise; then came the captains of the private ships, mostly American, with their "speculative cargoes"; but neither class could compete with the military and civil officers, who had official backing. Thus, as shipping to the colony increased, participation in trading by the few civil and military officers able to take advantage of it soon hardened into a systematic and rigid monopoly. The wife of one of them, Mrs John Macarthur, described the system in an artless letter to an old friend:

The officers in the Colony, with a few others possessed of money or credit in England, unite together and purchase the cargoes of such vessels as repair to this country from various quarters. Two or more are chosen from the number to bargain for the cargo offered for sale, which is then divided amongst them, in proportion to the amount of their subscriptions.

The encouragement of monopolistic trading was only one of the ways in which Grose allowed effective power in the colony to accumulate in the hands of officers of the New South Wales Corps. He approached matters from a different standpoint from that of Phillip. He was a man of narrower outlook, concerned only with immediate issues. He described himself as "unaccustomed to business," and admitted to Downing Street that he feared of acting on his own initiative. In general his attitude was one of disdain for "the people who had become settlers" (the first few free immigrants arrived in 1793) and he made no secret of the fact that he disliked having to deal with those who were neither military men nor cowed convicts. One of his earliest orders was that in future the duties of the civilian magistrates were to be taken over by the military officers; thus the administration of civil as well as of the criminal courtscame to rest with the Corps officers.

At the same time Grose's fellow officers received new privileges. In response to a request made earlier by Phillip, a dispatch conveying permission to make grants of land to serving military and civilian officers was received from London, and Grose was soon reporting happily that "I have allotted such officers as have asked one hundred acres which with great spirit they at their own expense are clearing." One of these officers was the ambitious, energetic, and able young lieutenant John Macarthur. It is probably significant of Macarthur's early appreciation of the careers open for talent in a new country that he was the first civil, naval, or military officer apart from Chaplain Johnson to bring his wife and family to the colony. Early in 1793 Grose appointed Macarthur Paymaster and Superintendent of Public Works in the farming area, and under his administration private farming gained new strength; a marked improvement was recorded in agricultural output and in the breeding of livestock.

The area under grain was steadily extended and the crop yields were improved by better farming methods instituted by individuals on larger farms. At the same time the government farms were allowed to fall into neglect. Captain Henry Waterhouse, a naval officer who arrived in the colony late in 1795, considered that Macarthur had remarkably fine farms, though (significantly) he could not so describe those of the government which Macarthur supervised around Parramatta and the Hawkesbury.

Macarthur's position made him virtual dictator of the colony's labour force. Following Phillip's urgent recommendations, the British authorities had allowed a certain amount of aid to farmers for their first year or so on the farm. Now the military and civil officer-farmers were allowed much greater concessions, particularly in the services of convict labourers. Besides three domestic convicts, each was allowed the full-time services of ten convict farm-labourers, who did not have to be paid but were fed and clothed from the commissariat stores for an indefinite period. This concession to the officers continued despite the instructions of the Secretary of State, who considered that they as employers, farming as a sideline to their ordinary duties, should feed and clothe all but two of their convict farm-labourers.

Grose's lax administration of the system of land grants played into the hands of the efficient and land-hungry officers. Land was granted freely, including town lands. Some of the senior officers gave even convicts still serving their sentence a paper certifying "X has my permission to settle," which was apparently an acceptable land title. Many of the ex-convicts asked for land only to sell it and raise the money for a return passage to England. Soldiers claimed land as a bonus. Reporting on the system that had prevailed under Grose, Governor Hunter wrote in 1796:

> I found that the late Lieutenant-Governor made it a rule to grant to every private soldier under his command 25 acres of land wherever he chose to have it. Those farms could not, as expected in the grant, be occupied and cultivated by the proprietor who in this case had other duty to do; this of course was understood; therefore they sold them and most of them were purchased by their own officers, some of whom have by this means considerable tracts.

Thus the efficient few were able to build up their holdings and, with a little enclosure movement under way, prosperous estates were established. Very soon more than a quarter of the acreage under cultivation around Sydney was held by a handful of civil and military officers. However, Grose settled a number of settlers—400 people including ten families—near the mouth of the Hawkesbury River.

The colony's livestock, which at one time had dwindled to 116 animals, increased rapidly during this period. More livestock was imported, both by the administration and directly by the officers, who on two occasions had the initiative to charter a storeship, which they sent to Bengal for cattle and other farm animals. (A sideline was the rest of the cargo, which they divided among themselves or sold at the usual monopolistic prices.) The officers were able to augment their flocks and herds by purchases from needy or improvident farmers; the sheep which Phillip had presented to settlers on his departure changed hands in this way. The principal concern was to produce meat, and special attention was given to goats, which also produced milk. Little attention was given to sheep at this time. Thus John Macarthur's stock in 1794 consisted of 2 mares, 2 cows, 130 goats, upwards of a 100 hogs, and "poultry in the greatest abundance." By the middle of 1795 the colony's total livestock had increased to 2,049 animals, including 832 sheep, 176 cattle, and nearly 1,000 goats; apart from the cattle, most animals were owned by the civil and military officer-farmers.

The capability displayed by the officer-farmers was bolstered by privilege. The only market for produce was the government store in the various farming districts, run by the commissariat under the ultimate control of the superintendent of public works. The governor fixed the price of grain, and it was left to the storekeepers to decide whose grain should be bought and whose refused. David Collins, who had been secretary to Governor Phillip, later described the way this operated:

> The delivery of grain into the public storehouses when open for that purpose was so completely monopolized that the settlers had but few opportunities of getting the full value of their crops. A few words will place this iniquitous combination in its proper light. The settler found himself thrust out from the granary by a man whose greater opulence created greater influence. He was then driven by his necessities to dispose of his grain for less than half its value. To whom did he dispose of it? To the very man whose greater opulence enabled him to purchase it and whose greater influence could get it received into the public store.

Following a good harvest early in 1792 the Lieutenant-Governor of Norfolk Island, Philip Gidley King, purchased 11,500 bushels of maize from the settlers on the island, making payment in bills drawn on the commissary, which had to be approved by Grose. The mainland stores were full, since two store ships had just arrived from England, plus another store ship which Grose had chartered at the end of the previous year; so he refused to approve the bills. The result was that a great many of the Norfolk Island farmers had to give up their farms. Grose could not be blamed for refusing to fill the stores with perishable grain in excess of requirements; but it was the small settlers, not the part-time gentleman farmers, who were forced to give up their land because of the refusal to buy their produce. More than a year later Grose received instructions from London to "make the best terms you can with the owners" but this was too late to save the farms.

The incident illustrates a fundamental weakness in the economy. Farming had to be expanded so that the community could become self-supporting; but since the demand was in fact small and inelastic, and there was no opportunity for export of grain, a glut could occur following a bountiful harvest. Because of the strictly limited demand, the wheat acreage could not be expanded too greatly; yet when two bad crops came in succession there were dangerous shortages, and the community had to revert to temporary dependence on imports.

Some farmers found an alternative outlet for their grain to selling it to the public store for milling into flour: they found it more profitable to use illicit stills to convert the grain into alcohol, thus supporting and extending the notorious trade based on supplies from occasional American vessels. It was inevitable that the unhappy wrecks of England's prison hulks and transports, who comprised such a large section of the community, should find their solace in drink. As time went on, rum came to assume a special place as an article of barter in a community deficient in money and means of exchange. Many commodities were used in barter, including wheat and meat; but rum assumed a role of importance as an inducement to convicts to work harder. It came to be used as an overtime payment by land-owners to encourage their assigned men to work beyond the normal hours, and it was the only type of wage with any attraction for these freed men who were able to work for wages. Thus from small beginnings, rum was to play an increasingly significant part in the colony's affairs.

After two years Grose returned to England because of illness brought about by an old war wound, and the lieutenant-governorship devolved on his successor in charge of the Corps, Captain William Paterson. Like Grose, the new administrator was personally honest—but he did even less to control the monopolistic activities of his subordinates.

Since the commencement of the war with France in 1793 the colony had enjoyed something of a breathing space. In contrast to the shiploads of sick convicts dumped on Phillip's quayside by the Second and Third Fleets, no more than four transports, bringing 404 convicts, arrived during the Grose-Paterson régime; in one year the only convict added to the population was a single Scottish political prisoner. The population was hardly greater than when Phillip left the colony, but the death roll was much smaller, only 158 people dying in 1793, 59 in 1794, and 24 adults in 1795. Ironically, since they were not so sorely needed, stores and provisions were sent from England much more regularly than in Phillip's time; during the Grose-Paterson interregnum ten provision ships and two store ships arrived from England. Meat was now much more of a problem than grain, since it was obviously unsound to kill breeding stock. On the occasions in which store ships were chartered by Grose and Paterson, it was mainly to obtain salt beef and pork, rather than grain.

As the output of farms increased and the landholders sold more to the government, they acquired greater funds (in the form of negotiable bills drawn on the Treasury) and so could more easily monopolize imports. The regimental funds of the New South Wales Corps, under the control of the able paymaster, John Macarthur, could also be called upon to consolidate the position of the only groups with capital and available credits. Money and negotiable credits were thus concentrated in the same hands—those of the officers and civilian officials—as organizing ability, with consequent development of trade and agricultural production.

The confidence of Grose and Paterson in the ability of these officers and officials to get the colony moving, in an economic sense, was well-placed; but this gain was offset by the social effects of their domination over all aspects of the colony's economy. The two lieutenant-governors had freely abrogated their own rights in favour of their subordinates; they were unable to foresee that the power which they had allowed to pass to the officers would grow in their hands beyond all reason.

By the time Captain John Hunter returned from London to take over the office of governor, domination by the military and civilian officers was well established. Hunter had applied for the governorship when he learnt that his old friend Phillip had resigned; he had received his appointment in February 1794, although he did not reach the colony until September of the next year. A seaman since the age of sixteen, Hunter had been a first fleeter and the first to chart Sydney Harbour; he was fifty-seven when he became governor. His instructions were strict and definite. He was to reinstate the civil magistracy, and to direct the judge-advocate to carry out his judicial duties. He was to control the importation of spirits, to enforce the land grant regulations strictly, to extend public agriculture, and in general to correct the abuses which Downing Street officials realized' had crept into the economy.

Hunter found it easy enough to issue general orders on these lines, but difficult to enforce them. Conditions were very different from those he had known in the earliest days of settlement. He faced the hostility of a military clique entrenched in power and able to exercise independent authority. As a naval officer he found the breakdown in the governor's control of affairs almost intolerable. He found that at every turn the officers of the New South Wales Corps and the civilian officers were resisting his efforts to re-establish the older order. They held jealously to their privileges and tenaciously to their profits. With no force to support him, Hunter could get nowhere in his efforts to reinstate the authority and independence of the governor's position as it had been in Phillip's day.

The new governor had to contend with greater numbers of convicts, many of whom represented a new and disruptive element: political prisoners from Ireland. Hunter wrote to London in November 1796 reporting that he had built a strong log prison "for the securing of turbulent and disobedient prisoners." It was needed, he said, "more particularly since it has been found necessary to send to this country such hard characters as the people called Irish Defenders who, I confess, my Lord, I wish had been sent either to the coast of Africa or some place as fit for them."

Hunter made voyages along the coast and undertook some land trips. He did what he could to encourage further discoveries. With him from England had come Matthew Flinders, a midshipman, and George Bass, a naval surgeon; within a month of their arrival these two young friends set out in the tiny *Tom Thumb* and explored George's River for a distance of 20 miles beyond earlier surveys. In March 1796 they put to sea in the 8-foot boat and explored the south shore of Botany Bay. Next year Lieutenant John Shortland, while pursuing some runaways, discovered a fine river—which he named the Hunter—entering the sea a 100 miles or so north of Port Jackson, and also a harbour with cliffs containing coal.

The continent's southern shoreline came under investigation during Hunter's term of office. Bass in 1797, sailing in a 27-foot whaleboat, explored far enough to make it appear likely that a strait separated Van Diemen's Land from the mainland. In February Matthew Flinders was sent in the schooner *Francis* to rescue some sailors who had been wrecked on the Furneaux Islands more than a year before. During a five-week voyage Flinders discovered some minor islands and noted the drift of the current westward, suggesting strongly that a strait existed, but he was not able to prove this point until later in the same year when he and Bass set out on a voyage which took them through Bass Strait, down the west coast of Van Diemen's Land, and around the southern limits of the island.

Hunter strongly supported a number of enterprises which gave prospects of making the colony more productive. He was convinced that the land had some useful products in its trees, furs, and minerals. He tested the suitability of native timbers for various purposes, concluding that some of the eucalypts produced hardwood similar in its properties to Indian teak. He considered that ship's timber could be obtained from some trees, and that there was material for gun carriages and other articles in which durability and strength were needed. He found the astringent bark of other trees suitable for use in tanning skins and hides, and he thought that iron-smelting might be possible with the abundant iron ore and coal. Coal from collieries near Botany Bay was sent to the Cape of Good Hope in 1800, and to India in the following year. Whaling and sealing were also begun.

Farming followed much the same lines as under Grose and Paterson. Increasing areas were brought under cultivation, more grain was produced; but drought, bush fires, and the flooding of the Hawkesbury River still made importation of grain necessary. The process by which the small farmers lost their farms to the favoured estate-holders continued. In 1798 Hunter appointed a two-man commission to report on conditions in the older farming districts. In each district it was the same: small settlers were forced to give up their farms because they had to pay extortionate prices for everything they bought. Of seventy-three farmers selected and settled by Phillip, only twenty-one remained on their farms.

The commissary store continued to be the centre of the colony's economic life. A great number of the population were still victualled from the store: these included the military and civil staff and their families; settlers with land grants, whether expirees or free, for their first two years on the farm; and convicts working for the government. Despite instructions to the contrary, Hunter at first continued to allow the officer-farmers to have thirteen assigned convicts victualled from the store since he considered "two men are not nearly enough for the clearing of heavy timber, attending a flock and cultivating the quantity of land allowed to the officers, all of which is done by manual labour." But the Secretary of State insisted, and regulations were issued in 1798 that all except two assigned convicts had to be clothed and fed by their masters. However, this order was not strictly enforced. Hunter's last muster of population (September 1800) showed that more than three-fourths of the total population of 4,930 were victualled by the government.

Clothing and provisions were still supplied from England with the incoming convict transports but, except in emergencies, by now the colony was expected to supply most of its own requirements in grain and meat, both being sold by the settler farmers to the storekeepers. This system placed great power in the hands of the commissariat staff, a power that was very often abused, despite the governor's orders that buying orders should be spread over a large number of suppliers, with preference to the small farmers.

In payment for grain and other purchases, the commissariat issued receipts, with the understanding that when a sufficient number of receipts had been accumulated, the holder would exchange them for bills in London. These "store receipts" circulated freely within the colony, and in fact approximated to currency.

Livestock continued to increase, especially on the larger farms. When Hunter left the colony, in September 1800, livestock included more than 6,000 sheep, 4,000 hogs, over 2,000 goats, and 1,044 cattle. The sheep, though mainly of the Cape and Bengal hairy breeds, included the colony's first merinos. The merinos had been brought from the Cape of Good Hope in 1797. Hunter had sent two ships to the Cape to buy cattle; the ships' captains, Waterhouse and Kent, also purchased a number of large-bodied sheep of merino type, which had originally come from the Netherlands and were owned by the Dutch commandant at Cape Town. Although those in the *Supply* died, more than half the original consignment in the *Reliance* was safely landed, after a dangerous passage that took seventy-eight days instead of the usual thirty-five to forty days. From this small flock a number of settlers, including John Macarthur, purchased their first merinos.

By this time the settled area around Port Jackson extended over a radius of some 30 miles. The little settlement around the mouth of the Hawkesbury was developing, though always liable to flooding. Hunter's last return of land under cultivation comprised 4,665 acres of wheat, almost 3,000 acres of maize, and 82 of barley. Government farms had been almost eliminated (only 280 acres were under cultivation in 1799), while over 1,200 acres were in the hands of officers and over 7,000 acres were held by settlers, mainly ex-convicts.

Hunter's first impressions on returning to the colony had been enthusiastic, but when he settled down to carry out his instructions and exercise control over the monopolists, he found himself thwarted at every turn. Officials received him with great respect but they were determined not to allow any interference with the trade practices that had grown up, and his orders were not carried out. "There exists, I believe, a jealous antipathy against naval government," he wrote; and he advised London that the New South Wales Corps should be withdrawn and the duties of the Corps taken over by a force of marines.

In the power struggle in which he found himself engaged, much of the management of the colony's affairs remained beyond his reach. He was unable to wrest control from the hands of the military officers and civilian officials, particularly those of the commissariat. He complained of the inferior type of official sent to the colony. He was aware of the unsatisfactory state of affairs and realized that control had to be restored to the governor; but he found the task beyond him. If his position in London had been stronger—or if his opponents had not possessed such powerful friends there—he would not have found himself so helplessly placed. He was not in a position to move directly against the officers, who were meanwhile spreading malicious reports in London, further undermining his authority.

Hunter defended himself against the charges made against him—and they included suggestions that he was participating in the very abuses he was striving to root out—but he was recalled in a dispatch sent from London in November 1799 which reached him five months later. By the same ship his successor Philip Gidley King arrived, with a dormant commission as Governor. King, like Hunter, was a first fleeter, and had shown administrative ability during his long period as Lieutenant-Governor of

Norfolk Island. When Phillip resigned he had recommended King as his successor.

Hunter was in no hurry to hand over the reins of office and, in spite of strained relations with King because of the delay, he retained the governorship until September 28, 1800. Three weeks later he sailed for England and on his arrival the following May he began an attempt to vindicate his character with the authorities. He was given no opportunity to do so, and he published a short booklet defending his actions. He also advocated a number of reforms, most of which were eventually carried into effect, though by others and many years later.

On assuming the governorship, Captain King was faced with opposition just as strong as that which had confronted Hunter. He was badgered on all sides as the military domination was exploited by vindictive and malicious individuals anxious to destroy his power. He had already antagonized the members of the New South Wales Corps during his lieutenant-governorship of Norfolk Island: members of the corps on the island had been so unruly and hard to control that he had sent them all back to the mainland and had replaced them by recruiting a guard of ex-marines and trustworthy settlers.

At first King made considerable headway in his efforts to break the power of the monopolists. He revived the public farms, tightened up the regulations on victualling, assigned labourers from the public stores, and issued orders that storekeepers must call for public tenders before making any purchases of grain. He induced the home government to send out regular cargoes of miscellaneous goods, for sale at fixed prices, and allowed independent importers to carry on business. The regular arrival of supplies overcame many shortages, and the position of the monopolists was gradually weakened as expansion of private trade followed. King also increased the number of pardons granted to convicts (adding to the growing numbers of those who became free by expiration of their sentences), thus helping to build up the independent forces within the community.

The land along the coastal strip on which wheat was being grown was not well suited to agriculture, and new troubles were appearing. Soil and climate were against good crops, and after a few years of tillage fields became unproductive. Governor King was aware of the danger of relying wholly on wheat "for the general support of any class of [the colony's] inhabitants." In a dispatch in 1806 he referred to the many difficulties, and noted the exhaustion of the land under successive crops:

> Wheat is seen destroyed in the fields by the blights, rust, smut, and caterpillars; also in this climate by fire, and in the stack by weevil, and by corn moths when in the granary, added to which, when the wheat is continually sown on the same land, it impoverishes so much that, if the crop is not destroyed by any of the above common evils, the produce will be small, and by no means equal to the expense of raising it.

Despite these drawbacks, King's energetic measures were very successful in increasing production. An exceptionally good harvest in 1802 resulted in a surplus of 14,000 bushels above the colony's requirements. If the government farms were continued in competition with the private settlers, there would clearly be over-production in good seasons; as a result government farming was discontinued in 1804. Even so, there was "upwards of two years' wheat in the stacks of the year's produce" at the end of 1804, and King raised the question of finding external markets. He had to arrange for the importation of grain on only one occasion, after disastrous flooding of the Hawkesbury in 1806; apart from this, the colony was quite independent of grain imports during his governorship. King also fostered sound farm practices by rewarding with a bonus of livestock those farmers who had shown the greatest success in growing grain, in the breeding of pigs, and in the production of flax.

In trying to increase and stabilize farm output, the government had by now become involved not only as a buyer of produce but also as a lender to suppliers of produce. The original nature of the official store as an organization for administering supplies in a penal colony had undergone marked change; the commissary had developed into a trading concern and as such it made advance payments to settlers for their produce wherever necessary, becoming in effect the core of a monetary system almost devoid of money.

Following the introduction of the merinos from the Cape in 1797, a number of sheep-owners had improved the wool-bearing qualities of their sheep; one of these owners was Macarthur, who decided to return to England in 1800, and offered his entire holdings to the government for purchase. King, a keen advocate of the development of wool-growing, referred the matter to London and sent a selection of eight fleeces in the hope of furthering the proposal. The sale fell through, Macarthur and King were soon at loggerheads, and late in 1802 Macarthur returned to England under arrest, after wounding his commanding officer in a duel, the cause of which was Colonel Paterson's refusal to join Macarthur's boycott of the governor. The military authorities in London considered that any court martial should be carried out in the colony, and released Macarthur from arrest.

By this time "some of the most eminent manufacturers of woollen cloth" had examined Macarthur's fleeces and reported them "equal to the very best we ever receive from Spain." A fellow officer reported that Macarthur was engaging the favourable attention in London of "the principal noblemen and gentlemen" as well as "the majority of the wool staplers." Macarthur was invited before the Privy Council's Committee of Trade and Foreign Plantations to give his views on how wool-growing in the colony could be encouraged. Having resigned his commission, he made a triumphant return to New South Wales in 1805 in his own ship the *Argo*, with the colony's first woolclasser in his entourage, some Spanish merinos from King George III's Windsor flocks in the hold, and the knowledge that the governor had been directed to make him a grant of 5,000 acres of land and allow him the services of thirty convict labourers.

At the time King assumed office the population was just over 5,000; with a sharp increase in the rate of transportation it passed 7,000 in 1802. The proportion of Irish among the convicts had increased steadily since

1791, when the first transport from Ireland, the *Queen* arrived with the Third Fleet; 41 per cent of the convicts who reached the colony from 1793 to 1802 were from Ireland. One reason for the Irish predominance was that during the war years many English able-bodied offenders were enlisted instead of transported. Throughout the 1790s the United Irishmen's campaign for freedom from English rule was gaining popular support, and the Irish transports included many political prisoners, their number increasing after the suppression of the rebellion of 1798. After the rebellion, many prisoners were transported without trial, under courts martial or summary convictions by magistrates; and even before this, the Irish convict ships very seldom carried any record of the sentence imposed upon the prisoners.

In both Hunter's and King's terms of office, there was a widespread fear of a rising of the Irish prisoners. A minor conspiracy was uncovered at the end of 1800, and four years later some of the Irish at Castle Hill did in fact attempt an armed rebellion. Their plans were betrayed, martial law was proclaimed, and the rising was quickly and easily subdued. Eight men were hanged and others flogged. King felt it desirable to remove the remaining ringleaders far from any contact with the general community, and he reoccupied Newcastle on the Hunter River, which had been temporarily settled in 1801 but abandoned the year after.

Around the turn of the century fears of French intentions caused the founding of new settlements and accelerated coastal exploration. England and France had been at war since 1793, and it was natural that any rumours of French naval activity in the Pacific should arouse suspicion. French privateers were active in the Indian Ocean, despite England's naval superiority. England's powerful East India Company was concerned lest the French should consider establishing a colony on the north coast of New Holland, which would have meant an addition to France's bases in the Indian Ocean. Englishmen in general lived in continuing fear of French attack—even fear of invasion over the Channel by the newly invented balloon, or of invasion by a secretly constructed tunnel beneath the Channel. This concern was transmitted to the utmost ends of the earth when the military genius of First Consul Napoleon Bonaparte tightened the French grip on Europe.

News of French plans for a scientific expedition to the South Seas, under Captain Nicholas Baudin, reached the Admiralty in 1799. As a result, preparations were advanced to send the *Lady Nelson* (under Lieutenant James Grant) to explore the coastlines of Bass Strait—shores only recently known to exist.

Meanwhile, Matthew Flinders had set out to explore the east coast of the continent. He sailed to Moreton Bay (named by Cook), and explored Glasshouse Bay and Hervey's Bay, but was forced to return to Sydney when his vessel sprang a leak. He sailed for England, arriving late in 1800. Baudin's expedition had just left for the South Seas, and Flinders found considerable interest in London in the idea of undertaking a detailed survey of the entire continental coastline. Early in 1801 Flinders was given command of the 334-ton *Investigator;* the East India Company was so interested in the voyage that it voted a sum of £600 to the captain, staff, and crew.

By this time Baudin's two vessels, *Le Géographe* and *Le Naturaliste,* which had set off in 1800, had reached the Western Australian coast near Cape Leeuwin. After some land exploration there, the vessels parted company on June 8 during a storm; *Le Géographe* went north and explored Shark's Bay while *Le Naturaliste* entered the Swan River, where it spent three weeks. After wintering at Timor the ships sailed to Van Diemen's Land, which they sighted on January 13, 1802.

When Flinders sailed from Spithead in July 1801, he began his greatest enterprise. Early in December he sighted Australian shores, and set about making a detailed survey of the southern coast. On December 8 he anchored in King George Sound (which had been discovered and named in 1791 by Captain George Vancouver in the *Discovery*). He sailed eastward, charting as he went; and as he did so he became the discoverer of the coastline from Fowler Bay, at the head of the Great Australian Bight (the farthest point reached by the *Gulden Zeepaard* in 1627), to Encounter Bay. He explored Spencer Gulf and St Vincent Gulf and demonstrated that neither penetrated deeply into the continent. In surveying this last unknown section of coastline Flinders proved that no channel divided New South Wales from New Holland.

A few days later, on April 8, a ship was sighted in Encounter Bay, east of Kangaroo Island. It proved to be Baudin's *Le Géographe.* After messages had been exchanged, Flinders had a boat hoisted out, and he called upon Baudin. The two navigators exchanged cordial reports on their activities to that point, and on the advice of Flinders, Baudin sailed for Sydney.

Flinders proceeded with his survey, though in fact he had been forestalled from this point; Baudin had preceded him from the mouth of the Murray eastward to Cape Banks, while Captain Grant in the *Lady Nelson* had charted the coast eastward from this point. Weather conditions now made it necessary for Flinders to keep clear of the coast, and his southerly course took him to King Island. He sailed to the mainland coast when the weather abated and came to Port Phillip, which he believed to be a new discovery. Again, however, he had been forestalled: some weeks earlier Lieutenant John Murray (in the *Lady Nelson*) had reached this point and recorded his findings. Flinders made a cursory examination of the bay but hurried on to Sydney because his stores were low.

Flinders reached Sydney six weeks before Baudin, who arrived on June 30. News of the signing of peace between Britain and France had just been received, and Baudin and his officers were soon on very friendly terms with Governor King. However, Baudin made pointed inquiries regarding the extent of British claims in the Pacific, and this led the governor to inform him that the whole of the continent and Van Diemen's Land were British territory—a claim which would have been hard to substantiate since discovery and proclamation were insufficient without settlement.

Governor King reported the French visit to London, stressing the rumour (which reached him only after Baudin's departure) that the French intended to select a place for a settlement in Van Diemen's Land. He also decided to send H.M.S. *Cumberland* to keep watch on the expedition's moves. The French vessels were overtaken at King Island in Bass Strait. Here the British colours were hoisted and then saluted daily as a sign of prior possession. Somewhat surprised by this flurry of activity, Baudin wrote to King confirming that he had no intention of annexing any territory, and that the expedition's interests were strictly scientific.

This assurance did not convince King, who decided that unless he forestalled them the French would probably claim northern Van Diemen's Land. Accordingly the governor sent Lieutenant John Bowen with fifty people to found a settlement on the Derwent in May 1803. At the same time he wrote to Lord Castlereagh explaining the necessity "of preventing the French gaining a foothold" in Van Diemen's Land. He referred also to the urgent need to forestall them on the mainland in the Port Phillip region.

Governor King's interpretation of French intentions made a deep impression in London, where suspicion of French motives in all things was stronger than ever since the failure of the Peace of Amiens and resumption of war in March 1803. There was no other reason for spread of settlement. When London heard of the existence of such fine harbours on the southern coastline of the continent and read King's dispatches which spoke of "the probability of the French having it in contemplation to make a settlement," action was taken. In October 1803, Lieutenant-Colonel David Collins arrived in Port Phillip from England with a force of marines, a civil staff including a Church of England chaplain, a few free settlers, and nearly 300 convicts.

Collins was no Phillip; he was unenthusiastic about the propsect and made no attempt to find a suitable site for the settlement. He took the company ashore on the barren tongue of land between the bay and the ocean, now Sorrento. Convinced that the whole venture was unsound, Collins sought permission to withdraw; he was instructed to take his whole company to the River Derwent, in Van Diemen's Land; here he joined forces with Lieutenant Bowen and the combined group transferred from Risdon Cove to a position on the foothill slopes of Mount Wellington, where Collins chose the site for a town which he named Hobart.

Meanwhile, after refitting the *Investigator*, Flinders had set out from Sydney on July 22, 1802, and had sailed north, to explore and chart the Gulf of Carpentaria and Torres Strait. Although his vessel's condition was deteriorating by the time he completed this undertaking, he continued on to Timor and then sailed completely around Australia, arriving back in Port Jackson on June 9, 1803, at the completion of the first circumnavigation of a continent ever made. Flinders knew the value of the work he had done, and he was eager to return home to complete his charts and journal; he wrote to a friend: "I am going home with the promise of being attended by fortune's smiles."

The *Investigator* could not be made ready for sea again. So Flinders took a passenger berth in another ship, which was unfortunately wrecked on the

Great Barrier Reef. After a hazardous journey by open boat he reached Sydney, where all that could be offered as a rescue ship to take off survivors and then continue the journey to England was a 29-ton cutter, the *Cumberland*.

Baudin meanwhile had spent a further six months on Australia's south coast, exploring and charting Spencer and St Vincent gulfs. He then sailed up the west coast, intending to make some further investigations in south-west New Guinea; but water was short, he himself was ill, and he decided to return to France. He got no further than Île de France (Mauritius), where he died in September 1803.

Three months later Flinders was forced to put in at the same island because of the bad state of the *Cumberland*. By now France and England were again at war; his ship was seized and he was held prisoner. By the time the French Government sent orders for his release (in 1806) he had been there so long and knew so much about the island's military weakness that the commander thought it unwise to let him go. Flinders worked on his charts while under detention; but before he could leave, an atlas published in Paris with the narrative of Baudin's expedition gave French names to some of the continental coastline. A section of the coastline along Bass Strait had been named Terre Napoleon.

Flinders was not released until 1810: he then took ship for England and prepared his reports and charts for publication. He wished to use the simple title Australia for the continent, but the publisher of the charts, advised by Banks and the Admiralty (which was paying for the publication), would not agree to this, and the book was entitled *Voyage to Terra Australis*. Flinders did not live to see the published book, which was issued in July 1814. When the first copy came from the publisher he was already unconscious, and he died the following day.

Since the start of the 1780s trade opportunities in the Pacific had been continually expanding; ships from New England ports led the way, ranging far and wide throughout the area in pursuit of furs. At first they had sought sea otter, whose fur the Chinese prized, in the northern Pacific; but soon the seals found on islands in southern latitudes became their objective. Sealing operations grew very rapidly in the South Pacific and in Antarctic waters, and after 1800 American sealers were collecting furs from points as distant as Africa's west coast, islands off Chile, and the northern coast of California, as well as from islands around Australia and New Zealand. In criss-crossing the Pacific many of the captains included Sydney among their ports of call. At the same time, following France's conquest of Spain and the consequent closing of Spanish ports in America which had formerly been used by British whaling ships, Port Jackson became a more important base for the British whalers who were becoming more active all the time. Maritime industries and island industries such as sandalwood and trepang (which were complementary to the fur trade with China) were expanding. Whaling and the kauri timber trade had been taking British vessels to New Zealand from the mid-1790s.

The Port Jackson settlements were still small, but as the only occupied harbour in this sector of the globe, Sydney quickly became a focal point for maritime activity. As early as 1802 Francois Peron, naturalist aboard *Le Géographe*, had written, probably with some exaggeration:

> In port we saw several vessels from different quarters of the world, the majority destined for new and hazardous voyages. Here were some from the banks of the Thames or the Shannon ready to proceed to the shores of New Zealand, and others after landing freight about to sail for the Yellow River of China; some laden with coal intended for the Cape of Good Hope and India. Many small vessels were ready to depart for Bass Strait to collect furs and skins, obtained by men left on different islands to capture the seals which make them their resort. Others of greater burden were intended for the western shores of America. Others again were busily fitting out as store ships for the Navigator or Friendly Islands and Society Islands to bring back pork for the colony. At the same time Captain Flinders was preparing to resume his great voyage round New Holland. This assemblage of operations, this constant movement of shipping impressed these shores with an activity which we were far from expecting in a country so lately revealed to Europe.

Less than twenty-five years after the first landing at Sydney Cove, New South Wales had progressed to such an extent that a few Sydney merchants were in a position to venture into the profitable Pacific trading. They faced stiff barriers: on the one hand the domination of local business by the New South Wales Corps, and on the other the restrictions on trade imposed by the East India Company's charter. Nevertheless, in 1801 export trade in coal had begun. Simeon Lord, an ex-convict merchant, began exporting coal from Sydney, and he also entered the trade in sealskins and whale oil, taking shares in American ships sealing and whaling in Bass Strait and holding the skins in his stores in Sydney pending reshipment with sandalwood to Canton. By using French or American ships (which were not bound by the East India Company's monopoly), it was possible for Lord to get around the restrictions against direct trade with China.

On the importing side, action had begun even earlier when, in 1798, Scottish-born Robert Campbell, a representative of the Calcutta trading firm of Campbell Clark and Company, had arrived in Sydney and, impressed with prospects for trade, had sought permission from Governor Hunter to build a warehouse and to supply the colony with goods of various kinds. On his return to Calcutta, Campbell stocked a ship with wine, spirits, sugar, tea, coffee, tobacco, and a wide range of household articles, and sailed back to Sydney with it, arriving in 1800.

Governor King, who had succeeded Hunter by this time, was anxious to see more vessels arrive with moderately priced cargoes. He replied favourably to Campbell's request for permission to land the cargo. He placed some limit on the amount of spirits landed (it was to be no more than that required for the domestic purposes of the officers and a few deserving settlers), and on other items he replied: "There can be no sort of objection to their being landed on complying with the regulations . . . in which the interest of the fair dealing merchants and rescuing the settlers and other inhabitants from the oppressive monopolies that have hitherto existed here, will be equally the subject of my attention." Campbell was soon selling livestock, grain, and general merchandise to the commissariat and private buyers; the government alone bought several thousands of pounds worth of goods from his firm each year.

Campbell also entered the whaling and sealing activities in Bass Strait, and in 1803 he sent a trial shipment of oil and sealskins to England. Governor King encouraged such trading. He was anxious to see the charter restrictions relaxed so that trade could develop normally, and he proposed that whale ships should be permitted to carry supplies instead of having to sail on ballast; the shipowners supported the pleas. King then went further; he suggested in 1804 that New South Wales merchants should be allowed to trade directly with Chinese ports, and followed this with a recommendation that oil and other produce owned by Sydney merchants should be free to go to China or England.

Before permission was received from the Colonial Office for such transactions, King authorized a shipment to London of sea elephant oil and sealskins, owned by Robert Campbell and other Sydney merchants; but on arrival the vessel, the *Lady Barlow*, was seized and the cargoes were declared contraband. Sir Joseph Banks supported the claims of the Sydney merchants, while the East India Company insisted that the law be enforced against them.

Eventually the vessel was released subject to the compulsory sale and forfeit of its cargo. Not only did the Sydney traders lose heavily but the episode resulted in Governor King being instructed to stop all such ventures. Accordingly in 1806 he published a proclamation forbidding British subjects in New South Wales from entering into any mercantile contact with foreigners. In spite of the efforts of Banks in London to secure some relaxation of the restrictions, and his advocacy of a complete change in trading policy under which the commerce of the colony might be developed, the situation remained unchanged. A bill was drawn up in 1806 to provide for "the opening of the trade of New South Wales under licences from the East India Company and the South Sea Company." However, a change of government occurred and the bill never became law. The restrictions remained in force, and local merchants had little opportunity to trade. Nevertheless, over the next five years, American trading ships visited Sydney frequently, and there were also a few voyages by independent British traders licensed by the East India Company.

The restrictions on commercial activities were becoming more irksome as the main settlements grew and activities sprang up along the coast. In Sydney and Parramatta, the community's activities were broadening. Besides the town and jail gangs and the farm-workers, a return of convicts employed on government service in King's last year of office listed brick and tile-makers, bricklayers, blacksmiths, shingle-, pale-, and lathe-splitters, sawyers, painters, lime- and charcoal-burners, shipwrights, wheelwrights, millwrights, millers, basket- and broom-makers, coopers, tanners, tailors, shoemakers, and boatbuilders. There were three natural history painters and botanists, one sailmaker, two printers and bookbinders, and forty-one flax dressers, wool carders, and weavers. King had established a "woollen and linen manufactory," which produced mainly "blanketting flannels and drugget"; fifty-eight women convicts were employed here, as well as "the aged, crippled and infirm."

When King left the colony more than 11,000 acres were under crop, including 6,075 acres under wheat, 3,876 acres under maize, and 1,000 acres under barley; in addition, more than 145,000 acres were held as pasture. Settlers and landholders numbered 689, including 43 officers. There had been a sharp advance in livestock numbers, partly from imports but mainly due to natural increase; sheep numbered over 21,000, and cattle over 5,200, while there were 552 horses. Of a population of 7,126 in the various mainland settlements (Sydney, Parramatta, the Hawkesbury, Toongabbie, and Castle Hill), less than one third were now victualled from the public stores.

King was greatly dissatisfied with the judicial system, with its criminal courts conducted by the judge-advocate and military and naval officers, and suggested it might be appropriate to institute trial by jury. He also spoke out in favour of recognition of the rights of emancipists—convicts who had served their sentence and were seeking to rehabilitate themselves as free citizens. In these recommendations King was influenced largely by his quarrels with the officers, and his desire to raise a counter force within the community. Although his price control measures and encouragement of legitimate merchants had made a considerable impression on the old rackets, as time went on enforcement of controls became less strict, and the traffic in rum continued to flourish.

This was the legacy left for King's successor, the irascible Captain William Bligh, when he was appointed to the governorship, at the age of fifty-one, in 1805. Bligh, who had survived mutiny on H.M.S. *Bounty* sixteen years before, was a man of great personal courage, as he had demonstrated in a life at sea which began at the age of seven. His resourcefulness in navigating an open boat over nearly 4,000 miles of ocean and treacherous seas after the *Bounty* mutiny, and his distinguished conduct when in command of ships during naval engagements, had won admiration. To administrators in London, and particularly to Sir Joseph Banks, the recognized authority on affairs in New South Wales, Bligh seemed to possess all the qualities needed to guide the Sydney settlement on its appointed course.

Bligh arrived in August 1806, after a tempestuous voyage, in which he quarrelled violently with the commander of the convoy. Just about the last action of Governor King was to make extensive grants of land to Bligh's daughter; just about the first action of the incoming governor was to make a land grant to his predecessor's wife.

Bligh quickly became aware of the difficulties arising from the colony's lack of normal trading facilities. He visited the various settlements and found that when the farmers had produce to dispose of there was no way in which they could sell it for coin; instead they had to barter their wheat for tea, sugar, and other commodities—or, more likely, for·rum—and in doing so they lost heavily while the dealers made immense profit from the transaction. Bligh decided to correct the situation. He received addresses from the settlers at Port Jackson and the Hawkesbury, who asked that all payments should be made in currency and that everyone should have the right to buy and sell in the open market. Bligh set about determining the commodities that the settlers needed and what produce they could supply to government stores in return. He then fixed rates at which the various items could be exchanged, and issued a general order prohibiting "exchange of spirits as payment for grain, animal food, labour, wearing apparel, or any other commodity whatever, to all descriptions of persons in the colony and its dependencies."

Although there was little or no coin available, anyone offering a bill of exchange for payment was henceforth obliged to state its value in terms of sterling. Individual settlers found these measures encouraging, and an address thanking the governor for having greatly improved conditions was signed by 835 settlers and presented to Bligh on January 1, 1808; but in other quarters the new measures stirred up resentment and resistance.

Bligh's actions, as well as his violent temper and arrogance, had quickly involved him with most of the leading people in the colony. These included merchant Simeon Lord and his emancipist partners (whom Bligh threw into jail), the few wealthy free settlers like the Blaxland brothers, to whom he refused a large land grant authorized by the Secretary of State, and the whole of the New South Wales Corps, whom he wanted to have withdrawn from the colony. His principal opponent was the formidable John Macarthur—wealthy, powerful, and as arrogant and quarrelsome as Bligh himself. Friction began when Bligh threatened to withdraw Macarthur's 5,000-acre land grant. Incident followed incident. The climax came when Bligh ordered Macarthur's trial on a variety of charges, including "deceitfully, wickedly and maliciously contriving and abetting against His Excellency to vilify and represent him and others as unjust officers."

The Criminal Court appointed to try Macarthur comprised six officers of the New South Wales Corps, under the presidency of Judge-Advocate Richard Atkins. Before Atkins could be sworn in, Macarthur protested against his acting as one of his judges, since a suit brought by him against Atkins was pending, and since he and Atkins had been inveterate enemies for twelve years. Atkins adjourned the court and withdrew, while the other members of the court upheld Macarthur's objections and asked the governor to appoint another judge-advocate. The officers remanded Macarthur on bail, but the provost marshall issued an escape warrant, and the haughty Macarthur found himself in the county jail. Bligh summoned the six officers to him, to answer the judge-advocate's memorial charging them with crimes that "amount to an usurpation of His Majesty's Government, and tend to incite or create rebellion or other outrageous treason in the people of this territory." This threat roused the Corps' acting commandant, Major George Johnston, who used his authority as lieutenant-governor to bail out the prisoner. Macarthur then drew up a document asking Johnston to place

Bligh under arrest, and pledging those who signed the petition to support him in this act.

Towards sundown on January 26, 1808, at Johnston's direction the New South Wales Corps marched to the governor's residence. From the windows Bligh saw them coming; a long search was needed to find him, but when found he was placed under arrest. Johnston assumed control as lieutenant-governor. Macarthur was taken before a substitute judge-advocate and retried; not surprisingly, he was acquitted of all charges. Johnston then created the administrative office of secretary to the colony and appointed Macarthur to it.

Bligh was confined at Government House for more than a year by a military guard. There he kept "a spy glass trained on the waters of Sydney Cove" in the hope that a ship would bring someone from London to overthrow the military régime and restore him to power. When Lieutenant-Colonel Joseph Foveaux arrived in July on his way to take up the governorship of Norfolk Island, he learnt with surprise of the turn events had taken and, as senior officer, assumed the government of the colony. He in turn was succeeded by Colonel Paterson who arrived from Van Diemen's Land, where he had been acting as commandant of a settlement at Port Dalrymple formed in 1805. However, neither Foveaux nor Paterson was willing to attempt to reinstate Bligh to power.

Bligh tried to win over some of the malcontents who had opposed him, but he realized that his position was hopeless. Finally he agreed to return to England on the *Porpoise*, and he undertook not to return to any part of the territory or interfere in any way with the government. He had no intention—he divulged later—of keeping this pact; he was again dealing with mutineers, and he signed the document because he felt it his duty to regain his ship. Once on board the *Porpoise* he assumed command and instead of sailing for England he attempted to begin a bombardment of Sydney in order to regain control there; when this notion proved impractical he decided to proceed to Hobart, where he expected to enlist support. The Lieutenant-Governor, Colonel Collins, received him with respect, but very soon relations cooled between the two men. Bligh then stationed the *Porpoise* near the Derwent River mouth where he remained, a brooding and bitter exile, for nine months, until a whaling ship arrived with news that his successor had been appointed, and was probably by now in Sydney.

The authorities in London, bewildered by such an unprecedented event as the overthrow of a governor, and concentrating on the war against Napoleon, had delayed action to deal with the confusion that had subsequently arisen in Sydney. It was not until early in 1809 that the government decided to recall Bligh and, subsequently, to appoint Lachlan Macquarie as his successor. Macquarie had instructions to arrest Major Johnston and send him to England for trial. With regard to Macarthur, the instructions were that "if examinations be sworn against him charging him with criminal acts against the governor and his authority," Macquarie should have him arrested and brought before the Criminal Court. When Macquarie reached Rio in August 1809 on his way to Sydney, he learnt that Johnston and Macarthur had sailed from that port on their way to London only a few days before. Macquarie also had instructions to reinstate Bligh as governor for one day; but when he arrived in Sydney in December, Bligh was far away in Van Diemen's Land, and it was impracticable to put the face-saving instructions into effect.

Bligh now returned to Sydney so that he might collect evidence to present against Johnston at the latter's trial. He sailed from the Derwent and reached Sydney in January 1810. Macquarie found it "extremely difficult to form a just judgement" on the causes of Bligh's arrest; he could not discover any action of Bligh's that could possibly justify the rebellion but—like the previous senior officers who at first had been prepared to support Bligh—he found his predecessor "certainly a most disagreeable person to have any dealings, or public business to transact with." After four months Macquarie was highly relieved when the farewells—including a ball which he gave in Bligh's honour—were concluded. Bligh sailed for London in May.

Johnston's court martial in May 1811 resulted in a verdict that he had been guilty of mutiny, and he was cashiered from the army; nevertheless he was allowed to return to the colony. He again took up land—he had been one of the first landholders from the officer class, having received a grant in 1793—and he farmed until his death. Bligh, though promoted to the rank of Rear-Admiral, was never again entrusted with public office. The other main figure of the crisis, Macarthur, was able to look to the support of influential friends once he was in London. No action was taken against him, but he felt it wiser to accept "exile" in England than risk a return to New South Wales. He stayed on in England learning all he could about the market requirements for fine wool, while his devoted and capable wife Elizabeth remained in New South Wales and established the merino flocks at Parramatta and Camden on an organized plan.

The Bligh episode finally convinced the British government that in a settlement of expanding horizons an impossible task had been given the governors. Since Hunter's time, governors had been pointing out the impossibility of administering the colony's affairs when the governor's authority could be nullified by the separate power residing in the New South Wales Corps. It was therefore decided that a soldier should be appointed governor.

Colonel Lachlan Macquarie was not the first choice for the governorship in succession to Bligh. Macquarie was commander of the 73rd Regiment, which was to accompany the original appointee, General Miles Nightingall; when Nightingall withdrew because of ill-health, Macquarie was elevated from Lieutenant-Governor-elect to Governor.

On arrival in Sydney, Macquarie found the little community riven by dissension and close to starvation. A capable and seasoned leader, he had been given a free hand and adequate means of carrying out the measures he deemed expedient. He had with him a force of 700 men personally loyal to him, and he put an end to the New South Wales Corps by disbanding it soon after he assumed office. A good segment of the Corps—about 300 in all—joined Macquarie's regiment, and nearly 400 members were sent home to England. All who remained were those who decided to stay on in the colony as civilians.

Shortly after his arrival, Macquarie dismissed all officers who had been appointed by Johnston, Foveaux, and Paterson, and reinstated those who had been dismissed in the two years since Bligh's overthrow. All trials and investigations held during the interregnum were declared invalid; all grants and leases of land were withdrawn and pardons revoked. However, to avoid chaos Macquarie found it expedient—and even necessary—to restitute many of the grants and pardons.

The days of turbulence were over. Macquarie was determined to bring order and progress out of the confusion he found. Members of his regiment had instructions not to engage in trade, and the prohibition was meant to be enforced. A firm and steady hand had come to rule the colony.

Consolidation   5
and expansion

When Lachlan Macquarie took up his duties as Governor of New South
Wales on the first day of 1810, he brought to the task considerable administrative ability and the experience gained in more than thirty years of
military service in America and Asia; for most of the period since the foundation of the settlement at Port Jackson he had been stationed in India, for
a time as military secretary to the Governor of Bengal. He was capable,
conscientious, vain, and obstinate; a humanitarian, with a strong sense of
duty, and an abnormal sensitiveness to criticism; he was forty-eight years of
age when he landed in Sydney, and had recently married for the second
time. He enjoyed the full support of the authorities in London, who were
anxious to see an end to the turbulence that had plagued the Sydney venture.

Macquarie found that the practical affairs of the colony had been seriously
neglected during the skirmishes between the main actors in the rebellion
drama. The community had suffered as a result; credit was short, and
confidence lacking. Sydney appeared to him to be "barely emerging from
infantile imbecility," and he determined to set the enterprise on a sounder
course. The immediate task was to bring factions into harmony and restore
a sense of unity, and he gave the lead by holding official functions and gatherings at which representation was as wide as possible.

With the main discordant elements out of the way, dissension abated
and Macquarie was able to devote his attention to the task of getting the
colony's affairs in order. It was not only a matter of restoring confidence
and correcting troubles arising directly from the Bligh episode and its
aftermath; there were many other matters to be improved if affairs were
to be set on a progressive course.

The town of Sydney had become a collection of mean tents and houses
scattered at random or huddled together in unplanned fashion; Macquarie

determined to give it wide, well ordered, named and numbered streets, and fine public buildings. Within a few months work had started on new barracks for officers and men, new granaries, and other public stores. Within a year there were turnpike roads from Sydney to the Hawkesbury and from Sydney to Parramatta, with extensions planned; several new schools had been started, and an "elegant racecourse" laid out; a contract had been let for a fine new hospital. The governor had made a tour of the farming districts, and had made plans for five townships in the neighbourhood of the Hawkesbury River (including Windsor and Richmond) and another, Liverpool, on the George's River; each township was to have its church, school, jail, and guardhouse.

Macquarie believed that roads and bridges should precede rather than follow settlement—that they were pointers to wealth and progress as well as aids to development. The existing rough winding tracks, made by horses and carts as they passed along a string of notched trees, were completely inadequate in his eyes. He believed that routes should be set by careful survey so that the shortest and best course would be followed, even if this meant that swamps had to be drained, tree stumps removed, soft patches filled in, and bridges built; when the whole road was cut level, it could be macadamized, its surface strewn with gravel and rolled hard. Macquarie was determined to build soundly for the future as well as for the day.

In the early years of Macquarie's governorship, the restrictions shackling the colony's trade remained in force, and it was largely American vessels that brought much-needed supplies. The East India Company's monopoly still excluded other British traders and, partly because of war exigencies, the volume of other shipping was so limited that provisions were frequently short in the colony. In 1813 the East India Company's rights and status were brought under review in London, and as a result its monopoly rights were reduced to a point where they applied only to trade with China and trade in tea; but in practice the growing numbers of Sydney merchants were still unable to benefit greatly. Under the new law, only ships of over 350 tons were permitted to operate freely, and—as London well knew—the colony was not capable of building such vessels.

The East India Company's monopoly had been broken, but the effect of the tonnage limitation was to favour British rather than colonial merchants. After the outbreak of war between Britain and the United States in 1812, American traders no longer visited Sydney, but sufficient shipping was arriving from London, Calcutta, and other ports to make it unnecessary for the government store to sell ordinary retail goods; and this was discontinued in 1815.

Foodstuffs and rum were still a medium of exchange, and Macquarie's huge 300-bed hospital, with surgeons' quarters, was built by contractors whose payment took the form of licences to import rum. Soon after his arrival, Macquarie reported to Lord Castlereagh, the Colonial Secretary, that agricultural and commercial pursuits were "much impeded and obstructed by the want of some adequately secured circulating medium." Macquarie noted that "the people have been in some degree forced on the expedient of issuing and receiving notes of hand to supply the place of real money, and this petty banking has thrown open a door to frauds and imposition of a most grievous nature to the country at large." In fact there was practically no currency in circulation, and coin was so scarce that substitutes had to be used as a means of exchange.

Originally authorities in London had frowned upon currency being taken into the colony in the belief that there was no need for it in a penal settlement. Only limited quantities of English shillings and bulky copper coins were available, and other coins in use—each with a value established officially in relation to the pound sterling—were Spanish, Dutch, Portuguese, or Indian. The "store receipts" issued by the commissary for its purchase of produce and goods were negotiable and circulated freely. In addition the system of issuing promissory notes which passed from hand to hand had grown up; this system was liable to abuse, many notes being issued with no backing other than the signatory's hopeful imagination.

During the period from 1810 to 1813 Macquarie issued a number of regulations designed to cut down the use of promissory notes. An early restriction was that the notes had to be written on printed forms; a later regulation provided that duty on goods entering the port of Sydney could not be paid in promissory notes but had to be paid "either in sterling money, dollars at five shillings, storekeeper's receipts or paymaster's bills." Subsequently the restriction on the "base colonial currency" was extended to cover fees paid to public departments.

To relieve the coin shortage, the governor had asked London to provide a copper coinage for use "in the lower branches of trade." However, England was suffering from a severe shortage of coin due in part to the extensive use of gold to finance the war effort, and it was some time before anything could be done to meet the request. In July 1811 a shipment of Spanish dollars from India was promised. The transfer could not be arranged immediately, but in 1812 the shipment of 10,000 gold dollars reached Sydney. In order to prevent their re-export to a gold-hungry world, a hole was punched in each dollar by a locally made machine. Each coin was stamped Five Shillings on one side and New South Wales, 1813, on the other, while the small piece—the dump—was stamped Fifteen Pence. The colony's shortage of coin was not greatly eased until after a great re-coinage was completed in Britain some years later. By this time Macquarie had succeeded in abolishing the system of barter for spirits that had been the cause of so much trouble and distress for more than twenty years; free importation of spirits was permitted from the beginning of 1815.

By 1816 it was clear that the regulatory measures were not in themselves sufficient to cure the currency troubles. Petty banking had not been eliminated, there was still a hodge-podge of coins in circulation, fluctuations were occurring in the value of "currency" compared with sterling, and fraudulent or unauthorized note issues continued; even officials of the commissariat were involved in currency frauds. The colony's internal and external trade had grown to a point where a properly constituted bank, competent to issue bank notes, was urgently needed. Macquarie had been aware all the while of the need for the creation of a bank as a means of overcoming the money problem. Soon after his arrival he put this proposal to London, but his plan was not acceptable; London had no wish to encourage ventures to change the character of the colony.

By late 1816, however, the situation was such that Macquarie was convinced action could no longer be delayed. Late in November he called together fourteen leading citizens, who thereupon agreed to become sponsors and financial backers of a bank. The governor immediately issued a proclamation invalidating all but sterling notes; at the same time the organizing of the bank went ahead. A few days later a public meeting was held at which £5,000 was subscribed to launch the bank; a committee was appointed to run affairs until directors could be formally elected. The directors took over in February 1817, and a charter was issued by the governor the following month. At this point Macquarie drafted a dispatch to London reporting and justifying his action. The bank opened for business on April 8, 1817 as the Bank of New South Wales. Subscribed capital was £12,600.

When Macquarie's dispatch reached the Colonial Office, his action was considered insupportable. Acting on legal advice, Lord Bathurst, who had become Secretary of State for War and the Colonies in 1814, refused to approve the charter to the bank, and he informed Macquarie accordingly. In his reply Macquarie played for time, and the bank remained in operation. Notes for half a crown, 5/–, 10/–, £1, and £5 were issued. As the notes of a bank with official backing (the backing of the governor, though this was not sanctioned by the home government) they had a solid support; but neither they nor the dollars wholly replaced barter, and all kinds of produce still changed hands at market value without the use of money. The bank's activity in discounting bills of exchange meant that promissory notes were soon outmoded, although store receipts were still being issued by the commissariat. The use of money continued to increase in relative importance, particularly in government finance.

Confidence in the bank grew quickly and, even though in its early years it had to go through some difficult times, its creation and operation had a significant effect in helping the colony outgrow the rigid and limited objectives of a large scale reformatory.

Numerically the colony was still dominated by the convict element. Largely because of wartime exigencies and partly because of the East India Company's monopoly, there had been very little shipping between England and the colony, so that the few would-be free emigrants had always found it as difficult to get to New South Wales as the time-expired convicts did to get back to England. Macquarie thus found that at least five out of every six of the population of under 12,000 were convicts or ex-convicts. Some of them had been free now for twenty years or more, had raised families, and were living perfectly normal and respectable lives. Some had come to the colony as mere children; many had been first offenders, sentenced to a seven-year term; some had been convicted on political, not on criminal, charges.

The emancipated convict was free to take up any occupation for which he had the training or capacity; this applied to those who had served their sentences, those freed by conditional or absolute pardon, and the large number holding tickets of leave (which meant that the holder was not liable to work for the government, nor to be assigned to one of the settlers). In the absence of free trained men, educated emancipists were necessarily appointed to minor administrative positions; the greater part of the commissariat staff, storekeepers, superintendents of convict work and jail gangs and government farms came from their ranks. Among the emancipists were several schoolmasters and lawyers, as well as an occasional doctor and clergyman. There were a number of shopkeepers and merchants, some of whom had made personal fortunes. Such men transacted daily commercial business with the free settlers as a matter of course; but the question of their social status was another matter.

Before he arrived in New South Wales Macquarie had held more or less the views that might be expected of an army officer of the day; his own association with the convicts or ex-convicts would be that of "control," he thought. Before long, however, his travels through the colony had convinced him that some of the emancipists had become not only respectable but in many ways extremely useful members of the community. He therefore determined to act on the principle that once a prisoner had become free "his former state should no longer be remembered, or allowed to act against him." In his first long dispatch to London he noted the need for great caution and delicacy in pursuing such a policy as he proposed, and went on to record that initially he had limited his dinner invitations—the seal of social approval—to four emancipists including the "opulent" merchant Simeon Lord and William Redfern, the assistant surgeon. He also reported that he had appointed one emancipist a justice of the peace and magistrate, and intended to confer the same "mark of respect" on two others when vacancies occurred.

This social recognition of the emancipists was greeted with horror by a small but influential section of the community, the ex-officers of the New South Wales Corps and the civil officials who had become wealthy through trade and the land, and the few free immigrant landowners. From his exile in London, John Macarthur wrote to his wife with incredulous amazement: "God alone knows how such a state of things as you describe may terminate. . . . Would to God I could withdraw you all from the colony."

One of the most bitter critics was the Reverend Samuel Marsden, trader, livestock- and land-owner, magistrate at Parramatta, and principal chaplain of the colony of which he had assumed the role of moral censor. Finding himself appointed to a new Road Board with two emancipists, Marsden wrote to the Colonial Office and the Archbishop of Canterbury about the "degradation to his office" and declined to take his seat on the board in such company. The officers of the garrison, who regarded themselves as setting the standards of society, were equally affronted by the Governor's attitude to emancipists; particularly was this true of the officers of the 46th Regiment, which replaced Macquarie's own 73rd Regiment in 1814. A few selected emancipists were welcomed to the drawing-room of Government House, but never in the officers' mess; and an officer was court martialled for ungentlemanly behaviour in sitting down with an emancipist.

Macquarie was prepared to appoint "meritorious men" to senior government offices when their talents justified it. Emancipists in such offices were the assistant surgeon, the deputy surveyor, the civil architect, one of the assistant chaplains, and the chief clerk in the office of the governor's secretary.

As his instructions enjoined him to do, Macquarie settled emancipists on the land, granting blocks of 30 or more acres, cleared from the forest if necessary, to men who had served their sentences. He believed that agricultural settlements formed in this way could best provide for the rehabilitation of those whom he considered to be the most deserving men in the colony. Besides the usual "indulgences" by which settlers received food and clothing from the government stores, plus the services of assigned convicts, he made gifts of cattle from the government herds to small settlers, with safeguards so that the cattle were not disposed of; previously cattle had been granted mainly to the settlers with capital.

Official opinion in London was naturally somewhat wary about Macquarie's pro-emancipist policy; but he had support in 1812 from a committee of the House of Commons appointed to review the transportation system, which cordially concurred with the governor's principle that "long-tried good conduct should lead a man back to the rank in society which he had forfeited." Encouraged by this, Macquarie suggested it might strengthen his position if he could be favoured with the Prince Regent's sentiments on the subject; this suggestion was ignored. Lord Bathurst took a cautious view; he wrote to Macquarie that while he agreed with the principle in general, it could be carried too far and too fast. He advised the governor to "trust to gradual effect." This Macquarie was unwilling to do. The continuing opposition in the colony only strengthened his belief in the humanity and wisdom of his policy; the result was a very serious crisis in the judicial system.

Until Macquarie's time there had been no change in the judicial system established in 1787. The Criminal Court had consisted of the judge-advocate, together with six officers of His Majesty's Forces, from the military garrison and (whenever a warship was in port) from the navy. The Civil Court consisted of the judge-advocate and two other persons appointed by the governor, while the judge-advocate and a justice of the peace formed the Bench of Magistrates. Appeals could be made to the governor. The first Judge-Advocate, Captain David Collins, was a marine corps officer without legal training. A lawyer, Richard Dore, was appointed to the position in 1789 but died the following year. The next Judge-Advocate was Richard Atkins, a habitual drunkard who, according to Bligh, "pronounced sentences of death in moments of intoxication," while his knowledge of the law was "insignificant and subservient to private inclination." Even without Atkins's inadequacies, the judicial system had long been unsatisfactory. Apart from the possibility of injustice to individuals from the lack of legal training on the part of the judge-advocate and members of the courts, the governor had no one on whom he could rely for legal advice as to the consitutionality of his actions and general orders. A big step forward came when a lawyer, Ellis Bent, was appointed Judge-Advocate; he reached the colony at the same time as Macquarie.

In its report the 1812 Committee of the House of Commons had condemned the colony's judicial system as being more like a court martial than an English court of justice, and soon afterwards the colonial office took steps to reorganize the system on the lines advocated by the committee. In future there were to be three courts of justice. A Governor's Court, presided over by the judge-advocate assisted by two "fit and proper persons" appointed by the governor, was to hear and determine minor civil cases. A similarly constituted court was to sit in Van Diemen's Land. And a Supreme Court, under a chief justice and two persons chosen by the governor in rotation from the magistrates of the colony, was to deal with all criminal cases, and all civil cases in which the sum at issue exceeded £50.

The emancipist question flared again in the new courts of justice. Up to this time the absence of lawyers in the colony had necessarily meant that emancipists had held minor court offices, as well as acting as solicitors under generalized powers of attorney from their clients. The question of the eligibility of emancipists to practise as attorneys was first raised by Bent; it was renewed when his more aggressive brother, Jeffrey Hart Bent, arrived in the colony in 1814 to take up his appointment as First Justice of the new Supreme Court. The Bents held the view that, according to both statute and case law, a man who had once been convicted of a felony could never again be allowed to practise as an attorney. On the other hand, the magistrates assisting the justices supported the governor's view, which was that such a deprivation would strip from the emancipist attorneys "the most active of all stimulus to reform," the hope of again practising their profession. However, when an emancipist attorney presented his petition, the two judges refused to open the courts, and a deadlock ensued. Both the judges and the governor appealed to the Secretary of State, pleading their viewpoints, while the courts of justice remained closed for over a year.

The Colonial Secretary's eventual decision favoured Macquarie, but not unreservedly. Lord Bathurst recalled the Bents (Ellis Bent was dead by the time the dispatch recalling him was received) and censured them severely for closing the courts, an action for which there could be no possible justification. He pointed out that as there was only one "free" attorney in the colony at the time, a litigant would have to conduct his case himself, or employ the same attorney as his opponent. At the same time he wrote to Macquarie that in the existing circumstances—there being only one attorney in the colony—the employment of "convict" attorneys (they were still convicts to him) could be sanctioned; but only under those exceptional circumstances, and not as a general and normal line of policy.

Most of Macquarie's predecessors had been naval men and had looked as much to the sea as the land. Macquarie had different ideas; he was not overawed by the wildness of the land but rather saw in its immensity and rawness a challenge. Quite soon after his arrival he visited Van Diemen's Land and there he made the overland journey from the Derwent settlement north to the Tamar on horseback. What he saw of the terrain away from the coast impressed him.

Back in Sydney, Macquarie discussed the possibility of breaking through the mountain barrier and finding a way westward. The settlement around Port Jackson was severely circumscribed by a tangle of ravines, gorges, and escarpments which barred the way inland. Sometimes an escaped prisoner in a desperate search of freedom, or a deluded visionary disappeared for ever in the labyrinth of rough vegetation and sandstone ridges. Many unsuccessful attempts had been made to cross this barrier westward, or to find a path through the Hawkesbury Ranges that hedged in the little settlement to the north.

Governor Phillip had first noticed the western range when exploring the shores of Port Jackson in April 1788, and within a few years the name Blue Mountains had become common. At first there had been no thought that it would be difficult to find a way inland; but soon the impenetrable nature of the barrier was realized as several capable men tried but each in turn failed. In 1793, 1794, and 1796, and again in 1802, 1804, and 1806, assaults were made. The broken plateau of sandstone was found to break up into sheer precipices, drop into deep gorges, and throw up rocky ribs across the gaps, blocking the path. After the long series of failures Governor King had suspended official attempts, and the territory beyond the western horizon remained a complete mystery. King had declared that the idea of attempting a crossing of such "a confused and barren assemblage of mountains with impassable chasms between" was as chimerical as it was useless.

Early in 1812 Macquarie decided to back another attempt, and when a serious drought made it imperative the next year to seek new pastures for the increasing numbers of sheep and cattle, he gave his support for a well-organized expedition. A party consisting of free settler Gregory Blaxland, army lieutenant William Lawson, and an Australian-born youth, William Charles Wentworth, set out on May 11, 1813, with four other men, five dogs, and four horses laden with provisions. By keeping to the ridges rather than the valleys (all of which had been found to end in sheer cliffs) the party was able to cut a path through thick underbrush and timber. Scrambling over the broken terrain, the men held to the ridge top and finally found a pass which led them through the last rocky barrier. Thus, after three weeks of arduous travel covering 50 miles or so, they had the satisfaction of seeing well-grassed woodlands stretching away to the west.

The group did not wait to explore the new territory. Instead they returned at once to Sydney with the good news that a path could in fact be found through that forbidding range, and that beyond lay fertile land for the farmer and stock-raiser—"forest or grassland, sufficient in extent to support the stock of the colony for the next thirty years," Blaxland wrote. Lawson noted that there should be no difficulty in building a good road for access, and he expressed the view that the ridge the party had travelled on would open the way also to the head of the Hunter River, "where, to my knowledge, is a large extent of grazing country."

Macquarie sent Surveyor George William Evans to survey a road through the range and to determine what lay beyond. Starting in November 1813, Evans followed the route of the three pathfinders. He proved that they had not reached the highest part of the range, and descending the western slope he pushed 85 miles beyond their limit point. He gave the names Macquarie River and Bathurst Plains to a fine river and the rich plains it watered, and penetrated to a point about 170 miles directly west of Sydney.

Evans found the region to be "a fine plain of rich land, the handsomest country I ever saw." He noted that the soil was exceedingly rich, and produced the finest grass intermixed with a variety of herbs. "The river winds through fine flats and round the points of small ridges which gradually descend towards it. I am more pleased with the country every day; it far outpasses in fertility and beauty any I have yet seen." On the way back to Sydney, Evans and his party met two Aboriginal women and four children —the first Aborigines encountered west of the mountains. On seeing the white people, the Aborigines fell down in fright, and on recovering made off quickly.

After the governor received Evans's report, he officially acknowledged the services of the three pioneers and granted each 1,000 acres of land as a reward. At the same time William Cox, ex-paymaster of the New South Wales Corps and now a leading stock-owner and magistrate at the Hawkesbury, volunteered to construct a road over the route. His work force was a superintendent and guide (both free men), eight soldiers to act as guards, and twenty-eight carefully selected convict volunteers, including a carpenter, blacksmith, overseer of tools, two bullock-drivers, and a doctor-constable. Within six months Cox had completed a dual carriageway, 20 feet wide, or 12 feet in the most difficult parts, without a single casualty. The road was open in January 1815, and a few months later the governor travelled over it, reaching the Macquarie River in nine days. He fixed the site for the erection of a town "at some future period," giving it the name Bathurst in honour of the Secretary of State. Cox received the first grant of land in the area; the convict work-force received free pardons; and in July 1815 Lawson set off with a 100 head of cattle for the land grant he had selected beyond the range.

As the Macquarie River flowed with such strong current and volume past the new outpost of Bathurst, Evans was sent to trace it and explore the area farther to the west and south-west. Evans and his companions succeeded in discovering a series of creeks along whose banks was fine grazing land. On a subsequent trip Evans came upon a watercourse with banks 80 feet apart. It was dry, but the trees lining the banks indicated that it was the bed of a large river; Evans named it the Lachlan.

The crossing of the Blue Mountains opened a way to a great new province containing lands upon which a grazing industry could be based. By the end of 1815 a number of stock-owners had sought permission to move their sheep and cattle to the new lands. Within a few years ten settlers (five of them Australian-born) were established and livestock belonging to another twenty owners, as well as some government flocks and herds, were being grazed on the pastures around Bathurst.

The year 1815 marked the end of the series of wars in which England had been engaged almost throughout the preceding twenty-three years. This landmark in European history had repercussions in Australia. There was extreme poverty and growing industrial unrest in England, and a great crime wave swept the country in the wake of the conflict; at the same time shipping was released from wartime patrol duties; the result was a very great increase in the number of convicts transported to Australia. A year after the war, the British government eased its restrictions on the free emigration of its citizens; at first there were not many individuals prepared to make the long voyage to New South Wales, but from an early trickle the number grew steadily. The rapid increase in population as more transports arrived, and the new factors introduced by the accelerated intake, which occurred just when pastoral expansion was beginning to open new horizons in the colony, aggravated the standing conflict of interest that rent the community.

With more labour available, the sheep-owners were anxious to extend their activities in wool-growing, and they wanted more land and more convict labour to develop it. The expectation that the new land would provide a growing volume of fine wool was also awakening interest in commercial places in England. Macquarie seemed to ignore the implications of this prospect, and gave little encouragement to the proposition that wool-growing would develop into a great industry that eventually might employ a large work force. He considered that the type of primary producers from which the community derived most benefit were the small yeoman-class farmers—the emancipists being the best of the class—while stock-owners benefited only themselves. His attitude was expressed in a complaint about the Blaxland brothers, pioneer stock-owners:

> Instead of contributing thus to the general welfare of the country and setting a good example of an improved style of farming and agriculture, they have turned their whole attention to the lazy object of rearing cattle. . . . They have sold eighty-eight thousand three hundred and ninety-six pounds of fresh meat to the government stores in two years and nine months . . . and within the same period they have not paid into the store one single bushel of any kind of grain whatever.

The fact that, as he saw it, most of the malcontents and turbulent individuals who had made trouble for all the governors from Hunter to himself came from the class of gentlemen-farmer/stock-owners contributed to his prejudice and sharpened his preference for small farmers, who could be expected to be less difficult to handle.

Up to 1817–18 Macquarie had been able to concentrate on the advancement of those in his charge within the framework of a comparatively compact penal establishment. He had settled numerous emancipists, the few incoming free settlers, and even some Aborigines on small farms, to grow the food the community needed. He had fixed the prices at which grain and meat would be bought for the government stores, and made sure that purchases were spread fairly over the suppliers; a system of purchase by tender and contract would favour a few "rich monopolizers," he thought. He had made sure that military and civil officers did not engage in trade, and had ended the practice by which grants of land were made to officers while they were still in government employ. The number of convicts arriving had varied between 200 and 630 a year, a number that could easily and profitably be absorbed into the community. When the convict ships arrived, most of the male convicts were assigned, as farm labourers or servants, to settlers, who had to feed and clothe their assigned men. Government gangs operated on the roads and wharves, and government convict-artisans worked in the Lumberyard, a series of sheds and yards surrounded by a high wall, in the heart of Sydney; but most of Macquarie's early roads and public buildings had been built by contractors, using convict labour.

All this was in the pattern of paternal administration; but its limitations were to become increasingly apparent.

With the sharp rise in convict intake that followed the restoration of peace in Europe—the number of arrivals rose to 1200 in 1816 and the following year exceeded 2000—many adjustments were called for to meet the new conditions in the colony. In May 1818 Macquarie reported the situation to Lord Bathurst and explained the measures taken to meet it:

> I am greatly grieved to say that I am as yet unable to make any considerable reduction in the public expenditure of this colony, owing principally to the vast number of convicts that have been sent out to it within the last two years and the settlers returning to government some hundreds of their convict servants whom they could not afford to maintain in consequence of the scarcity of provisions and other serious distress occasioned by the inundations of the Hawkesbury and Nepean Rivers in 1816 and 1817 . . . They [the settlers] are unable to take many convicts off the store so that the expense of maintaining the latter must for some time longer fall principally on the government. I am therefore obliged to employ at present strong gangs of convicts in the several public works in progress at Sydney and in constructing new and repairing old roads in the interior of the colony.

Armed with such justification, he happily embarked upon a spate of building. Government gangs were put to work on such structures as new barracks for convicts, a house and offices for the judge of the Supreme Court, soldiers' barracks in Sydney ("perhaps the best and most complete in His Majesty's foreign dominions"), a light-house at South Head, churches in Sydney, Windsor, and Liverpool, and schoolhouses which were used as Sunday chapels in the smaller townships. Road-building continued, the outlying districts being linked with Sydney and with each other. Macquarie the builder had the great good fortune to have at his disposal the services of Bristol-born architect Francis Howard Greenway, who arrived in the colony in 1814 under sentence for forging an endorsement on a contract. Macquarie put him to work reporting on the public works under construction, and in 1816 appointed him civil architect (granting him first a conditional and then, in 1819, a full pardon). The result was a series of simple, dignified, beautifully proportioned, and well-finished buildings and monuments, from Georgian churches and military barracks to the little stone obelisk from which were measured the roads that radiated south-west, north-west, and west of Sydney.

Even if private land-owners were unable to employ the whole of the labour force that entered the colony from 1817 onwards, the government's right to take the pick of the available workforce was a perpetual grievance. "Opulent men" who wanted to erect mansions for themselves complained that the government had first choice of all the best convict stonemasons and carpenters, and that the necessity to compete for available labour with the government forced up wages. Macquarie found himself beset with difficulties as opposition to his policies built up among the landed interests.

More importantly, he found himself increasingly out of step with London's attitudes. Quite suddenly, the state of the colony of New South Wales had become a matter of interest to Opposition members of the House of Commons. There were two distinct centres of dissatisfaction: the commercial and manufacturing interests, who wanted to see the way opened for increased wool-growing, and the evangelical—radicals, led by slave-trade abolitionist William Wilberforce, who were concerned to remedy tyranny and oppression wherever it occurred. Both groups were supplied with verbal ammunition by their friends in the colony—notably by Marsden, by now a leading sheep-owner for whom his chaplaincy appeared to be a sideline. There were anonymous letters, a petition that accused the governor alternately of tyranny and leniency, and a pamphlet-letter published by a member of parliament alleging "flagrant examples of misgovernment" by Macquarie. The administration of its penal colony was becoming a source of political embarrassment to the government.

The continuing increases in expenditure were a constant irritation. Colonial officials took the view that if the colonists were not able to pay for roads, bridges, and public buildings, the colony was not ready to receive these luxuries. Macquarie was reminded that colonial governors had to submit plans and estimates to the Treasury before expenses were incurred. His plans for erecting a new Government House (the existing Government House at Sydney dated back to Phillip's time and Macquarie considered the rooms were "so much decayed and rotten as to render them extremely unsafe any longer to live in") were sternly vetoed.

At first Macquarie's attitude to the rehabilitation of former convicts had been rather grudgingly supported by the London authorities; but as time went on and complaints about the governor's sponsorship of emancipists came from the colony in mounting numbers, there was a change of attitude. Macquarie was subordinating punishment to reformation, it was felt. Whitehall could not but approve of the reforms Macquarie and Redfern had made in the medical supervision and hygiene control on board convict transports, and they were prepared to accept the reduction in flogging. Yet all such reforms made transportation less of a deterrent to crime. There were numerous cases of convicts sentenced to lighter punishments appealing to have their sentences changed to the supposedly graver punishment of transportation; and an investigating committee heard from a Newgate prison orderly in 1818 that prisoners sentenced to transportation considered it "a party of pleasure—as going out to see the world."

In his continuing opposition to the encouragement of free immigration, Macquarie found himself increasingly out of step with attitudes developing in London. Every ship arriving in Sydney now brought its quota of free settlers—much to Macquarie's apprehension, for he could see that basic changes would follow.

One arrival was that turbulent individual John Macarthur, whose enforced exile in London from 1809 onwards was ended in 1817 when Earl Bathurst granted him a permit to return to New South Wales with "neither concession nor retraction demanded," but on the understanding that Macarthur would keep out of public affairs. For the second time Macarthur had returned in triumph from disgrace. While his wife Elizabeth had run his estates at Parramatta and Camden, Macarthur had used his time in London to study wool marketing, and he had become an expert in fibre qualities and in the procedures necessary for the selling of colonial wools. He had seen at first hand the incessant demand of Yorkshire wool spinners for fine wool, a demand that the war-ravaged traditional European sources were unable to supply in full. More than ever he believed that the colony's future lay in the growing of fine wool, and he wanted to see the way cleared for expansion of wool-growing. As a start, he pressed the governor to accept his proposal that he should become a monopoly provider of fine-wool rams in return for a grant of land and the exclusive use of 50,000 acres for pasture. Macquarie was not impressed by the artful suggestion that he might "procure the favourable opinions and interest of the commercial and manufacturing gentlemen at home" to oppose that of his "inveterate foes, the Saints."

Macquarie declined to do more than forward the details of Macarthur's grandiose plan to London. Thereafter Macarthur, through correspondence with his son John in London, did everything possible to undermine the governor's standing with the Colonial Office. Openly, however, he maintained good relations with Macquarie, who regarded him as a friend even if he could not see him as a prophet.

As early as April 1817 the British Government was considering the appointment of a Commissioner to investigate affairs in New South Wales, and early in 1819 the appointment was given to John Thomas Bigge, a barrister of thirty-nine and former chief justice in the slave plantation colony of Trinidad. Bigge was to investigate and report on the laws, regulations, and usages of the settlements in New South Wales and Van Diemen's Land; the principal point stressed in his instructions was that he was to "bear in mind that transportation is intended as a severe punishment . . . and as such must be rendered an object of real terror." The commissioner was empowered to recommend to Macquarie, for immediate adoption, any change which he might consider necessary either to remedy existing evils or to prevent future causes of complaint. If the governor declined to adopt any of the commissioner's suggestions, he was to report his reasons to London at once.

Macquarie had sent a letter of resignation to London in December 1817; on receiving it, Bathurst felt that the governor, with his extreme sensitiveness to criticism, had misinterpreted his strictures, and wrote asking him to reconsider his resignation. This letter was apparently lost in the mail, and Macquarie did not receive it. Instead he received news of the appointment of Bigge, and five days later the commissioner reached Sydney in person.

While the British government's new adviser on colonial affairs was on his way to Sydney, the *élite* among the colonists themselves had for the first time put on paper, for the consideration of the British government, their ideas about the colony's present and future.

With the governor's approval, a public meeting of "free settlers, merchants, land- and house-holders," both free immigrants and emancipists, was held in March 1819 and a memorial to the Prince Regent drafted. By far the greater part of the petition was concerned with trade and commerce. At this time the colony's "commercial marine" amounted to about twenty-nine vessels, the largest of which was 184 tons weight, seven of them not more than 15 tons weight. They were engaged in coastal and some island trade, carrying to Sydney such cargoes as timber from Shoalhaven, coal from Newcastle, sealskins from Macquarie Island, oil, grain, and salt meat from Van Diemen's Land, and pork meat from Tahiti.

Several leading traders—notably the enterprising Simeon Lord—had larger ambitions. The petitioners complained about the limitation of the right of navigation between England and New South Wales to ships of at least 350 tons, and pointed out that Sydney merchants did not have the capital for vessels of this size. Since 1813 local customs duties had been charged on sandalwood, pearlshell, bêche-de-mer, whale oil, sealskins, and similar products of the South Seas, as well as spars and timber from New Zealand; these duties (additional to those that would be charged if the goods were exported to England) were cited as a hindrance to trade, which would lead to the ruin of "our infant shipping interests, colonial coasting trade and fishery."

A reduction of English duties was sought on whale oil and other whale products, hides, hoofs and horns, and bark for tanning (on all of which the Australian colonies paid higher duties than other colonies) as well as on wool. The colonists boasted that "we can grow wool as fine as imported from Spain in considerable and rapidly increasing quantities," and looked forward confidently to a time when merino wool would be the principal staple export to the mother-country. They also asked for permission to erect a distillery, which would provide a market for surplus grain, and so lessen the alternations of glut and scarcity which continued to plague the farming industry.

The other principal question agitating the petitioners was the Criminal Court; they described it as "rather a court martial than a court of law" and urged that trial by jury be introduced. There was no mention of a legislative council, or any other political or consititutional question. There were well over 1,200 signatures to the petition; John Macarthur, who objected to the clause about trial by jury, was the only prominent individual not signing. In forwarding the petition, Macquarie declared himself in complete accord with the signatories; he had, in fact, made most of the same suggestions in dispatches to London.

Some of the grievances had already been remedied by the time the petition reached London; both the 350-ton restriction on shipping and the New South Wales duties on South Sea products had been removed; permission had also been granted for a distillery. The other points were held over pending receipt of Bigge's report.

Another petition, this time signed by emancipists only, was sent to London in the following year. Judicial verdicts in two court cases had held that persons holding absolute or conditional pardons from the governor were not thereby fully restored to the civil rights of free men. Faced with this threat to their future (it was interpreted as meaning that the emancipists could not hold or convey property, and could not sue or give evidence in a court of justice), the anxious emancipists drew up a petition, pointing out that since the foundation of the colony it had been assumed that those who obtained a pardon could acquire and possess land and enjoy all the civil rights of free citizens. They also quoted statistics on the amount of land, sums invested, and value of livestock and property owned by the emancipists and the "emigrant colonists" respectively. In every respect the 7,556 emancipists outweighed the 1,558 free settlers, holding nearly three times as much land under cultivation and having very much greater investment in trade and property.

The convict intake continued to increase. More than 5,500 convicts arrived in the colony during the two years and four months from September 1818 to December 1820—roughly half the number transported during the first twenty-two years of the colony (or up to the beginning of Macquarie's governorship). In 1821 another 2,200 arrived. This unprecedented influx intensified all the problems of the administration, as well as aggravating the differences between Macquarie and Bigge which were inevitable in view of the two men's completely divergent points of view. Macquarie was a humanitarian, who conceived he had a duty to the whole population of the colony, "be they bond or free, black or white." The fact that convicts, ex-convicts, and their children formed at least six-sevenths of the population seemed to him clear indication that his policies should be directed to their welfare. Bigge was concerned—by his instructions as well as his instincts and experience—with practical questions of how to make the colony pay for itself, and how to make transportation once again a deterrent to crime. There could be no reconciliation between two such opposites.

About the only thing the two men agreed upon was the damaging effect of the huge increase in the numbers transported. Though he criticized Macquarie's employment policies, Bigge admitted that the convict intake "had certainly exceeded, during the period of the last three years in New

South Wales and during that of two years in Van Diemen's Land, the positive demands of the settlers for labour."

Macquarie continued to employ the ever-increasing work force on public works; Greenway's fine churches at Windsor and Liverpool were completed in this period, together with Government House stables, a fort at Port Bennelong, and a factory and barracks for the female convicts at Parramatta. Macquarie sent to Van Diemen's Land as many convicts as the settlers and the public works programme there could absorb. In 1819 he started a government farm at Emu Plains, and in 1821 he established a new convict settlement 220 miles north of Sydney at Port Macquarie; this harbour had been discovered by Surveyor-General Oxley, who in 1818, starting from beyond the Blue Mountains, had found a way over the Liverpool Plains to the coast near the mouth of the Hastings River.

New areas were being opened for grazing and for the movement of stock. In the south, a free settler, Charles Throsby, had in 1819 discovered a way from the Cow Pastures to the Bathurst Plains; this was a much better route for stock to take than the track across the Blue Mountains. Further exploration penetrated as far south as Jervis Bay and the northern shores of Lake George. Macquarie proposed to reserve for the Aborigines 10,000 acres of the country discovered by Throsby, although more than 5,000 cattle and 6,000 sheep were already grazing there.

In spite of the opportunities for pastoral expansion offered by the new discoveries, Macquarie was still thinking of primary production mainly in terms of agriculture. In view of the numbers of convicts being sent to the colony, he naturally hoped that no more poor free settlers would be sent out, to add to his expenses; but he favoured the immigration of men with about £500 capital, to be laid out in agricultural pursuits in the colony. In his last year of office, when the numbers of free emigrants were greatly increasing (123 heads of families presented the Colonial Office's recommendation for land grants and "indulgences" to the governor in 1821), he drew up a scale for land grants in proportion to capital. The maximum was 2,000 acres, to be granted to men with £3,000 real capital, "that quantity being full as much as any individual can have occasion for, either for the purpose of grazing or cultivation, for many years."

John Macarthur, then grazing 7,000 sheep on 9,000 acres of land at the Cow Pastures, held very different views. He was delighted to find he had a disciple in Commissioner Bigge, who told a third party that he looked to Macarthur's evidence as "the key or touchstone of the truth of all he heard from other sources."

After two years in the colony, Bigge left in 1821 to return to London. By that time Macquarie, sick and tired, his spirit broken by continued policy and personal disagreements with the commissioner, and increasingly conscious that he was out of step with London, had repeated his resignation, which was accepted. In February 1822 Macquarie sailed for England, and presented his report on his administration to Lord Bathurst, who received it with thanks and praise, qualified by the observation that as a place of punishment, the colony had not answered all the purposes for which it was intended.

Very soon afterwards the Bigge reports were issued. The first was an account of the convict system (published in 1822), the second dealt with the judicial system (1823), and the third reviewed trade and agriculture (also 1823).

Bigge took exception to Macquarie's ambitious building programme; some of the buildings in which the governor affirmed his "pride and exultance", Bigge pronounced over-ornamented and extravagant, and "too grand for an infant colony." He condemned the governor's convict policy from beginning to end. The acceptance of emancipists as ordinary members of society was "recommended more by motives of humanity than those of reason." The result of Macquarie's excessive generosity in granting pardons and making land grants was that, at least for those serving seven-year terms, a sentence of transportation had become "more one of emigration than of punishment."

Bigge considered that the concentration of convicts in and near towns by Macquarie's public works policy was an inducement to crime, and recommended that new exclusively penal settlements should be formed at Moreton Bay, Port Curtis, and Port Bowen. On returning to the settled districts, the convicts should work for the landowners for some years, then should work out the balance of their sentences on tickets of leave. He considered that the nature of the land was such that a small settler without capital had no chance of making a profit from an allotment of 30 acres, so recommended that grants to time-expired convicts (unless they could prove they had capital of at least £20 in stock or implements) should be limited to 10 acres.

The core of Bigge's recommendations came in a section that could have been dictated by Macarthur. The commissioner pointed out that the country discovered to the west and north of Bathurst had already proved particularly suited for the feeding of sheep and cattle, especially for the "more delicate breeds [of sheep] that have hitherto attained their greatest perfection in the warmer climates of the south of Europe." He pointed to the improvement of Macarthur's fine-wool flocks as "unquestionable proof of the value of this branch of rural industry in New South Wales, both as with regard the employment of convicts, and the saving of all expense to government in their subsistence, as well as in the production of an article of export to Great Britain, that is indispensable to the progress of her great staple manufacture": an article that had the added merit of not competing with anything produced in England. To induce "persons of respectability" to engage in large scale rearing of sheep and cattle, "grants of land might be made to them, in proportion to the number of convicts that they engaged to employ, as well as to the numbers of sheep and cattle that the proprietors took with them in the first instance; a power being added of purchasing, at a low rate, such greater quantity as they might then require; and, with a further understanding, that as the number of their flocks and herds increased, a further augmentation of land would be made to them gratuitously."

Bigge's report was not confined to public policies, but contained many pages detailing scandals and complaints, some dating back to 1810. One young Australian, William Charles Wentworth, later described these sections as "all the dirt and filth, all the scandal, calumnies and lies, that were ever circulated in the Colony . . . evidence, too, not even taken under the sanction of an oath."

Macquarie was forbidden by the government to reply publicly to Bigge. Vainly he tried to get some public recognition that the government did not accept the strictures of what he called "this vile insidious Bigge Report," which "is everywhere, in the hands of everyone, and has gone all over the world." He died in a London lodging house, three years after giving up the glories and griefs of his antipodean viceroyalty; his replies to Bigge were not made public until four years after his death.

Bigge had not been instructed to make any recommendations on the machinery of government, which had not been altered since the foundation of the penal settlement at Port Jackson in 1788. The first influential suggestion for a change had been made by the House of Commons Committee on Transportation in 1812, which considered that no one man should have as much power as was in the hands of the governor of New South Wales, and made the recommendation that the governor should have a council to share his responsibilities. Lord Bathurst and Colonial Office officials had considered this premature, to Macquarie's great relief. Bathurst still held the same point of view in 1817, when he wrote to Jeffrey Bent:

> I am aware that it is a matter of some embarrassment to fix the precise moment at which a colony constituted, as that of New South Wales is, for the punishment of offenders ought to be released from that species of military government which the composition of its population is admitted in the first instance to have rendered indispensibly necessary. On such a question it is natural that the governor, responsible as he alone is for the security of the colony, should feel strongly the necessity of continuing the system that he found in force, and should incline to the opinion that the convenience of those who have freely placed themselves in a colony of such a description should be a secondary object when compared with the control which he considers necessary for the security and the proper government of the convicts.

This attitude began to change over the next few years. Then came the Bigge report. Its accumulation of factual statistical evidence about all aspects of life in New South Wales made it abundantly clear that the time had come for a change. A military autocracy was no longer adequate for a colony that had far outgrown the stature of a mere jail.

Accordingly the Colonial Office draftsmen set to work to provide the framework for a system of government for New South Wales more in keeping with the colony's new stature. They took into consideration not only the Bigge report but also the recommendations of the House of Commons committees of 1812 and 1818 on transportation, and the petitions of the Sydney merchants in 1918 and the emancipists in 1821. They also took some account of the views expressed by Wentworth, who for several years had been actively campaigning in London to raise the status of New South Wales in the eyes of important people. Wentworth, an author-lawyer of persuasive eloquence, wanted to see parliamentary government for New South Wales applied through a nominated council and an elected legislative assembly, and in a book on the colony, published in 1819, he had written: "The colony is, I believe, the only one of the British possessions inhabited by Englishmen in which there is not at least the shadow of free government."

A general policy of setting up legislative councils, with limited powers and nominated membership, to advise colonial governors on local matters, had been accepted by the British government. The changed circumstances in New South Wales now made it possible to liberalize the administration there. The result of the official deliberations was the New South Wales Judicature Act of 1823. Under this act, the governor was to have a nominee legislative council of from five to seven members with power to make laws for the peace, welfare, and good government of the colony, provided that such laws did not clash with English law. The governor would hold the power to nominate the members of the council, he alone could submit legislation to it, and he could override the council's objection to the extent that even if a majority of the council rejected a proposed law the governor could bring it into effect pending a decision from London on the matter.

For all its limitations, the council provided a certain degree of representative government. No longer was the governor's authority absolute; it was now subject to some measure of review, at least, within the colony. The question of emancipists' rights was covered in the act; the governor's pardons were to have the same force and effect in law as any general pardon issued in Britain under the Great Seal. The legal rights of the emancipists were thus protected in perpetuity. On judicial procedures, the act marked a notable step forward by providing for trial by jury in civil cases if both sides wanted it, and for the setting up of a Supreme Court presided over by a chief justice.

In introducing the bill in the House of Commons, the Parliamentary Under-Secretary for the Colonial Office emphasized the change in New South Wales' stature. He began his second reading speech by declaring that whereas in its numerous measures the government had always treated the settlement as the destination of certain individuals sentenced to transportation, the new bill treated New South Wales as a British colony.

In the progress towards that status, Macquarie's twelve-year term of office had provided a notable share of gains, some fortuitous and some the direct result of his administration. Macquarie had been sent out in 1809 to administer the affairs of a turbulent and disordered colony that was still seen by the British government as no more than an outlet for unwanted criminals. His innovations in the financial and commercial fields, his removal of monopolistic abuses, his town planning, his seventy or more public buildings and 210 miles of roads had laid a solid groundwork for the future growth of New South Wales: in his own words, "I found New South Wales a jail and left it a colony."

In summing up the gains of his administration, Macquarie quoted comparative statistics for the whole of the territory under his jurisdiction, which included Van Diemen's Land, at the time of his first population and property muster, in April 1810, and his last muster, in October 1821. During this period population had increased from 11,500 to nearly 30,000; cattle from 12,000 to 103,000; sheep from nearly 26,000 to 290,000; land under cultivation had increased more than fourfold, from less than 8,000 to 32,000 acres; the penetrated area had increased from 2,000 to 100,000 square miles.

This is how the population of New South Wales was made up in October 1821:

Came free (adults)		Born in colony (adults)		Free by servitude		Free by absolute pardon		Free by conditional pardon	
m	f	m	f	m	f	m	f	m	f
846	643	906	978	2174	1864	134	27	1023	90

Ticket of leave		Convicts		Children		On colonial vessels			
m	f	m	f	m	f				
1266	313	11,342	893	3762	3462		240	Total	29,963

Various systems and institutions begun by the earlier governors had developed considerably during the twelve years of Macquarie's governorship. Bigge in his comprehensive report touched on such matters as religion, education, revenue, and expenditure at this definitive stage in the colony's history.

From the start of the colony, a clergyman of the Church of England was a part of the governor's official establishment, with his house provided and his salary paid from the civil list. As new districts were settled, assistant chaplains were appointed and land set aside for churches and clerical homes. By the time Bigge made his report, the Church of England establishment consisted of a senior chaplain at Parramatta, two chaplains at Sydney and four at outer districts, with an assistant chaplain at Newcastle. This ecclesiastical organization was in keeping with conditions in England at the time; until the repeal of the Test Act in 1828 neither Catholics nor Protestant nonconformists were able to hold state or municipal office, while until 1829 Catholics were debarred from sitting in either House of Parliament.

Several other denominations had established themselves on a semi-official basis by the time of the Bigge Report. Presbyterian settlers on the Hawkesbury River built their first church at Ebenezer in 1809, although they had no minister at that time. Laymen Methodist settlers and emancipists formed religious study classes at Sydney and Windsor in 1812, and three years later the Reverend Samuel Leigh arrived to organize the practice of Methodism within the colony on English lines. By 1821 the Methodists had three chapels, built by private subscription, on land donated by individuals or by the governor.

Although two Roman Catholic priests had offered to accompany the convicts of the First Fleet, the offer was refused, and the Catholic story did not begin until 1800, when three Irish Roman Catholic priests reached the colony under sentence of transportation for actions during the 1798 rebellion. One of them, Father James Dixon, received a conditional pardon and was allowed to celebrate mass; but this permission was withdrawn after the Castle Hill rebellion in 1804. Another priest, Father Jeremiah O'Flynn, arrived in the colony in 1817 on his own initiative and without authorization from the Colonial Office. Macquarie, who regarded uniformity in religious matters as an important factor in maintaining law and order in the colony, had him deported. A more liberal attitude was gaining ground in England, however, and in 1819 the Colonial Office approved the appointment of two Catholic priests, Fathers Joseph Therry and Phillip Connolly. As they were to minister to their co-religionists among the convicts, their salaries were to be paid from the colonial funds. Father Connolly went to Hobart and Father Therry to Sydney, where the foundation stone of the first Roman Catholic church, provided by private subscriptions and built on land granted by the governor, was laid in 1820.

Education was more or less a sideline to religion, and the colony's first classes were held by the hard-working chaplain Reverend Richard Johnson. It was not long before a few small schools were established in the different districts, with emancipist or convict teachers. Governor King, shocked by the plight of many children in the colony, started a free boarding school for girls in 1801; although called the Girls' Orphan School, it was for neglected children generally. It was supported by an eighth part of the revenue from import duties, plus voluntary contributions and the profits from a herd of cattle. By the beginning of 1821, 217 girls had been admitted to the school, and 63 boys had been admitted to a similar school for boys which was started by Macquarie in 1819. The teachers of both schools were under the general supervision of the chaplains, while committees (mainly government officials for the boys and local ladies for the girls) helped with the administration. By 1821 there were eighteen schools established and partly supported by the government, besides twelve non-government schools, one of them run by Father Therry, and one regimental school. The well-to-do families mostly employed assigned convicts as private tutors and some, like the Macarthurs, sent their children to be educated in England. Only a very small proportion of the children of school age received any education whatsoever.

Macquarie took a particular interest in a school for Aboriginal boys and girls, which he established at Parramatta in 1814. The following year he settled sixteen Aboriginal families on a land grant; the "indulgences" granted to settlers included, in their case, a boat, as they were very fond of fishing. Relations with the Aborigines in the coastal fringe had improved considerably, and the unfortunate incidents of earlier days were not repeated in the first years of Macquarie's regime. However, as settlement spread, and men and livestock began to occupy new areas, open acts of hostility occurred. Farmers and stockmen were speared in attacks which became more frequent as more of the tribal hunting grounds were occupied. Macquarie decided to send out punitive military expeditions in 1816, and fourteen Aborigines were killed in the Appin district near the Nepean River, the principal trouble spot. In the following year the governor outlawed ten Aborigines, but no bloodshed followed. Although there were no more incidents in Macquarie's time, the conflict between the original occupiers of the land and the new claimants had begun, and Macquarie's palliative measures did not long outlast him.

The first voluntary charitable activities within the colony began when settlers in the Hawkesbury River district formed a Benevolent Association in 1819; sub-district committees, including both emancipists and free settlers, raised funds to supply medical aids and comforts to the sick and aged poor. Other districts soon followed.

Colonial revenue dated back to 1799, when Governor Hunter imposed wharfage dues and customs duties on imported goods in order to raise money for a new jail; the name "Gaol Fund" remained. King created the Orphan Fund, to support the Girls' Orphan School. Macquarie divided revenue into two funds; one-quarter went into the Orphan Fund, which was used to support the various government schools; by 1817 revenue had increased so considerably that a one-eighth share was sufficient for this purpose. The balance of revenue, usually called the Police Fund, was virtually a consolidated revenue fund. Principal outlay went towards costs of the jail and penal establishments; salaries for locally appointed civil officers; rations and clothing of convicts in government employ; victualling of troops, civil officers, and those free settlers still "on the store"; and purchase of materials for government works. By far the largest item of colonial revenue was the duty on imported liquor. Macquarie raised the duty progressively from 1/6 to 10/– per gallon, without any appreciable drop in consumption. Here is his statement of revenue for the year ended December 31, 1820:

	£.	s.	d.
Duties collected on wine, spirits, tobacco, foreign goods, on auctions, and on South Head lights, amounted to	30,550	14	6
Spirit, beer, and brewing licenses, to	1,527	10	0
Parramatta, Liverpool, and Windsor road tolls, to	569	0	0
Duties on slaughtering cattle at Sydney, to	418	0	10
Market duties at Sydney, to	357	0	0
Market duties at Parramatta, to	37	10	0
Hawker's license, to	20	0	0
Total	£33,479	15	4

Macquarie claimed that the costs of his public works were all met from colonial revenue, and that all the material for the buildings, except iron work, glass, and paint, was made or procured by government convict workers. This did not take into account the costs of feeding and clothing the convict workers who built the roads and buildings. Bigge quoted a figure of

5,135 convicts victualled in New South Wales at the end of December 1820, a year in which the cost of rations and slop clothing for each convict came to £24 14s. 10d. The greater part of the colonial government expenditure was met by the British Treasury. The governor had the authority to draw bills on the Treasury in payment for purchases from farmers, merchants, and shipowners. These bills amounted to £181,376 in 1820 (Van Diemen's Land expenditure being included) and represented a very considerable infusion of capital into the colony. The chairman of the Chamber of Commerce of New South Wales, writing in 1826, estimated that during the latter part of Macquarie's administration, the "circulating remittable currency of New South Wales" amounted to £210,000 sterling, of which not less than £150,000 consisted of drafts on the British Treasury.

The administration of government was no different in principle in Macquarie's time than in Phillip's; all officers were responsible to the governor, who was responsible only to the Secretary of State for the Colonies. The principal civil officers who came out with the First Fleet were the chaplain, surgeons, commissary, and surveyor and their deputies; all, except the chaplain, were army or naval officers. Some of the marines officers performed extra civilian duties for a small extra salary. Phillip added a provost-marshal, as well as a number of superintendents and storekeepers whom he recruited for his staff from the ranks of the crew of the *Sirius*. The total salary list, including the governor and lieutenant-governor, came to about £4,650 a year.

By the end of Macquarie's governorship the penal, judicial, medical, ecclesiastical, and survey departments had naturally all expanded considerably; there was also a police department, while the civil list included schoolmasters, a printer, a customs officer, a civil architect, and an inspector of public works. The branch of government with by far the greatest number of employees was the commissary, which had storekeepers and clerks throughout the colony, many of them convicts or ticket of leave men. Apart from the principal officers, who were sent out from England, appointments were made by the governor. Most of the general administrative work was carried on by the governor's secretary, assisted by twelve or so clerks. He prepared pardons and tickets of leave, mustered and interrogated the convicts on their arrival in the colony, edited the *Sydney Gazette* (which was a combined government gazette and newspaper), and prepared general orders and correspondence for the governor. The secretaryship was originally a personal appointment. Until 1820 Macquarie's secretary was John Thomas Campbell, whom the governor recruited from a banking position at Cape Colony; but in 1820 Frederick Goulburn, a brother of the Under-Secretary for the Colonies, was sent out to New South Wales as the first colonial secretary.

The civil salary list by this time (1821) amounted to £18,253 15s., more than half of which was paid out of colonial revenue; pensions to former governors or their widows were included. Government officers and their families were still rationed from the commissariat stores, and received free housing, the services of convict servants, firewood, and such perquisites. Salaries of some officers, like the governor's secretary and the surveyor, were supplemented by fees, while the customs officer received a percentage of customs duties in lieu of salary.

Although those born within the colony were still only a small proportion of the total population, already they were beginning to impress observers as a distinct type. Several observers noticed that the children of former convicts were often non-drinkers, seemingly in reaction against the example of their parents. Commissioner Bigge, no friend to convicts or emancipists, was impressed by their children, whom he considered "a remarkable exception to the moral and physical character of their parents." He described them as active, quick-tempered, and generally tall in person, of fair complexion and small features. They were keen on life at sea, and one of Bigge's reasons for recommending a reduction of commercial duties and encouraging growth of merchant shipping was that in these ways opportunities would be provided for employment of the young Australian-born; and though Bigge did not favour land grants to emancipists—or small settlers generally —he considered an exception could be made in the case of the Australian-born under twenty-five years of age.

Already the quiet new land was exerting its special spell over those who had grown up in it; in December 1817 Mrs Macarthur wrote to an English friend of the return of her two sons:

> They are delighted to return to their native land and breathe not a regret for the gay scenes of the English metropolis. Nothing they saw in France or Switzerland effaced the strong desire they had to return to their native wild woods in New South Wales.

For his part Macquarie had developed a feeling of pride in the colony; in 1818 he began the annual celebration of its founding and spoke to his secretary of the importance of collecting material for a history of the colony. He took a keen interest in the generation of young Australians now rising to manhood, appointing one, William Charles Wentworth, to a senior government position and helping his brother Darcy to obtain a commission in the British army; each was the first such appointment given to a native-born Australian. When Lord Bathurst sent him a copy of Flinders' charts of "New Holland," he acknowledged the receipt of charts of "Australia," and he continued to use the name in the dispatches which progressively showed the proud old Scot's growing sense of identification with the people and country of Australia.

Europeans who visited the colony were usually surprised by the signs of material progress. One of these was Jacques Arago, artist with the de Freycinet expedition of 1819–20. In his *Promenade autour du monde*, Arago described Sydney as a beautiful, large and populous town, with "magnificent town houses, majestic castles, houses of extraordinary taste and elegance, fountains ornamented with sculpture worthy of the chisel of our best artists, vast and airy apartments, splendid furniture, horses and carriages of the utmost elegance, immense shops." The country homes along the shores of the harbour reminded him of the chateaux around Bordeaux. He enjoyed the parties, balls, and lavish hospitality extended to members of the expedition by local society, and was impressed by the apparent reformation of former criminals:

> I have seen a swindler honoured with the just confidence of the government, imparting to the children of Sydney, as much by his example as by his lessons, the principles of the strictest virtue and honesty. It seems that the atmosphere of this country, although some wild people are breathing it, purifies their hearts and makes generous feelings grow in them.

New windows   6
on a continent

After the discovery of Bass Strait in 1797–98, vessels on their way to Sydney gave up the old southern course and took instead the shorter route through the strait, which quickly assumed a special significance. It was soon to become the object of marked attention when expeditions were dispatched to set up military outposts on its shores. Before the strait was known to exist, however, notable navigators had rounded Van Diemen's Land and put in at bays on its south-east coast, just as Tasman had done first in 1642. The island became something of a way station on South Seas voyages even before settlement was made at Port Jackson.

It was almost 130 years after Tasman's voyage to Van Diemen's Land that Marion du Fresne, the first to follow him, anchored in Frederich Henry Bay and found "savages with flat noses and woolly hair powdered with red chalk." Then came Cook, first in the *Resolution* in March 1773, and again (this time with young William Bligh as his sailing master) in January 1777. Five years after that Bligh anchored in Adventure Bay when the *Bounty* was on the way to Tahiti to pick up breadfruit trees for the West Indies. The next arrival was Captain John Henry Cox in the brig *Mercury;* he was interested in collecting sealskins as well as in adding to nautical knowledge, and he discovered Oyster Bay when on his way from the island of St Paul (where he gathered nearly a thousand sealskins) on the new all-season route to the northern Pacific and Canton. Bligh was back in February 1792, this time on his second (and successful) attempt to transplant breadfruit from Tahiti. Eight weeks later the French Rear-Admiral, Bruni d'Entrecasteaux, with his frigates *La Recherche* and *L'Espérance*, sent by his Government to seek evidence of the fate of La Pérouse and his men, sighted the coast of Van Diemen's Land and soon were at anchor in Recherche Bay, where wood and water were taken aboard; their search was fruitless for (as later evidence indicated) La Pérouse's vessels had not gone south after leaving Botany Bay in March 1788 but had headed for the Santa Cruz group and had been wrecked there. Then, following the discovery of Bass Strait, Bass and Flinders had circumnavigated the island in 1799.

After the outbreak of the French revolutionary wars it was inevitable that any further activity in the far southern waters would be watched closely in London as an indication of French intentions. Île de France (Mauritius), in the southern Indian Ocean, close to the sailing route between Britain and the distant struggling colony at Port Jackson, had been in French hands from 1715 and under direct French government control from 1767; it was a strongly fortified naval base, and Whitehall was aware that it could be a stepping stone to further conquests.

When the French expedition under Captain Nicholas Baudin, which left Le Havre in October 1800 on a voyage of discovery to southern lands, began a scientific examination of the coasts of New Holland and Van Diemen's Land, British concern was aroused. Baudin's assurance, when the expedition put into Port Jackson in 1802, that the expedition's purpose was scientific did not allay Governor King's fears, and when on his departure from Sydney Baudin sailed south and undertook a detailed investigation of Bass Strait, the governor decided to act directly to forestall any hopes the French might entertain of establishing themselves in the area, where they could have menaced the sailing route between England and Port Jackson. As a result, three outposts were set up—one on either side of Bass Strait, and the other on the Derwent River, in the south of Van Diemen's Land.

As soon as London received King's first reports, action was taken and an expedition dispatched from England with the express purpose of setting up a military outpost in the Bass Strait area. Lieutenant-Colonel David Collins, formerly the Judge-Advocate in Sydney, was in charge of the expedition. He landed his charges on the sandy peninsula enclosing the southeast sector of Port Phillip Bay, the present Sorrento. He was unaware that in May 1802 Flinders had visited the bay and from heights overlooking the western shore had noted "the goodness of the soil and natural advantages" of that area; nor did he know that in 1803 a complete survey of Port Phillip had been made by Charles Grimes and the Yarra River discovered. The report and chart had not reached London by the time Collins set sail with the *Calcutta* and *Ocean*, bearing nearly 400 people (300 of them specially selected convicts with experience of farming, or mechanics). Once ashore a few of the convicts escaped. After unsuccessful attempts to find fresh water on the Port Phillip shore, Collins secured permission from Governor King to transfer the group to Van Diemen's Land. The locality chosen for the new outpost was on the Derwent River.

Earlier, at King's direction, a small company—forty-nine in all, including twenty-one male and three female convicts—had been sent from Sydney under Lieutenant Bowen to occupy this southerly area. They arrived in August 1803. The first shipload of Collins' charges was taken from Port Phillip to the Derwent in February 1804, the second four months later, and they joined Bowen's group from Sydney; Collins chose a spot called Sullivan's

Cove as the best site and named the little camp Hobart Town in honour of Lord Hobart, the Secretary of State.

It was considered prudent also to set up an outpost on the northern shore of Van Diemen's Land and so, after he received an instruction from London, Governor King sent Lieutenant-Colonel William Paterson with a party of 181, including 75 convicts, to settle on the Tamar. The mouth of the river had recently been surveyed, and Paterson encamped at Port Dalrymple in 1804. After the river had been carefully examined, Paterson in 1806 moved part of his little establishment nearly 40 miles upstream to Launceston. Like Hobart Town, this was a small military post, in which a small number of convicts provided the labour necessary for maintenance.

In 1805 it was decided that the two outposts in Van Diemen's Land should be built up; instructions were given that people should be drawn from Norfolk Island, which was to be cleared first of free settlers (who at this time numbered several hundreds). In many cases the settlers were reluctant to make the move, however, and in 1806 the authorities decided to issue an order for Norfolk Island's immediate abandonment. As a result, a more rapid build up occurred in Van Diemen's Land as the settlers arrived with their livestock. Many settled on the upper Derwent, where the name New Norfolk marked the association with their former island home. Withdrawal of convicts from Norfolk Island began in 1808; five years later, when the last had gone, the settlement was totally abandoned.

Settlement spread out steadily from the two original centres in Van Diemen's Land. Officers and privates who wished to become permanent settlers were able to receive land grants in proportion to their capital; they were also encouraged by the grant of livestock and seed grain to help start their enterprise. Emancipists and the children of convicts were likewise assisted. Convicts were usually assigned to provide the necessary labour.

Hobart Town developed as a whaling centre after 1804 when whaling grounds were discovered. The estuary of the Derwent swarmed with whales, and soon whaling made Hobart Town a thriving port. Small ships were built and visiting ships repaired. Thus the little settlement came to divide its attention between the sea and the land. Recurrent shortages of food and supplies such as Sydney had suffered in the early years were repeated in Hobart and Launceston, and there were great privations in 1806 and 1807. The climate and soil generally made it easier to grow grain and other food than around Port Jackson, however, and the situation gradually improved. The more regular rainfall ensured that the colony would not suffer from the droughts that so often threatened Sydney's harvests. In 1812 the whole island was brought under the one administration, operating from Hobart Town. By 1813 there were more than 300 small farms, with 2,000 acres under cultivation. By 1815 the colony had become self-supporting in grain, but further expansion was hindered because there was no external market apart from Sydney.

By that time British naval supremacy had altered the whole strategic position in the Indian Ocean area. After the British capture of Mauritius and the Seychelles in 1810, the French no longer represented any threat. The original purpose of occupation had passed. From this point Van Diemen's Land, already the repository for convicts who had committed further offences after transportation, became a penal colony imposing the severest discipline.

At first the island's Aborigines showed no hostility to the settlers, but a clash occurred in the early days at Risdon Cove in which at least three tribesmen were killed (and perhaps many more). When the Derwent settlement was being established the local tribesmen were in their summer hunting areas along the central highlands, and when some months later they moved south again the loss of some of their hunting ground did not concern them greatly. However, with the occupation for settlement of the open forest lands—their best game areas—the situation changed and they began to show hostility.

By the 1820s, settlement had encroached seriously upon tribal lands, and traditional migrations of the Aborigines were upset. There had been occasional pilfering, and soon the settlers became intolerant. Open conflict began when the Oyster Bay tribesmen accepted as their leader an Aboriginal named Mosquito who had come from the Sydney area. Mosquito had been transported from New South Wales for a misdemeanor, and had been employed to assist in capturing escaped convicts—a task in which he showed remarkable skill. Soon he decided to revert to a tribal life and he was accepted as a leader. Under his direction the tribesmen grew violent, plundering, and counting every settler an enemy. There were attacks and ambushes. With only a few detachments of soldiers to protect them, the colonists became alarmed. Finally Mosquito was captured, charged with murder, and executed early in 1824. The bitterness engendered by these incidents was soon to reappear and develop on a larger scale as tension grew between the migratory tribesmen and the settlers who were steadily spreading into new areas of occupation.

In the early years the population of the Van Diemen's Land establishments increased slowly, and the number of people on the island did not pass 2,000 until 1816. From that year there was a much faster rate of growth as both convicts and free settlers arrived in greater numbers. The population more than doubled in four years. When Commissioner Bigge made his visit in 1820 the total population of the island was 4,968, of whom 2,600 were convicts and all but 1,200 of the remainder were ex-convicts. The rate of increase was maintained in the 1820s, and in 1824 the population numbered 12,000.

The turbulence of the first twenty years of settlement in New South Wales was not repeated in Van Diemen's Land. The slower pace of affairs came in great part from the tight rein maintained by the administrators. Rural industries were able to gain a foothold; potatoes were exported to Sydney in 1817, hops for beer a few years later, and large quantities of grain after 1820. Because of limited markets for grain, woolgrowing became more important than agriculture in the mid-1820s.

The first sheep were introduced into the colony in 1807. At first they were bred for mutton; their wool, if used at all, was used for stuffing mattresses. In 1820 Macquarie and the Van Diemen's Land Lieutenant-Governor, Lieutenant-Colonel William Sorrell, combined to purchase a consignment of merino rams from John Macarthur's "improved flocks." The 181 merinos that survived the voyage to the island were distributed among capable flockmasters. Sorrell, who was impressed by reports of the high quality of merino wool and convinced of the prospects, also imported considerable numbers of merinos from England and Saxony, and these were distributed. In 1820 there were already 180,000 sheep in the island's flocks, and more than 30,000 head of cattle. The island's wool was first exported to England in the same year.

Although the governor in far-off New South Wales had never exercised more than nominal control over Van Diemen's Land, by the beginning of the 1820s the people of the island were beginning to resent even this degree of dependence. On April 30, 1824 a public meeting held in Hobart resolved to petition the King asking that the island should be made a separate colony from New South Wales, with the right to administer its own affairs. Under the Judicature Act of 1825, Van Diemen's Land became a separate colony; the proclamation was published on December 3, 1825, and Colonel George Arthur, who had held the rank of Lieutenant-Governor when he succeeded Sorrell in 1824, became Governor.

Arthur was the first administrator in Van Diemen's Land to have responsibility direct to London. Under the Act of 1825, the administration was placed on a similar footing to that of New South Wales. A legislative council was provided for; it was to consist of from five to seven members, all nominated. The governor's power was supreme, however; policy was formulated by an executive council (consisting wholly of officials) in which the governor had the casting vote, and then given legal status by legislation in a docile legislative council. In practice there was no appreciable lessening of autocracy in the administration.

Meanwhile, exports of wool from the island were increasing steadily, and a bright future was opening up for the sheepowners. After 1819 land grants were made to people with capital. An indication of the colony's economic progress was the founding of the Bank of Van Diemen's Land in 1824. Interest in London in the island's potentialities was growing; some people felt that the mild climate, good soil, and steady rainfall assured a brighter future for the rural industries of Van Diemen's Land than for those of New South Wales. Investment interest was increasing; in 1825 the British government granted to the Van Diemen's Land Joint Stock Company 250,000 acres of land in the north-west sector of the island for pastoral and agricultural development. This grant, a parallel to that made to the Australian Agricultural Company in the same year, exemplified the British government's policy of encouragement to invest capital for the purpose of land development. It emphasized the fact that Van Diemen's Land, like

New South Wales, had passed out of its period of total dependence upon governmental activity.

In his report on colonial affairs, Commissioner Bigge had come out in favour of the special penal settlements existing for the severest possible treatment of convicts who had committed further crimes, and had recommended that such settlements be expanded. Hobart had originally absorbed convict groups from Norfolk Island, many of whom had been adjudged in need of intensified punishment because they had committed offences after transportation. In order to maintain the harshest discipline, a system of severe punishment became established. Bigge's approval of the general method of correction of desperate characters was the signal in 1821 for the setting-up of a grim last outpost from which all escape was impossible.

An ideal spot for such a prison stronghold had been discovered on the rugged western shores of Van Diemen's Land in 1815 when Captain James Kelly had sailed in a whaleboat from Hobart Town to the Tamar settlement and had named Port Davey and Macquarie Harbour. Bleak and rain-drenched, Macquarie Harbour became a place for the final banishment of the worst type of convict—where "man lost the aspect and the heart of man." The convicts were put to work felling the tall trees of the forbidding rain forest and dragging the huge logs to the shore. After eleven years in which terrible brutality prevailed, the Macquarie Harbour penitentiary was finally abandoned in 1833 in favour of the new prison, Port Arthur, on Tasman's Peninsula, which quickly gained a reputation for being equally grim and dreadful in its purpose.

Desperate convicts who had managed to escape were able to conceal themselves in the remote fastnesses of mountains or forest, away from the settled districts. Bushranging, as such activities came to be known, developed out of the conditions of the times; and in Van Diemen's Land (as in New South Wales) governors had to face the problem of dealing with desperate escapees dedicated to a life of plunder. At various times it was necessary to organize large-scale manhunts. Generally the bushranger was a man who had served his sentence, or had escaped, and decided to "take to the bush," where he might steal a horse and lead a life of excitement by waylaying travellers until he was shot or caught.

By Governor Arthur's time, bushranging had become a serious problem. Settlers' homes were barricaded against attack and loopholed for defence, while military detachments strengthened by armed settlers went out to hunt down the organized companies. Some of the desperadoes were shot; many more were captured, and in 1825 and 1826 more than a hundred were executed by order of the court. Even these measures did not eradicate bushranging from Van Diemen's Land, since the ranks of the malefactors were constantly being strengthened by new escapees; but by breaking up the organized gangs the worst aspects of the evil were suppressed.

The lawlessness that had been demonstrated, and the violent methods introduced to suppress it, helped to aggravate the conflict with the Aborigines.

These simple people, who differed fundamentally from the Aborigines of the Australian mainland and probably did not number more than eleven or twelve hundred in all, were caught between forces that they neither comprehended nor could cope with; and when depredations at the hands of bushrangers were added to oppression from sealers, convicts, and stockkeepers, unrelenting warfare naturally resulted.

As early as 1813 the lieutenant-governor had written of the resentment aroused among the Aborigines by the "barbarous and inhuman treatment" of the settlers, and by Arthur's day the situation was appalling as revenge was always met by more shootings and bayonetting of the Aborigines.

Governor Arthur proclaimed martial law in an effort to put an end to the killings. Under the proclamation, martial law was to be enforced against the Aborigines in all the settled sections and adjacent areas until "the cessation of hostilities." The tribesmen were prohibited from trespassing over a vast part of the island; those who did so were subject to the law. In one of his dispatches to London on the subject, Arthur declared his sincere hope "that the measure that has been resorted to, of treating them as open enemies, may be annulled"; but the intent was clear. Arthur's advisers were a good deal more bloodthirsty in their attitude than the governor himself, and they wanted no quarter given.

With the proclamation of martial law the destruction of the island's Aborigines began. The civil authorities, supported by a few soldiers, set out whenever occasion offered in search of the tribesmen. Few were brought in alive, even though from early in 1830 rewards were offered of £5 for every adult and £2 for each child brought in unharmed. The Hobart *Colonial Times* declared it was "like a warfare with the chamois goats of the Alps" to catch the Aborigines.

As the problem was still unresolved, the governor decided to set up a committee "to collect the most ample information and to consider what measures it would be necessary to pursue." The committee was made up of three clergymen and four laymen. After investigation, it reported that the instances of savage vengeance which the Aborigines had taken had resulted directly from injuries they had received; but the committee was powerless to prevent the violence on both sides. Finally the governor agreed to a plan for herding virtually all the island's Aborigines on to Tasman's Peninsula, in the far south-east, where they could be left to themselves and prevented from escaping.

In 1830, 300 soldiers and hundreds of settlers formed a cordon across the island, to drive the Aborigines south into their new territory. The undertaking was planned on military lines as if it were a great war in miniature. The Aborigines knew the terrain better than their pursuers, however, and they had no difficulty in eluding them and slipping through the cordon. After all the commotion, when the governor and his party arrived at the peninsula they had rounded up only two Aborigines; apart from two who had been shot, the rest were all behind them! The great manhunt had cost the colony over £30,000 in direct expenses.

The next effort to deal with the matter was quite different in nature.

George Augustus Robinson, a bricklayer and a lay preacher in the local Methodist church in Hobart, offered to gather the Aborigines together if the governor would provide them with a new home. With a companion and a few friendly Aborigines, Robinson set out and, by means of persuasive argument and kindness, gathered in many friendly groups. On Robinson's promises of fair treatment, some 300 native men, women and children were brought in peaceably between 1831 and 1835. "The Pacificater" had brought an end to the Black War. From time to time groups were taken to Bass Strait islands for resettlement. The first place chosen was Gun Carriage Island; it was only about two miles long and a mile and a half wide, but Robinson considered that here the Aborigines "would be enabled to fish, dance, sing and throw spears and amuse themselves in their usual way."

One voice raised against the proposal was that of the chief justice, who told the executive council that "however carefully these people might be supplied with food, they would soon begin to pine away when they found their situation one of hopeless imprisonment, within bounds so narrow as necessarily to deprive them of those habits and customs which are the charms of their savage life." Governor Arthur's view was that even if they should pine away in this manner, "it is better that they should meet with their death in that way, whilst every act of kindness is manifested towards them, than that they should fall a sacrifice to the inevitable consequence of their continued acts of outrage upon the white inhabitants." Sarcastically the *Colonial Times* invited the public "to enrol yourselves under the banner of the G.A. Robinson as aborigine tamers and instructors of our sable neighbours in all sorts of polite accomplishment!"

The settlement was formed in April 1831 as planned. Less than a year later it was transferred to the much larger Flinders Island. Meanwhile Robinson was busy rounding up new inmates, but in 1835 he took charge at Flinders Island. From time to time someone visited the island and made a report. Each time it was the same melancholy story of many deaths and few births; each time the inevitable prospect was that "their utter extinction may be looked forward to at no very distant period." In 1846 some of the survivors signed a petition, doubtless inspired by their superintendent but containing one phrase summing up the whole miserable story: "When we left one place we were plenty of people; we now but a little one." Within a few years their numbers were down to fifty. In 1847 the forty-four survivors were removed to Oyster Bay, not far from Hobart, where they were quartered in the remains of an old penal station. Here the last male survivor died in 1869. Seven years later Truganini, wife of a tribal chief, died in Hobart—the last of her race except one woman living on Kangaroo Island where she had been taken, along with three others, by sealers many years before.

Settlement of Van Diemen's Land had begun as a move to counter any designs France might have had at the beginning of the nineteenth century. During the first two decades of the century, Britain's mastery of the seas meant that there could be no serious danger of a rival power moving in to annex any part of Australia; yet new circumstances arose which made it desirable to rapidly bring the whole continent under British sovereignty.

Previously, the British government had not felt it necessary to put forward any claim to the unpromising western half of the continent (the New Holland section), and the western limit of the British territory of New South Wales remained the 135th parallel of latitude, as it had been in Phillip's day, even though Captain George Vancouver had visited various points along the south-west coast in 1791 and had taken formal possession of some hundreds of miles of coastline in the name of King George III. However, in the early 1820s, the old fears of French intentions were reawakened when it became known that the French government intended to send another exploratory expedition to the South Seas. These fears, combined with a new assessment in London of the worth of the continent, led to the annexation of the whole of the continent, and to the establishment of a new series of settlements at strategic points around the coast.

The East India Company had had a close-up inspection of the riches of the East Indies during the last five years of the Napoleonic wars, when Java and other Dutch-held islands had been captured. After the peace treaties of 1814 and 1815 these islands were returned to the Dutch, who soon reimposed the old restrictions on English trade with the area. The company was interested in securing new trading posts which would give it access to the rather loosely held easterly islands of the archipelago, and north-west Australia was an obvious possibility for such posts.

In 1817 the Admiralty ordered a thorough survey of the whole of the northern coast of the continent, entrusting the task to Lieutenant Phillip Parker King, the Australian-born son of the former governor. Before he started his surveys, King had an unofficial briefing from Stamford Raffles, who had governed Java during the British occupation. King spent more than four years on his surveys and took a much more favourable view of prospects than the old Dutch traders had done. He visited two islands off the continent's north-west extremity which he named Melville and Bathurst, and he concluded that they might be valuable possessions. Shortly after King's return to London, a suggestion was put to Lord Bathurst that a military station should be set up on the northern coast to protect trade routes and to develop trade with the East Indies; as an outcome both islands, and also the north coast of the mainland between 129° and 135° East, were annexed in September 1824 by Captain James Gordon Bremer, and on the larger of the two, Melville Island, a fortified military outpost and convict camp was established.

By this time a French expedition under Dumont d'Urville had set off on its scientific mission to the South Seas. In London, this venture aroused suspicion, and rumours—all of them false—were circulated that d'Urville's intention was to found a colony. The British authorities believed the stories, and word was sent to Sydney instructing the governor to prepare at once to form settlements at Western Port in the south-east, on the east coast well north of Sydney, and on the western side of New Holland.

After visiting various parts of the Australian coast, d'Urville spent almost

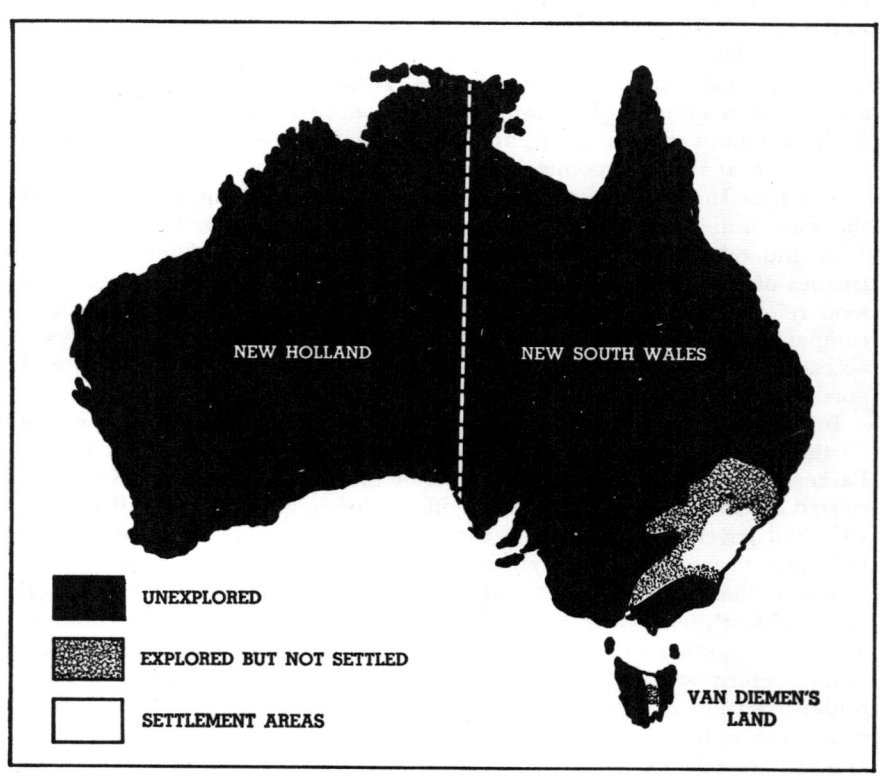

General sketch map showing exploration and settlement by 1824. Expansion inland from Sydney followed the crossing of the Blue Mountains in 1813; the Moreton Bay settlement was begun at the end of 1824. Settlement of Van Diemen's Land started in 1802, and by 1824 a broad band of country through the centre of the island had been explored.

a month in King George Sound in October 1826. At the same time, Governor Sir Ralph Darling dispatched Major Edmund Lockyer from Sydney to found a garrison settlement. With a detachment of soldiers, Lockyer landed on Christmas Day and set up an outpost at Albany, formally annexing the surrounding territory on January 21, 1827. He had been instructed that, should any discussions take place with the French, he and his officers were to take care "to avoid any expression of doubt of the whole of New Holland being considered within this government."

No meeting with the French occurred. Later in 1827 Captain James Stirling sailed from Sydney to examine the land adjoining the Swan River, where another settlement was contemplated. He explored the land on both sides of the river for some 60 miles inland and reported most favourably on it.

London decided to proceed with the Swan River venture, and on May 2, 1829 Captain Charles Fremantle arrived from the Cape of Good Hope, landed at the mouth of the Swan in H.M.S. *Challenger*, and took formal possession of "all that part of New Holland which is not included within the territory of New South Wales." With this annexation the whole of the continent formally became British territory, and instructions to the Governor of New South Wales were amended accordingly.

The attempt to establish an outpost at Western Port began in November 1826, when a party of about fifty people, half of them convicts, landed at a spot called Settlement Point. The area chosen proved unfavourable, and the undertaking turned out to be a total failure. The ship, *L'Astrolabe*, had already called at Western Port, collected the scientific data the French captains sought, and departed, and so there was no object in maintaining the settlement. The French scare having abated, the party was withdrawn after a little over a year's occupation. Similarly the Albany garrison was withdrawn in 1831.

The Melville Island outpost had fared little better; no trade developed, supplies were short, and two ships were captured by pirates. Late in 1828 it was decided to abandon the outpost, and transfer the garrison to a settlement that had been formed at Raffles Bay, on the mainland; this too was abandoned in mid-1829.

Fear of entry of the French into the English sphere of influence had inspired England to make settlements; similarly the English intrusion close to what Holland regarded as her own preserves aroused the apprehension of the Dutch, and inspired them to settlement plans.

In 1828 the Dutch took formal possession of western New Guinea from longitude 132°45 to 141° East. At the same time they established a settlement at Triton Bay, on the south coast of the island; but this was not much longer-lived than the English settlements in northern Australia, being abandoned in 1835.

One more strategic military outpost was established in 1835, following renewed fears of French interests in northern Australia. Captain Bremer was again given the task of forming a garrison post at Port Essington, on the Coburg Peninsula; this outpost was abandoned in 1849.

The decision to plant additional garrison outposts combined with the desire to segregate the worst of the convicts resulted in the establishment of Moreton Bay, on the east coast some 500 miles north of Sydney. Immigrant ships were arriving in Port Jackson more frequently now, and as the settlement there took on a new aspect it was clearly desirable to set up a new penal establishment elsewhere. Not only for strategic reasons but so that it would be beyond the reach of encroaching settlement, the location should be remote from Sydney; this had been one of Bigge's principal recommendations.

Newcastle, where convicts had cut timber and mined coal, had at first been used for the handling of bad cases, but free settlement had engulfed the area. The penal station had been moved farther north (to Port Macquarie) but this area, too, soon became too accessible. In 1823 John Oxley was sent with the *Mermaid* to find a remote spot where an outpost might be self-supporting. He went as far north as Port Curtis, which he examined but found unsuitable. He sailed back to Moreton Bay and there a surprising circumstance led him to the discovery of the largest river of Australia's eastern seaboard. Among the tribesmen who ran towards his vessel late on November 29, 1823 was a white man: Thomas Pamphlet, who had been living for some weeks with the Aboriginal tribe. Pamphlet had been one of a boat's crew blown out to sea from Port Jackson and wrecked on Moreton Island. Pamphlet led Oxley to a fine river entering Moreton Bay, and this Oxley named Brisbane after the Governor.

The following year Oxley returned to explore the river further; in company with Allan Cunningham, a botanist who had accompanied him on inland journeys, he chose a site for settlement on the north bank of the river at a point where fresh water was abundant. Here the commandant, the small detachment of soldiers, twenty convicts, and the storekeeper and his assistant were left encamped when Oxley and Cunningham returned to Sydney. A few weeks later the governor and a few leading citizens made the voyage north to the new outpost on the fringe of the tropics. Action to establish settlement had been hastened as a result of London's concern over the French; but once set up, the settlement was regarded as a convict outpost reserved for the punishment of those convicted of further crimes within the colony.

Norfolk Island was reoccupied for the same purpose in 1825, and here the conditions were of unmitigated severity. The decision of the governor (relayed to London) was that Moreton Bay would be used for runaways from other penal establishments, with Norfolk Island as the ultimate in convict punishment. From this time until the abolition of transportation, Norfolk Island represented the abysmal pit of the penal system. As at Macquarie Harbour (and after 1830 at Port Arthur) the work was unremitting, and the lash and irons were in frequent use. There were no inhabitants other than the prisoners and their warders.

Occupation of quite a different nature had by now been established in

New Zealand. Some early governors of New South Wales had interpreted their commissions to involve jurisdiction over New Zealand, but this was not altogether clear, and when pressed for clarification of the status of New Zealand the Colonial Secretary left the question open. From 1817, however, various acts of parliament specifically stated that New Zealand was "not within His Majesty's dominions." As early as 1792 sealers from Sydney had operated in the south-west, and soon the first whaling vessels were in New Zealand waters. By 1794 a landing had been made with the object of securing timber and also a quantity of the native flax; other visits soon followed as ships' captains began to develop the trade in timber. Whaling in the area was inhibited at first because of the East India Company's rights in the area; however, it developed after 1801, and when the sealing grounds of Bass Strait declined, activities of the sealers were transferred to islands adjacent to New Zealand.

Missionaries followed in the wake of the traders. The leading figure was Reverend Samuel Marsden, who in 1810 arranged to send a group of missionaries whom he had enlisted in England; but when a massacre occurred Governor Macquarie blocked the attempt to settle in New Zealand, and Marsden did not secure permission to proceed until 1813. The party of missionaries left Sydney in March 1814. A few months later they returned and took Marsden with them to the Bay of Islands where he traded a dozen axes for 200 acres of land. He returned to Sydney, then took back additional settlers, securing more land from the Maori chief Hongi, who became the missionaries' protector. Marsden refused to trade in firearms, which Hongi wanted. Hongi made a trip to England where he was given many presents, some money, implements, and other things, and when he reached Sydney on his return he traded all these goods for firearms and bullets which he took to New Zealand. He waged war on enemy tribes over many years, but he protected Marsden's group in spite of the lectures Marsden read to him.

The settlement barely survived during the 1820s; there were no capable farmers in the group, and food supplies had to come from Sydney or London. In 1830 farm land was acquired some miles from the coast, and later the land was ploughed and sown. By 1835 the farm was flourishing.

Missionaries of other denominations also established themselves. A Wesleyan mission was set up in 1822; but without the protection of a chief like Hongi its difficulties were great.

Attempts to set up trading outposts were hardly more successful. In 1825 a New Zealand settlement enterprise was formed in London and a few settlers arrived in two vessels; but the prospects seemed so bleak that they transferred to Sydney almost at once. The same year a boat-builder, Captain Thomas Raine, established a boatyard on the Hokianga River and began building schooners to export flax and timber for ships' spars. His business prospered for a few years.

As time went on, there was growing concern about the unsatisfactory state of affairs in New Zealand. There were continuing reports of massacres, and it was well known that the crews of visiting whaling ships were profligate and uncontrolled. In 1831 the *Sydney Gazette* spoke of the possibility of New

Zealand's becoming "an integral and productive part of a great Australian Empire" so long as it was not allowed to fall into foreign hands. Later the same year Sydney was buzzing with rumours that a French vessel had taken possession of the islands for France. Meanwhile, Governor Darling had urged the British government to intervene so that law and order could be restored. He suggested that an official, with a few troops, should be installed, or an armed vessel stationed on the coast. But not until 1833 was action taken. In that year James Busby was appointed by the Colonial Office as resident official, responsible to the Governor of New South Wales. No force was sent with Busby to maintain order; he was expected to use moral persuasion upon the chiefs, and he was without legal authority to arrest British offenders (including escaped convicts who were known to be in New Zealand).

Throughout the 1830s the confusion over New Zealand's status continued. Australian land sharks were trying to stake a claim to New Zealand land; one Sydney syndicate claimed to have bought the entire south island for a few hundred pounds. A French adventurer's plea to the British Crown for aid and protection in an ambitious enterprise was turned down in 1835, but various small groups steadily gained footholds on both the north and south islands and by 1837 there were nearly 2,000 settlers living in New Zealand.

With increased English interest in New Zealand, as well as in colonization in general, the idea of launching a settlement enterprise caught on in London. In 1837 the New Zealand Association was formed with the purpose of establishing a settlement. Two years later, after fruitless negotiations with the British government, the association dissolved and reformed itself as a joint-stock company under the title of the New Zealand Colonization Company. Soon afterwards a shipload of colonists was sent out in the *Tory*—a venture which led to the British government's assumption of sovereignty over New Zealand in 1840.

Meanwhile, British settlers had moved into the far west of the Australian continent to occupy lands which Dutch seamen had discovered two centuries before but had never colonized. By now Australia had a changed image in the eyes of British investors and emigrants; the sheep's conquest of the wide plains of New South Wales had roused an interest in Australian land development enterprises.

Reports made by Captain James Stirling in 1827 praising the country along the Swan River had created interest both in official quarters and among English investors. After his return to Sydney, Stirling had been sent to London to plead the case for another settlement in the west to supplement the little establishment at King George Sound; and although the British government showed no inclination to spend money on another venture so far from Sydney, in the end private capital made possible the establishment of a settlement on the Swan River. The undertaking was actually a combined effort by investors and the British government; and so, although in one way the western settlement looked back to the days of the French scare, in other and more important ways it was the first Australian colony to be set up with free emigrants and private capital.

The Swan River settlement was promoted largely by a syndicate of London investors who sought concessions of land in the area and in return offered to subscribe funds to send out emigrants. The suggestion that the enterprise could be privately financed appealed to the government, and even though many of the potential investors withdrew when the Colonial Office refused to grant the whole of the area requested, negotiations continued with Thomas Peel, one of the group, who was a cousin of the Home Secretary. There was considerable political criticism, and newspaper cartoons lampooned the arrangement, but modified proposals were accepted. The government agreed to provide the colony with a small civil administration and a military detachment; Peel was to receive a free grant of 250,000 acres in return for landing 400 settlers. Unlimited areas were to be granted to settlers at the rate of 40 acres for every £3 invested. Large grants were also to be made to officials in lieu of salary. It was intended that no convicts should be sent to the colony—the first such "free" settlement.

On June 1, 1829 Stirling arrived in the transport *Parmelia* in charge of the enterprise. From the moment of Stirling's landing at Fremantle it was clear there would be many difficulties in establishing the settlement. The first group of settlers, numbering about seventy people in all, arrived with Stirling; a few days later a detachment of troops landed, and on June 18 the colony was proclaimed. The town sites of Perth, the capital, and Fremantle, the port, were laid out. In December the *Gilmore* arrived with Peel and his retinue of yeomen farmers and workmen, bringing the arrivals to eighteen shiploads. As well as the official administrative group and Peel's party, there were many independent investors with their families and workmen. Some had invested quite heavily. Until land could be surveyed and allotted, the people lived on Garden Island, almost without shelter and in the most primitive conditions. In London, meanwhile, Peel's agents were still circulating encouraging reports, and more people were attracted. As ships continued to arrive, hundreds more hopeful settlers stepped ashore; soon the total exceeded 2,000. Livestock, fruit trees, seeds, and tools had been brought in, and everything needed to set up an active colony seemed to be at hand.

Few of the settlers had realized what pioneering a raw new land really meant; one settler wrote that many of his fellows "thought they had nothing more to do than scratch the ground and sow." For most of them, the attraction of plentiful and inexpensive land had proved deceptive. Land was so cheap—its cost was only eighteen pence an acre—that individuals had taken up far more than they could cultivate or had the capital to develop. It was very difficult land, with patchy soil and vegetation that was useless as fodder, and many settlers found they were unable to do anything with their holdings. Much of the equipment and material brought from London at considerable expense consisted of luxury goods that were useless in the new undertaking. The scattering of the settlers over large holdings added to the difficulties, making the whole enterprise unwieldy and unworkable.

Soon the settlers came to realize their terrible mistake. The tasks of building, clearing, cultivating, and caring for livestock proved beyond them. Many abandoned their sprawling properties and moved to Perth seeking work or food. Some decided to return to England, others to try their luck in other colonies. Peel proved to be one of the least competent, and his investment of £50,000 was lost. He was incapable of developing the tract awarded to him and had to dismiss the 300 workers he had brought with him.

By the end of 1830, when well over 1,000,000 acres had been allotted to settlers, less than 200 acres were under cultivation. Meanwhile the number of people in the colony fell from nearly 4,000 in 1830 to 1,500 in 1832.

At this point the drift was arrested. Largely thanks to Stirling's energy, resourcefulness, and administrative ability the colony had been kept afloat, and now the work of growing food was seriously tackled for the first time.

Instead of the large and indiscriminate land grants, the price of land was increased to three shillings an acre in 1831 and to five shillings the following year, when acreages were limited; though there were very few sales at these prices, as failed grantees were selling their land at a few pence an acre. Threats of penalties for non-cultivation of holdings were successful, and settlers began to make better use of the land. By the terms of the grants, the government could resume completely unimproved lands after either ten or twenty years. After 1838 some of the holdings granted earlier were re-claimed and released in smaller lots; as settlers in outlying areas exchanged their straggling holdings for better land the settlement became more com-pact and workable. Only the tenacious had held on, however, and no new settlers had been arriving.

It was not until 1837 that the population edged above 2,000. By that time land further inland had been occupied for grazing, wool was being produced in increasing quantities—sheep numbered over 10,000 head—and the colony was growing more wheat than its people could eat. Whaling operations were showing promise, and the exports of jarrah had begun. When Sir James Stirling retired in 1838, the colony had passed through its crisis years, though progress remained slow.

Another settlement enterprise involving the participation of private capital was responsible for the founding of South Australia. Inspiration for the experimental ideas that lay behind the plan came from Edward Gibbon Wakefield, a young diplomat and theorist who, while in prison following his conviction for abducting a young heiress, developed and propounded new theories for managing the settlement of "new" lands. He put forward his views, as coming from an anonymous immigrant to Australia, in a series of letters published serially in a London newspaper in 1829 and published in book form later the same year as *A Letter From Sydney*. Although the author had never been farther than Europe the book was accepted as being written by a genuine settler; it appeared at an opportune time, and attracted im-mediate attention.

The basic feature of Wakefield's theory of colonization was that the principal wealth of new countries, their land, could best be developed by achieving a balance between the demand for and the supply of labour. The key to this balance was the price of land. Wakefield argued that if the colony's land were too easily obtainable, whether by free grant or at a low price, every labourer would be able to buy land, and there would be no supply of labour, and thus no means of utilizing capital, which would be wasted. On the other hand, if the price of land were too high, the colony would not have any attraction for capitalists. What was needed was a sufficient price—"a just medium . . . [so] as to give the cheapest land a market value that would have the effect of compelling labourers to work for some considerable time for wages before they could become landowners."

The most beneficial way of using the proceeds of land sales would be as an emigration fund, to take working people from the mother-country to the colonies, thus greatly accelerating the development of the colony. This did not mean "pauper shovellings," but a balanced and selective emigration programme, with preference given to young married couples. Wakefield thus offered an alternative to the "penal slavery" of the existing convict labour system, which he attacked on a number of moral and social grounds, particularly the disproportion between the sexes which it caused. He envisaged a free colonial society, with the sexes numerically balanced, which would attract a high type of professional emigrant. People of such a society, "qualified, powerful, and entitled to govern themselves," would have every right to self-government, either by means of representatives in the British parliament or in their own colonial assembly, "whose secretaries, like the ministers of England, should be responsible to the people."

The full development of the Wakefield theory was worked out in reply to criticism of details, and was expressed in a number of books, published over a number of years. The main criticism was centred on how the exact "sufficient price" should be ascertained. Wakefield explained in a later book that this would depend on a great many local factors, including the rate of emigration, the rate of wages, the cost of living, the soil and climate, and the amount of land necessary for profitable production. He also explained that the sufficient price was intended to apply only to agricultural land, not to town lands or to pastoral land, which was not freehold and so did not affect the labour market. Pastoral land should be freely available, on a "first come, first served" basis, at a minimum rental; but such land should always be liable "to be brought into the Government sales [system] whenever anyone wished to obtain, by paying a sufficient price, the freehold property in the land."

Plans for a new colony in which Wakefield's principles could be put into effect were developed by Wakefield and his close associate, editor, and representative in public, Robert Gouger. For six years these two men formed associations and companies, wrote pamphlets, and canvassed public and parliamentary support for a model colony, which would embody the principles of planned emigration and sale of land at a sufficient price: a settlement that would be controlled by the promotors until such time as the colonists could form their own government. Their adherents represented many different shades of opinion and interest: those who saw in colonization the solution for England's problems of poverty and unemployment; radical Benthamite members of Parliament, seeking to promote the greatest happiness of the greatest number; economists and investors, democrats and dissenters—doctrinaires in the main, but with an admixture of businessmen seeking a profitable investment for capital.

Wakefield and Gouger soon decided upon a general location for the proposed colony: explorers and sea captains had described favourably Kangaroo Island and the neighbouring gulf country; here was virgin soil, far from the convict-tainted colonies in the east and the failing Swan River settlement in the west. The deciding factor was the news, which reached England late in 1830, that Captain Charles Sturt had discovered a magnificent river, and had followed it to its outlet near Gulf St Vincent.

Sometime before this, Wakefield and Gouger had formed the National Colonization Society to disseminate and, if possible, put into practice their ideas. Two draft proposals for a colony on the South Australian coast—the first by a Major Anthony Bacon, the second by the society—were submitted to the Colonial Office in 1831, but met with a lukewarm reception and were dropped. A fresh start was made in 1832, when the promotors formed the South Australian Land Company, a joint-stock enterprise which sought a charter giving it the right to found a Wakefield-type colony. This straight-out profit-seeking organization attracted many investors and would-be immigrants. By this time Wakefield's theories had won increased support among members of parliament, particularly among the followers of the radical philosopher, Jeremy Bentham. A committee of parliamentarians and bankers, representing the promotors, approached the Colonial Office for the necessary sanction and support of their plans; but so many objections to the company's "wild and impracticable" and republican proposals were raised by the department's counsel that approval was withheld, and finally the whole project was dropped.

In 1833 new interest was aroused by the publication of Wakefield's *England and America*, as well as by Sturt's arrival in England with first-hand descriptions of the discoveries he and other explorers had made. The next colonization organization to be set up, the South Australian Association, had a committee made up largely of bankers, merchants, and radical members of parliament. This time the idea of a profit-making joint-stock company was abandoned; instead the controlling body was to be a board which would act as trustees for both the promoters and the colonists. A parliamentary bill for the foundation of the province of South Australia was drafted by Edward Wakefield and his brother and, after skilful lobbying by the colonizers and their supporters, the bill passed through all stages and became law in August 1834.

Throughout the four years of planning and negotiations, a leading principle had been that the colony was to be free of control by the British government and that it should become self-governing at an early stage. The earliest rough draft proposal, dated May 1831, proposed control by a governor "instructed" by the Colonial Office only until the population reached 5,000 when a legislative assembly was to be chosen by the colonists. The more detailed proposal submitted to the Colonial Office in August 1831 provided for administration by a governor appointed by the King but nominated by the council and removable by it, while there was to be a legislative assembly, elected annually by manhood suffrage, as soon as the male adult population reached 10,000. (At this time reformers in England were still fighting for the abolition of the rotten and pocket boroughs; full manhood suffrage was not achieved in England until 1918). By 1834, the promoters had come to the conclusion that the Colonial Office would never sanction the foundation of a colony over which it had no political control, and decided, in Wakefield's words, "to abandon the political part of our scheme in the hope of being able to realize the economic part."

Another key principle was that the colony was to be a haven of religious liberty. In this the great appeal was to the Dissenters (members of various non-Anglican Protestant groups) who at this date were still subject to some minor restrictions in England. In the many books, pamphlets, advertisements, and newspaper paragraphs in which the new province was publicized, the "voluntary principle" was stressed: the colonists of each denomination were to support their own ministers of religion, and there was to be no Established Church as there was in the other Australian colonies. Despite the colonizers' intentions in this regard, a clause empowering the Crown to appoint chaplains and clergymen of the Established Church of England and Scotland was included in the act. This was only one of several clauses in which a compromise was reached between the colonizers and the Colonial Office.

Under the act, the Colonial Office had ultimate authority, although how this authority was to be exercised was not clearly defined. There was to be a governor, responsible to the Colonial Office, and appointed by the Crown on the recommendation of the South Australian Association. A board of commissioners, sitting in England, was to be appointed by the Crown on the recommendation of the association; this board was to have charge of all matters relating to land sales and emigration. The price of land was to be not less than 12/– an acre. Proceeds of land sales were to be devoted to sending out emigrants, who were to be as far as possible adults under thirty years of age, with equal numbers of men and women. For general administrative purposes the commissioners were authorized to raise loans up to a total of £200,000, on the security of future colonial revenue. No convicts were to be sent to the colony. Before the act could come into operation, the commissioners had to sell land to the value of £35,000, and to deposit an additional £20,000 with the Treasury as a guarantee fund.

The ten unpaid commissioners were not appointed until 1835, Robert Gouger having the principal say in the recommendations; the commissioners included political, banking, and mercantile members, all more or less devoted to the Wakefield system. Their first task was to sell land to the required amount, and they decided to fix the price at £1 an acre. This was not a sufficient price in Wakefield's eyes, and he therefore washed his hands of the province.

At this time Crown land was selling for 5/– an acre in New South Wales and Van Diemen's Land, while settlers who had failed were offering their land for a few pence an acre in the Swan River Settlement; so sales of land in this completely new and unknown area were naturally slow, and the whole project seemed in danger of collapsing. One of the commissioners, a merchant-shipowner-bank director and philanthropic Baptist, George Fife Angas, came to the rescue. He offered to form a joint-stock land company which would buy sufficient land at the concession price of 12/– an acre to bring the sales up to the required total. Soon afterwards a banker member of the board, John Wright, arranged for the raising of a loan and issue of bonds, giving the province a general expenses fund of £88,200. Since Angas and Wright (who received a commission on the transaction) now had a financial interest in the province, they both had to resign from the board, which thus lost two of its ablest and most influential members.

The board made its appointments to the principal offices; the governor-ship went to Captain John Hindmarsh, a veteran of forty years' naval service; ex-army officer Colonel William Light became Surveyor-General, and the indefatigable organizer Robert Gouger became Colonial Secretary. While the commissioners were still organizing matters in England, the South Australian Company was in action. Anxious to start whaling operations before the end of the whaling season, the company dispatched two shiploads of its employees to establish a whaling station on the north side of Kangaroo Island. Late in July 1836 these pioneer settlers landed at Nepean Bay where they mistook the laughter of kookaburras for that of attacking Aborigines. Three weeks later Colonel Light and the small survey party arrived, with the task of selecting a site for the principal settlement. Light soon decided that the east side of Gulf St Vincent was the most suitable general location, though in accordance with his instructions he examined possible sites at Port Lincoln, Kangaroo Island, and the mouth of the Murray River; discovery of a safe harbour, extensive plains, and a river determined his choice of the present site of Adelaide and its port.

When Governor Hindmarsh arrived in December 1836, fifty huts had been put up, and although the governor disagreed with the choice of the capital site, seven miles from the sea, Light held to his decision. Differences over this issue soon developed into quarrels on other matters of administration, and Governor Hindmarsh and the Resident Commissioner, James Hurtle Fisher, found themselves at loggerheads. Neither had clear authority over the other, and the result was the formation of factions among the officials, and general paralysis of administration; the local manager of the powerful South Australian Company was a third source of practical authority. According to the Crown law officials in England, the way in which the Foundation Act had been drafted gave the commissioners complete control of the finances of the colony, not merely of the land fund, as had been thought. Accordingly the Colonial Office passed the governor's dispatches on to the commissioners, and generally left the overall control to them.

In their efforts to attract capital, the commissioners had made generous concessions and lavish promises. Trying to keep these promises thrust an impossible burden on the hardworking staff in the colony, who soon learnt the difference between the theory of systematic colonization, as propounded in London, and the practical application of the enterprise in an untried setting, thousands of miles away. Chief victim was the surveyor-general. Intending settlers had been assured that land surveys would be well in advance of settlement; yet Light and his survey party arrived in South Australia, with detailed instructions that would have taken them up to two years to carry out in full, a mere twelve weeks before the first shipload of settlers. Other ships followed, full of settlers anxious to get settled on the land they had purchased; but this was impossible until extensive surveys had been carried out.

The original land orders, purchased in England, entitled the purchaser to a country section of 80 acres and a town allotment of one acre for the combined price of £81. (The "bonus" of the town allotment was considered a necessary bait to attract buyers.) The town sections were to be surveyed and distributed before the country ones. After the streets, squares, and government domain had been laid out, the town of Adelaide was to be divided into 1,042 blocks, each one acre in size; 437 of these were to be ballotted among the original purchasers, while the remainder were to be auctioned in the colony. The original purchasers were to have prior choice of the country sections, and had been promised "the most complete liberty of appropriation." This involved an exact trigonometrical survey of 150 square miles of country, in the area around Adelaide and the port. To carry out this task, Light had a staff of three officers and twenty men, and a budget of £3,000 a year.

The auction of town acres took place in May 1837, the allotments bringing an average of £6 per acre. By December, Light had trigonometrically surveyed 59,000 country acres—the exact number necessary for allotment to holders of the original land orders—within the 150 square miles inner area around Adelaide. Two-thirds of the holders were happy with the general area, and the sections were distributed by ballot in May 1838. By this time explorations had been carried out farther afield, revealing what seemed to be better land to the south of Adelaide, and a minority of the original purchasers insisted on their right to make their selection from a much wider area. In view of the commissioners' promise of the complete freedom of choice, this was acceded to, and it was agreed that an additional 1,000 square miles to the south of Adelaide should be included in the survey.

This placed an impossible burden on the small overworked survey staff. Long before this, Light had experienced the difficulties and frustrations of opening up a new country for settlement to meet theoretical targets. When the commissioners first realized how far the surveys were behind schedule, they asked the Royal Engineers Ordnance Survey Office for advice. Lieutenant Dawson replied that each survey officer should survey 100 to 200 acres a day, so that Light and his six assistants should get through 150 square miles in four to six months. When Light received a copy of this theoretical opinion in April 1838, he wrote to Fisher in terms that express very clearly the difference between the practice and the theory of colonization:

> Lieutenant Dawson has reckoned as if this survey should be made in England or Ireland where every facility is given by roads, carriages, provisions, lodgings, etc.; he could never have considered the difficulty of moving tents, provisions and even water over a country without roads and without proper conveniences, and that the surveys must necessarily be stopped until such conveyances were supplied. Lieutenant Dawson never once considered that without rations men will not work and that on first landing in a new colony they may be often exposed to such wants. . . . Lieutenant Dawson seems to have overlooked entirely (because perhaps he never served in a strange country) the difficulty of passing over high hills without a path, or going through long grass reaching nearly to one's chin, nor does Mr Hill or Lieutenant Dawson consider that in surveying, signals or some mark at different stations are absolutely necessary and that in fixing these it takes sometimes a whole week for one party without doing any other work (not in England or Ireland where very often church steeples, chimneys and various objects are stations already fixed for triangulations).

Light also pointed out that the Ordnance theorist had not allowed for bad weather, or for sickness among the surveyors, or for the shortage of equipment and vehicles.

The surveyor's resignation and suspension took place a few months later; most of his staff resigned in sympathy, and at times his successor worked almost single-handed, while the survey fell still farther behind.

The result of the breakdown in surveys was that very little land was brought under cultivation during the first two years of colonization, and the majority of settlers were forced to remain in Adelaide. The prices of town land at the May auction were soon exceeded as subdivisions were made and new settlers arrived. Seeing their capital dwindling, many people divided their town sections, selling part of their holdings. New arrivals bought town land as a speculation, or bought out the original purchasers to obtain their prior rights of selection. The South Australian Company subdivided and sold part of its town acres. Before the end of 1837, blocks in town allotments were changing hands for as much as £80 per acre, and speculation was rife.

This paper boom in land was merely symptomatic of failure to settle people on farms and represented a dangerous situation; but in London reports of the high prices being paid for town land suggested quick riches and the colony's stocks boomed. Nearly 40,000 acres of land were sold in 1838. The commissioners spent the proceeds on free passages for immigrants, without waiting for the surveys to catch up with land sales. During the year 3,500 people arrived in the province, nearly 3,000 of them having their passages paid for from the land fund. There was no work available in the country, so the assisted immigrants stayed in the town, those who could not obtain work being supported by the government. Imports were heavy and prices high. The newcomers with capital spent their money on town land, which before the end of 1838 had reached boom prices of up to £2,000 per acre.

This was the position when Colonel George Gawler arrived to take up the combined position of Governor and Resident Commissioner. The division of authority had thrown the colonial administration into such a state of confusion that the decision had been taken to recall Hindmarsh and combine the two chief administrative positions. Gawler found the province in a state of chaos. About four-fifths of the population was crowded in Adelaide; there was no work available and they clamoured at the doors of the government offices seeking the help of the guaranteed wage promised by the commissioners if private employment were not available. Gawler was faced with an empty treasury, and with officials and creditors demanding payment.

Gawler determined to strike boldly at the heart of the problem—the lag in surveys. He determined that the survey staff must at all costs be increased to the point where it could clean up the backwash of land orders, and cope with the new land orders which continued to be presented. He reinstated the survey staff, attracted surveyors from other colonies by increasing salaries, and let out survey work on contract. When an army survey team arrived from England, sent to replace the previous staff, he combined the two staffs. He also greatly simplified the survey procedures.

The speeding up of the survey work was all the more necessary because of the increased rate of land sales. Canada was out of favour with British investors because of the French-Canadian rebellion of 1837–38, and South Australia, widely and skilfully advertised, was a popular alternative. In 1839 sales of South Australian land exceeded £170,000; but the Survey Department was able to cope with the demand for extended surveys which this huge total demanded in the following year. In just over two years, 7,000 square miles of country were explored and mapped, a triangular survey of most of the southern area was carried out, and 500,000 acres were divided into sections. More country sections were made available for occupation each month. At the time Gawler arrived in Adelaide, only 1,000 people were on the land and more than 4,000 in Adelaide; by mid-1840 the population had more than doubled, but nearly 6,000 people were on the land; when Gawler left in May 1841, nearly 16,000 acres had been enclosed and nearly 7,000 acres were under crop.

The advance of the surveys pushed the squatter-pastoralists onwards into new country. Land for grazing was not included in the commissioners' regulations, and progress of the pastoral industry was rapid. The first sheep and cattle were brought from Van Diemen's Land, England, and Europe by the South Australian Company by ship, but stock losses were heavy, and the industry did not make much progress until the commencement of "overlanding." Early in 1838, the first overlanders drove cattle and sheep along the Murray from the Riverina District in New South Wales, and early next year the coastal route from Port Phillip was pioneered. By 1840 there were 200,000 sheep and 15,000 cattle in the province.

Gawler's speeding up of the surveys was extremely successful; but it was also costly. Another expensive item was public works—the provision of the "permanent outfit" which Gawler considered necessary since, as he argued later, "the public services of 2,000 to 5,000 souls can be carried on in cottages, and the imports landed in the mud of their harbours but colonies of 15,000 souls absolutely require public buildings, works and wharves." The public buildings which he erected included a jail, Government House, hospital, wharf, immigration depot, and government offices; most of them on a substantial scale, to allow for future increases of population. The work was done by private contractors. Roads were begun, to link the north, south, and eastern districts with Adelaide.

Still another expense was the police force. As settlement spread, there was increasing conflict with the Aborigines, and more police were needed to protect settlers against Aboriginal attack, as well as from bushrangers and convicts from the other colonies. All this time the commissioners were spending the proceeds of the land fund on assisting more migrants. In 1839 they sent out more than 5,000 people, far too great a number to be absorbed in employment. The commissioners had promised to support immigrants who could not get work, and the governor interpreted this promise as meaning that he had to provide them with "food, shelter, medical attendance and relief in destitution."

Gawler's whole extensive developmental programme was carried out without consideration of its cost. The result was bankruptcy.

Under the Foundation Act, the commissioners had been authorized to raise loans for general expenditure up to a total of £200,000. By the end of 1838, they had come to the end of the original loan money of £88,200; instead of floating another loan, they sought the passage of an amending act, which enabled them to transfer part of the land fund to general expenses. Throughout 1839, when the colony was high in popular favour, they made no attempt to raise another loan, with which to meet the mounting expenditure in the colony.

Apart from the sums raised by fees and customs duties, both Hindmarsh and Gawler had been authorized to draw bills on the commissioners up to a definite amount. Hindmarsh had drawn bills totalling £19,000 during his twenty months in office. Gawler was authorized to draw bills to the total of £12,000 a year, while a great number of specified additional expenses were sanctioned by the commissioners. As his expenditure mounted, he continued to draw bills far in excess of these limitations, while sending the commissioners only generalized warnings about the excessive expenditure he was incurring. He considered that all his expenditure was essential and unavoidable, a fact that justified his use of the emergency powers conferred upon him, and took it for granted that the commissioners would continue to honour the bills as they were presented; he relied also on assurances given him by the commissioners and a high official in the Colonial Office that the British government would support the colony in a crisis. By mid-1840 he was spending money at the rate of £140,000 a year.

In January 1840 the Colonial Secretary dismissed the original commissioners and appointed a new three-man salaried board. The new board thought there was no great need of funds and did not at first try to raise a new loan. When they did try, the attempt failed. The board continued to send out emigrant ships (nearly 4,500 assisted emigrants arrived in Adelaide in 1840) and continued to meet Gawler's bills as they were presented for payment until August 1840, when funds were exhausted. Then they refused payment of bills from the colony, wrote ordering Gawler not to draw any more bills, and appealed to the Colonial Office to save the colony from disaster.

In May 1841, the *Lord Glenelg* reached Port Adelaide with a dispatch for Gawler informing him that as he had drawn bills in excess of the authority given to him, he had been relieved of his office. His successor, Captain George Grey, arrived by the same ship, and took over the administration immediately.

When Parliament met, the Colonial Secretary arranged for a government loan of £155,000, to enable the board to meet Gawler's bills; he also arranged for a Parliamentary Committee of Enquiry into the affairs of the province. The committee declined to pass judgement on Gawler, who was not present to defend himself, but considered that none of the witnesses had been able to point out any specific items by which his expenditure could have been reduced without great public inconvenience, and that the state of the enterprise on his arrival had made it necessary for him to exceed his instructions. The original commissioners were blamed for making completely inadequate financial provisions. The chief and original error lay with the Foundation Act, which conferred enormous powers on a board of private gentlemen, without adequate provision for their control and supervision by the British government, and which laid down an expensive and precarious system for financing the general administration by the raising of loans.

The committee recommended that South Australia should be placed on the same footing as the other Australian colonies, and this was done in 1842. South Australia became a Crown Colony, with a governor and nominated legislative council; an elective legislative assembly was to be introduced when the population warranted it. Land and emigration matters were to be brought into line with the regulations in the other Australian colonies, while the loan of £155,000 was made an outright gift.

Grey's instructions had been to exercise the most rigid economy, and the twenty-seven year old army officer, a man of great administrative ability, self-confidence, and strength of character, carried out these instructions unflinchingly. Some of his economies were possible only because of the success of his predecessor's crash programme of development. The work of the Survey and Public Works Departments was so far advanced that cuts could be made in the activities of both departments without serious inconvenience. In all the government departments expenses were cut, staffs reduced, and fees and charges raised.

Some economies were possible because the province was now a Crown Colony; the Police Department could be reduced since Grey was able to replace the police by troops from Van Diemen's Land. Other economies were possible because the governor was not bound by the commissioners' promises as Gawler had been. The expenditure on arriving migrants was lessened now that no more assisted migrants were being sent to the colony.

The heavy cost of relief work for the unemployed was cut rigidly; the ration was discontinued, the wage rate reduced, and a means test introduced which withheld relief from many former recipients (although Grey was generous with private charity to the victims). Settlement of the claims upon the government by local creditors was postponed for the time being.

The result of this thorough deflationary policy was a violent and prolonged depression, with many bankruptcies, widespread unemployment, and universal distress.

Late in 1841, when the worst of the crisis seemed to be passing, Grey learnt that the British government was honouring Gawler's bills held by creditors in the United Kingdom, and he concluded he was free to take the same action in regard to the local creditors. He disallowed some of the claims, reduced some, converted others into debenture stock, and persuaded the largest creditor, the South Australian Company, to accept a land grant in lieu of its claim. For the balance he drew drafts of almost £14,000 on the Treasury, which disallowed the transaction, thus prolonging the crisis in the colony; eventually the amount was converted into debentures.

The benefits resulting from Gawler's accelerated programme of surveys were already being felt when the change of administration took place; thousands of settlers had already moved from Adelaide to occupation of their country land, and cultivation was well under way. Grey's curtailment of unemployment benefits forced workers out of the city, and those already settled on the land were helped by a supply of cheap labour, as well as by reduced prices for food and farm materials. Once the farmers could get to work, the quality of this natural grain country made it possible for excellent crops to be produced without great initial expenses. An excellent harvest was reaped at the end of 1841, from a total of about 8,000 acres under crop. Agricultural operations were further extended during 1842, and the harvest from 20,000 acres under crop was so abundant that troops and public officers had to help bring it in; in fact, twice as much grain as was necessary to feed the colony's population of 16,000 was harvested, raising the question of export markets. The pastoral industry was making similar progress; sheep numbered 340,000 in 1842, and 850,000 pounds weight of wool was exported. In January 1843 Grey could truthfully write to the Secretary of State: "I have now brought to a successful issue the task which was committed to my charge of equalizing the revenue and expenditure of this province."

The South Australian Company, which had shared the province's early years of boom and depression to the full, made its contribution to the recovery.

George Fife Angas, the founder and chairman of the company, was personally responsible for bringing to the colony several hundred Evangelical Lutheran religious refugees from northern Germany—the first European immigration to Australia on an organized and substantial basis. By the end of 1841 more than 500 Germans were settled on small leasehold farms in three separate self-supporting village communities. Each family farmed a plot of land, on which they cultivated vegetables, wheat, and maize, and kept a few cows. Their vegetables and dairy products—at first carried to the town market on the heads of the women—helped to ease early shortages. The village communities also contracted to shear sheep for the company and private settlers, as pioneer settler John Wrathall Bull remembered:

> The shearers, principally young women, were waited on by men of the village, who, when called upon, caught and carried the sheep to the shearer who was ready. The sheep was carefully laid down on its side; the young woman, without shoes and stockings, had a piece of thick, soft string tied to one of her great toes, and the other end was tied to the hind foot of the sheep; the girl's leg was then stretched out to extend the legs of the sheep; her knee or left hand was pressed on the neck or shoulder of the animal, which was then left to her charge, and she commenced her clipping work, most carefully avoiding any snips of the skin. The number shorn by one never exceeded thirty a day, but I was pleased to see how tenderly the sheep were handled. The wool was taken off very close.

These frugal, hard-working German Lutherans, who had emigrated at the dictates of their consciences, fitted admirably into the population pattern that gave South Australia its distinctive character among the Australian colonies.

Part
Three

The frontier phase

FROM THE BEGINNING OF THE 1820s, men on horseback, men on foot, and men driving drays and wagons were moving over the ranges and down into the broad valleys and wooded plains beyond—all part of the takeover of the land that was now beginning. Men were going wherever sheep led them. The moving settlement-frontier that had come into being drew them steadily inland from Sydney, spreading men and sheep across the face of the continent. Private capital moved into the colonial scene at an increased rate in the wake of the Bigge Report, spurring transition from an economy geared to convictism. Once prospects opened up for development of commercial enterprise, the relentless occupation of the land began.

In both New South Wales and Van Diemen's Land, the stimulus was a desire to secure pastures for ever-expanding flocks. A conjunction of forces had occurred to spur the drive inland. Success had been achieved in the breeding of fine-wool merino sheep; at the same time penetration inland away from the original coastal footholds had revealed new and seemingly limitless grasslands providing ideal pasture for merinos. The 1825 London reduction of customs duties on colonial-grown wools gave the sheepmen a sharp new cutting edge with which to reshape economic affairs in far-off New South Wales. In the same year, it was decreed that intending settlers no longer had to have the sanction of the Colonial Office. This opened the way for immigration. Machinery was coming into increasing use throughout the English woollen industry, spurring the textile manufacturers to demand ever-increasing quantities of fine fibres. Thanks to her industrial world leadership, England had a huge surplus of capital available for investment at home and abroad. Thus a variety of factors, operating in both England and Australia, combined to spur pastoral development in the Australian colonies.

In the early years, activities in each settlement had been dominated by government planning and government expenditure. In Sydney and Hobart Town the few locally grown products were brought in to feed the establishment; but, apart from timber and some coal, or whaling and associated activities of the sea, no product existed that could be exported and so support a viable economy for a growing colony. In order to set the stage for providing development, a commodity had to be found that would be capable of making its way in a world market. And only wool could amply fulfil this role.

With the establishment of sheep-raising and the export of wool, a move away from almost total dependence on government activities had begun. No longer would colonial officials in London have to rack their brains in conjuring up hopeful suggestions for agricultural products that might be tried, and no longer would they feel obliged to write dispatches solemnly instructing governors that indigo—or hemp, or rice—should be cultivated on the assumption that the country must surely be capable of growing whatever produce the home government thought desirable. The answer had been found.

Sheep-raising on the vast grasslands, where the climate was dry and rainfall variable, called for considerable capital. Recognizing this, the British government encouraged investment through large-scale grants of land to companies and individuals ready to spend money on developing it. The phase of capitalist immigration thus opening up gave new direction and dimension to the colonial economies.

Wherever in the great wooded pastureland promising land could be found, someone was ready to occupy more of this endless kingdom of grass over which scattered tribes of Aborigines wandered. The legendary quest for the golden fleece came to reality as there began a seemingly endless venture into new and unknown tracts. The movement accelerated as grand vistas and boundless ambitions overcame the restraints imposed by practical difficulties. Convinced that wealth could be gained by possession of the apparently limitless lands, men were prepared to turn their backs on the known world and to suffer isolation and loneliness in the hope of a rich future. In pushing forward the frontier of occupation, the pioneer faced a daily round requiring hardihood, determination, and self reliance—and although he faced little in the way of physical danger, the isolation in which he lived demanded of him a high degree of adaptability, robustness, and confidence.

Only by coming to grips with the land on its own terms could the pioneer hope to succeed. Yet the frontiersman's personal qualities would not have brought success had it not been for the equally robust nature of the sheep he took with him into the wilderness. The hardy merinos were quick to thrive in the surroundings in which they found themselves. For centuries flocks of these hardy sheep had moved each year across Spain between the northern mountains and the southern lowlands (where they spent the winters), and their abundant wool of fine quality was so important as a source of wealth that the sheep were carefully guarded.

Their export from Spain was permitted for the first time in 1765, when some favoured lands received drafts; after that the breed spread through Europe. In some areas the fine merino strain was absorbed and lost, but in Saxony, Silesia, and Mecklenburg, and in France, the breed was kept pure. The Dutch secured some, probably from Silesia, and small flocks of merinos were established at the Cape of Good Hope; in 1797 when an auction of a flock was held there, twenty-six were bought for shipment to Sydney. A few survived the journey and, after Governor Hunter refused to purchase them, they were dispersed among three or four landholders, including John Macarthur. A few years later Macarthur, then in London, secured seven rams and some ewes from the Royal flock which was being disbanded because the damp English climate had proved unsuitable for merinos; these were sent to Sydney to build up the growing flocks on the Macarthur farm at Camden.

By 1815, when the way was opened across the Blue Mountains, merino and other flocks were well established around Port Jackson and, with open grasslands revealed beyond the range, their spread began. After 1820, wool was being exported in reasonable volume, and English mill-owners were paying good prices for it. From Bathurst and adjoining districts, occupation spread like fingers that sometimes followed the tracks of explorers and sometimes felt out good land in unexplored territory. Explorers and land-hungry stockholders might move side by side; usually the sheepmen were the first to open up the land between the main thrusts of the explorers. Slowly they traced the complicated pattern of the westward flowing streams of the south-east sector of the continent. The answer to the principal riddle of what happened to the rivers came in 1830, when an army captain, Charles Sturt, made the long journey down the Murrumbidgee and then the Murray, and found that the river into which the other streams eventually flowed reached the sea on the continent's southern shore. Others—explorers and stockmen—added to Sturt's discoveries in the great saucer of pastoral lands across which all the rivers of the Murray-Darling system—tributaries of the Murray—were found to flow.

Drawn by the indefinable "opportunity" of an expanding frontier, ambitious people faced with relative equanimity the rigours—even the terrors—of an ocean voyage half-way around the world. They arrived wide-eyed and wondering, their clothes stiff with salt, heavy with the dampness of the sea. They felt a little uneasy at first, curious as they sought to define the differences between this land and their own. The sky was bluer, the sun brighter than in England or Scotland or Ireland; instead of the familiar trees and plants and birds there were weird and beautiful flowers, strange bright birds, and unbelievable animals. Naturalist John Gould and his artist wife Elizabeth were among those enchanted with the scene; from the late 1830s Elizabeth Gould's paintings appeared in her husband's *The Birds of Australia*, and this handsome publication, and *The Mammals of Australia* which followed, extended the interest of educated Englishmen in the Australian scene.

Books written by the explorers told of an enticing and unusual land.

Sir Thomas Mitchell, contemporary and rival of Sturt, declared that he had discovered an "Eden," to which he gave the name Australia Felix, south of the Murray River—extensive tracts of country "ready for the immediate reception of civilized man." The discoveries opened up new vistas to thinking Englishmen as London newspapers and magazines began to publish reports on the vast unoccupied territory where land could be obtained so readily and used so profitably. This seemed like Arcady, and immigration, both assisted and unassisted, grew.

Although the advance of the sheep was providing the main spur to settling more people in Australia, other factors were having an influence. From the 1820s, population pressures in the British Isles became an important force in colonial development plans. The feeling grew that emigration alone could relieve the problems of over-population, unemployment, and hopeless misery in the midst of increasing wealth. In Ireland, poverty was even worse than in England. Poorer classes had been emigrating in increasing numbers, drawn largely by the advancing prosperity of the United States and the North American colonies. Committees of the House of Commons in 1826 and 1827 approved the idea of emigration, but New South Wales and Van Diemen's Land were not given any special attention in this connection. The high cost of a passage to Australia was a deterrent; but although it was becoming obvious that only with a plan of assisted immigration could the far-off colonies attract a reasonable share of the emigrants, the British government was not prepared to place this added burden on the taxpayer.

It was Wakefield's plan that changed the scene. The Ripon regulations for sale of Crown land, which came into force early in 1831, quickly yielded funds, and within a few months a plan was in operation to assist those who had previously been held back by the expense of migrating to the colonies. As a result of worsening social conditions in the 1830s—widespread unemployment, rioting that followed the suppression of trade unionism, poverty and upheaval in Ireland, a badlyworking Poor Law system—pressure to increase the outflow grew in England. The prospect of relieving such problems by stepped-up emigration to the colonies came as a godsend to policy-makers in London. An emigration committee was set up to make funds available as passage money. This was a windfall for the shipping agents, who saw to it that the ships were filled.

The colonial administrators and the leading colonists were unhappy over the selection of immigrants; they wanted men who could relieve the shortage of labour on the grazing properties; instead, they saw the Land Fund being spent to bring unsuitable and unsavoury types to Australia. Many of the new arrivals were criminals or sick, or had no qualifications as domestics or farm workers; the *Sydney Herald* characterized "the great bulk of the kidnapped creatures" of the early phase of assisted migration as adding "pollution even to a society of convicts."

It was not until 1837 that the colonial administrators had any share in the control of the Land Fund; thereafter they were able to apply one-third of the funds available for emigration to bringing out people chosen by their own appointees, while the remaining two-thirds were selected by authorities appointed by the British government. The system still did not work to the satisfaction of the landholders, and the desire of the leading citizens of New South Wales to secure full colonial control of immigration through the associated Land Fund became a driving force in their efforts to achieve self-government.

Still sparsely populated, Australia was a land of strange appeal, offering a wild freedom. Although overland journeys were difficult and hazardous undertakings, the demand for livestock in newly established districts soon resulted in droving expeditions in which men might traverse 1,000 miles almost wholly through uninhabited country. The "overlanders" faced special dangers—bushfires or sudden floods, droughts or sickness or injury, the peril of attack by Aborigines. There were compensations for the hardy and the adventurous, however, as recorded in this description by a pioneering drover:

> "The earth for a bedstead, the heavens for curtains, and the wilderness for a bedroom, are fair qualities enough, and there is a charm about the whole affair quite enchanting to the wanderer, if he is not too hungry to be pleased, or too tired to be cheerful. . . .
>
> [You] travel through the almost untrodden wilds by day, passing through the bush hitherto unseen by the eyes of white men, now moving on through thick scrub, then emerging into the forest glades with free, untrained, untrammelled nature around about, no law of trespass to turn you back, no fences to enclose the land and bar progress . . . no dinners or lunches, or patent leather boots, or diamond studs with clean linen. Here in these wild regions the liberty of rags and the freedom of dirt."

Many of the new arrivals from England were, nevertheless, appalled by the immensity and emptiness of the land, and preferred to stay in Sydney rather than face the loneliness and isolation of the bush. It was the native-born who could more readily take to the bush life; lithe and strong and used to the outdoor life, they were the drovers, bullock drivers, and horse-breakers. The colonial scene did not always appeal to English visitors, and even as erudite an observer as Charles Darwin was inclined to flinch at the prospect. When Darwin visited Australia, during the memorable voyage of H.M.S. *Beagle*, he recorded that he was "filled with admiration" for "the fine town of Sydney" with its regular, broad, clean streets, but after a few weeks in Australian waters and at Australian ports he wrote, as the vessel left King George Sound in 1836:

> Farewell, Australia! You are a rising child, and doubtless some day will reign a great princess in the South: but you are too great and too ambitious for affection, yet not great enough for respect. I leave your shores without sorrow or regret.

The new wealth of wool was Australia's rising star. In the wool saga that was now opening, a major factor was the introduction to colonial flocks of merino strains from Saxony, Silesia, and Mecklenburg. In these dry northern lands near the Baltic, merinos had developed heavier fleeces and finer wool so that the new strains bred there proved superior, if anything, to the original Spanish types. From the mid-1820s sheep from these improved flocks were bought and sent to Australia by individual settlers and by syndicates and joint-stock companies; their introduction led to marked improvement of colonial flocks. Wool yields and fibre quality improved as the progeny of these sheep spread. The prophesy of Macarthur was fulfilled. Other flockmasters were now winning a place for themselves as new blood-lines were established. The development of improved flocks was no longer in a very few hands. Australian pastoralists were competing successfully for the finest of the merinos as they were released from German sources and before long Australian-grown merino fleeces were accepted by the English buyers as finer than all but the best fleeces from Saxony.

The system of free land grants, having served its purpose of encouraging capitalists to develop the land, ended in 1831. Henceforth a freehold title to land could be obtained only by purchase. Yet whether the official means of land-disposal was by free grant or by auction mattered nothing to the sheep and little more to many of the sheep-owners. Unauthorized persons moved across the grasslands with their flocks and took up holdings. They were known as "squatters," because they entered on land to which they had no title, built simple dwellings, and put sheep and cattle to pasture. In the open grasslands, ambition could set its own limits, and individuals moved on to occupy tens and even hundreds of thousands of acres.

The appetite of the sheep for grass and that of their owners for land was voracious. The British government, on the other hand, believed that settlement should not be allowed to spread far in advance of surveys, police, roads, and other government services. Successive Secretaries of State clung to the theory of concentration of settlement, in spite of the warnings of successive governors that there was no practical way to prevent spread of occupation. ("As well might it be attempted to confine the Arabs of the desert within a circle, traced upon their sands, as to confine the graziers or wool-growers of New South Wales within any bounds that can possibly be assigned to them" was Governor Sir George Gipps's assessment of the situation.)

Even the sea was no barrier to the onward march of the sheep. In the 1820s there was notable expansion of flocks in Van Diemen's Land, and by the 1830s the sheep had multiplied to a point where the pressure on the island's pastures turned stock-owners' thoughts to the unoccupied tracts across Bass Strait. Unauthorized, and frowned upon as illegal occupation, the move north across the Strait began in 1834, and in the following year the land around Port Phillip Bay was occupied. Overlanders from the districts farthest south also drove their flocks onward, eventually meeting with the northward thrusts from Port Phillip. In this rolling province of grass there were no barriers to settlement. Soon great holdings were taken up, and hundreds of thousands of sheep were being grazed.

Melbourne, the main entry point, quickly outgrew the status of a village, probably because it suffered none of the disturbing problems that plagued other settlements in their formative years. Port Phillip was in fact settled by Australians—the first such enterprise—and it was free of both official and English doctrinaire planning. Those of its founding fathers who were not Australian-born had been long enough in the colonies to be considered Australian. Their practical experience combined with initiative put the enterprise on its feet at once, so that by the time the facts of the occupation were realized by officialdom the Port Phillip settlement was already well established.

The enforced recognition of the squatter settlement of Port Phillip was a highlight of the series of victories which the squatters gained over the restrictive policies of the British government. In 1836 the squatting system was officially recognized and regulated by a licence system. Judicial decisions confirmed the squatters' rights over the runs they occupied while from time to time, as surveyors advanced, more and more squatting districts were officially declared open for pastoral occupation.

Squatting in the Australian bush was not what it was in the United States, where the squatter was the lowly and unauthorized occupier of 20 or 30 acres. The Australian squatter often occupied tens and even hundreds of thousands of acres. Practically all the landowners were part-squatters, pasturing some of their flocks beyond the boundaries of location under the management of their sons or overseers. As Governor Gipps noted in 1840, the ranks of the squatters included young Englishmen of good family, army and navy officers, university graduates, as well as some of the wealthiest men in the colony. The governor wrote that the squatters were "the real discoverers of the country, and they may be said to be in Australia (what the backwoodsmen are in America) the pioneers of civilization."

The pastoralists had wealth and social status: during the period from 1823 to 1842, when the governor of New South Wales was assisted by a nominated legislative council, it was natural that members of the council should be drawn almost exclusively from this group. From 1823 onwards the main thrust of colonial political development was towards meeting the demands of this numerically small but economically powerful minority of the population. Even after 1842, when the colony was given a two-thirds elective council, the restricted franchise and the high property qualification for membership had the effect of more or less reserving membership of the council for pastoralists. The influence of the pastoralists was bolstered by powerful interests in England. As wool exports continued to increase, and the colonies began to overtake Germany as the principal supplier of England's raw wool, the pastoralists were always able to call on the support of the English woollen manufacturers, importers, and shipping companies, and this powerful group exerted pressure on the colonial office to reject any moves that seemed likely to hinder the growth of Australia's wool industry.

Squatting flourished in the few years immediately following its recognition by the licence system in 1836; and squatters, with their status legalized and their contribution to the community's wealth beyond challenge, began to increase their demands. At first they had merely wanted to occupy the maximum area possible with available resources. They were prepared to endure personal discomfort and privation, and kept the outlays on their runs to a minimum, since there was no inducement to spend money on houses and improvements to land in which they had no secure tenure.

From the beginning of the 1840s the squatters' insistent demands for security of land tenure provided the principal issue in New South Wales politics. Governor Gipps favoured giving the squatters unrestricted rights to occupy land, but he was against making it easy for this small proportion of the population to gain what amounted to freehold possession of vast tracts of land at a low price. Such a policy would be, he believed, a betrayal of the future interests of the people as a whole. Accordingly, he worked out a policy by which the squatters could purchase their runs by instalments over a long period, but could not prevent other people buying the runs if they themselves were unable to do so.

The squatting interests were far too strong for the governor. A pastoralists' association headed by members of the legislative council was formed to oppose Gipps's proposed regulations, enlisting the active support of English woollen manufacturers, shippers, and importers, who brought pressure to bear on the Government. The Colonial Office, which had at first supported Gipps, changed its attitude, and his proposals were dropped. An Order in Council which came into effect in 1847 met most of the demands of the squatters. It divided pastoral land into three classes: settled, intermediate, and unsettled districts. In each district the land was to be leased with rights of purchase, the leases being for one, eight, and fourteen years; so that in the remote squatting lands where occupation was still proceeding, the lessee had security of tenure for fourteen years, during which he alone could purchase the land.

From this time onwards there was an air of permanence about the Australian rural scene. With it went a change in the nature of colonial society as family settlement began to merge with pioneering in its crudest form. Now that they could obtain secure titles to their land, the squatters began to lay out money for the improvements they had been reluctant to tackle before, and to build homesteads to which they could bring their wives and families. As temporary makeshift dwellings were replaced with larger houses of sawn timber, the rawness of the wilderness was somewhat reduced.

The increase of free immigration had brought about fundamental changes in colonial society, mainly because it watered down the proportion of ex-convicts in the population. Throughout the convict period far more men than women had been sent to Australia, and the social evils resulting from this had been one of the most cogent arguments put forward by opponents of the transportation system, such as Edward Gibbon Wakefield. One of Wakefield's most valubale contributions to Australian development was the impetus he gave to selective immigration, and particularly to the immigration of equal numbers of men and women. The commissioners and agents who made their selection from those wanting free passages to South Australia tried as much as possible to send out equal numbers of men and women, and as a result South Australian society never suffered from the high masculinity ratio that plagued the other colonies. Significant in correcting this imbalance was the work of Caroline Chisholm, whose campaigns for family colonization and for including women in assisted immigration plans helped redress the balance between the sexes in the older colonies.

Increasing pressure had been building up in England against the transportation of convicts; it was led by the churches, many liberal thinkers, and evangelical philanthropic opinion. Within the colonies, arguments against transportation had become stronger; as sheep numbers soared, the need for efficient labour increased, and it was clear that if convictism were maintained there would be insufficient incentive for free immigrants, for wages would continue to be depressed while assigned men were available. In 1837, instructions were sent to the Governor of New South Wales from London directing that measures be taken "for inducing the settlers generally to look for the future to emigration rather than to [convict] assignment" as a labour source. A House of Commons committee in 1838 came to the conclusion that if the colonies were to depend on British jails for their supply of labour, "their prosperity has reached its climax and must decline." The recommendation of this committee against the continuance of transportation to New South Wales represented a triumph for progressive forces in England and for enlightened colonial opinion. The committee did not suggest that transportation should be completely abandoned, but after 1840 it was confined to Van Diemen's Land and Norfolk Island, and there a modified system went into force.

Once transportation to New South Wales ended, political changes could not be long delayed. The way was opened for the granting of more power to the colonists, and political advancement taking place simultaneously in Canada provided both a spur and an example to follow. Lord Durham's report on the Canadian situation, following the French Canadian rebellion and widespread unrest, was issued in 1839; the consequent Union Act of 1840 provided for a union with a legislative council, with members nominated for life, and an elected legislative assembly. The new arrangement in turn ushered in responsible government, not through legislative action but as a means of making the system work. The development in Canada marked an important milestone in colonial government at the time when political horizons were opening in New South Wales.

The squatters were now secure in possession of their runs, but the right to dispose of Crown land and the use of the proceeds of sales and leases remained under the control of the governor, representing the Colonial Office. The continuing struggle of pastoralists to gain control of the colonial waste lands was a principal factor in the growing demands in the late 1840s for colonial self-government. In spite of severe depression in the early 1840s, Australia's exports of wool and the Australian percentage of England's wool imports had continued their spectacular increase. From a fraction of one per cent in 1820 and about 8 per cent in 1830, Australia's contribution to English raw wool imports had risen to 43 per cent of the total in 1850—by which time England's total volume of wool imports was nearly three times as great as it had been twenty years before.

The handling of wool was improving steadily. Wool stores were set up at the shipment ports. Like Sydney, Melbourne had become a solid town with prosperity based on its burgeoning trade in wool well before the extraordinary gold strikes near by in the early 1850s brought a horde of fortune seekers from around the world, and in London and Hamburg, Canton and Boston, the very word Australia came to acquire a magical aura as newspapers told of the astonishing discoveries. The sudden outpouring of gold changed the local economy. Within Victoria, separated from New South Wales in the gold-strike year of 1851 and created a separate colony, the wealth that came from gold stimulated economic growth, and this in turn led to political and social changes whose effects were to be felt beyond the new colony's borders.

The repercussions extended to world trade. In London, *The Times* was among the publications that conjectured upon the likely effects of Britain's acquisition of such unprecedented quantities of gold—enough, the paper declared early in 1853, "to justify the wildest speculations as to [its] commercial and social results." Year by year, as extraordinary quantities of Australian gold found their way to London and other centres, the effect was momentous.

The outpouring of Australian gold in the 1850s was so great that it was changing the monetary condition in Britain and other lands. The flow from Victorian fields and, to some extent, those of other colonies, was largely responsible for gold becoming a practical medium of exchange in the world's monetary systems. The great expansion in the world's supply of monetary gold dates from the time of the great Californian and the Australian discoveries, as this general table indicates:

Year	Australia	Rest of World	Total
1801–1840 (annual average)	nil	15	15
1841–1850 (annual average)	nil	54	54
1851	10	124	134
1852	102	117	219
1853	108	123	231
1854	80	120	200
1855	94	115	209
1856	102	116	218
1857	101	108	209
1858	94	112	206
1859	91	113	204
1860	89	103	192
1861	83	102	185

World's Output of Gold (1810–1861): Approximate production (in tons)

In the 1850s, by far the greatest period of gold production yet known, Australia and the United States shared more or less equally in the output (with American production slightly the greater). However, it was Australian gold that made the main impact on world trade, since much of the American output remained at home while gold from the Australian fields was almost all exported. Australian gold helped strengthen Britain's economic position, supporting the great boom which continued from the early 1850s to

1873. The bulk of the gold found its way to the Bank of England, whose holdings quickly doubled even as increased quantities of gold passed into circulation; by 1856 the Bank's gold holdings were seven times what they were a few years earlier. The gold could be freely coined (England had been on the gold standard since 1816) and huge sums were minted in London in 1852 and 1853—six and eight times, respectively, the amount coined in 1850. With a great flood of gold in its vaults, the Bank of England reduced interest rates sharply from 1852, and with abundant capital available at low rates British industry and trade were stimulated, and the way opened for continuing expansion of industry and international trade.

Australia, the once-unwanted land, now the frontiersman's realm, had proved to be a treasure-house of extraordinary value and great significance.

Sheep, land, and frontiersmen 7

When Governor Sir Thomas Brisbane took over the administration of New South Wales in 1821, settlers and their livestock were already spreading out quite rapidly on the western side of the mountain barrier that for so long had hedged in the settlement around Port Jackson. By 1820 the sheep in the Bathurst district numbered more than 11,000—not all merinos, but most of them bred from good stock. By this time the pastoral prospects of the hinterland, with its natural grasses and herbage, and fine dry climate, had been demonstrated. Not only were the sheep found to thrive, but their fleeces improved. Land was available for the expanding flocks, and the market for wool was growing all the time. England's insatiable demand for fine wool, coupled with the natural propensity of the newly opened land for growing it, induced the sheep men to move into the wilderness. The pioneer breeders of merino sheep in the confined area close to Sydney had laid the foundation for a wool-growing industry; but it was the opening of the hinterland that made possible the realization of the industry's great potential. Cattle could thrive on the extensive new pastures just as readily as sheep—but they could not be as profitable as sheep with their annual yield of a non-perishable commodity for which an eager demand existed abroad.

The prospects for the growing of fine wool in quantity on the inland plains were already attracting interest in England towards the end of Macquarie's régime, and increasing numbers of moneyed free settlers were presenting to the governor the Colonial Office recommendation for a grant of land in proportion to their capital. This system was expanded following publication of the Bigge Report. The practical ideas of John Macarthur and other successful sheepmen shone through the report; its theme was shaped largely by their views and objectives. Bigge had advocated extensive

165

land grants to men or companies with money to invest in pastoral activities, who would take the convict labour off the government's hands and thus lessen the heavy expenses of transportation at the same time as they developed a broad and efficient pastoral economy. This principle was taken up wholeheartedly by both the British government and the colonial administration, and every incentive was offered to people of means to interest themselves in the colony's pastoral development: the result was a new and constructive phase in the colony's growth.

Britain was entering the period of active investment abroad. The amount of money subscribed for large-scale Australian enterprises was insignificant compared with British investors' outpourings of capital to other overseas lands. Nevertheless, an accelerated inflow of capital into the Australian colonies began as companies were set up to invest in pastoral pursuits, and banks backed individuals with funds for such enterprises. The leaders and the principal beneficiaries of the great pastoral expansion were of necessity men possessing substantial capital. In the area around Sydney, impoverished emancipists by diligent effort might set up farms that would be self-supporting; in the great hinterland money was needed if the enterprise were to succeed.

The largest single venture was the Australian Agricultural Company, a joint-stock company with a capital of £1,000,000, incorporated under Royal charter by act of parliament in 1824. The company, intended mainly as a stock breeding and wool-growing enterprise, received a grant of a million acres of land in the hinterland behind Port Stephens, plus a coal monopoly at Newcastle, on condition that it became responsible for the maintenance of 1,400 convicts (then costing the administration £30,000 a year in upkeep). The company had financial backing from London and Sydney interests, and the shareholding was quite widespread, but one man's vision and drive dominated the enterprise.

The formation of the company represented the fulfilment of one of the oldest and most ambitious of the many projects put forward by John Macarthur. His first proposal for a large land grant to a joint-stock company for development of a pastoral industry had been made in 1802, when Australia's merino flocks numbered a few thousands, and he himself was a young army officer. The proposal he expounded to Macquarie and Bigge in 1819–20, that he should become the monopoly provider of merino rams for the colony, was a variant of the same idea. The new company was brought into being by an act of parliament mainly drafted by John Macarthur junior, who had been active in London throughout as a public relations man and lobbyist on his family's behalf. A local management committee of five, set up in Sydney, included John Macarthur's son James, his nephew Hannibal, and his son-in-law, Dr James Bowman. One of the main activities of the company in its early days was buying merino sheep and lambs from John Macarthur; this was done in order that it might develop as a major source of high-quality breeding stock.

Thus by the mid-1820s Macarthur's foresight, business acumen, and energetic promotion of his ideas before British manufacturers and government leaders had finally brought fulfilment of old dreams. Following Bigge's commendation he had received a grant of an additional 5,000 acres of land in the Cow Pastures. Every governor from King to Brisbane had demurred at giving Macarthur the rights to this picked land, where the progeny of the strayed First Fleet cattle had multiplied; Brisbane's efforts to divert Macarthur's attention to land elsewhere failed as completely as those of his predecessors. These were days of triumph for Macarthur: the governor offered him membership of the new legislative council; the Royal Society of Arts presented him with medals commemorating his pastoral successes; his sons were carrying on his work ably and well; his wool consistently sold for high prices, while the colony's second bank, the Bank of Australia, was established in Sydney in 1826, largely under the family's sponsorship. Macarthur had outfought all his opponents and he had outlived most of them, and now he could bask in absolute triumph—had his character made such basking possible.

It took some years for the Australian Agricultural Company to get on its feet, and its first successes were in the winning of coal. In its pastoral activities, early troubles were due largely to the choice of unsuitable land and to labour problems. After initial setbacks, the company's importation of Saxon and other German-bred rams, and the enclosing of its runs, were the forerunners of success gained through notable improvement of its livestock and more scientific methods of animal husbandry. By the early 1830s the company was running over 80,000 sheep and 5,000 head of cattle, and producing 16,000 tons of coal a year.

The Australian Agricultural Company had its counterpart in Van Diemen's Land, where wool-growing had developed significantly following the introduction of merinos from the Macarthur flock by Governor William Sorrell in 1820, and subsequent importations from Saxon flocks. In 1825 the Van Diemen's Land Company was granted a charter to raise stock, employ and maintain convicts, and develop a grant of 250,000 acres beyond "the ramparts of the unknown" in the unexplored north-west of the island. The company established headquarters at Burnie, but because of the nature of the land and the convict labour force, its progress was slow until the formation of settlements on the south coast of the mainland, which provided a market for the company's livestock.

The policy of encouragement to capitalists by large land grants (free except for small deferred quit rents) was not included in the instructions to the governor which had been drafted before receipt of the Bigge Report, but the Secretary of State's dispatches to Governor Brisbane expressed the policy clearly and definitely. The land grants were conditional upon the permanent maintenance of a certain number of convict labourers, one convict for every 100 acres being the normal proportion.

The instructions to the next Governor, Sir Ralph Darling, who succeeded Brisbane in 1825, marked the complete acceptance of the policy. The provision—in the instructions to all earlier governors—for settlement of ex-convicts on the land was omitted: instead land grants were to be not more than 2,560 acres, and not less than 320 acres (execpt near towns and villages), "it being our intention by the before-mentioned restrictions to prevent the increase and extension of farms and settlements too inconsiderable to replace with profit the capital to be expended in the cultivation thereof." Quit rents were to be paid for seven years after the execution of the grant.

Darling appointed a three-man Land Board to advise him on land grants and related matters, and it put into practice and systematized the procedures laid down in the governor's instructions. Henceforth each approved applicant for a land grant was entitled to 640 acres or one square mile for every £500 of his real capital, 320 acres being the smallest grant and four square miles the largest, although grants greatly in excess of this limitation continued to be approved by the Colonial Office.

Grantees included both those already in the colony and newcomers who were prepared to make the long and sometimes hazardous voyage to Australia. Nearly all of them based their applications for land grants on the grounds that the applicant had introduced or intended to introduce merino sheep into the colony. Among them was Alexander Riley, who had settled in New South Wales in 1804, and had been one of the contract-builders of Macquarie's hospital; he had acquired a large estate and imported a valuable flock of pure Saxon-bred merino sheep. The submission sent from Sydney in July 1825 reported that Riley had just bought 200 of the finest-fleeced sheep obtainable in Saxony for shipment to Port Jackson, a purchase that would bring his flocks up to 24,000. Riley supported his application with samples of his quality fleeces, and wrote:

> I shall in January next begin breeding from the pure ewes in distinct flocks and at the same time commence ennobling the produce of a thousand of the best ewes at present procurable in the colony; furnishing also after the first season such other sheepholders in the settlement as are desirous of improving their wools with rams of the full Electoral blood.

In consideration of the public benefit to the colony gained from Riley's importation, he was granted 5,000 acres of land, with a reserve of another 5,000 acres and he selected land on the banks of the Murrumbidgee River.

Riley was one of the first of the capitalists and great chartered companies to bring in merinos from the German flocks, then established as producers of the world's finest wool. As time went on many individuals, and the Australian Agricultural Company, the Van Diemen's Land Company, and Angas's South Australian Company all brought in these fine-wool sheep to enhance the quality of the Australian flocks. These importations proved to be one of the most significant factors in building the prosperity of the colonial wool industry in the years to come. Big investments were involved. Thomas Icely, who was connected with a sheep-exporting firm in England, reported when writing in 1825 to seek an additional land grant that he had "already spent £13,680 on agricultural and pastoral pursuits (in New South Wales), including importation of 1,500 improved merino sheep on board ready to sail for the colony." Others, like banker-merchant Richard Jones, imported Saxon merinos on a more or less regular basis to stock their runs and sell the progeny to other settlers. Some who had bought merino sheep from Saxony buttressed their applications for land on their experience of the German systems of sheep management; one such, James Atkinson, published the first pamphlet on agriculture and grazing in New South Wales.

Demobilized officers of the Napoleonic Wars were among the recipients of land grants. The Admiralty and War Office worked out a scheme by which retiring officers could sell their commissions, and one-third of the purchase money would be withheld until they reached the colony, when they could use the money to stock the land they had been granted. A syndicate of army officers was granted land in New South Wales and Van Diemen's Land on which to breed stud horses on a large scale, while a former West Indian planter wanted to grow cotton and sugar near Port Macquarie; but by far the greater number of grants were made to actual or intending pastoralists.

The alienation of land went on throughout the 1820s at an accelerated rate. At the end of Macquarie's régime, less than 1,000 square miles of land in all had been granted by governors; in the next four years, under Brisbane's administration, grants totalled almost as great an area, while in the three-year phase beginning with Darling's arrival something like 2,000,000 acres were granted, in addition to several hundred square miles of land sold.

The break with governmental authoritarian control and transition to a private enterprise system was evident in other branches of the economy during the 1820s. That private enterprise should relieve government of the expenses of convict maintenance was an essential feature of the system, according to Colonial Office thinking. In contrast with the last years of Macquarie's governorship, convict intake during Brisbane's régime was regulated in accordance with the demand of landholders for labour, and as a result the landholders were able to take all the convict labour (at least the able-bodied) off the government's hands. There was a resumption of large-scale transportation in the late 1820s; well over 3,000 convicts arrived in 1829, and greater numbers throughout the early and middle 1830s; by that time the development of the pastoral industry was such that the incoming convicts could be absorbed without strain. Most of the new transportees were at once assigned to pastoralists and private settlers, who were responsible for their maintenance, according to an organized system.

The need for public farms had passed. The last of the government-owned farms were disposed of, and the government stock sold, during Darling's term. Public tenders had to be called for all commissariat purchases, and after 1830 public works had to be tendered for and carried out by contractors instead of government gangs.

By this time New South Wales had developed into a wealthy colony with a substantial and growing export trade based mainly on the enterprise of sheepmen and whalers. The value of products from the sea—whale oil, whalebone, sealskins, spermaceti—exceeded that of the pastoral industries in most years from the mid-1820s up to 1833, and it was not until 1834 that wool began to race away from whaling. Whaling was the stimulus to a strong shipbuilding and repair industry, as well as to timber, cordage, and other subsidiary trades. By 1834 there was a veritable "whalemen's harbour" at the head of a sheltered cove on the north shore of Port Jackson, where merchant-shipowner Archibald Mossman had built a wharf and premises for barrel-making, processing whale oil, and careening and "heaving down" whaling ships. On the other side of the harbour, more and bigger storehouses were being built to hold wool awaiting export and to accommodate goods unloaded from incoming ships. The flow of merchandise was increasing each year to the enrichment of the traders. There was a strong pulse to commercial life; auctioneers, bankers, and brokers were doing good business, and there was an active chamber of commerce. Opulent houses were rising on the shores of Port Jackson as merchants and others gained wealth and gratified their desires to display it. A depression in the late 1820s, following the inflationary importation of capital and purchase of stock by the Australian Agricultural Company, was of short duration.

A petition from a number of landed proprietors in January 1830 described the "astonishing effects" of the removal of restraints on the colony's economic enterprise in the colony over the past eight or nine years:

> Ten years ago a ship of three hundred tons transported the whole of the exportable produce for that year to England. From the 18th June 1828 to the 18th June 1829, twenty-four vessels measuring 6,752 tons have cleared to various ports of the United Kingdom with cargoes of colonial produce to the value of £154,614. During the same period our exports to other places have amounted to £30,106, making a total of £184,720. Our principal mercantile relations besides England are with the Cape of Good Hope, Mauritius, China, and Van Diemen's Land.

The petition stated that seventy-four ships totalling 26,185 tons had entered from England within the previous twelve months (including twenty convict transports). The petition ended by contrasting the commissariat expenditure of £189,000 in 1821, the last year of Governor Macquarie's administration, when the country was "little more than an appendage to the English gaols," with the current commissariat expenditure of £140,000, although the prison population was twice as large as in 1821.

The social results of the policy were less happy. The restrictions on small settlers, whether free, emigrant, or emancipist, tended to perpetuate the original divisions between free-born and convict, and to create a plantation-type society. Principal spokesmen for the small settler was the radical newspaper editor Edward Smith Hall, who accused the local Land Board of showing preference to large land-owners in the distribution of convict labourers and of licences to pasture stock on Crown land, and claimed that the policy of preference to capitalists would alienate the affections of the native-born youth of the colony from the mother-country. Even the landed proprietors themselves, in their 1830 petition, showed some recognition of these drawbacks; they bolstered their arguments for the removal of England's protective tariffs on colonial-grown tobacco, on the grounds that a tobacco industry would be an inducement to emigrants of the small settler class, and said:

A wholesome admixture of society would result from this measure, and an intermediate class would rapidly spring up between the present extensive land proprietors and the prison population, a circumstance of much importance to the moral and political condition of this country.

The approaching end of the free grant system was foreshadowed as early as 1826, when Darling wrote to the Secretary of State that the settlers' demand for convict labour would soon exceed supply, and "it cannot therefore be necessary to hold out a reward to the settlers to take the convicts off the hands of the government." During the next few years it became increasingly evident that the system was being abused, and that many grantees had exaggerated their available capital and had taken up far larger holdings than they could possibly bring into profitable use. Quit rents were hard to collect, and brought in very little revenue.

The land grant system had served its purpose; it had encouraged companies and individuals to invest capital, take convict labour off the government's hands and develop the land. Now wool-growing was proving so profitable that people were prepared to pay for the land, and the British government saw in land sales a means of recouping its outlays in the colonies. The theories of Edward Gibbon Wakefield, who maintained that new colonies needed labour as well as land and capital, influenced policies at this point. Wakefield's argument that colonial land should be sold for a "sufficient price" and the proceeds used to finance immigration helped to shape the Ripon regulations of 1831. Under these regulations the system of free land grants was abolished; in future, Crown land in New South Wales and Van Diemen's Land was to be sold at auction, with a minimum price of five shillings an acre; part of the proceeds was to be used as an immigration fund, while it was hoped that the sale of land would encourage concentration of settlement and check the squatting movement, which was becoming a problem.

The need for some form of tenure other than freehold for grazing land had been apparent as soon as the colonial flocks had begun to show substantial increase. Since King's governorship, tickets of occupation had been issued, giving the holder the right to pasture his flocks on Crown land. In 1826 a new system of annual licences for grazing on Crown land was substituted; but no licence system could keep up with the outward march of the sheep and the sheepmen.

At first the squatters—those who occupied land to which they had no claim—were mainly escaped or ex-convicts who had stolen stock; as settlement moved closer to them, such men would drive their flocks deeper into the wilderness. More respectable colonists were inclined to imitate the process of occupying land without any authority to do so. If the government was prepared to give land freely to those who had capital, those with ambition but little money felt they had a right to stake a claim to land not already occupied. A small settler in the Hunter River valley expressed a widely held resentment when he asserted that "the government had no right to give so much land to free settlers and so little to those that are born in the country."

There was no one to dispute occupancy, and the squatters had little difficulty in persuading themselves that they had every right to the use of grass on land held in the name of an impersonal government. Challenges from the scattered tribes of Aborigines were not taken too seriously at first but before long in various districts white men were being speared. As the better hunting grounds were occupied, the Aborigines continued to kill stockmen and to pilfer livestock; in retaliation the tribesmen were slain in increasing numbers as the area of conflict widened with deeper penetration of the hinterland.

There were other causes for the decline in numbers of Aborigines in areas where settlement was consolidating. Some had fallen back to remoter areas, but white man's ways were proving dangerous; the decrease in numbers had been due in part to the introduction of alcohol, and to European diseases (even the milder diseases, such as measles, proving very destructive). Charles Darwin, during his visit to Sydney and the hinterland, noted these facts, and he recorded that while on a ride to Bathurst and back in January 1836 he saw only two parties, one of about twenty. Darwin gave a young man in one of the groups a shilling and in return the Aborigines threw their spears for his amusement. He was favourably impressed with their bearing, and reported:

> They were all partly clothed, and several could speak a little English; their countenances were good-humoured and pleasant, and they appeared far from being such utterly degraded beings as they have usually been represented. In their own arts they were admirable.

The Aborigines might be falling back before the sheepmen's advance, but it was not so easy for the graziers to persuade the British government that the appetite of their flocks for grass conferred rights of ownership to otherwise unoccupied land. Officials in Downing Street, used to the centuries-old land ownership system in England, with its time-honoured land titles, fenced or hedged agricultural blocks, and completely orderly land surveys, could not appreciate the totally different conditions of land occupation in the vast antipodean continent that none of them had ever visited. According to some Colonial Office theorists, there was no real difference between a New South Wales sheepowner who pastured his flocks on land to which he had no title and a Middlesex man who took his sheep to feed on the royal demesne at Hampton Court. Accordingly, in 1829 Governor Darling limited the area in which settlement was permitted to the Nineteen Counties which had already been surveyed, an area of about 22,000,000 acres; pastoral licences continued to be issued for grazing land within this area. At the time the limits were drawn, sheep were already grazing to the north and south of the defined limits.

In the following year the first eviction of squatters was carried out in the Tamworth-Quirindi district at the instigation of the Australian Agricultural Company, which chose this area as part of its land grant. The eviction was upheld against the recommendations of Governor Sir Richard Bourke, who had succeeded Darling in 1831; Bourke expressed the view that mere occupancy should confer some rights, and from time to time tried to explain to the Secretary of State that it was impossible to apply a policy of concentration of settlement in a colony like New South Wales, where "wool is our wealth."

The 1829 limits of the "boundaries of location" did not remain constant; as surveys extended, from time to time new districts were added to the areas officially approved for occupation; yet concentration of settlement remained the official policy, although it could not be enforced and the successive limits were always far behind the spread of pastoral settlement.

From the late 1820s the main squatting movement was in the Murrumbidgee area, at first along the river line, then backwards to take up land at first passed over, and outwards throughout the hinterland of the river. Hopeful new settlers, native-born and immigrant, were all the time moving out from Sydney and pushing their way into the wilderness. The more prudent got practical experience by working for some pastoralist before starting out on his own. Experienced squatters had plenty of practical advice for the newcomers. A prime consideration in the 1830s, according to Alexander Harris, who recorded his experiences as an "emigrant mechanic" in *Settlers and Convicts,* was that:

> ... the outskirts of the colony are the best tracts for occupation; the land is less picked; the expenses of fencing, etc., do not come so suddenly on you; and there is much more unoccupied land adjacent to you which you get the benefit of for some years. In making your selection, see to it that you combine high and low lands; the high for wet seasons, the low for times of drought. Take care to have a constant supply of water. It should be either a creek or river, or holes that never dry in any season.

If the land promised well, the new squatter decided how much he wanted as his run. He made a note of its natural boundaries, such as a creek, a hill or a ridge, and perhaps cut notches in a line of trees or later ran a single furrow with his plough to mark the edge. Since no one had any rights except those conferred by occupancy, there were frequent disputes over boundaries and ownership of waterholes. Sometimes it was necessary to clear heavily timbered land, but the first job usually was to cut timber and split posts to make a rough yard for sheep and/or cattle. Then a few days were required to build a rough hut from the materials at hand, mainly bark stripped from stringybark or similar trees. In some areas the local timber made this an easy task. The sheets of bark were stretched out and tied by strings of bullock hide to a framework composed of saplings, also tied together with strings of hide. Not a nail was used in the entire building. Inside, bunks and a table were also constructed of bark. The fireplace was put together from stones built up against the bark for protection. C.P. Hodgson gave this description of the construction of a more elaborate frontier dwelling in *Reminiscences of Australia:*

> In front, a large verandah eight feet wide is erected, both as a promenade and lounge, as also a shelter for the sitting-room. The huts generally face the south-east, to avoid the midday sun. The sides are built of large slabs, about nine feet

high, and of various breadths, fixed into large, heavy sleepers, top and bottom, which sleepers are dovetailed and spliced into each other at their extreme points. These slabs are run out of a large tree, and cut into the required length; the wood being very free, the labour is not great. A roof of bark or shingles is arranged from the face of the top sleeper, and forms nearly an equilateral triangle, to give the rain sufficient fall, and a proper elevation for the admission of air. The whole is therefore a compact body. . . . The inside is decorated according to the taste of its owners. Some have a light coat of osnaburg or canvas nailed inside to exclude the draught.

Apart from small yards of rough timber close to the huts, there was no other sign of settlement over great tracts of the new country. When streams dried up, or there was a bad drought or fire—or when flocks grew too large— the sheepmen simply took their stock farther out and found a new tract for themselves. Very few of the early squatters were prepared to spend time and money on making improvements to land for which they had no secure title; they preferred to spend all the money they had saved or could borrow on buying more sheep.

Each newcomer had to go through the same settling-in process; some pointers which could help him were set down by the "emigrant mechanic":

Having chosen your farm, buy a dray and team (say five or six bullocks) near Sydney and load it with necessaries. But for any future lot of stores you need from Sydney, pay for the carriage by one of the public carriers. Your own dray will be for several years in full occupation at home. Besides, not one bullock driver in ten is fit to be trusted with your team by himself in a three months' trip.

The same writer pointed out that it was necessary to hire a bullock driver and a night watchman (called the bullock-driver's mate) who would see that the bullocks did not stray. To take care of the stores and act as general assistant to the employer, an overseer was essential. Those completing the team were a hut keeper, two men to work as timber splitters, a hand for general work and—at the bottom of the working scale—the shepherds, whose duties consisted merely of wandering about with a flock by day and rounding up the sheep into a temporary fold to protect them at night from attacks by dingoes or the pilfering of Aborigines.

As the great onward sweep across the grasslands accelerated, the groups taken into the wilderness always included convicts. In 1836, out of a total of 27,000 assignees in private service, 8,000 were working as shepherds. In few cases were the assigned men satisfactory, and it was only the chronic shortage of labour that forced the landowners to take them.

In the bush it was a world of men, and they lived lonely, monotonous and sometimes brutish lives. Isolation engulfed them, and they became men apart. This is how an encampment of bullock drivers at a water hole struck a traveller in the 1840s:

A strange wildlooking, sunburnt race, strong, rough and taciturn, they appear as though they have never lived in crowds, and have lost the desire and even the power to converse. So deeply embrowned were the faces, naked breasts and arms of these men, and so shaggy the crops of hair and beard, that a stranger had to look twice to be certain they were not Aborigines.

Whatever his job, the bush worker was supplied by his employer with rations, including 10 lb or more of meat a week; the rest of his pay was given by cheque at the end of his term of work—usually six months, sometimes three or four months. When he received his wage cheque he would head for the nearest hotel or grog shop, where he would hand the cheque over to the publican and enjoy "a bright flareup for a few days" until he was told the money was gone. In some cases men worked on so that their cheque would build up and they could get to Sydney. As one observer wrote:

> After starving for ten or twenty months on salt beef and damper, and tea without milk, often without sugar, the bushman goes down to Sydney to spend, like an ass, in a month's revelry, money he has worked for like a horse or say a bullock.

The search for new pastoral land never ceased. Individual explorers might show the way but the settlers who followed (sometimes in their very wagon tracks) opened up as much or more land, pushing on into the unknown as they were lured by tales of better country farther out. Important exploratory expeditions were made during the governorships of Brisbane and Darling. Continuing on from the expeditions by John Oxley under Macquarie, the botanist Allan Cunningham in 1823 discovered Pandora's Pass, a convenient connection between the Bathurst Plains and the Liverpool Plains to the north. Four years later Cunningham struck north from the Liverpool Plains, reached the Gwyder River and then the Dumaresq, changed his course from north to north-east, and finally reached the rich Darling Downs. He pushed into the higher land and from a gap in the range was able to see the Moreton Bay district, where a penal outpost was already established. He noted that a route could be opened from the Darling Downs to Moreton Bay. He attempted to return due south over the tableland but this proved impossible because of the rugged nature of the terrain and the severity of the winter. Instead he returned by much the same route along the western foothills that he had followed on his outward journey. He had opened up what was to become the main stock route to Brisbane.

To the south, the Monaro Plains were reached for the first time by Captain Mark Currie, who struck out from south of Lake George in 1823. Attention had also been turned to the distant country lying between the southern limits of settlement and the Bass Strait area. For the task of driving through to Western Port on Bass Strait, where he was considering establishing a party of convicts, Governor Brisbane chose Hamilton Hume, a Parramatta-born settler in the Appin district who had the reputation of being a wonderful bushman, and William Hilton Hovell, a retired sea captain, who offered to contribute men and provisions to the expedition.

With six men who were prisoners of the Crown, two carts, five bullocks, and three horses, Hume and Hovell set off on October 14, 1824, from Hume's property at Lake George. The next day, they came to the Murrumbidgee River and found crossing difficult because of flood conditions. As they moved south they came to very hilly country and then reached a wide plateau. On November 8 they caught their first glimpse of snow-clad mountains which they named the Australian Alps—"a grand and beautiful spectacle." On November 16 they reached a great river that swept out of the foothills of the Alps and named it the Hume; but when Charles Sturt later reached the river downstream he did not know it was the same stream and he named it the Murray, the name by which it became known.

The party bore south-west, and during the next few days many smaller rivers were reached. After crossing the ranges the explorers passed through better districts, and when they reached the sea on December 17 they believed they had come to Western Port. They talked with some of the tribesmen, who described once seeing a vessel in their bay which they called Geelong.

Hume and Hovell retraced their steps back to Lake George in January and from there reached Sydney with news of fertile land between the Murrumbidgee and Bass Strait, much of it suitable for either grazing or the growing of crops. It was after receiving the explorers' favourable report on the land near what they thought was Western Port that Governor Brisbane, in the grip of one of the periodic French scares, sent off the group under Captain Samuel Wright to form the settlement there. What Hume and Hovell did not realize was that they had miscalculated their position by 1° of longitude, so that in fact they were far to the west of Western Port when they reached the sea. Wright's party of soldiers and convicts, landing at the real Western Port, found the land quite unsuited to farming and Wright abandoned the enterprise.

The mystery of where the inland rivers emptied their waters had not been solved by the Hume and Hovell expedition; it had, if anything, become greater since all the rivers Hume and Hovell crossed appeared to be flowing into the interior of the continent. The facts seemed to support the view that somewhere there must be either an inland sea or a great river outlet for all these waters. Meanwhile a severe drought had afflicted many settled areas, both coastal and inland, and for three years crops had failed and livestock died in districts where in normal seasons there was an abundance of grass and water. The need to find well watered areas was urgent, and in 1828 Governor Darling decided to equip an expedition for further inland exploration.

Captain Charles Sturt, a skilled surveyor, was chosen as leader, with Hume as his assistant. The expedition was quite an elaborate one; a doctor, two soldiers, and eight prisoners were included. The party set off in September 1828; its first task was to determine the course of the Macquarie in an effort to extend the boundaries of discovery westward; but like Oxley ten years before, the explorers were soon blocked by reed beds into which the Macquarie disappeared. Moving towards the north-west on horseback, they reached the Bogan River. They travelled for weeks over bare, dry, and scorching plains until suddenly they found themselves on precipitous banks 40 to 50 feet above the level of a river bed, the channel of which was 70 to 80 yards across. Sturt noted that the trees lining the banks were "of beautiful and gigantic growth," and he added: "Our difficulties seemed to be at an end."

When the men rushed to quench their thirst, however, they found to their amazement that the water was salt and unfit to drink. "Our hopes were annihilated at the moment of their apparent realization," Sturt recorded. By good fortune a pond of fresh water was found, and men and horses were refreshed. Brine springs feeding the river were discovered, and Sturt realized that there was no inland sea in this region. He named the river the Darling, and traced its course for some 70 miles before being forced to turn back. He picked up the course of the Castlereagh and followed its dry bed back to the Darling.

Sturt believed that the Darling was the main river into which all the westward-flowing streams emptied. It was important to find out where it flowed and to find its mouth. After a few months Sturt was instructed by the governor to tackle the river mystery from another point, and in November 1829 he set out on another major journey.

Settlers in the Yass district had reported that the Murrumbidgee flowed directly inland without showing any sign of diminution. Sturt was to trace its course and follow any other rivers with which it might be connected.

Sturt's party followed the river until it shallowed among reed beds. Then the 27-foot whaleboat that had been carried in sections on the drays was assembled, a small skiff was constructed from timber cut from the bush, and early on January 7, 1830, Sturt and seven of his men set sail, waving good-bye to those who were to remain with the drays. The current carried them on by day; each night they set up camp. Sturt noted a tributary which he believed to be the Lachlan; shortly below this point the skiff which was being towed struck a snag and sank. The cargo was recovered, but all the foodstuffs had been ruined.

After a week the whaleboat shot out into what Sturt described as "a broad and noble river." It was in fact the same broad stream that Hume and Hovell had crossed about five years before, but Sturt did not know this. As the journey continued along the great river, there were dangerous encounters with Aborigines. The first incident occurred on January 17 when a group of tribesmen appeared just after the tents had been pitched for the night, but Sturt pacified them and made friends with their chief. A few days later, while the boat was on the river, another big group appeared; Sturt moved in close to the opposite bank to keep clear, but the natives (who were armed for attack) kept pace with the boat and finally moved out on to a sandbank which narrowed the river ahead. Sturt was taking aim with his gun when four other tribesmen were seen running along the opposite bank; the leader rushed ahead, threw himself into the water, and on reaching the sandbank remonstrated with the hostile tribesmen and pushed them back. Sturt was able to make friends with them. To his amazement he found that the native who had interceded on his behalf was the chieftain to whom he had given presents a few days before.

On January 23, when Sturt came to the junction of "a new and beautiful stream coming apparently from the north," he named the main stream the Murray. The secondary river he identified correctly as the Darling, whose upper reaches he had discovered earlier. He sailed on, and on February 9 reached Lake Alexandrina and the Murray mouth. Then began the expedition's return up-river. The men were weak and exhausted, but they rowed against the stream to the junction with the Murrumbidgee in twenty-three days, then had to spend another seventeen days battling against a raging flood in the Murrumbidgee in order to get back to the depot. Their great journey of almost 2,000 miles had done much to explain the drainage of the continent's greatest river system and had revealed extensive areas of good land. Sturt's subsequent reports of the area along the lower reaches of the Murray aroused interest in London which spurred the South Australian Company's plans for land settlement.

Soon after Sturt's return to Sydney, Thomas Mitchell, who had become Surveyor-General in succession to Oxley, set off on the first of his expeditions into the Murray-Darling basin. Late in 1831 he went north in search of a large river reported by an escaped convict as flowing towards the north-west; this news seemed to substantiate the old belief that somewhere an inland sea existed or that a great river might carry all the inland waters west or north to the ocean. Mitchell crossed the Peel and Namoi rivers, reached the Gwydir, struck north, and in January 1832 discovered the Macintyre, a tributary of the Darling. At this point, two of his teamsters were killed in a brush with Aborigines, and Mitchell decided to return to Sydney. He had satisfied himself that all the inland rivers in this area joined the Darling.

Mitchell was not convinced that Sturt was right in believing that the southward-flowing river that joined the Murray far to the south-west was the same river whose headwaters he had reached. In 1835 he set off to confirm or disprove Sturt's opinion that the Darling flowed into the Murray. With a party of twenty-three, he started from Parramatta and followed the Bogan to the Darling, tracing the river's course for some 300 miles. It became increasingly clear that the river's south-west course would in fact take it to Sturt's Murray. At that point a clash with the warlike Darling tribe resulted in several Aborigines being shot, and Mitchell decided to return to Sydney.

The following year he set out again, this time going almost directly westward. From Orange he picked up the Lachlan and traced it to the Murrumbidgee, which he then followed to the Murray and continued downstream until he reached the junction of the Darling. The party went north along the river for some distance until Mitchell was convinced, by the noticeable similarities with the stream he had explored far to the north-west, that Sturt's surmise about the southward-flowing river's source had been correct.

On May 29, when he was encamped near the junction, he noted that "a line of yarra trees enveloped a dry creek, very much resembling the ones seen by us on the Darling," and the next day he recognized "several shrubs . . . seen before only on the Darling." Mitchell learnt from the Aborigines that "the channel we had reached contained all the waters of the Wambol (Macquarie) and Callewatta (the Upper Darling) and I accordingly determined to trace it up at least far enough to identify it with the latter, but I thought it right that we should endeavour first to recognize the junction with the Murray as described by Captain Sturt. . . . I pursued the river through a tortuous course until sunset when I was obliged to quit it and return to the camp by moonlight."

On June 1 Mitchell decided not to continue his search for the junction immediately but instead to strike out for the river and then follow it northward. The party soon found all the usual features of the Darling; the hills of soft red sand near the river covered with the same kind of shrubs seen farther upstream. Mitchell noted:

> The [Aborigines'] graves had no longer any resemblance to those on the Murrumbidgee and Murray but were precisely similar to the places of interment we had seen on the Darling, being mounds surrounded by and covered with dead branches and pieces of weed. On these lay the same singular casts of the head in white plaster which we had seen before only at Fort Bourke.

The river itself Mitchell found to be

> . . . only a chain of ponds, and I walked across its channel dry shod. . . . The width and depth between the immediate banks were about the same as I had found them in the most narrow and shallow parts during my former journey. While I sat on the adverse or right bank of this hopeless river, I began to think I had pursued its course far enough. The identity was no longer a question . . . and nothing was to be gained by following the river further.

From this point Mitchell turned back along the Murray which he followed to Mount Hope, east of the Murray's junction with the Loddon (which he named the Yarrayne). He decided to strike south and explore the attractive, well watered countryside which spread before him, and he named the paradisal region Australia Felix. He crossed numerous northward-flowing streams, and reached the Grampians—"a noble range of mountains rising in the south to a stupendous height and presenting as bold and picturesque an outline as ever painter imagined." Mitchell's enthusiasm for the countryside knew no bounds. He wrote:

> We had at length discovered a country ready for the immediate reception of civilized man, and destined perhaps to become eventually a portion of a great empire. Unencumbered by too much wood, it yet possessed enough for the purpose; it was bounded on three sides by the ocean; it was traversed by mighty rivers and watered by streams innumerable. Of this Eden I was the first European to explore its geological character—and by my survey to develop these natural advantages certain to become at no distant date of vast importance to a new people.

The party continued south, probed the Glenelg River, and finally marched east. When Mitchell looked down upon Portland Bay he found to his surprise that a brig lay at anchor there and buildings had been erected on the shore.

The settlers were the Henty brothers who had moved from Van Diemen's Land two years before to establish a pastoral settlement. Mitchell replenished his supplies of flour and was given fresh vegetables by Edward Henty; he rejoined the rest of his party, who were waiting for him, and struck northeast from Portland Bay, crossing rolling grassy plains and well watered open parklands.

When he got back to Sydney, his glowing account of the whole region excited great interest. His reports of a vast area of fertile land awaiting settlement resulted in a stream of "overlanders" from the expanding area of settlement on the western slopes of the range. They followed the track made by Mitchell's heavy cart as it trundled across the new land—the Major's Line, as it was called—in opening up the rich grazing land south of the Murray. Already settlers spilling into the great basin had established themselves in the region of the Upper Murray; they had followed the Hume and Hovell track. Sheep runs had already been established along the Murray at Wodonga and Bonegilla by the time Mitchell passed that way on his return to Sydney, and Joseph Howden and other overlanders setting out for Adelaide met him *en route*. Even as Mitchell was on his way to England to publish a book on his explorations, settlers in increasing numbers were moving with their sheep into the accessible land of the south-eastern crescent of the continent.

Not only was there infiltration south-west and then south from the established areas, but a new channel had been opened through which a flood of new and eager settlers from Van Diemen's Land was soon to pass; for where official attempts to plant settlements directly on the Bass Strait coastline had failed, individuals succeeded.

The success of the sheep raisers in Van Diemen's Land was the immediate cause of occupation of new land across the strait. Flocks had spread, exports of wool from the island continued to grow steadily, and the successful flock owners were keen to find new and bigger runs. By the mid 1830s there were nearly 1,000,000 sheep in the island, where the climate made it possible to develop sheep with special woolbearing qualities; even though they did not have the large frame of the mainland sheep they grew more wool, with longer fibre of good density.

The official policy of concentration of settlement did not deter pastoralists in search of good uncrowded grazing land. The first to make the move across Bass Strait were the Henty brothers, who established themselves at Portland Bay. The Hentys came from a family of Sussex farmers and sheep-breeders. Their father, Thomas, was England's leading breeder of merino sheep, and had sold merinos to most of the principal New South Wales breeders in the 1820s; he had been interested in emigration then, but had left his departure too late to secure a grant of land in New South Wales. Instead he and his sons obtained a grant of 80,000 acres when settlement was begun at the Swan River. After discouraging years at the western settlement, the Hentys decided to move to Van Diemen's Land, where they developed a fine flock of merinos. While still in Van Diemen's Land, they sought permission from the colonial authorities in London to buy a holding on the southern coast of the mainland; but this was refused. They were not easily thwarted. Edward Henty was so enthusiastic about the prospects of the land around Portland Bay (which he had visited) that he decided to settle there, even without official sanction. In 1834 he and his three brothers took all their livestock, farm implements, and fishing tackle, and crossed the strait. Very soon they had their houses built, their gardens under cultivation, and their livestock on good pasture, as Mitchell found.

The spread of settlement across Bass Strait owed even more to John Batman, who had a farm at Kingston, near Ben Lomond, and was interested in sheep-breeding. Batman was born in Parramatta, and had accompanied Hamilton Hume on some expeditions. Hume, who had crossed the Murray and made his way overland to Port Phillip in 1824, found that his enthusiasm for the land was shared by Batman. As early as 1827, after the short-lived settlement at Western Port, Batman had approached Governor Darling for permission to run sheep on pastoral lands there, but his request had been refused. In Launceston, Batman was one of the instigators of the Port Phillip Association—a syndicate of fifteen sheepmen and traders on the island—formed with the avowed purpose of occupying the land around Port Phillip. Batman and his supporters conceived the notion of acquiring a vast tract by direct negotiation with the Aboriginal tribal leaders in the area. They sought the land "upon equitable principles," and hoped that in the process of time the action "would lead to the civilization of a large portion of the Aboriginals." Batman had proved that he was a friend of the Aborigines; at the time of the war against the island tribesmen he had induced a number of Aborigines to come in, by peaceful means. Joseph Tice Gellibrand, who drew up the "treaty," was also a humanitarian sickened by the slaughter that had taken place in Van Diemen's Land.

On May 12, 1835, Batman sailed from Launceston in a 30-ton schooner, the *Rebecca*. In his party were seven Aborigines from the Sydney area. Batman sailed north into Port Phillip, and when he landed he traversed a green and well-grassed countryside. On several successive days he made excursions through areas around the head of the bay, and everything he saw pleased him. On May 31 he wrote in his journal:

> I never saw or could suppose there could be such extensive plains as I saw today; five thousand sheep would be almost lost upon them.

The next day, after climbing a hill, he wrote:

> I am sure from the top of these hills we could see thirty miles in every direction of plain land; this at least if not a considerable count more . . . a gig or carriage may be driven in any direction for twenty miles without the possibility of upsetting.

The Aborigines were friendly, and Batman presented eight of the tribal elders with a "treaty" under which they were to grant him two tracts of land, totalling some 600,000 acres, in return for blankets, knives, hand mirrors, tomahawks, scissors, flour, and trinkets, presented as payment, and a yearly tribute "payable for ever" to the value of at least £200. Batman recorded that the parchment was "signed" by the chiefs and that some of the soil from the tract of land of each was delivered to him as a token of possession, adding:

> This took place alongside of a little stream of water and from whence my land commences and where a tree is marked four ways to know the corner boundary.

... The country about here exceeds anything I ever saw both for grass and richness of soil. . . . My natives gave the chiefs and their tribe a grand corroboree
tonight. They seemed quite delighted with it.

Before returning to Launceston Batman rowed up the Yarra River to a
point where the stream ran over rocks with fresh water above the waterfall;
the gently rising hill sweeping back from the bank would be the "place
for a village," he noted. Batman left three white men and five of the Sydney
Aborigines to maintain possession. He was back in Launceston before the
end of June. He reported what he had done, and his backers were well
pleased.

Even as he returned, a rival group led by John Pascoe Fawkner was
already preparing to launch an expedition with occupation as its objective.
Fawkner (who as a boy of eleven had been in Colonel Collins's party when
the attempt was made in 1803 to settle on the shores of Port Phillip) now
hastened preparations, and on July 29 the schooner *Enterprise* sailed. Because
of illness, Fawkner himself could not make the trip. Hardly had the schooner
reached Port Phillip than Batman's representatives, in a whaleboat, intercepted the little vessel and warned the "trespassers" that they were not
welcome. No quarrel occurred, however, and the *Enterprise* proceeded up
the bay and into the Yarra, landing Fawkner's group close to the point
Batman had selected for his village.

News that the *Enterprise* has departed caused concern among Batman's
supporters, and they were able to prevail upon John Helder Wedge, who
was Assistant Surveyor-General of Van Diemen's Land as well as a member
of the syndicate, to remonstrate personally with Fawkner's group. He told
the interlopers that the land was already subject to Batman's "treaty";
but it had no effect. Fawkner's men remained, along with Batman's.

Batman and Fawkner each resented the presence of the other in the new
domain. Each did everything possible to maintain his group's position,
and both were still organizing the transfer of flocks to the new pasture
when a third claimant landed a flock on the eastern shores of Port Phillip.
Nothing could now stop the occupation. Soon more farmers were on the
move from Van Diemen's Land.

In the view of the Colonial Office and Governor Bourke, Batman, Fawkner, and any other settlers were all trespassers. In a solemn proclamation
Bourke warned them that they were liable to be dealt with "as other invaders
upon the vacant lands of the Crown." The prohibition had no effect, and
all the governor could do was to report to London that he simply could not
prevent settlers pasturing their flocks and herds outside the official boundaries
of settlement; he advised acceptance of the situation, and proposed that
townships should be marked out at Port Phillip and at Twofold Bay, where
a similar unauthorized occupation had taken place in 1834.

Very soon the situation at Port Phillip had gone too far for reversal, in
any case. People were setting sail from Van Diemen's Land intent on getting
their share of land, or going as servants to the more affluent. Governor
Bourke realized that an official representative must be appointed to keep
order. In May 1836 he sent a police magistrate to report on the situation

and three months later he appointed Captain William Lonsdale to exercise the functions of a magistrate and also to undertake "the general super-intendence of the new settlement of all such matters as require the immediate exercise of the authority of the Government."

The land around the shores of Port Phillip was quickly occupied. Beyond it lay a province, as big as France, of good grazing land which acted as a magnet. More settlers arrived, to stream outwards from Port Phillip and occupy as much land as each wanted. Livestock vessels from Launceston crossed and recrossed the strait, and soon runs had been established 80 miles inland. Before long the runs occupied by the overland settlers flowing in from the north were reached. It was great country for sheep. The pastures of the Port Phillip district were of sweet and ample grass; their quality was matched by the quality of the sheep being introduced to them. The men coming from across the Murray had with them valuable sheep from established New South Wales flocks, and many of the sheep from Van Diemen's Land had been bred from imported stock. The 40,000 or so taken in by sea or overlanded from the north by 1836 increased to 300,000 in the next two years.

By that time the township on the Yarra had been surveyed. Bourke visited the settlement in March 1837. He named the portside settlement Williamstown (believing this the more important centre) in honour of King William IV, and to the village he gave the name Melbourne, in honour of the Prime Minister. The surveyor, Robert Hoddle, who made the trip from Sydney with the governor, confirmed the town plan drawn up by Robert Russell, and the first land sale was held on June 1, 1837. Shortly afterward James Backhouse wrote that:

> The town of Melbourne, though scarcely more than 15 months old, consists of about 100 houses, among which are stores, inns, a jail, a barrack, and a school-house. A few of the inhabitants live in huts. There is much bustle and traffic.

Lonsdale continued to administer the Port Phillip district until 1839, when Charles Joseph La Trobe was appointed Superintendent. Commerce developed rapidly. Wool production increased as sheep spread across fertile grasslands. There seemed to be no obstacle to progress. The struggles faced by other settlements in their early days were absent. The whole enterprise was undertaken by men who had considerable resources behind them, and they were intent upon taking advantage of the opportunities for pro-fitable activity arising from Britain's insatiable demand for wool.

In the process they were prepared to live in the simplest way, dropping all pretence of comfort. Thomas Walker in 1838 recorded in *A Month in the Bush* his observations of early pastoralists on the Yarra:

> I think no class of people live in a rougher way than many of the settlers do here at present. Mr Mollison has erected a hut, which will be well enough when finished but in the meantime it is open and comfortless. No furniture has he, except a bench or stool, a broken cup or two, tin pannicans, a couple of knives and forks, and a plate or two. All he has to eat is Irish salted pork, damper and tea and sugar, and the light we had was produced by burning rags in pieces of fat pork. Upon

the whole, I have never met with people living in a style more rude and rough, or with less attention to comfort, but to that they seem perfectly indifferent, and aware it is only a temporary inconvenience.

Very soon there were signs that an important future was in store for the settlement. In 1839 immigrant Jonathon Binns Were was "perfectly astonished" to find that "one mast after another opened to view, and when we cast anchor we were as completely in a little fleet at the mouth of the Yarra as if we had been in Plymouth Sound." Were noted that eighteen vessels lay at anchor, all delivering goods or passengers for Melbourne. During the following ten days another seven vessels arrived. Melbourne was growing apace, and Were found

> ... good shops with Drugs, Groceries, Haberdashery, Ironmongery; indeed each shop seemed to be quite an emporium. But what struck my fancy was the many young men we met, dashing looking fellows, all with trousers lined with yellowish leather and having large riding whips in their hands; no braces on but coats of the most fantastical shapes and colours and their bearing being that of gentlemen, young and handsome.

The spread of settlement in the Port Phillip area was simply an example on a large scale of what was being done in other parts of eastern Australia; it was more spectacular because it involved crossing the sea, whereas sheep-men who opened up territory elsewhere without leave or licence from government merely had to drive their sheep farther onwards over the land. The British government still adhered to the policy of concentration of settlement that had produced the 1829 regulations limiting settlement in New South Wales to the 22,000,000 acres of the Nineteen Counties. As late as 1835, the Colonial Secretary was still warning Governor Bourke against countenancing any expansion of settlement, and complaining that

> ... if everyone were allowed to follow his own inclination by selecting a fit place of residence on the coast of New Holland, all hopes of restricting the limits of our settlements in that quarter must be at once abandoned.

This was, in fact, exactly what was happening, the Port Phillip settlement being the prime example. Efforts to restrict the spread of settlement there and elsewhere failed, as they were bound to do in an almost empty land when a product was involved that depended on broad acres and was of immense importance to the mother-land.

The occupation of Port Phillip brought to a head the whole question of what legal right the squatters had to the lands they occupied. In 1836 the Legislative Council of New South Wales, representing the sheep-owning interests, passed the first act to legalize the squatting system. Every stock-owner outside the boundaries was to pay £10 a year, in return for which he could stock as many acres as he pleased. Commissioners of Crown lands were supposed to check the licensing system, but they had little practical authority. In 1839 the law was amended so that the stock-owners paid tax on a sliding scale according to the number of livestock grazed, as well as the fixed licence fee; the revenue was used to establish a border police force which would support the authority of the commissioners. Port Phillip was named as one of the pastoral districts of New South Wales the same year, and other new squatting districts were also officially established. The squatters' position was further strengthened by a series of colonial judicial decisions, which upheld their rights of occupation against anyone except the Crown.

Squatting flourished under the licence system. By 1840 there were over 700 runs, with a population of nearly 8,000, where well over 1,000,000 sheep were grazed, in the region from New England in the north to Port Phillip district in the south. These were the officially accepted pastoral districts; but, as Governor Sir George Gipps (who succeeded Bourke in 1838) pointed out to the Secretary of State, "towards the north stations already extend to the country behind Moreton Bay, three hundred miles beyond the limits of location; to the south and west they extend beyond Port Phillip to the boundaries of South Australia."

The squatters' rights under the licence system were leasehold only, and did not confer a freehold title to the land. The system of selling Crown land by auction, with an upset or reserve price of 5/- an acre, was in operation from 1831 until 1839. Nearly 1,500,000 acres were sold in New South Wales at this price, as well as 239,000 acres in Van Diemen's Land and 22,000 acres at the Swan River. The situation was complicated by the foundation of the Wakefield-inspired settlement in South Australia, where land was offered for sale at a fixed price first of 12/- and later of £1 an acre; the South Australian land commissioners found it difficult to sell their land at this price when equally good land could be bought elsewhere in Australia for 5/- an acre. In addition, the increase of land values in the mother-colony appeared to justify a higher price. Accordingly the minimum price of New South Wales land was raised to 12/- an acre in 1839.

Wakefieldian theorists had a strong influence on parliament and the Colonial Office at this time. The British land and immigration commissioners, appointed in 1840 to administer land and immigration matters throughout the Australian colonies, considered that the fixed price system had worked well in South Australia, and recommended that a fixed price be substituted for the auction system in other parts of Australia. The old system of auction and the old reserve price were to be retained in the Central District of New South Wales (the original Nineteen Counties), but beyond this area Crown land was to be sold at the uniform price of £1 per acre. In addition, as an encouragement to capital investment, anyone willing to pay the uniform cash price for an 8 square-mile block could have an immediate "special survey" of his choice of land, the only restriction being that land previously advertised or within 5 miles of a town could not be included.

The special survey system led to windfalls for a few men who picked up blocks of eight square miles in South Australia (including mineral land) and in Port Phillip (including parts of the present Melbourne suburbs of Brighton and Kew). Special surveys were so unsound in principle that Governor Gipps refused to sanction further sales under the rule; his defiance of instructions was later recognized in London as being justified.

The financial collapse in South Australia further discredited the fixed price system. The committee of the House of Commons which investigated South Australian affairs in 1841 considered that in Port Phillip the system of sales by auction had resulted in prices in truer relation to land values. The Waste Lands Act of 1842, which came into operation in the colonies in the following year, provided for the auctioning of colonial land with a minimum price of £1 an acre. Although most colonists considered the price was far too high, the £1 minimum price remained in force until the colonies obtained control of land policy in the 1850s.

The Australian wool saga had captured the imagination of the British investor, and in the late 1830s capital poured into the country. Between 1833 and 1840 nine new banks were formed to operate in the Australian colonies; four had their head offices in London, two were Sydney-run banks, one had its headquarters in Bathurst, and the other two were based in Launceston and Melbourne. Paid-up bank capital rose fifteen-fold in the seven years. Legal restrictions on the rates of interest had been removed in Van Diemen's Land in 1830 and in New South Wales in 1834, enhancing attractions of the colonies to investors. Banks and mortgage companies lent money freely for pastoral ventures and land speculation. Land sales boomed, particularly after the occupation of the Port Phillip district, opened new horizons for the acquisitive. English merchants poured speculative cargoes into the colony, and imports continued to exceed exports by growing margins, while prices soared. Wool-growing was so profitable that some farmers gave up cereal crops to run sheep, and wheat imports increased.

Despite the boom, all was not well with the wool industry. The rapid build-up of colonial flocks had resulted in wool clips that outstripped demand, and wool prices fell from 1840 onwards. A prolonged and severe drought began in 1838, striking many areas in turn. Many flock-owners had recklessly overstocked, paying inflated prices for sheep and cattle, while their labour costs became higher after the abolition of transportation to the mainland in 1840. Heavy grain importations were necessary after two successive bad harvests. Thus the primary producers were already in severe straits when a financial crisis in Britain caused the curtailment of the flow of capital to Australia, resulting in a severe depression that reached its nadir in 1843. That year three banks failed, while there were hundreds of insolvencies. Country properties that had cost thousands of pounds were sold at auction for a few hundred, sheep brought a shilling or so a head. It was said that gentlemen with 10,000 sheep could not get credit for a bag of sugar or a chest of tea. Natural disasters contributed to the distress: floods along the tributaries of the Murray put large areas under several feet of water, while in the Port Phillip district there were frequent and severe bush fires.

By 1843 the sheepmen were desperately seeking a supplementary source of revenue, and those in the more accessible areas began sending large numbers of sheep to be killed and boiled down for their tallow, which met a ready market in London. The tallow and boiled fat was packed in the skins or casks for shipment; the trotters were boiled for their oil, the bones exported to make hafts for knives, and the wool was stripped from the skins, washed, and exported. Some of the mutton was sold locally, some salted and shipped to other colonies. The cash return from boiling-down was relatively high: the owner might get as much as five shillings a head instead of the very insignificant amount from wool. The sale of sheep for their tallow, though a makeshift solution, at least provided a minimum fixed value for sheep; but it was not avaliable to those men who had gone into the remoter areas, and their only solution was to increase wool output through larger flocks and access to greater areas of land.

The New South Wales Legislative Council passed several measures aimed at relieving the pastoralists' burdens, the most important being the Lien of Sheep Act, which permitted the legal registration of mortgage loans on the security of livestock and the next wool clip. Loans of this type were at first made by merchants rather than by the banks, but before long they had become regular banking practice.

In spite of the onward growth of the wool industry, there were many problems to be faced. There was an unmistakable need to keep costs down. It was undeniable that capital outlays had to remain low. In terms of land usage, wool was a low-yield "crop," and large tracts were needed to produce a reasonable return. Land had to be available at minimal outlay if the sheepmen were to achieve success. The landholder had been prepared to spend his money on buying all the sheep he could afford, in paying for essential improvements on his land, and on a few personal belongings; but all other outlays had been avoided. The struggle was for more land—at minimum cost—so that more sheep might be grazed and labour costs spread. Yet in the unrelenting scramble for pastures there was no sure formula for success. Inevitably in the dynamics of occupying vast acreages, the careful theorist was as vulnerable to failure as the most optimistic gambler.

Whenever one man failed, there were others ready to take his place. Above all, the drive was to secure land, even though it might be untried and deep in the wilderness.

Expanding horizons   8

The relaxation of authoritarian control that followed Macquarie's departure was evident in fields other than that of economic enterprise. The new concept of New South Wales as a colony where a free enterprise economy based on pastoral pursuits might flourish, side by side with penal institutions, implied other changes. The new Governor, Sir Thomas Brisbane, marked the transition from viceroy to something akin to a constitutional governor. He was admirably suited to smooth the transition to a broader economy and new objectives; as an army engineer he had travelled widely, and at the same time he was a scientist and a thinker, a man of wide interests and independent means. He manner was less formal and rigid than that of any of his predecessors and his control more flexible, while his urbanity made him less resentful of criticism. His attitudes and actions made simpler and more workable the transition towards the goal emerging in Downing Street for a free enterprise colony.

Halfway through Brisbane's term of office the change took definite constitutional form with the setting up in 1825 of the nominee Legislative Council of New South Wales; it put through the first acts passed by a legislative body in Australia. Another constitutional change was the creation of an executive council, consisting of the chief justice, the archdeacon, and the colonial secretary, all of whom were London appointees. By this time the affairs of government were becoming so complex that no governor could give the same close attention to matters of detail that Macquarie had done. As a result, the principal administrative officials, particularly the colonial secretary, acquired a good deal of power. Powers of both executive and legislative councils were limited to advising the governor—the one on matters of administration, the other on legislation. The legislative council consisted of seven members, four of them officials and three chosen by the governor from the "more intelligent, wealthy and respectable" members of the community. Only the governor could initiate legislation, and he could carry measures even if only one member of the council supported him, so that his power was very little limited by the community representatives. The chief limitations on the governor's power were legalistic; it was considered wise to entrust a veto power to a trained constitutional lawyer rather than to the politically inexperienced representatives of the community. All legislation and proclamations had to be submitted to the chief justice (a newly created position), so that he could certify that they were not repugnant to the laws of England; the final authorities in case of dispute were the English Crown Law officers (for legislation) and the Colonial Office (for proclamations). The act was something of an experiment, and after five years it was to be subject to renewal or revision. Its provisions applied in Van Diemen's Land as well as in New South Wales.

The original purpose of the Judicature Act of 1823 was mainly to reform the judicial system. The basic machinery of the judicial system was created by the act. A new Supreme Court was set up; it was presided over by the chief justice (who took the place of the former judge-advocate and judge of the old Supreme Court). The act separated the systems of civil and criminal law, created various legal offices, and established various courts. It also introduced the first instalment of trial by jury. A jury of seven civilians was permitted if both parties in a civil action requested one; a property qualification restricted the choice of jurors. Juries in criminal cases were restricted to military officers.

Demands for trial by jury and more widely representative government were the chief points on which political feeling developed during Brisbane's governorship, growing in strength in that of Governor Ralph Darling. Political attitudes and activities were becoming more complex; the main elements were liberal versus conservative thinking, native-born versus emigrant, would-be small settler versus capitalist landowner, while the sharpest division was that between the emancipists and their descendants on the one hand and the "exclusives" on the other.

The Bigge Report, by now practically the Bible of the Colonial Office, had strongly condemned Macquarie's emancipist policy, and henceforth no more emancipists were appointed to the magistracy, nor to leading civil service positions. In practice emancipists were not called for jury service, while there was not the slightest possibility of an emancipist being appointed to the legislative council. Socially the division between emancipists and exclusives was stronger than ever. The exclusives came from the same groups as had opposed Macquarie—the wealthy landowners, whether ex-officer or capitalist immigrant, or merchant-turned-landowner. All the nominated members of the legislative council were from this group, whose effective leadership came from the Macarthur family, while most of the civil service members had the same general viewpoint.

Probably the man who did most for the liberals' cause was Francis Forbes,

Chief Justice from 1824 to 1837. The popular leader, and the most aggressive personality on the liberals' side was the young William Charles Wentworth. Wentworth was born at Norfolk Island in 1790, the son of surgeon D'Arcy Wentworth and a woman who had been a convict. His father occupied an ambiguous position in colonial society: although he had come to the colony a free man, D'Arcy Wentworth had twice stood trial in England for highway robbery, and within the colony he was generally considered an emancipist. He quickly made money, and sent his sons to England for their education. Returning to Australia at the age of twenty, William was appointed Provost-Marshal by Macquarie and took part in the first crossing of the Blue Mountains before going back to England in 1816 to study law (and to absorb Whig principles). His was the first literate voice from the colony to express a patriotic devotion to Australia as a land with a great future and rightfully the inheritor of British rights to freedom and self-government. In 1819 he published a book on New South Wales, in which he demanded an elected legislative assembly and trial by jury for the colony, and extolled the new land's attractions for British emigrants. A friend and protégé of Macquarie, he bitterly attacked the Bigge Report (which described his father as an emancipist), and he was strongly critical of the limitations of the 1823 Act.

Wentworth returned to New South Wales in July 1824, entered his name on the colony's bar roll, and at once began his campaign for freer institutions by establishing an independent newspaper, the *Australian* (first published in October 1824). The only newspaper before this time was the government-run *Sydney Gazette*, established in 1803, which was mainly concerned with government official notices, though it carried general news also. The fiercely independent *Australian* defied local concepts of government authority over the press. Governor Brisbane was prepared to "try the experiment of full latitude of freedom of the Press"; but the newspaper quickly aroused official displeasure by campaigning openly and vigorously for self-government and trial by jury. Above all, it espoused the emancipist cause. In its columns, Wentworth and his editor, Robert Wardell, unleashed a torrent of criticism, something unknown in the colony before. Brisbane was taken aback by the thundering censure; he referred the matter to London in January 1825. Six months later Lord Bathurst directed in a dispatch that steps be taken at the earliest opportunity

> ... to initiate a measure to control the press, to extract a licence before publication, and to make the maximum term of licence one year.

It fell to Brisbane's successor, Governor Ralph Darling, to try to put the instructions into force.

At first Darling (who took over the governorship in December 1825), hoped it would be possible to remain aloof and impartial and that discord would subside. However, the new governor had quite a different character from his predecessor; a strict disciplinarian, he was soon taking a much stronger line against his opposition.

A new voice joined the anti-Darling chorus when Edward Smith Hall began publication of the *Monitor* in May 1826. The two newspapers waged a vigorous campaign for representative government and extension of the jury system, and directed their criticism mainly against Darling, although in these matters the governor was no more than the instrument of policies created in London. An incident that gave the editors a wonderful opportunity to attack the governor involved two soldiers, Sudds and Thompson, who had openly committed a petty larceny soon after their arrival in Sydney in the expectation that through this device they would receive an immediate discharge from the army, as other reluctant soldiers had done. The government and the military decided to make an example of Sudds and Thompson, and instead of being discharged they were arrested, charged, and sentenced. Darling commuted their seven-year transportation to labour on the roads. The men were stripped of their uniforms, fitted with heavy iron collars and great ankle irons, and drummed out of the garrison in convict garb. Sudds complained of illness; he soon collapsed and, within a few days of being admitted to hospital, died. The newspaper editors took advantage of Sudd's death to denounce the governor for callousness and maladministration.

Meanwhile, nettled by the barrage of criticism being levelled against his administration on many issues, Darling decided that Bathurst's directions for newspaper control must be put into effect and the "villainous editors" curbed. As a first step, the governor brought the matter to the notice of Chief Justice Forbes, but the chief justice was not satisfied that the issue of a revocable licence was permitted by English law, and he would not issue the necessary certification. Darling then asked the judge how far he felt himself "at liberty to sanction the measures directed by Lord Bathurst," to which Forbes replied that he was ready to certify any ordinance "as far as I am authorized by law." When two draft bills (for a licensing system and for a stamp tax on newspapers) were placed before him, Forbes declined to approve the first six clauses of the licensing bill, suggesting instead that the legislation be held over until law officers in London could be consulted. Darling replied that the safety of the colony was endangered by the "licentiousness of the press" and resubmitted the bills, with some amendments, to Forbes as urgent measures which he had been directed to initiate. He informed Forbes that he believed as chief justice he was "required" to sanction the measures; but this failed to pressure the chief justice into compliance.

Through the *Australian* Wentworth and Wardell challenged the validity of the Stamp Duties Act on the ground that it had been submitted for certification in an incomplete form since it had unfilled spaces left for the rates of duty which the council could fill in at its discretion. Forbes held the measure to be invalid, accepting Wentworth's points, and also noting that it failed to comply with the provisions of the 1823 Act which laid down that the purpose for which any tax or duty was being levied had to be stated in the law or ordinance imposing it. Forbes held that "if a tax be professedly imposed for one objective and covertly intended for another different objective, it is contrary to the letter of the Act, it is a breach of faith with Parliament, it is an abuse of the trust confided in the Council, it is derogatory to the Government." The legislation was dead; the act was suspended almost immediately. Late in May 1827, Macarthur wrote disconsolately to his son in London:

> Four newspapers are now published, all in the convict interest, and the editors all are desperate radicals, alike shameless and unprincipled. Our Chief Justice is their idol.

When law officers in London were asked to report upon the issue, they supported the chief justice's action in refusing to certify the controversial clauses of the licensing measure; they did not uphold his opinion on the Stamp Duties Act, but when this measure was sent to England for the royal assent, that assent was refused. The battle for a free press was virtually won, although the legal system, with its military juries in criminal cases, still gave the opportunity for curbing the activities of radical editors. Hall spent three years in gaol as the result of a long series of actions for criminal libel.

The British Government had been concerned about the differences that had arisen between the governor and chief justice over certification of proposed legislation. It was realized that the governor could be placed in the position of being unable to carry out his duties (as he saw them), or his instructions, if another official, the chief justice, holding a veto power, disputed the legality of the measure. On reflection it seemed to the colonial Office that adherence to the strict letter of the law was all very well, but such an approach was somewhat inappropriate where a military governor had to maintain control in a distant convict colony. Accordingly, in the Constitution Act of 1828 the duty of certifying the legality of proposed legislation was to be exercised by the whole body of justices, not the chief justice exclusively.

Although it added to the ranks of his enemies, Darling's most valuable contribution was his reform of the civil service. Several new positions had been created under Brisbane, including a colonial treasurer and an auditor, and something had been done towards raising salaries so that the out-worn system of fees and privileges in lieu of salary could be done away with; but the constant disputes between Brisbane and his colonial secretary (which eventually caused the recall of both) and the lack of control over departmental heads had led to anomalies, abuses, and general confusion. Darling, an able and conscientious administrator, appointed boards of inquiry to advise him on the reorganization of (in his own words) "every department and establishment without one single exception of the whole government"; he introduced business methods into the civil service, rationalized salaries and duties, reorganized the police force, commissariat, and post-office on sound lines. He organized a water supply system for Sydney, raising a loan for the purpose, and extended the substitution of reasonable salaries for the old system of privileges and fees; he created a new and efficient Customs Department in place of the old system which had left the collection of customs duties to a fee-collecting naval officer. Another sensible innovation was the separation of administration into two distinct branches, the departments dealing with the penal system, which was paid for by the British

Treasury, and those dealing with colonial affairs, whose expenses came out of colonial revenue.

The heads of department were in every case sent out from England, while the governor made local appointments, on the advice of the colonial secretary or departmental heads; in each case these appointees owed their position to patronage, as was the general custom at that period. Most men born in the colony preferred an outdoor life, and did not take up clerical jobs; and so emancipist or convict clerks still filled most minor positions. There was a great need for efficient and soundly trained civil servants to fill the middle ranks; Darling worked out a plan by which a few well-educated young gentlemen would be sent out as junior clerks, and would receive land grants and cash with which to buy livestock as part of their increments after every few years in the public service, but nothing came of this—mainly because any capable and well-educated young man who came to the colony was soon lured away from government service by the higher salaries offered by business firms or by the more attractive prospects of sheep-raising.

The arrival of men with capital had been creating new tensions as the Australian-born and the emancipists realized that the newcomers were rapidly taking over the available land and there was little hope that they could compete successfully with the new arrivals. During his struggle with Darling, Wentworth had developed a strong following among the emancipists and the generation descended from them. His party—for his following was by now virtually that—continued to campaign in the press and at public meetings with the object of influencing the Colonial Office when constitutional revision was being considered.

The propaganda methods of the Wentworth party and the violence of their attacks upon the governor were not likely to impress the British government, and the 1828 revision of the 1823 Act made few concessions to the popular party. In a purely constitutional sense, the colonists did gain a somewhat enhanced role in the government of the community. Council membership was increased to fifteen, with seven of them nominated non-officials. Summaries of new bills had to be published at least a week before the bill was brought before the council, a clause which gave some opportunity for the expression of public opinion in the newspapers, while the governor had to submit his annual estimates of expenditure to the council. The consent of the majority of the council members was necessary before a bill could become law.

Because of the non-representative nature of council membership—the governor was directed to choose five members from the landowners and two from the merchants, and Darling naturally chose those who shared his own conservative views—the progress resulting from the constitutional changes was slight. In practice only a small minority of the population gained. As Hall wrote in the *Monitor*:

> The power of a Governor is much greater with a Council to assist him, than it is without one. The acts of our new Council have proved this. The governor

would never have ventured without a Council to pass the oppressive and unconstitutional Acts that have been passed since the Council was given him.

On the judicial side, the 1828 Act retained the military juries for criminal
cases; at the same time the British government handed over to the governor
and council the responsibility for determining if and when full trial by
jury should be introduced, and whether emancipists should be eligible to
sit on juries. Darling and his conservative-minded council naturally took
no action to introduce the jury system.

The continuance of the transportation system was the vital point in
influencing the British government to withhold from both of the Australian
colonies the two key civil liberties—trial by jury and representative government—which were in operation in such colonies as Canada and the West
Indies islands. Darling's experience convinced him that "no colony, so long
as it continues to be a receptacle for convicts, can receive or be considered
eligible to the processes of the English constitution." Members of the
legislative council, canvassed by Darling, held the same view, one member
considering it impractical to introduce trial by jury "until the original free
and the freed bear almost an equal proportion in number, which is far from
the case at the present time." The British government, which by the early
1830s was sending between 3,000 and 4,000 convicts into the country each
year, saw no reason to disagree with this viewpoint. Although from its
foundation in 1830 the *Sydney Herald*, the most influential of the newspapers,
kept up a running fire of opposition to transportation, there was as yet no
general demand for abolition, and there was a strong body of opinion in
favour of the government's declared intention to continue the system.

Apart from its value in providing free labour for the pastoral industry,
transportation was far too convenient a means of ridding the mother-country
of its unwanted criminals for the British government to consider abolition
or limitation of transportation at this time. Most of the transportees became
assigned workers; the bulk of the others were segregated in penal establishments at Moreton Bay and Port Macquarie (in New South Wales), Norfolk
Island (which had been reoccupied in 1825), and Port Arthur and Macquarie Harbour (in Van Diemen's Land), all well away from the main
centres of population.

Even though the "freed" still outnumbered the "free immigrants," the
latter were constantly increasing in number. Australia's remoteness was
an effective deterrent to mass immigration, but the trickle of free settlers
of earlier years was steadily growing.

The British government had begun supporting working-class emigration in 1823 when the first of a series of small experiments were undertaken
and a few hundred emigrants sailed, with government subsidy, for Canada
and the Cape of Good Hope. The original and subsequent groups in the
1820s had not been directed to Australia because it was felt that any
build-up of free immigrants would disturb the convict system. In 1826
committees of the House of Commons had approved the idea of assisting

emigration on a more substantial scale as a means of relieving England's over-population. However, with the land policy in force in the Australian colonies at the time—that of reserving the land for men of substance—it was still not possible to encourage free immigration of working men since any substantial increase in the number of free labourers would throw the burden of convict support back upon the government. Special concessions offered by the British government to demobilized officers of the army, navy, and marines who were prepared to settle in the Australian colonies stimulated interest, and men of this class, and their families, were prominent among those who arrived as free settlers in New South Wales from the late 1820s. Efforts to include ex-privates in the programme proved unsuccessful, since the men had insufficient capital to acquire properties of their own, and they were unable to find satisfactory employment. Assistance was subsequently restricted to ex-officers.

The new arrivals in Sydney or Hobart around 1830 continued to be largely men of some property. Australia remained beyond the reach of the poorer Englishman. Few members of the working classes could meeet the expense of the passage which might exceed £200 for a family; the cost was six or eight times that of a crossing to Canada or the United States, and those lands attracted far greater numbers than the Australian colonies, which continued to rely on convicts and ex-convicts as the principal labour supply.

There had always been some humanitarians who loudly deplored the moral and social aspects of transportation; but it was not until Edward Gibbon Wakefield published his *Letter from Sydney* that anyone offered an alternative way of providing labour for the distant and not-too-attractive Australian colonies. Wakefield's alternative was that colonial land should be sold, not given away, and the proceeds used to bring working-class immigrants to the colonies.

Following Wakefield's proposals, part of the proceeds of sales of Crown land in New South Wales and Van Diemen's Land was used after 1831 to create a land and immigration fund, from which the government paid the passage money for labourers and female emigrants, or later paid a bounty to employers in the colonies (in practice, to shipowners) for bringing migrants to the colonies.

The first assisted migrants to New South Wales and Van Diemen's Land arrived in 1832. With the creation of the Land Fund in 1831, the British government appointed emigration commissioners to organize the assistance to migrants; the commissioners were soon replaced by an independent organization, the Emigration Committee. (South Australia had its own similar but separate Wakefieldian emigration organization.)

The first programme was directed towards reducing the great predominance of men in the population by sending to the colonies women between fifteen and thirty years of age. The government contributed £8, later £12, towards the passage money of from £30 to £40, with the balance provided by the emigrant or by a charity group. After 1835 the government paid the whole of the passage money, which had been reduced to £16. A good deal of discretion lay with ships' agents—and they were interested only in filling the ships. Some undesirable characters were among those who sailed. Colonial opinion was strongly critical; to the colonists, the selections were made "more with the view to relieve the Mother-Country than to benefit the colony," as a committee of the New South Wales Legislative Council put it in 1835. Following a recommendation by Governor Sir Richard Bourke that an independent officer have the final say in approving emigrants before their departure, agents were appointed in London and Liverpool in 1834; but this new procedure did little if anything to improve the quality of the new arrivals. Inmates of work-houses, whose will to work had been drained away, still predominated.

At this point the committee of the New South Wales Legislative Council insisted on "the necessity of appointing [immigration] agents well acquainted with the colony and responsible to the Colonial Government." In relaying this recommendation to London, Governor Bourke also proposed that the assisted migration programme be extended to include privately sponsored immigration. He believed that the bounty should be available to colonists who "have the means and would prefer to engage by their own agents, mechanics, or agricultural labourers." Settlers were to receive the bounty if they introduced married couples under thirty years of age, and others under thirty, who were passed as satisfactory by a board when they arrived. Bourke envisaged this private plan operating side by side with an improved governmental plan.

Emigration was becoming part of the ordinary business of government, and by the end of 1836 the inadequacy of the existing administration was apparent. Wakefield and his followers had the land emigration policy under persistent attack, and when a committee of the House of Commons inquired into the question of disposal of land in the British colonial possessions, Wakefield was an important witness. The committee recommended a uniform land emigration policy for the whole empire.

In 1837 the Colonial Office propounded a plan whereby governors of the Australian colonies were allowed to apply one-third of the funds available from emigration to the introduction of people under the bounty system, with selection of the remaining two-thirds still under the control of authorities appointed by the British government. Before these proposals reached Hobart, the Legislative Council of Van Diemen's Land had asked London to suspend immigration indefinitely, because transportation provided sufficient labour; but the system went into operation for the other colonies and Thomas Frederick Elliot was appointed Agent-General for Emigration in London. The work was too much for his small staff, and the operation did not work smoothly. The government system savoured of dictation from London and the colonists, determined now to press for full control of migration and the land policy with which it was linked, were louder than ever in their criticism of the choice of migrants. They had an alternative in the bounty system, which had been begun in a small way in 1835. Booming land sales were swelling the Land Fund, and by 1839 so many migrants were moving to the colony under the bounty system that the government system was suspended.

The settlers now had full opportunity to seek the migrants of their choice—but they were unable to hire capable and independent agents, and so the bounty system, which at first seemed so promising, soon fell into the hands of shipowners and speculators. As the rates of the bounty increased, more speculators were induced to enter the business of emigration.

Early in 1840 the agent-general's office was merged in a new board of Colonial Land and Emigration Commissioners, which also took over the South Australian system. They had supervisory authority over the bounty agents, and their attempts to check abuses and prevent fraud met with strong opposition, both from the shipowners and from the colonists, who resented their interference.

Before long the economic depression in the colonies had altered the whole migration picture. Land sales were no longer sufficient to provide funds for migration, and there was no demand for labour. Assisted migration was suspended in 1842, resumed early in 1844 and suspended again in 1846. By mid-1847 the economic prospects were so improved that land-owners and employers were asking that migration ships be sent to the colony on a fortnightly basis. Subsidized migration was accordingly resumed under new regulations; selection was now entirely in the hands of the Land and Emigration Commissioners, and the colonists continued to complain of the type of migrant sent out.

Members of the legislative council represented mainly one section of colonial opinion, the landowners whose main concerns were to have efficient pastoral and agricultural workers brought into the country, and to get control of the Land Fund and land policy; and on the issue of greater local autonomy the press sided with them. A more balanced verdict was that of Governor George Gipps. In 1844, after the failure of the land boom, Gipps wrote that

> ... the mania [for land speculation] while productive of many evils, has at least had the good effect of adding 50,000 souls to our population and of changing, in the almost incredibly short time of six years, the whole character of the colony, of converting it in fact from a convict colony into a free one.

Thus the Wakefield-inspired immigration fund helped to blot out convictism; the growth of the pastoral industry, by making the country wealthy, productive and attractive to free men, had been the economic driving force contributing to the same result.

In the early years of assisted migration, migrants paying their own way heavily outnumbered those who received assistance; but soon the proportions were reversed and after 1836 the bulk of the new arrivals were those who had received assistance. Over the 1830s and 1840s, almost half of all assisted migrants were of Irish origin; England and Wales provided about 40 per cent, and Scotland more than 12 per cent, with a negligible number from other countries. The total migrant intake into the three eastern colonies between 1831 and 1846 was as follows:

Immigration in the eastern colonies, 1831 to 1846

	New South Wales		Van Diemen's Land		South Australia	
	Assisted	Unassisted	Assisted	Unassisted	Assisted	Unassisted
1831–	—	457	—	697		
1832–1836	3,882	5,522	2,041	5,450	813 (1836 only)	—
1837–1841	43,922	8,503	629	3,106	11,391	856
1842–1846	11,471	4,843	918	1,575	2,158	7,527

Throughout the period the pastoralists had been the chief employers of labour, bond or free. In opening up new country the pioneer settler usually found it difficult to recruit labour, and he had to offer the inducement of high wages to the Australian-born to go into the more distant areas. New arrivals in the colony usually found the loneliness of the "bush" rather awesome, and very few were prepared to venture far into the unknown. Generally they preferred "lingering at lower wages in the settled districts." The job available to newcomers was usually that of shepherd; other bush workers—bullock drivers, stockmen, and shearers, mainly, who were very often former convicts or "old hands"—had already established their own superiority over the more lowly occupation of shepherd.

From the beginning there had been a preponderance of men in the colonial population. In the 1820s the masculinity ratio was generally as high as three to one; by the 1830s it had declined slightly, but throughout the decade there were still twice as many men and boys as women and girls, the excess of men being greater in the rural areas. Hardly any women had ventured into the hinterland. If the rawness of the frontier were to be broken down, it would be necessary for women to settle there and establish normal communities.

Pioneer work in helping to bring about this result was undertaken by Caroline Chisholm, wife of an officer in the East India Company, who arrived in Sydney in 1838 and was at once struck by the plight of unmarried girls, left penniless and friendless on arrival. At first she could do no more than shelter a few homeless immigrant girls in her own home and find jobs for them with her friends; but in 1841 she persuaded the governor to give her an old building in which she established a Female Immigrants' Home as a temporary shelter, and in one year she found employment for over 700 young women, nearly half in country districts. The young women hesitated to set out unaccompanied on the long journey by dray, and so Mrs Chisholm organized and led expeditions in which scores of girls and newly arrived families moved out into the sheep lands, some of the trips lasting four or five weeks. Displaying a remarkable ability, she enlisted public support and organized employment depots in many country districts. From farm to farm, homestead to homestead, she sought employment for her charges, judging the fitness of employer and servant, and drawing up employment contracts. Above all she saw the development of family life as the way to better living conditions and healthier social attitudes. She wrote:

For all the clergy you can dispatch, all the schoolmasters you can appoint, all the churches you can build and all the books you can export will never do much good without "God's police"—wives and little children.

Mrs Chisholm's example was an inspiration for a change in attitudes whereby the new frontier lands were drawn into the community. In 1846, with her organization for settling migrants in the colony widely established, Mrs Chisholm returned to England where she set up the Family Colonization Loan Society, which had the backing of philanthropists and social reformers. Interest in her plans was stimulated by widespread publicity, including several articles by Charles Dickens in his periodical, *Household Words*. The society not only chartered ships to take families to the colonies, and campaigned for improved conditions on board ship, but also persuaded the government to grant free passages to the wives and families of men sent out earlier. This, together with the improved balance of population within the colonies as a result of higher birth-rates, helped redress the striking disproportion between the sexes. By 1850 the ratio of males to females had fallen to 1.43 to one.

The aspects of a freer, less authoritarian and more cultivated society became apparent as early as the governorship of Sir Richard Bourke. An army man who was also a lawyer, an experienced colonial administrator and a genuine liberal, Bourke helped widen the horizons of the colonists by encouraging and initiating endeavours in educational and cultural matters. In Sydney, with its population of over 15,000, a Mechanics' School of Arts, with a library, lectures, classes, and debates, was set up under Bourke's patronage. Immigration was bringing people from higher educational backgrounds to the colony; Scottish settlers brought out under the auspices of the Reverend John Dunmore Lang, including Presbyterian ministers and teachers, formed a core of thinkers and speakers with whom others joined in the work of overcoming the prevailing cultural barrenness.

In both religion and education the demand was growing for changes in the privileged position of the established Church of England. Bourke considered that the exclusive privileges of the Church of England (land and houses for clergy, the major share of the government's grants for clerical salaries) were both unjust and impractical in a new country, where no more than half the population belonged to this church. He wrote in a long and thoughtful dispatch in September 1833:

I would observe that in a new country, to which persons of all religious denominations are permitted to resort, it will be impossible to establish a dominant and endorsed church without much hostility and great improbability of its being permanent. The inclination of these colonists, which keeps pace with the spirit of the age, is decidedly averse to such an institution.

Accordingly the governor proposed that wherever a "moderate congregation" of any of the colony's three main denominations (Church of England, Church of Scotland, and Roman Catholic) could be collected, and £300 contributed for building a place of worship and minister's dwelling, an equal sum should be paid by the colonial treasury, together with a "modest stipend" for a chaplain; this arrangement could be extended later to other denominations. Following this proposal, under the Church Act of 1836 the colonial government assumed the duty of paying salaries to clergymen and of subsidizing church buildings for the various denominations willing to accept this state aid.

Education was a much more controversial subject. The ragged and scanty educational system of Macquarie's day had been reorganized in the mid-1820s and a system of primary schools, run by the Anglican Church and School Corporation with governmental finance, established. As the population grew and liberal ideas strengthened, the demand by the other religious denominations for a breakdown of the Anglican monopoly of educational aid became a controversial issue in the press and in the legislative council. In the same dispatch that dealt with sharing government grants between the denominations, Bourke put forward a proposal for a system of state or national elementary schools providing general education without Bible reading, and with religious instruction given only outside school hours. This system was called the Irish national system because it had recently been introduced in Ireland, where the English government had come to realize that a school system featuring religious instruction according to the established Anglican church had to be modified for a country where that church had a minority of adherents. The system was to be introduced gradually, and support was not to be withdrawn from the existing denominational schools.

Bourke did not discuss the matter with local Church leaders, or seek support for the idea; instead he proposed directly to Secretary of State Lord Stanley that a plan based on the Irish system be introduced. When it became known locally, Bourke's proposal was strongly attacked on all sides. The able Bishop Broughton led the Anglicans in defence of their faith and their privileges, while the other Protestants were inclined to see the whole business as an excuse for helping Catholic schools. Most Dissenters, while favouring national schools, preferred the alternative British and Foreign Schools Society system (a Protestant system that excluded denominational religious teaching but included Bible reading). Bourke's plan had to be dropped, and a compromise system was adopted in 1836, whereby subsidies for land, school buildings, and teachers' salaries were divided between the four main denominations (Methodism being the fourth).

With the growing prosperity of the colony, there was a need for secondary education for those who could afford it, and by 1833 the colony could boast of the non-denominational Sydney College (later Sydney Grammar School), The King's School at Parramatta, run by the Anglican church on English public school lines, the ambitious Australian College, founded by Reverend John Dunmore Lang, with Scottish teachers and an advanced curriculum in the hope that it would develop into a university, and a Normal Institution for training teachers, run by one of Lang's migrant-teachers. Although the Australian College and the Normal Institution both ran into difficulties and had to close, they played important parts in raising educational standards.

By 1840 the demand was growing for a secular school system since, besides offending liberal and anti-clerical opinion, the denominational system was wastefully competitive, and was obviously failing to bring schooling to children beyond the main towns. Governor Gipps, a pragmatist for whom religious training was a sideline to the main issue of bringing education to as many children as possible, proposed a national system, with education on the lines of the British and Foreign School Society for the combined Protestants and a separate grant for Roman Catholic schools. This pleased practically none of the religious bodies; their opposition was well organized, and it was not until 1848 that the issue was resolved with a compromise system: two school boards (with part-time honorary commissioners) were set up, one with authority over the national elementary schools which were to be organized throughout the colony, and the other supervising and allocating government funds to the various church-sponsored schools.

The early national schools were developed on a local self-help basis. In 1849 the new national education board appointed two agents to get schools founded throughout the Port Phillip and Moreton Bay districts respectively. The agent for the Port Phillip district was an energetic and capable young organizer, George William Rusden. After advance letters to the towns on his itinerary, he would hold private and public meetings at which he would allay fears of the "godlessness" of the national school system, proclaim its advantages and explain the board's policy:

> In building school-houses, the National Board will contribute two-thirds of the total expenses—they will obtain a site from the Government—they will give a salary to the teacher of not less than £40, and they will confer their assistance wherever the number of thirty scholars can be brought together.

Before Rusden left the town, local "patrons" would often have been chosen; the responsibilities they took upon themselves were "to conduct the preliminary arrangements with the board, to supervise the fulfilment of the building contract, to fix the rate of fees to be paid by the parents, and otherwise to promote the interests of the school."

Where local public spirit was high, schools were started under this system—no less than thirty-one schools as a direct result of Rusden's two-year odyssey throughout Port Phillip and later Moreton Bay—but this initiative was not backed by any real organization, and at mid-century at least half the children of school age were growing up without any schooling whatever.

Because of the nature of council membership, the increased powers granted to the legislative council after 1828 were actually a hindrance to the introduction of liberal institutions. The council was made up of men appointed by the conservative Darling, and Bourke found that they stood against him in his efforts to introduce more liberal institutions. Bourke pointed out to the Secretary of State in 1833 the evils of a political system in which the community was divided into two parties, only one of which (and that a minority) was represented in the council; the result was that the council, with its members "all of one and the same political bias," was mistrusted by the community in general, not excepting "persons of integrity wealth and industry." The attitude of the popular press, which by now numbered eight periodicals, showed this. In an effort to achieve better balance in community representation, Bourke appointed the liberal landowner Sir John Jamison to the council, and offered membership to Wentworth, who declined to accept the appointment thinking it would tie his hands.

In 1833 and again in 1835 Bourke urged the Secretary of State to introduce a measure of elective government. In 1835 he made the suggestion that the council be increased to thirty-six members, two-thirds of them elected; he proposed also that a property qualification should be the only condition of franchise and that ex-convicts as such should not be disqualified from voting, although they should not be eligible for membership of the council. Bourke suggested that his proposals should be brought into operation in 1836, when the Constitution Act was due for renewal, and also advocated the abolition of transportation to the colony.

Full trial by jury was advocated by Forbes and the other judges and in 1833 Bourke used his casting vote to carry a Jury Act through the council. By this act trial by jury in criminal cases was introduced, where the accused demanded it, side by side with the old military juries for criminal cases, whose retention was a concession to the conservative members of the council. Emancipists were entitled to be chosen as jurors on the same basis—a small property qualification—as the rest of the community.

By this time Wentworth's demands for self-government had attracted very much greater public support. The Australian-born were developing pride in their homeland, and new arrivals from the British Isles wanted to improve a situation in which they found themselves unable to play any direct part in the government of the colony; neither group was truly represented by the landed interests dominating the legislative council as nonofficial representatives. In 1835 Wentworth and his supporters formed the Australian Patriotic Association, the first organized group in Australia's political history. Besides Wentworth, the leaders were Sir John Jamison and Dr William Bland (who had been transported for killing his man in a duel); "Monitor" Hall was the secretary. Although the association gained its main support from emancipists, Bland was the only emancipist among its leaders. The group had a radical wing, drawn from the immigrant mechanics and artisans.

The association's programme was aimed at the earliest possible introduction of self-government through representative institutions. To this end an active propaganda programme was carried out in the press and at public meetings, and petitions were drafted. A bill was prepared and this was sent to England by Bourke with his blessing. The association appointed a member of the House of Commons to express its point of view, and it tried actively to influence members of parliament. However, the time had not yet come for the change Wentworth's followers sought, and the association's House of Commons representative felt compelled to advise the group that the granting of self-government was completely incompatible with the continuance of transportation.

A year after the formation of the association, the landowning-magisterial group headed by James Macarthur (his father had died in 1834) sponsored a rival body, which became known as the Petition Committee. Macarthur claimed that its membership included six out of the seven non-official members of the legislative council and two-thirds of the magistrates.

In London, Edward and James Macarthur (the latter went to England for the purpose) aired this group's views before the officials of the Colonial Office and political leaders, James Macarthur publishing a book with detailed facts and figures supporting the petitioners' viewpoint. Macarthur's main argument was the desirability of withholding full civil rights, whether as jurymen, voters, or council members, from emancipists. He also suggested that the legislative council should be enlarged to thirty or thirty-five members, two-thirds or a half being elective from the members of the magistracy; and as a means of disqualifying emancipists in fact though not by name he suggested that the magistrates or returning officers should have the power of withholding the right to vote or serve on a jury from "any person, whether an immigrant, a native of the colony, or any other class whom the returning officers may find deficient in character or otherwise unfit."

The propaganda of the Wentworth and Macarthur factions was designed to influence the Colonial Office and the House of Commons when the Constitution Act came up in 1836 for its periodic revision. However, the Colonial Office decided to postpone any constitutional changes until after a committee of the House of Commons, appointed to consider the whole question of transportation to the Australian colonies, had completed its study and report. It had become clear that the convict issue had to be decided before other changes could be introduced.

The Wentworth party and the Macarthur faction both generally supported the continuance of transportation to New South Wales, but differences on the issue existed and these cut across party boundaries. Wentworth, whose inheritance of his father's properties in 1827 had made him one of the colony's largest landholders, continued to urge retention of the system (supporting the plan of assigning convicts to landholders). At the same time, many supporters of the Australian Patriotic Association—chiefly the immigrant working class members, who feared the competition of convict labour—held the opposite view, and soon divergence of opinion on this issue caused a split in the party. On the other hand, the Petition Committee's leader, James Macarthur, at first strongly in favour of transportation (believing that convicts should be put to work in gangs to clear the land for settlers or undertake public works), slowly changed his position on the issue; by the end of the 1830s he had come to believe that New South Wales had reached a stage of economic development where it was no longer dependent upon or in need of convict labour.

It had become clear that the legislative council was powerless on important matters while it remained without control over land policy, and only with self-government could that control be wrested away from the Colonial Office. This control was important to the landholders because they wanted to be able to assure themselves title to their holdings, and at the same time they sought control of the land fund so that the whole of the sales revenue, not merely part, would be devoted to bringing out immigrants. In turn they wanted control of immigration policy to make sure they got the types of immigrants they needed; it might suit the English authorities to clear out paupers, but the colonists wanted effective labour.

By 1840 Macarthur's advocacy was directed wholly towards self-government, and to achieve this goal he was prepared not only to support abolition of transportation but also to drop the emancipist issue which had been in contention for so long. By this time the emancipists were a smaller segment of the free community, they, like the convicts themselves, swamped by the new free settlers and Australian-born element. Many of the emancipists had prospered and were seen as allies in a common cause by the old landholding families. The emancipists still wanted to see status in the colony depend upon wealth rather than social background; but differences between them and the old landholders faded as common economic interests brought the factions closer. The last bastion of anti-emancipist feeling disappeared in 1839 with the abolition of military juries as an alternative to ordinary juries in criminal cases.

As early as 1836 the Colonial Office had come to the conclusion that transportation to New South Wales should cease as soon as practicable, and this view was supported in the two reports issued by the committee set up by the House of Commons to inquire into the transportation system; the committee, under the chairmanship of Sir William Molesworth, sat in 1837–38. The convict system was assailed by various witnesses who told the committee that, although the system was costing nearly £500,000 a year, it neither diminished crime in Britain nor assisted in the reformation of criminals, while it produced a disgraceful state of depravity in the colonies receiving the convicts; decent immigrants tended to become demoralized and "polluted." The assignment system made a lottery of a sentence of transportation. Following the Molesworth committee's report, an order-in-council in May 1840 put an end to transportation to New South Wales (though it was to be continued to Van Diemen's Land and Norfolk Island).

With the removal of the chief barrier to a more liberal constitution it was inevitable that the British government would soon grant wider powers to the colonists of New South Wales. In 1840, Sir John Russell, who as Secretary of State supported the concept of representative government for the colonies, introduced a measure designed to broaden the legislative council's membership and extend its powers. However, it was not until 1842, under his successor, Lord Stanley, that the bill was passed.

The act of 1842 owed far more to Sir Richard Bourke's proposals of a decade earlier than to those of the Australian parties headed by Wentworth and Macarthur. It enlarged the council to thirty-six members, twenty-four of them to be elected, while not more than six of the twelve nominated members were to be officials. For council membership the property quali-fication was £1,000 freehold or £100 annual rental, while those eligible to vote had to be £200 freeholders or £20 leaseholders. (A pastoral lease soon came to be accepted as a qualification for voting.) There was no restric-tion on emancipists, as such, voting or standing for election. Country dis-tricts returned three-quarters of the elected members, while the wealthy and independent-minded Port Phillip district, which had been demanding the right to secede from New South Wales, was to return six members.

Administrative officers were still responsible to the governor and not the council, and a scheduled annual grant of £81,600 made the governor financially independent of the council. Revenue from sale of Crown land and from the pastoral licence system remained under the control of the governor, although customs and other colonial revenue came under the council's authority. A Speaker was to be elected from and by the members; the governor thus ceased to preside over meetings. While the governor could still instruct the council to consider legislation, its members were granted the right to initiate legislation. The life of the council was fixed at a maximum of five years.

The act represented a step forward in transfer of power to the colonists themselves, though because of the property restrictions on franchise and membership and the preponderance of country electorates, only the property-owning classes were represented, and the landholders still had the upper hand in the council. Thus it was their interests and demands that con-tinued to dominate the scene for the remainder of the decade.

Leading colonists might be strongly urging the transfer of political power in the broad field of colonial affairs, but they were less than anxious to take over responsibilities in municipal or shire affairs. In 1840 Governor Gipps had introduced into the legislative council a measure designed to set up municipal institutions in the colony. Behind this move was the idea that the colonists would gain from the experience in self-government in wholly local matters. When the measure came before the council, however, issues of a general nature—including the political rights of emancipists and matters concerning control of land and the disposition of colonial revenues—intruded, and the governor ultimately withdrew the measure.

The Act of 1842 included a provision for the creation of district councils by legislative council action, and the necessary bills were introduced to constitute the municipalities. The City of Sydney was incorporated, but other bills were rejected by the legislative council. The main reason for rejection was that additional taxation would be involved. The timing of the move was bad; it came forward when wool prices had slumped, and landholders were seeking to reduce commitments and were unwilling to pay more money in taxes. Gipps was instructed from London to institute the district councils by letters patent against the wishes of the legislators; but both he and his successor felt this course unwise, and they took no action. It was to be another decade before municipal and shire administration became a reality in the colonies.

New South Wales was the only colony to receive a part-elective legislative council, a fact that is an indication of the much greater development of the mother-colony, and to a lesser extent, of the more insistent and turbulent interest in political affairs. Van Diemen's Land did not share in the change; transportation remained.

Van Diemen's Land, where rugged rain-soaked terrain and surrounding seas set an impassable limit to pastoral expansion, was already running practically the maximum number of sheep early in the 1830s, and so the island was unable to keep pace with the expansion of wool-growing that characterized New South Wales at this time. With the formation of the Port Phillip district, many of the island's most enterprising citizens, as well as livestock and capital, were drawn to the mainland. The penal establishments in New South Wales could be removed far from the main centres of population, but the taint of convictism seemed to pervade the whole of the island colony. By the late 1830s Van Diemen's Land was still unable to do without the economic basis of the convict system, whether from the standpoint of the British money involved in its upkeep or the use of convict labour by the landholders. The settlers had no wish to lose the convict labour or the assured market for their produce that the convict establishment provided, and the Molesworth Committee was pleased enough to be able to continue use of Van Diemen's Land when it recommended abolition of transportation to the mainland. In September 1840 Sir John Russell advised Governor Sir John Franklin that Tasman's Peninsula was to be retained as a convict station—one of only three in the Empire, Norfolk Island and Bermuda being the others.

Now that convicts were no longer to be sent to New South Wales, the number reaching Van Diemen's Land rose sharply to a rate far in excess of the island's ability to absorb them. In 1839 the governor had been advised from London to be prepared for the "immediate diminution and approaching discontinuance" of the practice of assigning convicts to settlers. In 1840 instructions arrived that the assignment system was to end forthwith— which meant that henceforward not even the employers of convict labour would gain any benefit from the system.

Under the new probationary system, the transported convict was to go through five stages of punishment and reform, passing on from one stage to another only if his conduct was satisfactory. The first stage was rigorous punishment, the second labour in government gangs; in the third stage, the convict could work for a private employer, who had to pay him a small wage; the fourth stage was ticket-of-leave; and pardon was the final stage.

After 1841, when the island's intake of convicts shot up to four thousand or more a year, the great weight of the influx of transportees stagnated the economy. Free immigration was held back and the glut of convict labour drove free workmen out of the colony. As convictism reached such proportions that it drenched the scene, the old free settlers in the land found that the "deadly shade of slave labour" had come to blight the island.

Nevertheless, education and cultural life advanced notably under Governor Franklin (1837–43) who reorganized the school system. Like Bourke in New South Wales, Franklin saw the need for a national system of elementary schools and favoured the Irish system, but instead it was the system of the British and Foreign School Society that was adopted. Under regulations published in 1839, undenominational schools could be established in Van Diemen's Land wherever ordained ministers, magistrates, or responsible citizens showed that there were sufficient children in the township or district to justify the establishment. The costs were met partly by fees (a few pence a week for each child) and partly from government funds; the government paid the schoolmaster's salary and gave a small grant for each child above the minimum. A board was appointed to organize the system, some trained teachers were brought out from England, and the number of children attending school increased. There was a great deal of clerical opposition to the system, however, especially from Church of England groups, and in 1848 the governor was directed to establish a dual system, like that of New South Wales, with grants both to denominational and national schools. This involved some trimming of grants to the national schools; they struggled on, but the parallel denominational (mainly Anglican) school system was much more extensive.

The community's interests were widening; a scientific society and a number of Mechanics' Institutes had been founded in the late 1820s and early 1830s, and Franklin had actively supported the establishment of the Natural History Society in 1839. Progress in other aspects of civil affairs also dated from this time. In 1840, trial by military court in criminal cases was replaced by civil jury; but the objective of a part-elective legislative council, as in New South Wales, was not likely to be achieved while Van Diemen's Land remained a penal colony.

The prosperity of Van Diemen's Land in 1839 and 1840 (when there were 1,000,000 sheep in the island's pastures) had come from an increasing export trade, particularly to the mainland colonies, as livestock and wheat were shipped out in considerable quantities. The prosperity induced large imports and active speculation in land; ten banks were operating by 1840, and considerable credit was available. The fall of wool prices in the early 1840s brought a sudden contraction; markets on the mainland were simultaneously shrinking as the colonies began to produce their own wheat, while in the Port Phillip district and in South Australia the growing demand for livestock was being met from local supplies as overlanders moved stock in from the older pastoral districts of New South Wales.

Van Diemen's Land whaling reached its peak in 1837, when the value of fishery products exceeded £135,000. The island whalers concentrated mainly on hunting black whales offshore, since this needed smaller ships and less capital than hunting sperm whales in the deep seas. In the bay whaling system the whalers established boat-stations in a coastal bay, with a look-out on the cliff to watch for whales. When one was sighted, three or four boats (35-footers with a crew of harpoonist, steersman, and five oarsmen) would row out, harpoon the whale and, if they were lucky, tow the carcass back to the shore, where they had the simple facilities needed for rendering down the blubber. By 1840 unrestrained slaughter had killed all the black whales or driven them from the coasts (the seals of Bass Strait had been exterminated nearly a decade earlier) but Van Diemen's larger shipowners were able to compete very successfully in sperm whaling, though the depression affected this industry also.

Only the requirements of the convict establishment for food remained buoyant; but the probation system was turning the colonists against transportation, and as the hopes of profit faded there was a growing agitation for abolition of the system. The burden of administrative costs was growing, and a sense of grievance against imposts became widespread. There was difficulty in raising revenue to balance the budget, and six of the non-official members of the legislative council refused to support the governor's proposals and resigned instead. In 1847 the anti-transportation movement was launched in earnest in Launceston; it soon gained public support throughout the island and later—following a series of tactless attempts by the British government to reintroduce a modified form of transportation to New South Wales—on the mainland.

The British government still considered it "indispensable" that a receptacle should be found in the Australian colonies for all the convicts England wished to dispose of; this was "so momentous an object of national policy" that no conflicting motive was considered of sufficient importance to supersede it. In the early 1840s, when Van Diemen's Land was congested with convicts, a policy was devised by which limited numbers of prisoners who had been "reformed" by preliminary punishment in English penitentiaries were to be sent to New South Wales, where they would be free under conditional pardons; they were to be known as "exiles" not convicts. Although most colonists regarded the introduction of "exiles" as a thinly disguised attempt to resume the transportation system "without its advantages, with all its evils and none of its benefits," the cheap labour was welcomed by many pastoralists, and more than 1,700 men were landed in the Port Phillip district during the period from 1844 to 1848.

During part of this time the Colonial Secretary was William Ewart Gladstone, who had a special interest in Australian affairs since he was part-owner of a sheep property in the Port Phillip district. The advice he received from private colonial sources was heavily weighted in favour of the landowners' viewpoint, and he continued to uphold policies which were completely outdated as far as general colonial opinion was concerned. Gladstone's idea was that a new penal colony, to be called North Australia, should be set up in the Port Curtis area, more than 300 miles to the north of Brisbane; "exiles" and convicts were to be set up on small blocks of land and transformed into farmers under the guidance of free settlers. A small advance party landed at Port Curtis in January 1847 but after three months, during which many difficulties were encountered and violent opposition expressed in Sydney, the whole project was abandoned. (Pastoralists successfully occupied the area soon after.)

Much more provocative was the decision by the next Colonial Secretary, Earl Grey, to send convicts to New South Wales under ticket-of-leave conditions of reporting regularly to the police. At first the legislative council assented to this resumption of convictism under certain conditions, but reversed its decision when the conditions were not being met. When the first ticket-of-leavers reached Melbourne in the *Hashemy* in June 1849, the demonstrations were so violent that the superintendent, Charles La Trobe, directed the captain not to debark his passengers but to take them on to Sydney. The same thing happened when a second convict ship arrived in August.

Grey's retrograde and tactless actions strengthened the hands of those who were working for the abolition of transportation to Van Diemen's Land. Meetings and petitions throughout the eastern colonies made clear the depth of public feeling on the issue. Anti-transportation associations in Launceston and Melbourne joined forces, and by the end of 1851 the Australian Anti-Transportation League had branches in all the colonies except Western Australia. London reversed its policy, and from this time there were no more attempts to lose England's unwanted prison population in the broad acres of eastern Australia. The British government was still reluctant to relinquish its right to send convicts to Van Diemen's Land, however, and the order in council ending transportation to the island was not signed until the end of 1853.

South Australia, which had become a Crown colony in 1842, was still too much involved in its financial depression, and its revenue was still too small for it to be considered ready for representative government. After 1842 the governor was assisted by a legislative council with a membership partly official and partly nominated; this was no consolation to colonists who had once rejoiced in their freedom from "Downing Street swaddling clothes."

The question of whether churches should accept government aid, important in South Australian affairs from the beginning, flared up with new intensity in the late 1840s. From its founding Adelaide had attracted many ministers and preachers representing a number of denominations and sects; at least twelve distinct church groups were active. Even though they were not in favour of establishing a dominant Church, successive governors viewed with apprehension the failure of the voluntary provision for the colonists' spiritual welfare.

In Gawler's time, those supporting the voluntary principle formed a society for the preservation of religious freedom, and strong pressure against state support continued. Grey's successor, Major Robe, after a "careful evaluation" of government aid in other colonies, considered that an appropriate plan would be to offer aid to churches according to the number of their adherents and "their zeal in all forms." He noted in 1846 that in his opinion the colony was the most backward of all in supplying from its public resources the means of worship, and the legislative council approved ordinances granting money, on a *per capita* basis, to the different churches in support of religion and education.

The Lutherans and other smaller groups refused to accept the aid, and an all denominations group, bringing together all who opposed the idea, was formed; it drew up a petition seeking withdrawal of the ordinance. The petition was rejected by the Secretary of State, on Governor Robe's recommendation, as not being truly representative of colonial opinion. In the early months only part of the available support money was taken up, however, and when renewal of the grant was under review Robe introduced a new Church Bill abandoning the *per capita* grant and offering instead state aid in proportion to the amounts subscribed voluntarily by each congregation (as in New South Wales). Again most denominations refused state aid or grants of land; but these same groups made rapid progress from their own resources. The antagonism remained, opening up deeper gulfs between the denominations and feeding sectarian bitterness.

Economically the corner had been turned in South Australia, where agricultural and pastoral production had increased, and by 1843 more wheat was being grown than the colony could consume. Copper mining was on the increase. Progress continued in the 1840s, though pastoral expansion was much slower than in the neighbouring Port Phillip district. Sheep in South Australia, numbering 200,000 in 1840, increased to nearly 500,000 in five years, so that by 1845 most grazing land along the Murray had been taken up as far as Lake Victoria, and sheep were spreading into the southeast corner of the colony.

Mining had also opened up new prospects. A discovery of copper was made on private land at Kapunda in 1842; three years later copper was found on Crown land near Burra Burra and colonists raised the money for a special survey so as to secure the copper lands. Two companies were formed; they operated profitably, and other companies were set up as experienced miners arrived from Cornwall and Germany. Before long hundreds of men and boys were working. In the late 1840s the value of minerals exported was greater than that of wheat and wool combined as the country's first mining boom developed.

South Australia's exports exceeded imports in value for the first time in 1848—a short-lived surplus, but an indication of the great strides the colony had made. After the early difficulties blighted the settlement, only one shipload of emigrants was sent from London even though sales of land in the colony had yielded more than £32,000 to the Emigration Fund, and by 1845 colonists were pressing for a full resumption of immigration—demands that were supported by Governors Grey and Robe.

Demands for labour in England were slackening, and from 1846 the number of assisted migrants reaching Adelaide from London rose sharply. Between 1847 and 1851 over 20,000 people were granted free or assisted passages from England under the provisions of the emigration fund, while nearly 4,000 came in from Germany, all with some form of assistance. Another 13,000 people, paying their own fares, arrived from Britain, and more than 12,000 moved in from neighbouring colonies. Over the same period there was also a considerable movement out of South Australia, but the five-year net gain of 30,000 new settlers helped lift the colony's population to 66,500 in 1851.

Although in 1842 there were no convicts in Western Australia, other basic standards tacitly set by the British government as prerequisites to the granting of representative institutions were still very far from attainment. These requirements were sufficiently advanced economic development and a sufficient revenue to support representative institutions. The part-official, part-nominee legislative council (first introduced in 1832) continued in operation. As in other colonies, wool appeared to offer the best prospects, but the difficulties of putting the colony on a wool economy were great. There had been wholesale desertion of livestock by shepherds and farm hands in the colony's early phase. Many sheep had wandered off, to be speared by Aborigines or die of thirst. Even the surviving flocks proved less profitable than their owners hoped. There was no available market for meat or skins, and transport and shipment of wool remained difficult and costly. The grass and scrubby herbage of most land afforded poor feed, carrying no more than a sheep to three or four acres, and some of the native plants were poisonous. Progress was slow; because of ignorance of local conditions, little had been done with the large areas under occupation.

It was 1842 before the number of sheep in the colony reached 60,000. The following year the fall in the price of wool came as a blow; but from this point sheep numbers began to rise steadily and the quality of wool improved as better sheep were introduced. By 1846 the Swan River colony was growing wool on a more substantial scale; nearly 300,000 pounds of wool was shipped—more than double the quantity of the previous year. Sheep numbered 141,000 when the colony's first official census was taken late in 1848, and 7,000 acres were being cropped, with almost half of the area under wheat.

Immigrants were still shunning the backward and isolated colony in the west; land sales brought in too little revenue for any appreciable numbers of assisted migrants to be brought into the colony and by 1848—almost twenty years after the first settlement—population was a mere 4,600. In addition to wool, there were some meagre exports—a few horses sent to India and cattle to Mauritius, whale products, and some timber and sandalwood—but the lack of population remained crippling. There were few properly cleared roads, no substantial public works, and little labour available for any task. There was a pressing need for labour to expand sheep-raising and for the government spending that had helped sustain New South Wales and Van Diemen's Land in their early years, and public opinion was behind the pastoralists who insisted that only the introduction of convict labour could get the colony on its feet.

In 1849 the legislative council petitioned that convicts should be sent to the colony. The British government was happy to oblige. An enabling order was published, and in June 1850 the first group of seventy-five convicts arrived at Fremantle. Thus the unfortunate Swan River colony reverted to the old dependence on convictism and government enterprise that the other colonies had outgrown.

Trial judge and jury had been introduced in 1837 when a civil court and a criminal court were established; improvement in social conditions generally had been slow, however. All during the 1840s educational facilities lagged; twelve new schools were opened in 1848, but as late as 1849 at least half the children went without schooling. Settlement was still confined to the south-west sector; and although by the late 1840s settlers had pushed out from Perth, they had generally found it necessary to keep close to the coast. There were some little pockets of settlement along the coast, and a few sheep stations inland. Encouraging discoveries of coal and lead were made, while exploration in the north-west revealed some useful pasture lands along the coastal rivers.

As elsewhere, the Aborigines took little or no part in activities. The native population in Western Australia was smaller in number, and generally the tribesmen were more docile than in most other parts of the continent; but as the tribal pattern of life was disturbed by occupation of land by the settlers, inevitably there were clashes which ended in the death of some Aborigines and the withdrawal of the tribe from the immediate area. In 1846 the first systematic attempt to help and educate the native people began when Benedictine missionaries arrived to found a monastery and mission at New Norcia, north of Perth.

In the eastern colonies, the quest for new pastures continued all through the 1840s. To the individual bent on securing a vast estate deeper inland, and spurred by the thought that land was there for the taking, the beckoning mirage that shimmered near the horizon could be a cruel lure; for the enticing "lake" with trees deceptively reflected in it moved back mockingly in step with the advancing pastoralist—just as his dreams might be shattered when streams dried up or flooded, or bushfires devastated the land on which he had settled with such high hopes. Yet for every man who pulled out, there were others eager to take his place. Always the drive was to secure more land, always the belief was that the new land would be better.

In 1840 pastoralists in South Australia subscribed to a fund to finance an exploration of a stock route along the shores of the Great Australian Bight, and Edward John Eyre (who at twenty-five had already undertaken exploration work in the interior of South Australia, discovering Lake Eyre) was chosen to lead the attempt. Setting out from Adelaide in January 1841, Eyre first struck north from Spencer Gulf in search of good pasture land, but he was soon driven back by heat and dryness. He then struck west—only to find himself in utterly desolate country and constantly in difficulty because of shortage of water and provisions. He sent three of his party back to Adelaide and pushed on with his foreman and three Aborigines, hoping that his eleven remaining packhorses could carry sufficient water and food to get the small group to Albany.

It was an exhausting journey as for months the little band toiled slowly along the waterless shoreline. Then Eyre's companion was speared by Aborigines, who took a quantity of provisions, leaving Eyre alone with one faithful Aborigine. The two struggled on across the desolate terrain, and after receiving some stores from a French whaler anchored near Esperance they were able to complete their journey in July. Eyre's great feat of endurance and courage—perhaps the most remarkable in the annals of Australian exploration—had no useful result except the negative one of showing that practically no good land existed anywhere along the Bight coastal area. Western Australia was still practically cut off from land communications with the eastern colonies.

As the quest for new pastures continued unabated in the eastern colonies, settlement was spreading over the inland plains. In New South Wales there were hundreds of stations scattered in the interior, with an average of ten or twelve people on each. The main drive was now northward as sheepmen worked their way along the western slopes of the main range. Squatters in the rich Darling Downs district forced the government's hand in the same way as in Port Phillip a few years before.

The first squatter, David Leslie, took up a run on the Darling Downs in 1840, and so many others followed that in 1842 Governor Gipps removed the ban on free settlers in the Moreton Bay area, sent in a survey team, and opened the area for pastoral occupation by licences, as in the other squatting districts of New South Wales. By 1844 there were seventeen large stations in the Moreton Bay area and twenty-six on the Darling Downs; the total number of sheep in these areas exceeded 180,000, and 13,000 cattle were grazed. During the pastoral depression, many sheepmen drove deeper into the hinterland, hoping to ease their difficulties by the acquisition of more land. The coastal runs were soon given over to cattle, while in the inland areas the sheep remained and slowly flockmasters moved north towards the tropics.

At this time there were fifteen official squatting districts extending in a great arc from the Glenelg River through Port Phillip, Bathurst, and Sydney, well to the north of Brisbane. In some of the areas already taken up by pastoralists, droughts and seasonal variability of rainfall were already causing concern. Early promise was not always fulfilled. It was natural to assume that good tracts of land could be found in the unknown interior. The North American continent seemed an enticing example of how fertile and well watered land might be found to extend far and wide; but Australia's basic geography was still unknown. The pastoralists—and even the explorers—who had helped open up the fertile south-eastern crescent of the continent buoyed their hopes in the expectation that unexplored regions would contain equally valuable land. However, the New South Wales Surveyor-General, Sir Thomas Mitchell, considered that unless exceptionally fertile land was found, expansion beyond the existing limits of pastoral occupation was not warranted. Mitchell's probing journeys into the interior, and those of Sturt and Eyre, had convinced him that good pastoral land was not likely to be found farther inland, and that only towards the Gulf of Carpentaria was further expansion feasible.

The idea of seeking new pastoral lands in the vast unknown areas excited a young German botanist, Ludwig Leichhardt, who had come to Australia in 1842 in the hope of finding employment as a naturalist in an exploring party. In 1843 Leichhardt travelled alone for 600 miles through settled areas on a trip from the Newcastle district to Brisbane; and he then made a number of shorter excursions inland during which he learnt of the interest of pastoralists in opening up the remote and unknown northern lands. Money was raised, and in August 1844 he set out in command of an overland expedition to cover almost 3,000 miles of uncharted country in the tropics. From the Darling Downs he moved north along the general line of the highlands, struck north-west from the Burdekin River, then skirted the head of the Gulf of Carpentaria, finally pushing along its western shore to the Roper River and on to Port Essington, his objective. The journey had taken nearly fifteen months, and many major streams had been discovered. Some good areas had been traversed which gave some promise of settlement.

As Leichhardt was leaving the Darling Downs in August 1844, Charles Sturt was setting off from Adelaide with a sixteen-man expedition which was to strike deep into the continent in the hopeful search for "a large body of inland waters." Sturt moved north along the Darling, following it to Menindee, then struck north-west across arid country to the Barrier Range. Here, trapped by appalling summer heat and debilitated by the general conditions, the party was forced to remain for six months (January-July 1845). Sturt decided to send most of the party back to Adelaide in order to save provisions; but when James Poole, his second in command who was to lead the group, died of scurvy, this plan was dropped. Instead, the expedition pressed on, striking north and then probing westward as it moved through a progressively more desolate area until it ran up against a salt-encrusted lake. Returning to the depot he had established in better-grassed country, Sturt with a small party moved north and then north-west. Sturt soon found himself in a stony desert covered with gibber scatter—"that iron region," as he described it—where occasional sandhills thrust above the barren surface. He wrote in his diary:

> It was not until we had run down every creek in our neighbourhood, and had traversed the country in every direction, that the truth flashed across my mind, and it became evident to me, that we were locked up in the desolate and heated region into which we had penetrated, as effectively as if we had wintered at the Pole.

In September Sturt reached his farthest point; he was in the heart of the Simpson Desert, and could proceed no further. His depot was over 440 miles away, and the tattered party barely struggled back to it.

Still unwilling to accept defeat, Sturt struck out once more, this time due north, but again the desolation was unrelieved. Returning across the stony desert, he discovered Cooper's Creek; he followed the watercourse eastward in the hope of finding better land, only to be confronted with unbearable conditions as desert temperatures soared with the onset of summer. By this time Sturt himself was at the point of collapse, and he decided to withdraw southward, by way of the Darling. It was January 19, 1846, when the party reached Adelaide after travelling more than 3,000 miles through unknown country. In spite of the tenacity and the daring shown by Sturt and his party, no good land had been found, and the theory of an inland sea had been exploded. Instead, the expedition had revealed a seemingly impenetrable barrier of desolation deep in the interior.

Mitchell, meanwhile, had been able to start his own exploration into the northern area. With a party of thirty-two he crossed the Macquarie and Barwon and reached the Condamine. A messenger from Sydney brought news of Leichhardt's success in reaching Port Essington and of the discoveries he had made. Moving on, Mitchell passed into the fertile Maranoa region, then crossed several streams flowing south-west. Mitchell now turned westward and the sight of a stream flowing north-west excited him as it gave support to his belief that a major river would be found running from the central area to the Gulf of Carpentaria. He named the river the Victoria, and returned to Sydney.

When Edmund Besley Kennedy was sent to trace the Victoria's course in March 1847, he found that it veered to the southwest and was in fact the Barcoo, a tributary of Cooper's Creek. The hopes that Mitchell had held for a great northward-flowing stream were shattered.

Meanwhile, Leichhardt had not been idle. He was capitalizing on the extravagant claims that had been aired about the discoveries made on the 1844 journey. His journal, when it was published, gave emphasis to the "extensive tracts of fertile country, watered by several large rivers" that had been traversed. The Geographical Society of London had awarded its medal to Leichhardt, and in a widely quoted speech to the society Lord Colchester had enlarged upon the significance of the venture. Lord Colchester described Leichhardt's 1,800 mile journey through a country previously altogether unknown, as having been "prosecuted with almost unexampled perseverance, and crowned with the most complete success," and declared that it opened to the settler in Australia

> ... new and extensive fields of enterprise, and connecting the remote settlements of New South Wales with a secure port on the confines of the Indian Archipelago, thus avoiding the circuitous and dangerous navigation through Torres Strait.

When Leichhardt sought support for his second expedition, funds were freely contributed. He had become a notable figure, and when he set off from the Darling Downs in December 1846 to cross the northern sector of the continent from east to west on a course somewhat south of the Tropic of Capricorn, he and his supporters had high hopes. But after eight months afield he returned, defeated; he had failed to travel more than 500 miles.

Undaunted, he prepared to make a second attempt to cross the continent, this time starting from Brisbane, westward through the Darling Downs. No really deep penetration of the continent had been made up to this time: the experienced Sturt—the pioneer explorer of the desert interior—had been driven back from the desolation of the stony desert between Cooper's Creek and the Diamantina in 1844, and Leichhardt was far less well equipped than Sturt, whether by knowledge, ability, or temperament, for such an exacting enterprise as he had embarked upon. He and his party of six, two of them Aborigines, struck westward from the outermost station (near Roma) early in April 1848. He wrote his last letter on April 4. From that time all trace of the party was lost, and its fate was to remain a mystery.

Various aspects of land policy came to the fore in the opening round of political activity in the new Legislative Council of New South Wales, which met for the first time in 1843. Land matters were dear to the hearts of the sheepmen who, as a direct result of the property qualifications for council membership and voting and the greater number of rural electorates, predominated in the two-thirds elective council, and it was inevitable that matters related to land disposal would provide the main political issues. Wool was the colony's great economic driving force, and sheep numbers were doubling every four or five years.

The pastoral industry was still regulated by the system of squatting licences, the squatter paying an annual licence of £10, no matter how large or small his run was, plus an agistment fee based on the number of stock grazed. This system had given the squatters more recognition than they had had in the past, but they had no real security since the licence gave them tenure over the land for a single year only. Without security of tenure, the squatter was disinclined to spend money to improve his run. The only form of building he was prepared to put up was a simple hut for himself and his overseer, and bark huts for the shepherds and stockmen. The squatters' demand was for security of tenure, with pre-emptive rights, and compensation for improvements if the land were bought by someone else. The real interests of squatters and landowners differed to a certain extent; but most landowners pastured some of their stock on squatting leases, so that the squatters' demands were favoured by most of the landowners also. Whatever the status of their holdings, both groups were essentially sheepmen, producing the real wealth of the colony, so that their claim to security could not be brushed aside.

The terms and operation of the Imperial Waste Lands Act of 1842 provided a source of irritation for most sections of the community. The minimum price of £1 an acre for sale of Crown land was regarded as too high; landowners and squatters argued that land for grazing was not worth anything like that sum; that a high price would result in less land being sold, which would mean a slackening in the rate of assisted immigration, as well as discouraging the import of capital from England; even the great depression of the early 1840s was blamed on the £1 minimum price. Many of the new immigrants of the radical working class attacked the £1 minimum price from a different standpoint; they saw it as an impassable barrier to fulfilment of their belief that there should be land for everyone in a new, vast, almost empty country. In 1843 these unenfranchised immigrants set up a Mutual Protection Association, one of whose aims was a return to the system of free land grants on a community settlement basis; but the association was short-lived, and its members had no influence on events. The objective of securing land remained impracticable for men without capital.

Though their economic grievances were uppermost, the sheepmen were fundamentally opposed to the whole system by which land policy in general, and especially the land fund, remained under the control of the British government, through its representative the governor, instead of coming under the authority of their elected representatives in the legislative council.

The governor was empowered by the British government to spend half the money on assisting immigration, and the other half on various administrative matters including the care of Aborigines. Only the unspent surplus of the fund, if any, was paid into the general revenue, which was controlled by the council. The revenue from pastoral licences and the stock tax was withheld from the council's control in the same way. This situation could be considered a case of taxation without representation, thus giving the landholders' demand to control land policy in their own interests a basis of theroretical principles, and tying their demand for greater economic security with the demand for colonial self-government as a matter of principle.

The pastoral and business depression of the early 1840s aggravated the pastoralists' grievances; while the depression lasted, payment of any licence fee was felt by many as a hardship.

Governor Sir George Gipps hoped to settle the land question once and for all. He favoured letting the squatters occupy and use pastoral land on the easiest terms, but was against giving them any freehold rights over such land unless they paid the normal price for it. He considered that the setting of a high minimum price for sale of Crown land was beneficial, since this prevented the premature alienation of land as yet valuable only as pasture, but which might be capable of more intensive development at some later period. He favoured the retention of such land by the Crown in trust for the future. In a dispatch to the Secretary of State in January, 1844, Gipps wrote:

> It seems to be premature to pronounce that land in Australia is valuable only with reference to its capacity for feeding sheep; and I see no reason to conclude that the proprietor of sheep that are fed upon any land, ought to be the proprietor also of the land itself. If indeed settlers were positively prohibited or effectively precluded from depasturing their stock on Crown lands without purchasing them, then there would be reason to demand that the price of Crown land should be reduced; but so long as the present system is followed which permits the occupation of Crown lands upon easy terms, the demand for a reduction in the price of them cannot in my opinion be supported. . . . It is undoubtedly very much to be desired that the colonists and even the squatters should possess a fixed interest in some portion of the lands they occupy, for otherwise they will have no inducement to improve them; but it is in my opinion, by no means desirable for them to become the proprietors of extensive tracts of land which they have no means whatever of improving. A high minimum price acts as an inhibition on the sale of land that is not worth improving.

Accordingly Gipps worked out a policy which would serve the dual purposes of raising revenue (with which to continue the policy of assisted immigration), and helping the sheepmen to secure their lands—but only on terms that would safeguard the interests of future generations. Under his proposed occupation regulations, published in April 1844, each £10 pastoral licence was to cover one run only, a run being defined for these purposes as an area of not more than 20 square miles. If a run carried more than 4,000 sheep, the amount of the licence would be increased by £1 for each additional 1,000 sheep over the 4,000. The regulations were not to come into operation for fifteen months, to allow time for full recovery from the depression.

There was a lapse of six weeks between issue of these proposals and publication of a set of associated regulations covering land purchase. Under these regulations, purchase of the homestead and 320 acres of the run, at the fixed price of £1 an acre, would give the squatter undisputed possession of the whole of the run for the next eight years; at the end of this period he could buy an additional 320 acres, which would continue his rights over the rest of the run, and so on until he had bought the whole of the run. If the squatter was unwilling or unable to buy the land at the end of each eight year period, it could be sold at auction, the original squatter receiving compensation for the value of any improvements he had made. This whole system of compulsory purchase by instalments was not to be put into operation until a run had been occupied for five years.

The two sets of regulations, taken together, presented a real threat to the larger squatters. A squatter occupying a run of 20 square miles could obtain his homestead and security of tenure for his whole run by annual instalments which worked out at an average of £40 a year, which was reasonable enough. However, the large squatters, if they wanted to keep the whole of their runs—amounting, in some cases, to as much as 1,000 square miles, or the equivalent of fifty runs in terms of the new occupation regulations—would have to pay considerably more. Disturbed by recent sharp fluctuations in wool prices, the pastoralists were looking for concessions, not new burdens, and all were prepared to make common cause against Gipps. The governor was an able adminsistrator but he was no politician; he considered that his position lifted him above political manoeuverings, and he made no attempt to get colonial backing for his proposals. He was content to demolish the arguments of his opponents in dispatches to the Secretary of State—but he underestimated the strength which their silent supporters, the sheep, gave to their pleadings, for even his most lucid dispatches could not overcome the basic facts of economic geography and land use in a pastoral economy.

It was the large squatters who led the bitter, widespread, and extremely well-organized opposition to the Governor's proposals. Most violent of them was Benjamin Boyd, representative of an English investment company, who had bought up so many properties during the depression that his combined squatting holdings covered some 1,200 square miles; he expressed the extreme and obviously untenable view that payment of a single £10 annual licence fee should give him freehold rights over this whole area, and demanded that squatting leases should be for twenty-one years. A leader with a less extreme viewpoint was William Charles Wentworth, now one of the elected legislative councillors for Sydney, whose combined squatting holdings totalled about 400 square miles. Boyd was chairman of the Pastoralists' Protection Association formed to fight the governor's proposals. The association carried on an anti-Gipps campaign in the press and at public meetings with a virulence that recalled the attacks on Governor Darling some fifteen years before: there was even talk of "Blighing" Gipps.

The main battleground was not in Sydney but in London. The legislative council, two-thirds of whose members belonged to the Pastoral Association, appointed a parliamentary agent to represent their interests, as distinct from those of the governor, in London. The demands of the pastoralists were supported by strong pressure from their allies the English wool importers manufacturers, textile exporters, shipping, and banking firms, all of which had a strong interest in opposing any measures that might result in lower wool production; a memorial from these interests favoured twenty-one year squatting licences. The Colonical Office had at first approved of Gipps' proposals, but Earl Grey bowed to the mounting pressures; Gipps' proposals were shelved, the governor resigned, and the British parliament soon afterwards passed legislation for licensing and purchase of pastoral land on terms that represented sweeping concessions to the squatters.

The Imperial Waste Lands Act of 1846, which came into force in the colony as the orders in council of 1847, divided pastoral land in New South Wales into three classes: in the settled districts, near towns and the coast, a pastoral lease had to be renewed annually; in the rather more populated "intermediate" pastoral districts, leases were for eight years; land here could be auctioned at the end of each year, the lessee having an option and receiving compensation for improvements if the land was sold to someone else; in the outback squatting lands, leases were for fourteen years, during which the lessee was the only one able to purchase the land. The minimum rental or licence fee in all districts was to be £10 per annum for a carrying capacity of 4,000 sheep, plus 50/– for every additional 1,000 sheep grazed.

Some of the results arising from the new regulations were described by one squatter, W.A. Brodribb, who pointed out attendant social benefits as well as economic gains:

> A new era [had] dawned upon the colony. The squatters commenced to erect permanent improvements on the squattages and they pushed farther into the interior, and occupied new country for their surplus stock. . . . In travelling through the far interior hundreds of miles from Sydney or Melbourne, the traveller would meet highly respectable ladies with their families located on their squattages in comfortable houses very happy and contented.

Less favourable effects were to be found in the speculation which followed the 1847 regulations, and in the merging of holdings into immense properties as a result of purchase for resale. Frequently the land fell to the control of absentee proprietors and mortgage holders, and the properties were held with a minimum of people working on them, at least in the outer districts. One of the results was the locking-up of the land in large estates held by a comparatively few people; a struggle to "unlock the lands" was to follow.

Similar legislation was brought into effect in Western Australia, where it resulted in a considerable amount of new grazing land being opened up. In South Australia, where the farmers and not pastoralists were in the ascendancy, and where climatic conditions made large areas eminently suitable for wheatgrowing, the orders in council of 1847 were not applied; instead the 1842 rules, under which squatters had to renew licences annually, remained until new pastoral regulations were issued in 1850. Under the revised regulations, in the areas "outside the hundreds" occupation leases for terms of up to fourteen years were granted, the rental being either 10/– or 15/– per square mile according to the quality of the run. Within the "hundreds" (where land had been surveyed and originally offered in 80-acre sections), licences were granted only on a year-to-year basis, at a rate of £1 per square mile. The governor reserved the right of proclaiming additional hundreds for division and sale at any time, and lessees whose runs were resumed were then to receive adequate compensation. These conditions, less conciliatory to the pastoralists than those applying in New South Wales, helped limit the growth of large estates in South Australia as compared with New South Wales and the two colonies—Victoria and Queensland—which were later carved out of the mother-colony.

Wondrous gold   9

Sheep flocks in the Australian colonies had multiplied to number more than 15,000,000 head when into the scene of active pastoral development suddenly came a new and startling factor: gold. The yellow metal lay hidden in the hills and valleys of the coastal ranges, and when the extent of the wealth in New South Wales and Victoria was revealed, the effect was dramatic. From all corners of the world people came flocking in, anxious to win some of the fabulous riches. In the decade ended December 1850, the population of all the Australian settlements had risen from 190,000 to 405,000; but the rush of people to the empty continent between 1851 and 1860 brought the astonishing increase of 740,000, so that by the end of 1860 the population exceeded 1,144,000—or nearly three times what it was ten years before. Thus the course of events was sharply changed as an amazingly rich source of immediate wealth was uncovered.

Long before the wonderful discoveries of the 1850s, small quantities of gold had come to light. As early as 1823 a government surveyor reported the discovery of alluvial gold in Fish River, in the Bathurst district, west of Sydney. The question of rights to minerals discovered was not covered in early land grants, but in 1828 the British government announced its intention to reserve to itself all gold and silver, and the land regulations of 1831 contained a statement that in all grants the Crown would reserve to itself "all mines of gold, silver and coals." Encouraging observations regarding minerals were made in 1839 by the Polish explorer, Count Paul Strzelecki, when he crossed the ranges and made the first discovery of eastern Gippsland in the far south-east of the continent. Although Strzelecki noticed particles of gold, at the time he recorded this discovery as being more of "a mineralogical curiosity than an economic element of value." The general prospect of mineral wealth was noted by Strzelecki, and he considered that the country probably contained gold, silver, and iron as well as valuable clays, coal, lime, serpentine, and earthy salts.

When he went to London in 1844 Strzelecki took with him some rock specimens he had collected on his journeys. These specimens proved of such interest that public discussion was aroused in London, and the eminent geologist Sir Roderick Impey Murchison suggested that the ranges of south-eastern Australia might be rich in minerals including gold. Murchison proposed that a mineral survey might profitably be undertaken; but the Colonial Office was not prepared to launch so costly a project in far off New South Wales on the available evidence.

Reverend William Clarke, who was a capable geologist, unearthed some gold in the Lithgow area in 1841 and followed this with other discoveries. He reported his casual finds and, although he did not believe he had found payable gold, in 1847 he wrote to the *Sydney Morning Herald* to say that he believed there was gold in quartz veins and pyrites in the Bathurst district.

Others who chanced upon gold did not report their finds. If a shepherd came across an isolated piece of gold in a creek bed or where the soil had been disturbed, he probably pocketed his find and said nothing about it. The discoveries that were made were accidental, and they were made mainly by shepherds. The fortunate finders did not wash for gold; rather they chanced upon it, or noticed it as tiny specks in quartz which they thought had no commercial value. One of the consistent finders was a shepherd named McGregor who from the mid-1840s quietly worked a legendary reef in the Wellington district, 250 miles west of Sydney.

Random discoveries continued throughout the 1840s, both on the mainland and in Van Diemen's Land. As hilly land around Melbourne was occupied, fragments of gold were occasionally unearthed. In 1847 a shepherd found some gold exposed among the roots of a tree blown down in a storm, and in 1848 and 1849 Melbourne goldsmiths were offered other pieces of gold found in similarly chance fashion—in a newly dug post-hole, in gravel near a creek, or lying partly uncovered in the topsoil where sheep were grazed. Those who found gold in this way were not inclined to pursue the search by digging; nor were they likely to discuss it with anyone. Rights to ownership of such gold were not clearly defined. The working man might think that the gold belonged to his employer, or at any rate feel that his master would be sure to claim it. An old legal maxim held that all gold or silver, wherever found, belonged to the Crown, and as any discoveries were in fact made on land owned by the Crown and leased to the holder, the shepherd or working man was in a weak position if he revealed his find.

Varying conditions as to restrictions on rights to minerals had been laid down in the series of regulations relating to the disposal of land in New South Wales and Van Diemen's Land. The provisions of the 1831 land regulations reserving to the Crown all gold, silver, and coal were operative in all land sales over the next decade. The regulations issued under the Imperial Waste Land Act of 1842 provided that in addition to coal "precious minerals and metals may also be reserved, if it be known that they greatly abound in any district, but not otherwise." It was because of the irregularity in the conditions of land disposal that Sir Roderick Murchison wrote to Earl Grey in 1848, to point out that a search for gold in Australia was not being undertaken because it was known that precious metals "necessarily lapse to the Crown."

Murchison's examination of Strzelecki's rock specimens made him feel optimistic that gold would be found. He pointed out the similarity the specimens bore to the auriferous rocks of the Ural Mountains; his associate at the Imperial Academy of St Petersburg had suggested that a careful search for gold in the Australian mountains would most probably lead to its detection in abundance. By the late 1840s Murchison's remarks were being noted in Australia; one who was interested in them was a landholder, W. J. Smith, who in 1849 forwarded to the Colonial Secretary a lump of gold embedded in quartz, offering to disclose the place where it was found if the government paid him a reward in advance. The offer was not accepted.

By this time, and before any concerted effort was made to test theories that the eastern ranges of Australia were rich in gold, the gold fever in California had diverted attention. News of the Californian strikes reached Australia late in 1848 and was greeted with some scepticism. Once it had been confirmed, however, there was an outbreak of gold-rush fever. In January 1849 eight ships carrying gold-seekers left Sydney, the forerunners of a wave of emigration which by mid-1850 was to take thousands of men to join the rush to the goldfields of central California. Among those who emigrated were a number of bounty immigrants, to the great disgust of members of the legislative council, who suggested that the immigrants should refund part of their passage money.

With those who joined in the trans-Pacific exodus was Edward Hargraves, owner of a sheep property on the Bathurst plains. His purpose was to study the nature of gold-yielding land in California—and what he saw there convinced him that the lands west of Sydney, where traces of gold had already been found, would indeed yield great wealth. On March 5, 1850, he wrote from San Francisco to a friend in Sydney, to report that he was "very forcibly impressed" from his observation that he had in fact been in a gold-bearing region in New South Wales.

Hargraves decided to return to New South Wales without delay and to begin a search in earnest, armed with knowledge of the Californian methods of panning and cradling for gold. Back in Sydney, he at once set off for Wellington, staying overnight at Lister's hotel in Guyong (15 miles beyond Bathurst). From the publican he picked up news of finds made by shepherds and others in the district; in the hotel he found that almost "every mantelpiece was crowded with specimens of ore." Hargraves decided to stay on in Guyong and prospect in the area; he enlisted the help of the publican's son and together they found a spot where panning soon yielded a few specks of gold. Hargraves then rode on to Wellington, but in spite of his high hopes he was unsuccessful there.

Hargraves realized that other searchers might follow his example; he wanted to forestall any miner from California who might make a similar discovery, so he hurried back to Sydney so that he would be able to collect a reward he expected from the government. In March 1851 he informed the Colonial Secretary, Edward Deas Thomson, that he had found pieces of gold over a wide area and showed him the specks of gold that had been unearthed. After a lengthy interview it was agreed that Hargraves would set down the terms on which he was prepared to reveal the gold-bearing area. "If this is gold country, Mr Hargraves, it will stop emigration to California—but it comes on us like a clap of thunder, and we are scarcely prepared to credit it," Deas Thomson said. Deas Thomson was unconvinced, however, and he decided to await a report from the government geologist before committing himself concerning a reward for Hargraves's discoveries.

The gold was there, in spite of the colonial official's hesitancy. In April Hargraves was informed that his erstwhile prospecting companion, young John Lister, had found a good 4 ounces of gold where the two had previously panned less successfully; he rode back to Guyong and bought the specimens, which he sent immediately to the colonial secretary. Hargraves was then taken to a secret new field deep in the hills which he named Ophir; the spot was 10 miles north-east of Orange. Here he issued the two discoverers of the field with a paper "authorizing" them to dig for gold. Shortly afterwards, the Government Geologist, Samuel Stutchbury, arrived at Ophir; in his presence Hargraves panned 21 grains of fine gold from a single washing. Hargraves then went on to wash several baskets of earth, and specks of the yellow metal appeared in each.

Stutchbury accepted this as evidence that Hargraves' undertaking had been fulfilled, and he signed the interim report to this effect which went forward to the governor so that Hargraves might collect his reward. His initial report reached Sydney on May 17; a few days later a fuller report arrived confirming the richness of the field. Before the government knew what was happening a small rush to Ophir was under way. There was confusion about how to control the situation. It was thought prudent to issue a proclamation threatening prosecution to all who mined gold without authority, but the governor still required legal opinion on the validity of such a step. A goldfield had not been discovered in a British country before; all that could be done was to enforce the Crown's right under common law to all gold mines and to threaten to prosecute all who searched for gold without permission. Governor Sir Charles FitzRoy, realizing that a rush was inevitable, turned his attention to ways in which some meausre of control might be invoked.

In California, where the state did not make any claim to ownership of minerals, the mere pegging out of a miner's claim (and the recording of it) was generally recognized as giving the holder rights to any minerals discovered by him. (In California, for the first time in history, the "Crown" or its equivalent had not made a claim to minerals uncovered; in Mexico and Peru the Crown had automatically taken the largest share.) Generally to gain rights on the Californian goldfields, a simple fee of $1 was payable for registration of every claim before the Recorder of the district. Stiffer levies were made on a regular basis on the Chinese, Mexicans, and other "undesirables," however; the impost was intended as a deterrent and was virtually in the form of a head tax, reducing the number of non-whites on the goldfields. Hargraves reported to the colonial secretary that the California" licence system worked well, and he advocated a general monthly licence fee for all miners. Governor FitzRoy decided to adopt a licensing procedure in New South Wales; it was a convenient way in which some limitation might be placed on the searchers. For a monthly fee of 30/-, any licence holder was granted rights of ownership to whatever gold he was able to unearth.

News of the Ophir discovery soon spread. In the Bathurst district itself the effect was immediate. Some looked on in horror as the great exodus took place to the diggings. A few speculated on the social and economic consequences of an Australian gold rush. The Commissioner for Lands in the Bathurst district itself was the first to express concern. He sent off a letter to the governor suggesting that Hargraves' activities called for "stringent measures" designed to restrain the labouring classes from leaving their employment tending sheep. His plea was in vain. The governor would have been hard put to it to restrain the activity, even if he had wished to do so. For several days the business in the town was utterly paralysed as people dashed off to Ophir or Summerhill Creek, now equally rewarding to the lucky. The Bathurst *Free Press* reported that "a complete mental madness appears to have seized almost every member of the community," and that there had been an almost universal rush to the diggings. Soon hundreds of men were at work panning or cradling for gold.

Sydney newspapers were carrying similar reports, and the excitement was spreading. An experienced Californian miner was soon at work and, according to the *Sydney Morning Herald*, several magistrates were "plying their picks and cradles most laboriously." Only the approach of winter seemed likely to do "something towards cooling the ardour of the excited multitude," the newspaper noted; but there seemed little hope that the excitement would ever end and the report foretold "the probability of a complete social revolution in the course of time."

In Melbourne, news of the Bathurst discoveries caused an immediate furore. Within a week of the first report being published in Melbourne, on May 21, 1851, every ship leaving for Sydney carried away a band of gold-seekers—civil servants, lawyers, clerks, plicemen, soldiers, and even doctors, all keen to join the throngs converging from the open lands and from the towns and cities. They set off to cross the Blue Mountains in search of El Dorado—

... new-made miners from every quarter, some armed with picks, others shouldering crowbars and shovels and not a few strung around with wash-hand basins, tin pots, and collenders, garden and agricultural instruments of every variety

—according to a newspaper reporter who watched the throng arrive in Bathurst. The report from the *Sydney Morning Herald*'s correspondent in Bathurst told how

. . . people of all trades, callings, and pursuits were quickly transformed into miners, and many a hand that had been trained to kid gloves or accustomed to wield nothing heavier than the grey goose quill became nervous to clutch the pick and crowbar or "rock the cradle" at our infant mines. The blacksmiths of the town could not turn off the picks fast enough, and the manufacture of cradles was the second biggest business of the place.

Correspondents from other towns hundreds of miles away had the same story as the hopeful gold-seekers converged on Bathurst. The *Herald*'s correspondent in Goulburn reported on June 7:

> Goulburn presented a most exciting appearance by the departure of seventy of our townsmen, principally mechanics, who left thus for the gold regions; there were six teams laden with plenty of horsepower. . . . This is the third batch that has left and a fourth goes on Friday. The town will in a few days be completely deserted.

Melbourne was not prepared to allow the great exodus to go unchallenged. Activity was all but paralysed as more and more people left. Melbourne's prosperous business community urged that a committee be set up to offer a reward for the discovery of gold in the district. A committee appointed by the mayor early in June reported that there was undoubted evidence of gold-bearing rocks; a reward was offered for a substantial discovery within 200 miles of Melbourne.

The hunt for gold was now on in earnest. First news of payable gold came in mid-July after James Esmond unearthed a small quantity of gold near Clunes; the discovery did not qualify for the bounty but it added a new element to the wild excitement that gripped Melbourne when news arrived of the granting of self-government to the newly created colony of Victoria. Rejoicing over gold blended with the celebration of "glorious separation." On July 29, a group of prospectors found specks of gold in a dish being panned in a small stream less than 20 miles from Melbourne; the creek was dammed and within a few hours forty pieces, some the size of marbles, came to light. News of this discovery spread quickly, and a minor rush began. In August a more notable discovery was made in the Buninyong area near Ballarat, 70 miles or so from Melbourne.

Elsewhere a fantastic treasure-house was beginning to unfold. Wherever men looked, it seemed, gold lay waiting for them along the arc of hills west, north-west, and north of Melbourne. The goldfields were at the very back door of the prosperous little city. Here, for the lucky ones, was the wealth of an Aladdin's cave awaiting finders.

In some places the gold was found in small round lumps, with now and then some larger pieces, but mostly the glittering harvest was gathered as tiny specks, scarcely perceptible to the eye until the gravel was washed away in pans or cradle. On some fields gold could be won both by simply skimming off a thin layer of gravel from the hill cover or by digging, in which the miner might go down 6, 10, or even 40 feet, near streams or between hills. Sometimes the gold lay spread beneath the surface in an array like that in a jeweller's showcase. Shepherds and farm hands rushed to the diggings; tradesmen left their jobs, bought picks and shovels, and hurried off to Ballarat, Castlemaine, or Bendigo. The fabulous strikes were already attracting attention in other lands, and people were pouring in.

London newspapers had first reported the Bathurst finds in September, and their attention was sustained as shipments of gold arrived at English ports. Satisfied that the seemingly incredible stories of tremendous finds were indeed true, *The Times* was able to declare with enthusiasm and some satisfaction, "We have a California of our own."

Soon the Victorian fields were outstripping those of California—for in the Victorian ranges lay hidden the world's most wondrous stores of easily won gold. In size and abundance of nuggets and in the accessibility of their riches, these fields were unique. Within a few months the number of licences granted to miners exceeded 12,000. A gold escort that reached Melbourne late in November 1851 brought in no less than half a ton of gold. Reports of men digging up gold in great lumps punctuated the activity. One man unearthed 12 lb. in two days, another 30 lb. in a single hour. Scenes like the encampment of armies were common. An eyewitness of the events at Ballarat declared that gold was "actually oozing from the earth." Describing the mine workings as a "honeycomb of holes," he said of Ballarat:

> The whole place swarmed with men; some at work in the pits; others carrying down the auriferous earth to be washed in the creek—in wheelbarrows, hand barrows, sacks, and tin dishes in their hands; in some of the holes I even saw men digging out bits of gold with a table knife.
>
> Busy as this scene was, I think the scene at the creek was busier. Both banks for half a mile were lined with men hard at work washing the earth in cradles. Each cradle employs three men; and all the cradles are placed close to one another, at intervals of not more than a yard. The noise produced by the incessant "rock-rock" of these cradles was like that of an immense factory.

Newspapers teemed with reports of the goldfield activities, and more and more men left for the diggings. The Victorian fields were yielding ten times as much gold as those of New South Wales. By the end of 1851 more than £1,000,000 had been won. Governor La Trobe caught the air of excitement in a dispatch sent late in December 1851, in which he said:

> Judging from the general prevalence of the geological formation in which the gold has hitherto been found so abundantly over the whole length and breadth of the colony, I can contemplate no limit to the discoveries, or to the results of the new fields.

La Trobe noted that the gold secured from the Mount Alexander fields was calculated by hundredweights and arrived in the cities at the rate of probably two tons a week. He estimated that 20,000 individuals were congregated at the four fields in the area. No less optimistic, the Chief Gold Commissioner injected an enthusiastic note into his official report when he said he could at present see no limit to the number of people that might be employed.

In many parts of Victoria, and in the other colonies, business came virtually to a standstill. Little communities melted away. To sheep-owners left without labour, the exodus was a calamity worse than drought or deluge. Men were reported to be earning wonderful wages at the fields, and no one could be induced to remain at humdrum tasks. In Melbourne, with quarrymen and dray drivers absent, prison authorities could not find stone for prisoners to break. For lack of a stable hand, Governor La Trobe had to groom his own horse and feed it.

Conditions elsewhere were no different. Lady Denison, wife of the governor of Van Diemen's Land, noted in her diary on January 25, 1852:

> Such numbers are gone to the diggings that it now becomes scarcely possible to get anything done here; if you happen to break or injure any of your goods and chattels, broken they must remain, for there is nobody left in the upholsterers' shops to mend them . . . . Archdeacon D. told me that the other day he found himself obliged to lay the cloth while Mrs D. cooked the dinner, every servant having gone. . . . The Bishop, who keeps a little yacht, has no longer a man left to take care of it; so he absolutely now paddles himself off to the yacht every night and sleeps on board and paddles back in the morning. He does it, I suppose, because he had already had one yacht stolen by some prisoners, who went off in it to California; but if another set should want to do the same, I do not see how he alone could hinder them, and they might carry off both yacht and Bishop.

The world continued to hear of the amazing treasure hunt taking place in the Australian bush. In the London weekly *Household Words*, the editor, Charles Dickens, wrote in July 1852 of the rush of "tens of thousands of Englishmen" who were off to the diggings

> . . . as fast as sailing ships and steam vessels can carry them to join the Golden Fair in Australia: the great South Land. There has not been such an exodus from London within the recollection of the oldest shipbrokers. . . . I cannot say how many youths at the Customs House and the Docks have drawn their last quarter's salary and now are expending the amounts on Guernsey shirts, canvas trousers, American boots and wide-awakes.

Dickens went on to report "the struggling and elbowing and beseeching for passages" that went on from ten o'clock each morning until six in the evening; two or three clerks took down the names of applicants as all day long the names of eager emigrants were posted in huge books. Trade was following the new settlers to Australia, and Dickens noted that every alternate shop near the London docks seemed to have been suddenly converted into an outfitting warehouse.

> What a sight there was upon the jetty! I could have fancied the whole export trade of the country had gone stark staring mad with the gold fever and had plunged out of bed and rushed down to the Docks. Boxes and cases, cartwheels, barrows, casks and barrels, ploughs, crates and bales were all lying about in wild disorder looking as though they would require a couple of years and a small army of labourers to stow them away.

Even prisoners in the hulks at Woolwich were affected by the reports that filtered through to them, according to a story in the *Illustrated London News*:

> It would appear as though the news of the gold discoveries have penetrated to

the wretched inmates of the hulks who have been sentenced to the penalty of transportation. . . . They have risen *en masse* aboard the *Warrior* at Woolwich and, armed with knives and other weapons, have mustered together in one part of the ship in a body numbering upwards of one hundred, and demanded to be immediately conveyed to the 'diggings.'

The chief grievance of the convicts was reported to be retention in England instead of being sent to Australia! Just a few days later the *Sydney Morning Herald* carried a report from London that another of the rumours current was that the Rothschilds were going to open a bank in New South Wales.

The torrent of gold was astonishing alike to Paris and London, and alike to Threadneedle Street and Fleet Street. On November 24, 1852 *The Times* noted that the previous day three vessels had berthed in the river Thames from Australia with the "extraordinary quantity" of over seven tons of gold on board. One of the ships, the *Eagle,* carried the greatest gold cargo ever known to arrive in one vessel, 150,000 ounces or over six tons, valued at more than £600,000. The newspaper added that the *Dido,* expected within a few days, had 200,000 ounces (more than ten tons) on board, and that other ships with great cargoes of the precious metal were following.

London newspapers were printing many extraordinarily enthusiastic reports on conditions in the gold-producing areas. A letter published by *The Times* on earnings of labouring men at the mines said that "a fair working man can make a full £1,200 a year on the ground, clear of his expenses at the present rate of food. Nine out of ten will do this readily, and some few here and there much more." The letter-writer's brother, a visitor to the Victorian fields, was quoted as saying that the mines were "inexhaustible for centuries."

Such unbridled enthusiasm helped to keep up the flow of hopeful immigrants. Ships arriving in Melbourne and Geelong were crowded. Just before the first gold strike, Victoria's population had been 77,000, of whom 46,000 were living outside the two centres of Melbourne and Geelong. Within a few months it had increased by more than 20,000. An American businessman arriving in Melbourne in May 1853 saw

. . . the bay was full of shipping, from Williamstown to Sandridge, nothing but one complete forest of masts. . . . Between 600 and 700 [vessels] were crowding each other for more room. All parts of the world were represented and every product of Christendom could be found among the cargoes.

Many of the new arrivals were unprepared for the kind of life that faced them. They had to find makeshift lodgings in Melbourne until they could equip themselves for the trip of a 100 miles or more to the diggings.

Some spent all their money before they set out. Day by day, endless lines of bullock drays and carts jolted their way along the tracks to the diggings, each piled with an assortment of household goods.

The claim allowed to each man was quite small, and luck varied. Sometimes adjoining claims produced very different results, one providing a small fortune and the others proving worthless. If a new field showed itself to be rich, the pace became frenetic as more miners arrived and those with claims worked harder. If the early promise was not sustained the men soon left to try their luck elsewhere. There were stories of unbelievable good fortune to sustain them. A nugget of over 1,000 ounces was unearthed at Canadian Gully, Ballarat, in 1853; other astounding finds quickly followed.

Overnight a secluded valley might become the scene of great activity. In the wake of the miners went more and more store-keepers who set up tents and makeshift shops. Money was freely spent, and many a trader did better than all but the luckiest miners. Butchers, grocers, barbers, auctioneers, printers, and a host of other tradesmen, were soon in business in each new gold centre. Nearly everyone lived in small calico tents set up in rows on slopes well away from the diggings. A few log huts sometimes were included. Stumps of trees served as chairs, and anything in the shape of a packing case or a tea chest was pressed into service as a table. Beds consisted of stretchers or bunks set up in a framework of forked stakes and saplings.

The rush to Australia had become world-wide, and it was centred on the Victorian fields. From London, Hamburg, San Francisco, and Canton came the hopeful. Soon the goldfields were thronged with as mixed assemblies as any on earth. In the first year, people from other countries outnumbered those arriving from the British Isles, but the balance was soon corrected.

Generally the settlements were orderly, but in some places a rough and unruly element quickly appeared and the police force was ineffectual. At Ballarat the situation was for the most part good; but in some camps chaos reigned and the government came in for criticism for its inability to suppress crime and violence. The Melbourne *Argus*, noting the condition in some camps, said that Lynch Law with all its terrors was being forced upon some mining communities "by the imbecility of our government."

The dislocation of society and the machinery of government was inevitable in a colony in which there was only one considerable centre of population, with a sparsely populated hinterland, and where the responsibilities of government had just been taken over by a newly constituted administration.

There were few roads, the police force was small, and the government revenue trifling. The flood of gold-seekers—eager, jostling, excited people— was as unexpected as it was overwhelming.

The landed interests set themselves against the upstart gold-mining industry from the beginning. The cost of maintaining law and order in the mining camps fell on the new administration, and La Trobe's ministry was informed from London that it was at liberty to make whatever regulations were necessary for deriving revenue from gold-mining.

The council adopted the same procedure as New South Wales, issuing miners' licences for 30/- a month. The collection of the fees was entrusted to the police. At first, in the eager anticipation of rich finds, the diggers paid without protest; but the flat fee was inherently unjust and to luckless men it became an irksome impost. Those whose efforts were not well rewarded could ill-afford to pay, since everything they bought on the goldfields was highly priced. Soon many of the diggers were grumbling. They charged that the police were rough and overbearing and were inclined to show more determination in collecting the fees than in dealing with crime. They branded the licence system as iniquitous, believing that an export duty (by which individual earnings would be the measure for the levy) would be preferable.

The justice of the miners' attitude was apparent. Governor La Trobe favoured the idea of an export levy and would have introduced the necessary changes, but he hesitated to place the revenue within the power of the inexperienced and rather stormy council. He was faced with the need to meet rising administrative costs, however, and he proposed to double the licence fee. The gold-miners, who were not entitled to the franchise and so had no representation in the council, protested hotly. The governor decided to withdraw the measure, whereupon the council passed a resolution favouring an export levy instead. A bill providing for an export duty, not as a substitute for licence fees but as an added impost, was proposed, only to be opposed by the chamber of commerce and general business interests and howled down on the goldfields. After passing the second reading, the bill was rejected by the council on the third reading.

The frenetic activity that characterized the gold-rushes in Victoria was not equalled in New South Wales. After the early flurry at Bathurst, the situation quietened down quickly; the long stretches of mountain road to the goldfields were a deterrent to many, and so the wild pressures that were part of the Victorian goldfields scene were not present in the older colony. Administrative costs for the goldfields were not very great in relation to the colonial administration's general outlays, and as revenue from other sources held up well, it was possible in June 1853 for the New South Wales Legislative Council to propose dropping the licence system in that colony. Immediately, diggers on the Victorian fields determined to press for abolition—or, at least, reduction—of the fee.

In Bendigo, which had attracted a great assemblage, a militant organization was formed to campaign against licensing. The anti-licence association quickly gained adherents; more than 5,000 men supported a petition. The demand for an end to licences was backed by passive resistance. The governor, sensing the danger inherent in the situation, allowed licences to remain unpaid. He ordered all available military forces into the Bendigo area to maintain order, at the same time writing to the Secretary of State to say that unless something was done there would inevitably be bloodshed there. In November the legislative council accepted the governor's Gold Fields Management Bill, under which the licence fees were reduced to £1 a month, or £2 a quarter. The Bendigo miners were not satisfied, and in January 1845 they were establishing a permanent Diggers' Congress when a new rush dispersed many of the most militant of the men. Governor La Trobe's capable handling of the situation had averted serious trouble.

The reduction in licence fees did not end the pressure for reform. The agitation had become intermingled with a demand for political reform as increasingly the miners sought to break down the power of the landed interests represented in the legislative council. It was the beginning of a fierce battle.

The miners based their claim for direct representation in the new Victorian legislature on the simple fact that gold-mining was furnishing about one half of the colony's total revenue. Even though the licence issue subsided, there was ferment everywhere, and rumours of threatened uprisings spread from time to time. For their part the members of the legislative council remained adamant in their stand against what they regarded as the riffraff element.

In spite of the tensions and the difficulty of maintaining law and order in such a volatile situation, there was relatively little violence. At one stage of the gold mania there had been less than fifty soldiers and only half a dozen policemen in the colony's service. Governor La Trobe sent off an urgent request to the Secretary of State in 1851 seeking at least a regiment of foot soldiers and two men-of-war; meanwhile he was able to secure thirty soldiers from Sydney and some from Van Diemen's Land. In 1852 a body of fifty of the London Metropolitan police and four companies of soldiers arrived. These acquisitions proved sufficient to restore normal security both in Melbourne and on the goldfields, though in some remoter parts highway robbery could not be suppressed.

The population of Victoria was growing as much as 50 per cent a year in the early 1850s. The ranks of the miners were constantly swelling as waves of new arrivals joined in the search for gold. Not all the diggers found their expectations fulfilled, and as extravagant hopes were sobered by realities, numbers of the men gave up prospecting and took jobs. The sudden expansion of the community created opportunities in many fields. The profits of carrying goods and provisions from Melbourne to the diggings were sufficient to lift some draymen and bullock drivers into the ranks of contractors for the public and private building that was required. Merchants and shipping firms, shopkeepers and publicans all profited handsomely. Prices rose and rents in Melbourne soared as the flood of arrivals continued.

By 1854, when Victoria surpassed New South Wales in population, the number of miners in the Victorian goldfields was nearly three times as great as it had been two years earlier—yet the amount of gold being won had fallen to half the 1852 total of £12 million. For many, prospects were fading. As failure rather than success became common, a sense of frustration came to dominate the miners' attitude. They were frontiersmen by adoption only; they had accepted the crude life in the mining camp in the belief that ultimately riches would be theirs. Now they saw only a grim prospect, and their tempers soured. No more than a spark was needed to stir mass resentment into a head-on collision with authority.

Early in 1854 Governor La Trobe resigned from office, depressed and disappointed by the never-ceasing problems of goldfields administration. The fiery mood of the diggers remained. The levying of licence fees continued to be contentious; the officious and arrogant way in which many of the police collected the fees roused the anger of the miners, while the system itself had failed to yield the added revenue needed for the administration of the rapidly expanding colony.

When La Trobe's successor, Sir Charles Hotham, arrived in Melbourne in June 1854, the city was suffering a sudden shrinking of its commercial boom and wool-growers were having difficulties because of higher costs and labour shortage. Hotham faced an empty treasury and, on the goldfields, an air of insurrection. He decided to correct both by stricter collection of miners' licence fees. He instructed the commissioners accordingly, even though it was clear that only one in four diggers could now hope to make an adequate living from gold-mining.

A new rush had attracted many disorderly groups to Eureka Valley, in the Ballarat area. Suddenly a wave of ill-feeling swept through the settlement. It was directed against the police, who continued to act as collectors of the licence fees but, in the miners' view at least, failed to protect individual rights. In October, a miner was stabbed during a bar-room incident, and tempers flared; and when the saloon-keeper was acquitted by a corrupt magistrate the miners took affairs into their own hands. Thousands converged upon the area, swept the police aside, and set fire to the saloon. Complaints were made about the magistrate, and after an inquiry Hotham decided to dismiss him, and to order a new trial. The saloon-keeper was now convicted; but three of the miners also found themselves sentenced to prison for their part in burning down the saloon. This the miners regarded as injustice, and tension mounted.

On November 11 the Ballarat Reform League was established. As with the Bendigo group, its call for correction of the miners' grievances was fused in its programme with purely political demands in the lines of the Chartist movement for political reform which had developed in England from 1837 and had as its objectives the introduction of universal suffrage, voting by ballot, and payment of members of parliament. The secretary of the League, Welshman John Basson Humffray, was a dedicated Chartist, more interested in political agitation than in the immediate issues of licensing and political arrogance; but his pleas for the exercise of "moral force" rather than violence, and his advocacy of political goals, were drowned out by noisy objections to licensing. The diggers had lost faith in the impartiality of justice; the licence hunts carried out by the police, sometimes with brutality, had stirred deep opposition, which was now set against all official authority. Every member of the Ballarat Reform League took a pledge to refuse payment of the obnoxious licence fees, and each man undertook to support all others in carrying out the pledge.

Hotham's orders to enforce the collection of licence fees now resulted in a provocative hunt for unlicensed diggers. This tactless act was all that was needed to turn irritation into rebellion. When the governor sent eighty soldiers to reinforce the police, an armed guard of diggers intercepted them in a skirmish in which the ammunition waggon was captured, the baggage cart overturned, and the troops, surprised and outnumbered, were scattered.

It was clear now that the situation was not likely to be resolved without a final clash. The government could not allow the challenge to its authority to remain unresolved, while the Eureka diggers would have to decide whether to submit or defend themselves. There could be no doubt of the defiant miners' decision. At a meeting on November 29, Peter Lalor, an impressive figure and a natural leader of the strong Irish element among the group, spoke for the first time in public; a motion was put that all licences should be burned as an act of defiance, and this motion was passed with very few dissenting. The following day the commissioner in charge of the goldfields ordered a licence hunt; when the miners heard of this decision they assembled at Bakery Hill. In the absence of other leaders, Lalor became the central figure; he mounted the stump and proclaimed liberty. The crowd moved to the Eureka lead and there a stockade composed of rocks, logs, broken carts, stakes, and rope, was thrown up to enclose an acre or so of land. Lalor was elected "commander-in-chief" by a council that gathered around him. Behind the barricade, companies of men drilled.

About 200 men were inside the stockade when, at four in the morning on Sunday, December 3, 1854, a company of 276 men, 182 of them soldiers and the rest police, marched quietly towards it. In the pale pre-dawn light the alarm was given by the sentry when they were about 300 yards away, and almost immediately a volley killed one of the officers and two soldiers. An answering volley came from the government forces, and the order to charge the barricade was given. The rough defences were quickly breached and in a few seconds hand-to-hand fighting was in progress. The defenders had no chance of success; within fifteen minutes or so, the diggers' blue flag displaying the Southern Cross in white stars had been torn down, and resistance was at an end. In the struggle, twenty-four of the insurgents were killed and many others wounded. The casualties among the troops numbered five killed and twelve wounded. Lalor, who was severely wounded in battle, was hidden by his comrades in a hole covered with bark and wood slabs where he remained undetected.

All the insurgents who could be rounded up—about 120 in all—were marched off to prison. The governor insisted that the ringleaders be tried for high treason—but there was widespread belief that ineptitude and provocation in the handling of the miners' claims had precipitated the issue and that the administration had been almost as much at fault in the whole affair as the miners. Juries refused to convict any of the thirteen men brought to trial. As each verdict was announced, there was loud cheering. The Melbourne *Argus* reported exultantly that in spite of bad weather, the prisoners were "escorted from the Court by a large company who frequently raised loud plaudits on their way down Stephen Street." Peter Lalor was not among those charged; in spite of the offer of a reward, he succeeded in evading arrest, and when the furore died down and the reward offer was withdrawn he reappeared and became a candidate for the legislative assembly, gaining a seat in November 1855.

On both sides—the legislative council and the executive, on the one hand, and the miners on the other—it was now realized that a more realistic approach was necessary. For its part the government set in motion an official inquiry into goldfields grievances which had been planned for some time.

The result was that the licence fee system was abolished; instead, a small export levy on gold was imposed and a miner's right granted for a fee of £1 a year whereby the holder was granted legal rights in his claim and the gold extracted from it. The export duty produced the revenue needed by the government without imposing hardship. As leaseholders of Crown lands, those who paid for a miner's right were given the right to vote. By 1855 these reforms—practically everything the diggers had asked for—were carried into effect. The *Argus* commented that it had long been recommending these very reforms.

The golden store continued to pour from the Victorian diggings, fluctuating as fields became exhausted and new ones opened. Some great nuggets were being unearthed. At Bakery Hill, Ballarat, the 2,195 oz. Welcome nugget was dug up in 1858 (the largest of all, with the exception of the 2,284 oz. Welcome Stranger, which came to light in 1869 at Moliagul, near Dunolly, from under its covering of a few inches of soil). However, generally less gold was being won from alluvial or surface mining, in which individual miners were involved; a steadily increasing proportion was being extracted by companies with sufficient money to install machinery capable of working the ground systematically. The readily accessible gold had been largely cleaned up; but the store was still extensive and in spite of difficulties the alluvial miners persisted—in fact, their numbers increased. In 1854 Victoria had 68,000 active alluvial miners; three years later the figure passed 82,000, and by 1861 it was slightly higher. But gold yields were not keeping pace. From about £11,700,000 in 1855, total output rose in value to almost £14 million the following year, then fell back to under £11 million in 1857, and declined from there to below £8 million in 1861.

Elsewhere, new fields had opened up to divert some attention. After the initial discoveries in the Bathurst district, interest in New South Wales fields had subsided somewhat as the dazzling treasure of Victoria was revealed; but activity was sustained, and as time went on many gold-seekers returned to the area. Production in New South Wales was valued at £670,000 in 1857, and output rose steadily to £1,800,000 four years later. A minor rush in 1858 took many miners to a promising field at Canoona on the Fitzroy River, well north of Moreton Bay. Here some of the early arrivals won fortunes, and Canoona soon had a population of 16,000; but the excitement was short-lived, and latecomers lost everything, for it was only a small rich pocket. It was some years before other far northern fields were opened.

In New South Wales, gold fever was kept alive by windfall finds and the opening of new fields. Hill End, situated in the rough bush country 180 miles north-west of Sydney, drew thousands of prospectors; by the time the rush reached its climax in 1872 the town had a mile of shops and 50 hotels to cater for the men scouring the dull red earth in search of fortunes. Many of the hopefuls won minor riches. The most fortunate were two German-born prospectors, Louis Beyers and Bernard Holtermann, who in 1872 unearthed a massive nugget which yielded £12,000 worth of gold when it was put through the crushing mill.

Under gold's impact, Victoria underwent very great change and rapid development. In the briefest possible time it was transformed from a prosperous land of sheepmen to a booming community with a mass of free-spending people. The colony's population rocketed to 538,000 by the end of 1860—a sevenfold increase in ten years which radically changed the balance of population among the colonies. At that time Victoria had almost half of all the people in Australia.

Among those drawn to the goldfields were some Chinese, and their presence quickly caused friction. Strong feeling developed, and in 1855 Victoria passed a measure restricting the immigration of Chinese. Similar restriction were imposed in 1858 by South Australia and three years later by New South Wales.

The great gold discoveries attracted attention and acted as a magnet not only overseas but, even sooner, in the neighbouring colonies; the fabulous wealth uncovered in the Victorian fields started a big emigration from Van Diemen's Land (where some small gold-finds made from 1850 failed to turn into a bonanza), and from South Australia. The ready availability of gold thus led to changes even in the colonies where no discoveries were made.

When news of the gold discoveries in near-by Victoria reached Adelaide, shops were quickly closed and "gone to the diggings" signs displayed. About 16,000 people quickly left the colony. Writing later, Thomas Worsnop, town clerk of Adelaide, noted:

> Everything came to a standstill. Trade was paralysed; all the available coin was taken away by the speculative diggers. So small was the amount of actual cash in circulation that several of the few storekeepers who did not or could not leave their business issued paper notes for sums as low as 2d. Sixpenny notes were quite common.

In January 1852, the Bullion Act of South Australia was passed as a means of coping with the run on bank depositors' funds which had accompanied the mass exodus. Its effect was to reverse the outward flow of funds by drawing into Adelaide a portion of the gold unearthed in the neighbouring colony. The act introduced a degree of independent action new to the colonies; its provisions were an example of the greater sophistication in financial matters made possible now that a ready source of gold had been uncovered.

The South Australian act provided for the assay of uncoined gold and restricted the use of bank notes; soon a government assayer had been appointed with authority to cast gold and stamp coins for currency. The two English-owned banks operating in Adelaide were authorized by the act to give notes in return for the gold, which was then bought at £3 11s. an ounce—a considerable premium on the price ruling on the goldfields, where dealers and banks usually bought at a 30 per cent discount on the ruling English price. Regular escorts were sent to the Victorian fields and as a result of the higher price being paid, one-fifth of the first year's outpouring of gold found its way to Adelaide; in two years £2 million worth of gold was handled under the act.

The directors of the Royal Mint were shocked by the action of the South Australian government but they could not prevent it. Eventually they came to the conclusion that a Royal mint should be set up, and in 1855 the mint was opened in Sydney. It turned out sovereigns marked "Australia." The operation of the mint had a steadying effect on exchanges with London; previously the tremendous outpouring of gold had tended to weaken the price of gold in the colonies.

The miners' earnings were freely spent, and in the wake of the gold-seekers themselves went many prepared to earn a livelihood by supplying the needs of the miners. The enormously increased purchasing power was a new colonial phenomenon. Unlike the hard-saving sheepmen who conserved every penny for investment in sheep and land, those attracted from abroad by gold were free spenders. The new arrivals were for the most part men of very limited capital, but many were not thinking in terms of permanent settlement; rather they were drawn by the prospect of quick riches, and their outlook was conditioned accordingly. As gold flowed and wages rose, caution was thrown to the winds, and soon the people of the Victorian goldfields (and Melbourne) had become the freest spending community to be found anywhere.

A great market for goods was created as people who had been of modest income and social standing at home found themselves in possession of relatively large amounts of money. With gold in their pockets the miners and those who were present to serve their needs could command purchases from the world at large—and a great surge of imports came in response to the expanded demand for goods.

Many of the diggers benefited less from the finds than did the men of commerce, the bankers, and shopkeepers. Merchants sold supplies to the goods-hungry community to advantage; the gold-buyers, and the growing number of banks, did well out of their handling of the precious metal. Yet, as wealth undreamt of previously in the colonies was released, poverty was present, too, and there were many who sought consolation in drunkenness and lawlessness. Side by side in the population were confidence men and solid traders—on the one hand the avaricious and lawless element, on the other ambitious and dynamic people of undoubted vigour and enterprise.

The Victorian fields were unique not only in their richness and the ease with which their golden bounty could be won, but also in the fact that they were located close to the seaboard in a fertile, well-watered region capable of immediate development. People drawn to the goldfields could stay on to turn their hands to other tasks if they were unlucky in the search for gold, or when the gold petered out. Melbourne, as the main centre through which the bulk of the gold was handled and the main entrepôt for all the goods needed by the hundreds of thousands of people moving into the new land, had become a great port and a city of extraordinary wealth.

The immense quantity of merchandise pouring in from many parts of the world was noted with amazement by George Francis Train, a young Boston-trained merchant who set up an American import agency. Train wrote in June 1853:

> I sincerely believe that the whole shipping world is mad; for it does really seem stark lunacy the way they are going on in England, and I cannot say much more for the U.S. With a population not exceeding 800,000 in all the colonies, we have been, are still receiving, and shall continue to receive goods for the next three months, for at least five millions of people.

A year later Train reported that:

> *Australian imports last year reached the enormous sum of 85 millions of dollars!* and the imports into this colony reached 300 dollars a head to each man, woman and child in Victoria! . . . The world never saw a parallel! . . . At one time [there were] 600 ships in Hobson's Bay deep-loaded with valuable cargoes all clamouring to be discharged.

The continuing output from the goldfields was sufficient to maintain the flood of imports, however, and the boom held almost to the end of the 1850s.

Included in the great influx of people from abroad was a significant American element. Most came as miners, some as merchants and engineers, and some were responsible for innovations that helped change the land. In a setting in many ways similar to that of their rapidly growing homeland, American businessmen could anticipate public demand. The free-spending attitudes of the community matched—and in some ways surpassed—those of Americans. The continuing influence of American ideas and "indomitable energy" on the community at large was very great. It was, in fact, out of all proportion to the number of Americans present, and some considered that Melbourne was fast becoming Americanized. Americans had won the contract to build the Hobson's Bay railroad and pier, and fire engines and watercarts from the United States were in use on Melbourne streets. There were scores of New York buggy waggons in and about the city, and an American was selling ice brought in from Boston at fifty cents a pound.

With the benefit of experience in broadly similar circumstances, American businessmen possessed an enterprising approach which gave new zest to local expansion. One of the enterprises backed by Americans was a coach service to the goldfields.

Freeman Cobb and others who had experience in this type of business established a short-run parcel service and the first regular coach service to the goldfields. Known as Cobb and Co., the organization was an immediate success. Later it extended to other colonies, providing a lifeline that reached to the very edge of the frontier of settlement.

In the period Melbourne became a great port and a wealthy city, the centre through which much of the vast amount of gold from the diggings was handled and finally shipped, and through it a constant stream of people passed. Building boomed. Wharves and warehouses multiplied, makeshift buildings were replaced by solid commercial offices. In one year more than 1,000 buildings were erected. There was work for tradesmen—carpenters, stone masons, slaters, glaziers—and jobs were available for grooms, chimney-sweeps, housemaids, cooks, gardeners, blacksmiths, and roadmakers as well as grocers and bankers. Wages were high—and so were prices. A university and other cultural institutions were founded. Streets were macadamized and footpaths paved, and telegraphs operated to the Heads. The first railway line, laid between the city of Melbourne and the port, was opened with a grand flourish in 1854.

Commerce was flourishing. Traders, bankers, and merchants developed great businesses as importers catered to the needs of a free-spending population in a land without manufacturing industries. The handful of merchants who had earlier founded a commercial exchange set up a chamber of commerce in 1851, and merchants and brokers met daily to discuss and publish prices of goods. A visiting judge compared the Melbourne of 1856 with that of 1845:

> In 1845 Bourke Street contained but a few scattered cottages, and sheep grazed on the thick grass in the street . . . [In 1856] this same Bourke Street was as crowded with fine buildings and as thronged and alive with the hurrying to and fro of busy people as one of London's busiest streets.

He noted that whereas in 1845 Melbourne's banking business was carried on a few hours a day by two branch banks, in 1856 eight banks could scarcely meet "the pecuniary exigencies of the community." In 1845 the judge had counted two large ships, three brigs, and a few small craft in the harbour; in 1856 that same harbour was filled with "about two hundred London and Liverpool A-1 ships and countless other vessels from America, New Zealand, and various other foreign parts."

Early in 1855 Melbourne was delighted by the announcement that the *James Baines* had completed the run from Liverpool with the December mails in sixty-five days—an "astonishing and unprecedented" performance. Because of the great build-up in its shipping links with England and the world, Melbourne came to handle a considerable volume of both imports and exports for South Australia and Van Diemen's Land. Within a few years Melbourne had become a major distribution centre and by the late 1850s was importing over £300,000 worth of goods a year on behalf of South Australia—three-fourths of that colony's tobacco imports, two-thirds of its tea and soap, half its coffee, a third of its rice, its spirits, and its sugar. Exports of almost equal value of South Australian origin were handled; they included wool, copper, and lead.

New South Wales and Sydney shared in the commercial and general benefits from the sustained outpouring of gold, although not to anything like the extent or at the same rate as Victoria and Melbourne. Sydney's population, 52,000 in 1850, moved up steadily and in a decade reached 95,000. From 1852 Sydney, previously little more than a port of casual freighters carrying wool, whalers and Pacific traders and immigrant ships, became a focal point of regular shipping routes as more wool was shipped each year and more goods arrived. Port facilities were improved as the wool trade consolidated; a great dock was excavated to serve Thomas Sutcliffe Mort's wool stores. That shrewd observer George Train noted that Sydney in 1854 had a "very English air" about it and that, with the rival of Port Phillip attracting the gaze of the whole world, the city would have to enliven itself. He wrote:

> Wake up, ye Sydney people, or Melbourne will take the bread from your mouths! The young giant is already boasting of his strength and your natural position will not offset his energy—socially you are a hospitable community, but commercially you do not keep up with the age in which you live.

For every ship in Port Jackson there were a dozen in Hobson's Bay. Nevertheless, Sydney's society impressed the visitor, who, after "a delightful time" at Government House, wrote:

> As the lackey announced name after name, some of them ringing with titles, I thought that Sydney boasted a society that Melbourne never dreamed of.

For all its bursting affluence, Melbourne was still little more than a centre for frontiersmen.

In spite of the greatly increased local demand for wheat, agriculture in both New South Wales and Victoria declined sharply in the early years of gold, the area of land under cultivation in Victoria falling 40 per cent in the first two years as the diggings attracted so many men. Yet there was an increased demand for agricultural products from which South Australia profited. In the early days of the gold-rush, many of the South Australian farmers had returned from the Victorian diggings at harvest time; later, when the price of wheat rose sharply to over 15/– a bushel, they found it more profitable to stay on their farms. Other men joined them, buying land with money gained from mining. South Australia soon became a granary; by 1855 there were well over 5,000 farmers and from 160,000 acres of land under cultivation the harvest exceeded 4,000,000 bushels. Much of the wheat they grew was needed on the goldfields and it was taken up the Murray by paddle-wheelers which began to operate after the first successful navigation of the river in 1853. Grain was also shipped to other markets by sea.

In 1850 the colony had been exporting breadstuffs and grain worth about £40,000; by 1859 the value of such exports exceeded £500,000; from 1,500 tons in 1850, flour exports rose to over 21,000 tons, while wheat exports went up from just over 100,000 bushels to 235,000 bushels. The largest customers for cereals were Victoria and New South Wales. The investment of capital brought from the goldfields or resulting from the high prices for exportable produce between 1852 and 1855 helped to bring about the great increase in South Australia's trade; a supporting factor was the purchase of land and the resulting increase in the Land Fund which in turn was used to bring out new settlers.

As South Australia's farms expanded, agricultural machinery as well as foodstuffs were produced in increasing quantity, so that the colony was soon able to export farm equipment to Victoria. Although some tradesmen and others were drawn from Adelaide to settle in Victoria, the large reserves which Adelaide banks held as a result of the Bullion Act provided funds for the rapid progress of the colony's agriculture. Van Diemen's Land, on the other hand, gained comparatively little from the demand for grain; in nine years the land under cultivation rose only slightly—from 168,000 acres to 208,000 in 1859. Colonial markets for grain that had previously belonged to Van Diemen's Land were lost to South Australian competition.

The loss of manpower from the island in the wake of gold retarded development for years to come; population remained almost stationary in the early 1850s, and did not pass 80,000 until 1857.

Meanwhile Western Australia remained in the doldrums, and even though its exports moved up in the mid-1850s, its trade was less than one per cent of that of Victoria in the 1850s.

In the decade of gold, imports of every colony except South Australia moved up even more sharply than colonial exports. As was natural in a rapidly developing country, articles and goods flooded in to meet demand for both consumer and capital goods.

As a result, imports ran at a consistently higher level than exports, the difference being made up by investment from abroad and by the funds brought in by some of the settlers. The steady investment reflected a growing confidence in the colonies' future as it was assessed in London and Glasgow and elsewhere.

The following figures show the imports and exports for each colony over the period:

Overseas Trade of the Australian Colonies, 1851–60

	NEW SOUTH WALES		VICTORIA		
	Imports £	Exports £	Imports £	Exports £	
1851	1,563,931	1,796,912	1,056,437	1,422,909	
52	1,900,436	4,604,034	4,069,742	7,451,549	
53	6,342,397	4,523,346	15,842,637	11,061,544	
54	5,981,063	4,050,126	17,659,051	11,775,204	
55	4,668,519	2,884,130	12,007,939	13,493,338	
56	5,460,971	3,430,880	14,962,269	15,489,760	
57	6,729,408	4,011,952	17,256,209	15,079,512	
58	6,059,336	4,186,277	15,108,249	13,989,209	
59	6,597,053	4,768,049	15,622,891	13,867,859	
60	7,519,285	5,072,020	15,093,730	12,962,704	

	SOUTH AUSTRALIA		VAN DIEMEN'S LAND		WESTERN AUSTRALIA	
	Imports £	Exports £	Imports £	Exports £	Imports £	Exports £
1851	690,777	602,087	641,609	665,790	56,598	26,870
52	798,811	1,787,741	860,488	1,509,883	97,304	24,181
53	2,336,290	2,241,814	2,273,397	1,756,316	126,735	31,645
54	2,147,107	1,322,822	2,604,680	1,433,021	128,260	34,109
55	1,370,938	988,215	1,559,797	1,428,629	105,320	46,314
56	1,366,529	1,665,740	1,442,106	1,207,802	122,938	44,740
57	1,623,052	1,958,572	1,271,087	1,354,655	94,532	59,947
58	1,769,351	1,512,185	1,328,612	1,151,609	144,932	78,649
59	1,507,494	1,655,876	1,163,907	1,193,898	125,315	93,037
60	1,639,591	1,783,716	1,068,411	962,170	169,075	89,247

Note: These are trade figures based on port of entry or export. Imports were not necessarily all consumed in the colony shown, nor were exports all produced there (e.g., Melbourne was the import point for goods destined for other colonies, and some minerals and wool from inland areas were exported from other than the colony of origin.)

The gold-rushes marked a watershed in colonial history. Before them, the various colonies were broadly similar in form and structure, relying for their export income largely on the earnings from wool; there were points of difference to distinguish each of the colonial enterprises but these were relatively minor. In drawing to Victoria a great mass of people and precipitating rapid economic change there, the gold discoveries and their influence were sufficient to give colonial development an entirely new direction. By creating its own reservoir of capital, Victoria became temporarily insulated as local capital arising from mining dominated the economic scene, and for a time the economy became less sensitive to London investment. Local investment companies sprang up as a logical outcome of the increased demands for finance by the government, by municipalities, by gold-mining enterprises, and by trade and industry.

Among the host of newcomers to Victoria were capable and enterprising individuals, including professional people and those with industrial and business skills superior to any earlier immigrants. Men from London and Glasgow arrived to open branches of the banks and mercantile firms which employed them; the publicity given the bonanza had its effect on writers, artists and lawyers, and businessmen, who did not necessarily wish to prospect for gold but were nevertheless attracted to the new type of colonial community.

Major changes in the distribution of population among the colonies were brought about as a result of the gold discoveries in Victoria. The following table shows the changes that took place between 1851 and 1860:

Australia: Population, 1851–1861

	New South Wales	Victoria	Queensland	South Australia	Western Australia	Tasmania	Australia
1851	197,265	97,489	(included in New South Wales)	66,538	7,186	69,187	437,665
1855	266,901	347,305		97,387	12,605	69,962	794,160
1860	348,546	538,234	28,056	125,582	15,346	89,821	1,145,585

Although it had fallen well below the two-to-one ratio of 1840, the excess of men over women in the community was still considerable when gold was first discovered. It averaged 142:100 for the colonial population as a whole. In Victoria, still in a pioneering pastoral phase, the masculinity ratio was slightly higher than in New South Wales. The sustained influx of men to the Victorian goldfields from 1851 lifted the numbers quite sharply, and over the 1850s Victoria's masculinity ratio was higher than that of any colony except Western Australia (still affected by convict intake). The population figures were affected by the new arrivals and by movements between the colonies, with men being drawn to Victoria from other colonies.

Masculinity of Australian Population

	New South Wales	Victoria	Queensland	South Australia	Western Australia	Tasmania	Australia
1851	134.53	148.35	(included in New South Wales)	127.74	181.47	170.73	143.20
1855	125.08	187.40		100.62	193.55	123.65	145.48
1860	131.29	146.61	153.52	106.32	167.29	119.95	134.20

Figures show number of males to every 100 females.

Even after 1860 the gold flow in Victoria was well sustained and in New South Wales it showed a slight rise. Nevertheless, even if gold might still be won, it was no longer to be picked up readily as in the 1850s. Once surface deposits were depleted, expensive machinery was required to deal with the deeper deposits, whether alluvial or quartz. This involved the outlay of considerable capital, and the working of the fields increasingly became the responsibility of companies. As this happened, the gold prospector with his eyes on quick riches was attracted to new prospects. In 1861 some rich fields were discovered in New Zealand, and an exodus from Victoria began, so that in that year almost 6,000 more people left Victoria than arrived and the natural increase of 28,500 showed up as a population gain of 22,500. But nothing could reverse the changes that had come in the dazzling decade of gold.

Part
Four

Part
Four

Colonial separatism

BOISTEROUS POLITICIANS AND RUGGED INDIVIDUALISTS set the tone of the period of rapid economic growth that opened in the eastern colonies with the gold-rushes. As the pace of life quickened, quiet colonial ways were soon being swamped—as much in torrents of oratory and advocacy, it seemed, as in the torrent of gold. A greater sense of urgency and expectation was in the air; new horizons were opening not only for the individual but for the colonial community at large. Tough energetic men, prepared to tackle challenging tasks and to risk everything they had in the hope of winning economic success, were being drawn to a land where opportunity seemed boundless. Along with the scurrying hordes of fortune-seekers bent on finding gold, went traders and others eager to cater to the needs of a new community of free spenders; and behind them in the seaports and at staging points businesses flourished as merchants and storekeepers met the surging demand for goods. Even in cities and towns tens of thousands were still living in huts or tents, but there could be no doubt that the raw frontier-land of mid-century was being transformed.

Self-government came to New South Wales, Victoria, South Australia, and Van Diemen's Land (renamed Tasmania) at the very time of the great ferment caused by gold. With the end of transportation to New South Wales the way had been cleared for transfer of control over local affairs to the colonists themselves. Secure behind the 1847 regulations granting the graziers rights to the land they occupied, many members of the pastoral oligarchy in New South Wales would have been content to see the 1842 "representation" Act stand; but William Charles Wentworth, as controversial and forthright as ever, had remained adamant that nothing short of responsible government for the colony would suffice. The pressure sustained by Wentworth and other political activists in Sydney during the late 1840s, and the loud demand from the Port Phillip district for separation finally led to the passage of the Act of 1850 for "the Better Government of Her Majesty's Australian Colonies."

This document did no more than sketch in a framework, and Lord Grey, the Secretary of State for the Colonies who guided the measure through the British parliament, was unwilling to modify the limits it set upon the powers to be transferred into the colonists' hands. When a change of government resulted in Lord Grey's replacement in 1852, his successor, Sir John Pakington, bowed to the insistent pressure from Sydney and extended the scope of powers granted to the colonial legislatures. Although the act provided that each colony was to shape its own parliamentary institutions, the Colonial Office could exercise a restraining hand on the constitutional plans which the colonial legislatures had to submit for approval. As things transpired, the principal effect of London's review of the recommendations was to bring the various colonial constitutions more into line with each other than they might otherwise have been. Nevertheless the proposals that emanated from the various legislative councils reflected to some degree the distinctive factors in each colony's economic and political scene.

Conservative elements, led by Wentworth, prevailed in New South Wales, whereas in Victoria landed interests were not so firmly entrenched and had to face a concerted attack by more radical elements, particularly those following Chartist principles. In South Australia the strongly independent and nonconformist background of the settlers prevailed and a most liberal constitution emerged, while in Tasmania conservative constitutional provisions maintained the strength of the island's freeholders.

By 1856 the four new constitutions had all been approved and the serious business of setting up colonial administrations subject to local parliamentary control had begun. For colonies founded only a few decades earlier, the power conferred upon the electorates was extraordinarily great.

In setting up parliamentary government, the colonists naturally looked to Westminster as the model. They were heir to existing British law, and they sought to follow the evolving British system of responsible government with the administration in the hands of the parliamentary group directly responsible to the lower house and liable to dismissal from office when it lost the confidence of that house. In seeking to follow the British system of the mid-nineteenth century, the colonial constitution-makers ran into special problems, many of which were due to the difficulty of transposing the unwritten and still evolving constitution under which the parliament at Westminster operated into a written constitution. Written documents sought to define various aspects but of necessity left untouched many subtle relationships which in practice were equally important to the running of the system. No machinery was laid down for what should be done in the case of disagreement between the two houses. Most of the framers of the colonial constitutions did not really intend the elective assembly to be the definitely dominant partner, even though this was inherent in the natural operation of responsible government.

The smooth operation of colonial self-government had to be worked out by trial and error, building up from precedent to precedent. In the different colonies arguments raged from time to time over various issues related to the operation of responsible government, and occasionally the business of administration was disrupted. An essentially British parliament had been set up in each colony; but the twig could not be a replica of the tree that had been growing for so long so far away. The new parliamentarians did not at first appreciate the need for restraint and good sense in the operation of the system. They could learn the mechanics of good government only in the workshop of parliament itself.

From colony to colony constitutional provisions varied to only a limited degree; but economic factors differentiated the colonies quite sharply. Victoria had become quite distinctive—in fact, a colonial phenomenon. Gold had concentrated half a million people within its borders—almost as many as there were in the other five colonies combined. The accumulation of capital taking place in Victoria, largely as a result of the riches won from gold, provided a means for the expansion of the economic base. The colony's relative independence of outside capital, and its hunger for goods, would soon be enough to make possible a move towards manufacturing on a simple scale. Even before this happened, conditions in Victoria were favourable to a sustained attack on the sheepmen's monopoly of the land.

It did not take very long for Victoria's fantastic accumulation of accessible surface gold to be gathered up by the eager men who scratched feverishly at the soil and turned over a myriad rocks and stones to expose it or washed it from the gravels of creeks and river beds. From the mid-1850s a sharp decline became evident in miners' earnings; from an average of £263 in 1852, income had fallen to less than £70 per man by 1858. There was still great treasure to be won but it was in inaccessible or hidden areas, or it lay deep in the earth, in auriferous rocks where it could be won only by those with capital to buy machinery and pay wages to miners. The day of the mining companies had arrived, and the independent miner with pick, shovel, and cradle no longer had much chance of survival. Gold yields were dwindling; from almost 3,000,000 ounces in 1856, output was down to 1,500,000 ounces nine years later. Fewer men could hope to earn a living on the goldfields, and from a peak of 150,000 diggers in 1854, the number dwindled to 80,000.

Sheep-grazing had given purpose and spur to the continent's settlement, and the drive continued. Farming had progressed slowly, and even the improved prospects for selling greater quantities of grain in Britain after the repeal of the Corn Laws in 1846 failed to stimulate much activity. Sheepmen had already come to monopolize practically all the good and accessible land. Farming had generally been difficult and unrewarding; but as the demand for basic foodstuffs increased greatly with the rapid rise in colonial populations, the land under cultivation proved inadequate to meet it. When the first waves of gold seekers arrived, food, including wheat and dairy produce, had to be imported; and even though the acreage under crop rose from 500,000 in all the eastern colonies in 1850 to more than 1,000,000 acres eight or nine years later, there were still not enough farms to feed the enlarged population. All the land seemed to be in the hands of the pastoralists, who were not interested in farming. A call to "unlock the land" was first raised by Melbourne newspapers in the early 1850s; it was soon to become insistent. The *Age*, edited by a political activist, Ebenezer Syme, for a partnership led by his brother, David Syme, raised the issue loudly.

The people drawn in by gold were an active force pressing for change; but the old wool economy had not been greatly disturbed in any of the colonies, and even in Victoria wool again established itself as the dominant factor once the gold flow subsided. Each successive year the wool clip rose: the land was becoming an even vaster sheepwalk as the industry organized itself to meet Britain's ever-increasing needs for fibre. Some of the diggers and new arrivals found employment in the pastoral industry; but this was no solution for men who wanted to set themselves up as independent farmers or for the many artisans and skilled men who had come hopefully in search of gold and the opportunities that went with it. New arrivals soon wanted to settle down in the new land where the climate was so benign and skies were bluer than the skies of England or Scotland or Ireland; but they were unprepared to accept the prevailing situation in which little was offering beyond the narrow choice of working for the government on public works, helping to fence the sheepmen's properties, or building stores for importers and mansions for successful merchants and businessmen.

Clearly, new activities had to be developed if the great numbers already in Victoria, and others still flocking in, were to be employed. One obvious answer seemed to lie in farming. Victoria was not growing enough grain to supply local needs, and wheat still had to be imported because a few thousand sheepmen were monopolizing the bulk of the arable land.

Now that the power over disposal of Crown land had been transferred to the colonial legislatures, the clamour to provide wider opportunities grew, in the other colonies as well as in Victoria. The sheepmen had won the battle against the governors and Colonial Office administrators; now they were faced by the land-hunger of the newly enfranchised people. The opening of new land for auction and settlement in the early 1850s did little to relieve the situation; in 1856 a parliamentary committee in New South Wales reported that it was very difficult for men of limited means to compete successfully against the graziers since the process of acquiring small holdings was complex and expensive. From this time, the hope of the reform elements in both New South Wales and Victoria was to remedy the situation by simple laws which would open up the land to farmers. The same drive was present in Queensland when that colony was created as a separate entity in 1859.

For their part, the woolmen wanted nothing more than to continue business as usual. They were gaining new successes; economies were introduced with the fencing of runs, sheep were growing more wool, and the prices received for the staple were again moving up after the low point of the mid-1850s. By 1860 the London price of Australian greasy wool had risen to a highly profitable fourteen pence a pound, and prices edged up throughout the 1860s to reach eighteen pence average in 1869. The woolmen felt they should be able to hold out against all comers.

It was at this point that David Syme, owner and editor of the Melbourne

Age, having succeeded in gaining purely political objectives relating to voting procedures and the franchise, began his perceptive campaigns on economic issues. Other newspaper editors were campaigning on the land issue, but Syme's advocacy was more sustained and it was part of a wider programme of development. His newspaper attracted as much attention for its policies as its news; it became the advocate of policies which appealed to middle-class people as well as to the working-man. Syme's main objectives were seen in two campaigns: one was aimed at opening the land to small settlers, and the other urged adoption of a selective tariff so designed that import duties on certain classes of goods would be raised to levels where local manufacturers and producers could compete successfully while paying their employees reasonable wages. Such policies seemed extremely radical at the time, but in both cases Syme's ideas coincided with developments actually taking place in the United States and Canada.

In the other colonies the old emphasis on shipping wool and bringing in consumer goods remained unchanged. From each colonial capital, the main arteries of a railway system were reaching out to the sheep-raising areas; the ports were growing as funnels through which commodities and goods passed. At the point from which transport facilities spread, each colonial capital was growing steadily as a commercial centre serving a vast hinterland. However, none had exuberance matching that of gold-rich Melbourne.

In his ambitions for expansion of Victoria's economy, Syme saw the need for the young community to modify the operation of "natural" economic laws. He challenged the prevailing concept that the sound thing to do was to concentrate on pastoral activity, keep wages low, and bring in from the cheapest market whatever goods were needed. Instead, he urged that legislative action be taken to moderate the effect of the prevailing economic forces and give the colony a chance to develop a more diversified economy. To Syme, and to those around him, it was not enough to leave Australia a continent of grass. The colonies must establish a more advanced and balanced economy—something that could not be done while they were being swamped by English goods that were the production surplus from big factories. His economic plans met bitter opposition; but through his unremitting campaigns in the *Age* Syme gathered an avid following.

Soon Syme was leading his growing readership in a crusade for policies which would make possible the settlement of more men on the land and the establishment of simple manufacturing industries. This crusade represents the first phase in the expression of a new Australian "frontier nationalism," with two main aspects: the determination that the colonists should manage their own affairs without English interference, direct or indirect; and the determination to have a hand in the shaping of the colony's destiny through active economic measures insead of letting things take their course. Victoria's "frontier nationalism" was exactly the same force that had brought about the American War of Independence: in both cases the colonists were determined to shape their country's future and to control the course of affairs through measures that suited them if not London. As time went on, similar broad objectives shaped thoughts in the other Australian colonies, and led eventually to a wider acceptance of the need for legislative action in economic affairs.

The struggle to "unlock the land" dominated politics in most of the colonies long before tariffs became an issue. It took a long while for politicians and voters to realize the bitter truth that "unlocking the land" was not the simple process it seemed. Much of the good land where tillage might have succeeded had already been sold under the old system. In many of the areas where land could be withdrawn from the big leaseholders, the climate was uncertain and conditions were generally such that agriculture was hazardous or doomed to failure. In New South Wales, John Robertson led the fight for opening up land to small settlers. He and his followers were obsessed with the idea of spreading farms deep into the country, in the same way that America's Middle West was being occupied by homesteaders. In offering land in relatively small acreages, much of the legislation in New South Wales and other colonies followed the homesteading laws of the United States quite closely. However, climatic conditions were very different in the Australian hinterland, and although parliamentarians might pass laws to divide up large holdings they could not legislate for rain, while high costs of transport, and other basic handicaps such as poor soil and unsuitable strains of wheat, made farming hazardous in many areas—even in some that had seemed promising at first.

Apart from different geographic and climatic conditions, there was another vital difference in land settlement in the two countries; under the United States Homesteading Act of 1861 a 160-acre allotment of arable land was available as a free grant to anyone who cared to settle on it, while in the Australian colonies the man who wanted land had to pay for it. Hence the Australian legislation to "unlock the land" did not attract immigrants in the way that the United States act did.

Most of the Australian legislation omitted to provide adequate safeguards for ensuring that land was bought and retained by small farmers and not by pastoralists. In many cases it was possible for the big landholders to manipulate the new land laws to their advantage. Sometimes under expensive terms as selectors were bought out, and frequently under chaotic conditions, ownership of millions of acres of Crown land passed into the sheepmen's hands over the 1860s and 1870s as former leaseholds were converted into freeholds. The farmer had little hope of competing with the infinitely greater financial resources of the pastoralist, especially while wool prices were buoyant. The small farmer inherited the United States: in Australia the pastoralist remained king, in a country of extensive freeholds tied to larger leaseholds. Climatic factors supported a big-man's frontier; this in turn meant that the majority would remain landless.

In spite of the absence of any special incentive to immigration in the form of free land, new settlers continued to arrive, and the population moved up at quite a rapid pace. The rate of growth far outstripped that in Canada at the same period; in 1851 Australia contained less than one-fifth as many people as the Canadian provinces but within a few decades the Australian colonies had almost two-thirds as many people as Canada, and colonial development had been set on a new course. Gold had acted like some all-powerful genie conjured from a void and creating wonders out of everything he touched.

In earlier days the colonial economies had been in no way diversified, and apart from whaling and sealing, mining coal, and more recently digging for gold, the object of almost every export activity had been to feed England's voracious appetite for wool. To serve the all-important pastoral activity, capital had been drawn from Britain either in the form of personal investment or (more generally) advances from banks or other lending institutions, or mercantile houses, supported from London. The London-controlled banks were naturally conservative in their approach; they preferred to back the sure and established industry, wool, which they did through traders.

With gold came a new source of investment money which could help support local business. Not all the great outpouring of gold was exported; some found its way into locally sponsored banks set up in Melbourne, where a considerable reservoir of money quickly built up, while Adelaide and Sydney also accumulated some capital resources (though of a relatively minor significance). As well as absorbing local investment money, some of the colonial banks drew supporting funds directly from England and Scottish sources.

Money under the control of men in Melbourne's Collins Street could be more readily directed to the support of new forms of colonial activity than the funds of London-controlled banks. Colonial banks were in fact anxious to find lucrative use of their funds; they were unable to do as well as their sponsors had hoped in the discounting of trade bills for importers and exporters, since the English-owned banks had little difficulty in maintaining their hold on this type of business (in which they had specialized for years). However, even though the pastoralists and the wool industry were so closely tied to sources of London-controlled capital, opportunities for employing the locally controlled money might be found in new fields of enterprise.

The expanding economy of the time brought the two forces of investment in the Australian scene into collision if not conflict—on the one hand British capital reaching out from London through banks, merchants and export houses, and shipping companies; and on the other the limited but assertive local capital, mainly centered in Collins Street, sometimes speculative and sometimes conservative but nearly always aggressive. There were fundamental differences in the type of economic activity each was prepared to support, and so representatives of the two forces seeking investment found themselves at odds over policies which could either secure more outlets for London-based capital or open new avenues for local capital. The local money could be more readily diverted to finance undertakings of significance in meeting local demand, and small settlers, men setting up in business, and traders, drew upon it. The new independence in finance, and the arrival of many people of independent means, soaring ambitions, and considerable business skill, combined to make possible the creation in Victoria of a remarkably urbanized society.

Reversing the dream of alchemists of old, abundant gold was being converted into less wondrous but more useful things. Railways were being built to serve the suburbs; water was being reticulated from the new Yan Yean supply, and gas lamps were being set aglow each night along Melbourne's paved streets. In 1860 Melbourne held more than 130,000 people; in numbers it was well ahead of Sydney. The building boom which had begun in the early 1850s continued; timber-walled, iron-roofed cottages went up at a great rate, though too slowly to take care of the great influx. At one stage there were 100,000 huts or tents, and throughout the 1860s the numbers remained high. By 1870 Melbourne's population had passed 200,000. Now the largest in all Britain's colonies, the city built on gold and wool had grown to be a significant financial centre in its own right.

It was also the scene of unrestrained struggles among politicians as the "popular will" was put to the test in a series of dramatic episodes. The *Age's* advocacy of popular causes had gained an extraordinary following, extending to include many people of independent means as well as the workingman. Syme's unremitting pressure for progressive measures was not confined to land legislation; he fervently believed in the need to get manufacturing activities started in order to give employment to the men (many of them from the industrial towns of England) who were leaving the diggings and clamouring for work. A Tariff League was formed in 1860, and soon after this Syme began his attack on the free trade defences of the merchants. He faced economic boycott, but he found support not only in Melbourne but also in the gold-towns, where American interest was strong and where many individuals were ready to support ideas for rapid development of a young country.

Taking their cue from what was being done to foster manufacturing in the United States and Canada, and in European countries, the protectionists advocated a system of higher customs duties on selected items which would protect local manufacturers of these products from outright competition from abroad. As the campaign developed and ran directly into the combined opposition of importers, businessmen, and sheepmen, the issue became one of the right of the legislative assembly, elected by manhood suffrage, to prevail over the will of the legislative council, which represented a much more restricted electorate.

Before long, serious constitutional crises were developing out of the struggle. In each, Syme's dedicated following made it possible for him to exert pressure in the legislative assembly to advance the policies of his choice. In the clash, all the radical and democratic groups came in beside the unattached city interests and those representing Australian capital to engage and oppose the pastoralists, who were backed by importers and exporters and other interests attached to English capital. The struggle went beyond mere politics: it was a clash of men fighting for their futures. They were not professional politicians, but men whose livelihood was wrapped up in the policies they espoused. Successive premiers were men who fervently believed that the rule of the majority of the assembly must be paramount; Syme, in his determination to break the power of the squattocracy and its supporters once and for all, fostered this conviction.

Serious constitutional deadlocks, involving the two houses of the Victorian Parliament and the governors, resulted from the test of will between the two groups. There were three such confrontations in all. They were spread over a dozen years, but each grew out of a sequence of events touched off by passage through the assembly of a bill arising from forcefully presented *Age* dogma.

In each of the crises, both houses acted stubbornly, each pressing to the extreme its legal powers regardless of the consequences to the community. The Council had the letter of the law on its side; but its action was out of step with the times, and in the long run the victory rested with the Assembly —and with Syme. Eventually electoral reform, which extended the franchise for the legislative council to a wider (though still restricted) electorate, produced councils less violently opposed to the will of the majority as represented in the assembly.

Similar constitutional crises occurred in several of the other colonies, but the issues were not so important, and the struggle was not so violent as in Victoria.

The driving force behind the tumult in the southern colony was to be found in the outpouring of energy by ambitious individuals bent on building a better world for themselves and their kind. In the early 1870s, English journalist and author Anthony Trollope wrote during a visit to Victoria of the transformation that had taken place in the twenty years since the gold bonanza began:

> Since that time have sprung up a people second to none in their own opinion, strong in energy, strong in industry; battling and grasping, making speeches and editing newspapers, governing themselves with more than ordinary bustle of Parliament and responsible ministers; often ignorant, always conceited, abusive among each other with more than British violence, but determined to succeed, determined to grow and to become rich—and succeeding, growing and becoming rich accordingly.

While expressing a dislike of the use of superlatives, Trollope said he felt bound to admit that probably no country had made quicker strides towards material comfort and well-being than had Victoria.

An undeniable aura of affluence and success permeated the rich men's ornate mansions that rose in spacious suburbs along the eastern bank of the Yarra. Public buildings were planned on spacious lines; the architect of Melbourne's new Government House was instructed to make the ballroom one-third bigger than that of Buckingham Palace. Local society supported theatre; the plays of Shakespeare, Sheridan, and Goldsmith were presented. In 1874 James Cassius Williamson arrived with his wife Maggie Moore to stage *Struck Oil*, the first of a long series of successes. A stream of impressarios and actors arrived; fine theatres were built as entrepreneurs organized companies. Soon other colonial capitals were sharing theatrical presentations with Melbourne.

Just as elegance was coming to the homes of the affluent, so improvements were being made in general living conditions. Gas and water supply had been introduced in Sydney, Brisbane, Adelaide, and many smaller towns, as well as in Melbourne, in the 1860s. The prosperity of the community was being consolidated. Blocks of plain and cramped terrace-houses, poorly built for the most part, were appearing in all the capitals; but generally the working-man was better housed than before, and modest villas, each with its picket fence and lawn and neat garden, were spreading. People spent freely and followed the dominant trends of the day; house interiors were cluttered with an assortment of highly ornamented vases and a mass of cushions, and romantic pictures dotted the walls.

People were still pouring in from Britain, and inbound and outbound freight was increasing steadily. Steamers—the first of them had appeared in 1856 under the Peninsular and Oriental company's flag to challenge the graceful clippers—were now dominating the passenger trade, and they were taking a large share of the cargo trade also. The opening of the Suez Canal in 1869 gave a new and somewhat shorter route than around Africa; the voyage time was cut so that it was possible to deliver mails in Adelaide or Melbourne thirty days or less after they left London. Links with the west coast of the United States—maintained as a valuable alternative means of fast communication with London—became less important as the Suez route developed and trade throughout the Empire grew.

Behind the protective security of British naval power, the colonists had no fear of being dispossessed of their inheritance. There were occasional rumours of invasion and fears of enemies, known and unknown, but war scares were short-lived. The visit of Queen Victoria's son, the Duke of Edinburgh, which began late in 1867, provided opportunities for enthusiastic demonstrations of loyalty to the Crown. Twenty huge bonfires in the Adelaide hills blazed into life to welcome him; colonial dignitaries in Adelaide, and in the other capitals, gave formal address of welcome against backgrounds of military pomp and civic splendour; there were endless agricultural and horticultural shows, sporting events, receptions, displays, and concerts to mark the Royal progress. In March 1868 an attempt to assassinate the Duke occurred at Clontarf, New South Wales, where a corroboree was being staged in his honour; an Irishman fired a revolver at short range, but the Duke's wound was not serious and he soon recovered. The attack was accepted as a crazed man's act: the Duke on his departure said the event could not "in any degree shake my conviction of the loyalty of the colonists at large—nor Her Majesty's confidence in her Australian subjects."

By the 1870s a sense of permanence had come to the frontier. For all practical purposes the territorial limits of the good land had been reached. The frontier still existed but it was no longer a moving zone. The emphasis was changing from expansion and penetration to improved use of the land already occupied. A better distribution of population was being achieved; by the late 1870s Victoria's share of the total population had been reduced to less than 40 per cent. At the same time, the increasing diversification of activities was apparent. In 1871, 44 per cent of all breadwinners had been engaged in primary industry. Within a decade the proportion had fallen to 39 per cent, with 29 per cent then engaged in industrial activities, 9 per cent in commerce, and 4.5 per cent in transport and communications, with 12 per cent in domestic service. The Australian-born had come to represent about 60 per cent of the population, and the proportion continued to rise. There were more young people in the community; four out of every ten were now under fifteen years of age. At the same time, immigration had increased and the total population rise of the 1870s, 784,000, was slightly greater than that of the 1850s and far above the half-million increase of the 1860s. The once-high ratio of males to females had been declining steadily as the growing proportion of women among the immigrants and the subsequent high rate of natural increase corrected the abnormal situation of earlier years and helped to provide the basis for a normal community.

Australians felt a growing sense of understanding and appreciation of their country. Explorers had criss-crossed the continent by the late 1860s and had revealed the general aspect of the land. The impressions of explorers, however, tended to be optimistic and were not always valid as a guide to the true nature of the country traversed. Many factors could colour individual judgements, and reports and impressions of the countryside in any area might vary greatly according to the explorer's own ideas or the season when the trip was made. Only sustained observations—impossible until permanent settlement was established—could produce sound assessments.

One of the men who did much to help developing a scientific appreciation of the nature of the land was Ferdinand von Mueller, who was both botanist and explorer. In the 1850s and 1860s he undertook a number of expeditions which greatly extended botanical knowledge. On trips in Victoria and across northern sectors of the continent, Mueller found many hundreds of new plant species, cataloguing them and noting their useful qualities. He did much to bring the value of eucalypts and acacias to the attention of experts in other countries, with the result that Australian plants were used in many lands for special purposes; but within Australia Mueller's enlightened views on afforestation were ignored as pastoralists and selectors continued to denude lands of their timber cover by ringbarking or felling trees over large areas.

Explorers were pushing deeper into the continent and penetrating new areas, their backers ever hopeful of bountiful discoveries. There was unending optimism that good land remained hidden beyond the known frontiers; but the practical boundaries of the sheep lands had been reached by 1860 and from that point it was the cattlemen who would take over to push the frontier of occupation deeper into the wilderness.

Greater numbers of men were living in the areas away from the coast; the men on horseback and the sheep dog had become symbolic. Across the pastoral lands, migratory teams of shearers and shed hands were passing from station to station in a cyclical sweep that started in Queensland early each year and moved south. Sheep stations were run as large-scale enterprises, yielding ever-increasing quantities of wool and employing a growing army of men. More and more bush workers were needed to carry out the various tasks. At the annual shearing the station hands were joined by the team of specialists, with the wool classer and the shearers enjoying favoured status among these seasonal workers and the retinue of other hands falling into place behind. By the end of the 1870s, carefully planned industrial methods were in force in the sheds; there was a clear division of duties and an assembly-line process applied.

The spread of settlement had precipitated prolonged and bitter clashes with the Aborigines. At first the tribes were able to fall back as more land was occupied, but with the quickening pace of occupation they found themselves cut off from their traditional areas of food gathering and social and ritual activities. Since the tribal groups had no permanent habitations and gave little sign of occupancy of the land, the question of dispossessing them hardly arose in the settler's mind—or if it did, the settler felt no qualms; yet the Aborigines had come to resent the intrusion of those who were moving in to occupy their traditional hunting grounds. It was an unequal struggle and the primitive tribesmen were doomed to failure in their efforts to stem the white man's encroachment.

In the south, where relatively small numbers ranged over vast areas, the Aborigines were at first docile and few direct clashes occurred. Nevertheless, the Aborigines were steadily eliminated—some of them shot by settlers in isolated encounters, many slowly pauperized and falling prey to newly introduced diseases. In the vicinity of white settlements they became unhealthily sedentary and relied more and more on the unbalanced diet of whatever they obtained from settlers and officials.

In the early years of settlement in South Australia, Western Australia, and in the Port Phillip district, Aboriginal protectorates were set up and missionary efforts to civilize and christianize the Aborigines were encouraged. In each colony some reserves, schools, farms, and food depots were set up; few of them lasted very long. In no case did these ventures—usually regarded with hostility by the settlers and with apathy by the colonial governments—succeed in arresting the decline in the Aboriginal population.

Away from the main centres, the fate of the Aboriginal groups was of necessity largely a matter of the whim of individual settlers. The Aborigines could not know anything of the great numbers of white men behind the few they saw, any more than they could comprehend the decisive firepower of the rifle or gun compared with their own primitive and expendable weapons. Across the vast and open land, minor thefts and nuisance tactics hardened to brutal assault and to killings on both sides. In the violence of attack and counter-attack, undertaken wherever and whenever opportunity presented itself, there was no means of establishing justice by punishment for the occurrences.

In the absence of law, the white settlers took vengeance in retaliation for Aboriginal attacks, and the piecemeal annihilation of tribes proceeded. In some areas (particularly in Queensland) the tribesmen's demise was accelerated by the destruction of forests that sheltered animals and birds, and various plants on which they relied for food. In one form or another, attrition continued, so that within a comparatively short time after the white settler's appearance on the scene the tribes were reduced to remnants.

It was only when settlement reached the dry lands, where the onrush of the pastoralist slowed and large areas remained untouched, that local tribes were able to adjust themselves to the new factor in their environment. In these less-favoured areas, where holdings were large and the pressure on land was less, the Aborigines could still go on living in much the same way as in the past. Over all the better pastoral lands, however, the Aboriginal way of life had been destroyed for ever.

Self-government 10

In placing in the colonists' hands the power to shape their own parliamentary institutions, the 1850 Act for "the Better Government of the Australian Colonies" proved to be a bridge to important political changes. Downing Street recognized the new status of the eastern colonies; and while the Colonial Office may not have appreciated just how quickly the Australian colonies were growing politically, the way in which the colonial legislatures set about moulding the provisions of the act soon showed that nothing less than self-government would be acceptable to ambitious colonial leaders. The act itself was a tentative step; but within five years the impediments imposed by it were swept aside and responsible government was in force.

The act arose primarily from the desire of New South Wales for a greater measure of local self-government, and from the increasingly loud demands of Port Phillip settlers for separation of their district from New South Wales. It did more than meet these demands. In addition to setting up Victoria as a separate colony and making provision for the future separation "upon the petition of the inhabitant house-holders" of any portion of the territory of New South Wales lying to the north of latitude 30° South, it gave Victoria, South Australia, and Van Diemen's Land each a legislative council two-thirds elective (as New South Wales had had since 1842). The franchise in New South Wales was greatly extended; it could now be exercised by owners of freeholds worth £100, occupiers of dwellings worth £10 a year, holders of pastoral leases, and leaseholders paying £10 a year: the same franchise applied to voters for the other legislative councils.

Each of the councils was empowered to make laws for "the peace, welfare and good government" of the colony concerned. Two important new provisions were that the colonial government could now levy non-differential customs duties (even on imports from England), and that the new Legislatures themselves could propose constitutional amendment (which would be subject to confirmation by the colonial authorities in London). Thus the council in each colony was granted the right to change the qualifications of electors and elected members, and to establish, instead of the existing legislative council, both a council and a house of representatives (or other separate legislative house) for the colony. Only in Western Australia was the transfer of power withheld; convictism had been introduced there and about half the colony's 20,000 people were convicts or ex-convicts, while trade was sluggish, with meagre exports of wool and timber; and the act therefore provided that the existing nominated council in Western Australia was to continue until a third of the inhabitants petitioned for a change, and until the colony's revenue was sufficient to meet its administrative expenses.

The act failed to provide the degree of self-government that Wentworth and his followers had sought. Wentworth's immediate reaction, when the act was received in Sydney in 1851, was that it failed to give the legislature of New South Wales full power over land policy, the appropriation of revenue raised in the colony, or the appointment of men whose salaries were paid from colonial revenue.

Moves to widen the powers granted the legislature began with the old council before it was dissolved. A remonstrance was drawn up asking for the transfer of full control over the colonial revenues (including land revenues) and over the civil service, and seeking abolition of the Crown's power to veto colonial acts, except in matters where Royal prerogatives or Imperial interests were concerned. The enlarged house, elected on the wider franchise, followed the remonstrance with a petition guaranteeing in return for these concessions to meet all costs of colonial government and to grant a generous civil list to take care of those who lost their jobs in the reorganization.

The remonstrance was received coldly at the Colonial Office. Convinced that the pastoralist-dominated legislative council could not be relied upon to dispose of Crown lands for the public good, Lord Grey refused to relinquish control of the disposal of the vast domains, and he rejected the other proposals included in the remonstrance. However, the new council's petition, which reached London in mid-1852, met with a different reception. By this time Lord John Russell's Liberal administration had been put out of office by the Tories, and Sir John Pakington had replaced Grey as Colonial Secretary. Pakington was quite prepared to grant the concessions, and the cabinet was quickly won over. Pakington notified the governors of the colonies that henceforth control of land, revenues, and civil service would be in the hands of the colonial legislatures (except in Western Australia). The decision to end transportation to Van Diemen's Land was taken at the same time.

In his dispatch, Pakington explained the policy reversal as being justified by the growing wealth and population of the colonies which had followed the discovery of gold, and noted that he considered it

> . . . a matter of justice, as well as expediency, that concessions made for some time in the principal North American colonies and recently in New Zealand, should no longer be withheld [from the colonies of eastern Australia].

Pakington expressed confidence in the colonists

... as English subjects and men accustomed to the freedom and institutions of this country which they claim the right to share and which they are so well entitled to possess.

Nevertheless, he found it desirable to impose one restriction: he would approve only a bi-cameral legislature in which the upper house was composed of members nominated by the Crown.

The Tory government did not last long; before the year was out the Whigs were back in office. The incoming Colonial Secretary, the Duke of Newcastle, did not upset Pakington's undertakings, however; he confirmed the concessions to colonial demands, and went further by dropping Pakington's restriction on the composition of the upper house, declaring that nobody was more competent than the local legislative councils to decide upon the best form of legislature.

The concessions applied not only to New South Wales but also to Victoria and South Australia, and they were extended shortly afterwards to Van Diemen's Land. The granting—in principle, at least—of self-government placed in the hands of the legislators effective power to shape future policies.

Attention in the colonies now turned from the question of what powers the legislatures held to an equally significant matter: the writing of the new constitution for each colony.

The lead was taken in New South Wales, the most politically experienced colony, where the pastoralists who had pressed so clamorously for colonial rights were now equally determined that those rights should not fall into the wrong hands. They hoped to maintain their ascendancy by restricting the right to vote and by weighting representation in parliament in favour of small numbers of rural electors as compared with electors in the populous towns. The Electoral Act of 1851 had incorporated these principles and the existing legislative council, elected under this act, was dominated by pastoral interests. Thus it was inevitable that any proposals for a constitution put forward by this council should maintain the claims of landed property to political authority, even though political agitation of a more radical kind was supported by the mass of working people, shopkeepers, and some of the less socially prominent merchants. Several small newspapers expressed the Chartist principle of equal parliamentary representation, notably *The Empire*, run by Henry Parkes, an immigrant working-man. As early as 1850 the *Empire* had proclaimed grandly:

Representation must be based solely on the basis of population, because we will never consent to be balancing houses and land or sheep and cattle against human beings.

Although Wentworth was losing popularity in the electorate (he almost lost his seat in the 1851 elections) the New South Wales Legislative Council remained firmly under his guidance, and his parliamentary skill and persuasive eloquence dominated the council's debates on the constitution. Wentworth had left behind his earlier ideas of support for emancipists and those of lesser privilege, and now he longed to see a colonial gentry of landed families leading the colonies in politics as well as in wealth and culture. He feared above all a "radical democracy" and sought to mould a community in which the pastoral interests would prevail against the increasing urban population. He believed that the essence of the British constitution was the weight it gave to the "great interests" of the community as compared with "mere population." In Australia, the "great interests"—the class that had brought prosperity to the colony—were the pastoralists,

> . . . a class which has been great and powerful in all ages and in all countries where it has existed; which must continue to be great and powerful here as long as the great interior wilds of this country can be applied to no other purpose than the sustenation of sheep and cattle.

The population of Sydney—the merchants and those they employed—were "productive of absolutely nothing to add to the real wealth of the colony" and therefore their representation in parliament should be limited. His broad aim was to establish an aristocracy based on the land, and he stated the case for the "shepherd kings" in glowing terms:

> If it had not been for these people, when transportation was discontinued to the colony it must have dwindled into insignificance, and they would have had the grass now growing in their streets. If it had not been for the squatting class their magnificent city would have shrunk into a small fishing town, unfamed, and disregarded by European nations. . . . It was this class that had caused the lofty warehouses to rise on their quays; it was this class that provided the splendid equipages that rolled through their streets, and afforded the means for all those appliances of wealth and splendour which abound in their dwellings.

As head of a committee of the legislative council that included James Macarthur and Edward Deas Thomson, Colonial Secretary since 1837, Wentworth set to work to draft a constitution which would carry into effect this concept of colonial society and best secure the future against the seemingly boundless demands of irresponsible newer elements for a say in affairs. The committee drew up a constitution in May 1853, before any of the other colonies had taken similar action. Provision was made for an upper house of members nominated for life (Wentworth had wanted an hereditary peerage, but a "bunyip aristocracy" was too much even for his supporters). Such men could be relied on to check any tendency to rash democracy in the lower house, where a fairly liberal franchise was proposed; but even in the lower house the rural element's ascendancy was to be assured by a distribution of electorates cutting down representation of the towns and enlarging that of rural districts. A further barrier against any subsequent liberalizing of the constitution was created in the proposal that major amendments could be carried only by a two to one majority.

The proposals were debated in the legislative council late in 1853. There was strong opposition from the popular party, which demanded an elective upper house, equal electorates, and abolition of the two-thirds majority clause. Henry Parkes denounced the bill as the product of a "class ascendancy" in the council, and asserted that if members weighed the fact that no less than thirty-three of the council's members had grazing interests and then looked at "the provisions Mr Wentworth has made to secure the possession of their lands in the hands of the squatting interests," they would see "that a deep design to exalt and aggrandize a class by the spoliation of the people is at the bottom of the present measure."

The council's grazier majority was not likely to be swayed by such arguments, and the committee's recommendations were carried. The draft constitution was submitted to the Colonial Office, Wentworth resigning from the council in order to go to London to plead the cause there.

In the other colonies the first round of constitution-building was hardly able to compete for attention against the dazzling spectacle of the gold bonanza, with turmoil in Victoria and a helter-skelter rush to that colony from South Australia and Van Diemen's Land. In Melbourne even news of "glorious separation" had to compete for public attention with successive reports of astonishing finds, and the details of how a separate parliament would be set up mattered little.

Colonial administrators in the three colonies, deluged beneath unexpected and onerous new tasks, wanted to see as little change as possible, and they almost dismissed such an abstract issue from their minds; when they thought about the matter they were inclined to fear the implications of introducing liberal constitutions at such a time, believing that in the gold-rush madness the less change in administrative machinery the better.

In South Australia the issue rousing excitement and controversy was that of state aid to religion. The strong nonconformist element in the community had continued to oppose the system, introduced by Governor Robe and his nominated council, of government grants to the Churches in proportion to the amounts raised by each congregation. The nonconformists, campaigning vigorously, made state aid to religion a key issue in the 1851 elections for the two-thirds elected legislative council, and enough of their supporters were returned to carry a motion for the withdrawal of all state aid to religious bodies. This made South Australia the first British colony completely to separate Church and State. One of those who helped carry the measure was the old Baptist businessman, George Fife Angas, who was elected to the council very soon after his arrival in the province.

The governor of South Australia, happy to discharge his obligations in the matter of constitution-making with a minimum of fuss, simply secured a copy of the New South Wales Constitution Bill, and used it as the basis for a bill which he introduced to his legislative council. In so doing he was ignoring the majority report of a committee of the council, which had recommended much more liberal provisions, including an elected upper house. In the governor's constitution there was to be a low property franchise for voters for the lower house, while the upper house was to have twelve members "summoned by the Crown, holding their seats for life independently of both government and people." After prolonged debates, the council finally passed the bill, which was sent to London in November 1853.

In Victoria, where preoccupation with gold obscured almost every other issue, a very conservative constitution was drawn up, largely by officials, and approved by a committee, a majority of whose members were determined to hold out strongly against any encroachment by democratic forces. In the proposal, an elective upper house was seen as a surer safeguard—because less likely to rouse popular disapproval—than a nominee one. Hugh C.E. Childers, the Auditor-General and a member of the committee that approved the proposed constitution, summed up the committee's viewpoint:

> If we establish a nominee upper house we shall have no element whatever to withstand that overwhelming democracy that from time to time every statesman must anticipate in these colonies, [and] no conservative barrier against the levelling flood of ignorance and prejudice to which every nation is subjected.

It was agreed that the basis for the legislative council franchise had to be wealth, although the unusual feature of an education qualification was added. The council was to consist of thirty members of at least thirty years of age and possessing freehold property worth £5,000. Voters for the council had to own or lease property worth £1,000; the right to vote was also extended to lawyers, clergymen, doctors, army and navy officers, and graduates of any university in the British dominions. Candidates for the lower house had to possess freehold property worth £2,000. Voters had to be able to read and write, and to own property worth £50, occupy property worth £10 a year, occupy Crown land, or have a salary of £100 a year. Voters could vote in every district in which they held property.

The draft constitution went to the legislative council for approval. In the debate, the four or five democrats accepted the "concession" of an elective upper house. There was some dissatisfaction over the property qualifications for members of the legislative assembly, but only one man spoke up for manhood suffrage. The council was determined that the miners should not be given the vote.

The other crucial question in Victoria was the distribution of seats, and the view that prevailed was that these should be based on representation of interests and not of population. A motion for creation of equal electoral districts was lost; it was calculated that on a basis of population Melbourne and Geelong would have to be given half the seats. Finally a compromise gave a break-up of twenty-six urban seats (of which Melbourne and Geelong had eighteen)with eleven mining, eleven agricultural, and twelve pastoral. In the legislative council there were to be six constituencies, of which Melbourne would be one.

Apart from heated debate, both within the council and outside, on the issue of provision for state aid to religion (to the extent of £50,000 a year) there was very little interest in the constitutional aspects; on the goldfields the matter was almost igrored. The draft was approved by the council and sent to London in March 1854.

The Colonial Office held up all three proposals while legal officers studied them. The legal view was that the clauses classifying colonial bills as either imperial or local, and limiting the governor's right of disallowance or reservation to bills of the former class, limited the Royal prerogative.

Meanwhile, in Van Diemen's Land the council had appointed a committee to prepare a constitution. The council drew upon the work done by Wentworth's committee, and the provisions of its recommended constitution varied little from those of the proposals framed in New South Wales, though they did include an upper house elected on a property franchise.

By this time the Colonial Office's comments on the measures from the three other colonies had reached Hobart, and the council therefore omitted the clauses which seemed to encroach on the Royal prerogative. With this contentious aspect cleared, the Colonial Office moved at once. It secured an Order in council confirming the Van Diemen's Land constitution; notification of this approval was sent to the colony by mid-1855 and, to mark the new status with convictism dropped, the colony was renamed Tasmania. The franchise adopted for the legislative council was severely restricted and heavily weighted in favour of landed interests (with some leavening of professional people); for the lower house the franchise was more liberal, but it still granted only about 40 per cent of men the right to vote.

The long delays in handling the constitutions submitted to London had naturally caused discontent in the other colonies. Instead of offending New South Wales and Victoria by returning their bills for redrafting, the Colonial Office decided to remove the clauses dealing with limitation of the Royal prerogative. To Wentworth's dismay, a section was inserted in the New South Wales Constitution Bill virtually permitting amendment of the constitution by simple majorities, instead of the two-thirds majorities which had been his main bulwark against change. The amended acts received parliamentary sanction and were given the Royal assent in July 1855.

Affairs followed a rather different course in South Australia. No sooner had the draft constitution left Adelaide than a petition was drawn up by indignant citizens, including diggers who had returned from the Victorian goldfields; the petition had 5,000 signatures. London's long delay in dealing with the South Australian Bill was largely due to the realization that it did not reflect the views of a large section of the community. It was not until July 1855 that the new Governor of South Australia, Sir Richard MacDonnell, received back his predecessor's Constitution Bill; in his dispatch Lord John Russell advised further consideration, preferably after public opinion had been consulted by a dissolution of the elective part of the legislative council. Lord John also pointed out that a Constitution Bill like that of Tasmania, without any clauses limiting the Crown's right of disallowance, could be accepted by the Imperial Parliament without any debate. The ensuing election greatly strengthened the radical-liberal element in the council; nevertheless the governor—accepting the broad hint from London—introduced into the council a Constitution Bill based on that of Tasmania. It was immediately evident that what was good enough for conservative Tasmania would never do for the radicals of South Australia! After considerable debate, the council passed a Constitution Bill which provided for an elective upper house, vote by ballot, triennnial parliaments, and adult manhood suffrage for the house of assembly. Plural voting was not permitted, and there was no property qualification for membership of either house.

The most interesting feature—and the one that distinguished South Australia from the other colonies—was the Electoral Law Bill. In working out the electoral districts for the house of assembly, a council committee acted on the principle that electoral districts should be as far as practicable based on population. There were to be seventeen districts, returning six, three, two, or one member according to population; the six-member district was of course Adelaide. This meant that by contrast with the planned preponderance given to conservative rural interests in the other colonial constitutions, South Australian towns would have the preponderance of seats to which they were entitled on a population basis. Although a low property qualification applied to voting for the legislative council, the whole colony was to vote as a single electorate, thus again ensuring representation according to population, which meant city dominance. A Colonial Office official considered this "the only thorough Benthamite constitution" yet enacted. The proposals were "laid upon the table" of both Houses of the Imperial Parliament, received the Royal assent, and duly became law.

South Australia was still so close to its origins that two of the province's original settlers held high office in the first parliament under responsible government; they were James Hurtle Fisher, Resident Commissioner in the early days, who became President of the Legislative Council, and George Strickland Kingston, Deputy Surveyor under Colonel Light and more recently sponsor of radical amendments to the Constitution Bill, who became Speaker of the House of Assembly.

Eighteen months passed before the dispatch of Victoria's draft constitution and its return from London in its final form. Before assent was received, the special goldfields commission (appointed late in 1854) had recommended electoral reforms which opened the way for additional representation in parliament of the non-propertied miners; eight goldfield members were added to the legislative council in 1855.

The constitution was proclaimed in November 1855 but it was nearly a year before an election was held. Preoccupation with insurgence on the goldfields contributed to the delay; but Governor Hotham and his officers did not press for the changeover, partly perhaps because they were not sure of what was involved in the transition to responsible government. The old legislative council continued in operation. Early in December 1855 the government brought in its electoral bills, and immediately it ran into a crisis. Public meetings were held on the issue of the secret ballot, for which there was strong support from the *Age* and *Argus*. A motion for adoption of the ballot system was carried in the council by a majority of eleven, the goldfields members all voting in favour. The upper house or legislative council was to consist of thirty members elected to represent six large provinces. Franchise for this house was severely restricted, while the property qualification for membership was set at a high figure—£5,000 freehold or £500 a year rental; tenure was for ten years. The provisions of the franchise for the lower house were liberal, but the electorates were far from equal: thirteen squatter seats represented not much more than 3,000 voters, whereas for eighteen seats in Melbourne and Geelong there were more than 14,000 voters.

In the Victorian elections of late 1856—the first to make use of the ballot system—there were no clear-cut party divisions. About half of those elected were merchants, traders, or professional men. Less than a quarter came from pastoral interests. Victoria's first settler, Edward Henty, won an Assembly seat, while two of his brothers were councillors, as was the live-wire publican and newspaper owner John Pascoe Fawkner. Two of the heroes of Eureka days, Peter Lalor and John Humffray, won goldfield seats.

Pressed by Ebenezer Syme—now an assemblyman—and the *Age*, measures were soon carried to extend the assembly franchise to all adult males (1857) and to make the electorates more equal in size (1858); but in abolishing the property qualification for assembly membership and accepting the Manhood Suffrage Bill, the legislative council insisted on reducing the number of goldfields seats. Plural voting remained, and electorates were still far from equal.

The New South Wales Parliament still contained a very strong party violently opposed to any such popular moves as representation by "bare numbers." Nevertheless, the two-thirds majority clause was repealed in 1857, and in the following year the secret ballot and manhood suffrage were adopted for legislative assembly elections. The weight of political power still remained with rural interests because of the distribution of electorates, which was described by Dr John Dunmore Lang, the influential Scottish ex-minister turned politician, author and publisher, as being "of the most barefaced, impudent, iniquitous description imaginable." Sydney, with a third of the voters, had very inadequate representation as compared with rural areas. This was no consolation to the frustrated Wentworth who, after a short period as President of the Legislative Council, retired in 1862, to live in England, spending the last ten years of his life far from the dangerous democracy which he was convinced was ruining the country of his birth.

Tasmania adopted the ballot in 1858, but did not introduce manhood suffrage until after federation.

The Australian colonies were in the van of progress towards an advanced form of parliamentary democracy, and were breaking down the strong barriers to fair representation which still characterized older and more economically advanced lands. Even the more conservative of them were decidedly more democratic than England, where the provisions of the 1832 Reform Act still virtually restricted the franchise to the middle class. England did not abolish property qualifications for members of parliament until 1859, while the introduction of the ballot was delayed until 1872 and adult male suffrage until 1918. Many migrants who had always been considered radicals in England were surprised to find themselves voting as conservatives in the more advanced political climate of the colonies.

One of many English politicians for whom the move to responsible government seemed to be a backward not a forward step was Lord Grey. He firmly believed that the constitution given New South Wales in 1842 (with a legislative council only, and one-third of that nominee) was better than the measure of 1850 under which democratic constitutions were granted to the colonies. In a letter written some years later Grey maintained that the 1842 provisions would have worked better, and he continued to hold that view.

Colonial parliamentary procedure was based from the beginning on the standing orders and accustomed forms of parliament at Westminster. The new legislatures had complete control of their affairs however. Further, they were empowered (subject to royal assent) to amend the Constitution Acts themselves by following procedures laid down—a two-thirds majority in each house in New South Wales, and an absolute majority in each house in the other colonies—and they had authority to amend these amendment procedures. (The two-thirds majority clause was soon amended, bringing New South Wales into line with the other colonies.)

There was no violent break with tradition involved in the change-over to responsible government. The heritage of British administrative skills was not lost, and administration remained largely undisturbed when political control passed to the colonists themselves. As things turned out, the transition brought to light some difference of opinion on the exact implications of responsible government. Sometimes the new colonial leaders, in their determination to press favoured policies, ran into obdurate opposition, and in the early years colonial self-rule produced some dramatic episodes before a balance was established between the various functions of government—executive, legislative, and judicial—in the light of the special obligations arising from unsevered links with London and uninterrupted integration with English law.

Policies were laid down by an executive drawn from the parliamentary representatives and holding power only so long as it had the support of a majority of members of the lower house; but there was no question of arbitrarily replacing administrative officials. Small as they were in population and new as they were in the right to self-government, the colonies thus had the benefit of continuity in administrative patterns and skills gained through the years of colonial rule and representative government.

Generally the officials were trained men of the utmost integrity, and some of them proved to be men of marked ability. Their quality had determined in large measure the effectiveness of government, in each of the colonies. Anti-English radicals might declare that it was the practice of the colonial office to send out men for even the highest appointments who were in fact "bankrupt alike in character and purse"; but by and large the officials, who had been the backbone of government, had provided effective and impartial administration. With self-government the colonies each acquired a civil service which, though small and sometimes subjected to parsimonious treatment, was efficient and knowledgeable. The existing administrative system was not seriously affected by the change-over, though adjustments had to be made to take into account the new status of the colonies.

The functions of the governor were completely altered with the coming of responsible government. As the *Sydney Morning Herald* put it,

Hitherto responsible solely for the conduct of legislation—himself the government—he now becomes one of the three recognized Estates. He will surround himself with men whose place and power will depend on support of the Assembly; who, if unable to maintain their position, will be obliged to yield up the staff and make way for more favoured successors.

At the same time as he lost practical power, there was a certain theoretical gain in status for the governor. He was still appointed from London, but he was now regarded as representing the Crown rather than the Secretary of State for the colonies. This was the view of the *Herald*:

> The Governor Sir William Denison has ascended to a loftier position. Formerly the servant of the Cabinet in England, he has become the representative of the Crown.

The link with the Crown was seen as the keystone of colonial self-government, and it preserved an association which was of paramount importance to the colonists. Self-government was regarded not as a measure of separation but as a means of preserving the link between the colonies and Britain, and it had been sought on that basis.

There could be no doubt about the strength and significance of the ties. In many important ways the influence of the immigrant still outweighed that of the Australian-born, though less so in New South Wales than in the younger colonies. The association with Britain was close through the personal influence of individuals as well as in economic matters; as yet among men in important positions—in politics, the judiciary and the civil service proper—only a very small proportion were native-born. Other community leaders—clergymen and journalists—were from overseas. Because of their educational background and broader experience, trained men had been sought from London for all the more important administrative posts; there were many ex-army officers and many men from the British colonial service among them. Among those who made their own way to the colonies were many whose education and social position helped give them advantages in the colonial scene. Success in business led naturally to public life. The gold-rushes attracted many men of outstanding ability and enterprise to Victoria in particular. In that colony's first parliament, against four native-born in the assembly there were twenty-eight English, sixteen Irish, and twelve Scots. The early premiers of each colony were immigrants; Victoria did not have an Australian-born premier until 1869, and South Australia until 1881.

Responsible government resulted in considerable reorganization at the highest administrative level, for the functions carried out formerly by an appointed official as department head now became a political responsibility. Before the granting of responsible government, the principal administrative officers in each of the colonies—the holders of such posts as colonial secretary, colonial treasurer, and attorney-general—had been sent out from England. These men had been ex-officio members of the executive councils and the representative legislative councils. The coming of responsible government meant that the new holders of these offices had to be chosen from among members of the colonial parliament. Sometimes the compulsorily retired officers resigned and stood for parliament, were elected, and were then chosen as members of the government. In both South Australia and Tasmania, former civil servants were the first premiers and ministers—though they were not able to hold office for more than a few months.

Those who lost their jobs as a result of the constitutional change were granted pensions, annuities, or compensation by the colonial parliaments; arguments in support of the principle of compensation were based on the point that the chief officers of the government were being called upon suddenly to surrender positions and incomes of immediate and prospective advantage as the price of great benefits accruing to the public. One of the men affected by the change summarized the position thus:

> The despatch of the Secretary of State proposing a change in the conditions of the colony required, as one of the conditions of the change, that there should be a civil list [providing pensions]; ... the constitution of the lower chamber by the new bill required that every member of the Government should gain his position or retain it by election to a seat in that chamber. ... Since it was almost a matter of certainty that some and perhaps all of the officers of Government would lose their present appointments ... it was necessary to provide for these officers, some of whom had abandoned professions and others [who] had devoted the best portion of their lives to the public service.

The offices to be held by members of parliament were listed in the various constitutions. That of New South Wales listed the attorney-general, solicitor-general, colonial secretary, treasurer, and auditor-general. Because of the predominance of legal men in this division, it was soon altered to four departments, under the control of the principal secretary, treasurer, attorney-general, and secretary for land and public works. Vigorous gold-rich Victoria started with seven political portfolios, South Australia and Tasmania, with smaller populations and less revenue, were content with five political portfolios apiece.

Below the level of political appointments, among those who were permanent civil servants in the modern sense, continuity was maintained. Most of the old appointments at the next level—the equivalent of the modern heads and deputy heads of government departments—were confirmed under the new arrangement whereby the governor (as advised by his ministers) and not the Colonial Office was responsible for the appointment. (Appointments below the higher levels had previously been made by the governor.) The continuity thus achieved was a remarkable tribute to the good sense of the men running affairs in the colonies. As in other countries at this time, civil service appointments were not made on an organized basis through competitive examination and promotion, but rather through patronage. This system continued to be the normal way of getting appointments under colonial self-government (even though it was now in different hands). Yet a spoils system did not develop, and there was no grab for offices and their perquisites. The old appointees throughout the ranks of the civil service were in general retained; by far the greater number were men who had been in the service for years—back to the 1830s in many cases in New South Wales, the 1840s in other cases.

In the case of the judiciary, the main appointments had been made from London, and again most of the appointees were confirmed in office after the 1856 change-over to self-government.

The coming of responsible government emphasized the need for an effective civil service. However, it was some years before constructive moves were made to classify the public service according to the duties performed by officers, to regulate salaries accordingly, and to create a just and uniform system of appointment. The first move came in Victoria, where a commission of inquiry was set up which led to legislation in 1862. However, it was another twenty years before the main principles of modern public service recruitment and control were introduced.

In the initial phase of self-government, there were many practical difficulties to be overcome in the transfer of power from the governors to elected representatives. The party system was not developed and the local leaders were new to political and parliamentary responsiblity. Sir William Denison, the Governor of New South Wales, a thoughtful and experienced administrator, wrote in a private letter in December 1855:

> I shall have a good deal of trouble in organizing anything like an effective government, whoever may be at the head; for in these colonies there is but little of the instinct of party. In Victoria the Government which was installed about three weeks ago has been ejected. I do not think that the persons who have come in to replace it will have a longer existence and amidst this chopping and changing of heads what is to become of the business of the country? It will take some time to teach these political neophytes that the details of the work of a government are not picked up in a week or so. In the meantime the subordinates by whom the regular business of the government must be conducted, who are to all intents and purposes irresponsible, will have the charge of what people choose to term a "responsible government."

The governor's concern on the issue of organizing a stable and effective government proved well founded. There were numerous changes and much bickering. Between June 1856 and January 1861 New South Wales had six separate ministries. Victoria had six ministries in the same period, and Tasmania and South Australia had five apiece. With no definite party system and no precedents, the groupings were necessarily erratic and unstable. A scornful observer commented on the political scene in South Australia in the 1860s:

> Parties are divided upon particular subjects. There is a squatting party and an anti-squatting party; a Government House party and a party opposed to Government House; a religious endowment party and a party unfavourable to religious endowments; but as to well-defined lines of political demarcation, you might as well look for ink spots on the moon.

The constitutions did not say the last word on colonial self-government; its operation had to be worked out by a process of trial and error, building up from precedent to precedent. The bare outline of constitutional clauses had to be interpreted in the light of day-to-day political practice. The relationships of the legislature with the governor and the judiciary had to be worked out, and inevitably there was room for disagreement in the process. Practical men tackling the problems of opening up a raw land were often impatient at the slow and legalistic aspects of the system they had inherited. The colonies were still tied to London by legal strings, and in practice the exercise of the self-government that had been granted in theory sometimes involved a struggle.

In the early years of self-government the two most important instances of this took place in New South Wales and South Australia.

The issue that developed in New South Wales in 1860 concerned the right of the governor to affix the Great Seal of the colony without the consent of his ministers. Governor Denison maintained that the letters patent creating his office conferred on him authority to keep, and use, the Great Seal; for their part the Premier and Colonial Secretary Charles Cowper and his cabinet insisted that it was constitutionally improper for the governor to act in the matter except on the advice of his executive council.

The issue arose out of a long drawn-out minor legal case involving transfer of land. In 1860 the London authorities instructed the governor to issue a deed conveying the property. On completion the deed was passed, at the governor's direction, to the premier for him to affix the Colonial Seal, which was in his custody; Cowper refused to seal the document on the grounds that he had reason to doubt the accuracy of the definition of the land referred to in the deed. The governor pressed for action, and asked for the Seal to be sent to him. Cowper deferred by handing over the instrument; but at the same time he affirmed a constitutional principle by submitting, with the Seal, his own resignation from office. Governor Denison refused to accept the resignation. Cowper next took the issue to the legislative assembly; he gave notice foreshadowing the creation of a select committee which would draw up an address to the Queen praying that she direct that the Great Seal should not be used "except with the advice and consent" of the responsible minister or of the executive council. The matter was not pressed, and shortly afterward Sir William Denison left Sydney to take up another appointment; but the strength of the support for Cowper in the assembly was fully evident, and by his assertive stand the premier had won his point.

In South Australia, about the same time, differences between legal men and legislature over land transfer laws had erupted into a bitter clash between parliament and Judge Benjamin Boothby. The battle was typical of the conflict between men who saw an empty land and wanted to do something with it for themselves and their children and those who were still thinking in terms of English traditions and the legal niceties of a dusty law library in London.

South Australia's founders had planned a central registry of land titles but nothing was done in the matter until the late 1850s. By that time practically all the colony's title deeds were either lost or held by absentees, and most of those remaining were so complicated that they were unusable as legal documents. As a result, transfers of land had become slow and very costly (as, indeed, they were in all the colonies). Lawyers had turned down every proposal for reform of the cumbersome process. In 1857 Robert Torrens, a former colonial administrator who had become Premier and Colonial Secretary, introduced legislation designed to clear the way for greatly simplified and improved land-transfer procedures. Torrens's ideas were strongly opposed by the legal profession in Adelaide (they saw their work diminishing), but the measure passed both houses of parliament and became law as the Real Property Act of 1858. Under it, an official registry was formed in the Land Titles Office, where a certificate was to be filed to record details of each pice of land; the owner of the land could then receive a copy of this certificate of title to his property. These procedures eliminated dangers inherent in the old method of land deeds, where it was necessary to undertake repeated examinations of titles. Torrens, determined that his legislation be given a fair trial, resigned from parliament in June 1858 to become head of the new Titles Department.

Opposition to Torrens's innovation was now taken to the colony's Supreme Court, where the act was challenged before Judge Boothby. Clearly the provisions of the act were unorthodox—it was intended to bring drastic change by doing away with outworn methods—and Boothby, already involved in disagreement with the colonial administration, declined to uphold the measure; he held it to be repugnant to English law and therefore invalid. Repeated amendments were made to meet the Judge's objections; but with each change Boothby moved his grounds for disavowal.

Boothby's obdurate stand against the act was entwined with other issues. The judge was already involved in disagreement with the colonial parliament, and in 1861 both houses petitioned the Queen for his removal from office. The judge maintained that since the governor had not reserved the Electoral Acts for the Royal assent, as his instructions obliged him to do, these acts were invalid; hence the Constitution Act passed by the parliament elected by this act was invalid, and so was the whole body of legislation passed by that parliament. This was a legalistic viewpoint, but it did highlight the pertinent question of whether acts passed by the colonial parliaments were valid if they conflicted with British law.

When the petition reached London the Secretary for Colonial Affairs was not prepared to cancel Boothby's appointment, but he secured the Imperial Parliament's approval for measures to validate specific acts challenged by Boothby. In 1865 the Colonial Laws Validity Act was passed; it provided that acts passed by the legislature of a self-governing colony were not invalidated by repugnancy to the fundamental principles of British law, but only to the extent that they conflicted with an Imperial statute "expressly or by intendment" applying to the colony.

The implacable Boothby still refused to review his decisions, and in 1867, after a second petition to the Queen for his removal had been refused, he was brought before the governor and executive council on five charges of judicial misbehaviour. He was found guilty and removed from office, and he died in 1868, before his appeal to the Privy Council had been set down for hearing.

By this time the Torrens land transfer system had been clearly shown to be a success, and the other Australian colonies had soon followed South Australia's lead. Queensland was the first to adopt the system (in 1861) and within a year or so Victoria, New South Wales, and Tasmania followed. Soon England began to adopt the idea, and over the next decade or so variants of the Torrens system spread to the Philippines, the United States and, indeed, to practically every English-speaking land.

In the thrust and parry of political jousting, the legislative councils still held a commanding position. The constitutions made no definite provision for the lower houses to have supremacy over the upper houses. They did not specify any procedure for breaking deadlocks between the two houses, although in their "compact of 1857" the two Houses of the South Australian Parliament worked out a compromise formula which kept the peace between them for more than fifty years. Just as the House of Commons had not yet gained the clear supremacy over the House of Lords that was to be embodied in the Parliament Act of 1912, so there was no clear intention in the minds of the framers of the colonial constitutions that the assembly should be the definitely dominant partner. In any case the Australian legislative councils— all except those of New South Wales and later Queensland being elective— did not consider themselves in the same position as the hereditary House of Lords, but more on a par with the House of Commons. Nevertheless the supremacy of the popularly elected lower house was inevitable as part of the operation of responsible government.

In Victoria sharp differences on constitutional questions did not arise in the early years of self-government, but they were to come later when the legislative assembly, bent on innovations, clashed with the conservative and unyielding council. Meanwhile, with gold still being garnered in great quantity, the pressure was towards carrying into effect advanced social objectives in the form of shorter hours of work. In the early phases of the colony's gold-rushes, working-class activity had been pushed into the background; but as carpenters and joiners, stonemasons, plasters, and brick-layers came in increasing numbers to fill jobs in the burgeoning community, trade unionism was strengthened. In 1856 the idea of a "National Trades Hall and Literary Institute" was born among Melbourne's building workers. A committee with Benjamin Douglass, a plasterer, at its head was formed to press the government for a grant of land. Douglass, whose father had been wounded in Chartist riots in England, had arrived in Melbourne in the gold-rush days; he was a forceful proponent of radical trade unionism. His committee's appeal to the government was successful; the unions were given a Crown grant of one acre, and in 1859 a small hall was completed.

Wages were considerably higher than in Britain, and the unions' pressure for improvement took the form of demands for shorter working hours. The case was argued largely on the grounds of climate and the workers' need of rest and relaxation. It was natural that the drive for reduced working hours should begin in the most economically advanced colony. The move gained wide support in Melbourne and soon spread to country towns. By mid-1856 the shop assistants' campaign for earlier closing had won general success, and by 1857 some shops were closing at midday on Saturday. In the building trades, claims for an eight-hour working day began early in 1856. An Eight Hours League was formed, and as men engaged in such activities as harness-making and coach-building joined the pioneer Operative Masons Society in the demand for shorter hours, agitation spread. Employers did not attack the principles but pointed out that it was impractical as even with the prevailing ten-hour day they were scarcely able to compete with imported goods. Some employers insisted on reducing wages in proportion to the cut in work-hours.

As the struggle went on, some strikes occurred, but within a few months a settlement was arrived at, and under it those sharing in the building boom were able to avoid the wage cuts which the coach builders had to accept. Before long bakers and butchers had agreed to reduce their employees' hours without wage loss, in line with the gains granted elsewhere. In 1859 the Political and Social Labour League was formed; its objectives included that of the legal enactment of the eight-hour working day. When the league's president won a seat in the legislative assembly he immediately started to work for this objective. The league was a natural outcome of the earlier moves for democratic rights, and in setting down a programme of popular radical demands it was the forerunner of a labour movement expressing political attitudes. The radicals in the Victorian Assembly, having gained some of their immediate objectives in terms of the original Chartist demands, were turning to legislative measures that would carry positive policies into effect.

The strong feelings aroused on the work-hours issue helped to colour attitudes to other matters related to working conditions, wage standards, and the objectives of the working man. One matter that came to the fore at this time was that of the Chinese who had begun to move into the goldfields in 1853 and soon represented a considerable proportion of the gold-seekers in some areas. They were law-abiding, but they worked long hours and much of the gold they won was sent home to China. They kept to themselves; many of them were bound financially to their own countrymen, and few understood English. Tension developed between them and the general body of miners, many of whom were quite intolerant; resentments were fanned by small incidents. Just as the presence of increasing numbers of Chinese on Californian goldfields a short time before had led to restrictive measures against their mining rights, so pressure built up to reduce the inflow into Victoria, where there was fear that the Californian experience of a massive influx might be repeated. To meet popular clamour, an Act was passed in 1855 to impose a £10 poll tax and directly limit the number of Chinese arriving on ships.

Nevertheless, by 1858 there were more than 25,000 Chinese in Victoria. Practically all of them were seeking alluvial gold, coming in to pick over old fields as the main body of miners moved on. In reworking the shafts and tailings worked by white men they generally had some success, though as surface gold deposits were exhausted their rewards dwindled. Resentment against the Chinese remained among the miners; they were regarded as mere parasites, and their presence was seen as a social evil. The poll tax was raised and, with the gold yield dwinding, the inflow of Chinese to Victoria stopped.

In 1858 South Australia, faced with the same issue, adopted similar legislation. By 1860, New South Wales, where a restrictive bill had earlier been passed by the legislative assembly but killed by the employer-dominated council, had 12,000 or more Chinese, most of them engaged in gold-mining. In 1861 an exclusion bill was presented again, and this time it was passed. An ugly incident had occurred when Chinese in search of gold swarmed to the new field at Lambing Flat, near Yass, and were driven from the diggings by the white miners.

In the competition for survival, the habits of the Chinese seemed to threaten the high wages and high standards of living that Australians were already determined to maintain and improve. The miners' strong feelings on the issue had a parallel in the attitudes prevailing on Californian goldfields in the 1850s. After the California State legislature's $20-a-month "foreign miners' licence" tax of 1850 was suspended, a wave of Chinese immigration began; by 1853 the influx was so great that the law was re-enacted, with the fee fixed at $4 a month. California was not a sovereign state and so could not totally prohibit the entry of Chinese, nor harass them, but in some mining districts it was specifically provided that "neither Asiatics nor South Sea islanders" would be allowed to mine for themselves or others. In other districts, prejudice against the Chinese strengthened among the independent miners, who continued to press for restrictive anti-Chinese legislation against the wishes of employers who favoured the immigration of cheap Chinese labour. Restrictive laws passed by the Californian State legislature (most of them imposing increased taxes on the Chinese) were declared unconstitutional and so invalid.

The question of the Australian colonies' rights to restrict immigration had not been finally confirmed, but meanwhile they were free to legislate on the subject, at least on a temporary or emergency basis. When it appeared that the flood of Chinese immigration had been deterred by poll taxes, the colonies' restrictive acts were repealed—by SouthAustralia in 1861, Victoria in 1865, and New South Wales in 1867. Nevertheless, a deep-seated animosity for the Chinese, based on economic grounds, remained among Australian workers. The feeling sprang from a fear that these people threatened to undercut wages. It was antagonism by a free-spending people against men who lived at subsistence level.

Even before the surface gold petered out, many of the Chinese took up market gardening—something quite new in a land where no small-scale tilling of the earth had been successful. The industrious and painstaking efforts of the Chinese market gardeners were rewarded, and vegetable-growing on small plots was established around Melbourne and elsewhere.

After the withdrawal of Gladstone's proposed colony at Port Curtis in

1847, and the tragedy of the Kennedy expedition up Cape York Peninsula a year later, it was some years before any concerted effort was made to create a new colony in the tropical and semi-tropical north. Kennedy's fate—he was speared by Aborigines, while nine others of his party of thirteen died of starvation or were lost without trace—was a grim deterrent to any thoughts of settlement in the far north. Meanwhile, Brisbane was growing as an export centre for wool, hides, tallow, sheepskins, beef, staves, and timber, as the pastoral invasion moved deeper into the hinterland; in the 1850s during over-landing activities vast holdings were taken up, and the occupation moved north and west. The pastoralist politicians dominating colonial affairs gave no support to the drive for separation which was developing as Brisbane interests pressed the issue. Under the 1850 Act power had been reserved to set up a new colony "northward of 30° South latitude." This limit had been defined to meet demands presented in a petition submitted in May 1850 by northern graziers, who wanted to see New England and the Macleay district included in a new colony; but powerful influences, including Governor Denison, wanted these districts kept in New South Wales, and as the popular cause gained increased parliamentary success, people in the main towns of the New England area began to oppose separation. Meanwhile, fears had grown among New England pastoralists that Brisbane influences would be inimical to their interests, and they dissociated themselves from the growing Brisbane clamour.

After the Brisbane separationists had produced figures to show that more was being contributed in revenue from taxes and customs duties than was being spent in the whole northern area, the Colonial Office agreed that a new colony should be set up. The southern boundary was set at the 28th parallel of latitude, leaving the contentious districts in New South Wales. Under letters patent of June 6, 1859, the Colony of Queensland was created, and Sir George Ferguson Bowen, who was appointed first Governor, arrived in Brisbane in December to take up his duties. The population of the new colony numbered 23,500. From the beginning Queensland was to have a parliament; modelled on the New South Wales legislature, its upper house was of nominated members, the lower house elective. The western boundary of the new colony, 141° East longitude, extended from the southernmost point of the Gulf of Carpentaria. In 1860 a request was sent to the Colonial Office asking that the boundary be moved westward to the 138th parallel of longitude, and approval was granted in 1862 for the annexation of the 120,000 square miles involved.

Meanwhile the north-central area of the continent remained attached to New South Wales, and the Speaker of the Queensland Legislative Assembly suggested to London that this additional area be annexed temporarily to Queensland; but, following reports of valuable grazing land there, the Governor of South Australia applied for the area on behalf of pastoralists under his jurisdiction, and in 1863 the 600,000 square-mile Northern Territory was placed by London authorities under the temporary administrative control of South Australia.

Three months elapsed between the arrival of the governor and the meeting of Queensland's first parliament. As the business of government had to be carried on Bowen appointed a caretaker ministry led by Robert Wyndham Herbert, the youthful former secretary to Gladstone, who had come out to the colony as Bowen's private secretary. Herbert and all Bowen's other appointees were duly elected. to parliament, and the makeshift Herbert ministry "weathered the storms of three parliamentary compaigns," attaining, as Bowen put it, "a patriarchal age for an Australian ministry." Herbert continued in office until he resigned in 1866, as he wanted to return to England.

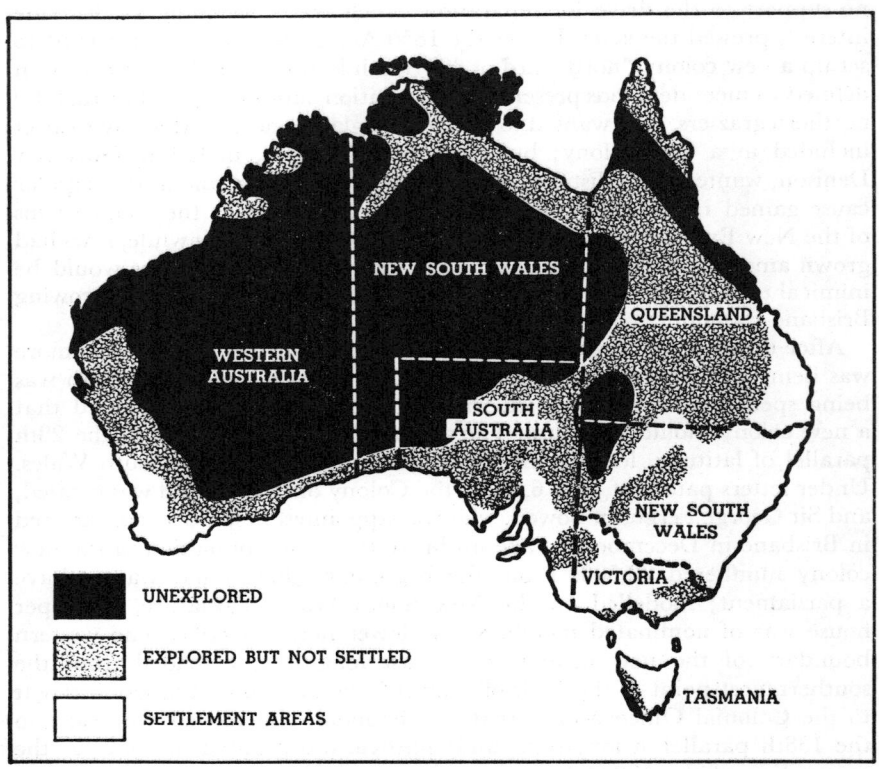

By 1859 little of eastern Australia remained unexplored, and most of the good land had been taken up by graziers. Victoria had been proclaimed a separate colony in 1851 and Queensland created eight years later. Tasmania was so named from 1853.

Queensland was bent on expansion. One of the earliest resolves of the new parliament had been to build up the population of the new colony as rapidly as possible. A land-order system was devised as part of a plan to attract new settlers with the prospect of their becoming landed proprietors with small outlay. Agents were appointed to tour Britain and Germany; in England and

Scotland the sign WANTED, YOUNG MEN FOR QUEENSLAND, attracted attention and many prospective settlers were interviewed. All who paid their passage to Queensland were assured of a land-order, worth £18, as part-payment for any land taken up in the colony. In three years or so, nearly 25,000 people landed in Queensland.

The five eastern colonies had gained control over their own affairs, but Western Australia remained under the old system, with the governor exercising policy control assisted by a part-official part-nominee legislative council. The stagnant settlement of the 1840s had barely begun to move forward when self-government was being introduced in the other colonies, and Western Australia was therefore excluded from the provisions of the Act of 1850 "for the time being." Discovery of lead and copper ore in 1848–49 in the Geraldton area had taken some people north, and elsewhere public buildings were beginning to take shape in various towns, but the vast colony was still almost untouched in 1850, when the first shipload of convicts arrived from England.

By this time the British government had learnt one lesson about the convict system, and the rate of transportation was strictly limited to the numbers that could be profitably employed; numbers sent to Western Australia in any one year were counted in hundreds, not thousands. In the ten years from mid-1850 more than 5,500 convicts, all men, were sent to the colony. Over the same period there were more than 3,000 free immigrants—either guards and their families, or assisted passage settlers. Increased expenditure by the administration gave an important lift to the economy; roads and buildings were constructed, and the amount of money in circulation increased. The farmers gained an increased market for sale of wheat and meat, while pastoralists and settlers benefited from the cheap labour force provided by the convict system. Throughout the 1850s there was steady progress; wool, copper, lead, hardwood sleepers for railway construction, sandalwood, pearlshell, and horses were exported. Although land utilization was still inhibited by the government's insistence on maintaining a uniform price for sale of Crown land (£1 an acre until 1859, then 10/– an acre,) new grazing country was opened up following the issue in 1849 of regulations permitting long-term pastoral leases. Reports of good pastoral country in some of the remoter areas were coming in, and there was speculation that the colony almost certainly had gold-bearing country. There was still no magnet to draw ambitious people, however, and Western Australia remained far behind the eastern colonies. By 1860 its population was no more than 15,000, and there were only 250,000 sheep and 30,000 cattle in the colony.

In 1868, when a total of almost 9,700 convicts had arrived, transportation was brought to an end. The colony was on its feet; pastoral expansion was accelerating, and larger areas were being sown to crop each year. By 1870 sheep flocks exceeded 600,000 head, and 50,000 acres were being farmed. A new eighteen-man legislative council, based on the two-thirds elective principle, was set up; it marked the introduction of representative government in the colony, lasting, with changes (including an increase in council membership to twenty-four, with sixteen of them elected, in 1882) until the granting of responsible government twenty years later.

With the expansion of activity in the eastern colonies in the early 1850s came the introduction of steam traction railways. The first moves were made in Sydney, but Melbourne led the way with the completion in September 1854 of a $2\frac{1}{2}$ mile line extending from the heart of the city to the pier at Sandridge (Port Melbourne). Constructed by the Hobson's Bay Railway Company, the line was of broad gauge (5 feet 3 inches); carriages and wagons were delivered from London but the locomotive was built locally. (It ran in fits and starts for a few months, until regular locomotives arrived from England.) Land for the line, and some money to finance the undertaking, were granted by the government. Other lines to the suburbs were built during the next few years by private companies, with official assistance; in the 1860s some lines were amalgamated, and finally the assets of the private companies were acquired by the government.

Construction of the first line in New South Wales—a 13-mile Sydney-Parramatta link—was begun by a private group in 1850, but after advancing large sums the government felt compelled to step in to complete the work. Of standard gauge (4 feet $8\frac{1}{2}$ inches), the line was operated from 1855 and was the first government-owned railway to be opened on British territory. Earlier, another company had begun construction of a line in the Newcastle area but in 1855 it was in financial difficulties and the government completed the line, which was opened in 1858. Subsequently construction under government direction became the practice in New South Wales and in other colonies.

Construction of railways in South Australia had been proposed first in 1846. A company formed in London proposed a 7-mile line between Adelaide and the port, but interest flagged. The government then voted funds for railway construction (thus setting a precedent for all colonies to follow in turn) and in 1851 began the building of a broad-gauge line which was opened five years later. In 1856 a board of railway commissioners was appointed to finance, construct, and operate railways. From the beginning railways in Queensland were built by the government. Construction of a line running inland from Ipswich began in 1863. For reasons of economy a narrow-gauge track (3 feet 6 inches) was adopted. A second line, extending from Rockhampton, was opened in 1867. By this time lines had been pushed inland in Victoria to reach the pastoral wealth of rich valleys north of the ranges, and to tap the agricultural potential there. In New South Wales the steep mountain country behind Sydney was still a barrier, but lines in the Newcastle-Maitland area were operating by 1857 and the mountains were soon crossed.

The extension of lines deeper into rural districts could not always be expected to be a profitable venture, but governments saw the need to develop railways as the backbone of a transport system to serve the rural economy, and they financed them accordingly. Thus, by circumstance, the practice developed of providing public funds for what was soon to become a basic form of transport and colonial governments found themselves operating large-scale railway enterprises.

With self government a reality, it was realized that educational facilities must be greatly extended and improved if manhood suffrage were to work satisfactorily. Apart from the enormous practical difficulties of keeping schooling not too hopelessly far behind the spread of settlement, there was room for wide difference of opinion on questions of governmental control and governmental aid for education, and from time to time these questions were the central issue of public controversy and political debate in each of the colonies.

The educational organization established in 1848 in New South Wales and Tasmania, with a state or national elementary school operating side by side with denominational schools, both systems being controlled by boards of education and both receiving financial aid from the government, remained in operation in these two colonies for some years. Victoria and Queensland, when they received their independence from New South Wales, both carried on with the dual system. South Australia's approach was rather different: in 1851 when the short-lived period of state aid to religious denominations came to an end, a central board of education was set up which saw to it that state aid was given only to licensed schools where non-denominational religious instruction was given. Although state aid was withdrawn from the churches in the other colonies—Tasmania and Queensland in 1859, New South Wales in 1862, Victoria in 1870—financial subsidies were still made to schools run by religious denominations, though increasingly with conditions attached.

The general trends in the late 1850s and 1860s were towards strengthening the state school systems, centralizing the educational organization, and bringing church schools more firmly under official supervision. Increasingly political controversy centered on whether state financial aid should be withdrawn from schools unwilling to follow the general line of basically-secular education. A single board or council of education replaced the two boards in Queensland in 1860, in Victoria in 1862, and in New South Wales in 1866. Under the new systems in the two latter colonies state aid was still available to existing denominational schools, but only under certain conditions, and new denominational schools qualified only if they were a set minimum distance from the nearest state schools.

The Protestant churches were able to accept the conditions laid down by the colonial governments for educational grants without conscientious scruples, but it was a different matter for the Catholic church. Because of the poverty in their flocks and the urgent need for schooling, the Catholic hierarchy had usually complied with governmental conditions, but its attitude became much more uncompromising after publication in 1864 of the papal Encyclical and Syllabus of Errors, which asserted Catholic educational ideals, condemned mixed schools, and declared that education should never be subjected to the civil-political power. Meeting in Provincial Council in 1869, Australian Catholic bishops issued a statement of education aims: they accepted the need for government inspection of schools, but maintained that the only type of school acceptable to their church was one in which there was complete freedom of denominational action; at the same time they asserted their right to their "just proportion of the public revenues which are yearly set apart for the education of the people." Back in their dioceses, the Bishops pressed forward with a vigorous educational campaign: new schools were built, Catholic children were withdrawn from non-Catholic schools, a newly-founded Australian teaching order (the Sisters of St Joseph) was extended from South Australia to other colonies, and the Catholic viewpoint on education was proclaimed in sermons, pastorals, and speeches.

The Protestant majority considered the new Catholic schools divisive and exclusive, and a portent of future political regimentation. The state was doing its best to build schools for all; why should a share of its funds be diverted towards schools that would hinder rather than help the achievement of democratic equality and social cohesion? Thus sectarianism came to the forefront among the many strands of opinion—the liberal belief in education as the birthright of citizenship, the democratic dislike of church schools as incubators of class privilege, the rationalism and agnosticism of the age of Darwin, the voluntary principle upheld by the more extreme Protestant denominations—which determined the mould in which the Australian educational system was to be cast.

Sectarianism was strongest in Victoria, which in 1872 passed a momentous Education Act setting up a system of free, compulsory and secular education. The whole system was to be administered by a central department of education under a minister responsible to parliament; all state aid was to be withdrawn from schools outside this system. Teachers were forbidden to give religious instruction (although later it was provided that such instruction could be given at the schools outside schools hours). The Victorian legislation set the pattern for the other colonies, although details of the clauses relating to religious instruction differed. In 1875 Queensland and South Australia both adopted a broadly-similar system, to be followed five years later by New South Wales and in 1885 by Tasmania. Western Australia—something of an odd-man-out in education policy—had withdrawn state aid from Catholic schools in 1855, but in 1871, following the reformed English systems of a year earlier, introduced a dual system of government and assisted (denominational) primary schools; after the granting of self government to the colony, this sysem came under popular fire, and a new education act (1895) put an end to state aid and brought education policies into line with those in the other colonies.

In each of the colonies, meanwhile, the Catholic church pushed on with the creation of a network of primary schools parallel with the state system. Fees were low, and teaching expenses were kept down since the teachers were unsalaried nuns and monks. Organization was on a parish basis. The other denominations closed down most of their primary schools, concentrating their efforts on secondary education to provide a prestigious, academic, Christian secondary education for the children of the upper and middle classes.

In the pioneer University of Sydney (1852) the sectarian issue had been avoided by confining theological studies to the affiliated colleges and seminaries, which were under denominational control. The same pattern was adopted when universities were founded in Melbourne (1855), Adelaide (1874), and Hobart (1890).

As yet most primary school teachers were inadequately trained. There were a few "model schools" and teachers' training institutions in the cities, but most teachers started their careers as fourteen-year-old pupil-teachers and learnt their jobs as they did them.

Although the sections of the education acts that created most controversy in press and parliament were those dealing with state aid and religious education, the free and compulsory clauses (which did not differ from colony to colony) were no less significant. They represented an Australian solution to the basic educational problems created by the thin spread of settlement over a vast continent, problems for which the English educational system, evolved in very different conditions, offered no precedents. The educators of the 1870s and 1880s were determined to face up squarely to these problems. As James Wilberforce Stephen said in introducing the Victorian Education Bill of 1872:

> We have been for years following a policy of spreading people over the land; some of our best immigrants are in remote districts. We have sent them out into all corners of the country, and it is our plain duty to follow them with schools.

Hence the need for free education and—since this alone was unlikely to provide sufficient inducement to parents in country districts who desperately needed their children's help with the farm work—the introduction ("in a very mild and gradual form") of the experiment of compulsory education.

The Education Acts heralded the one-teacher rural school; soon hundreds of these schools were appearing. This feature of the educational scene was paralleled in some parts of the United States, where similar settlement conditions prevailed. With an attendance of as few as ten pupils and nowhere more than thirty, spread over all grades, these schools were well-adapted to the needs of the day. Academic learning was not such an important factor; the emphasis was on practical subjects. However, under the control of an enthusiastic and capable teacher, such a school could provide a sound basic education and at the same time help the youngster appreciate the need for initiative and co-operation.

A strong democratic idealism inspired the Education Acts. Educators were insistent that their free schools were not to be looked at in the same light as English "charity schools" but—as Stephen put it—"as one of the advantages derived from living in a free country where all co-operate in supplying the common necessities." Henry Parkes, speaking of New South Wales developments, expressed the same ideal when he claimed that

> ... our system of education ... opens the door to every child without distinc-

tion as to creed, sect, country or colour. It abolishes once and for ever the idea that the public school is a poor man's school or a class school. It has so completely abolished that invidious distinction that the children of the poorest and the richest man can sit side by side receiving the same amount of instruction and yet feeling each his spirit of independence. . . . Instruction is given not only for the benefit of the children but also for the sake of society hereafter. It seeks to secure sound primary instruction to all as the basis of character and at the same time to familiarize the children with each other, so that whether they are rich or poor they should feel themselves members of the same human family and responsible members of society.

The effect of the spread of schooling to more and more children was to be reflected within a generation or so in a rising level of literacy and in new national attitudes.

On the sheep's back   11

When the first gold-rushes occurred, many of the sheepmen were convinced that disaster had struck the country. A Victorian pastoralist summed up their attitude in a letter to a relative:

> There have been most unfortunate circumstances ever since you left. In the first place, there was the greatest drought ever known, next the wettest season within the memory of man, and to crown all, the discovery of gold.

Certainly the immediate exodus from the land made life extremely difficult for the landowners. Men were no longer willing to work at humdrum tasks on the sheep runs when chances for winning quick riches on the goldfields seemed so bright. Even though wages went up, it was increasingly difficult to hold men to the monotonous life of tending flocks. In the first years of the gold-strikes, the pastoral industry almost stagnated, even though in Yorkshire the demand for Australian wool was still growing and, with greatly improved shipping services as an outcome of gold, shipping freight charges were considerably lower. The sheepowners, many of them with large investments in their holdings, had to find ways of solving the labour problem if they were to stay solvent. They did what they could to recruit labour. Wages rose to unheard-of levels, and the work was somehow done—by a combination of new arrivals and Aborigines and some old hands who remained. Nevertheless, the comparatively large force of shepherds and hutkeepers required for each unfenced run dwindled away; in the first five years of the gold-rushes the number of men engaged in the pastoral industry fell by more than one-fourth.

Simpler, less labour-consuming methods of sheep management had to be found. Meat prices were higher—mainly as a result of the new arrivals' appetite for meat—and the land was potentially more profitable than ever. If a way could be found by which the flocks could be guarded equally efficiently by fewer men, the graziers knew that the future would be bright.

Fencing of runs was the key. With more capital available, at reasonable interest rates, the pastoralists (enjoying security of tenure under the 1847 regulations) were prepared to fence their holdings. Once the land was fenced the sheep might be left unattended at night. The old shepherds could be replaced by fewer numbers of mounted boundary riders; Australian sheep-raising was beginning to take on its characteristic aspect of minimum use of labour.

The fencing of runs began in Victoria, close to the goldfields, in the late 1850s, and it spread steadily; wherever wages were highest it was quickly adopted. Contractors—mainly disappointed miners—were available for the work. In the 1860s wire fences began to spread their patterns across the New South Wales sheeplands, moving steadily northwards.

Fencing brought other gains. In the paddocks, the sheep were far less subject to disease than when they were herded together each night. Their fleeces remained cleaner, so that the traditional pre-shearing job of washing each sheep could be dropped. Roaming freely, the sheep cropped the grass more evenly; on richer lands the native grasses, many of them tussocky, were eaten down so that a better sward resulted.

Left to themselves within their sprawling paddocks, sheep became more robust and more active—and less accustomed to being yarded. Sheep dogs were now more important for the handling of sheep. The English breeds possessed patience and intelligence, but the open-paddock conditions were a-gainst dogs with long and hairy coats. Many breeds—even greyhounds—were tried in the effort to meet the need for a lithe and energetic sheep dog able to cope with these conditions. Finally a new strain, known as the kelpie, was developed in the 1860s. With fleetness of foot and the tireless endurance needed for the rounding-up of sheep and handling of large flocks, the kelpie breed soon won favour and was widely adopted as part of the new methods of sheep management.

Once the gold-fever subsided, more labour became available. When gold-seekers realized that the remaining gold lay too deep for the independent miner to reach, many of them began to look for a permanent life on the land. With wool output increasing so rapidly, it was not too difficult for them to find jobs in the pastoral industry, or to work on their own account. Some turned to shearing and some became teamsters who transported wool for shipment and carried in supplies to the stations; other became contractors specializing in such tasks as fencing or ringbarking trees to clear the land for pasture. The industry was becoming better organized.

More attention was being given to the breeding and selection of sheep as far-sighted property-owners became aware of a need to invest in the work of enhancing the wool-bearing characteristics of their flocks. Consequently, fleece weights began to increase.

By the end of the 1850s the wool industry had overcome the disruptions caused by gold and was beginning to move forward again. Over the whole decade, however, the number of sheep in all the colonies had increased by only three or four million, a much slower proportionate increase than in the previous decade. By 1860 there were 20,000,000 sheep in the colonial flocks.

To offset successes, graziers endured calamities, irritations, and annoyances. Among the natural disasters, bushfires or floods might punctuate the seasons, and dry spells were all too frequent. And no matter how the sheepman tried, he seemed unable to achieve a happy balance with nature; having succeeded in his efforts to eliminate the Aboriginal tribesmen and the dingoes from his chosen area, he might be faced with a new challenge to his sheep in the form of a plague of kangaroos, for these animals flourished when the consumers of kangaroo-meat were removed. One writer of the day, noting that where a few score had originally existed there were very soon a thousand once the Aborigines and dingoes had been disposed of, feared that in many places the kangaroos might "jostle the sheep and his master off the land." On some properties thousands of kangaroos were slaughtered year after year without any great effect on the numbers; but the sheepman was not likely to give up his land, no matter how persistent the kangaroo might be.

Outlaws appeared from time to time to steal horses, or, occasionally, to terrorize the station owners. From quite early days, individuals or gangs using the bush as a base for their operations had been robbing people and stealing stock. At first nearly all the bushrangers had been convicts who had managed to escape from custody, and although in Van Diemen's Land such men were a menace, they were of little consequence on the mainland. Then, with the discoveries on the Victorian goldfields, the temptation to seize gold as it was being transported over lonely roads induced free-born adventurers as well as ex-convicts to set themselves up as bushrangers in the lawless years. As security for the transport of gold improved, the hold-ups became fewer. A new outbreak of bushranging occurred in the early 1860s in Victoria, New South Wales, and Queensland; for the most part the bushrangers were the sons of poor settlers. The horses they stole from station properties gave them mobility to hold up coaches and to attack travellers or towns-people or to rob post offices and then gallop away. They were able to find refuge among friends, many of whom saw little wrong in their infamous adventures, and they relied upon the fear of reprisals to dissuade others from reporting their movements to the police.

The land was wide and almost empty, and bushranging seemed almost a natural part of its life. The pluck and daring of the swaggering young men who held up the rich—their stand as individuals against an increasingly affluent society—bathed them in an aura of romance. They were quick-witted, often courageous, and vain, and they possessed a spurious dignity. They lived for the day and were not always bloodthirsty, usually preferring to vanish into the bush with their booty and to rob another day, but even the petty thieves among them were prepared to kill those who got in their way. The names of such desperadoes as Daniel Morgan, Frank Gardiner, "Captain Thunderbolt" (Frederick Ward), "Captain Moonlight" (Andrew George Scott), Ben Hall, John Gilbert, and Alpin McPherson, struck fear in the hearts of many a family living away from police protection. Attacks on remote stations were by no means rare; and when the mounted troopers arrived it was usually too late to catch the bushranger.

After initial successes, the men became increasingly bold and desperate. Newspapers carried a stream of news about outlaws, highlighted by the occasional item on some individual's capture or demise, such as a message from Rockhampton in September 1864 presented under the headline, WRIGHT THE BUSHRANGER SHOT DEAD! Wright was one of twenty-three bush-rangers killed or hanged for their crimes between 1862 and 1867. In that period a score of men had been shot dead or had died from wounds inflicted by these men, and almost as many police had been wounded in encounters with them.

Throughout the 1860s the wool industry moved forward on a broad front; it was the decade of the sheepmen's most notable success. Behind the expansion was a surging demand for wool by British mills, resulting in higher prices. From a low of $9\frac{1}{2}$ pence a pound (greasy) in 1858, the price of Australian wool in London moved up to 14 pence in 1860. When the outbreak of the American Civil War in 1861 interrupted the supply of cotton, all fibre prices rose and requirements of British textile mills increased sharply. The fine wool of Australia and New Zealand won a larger proportion of the expanding fibres market, and purchases from these sources in 1865 were 70 per cent greater than five years earlier. By this time more than half of Britain's wool imports were coming from the southern lands.

As well as consolidating in the areas of earlier success, the sheepmen were now pushing on into new regions. They were thrusting north-west across Queensland, and moving in to occupy a broad tongue of land in the drier tracts of South Australia. At the same time, the north-west sector of New South Wales was taken up, and in Western Australia a coastal fringe running into the tropics was occupied. Much of this newly occupied land had low and uncertain rainfall, and it could be successfully worked only in vast holdings, but venturesome graziers were not easily dissuaded when new horizons opened.

While enterprising pastoralists were thrusting forward into new and drier lands, the main development still hugged the well-watered areas of the south-eastern sector of the continent, where wool output continued to rise. Along and across this fertile crescent, a well-organized stagecoach enterprise was conveying mail and goods and passengers along everlengthening routes; the firm that ran these services was Cobb & Co., which owed its origins to the gold-rush days.

Heavy coaches, either imported from England or built in Sydney to English design, had been in use for years previous to this in areas close to Sydney and, from the early 1850s, on runs which took them considerable distances inland. Similar services were fanning out (usually on shorter runs) from other colonial capitals when gold spurred the bigger enterprise in Victoria. In 1853 Freeman Cobb and three fellow Americans set up a coach service modelled on the lines of similar American operations; its immediate purpose was to serve the principal Victorian goldfields, and it linked Melbourne with Geelong, Ballarat, Bendigo, and Castlemaine.

Experience gained in working for the American organizations of Wells Fargo and the Adams Express Company helped Cobb and his associates to make a success of the venture from the start. The Victorian Government was soon supporting Cobb & Co. with a subsidy as well as granting it mail contracts. Its red-painted American-built coaches, their bodies suspended on leather straps to lessen jolting on rutted tracks, were eminently suited to the raw Australian bush. Teams of four to six horses were used; they were changed at halfway houses or 10-mile inns. "The regular bush inn" was described by a traveller as having similar characteristics far and wide; he noted that

> ... it is always a very long and low building, of brick or weatherboard, with a verandah along its whole front; above it stands a more or less ornamental signboard. Under the verandah, facing the front, there is a long series of doors—one leading to the bar, another to a billiard or bagatelle room; then come one or two private rooms, and then bedrooms *ad libitum*.

As more land was taken up, and the number of travellers rose, the call for coach services increased. Ownership of Cobb & Co. changed hands, but the company continued to prosper as it was reorganized and its operations expanded. For some years the Victorian goldfields traffic remained the backbone of the firm's activities, but when railways were extended to the mining districts (from the early 1860s), the head of Cobb & Co., James Rutherford, succeeded in persuading his partners that it would be best to transfer operations to New South Wales. The new headquarters were established with great fanfare in Bathurst in 1862. Rutherford, recording the invasion of New South Wales from Bendigo, noted that the cavalcade was "quite an imposing affair"—103 horses, of which 80 were in harness drawing ten scarlet coaches and two feed wagons. Bathurst was to remain the firm's centre of operations for more than fifty years, and it became a coachbuilding centre. The business of Cobb & Co. extended to Queensland in 1865, and it grew rapidly in the following years; its services reached more and more outlying centres and provided exssential communication links for isolated settlements scattered across 500,000 square miles of territory. By 1870 the Cobb & Co. organization in the three eastern colonies was harnessing 6,000 horses every day, and its coaches were travelling 28,000 miles a week.

Coaches were able to provide a mail service and to overcome isolation in many areas, but the product that dominated the life of the inland had to be moved by slower methods of transport. Bullock teams, or heavy horse teams, were needed to haul the great wagonloads of wool to port on journeys that might take weeks; but some of the wool men had been exploiting another channel that lay open: the river network of the Murray-Darling system, reaching deep into the back country. With paddle-steamers available to ship out the annual wool clip inexpensively, large new areas of remote but useful grazing land along the rivers could be occupied.

The early drive toward river navigation had come from South Australia in the early 1850s. Interested in drawing commerce to the colony, the Governor, Sir Henry Young, had encouraged the idea, and he had been largely responsible for the government's offer of a reward of £2,000 each for the first two iron steamers of not less than 40 horse-power to navigate the lower reaches of the Murray to its junction with the Darling. In 1853 Captain Francis Cadell, in the *Lady Augusta*, carried a party (including the governor) from South Australia upstream beyond the Murrumbidgee junction; above Swan Hill the steamer turned back, taking on a cargo of wool for the return voyage. A smaller steamer, built on the banks of the Murray by William Richard Randell, went 300 miles further to Moama. Cadell, on his return to Adelaide, formed the River Murray Navigating Company, and another group with rural interests set up the River Murray Company in competition. Thus began the commercial river trade.

Business was brisk for Cadell's fleet and a number of privately-owned boats. Paddle-steamers, each with a barge or two in tow, were soon moving out of the Murray itself and nosing their way along the Murrumbidgee, the Darling, and the Edward, to reach the isolated sheep stations, taking provisions to them and picking up their wool. At the point nearest the station shearing shed, wool bales were stacked on the bank for the river boat to pick up. The steamers, shallow of draught and broad of beam, were generally driven by side paddles, though a few were stern-wheelers. Many were built in the little towns that were springing up along the lower reaches of the Murray. The steamers were fired with timber cut along the banks, and before long there were woodcutters' huts at intervals along the river. Soon riverboat captains were running a thriving business and, like the Mississippi rivermen, were selling a wide variety of wares at each stopping place deep in the inland. The arrival of a steamer was an occasion of special interest and excitement for people in the river towns and for miles around.

As the river trade flourished, transit facilities were developed near the mouth of the Murray, where sandbars blocked direct navigation. Goolwa, the point on the river nearest the sea, became the trans-shipment point for wool brought out from the hinterland and for goods taken to the isolated stations and settlements. Governor Young considered the possibility of having a canal dug to link Goolwa with Port Elliot, on the coast, but this idea was dropped and instead a horse tramway was built and opened in 1854 to connect the ports.

River navigation could be greatly affected by seasonal conditions. The river flow was fickle, and in dry seasons and for much of the year sections of the streams were frequently too shallow for navigation; boats were sometimes stranded for months at a time. Everywhere the dangers of sandbars, hidden logs and snags, and floating debris created difficulties. Nevertheless, the river fleet grew and extended its range of operation; wool was not a perishable commodity and as more stations were established along the river frontages of the wide-ranging area and wool clips expanded, greater numbers of paddle-steamers nosed their way along the fitful rivers, either carrying in provisions and equipment or laden heavily with bales of wool starting the long journey to British mills.

If the river trade was profitable to the riverboat operators and vital to the owners of scattered and isolated stations, it also represented an important part of the commerce of the three colonies concerned. The Governments of New South Wales and Victoria saw the trade of the wool lands being captured by South Australia in ever greater volume. Victoria was the first to take steps to reverse the trend; her weapon was the railway. Some railway lines had been pushed well into the pastoral lands by the early 1860s, and the railway was at Sandhurst (Bendigo) early in 1864. By extending the line to Echuca, the nearest point to Melbourne on the river system, much of the wool grown in south western New South Wales could be siphoned off. As the line neared completion in September 1864 the *Sydney Morning Herald*, sensing that Victoria had won a rich prize, wrote:

> When the locomotive that has breathed itself by the run up from Melbourne slakes its thirst in the waters of the Murray—when the commerce of that river and of the Darling is sucked to the inland terminus of the railway . . . people will wake up to the commercial hold that Victoria has got over the southern and western parts of the Riverina. Sydney will be nowhere. Two neighbours (South Australia and Victoria) will be scrambling for the commerce of nearly half of our territory, and the metropolis of the colony to which the territory belongs will look hopelessly on at the division of the spoil.

The newspaper's fears were well founded. Very soon Echuca became a thriving river port for the Murray fleet. Through it was funnelled wool grown along the Darling, the Murrumbidgee, and the Lachlan as well as the Murray itself—wool sometimes carried long distances to river loading points by bullock team or camel train before being transported along hundreds of miles of waterways to the railhead. Just as it now handled the outgoing wool, Melbourne became the supplier of the equipment and provisions bought by the station owners. From a population of 300 in 1864, Echuca quickly grew to 1,500 as more men were engaged in handling wool and other cargo on the river wharves, and in boat-building; by 1866 the little town had become Victoria's second busiest port.

Elsewhere, railways were being thrust into the grasslands to provide better transport to the seaports, but as yet the lines were few, and much of the wool clip—now expanding at a tremendous rate—still had to be handled by the old method of bullock team.

After peace was re-established between the warring American States in 1865, the demand for wool did not slacken; instead it surged upward again as British textile mills won wider markets. The Australian and New Zealand sheepmen saw to it that their output of wool kept pace. As advances were made in methods of wool handling and, more notably, in flock management, the quest for ways to secure sheep able to produce more profitable fleeces became keener than ever.

The challenge was taken up by a few studmasters; their task was one for which, as Charles Darwin had once noted, perhaps one man in a thousand might have the requisite accuracy of eye and judgement. The studmaster's skill lay in selecting as breeding stock the sheep capable of handing on the most desirable characteristics, while at the same time he suppressed unwanted factors by culling the less favourable sheep from the flock. The objective was not merely to produce a few outstanding sheep; rather it was to raise the standard of whole flocks in a minimum of time. By selective breeding on a grand scale, the new flockmasters—most of them from English farming or stock raising families—were soon producing great numbers of sheep that grew fleeces of a quality and weight beyond the dreams of wool men of an earlier generation.

Early merino studs, in effect the foundation of the flocks that first spread into the inland plains, had been established in the 1840s in New South Wales and Victoria (where sheep bred in Van Diemen's Land had contributed to early success). However, the sheep had not been of uniform quality, and in succeeding generations flocks remained static or improved according to the knowledge and ability individual owners had of flock management. Among the most significant influences in the improvement that took place from the 1850s was that of Bristol-born Thomas Shaw, an accomplished wool expert. After helping to establish or enhance most of the important Victorian studs by classing the sheep and buying new breeding stock, Shaw became joint owner of a property in the Western District. He founded a small but successful stud, Wooriwyrite, based on the notable Ercildoune flock, in 1857. Fleeces from his sheep frequently topped the market. His *Practical Treatise on Sheep and Wool* (published in 1860) was read by many wool-growers. Shaw's sheep spread far and wide; he himself acquired properties in New South Wales and Queensland to which his sheep were sent.

In most years of the 1860s, about 2,000,000 sheep were added to the colonies' flocks, so that over the decade the total more than doubled, passing 41,000,000 head in 1870. New Zealand's flocks were also growing rapidly, and they exceeded 10,000,000 head by 1870. The industry become more competitive within itself, and even if dry spells and seasonal problems occasionally intruded and contributed to personal failures, the grip of the sheepmen on the land and on economic affairs was greater than ever. In 1870 the total outpouring of wool in the six Australian colonies exceeded 173,000,000 lb., and it continued to increase in volume each year.

Pacing the rapid expansion was a move into drier lands where a type of sheep adapted to the more rigorous conditions was needed. Success with fine-wool strains had demonstrated what might be done with the merino in the Australian environment; but as yet no general or standard type had been fixed, and although expensive sheep were being imported from European and American flocks there was still no notion of what constituted the most desirable features to be bred into the merino to meet special conditions of land and climate in different regions.

There was now a strong incentive to develop sheep capable of thriving on the great plains of the Murray-Darling basin, and it was here that the most notable development in the merino was to take place. Tens of millions of acres of this land were well-grassed—at least in good seasons—and, in spite of hot summers and dry spells, it was a region eminently suited to the grazing of sheep. In the 1860s it became the newest province of the wool men. The rich Riverina district, immediately north of the Murray, and adjoining areas (including northern Victoria and the central and south-western portions of New South Wales) of rolling plains and interspersed river flats—sections which had been settled from the 1830s and 1840s—formed the heart of this natural pastoral province. As the frontier of pastoral occupation was thrust deeper into the back country, the rich heartland became the locale for the intensive development of merino strains suited to conditions on the open plains.

The smaller and lighter types of merino that had flourished in cooler districts were not well suited to the dry and shadeless country, where the fine, short-staple wool was unable to withstand the ravages of heat and dust. Larger-framed, more robust sheep carrying a heavier fleece were needed. Flockmasters had to set about developing a hardier strain, able to stand up to summer heat and drought, if necessary, and still able to produce a heavy fleece of good quality wool.

The evolution of a new merino was the work of a handful of men who seized the opportunity first of all to advance the quality of their own flocks and then, by further investment of money and skill, to turn their properties into reservoirs of breeding stock on which other graziers could draw. As the demand for better-quality merinos extended, it also intensified, and prices paid for sheep of outstanding quality rose to unheard-of levels. Meanwhile the successful stud owners were enlarging their activities to cope with the ever-growing demand for selected ewes and rams.

With the establishment of new studs and, in many cases, the reorganization and improvement of the older studs, greater numbers of sheep of superior quality were available for breeding purposes. As more of the improved stud sheep were decanted into general flocks all through the sheep country, fleece weights rose steadily. Outsanding rams were bringing hundreds of pounds, and there was great rivalry among breeders for the accolade of success in the competitive sheep shows being held as part of the widened interest in sheep breeding. In 1860 a 10 lb. fleece had been considered good for a stud ram, a 6 lb. fleece reasonable for a stud ewe; ten years later these weights could be almost doubled. Over the same period the average fleece weight (for all sheep) of under 4 lb. had moved up to about $5\frac{1}{2}$ lb. A few rams could be found which shore as much as 25 lb. of wool—a fact which their owners advertised freely. As sheep lore gained a new importance among graziers, from time to time individual sheep in various studs around the country (and their progeny) came to be mentioned almost with a sense of awe; they included notable specimens with such imposing names as Prince Regent, President, Little Wonder, Emperor, King Billy, Wool King, and Napoleon.

The great studs through which consistent improvement was to be achieved were based on sheep from many of the older studs in the Mudgee district of New South Wales, or from the Western District and Northern Victoria, but as well they had important infusions of more recent importations of Saxon and Silesian merinos and of the more robust, large-framed, and

297

heavily-woolled French strain, the Rambouillet.

Outstanding among early studmasters who laid a foundation for establishing the bolder type of merino as the all-conquering strain for the drier districts was George Hall Peppin, a Somerset man who settled in the Deniliquin district of southern Riverina in 1858. Thomas Shaw was engaged by Peppin to select from the 8,000 sheep on Peppin's property the 300 ewes with which the Wanganella stud was founded in 1861. Peppin introduced Rambouillet rams, and there was an infusion of the American Vermont-type merino in 1866; from this time the Wanganella sheep were notable for their well-shaped frames and bulky fleeces of medium wool. After George Peppin's death in 1872 his sons continued to expand the enterprise, taking over adjoining Boonoke and establishing part of the stud there. Their sheep were cutting 20 per cent more wool, on the average, than the older-type merino still run by many of their neighbours. The Peppin brothers were stocking their own properties with their new-type sheep; but outside the district the Peppin success was practically unknown, and there was no great demand for their big-framed sheep: sheepmen generally were still thinking primarily in terms of finer wool.

In 1878 the Peppin brothers decided to sell off their holdings. Boonoke, with its stud, was bought by Franc Sadleir Falkiner, who set about building up the quality of his newly acquired sheep by a process of careful selection of breeding stock while avoiding the introduction of any new bloodlines. The Boonoke stud expanded steadily—the ewes were never sold—and it became an important source of first-quality sheep which went out in annual drafts to improve the flocks of many other breeders. Under George and Otway Falkiner and their successors, the family sheep-breeding enterprise extended and flourished to a remarkable degree; the Peppin strain was refined and improved, and as the Falkiners acquired new properties successful offshoot studs were established on each. The Wanganella stud, under its new ownership, also developed and, following distinctive lines, it too achieved great success and its sheep came to be distributed widely as the merit of the Peppin innovations came to be accepted by more graziers. The desirable fleece qualities of high density, long staple, good colour, and elasticity of fibre had all been retained in spite of change of style brought about by the hotter and drier climate.

During the 1860s other significant studs—though usually less successful— were being developed in the Riverina to help meet the greater demand for breeding stock for this region and the drier lands into which it faded. More and more stud owners, including men such as Samuel McCaughey of Coonong station, with its tens of thousands of sheep, and later Charles Mills of Uardry, bought drafts of the Peppin strain to build up their flocks.

Although various studmasters were inclined to follow distinctive lines of breeding, a more or less standard type of open-plains merino (with the Peppin sheep usually setting the style) was being established from a fusion of the various merino strains. The wool of these bold Riverina merinos was not as fine or as pure as that of sheep bred directly from Silesian or Saxon imports, and the new strain could not be universally successful; but because of their stamina and their ability to grow a heavy fleece of good commercial wool, the Riverina-type sheep came to be accepted far and wide. In the areas of cooler climate and higher rainfall, near the coast, sheep that produced fine or superfine wool were still preferred. On the other hand, in the marginal lands of the Darling, and in South Australia and elsewhere, with a short winter and dry exposed conditions most of the year, a still coarser-wool merino was needed, and such sheep were soon being bred from Riverina-type stock. Ultimately the Peppin strain was to find its way into the flocks of most of Australia's sheeplands (including those of Queensland and Western Australia) and to reach out to New Zealand, South Africa, and South America to improve merino quality there.

As the sheep saga of the 1860s and 1870s was unfolding, capable and fortunate landholders were amassing considerable wealth. Men who had made their way over trackless country to reach their chosen land, or their sons, now seemed close to establishing an aristocracy of wealth. Their properties were now run as large-scale enterprises. Fine station homesteads, some built in a lavish manner, had generally replaced the makeshift and modest dwellings of earlier days. Sometimes the homestead might be a great two-storied mansion, built in granite or bluestone with tall tower and slate roof; but mostly, particularly in the warmer areas, it was a sprawling building of local brick (sometimes only sun-dried), surrounded by a wide veranda to give shade and protection. Close by would be the separate buildings of the station: a cottage or barracks for the young men and for travelling guests; a hut for working men; a coach house, and stables.

Living conditions for the well-to-do were no longer primitive. One visitor to a Victorian sheep property wrote of her delight at finding the homestead so attractive:

> The house far exceeds my most sanguine expectations. . . . The sittingroom is so cool and pretty, with its piano, books and flowers. The house is all in the ground floor, no stairs. The fireplace in the sittingroom is as large as a closet.

Among those enjoying the greatest success were the families who had won the race for land in Victoria's rich and bounteous Western District, the broad strip of parklike land stretching back from the gold-bearing hills of the Ballarat area. Station owners who had come through earlier difficulties successfully now had established affluence; in their station homesteads—and the fine town houses they were building in Melbourne—they followed as best they could the manners and customs of English society, keeping up with affairs in the London weeklies. By circumstance such men watched the London wool market closely; by inclination and habit they invariably thought of the British Isles as "home," and in many cases they sent their sons to England to be educated. English journalist Anthony Trollope, after visiting the homesteads of the pastoral elite in Victoria in the early 1870s, found social significance in these "country gentlemen," who, he said,

> . . . now form an established aristocracy, with very conservative feelings, and are

very quickly becoming as firm a country party as that which is formed by our squirearchy at home.

The traditions and grand outlook of these Victorian shepherd kings also spread into the Riverina, and soon moved farther northward, as great stations were established by migrating families.

Ambitious but less fortunate men had long been clamouring for a share of the land monopolized by the sheepmen under pastoral leases in the eastern colonies. Tens of millions of acres of land in New South Wales and Victoria were locked away in the pastoralists' hands, and in the late 1850s there were increasing demands for a more equitable distribution of the Crown land under pastoral lease. Was Australia to remain one huge sheep run, men asked, forced to import wheat because would-be farmers could not get the chance to raise crops on good farming land? Surely if parliamentary democracy meant anything, it meant the opportunity for men to secure land on which to make a living. The clamour to "Unlock the Land" became the dominant political issue of the 1860s. Land act followed land act, amendments proliferated as idealistic or demagogic but always baffled politicians sought to cope with the central problem of selling land to small farmers while preventing established graziers from buying it. However, while wool prices remained so favourable, farmers were unable to wrest much land from the sheepmen.

It was in 1861 that the New South Wales Government introduced a policy of free-selection-before-survey in the sale of Crown lands as an alternative to the system of auctioning surveyed lands. The legislation was sponsored by John Robertson, a sheepman, whose avowed purpose was to help in the settling of farmers on the land. Under Robertson's Land Acts, anyone prepared to reside on the land for three years, and to make improvements, was permitted to select from 40 to 320 acres anywhere in the "settled" or "intermediate" districts of New South Wales. The land had to be selected prior to survey. The selector paid one-quarter of the purchase price of £1 an acre as a deposit and received a freehold title. All leases taken out or renewed in New South Wales since 1857 were reduced to a year's currency if within the "settled" districts, and to five years' currency if beyond these limits. The legislation was designed to allow small selectors to take up whatever land they wanted in the leasehold areas, bu in practice there were many barriers to this. Special provisions gave the established squatter the prior right to buy one twenty-fifth of his run; he was also allowed to buy certain lands which he had improved; in either case such purchases carried grazing rights over three times the freehold area. Amendments to the 1861 Acts were introduced later in an effort to prevent the original conditions being infringed, but the basic principles remained, and in practice the original landholder was usually successful in maintaining possession of his run against all comers. In many cases the smaller squatters lost their land to finance and pastoral companies.

In Victoria, where the pressure for land laws opening smallfarm areas was even greater than in New South Wales, William Nicholson's Act of 1860 provided for a system of selection-after-survey and imposed penal taxes on unimproved lands; but at the same time it conferred pre-emptive rights over three times the area purchased (and granted deferred payments) and not much land was wrested from the pastoralists. Legislation introduced by Charles Gavin Duffy in 1862 provided that squatters should be ejected from 10,000,000 acres of good country so that it could be thrown open for selection at £1 an acre, subject to improvement conditions. Again the pastoralists got the lion's share; of the 4,000,000 acres thrown open 1,000,000 acres fell into their hands against less than 500,000 acres secured by small holders.

It was only with James Macpherson Grant's Act of 1865 that the fundamental problem of selling land to farmers while preventing the big graziers from buying it was solved. Under this act selectors were limited to a single block of 320 acres; residential and improvement conditions had to be complied with over a three-year period before the land was alienated, and an independent board had to confirm that these provisions were met before the Minister for Lands would confirm selection. Soon 3,000,000 acres had been taken up, many of them by small selectors. A similar Act in 1869 opened nearly 11,000,000 acres in Gippsland and the north-west to selectors.

From the early days of separation, the Queensland Government had grappled with the problem of helping the poorer man obtain land in his own right. In a relatively empty colony this seemed to present less problems; in 1860 the first of a series of Land Acts was passed, introducing selection-before-survey, but restricting the right to certain areas designated as agricultural reserves. The Macalister Act of 1868 aimed at creating a new type of landholder, part farmer and part grazier, as a compromise—suitable to local conditions—between the small selector and the big grazier. The squatter, on surrendering half his run, could buy four square miles together with a secure tenure of the remainder. The act also provided for settling men on "agricultural homestead" blocks. Neither the liberal terms of payment nor the lavish distribution to immigrants resulted in any notable expansion of farming. Relatively few cared to take up the holdings open for cultivation, and most of the new arrivals simply sold out to pastoralists.

Tasmania had led the way with the experiment of free-selection-before-survey, having introduced it in the Waste Lands Act of 1858. Under the act 3,000,000 acres had already been sold and another 3,000,000 were under pastoral licence; but the areas held were generally not very large, and the 1858 measure made little change in the situation in the island.

Western Australia was still in a stage of development more or less comparable to that of the 1840s in the eastern colonies, with pastoral development encouraged as the obvious and inevitable of opening up new areas of country. In 1850 regulations had divided the colony's land into two parts, with yearly or eight-year leases, tillage leases of 120 to 320 acres of farming land being allowed in the south-west; but the pre-emptive privileges conceded to squatters made them the principal beneficiaries of the regulations. It was not until 1872 that certain areas were classified as farming land and terms of settlement laid down—again without any great increase in the numbers of selectors.

Western Australia was still without responsible government, so there was nothing like the clamour from press and voters that had pressured land reform in the eastern colonies. In any case, conditions were dissimilar. During the 1860s and 1870s important discoveries of good grazing land were made—in the well-watered Gascoyne and Murchison districts in the north, in the extreme south-east of the colony, and on the Hampton tableland—which offered prospects for opening up new territory by pastoral occupation. So at a time when the eastern governments were trying to resume the squatters' land, the West Australian Government passed legislation (in 1878) granting the pastoralists liberal fourteen-year leases, with certain pre-emptive rights, anywhere in the colony. This contributed to the West's great pastoral expansion.

In South Australia the prevailing egalitarianism contributed to the consistent growth of agriculture within the confining factors of geography and climate. Squatters were never strongly represented in the South Australian legislature, and at no period did the land regulations give the South Australian squatter the security which his counterpart enjoyed in New South Wales in the 1840s and 1850s. The main classification of land within the province was "hundreds" and "outside areas." Within the hundreds only yearly leases were granted, and they conferred no pre-emptive rights; outside the hundreds leases of up to fourteen years could be granted; but as any land could be declared a hundred at any time, a proceeding that automatically cancelled all leases there, the squatter had no security whatsoever, and the pastoral industry naturally lagged behind agriculture. When South Australia legislated in 1869 to let selectors buy pastoral land on credit, the Henry Strangways Act was based on the Victorian Land Act of 1865.

Each measure to open up the land caused sharp argument and bitter struggles within the legislatures, where sheepmen protested hotly. There were genuine attempts made to farm the land in many cases, and soon hundreds of rough-hewn cabins were standing where only sheep runs had existed before. Just as the original settlement had proceeded in waves across the south-east of the continent or out from the other cities, with the sheepmen moving in behind the explorers, so now the selectors followed in somewhat the same pattern. They were generally men with very limited capital, and they could borrow little. Some of them—but not very many—had wives and children to take with them as they started out on the great adventure. Fences were put up around each farm as the land was cleared. Horses were bought, and very soon ploughs were turning over the soil.

Closer settlement of the land was socially desirable, and the moves to support it were well-intentioned, but in practice it could not always be economically sound and it could not be sustained in quite the way the idealists or the hopful settlers themselves imagined. One reason for this was that much of the good land where tillage might have succeeded had already been sold to sheepmen under the old system. In many parts, climate was on the side of the big landholders; and farmers could not spread deep into the country, in the way that they could into America's Middle West. For the small settler, there were unsuspected dangers. Land which at first seemed promising might change completely when it had been cultivated for a few years. When crops failed or the price of wheat fell, the farmer seldom had the financial resources needed to tide him over the bad years.

Many established landholders, their personal desire to retain their estates buttressed by a practical sense that small settlers would fail or at best merely scrape along, found ways and means of holding on to their land. The Free Selection Acts gave them loopholes to achieve this result. One method used was to have sham selectors who were agents of the squatter himself apply for the best parts of the leased holding, leaving only the poorer sections; eventually the original holder would again consolidate his property, finishing up with freehold rights to the best of it. At other times the landholder would buy the strip of river frontage and by this "peacocking" method effectively block selectors from taking up the waterless land. Sometimes the selectors were not farmers but speculators, and they (as well as others) were interested only in using their selection rights to gain a quick profit by selling out to the pastoralist. A commission investigating the effect of the Robertson land legislation in New South Wales over twenty years or so considered that the history of its operation

> . . . has been an unintelligible chaos, in which the rights and interests of all concerned have been the sport of accident, political interest, and departmental disorder.

There could be no mistaking the practical effect of the legislation; by methods "sometimes ingenious and sometimes dependent for success on barefaced perjury," the big leaseholders of earlier years had emerged as big freeholders. Over twenty years, nearly 40,000,000 acres of Crown land in New South Wales had been disposed of, more than half by conditional purchases, yet the number of settlers had gone up by only 20,000 or so. The area under crop rose by less than 500,000 acres over the same period; instead of concentrating on farming, some of the new smallholders were doing their best to share in the wealth of wool. The new type of grazier-farmer bought a few sheep sold off from a big property and began to build up his own small flock. While seasons were good and the price of wool held he could succeed.

The period of the land laws was one of booming prosperity for the pastoral industry. Sheepmen were still a far better risk when it came to bank loans, and farmers able to offer little in the way of security were frequently charged exorbitant interest rates by rapacious storekeepers or money lending agents. Once the wheatgrower's prospects improved, he could get more financial help, and the increased availability of bank credit in the 1870s, following a liberalizing of the laws relating to mortgage lending, was a factor in the increased acreage brought under cultivation during that decade. The newer Australian-based banks spread their branches throughout the farming areas, practically monopolizing the banks' share of the risky backing of the farming industry.

In Victoria, where climate made much of the land better suited to holdings of small size, the plan for settling farmers on Crown land on easy terms proved more successful than in New South Wales; but in many cases a subterfuge, "dummying," was effectively used by the pastoral leaseholders to acquire land through nominees who put themselves forward as selectors but later handed back the land (as freehold) to the pastoralist. Successive measures were found to have weaknesses, but some loopholes were closed by revised legislation; the consolidating Land Act of 1869 brought about general improvement, and reduced the area offered as a homestead farm from a square mile to half a square mile, However, it was in terms of sheep-raising rather than cropping that more settlers might best gain a foothold; and the Land Tax Act of 1877 helped equalize matters for the small holder by placing a tax on pastoral land, based on its carrying capacity, equivalent to sixpence for each sheep that could be grazed on it. Within a few years the small grazier-farmer had been able to establish a place for himself and, in the words of an official handbook, by the mid-1880s

> ... the owners of small flocks are supplying the greater portion of the fat sheep sent to the Melbourne market, and fully one-half of the wool that is sold in Melbourne is from their flocks. The quality of their wool and stock is steadily improving and their business is eagerly sought by the stock agents.

By the 1870s the opportunities for the sale of wheat abroad had increased, and in step with demand and the opening of the land (both by railways and by legislation) the area under crop in Australia more than doubled between 1870 and 1880. South Australia and Victoria were responsible for most of the gain; their combined acreages represented four-fifths or so of the whole. This is how the area under crop increased from 1861 to 1881:

Australia: Area under crop, 1861–1881 (in acres).

	New South Wales	Victoria	Queensland	South Australia	Western Australia	Tasmania	Total
1861	246,143	387,283	3,353	359,284	24,705	152,860	1,173,628
1871	385,151	692,840	47,034	722,031	49,089	161,620	2,116,695
1881	606,277	1,548,809	113,978	2,087,237	63,902	140,788	4,560,991

Farming in South Australia had not gone back from the impetus it had received during the 1850s, when Victoria's soaring population was happy to pay high prices for South Australian grain. Grain output moved up steadily. Some of the gain came from the invention locally of a labour-saving machine to harvest the crop. The " stripper" harvester devised by John Ridley and first put into use in 1843 made it possible to gather in more of the grain at lowered cost. Although the new type machine was not accepted at first, the stripper was eventually used increasingly through the farming areas of South Australia, and by 1866 the machine was in use in Victoria. Equally important, since it helped open up large new areas to farming, was the invention of another South Australian farmer, Robert Bowyer Smith.

This was the stump-jump plough, which made it practical and profitable to move into mallee lands even before the gnarled stumps had been removed. Previously, mallee land had had to stand idle for years after the tough standing scrub had been cut, but Smith's invention made it possible to till the soil at once. With the plough he designed, each share was able to move independently, and when one share struck a stump it lifted until clear of the obstruction; after it had passed over the stump it returned to the soil.

As more elaborate stump-jump ploughs were built, the farming of South Australia's mallee lands grew apace. The new plough was also used in Victoria, where in the north-west there were great tracts of dense and uncharted scrub, and other land that might be brought into use if men were prepared to undertake the task of clearing it.

South Australia's wheat production equalled the combined harvest of the other colonies for the first years of the 1870s. Thanks to a variety of factors—some stemming from repeal of England's Corn Laws in 1846 and of the Navigation Acts three years later, and others attributable to adoption of a shorter sailing route between Australia and England and the switch to hardwood clipper ships—the province was able to export wheat to England on quite a substantial scale. Almost 3,500,000 bushels were sent to England in 1873.

The success of agriculture in South Australia meant that the pastoralists were forced into the drier areas; in the late 1850s the pastoral prospects of unoccupied tracts in the north of the colony had once again been seriously canvassed. Although Sturt and Eyre had encountered increasing aridity beyond the Port Augusta region, new reports gave more optimistc assessments. By his enthusiasm, George Woodroffe Goyder, the colony's competent and respected Surveyor-General, contributed to over-optimistic assessment of the hinterland; in 1857 (when deputy Surveyor-General) he saw the country north of Port Augusta after good rains—the plains clothed in grass and herbage—and he gained a mistaken impression of the land's stock-carrying capacity. Goyder's rosy report caused a rush of applications for pastoral leases. The rentals he fixed in his enthusiasm did not deter the sheepmen, but rather strengthened their hopes; yet before long it was apparent that the true nature of the area was one of almost unrelieved barrenness. After the severe drought of 1864–66 the pastoralists' protests on rentals became so numerous and so loud that the government appointed a commission to investigate; in the light of the commission's report relief was given to the leaseholders.

After the unfortunate experience of opening the dry north, the South Australian Government came to realize the danger of misconstruing the nature of the land. In 1866 Goyder was instructed to make a field trip to examine the extent of the drought-stricken country. On his return he set down on the map the limits of land enjoying fairly reliable rainfall. He chose the 10-inch isohyet, which became known as Goyder's Line; north of it agriculture was considered impractical.

There were still many practical problems to be overcome to improve the farmer's competitive position, even in South Australia. Strains of wheat available to farmers did not always thrive in new districts. Much of the farmed land tended to lose its fertility after a few seasons, and when it was exhausted the farmer wanted only to move on to another selection. The strains of wheat available were unsuited to some of the areas in which they were sown, and dwindling crops combined with other problems forced many off the land. With railways reaching out, the farmer would soon win greater success; it was to be dependent upon the development of new farming practices and the introduction of improved strains of wheat, and access to capital at reasonable interest rates.

As yet tropical agriculture had scarcely begun in Queensland. Only about 2,000 acres were under sugar cane in 1868, though after this the acreage increased steadily. The high prices for cotton and tobacco that resulted from shortages during the American Civil War encouraged production of these crops for a time. Cotton was grown in Queensland from 1860; in a few years about 14,000 acres were under cultivation but once American production was restored the Queensland plantings fell away. Similarly production of tobacco, grown in response to the special demand, died away once normal supplies were available.

Queensland was saved from depression by gold. Payable gold was first discovered to the north of Rockhampton and, after the discovery at Gympie in 1867, new strikes were made almost every year. The richest were at Charters Towers (1872) and in the following year at the Palmer River, 150 miles inland from the mouth of the Endeavour River, where Cook had careened his wrecked ship almost a hundred years before. The rush of ships bearing prospectors to the river mouth compelled the government to build a port there, which they named Cooktown. Thousands of prospectors passed through the port on to the tropical mud and slush of the trail to the diggings.

As in Victoria and New South Wales in earlier years, Chinese arrived in considerable numbers in the wake of the gold discoveries. Friction developed between them and the general body of miners, always on the same issues (which included the frugality and uncleanly habits of the Chinese) and attempts were made to restrict the movement of Chinese on the Queensland goldfields. A discriminatory act passed in 1878 was designed to prevent Chinese moving to a new fields for three years after its discovery. In spite of it Chinese greatly outnumbered whites on some fields, especially along the Palmer River.

Gold became a spur to development in Queensland, though on a much smaller scale than in Victoria two decades earlier. Value of gold production exceeded £1,000,000 each year from 1874 to 1879. After the rushes died out some gold towns remained, while new ports were founded or existing ports developed as harbours to the different goldfields, which were spread out on a 1,000-mile chain inland from the coast. Queensland's population rose from 28,000 in 1860 to 150,000 in 1870 and 211,000 in 1880. The increased population boosted the sheep and cattle industries, which were still completely dominant in the colony's economy.

Queensland sheepmen were finding to their surprise that their flocks were able to move successfully into warmer districts away from the coast. The dry air of the inland regions with low night-time temperatures, made it possible for fine wool to be grown. Expansive new pastures were opened up on vast plains covered with a variety of natural grasses—summer grasses and winter grasses, some annual, some perennial—on which sheep could thrive. Huge runs were taken up, in some instances 150,000 acres or more of fine country, or 1,000 square miles of drier or remote land.

The use of land as sheep pasture still dominated Australia's rural economy. All through the 1870s (and for years ahead) the wool men remained ascendant. Another 20,000,000 sheep were added to Australian flocks during the decade, so that by 1880 the number exceeded 64,000,000 head. By then the annual wool clip had risen to 354,000,000 lb., or twice the weight of wool produced in 1870.

Money and manufacturing 12

The sudden wealth won from gold and trade, and the extraordinary influx of people, combined to produce in Victoria a new colonial phenomenon. By 1855 there were more people in Victoria than the entire continent had held ten years before, and in a few years Melbourne had exploded from a solid town into a booming city. Bank deposits increased eightfold between 1851 and 1854, advances rose in even greater proportion, and the notes issued by the banks changed hands at an enormously increased rate. Melbourne now possessed quite considerable capital resources; the prosperity of its banks had become the envy of London and Glasgow bankers. Shipments of bullion gave the banks great reserves in London, and profits from gold-buying and discounting trade bills were substantial.

English promoters had established three new banks to handle this business, but Melbourne men were aware of the profits to be won and they decided to set up wholly local banks. In the early years of the gold rushes one locally-financed bank, the Bank of Victoria, was created; following its success, as more capital accumulated in the years that followed, other colonial banks were established. The locally-backed banks provided vigorous competition for the English-based banks, and they spread branches into the gold towns and into the rural centres.

Traditional banking practice with the colonies had its emphasis in the discounting of trade bills—a practice which served merchants shipping wool or other commodities, and traders importing goods. Merchants were used as intermediaries in advancing money to the sheepmen; the banks were reluctant to lend direct on the security of livestock or wool, but the alternative of export bills (secured by bills of lading) provided an acceptable security since it was a form traditional in banking practice. The London-backed banks continued to concentrate on this business, which they had handled throughout. On the other hand, the locally-financed banks, finding themselves with a surplus of funds, were prepared to be less orthodox in their approach. As the community's activity expanded, the more radical bankers found an outlet for their funds in backing the formation of many new enterprises in different fields of activity—building, importing, transport (including the railway companies), mining, various small manufactures connected with mining, and the retail trade. Thus, although British finance and British investment was still far more important, so far as money volume was concerned, local investment was now providing a spur to activities in many significant new fields. The Colonial Bank, in its prospectus of 1855, declared:

> ... the colonists of Victoria are in a position to enjoy and ought to receive whatever advantages can be derived from the employment of their own capital.

As Victoria's surface goldfields became exhausted, it was clear that new industries were needed if the loss of population were to be stemmed. In addition to pastoral activities, three avenues were open—farming, manufacturing, and deep mining for gold. All required capital. The bankers were called upon to provide a considerable part of the funds, and in breaking through legal restrictions which in effect blocked loans for such activities they opened a completely new phase in colonial enterprise.

The British government had frowned on mortgage-lending in the colonies. A circular from the Colonial Office in the early 1850s outlined for the governors of all the colonies the general principles to be observed in the preparation of Colonial Acts for the incorporation of banking companies. One of the regulations stated that no banking company was to be permitted

> ... to advance money on security of lands or houses or ships or on the pledge of merchandise, nor to hold lands or houses except for transaction of its business, nor own ships nor be engaged in trade, except as dealers in bullion or bills of exchange, but to confine its transactions to discounting commercial paper and negotiable securities and other legitimate banking business.

In legislation for the incorporation of banks set up in the colonies, local parliaments had accepted the provision, and banks were debarred from advancing money "in anticipation or expectation of receiving title deeds of land as security." Back in 1840, during the prolonged pastoral depression, the New South Wales Legislative Council had passed the Lien on Wool Act, which cleared the way for money to be advanced on wool or mortgages taken over livestock. This innovation became accepted banking practice in the various colonies—but bankers generally remained unwilling to lend without permanent security, and usually they worked through finance and other companies in advancing money to primary producers. By 1859 money was being advanced in South Australia on the security of land, and very soon afterwards the same procedure was followed in Victoria. It was not long before the limitations were practically ignored, with the concurrence of the courts, even though technically the bar remained and the colonial authorities in London continued to disapprove of the practice. The system of lending on the security of land spread and as the demands for money expanded the Australian banks were soon heavily involved, even though the way was not cleared legally for them until 1864, when a Victorian act gave new banks the right to lend on the security of land and buildings. Soon bank finance in the form of small loans was available to pastoralists, farmers, and selectors.

Money was being lent not only to support pastoral and farming activities but also to finance mining enterprises. Companies that located gold-bearing reefs and needed money to install engines and crushing plants drew on generous credit, and as a result more poppet heads and thundering stamp mills appeared in Victoria's gold-bearing districts in the 1860s. This investment made it possible for Victoria to retain gold output at a high level even though the surface fields had been depleted.

As the great bulk of machinery and manufactured goods were imported, there was scope for small factories and mills, and with gold employing fewer men the need to develop industrial activities in Victoria became apparent. At first the idea of protecting local industries by a selective tariff was only vaguely understood, but soon it became the burning issue within the electorates; Canada and the United States had provided signposts. Canada had adopted its first protective tariff in 1859 in a bill which was a landmark even though it provided only a mild measure of protection. In the United States, advocacy of high tariffs was attracting attention; it played a big part in the presidential campaign of 1860, with the result that the traditional policy of mild protection was drastically changed in 1861 when the victorious Repulicans under Lincoln introduced a structure of high tariffs to foster industrial development.

Faced with the pressing problems of a falling yield from gold, a rash of business insolvencies, and a great glut of imports, Victoria was virtually compelled to develop corrective policies. The mercantile collapse that began in 1859 directed attention to the need for a more balanced economy. In the search for a solution, the idea of a system of tariff reform emerged, and a Protectionist League was formed. The man who gave purpose and drive to the concept of a protective tariff for Victoria was David Syme, who became proprietor and editor of the *Age* in 1860 on the death of his brother, Ebenezer. The newspaper had campaigned for votes by ballot and other political reforms in the 1850s, winning great popular support. Its policies, broadly on Chartist lines, had been vigorous in support of the underdog in his fight for recognition in the burgeoning colony. The working man had reason to appreciate the *Age* policies, and he was prepared to listen when in the early 1860s David Syme moved from a fight for political principles to thundering advocacy of practical measures for the economic advancement of Victoria.

Syme had been brought up on the teachings of Bentham and of John Stuart Mill. In the *Principles of Political Economy* (published in 1848) Mill had laid down a detailed explanation of the principles which should guide a government in its control of the economy; and although he made a general argument for free trade, he had proposed that duties should be placed on imports to young countries in order to protect industries that had still to be "naturalized" there. Syme believed that this fitted Victoria's case perfectly. It was clear that manufacturing could be started only if the unequal competition of surplus goods pouring in from established industrial countries was reduced to reasonable levels.

Starting from this point and maintaining that free-traders had no answers to unemployment or to stemming the exodus from the colony, Syme began to develop his sustained campaign for protection of local manufacturing by selective tariffs. For some time the *Age* had been hinting at some form of protective tariff when in March 1860, it came out unequivocally in favour of holding back the flood of imported goods in order that local industry might have a chance to develop. There was an overwhelming competition, the *Age* said, in "the multitudinous, inferior low-priced (not cheap) articles, made of refuse material especially for the Australian market, with which we are inundated from crowded factories and workshops." The need to place restrictive duties on these goods was urged, since, the newspaper said, this naked competition prevented manufacturers from even making a beginning in the work of opening up new industrial endeavours. A few months later an *Age* leader declared:

> We cannot remain a race of gold diggers and mere traffickers of commerce, with a small sprinkling of tillers of the soil amongst us, and yet become a great nation.
> The arts of the mechanic and of the manufacturer must become domiciled amongst us if we are to provide for our future population becoming thriving, contented and good members of enlightened society. In fact if we would stave off poverty, barbarism and crime, we must seek to become a nation at all points— agriculture, mining, manufacturing, trading and shipping.

Syme was one of the few in the colony deeply versed in economics, and his interest was constantly in evidence in the stream of proposals for reform that appeared in the editorial columns of his newspaper.

Melbourne's other important newspaper, the *Argus*, was completely opposed to Syme's proposals, declaring that protection had failed in England and could not but fail "in any country and in any circumstances." The *Herald* referred to the protectionism as a "delusion," and thought it hardly possible that the "bad example" of other protectionist countries would be followed.

Ranged against the idea of a selective tariff were powerful forces. The great pastoral interests wanted to see the existing fiscal policy remain; as producers of raw materials they saw advantage only in their being able to buy in the cheapest markets and sell in the dearest. They were glad to join hands with the importers in the struggle to maintain a free and open market for imported goods. Most traders identified themselves with importing interests. Syme found himself opposed by a solid phalanx of those fighting to maintain their position of political and economic ascendancy in the colony. He flung himself into the struggle with all the fervour and drive of a dedicated political campaigner. Before long his tariff campaign seemed to be gaining so much support that the importing interests decided to withdraw all advertising support from the *Age*. Syme fought back by cutting the price of the paper from sixpence to threepence, a move that greatly increased its circulation. He held firm even when routine government notices in the newspaper's advertising columns were witheld in 1862 at the direction of a cabinet under pressure from importers, backed by pastoralists who were opposed to Syme's simultaneous campaign for opening the land to selectors. Syme brought the price of the *Age* down to twopence, and again circulation rose. The effort to silence the newspaper editor failed, as did the government's attempt to introduce a Newspaper Tax-and-Libel Bill. The bill had to be dropped, to the delight of the *Age*'s army of devoted readers.

Syme was bent on attracting and holding a mass readership on a scale that would ensure acceptance of his political aims. He sought to impose through his readers' votes the principles which he believed to be vital for the development of a colony 10,000 miles and more from the British homeland. Repeatedly the *Age* asserted that the free traders had no answers to unemployment and that they could not stem the exodus from the colony; a protective tariff was the only solution. The press campaigns aroused bitter opposition—but the editor was relying on mass support rather than sectional interest for his policies; if he had that, sectional interests could be ignored.

Tariff leagues throughout the colony were prepared to press the matter and, campaigning hard, the *Age* made tariff protection an issue in the 1864 election. A majority of those elected to the Victoria Assembly favoured a certain degree of protection, but the government was formed by James McCulloch. Syme's influence on members of the assembly was so strong that the premier (who had declared himself a free trader a short time before) introduced a mildly protectionist bill; it was primarily to obtain revenue but protection was involved in the incidence of specific import duties on simple articles which could be produced locally—clothing, textiles, boots, saddlery, and earthenware. At the same time the revenue duties on tea and sugar were to be reduced to avoid raising the total cost of living.

The tariff measure was passed by the legislative assembly in January 1865; but the legislative council was strongly in favour of free trade, and it was clear that the bill would be rejected by the council. In order to force the council's hand, McCulloch tacked the tariff measure to the Appropriations Bill in which money was to be voted for public expenditure; he also inserted a preamble which asserted the assembly's exclusive right to grant supply. These tactics aroused the council's anger, and were condemned as being unparliamentary; but McCulloch and his Cabinet refused to withdraw the clause. The council was debarred by the constitution from altering or deleting any clause of a money Bill, but it had the right to reject any bill. The Council did not go so far as rejection of the Appropriations/Tariff Bill; instead it laid the measure aside on the ground that inclusion of extraneous matter in an Appropriations Bill offended parliamentary usage.

In spite of strong attacks by the *Age*, the legislative council stood firm. The only significant editorial support for the council came from the *Argus*. Popular opposition to the squattocracy was strong, and McCulloch was seen as a great emancipator. The Premier, under strong pressure from Syme's supporters and aware that withdrawal of the bill would mean personal defeat, decided to defy the council. Acting on the assembly's passage of the Tariff Bill, Premier McCulloch ordered the immediate collection of customs duties.

The council's refusal to pass the Appropriations Bill had meant that government accounts and contingencies, and officials' salaries, could not be paid. The traders from whom customs duties were being collected began action against the government for recovery of the payments; and, since the duties were being collected without the sanction of both houses of parliament, the Supreme Court gave judgment in favour of the merchants. The premier then adopted an audacious expedient to sidetrack the council and make it possible for his administration to meet obligations.

McCulloch held the post of Melbourne director of a London bank, and in this capacity he was able to secure for the government a loan from the bank to enable salaries to be paid. When the money had been spent, the bank sued the government for recovery of the loan. The government, by consent, did not defend the court action and the Governor, Sir Charles Darling, acting on the advice of his ministers, signed a warrant authorising the Treasury to repay the bank in satisfaction of the claim. By repeating this procedure every few weeks, the administration was able to secure and spend funds without the sanction of parliament, and in doing so to hold its ground for four months in the battle with the legislative council. At the same time, McCulloch went on collecting the new duties in spite of the court's judgment denying the government this right.

McCulloch's loan-and-claim device was a very questionable practice, and the dangers inherent in its continuance were widely recognized. Anxious as he was to see the power of the legislative council curbed, David Syme was among those who recognized that such juggling of official finances was irresponsible, and he urged the government to give up the practice. Syme advised McCulloch to break the "tack" forthwith and send up the tariff measure as a separate bill in the anticipation that the council would reject it, thus making possible an appeal to the people. McCulloch followed this advice; the council rejected the bill, and a dissolution of the assembly followed.

The device by which funds had been secured and expended was scathingly attacked by Edward Cardwell, the Colonial Secretary, in London. In a dispatch to the governor he characterized the methods as "simply illegal evasion of parliamentary control of finance." At the same time he instructed Darling not to repeat such actions. Cardwell—an ardent free-trader—also stigmatized the collection of money from merchants under a measure passed by the assembly only; he recorded his "extreme apprehension" at the actions of the government "in collecting money by mere force from persons from whom the Supreme Court has declared it is not due."

Amid intense excitement a general election was held in January 1866. The protection issue was now clearly before the electors. Even more important, popular opposition to the squattocracy in the council, which did not have to face an election, was stronger than ever. The election resulted in an increased majority for McCulloch. The council had to accept the people's verdict. In the new parliament the council declared itself ready to accept protection, but insisted that the established parliamentary usage, by which extraneous material was not inserted in money Bills, must be strictly adhered to. The assembly was not to be dictated to in this manner, and promptly sent up a Tariff Bill which retained the contentious preamble and included a measure for repeal of gold duties. For the third time, the council rejected the Tariff Bill. The resignation of the ministry followed. The assembly for its part made it clear that it would not support any government that did not persist with the Tariff Bill, and McCulloch came back to office and reintroduced the contentious bill, which was passed for the fourth time and sent to the council. After a conference between members of both houses, a compromise was effected whereby McCulloch agreed to remove the tariff provisions from the Appropriations Bill and the council for its part undertook to pass the tariff measure if it was submitted as a separate bill with an amended preamble. Finally in 1866 the Tariff Bill became law. The *Age* summarized its stand thus:

> We have not advocated Protection for its own sake but as a means to an end. Our object has been to accelerate the progress of the country towards the manufacturing stage. As agriculture is in advance of the pastoral stage, so is the manufacturing in advance of both. A manufacturing system acts protectively in relation to the whole business of the country.

From a legalistic standpoint the outcome of the dispute was a tactical victory for the council; but in its broader effect it was a triumph for Syme. The protracted constitutional struggle had brought to light the tremendous political power wielded through the *Age* by its owner-editor. McCulloch's support had come from *Age* working-class readers; through the ballot box they had demonstrated their determination to force the issue against the merchants and landholders, who were so strongly represented in the council. Syme's dominance as a policy-maker had been established.

Neither Syme and his readers nor McCulloch and the majority of the legislative assembly could save Darling from the wrath of the Colonial Office. For his failure to step in and uphold the Court decision against the collection of duties, and for his authorization of the payment of government funds without a supporting vote of both houses of parliament, the governor was censured and recalled by the Colonial Secretary. Darling left Melbourne in May 1866 amid demonstrations of public affection and support. To many he had acted as the governor of a self-governing colony should, accepting the advice and supporting the actions of the leader of the popularly-elected lower house. On the other hand, his detractors pointed to the fact that he also had an obligation to uphold constitutional principles and enforce the law; and, since he was appointed by the Queen, he had responsibilities to the Queen's advisers in London as well as to his own advisers. Nor could there be any doubt that he had outspokenly come out in favour of his ministers against the legislative council.

The aftermath of the sharp disagreement between the two houses on the tariff issue was a new stuggle, no less intense in bitterness, which arose out of a grant the Legislative Assembly of Victoria wished to make to Governor Darling on his recall. When it became known that the govenor had incurred the censure of the Colonial Office for his part in affairs connected with the tariff issue, and that as a result he was unlikely to receive any further appointment, public sympathy was strong for Darling. The proposed grant was to take the form of a sum of £20,000 to be paid to Lady Darling. Events followed much the same course as before: the council rejected the Darling Grant Bill, an election followed, the ministry was returned with a strong majority, and the premier announced his intention of sending up the grant with the Appropriations Bill. At this stage the Colonial Secretary intervened, advising the governor not to permit the bill to go to the Council in this form. The ministry promptly resigned in protest at this interference in the affairs of a self-governing colony, but no one else was able to form a ministry and McCulloch returned to office. There was no sign that either council or assembly was likely to break down when the crisis was dissolved by the action of the British government in reinstating Darling in the colonial service on condition that he and his wife refused to accept the proposed grant. Syme and McCulloch could claim a clear victory for the assembly, not only over the council but over the Colonial Office, which had backed down by taking Darling back into the colonial civil service after dismissing him.

One of the effects in Victoria was that before long a measure was carrried which lowered by half the property qualifications for both council membership and franchise; the question of the upper house's constitutional powers was not dealt with.

The *Age* continued its political campaigning, and in 1868 the trading interests organized another boycott of its advertising columns. Syme reacted by reducing the price of the *Age* to a penny, so that it came within the means of every working man. Its circulation doubled immediately, moving ahead of that of any other newspaper in a British land except those published in London. The working man had come to regard the *Age* as his champion, and looked upon its policies as infallible. The merchants and squatters had to content themselves by reading an exposition of their views in the *Argus*.

With expanded readership, Syme's position was strengthened; he intensified his drive for reform of the upper house, more effective land settlement laws and, above all, more effective protectionist policies. The existing low tariff of 1866 was "merely a beginning," and the editor declared his determination never to rest

> ... until Victoria is encompassed with a tariff wall that will enable the local manufacturer to pay the local artisan a fair living wage and at the same time enable him successfully to compete in the local market with the imported products of underpaid foreign labour.

When McCulloch refused to impose higher duties, Syme wrote him out of office in 1871.

There were varying degrees of success for the protectionist cause in the following years as ministry succeeded ministry. In the election campaign of

1877, Graham Berry had the *Age's* backing. Berry, leader of the Radical party, was returned in May 1877 at the head of a solid body of sixty members; his opponent, a conservative who had gone to the electors with a considerable majority, was left with a following of a mere twenty-six.

The Berry Ministry's new Tariff Bill was a milestone. The tariff schedule was drafted with Syme's assistance; he intervened when Berry's first proposals failed to produce a protective as distinct from a revenue tariff. In its final form, as promulgated in January 1878, it imposed substantial duties on a long list of imported products and produce, and even on livestock, brought in across the colony's "frontier." As well as levies of 5/– a head on cattle and horses, and 9d each on sheep, and 2/– on pigs, a 20 per cent *ad valorem* duty applied to dozens of wholly or partly made up articles of apparel (ranging through such items as aprons, bonnets, breeches, crinolines, and frocks to pelisses, petticoats, tunics, and vests) and a great variety of simple mechanical and household items from axle blocks and barrow wheels to pulley blocks, troughs, and winches. Manufactured stationery, saddles and harness, and articles made of leather, a variety of woodenware, agricultural implements, and furniture were also subject to the 20 per cent duty, while boots and shoes, matches, nails, and window sashes were subject to specified *ad valorem* imposts. A duty of 2d a 1b. was imposed on produce such as butter, cheese, honey, hams and bacon, on made-up food items (including confectionery, jams, jellies, and macaroni), on ale and beer, and on dried or preserved fruit and vegetables, and nuts; a similar duty applied to household items such as candles, starch, and blue. Machinery and raw materials were admitted duty-free.

Henceforth the principle of protection was firmly established in Victoria, where it survived all challenges. By this time the colony's population exceeded 800,000, one-third of whom resided in Melbourne. Industrial activity had a firmer base.

Other progressive legislation had come as an outgrowth of the increased activity in manufacturing in Victoria. The number of factory workers had risen from 4,000 in 1860 to well over 20,000 in the 1870s, and in 1873 the first Victorian Factories Act was passed. Its principal purpose was to limit to eight hours a day the time women could be called upon to work in factories; its provisions were under the administration of local boards of health.

The bitterness engendered by the passage of the Tariff Bill of 1877 helped precipitate a third constitutional crisis in Victoria in which once again the two houses took extreme attitudes. The immediate cause of the crisis was a proposal (again advanced by Syme) to make payment of members the permanent rule in Victoria. Two acts had been passed previously, in 1870 and 1872, providing for payment on a temporary basis, but the council was very much opposed to a permanent measure. Berry, secure in his backing by the electorate, and prepared to exploit his popular support to force a showdown with the council, decided to revert to McCulloch's tactics of including the sum necessary for payment of members in an Appropriations Bill. The council accepted the challenge and laid the bill aside. Public feeling was intense; without an appropriation, the government could not pay salaries nor meet other commitments. In order to intensify the pressure on the council, Berry dismissed from office a large number of public servants, including departmental secretaries, judges, and magistrates. The dismissals were announced on January 8, 1878; the next day became known as Black Wednesday when the dismissals took effect.

The immediate effect of the wholesale dismissals was to cause a mild commercial panic in Melbourne; the value of property and securities dropped sharply. The *Age* admitted that the dismissals could be justified only because of the importance of the objective they were intended to gain; the real purpose of the step was to defend the constitutional right of the assembly and the people whom it represented. As long as the public was with it, a government need ask for no other justification of its conduct, the newspaper declared.

When the assembly met early in February, Berry secured the support of the assembly for a resolution declaring that

> . . . all votes or grants passed in Committee of Supply become legally available for expenditure immediately the resolutions are agreed to by the Assembly.

This expedient had been devised in New South Wales ten years before; now Premier Berry asked the Governor, Sir George Bowen, to sign Treasury warrants authorizing expenditure in accordance with the resolution. The governor, doubting the legality of the procedure, took the surprising step of seeking advice from the power behind the ministry, "King David" Syme. Syme disapproved of Berry's expedient, and suggested that the governor should seek legal opinion on the matter; meanwhile he urged Berry to drop the practice. The governor signed the warrants, accepting the assurance of the attorney-general that the procedure was legal; the colonial lawyers' verdict differed from that of the Crown law officers in England, who held that public officers were not warranted in making payments, apart from those of a routine nature, that had not been authorized by statute. (The colonial ministry maintained that the governor should have accepted the advice of his local law officers without question, and should not have sought further advice from the Crown law officers.)

The financial community was already faced with crises brought about by bank failures and fear of further runs on banks, and there was general relief when a compromise settlement was arranged. The assembly withdrew the item tacked to the Appropriations Bill, while the council in March passed the separate measure for the payment of members.

The council's obduracy was threatening to make parliamentary government in Victoria unworkable. Berry and his legal advisers considered that the only way of avoiding future deadlocks and securing the assembly's supremacy was by amendment of the Constitution Act; such amendment could only be carried with the consent of both houses, which was obviously impossible of achievement so, after the council had rejected an Amendment Bill, Berry took the extreme step of going in person to England to request passage of an Imperial Act of Parliament which would provide that bills passed by the

assembly at two consecutive sessions of parliament with an election intervening should become law, despite rejection by the council.

The Secretary of State, Sir Michael Hicks-Beach, turned down the request, considering that the Victorian Houses of Parliament had not yet explored all the avenues for reaching an agreement on their respective powers.
He urged that both houses follow the spirit of the English practice, the
upper house not interfering in financial matters proper and the lower house
not introducing new principles and extraneous material into supply bills.
He hoped that the council would "so transact its business that the wishes
of the people so clearly and repeatedly expressed shall ultimately prevail,"
but considered that none of the assembly's proposals for safeguarding its
ultimate conrtol of finance were "free from objection." He concluded by making it clear that Westminster would never consent to alter Victoria's constitution at the request of one house only.

The issue had to be resolved locally, but the council was still not prepared
to lower its colours, and it was not until 1881 that a bill for reform of the
council passed through both houses and became law. After Berry was defeated the incoming premier, James Service, introduced legislation for reform
of the council through a widening of its franchise. The property qualification
for both members and electors was reduced, membership was increased, and
the tenure of members was reduced from ten to six years. There was no
constitutional limitation of the council's powers; indeed, in a sense every
widening of the council's base brought it closer to equality with the assembly
as a representative elected house. However, the reforms did bring into the
council a membership more representative of public opinion than the
councils of the 1860s and 1870s, and there were no more deadlocks.

The payment of members deadlock had highlighted the role of the governor in a self-governing colony, raising the issue of how far he should go in
following the advice of his ministers where extreme measures were involved.
The Secretary of State considered that the governor should not have con-
sented to the dismissal of the civil servants. Governor Bowen, an experienced
officer with eighteen years gubernatorial service behind him, made a spirited
defence, based on precedent, the advice given him by the previous Secretary
of State in a parallel case, and the ministry's overwhelming electoral victory
only eight months before.

The governor's acceptance of his ministry's advice saved the Colonial
office from a serious collision with an important colony; but it involved
other dangers. Alfred Deakin, Attorney-General in later Victorian Governments, went so far as to say that it was not the governor's fault that a
revolution did not occur; he wrote later that:

> A strong and wise man in his position would have consented only to temporary
> suspension of the public servants, and have insisted upon guarantees that the public
> should not be made to suffer. . . . It was fortunate that [Berry] did not advise still
> more drastic measures than those actually adopted; for had he done so they would
> certainly have been countersigned by the Governor who at the time imposed no
> check whatever upon his Ministers.

During the years of crisis, all the major reforms advocated by David Syme had been carried; Syme's Victoria was firmly and strongly embarked on the courses which Australia's national development was to follow in years to come.

The other colonies were slow in following along the path to selective protection to foster industry. The balance of forces was different from that present in Victoria; in 1861 Melbourne, with 140,000 people, had increased its population sixfold in ten years and held more than a quarter of the colony's people. In no other colony was there such a concentration of population, and nowhere else was there pressure for the setting up of manufacturing activities to produce goods for local use.

In New South Wales, where wool-growing continued to expand, all the emphasis of pastoral and financial opinion supported a policy of keeping costs low to help production for export, and with sales of Crown land still providing abundant funds, there was no great need for a tariff on the grounds of revenue. Sir Henry Parkes, the dominant political figure throughout the 1870s and 1880s, was as earnest an advocate of free-trade as David Syme was of protection. Although protection became a leading political issue in New South Wales, the Protectionist party was never strong enough to enforce its policies. The presence of easily worked coal helped foster manufacturing as a natural rather than a protected development, however, and industrial progress in New South Wales was not far behind that of Victoria.

In South Australia, customs duties had been imposed on imported goods for some years, but although the tariff was amended from time to time it was not until the 1870s that a concerted move was made by manufacturing interests to secure exemptions so that raw materials could be admitted free as a benefit to local industry. These initial steps were strengthened in the 1880s by the introduction of a more studied system designed to provide selective protection for manufactures through higher duties on some imports.

A somewhat different form of protectionism appeared in Western Australia, still almost totally rural, when the question of customs duties on various items came under discussion in 1870. Up to this point duties had been imposed with the sole object of providing revenue. Most imports were subject to an *ad valorem* duty of 7 per cent; exceptions were grains for use as stock feed, flour and meal, agricultural implements and a few other items, all specifically exempted and admitted free; spirits and tobacco were subject to special duties. When a new bill was introduced in the legislative council to maintain a tariff on generally similar lines for 1871, several council members sought to have the exemption removed from flour and other products which might be processed locally. The council voted in favour of such duties being imposed, but the governor vetoed the proposal.

When the council was dissolved, tariff reform to provide protection for rural processing industries was the main issue during the election campaign, and representatives of rural districts, which were strongly protectionist, were returned in force. However, it was not until 1887 that a tariff commission recommended a general increase "to promote the establishment of new industries and encourage the development of industries and many factories already established." The Tariff Act of 1888 increased duties all round, but mainly to enlarge government revenue.

All these colonial tariffs were imposed not only on imports from other countries, but also on goods brought in from the other colonies. This course was dictated by the Australian Colonies Government Act of 1850, which limited the colonies' right to levy customs duties to those which did not discriminate between goods from any "countries or places," a term which applied to the other colonies.

From 1863 onwards several attempts were made at intercolonial conferences to have the prohibition on discriminatory tariffs withdrawn and to form an all-Australian customs union, without any internal tariff barriers; but the British government was unwilling to withdraw the prohibition, and in any case the tariff policies followed by the various colonies were so divergent that it is unlikely that any agreement could have been reached.

The prohibition on discriminatory tariffs was withdrawn in 1873; henceforth the colonies had full power to make intercolonial trade agreements. There were some retaliatory tariffs (against Victoria) and some reciprocal tariff agreements, but generally the barriers remained.

In the 1860s the Colonial Office showed concern over the attitude of the colonial legislatures to banking issues. Particularly significant was the question of maintaining the old Whitehall prohibition on mortgage-lending in the colonies by any bank.

In 1864 the Victorian Legislative Assembly had agreed to a charter conferring on a new bank the right to lend on the security of land. In a self-governing colony, Whitehall could not intervene; but when the same issue arose in Western Australia, the Colonial Office (which still had effective control of Western Australian affairs) refused to sanction the section of an ordinance incorporating a bank there which would have permitted the bank to accept land as security for advances. The issue had to be clarified. An anomaly had been created; banks with Victorian-approved unrestricted charters were by now active in Western Australia alongside the banks with London charters.

The Colonial Office wished to avoid the confusion and difficulty of a situation where the various colonial legislatures followed differing policies on the mortgage-lending issue. With an expanding and more diversified economy, pressure grew for more flexible banking policies. In practice the old legal restrictions against mortgage lending were not being enforced; but with the new colonial banks avid for business and prepared to support rural borrowers in spite of the risks entailed, the older banks (operating with London charters) began to find the restrictions damaging to their interests. Local banks were expanding rapidly in spite of occasional difficulties and setbacks, and the English-based banks came to feel a need for greater scope to compete with the aggressive newcomers. In 1869 Victoria removed the bars remaining on the older banks; the lifting of the restrictions was hailed as a sign that the colonial legislature held untrammelled power on a significant matter of concern to the colonists.

The greater availability of bank credit, particularly from the locally-based banks, was an important factor contributing to the increased number of individual farms and increased area under crop that occurred in all colonies during the 1870s.

Into the interior   13

Seventy years or so after Sydney was founded, and when Victoria had more than 500,000 people, only about one-fifth of the land area of Australia had been settled and half of the continent still remained unexplored. The urge to penetrate deeper into the hinterland was strong. The extent of the dry regions was not known as yet. In the late 1850s, there were still many who hoped that great tracts of good land remained to be discovered—even though it had already been demonstrated that the grasslands did not roll on endlessly across the continent, and although Eyre, Sturt, Mitchell, Kennedy, and Leichhardt had all been confronted with desolation, heat, and lack of water during their probing journeys into the interior.

The appeal of exploration was temporarily eclipsed by the excitement of the great gold discoveries, and it was not until after 1855 that interest was revived. Well-equipped expeditions were mounted as the second phase of Australian exploration opened with successive attempts to drive deeper into the interior and solve the mysteries of remote regions. The challenge of the unknown was now a strong spur to exploration in addition to the traditional impulse to uncover new pastureland.

Those who undertook the long, exhausting, and sometimes tragic journeys into the heart of the continent had to struggle against scorching heat and lack of water. J. Beete Jukes, after a visit to some northern areas in the late 1840s, had described the prevailing conditions thus:

> The open and scattered woodlands of Australia . . . offer no shelter to the ground from the rays of the sun. The small, thinly-disseminated leaves of the trees, instead of giving shade, become themselves as hot and parched as the rocks and sands beneath them. The ragged strips of dry and resinous bark hanging from the trunks of all the trees are like tinder, ever ready to catch fire from a spark, and the grass among the trees commonly resembles hay. Everything absorbs heat freely, and radiates it into the surrounding atmosphere.

There were perils for the traveller in this barren and uncharted country where the threat of surprise attacks by Aborigines was an added danger. Many of the expeditions by little bands of intrepid men, who toiled on across trackless wastes of hot, blinding red sand or parched and blistering land when worn out by exertion and fatigue, revealed extraordinary fortitude. Some of the leaders were ill-equipped for their tasks; but they and their companions frequently showed courage and hardihood of a very high order, and many of the journeys rank among the great feats of land exploration. In terms of practical results, however, the story is quite different; the toil and sacrifices of brave explorers were not greatly rewarded for the most part, and the sanguine hopes of visionaries were unfulfilled.

The first major effort of the post-gold days was the North Australian Expedition of 1855–56, led by Augustus Charles Gregory. The expedition was decided upon by the British government after the Royal Geographical Society had suggested that an extensive exploration should be undertaken in northern regions of Australia. A sum of £5,000 was voted for the purpose. Gregory, who earlier had led a successful expedition in Western Australia, sailed from Moreton Bay and landed at the mouth of the Victoria River with a party of eighteen men. The expedition's botanist was Baron Ferdinand von Mueller.

The party had 50 horses, and 200 sheep and provisions for eighteen months were taken. First, exploration of the area about the Victoria River itself was undertaken by Gregory, who followed the river to its source; then he moved along its tributary (a creek which he named after Sturt) and followed it south-west until it disappeared in the desert. Returning to the Victoria, Gregory struck east to Elsey Creek, where he discovered traces of the Leichhardt expedition; he then set off south-east and followed the line of the coast of the Gulf of Carpentaria, picking up the Gilbert River, and finally the Burdekin as he made his way to Rockhampton.

In 1858 Gregory made a second journey, this one with the specific purpose of determining the course followed by the Leichhardt expedition. With a party of eight, using forty horses, Gregory headed westward through the centre of present Queensland to the Barcoo (which he found to be identical with Coopers Creek), and although confronted by drought-seared lands, he struck south-west past Lake Torrens to Adelaide. From evidence of an old camp site and other signs discovered during the journey, Gregory concluded that Leichhardt had probably struck north-west and perished in the desert. On the broader canvas of explorations, Gregory's journey was important since it linked the explorations of Mitchell and Kennedy (in the southern Queensland area) with those of Sturt (in his 1845 expedition north to the Stony Desert).

In South Australia, interest in opening up the hinterland to the north remained strong in spite of setbacks received in earlier attempts. The enterprising merchant-pastoralist, Thomas Elder, had set up an agency and store at the head of Spencer Gulf in 1854, and small wool shipments were being made from there which gave promise of growth. The colony's Surveyor-General, Goyder, visiting the area in 1857, was greatly impressed; recent heavy rains had turned the area into a sea of grasslands, and he found Lake Torrens to be a vast sheet of water. Pastoralists were pressing northward, and as new tracts of pastoral country were desperately needed, private funds were subscribed in 1857 to support an expedition to investigate the area. It was led by John McDouall Stuart (who had been with Sturt in 1845), and as a result of it some 40,000 square miles of sparse but usable grazing land were revealed. The government had by this time offered special leasehold terms to successful explorers. In April 1859 Stuart undertook a second journey, and west of Lake Eyre he discovered a great expanse of dry plains covered with grass and saltbush.

A proposal to send an expedition more or less directly north from the head of Spencer Gulf to the northern coastline caught popular imagination, and the South Australian Government announced in 1859 that it would give £2,500 to the first man to make such a journey. Stuart made immediate preparations and left Adelaide in March 1860 with two companions and thirteen horses. Keeping to the west of the Torrens basin, the party came to the Macdonnell Range (which Stuart named). At a point which he believed to be the geographical centre of the continent, Stuart built a cairn on a red sandstone hill covered with scrub and spinifex and raised the flag as the party gave "three hearty cheers." Notions that the central area might contain an inland sea or instead might be wholly desert were dispelled. Instead, the central area was found to possess some fair, though sparse, grassland.

As the party moved on again, striking north-west, the aspect worsened; by the time another 150 miles had been covered there was nothing but spinifex to be seen. Rations were short, there was no water to be had, and severe fatigue and illness racked the men. Finally an attack by Aborigines in which some of the horses were lost convinced Stuart that he should turn back. He had covered 1,200 miles on the outward journey.

The South Australian Parliament at once voted Stuart £2,500 for equipping a larger expedition. In November 1860 he set out with eleven men. Traversing his former route, on April 25, 1861 he reached the farthest point of his previous journey. He drove on doggedly toward the north coast, but finally the dense scrub impeded progress to such an extent that on July 12 he had to beat a retreat. Ten weeks later he was back in Adelaide, his party intact.

In the following year, when Stuart made another attempt, his "South Australian Great Northern Exploring Expedition" was successful in achieving a south-north crossing. With eleven men he passed the central area in March 1862, reached the Roper on June 26, and moved on to the Adelaide River which he followed through good country. Skirting the coastal "marsh," Stuart and his party set off early on July 24 to make the final push to the sea; as he wanted to give the others a surprise upon reaching it, Stuart informed only two of his companions that he knew the sea to be so near. He wrote in his diary of that day:

At eight and a half miles came up a broad valley of black alluvial soil, covered with long grass; from this I can hear the wash of the sea. . . . Crossed the valley and entered the scrub [bordering the beach] which was a complete network of vines. Stopped the horses to clear the way, whilst I advanced a few yards to the beach, and was delighted and gratified to behold the water of the Indian Ocean.

Thring, who rode in advance of me, called out, "The sea!" which so took them all by surprise that he had to repeat the call before they fully understood what was meant; hearing which they immediately gave three long and hearty cheers. . . . I dipped my feet, and washed my face and hands in the sea.

The trip to Chambers Bay had covered some 2,000 miles; the great trans-continental crossing had been made.

After cutting the initials J McD S on a large tree, Stuart prepared to return, and on July 26 the southward journey bagan. It proved extremely arduous. A man of indomitable courage and tenacity, Stuart suffered severely and, in his own words, was reduced to "a perfect skeleton" by the privations. His reports on the country were optimistic, however; he reported he had passed through "one of the finest countries one could wish to see." He added:

If this country is settled, it will be one of the finest colonies under the Crown, suitable for the growth of any and everything. What a splendid country for producing cotton!

Stuart's journeys opened the way for South Australia's annexation of the Northern Territory in 1863 and for the building of the overland telegraph line. In time the southern section of the Northern Territory was to prove an asset to South Australia's cattlemen.

Stuart received £3,000 in government rewards, but he was not the first man to have crossed the continent. The expedition that achieved that distinction was that of Robert O'Hara Burke and William John Wills. That expedition set out from Melbourne on August 20, 1860, to the accompaniment of fanfare and excitement. It was the outcome of a growing interest in Victoria in matters related to exploration—an interest aroused by tales of what might lie hidden deep in the continent's interior and fostered by erudite men such as Ferdinand von Mueller. The expedition was to undertake scientific investigation and its personnel included a botanist, a geologist, an astronomer, and a meteorologist. When a public fund was opened, £12,000 was quickly raised, half of it from the government. Arrangements for the expedition were under the direction of the Royal Society of Victoria. The society was one of the groups which had taken an active part in creating enthusiasm for exploration in northern sectors of the continent to be undertaken by a party from Victoria.

Burke, who was chosen to lead the expedition, was a young police officer, courageous and confident but without experience of inland exploration and—as events showed—he had little aptitude for such an undertaking. George James Landells, who had brought a train of twenty-four camels from India expecially for the expedition's use, was second-in-charge, but the settled districts had been barely left behind when he quarrelled with Burke and returned to Melbourne. Wills, the gifted young meteorologist, then took over

as second in command; like Burke, he lacked the practical qualities demanded for success in such a venture.

The expedition made a slow journey to Menindee, on the Darling River.
Here Burke set up a depot; William Wright and most of the men and equipment were left to follow to Cooper's Creek as Burke and Wills struck north
with five companions and sixteen of the camels. Burke waited at Cooper's
Creek for thirty-four days—November 11 to December 16—and then, as
Wright had not arrived, he decided to hurry north with Wills and two
others. They took six camels and a packhorse, and three months' rations.
The three men left at the camp were instructed to wait three months and
then, if Burke and his party had not returned, to go south to Menindee.

Impatient to reach his objective, Burke set a fast pace when he reached the
northward-flowing Cloncurry River. His haste proved costly, since the camels
were too weak to respond. The party endured all manner of hardship, chiefly
lack of food since they had taken an absurdly insufficient quantity. Before
long, Burke found that only two camels and an emaciated packhorse
remained. He decided to make a final dash for the coast with Wills as his
companion; at last they reached the mangrove swamps bordering the
shoreline of the Gulf of Carpentaria but were too exhausted to push on,
even though they were so close that they could hear the sound of the sea.
Burke wrote in his diary:

> It would be as well to say that we reached the sea, but we could not obtain a
> view of the open ocean, although we made every endeavout to do so.

Having completed the transcontinental journey, they headed south on February 21, 1861, on the 700-mile journey back to Cooper's Creek. It became
a nightmare trek. The remaining animals were just able to stagger, and as
provisions ran low the four men were soon barely able to keep going. By
April 17 they were starving. One of the party—Charles Gray—died; the
survivors spent most of a day burying him. The tattered band struggled on
again; by April 20 they were within 30 miles of the Cooper's Creek camp.
By dusk the following evening the three men staggered to the spot, dragging
the last camel behind them. They found the camp deserted. There was no
sound in reply to their calls, but they found a sign chipped into the bark
of a coolibah tree beside the water course. It read:

DIG

3 FT NW

Apr 21 1861

It had been cut that very day—just before the depot party had left around
midday, only seven hours or so earlier. By the light of the moon the starving
men dug as directed and unearthed a wooden box with a small stock of provisions: flour, oatmeal, rice, and sugar. With no inkling that Burke and his
companions were so close, the depot party under William Brahe had set off
after overstaying by more than a month the time set down for them to remain.

After making a meal from the stores, the three men rested, completely
exhausted, while Burke tried to decide what should be done. In the letter
he left Brahe had given no hint that his progress would be impeded by the
weakness of his animals and the severe illness of one of his party, and Burke felt

sure there was no chance of catching up with him. As it happened, Brahe was only about 14 miles from the depot when Burke's party arrived there. Burke and his companions rested all that day and the next night; then Burke made the decision to go down Cooper's Creek in an attempt to reach Mount Hopeless. This was just one more irreversible mistake in a sequence of tragic errors of judgment that dogged the hapless little band playing out the sad drama of ultimate despair. Burke had failed to leave a blaze on the trees or any other indication that he had been at the depot camp; and a few days later, when Brahe rode back with Wright (who had inexplicably wasted months at Menindee) and reached the camp to make a final check they found no evidence that Burke and his companions had returned. The two men failed to discover that the food cache had been unearthed; instead, they hurried back to rejoin the group going south.

For the unfortunate Burke and Wills and their companion, John King, wandering in the bush, the final struggle for survival had begun. Day by day they grew weaker. They relied almost wholly on nardoo seeds and fish given to them by Aborigines. After two months of this hopeless wandering, both leaders died, Wills two days before Burke. Their last notes were written on June 28. King, who had shown amazing fortitude throughout, was befriended by an Aboriginal tribe, and somehow managed to survive.

Various expeditions were sent out to search for the lost explorers. In August 1861 the first, a group led by Alfred William Howitt, left Melbourne and soon afterwards met Brahe who was hurrying south with news of the party's disappearance; Brahe turned back and accompanied Howitt. Cooper's Creek was reached early in September; a few days later the party was at the old camp depot, and soon afterward King was found. Howitt recorded that King

> ... presented a melancholy appearance, wasted to a shadow, and hardly to be distinguished as a civilized being but by the remnants of clothes upon him.

King was in fact so weak that he was almost inarticulate; but slowly he told the whole story of the ill-starred enterprise, and guided Howitt to Wills' grave; Burke's body was found later.

The funeral of Burke and Wills was held in Melbourne on January 21, 1863. It attracted greater crowds to the city than any event before; tens of thousands of people flocked to pay their last respects.

Three other search parties had been hastily gathered and sent on their way. From Brisbane, William Landsborough was sent by sea with instructions to land at the head of the Gulf of Carpentaria and work south, while John McKinlay was to lead an expedition north-east from Adelaide, and a third party was to work its way eastward from Rockhampton.

Landsborough landed at the mouth of the Albert River; he discovered a new river which he named the Gregory and followed it south, and penetrated the Barkly Tableland for the first time. Returning to the Albert, he struck south-east to the Flinders and followed it through fine pastoral country which had not been entered before. Landsborough picked up the headwaters of the

Thomson and followed that river until he struck south across the Barcoo and reached the Warrego. In nine months he had traversed many important new areas, and his report led to the area being occupied as sheep and cattle stations.

When McKinlay and his party of ten men reached the Cooper's Creek area he spent some time investigating stories which the Aborigines told him of parties of white men who had passed that way; and after news reached him of the fate of Burke and Wills he decided to continue northward. As it was now midsummer he was held back by lack of water, but in February 1862 he was able to move off and soon he was in the channel country bordering a river which he named the Mueller (later known as the Diamantina). He followed the stream north beyond the tropic of Capricorn then found a way across the harsh hills to pick up the Leichhardt River. This he followed to the mangrove swamps lining the river's mouth. The party then struck east and struggled over 700 miles of wild terrain to reach the settled areas along the east coast of Queensland. McKinlay's persistence and his thorough methods had demonstrated that long journeys could be undertaken without undue risk, and he had shown by example that sheep and cattle could be driven across the continent.

The expedition from Rockhampton was under Frederick Walker and comprised four white men and seven Aboriginal troopers. During wanderings through central and northern Queensland the party found traces of the Burke and Wills party and also of Leichhardt, and revealed the existence of considerable areas of useful land.

Thus the search parties for Burke and Wills—costing only a fraction of the better-known expedition but led by experienced bushmen—succeeded in throwing open vast new areas of rich black soil plains and good pasture. The region discovered was much superior to the area (400 or 500 miles to the west) through which Stuart had passed.

Even after the major exploring journeys had been made, many pockets of fairly good land in Queensland still remained hidden. One by one these tracts were explored during the 1860s by expeditions finding ways through the formidable barriers—steep scrub-clad ranges, deep gorges and rocky ravines, or impenetrable brigalow—which barred the path to more fertile areas. It was not long before enterprising pastoralists were moving in to occupy the new land.

Just as a generation or more earlier, pioneers had gone into the newly opened areas in the south, ambitious men were moving into the wilds of Queensland; now they were cattlemen (almost invariably with Scottish or Irish names) rather than sheepmen. The first buildings erected on a new run were inevitably of a very primitive kind, the principal hut being made of roughhewn timber. James B. Stevenson, in *Seven Years in the Australian Bush*, gave this sketch of conditions in outback Queensland in the 1860s:

> B—'s was a regular old-fashioned cattle station. The hut was long and roomy, built of round logs, and roofed with ironbark. One end was entirely taken up with

a large fireplace, round which were placed large blocks of wood which served as seats. . . . Near the fireplace stood a large rough table made of slabs, and round the walls at regular intervals were bunks for the occupants. . .

There were four stockmen and a hutkeeper, who, with B—and his overseer, made up the complement of hands. They all messed together somewhat after the old baronial style, B—, the overseer and the visitors sitting, as it were, above the salt, the table being filled up by the stockmen and any hands in search of work who might have called for a night's lodging.

Stevenson noted that over each bunk hung a rifle and, here and there, an old sword, "though what the latter were for I never could find out, as for purposes of defence against the blacks they were useless."

In some areas the graziers themselves opened the way to new land. Elsewhere, in the forests clothing the coastal ranges of Queensland and New South Wales, as well as in the heavily forested areas of eastern Victoria, timber cutters were usually the pathfinders. In the northern forests their search was for stands of red cedar, a tree yielding a fine-quality, soft, and workable timber, now in keen demand by local as well as overseas furniture makers. The activity had begun in the early years of settlement but as the demand for fine timber grew, the search extended, and the more accessible cedar stands were depleted. The cedar-getters were now moving north in the heavy forests along the coastal fringe. Faced with loneliness and plagued by pests—mainly mosquitoes and snakes—the tree fellers became hard drinkers. They were noted as being improvident and reckless, and were described as being among "the roughest of rough fellows"; an observer of the day found the typical cedar-getter to be

. . . muscular as a mule, simple as a child, generous as a slave of Aladdin's lamp.

Such men were among those contributing to exploration by penetrating still-unknown areas. As one observer noted in 1869:

. . . the cedar-getters are no doubt the pioneers of civilization. They are the first to brave the dangers of the wilds, to penetrate the recesses of the forest and to find the excellence of the land.

By the late 1870s the axemen were busy in Queensland's coastal forests; they were soon to be found as far north as the Atherton Tableland, where they were working a great patch of red cedar, cutting huge logs which were dropped into the Barron River to float down to the sea coast.

In the north of the continent, vast tracts remained unoccupied. Every attempt to establish coastal settlements had failed; tropical vegetation had long since grown over the relics of the little settlements at Melville Island and Raffles Bay, and in 1849 the second of the two settlements at Port Essington was abandoned.

Nevertheless, after Stuart's penetration of the Centre and north of the continent, beginning in 1859, new enthusiasm for advancing settlement appeared in Adelaide. The north was not to be written off. In 1861 the proposal was put to the British government by the governor that South

Australia's northern boundary should be raised from the 26th parallel so that the colony would extend through to the north coast. Two years later London agreed to transfer jurisdiction over the 500,000 square-mile Northern Territory from New South Wales, although in doing so the Crown stipulated that South Australian control was to apply only "until we think fit to make other dispositions" of the area.

The South Australian authorities were anxious to consolidate their claim, and in 1863 moves were made to colonize the area. Offices were opened in London and Adelaide to sell land orders covering various northern sections. Some sales were made, and although generally the response was poor the South Australian Government decided to persist and to promote a settlement on the north coast as part of the overland telegraph project which it was backing. A survey team in 1864 proposed a township site at the mouth of the Adelaide River. A year later the occupying party tried to establish itself, but the site was unsuitable; it was surrounded by swamps, and soon mosquitoes, disease, and dissension proved so overwhelming that many members of the expedition left. The attempt was finally abandoned in 1867.

A year or so later Port Darwin was selected as the site for a town, and a burst of activity by a survey party produced surveys covering 1000 square miles and four township sites, including Palmerston, northern terminal of the telegraph line. Interest in settlement of the northern areas was already waning, however, and land-order holders were clamouring for return of their money. Arguments among litigants replaced enthusiasm.

About the time the overland telegraph line was opened in 1872, a new flurry of excitement was stirred up by news of gold discoveries in the Pine Creek area. In Adelaide and Melbourne speculators moved quickly; companies were formed, and men, managers, and machinery were sent north in the hope of winning great riches. It was not long before the excitement died away; the prevailing costs, and general conditions arising from remoteness and a bad climate, soon killed the mining enterprises.

In the west of the continent, the great inland plateau area remained empty and untouched; it was the only region still wholly unexplored. Attempts to penetrate it had failed from the early days of settlement in the west as hopeful explorers were driven back by its scorching heat and dryness. Expeditions in the late 1850s to the Murchison and Gascoyne had shown that some good pasture land existed along the upper reaches of the rivers, but the barren and waterless hinterland defied attempts to penetrate it. In 1861 Francis Thomas Gregory revealed the existence of some useful pasture lands in the coastal regions along the Ashburton, Fortescue, and De Grey rivers; and three years later the first shipment of wool was made from the Port Hedland area. Enthusiastic reports by small exploring parties resulted in new pastoral ventures, including those of the Roebuck Bay Pastoral and Agricultural Association and the Camden Harbour Pastoral Association. Attempts were also made to settle land in the Kimberley region, but these failed. By the mid-1860s an expedition had penetrated the Hampton Plains district east of the present Kalgoorlie. The land was found to be unattractive and without rivers.

A great area still had not been penetrated—including the hinterland to Western Australia and the land west of Stuart's north-south route—and so long as it remained a mystery there were those who liked to believe that well-watered regions probably lay hidden somewhere behind the forbidding fringes to the area. Aborigines had reported great waters inland, and the hope of finding some good rivers there obliterated more realistic assessments. The optimistic kept alive vague hopes that a secret river system might pour its waters into a vast inland sea or support an area of abundant tropical vegetation somewhere in the veiled interior. Only an excuse was needed to turn the urge to investigate the theories into exploratory enterprises.

In 1869 John Forrest made the first of his notable journeys. Vague reports had drifted into Perth that the long-lost Leichhardt party had reached Western Australia and that its members had been murdered there. Forrest was put in charge of an expedition to investigate the stories, and from Perth he went into unknown country to the north-east, reaching Lake Barlee and continuing eastward from there. Nothing was revealed or heard concerning Leichhardt's fate, but the expedition established Forrest's reputation. The following year he was sent on an expedition to find a usable overland route between west and east. As things turned out, it covered in reverse the route of Eyre's trip of 1840, but it was completed in only five months.

The overland telegraph line, linking Adelaide and Darwin and following Stuart's route of 1862, was opened in 1872, and from that time way-stations along it became starting points for westward expeditions.

In 1873 Ernest Giles, an accomplished bushman who placed his faith in horses even in the driest country, pressed west from the Finke River area to explore the country about Lake Amadeus. He saw and recorded Ayers Rock and the Olgas from a distance. Before he returned he met Major Peter Warburton and his party, then on a westward journey to seek new pastoral areas in the interior.

Warburton's objective was to drive across the continent to Perth. With twenty-one camels, the expedition left Alice Springs in April 1873 and from the northern side of the Macdonnells drove in a direction slightly north of west. Soon they were in waterless and totally barren country. The men became ill and weak, and even the camels were affected as conditions became unbearable. Determination alone drove Warburton on; he decided to cut down daytime travel because of the searing heat and to move mainly at night. The party had great difficulty in finding water and was compelled by this factor to travel north-west instead of south-west. The course was across the northern section of the Great Sandy Desert, and here the expedition was immobilized for two months while scouts searched for water. Eventually some was found 100 miles to the north-west, and the party could move on. The pitiless land took its toll, however, and as the weeks passed many of the camels died. Finally, when the men were at the point of complete collapse and seemed doomed to perish after having traversed some 1,500 miles of parched land, they reached better country at the head of the Oakover River. From there one member of the party was able to push on alone to seek help, covering 170 miles to the coast. A relief party went out for

Warburton, who struggled on and reached Roebourne early in 1874.

At the same time as Warburton left Alice Springs, William Christie Gosse, Deputy Surveyor-General of South Australia, set off on a journey with a similar objective, though the route he chose lay further south. Skirting Lake Amadeus, he struck west from the Musgrave Range. He reached Ayers Rock, describing it as "one immense rock rising abruptly from the plain." He tried to climb it but failed. As he moved on, he was soon pinned down by lack of water. The land was harsh and wholly unpromising. Finally at a point south of the Barrow Range he was forced to turn back.

By this time Ernest Giles was reaching out into the same area, having set out from Macumba (South Australia) in August 1873. On a track very close to that taken by Gosse, he penetrated further west than Gosse, but he too was forced back; he then moved directly north to the desolate Rawlinson Range before turning west again—only to be blocked finally by the waterless Gibson Desert.

Giles now realized that his only hope of success was to use camels for crossing the parched regions, and on his return to Adelaide he decided to approach Thomas Elder, the pastoralist, for financial support for such a venture. By May 1875 he was able to set off again, this time using camels and following a more southerly route (about 150 miles inland from the Bight). The camels made it possible to cover the long waterless stretches—one of over 300 miles. Giles reached Perth in November, having traversed 2,500 miles in six months.

Meanwhile John Forrest had completed a crossing through the Gibson Desert. He had left Geraldton in March 1874, picked up the Murchison River and followed it into the interior, then continued eastward through country of varying promise. The cooler weather of winter favoured him, and he was able to struggle on through waterless regions, finally reaching the area Giles had penetrated a year earlier. After enduring the horrors of thirst the party, skirting the Musgraves and then picking up the Macumba River, reached the telegraph line, north of Peake telegraph station, in September. His extraordinary journey had taken him through the very heart of the forbidding and terrible western central desert.

The fourth—and last—great overland journey across the arid western plateau was that undertaken by Giles at the conclusion of his 1875 crossing. After only two months in Perth, he was on his way again, this time crossing from west to east. He chose a route between that of Forrest in 1874 and Warburton in 1873. Leaving Geraldton in January 1876, he struck out to the north-east and reached the headwaters of the Ashburton, more than 400 miles from his starting point and nearly 300 miles inland, before turning almost due east for the attack on the heart of the dreaded Gibson Desert. The country he passed through was extremely arid, as he knew it would be, but he picked up his old route along the Murchison Range and by August he had reached Peake.

Giles took for himself the title of "the last of the Australian explorers." The only notable expedition of pioneer exploration after his time was that of John Forrest's brother, Alexander Forrest, who in 1879 led an expedition along the coast from the De Grey River to King Sound, and from there up the Fitzroy River on to the Leopold Ranges of the Kimberley district. He discovered the Ord River and crossed Nicholson Plains before eventually reaching the overland telegraph line near Daly Waters. This journey revealed some of the best grazing land in the far north-west of the continent. Others had examined large pockets of pastoral country there from the 1860s but Alexander Forrest's journey touched off a movement into the area. His brother John examined a large portion of the Kimberleys in 1883, confirming the view that this region contained useful cattle country.

Pastoralists who had pioneered the cattle country of Queensland twenty years before were now thinking in terms of new and larger holdings, and the reports brought back by Alexander Forrest in 1879 seemed to point the way to a grander future in the far north-west. The reports induced Patrick Durack, patriarch of a family of cattlemen, to overland large herds across northern Australia to the new leases offering in the Kimberleys. A great mustering of cattle on various Durack family properties around the Cooper's Creek area was begun, and soon four groups of cattle (ranging from 1,500 to well over 2,000 head) were headed on the great trek. The leading groups left in May 1883. Many misadventures were to occur before the great herds reached the Ord River two and a half years later. By that time the losses of stock had been heavy, but there were sufficient cattle left to found six great properties from which in years to come cattle would be overlanded for sale in the southern settlements.

Such grand adventures were for cattle kings, and for only a very few of them. In the main areas of rural development, the wool lands, the sheepmen generally had gone through difficult times in the 1870s. Although in the 1860s sheep numbers had rather more than doubled, in the 1870s new problems beset the woolgrower and expansion of the industry was on a more cautious scale. Numbers continued to rise, but the rate of increase had declined. Even with careful management, the woolmen found that difficulties were increasing. After a sharp setback in 1871, the London wool market improved but prices remained depressed and only by substantially increasing output and improving the handling methods could sheepmen remain solvent. Moreover, a new and unexpected scourge was soon spreading out over the sheep lands.

The lowly rabbit began to eat a way across Victoria and then north and north-west through the pastoral lands beyond. Rabbits had first established themselves around Sydney from the early days of settlement, but they did not become pests. The destructive element began after a shipment of rabbits arrived from England for a landowner in the Geelong district in 1859; once liberated, the rabbits multiplied rapidly. They soon spread across the well-grassed lands of the south, then began to move north in hordes, advancing from 50 to 70 miles a year on a broad front. They penetrated deeper and deeper into the interior, and became more numerous in the lands where they had first established themselves. They caused great damage, particularly in areas where friable soil was ideal for their burrows and the sweet grass provided ample feed. By the mid-1880s the active and prolific little newcomer was moving forward across the west of New South Wales and across South Australia into Western Australia; soon the advance guard had reached Queensland.

The destruction wrought by the new pest was incalculable. In good seasons the rabbits multiplied rapidly, sometimes assuming plague proportions. In dry years they robbed the sheep of needed forage and at the same time they did serious damage by biting off all the living plants and scratching into the topsoil in search of the roots of grass and herbage. The cost of employing men to keep down their numbers was often a serious drain on the landholder's resources—but to leave the rabbits unchecked would be to court disaster. Individual farmers tried as best they could to keep the rabbits in check by digging out the burrows; on station properties the rabbiter, equipped with traps and poison bait as well as shovels and accompanied by a mixed pack of terriers and greyhounds, soon took a place alongside the fencer and the boundary rider as a man with a defined role in the increasingly complex world of sheep.

Meanwhile, as settlement in the eastern colonies consolidated and extended, so transport facilities improved in the accessible and more developed areas, and penetrated deeper into the hinterland. Wherever men were winning wealth from the land or from the earth, the stagecoach could follow. After the stagecoach might come the railway; meanwhile, the growing fleet of river boats operating along the Murray and its tributaries looked after the transport of wool from a vast inland area. There were more than 100 steamboats (and even more of the attendant barges) operating over a network of waterways totalling some 4000 miles in extent. Providing inexpensive transport, the paddle-wheelers helped carry the wool industry along to greater things while at the same time they opened up a considerable area of the inland to pastoral settlement. All during the 1870s the trade flourished; bigger and more elaborate boats were built, some of them carrying many passengers, and there seemed every prospect that something like the fleet of Mississippi riverboats would be established. Wool from areas far back from the river network was carried in to river loading points by bullock wagon or, in some cases, by camel train. However, the sandbars at the Murray's mouth, which prevented outlet to the sea, and the variability of the river's flow were impediments to the further development of paddle-steamer traffic which, after the extension of the railway to Echuca in 1864, developed largely as a feeder to the rail system of Victoria through the river port of Echuca.

The early railways driven across Victoria had helped rather than hindered the river traffic which served the great wool province across which the Murray tributaries ran. In the deep hinterland, back along the Darling, dependence on riverboats remained and even grew. As time went on, however, the steel bands reaching out from Sydney and Adelaide, as well as new lines leading to Melbourne, were to strangle the river transport which at best remained an uncertain factor because of the drying-up of rivers during droughts. When New South Wales ran a line westward from Wagga Wagga to Narrandera (1881) and on to Hay (1882), the tapping of the Murrumbidgee was a first blow; within a short time the rail links with the Murray River areas (Albury, 1881, Yarrawonga, 1886, and Cobram, 1888) drew off a great deal of the rivermen's freight. The attack on the Darling River trade began in 1885 when the line to Bourke was opened. The doom of the paddle-steamer was sealed, even if the old captains held on doggedly to a dwindling traffic.

As sheep and cattle were spreading, sometimes into areas farther from rivers and sometimes deeper into the inland, the vital requirement was water. Surface supplies were often deficient, but this was soon being overcome by the tapping of underground supplies. Artesian water was first discovered in the north-west of New South Wales in 1878. There was speculation on the extent of the area over which artesian water might be found, and some scientific papers were prepared suggesting that the disappearance of the water flowing from the inner watershed of the eastern highlands of the continent would probably be explained by the existence of vast underground storages. Test holes were sunk, and in 1881 a successful bore was drilled in the Lake Eyre region. In Queensland free-flowing bores were in operation from the early 1880s, while in the dry north-western sector of Victoria supplies were tapped a few years later.

Slowly it was revealed that most of the drier lands of Queensland and New South Wales, and a large area adjoining in South Australia, overlay the Great Artesian Basin and other artesian areas producing mineralized but usable water. Elsewhere, subartesian wells (in which the water comes close to the surface but must be pumped from there) proved successful, and windmills raising water for livestock or for household supplies soon became a feature of the outback landscape.

Underground water made it possible to push the frontier of pastoral occupation deeper into the interior and farther north into the harsh regions. Eventually various artesian basins were found to underlie one-third of the continent's total area, and as these water-bearing regions included large areas possessing inadequate surface supplies, stock-raising could be extended over lands that at first had offered little promise.

By the 1870s life in the colonies was showing a greater sense of order and security than ever before; yet in a sudden reappearance of bushranging one element of violence remained and until it could be removed the confidence of the community was somewhat dimmed.

The banditry practised by ruffians and petty thieves in the 1860s seemed to have been stamped out when most of the notorious robbers were captured and hanged, or were shot in affrays. Bushranging had not been finally suppressed, however. Unresolved tensions between small settlers and wealthy pastoralists kept an air of social discord, and in the still-new, raw, and open land there were many opportunities to commit crimes and evade the law.

Out of these circumstances came the ingredients for a dramatic and violent flare-up in bushranging activity.

The final episode began with the formation in 1878 of the Kelly gang by four young desperadoes. The gang was led by Edward (Ned) Kelly; others were his brother Dan, Steve Hart, and Joe Byrne. Living with their widowed mother on a small property in wild country on the edge of Victoria's north-eastern ranges, the Kellys were the centre of antagonism between settlers and cattlemen. Cattle stealing was rife, and Ned Kelly, who had been in the hands of the police on various charges from the age of fourteen, was suspected. Kelly had been sent to jail for three years in 1871 for receiving a stolen mare; after his release he worked for two years, then in 1876 joined his stepfather in stealing horses. It was in the old pattern of men who stole horses in order that they might have mobility to waylay travellers or raid towns. When a warrant was issued for his arrest, he fled. At this point Dan Kelly (who was sixteen) was sent to jail briefly, and the next year (1878) a warrant was issued for his arrest on a horse-stealing charge. The two brothers set up a hiding place in the ranges; the other two members of the gang joined them there. In October 1878 when a police sergeant and three constables, disguised as miners, went out to arrest the Kellys, who were known to be lurking in the Wombat ranges, three of the policemen were shot dead; the fourth returned to Mansfield with the news of the affray.

Ned Kelly then vanished with his gang. On November 1, amid intense excitement, the Felons Apprehension Act was rushed through the Victorian Parliament. Two weeks later the four members of the gang were proclaimed outlaws, to be taken dead or alive by any citizen. Police were drawn from many stations to strengthen the force scouring the wild and forbidding ranges. While the search went on, the bandits struck back on December 10 in a daring hold-up of a bank at Euroa in which they took £20,000. Banks in Victoria's north-east were placed under the guard of militiamen as fear and excitement rose.

The Kellys, with Joe Byrne and Steve Hart, were already far afield, however. Early in 1879 they chose the little town of Jerilderie, on the southern plains of New South Wales, for their next sortie. Appearing suddenly, they calmly captured the police station and took over the town for two days, robbing the bank of more than £2,000. Melting once again into the obscurity of the broad landscape, the gang later returned to the rugged area where they had many sympathizers among the small settlers from whom they received food.

Months passed, and although nothing was heard of the bandits, the silence did not calm the fears of bankers or citizens. More police were drafted to the search area, but throughout 1879 the outlaws were at large. It was not until June 1880 that the gang was finally trapped in armed battle at the small town of Glenrowan, 40 miles north of Euroa. Here, under siege in the wooden hotel, Ned Kelly, clad in heavy armour, showed a desperate but futile bravery in walking out to meet the police barrage; he fell, shot in the legs. His brother Dan, with Hart, aged twenty, perished in the flames that razed the building; Byrne, aged twenty-three, had already been shot dead.

Ned Kelly alone faced the judge in Melbourne who sentenced him to death in November 1880; the last of the bushrangers was then twenty-five years of age.

With the end of the Kelly gang, order was finally established. The last of the individualists openly standing above the law had gone; the frontier phase, in which such banditry was possible, had closed. However, differences between the big landholders and the less fortunate members of the community had not been resolved.

Part Five

Part
Five

Creating a nation

INNOVATIONS THAT WERE RESHAPING IDEAS and habits in older nations were bringing changes in the lives of people in the new land of Australia, where great distances and the sparsity of population added point to the urge to secure better transport and communications. Rail lines radiating from the main cities, and coach services extending deeper inland, were breaking down the physical isolation that had enshrouded men and women from the time they moved into the hinterland. The advancing steel tracks, and the trains that ran on them, pointed the way for new settlers. The trains not only carried regular mails but by lowering freight costs they opened the prospect of a wider range of rural activities. A plume of locomotive smoke rising above a broad valley or filtering through scattered gum trees was a herald of change for increasing numbers of people in the colonies in the 1880s.

Meanwhile, communications within the colonies, and the news link with the world, had been strengthened, too. Between 1881 and 1891 the number of those engaged in the transport and communication industries more than doubled—it rose from some 41,000 to around 92,000—and in the 1890s another 30,000 people were added. The telegraph now carried messages over an ever-growing network. From the 1860s telegraphic services had brought the eastern colonial capitals into closer touch with each other, and with the completion of the Darwin-Adelaide link in 1872 news of world affairs streamed in; it had an immediacy not previously experienced, and its impact was something quite startling on people previously out of touch with developments in the world at large. By 1877 the telegraph service was extended from Adelaide to Perth, bringing the isolated western capital into the intercolonial network. Henceforth the businessmen of Melbourne or Brisbane or Perth, and the farmers of South Australia or Tasmania, or the sheepmen of New South Wales, could keep more closely in touch with what was happening elsewhere.

As improved transport services brought the people of the inland into closer contact with the cities, newspapers could be delivered more promptly to more people; the men of the inland, the men working on the railroads and in the mines and shearing sheds could learn of the ideas and views held by others in similar circumstances. New publications were soon created to serve the scattered readership of men who revelled in their new-found freedom from isolation.

In the 1870s the Australian colonies had increased railway mileage fourfold; but in 1880 there was still only 4000 miles of track laid, and between them Victoria and New South Wales had much of this. From that point a stronger effort was made to extend the railways by thrusting lines deeper into the land and by forming a closer network to serve the seaports. Soon active railway building programmes were in force; thousands of men were engaged to cut sleepers, cut-and-fill, and lay tracks. Over the 1880s, an average of 50 miles or more of new line was laid each month; the total track mileage for all colonies moved past 10,000 by 1890. Beyond the reach of the railway, coaches or river steamers or lone riders took over to extend the transportation of mail and goods.

Because of the limited population to be served and the low yield of the land, there was little incentive for private companies to undertake railway operations, and so the activity was mainly undertaken by government. Funds for railway construction were raised in Britain, in a development roughly parallel with what was taking place at the same time in Argentina, Canada, the United States, South Africa, and other "new" lands, where money from British and European sources was converting pampas and prairie and veldt from raw land into railway-netted productive tracts; but the private rail developers elsewhere were not duplicated since the colonial governments raised guaranteed loans for public works.

Much remained to be revealed about the exact nature of the continent but there were very few truly "unknown" areas. With Ernest Giles' memorable expedition of 1875–76 in which he had traversed the desert westward of Lake Torrens and reached Perth, then doubled back (somewhat to the north) in a 4000-mile swing that established the hopeless nature of an area long thought to hold some promise, the era of great expeditions and great exploration was at an end. Indomitable explorers had been toiling across the continent's inner regions, but they had discovered almost nothing except a vacant brooding land, largely featureless. They hoped always, decade after decade, for some great central sea or lake, some sweeping Mississippi, some fertile green bowl or towering mountain range; but the whole of the Australian interior, half the continent or more in area, had turned out to be a huge wilderness. It was already clear that an end had come to the prospect of deeper penetration and steady absorption of new tracts for grazing. Except for the most adventurous or the wildly ambitious, the sprawling interior was unattractive and unworkable; it could be left to the Aboriginal tribes who wandered over it. It was only the rim, mainly the fertile crescent of the south-east, that offered hope for consistent development in a strip of fertile land around the western, southern, and eastern shores.

Even as the apparent limits of the pastoral frontier were set, more accessible lands began to take on a new significance. If explorers and graziers in earlier days had been forerunners, now men of practical farming experience were beginning to add a new dimension to knowledge and understanding of the occupied areas. Perhaps it could be more than a continent of grass and scrub. The drive to settle more men on the land, which had inspired land legislation of the 1860s, remained a potent factor. In New South Wales, wheat-growing on the plains and riverine areas now drew in large numbers of would-be independent men. In Victoria and South Australia, governments backed moves to set up organized projects which would establish cultivators on irrigated lands.

In his struggle for land in competition with the grazier, the farmer found his position strengthened when railways crossed the coastal ranges; but his success was dependent upon such immediate matters as improved machinery and a clearer understanding of environmental factors, leading in turn to better farming methods. When the demand for wheat became firm and wool prices declined, crop growers quickly expanded their acreages. Better varieties of grain helped to increase yields, and the farmers now moved in alongside graziers, sometimes taking over some of the sheepmen's lands on a share-farming basis or in other cases spreading into unsought-after areas of scrub land where it was uneconomic to clear the land for grazing. Elsewhere dairy farmers found in heavy-rainfall tracts opportunities to set up dairying operations once the land was cleared and sown with nutritious newly imported fodder grasses. The clearing of such land was a back-breaking task; it might be worthwhile for a man who was prepared to put his own time and effort into it, opening up a small tract piecemeal, spurred on by the thought that he would create something of value for himself and his children out of otherwise worthless land.

Across the land the Australians were the same people, essentially. They were almost exclusively of British descent, and spoke one language. All were bound together by a single loyalty to the Crown and by acceptance of compatible ideas and ideals. Whether native-born or new settler, all were shaped largely by the circumstances of life in actively growing but sparsely settled colonies. As closer contact was established with the world at large and men who were previously isolated were put in touch with events, the individual's horizons expanded and there was a greater sense of immediacy. Great clusterings of population existed in Melbourne and Sydney— and, to a lesser extent, in the other colonial capitals—to serve hinterlands of growing productivity. Cohesive forces were developing to counter the old dispersion produced by remoteness. The individual could feel part of a community; as the links of telegraph and rail grew and the pervading isolation was dispelled, a feeling of "belonging" came to replace the remoteness.

Men were now moving from colony to colony in greater numbers. Commercial ties were knitting the colonies together, and improved transport facilities—particularly the opening of Sydney-Melbourne and Melbourne-Adelaide railway services—were providing new and significant links of a practical nature. Increasingly there was need for uniform legislation on social and industrial questions, and the matter of fiscal union was becoming more pressing.

With their strengthened economies and improved communications, the colonies were growing up; now they were more prepared to grow together. A generation had passed since Victoria and Queensland had separated from New South Wales and set up their own administrations; now there were reasons to reverse the fragmentation and draw all the colonies closer.

From the 1840s there had been occasional vague talk about the benefits of some form of federation, but it was no more than talk. Even after the attainment of self-government the colonial capitals had remained in closer contact with London than with each other. The protecting shield of Britain's sea supremacy remained, and there had been no need to develop a sense of national unity on the basis of security. There were many barriers, real or imagined, to any form of political union. Local jealousies and pretensions divided the colonies, and these were sometimes magnified by strong-willed politicians. Against these divisive forces stood the common ancestry, common language and traditions, and the unifying influence of British law.

Basic to the growing national consciousness was a deepening sense of attachment to Australia. There were now many who could claim to be second or third generation Australians, proud of their pioneer forebears. These people were seeing the land with different eyes from those of the newcomer. It was not an alien land to which sharp adjustment had to be made: instead it was a familiar setting that had positive qualities to be treated with understanding. The harsh realities of the new land had tempered both the idealism and the radical outlook of many who had come hoping to witness the creation of a new Utopia; now these factors were merging into a new sentiment as the Australian-born came to grips with their environment.

There were nearly 3,000,000 people in Australia by the late 1880s, and two out of every three were Australian-born. They were coming to realize that they were creating a civilization rather different from that of their forebears. The idea of being a separate country, of having a separate existence and an image different from "home," had begun to emerge.

One element in this increased awareness was the fact that education was being extended to greater numbers. The Victorian Education Act of 1872 had ushered in the era of state-run schools under the system of free, compulsory, and secular education which extended to all colonies in the 1870s. Increasingly the Australian-born were able to secure the education needed to fit them for a constructive role in affairs—a development that had been urged by William Charles Wentworth, one of the founders of Australia's first University, as essential if self-government were not to be "a useless boon." More and more Australian-born were occupying the higher ranks in all sorts of activities. Local institutions of higher education—the universities of Sydney and Melbourne, the various technical and teachers' training colleges and the church-run private secondary schools in the various colonies—were turning out increasing numbers of doctors, lawyers, engineers, teachers, administrators, journalists, and men qualified by education and training to be community leaders. All over the country, Australian born and Australian-trained men were moving into positions of influence in affairs.

Meanwhile, the settlement of growing numbers of people in areas away from the coast had contributed not only to a closer understanding of the nature of the country but also to a growing sense of unity. Basically the occupied land was much the same everywhere, and men did the same jobs, going from New South Wales to Queensland or Victoria, or to South Australia, and back again, as work was available, without worrying about colonial borders. Railways were moving out from the cities, but even without them the station owners and their families travelled over the land in their buggies, and so did men on horseback or on foot who helped take care of the rapidly expanding flocks or sought a job at one of the great stations on broad pasture lands that stretched back from streams of the great Murray-Darling river system. In all the land there were no great natural barriers; a man could, if need be, cross the region on foot, just as livestock did when they were sold or were on their way to market. In good seasons the land was generally bountiful and serene; and although during droughts, or when fire raced across the plains, or river waters rose suddenly and spread themselves far and wide, it was a cruel land, there was a sense of spaciousness and quietude in which a man born in this environment could feel strong and unfettered.

The men who lived in the sheep lands were inclined to think of the continent as a whole rather than in terms of the colony in which they happened to be. Station owners sold sheep to fellow pastoralists up and down the country; and in their struggles against governments that seemed unsympathetic and increasingly intrusive, they naturally felt that their associates in other colonies were much closer to them in sentiment than were the bulk of city-dwellers of their own colony, who seemed to espouse radical causes. At the same time, since the most important product the pastoralists had to sell—wool—kept them in touch with a market far from Australia's shores, their eyes were on London, and they thought of the seaport through which their wool was exported as little more than a handling point or way station. City dwellers, with less cause to see things against a background of the land as a whole, were more inclined to think in terms of their immediate surroundings and so to concentrate on their own colony.

It took time—and it needed leadership and understanding—for the concept of nationhood to develop, and for that concept to be given political expression; only when successive episodes related to the encroachment of European powers into the south Pacific showed that a national approach was needed to cope with the situation was any concerted move made. The groundwork had been laid by an awareness of Australian unity at the community rather than the administrative level. An atmosphere had been created from public discussion and contact among men of like mind which brought the issue of nationhood to the forefront of political thought. In calling intercolonial conferences from the late 1870s. the trade union movement showed the growing affinity between the colonies that arose naturally as communications improved, and in the same way employers combating the unions' demands planned action on a basis that transcended the boundaries of any colony. Political leaders in the colonial capitals still tended to address themselves to London on matters going beyond their colonial borders; but for many years there had been men anxious to see some sort of federation and as community support for such a move grew, the politicians showed more interest in working towards it.

Political action was difficult, nevertheless. There were many barriers, real or imagined, to any form of federal union. The governments of the separate colonies had each accepted considerable responsibilities, and the political leaders were not likely to surrender power without compelling reason. The long absence of any strong external pressures had slowed up the process of working towards national unity, while the fact that there was no serious internal discord meant that any moves towards nationhood would be slow and carefully planned. The colonies had been free to work out their own political destinies; they had been able to develop their resources and shape their institutions without ever having any serious anxiety about their safety.

That happy situation could not last for ever, and as France and then Germany began to take over island territories in the south Pacific, the nakedness of Australia from a defence standpoint first caused concern and then fear. When it became evident that such annexations could not be prevented through pressure on London, the drive towards national unity accelerated. The British government's willingness to accept German assurances in spite of the evidence of German expansion caused consternation among the colonists in the 1880s. Soon there was a growing sense of alarm; it arose largely from the rising tide of anti-British sentiment within Germany, where the writings of historian Heinrich von Trietschke were inspiring mass adulation of all things German and a hatred of Britain as a barrier to pan-Germanism. Australians shared Britain's sense of danger in the growing militarism within Germany, and soon expansion of German trade and German territorial encroachment in the south Pacific came to be viewed with the greatest suspicion and apprehension.

Another compelling force to unity was the strong sentiment for the exclusion of Asian labourers and a revulsion against the importation of "kanaka" or South Sea island labour. Fear that Australian living standards would be jeopardized by low-wage labour lay behind these feelings, but backing up the exclusion sentiment was a determination to maintain the essential unity of the Australian race. As Alfred Deakin, one of the leaders of the federalist movement, noted, no other aspiration or interest so wrought for federation as "the desire that we should be one people, and remain one people, without the admixture of other races." On this issue an increasing number of middle-class voters held the same view as the growing Labour movement.

Meanwhile, in their struggle for better conditions and higher wages, working men were influenced by ideas of social change introduced from abroad. In English-speaking countries generally, socialist ideas were acquiring a strengthened following as Karl Marx's *Das Kapital* and Henry George's *Progress and Poverty* attracted wider attention. In Britain, numbers of middle-class intellectuals supported groups dedicated to the building of a new society in which the working man would have a better deal. Although the underdog in a new land was inclined to put his own interpretation on programmes for slow and evolutionary betterment such as put forward by the academic Fabian group in London, and although his attitudes were mainly shaped by his own experience and the conditions of life in a rapidly expanding new land, streams of thought from the great social reformers were being blended into his search for Utopia.

It was a time when individual freedom was acquiring new meaning. Old restraints had been under attack from many quarters. In political discussions, thought had been given to the view of John Stuart Mill, expressed in his essay *On Liberty* in 1859, that "the only purpose for which power can be rightfully exercised over any member of a civilized community, against his will, is to prevent harm to others." This concept had influenced attitudes in English-speaking lands, opening the way for new interpretations of individual freedom, and even though Mill himself acknowledged the need for refinement of his views and found many permissible exceptions to the "non-interference principle," the ordinary man was hard to shake from his new-found belief in the form of liberalism which cut to a minimum the checks on the individual's freedom. Over the same period, in the United States the writings of the "herald of profound discount," Ralph Waldo Emerson, and of Henry David Thoreau, who added pungent philosophic overtones to his rustic writings about nature, had drawn together a coterie seeking an economy which would not hinder the highest spiritual development of the individual.

In older countries, questions related to defining the individual's rights and balancing individual freedom against individual responsibility might be resolved slowly; but in the hinterland of Australia, where the emptiness of the land seemed to create its own licence, the issue was developing special urgency. In a society that was growing and changing quite rapidly, it was natural that each man, whether employer or worker, would give himself all the leeway possible in interpreting ideas about the freedom and rights of the individual, and in applying these in his daily life. The working man was bent upon emphasizing his rights as he saw them; the employer was holding to the established rights of property as well as his own individual freedom. Similar active conflicts of interest had been coming to a head in the United States, and just as in the United States, many of the most active social reformers in the Australian scene were to be found among the journalists. When improved transport facilities made it possible for newspapers to reach the scattered back-country readership these campaigners had a wider audience among men who filled in lonely hours in reading or in discussion with their mates. The editors who carried a new gospel to men living isolated lives did not think of themselves as social reformers, but they filled this role in a country going through a period of change and adjustment.

As the country's frontier phase ended, the working man's drive for better wages and conditions was fired by a lingering discontent springing from a feeling among the have-nots that a comparatively few fortunate but greedy men had grabbed all the land. Men trudging along hot and dusty tracks in their search for work naturally challenged in their minds the right of others to the possession of vast acreages. They saw no future for themselves, or for others like them. To some, a new social order seemed the only solution; to others, the answer lay in fighting for higher wages and better working conditions through concerted action. The fierce independence of the self-sufficient outdoorsman ran counter to the obvious need for solidarity if any objective were to be achieved; and only in the old concept of mateship was it possible for such men to find the bridge that would carry them to unionism.

The chief guide to the promised land was William Guthrie Spence, a dedicated unionist who had organized his first trade union among miners on the Victorian goldfields area in 1878. Spence showed a missionary zeal as he led the crusade among miners and shearers, and other rural workers, through which he was largely instrumental in developing a type of unionism indigenous to Australia. The old Chartist spirit of reform was now joined by new streams of thought appropriate to the underdog in a "new" land passing from its frontier phase. The new prophets included a succession of American writers evangelizing for a better world.

To stir the minds of the sincere and often introspective men came the challenging theorizing of Henry George, a newspaperman and self-taught social philosopher of San Francisco who had visited Australia as a boy. Almost simultaneously with its publication in New York, George's *Progress and Poverty* was published as a serial in Sydney, and very soon copies of the hardbound book were being carried by Spence's followers and by union organizers as they visited remote shearing camps along the Darling and the Lachlan. Just as George's interpretation of the contemporary social and economic scene was attracting a following among working men in the United States and in England, his ideas, expressed in eloquent prose, began to cast a spell over the simple, earnest men of the bushland. George's disgust at the callousness he had found among the wealthy people in New York, and his attacks on the viciousness of all great cities, found an echo in the hearts of countrymen. Here was a man who had suffered as they—and now offered a solution.

George based his conclusions on an engagingly simple presentation of what he called "facts of common observation and common knowledge, which every reader can verify for himself, just as he can decide whether the reasoning for them is or is not valid." His dedicated but deludingly plausible approach to matters concerning the corruption to be found in great cities, and the need for social adjustment and a better deal for the underdog, could not fail to make a deep impression on the simple men of little education who had shown no interest in (and had no access to) more learned and difficult books on economics and sociology. Such men had every confidence in George's belief that he had found a way to overcome the evils and problems of a materialist society; but his broad general principles were more significant and understandable to the men than his panacea of a single tax on land. *Progress and Poverty* quickly came to be accepted as an authoritative peg on which to hang discussions in the shearers' hut or around the camp fire; and although George's central theme was the urgent need for tax reform, those who read the book were more inclined to see a more realistic solution in the realization of what George called "the noble dreams of socialism."

The spread of unionism and a widening readership of *Progress and Poverty* advanced together. The new unionists in the Australian bushland were largely miners or shearers or rural workers. Whether migratory workers (in rural activities) or as company employees (in the mines) such men felt no strong attachment to their boss; theirs was a job, and nothing more. Trade unions based on antecedents in urban England might attract a membership of craftsmen or tradesmen in the cities or larger towns; but the more traditional aspects of unionism had little application in the Australian pastoral lands, where the workers were unskilled or, at best, semi-skilled. Here, as in New Zealand, the example of a new form of unionism that had gained a following among miscellaneous unskilled or semi-skilled workers in the United States was a more apposite model; and it was the American example of the Knights of Labor (with whose organizers New Zealand and Australian labour groups developed contact) that came to be followed by the rural workers.

As their grievances grew more pressing, such men, used to the rough and ready ways of the camp or shearing shed, were not prepared to compromise on issues that were important to them. A head-on collision was inevitable once the sheepmen decided to reverse the upward trend in shearers' pay. Other employers followed the same unyielding line. In the pastoral industry the situation had been aggravated because some employers had shown an almost callous disregard for the men's welfare and others had been unprepared to do anything to alleviate poor conditions. In many cases part of the cause for the men's discontent lay in general conditions; since any sizable outlay for accommodation which would be used only three or four weeks a year seemed quite unthinkable, station owners usually provided shearers with little more than a roof to shelter them, and in their combined eating and sleeping quarters they had to sleep on boards.

Unions became openly militant, partly because of the character of the men involved in them and partly because of the uncompromising attitude of employers. The result was a situation in which the men were adamant in their demand for strike action; they showed blind faith in the ultimate success of their cause, and they stood together accordingly. For their part, the employers had, in non-union labour and the lock-out, an answer to the men's solidarity, and they decided to organize themselves into a federation, which gave them the strength to oppose the men's demands.

The spread of unionism among miscellaneous workers and the methods adopted by the new unionists were following patterns that had emerged in the United States a decade or so earlier with the formation and growth of the Knights of Labor. This organization, founded in 1869, had as its immediate goal "organized effort and cooperation" to obtain and retain both employment and just remuneration for its members, who included the unskilled and semi-skilled. Although opposed initially to the calling of strikes, the Knights had soon created a strike fund and the pressure from members had forced strike action; membership grew rapidly after successful strikes against leading railroads, and in the early 1880s the Knights were dominant in the American labour scene. As the years passed, strike failures were to bring a decline in membership in the American organization, while the increased vigour of the employers' attacks finally destroyed the effectiveness of America's first militant trade union by the late 1880s. Meanwhile, an offshoot of the Knights had been established in New Zealand, while in Australia, trade unions that followed the Knights' general principle of admitting a wide membership of unskilled workers were moving to a position of strength and influence.

"Unionism came to the Australian bushman as a religion," Spence recalled later. "It came bringing salvation from years of tyranny. It had in it that feeling of mateship that he understood already which always characterized the action of one white man to another. Unionism extended the idea, so a man's character was gauged by whether he stood true to union rules."

Strikes had taken hold and employer-worker relationships were already inflamed when another forceful book by an American social reformer came into the purview of the Australian working man. In *Looking Backward, 2000–1887* (published in the United States in 1888 and serialized in the *Worker*, Brisbane, in 1890), Boston-born journalist Edward Bellamy launched a blistering attack on contemporary capitalism. He claimed that under this system the masses of humanity were chained to a great coach along a very hilly and sandy road under an unrelenting driver, hunger, while a few privileged passengers on top of the coach never got down. By contrast he painted the picture of an ideal society which he set in the year 2000; looking backwards to the 1880s he showed how the evils of the plutocratic society of the day might be overcome. Bellamy the Prophet set out also to create the ideal society, and chose for it a system which he called "Nationalism." This industrial democracy was in essence a form of socialism, but Bellamy rejected all ideas of class conflict; and whereas other socialist writers had advocated collective ownership of the means of production, he found a solution in government ownership and control. Bellamy took issue with the Marxists because of their advocacy of class warfare, and because of their ill-defined objectives, indicated that a selfish group would still retain power over others, a state of affairs he deplored; but to impatient and unhappy men in the bush reading his book, the short cut to his Utopian world still seemed to lie through strike action. There were still only a handful of wage-earners in Australia who were members of trade unions; they numbered less than 50,000 in 1890 and they were spread through 174 different unions—but they were earnest and dedicated, and their numbers were to grow steadily.

Meanwhile the great Bellamy debate in England and the United States and elsewhere was running its course, bringing in fervent adherents and at the same time creating a strong opposition among those who for one reason or another were against the idea of a centralized, all-powerful government to watch over and guide the destinies of individuals. Numberless articles and books appeared in support of Bellamy's concept, while in many lands critics were equally vocal (as, indeed, they were in Australia and New Zealand). Catholic commentators were among those who attacked *Looking Backward*; they generally labelled Bellamy's ideas impracticably useless, and politically and philosophically unsound. Poverty might be alleviated but it could never be abolished, they maintained; the poor would be always with us.

In the world at large, many significant voices were now being heard on social questions, and many differing proposals for dealing with the pressing social problems of the day were forthcoming. Of special importance was Pope Leo XIII's most celebrated encyclical, *Rerum novarum* (1891), dealing with the relations of capital and labour as essentially a moral question and calling for justice animated by charity as the basis for social relations.

Some exhortations that had special significance to wider audiences in countries abroad appealed to many city workers and city dwellers generally in Australia; but among outdoorsmen—the shearers and the boundary riders, the teamsters and the timber-getters—and the miners, Bellamy's ideas were more acceptable, and his vision had gained a special lustre. Even Henry George, visiting Australia with his Sydney-born wife in 1890, failed to discredit *Looking Backward*, though he tried hard to do so. By camp fire or under the stars, men took sides for Bellamy or George in arguments that went on far into the night. Bellamy's message—that of building a better world through government intervention—would not be quickly forgotten; it gave direction to the unionists' ideas, providing justification for immediate goals and long-range aspirations, and it became an important feature of a montage of ideas built up with elements from *Progress and Poverty* and Laurence Gronlund's verbose *Co-operative Commonwealth* (which presented an American case for socialism in the Fabian idiom). As these and other books were bought by unionists and carried by union organizers into the back country, access to them was credited with improving "the character of discussion" among shearers and rural workers. A home-grown, Australian version of socialism was emerging, drawing strength from the conviction that everyone should have a fair share and that no man should be denied the right or means to live. Mateship was taking on a new meaning.

Meanwhile, as Spence gained new converts for trade unionism he was assiduously linking the rural unions into an amalgamated body under his presidency.

The various theories on social change were part of the background against which increasingly violent action was taken by the trade unionists in support of their cause. What had begun in 1886 as an effort to hold shearers' wage levels had developed by the early 1890s into a major struggle in which the unionists were defending their right to work. The great strikes precipitated by the sheepmen's determination to insist on their right to employ non-union labour if they so determined, dragged on through a succession of employers' lock-outs and sympathy strikes until, piecemeal, the unionists were defeated. Social tension was increased when financial panic swept Melbourne and a great depression set in which soon afflicted other cities and, in fact, the whole land. As businesses closed and investment fell away, jobs could no longer be found in the cities; men walked the streets at first, then sought work—any work—in the country, thus intensifying rural unionists' problems. In the drawn-out struggle, individuals increasingly came to feel that they were in direct conflict with the pastoralists and company owners in possession of land and resources which well might have been the birthright of all. Sometimes unionists were fleetingly sustained by a wild hope or a vague belief that somehow through their stand they might turn Australia into a classless Utopia, free from the pressures of competition and operating on an idealistic formula. Union leaders, who were closer to the real issues, were generally less inclined to be carried away by such ideas than were the idealists in the union membership or the writers who blossomed in the trade union newspapers.

Slowly it became evident that things were not to be changed overnight. Men who had been striving blindly for a better world and believed they could reach it through strikes, now began to see that strike action was not a solution. When the strikes failed they were ready to turn to political means, and their objective was now clearer: they wanted to do away with the evils of a materialist society, as George had described them, and create a world closer to the ideals of Bellamy and Gronlund.

Although the strikes ended in failure for the unionists, the unity gained in the struggle made possible the next phase: political labour. The solidarity achieved in support of trade union activities could be made effective in parliamentary elections once workmen as a class began to realize their power at the ballot box. The outdoorsman, no longer fired with an evangelist's zeal for trade unionism, turned to the new form of political action; and although as migratory workers, shearers, and other rural workers were still without a vote in some cases, the basis for a political party to represent wage-earners existed. In the cities and towns, unionists might also be enlisted to the labour cause. In Queensland, the Australian Labor Federation was formed in 1889; two years later the Sydney Trades and Labor Council promoted an electoral league which drew up a platform and selected parliamentary candidates. Similar action was taken in other colonies. The separate Labor leagues thus formed kept closely in touch through inter-colonial conferences.

The pattern of rural development was characterized by the employment of increasing numbers of men by big landholders (and by mining companies). At the same time there was a noticeably high degree of urban development based on new activities in the main cities. In each colony, administrative activities had remained concentrated in the original coastal settlement; and by now some of the colonial capitals had outgrown their trade and transportation role to become significant centres for processing and manu-facturing activities. The proportion of urban dwellers already surpassed anything to be found in Europe or the United States. Melbourne had led this trend; from one in four of Victoria's population in 1861, Melbourne increased its share to over 40 per cent in the mid-1880s. Adelaide's pro-portionate rate of growth almost kept pace with Melbourne's. Sydney had about one in four of the New South Wales population in 1861 and reached one in three in 1891; Brisbane moved from one in eight in 1871 to about one in four of Queensland's population in the 1890s; only Tasmania and Western Australia kept their ratios at about one urban dweller in five. As suburban transport facilities improved, the old city boundaries had been breached; now a rash of red-brick and red-tile villas was beginning to spread across suburban hills in the larger capitals. The number of wage-earners was moving up steadily, and so was trade union membership.

One of the compelling reasons for the emergence of labour as a political force was the widely held belief that in the great struggle between capital and labour the colonial governments had thrown their weight to the em-ployers, and that this had been a decisive factor affecting the outcome. Aggrieved by a seeming injustice, and aware that labour could never hope to win out against the combined power of the employers and the govern-ment, unionists came to the conclusion that the situation could be corrected only if political action backed up their industrial action. A party made up of trusted labour men, individually endorsed by the movement as the most dedicated and worthy men among those offering, alone could achieve the result.

The course of events following the strikes was in marked contrast to what was happening over much the same period in the United States, where convulsive strikes embroiling the Knights of Labor and other union groups resulted in the virtual smashing of the union organization. Striking American unionists consistently found themselves in open conflict with sheriffs and marshals who aided in the employers' strike-breaking tactics, and after a series of confrontations ended in defeat, union membership fell precipi-tously. The isolation of the unionist was not nearly so pronounced in Aus-tralia, where there was far wider sympathy with egalitarian objectives. Thus the determination, unity, and burning zeal of Australian unionists, combined with the community's greater willingness to tolerate active union-ism, opened the way for the emergence of the Labor party as a political force.

The first trade unionists had been elected (as individuals, not party men) to colonial parliaments as far back as 1859 in Victoria, 1874 in New South Wales, and 1884 in South Australia. In the 1890s, after the Labor leagues had been created, more and more of the members of parliament arriving in Sydney or Brisbane to attend parliamentary sessions were men who had *Looking Backward* or *Progress and Poverty* packed away in their grips. At first the dabor group worked in parliament on the basis of pressure politics, assisting any political group that would serve the movement's interests, but by 1899 a Labor Ministry—the first ever commissioned anywhere—held office in Queensland for a short time.

Labor by now had become dedicated to the proposition that officially sponsored arbitration and conciliation boards or courts should regulate wages and general conditions of employment. Such bodies had been set up in New South Wales in 1892 and Victoria in 1896; subsequently they were created in South Australia and Western Australia (1900), Queensland (1907) and Tasmania (1910). In supporting officially regulated arbitration of employment matters, the Labor leaders earnestly believed that in any argument the weight of government would no longer be thrown against labour but (because of the justice of the cause) would come down on the working man's side. In their zeal, trade unionists failed to realize that there were obligations to the community at large to be taken into account, and law and order to uphold, and that in considering the two sides of any case official courts would give full weight to these wider obligations, which would not always coincide with labour's demands.

Concerned with more immediate issues, the Labor party did not actively campaign for federation, and even had some reservations on the issue. However, there were other groups (as well as influential individuals and newspapers) to carry forward the idea. Various influences contributed to the momentum now gained. The radical nationalism of the violently partisan *Bulletin* helped to further the objective, as much through the reaction of those determined to counteract the "republican" concepts tinging *Bulletin* proposals with a thoroughly British federation as those who saw merit in federation as a part of the building of a new social order.

Impetus gained from public discussion led by non-party federation leagues and other organizations dedicated to the cause of federal union soon forced the issue at a political level. After a series of formal convntions attended by the colonial parliamentary leaders, and many informal discussions, a constitution was written and submitted to the colonial parliaments and then to the electorate; after its approval by the voters, the Parliament at Westminster passed the necessary legislation to create the Commonwealth of Australia, which came into being on January 1, 1901.

The new parliament was divided more or less on the lines of free-traders and those who supported protection, with the Labor party a third force. As time went on, the constant pressure on the Liberals exercised by the tightly disciplined Labor party succeeded in securing the passage of legislation in line with various objectives of Labor. Measures were approved for setting up a federal Arbitration Court and for the exclusion of Asian and kanaka labour (on which the party had become vociferous). Support for a soundly protective tariff came after Labor party men accepted the concept that since wage levels were essentially linked with industry's ability to pay, wages would be in jeopardy without adequate protection against the competition of lower-priced goods from abroad. The Immigration Act protected the working man against cheap labour; this not only removed the danger of a two-wage system but also guaranteed a homogeneous population. When industry had tariff protection so that manufacturing survived against competition from low-wage countries, it was possible to move on and put into force the concept of a minimum living wage for all workmen. The Arbitration Court's basic wage determination of 1908 was a landmark. Thus, although in the early years of federation there seemed to be little change in everyday affairs as a result of the setting-up of a national parliament and a federal administration, the structure to support an Australian way of life was being erected piece by piece.

Innovations more startling than any yet seen were being introduced. From the rare examples of imported horseless carriages that had appeared on city streets from 1896, self-propelled vehicles were growing in number and were gaining in scope of operation; in 1900 the first overland journey, nearly 500 miles from Bathurst to Melbourne, was made by Herbert Thomson in a steam-driven vehicle made in Thomson's Melbourne workshops and exhibited before enthusiastic crowds in Sydney. At the same time Harley Tarrant, teamed with a bicycle manufacturer, was working to complete the first Australian petrol-driven car; powered by an imported motor, it was spluttering its way around Melbourne streets in 1901, and four years later and again in 1906 a Tarrant car won success in long cross-country trials for motor vehicles. By 1908 a transcontinental run (from Adelaide to Darwin) had put the seal of success on motor transport under Australian conditions.

Meanwhile, electricity was being used to light city streets and suburban homes, and telephones were coming into more widespread use. By 1909 a new wonder was in evidence: the aeroplane. The first public exhibition of flying took place at Narrabean Beach, near Sydney, when George Augustine Taylor piloted a biplane glider of his own design in a series of flights. In July 1910 John Duigan flew a powered machine, which he had built on his property, at Mia Mia, Victoria. In 1911 the first public flights were made with Voisin and Bristol planes. Soon a Sydney dentist, William Ewart Hart, holder of the first pilot licence issued by the Aerial League of Australia, was sporting his Bristol in flights in the Sydney area, and in 1912 he tested his flying skill against that of visiting American stuntman Eugene (Wizard) Stone in an air race from Surrey Park to Parramatta, which Hart won with a 23 minutes' flight. As one newspaper commented discerningly, "Mr Hart's amazing high speed flight from Sydney to Parramatta brings closer the day when the horse and buggy will completely disappear as a means of travelling to and from Sydney."

Pacing an expansion of rural industries and the growth of manufacturing was trade unionism. The number of trade unionists was rising rapidly—total membership moved up from 97,000 (6 per cent of all employees) in 1901 to 364,000 (almost 28 per cent) in 1911—and in the political sphere Labor was moving towards an ascendancy. The Australian Labor Party was determined to impose its own discipline over its chosen and elected representatives (as it saw Labor members), and moves towards stronger party discipline were favoured as Labor developed an effective political machine in the federal sphere. At first the other political groups lacked Labor's unity of purpose and Labor's zeal, and they were without political organizations; but the challenge presented by a rising Labor party, with a new sense of destiny and strengthened discipline, caused a shift in alignments within the federal parliament in 1910 (and later within the state parliaments as Labor gained strength in each of them in turn). By now reformers were pinning their hopes on Labor's ability to reshape affairs through federal action, and they avidly supported proposals for constitutional amendments which the Labor party brought forward to confer upon the Federal Parliament quite sweeping powers over economic affairs. The rejection of these proposals by the voters in 1911 and again when they were re-submitted in 1913, stemmed at least in part from lack of unity on the issue within the various facets of the Labour movement.

With a federal election in the offing, politics occupied much of the stage for Australians in mid-1914, and little heed was given at first to news of the assassination of the heir apparent to the Austro-Hungarian throne on the summer morning of June 28. As the days quietly passed and Europe blundered towards war, there was little to indicate that Europe was on the edge of the greatest conflagration the world had ever seen. The weeks passed. An election campaign went on across Australia; politicians pledged support for England in the event of war, but people were not convinced of the danger and there was time to give attention to other events. Audiences in the King's Theatre, Melbourne, were listening to Harry Lauder's broguish songs, and in Sydney, crowds were attending a series of wrestling and boxing tournaments held to raise funds to send a team to the 1916 Berlin Olympic Games. The return after two years abroad of Nellie Melba evoked great enthusiasm in Melbourne, and in reporting what seemed like the triumphal procession of a conqueror, the *Argus* noted with nostalgia that as the great soprano drove through her home town of Lilydale, "the golden wattle filled the air with its perfume, and down the hills crept the scent of Australian wood fires—a scent that no one ever smells save in Australia."

By the beginning of August, war fears were beginning to blot out all other thoughts. The tone of newspapers had changed; all forts and military outposts were manned, and on August 3 special prayers for peace were said in churches throughout Australia. Two days later the evening newspapers carried the stark headlines, ENGLAND DECLARES WAR ON GERMANY.

Six weeks after the Archduke's assassination, full-scale war had begun. Growing behind a wall of steel, Germany's increasing nationalism, now personified by the temperamental Kaiser Wilhelm, had been a cause of concern in many countries; but it had seemed improbable that Britain would be in open conflict with the land ruled by one of Queen Victoria's grandsons, and none could possibly foresee that the conflict would turn into a holocaust which would claim close to 38,000,000 casualties over more than four years of fighting on land and sea and in the air.

Even though it was fought so far away, the war that came unexpectedly to Australians was to bring profound changes in their lives and reshape national affairs. At first, a wild, untried patriotism and the confident belief that the war would be over by Christmas, carried everyone along. When the great expeditionary force, the Australian Imperial Force, was efficiently mustered and rapidly prepared, it seemed as though a great adventure, a fine crusade, had been launched. The Anzacs' Gallipoli landing of April 15, 1915, with its unmatched valour and heroism, vindicated a new nation's willingness to help preserve the old values of a world which (though few could realize it) was already crumbling.

As the blood of Australians began to spill in the cause of nation and Empire, there was a sense of awe; the *Sydney Morning Herald* spoke of the landing as "a searching test of character," and preachers and politicians saw in it proof that the nation had come of age. The real shock of war came with the publication of the growing casualty lists and the return of wounded men. The fine adventure of the Dardanelles campaign ended in withdrawal as, in the words of John Masefield, "in the haze of the full moon [the last of the] men filed off from the trenches down to the beaches and passed away from Gallipoli." Deeper involvement came as Australian troops moved into the morass of European battlefields, where terrible losses had been suffered by the Allies. What had begun as an old-fashioned campaign had taken on a nightmarish quality; it was total war, and it was more demanding, more terrible, more futile than anyone could have imagined. Furthermore, it seemed interminable.

Increasingly, Australians at home began to wonder about it all; those opposed on specific grounds were joined by many who questioned Australia's ability to sustain losses of men on the scale involved in war in Europe. Meanwhile the government, now under the forceful Labor leader William Morris Hughes, pushed for a more intensive war effort and greater commitment. The issue finally resolved itself around Hughes' proposal to introduce conscription of men for service overseas. That proposal split the Labor Party; Hughes and a group left the party and gained other support; but on the conscription proposal not only Labor but the whole community was sharply divided—even different members of a family would take opposing sides and friends began to question each other's loyalty—and the majority opposed the idea. There was considerable concern at the fast and extensive spread of federal powers already evident, and resistance to further encroachment was strong among individuals who felt sure that, whatever the merits of the conscription issue, there would be danger in granting the government any additional control over the lives of citizens. Even among volunteers serving abroad there was no overwhelming support for conscription. The total vote each time the issue was put to a nationwide referendum (as it was on two occasions) came out against conscription. The inference was that people felt that what a man did about military service was his own business, war or no war.

The bitterly contested conscription campaigns revealed the depth of feeling that existed in the community, and in his efforts to take the electorate with him on an issue which he felt touched upon his and his country's honour, Hughes opened cracks that could not easily be resealed. Nonetheless, the electorate recognized Hughes' individual worth as a wartime leader, and by keeping him in power it demonstrated its conviction that he should go ahead and do the best he could with what he had, without asking for more power.

Hughes' vigour and single purposeness impressed men in London and New York and Washington, and he emerged as the first Australian leader ever to have a voice in his own right in world councils. Within Australia he showed by his forthright and strongly national call for a greater war effort that in spite of his divisive capability he was a leader of outstanding character. He was ahead of others in foreseeing the need for Australia to be in a position to put forward and press separate and perhaps distinctive policies in international affairs when the war ended; the first step towards such freedom of action, he felt, was to maximize Australia's role during the war. Australia's record in terms of war casualties helped achieve the result Hughes saw as crucial to the national future. Sacrifices had not been in vain; by their valour Australians had won a special place among fighting men, and Australia's contribution to victory was acknowledged among world leaders.

A great change had come over Australia. As Charles Bean, official war historian, noted, when the A.I.F. sailed it left a nation "which did not yet know itself"; but through the valour of these fighting men in war, Australians were able to watch the name of their country "rise high in the esteem of the world's oldest and greatest nations."

By war's end the Commonwealth so proudly proclaimed in 1901 had in fact become a nation—and a nation still firmly within the British Empire.

Economic growth 14

The man with the plough was coming into his own by the 1880s. Wool was being garnered and shipped in greater quantities than ever, and as a single commodity it was still dominant; but other products of the land were beginning to assume importance as increasing attention was given to new types of production. From the gold-rush days, when some shrewd miners (and most of the Chinese who found themselves thwarted in their hopes for gold) first turned their attention to growing vegetables and other small-scale crops, more men had been battling with the problems of agriculture; but generally farming had not been sufficiently profitable for them to be able to wrest land from the sheepmen. Now, with the expansion of railways, and with new arrivals and investment funds pouring in from Britain, the situation was changing; henceforth the balance in the old farmer-pastoralist struggle was somewhat less heavily weighted against the cultivator of the land.

By 1877 the population in the six colonies had passed 2,000,000, with about 55 per cent of the entire population living in cities or towns of more than 500 people. The seaport capitals, drawing upon the overflow of England's industrial cities, were growing rapidly. The demand for food-stuffs had increased, and farmers could get funds more readily to set themselves up as producers. As sheepmen and cattlemen filtered deeper into the hinterland, farmers found ways to open up lands to agriculture in areas closer to the rail lines radiating from the main cities and in districts accessible to Gulf ports in South Australia.

Many difficulties, however, remained to dog the farmer. Droughts, crop diseases, unsuitable wheat strains, and inadequate preparation of the land all placed severe limitations upon his efforts. The pioneers who cleared the land had little knowledge of their new farming environment; such knowledge could be built up only by patient investigation, experiment, and research. Even the hardest working and most conscientious farmers ran into pitfalls. Very few yet realized it, but better farming methods, based on scientific principles, would have to be developed. Meanwhile, an air of expansion and the achievement of limited success were enough to spur men on; it took some time for them to appreciate that serious problems remained unsolved. For the pioneer the bringing of virgin land into production was a heavy task, and he could give little thought to anything but cropping the land constantly. Tradition and prejudice tended to concentrate the effort on wheat in many cases. Without proper crop rotation or a system of fallow, exhaustion of the soil was inevitable—yet ceaseless cropping was often the individual's only means of survival.

It was in South Australia that the farmer had his initial success—and waged his greatest battle. The colony had really been the farming frontier from the 1850s, and farmers in South Australia were well qualified to take advantage of the greater demand for grain. In their quest for new horizons, however, the South Australians had to face a mixture of failure and success.

In 1874, wheat men broke through the so-called Goyder "line" (the 10-inch isohyet) to take up land to the north, and some high yields were recorded in the new districts in the next few years. By 1880 Port Augusta had its own flour mill and was shipping wheat as grain. Good seasons favoured the expansion, and yields as high as 15 bushels an acre and more convinced some enthusiastic land-hungry men that even saltbush country could be turned to wheat. Land was ploughed and sown, and crops were harvested, where the average rainfall was only 8 inches or so a year. Confidence ran high; newspaper editorials hailed the extension of the farming frontier, one writer finding in the breakthrough into the dry north "additional proof that South Australia is destined to become one of the finest agricultural colonies in the world." Many pooh-poohed Goyder's restrictive "line" as a ridiculous concept; it was held that there had been a change of seasons. However, it did not take long for the situation to revert to normal; the exceptional run of good seasons—for such it was—soon ended. The harsher conditions which came to the newly opened wheat lands in 1881 and 1882 were enough to break the hearts and destroy the solvency of those who had a minimum of capital and limited experience of this kind of farming. Some of the farmers managed to hold on, and the blaze of early success convinced others that the gamble was still worthwhile. By 1884 South Australia had nearly 2,000,000 acres under crop—close to two-thirds the acreage of all Australia.

But average yields were falling disastrously, and from this point South Australia's wheat acreage declined steadily for a generation. As recurring droughts hit the northern districts, much of the farm land was abandoned. Elsewhere, loss of soil fertility and an increase in the ravages of plant diseases caused crops to fail and yields to decline.

Years before this happened there had been many who sensed the danger signs in South Australia's agriculture and realized the need for improved farming practices. The soil was being steadily impoverished by the ceaseless cropping of the ground with cereals; nothing was being returned to the land in the form of fertilizer or by way of alternate crops or fallow. A commission was appointed in 1875 to look into the matter and to suggest ways to help promote the well-being of the agricultural community through better farming methods. The commission suggested the appointment of a professor of agricultural science and the setting-up of experimental farms as well as the creation of a department of agriculture; but its recommendations were laid aside.

In 1881 the first issue of *The Garden and Field* was published in Adelaide; its editor, Albert Molineux, pointed to what he called "a total absence of any scientific principle in the method of farming" undertaken in South Australia. By now the government was prepared to act; it bought a property at Roseworthy for use as an experimental farm, and after two years a college was established there. The first group of students began their studies in 1884. However, the newly appointed professor's sharp criticism of agricultural methods did nothing to endear him to the farmers. Professor John Custance, brought up in the atmosphere of English farming and wholly scientific in his approach, characterized the colonial farming methods as "slovenly," saying that farmers were only "scratching the soil." Harassed and hard-working, the men whose efforts he was criticizing resented the charge by an English "new chum," and they replied with equal frankness.

At Roseworthy Custance began research into the causes of crop failures and yield decline; but because of the running battle of words between him and the farming community, the professor convinced very few men on the land of the facts they needed to know. His successor, a Scot, William Lowrie, had more success when he arrived in 1887. By this time the problems were more pressing and farmers were coming to realize that they must be prepared to listen to advice. There were enlightened voices. *The Garden and Field* continued to stress the need to devote greater attention to scientific agriculture, and at the same time urged farmers to diversify production. Farmers themselves were seeking precise information and many were ready to pool their knowledge. In 1888 the agricultural bureau system was instituted so that they might be grouped together in local branches for the exchange of information applying to their particular problems. The experiments made at Roseworthy, and the training given there, were important in adding to the store of knowledge and experience covering farm activities in the colony. With the founding of South Australia's Department of Agriculture in 1894 it was possible to build up a valuable two-way traffic in ideas and experience between the experts and the men on the land.

Investigations begun by Custance had shown meanwhile that many crop failures arose from deficiencies of phosphate in the soil. Custance's early experiments were followed up by Lowrie, who soon became an ardent advocate of the use of superphosphate, a soil fertilizer coming into use at this time as an effective means of improving yields and lifting farmers' cash returns. At first the hard-pressed farmers were sceptical about the value of superphosphate, but soon the remarkable results achieved with test plots gave convincing proof of the value of the innovation; and once ways were found to drill it in with the seed wheat, superphosphate became more widely used as an adjunct to good farming. Improved types of cultivation implements made it possible to hold more moisture in fallow land and helped keep down weeds in the crop. The decline in wheat had been halted, and from the mid-1890s when farmers adopted these new practices yields began to rise. At the same time, strains and varieties of wheat which did better in particular districts and showed some measure of disease-resistance were being selected for their superior qualities by local farmers. Among the most successful of the many farmers developing new strains was Richard Marshall, of Wasleys, who was responsible for selecting two natural hybrids of considerable value—Marshall's No. 3 and Yandhilla King. Grading of the grain was made more efficient by the use of better machines, and more even germination was achieved through improved methods of treating seed-wheat by "pickling" it to counter smut disease.

These innovations meant that shrinkages in South Australia's total acreage were offset by improved yields on the cropped land. Yet for individual farmers difficulties remained, and farming families sometimes felt themselves fortunate if they achieved anything above a subsistence living. There were many insolvencies in the 1890s among farmers who had struggled through earlier difficulties in the hope that things would improve; even the more fortunate could barely afford outlays on superphosphate or for machines. By 1900 superphosphate was being applied to more than one-quarter of the wheat acreage in South Australia; but even though wheat-growing was by now a less hazardous occupation, basic limitations of South Australia's wheat land soils remained and the fallow-wheat rotation which became widely adopted provided no more than an interim answer to the dangers of soil exhaustion resulting from continuous cropping.

In other colonies there was less emphasis on wheat-growing than in South Australia, where wheat was twice as valuable a crop as wool; but while in New South Wales and Queensland the great concentration was still on pastoral expansion, wheat lands were being opened up quite rapidly in Victoria as part of a movement towards a more diversified economy. Some wheat had been grown in the central and western districts of Victoria from the early 1860s, and after railways were taken north of the ranges wheat acreages increased steadily in the 1870s; from 1875 Victoria was self-supporting in wheat. Attention had been given to the Wimmera district, but at first the rich clay soils proved difficult to work, and the main expansion came when farmers from South Australia, with advanced methods of fallowing, found ways to bring the Mallee and Wimmera lands into use. By the mid-1880s, Victoria, with more than 1,500,000 acres under wheat, was beginning to overhaul South Australia in wheat production. In addition, Victoria had another 700,000 acres under other crops. Some dry seasons and the ravages of rabbits slowed progress but expansion continued. By the late 1890s, when superphosphate was coming into use and the Wimmera was highly productive, Victoria had 2,000,000 acres under wheat and was the leading wheat producing colony. Two agricultural training colleges, Dookie and Longerenong, set up to advance training in rural pursuits, were offering education in the fundamental principles and the most up-to-date practice of agriculture and animal husbandry.

In other colonies, similar colleges for educating future farmers and farmers' advisers were set up in the 1890s. Hawkesbury Agricultural College was opened in 1891, the year after the New South Wales Department of Agriculture was established, and Queensland followed in 1897. By the close of the century each colony had at least the nucleus of an Agricultural Department.

Improved machinery had helped wheat's advance. Notable among labour-saving devices was a machine able to cut off the heads of a standing crop and thresh the grain in a continuous operation as it moved through the wheat field—a marked improvement on the stripper with separate winnowing operation. The young man who contrived the new machine, Hugh Victor McKay, developed the idea in the early 1880s as he drove a stripper on his father's farm near Raywood, in Victoria. McKay's first stripper-harvester was an improvised affair, assembled from parts taken from disused machinery or fashioned out of rough materials that were available on the farm; yet when it was tested in February 1884 it worked faultlessly. It took some years for the stripper-harvester to win wide acceptance, but a few implement-makers in Victoria were soon building machines to McKay's design and by 1894 McKay was in business in Ballarat as a manufacturer. By this time the "permanent" design had taken shape, and the machine was being widely acclaimed.

As farming methods were improved, wheat-growing was consolidated on the inland plains; this in turn called for new varieties of wheat able to withstand the drier conditions. Experiments to develop suitable strains were begun in 1886 by William James Farrer, an Englishman who had a scientific training before he settled on the land near Queanbeyan. He set about cross-breeding wheats to produce a type that would stand up to hot, dry summers, and have natural resistance to rust and other diseases that attacked existing strains. Some farmers scoffed at Farrer's experiments, but others encouraged him. Interest in the results of his experiments spread, and soon his work was given official backing. By the late 1890s new wheats were appearing to replace the older varieties; they were strains which matured quickly and were disease-resistant. Farrer's greatest achievement was in the development of an early-maturing, strong-strawed wheat which he named Federation when it was released in 1901. It helped to open up new areas to wheat, particularly on the plains of the Murray basin.

Victoria led the way in the development of irrigation. The initiative came in the early 1880s when Alfred Deakin, a prominent member of the Victorian legislature and from 1883 Minister for Water Supply, took up the matter of water resources and their use. A Royal Commission set up in 1884, over which Deakin presided as Minister for Development, declared:

It is essential that the state should exercise the supreme control of ownership over all rivers, lakes, streams, and sources of water supply.

Deakin encouraged the introduction of improved water storages for small towns, and from this point the prospect of large-scale irrigation was developed. He visited the United States, India, Egypt, and Italy to study irrigation systems, and wrote in glowing terms in his official report, *Irrigation in Western America*, on the work of George Chaffey and his brother, two young Canadians who had already established successful fruitgrowing irrigation settlements in the dry lands of southern California. During his tour Deakin met George Chaffey and they discussed irrigation, but it was after Deakin left that the thought of a Chaffey enterprise in Australia developed. As a follow-up to Deakin's visit, a California newspaperman, Stephen Cureton, made the trip to Melbourne to interview Deakin, and his report that almost limitless land could be obtained from the Government of Victoria for the introduction of scientific irrigation brought Chaffey to Australia early in 1886; his family, and his brother William Benjamin Chaffey, arrived a few months later.

George Chaffey reconnoitred the central reaches of the Murray. He called at drought-stricken Mildura station, a 250,000-acre wasteland where no more than about 20,000 sheep might be run even in a normal season. Wholly unpromising as the property seemed—at an annual rental of 4/- a square mile the owner had been losing money—its watered garden contained flourishing fruit trees, indicating that its red soil was inherently fertile. The land was flat, the climate was dry with abundant sunshine to mature fruit (or to dry it without artificial means), and once raised from the river water could be reticulated relatively easily. Chaffey sensed at once that the land fulfilled the requirements for fruit-growing under irrigation, and he decided to look no further.

In October 1886 an interim agreement was reached between Deakin and Chaffey under which the Chaffey brothers were to be given rights to the Mildura tract (and to water from the Murray) in return for their undertaking large outlays on irrigation works and improvements. The government was to build a railway line to Mildura. The Chaffeys were to acquire 50,000 acres in fee simple by spending £5 an acre on the enterprise; a further 200,000 acres were to be released to them in return for £1 purchase price and £1 per acre spent on improvements. Their profit was to come from the sale of the land when developed and productive.

The two men were bringing not only money but unique experience and technical skill to the enterprise—yet many Victorian parliamentarians were cold and stubbornly critical. A feeling that outsiders were being unfairly granted a great concession permeated the discussions, and the opposition insisted that the whole arrangement be thrown open and made subject to tender.

At this point the South Australian Government became interested in attracting the Chaffeys, and George Chaffey was invited to investigate land for an irrigation project in the colony. Renmark, 90 miles downstream from Mildura, appealed to him as a suitable site, and a firm agreement was signed under which the Chaffeys were to promote an irrigation settlement there.

Great consternation was expressed in Victoria as soon as it became known that the Chaffeys, committed to the development of Renmark, refused to tender for the Mildura project. When the time for tenders expired without any offer being received, it became clear to all that the Chaffeys alone had the knowhow which would make success possible in the difficult task. The Government of Victoria made a new approach and the Chaffeys agreed to adopt the original arrangement for Mildura. The document was finally signed on May 31 1887 and a company was formed with £350,000 capital. The practical work could now begin. Gear for clearing and grading the land, and for the construction of miles of irrigation channels, was assembled. Mildura itself was mapped on a modern plan, and the work of laying out the whole irrigable area began. Early in 1888 eager men began to pour in. Splendid but tendentious brochures on the project distributed in England had attracted many of the settlers. There were people from other lands as well; the water-master was a Swede, the head planter a Swiss, and there were Canadians and Americans as well. It was a matter of pride that those who were in charge of many of the activities were Australian-born; *The Bulletin* noted exultantly in 1891 that the head accountant, the four surveyors, the auctioners, the four architects, and the station manager were all Australians; so, too, were the two editors, the bank manager, lawyer, schoolmaster, and one of the doctors.

Among the technical problems faced at Mildura was that of raising water to irrigate land set high above the river level; it was necessary to design a special pumping-plant for the purpose, and this George Chaffey did. As a temporary substitute, for use while the plant was being built in England, an old river-steamer was converted into a pumping barge and pressed into service to initiate the irrigation system. Meanwhile the irrigation settlement at Renmark was also launched; it presented less involved problems, was more accessible and, as it proved, ran into fewer difficulties.

By 1890 the population at Mildura exceeded 3000, including almost 1000 who were resident settlers and their families; more than 6000 acres of land had been cleared, with nearly 5000 acres of it under cultivation. Almost 1000 acres were planted with vines or fruit trees. In the hot, clear air fruit growth was phenomenal, and all seemed well; but the plan for the promised rail line to Mildura lay pigeonholed in Melbourne. Early in 1893, just as the fruit was ripening in the first general harvest—a great outpouring of oranges, grapes, peaches, plums, apricots, and other fruits—the river level fell to a point where the paddle-steamers could no longer get through and Mildura was cut off. No amount of recrimination could overcome the absence of a railway. A ready market for the Mildura crop existed in Melbourne, but the perishable fruit could not stand the jolting by dray or waggon on the long overland journey to the railhead at Swan Hill. Much of it remained to rot on the trees or vines.

This initial setback was but the first of a series of disasters that struck Mildura. The irrigation channels were already leaking, many earthen banks caving in or falling away; soon other problems, including excess salinity in the soil and waterlogging, were added. Most of the vines that had been planted produced table grapes and these could not be dried successfully. The raisin crop could not be marketed because there were no facilities for stemming the fruit. The sultana had not yet been planted; it was later to be a saving factor after experimental plantings of a few acres proved successful (beginning in 1893). By 1895 Mildura's fortunes were at their lowest ebb, with debts mounting and a rash of abandoned blocks. Land sales were at an end.

The Chaffeys were unable to keep the sagging settlement afloat; the whole enterprise had to be reconstructed financially. In 1895 the Mildura Dried Fruits Trust was formed as a cooperative enterprise, and the following year the First Mildura Irrigation Trust was established. Meanwhile, through bitter experience, the surviving blockholders had developed sounder technical knowledge and dried fruits production was increasing steadily. In 1896 the Greek secret of cincturing currants was discovered. By 1900 nearly 4,000,000 lb. of raisins and 5,000,000 lb. of currants were being processed annually, and by 1903—when the railway finally reached Mildura, amid rejoicing—the value of the products of the irrigated land exceeded £250,000. Long before this the Chaffey company had been forced into liquidation as part of the reconstruction process. George Chaffey was able to raise enough money to return to California (there to launch his most successful enterprise); W.B. Chaffey had stayed on in Mildura and was largely responsible for the successful development of the dried fruits industry.

Renmark shared some of Mildura's early troubles, but being closer to markets it was less seriously affected and the initial setbacks were more easily corrected. The raisin trust, formed in 1895, was the beginning of cooperative enterprise among the growers there. In both Mildura and Renmark, the new productive resources provided through irrigation represented an important gain in the community's real wealth.

Elsewhere, important new rural industries, made possible by other innovations, were bringing enhanced opportunity and helping to lift export earnings. Refrigeration opened the way for the development of a significant new activity in the shipment of frozen meat. Proposals for sending frozen meat to England had been talked of hopefully from the time Scottish-born James Harrison, a self-taught engineer, set up the first artificial ice-making factory in Geelong in 1852. Harrison's discovery of the coolant properties of a mixture of sulphuric ether and ammonia led him to develop a refrigerating compressor, and he patented the process in 1856. Harrison went to London and supervised the construction of a large ice-making machine which he installed in a Melbourne factory in 1859; but the venture proved unprofitable. The Sydney Ice Company was formed in 1860 and at first used Harrison's machine, but later the company adopted a process developed by Eugene Dominique Nicolle, a French-born engineer living in Sydney. Joining forces with Nicolle, Thomas Sutcliffe Mort, a successful broker and shipper of wool, soon succeeded in the important objective: preservation of meat for export. Independently, a small freezing works was set up in Rockhampton, Queensland, in 1871; but it was Mort's backing of the enterprise in Sydney that led directly to commercial success. Over some years, Mort made a heavy investment in experiments in refrigeration. He set up a freezing plant at Lithgow, where the slaughtering was to be undertaken, and one at Darling Harbour, where the refrigerated carcasses were to be taken and held for shipment.

A freezing plant was installed (at Mort's expense) on a ship in 1877; a defect developed in the equipment, however, and Mort died before the first consignment of frozen meat left for England in 1879.

The shipment, made in the *Strathleven*, was refrigerated by apparatus designed and fitted in England, and it reached London in good condition (as had the first shipment of frozen meat, from Buenos Aires to Marseilles, in 1877–78). This success of the *Strathleven* enterprise was the signal for the organization of a new branch of the pastoral industry. Leading graziers were now ready to back the enterprise; a company was formed in Victoria in 1880, and the first inland freezing works in New South Wales was opened at Orange in 1881. The sale of livestock for meat export grew quickly as a lucrative adjunct to pastoral activity. The number of cattle raised for beef increased. In 1890 there were more than 10,000,000 head of cattle in Australia (most of them raised for beef) and although the numbers fell later with prolonged droughts, by the mid-1890s substantial exports of beef and mutton were being made. Cattlemen were pressing deeper into northern inland regions, although after a peak in 1904 cattle numbers in the north declined for ten years and remained low for two decades.

Another industry that expanded and gained export markets with the introduction of refrigeration was dairying. The *Strathleven* had also carried an experimental consignment of butter, and this became the forerunner of shipments of dairy products that were to develop into a great trade. Dairying was mainly located in south-eastern coastal areas of assured rainfall and close to the principal centres of population. From the early 1880s the introduction of cream separators eased the dairy farmer's worries and, coming at a time of new export opportunities, helped transform the industry. Forested areas of Gippsland in south-eastern Victoria were soon being opened up; the land was made available at low cost (£1 an acre) with payment spread over many years. A new phase of pioneering began. Men moved into the densely-timbered districts, chopped out small patches, ringbarked the larger trees, and began to plant grasses and clovers. Tracks were cleared and rough roads were slowly developed. Soon Gippsland was a major dairying area. By the early 1890s butter factories were operating there.

Other high-rainfall areas that were similarly developed as a result of dairying were north of Sydney, in the Hunter and other valleys, and along the coast south of Sydney, and in the Darling Downs in southern Queensland.

Some of the dairy farmers found the going too hard and abandoned their blocks, but thousands struggled on in an effort to fulfil their dreams of independence. Hard work alone could not bring them success; in order to have productive cows they had to maintain good pastures, and so native grasses had to be replaced by forage that was nutritious and permanent. Dairy pasture plants were drawn from various parts of the world, with Europe providing a number of valuable species of grasses and various clovers and Africa and America each supplying at least two important grasses. Some of the introduced plants—including lucerne, which was already widely cultivated in the United States—were found to flourish in widely separated districts, but generally soil and climatic conditions imposed clear limits on the effective cultivation of any particular species. In the Lismore district, in northern New South Wales, Edwin Seccombe ended a long search for a pasture grass which would respond to local conditions, when he demonstrated the superiority of paspalum. In the early 1890s plants grown from seeds brought in from Brazil were found to flourish, and soon thousands of acres in dairying districts were sown to this tough and nutritious grass which assured summer feed.

A species of clover that was soon to spread through the cooler areas of Australia came from a chance discovery. A clump of subterranean clover—a plant of Mediterranean origin which probably was introduced as seed brought in with meadowhay used as packing for chinaware—was first noticed growing by the wayside in the rolling hills near Adelaide by Amos William Howard, a Hertfordshire-born nurseryman. He collected some seed and began propagating the plant in 1889; very soon his clover plots were flourishing. Howard found that the plants grew and spread profusely when superphosphate was added to the soil. After a few years Howard released seeds from his new plant, and soon farmers were sowing the rich clover as a supplement to or replacement for native and introduced grasses.

The search for new and better grasses and herbage plants to supplement native species had been encouraged and assisted by Ferdinand von Mueller, whose botanical knowledge had been extended by field trips over almost all Victoria and into many other parts of the continent from the 1860s. Mueller was interested not only in the introduction of new plants into Australia, and his study of the native flora took a practical turn. In treatises he extolled the many extraordinary qualities of the pungent and protean eucalypt as a hardy form of tree possessing special value if left standing. Not only did he laud the use of eucalypts for soil preservation and land reclamation in dry areas, but also as a source of timber, charcoal, oil, and honey. Soon seeds of many species of eucalypts were being exported to scores of countries—and although these exports did not contribute significantly to trade revenue, before long the hardy "gum tree" had appeared to grace landscapes in hot or dry lands across the world from the Levant to South America. Eucalypts were introduced to California with the hope that they would provide rail sleepers, but the species chosen was useless for that purpose.

At the same time, close to Mueller's home base in Melbourne, large areas were being cleared by farmers chopping a way into dense forests clothing hillsides and valleys. Even in more open lands of the southern sectors of the continent, trees were ringbarked so that they could not rob the soil of moisture and nutrients needed for grass or grain crops; soon their gaunt skeletons were to disfigure many a landscape. Elsewhere, along the rivers, red gum and other hardwood forests were being cut to yield railway sleepers, or wood blocks to pave streets in London and European cities, or for charcoal. In the same forests and woodlands, and on the plains, hunters were at work to supply the demand for the skins of native animals, including koalas, platypuses, opossums, and kangaroos.

Far to the north, a different climate was shaping affairs in a distinctive mould. Queensland was still mainly a wool-and-beef country; the explosion in population from 28,000 in 1860 to over 200,000 in 1880 had gone hand-in-hand with a doubling of sheep numbers (to 7,000,000) and a sixfold increase in cattle (to 3,000,000). Along the coastal strip plantation-type agriculture had been established—a feature distinguishing Queensland from the other colonies. As sugar and banana growing areas were extended, increasing numbers of islanders were imported as indentured labour, and this coastal development began to assume the character of a typical tropical land, with white overseers and massed native labour.

Kanaka or South Sea Islands labourers had been used on cotton and sugar plantations since the 1860s. Captain Robert Towns, a merchant and pastoralist who established a cotton plantation to take advantage of the high prices ruling for cotton during the U.S. Civil War, introduced the first kanakas, sixty-seven in all, into Queensland in 1863. They were recruited at 10/– a month, plus rations, to do "light field work or what may be required of them." In reply to a barrage of newspaper criticism of Towns for "blackbirding" and introducing the slave trade to Queensland, Towns maintained that the islanders had been properly hired and well provided for in barracks he had built. The practice continued, and (when cotton planting fell away after 1865) was extended; kanaka labourers were used as cultivators and cane cutters in the expanding sugar industry and as station hands. The islanders were recruited (for Peru, Fiji, and Samoa, as well as for Queensland) by the owners of luggers who promised that after serving a fixed period in the plantations they would be returned safely to their homes; but there were many abuses, and as the number of kanaka labourers rose the system came in for more widespread criticism.

Sugar had become the main product of tropical agriculture. As early as the 1840s some sugar had been grown in coastal New South Wales, and a refining operation begun (in Sydney); the area under cane rose slowly to 2000 acres by 1868, when a few mills were operating. In the next twenty-five years, when Queensland acreages expanded, production grew to 15,000 tons a year—still only a fraction of the requirements of the colonies, but a start in meeting Australian demand. During the 1880s the area planted with sugar expanded steadily and more island labour was required. An official inquiry instituted in 1884 into the methods used in recruiting kanakas in the islands provided a terrible indictment: "deceit, cruelty, treachery, deliberate kidnapping, and cold-blooded murder." After this, stricter supervision by government inspectors removed some of the worst abuses of the system, but the traffic was not stopped. The kanakas were still being paid a wage far below that of the poorest Australian labourer, and both on humanitarian grounds and as a matter of self-interest in protecting wage standards, the public became strongly opposed to the kanaka system.

Mining had meanwhile drawn great numbers to Queensland, and although some transients moved on again as soon as the mines became exhausted, many others stayed. Those with money were able to invest in pastoral and other activities, while thousands of unskilled labourers and men without money began to compete with the kanakas for a livelihood and to demand that in the land of their birth (or adoption) they should have the right to earn a living at a reasonable wage. It was a new concept: nowhere else had white men been prepared to undertake the heavy labour of plantation work. The experience in Queensland had not been promising. Diseases such as malaria, filariasis, and hookworm had been common; the kanakas had died in great numbers, and among white men the death rate was so excessively high that in the 1880s life expectancy (at birth) averaged only forty-one years—six years lower than for the Australian colonial population as a whole. As adequate measures of preventive medicine were instituted the outlook changed, and during the decade of the 1890s the average life expectancy for men in the colony moved up by almost nine years.

Meanwhile, as a counterforce to the incipient "plantation economy," Labor in Queensland had come to hold more extreme views than in other colonies, where such an acrimonious issue was not present. Strong opposition to the admission of kanakas and the use of kanaka labour was a rallying point for strong antagonisms. In 1893 the sugar planters of the north came to the conclusion that their only hope was to detach themselves from the seat of opposition, and they petitioned for separation and autonomy. But theirs was a lost cause. Stricter controls were already being applied. By the end of the decade there were still some islanders on the canefields, but the proportion had fallen sharply, and before long the activity would be wholly in the hands of white labour.

Drought burned its way over plain and valley alike when rains failed over most of the occupied land of the southern and eastern sectors of the continent during the 1880s. There had been dry times in many pastoral areas before, even in districts quite close to the coast, but these had usually been shortlived and had affected only limited areas at any time. The drought years that began in the 1880s set a new and terrifying precedent as rivers dried and the cover of ground plants withered away. No relief came from the cloudless sky. Seared landscapes like those described by explorers deep in the arid inland were spreading far and wide, eating their way back into once good districts. Rabbits were adding to the destruction in many parts, stripping living plants and killing the permanent roots. Winds began to lift the surface of the land, whipping up duststorms that obliterated the sun.

The worst year yet known was 1888—and yet in the following years the conditions became increasingly severe. Great areas were stricken as drought seared and bleached districts where rain had been sufficient in all previous years of settlement. From 1891 devastating conditions were widespread, and added to the sheepmen's worries was a wool market which slipped to its lowest level in forty years. From nearly 100,000,000 in 1890, sheep numbers fell steadily and over twelve years were reduced to 55,000,000; cattle numbers went well below 9,000,000. Part of the loss had come as a result of over-stocking; great areas of marginal land had been taken up and, without the benefit of experience to guide them, owners or managers had often been far too optimistic in assessing the carrying capacity of the properties. In many areas, valuable herbage plants had been eaten out or seriously depleted.

With their financial resources steadily drained by the prolonged drought, many pastoralists were unable to keep going, and they lost everything. Some properties were taken over or bought by companies. In other cases individuals prepared to speculate on the outcome of the season moved in and secured land for a fraction of its earlier price; their success or failure depended on just how soon the drought broke.

It was natural that pastoralists should feel that in a land where drought or poor seasons might come at any time, large holdings were needed for successful grazing. At the same time, it was not always recognized that survival was not guaranteed by vast acreages. Ambitious men, successful on smaller properties, had been induced to seek the greater freedom and brighter prospects that large estates seemed to offer. In this testing time, many failed tragically. Drovers who had started overlanding into remote districts were sometimes able to raise the capital needed to set themselves up as pioneer cattlemen. To succeed in such ventures they needed skill and a gambler's luck. One of the men who put together a cattle empire was Sidney Kidman, a speculator who by ventures in the ownership of land and cattle was able to convert relatively limited initial capital into a fortune. Kidman's success began when he bought Owen Springs station (south-west of Alice Springs) in 1880; it was the first phase in a series of moves which eventually gave him control of tens of thousands of square miles of cattle country in the dry lands of Queensland and New South Wales.

Yet, in spite of individual successes, this was over-all a tougher frontier than anyone could judge without first-hand experience, and even the most prescient could be deluded. Livestock losses due to drought could be stag-geringly heavy; and usually there were no buyers for the surviving stock.

The need for reserve capital was greater than even the prudent realized— capital sufficient not only to run a big enterprise but sufficient also to keep it afloat in periods of low wool prices and over a number of adverse seasons. Sometimes by good management and a determination to win through against any odds, and sometimes by sheer good fortune, holders of marginal lands survived the terrible years of drought and went on to win success. Speculation on the breaking of the drought itself might pay handsome dividends, or mark final disaster. The smaller settler however had virtually no hope of survival under such really adverse conditions; the drier lands could be taken up successfully only by those with large resources.

For many farmers on the fringe wheat lands, the drought years spelt misery and doom. Again, the prudent and the fortunate pulled through, but in the process they were reduced to mere subsistence in many cases, and the survivors accumulated a heavy load of debt.

Nevertheless, new prospects were opening for the farmer. As wool prices slipped in the late 1880s, a new trend appeared—graziers found it desirable to supplement their income from sheep by making some of their land available for cropping on a share basis. In this way land in the better rainfall areas that had previously been tightly held as sheep pasture was turned over to wheat.

Railways that had been pushed into the open grasslands of Riverina and the central districts of New South Wales now became ribbons of steel to support share-farming and wheat-growing by individual settlers who bought "homestead" blocks opened up originally in the days of land legislation (the terms of which were still operative). With the further decline of wool prices to a low point in 1894, farmers were better able to win a place for themselves in competition with the sheepmen.

New mechanical aids and the more widespread adoption of large-scale dry farming methods (largely developed in South Australia a few years earlier) were helping to make wheat-growers' operations more successful, even though wheat prices were generally low. They fell from about 5/– a bushel in 1891 to 3/– a bushel in 1894 and rose only slowly from that point. In the 1890s New South Wales tripled the acreage sown to wheat. The 1,000,000-acre mark was passed in 1897, and from about one-seventh of the total Australian wheat acreage in 1891, New South Wales moved up to almost 28 per cent of the total acreage in 1901. In Victoria, the active railway-building programme made it possible for farmers to push the limits of the wheat belt into the Mallee. Improvements in machinery, wheat varieties, and methods of cultivation all helped to strengthen the farmer's grip on the land and, combined with the improved competitive position of wheat due to price changes, did what the parliamentarians had been unable to bring about by direct legislative action.

Changing patterns in economic activity were being reflected in differing rates of population growth in the various colonies. People were going where opportunity seemed brightest, and Victoria, once the great magnet, no longer held its previous dominance in the economic scene. The great expansion of sheep flocks and wool output was taking place in states other than victoria.

During the phenomenal development of the wool industry in the 1870s and 1880s (when output increased two-and-a-half times), New South Wales showed the greatest rise, much of it due to the success of large stud owners in improving merino fleece quality. The relative positions of the colonies underwent dramatic change during this period of all-round growth, as this table shows:

Growth in Australia's Wool Output, and Proportion of Output Produced in Each of the Colonies, 1861–1891.

	Total wool output (all colonies)	New South Wales	Victoria	Queensland	South Australia	West Australia	Tasmania
				percentage			
1861	78,000,000 lb.	24	36	15	18	1	6
1871	212,000,000 lb.	35	30	17	13	2	3
1881	325,000,000 lb.	50	21	10	14	2	3
1891	543,000,000 lb.	59	13	15	9	2	2

After 1870 Victoria's wool exports showed little absolute increase, while gold production began to decline noticeably in the middle of the decade. Even the expanded activity in farming and in small-scale manufacturing in Melbourne, Ballarat, Geelong, and Bendigo, and the big programme of public works, did little more than delay the dispersion of the people who had flocked into Victoria over the previous two decades of gold and wool. Meanwhile, New South Wales was forging ahead on enhanced returns from wool; as railways reached out to tap the large areas from which much wool had previously been drawn to Victoria or South Australia by river steamers, the astonishing increase in the colony's wool clip was even more directly Sydney's gain. South Australia began to show a faster rate of population increase from the late 1870s, and the colony had 276,000 people by 1880. There was considerable progress in Queensland as pastoral activities expanded, and in the 1880s, when artesian bores opened new lands for livestock raising; but Queensland's fortunes as a wool producer were related closely to the incidence of drought conditions over wide areas of subtropical pasture. With important mineral discoveries in the 1880s the northern colony added new population, its numbers almost doubling from 211,000 in 1880 to nearly 400,000 in 1890. There was limited growth in Tasmania, where usable land had long been taken up, and from 100,000 in 1870 the population moved up to 114,000 ten years later. In Western Australia progress was slow, and it was 1881 before the 30,000 mark in population was passed.

In 1887 Victoria and New South Wales each passed the 1,000,000 mark in population, and five years later New South Wales moved ahead of Victoria to show a clear lead. The following table shows how the population pattern changed in the period between 1871 and 1891:

Proportion of Australia's Population in Each of the Colonies, 1871–91.

	Total Australian Population	New South Wales	Victoria	Queensland	South Australia	Western Australia	Tasmania
				percentage			
1871	1,700,888	30.4	43.9	7.2	11.1	1.5	6.0
1881	2,306,736	33.7	37.9	9.6	12.4	1.3	5.1
1891	3,240,985	35.7	35.7	12.3	10.0	1.6	4.7

Important new mineral deposits had been uncovered in remote parts of the continent. The prospect of gaining quick riches drew men to the new field, which contained a variety of mineral ores, but because of the nature of most of the deposits the exploration of the fields generally called for big investment. As long-life mines, some of the great new discoveries were to create centres of population, and eventually towns, in some isolated areas.

Silver-lead ore was first found in the Barrier Ranges of western New South Wales in 1875. A shipment sent to England in 1880 for assay proved to be so rich in minerals that minor rushes began. Then in 1883 a boundary rider in the same area found rich silver on a rocky outcrop, and pegged out a 40 acre claim; soon a syndicate was formed to mine the "broken hill." Chloride of silver was found about a 100 feet below the surface, and further rich ore was soon revealed. The rush to Broken Hill began. Visions of a silver deposit rivalling Nevada's Comstock lode drew eager miners to the hot and dusty area. Tents and iron huts were erected, and bullock teams from South Australia began arriving with machinery and stores. Soon shallow mines were being worked over a wide sweep of the desolate range; but the riches of Broken Hill lay deep, and it was to take great investment to unearth them.

There was considerable expansion of the coal trade in New South Wales as railways increased their operations and export demand grew. Also in the 1880s rich copper deposits and some gold were uncovered at Mount Lyell, on Tasmania's west coast, and silver-lead deposits at Mount Zeehan. In Queensland, the Mount Morgan goldfield was discovered in July 1882.

After years of unfulfilled hopes for gold discoveries in Western Australia, in the 1880s a region in the desolate northern inland was found to be gold-bearing. In 1885 Charles Hall and a companion turned up payable gold at Hall's Creek, and the following year the Kimberley goldfield was proclaimed. Hundreds of men joined in the rush, many of them experienced prospectors. Other discoveries were made—in the Pilbara district and along the Ashburton and Murchison rivers—but the rushes were shortlived. From 1887, prospecting far to the east of Perth was producing occasional strikes around Southern Cross, but it was not until Arthur Bayley and William Ford made their great finds at Coolgardie that the first evidence of the fabulous wealth of the desert lands was revealed. When, early in September 1892, Bayley rode the 125 miles into Southern Cross with 534 ounces of gold, the news was flashed around the world, touching off a wild rush to Coolgardie. Within a few months hundreds of men were on the field and a coach firm was running Cobb & Co. coaches, sent from Victoria, out from Southern Cross. As a growing horde of men probed into the bush, some exciting strikes were made.

In June 1893 Irish-born Patrick Hannan (who had worked in the mines at Ballarat) and his companion Thomas Flanagan pushed eastward from Coolgardie with a few horses. Three days out they camped near some low, scrub-covered hills. Soon they were picking up small nuggets, and within a few days they had 100 ounces of gold. Word of this was posted at the warden's tent at Coolgardie late on June 17, and a wild exodus to Hannan's

Find began. Great nuggets were quickly unearthed. As the surface treasure was depleted, well-backed companies were formed so that the search could go deep into the earth. The Golden Mile of Boulder became the subject of conversation far and wide; the city of Kalgoorlie sprang up, to mark the bonanza. In eight years gold worth over £20 million was taken from the new mines.

Gold was a catalyst of change in Western Australia, as elsewhere. The colony which to this point had relatively little in common with the other Australian colonies, was drawn closer to them. The crowds of miners and speculators—many of them from Victoria—flocking to Western Australia helped to change the social and political complexion of the colony. The landowning oligarchy—which held effective power after the granting of responsible government in 1890—did everything possible to retain its grip over affairs, withholding the franchise from the miners and also maintaining a weighted-vote system in which one rural voter had as much say as six or eight voters in mining districts. It did not take long however; for immigration to redress the balance, from under 50,000 in 1891 the population moved over the 100,000 mark in 1895 and added 35,000 in 1896, so that the land-owning group was being effectively swamped by new and more progressive elements.

During the 1880s there was a marked increase in employment; the number of breadwinners rose by almost 50 per cent between 1881 and 1891. However, economic conditions in most of the colonies began to take an unfavourable turn. A downturn came as wool prices dipped and droughts became widespread and severe; and the adverse conditions in rural affairs were soon eclipsed by a series of events in Victoria which had their origin in unbridled investment and a speculative boom in Melbourne real estate.

The country man might be living a life close to reality as independent farmer, as shearer, fencer, rabbiter, sleeper-cutter or rail-layer, or as teamster; but in Melbourne an air of expansion was abroad and a frenzy of speculation had begun. For many years enthusiastic writers who visited Australia—and many of them saw practically only Victoria—had been sending back to London glowing reports and optimistic forecasts. The colonies had assumed a new status in the eyes of stay-at-home Englishmen, and the way was open for increased attention to the far-off land. More books on Australia began to appear in England in the 1870s. In one, *Australia Illustrated*, Edwin Carton Booth gave rosy descriptions and spoke of bright prospects; elsewhere Anthony Trollope wrote a series of newspaper reports in which he painted an optimistic picture as he regaled his English readers with episodes from the spacious life of wealthy station owners. Trollope was greatly impressed by the evidence he found on all sides of progress and prosperity. His reports were hardly more enthusiastic than the stories of other English visitors introduced to the affluence of successful wool growers. By the 1880s all this had convinced moneyed people in London and elsewhere that investment in Australia would produce handsome rewards.

British investment in banks and companies created to channel money from London to developing lands abroad, including the colonies, found its way to Victoria in a flood in the 1880s.

Melbourne itself was aglow with confidence. Office buildings of ten and twelve floors appeared in the city, challenging the world's tallest. There were renewed bursts of spending as Melbourne broke its old bounds and suburbs spread across the rolling hills to the east of the city. Expensive building stone and rich timbers were imported to garnish the great new mansions and the fine city edifices. Huge theatres were built. City land values soared. Queen Victoria's Diamond Jubilee was celebrated in 1887 with great enthusiasm and extraordinary extravagance; the Great Exhibition organized for that year marked the peak of the city's exuberance.

Pressure for unrestricted bank lending resulted in the removal by the Victorian government in 1888 of all remaining barriers to mortgage loans (or lending on the security of land) by trading banks. Fearing an incipient boom, some of the banks at once adopted a cautious lending policy, but there were others prepared to feed the inflation. Share prices were at record levels. Money was still pouring in from London. For years there had been extensive private investment. Development of rural industries and the building boom absorbed the great bulk of available local capital. Colonial governments financed railway construction (and some other needed public works) by loans raised in London which were fully subscribed by confident British investors. By 1890, with nearly 11,000 miles of track open to traffic, the Australian colonies had aggregate public debts of close to £160 million.

Mushrooming share lists in Melbourne and Ballarat (when the Mining Exchange, set up in 1881, merged in 1885 with Ballarat's older Stock Exchange) fed speculation as prices shot upward. Mining companies absorbed large funds and shares rocketed in price. Victoria was in the vortex of an inflationary boom. Confidence was buoyed up by hopeful assessments of new ventures. The proposals of the Chaffey brothers for the Mildura irrigation project inspired hope and augured well; new wealth was being opened up at Broken Hill, gold was coming from mines in Victoria and Queensland, wheat farming, dairy farming and timbergetting were moving forward, and money was being spent on railway construction and city development. For Victoria, the Golden Age seemed to have dawned. Expansion, and certainty that the future was limitless, coloured discussions and decisions. Banking advances moved up to levels undreamed of in the past; loan companies sprang up in great numbers, all actively extending credit.

The colonies were indulging in an orgy of importing. Money pouring in for speculative purposes in Melbourne (which had become both a centre for investment and a source of investment funds) was helping to sustain a flood of importing by all the colonies. Over the decade of the 1880s, investment capital from overseas represented some 40 per cent of all the private investment undertaken in Australia. The airy nature of the enterprises in which investment money was being absorbed—particularly in speculative real estate—increased the risk element, but prospects seemed so promising that there was boundless confidence in investing.

Drought conditions in some areas helped to bring a general tightness of money early in 1891. Suddenly pastoralists were unable to meet their debts; the fiasco at Mildura was becoming apparent; businessmen were overdrawn. An air of nervousness was now abroad. Banks were already in trouble, and by August the first bank closed; it was the Bank of Van Diemen's Land, in Tasmania, and its demise hastened a depression in Melbourne as frenzied efforts began to recall loans made when credit was flowing freely. The boom was over. Soon a run began on the land-banks. As each closed its doors, greater sums were locked up, adding to the public concern and intensifying the sudden shrinkage. Men lost fortunes overnight. The city and suburban land and building boom collapsed. Only the main trading banks remained secure, though their position gradually became less assured as more financial institutions went down. An immediate shrinkage of demand occurred, and trade shrivelled

Banking affairs in Melbourne were becoming ever more chaotic. Depositors continued to withdraw funds, adding to the general problem as they did so. The first of the local trading banks of repute to go under closed its doors in January 1893, ushering in the final phase. The government urged the remaining banks to form an alliance so that any bank on which a run might occur would have the support of all—but the proposal came too late. A financial crisis had also struck London, and already British depositors were withdrawing funds there, adding pressure to the panic in which money was being taken from the banks in Melbourne and elsewhere so that it might be hidden or buried, or locked away. Fears spread. One by one banks in Melbourne and Sydney were forced to close; by April 1893 hysteria gripped Melbourne, where a dozen banks closed in six weeks, and Adelaide and Perth were caught up in the crisis. Finally the Victorian government stepped in to declare a five-day bank holiday in the colony. Not every bank had to observe it, for those who had followed conservative policies and had limited their lending were able to keep afloat. Few however survived unscathed and banks with head offices in Melbourne were particularly heavily hit. Imports were soon reduced.

When the bubble of speculation was pricked, real estate values in Melbourne fell precipitously, debts could not be paid, business was at a standstill, and factories struggled to remain open with lessened staffs. A procession of men streamed out in search of work in the country; on their trudge they were sustained by the meagre rations doled out at homesteads. The destitute included men who had lost everything in the debacle; most would never regain their financial standing. Jobs were not easy to find, even in the bush. Railway building had eased back and, with returns from wool at their nadir because of drought and low prices, sheepmen were disinclined to employ men. Even though a necessitous man might range far afield in his search, his chances of success in finding work were slim. Around the wanderings of the unhappy men legends were woven. The swagman became the archtype of the dispossessed, and soon emerged as the hero of *Waltzing Matilda* and of the poetry of Henry Lawson.

Personal calamities and individual setbacks might be permanent, but slowly the general scene improved and there was more chance for some, at least, to rehabilitate themselves. Soon there were increasingly encouraging signs in the expansion of farming, while the prevailing air of stagnation was reversed also in mining. Victoria's gold output remained significant throughout, while the important mineral discoveries of the 1880s in Queensland and Tasmania were providing great new sources of wealth. On Tasmania's west coast, a treasure trove was being revealed at Mount Lyell, where in the 1890s a large copper ore body was first turned to account and silver was extracted. At Zeehan silver-lead deposits were under rapid development after 1893. Broken Hill, in the far west of New South Wales, was yielding even greater riches in silver and lead, pouring profits back into Melbourne, source of its original mine investment, while Mount Morgan, in central Queensland, was being tapped of its great golden store. Men followed the discoveries, setting up new pockets of population requiring food and goods. A minor wave of development followed the mining expansion in western Tasmania; railway construction began, men moved in, production increased, and new crops, including apples and potatoes, were grown. Soon these products of intensive cultivation, well suited to the climate, were being exported.

Coal helped New South Wales stave off the worst of the effects of the Victorian depression. Coal mining had been growing steadily since the 1850s, and at the time of the crash the coal output was well over 2,000,000 tons a year, of which more than half was exported. A growing fleet of locomotives and the requirements of an active bunker trade absorbed increasing quantities, while industrial demands were expanding steadily. With Victoria stagnating, rich and abundant coalfields made it possible for New South Wales to catch up in manufacturing activity. Over the 1890s the two colonies were more or less equal in numbers of factories (slightly over 3000 in each colony, rising slightly over the period), and in employees—53,000 in Victoria in 1891 and 51,000 in New South Wales against 66,000 in each colony ten years later. However, for all the colonies the trend was back to the land; the number of people engaged in rural activities rose with the expansion of wheatgrowing and farming generally, so that although in 1891 no less than 31 per cent of breadwinners were employed in manufacturing industry of some kind, within a decade the proportion had slipped back to 26 per cent. The percentage engaged in rural pursuits held firm at over 30 per cent.

The terrible collapse in Victoria darkened all other colonial economies. There was no comparable bank crisis in Sydney or elsewhere, yet the impact of the Melbourne financial debacle was so severe that all the colonies were seriously and deeply affected. Deflation became acute. Local sources of capital, which had been growing during the boom period, particularly in the 1880s, and had then represented about 60 per cent of all the private investment funds, dried up suddenly. Building was brought to a complete standstill; buyers for property could not be found, even at bedrock prices, and jobs were no longer available.

While within the colonies the depression hardened and deepened, the shattering of the bubble shook Australia's credit abroad. Loan funds could no longer be raised in London by colonial governments, and private investment from abroad dried up. Confidence had been destroyed, and it was to take years for faith in the colonial future to be rebuilt among British investors.

Balladists and unionists   15

From childhood, the Australian on the farm or in the remoter and isolated areas spent a great deal of time outdoors. By the time they were twelve or thirteen, many children were at work. Children had to do things they might not want to do but which were necessary; and in doing anything and everything that came to hand they became practical, serious people. The vastness of the surroundings gave its own sense of freedom, and the individual developed self reliance, and an unquenchable independence.

In the 1870s and 1880s the great hinterland was still a world of men—now discontented men, for the most part; men who moved from job to job and and developed an allegiance to each other rather than to their employer. A greater gulf than ever divided the landless majority from those who had won the race for the land. In the pioneering days the landholder and his men might have slept under the stars or in the roughest shelter and shared hardships in the wholly primitive conditions. The close relationship that once existed between the sheep owner in the wilderness and his few trusty retainers was no longer present. Now the established station owner lived in affluence, while those who worked for him had to put up with poor conditions, earned little, and had little hope of ever attaining the independence for which they yearned. Around the campfire they exchanged reminiscences, told of their ambitions, discussed ideas on many subjects, and developed a distinctive philosophy of life.

The life in the railway gangs, in the small towns where teamsters and wool-carters and wool-lumpers met, and on the large sheep stations where shearers and permanent station hands mingled at shearing time, developed special characteristics. It was a hard life as well as a lonely one. The zeal of many of the men for a new-found solidarity in trade unionism was fuel to set ablaze their determination to stand by each other at any cost.

As the wool clip grew, techniques of wool handling from sheep's back to dockside improved. The big man's frontier was producing its own form of industrial organization and its chief operatives were showing a greater degree of skill and specialization. For most of the year the big pastoral properties might employ relatively few men; but for a brief period each in turn became a factory of a type, with assembly-line techniques. Shearing teams, compact within themselves and sometimes numbering dozens of men, moved across the land, working for a few weeks at each property they visited. As a seasonal job, shearing drew many miners who were glad to spend part of the year at this work. They were capable men—rough and ready in their approach, proud and fiercely independent in spirit. An attitude that ranged from manly independence to defiance was naturally present among such men.

Just as in the frontier society the pastoralist was the aristocrat, so those who had anything to do with wool regarded themselves as a cut above any other type of worker, and in the bushman's hierarchy the shearer maintained a position of absolute superiority. The shearer's prowess was greatly admired, and it was given something of a sporting aura through the competitive spirit that developed among shearers. There was always keen rivalry among the men to become the "ringer" or fastest member of the shearing team. As the techniques of shearing improved, making it possible for men to shear a greater number of sheep in a day than ever before, a hero worship began to develop; shearing contests were more and more widely held, and the winners were acclaimed by their rivals as well as their supporters. The shearer-hero had become established in the rural scene.

In their relationships with the station owners, shearers had become increasingly independent. An observer who spent some years in the pastoral lands in the 1870s, noted this and wrote that shearers were "perfect masters of the situation." As he saw the contest between station owner and shearers, the shearers

> ... dictated their own terms, and if the squatter refused to accede to them, they simply saddled up, and told him in language more forcible than polite, to shear his sheep himself. The unfortunate man ... dared scarcely speak in his own shed, and if he ventured to remonstrate with one of them, even if the shearing was disgracefully bad, a general throwing down of shears, and preparation to go were the consequence.

The writer's host had to undergo this "impertinence" in his turn, and when the shearers actually did go, he had to follow them with a case of brandy (which he was reserving for emergencies), the whole of which was consumed by the men before they would consent to return.

More men were working in the back country far from the sea coast, and increasingly they were coming within the reach of railways or coach services or river boats. New publications were being established to interpret the bushworker to himself and incidentally to place before him advertisements for pills or salves or herbal remedies promising to cure backache, skin diseases, fits, and a multitude of other ills.

The new publications were beginning to give men who were participating in the rigorous pioneering of the land, and undertaking its day-to-day tasks, an opportunity to contribute. A few among the chroniclers were to rise to eminence. A new literature was beginning; it was rough and raw but it had a genuine feeling for the land. Naturally writers who were facing the hardships of the life of the itinerant pastoral worker or miner were the champions of the individual; their own experience in facing the almost unalloyed hardships of the marginal lands brought sincerity to their portrayals.

The imaginative life of a whole continent—of necessity a chorus of many voices—could not be reduced to a single note; yet the voices from the wilderness seemed suddenly to produce a dominant theme. Much of what was being written reflected the earnestness and pathos of life in the back country, and practically all of it carried a sense of social consciousness and a sympathy for the bush worker. Its realism, stiffened by the writer's experience on the dusty tracks and in the shearing sheds or mining camps, contrasted sharply with the romanticism that had coloured so much of the earlier writing about the Australian rural scene.

Australia's real potentialities as a source of literary inspiration were not realized by the early colonial writers and poets—or at least the writers did not respond to the environment with close identification even though they experienced the life of which they wrote. Rather they tended to follow in the tradition of visiting observers who saw things through English eyes and wrote their impressions with English readers in mind. Such visiting writers were generally taken up with the pleasant, mellow world of the station owner and his family, and were barely conscious of the harsh, bare-boards world of the bush worker; they could not disguise their bemused satisfaction at finding the old world so faithfully reproduced in the antipodes. The English writer J.A. Froude recorded his delight at finding such elegance in the homestead at Ercildoun, a station in Victoria's Western District, where he was a guest. He noted that the homestead had a fine gate

> . . . which needed only a lodge to be like the entrance to a great English domain . . . A moment more and we were at the door of what might have been an ancient Scotch manor house, solidly built of rough-hewn granite, the walls overrun with ivy, climbing roses, and other multitudinous creepers which formed a border to the diamond-paned old-fashioned windows. On the north side was a clean-mown and carefully-watered lawn with tennis ground and croquet ground, flower beds bright with scarlet geraniums, heliotropes, verbenas, fuchsias—we had arrived in fact at an English aristocrat's country house reproduced in another hemisphere. . .
>
> Inside the illusion was even more complete . . . We found a high-bred English family—English in everything except that they were Australian-born and cultivated perhaps above the English average . . . Good pictures hung round the rooms. Books, reviews, newspapers—all English—and "the latest publications" were strewed about the tables—the *Saturday*, the *Spectator*, and the rest of them. The contrast between the scene that I had expected and the scene that I found took my breath away . . . Here was not England only but old fashioned baronial England, renewing itself spontaneously in a land of gold and diggers.

Henry Kingsley, who had spent five years in Australia and had begun his career as a writer in England with the publication in 1859 of *The Recollection of Geoffery Hamlyn*, had given no more than idealistic interpretation to the pioneering life in Australia. Marcus Clarke, in reconstructing the early convict days in *For the Term of His Natural Life* (published in 1874) provided authentic backgrounds but failed to show any adjustment of his characters to the Australian scene. Yet the fact was that over the years habits of life and thought brought from the British Isles had undergone cumulative change, and the emergence of a national consciousness had already begun. Creative writing based on the new concept of Australia as a separate land could not be long delayed.

The first notable Australian literary form was the bush ballad. The new writing came from practical men of the bush environment; it was individual and, above all, vital. Among the first balladists was Adam Lindsay Gordon; his poetry contained very little of the old-world imagery that had been dominant in the work of poets like Charles Harpur and Henry Kendall who had preceded him. Gordon had arrived in Australia in 1853 at the age of twenty. His successive occupations as horsebreaker and trooper gave him the opportunity to participate in the open-air life, and as years went on his influence as a writer on those who followed was strong. His lilting poems were recited around campfires and in shearers' huts inspiring other ballads which introspective men created and passed on to their group. Sometimes these poems gained widespread circulation as they were repeated wherever men foregathered in the back country.

It was the launching of *The Bulletin* as a "national Australian newspaper" in 1880 that opened the way for a later flood of poetry (particularly in the "ballad" form of narrative verse), anecdotes, and stories, all concerned with life in the pastoral lands and genuinely Australian in sentiment. In this aggressive Australianism and its refusal to be bound by English prejudices and attitudes, *The Bulletin* from its first issue was the voice of the growing "frontier nationalism" permeating the land. The publication had its strongest following in New South Wales but it reached out to all the hinterland; in its own words, *The Bulletin's* red cover was "equally familiar to the bushman of the Far North, the stockman of Central Australia, the pearl sheller of Torres Strait, and the digger of the New Zealand Ranges."

Lively and irreverent, with the motto "Australia for the Australians," *The Bulletin* thundered in support of many causes but reiterated the basic conviction that

> . . . a hundred years of ceaseless salaaming to the beloved motherland has inspired her [Australia] with a servile reverence for everything that affects to be English,

and that this must stop. In cheeky cartoon, witty paragraph, and hard-hitting editorial, the little newspaper was soon ridiculing the established institutions—"foreign" (i.e., English) titles, English governors, and even the Royal family (its name for the Prince of Wales was H.R.H. Tummy). It debunked the bias in history-teaching that glorified British heroics at Agincourt and Waterloo, and inveighed against Australian troops being used to fight England's Imperialist wars. Among its many hates were Chinese immigration, capital punishment, the rest of the Australian press, religious interference in politics, and the big landowners. Among the things it supported—rather fewer than its hates—were "the coming Australian Federation Republic," home rule for Ireland, Australian symbolism in art, and the sanctity of the Eureka stockade incident. While the rest of the New South Wales press was celebrating a hundred years of British settlement in Australia, *The Bulletin* claimed the day that the community ought to be celebrating was December 3, 1854, "the day that Australia set her teeth in the face of the British lion" at Eureka. Above all, *The Bulletin* called on Australians to form their own attitudes and policies not as colonial Englishmen but as Australians, and it presented them with the opportunity to express the Australian viewpoint.

Steadily a national spirit was in the making. All this time the feeling of unity had been gathering strength among Australians. As early as 1877, Scottish-born teacher-writer James Brunton Stephens, in a prophetic poem, "The Dominion of Australia," had captured the notion of federation and spoken of the presence of a spiritual force, "already here to hearts intense" which heralded the creation of a nation. In the attainment of this unity, Stephens had concluded,

> Our bounds shall be the girdling seas alone.

James Bonwick, visiting Australia a few years later, noted "a common interest gradually binding the several colonies," and he felt that a great future was "preparing for Australasia."

Writers with socialist leanings were linking ideas of the emergence of the new nation with the creation of an "ideal" unattached republic. To the English-born radical, John Norton, who found Australia's easy-going egalitarianism to his liking and became editor of the Newcastle *Morning Herald* in 1887, the portents were clear: Australia was standing "on the very threshold of a glorious career" in which nationhood and socialism would be attained together. In a review for the trade unions' ambitious *History of Capital and Labour*, published in 1888, Norton wrote:

> Milton, with prophetic precision, has unconsciously forecast Australia's future when he likens a young nation awakening to a full sense of destiny to a strong man rousing himself after sleep and to the soaring eagle mewing her mighty youth in the ethereal regions of light and liberty.

Two of the most notable poets of the day were Andrew Barton ("Banjo") Paterson and Henry Lawson. Both wrote of the bush, but their viewpoint was quite different. Paterson came from a pastoral family and attended Sydney Grammar School; the picture he drew was one of optimism. On the other hand, Lawson, the son of a poor immigrant, showed an introspection which was reinforced by his sojourns in the dry inland, with its drought and desolation and its parade of indigent bush workers and swagmen.

Paterson delighted in writing of the bushmen who "love hard riding where the wild bush horses are," and many of his verse-tales were set in the mountains and spoke of stockmen and their horses. He revelled in the friendships and the good fellowship of the bush, and although he wrote feelingly of the hardships that all had to share in pioneering the land, he rarely expressed resentment against privilege. His writing reflected the interest of the independent, struggling man pitted against Nature but not that of the embittered man struggling against a landed master. To Paterson adversity was not overwhelming—rather it was something to be accepted as part of the bush life. A warm and bland approach to the outback shone through almost everything he wrote, as in "A Bushman's Story":

> I'm travelling down the Castlereagh, and I'm a station-hand,
> I'm handy with a roping pole, I'm handy with the brand,
> And I can ride a rowdy colt, or swing the axe all day,
> But there's no demand for a station-hand along the Castlereagh.
>
> So it's shift, boys, shift, for there isn't the slightest doubt
> That we've got to make a shift to stations further out;
> With the pack-horse runnin' after, for he follows like a dog,
> We must strike across the country at the old jig-jog.

Paterson captured the excitement of bush activities in rollicking verse, as in "Shearing at Castlereagh," in which he told of shearers vying for the honour of being the "ringer".

> The man that "rung" the Tubbo shed is not the ringer here,
> That stripling from the Cooma-side can teach him how to shear.
> They turn away the ragged locks, and rip the cutter goes
> And leaves a track of snowy fleece from brisket to the nose;
> It's lovely how they peel it off with never stop or stay,
> They're racing for the ringer's place this year at Castlereagh.

He could also write feelingly of the "great, dark bush, with arms of night [that] folds every hearer in its spell" when bushmen met and campfires blazed.

In Lawson's writing, with its deep involvement with the problems of the underdog, an air of foreboding or of outright pessimism was often dominant. Influenced by the writing of Bret Harte, he showed early promise and at twenty he had his first verse published by *The Bulletin*. His approach was more penetrating than Paterson's, however, and in his hostility to privilege Lawson was closer to the prevailing mood. His visit to western New South Wales (in 1892) opened new horizons and in his subsequent writing he drew heavily upon his impressions of the back country. In his poem "Out Back" he told in his typical way of the trials faced by the landless, jobless man, as indicated by these extracts.

> The old year went, and the new returned, in the
> withering weeks of drought;
> The cheque was spent that the shearer earned, and
> the sheds were all cut out;

The publican's words were short and few, and the
  publican's looks were black—
And the time had come, as the shearer knew, to carry
  his swag Out Back.

For time means tucker, and tramp you must, where
  the scrubs and plains are wide,
With seldom a track that a man can trust, or
  a mountain peak to guide;
All day long in the dust and heat—when summer
  is on the track—
With stinted stomachs and blistered feet, they
  carry their swags Out Back.

He begged his way on the parched Paroo and the
  Warrego tracks once more,
And lived like a dog, as the swagmen do, till the
  Western stations shore;
But men were many, and sheds were full, for work
  in the town was slack—
The traveller never got hands in wool, though he
  tramped for a year Out Back.

Through his compassion and realism Lawson helped define the outlines
of the Australian ethos as it was emerging. A generation later it was being
said of his work that "all Australia is there, painted with a big brush in the
colours in which its people see it." Many of his poems had a simple lyric
quality of great beauty, and he excelled in short-story writing; in each field
he wrote of life in both city and country, and his sympathies were always
with the underdog. He was to be followed by others including Joseph Furphy
(Tom Collins) whose *Such is Life* was later to epitomize the Australian's
egalitarian approach.

Meanwhile, *The Bulletin* had begun to support a group of first-rate car-
toonists whose work of social satire reflected a strong concern with Australia's social problems. By vivid lampoon they not only launched barbed
attacks on injustice but they also reflected other *Bulletin* ideals. Thus what
Lawson and others were doing with their writings to stimulate a national
sentiment, Frank Mahony, "Hop" (Livingston Hopkins), and others furthered in black and white drawings.

By the late 1880s there were also signs of the emergence of a national
approach in landscape painting as artists began to succeed in the difficult
task of defining the Australian landscape with authenticity and insight.
Soon after Tom Roberts returned from Europe (where he had studied French
impressionists after enrolling in Royal Academy classes) he was joined by other
painters including Frederick McCubbin, Arthur Streeton, Charles Conder,
and John Longstaff, in the creation of a distinctive approach. The so-called
Heidelberg School, which over the years was to become a dominant factor

among Australian landscapists, was the outcome. Roberts' most notable paintings, "The Breakaway" and "Shearing the Rams," drew their inspiration from the picturesque life of the sheep country.

Out in the open lands, the mateship of earlier years had turned into active support for unionism by the 1880s, and many of the miners and rural workers had come under the dynamic influence of William Guthrie Spence, a trade union organizer who was convinced that "organization is the first step essential to society's salvation." Spence, who was born in the Orkney islands and came to Australia as a boy, worked from the age of twelve in the gold mines at Creswick, in Victoria, and became an effective group leader.

The first union group to be expanded under Spence's influence was the Amalgamated Miners' Association. This organization had developed from small beginnings; it came into being in 1874 when gold miners in the deep mines of Bendigo (who had formed a union in 1872) took the initiative in sponsoring the amalgamation of a dozen mining unions in Victoria. The combined organization made little progress at first, and by the late 1870s, with only a few hundred members, it was becoming inactive. Spence (who was no longer able to secure work in the mines once his union activities became known) was elected secretary of the association in 1882; immediately he set about building it into a strong body. Soon he was able to turn his attention to affiliating the group with miners' unions in the other colonies. The Newcastle coalminers' union (a strong group, with a continuous history from 1854) was affiliated in 1885, and other New South Wales miners were also absorbed. The Amalgamated Miners' Association membership quickly soared to tens of thousands; there were branches in Western Australia and Tasmania, and in New Zealand. In 1886, the silver-lead miners working at Broken Hill, their ranks increasing rapidly after the promotion of the Broken Hill Proprietary Company, joined Spence's association.

At this point Spence turned his great ability to organizing workers in the pastoral industry. Since many miners worked seasonally as shearers, he realized that it would be relatively simple to move into the new sphere even though the itinerant nature of the work added to the organizational problems. The opportunity came in 1886 when, following a fall in the price of wool and a tightening of credit, pastoralists attempted to reduce the contract rates paid for shearing from £1 to 17/6 for each hundred sheep shorn.

The shearers' grievances involved more than wage levels. The accommodation provided at shearing time was crude; Spence later said it was "something awful" and quite unfit for human beings. Mostly the quarters consisted of long draughty buildings without windows, with two or three tiers of bunks one above the other ranged around the walls and a table in the centre so that the men had to dress and undress, eat and sleep all in the one narrow hut. To men forced to live under such conditions unionism came as "a new religion."

Under the influence of part-time miners/part-time shearers, the first shearers' union was formed at Ballarat to meet the threat of reduced earnings; about the same time similar bodies were set up in the Wagga Wagga and Bourke districts of New South Wales. Spence was elected chairman of the Ballarat group and immediately set about creating an intercolonial organization, ignoring political boundaries. By January 1887 the Amalgamated Shearers' Union, with Spence as its president, had a membership of over 9,000—and the list was growing by the hundred every week. At first, station workers generally could join, but as they were somewhat reluctant to enrol, the union was made an organization for shearers exclusively. Within three or four years the organization had spread to encompass the great majority of shearers in Victoria, New South Wales, and South Australia. In 1890 membership passed 25,000. All but 400 or so of the 3,000 shearing sheds of the eastern colonies were now union sheds, and shedhands had formed a union of their own. Queensland's shearers had by this time become well unionized, but in a separate organization from that run by Spence.

Unionism had earlier gained a hold in more traditional fields, following English practice, but most of the craft unions had small memberships. Some transport workers had been organized from the early 1870s; the Federated Seamen's Union of Australasia, the first union among transport workers, had come into being in Melbourne in 1872, and two years later a similar union had been formed in Sydney; by 1876 the two groups had been loosely federated. During the 1880s, stewards and clerks, wharf labourers, trolley, and dray men in Sydney and Melbourne formed union groups. With increasing numbers of women finding employment in the clothing trade, the Tailoresses' Union was formed in Melbourne in 1882 following a strike brought about by intolerable conditions of "sweating," and very soon 3000 of the 4000 women and girls employed in the trade were enrolled.

Meanwhile intercolonial trade union congresses had been held; the first, which met in Sydney in 1879, had limited aims, but at the second, held in Melbourne in 1884, ideas had been exchanged on the possibility of creating a "federation of labour," and a committee was set up to lobby in the interests of organized labour. At subsequent congresses (Sydney, 1885 and Adelaide, 1886) increasing attention was given to a broader range of subjects. Trade unionism had become established and was consolidating; and although the numbers of unions and of unionists were still relatively small and unionism had not been widely accepted, the effectiveness of the unions was greater than enrolments might suggest. A sharp edge was given to their operation by the important nature of the unionised industries and by the very nature of the outdoorsmen as unionists.

Strengthened in their determination by a new-found feeling of solidarity, rural workers were ready to threaten strike action. The more the shearer or shedhand read, and the more the men exchanged views, the more they became convinced of the justice of the working man's cause. Political discussion among the men was unending. Newspapers arrived regularly, and often they were read aloud as groups gathered around the fire or in the summer twilight, so that even those who were unable to read were kept in touch. An Englishman, Francis Adams, observing the zeal with which the shearer kept up to date with affairs, wrote:

> At the different "sheds" at which [the shearer] works each year, in his more or less regular nomadic cycle, his letters and newspapers are awaiting him. Frequently he is party to an arrangement whereby all the papers that could possibly interest him and his friends are mutually subscribed for. Many sheds are better provided with "current literature" than town mechanics' institutes and schools of art, which are subsidized by the government. The political discussion among the men when they have "knocked off" work is perpetual, and its intelligence is yet more astonishing than its earnestness.

The Bulletin, with a growing readership, was one of the influences giving direction to the workingman's cause. Its forceful advocacy of certain issues helped give cohesion and direction to the labour movement which was now taking shape. It supported payment of salaries to parliamentarians and advocated "one person, one vote" (as a means of breaking the persistent power of upper houses), and direct taxation of land (as a means of breaking up large estates).

By this time even more radical journals—the first out-and-out working-man's newspapers—were beginning to pour out a ferment of challenging ideas and unorthodox proposals. In Queensland, the *Worker*, edited from its inception in 1890 by a Utopian Socialist, William Lane, was actively crusading for socialism and the "new unionism," while the *Hummer*, started in Wagga Wagga in 1891, became the *Worker* in 1892 and was transferred to Sydney as the forerunner of Labor party publications. Among the latter's most avid readers were the men working for the mining enterprises opening up great deposits of silver, lead, and zinc revealed in the Barrier Ranges, in the far west of New South Wales. Shallow mines along the Barrier were soon exhausted, and miners who had hoped to win quick fortunes had to content themselves with wage-paying jobs with Melbourne-backed mining companies. Similarly on Tasmania's west coast and, later, in Western Australia, there was no place for the lone prospector. Instead there were large-scale enterprises and wage-earning miners. These men were new prospects for union organizers.

Among city workers unionism generally took on a rather slower pace and followed traditional lines. Contact was maintained with British unions, and affiliations were established. More concern was shown over details of working conditions and wages and less attention given to the general problems of social reform, than among rural workers, for whom unionism was of political as well as industrial significance.

It was a time when airy ideas of a stateless society without government and without ownership of property were attracting followers in various industrial countries of Europe and in parts of the United States; poverty and degradation in many crowded cities had resulted in impulsive and deluded men coming out in support of what has been called "a daydream of desperate romantics." Conditions that produced bitterness in industrialized Europe and the United States were not present in the quiet and open grasslands of Australia, yet social tensions existed there which fed upon the writings of agitators as well as serious and constructive reformers. In the boisterous atmosphere of shearers' hut or mining town, the practical objectives of unionism and visions of social reform blended naturally and the boss *per se* was identified as the enemy of the working class.

The bush worker was unwilling to reconcile himself to a situation in which the bulk of the land was still held by the pastoralists; rather, he felt cheated. For democrats who had achieved success in the creation of legislative processes placing all effective power in the hands of the people at large, it was galling to find that political decisions could not immediately create the promised land. For the big landholder it was equally true (though perhaps less apparent to him) that the individual, no matter how much land he might possess, could not be a law unto himself. Thus the problem was to avoid anarchy on the one hand and despotism on the other. In the absence of experience establishing where the balance might be struck between land-owning employers and their awakened men, sharp differences arose.

In both Australia and New Zealand, contact with American influences in trade unionism and in social reform had been noticeably strong. Henry George's *Progress and Poverty* gained a great following in New Zealand, and in 1887 George's adherents in Auckland formed themselves into the Anti-Poverty Society. This group, which included parliamentarians, clerics and prosperous businessmen, shared sponsorship of a monthly journal with a group known as the Knights of Labor. Formed in 1887, this body grew out of a small organization of unemployed men (whose leaders affiliated with the Knights of Labor with headquarters in Philadelphia, in the United States). Various progressive bodies worked with the new group, which became the first political body to operate throughout New Zealand; the interchange of ideas it generated helped strengthen moves by unionists in Australia as well as in New Zealand in their efforts to create a workingman's party.

In its early years the shearers' union had a succession of victories and few setbacks. Sometimes with the threat of a strike, sometimes after outright strike action, favourable agreements were made with pastoralists in district after district in New South Wales and Queensland; they provided for an eight hour work day and the employment of all-union labour in the sheds. By 1889 the ascendant unionists were convinced of the unbreakable power they had won through unity. Only in Victoria's Western District were they unable to gain their way. The success had come in many cases by straightforward negotiation, but strikes were becoming more frequent, and in the three years from the foundation of the union in 1886 more strikes occurred in the pastoral industry than in all other industries combined. A trial of strength was in the making once the employers decided to make common cause, as they did in 1888 with the formation of the Australian Federation of Employers.

The shearers' gains and similar success won by the miners' union were sufficient to encourage more ambitious projects to further the working man's objectives. At the fifth Intercolonial Trades Union Congress, held in Brisbane in 1888, it was agreed that a plan should be drawn up for the creation of an Australian labour federation which would bring together all trades unions throughout the country and give central direction for both industrial and political activity. The Brisbane Trades and Labour Council was entrusted with the task of preparing the plan.

The move was an outgrowth of the new attitudes that were emerging under the influence of ideas expressed by social reformers such as Henry George and Alfred Russell Wallace, whose forecasts of impending catastrophe were making a strong impression in all English speaking countries. For many, the writings of these persuasive and earnest men showed a path leading from the liberal individualism they accepted to new socialist objectives.

Under the shaping hand of William Lane, dominant in Brisbane labour circles, a constitution for a Labor federation was developed. The proposal was for a Labor organization which would give a greater degree of unity to the trade union movement than had yet existed in any country. The federation's constitution provided that all unions were to be run by district councils but brought together in provincial (i.e., single colony) and national councils; although each union was to retain a degree of autonomy, important matters were to be decided at the national level. The 1889 Intercolonial Congress was not in favour of the proposed constitution, which it felt left too little power in the hands of the constituent unions, and accordingly the congress shelved the plan. Two years later, however, the proposal was brought forward again and this time it was adopted. Queensland unions had already fallen into line with the plan and by 1890 the unions of six districts of that colony had federated under the original title of the Australian Labor Federation. The Federation was never to function on a nation-wide scale, however.

By this time many streams of thought were affecting the Australian labour movement. As well as the writings of Wallace and George (who visited Sydney in 1890 and impressed even Henry Parkes), books by Laurence Gronlund, Sidney Webb, and Edward Bellamy were shaping thoughts on the need for social justice.

George's followers, the "single taxers"—who, as well as running their own newspaper, had their own independent political party by 1889—were among the strongest influences behind the new party; they provided one member of the three-man constitution-writing committee. Bellamy's views had also made a deep impression; hundreds of copies of *Looking Backward* had been bought by Spence's union and distributed to members, and the book had appeared as a serial in Lane's *Worker*. The stark picture Bellamy painted of contemporary society was horrifying, though he placed the blame on the system, not individuals. His beguiling story showed that all this could be corrected if the government would move in and take over all property and direct all human activity. He set the goal of a benign but all-powerful state—the cooperative commonwealth—to which all would contribute skill, energy, and work according to individual ability, and under which all would be cared for, each drawing equally since those unable to work were deserving of the full right to live on the produce of those who could. Bellamy's belief in the essential dignity of labour shone throughout his writing. His idealism was stated in the proposition that the title of every man, woman, and child to the means of existence "rests on no basis less plain, broad and simple than the fact that they are fellows of one race—members of one human family." He sought to show how all the social, ethical, political and economic problems of the day could be solved and a true government of, by, and for the people introduced through a peaceful, evolutionary, legal process, and maintained that once all means of production and distribution had been taken over by the state, unemployment, panics, depressions, and labour-capital conflicts would vanish.

Sentiments allied to Bellamy's were echoed in the trade union newspapers going out to bush and city workers. To many unionists, however, direct action seemed to be the only way to gain immediate ends, and theories of gradualism slipped steadily in to the background, while increasingly violent action was taken by unionists in support of their cause.

Social idealism was to the fore in the political programme which the first general council of the labour body in Queensland adopted in 1890. The preamble obviously owed much to Bellamy's views: it described competitive society as one in which the wealth of the few was constantly increasing while the poverty of the many was becoming ever deeper, and said that inevitably under such a system good times were followed by depression. The lives of the mass of the people could not be improved, it went on, until the existing system had been replaced. Accordingly the aims of the Federation were to include the nationalization of the means of production and exchange, as well as welfare provision for children, the invalid, and the aged.

Before the programme could be adopted on a wider scale, new forces had been unleashed. Early in 1890 the Queensland labour group had given notice to the pastoralists that only wool shorn under union conditions would be handled and shipped, and a conference between unionists and employers had been sought so that an agreement binding on the whole industry might be reached. The Pastoralists' Union—the organization that was now in control of negotiations on the graziers' behalf—rejected the request for a meeting and instead countered the union claim by asserting the principle of freedom-of-contract in their employment of labour. In reply, the Labor federation at once organized a boycott, and when wool shorn by non-union labour arrived in Brisbane the wharf labourers refused to handle it. Temporarily thwarted, the pastoralists accepted a conference and at it they agreed to the union terms, which included a clause stating that the graziers would employ only unionist shearers.

It seemed like another victory for unionism—but the pastoralists, by now deeply concerned over their shrinking wool cheques and alarmed at the tightening grip of the unions, had already agreed among themselves to set up a national federation in order to counter the unions in their demands.

A major clash was now inevitable, and both the men and the employers were well organized for it.

A great gulf separated the two sides. From the employers' viewpoint the issue was simple: it was freedom-of-contract. This principle cut across the recognition of unionism as understood by unionists, who believed that they had the right to form a union and to set down its rules (including the rule that unionists would not work with non-unionists), and that Labor organizations had the right to affiliate with one another. By mid-1890 the pastoral workers of eastern Australia were convinced that the employers were organizing to break the unions; a manifesto was issued calling on "united Labor" to accept the challenge and "settle once and forever the question of the right to unite for mutual benefit and the protection of the rights of Labor," and declaring that a cordon of unionism would be thrown around the continent to prevent shipment of any non-union wool.

In August, Spence and the shearers' assistant secretary met the pastoralists of the Upper Hunter valley, but the conference got nowhere; Spence's terms were "scornfully rejected" by the graziers' chosen negotiator, as the pastoralists' spokesman noted. The issues were left unsolved.

The centre of interest now shifted from the shearers to the seamen. Issue was joined in August 1890 when an association of mercantile marine officers decided to affiliate with the Trades Hall Council in Melbourne (which had been organized under that name for nearly twenty years). The shipowners took exception to officers belonging to the same organization as seamen on the grounds that difficult questions of discipline would arise, and they refused to sanction the affiliation. For their part, the marine officers' and the seamen's groups considered this refusal a denial of their rights of association. Furthermore, notices had been posted on the wharves calling for men to load wool from non-union sheds. Quickly wharf labourers and coal handlers were on strike. At this point the marine officers' decision to persist with the affiliation brought the threat of dismissal from the shipowners. The officers retaliated by resigning instead, and the seamen decided to go on strike as a gesture of solidarity. Strike-breakers were brought in by the shipowners, but this only widened and intensified the conflict. Coal miners went on strike in sympathy with transport unions. Tens of thousands of men were now involved.

As *The Bulletin* noted, "an undisputed rallying and mustering of forces" on both sides now took place. The employers formed an intercolonial committee (including representatives from New Zealand) and set up headquarters at the Sydney Chamber of Commerce, to plan and execute strategy on their behalf. For their part, the trade unionists drew closer, setting up an intercolonial committee with Spence as secretary. When the union committee ordered the shearers to cease work, Spence—always the realist as well as the visionary—was one of only two men to vote in the committee in opposition, but there was a strong determination among members of the shearers' union to enforce the union form of agreement in all sheds.

The unionists were confident of victory; but the employers were equally determined, and they had many factors in their favour. In spite of the shearers' boasts that without them there would be insufficient skilled labour available, unemployed men in the cities were only too anxious to step in, while employers were quite prepared to overlook the non-unionists' short-comings. Non-union labour was used increasingly, often with the protection of troops and police. The *Worker* declared on November 1, 1890:

> Unorganized labour broke the strike and not only unorganized labour but unskilled labour. Men who in ordinary times would have been considered unfit by shipowners, unions, and shipping offices, have manned the companies' fleets and been winked at by the law; raw lads have worked on the wharves and drunken boozers have been at a premium.

Union resistance was broken piecemeal, at place after place. By early November the last of the holdouts (miners at Newcastle) had returned to work.

It was no more than an uneasy truce. The employers' organizations were being strengthened. The next phase of the struggle centred in Queensland. Late in 1890 the pastoralists' organizations of New South Wales, Victoria, South Australia, and Queensland, meeting at an intercolonial conference, decided upon the form of shearing agreement they would offer for the coming season. It gave no undertaking on union labour, nor on hours of work. The graziers now had a publication to represent their viewpoint, *The Australasian Pastoralists' Review*, and it berated the unionists for their "bullying tactics." The struggle, the journal admitted, was one of employers versus trade unionists, but

> ... the employers have been compelled to enter the campaign simply by the instinct of self-preservation. They have been goaded by the aggressiveness of certain agitators to take up the cudgels and make a stand for liberty. To have attempted this individually would have been a hopeless task.

The union leaders' ultimate aim was seen by the journal as enrolling all labour so that a "ring" might be established to dictate to employers what terms it chose.

Immediately the new season opened non-union labour was gathered from the southern colonies for the early shearing in the central districts of Queensland; union picketing of stations against the free labour began. It was ineffectual, however. Troops and police were sent in by the government as protection, and among the non-union shearers were many who were armed and registered as special constables; against this force, the unionists were helpless—yet they still refused to accept work on the station owners' terms. Instead, they massed in a score of camps, the largest, with more than a thousand men, at Barcaldine. Some of the men in the great camp were armed; there was heady talk of using force if necessary; a blue flag with the Southern Cross picked out in white stars was flown as a reminder of the old Eureka episode. Members of the strike committee at Barcaldine and at Clermont (another shearers' camp) were arrested and charged under an act of George IV (which had been repealed in Britain but not in Queensland) with unlawful assemblage, riot and tumult, and other offences When the men were acquitted they were rearrested on charges related to conspiracy, and twelve men were convicted and sentenced to three years' imprisonment.

There were plenty of unemployed men to draw upon—more than ever as economic conditions hardened further with greater financial stringency in the cities and deepening drought in the sheep lands. Spence wrote later that "all sorts of characters were raked up out of city slums to fill the place of unionists."

In August 1891 a conference took place between the pastoralists and the shearers—this one with the graziers' representative in the chair—at which Spence finally accepted the principle of freedom-of-contract and the right of non-union shearers to work side by side with unionists. The victory was taken by the *Pastoralists' Review* to exemplify "the powerful effect of the sturdy combination of pastoralists" after one year of unity. The terms accepted at the conference by the "previously belligerent" Spence were taken to show any apathetic sheepowners the value of the organization and to underscore the necessity for keeping it alive and strong.

For the unionists the position became steadily grimmer. A lockout had followed when miners at Broken Hill voted in favour of subscribing to the Labor defence committee's fund in support of strikers and tension remained. Disputes in the Barrier mines reached a climax in 1892, when the mining companies' association notified the union that the uniform day wage would be abolished. The unionists walked out—only to find their places taken by non-unionists, who had military and police protection. The strike was called off in November 1892, but the Amalgamated Miners' Association never regained its hold for its Barrier membership fell to about 300, or only a tenth of what it was in pre-strike days.

A running battle between bush workers and pastoralists continued in spite of the general settlement that had been reached; a truce had not yet been called in the great struggle. A dramatic incident in the final phase was the burning on the River Darling of the paddle-steamer *Rodney*, on its way from Echuca with a group of non-unionists headed for Darling stations in 1894. The steamer was moored overnight at a small island in a reedy swamp; before dawn a dozen unionists with their clothing turned inside out, and face, head, and hair plastered with mud for disguise, waded to the *Rodney's* side, and in a few minutes they took over the craft. The men aboard were hustled ashore without harm, after which the unionists set fire to the boat. The perpetrators escaped detection and were never apprehended.

One of the factors that delayed a settlement of the shearer-grazier dispute —and an important factor in the unionists' defeat—was the "reference system" which the pastoralists introduced when they began to engage men through special recruitment offices. The so-called references issued by employers to the non-union men were often far more effective in getting a shearer a job than a union ticket since many graziers refused to employ a man without a "reference." Early in 1894 Spence met the organized pastoralists in the hope of getting them to drop their hated reference system, but his efforts were of no avail. The graziers had already won the day.

For all their solidarity and dedication to their cause, the unionists could not match the strength or resources of the forces ranged against them. Their hopes for outside support for their cause were dashed. The unionists had believed that their actions were legal and that they had the right of protection under the laws; but a decisive factor was that governments protected property and the non-unionist's right to work. A sardonic comment on the attitude of governments was made by *The Bulletin* in reply to a statement in the Sydney *Daily Telegraph* that not one government of any Australian colony had taken even "the smallest action" during the progress of the strikes on one side or the other; *The Bulletin* replied:

> Of course not. The governments' gatling guns have always equally been at the disposal of the unionist shearer as of the unionist pastoralists—the only monotonous peculiarity being that the muzzles were always pointed at the shearers while the breeches were the exclusive property of the pastoralists.

In fact, however, the governments generally had done no more than preserve the rights of private property and the right of owners to employ whom they chose. The only colony where a pro-Labor attitude was enforced was South Australia; here the political atmosphere tended to favour the strikers. Charles Cameron Kingston, a Liberal of persuasive power (he was Attorney-General in the colony 1884–85, Chief Secretary in 1892, and Premier 1893–99) declared early in 1891 that "the last strike was provoked and continued by the masters." Throughout, the South Australian Government refused to bring out the military.

The unions themselves had been badly shaken by the prolonged industrial struggle and its outcome. Reconstruction was called for, particularly among the rural unions. In 1893 the powerful Australian Workers' Union was formed from the former Shearers' Union and shedhands' organizations. It brought together shearers, shedhands, and other rural workers in New South Wales, Victoria, South Australia, and New Zealand. Later it was joined by the Queensland Shearers' Union, so that its 50,000 members were spread through most of the colonies.

Largely influenced by New Zealand attitudes, emphasis was henceforth placed by Labor men and unionists on the merits of compulsory negotiation as a means of solving industrial disputes. However, it was some time before success could be achieved in the creation of machinery to carry out this objective.

Utopian socialism had its final fling when a group of ardent supporters of William Lane joined him in the founding of a settlement in South America in 1893. Lane, convinced that socialism was not possible in the existing state of society in Australia, had founded the New Australia Cooperative Settlement Association, with the object of creating a society based on "communal ownership and control of the means of production, distribution, and exchange." The outcome was a settlement in the wilds of Paraguay. The government of Paraguay had constituted New Australia a separate region, and Lane and his ardent followers sailed with high hopes. The rules for the settlement's operation were elaborately set forth, but the altruistic experiment under Lane's administration failed dismally. There was disunity from the beginning and this increased when a second group arrived from Australia. Disagreement on the essentials of a cooperative community proved too strong, and even Lane had to admit defeat. He left in 1899 to return to Australia, and soon the settlement disintegrated.

The failure of the strikes had demonstrated that the unionist was unable to impose his will on the community through industrial action alone. The need for unified political action had emerged even earlier. A start had been made on the creation of a political party in 1890. In Queensland, the *Worker*, edited by William Lane, urged the use of the ballot box as a solution for unionists' problems; in New South Wales the Sydney *Worker* carried the crusade for a Labor political federation to its dedicated readers. The division between men and employers, between union and authority, had sharpened into a class-conscious struggle. The attempt to achieve industrial objectives had failed, and it remained for political action to be developed out of the common sense of grievance. Trade unionism became the starting point for political action. Payment of members (which spread from Victoria to all other colonies except Western Australia by 1890) had made it feasible for working men to run for parliament. It was argued that if men gave their vote to a candidate they had selected, and if he were pledged to set policies, their will would surely prevail.

A plaintive call to the workers to exercise their rights to vote came after the Barcaldine arrests, made under the Riot Act of George IV, in a sardonic poem signed by W. Kidston which was circulating among the shearers in Queensland and elsewhere. It ran, in part:

Oh comrades dear! and did you hear the news that's going round:
The shearer is by law debarred to tent on camping ground.
Unto the chain-gang's clank again Australia's woods shall ring
For they have found a law made when George the Fourth was king.
It makes the Squatters sing, oh, it makes the Squatters sing!
This vile old law that once was made when George the Fourth
was king.

Then keep your heads I say, my boys; your comrades in the town
Will help you yet to win a vote and put your tyrants down.
Throw your old guns aside, my boys, the ballot is the thing
They did not have to reckon with when George the Fourth was king.
The ballot is the thing, boys, the ballot is the thing.
We'll show these men how long it is since George the Fourth was king.

In fact, however, most of the shearers, as itinerants, were voteless. Another stumbling block in some colonies was electoral laws which provided for plural voting. *The Bulletin* attacking a "political system where the man owing to residential qualifications, possesses less voting power than an unimproved allotment of stony earth," urged trade unionists to give first attention to constitutional reform and, particularly, to abolition of plural voting. In August 1890, on the eve of the first great strike, *The Bulletin* had written:

At the present time the mere people are deluded and fooled by a spurious "manhood suffrage." Every man has a vote but a particular class of man has several votes. . . When it is considered that there are men who possess property votes in as many as 30 different constituencies, it will be comprehended that even five thousand men of the employer class in the metropolis may be in a position to counterbalance the direct political power of all the trade unions in the colony. The very first step therefore that Trades Unionists and their sympathizers should take . . . should be to concentrate all their political energies upon securing the passing of a bill to abolish plural voting.

The Intercolonial Trade Union Congress of 1891 decided to organize politically on a national scale, and a plan was prepared for the selection of men to run as Labor candidates. A series of questions had to be answered by each candidate, and local committees were to decide upon the suitability of the candidates for endorsement. Out of this came Labor's first platform and basic party structure.

In practice the party was organized by independent action in various colonies. In New South Wales the Sydney Trades and Labour Council moved to create the Labor Electoral League, which had a branch in each electorate; it was open to all who subscribed to its tenets. The timing and the length of the period required for the creation of a party structure varied from colony to colony, but sooner or later the same issues came to the fore and broadly the same solutions were found as Labor moved from pressure group to political party.

With the decision to form a separate political party instead of merely supporting individual members of parliament—Labor members were pledged to sit as a group on the parliamentary cross benches—came a determination to build a better world. The sharpened conflict represented a clear break with older methods and ideas. There could be no mistaking the fact that many in the party were determined to produce changes in the existing social structure. How far those changes should go was a matter of opinion, and among the unionist politicians there were many views. The *Sydney Morning Herald* declared that the New South Wales Labor platform of 1891 embodied a new creed, if indeed it did not proclaim a new gospel.

In spite of the setbacks their cause had suffered, bush workers generally retained all their earlier enthusiasm and loyalty to the principles of Labor. There were endless instances of the devotion shown the cause; men were prepared to make sacrifices to support their chosen candidate. In one instance noted by Spence, some eighty men eligible to vote found that the nearest polling place was 80 miles from their work; they mustered horses, made the trip to record their votes for the Labor candidate, and rode the 80 miles back.

The carry-over of enthusiasm from the trade union organization was one element in the rapid rise of the Labor party in the eastern colonies. The party brought together both those who were interested primarily in doctrine and those who insisted on action; yet among the more capable and realistic, the emphasis was on social reform rather than social reconstruction. The slogan, Socialism in Our Time, most nearly defined the objective—a doctrinal influence that owed most perhaps to Bellamy's Utopian solutions to problems of mankind. Writings of philosophical radicals, land nationalizers and social reformers had been read by the men shaping the new party, and their influence had permeated. Various aspects of Labor's plan were drawn from different sources; yet a broad common ideal drew together the men who founded the party, and it was accepted that diversities of belief could be resolved through the commonsense and judgment of the party membership. Included in the party's constitution was acceptance of the principle that "one collective membership is sovereign." This meant that decisions were to be taken by majority vote, and that all party members must abide by a decision once taken.

The points laid down in the New South Wales Labor league's platform of 1891 stressed matters related directly to protective legislation for the working man and woman. The objective on which all were determined was to "secure for the wage-earner a fair and equitable return for his or her labour." However, broader implications were to be drawn, and many members stressed the need for the party to introduce some fundamental changes. *The Bulletin* wrote with enthusiasm about Labor's desire "to wipe out the great act and swindle of politics," and saw the main objectives in general terms. *The Bulletin* declared

> . . . Labor wants co-operation in place of capitalism, national insurance [instead] of relief works and benevolent asylums, [and] a universal eight hours system.

A little later, a Socialist publicist expressed the same concept in the *Hummer* in this naive, sentimental way:

> Socialism . . . is the desire to be mates, the ideal of living together in harmony and brotherhood and loving kindness; and socialist writers agree in holding that this desire for harmony, for brotherhood, cannot have free play as long as some men, practically monopolizing the means of living, deny to other men the right to live. They say, and I say, that the workers must own cooperatively, that is, in common between them, the land and machinery used in producing wealth, and must arrange themselves for working, and must divide fairly the wealth produced . . . Those who cannot work should share with us, because they are our mates just the same, and because we'd be pretty low down if we'd see our mates sick or crippled or helpless and not stand by them.

Electorally, Labor party candidates had immediate and remarkable success. Thirty-six out of forty-five Labor candidates won seats in the New South Wales Legislative Assembly in 1891. One resigned from the new party at its first meeting but the remaining thirty-five held the balance of power in the Legislative Assembly of one hundred and forty-four members. Their effectiveness was lessened by divisions within the party—differences aroused particularly by the issue of "solidarity," or majority rule within the party. In November 1893, a conference decided that "only those men will be accepted as Labor candidates who can consistently pledge themselves to put the Labor platform before everything else." The conference threatened repudiation by all Labor bodies of any man "turning from the straight path" laid down whenever a question affecting the life of a government might arise in a colonial parliament.

Labor's "solidarity" represented something new in Australian politics; it was closely linked with trade union principles with their basic emphasis on presenting a united front. Labor introduced a much more thorough degree of political organization than any earlier political party or pressure group had achieved. In this, too, unionism and political Labor were interwoven; expenses to take speakers to Labor's public meetings and to party conferences were usually met from union funds. Agents were appointed in country towns wherever possible. By putting forward a "platform" setting down a series of points (or "planks") for which it stood, Labor gained a degree of cohesion. Not only were pledges demanded of all candidates, but candidates were chosen with care so that they might truly reflect the views of those supporting them and voting for them.

In the various colonies, political reform, including reform or abolition of the legislative council, was a prominent feature in the party platform; other demands were for restrictions on immigration, and arbitration of industrial issues. The New South Wales platform of 1891 had sixteen "planks," with the first one, electoral reform, covering almost a dozen different aspects, such as the abolition of plural voting, and extension of the franchise to seamen, shearers, and general labourers, by the registration of voters. Repeal of the Masters and Servants Act was also prominent, and the need for a "fair and equitable return" for labour was stressed. Three years later the platform was revised and made more practical; it was reduced to cover only six points.

The objectives of Labor in Queensland (as stated late in 1892) placed emphasis on electoral reform and improved working conditions. There was not the same need for electoral reform or social legislation in South Australia, where the Labor party sought to have the franchise extended to all adult women, and advocated tariff protection "for the purpose of encouraging local industries." In Western Australia, Labor-minded miners provided some strength to the party, which was formed in 1896, and objectives included conciliation and arbitration laws, and payment of members of parliament.

In Victoria, as in South Australia, many of the points the other Labor parties were asking for had already been granted; thus the early development of liberalism in the two southern colonies tended to blunt Labor's early drive there. However, Victoria, with the oldest Labor representation tradition of any colony, had returned two men of Labor persuasion in 1889; in 1892, when "political leagues" were organized, ten Labor men were returned in a lower house of ninety, and eight Labor candidates were returned to the South Australian Assembly in 1893. In Queensland, where local leagues operated from 1891, four Labor candidates were returned in 1892 and sixteen in 1893.

After Labor men undertook above all to support the party platform (the 1894 pledge) and in so doing to forgo their old allegiances as free-traders or protectionists, the party gained new strength in the colonies in which it was active. It held the balance of power in the New South Wales Legislative Assembly for considerable periods in the 1890s and was able to gain major concessions as a result. With George Reid as premier, many of the party's objectives were carried into effect. Taxes were levied on land and incomes; the electoral act was amended to reduce the period of residence in a constituency required as qualification for the franchise; mining regulations were tightened up; a nine-hour work day was established as the legal maximum, and a Factory and Shops Act was passed enforcing protection of workers from dangerous machinery and fixing maximum hours for the employment of children in factories. In addition, restrictions on immigrant Chinese were extended to all coloured races (except American Negroes).

All this was done in the face of a hostile legislative council. Conservative elements in the council led a fight to reduce some earlier concessions, and succeeded in frustrating attempts to secure legislation for the early closing of shops, and compulsory arbitration in industrial disputes, as well as for probate duties.

A switch of Labor allegiance from Reid to the opposition leader, William Lyne, took place when Lyne promised the Labor party that he would fight more actively against the legislative council's stand-fast tactics on measures relating to working conditions. Under Lyne's premiership, the council no longer obstructed the early-closing legislation; an act was passed for six o'clock closing of shops on four evenings a week, ten o'clock on one night, and one o'clock closing on Saturday afternoon. Probate duties were increased, and a plan for compensation covering mining accident injuries introduced. Legal machinery for an arbitration system was delayed until 1901, when Labor assumed office in its own right.

Under pressure from Labor, minimum-wage laws were introduced in Victoria in 1896 to apply in six trades (baking, bootmaking, furniture-making, men's and boys' clothing and underclothing). Two years later, the law was extended to include some other city trades and provision was made for the appointment of a special board with the function of fixing the minimum rate of pay and the maximum number of working hours in any other industry. The English Socialist writers Sidney and Beatrice Webb (who visited Melbourne in 1898) noted in the preface to *Industrial Democracy* that when the employers found themselves compelled to pay a standard wage to all, they increased efficiency by making labour as productive as possible and introducing new processes and machinery. The Webbs found the Victorian law "by no means perfect" (largely because it was evaded or disobeyed in particular cases), but at the same time they considered that the system whereby impartial factory inspectors enforced the common rule was in fact "a distinct advance on the anarchic private war to which the settlement of the conditions of employment is otherwise abandoned."

Towards   16
nationhood

After self-government was granted to the colonies, London remained responsible for their external relationships and their defence. The continuing protection afforded by the Royal Navy removed any danger of encroachment, and remoteness provided its own effective screen of security; but as time went on isolation was seen less as a shield and more as a danger. The colonial populations were so small—and the area they occupied so large—that the colonists were extremely sensitive to the threat, as they saw it, posed when European powers began to show overt interest in the southwest Pacific. This apprehension over foreign "intrusion" was in turn to act as an important stimulus in building a greater sense of unity among the colonies.

From the earliest days of Australia's settlement, the scope of British claims in the islands of the south Pacific had been vague. From time to time governors in Sydney sought clarification of the position, but London showed no inclination to extend sovereignty to take in any of the islands. The War of 1812 brought the first United States ship of war into the Pacific, but although the American flag was raised in the Marquesas by its captain in 1813, no territorial claims followed. As more ships were engaged in the search for whales and in sealing, islands ranging far and wide south of the Equator and variously populated by Polynesian and Melanesian groups, were visited more frequently. Already ships' deserters—and some runaway convicts—had established themselves as beachcombers in some places. In 1817 all the unattached islands were brought under the provision of a British law which dealt with them as no-man's lands; the islands were considered as being part of the high seas and henceforth British subjects committing crimes on them were subject to trial under British law. Fundamental responsibility for law and order remained with the islanders under the theory of "native sovereignty."

This may have detached the far-flung islands in a legal sense; but soon random contacts were increasing as growing interest in the South Seas resulted in important voyages of scientific investigation being undertaken by various nations. One of the earliest of these was the expedition under the Russian Admiral Fabian Bellingshausen in 1819–21; after him came the Frenchman Dumont d'Urville (in 1826–29 and again in 1837–41), and the English Captain Robert Fitzroy who in 1835 crossed the south Pacific in H.M.S. *Beagle*. Calls by foreign vessels were made more frequently at Sydney and Hobart, both of which had developed as important centres for whaling and sealing operations over large areas of the Pacific.

Even though Americans largely dominated whaling activities, theirs was a restricted, largely commercial interest and it did not affect the general acceptance of Britain's position of superiority in the south Pacific. A Royal Navy vessel for service in the waters of New South Wales arrived in 1821 and, later, ships from the British naval station on the west coast of South America were used on occasional visits to the scattered islands. Already Protestant missionaries, some sent direct from London and others from Sydney, were active. Generally the missionaries welcomed the visits of the British vessels as support for their efforts to deal with "difficult" islanders and heedless white men. The islanders were being taught English by the missionaries, and brought into touch with English ways. The missionaries, many of whom were trained as artisans rather than clerics, introduced trading concepts and often they were openly associated with trading activities. They believed it was important to convert the islanders to Christianity and indoctrinate them with the concept of work and the returns it might bring. Accordingly they set them tasks in gathering arrowroot and coconuts for trade.

At first the English or Scottish or Australian missionaries had generally favoured no more than token protection while they went about the work of converting the islanders and introducing them to new ways and new social values. They could not remain unconcerned, however, when French Catholic missionary groups appeared as a rival force. The clash of religion reinforced their belief that France's imperial causes were being furthered, and fears on this score were substantiated as the French government was obviously anxious to protect and advance the Catholic cause in the islands.

London showed no inclination to take over any of the south Pacific islands, even though by the 1850s the occasional visits of explorers and the subsequent sporadic contact by sealers and whalers or by those gathering bêche-de-mer, or pearlshell, or fragrant sandalwood had grown into regular trading calls and resident traders were establishing themselves. With the attainment of self-government, however, the Australian colonists had reason to interest themselves in the political future of the islands. Following the introduction of tropical agriculture to the islands and in Queensland on the plantation system, involving use of transplanted native labour, that interest was to grow into direct involvement.

From the earliest days of settlement there had been concern among colonial officials about French intentions, and these were never quite calmed.

There were signs of a definite revival of French interest in the area after the accession of Louis Philippe (1830–48) when new French colonizing activities began in Africa and elsewhere. The possibility of active trade being developed in the south Pacific was linked in French minds with the idea that a canal could be cut across the isthmus of Panama—a project that had been attracting attention for some years in France as well as in the United States— and this led the French to think in terms of acquiring stepping stones across the south Pacific to Australia and New Zealand. France declared protectorates over the Society Islands, including Tahiti and the Marquesas, in 1842.

The next French move was much closer to Australia's shores. In contention was the island of New Caledonia (on which Bougainville had been the first to land). From the early 1840s, sandalwood had drawn occasional "gatherers" and traders to New Caledonia and the neighbouring Isle of Pines, but the ferocious Melanesian inhabitants had struck down (and eaten) members of various crews, both French and Australian. French Catholic missionaries faced the challenge and established themselves on the islands by the mid-1840s, and a French exploring expedition in the 1850s surveyed New Caledonia's coast and penetrated the interior. On assuming power, Napoleon III reasoned that the British government had no intention of taking over the group and would accept (although, perhaps, grudgingly) a French move to assume sovereignty. Orders were sent out to French naval commanders to proceed accordingly. In September 1853 New Caledonia (with its outlying islands) was annexed. At the neighbouring Isle of Pines the French commander found a British naval expedition on hand, but the influence of the missionaries proved decisive: the islanders gave their support to the French, and the annexation was carried through.

Even if England, firmly allied with France against Russia, was in no position to resist the incursion into the area, France's imperialist designs were not overlooked in the Australian colonies or in New Zealand. The annexation was hotly resented in Sydney. Australian traders continued to operate in New Caledonia, drawing off such exports as became available—sandalwood, coconut oil, and a few sea products.

As the French grip tightened on New Caledonia, however, the new situation began to arouse concern with the weakness of Australia's defence. When he spoke in the New South Wales Legislative Assembly in December 1859 to urge establishment of a national militia, Henry Parkes, then an independent member, declared:

> We know no power in the world has greater means than France has of providing the necessary forces for a successful attack upon the Australian colonies; nor is there any other power so well protected in the Australian seas, as she always has the convenience for a hostile force in a port as contiguous to our shores as an enemy could wish it to be . . . France has [in the harbour of New Caledonia] a port of refuge within a very few days' sail from our own harbour—a port of refuge which I am given to understand is so well protected by forts that it would be almost impossible to follow vessels into the harbour.

In spite of London's mild response to events in New Caledonia, concern in Sydney remained strong. Another wave of apprehension came after New Caledonia was designated as a place to which convicts might be transported from France and, in 1864, the first transportees reached the island. Most of France's long-term political prisoners were sent there, and stories of the horrors of the notorious penal system spread as escapees found their way to Australia. In all, about 100,000 prisoners were transported from French jails over thirty years; at the peak there were about 7,000 convicts in New Caledonia. In the Australian colonies, particularly those where the stigma of the old convict system was still remembered, the consolidation of a large-scale foreign penal colony near by became a matter of deep concern. But nothing could be done to correct the situation; foreign affairs were not the responsibility of the colonies.

Apprehension was also aroused by Germany's entry into the area. This began in 1856, when a representative of a great Hamburg trading and shipping firm, J.C. Godeffroy und Sohn, arrived in Samoa, where a British consul and a commercial agent of the United States were already stationed. The Hamburg firm had a world-wide trade; its first incursion into the Pacific had been made in 1845 when a trial cargo was sent to the Marquesas and Hawaii, and this was followed by shipments to California and to the Victorian goldfields in the 1850s. The firm's representative visited Tonga, Fiji, and the Carolines, as well as Samoa, and chose Apia as the most suitable place for the agency. By 1860 British and American ships in Apia harbour were outnumbered by those of the Hamburg company, which was soon setting up commercial ventures in other Pacific islands. In 1861 a consul for the free city of Hamburg was appointed in Apia; he was Theodor Weber, an energetic and capable administrator who took charge of Godeffroy's commercial operations in the whole area in 1864. By 1871 Weber (now consul for the North Germanic Confederation) had extended the firm's trading business far and wide to the central and western Pacific, including the Fiji islands, Tonga, Niue and the Tokelaus, Wallis and Fortuna, the Gilberts and the Ellice group, New Britain and the New Hebrides, Nauru, the northern Solomons, and the Marshalls, Carolines, and Marianas. Apia was by now a staging point for trade with many islands in pearlshell, tortoiseshell, and coconut products. Weber had developed the idea of collecting dried coconut, or copra, and sending it to Europe for extraction of the oil there. A ship called at the various islands, picked up material collected by the chief or his representatives, and took it to the central station for transhipment to Europe in larger vessels.

The spread of German commercial activity coincided with the emergence of Prussian military might on the European continent in the 1860s. While the Prussian Chancellor, Otto von Bismarck, schemed the schemes and fought the wars from which came a united Germany under Prussian leadership, Weber in Samoa was preparing a comprehensive plan for German trade and colonization in the Pacific. Weber's plan was not carried fully into effect; instead the Franco-Prussian war of 1870 brought about a curtailment of the Godeffroy operations. However, Weber had already started the first coconut plantations in Samoa; and while waiting the eight years required for the palms to come to harvest he had planted cotton as a cash crop.

The coming of the planter to the south Pacific islands was a significant development. It opened the way for agricultural exploitation, which in turn established a new relationship between the European and the islander and in most cases led quickly to colonization and annexation.

Plantations were begun in the Fiji islands in 1864 as a result of the disruption of the cotton trade arising from the civil war in America. British influence had begun in Fiji with the arrival of missionaries in the 1830s. Tribal wars had continued intermittently until in 1858 the first British consul arrived and made peace between the tribal factions. The foremost chief was Thakombau, who was recognized by the various foreign powers as king; but his power was limited and no effective native government had been established. When a group of Americans claimed £9,000 damages from Thakombau and the demand for payment was backed by the United States government, the chieftain (who had been converted to Christianity) offered in 1858 to cede the islands to Britain in return for payment of the indemnity. The British government, with an expensive Maori war in New Zealand on its hands, wanted no more commitments in the south Pacific, and declined. However, affairs in Fiji had assumed a new urgency. Encouraged by a rumour that a large-scale cotton growing industry was to be established, settlers were moving in, without waiting for a British protectorate to be set up; they were mainly from Australia and New Zealand but included British, Americans, and Germans. When the Fiji islanders refused to accept the jobs the settlers offered them, the planters began in 1864 to import labourers, mainly from the New Hebrides. After repeated attempts to form some sort of regular government had failed, the question of Fiji's future came up again a few years later. Australian interest in Fiji was growing all the time, and the idea of annexing the islands had been gaining support. An English visitor to Victoria was surprised to find how much attention "the Feejee Islands" were attracting there. He wrote:

> Though of small extent, and peopled by not the most agreeable of savages, they offer singularly brilliant prospects for cotton growers; and the more enthusiastic Melbournites have already started the idea of planting there a Victorian colony; while, among the men of Sydney, are some who look forward to the profitable annexation of these fertile islands.

An intercolonial conference in Melbourne in 1870 passed a resolution in favour of Britain's assumption of sovereignty, but London again refused to act.

In 1872 the local leaders in Fiji agreed to offer a protectorate over the islands to Germany; this time it was Bismarck who declined.

The confusion into which Fiji was falling and the problem of the trade in labourers forced the British's government's hand. In 1872 the Pacific Islanders Protection Act was passed, limiting the transportation of native labourers in British vessels to those specially licensed for the purpose. This was inadequate to curb the "blackbirding" (kidnapping of islanders for use as plantation labourers) and in 1873 the Colonial Secretary, Lord

Kimberley, ordered a full inquiry; his instructions expressed the government viewpoint. He wrote:

> Her Majesty's government is not only far from desiring any increase of British territory, but would regard the extension of British sovereignty to Fiji as a measure which could in no case be adopted unless it were proved to be the only means of escape from evils for which this country might be justly held to be bound to provide an adequate remedy.

In August 1873 the British consul and the squadron commander stationed in Fiji were instructed to investigate and report on the matter. This report recommended annexation as the only realistic course; the alternative was said to be ruin and confusion. Disraeli had meanwhile become Prime Minister, and he had no qualms about extension of empire. In March 1874 a preliminary agreement was reached with the chieftains for handing over the sovereignty of the islands; certain terms were left for negotiation until Sir Hercules Robinson, newly-appointed Governor of New South Wales, took office a few months later. Under the charter drawn up in October 1874, the islands became a British colony.

Shortly after the annexation, a new act replaced the Pacific Islanders Protection Act of 1872. The 1875 Act reaffirmed British jurisdiction over British subjects in the islands of the Pacific not within the Queen's dominions nor within the jurisdiction of any civilized power; it also set up the office of High Commissioner and a court of justice. Fiji was made the headquarters and in June 1875 Sir Arthur Gordon took up duties as first governor of the islands and High Commissioner of the Western Pacific.

From this point, the political situation in the south Pacific changed radically as practically all the unattached islands of any consequence were absorbed by European powers. The vigorous trading policy initiated by Weber on Germany's behalf had resulted in various treaties being signed in the 1870s. In 1876 Germany concluded a treaty of friendship with Tonga, gaining most-favoured-nation treatment. Three years later a treaty with the Samoans granted the Germans use of the harbour of Saluafata, near Apia, as a naval station, and and included provisions for the protection of the lives and property of German nationals.

Australian interest in missionary work in the islands was extending steadily, and trading activities were developing. At the same time, the use of islanders as labourers had begun in Queensland with the development there of tropical agriculture. When the price of cotton rose after 1860, cotton planations were established. The first was started in 1863 by Captain Robert Towns, a Sydney merchant and shipowner, who brought in sixty labourers, chiefly from the New Hebrides, to do the cultivating and picking on his 2000 acre property near Brisbane. Towns's example was quickly followed by others. Native labourers (or kanakas) were soon to be found on newly-established sugar plantations in Queensland as well as in cotton growing.

The question of sovereignty of islands close to Australia became bound up with the matter of fixing Queensland's maritime boundaries. When Queensland became a separate colony in 1859, rights to "all and every adjacent island etc." were included in the colony's jurisdiction, but defined limits were not set, and it was not until 1872 that the boundary was defined as including all islands within 60 miles of the coast. A government station, established on Cape York in 1862, gave police surveillance to Torres Strait waters; it was of assistance to shipping passing through the strait. The pearling industry began in the late 1860s; within a few years there were scores of luggers operating in the strait, most of them working out of Queensland ports. In 1873 the importance of Torres Strait as a maritime route was emphasized by the establishment of the first regular mail service through the strait to connect the eastern cities of Australia with England by way of India and the Suez canal; the operators received a subsidy of £20,000 a year from the Queensland government.

In 1879 Queensland's boundaries were redefined to include all islands of the Great Barrier Reef, and those within the Gulf of Carpentaria and Torres Strait. This extended sovereignty to islands within sight of the southern shores of the great island of New Guinea.

The coastline of New Guinea had been charted early in the nineteenth century, but the island's interior remained hidden, locked in by mangrove swamps and jungles and mountain walls reaching to the clouds. An attempt in 1793 by John Hayes and John McCluer, two officers of the Bombay Marine (the naval arm of the English East India Company), to take over the northern coast of western New Guinea for Britain had failed; London had refused to recognize the move, and the Governor of the East India Company was not inclined to offer support to a venture so far from the centre of the company's operations in India. The little stockaded settlement, built in an area which Hayes and McCluer hopefully named New Albion, had to be abandoned within two years, and the great island remained free of European attention from 1795 until the 1820s. Then the Dutch, re-established in the Indies after the territorial restorations following the Napoleonic wars, resumed active competition with English traders; to compete, British merchants wanted to see a trading station established in an area that would give access to the Dutch-held islands. This rivalry resulted in the starting of the Bremer settlement on Melville Island, off northern Australia, in 1824 —a move which, in turn, provoked Dutch reaction. In 1828 a small Dutch settlement was set up at Triton Bay, on the western end of New Guinea, and a military outpost established on the southwest coast as formal possession was taken of the southern coast as far east as 140° East longitude.

The Dutch-annexed territory, like the eastern half of the island, attracted very little attention until the 1870s. In 1873 Captain John Moresby, during an Admiralty survey voyage in the Torres Strait, sailed eastward into a fine sheltered harbour on the southern coast (which he named Port Moresby in honour of his father). The following year Francis Labilliere, an Australian barrister resident in London, wrote to Lord Carnarvon, the Colonial Secretary in the Disraeli government, urging annexation of eastern New Guinea, and the Secretary was sufficiently interested to seek the views of the various Australian colonial governments. Their replies were generally cautious. Only the Parkes Cabinet of New South Wales came out strongly in favour of British action to forestall any foreign power's colonizing the island. Sydney's deep interest arose in part from the fact that a great proportion of the trade with all the islands of the southwest Pacific was passing through the port of Sydney; this trade was now worth about £50,000 a year.

Meanwhile, in London, the Royal Colonial Institute was urging the government to annex eastern New Guinea without delay. The plea was backed up by statements by Captain Moresby reporting that on his tour of duty in the area he had heard of various French, American and Russian projects for the exploitation of New Guinea resources.

By this time the German Pacific traders had begun to move into the islands just to the east of New Guinea; Goddefroy's traders had first landed at points in New Britain in 1873, while two years later a German warship visited New Hanover, New Ireland, and Bougainville; although there was no talk of Germany forming colonies in the Pacific, widespread trading activities were bringing her ever closer to New Guinea.

Among the people in Australia who kept interest alive in New Guinea was William John Macleay, a scientist and successful pastoralist, who decided to set up an expedition to study and collect natural history specimens. Enthusiasts in Sydney supporting establishment of a trading settlement somewhere on the island felt sure Macleay would report favourably on trading prospects. In May 1875 a meeting in Sydney attended by many influential people carried a resolution expressing the view that New Guinea's resources "should not remain beyond the reach of legitimate and commercial enterprise," and that "immediate occupation . . . by a civilized power is expedient, alike in the interests of humanity and commerce." With the Queensland government's recent establishment of a steamship route through the Torres Strait, another resolution said, the annexation of the territory not yet occupied by a foreign power was desirable "in the interests of the whole Empire as well as those of the Australian colonies." The cabinet of John Robertson, who had succeeded Parkes as Premier of New South Wales, was in wholehearted agreement with the popular sentiment; it forwarded a memorandum (couched in much the same language as the meeting's resolutions) urging the British government to assume sovereignty not only over eastern New Guinea but also over New Britain, New Ireland, the Solomons, the New Hebrides, and the Gilbert, Marshall, and Ellice island groups.

These grandiose proposals met with a cool reception in Whitehall. Neither the Colonial Institute's urgings in London nor the unquenched enthusiasm showed by Robertson and his supporters in Sydney could spur the British government to undertake new territorial acquisitions.

The Disraeli administration would perhaps have been less reluctant to intervene in New Guinea had the Australian colonies been united in their attitude. The cautious replies of the governors to Lord Carnarvon's question had not indicated any strong feelings about annexation among colonial cabinets; only the New South Wales cabinet, taking a different line from the governor of the colony, had supported immediate annexation. One important element in the British attitude stemmed from dislike of Queensland's use of kanaka labour, brought to Australia in local ships; although the point was not openly stated, there was a great reluctance in London to allow a colony where the kanaka traffic was operating to gain control of natives of another colony. Finance was another factor: Lord Carnarvon and the Colonial Office took the view that if the colonies desired annexation, it was for them to provide the funds for administration of the new territories. The protectorate over Fiji had been established reluctantly and under great pressure from the southern colonies, but they had refused to contribute towards its cost. Self-government in the colonies had posed an unexpected problem; it was the colonists who sought action by Britain, but who was to pay for the expenditure involved? Whitehall would not willingly extend the burden on British taxpayers. Nevertheless desultory discussion on the issue continued, with Whitehall holding to its refusal to annex without colonial subsidy and at the same time proposing to exclude the colonies from any control of government in annexed areas.

Although the report of the Macleay expedition to New Guinea dampened would-be traders' enthusiasm a little, since it emphasized the difficulties that settlers would surely face, this was only a temporary setback. Missionaries, prospectors, and traders were drifting into New Guinea through Port Moresby, and a business group was formed in London with colonizing plans. At the same time, the Queensland government was prepared to act independently. In 1877 a "confidential agent" was appointed by Queensland to maintain order, to report on mining and agricultural prospects, and to keep a register of land "purchases" in Port Moresby. Late in 1877, Henry Chester, the police magistrate at Thursday Island (which had replaced Cape York as the police post) was sent by the Queensland cabinet to investigate the position. A few months later a British warship arrived on the scene; but Whitehall refused to intervene directly. From Fiji, Gordon, the High Commissioner of the Western Pacific, reported that "a practical though informal" assumption of control over New Guinea territory was going on, with Queensland's "confidential agent," William Bairstow Ingham, holding courts and parading an armed force as well as registering land titles.

When Gordon returned to England for consultation in mid-1878, Sir Michael Hicks-Beach, who had succeeded Carnarvon as Colonial Secretary in the Disraeli government, sought his opinion on the advisability of annexing eastern New Guinea. The immediate reason for the new interest in the question was that gold had been discovered on the island. In November, Gordon informed the Colonial Secretary that after a study of the situation he was "forced to the reluctant conclusion" that annexation of at least certain portions of New Guinea was inevitable, mainly because a rush of miners to the areas where gold had been discovered seemed certain. Gordon was opposed to the idea of having the Australian colonies contribute to any administrative cost, however; he feared that this might open the way for them to have a voice in administrative policy—a notion he deprecated on the ground that it was unwise to give any colonial ministry control over relations between Europeans and native peoples. The expected gold rush did not eventuate; instead the advance prospectors struggled back to Australia. The immediate need for annexation passed, and no action was taken in London.

With the next change of government at Westminster, when Gladstone's Liberals took over in 1880 for a five-year term, colonial policy swung away completely from the Disraeli government's empire-mindedness to a concept opposing any extension of colonial possessions. Gladstone, a strong churchman, did not want to see more native peoples brought under white domination; he was particularly opposed to allowing Queensland, with its kanaka labour record, to gain control over native labourers from New Guinea.

Meanwhile, Godeffroy und Sohn had gone bankrupt and the firm's assets had passed to other hands. The rapid growth of German industry called for new sources of raw materials, however, and before long the idea of Pacific colonization was revived, this time with wider support within Germany.

In November 1882, an influential German newspaper, the Augsburg *Deutsche Allgemeine Zeitung*, came out in favour of immediate annexation, declaring that in the event of the German government attempting ("as many wish it would") to acquire New Guinea, "we might perhaps, in the interest of the nation, congratulate ourselves on the acquisition." The article went on to speculate that

> . . . it might be possible to create out of the island a German Java, a great trade and plantation colony which would form a stately foundation stone for a German colonial kingdom of the future.

The newspaper went on to declare it the duty of the German nation to take a hand in New Guinea's colonization.

The Royal Colonial Institute, in London, brought the article to the attention of the Colonial Office, but the Colonial Secretary, Lord Derby, affirmed that the government had no reason to suppose that the German government contemplated annexation.

The article was widely republished in the Australian press, stirring many fears. Soon it was reported from Brussels that a German New Guinea company was being formed. Meanwhile, there were signs that German-run plantations on Samoa had been expanding and were in need of more labour.

In Sydney as well as in Brisbane the movement of German vessels in and out of Australian ports was attracting attention and arousing suspicions. The governor of New South Wales early in 1883 wrote to Lord Derby to say he was now inclined to favour the establishment of a British protectorate over eastern New Guinea. Lord Derby had been soothed by Bismarck's assurances, however, and he confirmed that the government had no reason to suppose that the German government intended to take any action concerning New Guinea.

In February 1883 the Queensland Premier, Sir Thomas McIlwraith, drew up a long memorandum to the Governor of Queensland on the issue, stressing his view that British occupation of eastern New Guinea was vital and an urgent matter. He also cabled the Queensland agent-general in London:

> Urge Imperial Government annex New Guinea to Queensland. Reasons: large increase steam traffic through Torres Strait; population settled there requires government; Imperial coaling depot established; danger to colonies if other powers take possession. Queensland will bear expense of government and take formal possession on receipt of Imperial authority by cable.

McIlwraith did not mention the important point of the growing competition for kanaka labour between Queensland and German planters. The Germans were anxious to maintain New Britain and New Ireland as a reserve of labour for their Samoa plantations; meanwhile the number of Queensland traffickers seeking kanakas was growing rapidly.

McIlwraith had asked for a reply to his proposition by cable; but days passed and no cable came. Instead, word was received from Sydney that a German warship was on the point of leaving to annex various islands. On March 15 the Executive Council, meeting in Brisbane, decided to send an officer to New Guinea so that he would be on hand to act immediately authority was granted from London; a few days later, when news arrived that the German warship was already steaming north, Henry Chester was ordered to establish a preferential claim to New Guinea. On April 4, at Port Moresby, he hoisted the British flag and took possession of "all that portion of New Guinea and the islands and islets adjacent thereto lying between the 141st and 155th meridians of East longitude."

Greatly disturbed, Lord Derby demanded a "telegraphic explanation" of the Queensland action. When he received the reply he remained unprepared to support McIlwraith, even though he said the British Cabinet "would doubtless wish to arrange the matter in accordance with the wishes of the colonies." However, when the matter came before the British Cabinet Gladstone spoke of Queensland as not being "fit to rule" colonial areas and refused to ratify the Queensland annexation. "It cannot be denied that questions of this kind are questions on which the Imperial Government ought to have, as it actually has, a controlling power," Lord Derby said in explanation of this stand.

Word of the disallowance came as a tremendous shock in Australia. Although Queensland's move had been inspired principally by McIlwraith as the representative of the local plantation owners' politics, it had been applauded throughout the country, and the colonies had gone so far as to agree to a sharing of the administrative costs—an original bone of contention with London. The colonists had no doubts that their vital interests were being sacrificed to Britain's broader policies. They voiced their criticism of British policy freely in what was the first major difference of opinion to arise between the colonial capitals and London on matters related to external affairs. "The exasperation here is boundless," James Service, the Premier of Victoria, cabled London.

At a meeting of representatives of all the colonies, including New Zealand and Fiji, held late in 1883, a unanimous resolution urged the immediate incorporation within the British Empire of the whole non-Dutch area of New Guinea. Another resolution declared that the further acquisition of dominions in the western Pacific south of the Equator by any foreign power would be highly detrimental to the safety and well-being of the British possessions.

The Bulletin was scornful of the colonial attitude. A cartoon showed Gladstone pointing to a map of Australia labelled with notices—Vacant, To Let, Unexplored, Explorer Wanted—and asking, "Hadn't you better annex that first?" In a surprisingly bitter editorial the magazine said that the world had lately seen "no more ridiculous sight than a continent trembling with apprehension lest a few coral rocks thousands of miles away should pass under a strange flag." Others saw the situation differently. *The Age* commented—extremely acutely, as it happened—on the power play then taking place:

> A mere resolution affirming that Australia does not wish any foreign power to acquire further dominions in the western Pacific is a little like an intimation that they had better take what they are likely to want while we are too weak to prevent it.

It was one thing for the colonies to enunciate a "Monroe Doctrine" for the south-west Pacific, another to have it enforced. In June 1884, Bismarck made a speech rejecting the colonies' conference resolutions and promising that the German system of granting protection to overseas traders and settlers would eventually be extended to the South Seas. Two months later the British cabinet decided at last to accede to Australian demands to establish a protectorate over the whole of eastern New Guinea. When this decision became known to the German ambassador in London he protested to the Foreign Secretary against the inclusion of any of the north littoral in the protectorate and the British government agreed to withhold action on this sector pending diplomatic discussions with Germany. Whatever initiative London may have had in the matter was now wholly lost.

On October 23 and on November 6, and again later at nine different villages, a British protectorate was proclaimed over the southern shore of New Guinea from 141° East longitude eastward to East Cape. Two weeks later, German warships which had been steaming toward eastern New Guinea hoisted the German flag on the north coast. Bismarck, who had outwitted Lord Derby in negotiations regarding territories in the southern sector of Africa, had hoodwinked him also regarding New Guinea.

The British-protected territory was placed under a special commissioner, and the administrative headquarters were set up at Port Moresby. Subsequently the boundaries between the British protectorate and the German territory were adjusted by negotiation. In 1888 the protectorate was formally annexed. As a Crown colony, British New Guinea (or Papua) was governed by an administrator appointed from London but subject to the instructions of the

Queensland government—not that this was any consolation to the frustrated and furious colonists.

Australians learnt a lesson from the episode. Awareness grew that issues of prime concern to Australia might sometimes have to take second place to Britain's broader interests. The colonies had seen just how little they could do because of disunion; henceforth they must learn to work together. The half-formed objective of a united land gained strength.

Not only New Guinea and the tropical islands to Australia's northeast, but also the frigid regions to the south came in for greater attention in the 1880s. The feeling that Australia had some presumptive rights in the area was freely expressed.

Interest in the Antarctic regions had waxed and waned ever since the early days of the century when Frederick Hasselburgh, a sealer working out of Sydney, had reached Macquarie Island to begin a slaughter of seals which in a few decades decimated the island's prolific rookeries. The 1840s had marked a high point in activity as expeditions used Australian ports as starting points for incursions into the forbidding region. Dumont d'Urville had led a French expedition which sailed from Hobart and sighted the icebound land; Charles Wilkes had used Sydney as a base for his United States-sponsored expedition; the British ships *Erebus* and *Terror* had been fitted out in Hobart and they had sailed along the 170° East meridian through the icepack and into the sea named in honour of the expedition commander, Lieutenant James Clark Ross. From the late 1850s the Australian whaling industry had declined, after many years of activity, as petroleum products replaced whale oil as an illuminant and a lubricant; in 1866 the Hobart fleet was down to only nine vessels. Inducements were proposed in order to attract whalers to Melbourne, but with declining demand for whale products interest in the Antarctic was turning from commercial exploitation to scientific exploration. By the early 1880s Matthew Fontaine Maury, superintendent of the United States Hydrographic Office, the oceanographer who plotted the great-circle route which tooks ships plying to and from Australia to the very borders of Antarctica, was suggesting that Melbourne would be outstanding as a base for exploration in the far south, and one of Maury's disciples, the German oceanographer Georg von Neumayer (who had spent some time on Victorian goldfields) was able to influence the German Society for Polar Navigation to send an expedition south in 1882–83.

Scientists had designated the period as the first International Polar Year, and in Sydney and Melbourne discussion of Antarctica was given more attention as scientists and enterprising men supported proposals for an intensified effort at Antarctic exploration. The existence of a continent behind the great ice barrier was now suspected, but there was room for conjecture about the ice-covered wastes. In 1884, at the inaugural meeting of the Victorian branch of the Royal Geographical Society of Australasia, the erudite Ferdinand von Mueller directed attention to the Antarctic region as an area likely to yield "some of the grandest results for geographical science." Two years later a speaker addressing the Royal Society of Tasmania declared it to be "incumbent upon Australia" to take part in the exploration of the region. The speaker added:

> We aspire to be the leading power in these southern seas. We are gradually setting up a Monroe Doctrine of our own . . . If we expect to be the ruling power in these seas, the sooner we show ourselves upon them the sooner we shall see our claims recognised.

In Melbourne, also in 1886, an Antarctic committee with a distinguished membership was set up jointly by the Royal Society of Victoria and the Geographical Society. At the meeting in 1888 of the Australasian Association for the Advancement of Science a paper pointed to the effect the Antarctic had upon Australia's climate and weather conditions; exploration of the region was urged as "an inescapable duty." If a move were not made speedily, the speaker feared, "Germany will forestall us to our mortification and disgrace."

Nothing came of either the Australian or German initiatives at this time, however. There were more immediate and pressing matters for attention in warmer climates, and funds could not be gathered for expeditions into the frozen Antarctic wasteland.

In July 1883, in explaining the government's reasons for refusing to sanction Queensland's annexation of eastern New Guinea Lord Derby had drawn attention to the question of federation. He had said:

> If the Australian people desire an extension beyond their present limits, the most practical step that they could take, and one which will most facilitate any operation of that kind and diminish, in the greatest degree, the responsibilities of the Mother Country, would be the confederation of those colonies in one united whole, which would be powerful enough to undertake and to carry through tasks for which no one colony is at present sufficient.

It did not take long for the idea to take root. No sooner had Queensland's annexation move been rejected than a new initiative toward federation was taken by McIlwraith, who proposed that a convention of delegates should be held "to discuss the basis upon which a federal government could be constituted." He declared,

> Such a government, adapted to Australia's special requirements. would give life to national aspirations without repressing the autonomous governments of the colonies.

McIlwraith added that the united voice of the colonies should ask London to move towards providing a federal government.

Moves designed to bring about some type of federal union had been going on for many years without any marked effect. In the 1840s there had been suggestions in official quarters for some central authority (or "super functionary," as he was dubbed) to deal with matters of common concern to the colonies. In 1849 a committee of the Privy Council inquiring into constitutional changes which might be feasible for the Australian colonies, canvassed the idea of a uniform tariff, with intercolonial free trade, and suggested that one of the governors should be granted a commission whereby he would be Governor of Australia; he should be authorized to call a general assembly of legislators elected by the existing colonial parliaments. The value of having some central authority might be apparent in London, but the local legislators were more concerned with increasing their powers than with setting up any new and over-all authority. The Port Phillip people wanted to get away from New South Wales and form their own administration, and in other colonies local ambitions were strong. Nevertheless, as Colonial Secretary, Earl Grey held to the idea, and in 1851 he sent to the Governor of New South Wales, Sir Charles FitzRoy, a commission declaring him "Governor-General of all her Majesty's Australian possessions." The gesture had no practical effect, however; there was no desire among legislators or public in other colonies to go back under New South Wales.

Wentworth, while in London in 1854 to see the New South Wales constitution through the legislature, submitted to the Colonial Office a memorial referring to the necessity of creating a federal authority. The Colonial Office doubted whether the idea would be acceptable in Australia, and the matter was merely referred to the various governors. During the 1850s, select committees of the legislatures in Victoria, New South Wales, and South Australia inquired into and reported upon the necessity of a federal union, but nothing came of these inquiries.

In spite of the colonial separatism so clearly evident, the prospect of a federal union was kept alive. Matters requiring concerted action were arising more frequently from 1860, and occasional intercolonial conferences were held. At the 1867 intercolonial meeting in Melbourne, Henry Parkes spoke of the need for the colonies to be "united in some federal bond of connection," and within a few years the question of the Pacific islands began to bring the colonies together with a greater degree of unanimity and urgency. Constructive cooperation was another thing, however.

It was not until 1880 that a conference (held in Melbourne) got so far as to discuss the subject of a uniform tariff, and a resolution sponsored by Parkes affirmed the desirability of setting up a federal council. A draft bill, drawn up by Samuel Taylor Griffith of Queensland and submitted later to the conference (January 1881), was accompanied by a paper setting out a number of basic general principles which were assumed to be acceptable to all the colonial governments. These points were that the time had come for the creation of a federal constitution with an Australian parliament; that matters of concern to all the colonies could best be dealt with by a federal authority rather than by the colonies separately, and that an organization which would "lead men to think in the direction of federation" would be the best next step. When they were polled on the proposal, delegates were divided, however; those from three colonies (New South Wales, South Australia, and Tasmania) were in favour of the proposed bill, and three (Victoria, Queensland, and New Zealand) were against, while Western Australia abstained. The proposal had to be abandoned.

Far greater earnestness and urgency than ever before for creating a national voice came as a reaction to moves by foreign powers in the islands. At the intercolonial conference which convened in Sydney on November 23, 1883, after the British government's disallowance of McIlwraith's annexation of New Guinea, proposals for federation were discussed with the knowledge that until they spoke with a united voice London would take little notice of their views. The conference agreed to a proposal that the British government be asked to legislate for the establishment of a federal council. Accordingly an Act of 1885 authorized the Australian colonies, New Zealand and Fiji to set up a joint body to which two representatives would be sent by each colony. The scope of the council's power was to be limited and its authority slight. The legislative power was confined to a few subjects, mainly in the field of external affairs, such as relations with Pacific islands, quarantine, and fisheries beyond territorial limits; even after the council had passed any legislation on such subjects the individual colonies were still to be the ones to enforce such laws. The council's proposed powers excluded the significant matters of defence and, most importantly, the question of tariffs.

The whole enterprise was endangered by the founders' efforts to include New Zealand and Fiji in a comprehensive unit, since their problems and attitudes were distinctive. New Zealand was not represented at the initial meeting of the council, held in Hobart in January 1886.

Henry Parkes, head of the government in New South Wales, had been in England in 1883–84 while his colleagues were drafting the constitution of the new body, and because it failed to measure up to the organization he had proposed earlier, New South Wales was not represented on the new council. Parkes objected to the limitations on the council's authority, and —of more importance politically—he was aware that the idea of the council had not been well received in New South Wales. The conference was no sooner over than Parkes announced that New South Wales intended to adopt the name Australia for that colony—a proposal that met a strong joint protest from Victoria, Queensland, and South Australia.

In spite of the immediate problems, the real move towards federation had begun. Matters related to external affairs and defence provided important reasons for the colonies to come together initially; there were developments in many other fields to strengthen the movement and, as time went on, to give it deeper significance. At the same time, a major obstacle to federation was to be found in the widely-divergent individual viewpoints held by the colonial politicians on a great variety of issues. Naturally enough, the thought of voluntary surrender of power to a federal authority had little appeal to most legislators.

Much of the drive for a national parliament came from ordinary citizens and arose from simple issues. Men were moving from colony to colony more than ever before, strengthening the feeling that it was one country and that colonial boundaries were meaningless. In countless fields, there was evidence of closer contact. All the leading banks, insurance and pastoral companies, and many business organizations had branches in all or most of the colonial capitals. Theatrical companies toured from colony to colony. There was common action in many fields—from gathering statistics on a uniform basis to the fielding of sports teams. Old rivalries could subside when cricketers from various colonies joined against an English eleven in 1877 and the first "test" match took place; the following year an Australian team invaded hallowed ground and defeated the M.C.C. team (including W.G. Grace) at Lord's.

What was growing all through the 1880s was the view that an Australian nation might emerge. Various groups saw the need for this development in different ways, but in the country, in towns and cities there was increasing support for the idea among many public-spirited citizens and groups representing their views.

Intercolonial trade union conferences, which grew in number and importance in the 1880s, and action by employers on an intercolonial basis in response to unionists' demands, helped demonstrate that there were matters of a practical nature common to people in the various colonies. There was growing evidence that development would be much more rapid if the colonies were united. At the political level, the Australian Natives' Association, an organization originally formed in the early 1870s principally as a mutual benefit society for Australian-born citizens, came under the dynamic leadership in 1880 of Thomas Hart and soon acquired a national patriotic following. In the group's rapidly multiplying branches, federation was a principal topic, and the association's voice was increasingly heard in discussions of federation.

As new ideas were emerging, so were communications improving. By 1877 all the mainland capitals were linked by telegraph, and a cable to New Zealand was open. The railway lines of New South Wales and Victoria met at Albury in 1883, and the occasion provided an opportunity for intercolonial contact. Three special trains from Melbourne and two from Sydney carried the country's most prominent men to the grand functions at which orators addressed more than a thousand assembled guests. Albury was decorated from end to end with bunting, and was widely discussed as the future capital of Australia. "The difficulties which at present operate to keep the colonies apart will melt like snow on the Australian Alps," one speaker said. James Service, Premier of Victoria, declared, "We want federation, and we want it now!" The Melbourne *Argus* commented that some of the enthusiasm was sham and some of the sentiment spurious; but making allowance for all the platitudes, it said, there undoubtedly remained "some good union feeling."

An issue of immediate concern was Victoria's deepening involvement with a system of protective tariffs. Customs houses at the various border crossing points offended the growing feeling that it was, after all, one land, and brought clearly into focus the increasingly divergent policies being followed by various colonies. However, if reaction against Victoria's protectionist policy produced an impulse driving the colonies towards federation, the issue of protection as opposed to free trade at once became a divisive influence among the politicians groping towards some form of national union. Dominant politicians in New South Wales were as strongly attached to a so-called free trade policy as Victoria was wedded to protective tariffs, and they would not contemplate a union unless they could be sure the union would follow free-trade principles, while Victoria would not have a union unless it was protectionist.

At this point a strong motive for federation developed out of the question of immigration into Australia of non-Europeans. A mild but lingering resentment against the Chinese dated back to the days of the gold-rush influx, when restrictive measures had been enacted first in Victoria and then in South Australia and New South Wales. The number of Chinese declined, and the temporary restrictions were lifted in the 1860s; but the issue of Chinese immigration was revived with the opening-up in the 1870s of important gold and tin mines in Queensland. Indignation meetings were held in Queensland towns when hundreds of Chinese arrived; in 1875 more than 3000 Chinese landed at Cooktown, and before long the newspapers were reporting that as hundreds more were arriving others were departing from Cooktown with thousands of ounces of gold.

Public opinion hardened steadily on the question of exclusion of Chinese, and in the 1880s there was a revival of anti-Chinese legislation; between 1882 and 1887 all colonies fell into line and imposed a £10 head tax while further limiting the number of immigrants admitted according to the tonnage of the carrying vessel. Executive action was taken by the governments of Victoria and New South Wales to prohibit the admission of Chinese when vessels arrived carrying more Chinese than permitted by the statutes. On the matter going to court, the Supreme Court of New South Wales found that such immigrants could not be refused permission to land, and went on to deny the government the opportunity to appeal the case to the Privy Council; but in a similar case in Victoria legal proceedings finally established that the exclusion acts were enforceable in law. The latter case arose when the collector of customs in Victoria was sued by a Chinese immigrant for having prevented his landing; it was contended that this exclusion was illegal both as a proper construction of the Chinese exclusion acts in force and at common law. The Supreme Court of Victoria upheld the petitioner's view but granted the government leave to appeal and the case went to London. The Privy Council reversed the Victorian court's judgment on the question of interpretation of the statutes and further held that an alien had under the general law no legal rights, enforceable by action, to enter British territory.

All colonial administrations saw more or less eye to eye on blocking Chinese immigration, but on an equally important issue, that of the kanaka traffic, there was sharp division. In the 1890s, Queensland's readiness to admit thousands of Pacific islanders, and also Japanese, was a source of concern not only to the Labor movement and to Liberals in Queensland but to people of all parties in the various colonies. Increasingly the issue posed by the admission of cheap labour aroused discussion and caused irritation, forming a bond between groups throughout the country and underscoring the need for a national approach to immigration. Even within Queensland the matter was hotly contested. Most of the northern planters wanted to continue with coloured labour, but they realized that the majority of people in the colony (those living in the south) were opposed. The two political leaders were McIlwraith, who was receptive to the planters' views, and Samuel Griffith, a Liberal who wanted to see the end of the kanaka traffic, at least; with these two alternating in office the official attitude varied accordingly. As time went on it became clear to southern Queenslanders that the soundest way of assuring an end to kanaka and Japanese immigration to their colony was through the creation of a federation of all the colonies, with a nationally-controlled exclusion policy.

By now, matters related to external security were causing more acute concern to the political leaders, who sensed a dangerous situation. Britain had been assuming world-wide responsibilities; with the partitioning of tropical Africa her territorial possessions had increased, while there were also new commitments of British power in Asia. The concern felt in Australia and New Zealand became stronger when the British and German governments reached an agreement on their respective spheres of interest in the western Pacific in 1886; the colonists had set their face against encroachment by foreign powers, and this tacit recognition of the rights of foreigners in the islands confirmed their fears. The need for more adequate defence forces became obvious.

Since 1870, when all British military units were withdrawn, the colonies had each been looking after its own land defences, but the transfer of responsibility in naval defence naturally had been delayed. The British naval force in the area, originally part of the East Indian station, had been strengthened in 1859 and set up as a separate Australian squadron, and from the 1860s the various colonies were able to participate directly by providing and manning their own ships and by raising volunteers for the Royal Naval Reserve. The Russian scare of 1878, arising from fears that Britain might become involved in the Russo-Turkish war in the Balkans, had touched off discussion on the condition of empire defences, and this had led to the setting up in London of a commission of inquiry in 1879. Some of the colonies had sent delegates to participate in the commission's deliberations. The commission had found the attenuation of British strength to be such that almost any British harbour overseas would be in danger from a moderately-armed raiding force, and it not only recommended large additions to naval squadrons abroad and the strengthening of armaments at strategic points but also proposed that because of the expensive nature of the programme the colonies might share the cost. Subsequently, at a conference between the premiers of New South Wales, Victoria, and Queensland, and the British naval representative, in 1886, it was agreed that the colonies should contribute to the cost of additional ships for an Australian squadron.

Although *The Bulletin* spoke for a strident republican minority, there was a strong and fundamental feeling of loyalty which had resulted in successive offers of military assistance to the mother-country. In 1881 a volunteer force had been raised in South Australia for service in South Africa, and four years later a contingent of artillery and infantry was raised in New South Wales for service in Egypt. Patriotism and love of Empire was in the air.

Meanwhile the breakneck colonial expansion of Germany and the growing pro-Empire feeling in London had resulted in the calling by conservative Prime Minister Lord Salisbury of a conference of the self-governing colonies at the time of Queen Victoria's Jubilee in 1887. The conference, a "purely consultative" meeting, was an impressive assembly, with representatives from nine self-governing and two Crown colonies. The Australian delegates accepted the essentials of the proposals for enlarged naval defence and agreed to contribute, jointly with New Zealand, the sum of £126,000 a year for ten years, to be used purely for local defence. The British squadron in Australian waters was henceforth supplemented by an auxiliary squadron of five fast cruisers and two gunboats. The colonies paid part of the original cost of acquiring the vessels, and part of the cost of maintaining them as a local defence force.

The London Colonial Conference of 1887 strengthened the conviction that the Australian colonies would get nowhere with appeals or protests on British policies in the south Pacific. During the discussions, Alfred Deakin, representing Victoria, had criticized the lack of a constructive British policy in New Guinea and the New Hebrides and had contrasted it with the active colonial policies of the French and German governments. He had also expressed the hope that British policy would change, so that

> ... from this time forward colonial policy will be considered Imperial policy; that colonial interests will be considered and felt to be Imperial interests; that they will be carefully studied and that, when once they are understood, they will be most determinedly upheld.

Most delegates felt that Deakin's was a rather pious hope, and the consensus was that henceforth the colonies would have to be more zealous of their own interests. On his return to Melbourne, Deakin said he favoured "a fleet built, manned, and owned by Australia itself," and added:

> When the colonies are larger, wealthier, and more powerful they will then no doubt obtain and maintain a squadron of their own in these seas.

Before long there were new rumours of French preparation for seizure of the New Hebrides, and the three-man inner cabinet of Victoria's government decided to forestall the move by sending a detachment of the colony's permanent military forces to the island with instructions to hoist the British flag there and keep it flying. There was no supporting evidence that the French intended to move, however, and the secret plan was abandoned just before the vessel carrying the annexation party was about to leave. Nevertheless, the fact that such action was contemplated in 1888 was an indication of the growing determination that Australians must be strong enough to act for themselves if necessary.

In 1889 a report on the military forces and defences of the colonies was prepared by Major-General Bevan Edwards, who said flatly that if the colonies had to rely on their individual defence resources their position would be dangerous; his recommendation was that the colonial forces should be placed under unified or federal command. Parkes, sensing the growth of a national sentiment, spoke at Tenterfield on October 24, 1889, and stressed the urgency of the defence issue. He said he believed that to preserve the security and integrity of the country it was essential that all their defence forces should be amalgamated into one great federal army, whenever necessary, and it seemed to him

> . . . that the time is close at hand when the colonies ought to set about creating this great national government of all Australia.

Parkes spoke also of the need for unification of railways, and advocated the creation of a national parliament with a strong central executive to deal with matters of common concern. The time had come, he said, for the calling of a convention of leading men from all the colonies to draft a federal constitution.

Parkes's speech attracted considerable attention in all the colonies, and popular support for a federal movement grew. However, Parkes's earlier equivocation, and the strong antipathies he had generated, caused some colonial leaders to approach the proposal somewhat cautiously.

After some hesitancy the first conference of ministers representing all the Australian colonies and New Zealand met in Melbourne in February 1890. Following a notable debate, the conference unanimously resolved in favour of a union of "the Australasian colonies," and approved the summoning of a convention to achieve this objective. All the parliaments endorsed this proposal and elected representatives to the National Australasian Convention which met in Sydney in March 1891.

The convention's membership of forty-five leading parliamentarians represented both political sides in each colony. Although at first objectives seemed as ill-defined as delegates' ideas on how to achieve them, significant issues steadily emerged, and the convention got down to the work of framing a first-draft constitution. The ideas embodied in the proposal were discussed in open meeting; but the preparation of the actual written clauses was the work of a small group of influential lawyer-politicians. Parkes suggested the title Commonwealth—a controversial proposal (with echoes of Cromwell and the regicides of 1649) that received little support and was at first turned down by the drafting committee; only when Deakin urged its acceptance was it finally agreed to by a one-vote majority.

Adoption of a proposed constitution was a significant achievement; it at once changed the concept of federation from a nebulous dream into a firm proposal that outlined the full meaning of federal union. The provisions of the document turned out by the convention contained the essence of federation and formed the basis of work undertaken at later conventions, even though not all the provisions were preserved. The convention's weakness lay in the fact that no procedural steps had been laid down in advance to ensure that its recommendations would not be lost through accidents or delay of political opportunity.

The convention's proposals had to be ratified, and the battle now moved to the colonial parliaments. The attitude of New South Wales was crucial; and in the political quicksands developing in the New South Wales Legislative Assembly with the emergence of the Labor party, the proposal bogged down. Resolutions on the draft constitution were promised in the governor's speech when the parliament opened on May 19, 1891; on that day Parkes gave notice of supporting a motion, while reserving to the House the right to propose amendments—but by early June the assembly had been dissolved in preparation for a general election. In the new House, which convened in July, the Labor party was a force to be reckoned with, and its distrust of federation delayed action by the ministry, which was prepared to make this concession for Labor support. Meanwhile the parliaments of Victoria, Tasmania, and South Australia had given general approval and were awaiting similar action from New South Wales; the parliaments of Queensland, Western Australia, and New Zealand did nothing on the Commonwealth Bill. Queensland, divided on the immigration issue, was waiting to see what New South Wales might do; Western Australia, having just been granted responsible government after many years of agitation, was in no mood to become a junior partner in a federation.

With Parkes's retirement, an anti-federalist premier took office, and the prospects for revival in New South Wales declined further, even though Edmund Barton and Richard Edward O'Connor, two members of the new cabinet, who were pledged to federation, persisted with efforts to interest parliament and public in the subject. The Labor party's singleminded drive for legislation on social and economic matters meant that a government dependent on Labor support had to be prepared to push the federation issue into the background. For its part, the Labor party feared that federation might be a step towards an "imperial federation" which in turn would lead to partial loss of Australia's self-governing status. More generally, the draft constitution from the 1891 Convention ran into Labor criticism on the basis that it offered more to the "classes" than to the "masses"; since it was receiving some support from businessmen and men of wealth, the proposal was also claimed by the new party to serve the purpose of those who were concerned about the rising tide of Labor in New South Wales.

Without a lead from New South Wales, the interest of other parliaments waned. Slowly the initiative created at the political level by the convention was dissipated, an apparent waste.

Public interest in the question of federation was steadily growing, however, particularly in Victoria, and new impetus was given the movement by the formation of active local groups and organizations. The Australian Natives' Association sparked off many federation leagues in city and country centres in Victoria and elsewhere, and in July 1893 a conference of these groups and others interested in the federal movement was held at Corowa, on the

Murray River. The choice of Corowa as the venue was significant since it emphasized the frustrations suffered by farmers and businessmen in the border districts who were particularly affected by intercolonial tariffs.

The conference drew up a programme which featured some new points. The key change proposed was that a constitution should be drafted by a convention elected directly by the people instead of one made up of men appointed by and representing the colonial governments. In addition, it recommended that the constitution, when drafted, should be submitted to the people for acceptance or rejection and that if accepted by three or more colonies it should be sent to the British parliament with the request for legislation to give it effect. By mapping out in advance the course to be followed from the electing of the proposed new convention to the final acceptance of its recommendations, the delegates laid down a practical procedure for constitution building.

There was still criticism of the federal objective as well as political in-difference to it. Party leaders, and politicians generally, stuck closely to old issues—particularly free-trade versus protection—while economic difficulties arising from the bank crash in Victoria and the subsequent widespread depression diverted attention. In New South Wales, Labor persisted in its niggling objections to federation—objections now based on a fear that in a federal plan conservative states might outvote Labor and continue a taxing system based on customs and excise duties rather than on direct taxation (which the party favoured). The objective of federal union was more widely understood, however, and the movement was slowly on the march in spite of immediate difficulties.

It took the New South Wales Parliament over two years to pass its enabling Act (December 1895); once that affirmative vote came, South Australia, Tasmania, and Victoria promptly passed similar measures providing for the election of ten representatives from each colony as convention delegates. Western Australia decided to send representatives who had been named by parliament instead of being directly elected. In Queensland the question of possible secession of the northern section of the colony intruded into the discussions, and nothing was done about the Commonwealth Bill.

When the poll of delegates was taken in the eastern colonies, the support for federation generated through the Australian Natives' Association advocacy was reflected in a vote which cut across party lines. The electors came out strongly in favour of staunch federalists. The Labor party had put forward a spate of delegates, but no Labor man was elected from New South Wales and the only Labor representative in the gathering was from Victoria. The convention met for the first time on March 22, 1897, at Adelaide. It divided itself into three working groups: constitutional, financial and judicial committees. The draft of 1891 was taken as a basis on which to work, but every example of federation known to history was examined and features that seemed best to fit Australia's needs were adapted; however, relatively few changes of a substantial nature were found to be necessary.

A central problem was how to reconcile the consensus in the larger colonies that the controlling power in the new federation should rest with the majority of the people, with the demand of the smaller colonies for an influence as equal partners in the union. Interests concerned to maintain state rights saw the solution in a strong Senate, and conservatives generally supported this solution. Liberals and Labor men were instinctively opposed; they could see a federal Senate functioning in the same way as the colonial upper houses had functioned for decades in buttressing the interests of propertied men.

Convinced of the danger to its cause, Labor was particularly opposed to a second chamber with representation on a State basis. William Holman, the leading Labor parliamentarian in New South Wales, declared:

> We are not Federationists at any price. We lay down our own terms, the other colonies can please themselves whether they accept them or not. The terms are perfectly fair. Every man and woman in any colony has just the same power in electing representatives—no more, no less. Under our idea, a Tasmanian would have one vote, and only one—just like the inhabitant of New South Wales. Under the scheme of our opponents, a Tasmanian would have five votes to a New South Welshman's one.

There were other stumbling blocks. Each of the colonies had enjoyed a large measure of self-government for a considerable time; yet these colonial administrations would have to agree to surrender certain of their powers to the proposed new national government. Their independence would not allow them to accept an arrangement similar to that adopted by Canada thirty years earlier in which the provincial administrations became subordinate to the new central government. Rather than such a confederate arrangement it was the form of federation adopted in the United States that most nearly filled the requirement—with power over all matters not specifically transferred to the federal body remaining within the jurisdiction of each state. Admirers of the United States Constitution with its separation of executive and legislative branches—providing the basis for representative government—favoured an upper house with strong powers; but the prevailing desire to retain the British practice of responsible government inevitably placed the emphasis upon the lower house. The American titles of Senate and House of Representatives were adopted, but with them went the British form of administration, already operating within each colony, so that a prime minister and his cabinet could remain in power only so long as they held the support of a majority of the members of the lower house. The range of subjects to be transferred to the federal sphere covered matters related to defence, external relationships, immigration, banking and currency, foreign and interstate trade, conciliation and arbitration in industrial disputes, taxation, and postal, telegraphic, telephonic, and similar services. To head the judicial branch, a High Court was recommended; it was to be the guardian of the constitution.

The draft constitution was passed to the various colonies for comment, and by the end of 1897 the convention was again in session, sifting the suggestions (nearly 300 in number) made by the colonial legislatures and revising the whole draft. A final session was held early in 1898, the convention gathering in Melbourne. By March the task of revision was completed and the convention was able to adopt a draft constitution.

It had been finally agreed that in general legislation the Senate and the House of Representatives should have equal power, but that in the case of money bills the South Australian practice should be followed and the upper chamber should not be permitted to originate or amend money bills (though it might suggest amendments for the consideration of the lower house).

The work of the 1897–98 Convention put the seal on what had been done (and temporarily lost) at the 1891 Convention. Deakin wrote later:

> The bold outline of the form of government then adopted (1891) was reproduced in 1897/8, the only important changes being the substitution of an elective Senate for a body chosen by the State parliaments and the revival of the right to appeal to the Privy Council. . . By the introduction of the single vote [of Senate and House of Representatives] and a means of terminating deadlocks which included a dissolution of the Senate, the whole measure was given a more decidedly democratic development.

The bill was "in style and spirit" Griffith's creation, in Deakin's view. Certainly Griffith had, by his insight and his clarity of style, been a dominant factor in moulding its provisions; his influence had been a continuing thread over the years of effort to achieve federation.

After the constitution had been accepted by the convention, it had to go before the electors in each colony. There were still many who were opposed to the whole concept of federation, and others who took exception to particular provisions.

Each opponent of the measure was ready to seize upon some particular aspect that displeased him. Opposition in New South Wales remained strong, and this colony was the key to the whole proposal. During the sitting of the convention the anti-federalists had scored a technical advantage by securing passage of a bill which provided that for acceptance of the constitution at least 80,000 affirmative votes were needed; this meant that supporters of the proposal faced a severe handicap. There was some criticism of the provision which would have enabled the federal parliament to exercise a free choice in the selection of a federal capital, but more serious points of criticism were involved. These were, first, the principle of equal representation of the states in the Senate, and the powers given to the Senate, which were held to be such that the will of the majority would be thwarted, and secondly, the financial provisions (which were seen as involving great increases in revenue and therefore in taxation). To Labor the whole constitution smacked too much of conservatism and states' rights.

At the first referendum, in 1898, New South Wales failed to give the 80,000 affirmative votes required; the votes cast were 71,965 for and 66,228 against the proposal. In Victoria, however, the majority in favour was overwhelming—100,520 affirmative and only 22,090 negative—and equally strong 'yes' votes were recorded in South Australia and Tasmania.

Matters were brought to a standstill; but the moral effect of the majority of 'yes' votes in New South Wales, though small, encouraged the federalists there. The *Sydney Morning Herald*, edited by Henry Gullett, was campaigning on their behalf. The Premier, George Reid, about to face a general election, came out strongly in favour of federation, at the same time suggesting a series of amendments to the proposed constitution. Reid won the election, and then arranged a conference of premiers of all six colonies. The meeting, early in 1899, agreed to submit the proposal again to the electors with a number of amendments on purely parliamentary matters and other relatively minor changes. The premiers also agreed that the location of the federal capital territory—long a contentious issue—should be within New South Wales but at least 100 miles from Sydney; until the federal parliament could be established there, Melbourne would be the temporary capital.

The proposals were again submitted to the electors in mid-1899. This time the majorities in favour were larger than ever in Victoria (sixteen-to-one), South Australia, and Tasmania, while in New South Wales and Queensland (voting on the issue for the first time) there were big affirmative majorities.

Again, Western Australians were not given the opportunity to vote; members of the colonial parliament were still disinclined to support any move for federation. There was a strong fear that local industries established under cover of a protective tariff would not survive the strong competition from eastern manufacturers under a system of intercolonial free trade. Up to this time the entrenched rural interests had been successfully resisting the enfranchisement of the gold-mining community which had sprung up; with the rapid growth of the Labor party after its creation in 1896, the new forces were strengthened in their challenge to the establishment. Labor was the first political party in the colony, and it helped change the balance of power there, so that eventually the Western Australian government was forced to put the question to a referendum (July 1900). All six colonies had now agreed. Only New Zealand held aloof; it was developing along its own lines and, never more than half-hearted about the proposals, was not prepared to join the Australian federation.

Meanwhile, a delegation from the five eastern colonies left for London with the bill for the creation of the Commonwealth. Discussions and negotiations were undertaken in London with the British Colonial Secretary, Joseph Chamberlain, who had come to the conclusion that it would be necessary to amend the proposals as approved by Australian voters. Chamberlain had suggested that representatives of the colonies should be on hand in case amendments were moved during the debate on the measure. Chamberlain made it clear that the British government had no desire to interfere with Australian interests; its province was only to protect Imperial interests. One of the questions about which he was most concerned was the matter of the right to appeal to the Privy Council against decisions of the High Court of Australia. Chamberlain did not want to see the right of appeal in private cases dropped; on the other hand the colonists wanted to see the High Court as the final authority in cases related to Australia's own constitutional affairs. Finally the issue was solved by a provision making it possible for the High Court to grant leave to appeal from itself or from a subordinate court to the Privy Council, but this was to apply only in certain classes of constitutional questions.

British politicians waxed eloquent in praise of the constitution's framers, and none of its provisions was subjected to strong criticism. Chamberlain warmly commended the framers of the measure, declaring that "no praise can be too high for those whose moderation, patience, skill, mutual consideration and patriotism have been able to produce so great a result."

The parliament of Western Australia had meanwhile passed the enabling Act (in May), and when the referendum was held in July the voting was more than two to one in favour of joining the federation.

The bill to create the Commonwealth of Australia passed both houses of the British parliament, and on July 9 Queen Victoria gave the Act her Royal Assent. The federation was to come into being on January 1, 1901.

The Boer War, which had broken out in October 1899, had meanwhile intensified patriotic fervour. In some quarters there was sympathy for the Boers, and a number of newspapers had condemned the war; but in the cause of Empire Australian opinion had generally ranged itself behind British policy, and young men had volunteered in all the colonies. Before that war ended in May 1902, over 16,000 Australians sailed to fight alongside Britain's professional army and units from Canada and New Zealand.

A new 17
commonwealth

When the Commonwealth of Australia came into being on January 1, 1901, the population totalled 3,765,339, of whom New South Wales and Victoria each had about one third, with New South Wales slightly the more populous. After nearly forty years with a population less than Victoria's, New South Wales had regained first place in 1892; in the decade leading to federation an increase of 247,000 people in New South Wales contrasted sharply with Victoria's meagre gain of only 62,000.

Prosperity was returning to the colonies by the late 1890s, and even though memories of the bitter experiences of the early part of the decade remained, the creation of the new nation was exciting enough to capture popular imagination and make this a time for rejoicing. Dissentients no longer mattered; those in opposition to the federal concept now turned their attention to the terms of the constitution rather than the broad objective. Enthusiastic crowds hailed the occasion with patriotic fervour. The seemingly unattainable had been won: in spite of the sceptics, federation had been achieved. The people's joy (as one observer noted) was reflected in

> ... the pomp of military and civil display, the blare of trumpets, the roar of artillery, the fluttering of flags, the brilliancy of the illuminations in cities, [and] the glare of bonfires on hundreds of hills.

Even before the formal inauguration of the Commonwealth, a cabinet had been formed. The Governor-General, the Earl of Hopetoun, was appointed by the Queen in October 1900, and since it was generally conceded that first consideration for the prime-ministership should be given to the premier of the senior colony, Sir William John Lyne was asked if he could gain sufficient support. Lyne had led the anti-federation forces in New South Wales, and since the politicians who were moving into the federal sphere were predominantly federalists, he found himself unable to form a ministry.

The Governor-General then handed the task to fifty-one-year-old Edmund Barton, the key figure of the 1897–98 Convention vote in favour of federation. By December 31 Barton had formed a government. His interim cabinet was selected largely on the basis of balanced representation; of the nine members, three were from New South Wales, two from Victoria, and one from each of the other states. Lyne was included as Minister for Home Affairs, and Richard Edward O'Connor, a staunch federalist, was made Vice-President of the Executive Council. From Victoria, Sir George Turner (Premier) became Treasurer and Alfred Deakin the Attorney-General, from South Australia, Charles Cameron Kingston (Premier) became Minister for Trade and Customs, and from Western Australia, Sir John Forrest (Premier) was appointed Minister for Defence. The premiers of Queensland and Tasmania were included in the formally-declared ministry but neither played any active role. Sir James Dickson (Queensland premier) died before the elections, and Neil Lewis (Tasmania) did not seek election; later their places were taken by James George Drake, who as a senator from Queensland became Postmaster-General, and Sir Philip Fysh (of Tasmania) who was appointed Minister without portfolio.

Elections for the Senate and the House of Representatives were held on March 31, 1901. On May 9 the parliament was formally declared open by the Duke of Cornwall and York (later to become King George V) in ceremonies in Melbourne's spacious Exhibition building, lavishly decked out for the occasion. At the conclusion of his formal address, the Duke read a cable from his father, King Edward VII, expressing fervent wishes for the new nation's "prosperity and great happiness"; at that point a wild burst of cheering broke from the 12,000 people present. Formalities were soon completed, and the ceremony ended as the rolling strains of *Rule Britannia* echoing through the cavernous building were drowned by rounds of tempestuous cheering. The scene of activity moved to the nearby parliament building (made available, for as long as need be, by the Victorian legislature as a temporary venue for the federal meetings). There, business began with the election of parliamentary office bearers.

The following day, the legislators assembled to hear Lord Hopetoun's speech foreshadowing measures which would put into effect the provisions of the constitution—the creation of a High Court, and the setting-up of departments or commissions to deal with matters related to defence, customs and excise, trade and commerce, conciliation and arbitration in industrial disputes, pensions, and other activities for which the federal administration was to assume responsibility. The Governor-General also indicated the government's proposals in the legislative field. Restrictions were to be placed on the admission of Asians, and action taken to phase out employment of kanaka labour on Queensland plantations. The long list of other subjects to be dealt with included the framing of a tariff, legislation on banking, shipping, and quarantine, and the selection of a federal capital territory; some of these issues would not come to the point of action for ten years or so, although in these buoyant early days there was hope that they would be resolved quite simply.

Political rivalries carried over from the separate colonies contributed to the early groups in the federal parliament. Prime Minister Barton's supporters in the house numbered forty-two against thirty-two on the Speaker's left. In the Senate—where the special interests of the senator's state rather than his party affiliations were expected to be paramount—support for Barton was weaker; he had only fourteen avowed followers against twenty-one in opposition (including all six senators from Western Australia). Groupings polarized around protection/free trade, but they were somewhat fluid. Barton's supporters, who were protectionists, and the supporters of George Reid, the Opposition leader, each presented a united front on the tariff issue, but the groups were internally divided on other questions. Barton's majority of ten in the house was subject to the qualification that at least five were pledged to the Labor party, while another ten Labor men sat with the Opposition. The Parliamentary Labor party was constituted, with John Christian Watson as its leader. Labor men had freedom of action on the protection/free trade issue (on which party membership was sharply divided) and sectional differences between the separate state Labor parties remained; yet on issues other than the tariff the Labor parliamentarians voted as a bloc, throwing weight to any ministry prepared to proffer measures in line with Labor ideas. Labor men in the New South Wales parliament had learnt to extract favourable legislation from unstable ministries; now the same effective tactics of "support in return for concessions" could be adopted in the federal sphere.

Not only political figures but the new federal administrators were drawn directly from the colonial sphere. The whole of the staffs of the colonial departments of Trade and Customs (that is, the old customs and excise departments), the Postmaster-General Department (the old post, telephones, and telegraph departments), and Defence (naval and military) were transferred to Commonwealth control. In the new federal public service recruitment was by competitive examination; the code of public service regulations, was based generally upon colonial legislation (especially that of New South Wales, Victoria, and Queensland, where reforms and improvements had been carried through in the 1880s and 1890s). The number of permanent officials transferred in 1901 was just over 11,000; in addition about 72,000 other employees were involved. In 1904, when the Commonwealth Public Service Act came into force, there were less than 12,000 permanent officials, although by then the departments of the Attorney-General and of External Affairs, Home Affairs, and the Treasury had been added to the original four.

After legislation related to the business of establishing the necessary machinery for the federal administration was completed, some other measures upon which there was clear and general agreement were carried into effect.

Universal adult suffrage was adopted under the Electoral Act of 1902. In giving women the right to vote the Commonwealth was following the example set by South Australia in 1894 and Western Australia in 1899 (New Zealand having been the pioneer in 1893). The constitution guaranteed the federal franchise to all those in a particular state entitled to vote for that state's lower house, and since the federal parliament wished to

establish a uniform franchise the women of all states were included. New
South Wales took action to enfranchise women for state voting in 1902
and Tasmania followed the next year. Only in Queensland (1905) and
Victoria (1908) were similar state provisions delayed.

By June 1901 the parliament had before it its first significant legislation.
Two bills (introduced on June 5) dealing with immigration matters were,
in Prime Minister Barton's words, of "definite and high policy," and
"important with regard to the future of Australia." One dealt with the
exclusion of people from Asian lands, and the other with the problem posed
by Pacific islands labourers brought in to work in the canefields of
Queensland.

In acting to block immigration from lands lying to Australia's north, the
government was carrying into effect on a national scale a policy in line with
practices in force since the days of the Chinese exclusion in all individual
colonies except Queensland. Because the colonial laws preventing the entry
of Chinese, Japanese, and Indians had proved an embarrassment to
Whitehall in its dealings in Asian countries, the suggestion had been made
that a language test might be adopted as an exclusion device; such a test
had been used in the colony of Natal (in southern Africa) and had been
found to be effective in keeping out unwanted people without any direct
affront to the Queen's subjects in India or to nations with which the British
government maintained friendly relations. The Colonial Secretary, Joseph
Chamberlain, had advised Barton that exclusion based on race or colour
was "not only offensive to a friendly power, but contrary to the general
conceptions of equality which have ever been the guiding principle of
British rule throughout the Empire"; but, he added, there could be no affront
taken at a dictation test such as that used in Natal, where a person wishing
to enter the country was denied entry if he or she failed to write out and
sign, in a European language, an application for admission. In the debate
on the bill, there was hardly a voice raised against a restrictive policy in
general; method rather than intent was reviewed. Some parliamentarians
thought the exclusion of Asians should be more precisely spelt out, and in the
debate on the bill they expressed resentment at being hampered in their
desire simply in order to suit Britain's convenience. Labor members were
vehement on the issue. Watson, their leader, moved for an amendment
directly prohibiting from entry to Australia "any person who is an aboriginal
native of Asia, Africa, or the islands thereof." He feared any influx, saying:

> The objection I have to the mixing of these coloured people with the white
> people of Australia—although I admit it is to a large extent tinged with considera-
> tions of an industrial nature—lies in the main in the possibility and probability
> of racial contamination.

Other legislators spoke at length of dangers in admitting those of "inferior
races," but Watson stressed the fear that Australians would most likely come
off second best in competition with such immigrants. He discoursed on the

guile of the Oriental, and declared that "as a rule, the more he is educated the worse man he is likely to be from our point of view."

Deakin, in charge of the bill, beat off attacks by members who repeatedly charged the government with undue subservience to London's views on the best exclusion method. Deakin defended the provisions of the bill as it stood, pointing out that it would achieve the purpose for which it was intended. The Japanese consul in Sydney, meanwhile, drew the Prime Minister's attention to the fact that while the Japanese government fully recognized Australia's right to limit "in any way it thinks fit" the number of settlers it admitted, there was room for concern because by the provisions of the bill his people were being classed with Negroes and kanakas. The consul appealed for treatment of Japanese on the same basis as Russians, Turks, or Greeks; but his plea was not accepted. Instead, Deakin emphasized in debate that the Japanese were the main threat and they had to be "absolutely excluded." Deakin saw the Japanese as dangerous competitors because of "their inexhaustible energy, their power of applying themselves to new tasks, their endurance, and low standards of living."

The bill passed the lower house thirty-six to thirty-one. In the Senate, an attempt to turn to a colour line of prohibition almost succeeded; but the government's bill was passed in December 1901 by a one-vote margin. Its sole exclusion provision was the dictation test whereby any applicant for admission to Australia would be asked to write down what was said to him in any European language of the examining officer's choosing; if the applicant failed he had no right to admission. This method became the principal means of enforcing a policy designed to control the sources from which immigrants would be acceptable. Being flexible, it could be used against anyone whom the government wished to exclude.

Associated with the Immigration Restriction Bill, but less contentious, was the measure to deal with the kanaka problem. In introducing the bill, Barton pointed to the grave scandals that had attended recruitment of the islanders, and he said that, although more active supervision by the Queensland government had greatly ameliorated the conditions, the traffic still represented a "veiled form of slavery" which could not be tolerated; the only solution was to end the system and return the kanakas to their home island. In rebuttal, petitions poured in from plantation owners and representatives of shipping and allied firms and other business interests. Unanimously they declared that removal of the island labourers would spell extinction for Queensland's sugar industry. An official report prepared at this time supported the sugar planters' argument; but the weight of public opinion so strongly opposed continuance that clearly the system would have to go, no matter what the cost. The bill which finally passed the Senate in December 1901 prohibited the further entry of Pacific islands labourers after March 31, 1904, and provided for the repatriation of all those who had worked on the canefields. It was recognized that the sugar industry should be given special assistance to make up for its loss of cheap labour, and the Sugar Bounties Act of 1903 provided a rebate of excise on all sugar grown by white labour. This, together with tariff protection, made it possible for the sugar industry to survive and expand.

The creation of a general tariff structure for the new nation was called for under the constitution, and it had to be completed within twenty-one months of federation. In his opening address to the business session of the parliament, the Governor-General had foreshadowed the legislation when he said of the tariff:

> Revenue must, of course, be the first consideration; but existing tariffs have in all the States given rise to industries, many of which are so substantial that my advisers consider that any policy tending to destroy them is inadmissible.

The Tariff Bill carried in 1902 was little more than a stopgap measure. It provided a mixture of protectionist and revenue-inspired duties, and it left in abeyance the real issue of the level of protection to be afforded Australian manufacturing industry. Nevertheless, it sketched a course for the new nation. When Barton attended the Colonial Conference which coincided with Edward VII's Coronation late in 1902, he was able to point to the existence of the Act as a reason for rejecting Joseph Chamberlain's bid to develop a system of free trade among all British lands.

Those convinced of the need to provide a reasonable level of protection for the development of Australian consumer industries were determined to pursue the matter and improve upon the initial Tariff Act. In this drive for more effective protection, as in many other basic issues, the objectives consistently advocated for so long by *The Age* were eventually to be adopted and become absorbed within the concept of national policy. Underlying the measures was the genuine middle-class liberalism which had started so much social legislation in Victoria and New South Wales in pre-federation days; but it was David Syme's cogent and consistent advocacy that remained as a potent force to carry this approach over from colonial Victoria to the national sphere; editorials written under his direction continued to support protectionist policies with the same uncompromising attitude he had adopted in the 1860s and 1870s when urging a system of selective tariffs for Victoria. With the creation under the constitution of free-trade between the states, it was almost inevitable that a protectionist policy should be adopted for Australia as a whole; but the strong political divisions that the issue had aroused earlier now made constructive debate on the matter difficult. Instead, vehement discussion and wild argument raged.

In September 1903 Alfred Deakin, who had once been a leader-writer for Syme, took over the leadership of the protectionists when Barton resigned (to take a seat on the newly-constituted High Court under Chief Justice Sir Samuel Griffith). Protection had the active support of advanced liberals including Isaac Isaacs and Henry Bournes Higgins, and Charles Cameron Kingston (of South Australia), whose views were very close to those of Labor, and of some staunch conservatives including John Forrest. Naturally Victoria remained the stronghold of protectionist sympathy. In New South Wales the *Sydney Morning Herald* backed Reid and the importers, merchants, and pastoralists who formed the core of the anti-protection forces.

The issue of a firm protectionist policy came to a head in the elections of

December 1903. As a result of the poll, Deakin and his protectionists, Reid and his free-traders, and the Labor party under Watson were all of near-equal strength. The three-way split led Deakin to declare that it was impossible for responsible government to function under such circumstances and that some sort of amalgamation was imperative. Deakin endeavoured to gain Labor's support with an advanced social programme, while at the same time he tried to break Labor party solidarity through attacks on the caucus principle (the system of party pledge which Labor enforced on its elected representatives). Labor had grown stronger, however; the party, more unified than ever before, was developing an effective political machine in the federal sphere—the first party to do so—and was on the way to domination of the political scene. For a short time Labor backed Deakin's programme, but in April 1904 the support was withdrawn because of differences on an arbitration issue. Labor wanted the federal Arbitration Court to have jurisdiction over the public servants of the states; Deakin believed this would be against the spirit of the constitution, and refused to agree to the demand. With Deakin's resignation, Watson formed a ministry which brought Labor to power for the first time. Apart from the six-day Labor administration in Queensland in 1899, this was the first ministry formed in any parliament by and in the interests of Labor; but it could not hope to survive for long. In the house it had a minority of followers and no firm ally. Support by Reid and his group was out of the question, and Deakin (whose supporters backed the Labor ministry on a temporary basis) soon showed fright, believing there was danger in supporting a party which he considered to be "destroying the life of the tree of constitutional liberty." After three months Watson was forced to resign and Reid took over as Prime Minister.

Reid's tenure of office was dependent upon support from some protectionists and so he was unable to enforce his own free-trade policies; nevertheless some of the liberal protectionists felt alarm and they decided to work with Labor under an arrangement which set out specific issues on which they would maintain a united front while allowing freedom of action on others. The group formed a bridge to Labor and, although small in numbers, it included extremely able men whose advice strengthened Watson, now leader of the Opposition.

Deakin, looking to the time when the protection/free-trade feud would be at an end, spoke of an independent Liberal programme. His speech at Ballarat was widely interpreted as a withdrawal of support and a "notice to quit," and Reid unexpectedly took him up on this basis, even though the intention behind Deakin's speech was rather different. Reid threatened an immediate dissolution. Deakin, meanwhile, had received an assurance of general support from the Labor party, and when Reid resigned Deakin was able to take over the prime ministership. In an arrangement accepted by the Labor caucus, Deakin undertook to legislate for preferential trade and control of trusts and monopolies as well as for higher protection and industrial laws whereby more of the benefits gained through tariffs would be passed on to the workers. There was no formal coalition; each of the three parties remained separate. Labor's support of Deakin was a matter of convenience, sometimes grudging and generally fitful.

In retaliation to Deakin's strong attack on him, Reid began a strident campaign against Labor (which he characterized as the "socialist tiger") and against Deakin, whom he declared to be a puppet in Labor's hands. Describing Deakin's proposals as radical in the extreme, Reid managed to frighten some of Deakin's more conservative followers; but his bitter attacks had the over-all effect of bringing the Liberals and Labor closer together. Deakin continued to emphasize the need for more effective protection for manufacturing industries, arguing that such a policy would benefit workers as well as manufacturers. The Labor party for its part was greatly concerned with immediate objectives, and pressed for social legislation. Only mutual dislike and fear of Reid's policies held Deakin's followers and Labor together.

The Sugar Bounty Act of 1905, providing generous bounties for sugar grown by white labour, was a herald of the "new protection" under which benefits were to flow to the worker as well as the factory owner. Speaking in October 1906, Labor Senator George Foster Pearce castigated the opponents of such measures, and he added:

> They are concerned because an attempt is being made for the first time in the history of protectionist legislation to pass a little of the advantages of protection on to the man with the hoe; that when privileges are to be conferred by a protective duty the man who creates the wealth is to get a little better share of it; that when the legislative wall of protection is raised it is not to be merely on behalf of the manufacturer and the capitalist, but on behalf of the worker also.

The sugar bill was carried, and its provisions could be enforced; but other measures designed to afford greater protection to the Australian worker failed for one reason or another. Some were defeated in parliament and others which got through the legislature were declared unconstitutional by the High Court, where Chief Justice Griffith consistently gave narrower interpretation of federal powers than pleased Liberal-Labor supporters. Legislation was introduced in 1906 to extend the bounty system to other industries based on products of the soil, including cotton, flax, and dried fruits, but this bill was defeated. The Australian Industries Preservation Bill (1906), the most contentious to be introduced to parliament since the Tariff Act of 1902, was designed to prevent "dumping" of surplus goods from abroad at prices which would "destroy or injure any Australian industry," and to repress monopolist practices by firms. Some provisions of the act were later declared invalid by the High Court and the measure as a whole was not enforced. A private member's bill designed to effect the nationalization of monopolies was defeated, while an act to permit use of a "union label" on goods manufactured by firms employing trade unionists was declared unconstitutional by the High Court.

The federal parliamentarians were trying to legislate into being laws ideal for trade unionists and for free and enterprising men. Legal entanglements, and differences with state administrations were piling up, however. To deal with the increasing number of cases, Chief Justice Griffith asked that the High Court be enlarged so that its business might be dealt with more expeditiously. Two more justices were appointed to the bench. The court's decisions continued to curb federal power in favour of states' rights.

The 1906 elections did not greatly alter the balance between the parties, but Labor had moved steadily towards the doctrine of "new protection" (offering mutual benefit to the factory owner and the worker), and Deakin was able to gain parliamentary support for his programme. As well as increasing duties on manufactured goods, he saw to it that arbitration machinery was set up to mitigate the dangers and disruption of the industrial struggle.

With the enactment of Deakin's tariff of 1908, the nation embarked on a clearly defined protectionist course. The tariff provisions included sharp increases in the rates of duty on a wide range of articles. As well as protecting local industries, the tariff structure was designed to give preference to goods of British origin over those from foreign countries—a move in line with the ideas first advanced by Joseph Chamberlain in 1902. Meanwhile, the concept of "fair and reasonable" wages for all people in employment was being carried into effect through judgments of the Commonwealth Court of Conciliation and Arbitration (following the passage of a series of enactments beginning in 1904). One of the first fruits of this policy came in 1907 when Mr Justice Higgins delivered a landmark judgment establishing the principle of a minimum or basic wage which would reflect "the normal needs of the average employee regarded as a human being in a civilized community." Higgins' "harvester award" was made as part of a judgment involving the implement-making firm of H.V. McKay, and arose from provisions of the act which laid down that manufacturers were entitled to tariff protection only if they paid employees satisfactory wages. The wage was to be subject to adjustment; initially it was set at £2/2/– a week.

At the same time pensions were provided for invalids and the aged, marking the first involvement of the federal administration in the field of social services. There was general agreement that a federal welfare programme was desirable and that it should be based on the principle that pensions for the aged were not charity but recognition of past services to the community.

The creation of a relatively high tariff structure and the setting of wage standards by an official agency put the nation on a course involving active intervention by the federal government in matters significantly related to the general structure of the economy. Thus by 1908 Deakin, with Labor party co-operation, had largely molded the pattern in which Australia's future development would be cast. The High Court's judgments had frustrated some of the headlong attempts to legislate for the betterment of the working man, and other proposals failed to pass the legislature; but through the decisions of the Conciliation Court, or as a result of tariff measures, the broad aims of the "new protection" were being achieved.

External issues and defence were also being set on a new course. Australians saw their country (with New Zealand) as an outpost of British culture in a far distant setting, and they became ever more conscious of their remoteness from powerful friends. Since the 1880s, when the colonies had first come to realize that British policy in the Pacific had to take into account more factors than those of supreme importance to Australians, a feeling of closer attachment to the United States had been growing. Australian sympathies in 1898 were entirely on the side of the United States in the Spanish-American war, and American entry into the Philippines and Guam was welcomed.

Among Australians, an even closer identity of interest with Americans was clearly in evidence from the opening of the twentieth century. The natural and loyal association with Britain and other British lands still dominated the scene, but the sense of isolation within the Pacific basin which Australians had come to feel would increasingly affect national policy and draw the nation closer to the United States. At the same time, the burgeoning in the United States of an intensified spirit of national destiny was based on the Anglo-Saxon cult which was growing up, and it recognized a powerful bond of race and culture with Britain. The New Manifest Destiny (as the theory was called) was an attractive doctrine for a young and expanding nation, and writers and lecturers had expounded it to their American audiences so that it became part of the attitude of the day and thereby affected United States relationships with foreign countries. The unwritten alliance between the United States and Britain had sprung largely from it.

The Anglo-Japanese Alliance of 1902, which stemmed from England's desire to concentrate her resources against the menace of the German fleet, and Japanese fears of Russian expansion, caused mixed reaction in Australia. When American attitudes toward Japan hardened appreciably following Japan's victory in the Russo-Japanese war of 1904, Australians felt reassured; it was clear that on this issue the United States had a viewpoint akin to their own. Attitudes in the United States had been coloured by the problem of immigration from Asian lands, and similarly the fear of a flood of people pouring in from this area remained a vague but persistent factor in Australian considerations. Australian attitudes towards the United States became directly involved with Japan's emergence as a world power. Still wary about their ability to enforce demands on Russia in spite of their 1904 naval victory, the Japanese invited President Theodore Roosevelt to propose negotiations. He mediated the outstanding issues, and in the settlement reached at Portsmouth, New Hampshire, in September 1905, victorious Japan reduced some earlier demands. Roosevelt's successful mediation lifted American prestige to new heights—but the Japanese people did not share the world's acclaim for Roosevelt's peacemaking, and there were anti-American riots in many places in Japan. In turn, Americans began very quickly to lose any lingering sympathy for Japan, and relations between the two countries deteriorated.

Japan's defeat of Russia marked a turning point in the affairs of the Pacific. For the first time an Asian nation had defeated a major European power. The effect of the Treaty of Portsmouth was to establish Japan as a world power—and Australia was acutely aware of the change in Japan's status.

Australia might not be able to affect broader policies but there was a growing feeling that the Australian voice should be heard in matters related to British policies in the south Pacific. The issue of Australia's special interests arose over the handling of negotiations by Britain on the administration of the New Hebrides in 1905. The agreement reached in Paris in 1887 whereby a joint British-French naval commission was to watch over the islands and protect British and French lives and property there, had not worked out satisfactorily; affairs in the New Hebrides were more or less chaotic. Throughout, links had been maintained by Australian missionaries and trading interests, and the Australian government assumed that it would be consulted when the joint commission agreement was under review, especially since its information on conditions in the islands was believed to be much fuller and more up-to-date than that available to the British government through its High Commissioner in Fiji. In mid-1905 Australia asked the British government whether it would be possible to arrange a joint protectorate with France, and if so, on what terms, but no reply was received. Instead, according to Prime Minister Alfred Deakin,

> . . . in March 1906 a convention with France was suddenly thrown, as it were, at the head of the Commonwealth government, with an intimation that it must be accepted or rejected practically as it stood.

At the next Imperial Conference, held in London in 1907, Deakin protested strongly. Friction between the Australian government and the Colonial Office had come about, Deakin said, because of a fundamental difference of standpoint. Australians had been aggravated by a series of "exasperating losses" of island territories for some twenty years, and it was reasonable to expect that the Commonwealth should have been consulted in any negotiations.

In addition, Deakin said, Winston Churchill, speaking in the House of Commons as Under-Secretary for Colonial Affairs, had flagrantly misrepresented Australian policy, thereby setting public opinion in Australia unanimously against the government and rendering it impossible "to follow the traditional practice of trying to support statements made on behalf of the British government."

Replying, Lord Elgin, the Colonial Secretary, could say only that the British government had not meant the oversight and everything would be done to avoid any repetition of the misunderstanding. He explained the circumstances of a change of government midway in the negotiations with France as something that may have occasioned some oversight in neglecting to keep Australia informed of what was going on.

By this time, the growing stature and soaring ambitions of the Dominions, notably Australia and Canada, were beginning to have a marked effect on relationships. Whitehall found the new attitudes disconcerting; although they showed undiminished loyalty to the Crown, the Dominions were striking out on their own, no longer prepared to follow meekly the British government's policies on foreign affairs. The need to reconcile local autonomy with Imperial unity had come to the surface.

Deakin reflected the new spirit of independence; at the same time he never lost sight of the importance of the interdependence that he felt must be maintained among units of the British Empire. He believed the time had come for the Dominions to be consulted on foreign affairs. Cautiously he raised the question at the 1907 Conference, suggesting that a permanent Imperial secretariat would be one way to bring the Empire units closer. Noting that matters of foreign politics occasionally touched closely some or all of the "dependencies of the Empire" and among them some or all of the self-governing communites, Deakin said:

> At the present time any commission on these matters is indirect of necessity but it is also impeded by other considerations. We may appear officious;... [but] we desire to be in a position to be able to make such necessary inquiries in regard to foreign policies as may appear to us to be urgent and important, to make them direct, to obtain a reply, and, if that reply [warrants it], to communicate through a secretariat [set up with] the other self-governing communities.

The need for the Dominions to raise matters or consult on special problems might rarely arise, Deakin conceded, but when these issues did arise, "they might be vital indeed to some or all of us."

Deakin's proposal for an Empire secretariat was not well received, and nothing was done.

Deakin had done what he could to impress on London facts and attitudes arising from Australia's position as an outpost, but the degree of independent initiative in foreign affairs open to Australia within the framework of the British association was limited. For Australians at large it was the appearance in Australian ports of Roosevelt's Great White Fleet that provided practical reassurance; the fleet's tour of duty in 1908 was largely an outcome of tension that existed between Japan and the United States.

A major transfer of power was taking place in the Pacific. British naval strength in that area had been seriously reduced after 1905; the decision had been made at that time to concentrate on countering the menace to Britain of a growing German fleet, and all the Royal Navy's battleships in eastern waters had been withdrawn to bolster the North Sea fleet; all the powerful new Dreadnought additions to the fleet were similarly stationed in home waters. The safety of the British possessions in Asia and the Pacific, although no longer directly secured by the presence of the British Navy, was considered to be secured by the goodwill of Britain's ally, Japan, as guaranteed by the Anglo-Japanese Alliance. As one English writer put it, the bulk of the British navy could not proceed with the defence of the outlying parts of the Empire "until the safety of the heart was assured."

Many Australians did not see things in quite the British way; living in an almost defenceless country, they were far from happy with the security arrangements England had made for them. Their hope was that American interest would grow—and that American friendship might be redeemed in the form of protection. Signs of closer relationships and a growing identity of interest were welcomed. At the time of the United States fleet's visit a warmth of feeling for Australia was being expressed in the United States. The *New York Times* supported the concept of a separate Australian identity by declaring that in future, affairs in the Pacific could not be settled without regard for Australia, and went even further by adding that to an extent America's problems were identical with those of Australia. Other newspapers acknowledged the importance of Australia's potential and argued that its future had to be assured. "The United States will use its mighty power if need be to help preserve Australia's interests," the New York *Herald Tribune* declared.

The practical reassurance provided by the visit of the United States fleet to Sydney, Melbourne, and Albany, was demonstrated by the tumultuous welcome given to the visitors. In Sydney the fleet's arrival was greeted as an event which had been anticipated (as the *Sydney Morning Herald* said) "with an eagerness and enthusiasm without limit and in many respects without precedent in our history." The law courts were adjourned for the whole week of the visit, and a public holiday was gazetted. People poured in from even the remoter parts. A newspaper report said:

> There is not a township or district in New South Wales in which men have not for weeks past been preparing to set their businesses aside and join in the celebrations.

Cardinal Moran announced that he would excuse Catholics from the obligation of abstinence on the coming Friday because of the difficulty of providing fasting fare for such multitudes. There were tableaux in shop windows, illuminations in the streets, stands at vantage points. Around the foreshores and heights of the great harbour, 500,000 people were on hand to greet the fleet as ferryboats, tugs, yachts, launches and coasters all intermingled on the waters of the harbour. "Only one other event in our history has attracted a gathering so representative in character and so united in sentiment; this was the inauguration of the Commonwealth," the *Sydney Morning Herald* declared. American newspapers carried reports of the visit and the warm welcome accorded the visitors. "It was a manifestation of friendship that would not be forgotten," the *New York Times* concluded.

Underlying the festivities and the platitudinous speech-making was the comforting feeling that the warships' presence was proof of a solidarity existing between the two nations and recognition of a mutually-held view on the need to restrain Japan.

The United States fleet's visit had set Australians thinking about the great world beyond their shores. The visit clearly underscored the need for the new nation to develop naval power under its own control. This issue had been to the fore over many years. In 1902, at the time of the signing of the Anglo-Japanese Alliance, Sir Edmund Barton took to an Imperial Conference in London a submission proposing that an Australian navy should be created. The proposal got nowhere. At the meeting the British authorities advocated not only a "single navy under one control" (though with contributions of men and money from the Dominions) but went further, putting forward the idea of a single Imperial army, with headquarters in England and divisions throughout the Empire; and although the one-army proposal was castigated by the Canadian and Australian representatives as objectionable in principle, since it derogated from the powers of self-government enjoyed by the Dominions, the plan for a separate Australian navy was not pressed by Barton. Instead he agreed to Australia's contributing £200,000 a year as part of the cost of keeping a British squadron in Australian waters; he also undertook to supply crews for four ships. The agreement won little support, and in the general election of 1903 Barton's government was defeated.

Deakin, Barton's successor, took a stronger line. In 1907 at another London conference which explored some of the defence problems of the Pacific, Deakin revived the earlier proposal for an Australian naval squadron, proposing that the existing arrangement be reconsidered. His advocacy of more adequate defence for Australia was something that Australians themselves had to act upon, however, since it involved the creation of an Australian squadron paid for by the Australian taxpayer and controlled by the Australian government. As concern over defence matters intensified, Deakin ardently supported the creation of a separate Australian naval force.

At the next Imperial Conference on defence matters, held in London in 1909, Australia undertook to set up a wholly Australian fleet paid for, controlled, and manned by Australians. The proposal was accepted. The Naval Defence Act was passed in 1910; by that time the first three destroyers were on order. Other ships—a battle cruiser and two light cruisers—and two submarines were ordered from Britain for the force whose approved title was the Royal Australian Navy. The Labor party had taken over by this time, and the party's strong national sentiment helped spur the drive for an Australian defence effort. There was a mild sense of relief when vessels ordered in Britain arrived in Australian waters, and when the destroyer *Warrego* was launched from a Sydney dockyard in April 1911; it was the first ship of war ever built in Australia and the occasion was noted at the time as "naturally one of considerable jubilation."

As tension mounted in Europe, greater attention was given to strengthening military as well as naval defence. Generally there had been growing political pressure for stronger military forces and, in spite of problems posed by the split authority held by the Council for Defence and the Military Board, there were signs of an improved military organization. As early as 1903 the Labor party had advocated formation of a citizen defence force, and Deakin's call in 1907 for a "citizen soldiery inspired by patriotism" (and based on the Swiss model) had gained all-party support. Lord Kitchener reported on defence matters in 1909, and Imperial Defence Conferences in 1909 and 1911 furthered the formation of an organization able to give effective service in war and to co-operate with the British army. Australia was represented on the Imperial General Staff at its headquarters in London. Before long a citizen force was in being, and by 1912 more than 100,000 boys had also been drawn into a programme under which they were taught the elements of drill. In 1911 the Royal Military College was established at Duntroon to provide a nucleus of professionally trained soldiers.

From 1911, Britain's increasing involvement with Japan as an ally caused deepening concern in Australia. It was apparent that with the completion of the Panama Canal (under active construction from 1907) the United States would be prepared to play a larger role in the Pacific, and as fear of a "yellow peril" grew there was evidence of a stiffening of American attitude toward Japan, whose aggrandisement was widely opposed in the United States and Canada. California's open discrimination against Japanese in matters of land ownership continued to attract attention in Japan, leading to mounting tensions which newspapers openly expressed. Canada had been alert to the dangers of Japanese migration and, with the assistance of the British Ambassador in Tokyo, a special Canadian representative had negotiated arrangements with Japan about immigration into British Columbia, a *modus operandi* indicating a greater degree of independence in foreign relationships than Australia had yet achieved. Canadian initiatives in foreign affairs had been apparent for some time; commercial treaties had also been negotiated with foreign powers, and for years Canada had had a High Commissioner in London—a move which Australia followed with the appointment of George Reid late in 1909.

Dangerous implications arising from the growing divergence between the Pacific policies of Britain and the United States were somewhat lessened when the Anglo-Japanese treaty was rewritten in 1911 so that Britain would not have to go to war on behalf of Japan against the United States; however, for Australia the dilemma remained. From Australia's viewpoint, the Anglo-Japanese Alliance could be rationalized only on the basis that it was better to have Japan as an ally than as an assailant (which some politicians had spoken of as a distinct possibility). What was feared most was that population pressures in Japan might result in a tide of immigration and that the onus of defending Australia against possible Japanese immigration would be something that would have to be borne by Australia alone.

A forceful article in the Imperial affairs periodical, *The Round Table* (June 1912) drew attention to the Australian point of view on defence matters and the dangers of the Anglo-Japanese treaty. The writer claimed that England was notoriously out of sympathy with, and did not understand, Australia's exclusion policy, and pointed out that, under the existing arrangement, if Japan were to demand that her subjects should be admitted to Australia, England could not but allow the request. The alliance was no more than a "paper barrier" against the tremendous forces involved, since

> ... if the present Australian policy has any validity at all, it means that there is a fundamental diversity of interest between Japan and Australia... The alliance does not contain any settlement of the question of alien exclusion between Japan and any part of the Empire. Such questions are assumed not to exist or are left

without settlement and there is nothing to prevent Japan from raising them when the appropriate time arises.

The writer went on to describe Australia as a "lonely outpost of European civilization in a region which is profoundly alien," and while he admitted that the Anglo-Japanese treaty might afford protection for "several years," he stressed that Australia had to realize the necessity to shoulder the burden of nationhood.

He set out an ideal "Australian policy" calling for naval construction and creation of bases and involving close co-operation with New Zealand and other Dominions and India on matters of naval defence, an understanding with the United States "as to mutual protection of interests," administration of British colonies in the South Seas by and from Australia, and purchase of foreign-held islands which might be used as operational bases for an offensive against Australia, as well as domestic policies designed to greatly improve economic development and foster the growth of internal unity.

In the first decade of federation, Australians regained the prosperity that had fallen from their grasp in the early 1890s. Good seasons restored the land, improved techniques were introduced in the great primary industries, and the economic fabric of the nation was repaired. Exports moved up to exceed £60 million in value annually, while imports were averaging slightly above £40 million a year. After near-stagnation in railway construction during the late 1890s, a total of some 4400 miles of new track was opened between 1901 and 1911, much of it in Queensland and Western Australia. Money was being found from Australian sources to finance expansion in rural and manufacturing activities; the area under crop increased to almost 12,000,000 acres in 1911, and although sheep numbers at 97,000,000 were still almost 10,000,000 below the 1891 record, wool production had passed the previous peak. Just over half the nation's sheep were being grazed in New South Wales, with 20,000,000 in Queensland, 13,000,000 in Victoria, 6,000,000 in South Australia, 5,000,000 in Western Australia, and less than 2,000,000 in Tasmania. The national wool clip had risen in value to over £30 million a year. Not only had sheep flocks been built up after the precipitous fall of the drought years but cattle numbers, which had been quite severely affected, were rising steadily.

New activities were fostering the growth of the cities; the proportion of the population living in metropolitan areas exceeded 38 per cent by 1911. Trade union membership, about 97,000 at federation, had increased to exceed 360,000 ten years later, and it was still rising rapidly. Among breadwinners, those engaged in primary industry numbered three in ten; there had been a solid swing to commercial activities and new jobs had opened up in transport and communications as well as in the growing number of industrial activities.

Population growth rates in the different cities had varied considerably; the "new" and undeveloped areas were absorbing people more rapidly as resources were opened up. In the first decade of federation, Western Australia was producing almost as much gold as Victoria had done in the fabulous 1850s, and a 53 per cent increase in population occurred in the western state; in the same decade the population of Queensland went up $21\frac{1}{2}$ per cent, and that of New South Wales $20\frac{1}{2}$ per cent, while both South Australia (14 per cent) and Tasmania (12 per cent) were well ahead of Victoria's very low rate of under 9 per cent in the ten years. Mining had fallen away sharply in Victoria, and economic recovery had remained slow and hesitant, even though the state's factories increased their employment figures from 60,000 to 112,000 as protection became effective as a national (rather than as a purely Victorian) policy.

Australia's open spaces were causing concern among many; the dangers of an empty land were obvious. From 1906 there were active state-run programmes to attract migrants from Britain. Hopes for a co-ordinated Commonwealth-States policy to tackle immigration on a grander scale were dashed when the individual states, convinced that immigration was wholly their preserve, resisted Deakin's persistent efforts to establish a national office in London with the function of attracting more migrants and advising prospective settlers. Nevertheless, as tensions mounted in Europe and war fears grew, more people were inclined to uproot themselves and settle in new lands, and just as a great wave of emigration was directed to the United States and Canada, so Australia attracted greater numbers. After 1910 the trickle of immigration became a stream; in 1911, 1912, and 1913 the numbers swelled to a total of well over 200,000 new settlers, nearly all from Britain but some from the Continent.

This substantial intake of migrants was matched by further gains in the economy. The 1908 tariff was encouraging local industries as existing workshops were enlarged and improved and new factories were set up to produce a wider range of products. In the five-year period ending in 1913, the number of factories increased by a little over 20 per cent, while the number of hands engaged in them went up by 31 per cent.

At the same time, the value of production of the manufacturing industries, and the total value of their output each rose at the rate of approximately 9 per cent per annum. Most of the manufacturing was on a small scale; in practically all cases the activity was in the processing of commodities directly related to primary industry as well as being tied to immediate domestic needs in clothing, food and drink, vehicles and fittings, and metal items or machinery.

An increasing number of opportunities were presenting themselves for the development of more substantial forms of industry. Tariff duties were in force on imported iron and steel and a bounty was payable on Australian-produced iron and steel, though production was practically limited to a small plant at Lithgow.

The following are the figures recording the growth of manufacturing over the period:

Numbers of Factories and Numbers of Factory Employees, 1908–1913.

FACTORIES

	New South Wales	Victoria	Queens-land	South Australia	Western Australia	Tas-mania	Total
1908	4,453	4,608	1,371	1,243	627	557	12,859
1913	5,346	5,613	1,838	1,353	763	623	15,536

FACTORY EMPLOYEES

1908	89,098	93,808	29,200	24,268	12,425	8,727	257,526
1913	120,400	118,744	42,363	28,511	17,299	9,784	337,101

Meanwhile the extension of the rail network, coinciding with the introduction of new strains of wheat and improved tillage methods, made it possible for farmers to take up greater areas in the Riverina and in Victoria's Wimmera and Mallee, and to reap far heavier crops. The area under wheat in all states had expanded from the 6,000,000 acres or so of the early 1890s to exceed 12,000,000; and because of improved yields, the harvest was now three times that of twenty years before. More farmers had been able to establish themselves on the land; governments had assisted in the effort, especially in Victoria, after 1900, as some large estates were bought for agricultural subdivision. Irrigation was being extended along the Murray and its tributaries.

Production of gold, which had given a spurt to development in Western Australia and had strengthened the national economy over-all, was declining somewhat, but new prospects were opening for other minerals. The Broken Hill mines were active, supporting a population of almost 30,000; so were the copper mines at Mount Lyell, Tasmania, and Mount Morgan, Queensland. Enterprising mine interests were able to expand output from the Barrier mines as a result of the successful development of an important advance in metallurgical technology—the flotation process for the separation of zinc from ore—and, simultaneously, the discovery that the line of lode extended far to the north and south of the original Broken Hill workings. The new treatment process, conceived in Melbourne in 1905 by a Belgian-born brewer, Auguste de Bavay, made possible the extraction of zinc from Broken Hill ores already yielding lead and silver; before long the process was to create new prospects for Australian non-ferrous mining enterprises in general.

Education was being given greater attention by the various state administrations. In reaction to the depression of the 1890s, when expenditure on teacher training and school building had been severely curtailed, the first decade of federation was a period of educational reform. The return of prosperity, the pride of new nationhood, the demand of growing industries and businesses for better-educated staff, the needs of the public services (for all of which, recruitment was now by public examination) were creating a climate of opinion critical of the inadequacies of the existing educational systems. Expert commissions had made a thorough examination in three states—in Victoria from 1899 to 1901, in New South Wales from 1903 to 1904, and in Tasmania in 1904—and the findings of these commissions were extended to the other states through the state directors of education, who met regularly after 1906. New administrative leaders, most of them born and educated in Australia, carried out the reforms in teacher training, including substitution of training in teachers' colleges for the pupil-teacher system, and in many other aspects of education. Fresh and determined efforts were made to put into practice the ideal of equal educational opportunity by the state governments' assumption of increased responsibility for secondary schools, and by the introduction of unique methods of teaching by correspondence.

Up to this time the states (except Queensland) had left all responsibility for secondary education to the Church schools. Besides perpetuating a system of class privilege, this arrangement produced inadequate supplies of recruits with higher educational qualifications for the teaching profession and the universities. Queensland had pioneered the state secondary system in the early 1860s, with a plan of subsidies to municipalities able to set up grammar schools; this pioneering effort had been brought about by the fact that in Queensland church schools were fewer than in the southern colonies and there was a special need to improve and extend them. In New South Wales a few high schools were founded after 1880, and secondary subjects were introduced into a considerable number of primary schools, which were then called "superior" schools. Victoria and Tasmania preferred to encourage talent by a system of state scholarships to church secondary schools. After 1906 there was a great increase in the number of state secondary schools, with all states sharing in the expansion; it included not only academic high schools but also junior technical, commercial, and various other types of vocational schools.

Not to be left behind in the search for higher education, Catholic educationists also greatly increased and extended their secondary school systems.

University education was extended to two more states with the founding of universities in Brisbane (1911) and Perth (1913), the latter the first university in any British land to provide free tuition.

Unorthodox methods had to be adopted to help children in remote areas —children whose nearest neighbours might live scores of miles away. The correspondence system of education began more or less by accident when a country mother living more than eight miles from the nearest school wrote to the education department, in Melbourne, for advice about teaching her sons. The question was turned over to the teacher-training college, where a group of trainees was deputed to try to teach the children by correspondence. Their success with these and other country pupils made it clear that, provided there was a literate parent (or even a literate neighbour) it was possible to instruct by mail children who had never seen the inside of a schoolhouse. A full-time correspondence school was established in Victoria in 1917, and it was followed shortly by similar schools in other states. Teaching methods and procedures worked out in these institutions were to give practical meaning to the democratic ideal of equal educational opportunity for all children.

Labor parliamentary representation increased at each federal election. Elements in the party were becoming increasingly restive at maintaining a minority party—the Liberals—in power, and by 1908 Andrew Fisher, who had succeeded to the party leadership, was able to form a government. William Morris Hughes, the most vital influence in the party, became Attorney-General. However, within a year, Deakin was back—this time supported by some of his erstwhile opponents among the free-traders. Public reaction to the blatant opportunism of the manoeuvre that brought Deakin back to power, coupled with Labor's vigorous campaign tactics, resulted in a decisive electoral swing in 1910 which for the first time gave the Labor party a clear-cut majority in both the House of Representatives and the Senate.

Zeal and purpose had carried Labor to success, scattering the opposing groups, including the once-great Liberal party, in the process. The challenge presented by the rising Labor party, with a new sense of destiny and strengthened discipline, had been sufficient to cause a shift in political alignments. Deakin the Liberal, and his party, had been happy to support legislation designed to curb abuses apparent in the industrial system, and to work towards removal of gross inequalities in society; but the Liberals' drive to break down causes of class bitterness had always been held in check by their equally deep concern to avoid action which might result in loss of individual freedom or the submergence of the individual to the state. Even though their objectives sometimes seemed much the same, Liberals and Labor had harboured subtle but clearcut differences in outlook on many issues, and in time these came to the surface. Labor's loudly proclaimed objective of control (if not acquisition) of large-scale private industry, and other proposals smacking of socialist doctrine, alienated Deakin and his followers, and brought about a fusion with other elements. As liberal and conservative groups coalesced and many factions, some of which had previously been in violent opposition, were thrown together, Hughes twitted the newly-formed coalition as one which "is just now known as the Anti-Socialist party." Hughes was shrewdly foretelling that henceforth political alignments would be on a new basis: Labor on the one hand, and on the other a combination of the forces in opposition to Labor.

Hughes had done much to make Labor acceptable to a wide following. He was in the vanguard of Labor leaders who advanced the cause of legislative improvement while deriding strike action. He attempted to show that the old days of industrial anarchy would not be repeated; the party was actively suggesting remedies for social ills, and was developing legislative programmes to put the remedies into effect. In his persuasive and forcefully-written *The Case for Labour*, published in 1910, he said:

> Now the whole effort of the Labor Party is to substitute order for chaos in the industrial and economic spheres, and that section—an overwhelming majority—of unionists who support the Labor movement is in accord with [the Party] in this effort.

The 1910 poll resulted in forty-two Labor men (with two pro-Labor independents) being returned in a house of seventy-five; in the Senate, Labor won all eighteen contested seats. Caucus ballotted for the ten Labor ministers and Fisher then allotted the portfolios.

Control of the party was in moderate and responsible hands, and in spite of grim forebodings from opponents, Labor's assumption of power under Andrew Fisher brought few radical changes even though there was some progressive legislation. There were some increases in pensions, maternity bonuses were introduced, and measures were taken to strengthen the defence forces in line with earlier pledges. The Navigation Act was strengthened to give greater protection to Australian shipping and the seamen involved in it. The sphere of arbitration was significantly extended when the government decided to authorize federal employees to approach the court for a determination of wages and conditions of employment. However, conservative elements were able to find targets for strong criticism in the federal land tax (1910) and the measure to set up the Commonwealth Bank.

The land tax was levied on the unimproved value of land in excess of £5000 and on all land owned by absentee owners. Hughes, reflecting the strong influence in the Labor party still exerted by Henry George's theories, had foreshadowed land-tax legislation when he wrote in 1909 that such a tax was the main plank in Labor's platform, adding that the land, which belonged to the whole people, should be available to them, whereas at present it was monopolized by a few. In spite of Labor's hopes, the measure had little effect in breaking up the large estates and, since it was not the only tax imposed, it did not satisfy the purists among George's followers.

The banking proposal arose from the provision in the constitution which conferred on the federal parliament power to make laws on banking and on the issue of paper money. Interest in the setting-up of a "people's bank" had been strong within the Labor movement for some years; from 1905 the Labor platform had advocated a bank under government ownership, and establishment of a government-owned bank was included in the party's electioneering proposals in 1908. The Barton ministry had promised banking legislation without doing anything about it, and as the years passed without action conservative groups had been encouraged to hope that the matter would remain dormant; but since the constitution placed control of the currency and the issuance of bank notes in the federal sphere, some positive action was inevitable.

From the early days various Australian banks had issued their own notes as a convenience. In the case of banks in Victoria the notes had to have the backing of an equal value of coin, bullion, or government bonds, and elsewhere there were somewhat similar (though less rigid) requirements. The bank crashes of the 1890s brought to the fore the proposal that notes might be issued freely by a government as a counter measure to any "run" on the banks. Among the many proposals for financial reform that blossomed after the crisis were suggestions that governments should become responsible for the note issues. The only colony to act was Queensland, where the government took control of the note issue in 1893 by enforcing a prohibitive tax on private bank issues. By that time the premiers of New South Wales, Victoria, and South Australia had met and declared themselves in favour of some measure of control over note issues and also in favour of uniform banking laws. Since the profit on issuance of bank notes was negligible, many private bankers were inclined to welcome proposals for a soundly-planned official note issue. Meeting in 1895, leading bankers expressed varying views on how best the matter might be resolved. Although there was no strong opposition to reform, it was generally felt that the question should be held over until it could be handled on a national basis; some bankers still had serious misgivings, and these were again expressed at a further meeting in 1901.

Soon the bankers had reason to fear federal control of the note issue. Wildcat schemes were afoot; some who backed the proposal for a federal note issue saw in it a panacea for all ills. Political theorists put forward the engaging delusion that the printing press might be used to do away with the need for borrowing money from abroad. With equal vigour, those who opposed the contentious move to establish a federal note issue expressed their fears of devastating inflation if control of the currency passed into hands where it would be subject to political control.

There were sound reasons for instituting an official note issue, but nevertheless the first Commonwealth parliament was too busy to take up the proposals prepared by the Treasurer, Sir George Turner, which followed Canadian legislation on the subject. When the matter came up again, in 1907, bankers were fearful of the outcome, and they expressed such strong opposition that Deakin dropped a draft bill. The Labor party's attitude was hardening, however, and in 1909 Fisher promised legislation to allow the federal treasurer to issue notes. The measure was enacted in 1910. Gold backing had to be maintained to the extent of one fourth of the value of notes issued up to £7 million and to the extent of a sovereign for each £1 note in excess of this amount. The banks had to withdraw their notes by July 1911 or incur a tax of 10 per cent a year on them. The measure provided sound safeguards, and it was accepted without great public interest; even banking groups were unable to muster any strong opposition. The amount of gold coinage in use in Australia was greater than in any other country, on a population basis, and the expectation was that the circulation of notes would remain relatively limited. By late 1911 the bulk of the old bank notes had been withdrawn from circulation, to be replaced by official notes; at first these were no more than unissued notes which the trading banks had on hand overprinted with the words "Australian Note" and the signature of two Treasury officials. It was not until 1913 that the Commonwealth's own notes, strangely austere by comparison with some of the trading banks' flamboyant designs, were released.

In December 1911 the government dropped the restrictive provisions applying to its note issue when new legislation permitted an issue of any size with 25 per cent gold backing against the whole. Bankers and commercial interests expressed alarm; they regarded this move as a breach of an undertaking recently given, and they feared the consequences of the move as opening the door to inflationary practices.

Pressure from within the Labor party for creation of a government bank induced the Fisher ministry to introduce the Commonwealth Bank Bill in October 1911; the bill was passed eight weeks later. Some radicals hoped that by its superior backing and untarnished appeal it would be able to overwhelm the existing banks; but the legislation did not provide for central bank functions and in fact it did no more than provide for the creation of a trading bank and a savings bank—the latter to operate in opposition to state-owned savings banks. Some professional bankers professed to believe that the new bank would be controlled by political amateur financiers and that it would do nothing for the well-being of the community; but the moderation evident in Fisher's handling of the issue disposed of much of the criticism, and when a leading banker, Denison Miller, was appointed as its first governor there was little further that could be said against the move. The act fixed the capital of the bank at £1,000,900, but this capital was not raised. The bank's initial funds were provided by an advance of £10,000 from the Treasury, and between July and September 1912, agencies were opened in Victoria, Queensland, and the Northern Territory to handle savings accounts. Within six months the new bank had begun its trading activities, with an office in each state capital. Events were soon to give it a significance that none could truly foresee at its initiation.

If the first decade of the Commonwealth's existence had been a period of adjustment and somewhat slow advance because of economic conditions, the first period of Labor power (1910–13) was one of more rapid progress. The groundwork already laid was proving effective, and national income was rising. In its endeavours to press on with its aims of social advancement, however, Labor found that the constitution curbed some of the party's ambitions by placing definite limits on its legislative freedom.

Labor had come to support the idea of a federal system with greater centralized power. After a series of measures had been declared invalid by the High Court, the party decided to seek constitutional amendments which would clear the way for more sweeping social and economic programmes. In 1911 and again in 1913, Labor sponsored referendums which would have transferred significant additional powers in industrial and economic matters to the federal sphere. The proposed extension to the Commonwealth's powers were in connection with trade and commerce, and they would have provided for control of corporations, labour, and employment (including wages and conditions of labour and the settlement of disputes) and of "combinations and monopolies"; a second amendment was to give the Commonwealth power to nationalize any industry declared by parliament to be the subject of a monopoly. The proposals were rejected by the electors. This defeat of the proposals set limits to the degree of social experiment that the federal parliament could undertake.

On matters of revenue-raising, however, the federal legislature's powers were extremely wide. In its financial provisions the constitution placed the Commonwealth in a dominant financial position since the federal parliament held the power to tax in any field and the exclusive right to impose customs and excise duties (which had been the most lucrative source of income to the colonies). For the first ten years the Commonwealth was obliged to refund to the states three quarters of customs-excise revenue it garnered, and there was a further provision for any federal surplus to go back to the states; with federal departments multiplying and expenditure increasing, the latter provision was meaningless. Under a federal-states financial agreement in 1910, state debts were to be taken over by the Commonwealth and the states were to receive a fixed annual payment of 25/– per head of population; of the two constitutional amendments to seal this, only that related to states' debts was approved by the electors. The Fisher government then introduced a "surplus revenue" act which provided for per capita payment to the states at the rate of £1 per head, and per capita payments continued until a new arrangement was arrived at in 1927.

Meanwhile after a protracted search and much bickering, the location of a federal capital territory had been agreed upon: the choice was 911 square miles of hills and valleys locked away in the eastern ranges of New South Wales where the Cotter, Murrumbidgee, and Molonglo rivers converge. The site was agreed upon in 1909, and two years later the Fisher government called for designs for the new city. In 1912 a rambling plan by Chicago architect, Walter Burley Griffin was chosen for Canberra's development. In the same year construction began on the 1,000 mile trans-Australia railway between Kalgoorlie and Port Augusta which Western Australians had demanded as a price for joining the federation.

The general elections of 1913 produced a political deadlock; Joseph Cook, successor to Deakin on the latter's retirement, gained a majority of one in the House of Representatives but was in a minority in the Senate. In mid-1914 the Governor-General granted a dissolution of both houses, and a new election was set for September 5. By that time, war had broken out in Europe, and this gave a new direction to affairs.

World War I 18

Australia was in the throes of an election campaign during the rapidly mounting crisis in Europe which followed the assassination on June 28, 1914, of the Archduke Franz Ferdinand of Austria; but there was never any doubt about where Australia stood in relation to that struggle-in-the-making. Both political parties were unequivocally pledged to fight by Britain's side, and it would not be a token effort. "If it is to be war, you and I shall be in it," Joseph Cook, the outgoing Prime Minister, told his countrymen, adding,

> If the old country is at war so are we . . . I hope there will be no need for our brave men to leave our shores, but I am perfectly certain, if the need arises, we shall see a response as spontaneous and complete as at any time in our history.

The Labor leader, Andrew Fisher, was equally outspoken. "Should the worst happen after everything has been done that honour will permit," he declared, "we Australians will help and defend the mother-country to our last man and our last shilling." In the election (held on September 14) the Labor party made considerable gains, and Fisher became Prime Minister.

The war moves in Europe came at a time when concern over Japanese intentions was still intense in Australia. The country's forces were limited, and reports that Japan might use the occasion to force a way south and so relieve its population pressures were frequently quoted. In May 1914 the *Sydney Morning Herald* had declared that

> . . . here at the very gateway to Asia we may be pardoned if we do not view the future concerning the Anglo-Japanese alliance with such complacency as do some British statesmen.

Nevertheless, as war exploded in Europe, whatever fears Australians might have held were swept away in the enthusiasm of support for the patriotic cause. Few seriously believed that "the Kaiser's war" would last long; there was supreme faith in the Allies' ability to maintain "business as usual" and at the same time dispose quickly of the threat to a secure way of life.

At noon on August 5, Prime Minister Cook announced that he had received through the Governor-General a dispatch from the Colonial Secretary stating that war had broken out with Germany. As a unit of the British Empire, Australia technically was at war from the same moment as Britain, but the extent of participation was a matter for Australia to decide. There was no doubt of the response. Melbourne *Punch* wrote that in this "greatest crisis of our history," Australia

> ... must face the present with readiness for every service and the future with fortitude and faith. It has not been by choice that we have entered into the desperate life struggles of the white nations. The hell is none of our making. No vote that we have cast has helped it. But we are in it, and the time for regret has passed. ...
>
> There has been no argument about the justness of Britain's cause, no doubts about the sincerity of her disinterested spirit. We are fighting to secure the honourable fulfilment of international contracts, and to protect small peoples from the greed of their neighbours.

Even as the thunder of war broke across Europe the government had cabled the Colonial Office on August 3:

> The Government is prepared to place the vessels of the Australian navy under the control of the Admiralty. The Government is further prepared to dispatch an expeditionary force of 20,000 men of any suggested composition to any destination desired by the home government, the force to be at the complete disposal of the home government.

The offer was accepted, and in Melbourne Sir William Throsby Bridges, the Inspector-General of the military forces, set about organizing the expeditionary force. The British authorities had been thinking earlier in terms of an Australian force organized in brigades which could be split up among existing British units; but Bridges had been against this idea of fragmentation and loss of national identity of Australian soldiers, and he had persuaded the government to offer a complete division so that the Australian troops could be kept together as a separate entity in the field.

There were home-front problems to be tackled. At first, pastoralists and farmers feared that the wool and wheat they were producing might be valueless because markets would be cut off; the great base metal mines (whose ores had been sold to Germany) were in imminent danger of closing. Action had already been taken to put the country on a war footing, however. The stock exchanges were closed temporarily to prevent panic selling. The premiers were asked to limit their borrowing for public works but at the same time they were assured that the Federal Treasury would make some money available to maintain essential public works programmes. To safeguard internal security, all aliens were obliged to register. To sustain morale, the government imposed a strict censorship on the press. Soon the Federal

Treasury was calling in sovereigns held by banks and replacing them with the notes it was printing; to many this seemed a drastic step, but even conservative bankers agreed with the move, some going so far as to urge that for the duration of the war the notes should be made inconvertible to gold. It was only one of a succession of measures that were to affect the lives of individuals and reshape financial and economic affairs over the coming years.

Men sought leave from business firms or rushed from country jobs to enlist in the army. Within four days of the outbreak of war, details had been worked out by Bridges and his staff for the raising of an Australian expeditionary force. Ships were chartered to transport men and horses and equipment, and within eight weeks an army was equipped and ready to move off for distant battlefields. It was decided that Bridges should be given command of the overseas contingent which he had created—and named, by him, the Australian Imperial Forces. New Zealand was also enlisting volunteers; the departure of the New Zealand force was delayed by fears of German raiders, but on October 16 ten transports left Wellington to join the Australian force assembled at Albany, Western Australia. By November the combined force of thirty-eight transports was steaming across the Indian Ocean, with an escort of four cruisers—the British battle cruiser *Minotaur*, the Japanese battle cruiser *Ibuki*, and the light cruisers *Sydney* and *Melbourne*.

At Point Cook, in Victoria, a few men were undergoing training at the newly-established flying school. Two English airmen were acting as instructors, and five training planes were in use; but as yet no airmen were available to join the land forces.

By this time all the German island possessions in the Pacific had been occupied. The first move came when New Zealand troops were sent to German Samoa; accompanied by the battle cruiser *Australia* and the French cruiser *Montcalm*, the force occupied the territory on August 30. An expedition from Australia (escorted by the light cruisers *Sydney* and *Encounter*, which were joined by *Australia*) then moved to take over German New Guinea. Early in September the German headquarters at Rabaul were occupied. Very soon outposts on the main island and all the near by German islands of the Bismarck Archipelago were taken over; all opposition was overcome by September 24.

It was decided that *Australia* and *Montcalm* should at once hunt for two German cruisers believed to be operating in the region of the Marshall Islands—a decision which changed the composition of the escort of the main Australian-New Zealand convoy. *Australia* not being available, the convoy's protection depended largely on the Japanese cruiser *Ibuki*. As the convoy steamed across the Indian Ocean and passed the Cocos Islands (at a distance of 90 miles or so) a radio message from the Australian-operated signal station on November 8 reported the presence of a strange ship of war. The British officer in command of the convoy assigned *Sydney* the task of pursuit and attack; at nine o'clock on November 9 the German cruiser *Emden* was sighted, and the first sea fight in the history of the Australian Navy began. A landing party from *Emden* had by then completed the destruction of the installation on Cocos; as *Sydney* hove in sight the cruiser put to sea and on clearing the island opened the action. It was a running fight at long range. Before eleven o'clock the German cruiser which had sunk or captured seventeen British merchant vessels and torpedoed other Allied ships, was beached, a flaming mass of twisted metal, on Cocos.

With *Emden* out of the way, the whole of the Indian Ocean was safe; meanwhile, the danger of German raiders in the Pacific had been further reduced as the Japanese moved to take over the Caroline, Marshall, and Mariana Islands, and Nauru was occupied by an Australian detachment sent from Rabaul.

It was initially intended that the Australian and New Zealand expeditionary forces would be trained in England; but with the onset of a cold winter there this plan was changed before the expedition reached Suez. It was decided that training would be completed in Egypt. The first units reached Alexandria on December 3, and soon the infantrymen and cavalrymen were on manoeuvres in the desert. Under the over-all command of General Sir William Riddell Birdwood, a British officer, they were formed into the Australian and New Zealand Army Corps. In November, Turkey joined Germany, and from this moment the Allies feared that Russia, short of supplies, might collapse. As the war in Europe ground to a frightening stalemate after stunning German successes, a plan was developed to force the Dardanelles so that the way could be opened for the Allied powers to reach Russia's southern flank: if the Dardanelles route could be opened, guns and ammunition and supplies could reach the hard-pressed Russian forces and the grain supplies of southern Russia would be available to the Allies. Furthermore, there was the hope that a sharp blow might drive Turkey out of the war, making possible an attack through the Balkans and along the Danube.

An attempt was made (in February-March, 1915) to force the Dardanelles by British and French warships, but it failed when three battleships were sunk by mines or by torpedoes fired from the well-protected shore batteries. A second naval attack failed; but it alerted the Turks to the likelihood of a land assault. The decision was taken in London to launch a great military attack on the peninsula of Gallipoli, and accordingly the Mediterranean expeditionary force, assembled in Egypt, was prepared for invasion. The Australian and New Zealand troops—who by now had become known as Anzacs, a term coined from the initials of the Australia-New Zealand Army Corps—were to be the principal assault group to effect a landing. In addition to the nearly 20,000 Australians and 10,000 New Zealanders, there were over 20,000 British and Indian troops and 16,000 French soldiers in the force. This army with its guns and supplies was to be landed, under enemy fire, on the Gallipoli shore. Never before had an amphibious operation been carried out on such a scale. The main force for the assault was assembled on Lemnos, a Greek island about 40 miles from Gallipoli, and here an armada of 200 ships gathered. The assault troops completed their training, practising every phase of the undertaking, and on April 24 the invasion fleet steamed from Lemnos.

In the early hours of April 25, under cover of darkness, the 1,500 Australians who were to make the first landing took their places in the boats, and by dawn the assault had begun. Only as the men reached the rugged shore was it realized that the flotilla had been carried north of the intended landing spot; instead of fairly level land they faced rough slopes rising 300 feet, and tangled ridges. The landing was made over mined and wired waters, and in the face of withering crossfire. Hidden snipers were able to pick off the men as they struggled to gain a foothold.

Throughout the day the invasion continued as other groups joined the invading forces. A war correspondent wrote of this heroic assault: "Across the valley they struggled, shouting their battle song: 'Australia will be there'." By nightfall some 16,000 Anzacs, including Bridges, had landed and the beachhead was crowded with stores and equipment. There were countless examples of personal gallantry. The landing had been achieved; but the losses had been heavy—more than 2300 men were dead, and nearly 6000 more had been wounded. An immediate evacuation was considered, but the thought of withdrawal after so great a sacrifice was unacceptable, and instead the troops on the beachhead were ordered to dig in. The next day the first field gun was taken ashore and set up. The Turks launched counter-attacks but their fire failed to daunt the invaders.

As the days passed the Anzacs repelled attack after attack. A correspondent of *The Times* reported:

> No finer feat of arms has been recorded in the war than the Australians' sudden landing in the dark, the storming of the heights, and the holding of the position won by these raw colonials.

For all their heroism, however, there was no hope of success in the major objective—capture of the peninsula. Thirteen miles south of Anzac Cove (as the small bay of Ari Burnu was by now called), British troops who landed on the tip of the peninsula at the time of the first Anzac assault were unable to make headway with what was intended to be the main offensive of the Gallipoli campaign. They faced impossible objectives and their casualties were heavy; an Anzac brigade was sent as reinforcements for a new offensive in May, but in spite of its heroism the charge wilted in the face of devastating fire. The survivors were taken back to Anzac Cove. Here, the shallow triangle running in from the beach less than a quarter mile was still dominated from strongly-held heights; its total extent remained well under a square mile. In this confined space there was ceaseless activity as well as the "radiant force of camaraderie in action." Water and supplies were constantly short, however, and medical arrangements were primitive. No one lost heart, but little could be done. A "factory" had been set up to make hand-grenades and other small bombs—some of which were built up from scrap material. Other improvised forms included the periscope rifle developed for the close-range trench warfare, with the enemy only a few yards from the forward positions. The Turks for their part showed desperate courage in their all-out efforts to drive the Anzacs into the sea. During July, ten Turkish divisions or their equivalents were sent to strengthen the defenders of the peninsula.

Neither side could gain ground, nor would either side yield any. After tremendous sacrifices, a stalemate had been reached.

In August the Anzacs were reinforced by British troops, and a determined effort was made to seize the dominating heights. The climax of the campaign was an engagement in a tangle of crags and gullies with bitter hand-to-hand fighting. Four thousand Anzacs were killed in the fierce battle for Sari Bair, fought in blistering heat. At one point an assault carried New Zealand and British troops to the ridge from which the Narrows of the Dardanelles could be seen—but the position could not be held. A third beachhead was meanwhile established at Suvla Bay, a few miles north of Anzac Cove, by British troops. This landing was made by 20,000 men without opposition, but from that point they could make no significant gains.

As the months passed and it became clear that the whole Gallipoli venture was a fiasco, there was widespread criticism. It was evident that the Dardanelles plan could not be carried through successfully without more troops than could be spared from the fighting in Europe. By October the idea of evacuation was under discussion in London. From the blazing heat of summer, the weather on Gallipoli was turning cold; soon bitter winds whipped up from ice and snow. In November Field Marshal Lord Kitchener, Britain's Secretary for War, visited the Gallipoli beachheads, and from his observations reluctantly confirmed the opinion that evacuation was necessary. Kitchener reported that "with the exception of the New Zealand and Australian Army Corps, the troops are not equal to a sustained effort."

Plans were drawn up for the evacuation of the 130,000 men still on the peninsula, together with their horses, vehicles, guns, equipment, and stores. The withdrawal was to be gradual, and with secrecy and good weather to aid it disaster might be averted.

The Turks in their trenches remained unaware of the elaborate withdrawal plan that was soon under way. In less than two weeks, 40,000 Anzacs were taken off. No hint was given to the Turks that the forces opposing them were being reduced each night as men made their way stealthily to the boats, and no attack came. Little of value was left behind: millions of rounds of ammunition went into the sea, guns were rendered unusable, food and stores were destroyed, machinery was put out of action, and arrangements made for supply dumps to be destroyed as the last men left. The great casualties feared by some military leaders did not occur as the peninsula was evacuated.

Early on December 20 the last boat pulled out from the shore. The vain endeavour was at an end. Australia had suffered over 26,000 casualties, with more than 7000 killed. Among the casualties was General Bridges, who had died of wounds received in the first weeks of the assault.

The Australian community was now beginning to realize what was involved in participation in a major war—something that neither the people generally nor the government itself had to this time seriously evaluated—and to count the cost not only in lives but in individual liberty. The losses on Gallipoli brought the war home as the casualty lists lengthened. Under the Defence Act, men were liable to serve within Australia and its territories in the Australian military forces, but since the war was remote from Australia the numbers required for this defence were few. As front line losses mounted, the serious depletion of the volunteer ranks meant that it was now necessary to consider ways to step up the rate of enlistment for duty overseas, and suggestions were put forward that it might be essential to make military service abroad a compulsory duty instead of a voluntary undertaking as it had been. The reaction of many groups to the suggestion was strong and immediate. Various trade unions sought specific declarations from the Prime Minister that there would be no move to introduce compulsory military service abroad. With the prevailing tension, the thought of conscription seemed to be the last straw.

In organizing the country for war, the Labor administration had assumed an increasing measure of control over the lives of the citizens, and in a land where the utmost individual freedom had prevailed this caused a growing sense of irritation and unhappiness. Two acts passed in the early days of the war had conferred sweeping powers upon the federal administration: the Trading with the Enemy Act and the War Precautions Act had been accepted as essential to the efficient war effort, although they contained none of the usual safeguards against arbitrary use of executive power. As the pressure of irksome restrictions grew, changes in community attitudes soon put an end to the old unanimity, and divisions quickly spread to the political sphere.

In the early months of the war, party politics had been put aside; the war came first in everyone's mind, and there was general agreement in state and federal spheres that contentious or party-inspired measures should be avoided. This meant that Labor had to forgo the opportunity to further party objectives at the very moment when electoral victory in the federal campaign and in New South Wales seemed to place them within grasp. The government of William Arthur Holman (in office in New South Wales for fourteen months when war broke out) was preparing various long-promised social and economic measures conforming to Labor doctrine when the informal political truce came into effect. Soon Holman was under strong pressure from his supporters to proceed, since it seemed irrelevant for state legislation to be set aside because of war. At the annual Labor conference of April 1915 Holman was accused of jettisoning Labor's platform. This call by industrial Labour was the first outward sign of a serious split developing in the party's ranks—a split caused by differences of viewpoint between Labor's parliamentary representatives, with their wider responsibilities, and the labour movement in general. In the federal sphere, where war matters were clearly paramount, Fisher was under less pressure, but growing disaffection among his party supporters convinced the mild Fisher that he could better leave the conduct of the war to his fiery and able attorney-general, William Morris Hughes. The division between Labor's industrial and parliamentary representatives was widening as viewpoints hardened on the crucial issue: reconciling the party interest to the national interest as the parliamentary leaders saw it.

Late in October 1915 Fisher resigned to become High Commissioner in London, and Hughes succeeded him as Prime Minister. Senator George Pearce, who had been Minister for Defence during the Labor administration, remained, and King O'Malley returned as Minister for Home Affairs. Hughes did not immediately advocate conscription but instead he attempted to induce a higher enlistment rate by more active recruitment backed by a crescendo of publicity. There were those who criticized this intensified recruiting as indicating a drift towards militarism; nevertheless at first these methods succeeded in lifting enlistment figures appreciably. When by mid-1916 advocacy and the other measures were losing effect, a campaign by private groups urging conscription gained support as the only practical means of providing reinforcements for the five Australian divisions overseas. Some Labor leaders were moving towards acceptance of policies of direction, but others—including Hughes—remained opposed. "So far as I know, I believe, and I hope, no circumstances will compel the adoption of conscription," Hughes declared on the eve of his departure for London early in 1916.

Unremitting opposition to conscription was expressed by small but active groups. Some unionists were critical of the measures being taken to strengthen the war effort; on the other hand there were Labor parliamentarians prepared to support bodies such as the Universal Service League in its advocacy of compulsory universal service, military and civilian.

While abroad Hughes became convinced of the need for a greater Australian war effort; he attended meetings of the British cabinet, and saw the workings of conscription in Britain. He could see the seriousness of the war situation in Europe. On his return to Australia he was determined to introduce conscription in spite of his former stand and the continuing opposition of many of his supporters. Losses in the battles being fought along the Somme were an immediate cause for concern. Hughes was prepared to accept the war council's estimates of the needed reinforcements, and he defended these figures when they were assailed as being greatly inflated. On September 1, 1916, he informed members of parliament in a secret session that he intended to put to the people the question of compulsory overseas service.

For Labor, Hughes' ascendancy had opened a new phase. The harmonious relationship that had existed between the party in general and the parliamentary leadership under Fisher was no longer maintained. Even before the conscription issue emerged there had been sharp criticism within the party of Hughes' action in abandoning a referendum for extension of federal powers (recommended by the 1915 Labor Party Conference) and accepting instead an agreement with the States for voluntary transfer of certain powers for the duration. His autocratic methods alienated many.

When Hughes advocated compulsory military service abroad, an open breach occurred within the party. Always audacious, Hughes was prepared to accept the consequences. He maintained that as parliamentary leader he had national responsibilities which had to take precedence over party policy and Labor's struggle to gain its objectives. Nevertheless, to many it was hypocrisy to talk about fighting a war for freedom and democracy if workers had to abandon the struggle to improve their lot. Labor party stalwarts maintained their opposition, and at state level party conferences and councils declared against conscription. The members of the party were disillusioned with a Prime Minister who not only asked them to postpone sound reform but sanctioned the jailing of workers and the silencing of Socialist journals because they were prejudicing recruiting. Opposition among non-committed groups was consolidated.

Hughes had support for his policies among most members of his cabinet, and, although he had one resignation from the cabinet, he was able to exert sufficient influence on the Labor federal executive to prevent it making any declaration of policy. Nevertheless, the conscription issue was so clearly divisive that Hughes considered it more prudent to put the issue to the people than to take executive action or bring forward a bill. Shrewdly he surmised that parliament would not refuse a referendum but would reject direct legislation.

The referendum on conscription held late in October 1916 resulted in 1,087,557 votes for and 1,160,033 against, with New South Wales, Queensland, and South Australia returning "no" majorities. The votes of the fighting men themselves showed only a slight majority in favour of the proposal. It was a defeat for Hughes, and it widened the break between him and his party. Opposition among Labor parliamentarians grew. On November 16, at a meeting of the party's parliamentary group, it was moved

> . . . that the Prime Minister, Mr Hughes, no longer possesses the confidence of the Party as leader, and the office of chairman be and is hereby declared vacant.

In a rage Hughes stood up and asked his supporters to follow him from the room. Four ministers and twenty-six back-benchers walked out with him; among them were former Prime Minister Watson, union organizer Spence, and Senator Pearce. With them went Holman, premier of New South Wales. All were then expelled. The Labor party had lost its most able men.

Hughes assured the Governor-General that he could still command a parliamentary majority, and a new commission was issued. He was able to form a new cabinet, and to continue in office with Liberal party support. He adopted the title of National Labor for his new cabinet.

Anti-conscription feeling in the community was conditioned to a considerable extent by extremist and sectional opinion that the war was an Imperialist adventure and that Australians' loyalties were being exploited. Those who sought to see the fighting halted noted that both the Pope and President Wilson had called for a negotiated peace, and that some German politicians were now declaring that the Allies alone were responsible for continuing the war, which could be ended, they said, any time the Allies wished.

Outspoken factions in Australia opposed to active participation in the war used the conscription issue as a rallying point. The principal anti-conscription figure to emerge was Dr Daniel Mannix, Melbourne's leading Roman Catholic prelate, whose unalloyed attachment to his native Ireland and fierce denunciations of the English as oppressors soon brought to the surface deeply divisive influences in his adopted country. To a nation crying out for reassurance that its sacrifices were not in vain, his jibe that the war, after all, was "like most wars: just an ordinary trade war" was deeply wounding and hurtful. In Sydney, a prominent judge was among the Catholic clerics and laymen who dissociated themselves from Dr Mannix's attacks; he wrote to a newspaper to express his view "in behalf of fellow Catholics" that

> ...such hatreds and such treasons, though they may be cherished by individuals, are no part and no fruit of the Catholic teachings, but have their root quite otherwise.

In spite of such general protests, and the strong opposition to him within the Church itself, Dr Mannix was obdurate. As unofficial leader of the anti-conscription forces, he continued his acid-tongued attacks, leaving behind him a trail of bitterness and controversy not only in Melbourne but throughout the country, for his speaking tours over wide areas were nationally reported.

From the Socialists there was an equally dedicated opposition to conscription. An extremist faction, the Industrial Workers of the World, or I.W.W., an offshoot of a body formed originally in Chicago in 1905 to bring together "all class-conscious workers," was active. Shortly before the outbreak of war the I.W.W., closely allied to the Socialist Labor party and operating through several small clubs in industrial centres around Sydney, had launched a publication, *Direct Action;* when the publication took a strong stand against recruiting, its editor was jailed. Members of the anti-war group campaigned against conscription and against the war effort in general, and immediately after the conscription referendum twelve were charged with (among other things) conspiring to incite sedition. All twelve men were found guilty and sentenced to long prison terms. In 1917 some additional members of the organization were convicted and jailed on charges of making statements prejudicial to recruiting. Bitterness remained; and the feeling of martyrdom left by the incidents was to remain as part of Labor's attitude of resisting conscription of Australians for military service abroad.

Hughes did not accept the referendum rebuff of October 1916 as final. In January 1917 Hughes' National Labor group and the Liberals joined forces and this fusion created the National Party. Hughes remained as Prime Minister, but in the reconstituted cabinet six of the ministers were former Liberals and only five were from the group originally led by Hughes. A general election in May 1917 confirmed the new party in power. Hughes had made the difficult transition from leading Labor to leading what was formerly the opposition party; he now determined to step up the war effort and, particularly, the enlistment rate.

Continuing controversy over the conscription issue, and a growing disenchantment, made it more and more difficult to sustain enthusiasm for enlistment, and in spite of more elaborate methods introduced to stimulate recruiting the enlistment rate in 1917 failed to reach the targets set by military authorities. There were many who felt that the government should itself take the responsibility for introducing conscription; but once again Hughes decided to put the issue to a vote instead.

Hughes had impressive support from most of the prominent men in the community. Able publicists worked with him, and the daily newspapers were all ardently favourable. At the same time, opposition was strong, and new bitterness was injected into the campaign. Dr Mannix again stirred emotions on the Irish question, and there were people to whom the ill-starred Dublin riots of Easter 1916 seemed more important than the climactic struggle taking place in France and Flanders. A pivotal question was the thorny one related to the level of recruitment essential to maintain the overseas forces, and protagonists argued it endlessly.

Throughout the bitter campaign Hughes seemed determined to court opposition in order to override it, and his oratory—often frenzied—was pungent and purposeful. Passions had been aroused, families had been divided, and political parties and religious groupings split; the issue had even been made a test of loyalty. Yet the decision of the second referendum, held on December 20, 1917, was a more decisive rejection of conscription than the first, even though there was a 10 per cent margin among servicemen overseas in favour of the proposal.

With this defeat, Hughes found himself under great political pressure. The realignment of political forces was still unstable. The endorsement Hughes's newly-contrived alliance received in the general election of May 1917 reflected the electorate's feeling that, although it did not want conscription, it wanted the "get-on-with-the-war" party to govern rather than a partially anti-war party. During the campaign leading to the referendum of December 1917 Hughes gave repeated assurances that he would resign the prime ministership if defeated, and he went through the formality of doing so early in January 1918; but the Labor party had lost every seat in the Senate and had a reduced following in the House of Representatives, and so after he had had discussions with various members of the House the Governor-General took the view that there was no reasonable prospect that anyone else could command the necessary support to form an alternative government. Accordingly Hughes and his cabinet were reinstated at once. The Governor-General took the unusual step of explaining to parliament in a memorandum that Hughes "had the best prospect of securing unity" in the National party and, therefore, of being able to form a government "having those elements of permanence so essential to the conduct of affairs during war." At this point the Nationalists unequivocally accepted Hughes as their party leader.

On the war fronts, Australian soldiers had made a name for themselves and developed a lasting reputation for bravery, initiative and endurance.

After the evacuation from Gallipoli, the Australians and New Zealanders had gone back to Egypt to prepare for new assignments. The main task lay in reorganizing the forces, which were being constantly reinforced, and in preparing for their expected transfer to the Western Front. It was decided that the infantry should go to France, while other branches—the Light Horse, the Camel Corps and the Flying Corps—remained. Their first task was to guard the Suez Canal, and it became obvious that offensive rather than defensive tactics were necessary. General Henry George Chauvel led his mounted brigade over the canal eastward into Sinai, and by defeating the Turks at Romani ended any fear of a Turkish invasion of Egypt or capture of the canal. Gradually the Sinai peninsula was cleared of the enemy and soon the Australian and New Zealand forces broke through the waste of sand dunes and were ready to drive on into Palestine. The initial objective was to encircle Gaza; the first battle of Gaza developed into a stalemate, and a second attempt (in April 1917) failed; the Australian and New Zealand forces had borne the brunt of the long, gruelling campaign, and reinforcements were needed.

General Sir Edmund Allenby was appointed to command and, with reinforcements, he turned the attack to the eastern end of the Turkish line, using the Light Horse as his spearhead. Beersheba was captured, and then Gaza fell, opening the way for Allenby's forces to drive deep into Palestine; Jerusalem was captured on December 9, 1917, and the following month the Australian division occupied Jericho. The Turks were now stiffened by German leadership and troops, while the Arabs had joined the Allies. Allenby's offensive succeeded; Tiberias was taken and Damascus was captured; the army swept on to Beirut and Tripoli (Lebanon). The Turkish army signed an armistice on October 31, 1918.

In the prolonged and difficult desert campaign, a major factor in the final success had been the superiority in the air gained by Allied squadrons, to which No. 1 Squadron of the Australian Flying Corps contributed notably. This squadron had been formed early in 1916 when Australia took up the suggestion put forward by the British Government that the Dominions might raise complete aviation units, and sent volunteers, mainly untrained, to Egypt. It was not long before the squadron began operating in support of the ground units in Sinai; in January 1918 it was re-equipped and from that time it was the star squadron among those operating against the Turks. Meanwhile a second squadron had been quickly raised in Australia; it was transferred to England, where it was joined in 1917 by two additional squadrons.

On the Western Front, the Australian infantry divisions (1st Anzac Corps) entered the line near Armentieres from April 1916, and were soon engaged, farther south, in the first Battle of the Somme, where an Allied offensive began in July. In five weeks' fighting, nineteen heavy attacks were launched, nearly all at night and on narrow fronts; the three Australian divisions participating in them suffered heavily. After a brief respite, the

1st Anzac Corps, reinforced by the 5th Australian division, was back on the Somme battlefield to hold the line during the severe winter, when mud and cold were hazards to test even the toughest will and strongest body. By March 1917, the Australians were moving forward against strong rearguard action by the Germans, who were withdrawing to shorten their lines. In sharp fighting, the Corps was soon in contact with the Germans' main position, the Siegfried (or Hindenburg) line at Bullecourt. The Allied plan for a spring offensive against the entrenched positions failed, however, when tanks were unable to open the way for the infantry. In spite of massive efforts over some weeks and heavy casualties, the gains were relatively slight.

Meanwhile the French army, dispirited by its defeat on the Aisne and affected by mutinies, was leaving the main fighting to the British. Britain's war potential had reached its peak, with 2,000,000 men in the field in July 1917, and factories turning out munitions to meet all needs. Recognized by the Allied generalissimo, Marshal Ferdinand Foch, as "shock troops of the first order," Australian infantrymen were soon to have a special role to play as the war in Europe moved into its final phases.

While the 1st Anzac Corps rested after Bullecourt, the 2nd Corps was with the 2nd British Army, then preparing for attack on the Messines ridge (which dominated the plain of west Flanders), and in the successful battle of June 7–8 the Corps was heavily engaged. The collapse of Russia made it imperative to strike a vital blow on the western front before German strength could be transferred from the Russian front, and with the Messines ridge cleared the Allied attack could be launched; the third battle of Ypres (also called the battle of Passchendaele) began on July 31—a titanic engagement which lasted until November 6, when the village of Passchendaele was captured. In that long and costly engagement, the 1st Anzac Corps was prominent from September; nearly 100,000 Australian troops took part in the final assault, and losses were heavy. About 30,000 men were lost in three weeks' fighting.

On January 1, 1918, all five Australian divisions in France were brought together as the Australian Corps. Together with a squadron of the Australian Flying Corps, the consolidated corps spent the winter in the new line at Messines. Defences were built up in preparation for the major German offensive expected in the European spring as a result of Russia's defection and Italy's near-collapse, which together made it possible for the Germans to bring an additional 500,000 men to the Western front. When the great German assault was launched along the Somme in March, forty highly-trained divisions were thrown against the British 5th Army, which held a front over 140 miles long with only eleven divisions forward and three in reserve. The 3rd and 4th Australian divisions were at once moved, with many British divisions, to the Cambrai-St Quentin sector, the main objective of the enemy's massive Somme offensive. Tunnelling companies as well as field and heavy battery units were involved along with infantry brigades in the heavy counter-attack which finally held the German advance. During the bitter fighting, Amiens and Villers-Bretonneux were added to the Australians' battle honours. In May, General John Monash, formerly a divisional commander, was placed in charge of the Australian Corps, and he developed a constant series of small offensives which greatly weakened the German strength while gaining valuable though limited objectives.

When the time came for the Allied offensive to be launched, the initial thrust was made in the sector where the Australian Corps had strained German nerves to breaking point. August 8, the day the Australian and Canadian breakthrough was achieved, was described by the German commander, Ludendorff, as "the black day of the German army in this war." As well as four Australian divisions there were four from Canada and two British divisions (with three more in reserve) and they and the cavalry corps advanced, with British tanks, all along the line. The smashing gain was in the centre of the line where the Australians and Canadians fought. The advance brought Chaulnes junction under close fire, destroying German communications over a large sector—a decisive blow.

The breakthrough opened the way for the train of operations that quickly led to the launching of the general Allied offensive—an offensive made possible by the general strengthening of the Allied front, along which the American forces were now heavily engaged. The Australian troops continued to be in the forefront of the assault. On August 31, Australian infantry captured important German outposts, opening the way for the assault on the Hindenburg line itself. Late in September, when the general offensive began, a determined attack by British, Australian, and American troops caused panic among the Germans in the St Quentin sector; and from this point a slow but inexorable advance began which led to the final Allied victory and the armistice of November 11.

During the terrible four-year conflict, Australia had sent almost 330,000 soldiers abroad—all of them volunteers—and of them almost 60,000 had been killed and 166,000 wounded or affected by gas.

Profound changes had taken place in the economic and social scene as progressively the demands of war made it necessary to replace many older concepts and forgo the easy life in which the entire accent was on the individual's liberty of action. In order that the war might be prosecuted more effectively, the federal administration found it necessary to assume responsibility on a considerably enlarged scale, and the machinery of government was enlarged accordingly. The government moved to control the prices of many goods so that wartime shortages would not be reflected in wildly soaring prices. At the same time it had to arrange for the orderly disposal of important bulk products. Its role in financing the war effort at home and overseas meant greater involvement than before in financial matters. For the first time, the federal government began to take action directly affecting the lives and the livelihood of individuals. Significant strengthening of the federal government's powers had come in 1916 as a result of decisions of the High Court, which held that in time of war the overriding "defence" power could be given extremely wide interpretation; the Commonwealth was found to possess the right to regulate or direct many activities which had not been previously subject to such regulation.

Economic problems remained to the fore throughout, even though high prices and assured markets for exports were underpinning the nation's basic prosperity and its ability to prosecute the war. There was an upward sweep in taxation, and in addition a considerable part of the cost of the war effort was hidden in inflation which forced prices up in spite of official measures to curb increases. It was natural that with the disruption of normal trade, and consequent shortages of goods, pressure on prices should be great.

An aggravating factor in the early phase was the great searing drought of 1914–15 which cut deeply into every form of rural production; wheat output was halved, sheep numbers declined considerably, and output of dairy produce dropped away sharply. A conference of federal and state ministers in 1914 agreed that all state governments should pass uniform legislation to place foodstuffs under price control. The legislation passed by the various administrations, and the action arising from it, varied greatly from state to state, however, and with shortages caused by drought many items rose quite sharply in price. Within a year of the outbreak of war wholesale prices had risen 40 per cent.

It was clear that to be effective, price control would have to be on a uniform basis, and in July 1916 the price of foodstuffs and necessary commodities, and shipping freights, were brought under federal control as action by the individual states was superseded. Price increases could not be eliminated, but the rate of increase was held down, and in the final three years the wholesale price index rose only 25 per cent.

The net effect of the 47 per cent increase that took place in retail prices during the war was a decline in real wages. This became a major cause of disillusionment that swept the Labor movement in particular. The discontent found an outlet in industrial disputes. In 1916 a major disruption occurred in the coal industry; soon afterwards this was extended to a dispute among waterside workers which in turn merged with a railway strike in New South Wales. However, Hughes used the provisions of the War Precautions Act to stop the spread of the trouble, and a threatened general strike was averted.

Australian purchases of British goods were kept low by the acute wartime shortages in England, as well as by high prices and the shortage of shipping. As time went on Australian banks accumulated large credits in London as a result of payments made for Australian exports. Since these funds could not be readily transferred, the federal government met the situation by lending money (in the form of notes) to the banks in Australia in return for the funds held in London. The practice grew for the banks to adopt Australian notes as a basis for the settlement of debts among themselves.

Developments in finance and banking included a rapid expansion of the note issue and an embargo on the free transfer of gold. Gold was being mined in great quantity at the time of the outbreak of war; its shipment became impractical under war conditions, and from 1914 gold was held by the Commonwealth Bank and where necessary the Bank of England advanced money in London to Australian banks in payment. At war's outbreak Australians were carrying more gold coins in their pockets than were any other people; but as the sovereigns found their way to banks they were not reissued. Quickly sovereigns went out of general use as a flood of paper money was released; from about £10 million at the outbreak of war, notes in circulation increased threefold within a year. In the first few months of the war imports from Britain were heavy, and there were exceptional drains on London funds accordingly; this had the effect of reducing the trading banks' holdings of gold in Australia. On July 14, 1915, the export of gold was forbidden by government order and, technically, Australia went off the gold standard. The government took the step of blocking the free export of gold because the gold was needed in official coffers to maintain sound backing for the expanding note issue. Furthermore, the gold reserves were a safeguard in case overseas funds became depleted. As things turned out, good export prices for the products of the land maintained the London balances throughout the war; there were adequate funds at all times for all banks, and large exports of gold were not necessary. The Treasury continued to take in all available gold, on the understanding that it would be returned to the banks at the end of the war. The rapid expansion of the note issue meant that the notes' gold backing fell consistently.

Financial measures were directed to the diversion of resources to the war effort; at the same time, basic development projects arising from the community's normal needs and not directly related to war purposes had to be taken into account. In adjustments to the nation's economy, the problem of an over-all manpower shortage placed strict limits on what could be done. At war's outbreak the state governments were all committed to public works involving the expenditure of considerable loan money, and for the first two years of war they continued to spend at a total rate of over £20 million a year, with money advanced by the Commonwealth in all cases except that of New South Wales, which alone did not accept the federal undertaking to borrow on behalf of the states.

Direct war expenditure was met almost wholly from special loans which the Commonwealth raised. To meet overseas commitments, the British government lent large sums from the early days of the war; in all, some £92 million were borrowed in London. Locally, a succession of war loans raised in all more than £190 million, involving financial transactions on a scale unprecedented for Australia. To meet revenue requirements, taxation was increased, so that by the war's end the federal government was levying a number of direct and indirect taxes. Succession duties were introduced in 1914; income tax—described as a temporary measure—followed in 1915, and the rates increased as the war progressed. A wartime profits tax on businesses was introduced in 1917. Land tax rates were pushed up, the tariff was revised to yield greater revenue, and an entertainment tax was introduced. However, out of a total war expenditure of £311,452,248 at June 30, 1919, slightly less than £46 million had been paid out of revenue, and almost the whole of this amount represented outlays incurred in borrowing charges, interest, sinking fund payments, war pensions and repatriation costs. The great bulk of war expenditures had been met by loan money raised in Australia or Britain.

Other aspects of trade and commerce, including the marketing abroad of products of Australia's stations, farms, and mines, also came under federal direction. Export of many products deemed to be of importance for war purposes was prohibited from the outbreak of war; within a few days additional items (including copper and tin) were listed and could not be sent out except to ports in Allied countries. Australia was able to grow large quantities of wool and wheat, as well as meat—three commodities of special importance in the waging of war—and their export was reserved for Britain. To provide for the orderly disposal of these products, official agencies were set up to supervise their sale and transport to London.

Wool auctions continued until November 1916, after which the clip was taken over at an agreed price and London undertook to ship the wool. A central committee representing wool growers, brokers, buyers, and manufacturers, under an officially appointed chairman, was set up to arrange for appraisal and shipment of all wool. Payment of 90 per cent of the appraised price was made at once to the grower, with the remaining 10 per cent withheld for later adjustment. The acquisition price represented an increase of about 55 per cent over the rate ruling before the outbreak of war.

Wheat, more perishable than wool, was a more difficult problem. Shipping was soon short, and although the first summer of war was a severe drought period, wheat stocks began to accumulate after the bountiful harvest of 1915–16. It was decided to set up a wheat board and to institute a wheat pool under the control of federal and state ministers, who called upon the advice of wheat-handling firms. Farmers were assured of 4/– a bushel for all their wheat. Mice and weevils damaged considerable quantities of stacked grain while it was awaiting shipment. Eventually, however, purchasers were found in London who were able to provide the necessary shipping, and the wheat board was able to dispose of accumulated stocks. Similar officially-sponsored marketing programmes were set up to dispose of the exportable surpluses of dairy products and meat, with Britain contracting to take the products at a guaranteed price and to provide the necessary shipping.

The control of important mineral ores and metals produced in Australia was a more complex matter. The principal market for lead and zinc concentrates had been in Germany, and German interests had been dominant also in copper, molybdenite, wolfram, and other non-ferrous minerals. All export ceased when war broke out, and in September 1915 a metals exchange was set up under federal authority to assume control over the disposal of all the base metals. The prime object of the group was to prevent metals of war value reaching enemy countries by roundabout routes, and a strict check was maintained on exports. Zinc and copper were sold only to Britain.

To assist further in meeting wartime demands, the smelting of ores and the processing of metals was encouraged. The Broken Hill Associated Smelters was formed in 1915, with financier William Sydney Robinson as managing director, to undertake the smelting of silver and lead ores. The company took over and expanded a small lead smelter at Port Pirie, South

Australia. The Electrolytic Zinc Company's zinc smelter was established in 1916 at Risdon, Tasmania, using hydro-electric power, and non-ferrous fabricating works were set up at Port Kembla, New South Wales. Government-sponsored zinc and copper groups were set up, with boards of directors who were government officials able to draw upon Treasury funds to finance new activity. In 1916 Robinson went to London to become controller of Australian exports of non-ferrous metals; his work had the effect of developing closer integration of the Australian producer groups with the British non-ferrous industry, and Australian capital was introduced to help finance the expansion of zinc smelting in Britain. By 1918, production of refined lead, copper, and zinc in Australia exceeded 200,000 tons—more than double the 1914 output.

During the war years, the curbs on imports provided a stimulus and a form of natural protection to local industry, and manufacturing expanded to meet the demand for consumer goods, particularly in the later war years. A limiting factor was the difficulty of obtaining machinery, and this held the expansion in check. The textile and clothing industries expanded to supply the needs of the armed forces for uniforms, blankets, and some other types of equipment, and at the same time were able to meet civilian requirements. Some industries fell away as supplies of raw materials were cut off, and there were some fields of activity that suffered as markets abroad were lost. Among those that gained quickly after troubles caused by drought were overcome were the food processing industries (including canning and jam-making) which provided rations for the forces and for export. Grain and flour were made available to help feed Allied nations. Many men who had been employed in some form of processing or manufacturing activity went overseas; their places were taken by others. Women appeared in numbers for the first time in industry as well as in shops and offices.

Successive adjustments took place as shipping dwindled and supplies of goods from overseas were cut further. Manufacturers were soon lamenting a lack of foresight in failing to import machinery while it was still available. Nevertheless, the range of manufactures widened.

The chemical industry moved to the production of explosives, ether, oxygen and other gases, phenol, creosols and naphthalene, acetone and methyl-alcohol, all of which had previously been imported. Manufacture of communications equipment was expanded. The range of weapons produced was small, but about 3000 people worked in small-arms factories and in associated activities. Throughout, some 4000 men were employed in ship repair and construction work. In mid-1917, Hughes, noting that the need for shipping was growing "with every passing day" as products for export were heaping up, announced that a ship-building programme would be undertaken. As events turned out, it was too late to have much effect, but two cruisers of about 5000 tons were built, as well as other craft for war purposes, and experience was gained in ship construction which later would be turned to peacetime use.

Of major significance was the launching of steel production early in 1915 when a modern iron and steel plant was brought into operation at Newcastle, New South Wales. This enterprise was the result of initiatives taken by the Melbourne-based Broken Hill Proprietary Company Ltd, which had its origins in 1885 as a company floated to develop silver ore at Broken Hill but had now moved out of this field. Great deposits of iron ore around Whyalla, in South Australia, were under the company's control, and by 1911 the BHP management was convinced that these deposits could be used to support an integrated iron and steel industry. General Manager Guillaume Daniel Delprat then went abroad to investigate the technical aspects and after discussions brought back an American expert, David Baker, to work on the project. Meanwhile the New South Wales government had been studying the possibility of setting up its own steel-making operation; but when in 1912 the BHP board accepted the proposal of Baker and Delprat that a plant should be set up near Newcastle's high grade coal deposits, the state-sponsored project was shelved.

Construction of the Newcastle steelworks was started in 1913, and the plant was opened two years later as a blast furnace, three open-hearth steel furnaces, a blowing mill, and a heavy rail mill came into operation. With the backing of adequate capital, and with a sheltered market, the new enterprise was free from problems that had plagued a smaller plant set up some years before in Lithgow and operated by Hosking Bros with the help of a federal bounty. BHP saw to it that the most up-to-date plant was installed. American steelmakers were brought in to man key positions and to train Australian tradesmen in production techniques. In 1917 a second blast furnace was begun, and with new open-hearth furnaces, rolling mills, and coke ovens, a greatly-enhanced plant was in operation by war's end, when some 4000 men were employed.

Side by side with the development of steelmaking capacity came other notable advances in the industrial sphere as efforts were made to overcome the increasingly severe shortages. Most of the older engineering shops, employing a few hundred men in most cases, and making such items of equipment as steam engines, agricultural or mining machinery, road rollers, pumps, winches, wheels and castings, were able to expand their operations. Everything from screws and bicycle spindles to engineers' studs and typewriter parts, was included in the new range of products. The engineering industry was still short of materials, as one of its leaders was painfully aware in 1917 when he criticized the government for not doing more to foster production of the materials needed. They could be produced locally, he declared, adding:

> We are metaphorically wringing our hands and crying out for materials that under efficient exploitation are available in illimitable quantities within our own borders.

The same theme of expanding the nation's resources was being heard also from the Prime Minister himself. Faced with a rising import bill for "luxuries" or non-essential items coming in from Japan and the United States, Hughes found new scope for the development of his nationalist policies; and he had an ally in the Melbourne *Argus*, traditionally in favour of imports (when available from Britain) but now suddenly protectionist. Prodded by confidants, Hughes began the regulation of imports in conformity with a policy designed to keep

> ... the wealth of the country within the country and the Empire ... [and] encourage as far as is humanly possible the industries of Australia, and increase the opportunities of employment of our own citizens.

Among the items whose importation was prohibited or limited from August 1917 were various alcoholic and other drinks, biscuits, confectionery, furs, jewellery, perfumes and motor bodies. In some cases, new plants were set up to produce the banned goods, or small activities were expanded to cater for the now-unfilled demand. Already the general difficulties surrounding importation had helped lengthen the list of products made locally. Under the spur of necessity, items such as surgical, optical, and scientific instruments of a more or less simple nature, paints, varnishes and by-products, and glass, were being made for the first time. In the years to come the ability of these industries to survive would be at stake; the test would arise when traditional suppliers wanted to get back in the market.

The war did not bring prosperity, and throughout unemployment remained high, always over 6 per cent and sometimes above 7 per cent of the available work force. The demands on industry for the production of war equipment were limited; general expansion was retarded by industry's limited state of development and the shortage of raw materials. Nevertheless, there was an acceleration in the trend towards greater industrial activity. In the realignment, rural activities retained their special importance as the producers of exportable commodities, but secondary industry moved forward to a point where it was again employing more than 30 per cent of the work force and— something it had not done before—producing almost a third of the national wealth.

Out of the disruption and turmoil of war, divisive as it had been, Australians had gained an understanding of nationhood. It had been built on common sacrifice as the people had gone through their testing time and emerged as a nation.

Part
Six

Growing up

THE FOUR-YEAR WAR that had started out in 1914 as a "romantic" old-style war and then developed into the horror of deadlocked trench warfare (with such unprecedented weapons as tanks and poison gas and bomb-dropping airships) had done more than obliterate individual men and women and children; it had corroded the established fabric in Europe and beyond, opened the way for the onrush of violence and the emergence of new social orders, and changed the balance of power throughout the world.

Begun as a conflict of competing old-style imperialisms, it had pursued its destructive course until it had finally extinguished four major dynasties: the Hohenzollern, Hapsburg, Romanov, and Ottoman. Before their defeat, the German militarists had brought Nikolai Lenin forward to set up a Communist regime in Russia following the October Revolution of 1917 at St Petersburg—a signal and unexpected victory for Marxist theory which was to have momentous effects on the future course of history. Changes had come in the Middle East, but, through the creation of a network of lesser kingdoms and protectorates in the lands of the former Ottoman empire, Britain's position had been secured. Clearly the United States had emerged as a front-rank power; and if America's voice was muffled somewhat because of political disagreements in Washington, rapid development of the nation's industrial and armament-making capacity had gone hand in hand with new naval-military strength acquired through the expansion of a two-ocean navy able to make use of the Panama Canal (opened in 1915).

Less obvious but nonetheless real was Japan's enhanced status in the world scene. Japan had quietly gained a commanding position in the western Pacific in trade and in diplomacy as a result of the disruptions caused by war. In China, Japanese goods had supplanted goods from Britain and Europe, and the United States had already acknowledged that Japan had special interests in China. The role of a virtually non-combatant Ally had paid handsome dividends. Viewing the war less as a crusade against Prussianism than an opportunity to suppress republican China, Japan had gained a position of dominance in the western Pacific-China region. With maritime losses and war casualties at a minimum, the Japanese had made immense wartime trading profits which were now available for investment in further rearmament; already Japan ranked among the Big Five (with the United States, Britain, France and Italy).

It was to be some time before the realities of the new line-up were apparent or the implications could be realized in British lands. For the time being there was little other than relief that the most terrible war yet fought had come to an end. The prevailing hope was that the irksome restrictions of the war years might be left behind and that the clock might be put back to the more prosperous pre-war years.

Some of Australia's wrappings of insulation were already being removed, however, and closer involvement with world affairs was made inevitable as a result of the relative decline in Britain's power and the emergence of a greatly strengthened Japan as well as a more powerful United States of America. Imperial ties had been drawn closer by the wartime association and in the rejoicing at common victory: and although Hughes sometimes spoke stridently in expressing Australian interests he was a firm believer in the concept of close and active interdependence among the British lands as the keystone of Australian policy.

Australia was being drawn closer to the main stream; and even before matters of imperial or international relationships came to the fore, the traditional barriers of distance were being lowered as a result of developments spurred by wartime research. Britain seemed nearer after the first experiments in Australia in long-range radio communication undertaken in September 1918, when a Morse code message tapped out in England was monitored successfully in a shed behind the home of the pioneer radio engineer, Ernest Fisk, in Sydney. Intercontinental flights became possible with the biggest and most powerful of the wartime aircraft, and in March 1919, three months before the Atlantic was spanned, Prime Minister William Morris Hughes announced £10,000 prize money to the first Australian to fly a British aircraft from England to Australia in a thirty-day period. When the cumbersome Vickers Vimy bi-plane piloted by Captain Ross Smith and his brother Keith reached Australia late in 1919 after a twenty-eight day flight from London to Darwin, it seemed to many almost as though Australia had moved to within sight of the world at large, and could draw closer to the heart of the Empire.

In a disturbed, overcrowded world in which nationalism was rife, Australians faced long-term but real challenges. In spite of wartime exertions and the heroism of the Anzacs it was clear to the perceptive that Australia with its 3,000,000 square miles of territory and its population of 5,000,000 invited the attention of overcrowded lands of Europe and Asia. Prudence suggested that population-building be undertaken as an urgent national task.

Thus, Australians, although not fully aware of the changes that had taken place in the world power balance (and determined not to acknowledge any weakening of Britain's position) were soon awakened to the danger of an unguarded continent. Soon after the war ended, the distinguished journalist-war correspondent Henry Somer Gullett began proselytizing in favour of an active immigration policy to bring more Britons to Australia. Gullett's zeal soon had its effect on opinion-formers and policy makers alike.

Concern about the nation's future became a guiding factor in national policy and since Britain was anxious to find outlets for excess population, Australia was soon being given a special place in the grand plan for redistribution of population within the Empire.

Meanwhile, as earnest men at home set about trying to understand and evaluate the problems to be faced in the postwar world, Prime Minister Hughes had been staking a claim for a bigger voice in Pacific affairs for Australia and New Zealand. In his view there could be no rest until the island screen to the north-east of Australia had been secured, and Hughes was determined to see that Australia's voice would be heard and heeded in the final disposition of the former German island territories in the Pacific, some of which had been taken over by Australian and New Zealand forces at the outbreak of war, and others (north of the Equator) occupied by Japan.

Even before the war ended Hughes had begun to wage a war of words in the United States and Britain (where the future dispositions of the former German possessions would inevitably be determined), to stress Australia's national interests. At first Prime Minister David Lloyd George and other British leaders had shown no inclination to strip Germany of its territories as a result of its defeat in war, and certainly there was a disinclination in London to allow any single British country to impose special terms. Nevertheless, a subcommittee of the Imperial war cabinet, set up in 1917 to deal with territorial issues, decided to recommend the transfer of German New Guinea and the Solomon Islands to Australia as part of a peace settlement, and it was then agreed that the British delegates to a peace conference should be guided by these proposals. Australians saw this as an opportunity to correct a blunder of more than thirty years' standing; Hughes now strongly advanced the principle that none of Germany's former colonies should be returned, and asserted that the disposition of the German Pacific colonies would be of cardinal importance to the future peace of the area.

Japan's involvement as occupier of some of the islands was an embarrassing factor, since it was clear that Japan could not be expected to relinquish control. Nevertheless, Hughes began to work relentlessly both in public and private discussions on the issue, seeking outright control by Australia of former German-held territories closely associated with the country's future security.

In May 1918 Hughes visited Washington on his way to London to participate in a meeting of the Imperial War Cabinet. He called upon President Woodrow Wilson, saw members of his cabinet, and met congressional committees on foreign relations to press the Australian viewpoint concerning the Pacific islands. "Australia's demands are not made in the interests of empire but for security," the Prime Minister said publicly, adding: "The Australian continent could be swallowed up unless this safeguard is granted."

In New York, Hughes spoke of the Pacific islands issue as "a matter of life and death importance to Australia." The *New York Times* was among the newspapers that gave prominence to his spirited call for support for an Australian Monroe Doctrine when he spoke on May 31. Hughes declared that America, Australia, and New Zealand had common interests in the Pacific. "We must have guarantees against enemy aggression in the future," he said. "'Hands off the Australian Pacific' is the doctrine to which by inexorable circumstances we are committed." In London, Hughes continued his crusade, trumpeting loudly about Australia's role. He had a remarkably attentive press. *The Times* and *Daily Telegraph* found much to approve in the idea of a hands-off doctrine. Hughes pressed his views at every opportunity and worked determinedly for their adoption by the Imperial war cabinet, and although he failed to get far with his Monroe Doctrine theory he gained acceptance for the idea that peace terms should include the permanent ceding of German New Guinea to Australia and of Samoa to New Zealand. Australia was now gaining notice in the world capitals as a truly national entity, with a strident national voice, and involved for the first time in trying to play an individual, if circumscribed, role in international affairs.

Other self-governing units of the British Empire were also taking a more active role in foreign affairs. Sir Robert Borden, Prime Minister of Canada, had pressed the cause of the Dominions in foreign policy creation; in Imperial war cabinet discussions his persuasive overtures were backed by South Africa's General Jan Christian Smuts as well as Hughes. The result was that the British government agreed to accept separate Dominion groups within the British delegation to the peace conference that convened in Paris in January 1919. Each Dominion was granted the right to sign the peace treaty, with treaty approval subject to the Dominion parliaments no less than Westminster.

Through pre-armistice negotiations, President Wilson had gained agreement from the Allies that the peace should be based on the general points and principles—the Fourteen Points—he had enunciated, including the creation of a post-war League of Nations, and his ideals had been hailed by spokesmen for public opinion in all the Allied nations. In Paris, Wilson quickly won agreement for his view that the League he proposed must be created as an integral part of the peace treaties; at the same time he urged —and won agreement for his view—that absolute priority should be given in the conference to the framing of a charter or covenant for the League. As chairman of the group formed to draft the covenant, Wilson saw to it that no single aspect came to a point of decision before work on the covenant was finished.

To Hughes, ever the realist, the most pressing matter for decision concerned the fate of the German territories in the Pacific, and he was unprepared to fall in with Wilson's proposal that all former German possessions should be transferred to the proposed League under a system of administration by the smaller powers. Hughes sensed danger in placing responsibility for Pacific islands in the hands of an untried organization and, much to Wilson's displeasure, he worked ceaselessly—both within the British Empire delegation and beyond it—against acceptance of the proposal. He gained support from other participants, including General Smuts.

When the question of the disposition of the German colonies came under direct review, Hughes pleaded the cause for Australian sovereignty over the Pacific islands. Strategically the islands encompassed Australia like fortresses, he said; New Guinea lay only 82 miles from Australian shores, while to the south-east spread a string of islands useful as bases for attack. Australia could never feel safe with potential or actual enemies at its very doors—but Australia's security would constitute a threat to no one. In reply, President Wilson, taking the position that while colonies could not be returned to Germany they should not be treated as spoils of war, rejected all of Hughes' arguments and accused the Australian Prime Minister of lack of faith in the proposed League, which he was certain would be able to offer protection against any "outlaws."

However, Hughes remained unmoved, and there were others who took a similar stand against Wilson. Japan desired the German Pacific islands north of the Equator and the former German leasehold of Kiaochow in China, and the Union of South Africa wanted to annex outright the German Southwest African Territory. When Wilson pointed out how serious it would be to defy world opinion on the issue and hand over the German possessions to individual governments, an open break developed. Hughes led the attack against Wilson's views, openly expressing the fear that mandates without sovereign rights (including the right to control immigration into the territory concerned) would simply open the way for Japan to overrun the islands of the Pacific by a process of infiltration.

No meeting of the minds seemed possible until General Smuts devised a compromise formula. He proposed that all the former German colonies be transferred to the League but that the League assign a mandate for the administration of each one to some member nation, and that mandated territories be divided into three classifications; (a) those capable of eventual independence, in which the mandatory power would merely render "administrative advice and assistance"; (b) those, particularly in central Africa, where the mandatory power would have to take responsibility for administration; and (c) territories which could "best be administered under the laws of the Mandatory as integral parts of its territory." Included in the C-class mandates were to be Southwest Africa and the south Pacific islands—territories so designated, it was noted, because of "the sparseness of their population, or their small size, or their remoteness from the centres of civilization, or their geographical contiguity to the territory of the Mandatory." The mandatory was to be subject only to the requirement that it submit an annual report to the League on conditions in the territory under mandate. Although it seemed that the C-class mandate might open the way for virtual annexation, the proposal proved acceptable to Wilson, who feared that

Australia, South Africa, and Japan might refuse to endorse the covenant unless their interests were safeguarded in this way.

Hughes had won his demand for control over immigration to the mandated territory. Australia accepted C-class mandates for German New Guinea, including the northern Solomons, and the island of Nauru. Although at the same time Japan became the mandatory power in the islands of Micronesia, spread across some 3,000,000 square miles of ocean to the north of New Guinea, Hughes could return to Australia satisfied that the territories of more immediate concern to Australia would remain free from the danger of infiltration. His advocacy in world councils had brought success in a matter of vital significance to the British lands of the south-west Pacific.

Meanwhile, President Wilson's plan for American involvement in world affairs through leadership in the League of Nations was being torpedoed as a result of bitter opposition from isolationists at home. Even before Wilson returned to the United States, powerful political voices were being raised against his proposals for American involvement in the League as a peace-keeping body; yet American leadership in the League was the cornerstone of Wilson's plan for an international body to keep the peace.

By the time President Wilson presented the treaty for Senate ratification in July 1919, isolationist Republicans were demanding explicit disavowal of the commitment to collective security contained in the League covenant. The President countered by undertaking a long speaking tour in which he delivered forty addresses stressing the view that future peace and American security depended upon American leadership in the new world community. Then, on his return to Washington, at the very time when his leadership was most needed, Wilson suffered a crippling stroke. Only a small minority of the Senate (the "bitter-enders") opposed the covenant in principle, but the division between those supporting the covenant as drafted and those seeking greater protection for United States sovereign rights resulted in rejection when the United States Senate voted on ratification in November 1919 and again when the proposal was resubmitted four months later. Throughout, Senator Henry Cabot Lodge, Foreign Relations Committee chairman, an implacable foe of both Wilson and the treaty, insisted on reservations to reduce American responsibility to the League. Wilson, gravely ill, urged his party followers to vote for rejection rather than accept what he considered to be nullification. Neither side would budge. Wilson was pinning his hopes on the presidential election due in November 1920—but after a bitter campaign the election resulted in a resounding victory for the Republicans, and the new president, Warren Gamaliel Harding, lost no time in concluding a separate peace with Germany and making it plain that the United States would never enter the League.

The League came into existence in January 1920 with forty-nine members. Just as each Dominion had its separate representation at the peace conference and signed the peace treaties, so Australia and each of the other British lands was granted a seat in the League assembly and the right to election to the more powerful League Council (which at first was composed of four permanent members and four members elected by the Assembly).

In spite of the failure of the United States to join, and the hostile attitudes of defeated Germany and revolutionary Russia, the League settled down to its basic job of helping to solve political disputes and contributing to the economic reconstruction of Europe.

Close involvement with the great world had little appeal to Australians in general; from the remoteness and security of the antipodes they could look at the world's trouble spots from afar. Hughes had gained what he wanted most—control of a protective screen of islands north of the Equator. His incursion into the crucible of world politics struck more staid Australians as an unnecessary display of braggadocio. In any case the initiative was largely a personal one; it had limited objectives, and it was shortlived A long tradition of preoccupation with domestic affairs remained undisturbed. The creation of the League as a new experiment in international organization seemed a happy solution to other people's troubles, and Australians sought only to be left alone to concentrate on their efforts to develop national resources and push forward with social betterment. Britain's significant role in the League lent weight to the belief that the League's orderly system of international relations would make the world safe for smaller nations; and in spite of the scepticism of some on the question of the League's ability to guarantee Australia's security there seemed no valid reason why Britain's old guardian role should not be taken over by the new international body.

The League, with its emphasis on interdependence and collective security, might appeal to Australian idealism, but Hughes was still not satisfied with the League's guardianship. The Prime Minister realized that the participation of the United States in western Pacific security represented Australia's only hope of survival now that membership in the British fraternity placed an emphasis on co-operation and interdependence among British lands rather than protection for Australia. In the new world of shifting power balances, it was necessary to find a way for Australia to retain friendly relations with the Japanese as well as the Americans, even though relations between the United States and Japan were already being affected by American concern at pressures building up between Japan and China.

In this dilemma, Hughes, commenting on the projected renewal of the Anglo-Japanese Alliance, insisted that any such arrangement "must be absolutely satisfactory to the United States." The Labor party, in parliamentary opposition, was inclined to go further—even to the point of sacrificing the Anglo-Japanese Alliance, which it had never liked. When he went to London to represent Australia in the Imperial Conference of 1921, Hughes was determined to fight for continuation of the alliance. New Zealand supported his stand; Canada opposed it. From off stage, American voices were also raised against continuation of the alliance.

The meeting was the first Imperial Conference called to advise the British government on imperial policy rather than to act as a forum for discussion of each Dominion's views and policies, and with the apparent confusion of interests it seemed best to leave the matter of renewal of the Anglo-Japanese Alliance in abeyance until related matters, particularly those affecting naval forces in the Pacific, could be settled.

The British, war-weary and heavily in debt, were anxious to secure relief from their crushing naval expenditures. This seemed possible since the German fleet, against which they had strained every effort since 1900, was captive at Scapa Flow and doomed to destruction; but, to London's dismay, other contenders for naval power had appeared. In 1916 the United States. Congress had voted to build a navy "second to none," including several powerful battleships. These ships were designed primarily to check the Japanese, whose navy had been expanding rapidly. In 1919 the United States Navy had sent half of all its vessels through the Panama Canal into the Pacific. Although the naval programmes of the American and Japanese were counter-balancing, the intensification of foreign naval building struck at one of the cardinal points of British policy. In straitened economic circumstances, Britain was anxious to avoid a race in capital ship construction; but Britain's prosperity and safety (and the security of the Empire in general) remained so dependent on control of long sea lanes that London believed Britain had a right to a stronger navy than any other power. One of the main causes of misunderstanding over the American naval programme was that while the United States navy was concerned primarily with offsetting Japan's increasing influence in the Pacific, to British eyes this build-up could mean an American naval force strong enough to be a challenge to Britain's traditional maritime supremacy.

In pressing forward with its desire to do something tangible about disarmament, the new Republican administration which came to power in Washington in March 1921 decided to call a conference to discuss naval limitations. Occupied with redrawing the map of Europe, the peace conference at Versailles did not touch upon the problems of the Pacific; but the United States felt uneasy about the expansion of Japanese power, and decided to call a conference to settle outstanding issues. Policy was no longer in the hands of Europe-first Democrats; the Republicans had traditionally placed greater emphasis on the Pacific, and the Harding administration was acutely aware of the growth of Japanese power during the war years. Invitations to the naval conference were issued to Britain, Japan, France, and Italy, while invitations to a discussion of western Pacific problems went also to Belgium, the Netherlands, Portugal, and China.

All the British countries welcomed the American initiative in calling the talks. Australia and New Zealand were anxious to have a meeting on Pacific matters as a preliminary to the main disarmament conference; part of the appeal of the proposal was that such a conference might afford an opportunity for the Dominions to exercise rights to individual representation. The American view was that a preliminary conference on the Pacific was unnecessary.

The Dominions were not invited to attend the Washington conference as separate nations, but—again largely as a result of Canadian and South African initiative—Dominion representatives were included within the British delegation. It was agreed, however, that each Dominion would have the right to sign the resulting treaty, and for each Dominion parliament to approve it.

The formula proposed by the United States related to a ten-year "naval holiday" in which no new capital ships would be constructed except to maintain a five-five-three ratio in battle tonnage, with Britain and the United States allowed 525,000 tons each, 315,000 tons for Japan, and 175,000 tons each for France and Italy. The United States undertook to scrap various large vessels in existence or under construction—ships which would have made the United States Navy the mightiest afloat.

The partly-completed vessels were not the only sacrifices. The Japanese were unwilling to accept their 60 per cent quota of British and American battle strength until these nations agreed not to strengthen any of their existing defences in the western Pacific. This left the Philippines, Guam, and Hong Kong virtual hostages to the Japanese, with no significant British or American bases closer than Singapore or Pearl Harbour. In addition to these various naval agreements embodied in a treaty in February 1922, the conference produced a Four-Power Treaty in December 1921 of the United States, Britain, Japan, and France, supplanting the old Anglo-Japanese Alliance of 1902. At the same time, a nine-power Treaty was signed to guarantee the territorial integrity and administrative independence of China while repeating the traditional "open door" principle.

The Washington agreements really satisfied no one. The Americans had gained recognition of parity with Britain and had broken up the Anglo-Japanese Alliance, but had scrapped ships which would have given them an adequate deterrent to Japan. The British had prevented the Americans from outbuilding them but for the first time they had formally agreed that the Royal Navy's strength could be matched. The Japanese had prevented others from building up powerful bases within striking distance of Japan (while at the same time their own penetration of the central Pacific extended through mandates); but their national pride had been sacrificed in their agreeing to the 60 per cent ratio in capital ships.

If Britain's old allegiance with Japan had dangerous overtones for Australia-New Zealand, particularly in the light of American uneasiness about it, the new balance of power in the Pacific was not completely satisfactory. The plain fact was that with the diminished strength of Britain's battle fleet, naval supremacy in the western Pacific was passing to Japan. However, for Australians, external affairs no longer seemed so important.

The world appeared to be finding a new security; and most Australians clung tenaciously to the belief that through sound British leadership, all the nagging international problems would be dispelled. Talk of disarmament was in the air, the League of Nations appeared to be functioning satisfactorily, and in affairs directly related to the Pacific the Republican administration in Washington was obviously committed to a degree of American involvement that would surely be sufficient to neutralize any Japanese threat. For Australians, a renewed sense of identification with all things British had resulted from the four-month visit of Edward, Prince of Wales, in 1920. With the big issues in others' hands, it was for Australia to fit snugly into place in the Imperial family.

Political developments within Australia reinforced the natural trend to withdraw from the international scene, and leave foreign affairs wholly in London's hands. Some parliamentarians even begrudged the time taken to debate the peace treaties, implying that the country's economic affairs should be given attention instead. Some Labor men denounced war and sought to ignore matters connected with international affairs; and an important new political force, the Country party, had risen to voice the views of wheat farmers and other rural producers to the exclusion of broader issues.

In 1922, a handful of activists within the Labour movement who saw all of society's problems in terms of Marxist theory, formed the Communist Party as a unit of the world-wide movement anxious to see an end to the "capitalist system."

By 1922 the Country party held a balance of power in the House of Representatives, and under the driving leadership of Earle Grafton Page the group gained dominance in the non-Labor forces. Hughes was replaced as Prime Minister by a political neophyte of his party, Stanley Melbourne Bruce, but in the new Nationalist-Country party cabinet, representation was almost equally divided (six to five) and it was in fact, as well as in name, the Bruce-Page ministry.

Hughes' departure marked a new approach to Australia's external relationships. Bruce was mild where Hughes was tempestuous, and by training, background, and inclination he favoured a close, harmonious relationship in which Britain's leadership was accepted without question. He believed it essential to rebuild Britain's strength by "all pulling together" in the Empire cause, and he saw the future as being best safeguarded by a secure, unquestioning relationship with Britain in which—he hoped—the old Imperial protection might re-emerge. Hughes' policy of national self-assertion was in the discard; Bruce followed an Empire-first approach in which Australia might be seen but should not be heard.

In domestic affairs, the new ministry's policies were largely taken over from Hughes' administration, but they were intensified so as to place greater emphasis on material progress through an accelerated development of resources. By now there had been total acceptance of the concept that Australia must expand its population rapidly by absorbing more migrants from Britain, with the emphasis on rural development. Trade union opinion was still unfavourable to immigration in general—newcomers were seen as a threat to job holders and job seekers alike—but there was no concerted opposition to placing men on the land since a "drift to the cities" was already causing concern. Similarly, in gratitude for their services to the nation, returned soldiers were assisted to take up land under elaborate "closer settlement" plans. To help Australian producers of primary products compete against increasingly tough competition in world markets, boards were set up to control the marketing of various commodities. At the same time, through tariffs Australian manufacturing industry was given greater protection from imports.

Money flowed freely in the early 1920s. The wool market remained buoyant as the world's wardrobes were restocked, and other rural products found ready markets. Confidence was the keynote of political speeches; newspaper editorialists supported the concept that the country was great and could be made greater.

In the mid-1920s the great burst of activity in the provision of services for the public provided a basis for expansion of the national economy; but in the proliferation of boards, commissions, the other agencies bent on investigating or implementing expansion plans, governments were creating a system which was soon to give its own self-generating impetus and support to expansion without regard to the economic factors involved. Sometimes the price paid for that expansion was high.

The desire to break through old barriers and press on with development was heady wine. American firms began to invest; British firms expanded their activities, and many small enterprises based on local capital were begun. The economy was being distorted, however; money borrowed overseas was mainly being converted into goods which Australian consumers were using up, but there was still insufficient investment in Australian industry from any source, and production was not expanding. Above all, earnings from the sale of Australian produce abroad remained low. Debts were growing, but the means of paying interest (much less repaying capital) was diminishing as world prices for rural products drifted slowly downward. The forced development was deceptive; the fact was that inflationary policies were being adopted abroad—particularly in Britain, where Winston Churchill's unhappy term as Chancellor of the Exchequer was marked in 1925 by restoration of sterling to the gold standard at the old parity. The state governments vied with each other to draw in loan moneys from abroad; from 1926 they were encouraged to find a new source of funds in the New York money market to back ambitious public works as construction of roads and powerhouses and irrigation works now replaced the building of railways as state-sponsored enterprises. Price levels were rising in Australia even though they were falling elsewhere; it could not be long before the shock waves of the over-valuing of the pound and other heralds of world economic turmoil were felt. Economic good sense was being overwhelmed in Australians' exuberance of rapid expansion based on over-confident expectations.

Even before the world economic depression annihilated markets for rural produce, there were signs of trouble. Some rural industries had been expanded far beyond their natural limits, and production could be sustained only by means of subsidies. Yet land values had moved up in accordance with the fictitious "profitability." Considerable areas of land had been resumed by state governments and made available as farms to ex-soldiers; but in some areas the land was unsuited to closer settlement, and many of the soldier settlers, their debts mounting, found themselves saddled with problems beyond their control.

There were other signs of economic imbalance, After hovering around 8 per cent for some years, unemployment moved up to 11 per cent in 1928. Investment in industry had tapered off. Statistical information was not avaliable to provide a basis for understanding and interpreting the nation's financial affairs or the national economy as a whole, and politicians, convinced that the facile slogans they repeated monotonously would work magic, turned a deaf ear to the few experts who were beginning to sound warnings. Enthusiasm for an admirable cause had obscured the need for practical planning and careful administration, and as a result immigration had run into serious problems.

Bruce did not appear to share the prevailing distrust of the expert, but although he believed that scientific and technical knowledge should be mobilized so that it could play a greater role in the formulation of national policies, he had little time for economists. Bruce could see no merit in direct intervention in economic affairs, and although he spoke frequently of the need for national leadership in the investigation and solving of nationwide problems, an ingrained dislike of centralized power led him to the conclusion that such matters should be left to independently-run bodies (with government backing). The result was that many of the commissions, boards, and other bodies he created developed policies which, while admirable in themselves, were mutually conflicting in operation or failed because they were out of step with prevailing trends.

This was painfully apparent when the world financial crash came in 1929, and the resulting depression robbed Australia of much of its earning capacity abroad. Accumulated indebtedness overseas then placed crippling burdens on the economy. A newly-elected Labor government grappled with the problems, as great dislocation followed the collapse; values tumbled, wages were reduced, and demand for all goods and services fell away sharply; in three years national income fell by almost one third. Intensified problems in Britain, when in 1931 heavy withdrawals of foreign deposits caused a near-panic, added to Australia's difficulties in trying to stem the disaster. Faced with the effects of a deflation of extreme intensity, British interests were withdrawing money from Australia at the very time when export commodities were at rock-bottom prices and almost unsaleable. The depression moved to its blackest phase in mid-1932. Manufacturing industries were withering away as total unemployment reached 30 per cent of the work force. Holdings of international funds were drained to low levels as Australia struggled to meet its international obligations. The spread of responsibility for policy in vital economic fields among autonomous or semi-autonomous bodies now added to the problems of trying to cope with the situation.

First attention had to be given to direct measures designed to curb the flow of imports; at the same time ways had to be found to enable rural production to be made profitable even though overseas prices for Australian commodities were lower. A series of protective devices aimed at reducing overseas spending and building up local industry was introduced. These included sharp increases in tariffs and outright prohibition of some imports. Perhaps the most effective of all the measures was one initiated not by the government but by the Bank of New South Wales (against the wishes of the central banking authority) in the face of a sharp rundown of funds overseas: this was the devaluation of the Australian currency, whereby the Australian pound was given a value which eventually stabilized at 20 per cent less than the pound sterling. The devaluation in effect gave Australian primary producers a premium on their sales abroad and at the same time raised the cost, in Australian money values, of imported goods.

At the same time, the prevailing economic orthodoxy among politicians and financiers precluded the acceptance of budgetary measures to counter the general deflation.

Economic improvement was necessarily slow. Local measures could not overcome the whole trade problem. The British countries, now drawn closer together than at any time in decades, met in conference in 1932 to stimulate trade, at least among member countries. Concessions made to this end, embodied in the Ottawa agreement, met with a mixed reception in Australia; but before the four-year agreement had run its course changes were afoot which called for reappraisal of the nation's trade policies. One of these was the increasing significance of new markets for Australian products being developed in Europe and the western Pacific and Asian areas, arising from a policy of trade diversification. Another was the rapid growth of manufacturing activity in Australia induced and stimulated by the exigencies of the trade situation.

After its sharp initial depression setback, manufacturing began to strengthen, and by 1935 factory production had regained its pre-depression levels. Thereafter it made a steady advance. Once again overseas industrialists were among those who led the way with confident predictions of future growth, and private capital from Britain and the United States began to come in again at an appreciable rate. There was a general rise in efficiency in both management and labour.

Preoccupation with the state of the nation's economy meant that Australians took little notice of the serious deterioration occurring in international affairs. Militarists had been moving into positions of control in Japan, and Japan's invasion of Manchuria in 1931 marked the beginning of a new phase in which ultranationalist forces were able to defy world opinion and succeed in aggressions against neighbours with no more than a verbal rebuke from the League. A period of dual diplomacy began in which the Japanese foreign office placated the Western powers by statements disclaiming any aggressive intention in Asia while the military steadily expanded their control through intrigue and military campaigns. The League's adoption in 1933 of the report of its investigating commission, pinning Japan with the blame for aggression in Manchuria, was met by Japan's withdrawal from the League. Japanese militarists were bent on setting up a mighty empire stretching throughout east Asia and the western Pacific; absorption of the former German islands of Micronesia (the Japanese mandates) was under way, and development of naval and air bases on the islands proceeded rapidly. On the Asian mainland the Japanese militarists had set up a puppet government in Manchuria. They were soon extending their aggressions as they steadily tightened their grip on China. The first skirmishes of the Sino-Japanese war took place near Peking in mid-1937. The League

Assembly passed a pious resolution of disapproval and criticism of Japan, and the United States expressed its concurrence; but the efforts of a nineteen-nation conference late in 1937 which sought to bring the aggression to an end were brushed aside by the Japanese. The system of collective security had failed in this crucial test. China was left to fight on alone.

Japan had long since broken loose from the old five-five-three formula of the 1922 naval agreement. The Americans had sought in Geneva in 1927 to have the formula extended to all naval categories but had failed to secure agreement, and three years later when a further conference (in London) had carried into effect a depression-inspired plan for further reduction in American and British tonnages, the Japanese had managed to secure a ten-ten-seven ratio in cruisers and parity with the United States and Britain in submarines. The Japanese naval building programme gathered pace steadily, while American naval construction virtually ceased. Throughout, the United States had been falling farther behind the quotas permitted by the conference agreements, and Japan had been forging ahead, with heavy emphasis on aircraft carrier construction. The United States Navy began construction in 1934 in an effort to catch up on its quota; but after 1935 limitations no longer applied; in the conference that year Japan demanded full parity with America and Britain in all categories of ships, and when objections were raised Japan simply withdrew from the conference and announced an end to limitation pacts. By 1936 Britain was introducing its heaviest building programme since 1921 and America was stepping up its efforts. France and Italy had launched big naval programmes and Germany was back in the race.

Militarism had reappeared in Europe. In Germany, Adolf Hitler's National Socialist German Workers party had been growing in strength since 1930, when the multiplicity of political groups in the Reichstag had paved the way for the emergence of extremist parties openly hostile to parliamentary institutions. By 1933 Hitler was able to institute a totalitarian dictatorship; its backing of popular support was gained through a mixture of party allegiance and mass hysteria induced by shrewd propaganda techniques.

In his policy of cynical opportunism combined with intrigue and terror, Hitler was following closely a pattern set by Benito Mussolini in Italy, where the Fascist movement had developed in the 1920s as a totalitarian dictatorship which offered itself as the nation's saviour from communism but in fact used catchcries and slogans to disguise its ruthless destruction of civil liberties. Hitler bluffed and bullied his way to power in his own country, then used the same tactics in international affairs. By 1935, Britain and France had allowed air superiority to pass to the Germans.

Italy's attack on Ethiopia in October 1935 was the start of an aggressive foreign programme by Mussolini which dramatized for many Australians the nature of the threat now facing the world. After long debate the League decided to impose economic sanctions against Italy; but Mussolini, already allied secretly with Hitler, contemptuously defied the world organization and withdrew Italy from membership in December 1937.

The news was growing more ominous, headlines were becoming blacker, as Hitler precipitated a succession of diplomatic crises. In the face of aggression, the League and its component nations seemed powerless and the United States unwilling to commit itself. As it became clear that the initiative was now in the hands of dictators who felt free to grab what they wanted and trample all opposition underfoot, there was mounting concern in Australia.

The prime ministers of all the British countries met in London in May 1937 to discuss and analyse the nature of the world threat, and to plan the strengthening of defences with which the challenge might be met. On his return from the two-month conference, Prime Minister Joseph Aloysius Lyons made it clear that more attention would have to be given to military defence. Australia's contribution, while significant, could not be great; but for Australia the decisions taken at the 1937 meeting proved to be a turning point. As the political situation in Europe worsened, the old detachment was replaced by an awareness that the nation's future was directly involved and that Australians were no longer able to remain shut away in a sheltered corner of the world. The new defence plan took into account the possibility that Australia might come under attack, or at least that direct attempts might be made to limit the effectiveness of the nation's aid to Britain and her allies in the war that now appeared inevitable.

When war came in September 1939, it seemed to most Australians that the conflict would probably be confined to traditional areas. In the early stages, Australia's participation was on more or less the same pattern as in World War I, with an expeditionary force sent to the Middle East and special units sent elsewhere, and with the Royal Australian Navy operating in many theatres; but the training of large numbers of aircrew under the Empire air training plan was an outgrowth of the new age of air warfare.

The war against Germany and Italy had gone through alternating phases of despair and heartening success when the unleashing of war in the Pacific by Japan in December 1941 introduced entirely new factors. The urgency of the threat to Australia's own security posed by Japan's sweep southward early in 1942, culminating in air attacks on the Australian mainland, brought home to Australians an appreciation of how great a stake they had in the affairs of the western Pacific. From this point on, Australia became largely preoccupied with the war against the Japanese, even though gargantuan battles being fought between German and Russian forces might still feature in the war news. Involvement with the island fighting in the Pacific, and the association with United States air-sea-land forces continued to claim most attention as the European struggle neared its climax.

When the second of two atomic bombs dropped on Japan brought a swift end to the war in the Pacific, Australians were living in a new world and had a new sense of involvement in it.

Problems with prosperity

19

At eleven o'clock on November 11, 1918, the guns on the battle-fields of Europe fell silent on a world vastly changed by the violence and destruction that had begun four years and three months before.

Australia had suffered heavy casualties but had been spared the main horrors of war. For Australians, the burdens of a high cost of living and heavy national war debts were temporarily offset by the new feeling of pride and a deep sense of satisfaction that their countrymen had shown themselves fit and able to walk with the great. Now, it seemed to thinking men, the sacrifices of the fighting man must be justified by the creation of a better, safer, and more just world. The task seemed simple—at least if pious words could assure success. "Liberty is now assured to us and all men," Prime Minister Hughes declared with resounding rhetoric; "upon the foundations of victory we will build the new temple of our choice." Inspirational messages in similar vein were being offered by other politicians; and, if there was little agreement when it came to the question of what the new and better world should be like—and even less unity on practical issues of how it might be built—the drive to develop Australia, and expand the opportunities it offered, had been started.

To those who returned from the battlefronts, memories of the troubled outside world, with its sharp national and social divisions and its harsh cold ways, made Australia seem more attractive than ever—a land to be treasured and served in a spirit of dedication. Yet Australia's future would remain clouded unless it could be made strong and, above all, kept free from war. The brilliant soldier-leader Sir John Monash felt moved at war's end to recall to a member of his family that from "the far-off days of 1914 when the first call came, until the last shot was fired," every day had been filled with loathing, horror, and distress; he deplored the loss of precious life and waste of human effort, "Yet it had to be," he wrote; "and the thought uppermost was the earnest prayer that Australia might for ever be spared such a horror on her own soil."

Even as pride of nationhood crystallized (quite naturally) around the exploits of the digger, a feeling grew that the Australian way of life might one day be under deadly challenge. The continent's emptiness aroused fears about future security that soon became deep-etched in the thoughts of perceptive men. As men began to think more seriously than ever before about the problems, they realized the need for them to do more to evaluate their country, understand it, and build its longterm security.

It was clear that covetous eyes would be turned on Australia so long as its population remained insignificant. The ultimate population-carrying capacity of the country had long been the subject of speculative estimates by experts, and there was a great diversity of opinion on the matter of the "optimum" population level. As early as 1911, the geographer Griffith Taylor had begun to direct attention to the subject of the country's population potential and to prepare well-reasoned yardsticks by which to measure prospects. There was much speculation on the subject, since any projection was of necessity qualified by many factors, including the standpoint of the man making the estimate. German geographer Albrect Penck, who visited Australia in 1914, came out with an estimate of his own that Australia, New Zealand, and the islands of the south-west Pacific together might eventually hold 480,000,000 people. Others were more conservative in their estimates, but in spite of Griffith Taylor's efforts to inject more realism into the forecasting, estimates as high as 100,000,000, became established as "reasonable." The Queensland government had felt moved to speculate on the population prospects; in an official publication issued in 1915 at the time of the Pacific International Exposition in San Francisco, it pointed out that while the state's population was then only 660,000 there was "room and opportunity" for a population of 50,000,000 in "this vast territory" alone.

The theme of a stronger Australia was taken up by a prescient journalist, Henry Somer Gullett, immediately at the war's end; in *Unguarded Australia*, published in 1919, he pointed to the fact that Australia was a large, highly-favoured but empty land set in a small, overcrowded world which would not indefinitely tolerate so few people holding a continent largely unproductive. Britain was financially exhausted, the future uncertain. Australia had never had "munitions enough to keep a quarter of a million men fighting in a modern battle for half an hour"; yet crowded nations—and there were such nations to Australia's north—had always been prepared to fight for expansion. The only solution, Gullett considered, was a greatly expanded population; immigration alone could make the country independent of outside help in time of trouble. Australia's immediate safety and its future as a nation demanded a build-up in population to 15 or 20 million "at the earliest possible moment."

Gullett considered it was essential that the immigration issue be lifted above partisanship. It must be made a matter of "national policy, with the support of all classes"; there should be no regression to the approach of pre-war years when immigration policy had been "the plaything of politics and politicians," spasmodic in its operation, and "reduced almost to a farce by State working against State and the Commonwealth clumsily interfering." What was needed was a programme to draw men and women and children by the scores of thousands each year; they should be from the labouring classes, and should be drawn first from Britain and subsequently from Europe. There was a special need to embark upon "a great constructive policy of reproductive public works." Among such undertakings Gullett listed the building of strategic railways to aid in defence, development of irrigation ("the field of extension here is indefinite"), and improvement of major roads and the public services of cities and towns.

In many ways Gullett's blueprint for national expansion was to become the central feature of national policy in the 1920s. The inspiration of the nation-building theme was widely shared, and as time went on it was echoed in journals and newspapers. Steadily the theme of a stronger Australia was blended with the message of Anzac and the fighting man's sacrifice. It became a subject for contemplation when the Gallipoli landing came to be commemorated on April 25 each year with marches by long lines of returned men and with services at war momorials. Speaking at one such service in 1922, a returned commander declared:

> If every Australian would only emulate the spirit of the Anzacs and do the best for their country, there would be no fear for the future of Australia. The spirit of the Anzacs stands for the growth of Australia and forgetfulness of the provincial spirit; for friendships and common aspirations of the people; for the benefit of the world.

Along with population-building, the need to expand manufacturing was stressed, not only by Gullett but by many editorial writers. Australia, Gullett had said, could not remain dependent upon an uninterrupted flow of munitions in the event of a future war. The Australian Industries Protection League, formed in Melbourne in 1919 by manufacturing interests, strongly supported this view.

The drive to expand industrial enterprise was widely supported. Almost as the armistice went into effect, editorial writers were calling for national policies which would encourage development of manufacturing. According to Melbourne *Punch*, the war had made it clear that Australia to this point had "just lazed along" and had taken the line of least resistance. The war had cut off supplies of goods, which the public had previously regarded as everyday needs, and for four years or more the country had gone short; surely there was an opportunity to step up manufacturing. *Punch* continued:

> [During the war] we found that whilst we were the producers of the raw materials for some of the commodities no longer available, we had not the means, lacking the inclination, to prepare the manufactured article . . . Now this truth has been borne upon us, there is every likelihood that enterprise will not any longer be

neglectful of these gaping avenues for the employment of brains, labour. and capital.

Economic conditions, highly favourable to business interests, encouraged plans for rapid development. Inflationary pressures created by wartime conditions and shortages of goods remained unrelieved. Underlying causes for the immediate post-war boom were to be found in the soaring prices for export commodities which released great sums into the community, the increasing capital investment in secondary industries, and the expanding expenditure of loan money by government. State governments' outlay had gone unchecked during the war; this was reflected in a 50 per cent rise in the total debts of the states over the war and immediate post-war years (with a comparable rise in interest payments). The Commonwealth's debt had risen enormously, and was rapidly overtaking the total states' debts. Other factors aggravating the inflationary situation were the relatively low interest rates and a concomitant expansion of bank credit, and the use of notes instead of gold as a basis of currency.

In each of the last two war years there had been a very favourable trade balance, and this continued immediately after the war. In the year ended mid-1920, the excess of overseas earnings over outlays was more than £50 million. Wholesale price levels had been moving up; the peak was reached in August 1920. At that point a sharp break came, and bank advances were trimmed; price levels went down 38 per cent over the next sixteen months. Britain, anxious to rebuild export markets, was by now turning out goods for shipment, and when a deluge of imports—many of them on overdue orders—arrived at Australian ports commerce was thrown into confusion. In the year to June 1921, when bank advances increased markedly, the value of imports rose by £30 million, while over the same period export returns fell by £15 million. This sudden reversal of the trade balance brought about a sharp recession as banks again reduced credit, and interest rates rose. The deflation taking place in Britain and the United States had resulted in decreased spending in the importing countries; as a result, Australia's exports of wool, agricultural products, meat, and metals all suffered from the severe price reductions at a time when export volume of agricultural products had been reduced by a poor season.

Coming at a time when escalation of prices seemed to have become a permanent feature of the economy, the setback caused a sharp psychological reaction. In the confusion, the government moved to give further tariff protection to local industries, and at the same time, tried desperately to pacify the working man by meeting his demands for higher wages.

In his endeavours to meet each emergent problem by executive or legislative action, Hughes now found that his autocratic methods, barely tolerable in war, were arousing greater hostility. The war over, people wanted to be able to plan their own lives and run their own affairs. They were no longer prepared to accept government direction—particularly since policy-making was so frequently erratic and policies were becoming increasingly muddled and even mutually conflicting. On his return to Australia in August 1919, after an absence of sixteen months at the peace talks, "Little Digger" Hughes had been hailed as a conquering hero; but although the feeling was general that he had served Australia well while abroad, disenchantment came quickly once it became apparent that the Prime Minister was in no hurry to relinquish the sweeping power which the War Precautions Act provided. Dissension appeared within the coalition which he led. The irascible Prime Minister was not only failing to conciliate enemies: he was alienating friends.

Pressure on Hughes was greatest in two areas. One related to the persistent industrial unrest and associated wage determination problems, and the other stemmed from the rapidly rising political power of rural interests— particularly the farmers—who now spoke for the first time with a unified voice.

The methods he had adopted to settle wage issues in some industries created many problems for Hughes. In his attempt to hold down both wages and prices he had the support of nearly all the newspapers and of employers, but nevertheless discontent was widespread. Hughes had become directly involved in the handling of industrial disputes, when newspapers and employers had begun in 1915 to attack actions of the Court of Concilia-tion, accusing the court of encouraging men to strike for higher wages at a time when the national interest demanded wage stability. For his part, the president of the court, Justice Higgins, maintained that in fact the court was doing no more than upholding the right of a man to refuse to accept work at a minimum rate set by the court. The court (and the High Court, in an opinion) had upheld the view that while the employer remained free to give or refuse employment at a minimum rate, the employee was not bound to take employment at that rate. Justice Higgins had been pre-pared to allow the worker this discretion; but to the government it was imperative that key industries should be kept going, and when a dispute occurred in the coal industry in 1916 Hughes took the matter out of the hands of the Court of Conciliation by setting up a special tribunal to deter-mine an award. The tribunal consisted of an employer representative, an employee representative, and a neutral chairman. The court was very much opposed to the creation of such tribunals which, in the view of Justice Higgins, "in order to get temporary relief for the public, are constrained to yield anything that will put an end to the strike." Steadily, however, supplementary tribunals were appointed until finally a dual system was in operation, with the Conciliation Court's sphere of influence diminished accordingly.

The judicial approach to wage determination had been a relatively simple thing in earlier years, but in what Justice Higgins admitted to be "the whirling confusion of the times" the difficulties were greatly magnified. In seeking to create stability, the court had to face special problems: sharply fluctuating employment levels in industry, these in turn being affected by competition from goods coming in from abroad, and the prosperity (or ability to pay) of rural industries.

The president of the court and his deputies had shown an increasing tendency to stress general principles in giving reasons for each decision, and with the emergence of the matter of weekly hours of work ("the forty-hour week inquiry") as a matter of major concern, representatives of employers and employees in other industries were represented in the court proceedings.

The criticism levelled at the court centred around its willingness to increase wages to meet demonstrable rises in the cost of living. Newspapers and journals attacked the court on the ground that in approving wage increases it was itself the cause of the increase in the cost of living—the "vicious circle" theory which Justice Higgins debunked as a fallacy when he took to task those who "diligently instructed" worried housewives that prices would not rise further if the court granted no increase in wages. The court saw the price rises as a simple reflection of the fall in the value of money resulting inevitably from the war, and it approved wage increases in an attempt to maintain the wage-earner's purchasing power.

By 1920, rumblings of discontent over prices and wages had become louder than ever. The Government and the court were at odds over a solution; the court was maintaining its old function of setting the minimum wage level, and advocating the holding of "a full inquiry on scientific lines" into the cost of living (on the basis of distinct regimens), while the Government was intervening with special tribunals. Meanwhile the public was faced with a serious wage-price squeeze. Hughes and those around him were encouraging a breakdown in the overriding power of the court; the court for its part was opposed to the interference. Justice Higgins wrote of the situation:

> To purchase present relief from strike pressure by tampering with the balanced system of the legitimate tribunal invites further strikes... It is not only illegal, it is an encouragement of strikes to create or purport to create a special tribunal to overrule the legitimate tribunal... An Executive Government, from its very nature, is the worst arbiter or intermediary that can be conceived in industrial disputes.

In March 1920 a correspondent of *The Times*, reviewing the Australian scene, reported that there was "much discontent" with the whole arbitration system. *The Times* report added that the labour movement "roundly condemned" the system as a failure. This brought an immediate rebuttal from the general secretary of the Australian Workers' Union who said that there had been no such declaration by official labour. On the contrary, he added, by far the majority of the unions favoured arbitration, which was "infinitely better than the method of direct action."

The government was determined to perpetuate the special tribunals, and these were given formal status in the Industrial Peace Act of July 1920. This was too much for Justice Higgins, and he resigned shortly afterwards, castigating the Prime Minister for having undermined the influence and usefulness of the court. The judge declared that the permanent court (which sought to provide "a just and balanced system which shall tend to continuity of work in industry generally") and the special tribunals (which sought "to prevent or end an existing strike in one industry") were so different in objective that the two could not "function in competition." He suggested that if they must be kept, the tribunals should at least be integrated with the existing court system.

One factor that had some bearing on the number of post-war strikes was that most of them occurred in industries outside the court's jurisdiction, which was confined to cases of industrial dispute extending beyond one state.

The limitations placed by the terms of the constitution on the powers of the federal court were soon to be whittled down by judicial decisions, however. The most important was the High Court's decision in the engineers' case of 1920, which extended the jurisdiction of the federal Arbitration Court to state-owned industrial enterprises; the principle was applied and extended in other cases. Another factor contributing to the growth of the federal Court's over-all influence was the tendency of the unions to by-pass state tribunals in favour of federal jurisdiction wherever possible.

The strains on the arbitration system were increased as the economy underwent further adjustment in 1921. With depressed wool prices and sagging markets for other export commodities, wage determination was a major problem. The court could not see its way to grant any major wage increases, and there was widespread grumbling. Soon after the war, the government had appointed a Royal Commission to assess to what extent the "fair wage" principles enunciated by Justice Higgins were being carried out in the changed conditions. The Commission's report, published in November 1920, gave the figure of £5/15/8 (a weighted average figure for the six capital cities) as the wage necessary to sustain a man, his wife, and three children at a reasonable standard of comfort. At this time the basic wage was not much more than £4/0/0. Next year, when the unions sought to have the commission's findings made the basis for a new wage determination, they quickly discovered that in the court's view the commission had been unrealistic. Justice Powers's assumption of the court presidency had brought a strong swing to conservatism; Justice Powers stated that while the court's duty was to arrive at a minimum wage for unskilled workers, the commission's finding was not based on this principle; further, it was beyond the capacity of Australian industry to bear the increased wage burden.

In refusing the union's application, the court acknowledged that there had been a decline in real wages, and it attempted to meet this by the addition of sixpence a day to the basic wage. Two principles had been added to the old subsistence concept: that of tying wage adjustments directly to fluctuations in the cost of living and that of capacity-to-pay. In order that wages would not lag too far behind prices, a provision for automatic adjustments, based on the prices for basic commodities in the preceding quarter, was made in all federal awards after 1921.

The fiasco of the commission did nothing to increase Hughes' popularity. Wage determination remained a major problem. The prescient were coming to realize that it could be effective only within limits determined by government policies in other areas—including the level of tariff protection to be afforded industry—and the availability of markets for rural products.

The tremendous flow of imports landed in 1921 touched off demands for a greater measure of protection for local industry. A new tariff introduced by Walter Massy Greene as Minister for Customs provided a much higher scale of duties as well as a new system of classification of imported goods. In addition to the new general tariff, the act brought into being a new intermediate tariff designed to maintain the preferential treatment of British goods and at the same time provide a basis for reciprocal trade agreements. The general purpose of the act was to "protect industries born during the war, encourage others that are desirable, and diversify and extend existing [manufacturing] industries." Although nearly 400,000 men and women were now employed in industry, the limitations of a small market were still painfully apparent, and overseas goods would have quickly swamped the market if new tariff levels had not been established. The act set up a special board to hear claims for additional tariff protection for newly established industries as well as to watch consumers' interests.

In introducing the measure, Massy Greene noted that the war had not only found Australia lacking in many of the essentials of modern life, but it had led to Australia's being "bled to an almost unlimited extent by profiteers on the other side of the world." He added:

> The war has taught us . . . that Australia is lacking in many of those thing which are absolutely essential for her defence. . . Perhaps this time it did not matter much; but should we not reflect that some day the war may not be twelve thousand miles away from us? We may be called upon to defend this country, and the lines of sea communication may not be kept open. From the point of view of defence alone, Australia has a duty to fit herself to equip her troops with everything that a modern army requires.

There could be no longer any doubt that Australia was committed to a high degree of tariff protection as an aid to the expansion of industry. The president of the Associated Chambers of Manufactures was by now speaking of the day when there would be "a million workers in our factories."

Not everyone was prepared to allow the government's strong support for city-based industry to go unchallenged. Hughes found that there was an increasing weight of rural opinion against him to add to other dissatisfied groups. Farmers and pastoralists were grumbling loudly because they believed they were bearing a disproportionate share of the cost of the economic and social legislation. Rural men had for many years supported the creation of new and smaller states as a solution to their problems (most of which they associated with the dominance exercised in political affairs by city interests), and they had formed "new states leagues" as a result; these leagues were sounding boards for rural interests, and provided an organizational pattern out of which a rural party could grow. Interstate conferences among farmer organizations had been held from 1906, and state country parties were evolving from that time; in 1914 the first parliamentary representatives of the countryman's group entered the legislature of Western Australia, to be followed in 1915 by a similar group in the Queensland parliament. In 1916 the Australian Farmers' Federal Organization came into existence; its purpose was to counteract what the countryman considered to be a pampering of city interests.

Formed on an industry basis, the rural party derived financial and general support from primary producers' industrial bodies, but it sprang into being as a result of the countryman's alarm at the policies espoused by Labor (with a new emphasis on socialization) and by Hughes's Nationalists (advocating higher tariffs). Its aim was to counter the dominance of the political field by the representatives of city interests.

By the end of the war the farmers were determined to have their say as a unified political force; they had come to the conclusion that in this way alone they could correct the disabilities they felt they had suffered in the handling of wartime marketing of their products, and in the instability of the price structure and fluctuating demand. Candidates adhering to the new philosophy appeared in the federal sphere for the first time in 1919 when twenty-six men endorsed by the Australian Farmers' Federal Organization stood for election. Some of the candidates saw themselves as members of a rural wing of the Nationalists, and they sought—and in some cases secured—endorsement by the Nationalist party even though Hughes did all he could to belittle the new political group. In spite of Hughes's disparagement, fifteen of these Farmers' candidates were returned. Such a result had not been anticipated, and the surprising success led quickly to a move, headed by grazier Edmund Jowett, to form a separate Country party which would "act independently of all other political organizations." When the House met early in 1920, Hughes' thirty-seven Nationalists faced twenty-seven Labor representatives, while the Country party members numbered ten. The Country party gain had been at the expense, almost exclusively, of the Nationalists. Political commentators noted that probably the Nationalists' majority would have been even slimmer but for the switch from the "first past the post" system of vote-counting to the preferential election system.

Hughes' leadership, once the Nationalists' cornerstone of strength, was becoming an embarrassment to the party. As the political current continued to run against the Nationalists, Hughes found himself fighting to retain power within his own party, where increasing numbers found his personality and his policies obnoxious. His energy and personal drive, and the following he had acquired as a result of his forceful wartime leadership, no longer sufficed as pressure built up against him. His foreign/defence policy had pleased the conservative, Empire-minded groups; but in domestic affairs his persistence with policies held over from his Labor days displeased many in his party.

In political affairs, the old free-and-easy ways of non-Labor groups had been replaced by a new zeal. Political faiths were being loudly proclaimed, and coteries were sharpening the issues around which party support would polarise. More effective party organization was initiated by the Nationalists when Hughes and his followers transferred from the Labor banner, while the Country party was a well disciplined force from the beginning.

New alignments were gaining expression in changing political fortunes. State elections revealed declining support for the Nationalists, and this trend was confirmed dramatically in the results of the federal election of 1922: Hughes' lustre as a political figure had dimmed. In spite of an enlarged party organization to back them, the Nationalists came back with only twenty-nine members in the House of Representatives, a strength equalled by Labor. The balance of power was held by the Country party, with fourteen members.

The Country party adopted the policy of "support in return for concessions." It had no prospect of governing in its own right; instead it sought measures which would further the countryman's cause and preserve the special values in the rural way of life. Politically it was generally conservative, and it could not support Labor.

The Nationalists now required Country party backing to remain in office, and the Country party leadership was determined to drive a hard bargain. The Prime Minister's radical background, and his continued support for many of the policies he had so long espoused, made him the target of attack. Allying itself with the more conservative elements within the councils of the Nationalists, the Country party pressed for Hughes' replacement; Earle Page, the party's parliamentary leader, made it clear that Hughes had to make way for "a more acceptable person."

In spite of persistent efforts by his supporters to sway the negotiations Hughes was left with no alternative and in February 1923 he resigned. The man chosen as the new leader was Hughes' erstwhile treasurer, Stanley Melbourne Bruce, who had come into politics in 1919.

The new ministry, in which Bruce was Prime Minister, was a composite one; Page was recognized as "joint leader," and he became Deputy Prime Minister as well as Treasurer, while the Nationalists held six portfolios to the Country party's five. It was inevitable that under such an arrangement, weight would be given to rural interests out of proportion alike to the numerical strength of the Country party in parliament and to its following in the electorate.

In the early days the Country party had expressed itself against high tariffs, and in favour of lessening the role of government. Once in office, however, it was more interested in gaining "protection" for the farmer, and it refrained from pressing for less federal intervention in everyday affairs. Its policy became one of support for a syndicalist type of control of production and marketing of various rural products through boards under federal auspices (on which producers' representatives were in the majority) with the government providing support where necessary. Thus, although farmers had been loud critics of wartime marketing arrangements, they had come to the conclusion that some kind of orderly marketing was necessary. The Country party became the avid advocate of measures aiding the marketing of wheat and other agricultural products. The farmers' representatives had come to accept the view that "the morrow's breakfast is of more immediate concern than the millenium."

By 1920 Empire migration was becoming a dominant note in the Imperial theme.

Immigration to Australia had been practically suspended during the war years, but in 1920 Henry Gullett had been appointed director of the newly established Immigration Bureau, with headquarters in Melbourne. In 1921 an agreement between the federal government and the states gave the Commonwealth responsibility for recruiting the new settlers required by the states, and for their transport to Australia, while the state governments undertook to inform the Commonwealth of the numbers and classes of immigrants they were prepared to receive and place in employment or on the land. Those entitled to receive assistance included "selected" immigrants (farm labourers and domestic servants and others recruited on the initiative of a state government) and those "nominated" by Australian residents who undertook to care for the newcomer on arrival. From 1921 the new system of government-assisted immigration was further extended by an agreement with the British government.

Gullett's picture of an unguarded, empty Australia now fitted neatly into a larger Imperial scene in which the nagging problem of unemployment and "excess" population in Britain might be solved by large-scale transfers to the Dominions where the new settlers could grow food and fibre to swell Empire trade.

Concern had long been expressed in the inner councils of the Empire on issues connected with trade and defence and related matters. The Dominions Royal Commission (set up in 1912 as a result of the Imperial Conference of 1911) presented its first report in 1917; after cataloguing the natural resources in British lands it went on to recommend methods whereby trade within the Empire could be improved and extended. The commission pointed to a lack of co-ordination of economic effort—it believed the Dominions should concentrate on the production of raw materials, and Britain on manufacturing—and took the view that existing organizations for consultation were inadequate to deal with matters related to the Empire's economic prosperity. The report stressed the need for a new Imperial development board (to sit in London), and advocated a preliminary survey "of the relations between Empire production and Empire requirements throughout the whole range of articles needed for the sustenance or well-being of the people, for the maintenance of industry, and for the production of munitions of war."

These matters were very much in mind when the 1921 Imperial conference on emigration recommended financial co-operation between the British and Dominion governments in support of land settlement projects as part of a comprehensive plan for redistributing population. The Empire Settlement Act passed by the British parliament in 1922 opened the way for finanical co-operation in mutually approved plans which would help fill up the "empty" lands.

The proposal for closer ties between Britain and the British Dominions (now being given the title of the British Commonwealth of Nations with increasing frequency) was the key topic at the Imperial Conference in 1923, which Prime Minister Bruce attended. Associated with the main conference was a conference devoted to economic affairs, and in this the theme of a new "constructive imperialism" was stressed. All those attending the meetings were impressed by the possibilities opened up by a policy of Imperial consolidation. With the recent introduction by Stanley Baldwin's Conservative government of a system of protective tariffs, Britain had swung away from the traditional free-trade policy. A widely held view of the need for British solidarity and integration was expressed by the Prince of Wales when he wrote at this time:

> We are all proud of the British Empire, embracing more than a quarter of the world's land area and a similar proportion of its inhabitants, but very many of us fail to realize the infinite variety and vast extent of the Empire's natural products, which are capable of being made self-sufficing.

When the defeat (in December 1923) of the Conservatives gave Britain its first Labour party government, under James Ramsay MacDonald, all the economic resolutions that had been formulated at the 1923 conference were placed in the melting pot; but as well as accepting resolutions about improving trade among British lands, the conference had established a philosophy of greater and more rapid settlement of British people within the Empire and had produced pledges of London's willingness to provide financial assistance for land settlement schemes in the Dominions, and these were not affected by Britain's change of government.

By instinct and persuasion, both Bruce and Page were dedicated to policies of the closest co-operation with Britain. If others had been inclined to see Australia's manifest destiny in terms of a robust independence within the British Empire, Bruce was insistent that the primary emphasis should be interdependence. The great future he saw for Australia could be attained only in the most complete concert with Britain—and he saw the interdependence of the two countries, and of the Empire, as leading from consultation to integration of policies in all possible fields. In the light of Britain's straitened circumstances, Empire unity seemed to be essential if the British voice was to be heard and the British peoples were to prosper, and Bruce and his government shared the prevailing view that the best way to achieve this was by the development of an Imperially-inspired migration plan. Page and his followers saw the merits of this, provided it included an assured place on British tables for food produced on Australian soil.

In London, the words of Thomas Carlyle in calling for the establishment of an emigration service, "Our little Isle has grown too small for us," were being repeated by those who saw the need to rebuild the Empire through a great, planned dispersal effort. The Imperial Studies Committee of the Royal Colonial Institute was surveying the growth and development of the "far-flung congeries of countries and peoples that is called the British Commonwealth of Nations," and publicising its conclusions. The consensus was that an effort must be made, and made quickly, to replace "scores of watertight schemes, fatally unco-ordinated," with something massive in concept and officially planned and directed. The authors of the extensive study, *Migration within the Empire*, published in 1924, wrote:

Colonial Governments have worked manfully to discharge their particular trusts, the Colonial Office has taken a hand fitfully and without continuity of effort, philanthropists have pursued their noble designs, the mere crank has been often in evidence; but the guiding hand of an Imperial policy has been withheld.

The authors called for this omission to be rectified. The British Isles now held 50 million people "gasping for room and opportunity"; all that was needed was a bold and imaginative policy. Side by side with stupendous figures of national expenditure in Britain—including expenditure of £100 million a year to alleviate unemployment—only a tiny sum, £400,000, was being spent on migration. The real problem, it was concluded, was that "the great public" had not yet been stirred; but the problem was urgent for both Britain and the Dominions. To fill the empty spaces of the Empire it was necessary to find people, increase the productivity of the settled land, and find markets for the exportable surplus of production which would follow. As the authors put it,

"Ships, Colonies, Commerce" was the nineteenth-century motto of Wakefield. "Men, Money, Markets" should be the motto of to-day. These are three parallel problems, and the solution must be parallel.

Bruce happily adopted this slogan. For Australia, prospects in the drive to speed up national development were clearly related to attaining a larger population—the population was still under 6,000,000—and to achieving a marked expansion of rural and secondary industries. These objectives were to be gained without any sacrifice in living standards—in fact, the belief and expectation was that as well as advancing national security their attainment would mean betterment for the individual. Policies in support of closer settlement, organized marketing of primary products, large-scale developmental projects (undertaken, at public expense, on borrowed money), protection of manufacturing, and—above all—an expanded immigration programme, were natural outgrowths of the drive to accelerate development.

The only large-scale project undertaken by an Australian state with direct assistance under the Empire Settlement Act of 1922 had been a group settlement plan in Western Australia, which quickly ran into difficulties. The state undertook to place 6,000 settlers with their families on farms of their own at an estimated cost of £6 million, excluding passage costs. The federal government was to raise the necessary loans, with London contributing a sum equivalent to a third of the interest for five years. Administrative weaknesses were soon showing up; by the time 1300 or so settlers had arrived and been accommodated in the heavily timbered south-western district, troubles were multiplying rapidly. A Royal Commission noted that the farms, which the state undertook to provide for £1000 each, were costing close to £1,500, a sum considerably in excess of their market value. At the base of other difficulties was the fact that many of the settlers were inexperienced in agricultural work. The programme was tapered off, and before long it was brought to an end.

In the other states, where the land hunger of Australians themselves was more pressing, governments held back, and no large-scale move was made to draw upon the financial assistance available from London. The state governments considered that securing land on which returned soldiers could settle was a prior responsibility; plans in most states devolved upon taking over large pastoral properties which could be subdivided into farm blocks for soldier settlement.

Among the Imperially-minded, hopes were still high, however, and the nagging problems already accumulating around the immigration effort were shrugged off as inconsequential.

In 1925 a new and more ambitious agreement was worked out under which British loan money would be made available to state governments, at very low interest to be used for settlement or for public works designed to develop settlement areas or increase their capacity to support a greater population. Under the plan, up to £34 million might be provided over a ten-year period. Up to half the funds could be used for the settlement of Australians on the land, but for every £75 received by a state government under the agreement at least one assisted immigrant was to sail direct from Britain and be settled in Australia, though not necessarily on the land. Of all assisted migrants, a third might be people without any capital.

In 1925, almost 18,000 British migrants arrived in Australia; the number was close to 22,000 the following year. Two out of every three were "assisted," and the proportion was rising. As the programme gathered pace, the absorptive capacity of the country loomed larger in discussions related to rapid population growth. Distance from markets, transport costs, and the heavy investment needed to develop the land were practical matters that could not be overcome by mere enthusiasm; accelerated development of the land was not the easy thing it seemed on paper.

As in the early days, theoretical schemes to tap "vast and undeveloped resources" did not run according to plan. The plain fact was that a hard core of unemployment within Australia, coupled with large numbers of school-leavers seeking employment each year, was taxing the country's capacity to absorb those coming in from abroad. The economy was being choked. More and more imports, paid for abroad with borrowed money, were flooding in; but investment in employment-producing industry was falling away. It was no longer possible to absorb either the newcomers or the existing unemployed.

The drive to add rapidly to Australia's population remained strong, however. Henry Gullett, now a member of the House of Representatives, called for a more determined effort when he spoke of the need to double Australia's population within twenty years. The Bruce-Page government saw the solution in the creation of a commission of four members charged with the duty of stimulating the development of resources as a preliminary to attracting increased numbers of new settlers. In 1926 the Development and Migration Act was passed to carry into effect the comprehensive Imperial plan within Australia. The commission, working within the framework of the act, was under the chairmanship of a dynamic visionary, Herbert Gepp, a chemical engineer-turned-businessman. The commission's first task was to organize a body of scientists who in turn were to proceed with a survey of the resources of what the Prime Minister, in introducing the measure, described as "the greatest undeveloped country in the world." The commission was then to formulate plans for "utilizing our resources and the most effective and rapid method of dealing with them"; it was to act as a clearing house through which the needs for labour, on a nationwide basis, could be dealt with, and at the same time it was to advise on the possibilities of absorbing overseas capital. Bruce was convinced that adoption of "a scientific basis" for dealing with the problems of migration and settlement would assure the success of the undertaking.

As well as being responsible for activities related to men and money, the commission was to run the federal government's migration office in London, co-operate with the state governments in all their developmental projects, and have a hand in finding overseas markets for Australian products.

The problems were manifold, however. In its investigations the commission turned up more barriers to large-scale immigration than had been suspected, and it spent much of its time rejecting ambitious and impractical schemes put forward by state governments for endorsement. Earlier plans had resulted in migrants arriving at an average rate of about 21,000 a year, and under the "£34 million agreement" the intake rose by only 3000 to 4000 a year above this rate.

There were already misgivings in many quarters about the wisdom of the effort, particularly the heavy involvement of governments as sponsors and supporters of so much of the migration programme. Putting men on the land was no easy matter; land settlement was now mainly a matter of subdivision and resettlement, and there were still returned servicemen eager to take over any land offering under government-sponsored development schemes.

In spite of the commission's wide field of action, many administrative weaknesses remained. The division of functions between the federal authorities and the states in securing and placing the new settlers meant that there was frequently a serious lack of cohesion. Australia was trying to reverse a well-defined trend and put more men on the land when greater mechanization and steady improvement in technical aspects of rural industries were resulting in increased productivity; with the limited markets open to Australian produce it was becoming harder to sell the products available. In five years to the end of 1926, when the natural increase in population, without immigration, was over 10 per cent, the number of men employed principally in farming and dairying rose by less than 6 per cent, while the number of men employed in factories went up over 16 per cent. What increase there was in farm work took place in Queensland and Western Australia. Most of the immigrants had been drawn from industrial towns of Britain, and after a longer or shorter trial of the new conditions many of them reverted to industrial occupations in the Australian capital cities. Here they competed with established workers for the available jobs in factories or in transport or commerce. With the labour market oversupplied, opposition to immigration grew in the trade unions.

As a constructive advocate of an active immigration policy, Gullett had consistently maintained that migration could never flourish as a national movement until it enjoyed "the co-operation and blessing of organized labour," but the government had given little consideration to his call for special efforts to gain Trades Hall support for the migration programme.

Among policy-makers there was insufficient appreciation of the real problems to be faced and overcome if accelerated growth were to be maintained without dislocation. Special difficulties were posed in a country which insisted on holding its standard of living for all workers and at the same time was not (and could not be) self-sufficing. If a sound balance were to be struck in the economy during the expansion, it would involve blending the right proportions of land, labour, and capital in all Australian industries.

In spite of much discussion on the subject, little was known on which solid conclusions could be based. What was needed most, as one economist pointed out, was a series of preliminary surveys so that policies might be arrived at from knowledge and not merely hope. Such investigation should cover basic aspects of the problem. Starting with a comprehensive soil survey, research was needed also into matters related to raw materials, transport needs and facilities, power supply, the capacity of individual industries for absorbing labour and, perhaps most importantly, "all the problems of product marketing as a means of expanding both primary and secondary industries." Economist Gordon Leslie Wood, noting in 1928 that there was still an apparent disinclination, both in Australia and overseas, to admit the limitations imposed upon closer settlement by the country's climatic conditions, wrote of the danger of diminished prosperity if expansion continued to be based on "deficient knowledge and inaccurate data."

Settlement was advancing dangerously into marginal lands as a result of the flow of money made available under government auspices; but natural barriers to land utilization could not be overcome. Many of the soldier settlers placed on land as farmers as part of closer settlement projects were running into ruin. In some cases the outlays involved in bringing the land to a productive condition had been too high; but generally the problem was that the return from the crop was insufficient to give a reasonable margin of profit after costs of carriage to its overseas market, and the expenses of working the land, had been met.

The price of wool remained high enough for sheepmen to retain their grip on large acreages. As a result, transition from pasture to agriculture was still not the simple process many believed it to be. The acreage under crop in the 1925–26 season showed only slight expansion beyond the 1914–15 area (slightly less than 17,000,000 acres against 15,500,000 acres). The total area sown fluctuated from year to year under seasonal influences, but the limits of cultivation seemed to have been reached. The average output of wheat per acre, at 13 bushels, was well below that of other wheat producing countries' average yields.

Brighter prospects seemed to be opening up with the conversion from pasture land to intensive cultivation made possible through irrigation, and the irrigated area was being expanded as a consequence. Success achieved along the Murray in the older settlements had suggested that a more diversified pattern of production could be achieved, adding to the nation's agricultural products; and although expansion of irrigation areas involved heavy public expenditure, for the individual blockholder it seemed a less hazardous undertaking than dry farming. The storing and distribution of the waters of the Murray and its tributaries, long under discussion, had come under direct review at a conference of experts from Victoria, New South Wales, and South Australia as early as 1913, when it was agreed that a river-control plan was of joint interest. When, as a result, the River Murray Commission was set up in 1915, the federal government (which offered financial assistance for the project) was also represented on it. The commission at once recommended the building of large storages and a system of weirs along the Murray to maintain water levels in the river, and the first of the weirs (at Blanchetown, South Australia) was completed in 1922. Two years later another weir (Torrumbarry) was added, and five more over the next four years; each was intended to maintain river pools at a key point; but apart from pilot work on a dam above Albury, little was done to develop or plan catchment storages.

Victoria and New South Wales had rivers of their own on which irrigation could be expanded. On the Goulburn River, in Victoria, development was centred around Shepparton, where blocks were planted to stone-fruit and various types of vegetables; the Goulburn weir, completed in the 1890s, provided water for an expanding reticulation system in northern Victoria, and the Eildon reservoir, completed in the mid-1920s, provided water for further extension of the irrigation area. Along the Murrumbidgee, the New South Wales government was supporting new projects around Leeton, Griffith, and Yanco, as orchards and rice farms were established under irrigation.

The boundless enthusiasms of a Mildura-born promoter were a major factor in rivetting public attention on some of the products of the irrigated lands and in extending irrigation to Western Australia. Clement John De Garis, who first gained a following among the dried fruits growers in Mildura when he introduced modern packaging methods and improved viticultural techniques, in 1919 started an intensive publicity campaign on behalf of the dried fruits growers, establishing "Sunraysia" as a household name in the process. A visit to Western Australia in 1920 convinced De Garis that an irrigation settlement could profitably be established there, and he decided to take over a 50,000 acre property, Kendenup, out from Albany. His other ventures were prospering, and through his persuasiveness and enthusiasm he sold many blocks in anticipation of the completion of the Kendenup development. When local funds dried up he went to the United States to borrow more. At this point the promoter's costs outran his assets, and in 1925 the unfortunate episode ended in personal tragedy when De Garis committed suicide; it was many years later that his vision of a flourishing Kendenup settlement was vindicated.

In the days when enthusiasm for closer settlement was infectious, there were also those who pressed for something to be done about the continent's outlying and almost untouched areas. Under federal control since 1911, the Northern Territory had remained an empty land; its white population in the mid-1920s still barely exceeded 2000, and (as a writer of the day noted) it was still variously regarded as "a White Elephant, an Untamed Territory, or as a convenient barrier against Asiatic invasion." In 1926 the federal government authorized construction of a rail line from Oodnadatta to Alice Springs (a line which was completed three years later) as the first section of a through north-south railway. At the same time, a three-man North Australian Commission was created; among other things, it was to draw up a comprehensive plan for northern development.

During the war years the federal government's overriding defence power had prevailed, overshadowing the states' authority in important fields. There were many people who believed fervently that the wartime experience had not only demonstrated the benefits to be derived from having a more dominant federal administration but had further substantiated a need for continuation of an expanded federal role in economic affairs as part of a process inherent in an industrial economy. Those supporting centralizing trends polarised around Labor (and former Labor) men; those most strongly opposed were the conservatives, while many of liberal persuasion also feared any permanent strengthening of bureaucratic control.

The conflict of opinion between the states-righters and the centralizers had been illustrated by the referendum of 1919, when voters were asked to approve two constitutional amendments aimed at extending the Commonwealth's legislative power over industry and commerce. The proposals, sponsored by Hughes, were basically the same as those put to referendum in 1911 and 1913 under Labor's sponsorship. One would have extended temporarily the federal powers in respect to trade and commerce, corporations, industrial matters and trusts, and the second would have given the Commonwealth power to nationalise any industry "declared" by both houses of parliament to be the subject of a monopoly. Both proposals were rejected, although the vote in each case was close and in three states a majority favoured the proposals.

The happy abandon that had come in the 1920s as a natural reaction to the violent dislocations of wartime control could not last. In the more complex postwar world, hard-and-fast divisions between government and industry were no longer possible, and by the mid-1920s it had become evident that regulatory action would have to be taken in some fields traditionally beyond the scope of government. As Herbert Gepp noted, the time had come for Australia to "learn how to take conscious control of its economic destinies." Major and fundamental problems were in a no-man's land; the business community had no means of coping with many basic matters, nor were these matters under the proper control of the federal government. Bruce, unwilling to see the government intervene directly, believed there was a happy and practical solution which would achieve the desired result without a build-up in political power over everyday affairs. The answer, as he conceived it, was to set up independent advisory or regulatory commissions, composed of experts, to deal with the major national problems and proffer sound non-partisan solutions to them, or to grant additional money to the states (as was done from 1923 when a federal-support plan for road-building was initiated).

Bruce and Treasurer Page were determined that the government would divest itself of the remnant of enterprises set up during the war to produce urgently needed goods, and also of the government-owned shipping line. There was a sense of unholy glee at being able to clean up what Page described as "the mess which has been caused by the various socialistic ventures that have been left to us as a legacy of the war." The spring-cleaning resulted in the disposal of various enterprises ranging from the Commonwealth harness factory and the woollen mills to the Commonwealth shipping line, created in 1916 and consisting (at the time of its disbandment in 1928) of a fleet of over fifty steamers providing regular passenger-cargo services between Australia and Britain. As these and other enterprises were sold off—they included the Williamstown dockyard—Page felt he could take credit for adopting "sound business principles" in the divestment; but Labor claimed it was nothing more than a sell-out to commercial interests of ventures which could well be maintained in the public interest.

Thus in matters related to the federal government's role in all internal matters, the Bruce-Page government tended to reduce direct federal intervention or involvement wherever this could be done. It wanted to decentralize power, and it maintained this approach in spite of the fact that the more complex issues of an expanding nation demanded firmer federal policies if proper co-ordination of the states' varying policies was to be achieved; it refused to assume a more dominant position for the Commonwealth, holding to this view even though the High Court, long an unyielding guardian of states' rights, now appeared willing to favour a greater federal role.

The question of where the balance between federal and state powers should lie came down to legal, as well as political judgment. All through the first two decades of the Commonwealth, the High Court had held federal power in check; as Chief Justice from 1903, Sir Samuel Griffith had consistently opposed any peacetime expansion of the federal role by rigorously refusing to diminish the powers of the states. Where a federal power could be given a wider or a narrower meaning, the court under Griffith had generally accepted the narrower interpretation as a means of preserving the assured minimum of state competence. An exception to the general rule was in arbitration matters, where court decisions had tended to favour an increased federal role.

The balance in federal-states powers had been upset by wartime conditions; following Griffith's retirement in 1919, a basis for future legal relationships between the Commonwealth and the states had to be established and the degree of local independence in economic affairs determined.

Although Justice Isaac (a member of the court since 1906) had long favoured the recognition of wider powers for the Commonwealth, it was not until Griffith's retirement that any change in outlook was apparent in the High Court's pronouncements. In 1920 judgments were tending to suggest that a considerably broader interpretation of federal powers might be anticipated. Griffith's successor as Chief Justice, Sir Adrian Knox, headed a court which was inclined to reduce the old states-rightism.

At this very time, however, the community was in no mood to give approval to the growing powers and pretensions of the federal government, as was shown by the rejection of the referendum to extend federal powers. Wartime experience had suggested to the public that federal power was arbitrary, restrictive, and in conflict with old ideas of personal freedom. As a matter of political preference, voters were seeking to block any growth of bureaucracy, which they felt would be the inevitable result of any increase in federal powers. Ideas of local independence and the merits of personal action were most admired. Justice Isaacs might speak of the court's obligation in interpreting the law "to recognize the advancing frontiers of public thought and public activity" in relation to government intervention in affairs, and in general the High Court might be tending consistently towards a more expansive legal interpretation of the federal power—but to the conservative politicians and their backers federal powers needed pruning rather than expanding. In the absence of federal initiative, the states were firmly back in the saddle.

In financial matters, the policy of the Bruce-Page administration was complex. The difficult problem of financial relations with the states had to be faced, and there was obviously a need to co-ordinate loan policy. In addition, banking organization and practice seemed to call for modification.

Important amendments to the Commonwealth Bank Act were brought forward by Page, as Treasurer, in 1924. Under the capable control of Denison Miller, who had been governor from the bank's inception, the Commonwealth Bank had come to play an increasingly important part in the financial affairs of the country; not only had it acted since 1915 as agent in raising loans on behalf of the state governments, but its total deposits (trading and savings) had grown to a point where its holdings were equal to about a quarter of the deposits of all private trading banks combined. With Miller's death, late in 1923, it seemed appropriate to swing from one-man control to policy management by a board. The government decided on an eight-man board (to include the governor, under whose chairmanship the board would meet, and the secretary of the Treasury) on which there would be six private citizens whose careers had been in agriculture, commerce, finance or industry. The government believed that the creation of a board lessened the chances of direct political control of the bank and would place "independent expert advice at the disposal of the various governments and. . . assist in harmonizing, and, if necessary, in curtailing their loan operations." Labor was vocal in its criticism, seeing the move as "nothing less than an attempt to kill the bank," since the proposed board would have on it "men altogether out of sympathy with the objects of a real national bank." Instead, Labor wanted financial experts who were fully employed in the service of the bank appointed to its management as the only available safeguard against what Labor saw as political interference in the bank's affairs. The government's proposals, however, were carried in spite of Labor's objections.

The measure also contained provisions which took the Commonwealth Bank farther in the direction of central banking. It was, in the Treasurer's words, to become "the keystone of the financial arch" and "the pivot of Australian banking—a bank of issue, deposit, discount, exchange and reserve." The measure transferred control of the note issue from a special board within the bank to the full board. It also called for the compulsory settling of all banks' clearing balances through the Commonwealth Bank, and authorized the board to fix and publish the discount rate of the bank. In addition it proposed to set up local boards of advice in the principal cities, but this provision lapsed.

It was clear that the government hoped the Commonwealth Bank under its board would operate within definite limits and would not become a serious competitor of the other banks—which it might well have done now that it was clothed with power additional to the normal banking functions which it was still undertaking. Labor regarded any hobbling of the bank as a denial of one of the original purposes for which the bank was created; but the legislation was in fact an attempt to move the bank closer to what were believed to be appropriate central-banking functions. If such a role were to be pursued successfully, even to the limited degree considered necessary, obviously restraint would be essential in carrying out the bank's other functions. However, there was as much timidity as conservatism in the board's approach, and since to be successful a central banking function required strong leadership, no great change resulted from the legislation.

Subsequent amendments established a rural credits department within the bank (1925) and defined the manner in which funds might be advanced by the newly established savings bank division for house-building purposes (1927). For years Country party members had been pressing claims for special credit facilities to assist primary producers; the measure of 1925 provided that such advances could be made to other banks, or to co-operatives or other organizations, though not to individuals. Once again Labor attacked the restricted approach, urging direct loans, but the indirect method suited most Country party men, as well as the Nationalists, and under its provisions industry co-operatives concerned with the marketing of wheat and other products were able to function satisfactorily and strengthen their grip. The original list of products eligible for special credit facilities included wool, grain, butter, fish, preserved or dried fruits, hops, sugar, and cotton; subsequently it was extended to timber, precious and other metals, and superphosphate as well as wine, meat, eggs, peanuts, and fodder.

Savings bank business was separated from the Commonwealth Bank in 1927 at the same time as the Federal Housing Act was under consideration.

Provision of finance for home-building was an important role of the new savings bank, which was also authorized to invest in any government security, in loans on the security of land, and in loans for the erection of warehouses or storages for primary products. At the time the act was proclaimed in June 1928 the savings bank had nearly £50 million in deposits and 1,000,000 of the 4,000,000 depositors with all savings banks. Labor sought at once to have a rural credit branch established which might assist in land settlement and development, and to provide relief to necessitous primary producers, but this move was defeated.

Federal-state loan-raising and financial relationships were being clarified by this time. The Bruce-Page administration had been anxious to bring some sense of order into government borrowing; the competition among state governments for loan funds had raised interest rates, particularly for borrowings by the less developed states. Page proposed in 1923 that a loan council be formed to co-ordinate all government borrowing by laying down the order in which the the Commonwealth, the states, and various state-controlled bodies should seek funds on the market. After meeting in 1924 on an informal basis, the Australian Loan Council became the official borrowing authority in 1925; and although New South Wales refused to accept the restriction on its autonomy the council functioned satisfactorily.

Taxation and tax reimbursements to the states were also under review. Discussions on allocation of revenue between the Commonwealth and the states had been going on intermittently, with suggestions from all sides. Concerned that the allocation of revenue between the Commonwealth and the states now so heavily favoured the Commonwealth, Bruce decided to abolish the system of *per capita* payments and to introduce a new system of state grants. At a conference in June 1926 his proposal to substitute a permanent formula laying down the actual amounts to be paid to the states was approved, after minor modifications, by the states. Later, the new system, known as the Financial Agreement, was incorporated in the constitution following a referendum; it went into effect on July 1, 1928.

Not only had all states expressed dissatisfaction with the financial resources allocated to them by the Commonwealth, but a sense of grievance had developed among some state governments on broader issues related to the states' positions within the federation. Even in the populous and prosperous states some annoyance was evident, while in states with smaller populations and less development—Western Australia, Tasmania, and South Australia—the situation was becoming intolerable. Antagonism was greatest in the west; the very question of continued participation in the federation was under debate there. In 1927 Bruce appointed a Royal Commission to investigate federal-states relationships and to review the constitution. By the time the commission's report was completed (in 1929) other issues had come to the fore.

Wartime developments in aircraft design and construction had opened the way for the advance of aviation. Pilots trained for duty in the flying corps had shown themselves to be capable as well as daring, and for people living in a vast country set far from world centres the prospect of turning the longrange plane to account in peacetime uses was an exciting one. The thrill of personal adventure proved to be an irresistible magnet for wartime-trained flyers, while the public built up hopes of practical gain in mobility and accessibility—not to mention defence—from the development of air services.

The first transcontinental flight was made from Point Cook, Victoria, the flying corps training centre, to Darwin, in November-December 1919—a 2,500 mile flight which took forty-six flying hours. Soon afterwards, just to show that dependence on overseas plane builders was not complete, a home-made machine, 18 feet in wingspan, was flown across Bass Strait in the first crossing.

By this time the great saga of Australia-bound flights from half-way round the world was opening. At war's end Hughes' government had been quick to offer £10,000 for a successful England-Australia flight, and this handsome prize had attracted the attention of Australian airmen still in Britain. A number of teams gathered to attempt the long and hazardous adventure; but only one aircraft, a big Vickers Vimy, with a four-man crew led by Captain Ross Smith and Lieutenant Keith Smith, fulfilled all conditions of the award, including completion of the flight to Darwin within thirty days. The achievement of the Smith brothers and their companions, Flight Sergeants Bennett and Shiers, was hailed throughout Australia as they continued on from Darwin to Melbourne, where they were presented with their prize. In 1920, Lieutenants Raymond John Parer and John Cowe McIntosh made the England-Australia flight in a much less elaborate DH9 biplane in seven months.

Encouragement of aviation within Australia was Hughes' next objective. The federal government recognized that air services could be important in the development and defence of the remote and sparsely-populated northern areas of the continent. A civil aviation unit was formed in 1920 as part of the department of defence; it was authorized to assist in promoting operations to selected areas. The route had to be one inadequately served by existing transport and yet able to provide sufficient mail to warrant the experiment. The 1200 mile Geraldton-Derby run was chosen, and in December 1921 a weekly service was established by West Australian Airways Ltd. One of the pilots was a former A.F.C. Lieutenant named Charles Kingsford Smith, a Distinguished Flying Cross winner with an insatiable love of flying.

In western Queensland, interest in aviation's potential had been stirred in 1919 when the Smith brothers, flying on from Darwin, had put in at Cloncurry and at Longreach on their way south. Two other ex-war pilots, Lieutenants Paul Joseph McGinness and Wilmot Hudson Fysh, had visited these towns during a ground-survey by motor-car of the Darwin-Brisbane route in anticipation of the England-Australia "race" competitors, and the Point Cook-Darwin flight had passed this way. Out of discussion on the merits of air transportation had come the idea of a commercial air operation in western Queensland. Two outback pastoralists, Fergus McMaster and Alexander Kennedy, were among those who subscribed the initial capital to establish Queensland and Northern Territory Aerial Services in 1920. The promoters sensed that the men of the inland would quickly take to flying. They saw immediate prospects for revenue in air-taxi work and in providing joyrides to outback townspeople (at £3/3/– for a ten-minute flight), and they planned also to operate between Longreach and Winton railheads and to provide regular services between the main centres of western Queensland. Eventually, they hoped, links would be established from Charleville to Brisbane and across the Barkly Tableland to Darwin.

Delays occurred while a mail contract was negotiated; then on November 2, 1922, the Armstrong-Whitworth plane rose from Charleville to begin the new airline's first regular passenger flight. With stops at Winton and Longreach, it covered the 577 miles from Charleville to Cloncurry in less time than it would take a man to ride 30 miles on horseback. The Longreach-Cloncurry hop took four and a half hours; and in the passenger seat eighty-seven-year-old Alexander Kennedy remembered another journey he had made between these two towns fifty-three years before: it had been by bullock waggon and had taken eight months. The air age had begun for the people of the inland, bringing them a new mobility. As Fysh saw it, gone were the days of groping through hills on horseback; and gone were the days "when the grim edge of life or death was decided by [one's] bushcraft in locating a waterhole."

Air services were slower to get a footing in areas where ground transport was relatively well developed. In 1922, a firm was set up to operate services between Brisbane, Sydney, and Adelaide, but it was not until mid-1924 that the first route of Australia Aerial Services Ltd opened; it linked Sydney and Adelaide by way of Cootamundra-Narrandera-Hay-Mildura. A year later, a Melbourne-Echuca-Deniliquin-Hay service and a Mildura-Broken Hill link were added to create a network.

Two official round-Australia flights had already been made—the first when Squadron Leader Stanley James Goble and Flight Lieutenant Ivor Ewing McIntyre, distinguished members of the newly-formed Royal Australian Air Force, made the circuit in a seaplane in forty-four days (April-May, 1924), and the second shortly afterwards when the controller of civil aviation, Colonel Horace Clowes Brinstead, made a tour of inspection in a DH50 piloted by Captain George Jones. Late in 1926 the head of the R.A.A.F., Group Captain Richard Williams, and Flight Lieutenant McIntyre flew from Melbourne to New Guinea, New Britain, and the Solomons, and back, in a DH50 seaplane. It was the first flight into the Pacific islands.

By this time, English aviator Alan Cobham had flown from England to open a new phase of the spectacular long-distance flights which were to converge on Australia over the next six or eight years. Cobham had been selected by Imperial Airways (Britain's international commercial airline) to make survey flights over Empire routes preparatory to regular commercial flights.

Early in 1928 Bundaberg-born Bert Hinkler flew a solo Avro Avian from

Croydon, England, to Darwin, in fifteen days. Then came the astonishing flight of Charles Kingsford Smith, with Charles Ulm as co-pilot and two Americans, Harry Lyon and James Warner, as navigator and radio operator, from Oakland, California, to Brisbane. Flying the Fokker FVII *Southern Cross*, Kingsford Smith made the 7400 mile flight by way of Honolulu and Suva (Fiji), in eighty three hours, thirty eight minutes' flying time. The crossing included the longest single flight made to this time—the 2740 mile hop from Honolulu to Suva. The arrival of the Southern Cross at Eagle Farm, Brisbane, on June 10, 1928 started a round of uninhibited welcomes for the incomparable "Smithy" and his companions as they flew the Old Bus from city to city.

Kingsford Smith and Ulm soon followed up this memorable crossing with a non-stop trans-Australia flight (Point Cook-Perth), and then with the first trans-Tasman crossing and return.

As the target for great flights from half-way round the earth, Australia was being brought closer to the world at large. At the same time, within Australia, the individual's old sense of isloation was being steadily reduced.

In its various forms, the internal combustion engine was beginning to ring changes in the lives of country settlers and city families alike even by the war's end, and this was accelerated as motor-cars, trucks, and buses appeared on the roads and the farm tractor became an accepted substitute for the draught-horse team. At the same time the new wonder of cat's whisker radio was gaining acceptance, at least among young people in the cities; by 1922 the first sporadic "commercial" broadcasts were being made in Melbourne and Sydney, and from then on the wireless fad steadily gained adherents as the experimental broadcasters put the muffled sounds of the recorded Caruso or Lauder on the air.

The automobile age was ushered in by the T-model Ford. Before its advent, early motor vehicles with their large brass lamps and running-board tool boxes, had appeared in the big cities, and as early as 1908 one had succeeded in crossing the continent from Adelaide to Darwin—2,000 miles covered in forty days in a remarkable endurance test. By the 1920s the "Tin Lizzie" and its contemporaries were nosing their way along unpaved roads in the bush, jolting over bumps or becoming caught in impassable gluepots after sudden or heavy rains—sometimes causing frustration and anguish through mechanical failure, but increasingly seen as a boon to people scattered over a sprawling land.

Just as coaches and waggons of American design had proved best suited to local conditions, so the products of the American motor-car manufacturers had the characteristics that most Australians sought for out-of-town travel. Competitively the American makes, Ford, Graham-Paige, Chevrolet, Dodge, Chrysler, Buick, and others won greater public approval than the many British and European makes—including Vauxhalls, Bugattis, and Lancias—which were competing for the market. In 1924 the Ford Motor Company began assembling motor-cars for the first time at a plant near

Geelong; two years later General Motors began shipping in parts for assembly and launched a body-building operation.

As the number of motor-cars climbed, the blacksmith's shop was falling into disuse, The "garage" was becoming a feature of even the remoter town; and although the garage owner might rely on a well-thumbed handbook to explain the intricacies of four-cylinder motors and steering mechanisms, the farmer found out as much by trial and error. International oil companies, competing for a growing volume of business, were tackling the petrol distribution problems; they were making greater investment in storage installations for the petrol they imported, and in vehicles to transport it. The four gallon "tin" (the method by which petrol had been sold from earlier days) was no longer the only means of delivery; from the mid-1920s the motorist could drive up beside a tall roadside "bowser" and see the petrol hand-pumped into the graduated glass bowl before it gravitated down into the petrol tank.

The decline of the horse—Australia's peak of 2,500,000 was reached in the late war years—was concurrent with other significant changes; for as mechanical transport replaced the horse team so the build-up of city populations was accelerated. The new economics of farming strengthened the trend to larger farms where labour might be replaced by machinery. Other changes in the economy helped to expand city employment at the expense of rural employment, particularly in the already-developed states.

The trend to urbanization became the subject of political and editorial attention. Measuring the situation against the past, and convinced that the percentage of people living in urban areas compared with those in rural areas (62:38 in 1921) had risen to a danger point, many who spoke out on the subject professed to see evil consequences in the relative decline in rural population. The strictures of Henry George and Edward Bellamy on the menace of "bloated" cities had not been forgotten. As early as 1918 a select committee of the Victorian parliament had investigated "the drift of population from the country districts" and had set down causes (and symptoms). People were being drawn to the cities by the better opportunities for employment, at higher wages and under better conditions, that existed there. Fundamental to the reduced proportion of people in the rural areas was the same factor that was applying in other advancing economies: as the productive power of each individual engaged in the production of food increased, the percentage of people in the community needed for rural activities could decline without impairing output. In Victoria, where some 15,000 "new settlers" had been placed on the land under various closer settlement programmes put forward between 1904 and 1927, a total of about 14,000 people left rural occupations for towns and cities between 1922 and 1927. Policies which governments were stubbornly pursuing to direct immigration into channels of land settlement were in fact running counter to the economic facts.

The settlement of people from abroad was entailing a high level of investment. Divided almost equally between public works expenditure and private investment, capital outlays were absorbing an average of about 18 per cent of gross national product. Expenditure by public authorities was supported largely from borrowings in London and New York, while capital from abroad represented about one-fifth of all private investment.

The great building boom in the cities was absorbing close to 50 per cent of all private investment money in most years. Associated with the urban growth, manufacturing absorbed about 25 per cent of investment capital, while other urban expansion involved another 20 per cent or so. Less than one-tenth of private investment was devoted to developing the land, whether for pastoral or agricultural use. As the cities grew and better services were demanded, governments and local authorities had to find money for the expansion of electricity and water supply and sewerage facilities, as well as improved roads and new or improved transport services. In rural areas, in support of closer settlement, railway building had acquired an impetus of its own; and if governments were generally slow to recognize the role that motor transport would play, they were even less inclined to acknowledge the degree to which road and rail facilities could be complementary rather than competitive. Many uneconomic lines had been laid before ever-mounting interest charges on the rail debts, and the extinction of loan sources, finally forced a review.

Investment was weighted to meet the demands of a rapidly increasing population. Under these circumstances it was taking somewhat different lines from those it would have followed in simply improving the rate of growth of income per head of the natural-born population. Governments were in fact borrowing heavily abroad simply to avoid lowering the existing levels of consumption.

In matters of social welfare, there was little significant advance, and other nations were now overtaking (or surpassing) the progress Australia had made earlier. With nation-building on its mind, Australia was no longer a "laboratory of social experiment," No federal initiative in social welfare had been taken since the introduction of maternity allowances in 1912—a move which had led the non-Labor parties to adopt a more definite attitude to the method of financing social services. Insistence that all such programmes should be on a contributory basis led to various proposals being shelved by the federal government in the 1920s.

In individual states, however, some gains in social welfare were made. New South wales, which had been a pioneer with legislation for a non-contributory old-age pension programme at the turn of the century, introduced widows' pensions in 1926 and child endowment the following year. Queensland put an unemployment insurance plan into force in 1923; it was on a contributory basis and covered seasonal or intermittent workers as well as those in steady employment. Elsewhere, charitable relief systems were still generally relied upon to take care of needy cases. Following the action by New South Wales, the Bruce-Page government appointed a Royal Commission to report on the feasibility of federal child endowment on a general scale (the Commonwealth had instituted such a plan for those on its own payroll seven years before), and a national insurance plan to cover unemployment and sickness was considered in 1928; but the initiative lapsed.

From the beginning of the Bruce-Page regime, people and money pouring in from overseas had been effective pump-primers to the economy. Heavy investment was needed in housing and in services required to meet the needs of a fast-growing population; in the carefree atmosphere of an expansive world, overseas borrowing presented no great problem. The money went to finance a great stream of imports. Australia's reputation was high, and in this golden age of United States foreign lending, Australia received a flow of dollar funds from New York which totalled £48 million by June 1928.

Nation-building had become an inspiration in official policies. Politicians and newspapers outdid each other in the glowing word pictures they painted of a great future.

In the busy, restless world, money moved freely and thrift was no longer held in high regard. Attendance at sports events and at entertainment soared. There was less time to be devoted to reading or discussion or contemplation. In the newspapers, display advertisements offering new products and wares of all kinds seemed to be crowding out the news; and the briefer reports were sometimes supplemented by photographs of the happening described or the personage involved. Crossword puzzles and other word games had come into vogue; they provided a happy diversion for the train or tram traveller on the way to or from the office. The gramophone had displaced the piano, and jazz was making its début. At the head of all the new delights, "the flicks" were opening up new worlds of entertainment and escape.

Everywhere the silver screen was winning converts as the multiple-reel or feature film came into its own. Early enthusiasm for film-making—the first feature film, *The Early Christian Martyrs*, was made in Melbourne in 1899—had long since waned after a crop of outdoor adventure films featuring bushrangers and cattlemen. As more prestigious American-produced films appeared and movie-going became a habit, the competition of the overseas product was overwhelming alike to Australian-made films and to the local performing arts. Some city theatres were converted to film showings. In most cases suburban movie houses were built specially for the purpose; but in the country towns and even in outer suburbs where old halls were used, the limitations of reel-changing remained such that scenes of Charles Chaplin, Mary Pickford, or Rudolph Valentino were punctuated by blank periods between reels.

Overwhelmed by standardizing influences, the national movement in the arts had run its course. An effort was being made to develop Australian culture beyond its pioneering levels; but in the transition phase, creative expression tended to lose direction. Talent was still going abroad to join in the search for a more profound expression.

In verse writing, *The Song of a Sentimental Bloke*, published in 1915, and *Ginger Mick* (1916) had enshrined a vanishing idiom. These verse narratives were entrancing in their day to people throughout the land, and the name of their author, C.J. (Charles Michael James) Dennis became familiar to country- and city-dweller alike; but by the 1920s the old provincialism was no longer captivating readers. The visionary, Bernard O'Dowd, whose poem, *The Bush* (1912) had been the best known Australian poem until the appearance of *The Sentimental Bloke,* was still writing sensitive and scholarly verse, but his work no longer commanded great attention. Similarly, Christopher John Brennan, who a generation or so earlier had drawn inspiration from classical rather than Australian themes at a time of enthusiastic nationalism in writing, had virtually retired from the scene to concentrate on study of European literature. Thus, neither Brennan's extraordinary quality as a writer of romantic poetry, nor O'Dowd's clamant Australianism, aroused any great support. A coterie in Sydney, inspired largely by the work and outlook of artist-writer Norman Lindsay, launched the literary magazine *Vision* in 1923 as the banner around which nationalism-repudiating writers might rally; in the magazine the new poets tended to escape to Old World mythology and a world of fauns and pirates and masked balls in a search for a renewal of youth. Those who drew inspiration from the new worldliness included Hugh McRae and Kenneth Slessor, each of them a poet of considerable power. At the same time, both John Shaw Nielson and Frank Wilmot (whose work appeared under the pseudonym of Furnley Maurice) were writing fine verse, not particularly Australian in theme but always perceptive, lyrical, and close to the heart of nature.

In 1925 the notable literary review, the *Bookfellow,* had to close, going the way of the earlier *Triad* and *Lone Hand,* and marking a further retreat from the bush idiom. At the same time, Steele Rudd's *On Our Selection* and *Grandpa's Selection* maintained a big following; his upcountry characters now appeared comical against the modernity of suburbia.

If Australian subjects were no longer stirring old enthusisams among poets, much the same was true of other writers. In London, expatriate Henry Handel Richardson was at work completing her great trilogy dealing with the gold-rush days, *The Fortunes of Richard Mahoney*; but in Australia few significant novels were appearing. Among the few writers establishing themselves were Katherine Susannah Prichard (whose *Black Opals* and *Working Bullocks* won recognition), and Vance Palmer, who first gained attention in 1924 with his novel *Cronulla.*

Meanwhile, the few visiting authors found it very difficult to draw inspiration from the Australian scene. English novelist, D.H. Lawrence, after visiting Australia, gave some interesting reflections on Australian life and landscape in *Kangaroo* (1923). He described Australia as a "vast, uninhabited land, so hoary and lost, so unapproachable." The bush he found to be "so phantom-like, so ghostly, with its tall pale trees and many dead trees, like corpses, partly charred by bushfires" and, above all, so deathly still—waiting, waiting, Lawrence felt; but for what, he wondered, was it waiting? The emptiness he discerned went deeper than its manifestation in the landscape; Australians, though trustful and kind seemed to Lawrence to live lives without true meaning. In a private letter he wrote:

[Australians] are always vaguely and meaninglessly on the go. . . They are healthy, and to my thinking almost imbecile. That's what the life in a new country does for you: it makes you so material, so *outward*, that your real inner self dies out, and you clatter around like so many mechanical animals.

If local writers and those in the performing arts were in eclipse, the architecture of the time offered no relief. In painting, the first fine flush of a national school had lost some of its inspiration, and even though very fine work was being done by the leading landscapists and their followers, the Australian style had already become something of a stereotype. Arthur Streeton and John Longstaff, two of the men whose inspiration and great talent had helped to shape the Australian impressionist school, were no longer innovators. Other notable landscapists were now consolidating their position, some making contribution in the improvement of colour treatment and some developing new and improved composition; they included Hans Heysen, Blamire Young, George Lambert, Eliot Gruner, and Will Ashton. Their work, like that of others engaged in portraiture and still life painting, remained representational.

In 1925 a new element was introduced when the Contemporary Group was formed in Sydney. The new group was ignored by all but a small following; but there was already a stirring, and within a few years the results of fresh influences were to be seen as experimentalists seized on new ideas of colour and form.

In the detached world in which Australians lived, international affairs held little significance for the citizen. Nor did the creation of a national capital excite any great enthusiasm; even those who had raised no voice against the expenditure found the whole idea of an artificially-created Canberra rather incongruous. Nevertheless, by 1925 a date had been set for the opening of the federal parliament in its new setting, and work was hurried ahead so that the transfer from Melbourne could take place on time. On May 9, 1927, the efforts of years were vindicated when the Duke of York turned the key of the new parliament building on the bank of the Molonglo. From the steps, Dame Nellie Melba sang "God Save the King": the refrain was taken up by the assembled group below. The Governor-General, Lord Stonehaven, and the governors of the states were present; they, as well as all the notable political figures of the day and those who had played a part in the creation of Canberra, were received by the Duke and Duchess. Two thousand troops were drawn up for review, and a flight of Avro 504Ks roared overhead.

Canberra's main avenues and thoroughfares had been laid down, and hundreds of thousands of trees and shrubs had been planted; but the model city which Walter Burley Griffin visualized for the "irregular amphitheatre," with its formalized road patterns of grids and circles, was still little more than a dream. Nevertheless, parliament could now function there, and some small departmental secretariats were established. A few hundred key departmental employees had been transferred, and Canberra, although only a tiny place as yet, was now the seat of government. Its establishment exemplified the confidence that Australians felt in the greatness of their national future. There were still those who liked to scoff at the whole idea, and peripatetic newspapermen were acid in their comments—particularly those assigned to report the parliamentary proceedings. When entries were received in the public contest for design for Canberra's coat of arms, one sceptic wrote:

> The only design missing is one of a civil servant rampant on a field of red dust which is about the most conspicuous object on the capital city landscape today.

The seed had been planted, however, and in spite of its critics, Canberra would vindicate the faith of its founders.

Economic setback 20

The bright glow of prosperity was present when the national parliament moved to Canberra; but it was already twilight and not the dawn that many believed it to be. The economic base was shrinking. The hoped-for markets had not eventuated along with the men and the money from abroad; Britain was buying less, not more, as English belt-tightening followed the sharply deflationary policies initiated in 1925 by Winston Churchill as Chancellor of the Exchequer. By 1926 the terms of trade had turned quite strongly against Australia. With drought or dry conditions affecting many areas in 1927, hard times were on the way. In 1926–27 wheat prices fell noticeably in an erratic market, while the return from wool exports—the real barometer—declined quite sharply; from an average price of 27 pence a pound in the 1924–25 season, wool was now down to an average of under 18 pence a pound, and there were reduced quantities available for export because of seasonal conditions. The producers of other export products were suffering, too. Returns from sugar and meat were lower, and coal exports had dwindled.

The scene was deceptively rosy because of the heavy capital expenditures associated with the immigration programme and land development undertakings. Governments were borrowing heavily overseas, and locally, to sustain their programmes. As one observer commented acidly, Australia had a champagne ambition on a beer population. The objective of building a greater Australia had come to blind even the practical to the real problems. The economy was being extended by the investment of money beyond the level of productive works, and the heavy involvement of governments in the development process tended to obscure the fact that so many of the undertakings, though well intentioned, were not only unprofitable but, at the time, unsound.

Over the seven years 1920 to 1926, the states' loan expenditures had averaged £32 million a year, largely designed to support an expanding population and most of it borrowed abroad. In the year ended June 1928 the overseas debt rose by £54 million. As a new country, Australia was still in the same position as a business undergoing capital construction; but an unprecedented proportion of the capital investment was being undertaken by government—a result due in part to the fact that private investments were unprofitable. The dangers inherent in this situation were seen by Professor James Bristock Brigden, who pointed to its significance in *The Peopling of Australia*. While the capital construction continued, employment continued, he noted, adding:

> When a road or a railway is completed some of the workmen who have been employed on its construction may go on the land it makes profitable, or into the industries which expand elsewhere in consequence of extended settlement; or if they do not go, others may go in their place. But the slowness of the increase in farm workers does not suggest that the land opened up absorbs the same number of men as are occupied in its "development."

Professor Brigden foresaw an end to the rapid absorption of new settlers whenever "the present abnormal conditions" ended; these conditions were created and sustained by the heavy loan expenditures, the expansion of secondary industries, and the expansion of farming on the richer lands in Western Australia and Queensland (as "relatively undeveloped" states).

A policy of "protection all round" had also been accepted, so that some primary industries might be assisted. The sheepmen were left to themselves, and little was done for wheatfarmers; but the dairy, sugar, and fruit industries (all of which faced heavy competition in the British market) became the special responsibility of the Country party. Aid to them took the form of prohibitive duties on imports and export subsidies. Money for the subsidies came from levies on the part of the crop or produce sold locally, so that the consumers in Australia made up the difference between world prices and the local price. To meet the rising prices, unionists were pressing for higher wages. Where these were granted, costs moved upward. An escalation of prices and cost of production was occurring at the very time when world prices were falling and markets for food and fibre were shrinking.

In spite of his desire to keep the federal government aloof from entanglements, Bruce found himself in the centre of more and more problems as uneasiness aroused by the worsening economic situation turned to vehement criticism. The Prime Minister had put his faith in a multitude of commissions, boards, and other officially-sponsored organizations, set up for purposes of investigation or regulation; and he had not been able to bridle exuberant state politicians bent on expansion. In the good days of easy money, the government's belief that the greatest wisdom lay in "outside" advisory groups was matched by a willingness on the part of the community to back the findings of such bodies and to decry any suggestion of direct intervention by government. Now that new pressures were developing the government could not escape behind the protective screen it had thrown up.

The problems were clearly mounting. Clamour by various groups of primary producers for more assistance by way of price increases and export bounties had been met; but the high interest rates and over-valuing of land (itself a result of assured returns under price-support arrangements) meant that in attempts to cure problems official policies were creating new ills. Faced with mounting costs, primary producers preferred to seek assistance through controlled marketing arrangements rather than lower their costs by increased efficiency. While this helped to keep the grower solvent, costs were being forced up at a time when the world price trend was downward; and there were limits to what the home consumer could pay.

Matters related to arbitration, industrial legislation, and wages policy generally were no less baffling a problem to the Bruce-Page government than they had been to its predecessor. It was impossible to find middle ground for amicable settlement of the continuing wage problem in the face of steadily rising prices and costs.

The scope and over-all influence of the Federal Arbitration Court continued to grow. The inclusion in all federal awards after 1921 of automatic quarterly wage adjustments according to the price of basic commodities in the previous quarter gave the unions an increased incentive to approach the federal court, and the trend continued even though the state tribunals soon became influenced by the new federal practice. Following the precedent of the engineers' case in 1920, judicial decisions continued to enlarge the jurisdiction of the Federal Court. In 1923 the High Court held that banking and insurance were "industries" in the sense intended in the constitution, which meant that interstate disputes in those occupations could come within the scope of the federal court. Then in 1926 the principle was established that federal awards were to take precedence over wage decisions made at state level where parallel conditions operated. By this time the great majority of unionists were subject directly to the federal court's jurisdiction through membership in federal unions.

The various sections of the community were all feeling the squeeze from rising prices by 1927. A rigidity had entered the arbitration system which satisfied nobody. The wage level was creating alarm among employers and in government, while unions were criticizing as inadequate the increases they were receiving. Whatever the merits of conflicting arguments on whether the wage increases were a symptom or the cause of the price rises they were attempting to match, there could be no escape from the fact that the spiralling costs were increasingly a brake on industry. At the same time, with prices of food and goods rising steadily, the working man and woman were finding that their wages were less and less adequate. To wage earners it seemed as though Bruce, in his expansive word pictures of Australia as a land of plenty, was speaking of another land; where was the largess of which he spoke? Slowly but unmistakably the standard of living was slipping back, and the unionist at least was not prepared to see that happen without protest and action.

To the government, a fundamental obstacle to stability was the determination of the unions to press for higher wages and maintain short working hours. At the same time, as industrial unrest spread in key industries, militant union leaders were seen as playing a dangerous role. When production was interrupted, costs rose and hopes for expanding markets abroad were dashed. The situation was particularly bad in shipping; the seamen's union was run by men who exploited trivial disputes to disrupt sailings and generally did everything possible to by-pass the arbitration system, while the wharf labourers were equally disruptive. As alarm intensified over the unchecked industrial disorder, there was increased pressure, particularly from the Country party, to deal directly with "saboteurs" within the unions. The threat was seen as coming from Communist doctrine, and while wooing the "solid" unionist the government directed its criticism against union leaders said to be fomenting discontent.

A long period of industrial unrest on the waterfront reached a climax in June 1925 when the Arbitration Court took action to de-register the seamen's union. The interstate shipping companies then refused to sign a collective agreement, and the union called out its men, immobilizing all Australian shipping. The government determined on stringent action, and introduced two major measures to cope with the situation—the Navigation and Immigration Acts of 1925. The Navigation Act authorized suspension of the coasting-trade clauses of the principal Act so that the government could allow British and foreign ships to operate in local trade, while under the new immigration law the government was empowered to move for the summary deportation of any person not born in Australia who had been convicted of an offence against the laws of the Commonwealth relating to trade and commerce or arbitration and conciliation. The latter measure had direct application to the situation, since among the seamen's leaders were at least two men not born in Australia.

During the entire period of industrial tension, and particularly in parliamentary debates on the main measures, the Labor party was intensely embarrassed. Labor leaders in general did not condone the tactics of the militants, who were as contemptuous of the party as they were of the arbitration system; yet they and the party in general were strongly opposed to the government's actions in coercing the union leaders. In the end, Labor men were bound to defend the "right to strike" and thus to come out publicly in favour of a strike which many Labor stalwarts heartily condemned in private.

The Bruce-Page government took the opportunity to dissolve parliament prematurely and to fight the election on the issue of its industrial policy, placing the emphasis on a need to deal with Communist influence in the unions. The slogan "Kill that Snake," referring to the menace of "the Reds," was freely used. The government had a clear-cut electoral victory; nevertheless, the basic problem remained unsolved. The government and the unionists seemed to be out of sympathy, just as were employers and unionists, and in spite of the government's attempts to gain support among rank and file unionists for more moderate policies, industrial troubles persisted. Machinery existed for the settlement of all disputes, but legal determinations could not be the whole answer when no spirit of understanding and cooperation existed and each side was intent on pressing its point without taking into account its opponent's problems.

In trying to cope with the situation the government had been swinging from one approach to another. When the Waterside Workers' Federation struck again in 1927, the government proposed that an "industrial peace" conference should be held. Its hope was to work closely with the newly-established Australian Council of Trade Unions; but this body, engaged in an internecine struggle within the labour movement, could not forgo the opportunity for political bargaining. The A.C.T.U. stipulated that it would participate only if two conditions were met: that it would have the right to endorse all employee delegates, and that the government would agree not to proceed with its proposed amendment of the Arbitration Act. The government, rather than agree to these terms, dropped the idea of the conference.

Serious unemployment was being added to Bruce's other worries. In fact, part of the industrial discontent was arising from this cause. It seemed incongruous to the working man out of a job, or threatened with unemployment, that immigration should be continued with its attendant danger of a flooded labour market.

The ambitious ten-year Imperial programme agreed to in 1925 was beginning to gather momentum. In Britain, Australia was being actively advertised and promoted as the land of opportunity. In 1926, 31,000 settlers arrived under the migrant-assistance plan, and the total net immigration for the year exceeded 42,000 people (a 23 per cent increase over the preceding five years' average intake). As well as those from Britain, numbers from north-western Europe were arriving—and a few were coming in, barely tolerated, from southern Europe. In 1927, the total of new arrivals reached 49,000, exceeding the record 1912 figure for the first time. Then immigration dropped back sharply.

By early 1928 the unemployment figure had reached nearly 11 per cent of those registered with reporting unions. Debates turned more and more to this issue. A Labor-sponsored censure motion in the House of Representatives criticised the government

> ... for its failure to adequately protect Australian industries and to limit migration to the nation's ability to absorb new arrivals, together with its neglect to formulate proposals to deal with unemployment.

The motion was defeated; but, although the federal government was at pains to deny any connection between unemployment and immigration, the various state governments (who were responsible for handling the newcomers as well as requisitioning for them) began to cut back sharply on the number of new settlers they sought in Britain.

The boom had run its course, and reaction was setting in. The dangers of an empty land might be undiminished—in fact, more than ever pressing in the light of world tensions and pressures—but the great experiment was grinding to a halt. The simple fact was that markets were not to be found for Australian produce. Purchases by Britain, already in the throes of economic trouble, were easing back rather than increasing.

Meanwhile the Australian Labor party, in the wilderness for ten years or more, was reappearing as a strong political force. Scorned by many soldiers and by ultra-patriots for its anti-conscription stand, Labor had slipped into disfavour in the final war years, and in the early 1920s the federal party had failed to regain public favour as extremists assumed greater power within the organization. A federal conference in 1921 had adopted a clearly defined doctrine of "socialization of industry, production, distribution, and exchange," in which workers' control rather than nationalization of industry was stressed. The socialist objective had first been put forward at an all-Australian industrial conference in Melbourne in June 1921. At that meeting the federal president of the A.L.P. executive spoke of "lightning changes" taking place all over the world and the need to bring the party's programme into line with "the new psychology and mental revolution which has taken place among the workers throughout the world." Shortly after adoption at this meeting, the "socialization" objective was written into Labor's official platform.

At the conference, the A.L.P. had repudiated both the revolutionary tactics of the Communists and the direct-action methods advocated by the Industrial Workers of the World, and its statement of a general socialist objective had been modified by a resolution explaining that the party did not seek to abolish private ownership of any of the instruments of production "where such instrument is utilized by its owner in a socially useful manner and without exploitation." In spite of these hedges, the effect on the electorate at large of Labor's adoption of an out-and-out socialist objective was to alienate the important middle-of-the-road voter, who was inclined to agree with one Labor premier's description of the proposal as a proposition to "sovietize" industry.

In state politics, where Labor men were advocating less extreme policies, Labor had remained a strong force, and even while the federal party languished in the wilderness there had been Labor party governments in most of the states over considerable periods. Nevertheless, strains within the party had remained, and internal divisions continued to manifest themselves in endless factional struggles at various levels within the party. In the background was the continuing friction between the older (and now more moderate) Australian Workers' Union and the new industrial unions. There were sharp differences between the political and industrial wings of the party. Conferences became involved in the technical problem of policy-making method, and loud claims that high-handed tactics were being adopted by one or other faction punctuated meetings as men of principle struggled to develop policy within the party by democratic processes. The relative strengths of the "industrial section" of newer industrial unions, the moderates of the Australian Workers' Union, and pro-Communist elements, constantly changed. However, intrigues for personal power within the party were mainly confined to New South Wales. Divided and still warring, Labor under John Thomas Lang went down to defeat in the 1927 New South Wales elections; but the state party machine had become Lang's captive and he quickly tightened his personal dictatorship over it in preparation for what has more recently been described as a "terrifying example of the corruption of democratic methods and slogans for totalitarian ends."

So long as the socialization aim was stressed the A.L.P. remained unacceptable to the voters at large, as the results of successive federal elections of the early 1920s showed. These electoral defeats helped bring about a change of outlook. Bit by bit moderates regained control of the party, and after the heavy Labor defeat in 1926 they were able to win approval for the deletion of all references in the party platform to workers' control and "an elective Supreme Economic Council" to run nationalized industry. Instead, a bland platform which emphasized generalities and played down the 1921 socialism plank was adopted. This did little to calm newspaper criticism of Labor, but meanwhile the public's disenchantment with the Bruce-Page regime was growing apace as a result of the government's failure to find any workable solution to persistent industrial discord.

Quite unexpectedly, the Labor party suddenly found an opening to power as a result of a change of heart in the mercurial Hughes, so long regarded by Labor men as a renegade but now, unpredictably, ready to turn disillusionment with Bruce's handling of the arbitration issue into open opposition. When an opportunity came to turn the tables on the man who had put him on the back benches, Hughes, well into his sixties but still ambitious, spearheaded the move which was to oust the Prime Minister.

The storm over the machinery of arbitration had been gathering steadily. For some time many people had been moving towards a belief that one of the main threats to arbitration in general was to be found in the overlapping and duplication of awards, and the resulting confusion in authorities. Moves had been made to overcome this. One proposal had been that every industry should be classified as either "federal" or "local," the Commonwealth Court having complete authority over federal industries while the state tribunals had unrestricted powers over local industries; but it proved impossible to divide industries according to such a formula, and the idea came to nothing. The need for constitutional amendment seemed the more urgent when the Federal Arbitration Court was reconstituted following the resignation of Justice Powers in 1926. Bruce secured the approval of the Nationalist party to seek by referendum transfer to the Commonwealth of full control over industrial legislation. This was one of the two measures placed before the electors in September 1926, along with provision for an extension of federal power to legislate with regard to corporations and trusts; the second proposal sought for the Commonwealth power to protect the public against the "interruption of any essential service."

There had been sharp opposition to the referendum proposal within the labour movement where the government's intentions were construed as being coercive. Opposition came from varied interests as well; some important newspapers, normally pro-Nationalist, came out strongly for a "no" vote, and many state politicians were against the amendments. The final vote showed that these influences had been strong enough to sway a majority of electors, and both proposals were defeated.

The government's next effort was to frame new legislation within the limits of existing conciliation-arbitration powers. Its purpose was to salvage the system of compulsory arbitration—a "great experiment" which, Bruce declared, must be continued. The Prime Minister was convinced that the system could be preserved only if both sides were prepared to obey the law, which "must bind and be observed by" employers and wage earners alike. The government believed (in the words of the Attorney-General, John Greig Latham) that acceptance of the benefits of awards implied a corresponding responsibility. In his dedication to the sanctity of the law, Latham was coldly righteous; other members of the government were equally determined that arbitration was not to become a one-way street for the wage-earner's benefit. As well as attempting to deal with the central problem arising from the diffusion of the arbitration power between federal and state jurisdiction, the measure sought to reduce the legalism of the system by encouraging conciliation in the settlement of disputes and to enforce observance of the industrial law. With the object of fixing responsibility for the conduct of their members and officials on the organizations concerned, specific provisions related to the election of union officers, which was to be by secret ballot, while other clauses gave formal status to the position of the trade union in industrial law.

In framing the bill the government had been concerned with the persistent rises in wage rates, which were seen as undermining the capacity of many industries to operate competitively. The court was therefore cautioned to consider the possible effect of any award or wage agreement it endorsed on the industry or industries concerned as well as upon the community in general. Concern had grown over the existing system because, in prescribing wages and conditions, the court had come to play an important role in determining economic policy, yet it was left to the government and the parliament (through enactment of tariff duty or bounty on export or production) to find means whereby the industry concerned might meet the award. Experience had shown that whenever the Tariff Board had granted increased protection to an industry an application to the court for higher wages for workers in that industry followed; and when granted (as they inevitably were) these increases tended to nullify the effect of the customs rise and led to requests for a higher tariff. For his part, Bruce now made it clear that in fixing wage levels in future, the arbitration authorities were to consider not only the social question of a reasonable standard of living for the wage earner but also the economic effects on industry of any wage determination. Such an attitude seemed inconsistent with the Prime Minister's undiminished claims regarding Australia's continuing prosperity and expansion, and political and industial labour leaders were quick to seize on the inconsistency.

The Labor party was rising above the internal discords that had weakened it and minimized its effectiveness for years. Behind the scenes, rival factions were still struggling for power as the conservative A.W.U. faction withstood attacks by the representatives of industrial unions, but a semblance of solidarity had been attained. New South Wales representatives held the key to the power struggle within the federal party, and in 1927 Labor's federal conference adopted an elaborate plan to re-establish harmony; subsequently a "unity" conference bringing both factions together succeeded in papering over the most obvious rifts. A new figure had come forward to invigorate Labor's parliamentary attacks: this was James Henry Scullin, who succeeded to the leadership in 1928. His oratory sometimes stung even the suave Prime Minister. Having turned aside from much of its socialist doctrine to adopt a statement of glittering generalities, the party quickly found new strength as Scullin capably exploited the confusions increasingly apparent in the Bruce-Page administration's handling of major issues.

The government's greatest weakness was still in its dealings with the maritime unions. In September 1928, when the waterside workers objected to certain clauses in their award relating to the engagement of labour, the final phase of the coalition's long battle with the maritime unions opened. When the wharf men refused to work—at the height of the export season— the disruption to shipping was serious, and summonses were issued against the Waterside Workers Federation. A fine of £1000 was imposed on the union. This was the signal for shipowners to engage non-union labour on the wharves, and the government at once introduced a measure providing that any man seeking work was to be issued with a licence by officials of the Customs Department. In support of the measure, Attorney-General Latham said that industrial awards were being almost universally obeyed; the transport unions were the sole exception. He declared that the rights of non-unionists must be preserved.

In denouncing the government's action as provocative, Labor men emphasized that difficulties in the transport industry arose from the casual nature of employment in the industry, and they contended that the government was out to provoke a general upheaval so that it could exploit the issue of industrial peace in the coming election. Whether or not this was so, the waterside bill was passed, and non-unionists continued to come forward for work at the various ports. Clashes between them and unionists were frequent; many arrests were made as a result of the fracas. There was growing unemployment, and as the weeks wore on the pressures were too great for the unionists to resist. Members of the watersiders' federation decided on a return to work and they were prepared to take out the necessary licences to do so; but by the time the strike was declared off, practically all the jobs had been filled, and there was little work left for members of the federation.

As the elections of November 1928 drew near, the community was sharply divided on the central issue of industrial discipline versus the rights of the individual—the issue at the centre of the stage. In his policy speech, Bruce again brought to the fore his old theme of the danger to Australia existing in the work of extremists. The government, he said, would take up the challenge from these elements on its return. Scullin, campaigning vigorously and addressing large audiences with effect, attacked his opponents with broadsides aimed at their financial and general policies; he called for an extension of social benefits and the dropping of compulsory military training, denied that the A.L.P. was subject to "outside" dictation (as Bruce alleged it to be), and laughed at the ministerial statement that Australia was in danger from Communists.

The elections showed sharply reduced support for Nationalist-Country party policies; Labor gained eight seats in the House and reappeared in strength in the Senate. However, Labor was still in a minority in both houses of the legislature which met for the first time in February 1929, holding thirty-one seats in the House of Representatives to forty-four of the Nationalists and Country party combined.

Between the election and parliament's reassembly, the timberworkers, whose request for a forty-four hour work week had been refused in the Arbitration Court on the grounds that the industry could not afford a reduction from forty-eight hours, had been dismissed when they arrived at the mills at the hour fixed for the shorter week. Other unionists were called out, and the building trade was affected. The court declared that a strike existed, and on summons the timberworkers' union was fined £1,000. In Sydney, non-unionists were invited to apply for work; some who did so were made the target of physical attack. When parliament met, Scullin moved that the government be censured for its class legislation and partisan administration which had caused a dislocation of industry, but the motion was lost. The Arbitration Court ordered a ballot of members to determine whether they were in favour of the strike; in a skirmish in Sydney at a protest meeting, some ballot papers were burned. The final count showed only 6000 of the union's 15,000 members as having voted; and of these an overwhelming majority refused to resume work under the award. The judge in charge of the award said it was clear that secrecy had not been observed, and that the ballot had been manipulated.

After weeks of idleness the employers reopened their mills, but there was little response until a conference was held and it was agreed to have a public accountant determine whether a forty-four hour week was feasible. When some concessions on other issues were made by the employers, a joint application to the Arbitration Court was made to vary the terms of the award, and the strike ended.

The federal government was less eager to enter the lists against the coalmine operators of northern New South Wales when, in defiance of existing awards, employees were locked out and their wages lowered. Labor by now was thoroughly aroused, and freely expressed the view that it was no more than sophism when Bruce pointed to divided control in industrial affairs as the cause of the serious drift in events. For Bruce, the final straw was the decision of New South Wales, where Lang was Premier, to enact a forty-four hour work week at the very time the federal court had refused a similar reduction in hours.

In Bruce's view these events had brought the arbitration system to a crossroads. He believed that the existing duplication of powers between

Commonwealth and the states was unnecessary, and should be corrected; accordingly, at the premiers' conference held in Canberra in May 1929, Bruce declared that unless the state parliaments were willing to transfer full powers of industrial legislation to the Commonwealth he would ask the federal parliament to repeal all the acts relating to conciliation and arbitration in order to leave that sphere of legislation to the states. When each of the premiers in turn said he was not prepared to ask his parliament to pass legislation for the surrender of the industrial powers, the Prime Minister indicated that he would submit a proposal to the federal parliament to cancel legislation in all industrial fields except those related to maritime and waterside activities (which would be dealt with under the trade and commerce powers of the constitution).

In deciding to recast the nation's industrial legislation, the government had undergone a rapid change of front. There was more than an overlapping of awards involved. Much of the policy contained in the 1928 Act had proved unworkable, and there was no doubt that industrial unrest remained undiminished. Nevertheless, it appeared to many that the government was merely running away from a difficult issue, and that its decision had been mainly influenced by the increasingly strong criticisms it was facing for its handling of industrial matters.

The suggestion that the clock should be turned back a quarter-century by abandonment of federal jurisdiction came as a shock and an outrage to most working men. The A.L.P. protested loudly, and so did some members who sat behind Bruce. Hughes led the dissident Nationalists. He had never lost faith in the Arbitration Act, which he had helped to write a generation earlier; and if Justice Higgins had been caustic in his castigation of Hughes as a wrecker of the arbitration system in the immediate post-war years, Hughes was now no less vitriolic in his condemnation of the Bruce-Page proposal. Speaking to the Sydney Chamber of Manufactures, Hughes said that federal arbitration might have serious defects but it was the business of the captain of a ship to make the best use of his vessel—whereas in the height and fury of the tempest the Prime Minister had left the bridge.

Pressure was building up in Labor circles. Representatives of the nation's trade unions met in Melbourne and condemned the government's proposals. Resolutions were carried that the move had been made without a mandate from the people, that it was part of a general offensive by the government to lower wages and worsen conditions, and that abandonment of a federal system would not only cause unfair competition between states but would lead to the strife and turmoil of pre-arbitration days. Distrust of the Arbitration Court was attributed to the government's handling of measures related to the transport workers and the maritime industry, and to the provisions of the new Crimes Act passed in 1926 which were aimed at preventing use by the trade unions of the strike weapon. Leading Labor's political attack, Scullin pointed out that in spite of the difficulties under which the Arbitration Court had to work, 140 unions, representing four-fifths of the wage-earners, were registered with it. He also made the point that because some of the maritime unions had disobeyed awards all the unions that had observed them for many years were to be penalized. The timberworkers' union had been heavily fined; yet, he noted, when New South Wales coalmine owners had locked out 12,000 men a prosecution launched against one of the mine owners had been withdrawn by direction of the Prime Minister.

When parliament reassembled in mid-August 1929, Scullin's deputy, Edward Granville Theodore, moved that the government be censured for having withdrawn a prosecution of John Brown, the mine-owner in question. The Prime Minister, in reply, said that it had been difficult to secure evidence of a lockout; a conference had been pending between owners and men and continuance of the prosecution would have prejudiced its outcome. Hughes, whose hostility to the government was growing daily, described the reply as "utterly unconvincing." There were others sitting behind the Prime Minister who shared Hughes' view, and when the motion was put it was defeated by only a four vote margin, indicating reduced support for the government.

A week later Page, as Treasurer, introduced a budget in which extra taxation was proposed; it included a slight increase in income tax, higher entertainment admission taxes, and other increased imposts.

Before the shock of the budget had subsided, Bruce introduced the measure to repeal the Arbitration Acts; it bore the misleading title of the Maritime Industries Bill. It provided that all federal awards should expire on June 30, 1930. A maritime industrial court was to be instituted, and conciliation committees were to be created. In introducing the bill, the Prime Minister said that the Commonwealth was not endeavouring to abolish arbitration, but rather wanted to see it under the states' jurisdiction.

The debate revealed the solid opposition to the measure. Theodore launched Labor's attack, declaring that unemployment was a far more serious problem than the occasional industrial upheavals; but it was Hughes who was most devastating, and several other Nationalists were openly against the proposal. With fiery phrases, Hughes ridiculed Bruce's two claims that round-table conferences would work more efficiently and that uniformity could be obtained by states co-operating, and went on to attack the bill as one that

> . . . leaves no stone standing upon another of that temple of industrial legislation slowly and painfully reared by successive governments. And it does this in the name of industrial peace!

Hughes gave notice that in the committee stage he would move that the proposal remain in abeyance until the people had been given a chance to vote on the issue. Bruce and his supporters were determined to maintain the pressure; they believed that party solidarity would prevail in the end.

A new complication arose before the committee stage of the bill was reached. A special commission, appointed two years earlier to inquire into the working of the constitution, presented its voluminous report. The commission put forward a case for an increase in the power and responsibility of

the national parliament in certain directions; but it recommended the deletion from the constitution of the section relating to conciliation and arbitration of industrial disputes, and suggested that industrial legislation should
be left wholly to the states.

The government succeeded in having the Maritime Industries Bill declared
urgent. When the House went into committee on September 15, 1929, Hughes
moved his amendment; it was carried by the narrowest margin, thirty-five
votes to thirty-four. Although pressed by the government to do so, the
Speaker, Sir Littleton Groom, refused to vote, since he considered such
participation was against the best traditions of parliamentary practice in
which the Speaker remained aloof from party politics.

The day following this defeat for the government a meeting of cabinet
was held, after which the Prime Minister waited upon the Governor-
General, Lord Stonehaven, and advised that the House of Representatives
be dissolved. The dissolution was granted, and arrangements were made
to hold the election on October 12.

The issue was clearly and unmistakably that of the future of the arbitration system. This was underlined in the leaders' policy speeches—which,
for the first time, were broadcast.

In spite of the intensive electioneering efforts by Bruce and his supporters,
it soon became evident that the government had misjudged sentiment on
the issue. Salaried men saw their future threatened and in their uncertainty
they, along with many other middle-of-the-road voters, turned to Labor.

The election result was a landslide victory for Labor. In industrial
electorates, Labor candidates' majorities reached overwhelming proportions;
in conservative divisions support for the Bruce-Page coalition fell sharply,
and there were upsets in the "safest" seats. The crowning blow was reserved
for the Prime Minister himself: in his electorate of Flinders, Bruce was
defeated by a Labor candidate in the most galling upset of all. Hughes,
who had been confident that he would emerge in a controlling position with
a balance-of-power in the new House, also found his hopes dashed. He and
other "rebel" Nationalists who had come out against the Arbitration bill,
were all returned with handsome majorities—but Hughes had no hope of
regaining the party leadership, which now fell to Latham. Hughes and
those who had supported his stand were not even invited to party meetings.

Scullin became Prime Minister on October 22, 1929. In the House, he
held a forty-six to twenty-nine majority, but Labor was in the minority in
the Senate.

Electoral victory had been gained on the single issue of federal arbitration.
Labor had not sought a mandate on any major programme—indeed many
of the old objectives related to social betterment seemed to have faded into
the background—but rather had given a general pledge to safeguard the
existing standard of living (which had seemed to be under attack in the
proposal to do away with the Commonwealth Arbitration Court).

The sweeping proportions of the party's victory might have been expected to open the way for a constructive period for Labor; but the new government at once found itself in a millrace of problems—many of them arising from matters which had been ignored or glossed over in the concentration upon political and industrial issues. In such swirling waters, greater men than Scullin would have been overwhelmed. As it was, the journalist-turned-party-functionary struggled to keep abreast of a bewildering series of crises. It was the first A.L.P. ministry in the federal sphere since 1917, and although some cabinet members had held high office in state governments, all were quite inexperienced in national administration.

Australia had come to the end of a cycle of high export prices for raw materials and foodstuffs, of buoyant conditions in the overseas loan markets, and of great capital expenditure. Over the years, rural land had become dangerously over-valued as a result of contributing and interlocking factors— unsound credit policies followed by governments and banks alike, and over-optimism among individuals who were prepared to accept commitments beyond their capacity to discharge. Undue emphasis had been placed by borrowers and lenders on the current market value of the property, rather than on its earning capacity. Fired by the old land hunger, a chain reaction had been in process; as land was taken over for closer settlement the old owners joined those searching for other properties to buy, and each successive sale put another potential buyer into the market. Land values reached inflated levels which could be sustained only if prices of rural products moved up; instead, producers faced increased competition not only from newly-opened areas within Australia but from similar farm expansion in Canada and Argentina and elsewhere—expansion resulting in enhanced production which in turn forced a decline in world commodity prices. In the scurry to acquire land, true earning power was often overlooked, and as inflation of land values gained its own momentum, individuals had saddled themselves with disastrous debt loads.

By November a sharp deflation and calamitous business depression were obvious to all—a depression made unusually severe, as Professor Douglas Copland noted, not only because it came when Australia was about to meet the costs of mistakes in her economic policy, but because the external forces that caused the depression were much stronger than usual. As a producer of primary products and a market for capital, the country had responded strongly to boom conditions; now, in a severe slump, the economy was about to react with dramatic swiftness.

Both in the world at large and at home, exceptionally severe economic dislocation had occurred; the Great Depression had begun. Scullin faced an accumulated federal deficit of £5 million (reflecting falling customs revenue), and the deficit was mounting daily. Even before the election had been called in August, wool prices at the new season's sales had slid to new lows. Long term borrowing had ceased abroad some months before; Australia's credit rating had declined sharply from the beginning of 1929 and Australian bonds were selling at heavy discounts in London and New York. Now, even emergency help was impossible in these markets, for panic had followed the financial blood-letting which began with the decline and fall of American security prices on Wall Street early in September. Prices of the great staple commodities had already collapsed—cotton, rubber, the base metals, hides, and wheat were all almost unsalable, even at the sharply-discounted prices. Wool, which suffered less than most commodities, was down 30 per cent from the price levels of a year before. Because practically all nations had become interdependent, the depression was world-wide.

Throughout Australia, economic paralysis was spreading and unemployment growing as more and more individuals and businesses found themselves unable to meet their obligations. As confidence faded, buyers could no longer be found for houses or for goods; at once there was a sharp fall in building and in manufacturing. Bankers, sensing the coming storm, were withdrawing or withholding credit. Men thrown out of work were now unable to find other jobs. Purchasing power fell back, compounding the effect of the recession. Unemployment began to be widely discussed, and newspapers began to report individual cases of extreme hardship. No longer was it regarded as a man's own fault if he were unable to find work. The community had not anticipated such a development, and relief for the individual was not in sight. There were reports of unrelieved hardship, like that published in the Melbourne *Herald* under the title, "The Man who got Himself Locked up."

> One Walter Robertson, a 43-year old A.I.F. veteran, had shambled into Footscray (Vic.) police station clad in rags, and asked a constable to lock him up. "I have not been able to get work for 12 months. I have had nothing to eat for three days," he told police. When they refused to put him in the cells, he staggered outside, picked up a rock, and smashed the police station window. They locked him up and fed him. "He ate like a wolf," said the constable.

The terrible facts were being brought home to the community at large. The *Herald*, noting that 20,000 men were unemployed in Melbourne, considered that the ponderously-discussed plans for municipal relief were far from sufficient to meet the situation. With heavy sarcasm, its leader-writer commented on the slowness and paucity of the effort, declaring:

> If by some miracle the deserving unemployed could curb their hunger for another nine or ten weeks they could be assured of some relief by that time. This is poor solace to those men urgently wanting work now.

Professor Lyndhurst Falkiner Giblin, notable alike for his humanist philosophy and his penetrating economic analyses, declared that employers should wear hair shirts to remind them of "their responsibility to provide work." This, and his other startling proposal that all pleasure motor-cars should be scrapped to help in the economies, were lost in the welter of problems and possible solutions.

For Scullin and his Treasurer, Theodore, financial matters were pressing. Loans were maturing which had to be converted or repaid, and the state governments had partially-completed public works for which additional funds were required. Investors were wary, but the reservoir of local investment money had not dried up, and the security of government loans attracted the cautious. The government had little difficulty in raising a £10 million loan.

Economies were the order of the day, however, and there was need to take urgent action on other issues. By the time parliament met on November 20 the government had asked the British government to suspend migration, and even plans to set up a council for economic research (provided for in recent legislation) had been shelved. Higher income taxes and increased customs duties were introduced to deal with the widening gap between expenditure and revenue—a deficiency, the Treasurer said, arising from the previous government's "gross miscalculation" of expenditure estimates. To cope with the growing unemployment, a grant of £1 million was made to the states from the roads fund.

The flow of imports had not been stemmed, and with export earnings severely curtailed the trade balance was extremely adverse. Heavy exports of gold reserves began so that obligations could be met. Nevertheless, by the end of the year, the exchange rate on London placed sterling at a market premium for the first time. As pressure increased and commitments continued to outstrip earnings from exports, the exchange rate dropped to 106:100, reflecting the weakening of Australia's position in international trade. Sharp correctives were necessary.

When parliament resumed in February 1930 Scullin pointed to the fact that the balance of payments problem had been building up for some time: in six years, he said, the excess of imports and interest payments over exports had amounted to £193 million. Stringent measures would be necessary to adjust the trade balance. The first measure introduced was an emergency tariff intended to cut imports by £10 million or more a year. Certain luxury goods were prohibited, customs duties were raised by 50 per cent on other items, and quantitative restrictions were placed on a third list.

Among commercial interests there was strong criticism of the government for this "bombshell." Some contended that the higher import duties merely placed added cost burdens on exporters. The official justification for the step was that it would both check imports and stimulate employment by advancing local manufacturing. Some economists were quick to point out that probably imports would have tapered off even more rapidly if the exchange rate had been left to drift from the beginning of the crisis (by withholding the immediate support-shipments of gold) and if the volume of credit for importers had been restricted earlier.

The stark fact was that in two years national income had fallen precipitously with the export price collapse. Between January 1929 and December 1930 export prices (expressed in Australian currency) had gone down 45 per cent; devaluation checked the decline in earnings thereafter, but in gold values, the decline continued and if devaluation had not been undertaken by 1933 export prices would have been only about 30 per cent of those ruling in 1928.

Although in 1929 the chairman of the Commonwealth Bank board, Sir Robert Gibson, had spoken out strongly against even a temporary departure from the gold standard, events had quickly overtaken piously-expressed policy in this as in other fields. The Australian pound, discounted more than £6 per cent by March 1930, went lower still now that London loan sources had dried up completely.

In July the Loan Council and the banks, including the Commonwealth Bank, agreed to find the exchange needed for government interest requirements on a priority basis; only after £3 million a month had been provided for this purpose was provision to be made for import payments. By October the exchange rate had reached £9 per cent. The Australian pound was still over-valued, however, and a large market developed in exchange outside the banks, while at the same time it was almost impossible to obtain London funds from the banks. The demand for English pounds became so great that under pressure from the Bank of New South Wales banks found it necessary in January 1931 to increase the rate on London to £115:£100, then to £130:£100. This was followed by a movement outside to still higher rates—at one point close to £140:£100.

The effect of reduced imports and the stimulus to exports stabilized the situation at this point, and as the speculative element was reduced the outside exchange rate came back to that of the banks. Britain's flight from the gold standard in September 1931 further eased the pressure on the Australian pound. Since Australian exchange was mostly sterling exchange, the rate on London was now the index of Australian exchange, and the banks decided to adjust the Australian pound according to the condition of their London balances rather than according to its purchasing power in gold.

Among proposals brought forward to deal with the general crisis had been a number designed to expand credit and the money supply in Australia. Such proposals struck fear in the hearts of bankers and orthodox financiers, but they had many advocates. The government was prepared to back one such proposal. On April 2, 1930, Theodore had introduced a bill to expand the note issue by £18 million to £60 million. A third of the new money was to be used to aid wheat growers and the rest was to be applied to relieving unemployment by creating jobs. This proposal for a fiduciary issue, emanating from Labor, brought unrestrained criticism from some quarters. The measure was condemned as dangerously inflationary and a certain step on the path to ruin. Fears were expressed that, once launched, the process of creating "printing-press" money would continue; the £18 million would be the thin end of the wedge. After delaying tactics which lasted many months, in October 1930 the Nationalist-dominated Senate finally killed the bill twenty-one to six.

By this time, however, the legal minimum of 25 per cent gold backing for the note issue was under attack from another quarter, since the government had by now shipped its last exportable surplus of gold. To avoid outright default in London, it had to ship £5 million of the £15 million gold reserve held as backing for the note issue. In view of this, when the shipment was authorized, the government stipulated that the gold reserve behind the total note issue would be restored in stages to the original 25 per cent.

In trying to cope with the immediate effects of the depression, the government had taken what measures it could to alleviate the profusion of problems. The first corrective phase necessarily involved a series of hastily-devised expedients. It was only after the experts had diagnosed (with personal variations) the nature and extent of the malaise that remedies could be prescribed. And there were many contradictory voices, offering every type of "solution" from the severest forms of deflation to the wildest panaceas. As yet there was practically no understanding of the proposition that budget deficits could be safely and intelligently used to counter economic slump and reduce unemployment.

At this time Sir Robert Gibson, in his role as chairman of the Commonwealth Bank board, was wielding extraordinary power. He was, as news correspondent Warren Denning wrote, "more definitely Prime Minister of Australia than Mr Scullin was at any time." A cautious Scotsman, Gibson held to the most conservative principles of finance; and he possessed just those rigid qualities which Scullin lacked—in Denning's words,

> . . . a supreme confidence in his own opinion and a granite-like capacity to withstand every assault on any position of principle which he took up. He maintained throughout the independence of the Commonwealth Bank Board, refusing to submit to anything that savoured of political domination, and . . . . [he] hardly ever attempted to conceal his belief that the Labor government was a meddlesome and incompetent body.

Brooking no interference either from his own board members or the government, Gibson was adamant in his determination neither to adopt nor permit temporizing measures in the financial sphere. Yet economists were suggesting lines of constructive action.

To the panel of experts called in to advise the government late in 1929, the problem of the crisis for Australia was basically one of loss of national income from exports. In a memorandum to the federal Treasurer, in September 1930, the three economists concerned—Professors Copland and Giblin and Edward Clarence Dyason—expressed the view that a first principle of economic readjustment should be to distribute the loss of national income fairly among all classes according to their capacity to bear the burden. Their recommendations however, were shelved.

The man whose views caused the bitterest controversy was Sir Otto Niemeyer, a British banking expert. His visit followed conversations which began in March 1930, when difficulties in meeting interest payments due to the British government became pressing. The suggestion that a representative of the Bank of England might visit Australia to investigate the economic problems had been welcomed by Scullin. At the Prime Minister's invitation, Niemeyer attended the premiers' conference in Melbourne in August 1930; the hard line of retrenchment which he put forward contrasted sharply with the views of others, and discussion led to violent disagreement over proposed "cures." However, all member governments agreed to reduce the joint loan programme for 1930–31 from £24 million to £15 million and to move towards balanced budgets.

Niemeyer's reading of the economic situation was that in the long run the Australian policy of protective tariffs and heavy borrowing was no more than an attempt to maintain a standard of living which was out of step with economic conditions abroad and unjustifiable in terms of the national level of production. In these circumstances, he maintained, there was no alternative but to accept a lowered standard. It was a banker's plan—harsh and uncompromising, and suggesting no escape from the effects of the depression except deflation and retrenchment—and it placed special emphasis on the need for the Commonwealth and states to balance their budgets at any sacrifice. Looking at Australia's problem with an English banker's eyes—and evaluating it with an English banker's mind—Niemeyer was convinced that depreciation of the currency in terms of sterling was an error of the first magnitude; in his view, raising exchange rates could only "prejudice the whole fabric of national finance." To economists closer to the problem, and more attuned to the economy of a primary-producing country, the dictum was invalid. As Copland noted, in rebuttal, in an international setting of heavy deflation and faced with a drastic fall in the prices of its export products, Australia had to find part of the solution in devaluation, which was essential if the problems of a primary-producing country with rigid costs in exporting industries were to be eased. On these grounds, the leading Australian economists in 1930 urged a substantial devaluation, in terms of sterling, resting their case

> . . . on the fact that it reduced the magnitude of the monetary adjustment required and added much more to exporters' prices in local currency than to exporters' costs.

While the "battle of the plans" proceeded, Labor suffered a severe blow when a commissioner's report (claimed by many to have been politically inspired) asserted that, while a minister in the Queensland government, Theodore had been involved in improper practices and the "grossest impropriety" in the handling of certain transactions. Theodore, anxious to clear his name, resigned the treasureship in order that charges might be laid and the case tested; but the Nationalist Premier of Queensland refused to take the matter to court. The shadow cast over Theodore spread to his plans for an expanded money supply.

While learned solutions to the general economic impasse were being offered by the experts, there could be no doubt about the extent or the intensity of the suffering caused by the economic chaos now prevailing. To ordinary citizens the discussion raging over various plans and measures seemed remote from the fundamental question of how to secure a job and pay one's way. It seemed as though officialdom was standing aloof while ordinary citizens suffered near-starvation and faced no prospect but a quicksand of disaster and despair. Newspapers were now calling for more direct and positive action, but mostly they urged caution, too, lest the dire situation be made worse; and in the welter of advocacy and contradictory ideas the depression deepened. The bankers saw it as their overriding duty to remain solvent; and although they did what they could to help old clients they found themselves forced to take measures which further tightened credit and reduced spending power. More businesses closed, shops were locked up, farms abandoned; rents remained unpaid, and debts mounted. As returns from sales abroad of wool and wheat sank to new lows, credit and spending shrank still further. In some places barter replaced cash selling.

By mid-1930 one out of every five workmen was out of work; among building tradesmen and in some branches of manufacturing the proportion of unemployed was already as high as one-in-three. The "Army of the Unemployed" was still growing. A queue of men would form whenever some casual job became available. The classified advertising columns of newspapers were almost bereft of employment offerings but filled instead with "for sale" notices; motor-cars and vacuum cleaners and pianos and other household items were being offered for next to nothing. In the country, mortgage sales were being arranged—only to collapse when no one could be found to bid for the property or the farmer's goods. Even before moratorium legislation was passed, banks and mortgagors were giving up the practice of forced sales since it did not pay.

The dole had been introduced to help keep the workless alive. As author George Johnston, in *My Brother Jack*, was later to re-create the scene, the authorities

> ... unlocked the Defence Department warehouses, and out of the mothballs they took the old surplus great-coats and tunics and they dyed them a dull black— all that brave khaki of 1914–18—and against the contingency of a Melbourne winter issued them out as a charity to keep the workless warm. So that as the unemployed grew in number the black army coats became a kind of badge of adversity, a stigma of suffering. .... As the situation grew worse desperate attempts were made towards alleviation, and the "black coats" moved then in the more regimented bands of the "sustenance-workers" and you would see them with their brooms and picks and shovels and council tip-drays working in slovenly unison on pointless municipal projects.

The struggle within Labor (and within the community) to find effective ways to cope with the deepening depression was at its height when Scullin left for London in August 1930. The strongest resistance to retrenchment was in New South Wales, where under Lang's leadership of the Labor party a faction had developed which was prepared to support not only inflation but an arbitrary reduction in interest payments. Advocates of the Lang stand were asking why wage cuts should be imposed on Australian workers while interest rates—and especially interest rates paid to overseas bondholders—remained sacrosanct. Lang himself attacked "the newspapers and many leaders of government in Australia" who saw the claims of the London financiers as paramount; he declared that it was the soldier, the war widow, the sick poor, the worker, all without a bondholders' association behind them, who were to be mulct "so that the extortionate demands of the overseas financial interests may be satisfied." After an election campaign fought on the issue of abandoning the austerity programme which was the basis of the Premiers' Melbourne agreement, Lang won a sweeping victory. It was the first test of Niemeyer's plan, and Lang's victory opened the rift between the New South Wales State Labor party and the A.L.P. as a whole. As Premier, Lang stated that there would be no repudiation; but rumours persisted that extreme measures might follow.

In the confusion, measures were being taken to deal with new situations as they arose. State governments and the federal government had their own immediate problems, largely related to financial exigencies. Special taxation was imposed so that the destitute might be fed. At a personal level, it was natural that in a catastrophe of this magnitude everyone should do what he could to protect his own interests. Men were walking the streets in search of work or tramping through the bush in the hope of finding a subsistence living; others were able to meet their obligations and hold on; the lucky ones were those in jobs that were unaffected. The immediate task of government was to find ways to ameliorate the severest hardships by balancing out the losses and sacrifices, at least to some extent. It was for the experts to propose ways to achieve this and to help get the economy back on a sound basis; and it was for legislators to approve measures that would carry these proposals into effect.

According to their personal viewpoint and their place in the community, people were inclined to have very different views on the most desirable course. Traditionalists, and those who had come through the crisis, talked as though the depression had been caused by Australia's own excesses and declared that Australians would have to accept a different standard of living in the future, while those who believed that they were living through the vicious turbulence of a world business cycle took the view that any remedial measure, no matter how unorthodox, was acceptable.

There were many trade unionists who believed that Lang alone among Labor leaders had not compromised with those fighting to destroy the workers. Determined, ruthless, and supremely self-confident, the Premier of New South Wales stood like a colossus at the head of a well-disciplined party organization, drawing support directly from the industrial wing of the movement, and particularly from its most intransigent members. He played constantly on the fears and resentments of the underprivileged, and by his fierce denunciations of those whom he opposed, he appeared to his followers as the only champion of Labor who had not capitulated to the financier or the employer. In Scullin, an equally staunch Labor man, he found a mild yet determined opponent, and there were others around Scullin who would have no part of the radical proposals Lang formulated. While opposition to retrenchment was being fostered by Lang in New South Wales, and support for postponement of interest payments on loans was growing there, the Scullin government was moving slowly and fearfully in the direction of salary and wage cuts.

A meeting of the federal Labor party revealed the depth of the split that had developed within Labor over the handling of the crisis. Lang had won success at the polls; members representing electorates in New South Wales felt the influence of this strong political wind, and they loudly denounced the ministry's retrenchment plans (based on the "sound finance" proposals of the Melbourne agreement). As an alternative they advocated an expansion of the money supply to finance additional public works. Caucus was swayed by their argument, even though it was strenuously opposed by James Edward Fenton, acting Prime Minister in Scullin's absence in London, and Joseph Aloysius Lyons, a former Tasmanian premier who was gaining increasing stature as acting Treasurer (while Theodore stood down). Lyons finally succeeded in effecting a compromise within caucus, and it was agreed that the tax on "sheltered" incomes should be raised, that higher-paid public servants and members of parliament should take a 10 per cent salary cut, and that incomes over £750 should be subject to a super tax. Very soon the Arbitration Court, hearing a case involving railway men, ordered a 10 per cent reduction in wages in addition to the normal adjustment of the wage to quarterly decreases in the cost of living. The court made its decision in January 1931 after hearing evidence that covered the whole economic position of the country and finding that there had been a real loss in national income of £70 million or more a year. The 10 per cent formula was quickly extended to practically all other industries under the court's authority. The basic wage was brought down to £3/17/0 a week (weighted average of six capital cities); it was as low as £3/7/6 in Brisbane, and £4/2/6 in Sydney. The reduction took the real wage level back to that prevailing in 1907.

A new warning came from Copland, Giblin, and Dyason; in a second manifesto they urged that constructive measures be taken. As a committee of advisers to the Treasury, the three economists then drew up a series of recommendations, taking into account the conclusions of the Arbitration Court, in order to reduce costs and charges throughout the economy in line with the wages cut. They emphasized that while the restoration of economic equilibrium was largely a matter of lifting the burden of loss from export producers, the attainment of budget equilibrium depended in part on economies and in part upon a restoration of money income. Thus, as Copland expressed it,

> ... advances are necessary along two main fronts, the direct attack on costs and the exploitation of monetary policy. In the first we have the pruning of government expenditure and the reduction in real wages and fixed charges of 10 per cent. In the second we have currency depreciation and the expansion of central bank credit.

Behind this concept for reconstruction was a mingling of deflation and inflation, aimed at limiting the loss of money income and spreading that loss as rapidly and equitably as possible over various sections of the community.

Premier Lang at this point decided that New South Wales should withdraw from the federal-states Loan Council. He believed that if he were freed from the joint plan for borrowing he could raise money with which to ease the strain on the 100,000 unemployed in New South Wales.

Meanwhile a federal loan of £28 million for the conversion and redemption of maturing loans was oversubscribed. The drastic tariff measures, and the effect of the devaluation of the Australian pound, had resulted in a striking improvement in the overseas trade picture; in the six months to

September 1930, a favourable trade balance of £6 million was recorded as the import flood was stemmed.

The outlook was still gloomy, but excitement over the wonder horse Phar Lap and his victory in the Melbourne Cup of November 1930 temporarily turned conversation into new channels, and the visit of the first West Indies cricket team, coming after Woodfull's team regained the Ashes in England a few months before showed that things other than budgets and balance sheets could be important. Record run-making on tricky English wickets had elevated Don Bradman from the status of a schoolboy's idol to that of a national hero; his brillance as a batsman had already won him a place in the galaxy of outstanding performers which he sustained by breaking record after record in Test and other first-class cricket. Perhaps as an antidote to economic tragedy, sporting achievement was acclaimed with greater enthusiasm than ever, and individuals seemed to accept this as a spur to greater effort. In many lines of endeavour Australian sportsmen were scoring signal successes. Walter Lindrum was astonishing the world with his unexcelled wizardry with a billiard cue; Hubert Opperman was establishing a reputation as a road cycling champion of extraordinary skill and stamina, and sculler Bobby Pearce was an acknowledged champion. Fifteen-year-old Jim Ferrier was making a name for himself as a golfer, breaststroke swimmer Claire Dennis was already considered likely to outclass Olympic competitors, and in tennis Jack Crawford and Harry Hopman were astonishing their opponents and delighting their admirers with unbeatable doubles play. Sportswriters were recording outstanding achievements by Australians in many other fields.

The political situation that greeted Scullin on his return to Australia in January 1931 after a five-months' absence abroad was extremely unfavourable. The announcement by the King that on the Prime Minister's advice he had appointed Sir Isaac Isaacs to the office of Governor-General had awakened hostility against Scullin among traditionalists, who considered it an unspeakable affront to depart from all precedent and advise the King to appoint an Australian to this post. Scullin also found that the Labor party was rapidly disintegrating as its moderate section urged measures to correct a more than ever out-of-balance budget, while others stressed the need for succouring those caught in the tempest. The civic reception accorded Scullin in Melbourne gave him little solace as he struggled to maintain control of the situation. In Sydney he met Lang's criticism head on: although the world depression had caught Australia unprepared, short in finance, and with huge debts at home and abroad, the Prime Minister said, all its obligations would be met—and there would be no issue of bank notes for the construction of public works.

At a meeting of the federal Labor party in January 1931, Scullin initiated a move to reinstate Theodore as Treasurer. This was accepted, since, it was said, the failure of the Queensland government to take action against him practically exonerated him. Clearly the party was in need of his experience and debating power on the Treasury bench. However, Theodore's re-emergence was the signal, for immediate disruption within the cabinet. Lyons and Fenton, who had become the new idols of the press as sound middle-of-the-roaders, and two other members close to them, left the party forthwith, protesting that they could not sanction Theodore's reinstatement to cabinet until he had been cleared of charges made against him. Lyons was also openly opposed to Theodore's plans for an enlarged note issue.

By the time the federal Labor party met again in March, Lyons was already in close touch with spokesmen for the Nationalist party.

In the House, Opposition Leader Latham took the opportunity to castigate the government, moving that it no longer held the House's confidence. He attacked the Labor administration and declared that Theodore's reinstatement had caused "a shock of indignation" throughout the country; furthermore, the government had wholly failed to abolish unemployment. In his reply Scullin took Latham to task for having failed at a time of serious crisis to make even one helpful suggestion; the opposition leader's speech, he said, was a diatribe of abuse, sneers, insinuations, and repetitions. The previous government had not been able to balance the budget, even in good years; in spite of the crisis since his government had come into office, loans to the amount of £100 million had been converted or redeemed, and the government had cut administration costs by £2,600,000 a year.

Latham's motion was defeated—but the margin, thirty-eight to thirty-three—reflected Scullin's declining support. Lyons, Fenton, and three other former Labor men had crossed the floor to vote with the opposition.

Against strong opposition from all the financial institutions of the country, including the Commonwealth Bank, Theodore had continued to advocate an expansion of the money supply. At the February meeting of the premiers, he had broached a proposal that, in order to halt the inflation and provide employment, money should be provided through central bank credit; he believed that at the same time a sharp cut should be made in interest rates, and that the Commonwealth Bank should make large purchases of government securities, printing additional currency for the purpose. Sir Robert Gibson replied with a firm, "Not a penny, gentlemen," and the trading banks (whose co-operation would have been needed) also refused support. The decision was then taken to implement the monetary programme by direct legislative process, and in March Theodore introduced a series of measures designed to carry the plan into effect. A fiduciary currency bill to provide for the issue of Treasury notes to the amount of £18 million was carried in the House by a five-vote margin; but it went down to defeat in the Senate. Associated measures, including one designed to create a central reserve bank, with wider lending powers and subject to a greater degree of government regulation, were similarly passed by the House but defeated in the Senate. The impasse was complete.

Lang's policies and actions not only weakened the federal government's position but also aggravated the difference of opinion within the federal A.L.P. Lang supporters—a small band but important now that Lyons and his group had taken the "fatal step" of outright opposition—met separately from Scullin and the main body after a federal by-election (in March 1931) brought Edward John Ward into parliament for a New South Wales seat. Ward had fought the election on the Lang policy, and was strongly opposed to Theodore, Lang's openly declared political enemy. In the bitterly fought power struggle, Lang pitted his state Labor machine against the Australian Workers' Union, whose executive had come out in opposition to his policy. Henceforth "Lang Labor" was to become an established political force in the federal sphere as Lang, determined to capture greater power, decided that in the ensuing general election his chosen followers would run in opposition to all federal ministers seeking re-election for constituencies in New South Wales.

By this time Lang's go-it-alone plan was running into difficulties. Speaking to a deputation of unemployed, Lang said that if his government met its interest bill there would be no more food relief, and relief works would have to be closed. He followed this with an announcement that he had unhesitatingly chosen to stick to the people of his own state in preference to overseas bondholders. As Australian bonds sank in price in London and New York, the federal government decided that under the financial agreement the payment of interest on state borrowings was a national obligation, and that it would be met.

When the interest payment due on April 1 fell into default, the Commonwealth met the instalment. Then, to recover the amount, the governments of the Commonwealth and of the five other states issued a writ against New South Wales for £557,000. At this point the New South Wales Savings Bank faced a crisis; there had been strong withdrawals in March following the state's default overseas, creating a liquidity problem which was aggravated when the state treasury failed to meet its debts to the bank. The Commonwealth Bank, after refusing any additional advance, suggested amalgamation and Lang was so informed. On April 22 Lang issued a statement supporting the idea that the Savings Bank should be absorbed by the Commonwealth Bank; but immediately a "run" on the state bank caused it to close its doors and suspend payments. It was some time before the general body of depositors could withdraw money; but the Commonwealth Bank accepted responsibility for the deposits and all accounts were honoured.

By now Lyons had been encouraged to see himself as the future national leader. A meeting of public men was called at his instigation and a new political body was formed with the ringing title, The All-for-Australia League. Warming to the prospects of routing Labor, the Nationalist organization encouraged discussions which might lead to the creation of a single party able to draw in the defectors and absorb all non-Labor forces; it already recognized in Lyons a great popular vote winner. The Country party refused to sink its identity, and it held aloof. Nevertheless a conference of delegates representing all the other non-Labor groups, meeting in Melbourne, decided to form the United Australia Party. Although during two stormy years he had led the depleted Nationalist forces with great skill,

Latham recognized what his own party knew: that because of his austerity, his conservatism, and his legalist manner, he could never be a popular figure. Latham bowed out of the leadership of the new party, and Lyons accepted it. His first action in the House was to move a vote of no-confidence in the government; this motion was defeated, though narrowly.

Scullin was trying to arrange a round-table conference of leaders of all parties, but this proposal was not taken up, even though suggestions for an all-party government had been canvassed earlier from the opposition side.

By the time the Loan Council meeting opened on May 25, 1931, the need for a well-ordered approach to the economic impasse was widely accepted. Various committees were appointed to consider financial, economic, legal, and other aspects, and later in the conference Lyons, Latham, and Senate Opposition Leader Sir George Pearce attended by invitation. Hopes for reconstruction crystallized around a comprehensive plan developed by economists Copland, Giblin, and Dyason, and other experts, and this, as the "premiers' plan," was eventually accepted as a blueprint for national action. Even Lang fell into line—"somewhat wryly," it was noted.

Within the A.L.P. there were those who realized that adoption of the plan would be fatal to Labor, both as a party and electorally because of the inevitable loss of confidence and the bewilderment if would engender throughout the labour movement. One such opponent was John Curtin, a backbencher who had political acumen but little prestige within the party. Curtin's view was that if no alternative existed to adoption of the plan, an election should be called in which a specific mandate could be sought on backing reform as a means to resolving the financial impasse; if Labor went down to defeat in such an election, Curtin said, it would fall to the non-Labor parties to put the plan into effect. "If the present plan is the only alternative to national collapse," he declared, "then let the plan be directed by its authors and advocates." Curtin believed that it was "brazenly treacherous" for a Labor government to legalize coercion on wage-earners and pensioners without compulsion on bondholders, and to meet this criticism, Scullin introduced an all round reduction of interest rates in Australia, pointing to this reduction as justification for Labor's backing of the plan.

The plan called for a reduction of all adjustable expenditure, including salaries and wages, the conversion of all internal loans at a reduction of interest, additional taxation, lowered bank interest rates, and the relief of private mortgagors. There would still be a total budget gap of close to £15 million which would have to be covered by borrowing, but each government undertook to balance its budget within three years.

The New South Wales treasury had by now exhausted its funds, and Lang sought an advance to cover expenditure for July. Scullin canvassed the other states asking if they would agree to the issue of federal Treasury bills for the amount provided Lang undertook to rejoin the Loan Council, assumed responsibility for his state's overseas debts and adopted the premiers' plan. The premiers all agreed, and Lang accepted the conditions.

The Theodore case now came to a head. The Queensland government sued Theodore (and other defendants) for damages related to the mine-sale case which had produced the unfavourable commission report of twelve months before. The case came before the Chief Justice of Queensland, and a jury; after considering a mass of evidence the jury found in favour of all the defendants on all counts.

Time was already running out for the Scullin government, however. Theodore was again the target of attack when parliament resumed in November. The leader of the five-man Lang faction within the federal Labor parliamentary group moved the adjournment of the House to call attention to proceedings (in connection with the unemployment grant) which he considered to be improper. Theodore hotly denied the imputation. Scullin said he would regard the adjournment motion as vital. Lyons said he considered that enough had been indicated to show that the spending of the grant had been mismanaged. Page said that as the government had refused an inquiry he would vote for the motion.

Lang had engineered the attack on the Scullin government, and the five members of the Lang group who crossed the floor to vote for the motion were sufficient to carry it. Scullin advised the Governor-General that parliament should be dissolved. The elections were set for December 19.

The campaign was a hurried one but there were many well-attended meetings. Political interest was high and there was a record number of nominations (including many from non-party candidates). Lyons in his policy speech played on the danger that Theodore would "smash the financial system of the whole Commonwealth"; at the same time, he refused to bid for votes for his party by making promises. Instead, Lyons asked voters

> ... to trust us to meet difficult situations as they arise with such action as we consider necessary in the interests of the people of Australia as a whole. In return for that confidence I will pledge my Party to serve the people of Australia sympathetically, and to avoid the imposition of hardship on any one section of the community as against any other.

In all states the daily newspapers ran editorials almost universally scathing in their denunciation of Labor; the imputation was that the "once great" party had become a rabble.

The election returns showed that Labor had been utterly rejected. It was a crushing defeat. Six ministers lost their seats; in the seventy-five member House, non-Labor parties held fifty-six seats and in the Senate they won fifteen out of eighteen vacancies. Some of the majorities gained by non-Labor men were overwhelming. Only in Queensland was the rout stemmed; here local issues helped Labor. The United Australia party had thirty-seven members in the new House, the Country party seventeen, and there were two independents. The Australian Labor party had only fourteen, the Lang group five.

Labor's annihilation had come from the protest vote. As political correspondent Arthur Norman Smith noted,

> The voter whose income tax had been raised, the trader vexed by sales tax,

the importer called upon for primage duty and the small investor whose interest had been cut down coalesced with the public servant made subject to a percentage reduction [in salary], the old age and invalid pensioner whose allowance had been lowered, and the primary producer whose returns had been halved.

Scullin had perhaps shown poor political judgment in calling an election at this time. There were many observers who believed that he would have been wiser to have resigned and allowed Lyons to form a government without an election. Smith commented at the time that under these circumstances "every week would have strengthened the Labor Party and weakened the new Ministry, which would have had to do, or at least continue, all the unpopular things that Labor had initiated."

The cold fact was, however, that Labor had been unfortunate enough to be in office when the storm broke, and the party's political opponents had been able to sit comfortably on the opposition benches through the worst of the debacle.

Recovery   21

From the early days of the financial crisis, there had been those who saw in devaluation a measure to help Australia over an immediate impasse. Sir Otto Niemeyer had been strongly opposed to such a move, however, and the Commonwealth Bank board had striven to maintain parity with sterling, shipping out all available gold to do so. It was only when events left no other course open that the independent bankers (and particularly those whose policies were under Australian control) accepted the realities of the situation, and the Australian pound was allowed to find a more natural level. Australian economists saw in this device a useful addition to the armoury of assistance to and protection for the Australian economy as a whole. Shortly before Lyons and his United Australia party swept the polls, the Commonwealth Bank board had come to accept the same general view.

From December 2, 1931, when the Commonwealth Bank accepted responsibility for fixing the rate of exchange on sterling (and simultaneously undertook to purchase the trading banks' surplus London funds), the Australian pound was stabilized on the basis of £125:£100. By setting a value on Australian currency 20 per cent below that of sterling, official policy put its seal of approval on a reasonable level of depreciation and retained for Australian producers an effective protection of 20 per cent.

Like the tariff structure which had been established earlier, the devalued currency helped buttress the economy in a special way. Through the application of a favourable exchange rate it became possible for Australia to relate its economy to international economies at a point of its own choosing. The discount was, in fact, a new and special form of economic protection required by a country struggling to grow up in the twentieth century.

It was intended at first that the actual ratio of depreciation should be flexible, and although some observers still believed that the Australian pound ought quickly to be restored to parity with sterling, the 20 per cent depreciation soon became permanent. The rate met the basic requirement of a depreciated exchange for Australia as defined by Professor Copland: it was a rate which could be expected to "restore profit in industry at a level of costs that can be maintained [in Australia] without economic or social distress."

The move to a depreciated currency was a natural consequence of long-term trends in the Australian economy and the nation's trading position. In the coming years the exchange differential was to assist to a significant degree in Australia's endeavours to maintain a place in the international environment while at the same time pursuing chosen national objectives.

Even before the depression holocaust, Australia, the last of the great "new" lands, was pressing development policies against special but largely unsuspected odds. The comfortable days when growth could be financed against a background of buoyant markets for rural products were now far behind. In the changed post-war world, the terms of trade had turned sharply against Australia as prices for primary products failed to move up with prices for imported goods. The production of rural products was no longer so profitable, even with greater efficiency and higher productivity. Faced with an over-supplied world market for food and fibre, the Australian primary producer had also been suffering disadvantages arising from the great distance that separated him from markets overseas. In pre-war days Australia had lived handsomely on the returns from wool, foodstuffs, and minerals, in a world that paid well for raw materials; now against keener competition the Australian producer found that his returns were insufficient to meet inflated costs.

If the added money which the Australian producer of wool, food, or minerals received as a result of the exchange premium acted as a bonus in his hands, at the same time the reduced purchasing power of the Australian pound in international markets was effective in providing local manufacturers with an edge over their rivals abroad. Plagued with the problems of a small home market with strong competition from mass-production countries where Australia's requirements often represented no more than a production "surplus," Australian manufacturers desperately needed this extra help.

The move away from parity with sterling was confirmed in 1932 when another measure further reduced the gold backing behind Australian currency. A formal move was made to confirm what had been practice; henceforth no claim was made that notes were convertible into gold, and all restrictions on the use of notes as legal tender were removed. At the same time, Australian currency became tied even more closely to sterling since the backing of the note issue henceforth might be held by the Commonwealth Bank in the form of sterling (which meant London securities) equally with gold.

In supporting the legislation of May 1932 which confirmed Australia's retreat from gold, the Commonwealth Bank board gave three reasons to back the move. First, it believed retention of physical gold reserves was "a luxury that Australia could not afford" under existing conditions. Second, it considered that as settlements for external debts required a sterling basis, the holding of note reserves in sterling would provide more flexibility in dealing with external financial matters and "should not be inimical" to Australia's external credit. Finally, the bank felt that conversion of Australia's gold into sterling would turn a frozen asset into a working asset, thereby increasing national income.

The net effect of the legislation was to tie the Australian pound directly to sterling instead of to gold. The hard realities met in grappling with problems of a country in the throes of a great depression had caused Bank board chairman Sir Robert Gibson to modify his once rigid ideas, and on the currency issue, at least, he had moved some distance from his old economic orthodoxy.

The benefits gained by the stabilization of the exchange rate, combined with consequent improvement in Australia's trading position, were soon reflected in a build-up in Australia's external reserves. This improvement stemmed from a now favourable balance of trade, the return of capital to Australia, and the transfer of gold into sterling assets. London funds, which had fallen below £30 million at July 1, 1931, were more than 10 per cent higher twelve months later and in addition gold reserves in Australia stood at £13,500,000. By that time the Prime Minister and the Premiers, at a formal meeting, had endorsed the Commonwealth Bank's handling of the exchange.

Before long other countries with similar export problems (including New Zealand and Argentina) had placed their currencies at a discount with sterling, thus lessening Australia's competitive advantage; but the general gain from a realistic exchange rate remained for Australia.

In sweeping the United Australia party into power, the general election of December 1931 gave new direction to the nation's political affairs, for it was those supporting a middle-of-the-road policy, and not the conservatives, who were in control of the party's affairs. Lyons and five close associates who left Labor with him carried into non-Labor ranks a progressive viewpoint which, blended with other constructive elements, was to play a significant part in the reshaping of political thought. Reasonable men had come to see that in the economic boilover much had happened which could not be reversed, and that practical measures were needed to restore economic activity. Lyons was more than a politician with sufficient popular appeal to win the election; in the places where influential men gathered and behind-the-scenes discussions were held, he was recognized as a sound leader who could restore the confidence needed to get things moving again. There were many non-Labor people ready and anxious to break with the past; the emergence of the new party headed by Lyons was an outward sign of the shift in the balance of power within non-Labor groups.

The most important single question dividing the United Australia party and the Country party was the tariff. The Scullin government had raised the tariff wall to unprecedented heights, and the added imposts on a wide range of goods had incurred the great hostility of the farming community. In the "unity" talks between the two non-Labor parties which had preceded the election, the tariff issue had been glossed over; it was simply agreed that the tariff should be revised on "scientific" lines, that only "efficient" local industry should be encouraged, and that a series of reciprocal trade treaties should be negotiated.

The inter-party agreement was attacked by manufacturers' organizations. Lyons, dependent on the support of king-makers in Melbourne who in turn were sensitive to pressure from manufacturing interests, explained in support of the joint policy that the United Australia party was not a low-tariff party. A joint advisory group formed to supervise the election campaign failed to stem the growing divergence of opinion between the two parties on the issue. By this time the Melbourne *Herald*, which had come out strongly in favour of Lyons as leader and was a vocal protagonist for Lyons' policies, soft-pedalled the tariff issue, saying that Lyons could be trusted as "a Protectionist." In his policy speech Lyons pointed out that the United Australia party was heir to the old Liberal party, which had been responsible for protection; and while he undertook that the Scullin government's high duties would be submitted to the Tariff Board for review, he said flatly that there would be no arbitrary ministerial decisions on tariff matters. Simultaneously Page was laying down Country party policy: immediate reductions in the tariff, and ratification by parliament of all tariffs.

The voters overcame the problem of the obvious contradiction in policy views between the two parties by giving the United Australia party a landslide victory and a clear-cut majority in the House, so that a composite ministry was not needed. Nevertheless, Lyons continued to state his hope that the Country party would join forces with him. Page, always suspicious of other than dyed-in-the-wool conservatives, stood out for concessions from Lyons, and in a conference to discuss a possible coalition, Page insisted that the portfolio of Trade and Customs be given to a Country party minister, that the Scullin tariffs be abandoned, and that the 1928 schedules be taken as the basis for tariff revision. These demands were unacceptable to the triumphant United Australia party, and Lyons assembled a cabinet made up wholly of men from his own party. One of his first moves, however, was to do away with prohibitions on imports and to set in motion a revision of the tariff.

As things turned out, the corrective measures initiated by the Scullin government were in the main sufficient to carry the economy back into calmer waters. Lyons had made no rash promises, and once in office he made no dramatic changes. Rather he relied on a rebuilding of confidence within the community. In external trade, export earnings had been stabilized and with the sharp fall in imports the trade balance had been markedly favourable for some months. The unemployment problem remained unsolved, however. Throughout 1932 unemployment was greater than at any other time; before the corner was turned the unemployment figure reached 30 per cent of those in reporting unions in the April–June period. Many people still hardly knew where their next meal was coming from—yet somehow men and women went about their affairs, chastened, downcast, almost without hope in many cases, but persisting.

When the Lyons government assumed office, Lang was still following his chosen path to chaos in New South Wales. All other governments, federal and state, had accepted the inevitable and were faithfully adhering to the premiers' plan, and so long as Lang continued to play the role of rogue elephant a direct confrontation between the Lyons government and him was inevitable. The struggle was short, sharp and decisive. At a meeting of the Loan Council held in January 1932 it was noted that New South Wales alone had failed to introduce economies on an appropriate scale; when the following month Lang was again unable to meet overseas interest payments on state debts, the Loan Council refused to assist him to do so. To avoid the scandal of default, the Commonwealth paid up and immediately took legal steps to recover the money from New South Wales. The federal parliament passed the Financial Agreement Enforcement Act requiring that certain state revenues be paid to the Commonwealth (in conformity with the Financial Agreement between the states and the federal government which had been inserted in the Constitution in 1928). The Act also provided that certain moneys held by the banks on behalf of the state should be garnisheed. The application of the legislation was widened so that new classes of New South Wales revenue could be appropriated under it.

Lang decided to defy the Commonwealth by attempting to frustrate the provisions of the Act. This course led him from defiance of the federal law to a breach of the law of his own state, as he quickly learnt. The Premier arranged for a circular to be sent to all New South Wales departments instructing them to cease operating government bank accounts and to pay all moneys direct to the state Treasury instead. At the same time Lang directed that the Treasury be barricaded so that federal officers could not gain access to its records. The Governor, Sir Philip Game, requested that Lang withdraw the circular, on the grounds that it placed the Crown in the position of breaking the law (specifically, the state Audit Act).

The struggle threatened to go on for some time; but already the possibility of the Lang government's being dismissed had been canvassed. The governor had been petitioned to depose the premier; 400,000 signatures were on the petition. With public opinion so strongly against Lang, the governor felt that Lang had lost the confidence of the electorate, and at this point when Lang refused to accede to the governor's request for compliance with the law, Sir Philip asked for the premier's resignation. Lang believed he had the constitutional right to remain in office but the governor sent him a letter on May 13 informing him that his commission had been withdrawn. Lang's dismissal by the governor was bitterly attacked, Lang's followers accusing the governor of political partisanship and "a repudiation of the State's charter of responsible government"; but the governor had done what he believed to be his "bounden duty" under circumstances which had not arisen before and, with stricter observance of constitutional proprieties, were unlikely to be repeated. For the majority of citizens the governor's action was accepted as a welcome conclusion to a futile and dangerous impasse.

Lang's partisanship had resulted in the formation in February 1931 of a quasi-military anti-Lang organization, the "New Guard," pledged to oust him forcibly if need be, and 50,000 political extremists had rallied to it. In March 1932, a New Guard member had been the centre of a dramatic incident during the ceremony for the opening of the great Sydney harbour bridge when Francis De Groot, feigning the role of a cavalry officer in order to secrete himself in the official military escort party stationed near Lang, had dashed forward on his shaggy charger to slash the ribbon with a sword just seconds before the scissors-wielding premier could reach the ribbon.

In the election resulting from Governor Game's dismissal of Lang, which was held in June, the verdict was a heavy defeat for Lang, whose fifty-five followers in the old House went down to twenty-four in the new. Five of Lang's ministers were among those defeated. The Labor party had been reduced to less than its strength of 1891 when it was first represented. The *Sydney Morning Herald* said:

> The New South Wales people have re-iterated their earlier verdicts against Langism; and they have notably upheld the Governor's action in dismissing the outlaw and rebel Government.

Lang himself narrowly missed being defeated in his own electorate.

The drama of the Lang regime had ended; the hatreds the Big Fella had engendered while premier could now begin to subside.

In other directions, the Lyons government had been moving cautiously. Federal revenues were recovering, but in spite of innumerable political premonitions of its imminent appearance, prosperity remained behind an elusive corner. The world economic crisis remained, and export prices (and returns) were only creeping forward. The Commonwealth Arbitration Court refused to restore the special 10 per cent reduction to the basic wage; action on a wage cut in New South Wales, delayed at the Lang government's insistence, was now taken and the state wage went down by some 15 per cent to £3/10/0 a week.

This was the last downward adjustment to be made. More credit was being released, and interest rates were being lowered in order to help stimulate expenditures. Before the end of 1932 the bond rate on new loans was down to $3\frac{3}{4}$ per cent, and the Treasury bill rate had been cut from 4 to $3\frac{1}{2}$ per cent. This was the first of a series of interest-lowering measures which continued to trim rates for another year or more.

The simple and unacceptable expedient put forward in the so-called

"Lang plan" for reducing costs and balancing budgets simply by a compulsory slashing of interest rates had not been adopted; yet in calling attention to the interest problem Lang had to a certain degree made possible the initial reduction in interest rates and the continuation of a policy of lowered rates as part of the rebuilding process. Economists had rephrased Lang's churlish and strident early outbursts against "Shylocks" and "interest slavery" to urbane suggestions that holders of fixed money claims might in fact find a voluntarily-accepted "variation of their interest contracts" preferable to alternatives available during the initial crisis. Later, when wages had been reduced all round, the same economists had returned to the subject to urge the merits of lower interest rates generally as a factor in the regrowth of economic activity. Startling as they had been, Lang's tirades had turned the spotlight on a significant aspect of financial policy, and thus were not without effect.

The premiers' conference of June–July 1932 (with Bertram Sydney Stevens attending as New South Wales Premier) set a limit on the states' deficits for 1932–33 at £9 million (compared with actual deficits totalling £31 million in 1931–32). At the same time the conference agreed to a works programme for the year amounting to £6 million and a three-year special unemployment relief plan of £15 million.

By mid-1933, when the budget targets had been met, and wool prices were moving up from the pit, a start had been made on the long road back to prosperity. In the budget, Lyons as federal Treasurer confirmed the £125:100 rate on sterling, and noted that

> ... it is important that we should retain our own right to fix our monetary unit at the point which is consistent with our own price level.

Meanwhile, the tariff board had concluded that costs generally in industry had fallen to a point where it could safely recommend a substantial reduction in duties. The government accepted the recommendation, dovetailing it with the Empire-preference provisions of the agreement reached at the Imperial economic conference in Ottawa. With the resulting cuts in tariffs, British goods were again competitive on the Australian market; yet the value of the output of factories within Australia was now running at half as much again as the value of imported goods, and Australian-made articles were able to hold their own in the growing market over the next few years. There had been a general rise in efficiency in both management and labour (even though by world standards, machinery and methods in many plants were still disappointingly poor), and the policy of replacing imports by articles of domestic manufacture was succeeding. In 1934–35, factory production was valued at £143,800,000 and imported goods were valued at £90,500,000; two years later the value of local manfactures had moved up to £177,600,000 and that of imported goods to £113,300,000.

Overseas industrialists were among those who led the way in the industrial field with more confident predictions of future growth. Motor-car manufacturers were increasing output; Ford's Tin Lizzie, which in the 1920s had been flowing from assembly lines in five states, and its Model A successor, had both been superseded by the V8, a sensation from the time of its introduction in 1932. An innovation of a distinctive kind came in 1934, with the first coupé "utility," a wholly-Australian style of vehicle which caught on quickly. With it the man on the land could take his wife to the Country Women's Association meeting, pick up a delivery of machine parts, do the rounds of his property, and carry the light goods he needed.

Meanwhile aviation continued to bring Australia closer to the rest of the world. Experimental mail flights had been made by Imperial Airways from London to Darwin, with Queensland and Northern Territory Aerial Services taking over at Darwin. After 1934 the interests of the two lines were linked and a weekly service opened to Singapore.

Late that year the sleek, fast aircraft of a new phase of aviation thrust themselves into the Australian scene as a result of the great London-Melbourne air race, for which industrialist Macpherson Robertson donated handsome prizes. The winning aircraft—a British Comet—arrived 70 hours 54 minutes out from London; and the next day the *Argus* reported that Melbourne had seen history being made at 200 miles an hour, with the Comet a symbol of the air age. "If the conquest of speed be maintained at its present rate," the newspaper added, "an air journey to England in three days will be a commonplace; and Australia, that vast land over the edge of beyond, will become part of the great world metropolis."

By the early 1930s trends towards greater rural production begun a decade earlier were coming to fruition. Many farmers had walked off their farms penniless, and others among those who held on were saddled with debt—yet, national output was gaining from some of the over-expensive closer settlement projects of earlier years. The price had been high, but new districts had come into production. Large grazing properties had been subdivided into wheat farms—many in areas of less reliable rainfall—forest land had been converted into dairy farms, and the creation of new irrigation areas had brought new productivity to fertile but under-watered regions. In Western Australia, rural expansion was particularly marked; wheat-growing areas were pushed eastward beyond Merredin, northwards beyond Geraldton, and into the more isolated Esperance area, while dairying was extending in the high-rainfall southwest. In Queensland, sugar-growing extended farther north along the coast.

If the fundamentals of rural economics had been largely ignored in the early 1920s and insufficient research had been undertaken into practical issues in agriculture and pastoral pursuits, some notable advances had been made in the art and science of land management largely through the efforts of individual farmers or graziers. By that time the need for expert and detailed analysis of such fundamental factors as soils, pastures, crop rotation, and climatology, and the associated matters of plant pathology and entomology, and for more down-to-earth planning, was slowly being realized, but acceptance of the place of the trained agriculturist came only after major projects in land settlement failed. In some cases that failure was due in considerable degree to an aspect as fundamental to success as suitability of soil or climate; yet proper investigation of such matters had frequently been neglected. In other fields the expert was not called in to advise until a crisis arose which affected large numbers of people or an entire industry.

A Chair of Agriculture—the first in Australia—had been established at Sydney University in 1910, and soon faculties had been set up also in Melbourne (1911) and Perth (1914), but relatively little could be done by graduates until after 1920. The Waite Institute, in Adelaide, founded in 1925, brought together well-trained groups of workers, and in Queensland active work began in 1927. There were still far too few men for the real tasks, and there was still only the sketchiest appreciation among policy-makers of the scope of the expert-technical skills needed to cope with pastoral and agricultural developments. The numbers graduating in agricultural science were insufficient to fill all the positions offering; as well as in research there were demands in teaching and in administrative positions in state and federal government departments and institutions.

A better understanding of the role that could be played by skilled and trained men had come as a result of the work of an Advisory Council of Science and Industry which Hughes had called into being in the late war years. The council could not expect to do more than scratch the surface: the task of bringing applied science to the aid of rural and industrial efforts was far beyond its resources, even if it dared try to undertake it. Instead the council concentrated on setting up a series of committees in the various states, and then it set about doing what it could to evaluate the situation so that action might be taken on a few problems chosen from a vast array. Concentrating on rural matters, the council decided that priority should be given to problems of national importance; a soils survey, cattle ticks, sheep blowflies, the prickly pear pest, and products which might be produced from hardwood forests.

By 1920 the council had been replaced by the Institute of Science and Industry, with headquarters in Melbourne, operated with a director and technical staff. It investigated ways of using hardwoods, and went to work to control a disease which had attacked hundreds of banana plantations in Queensland. This disease, known as "bunchy top," had brought sudden ruin to many settlers, including scores who had extended the banana acreage during the wave of soldier-settlement projects immediately after the war. Until a way of reducing the spread of the disease was found and put into operation in 1927, the entire banana-growing activity was threatened with extinction.

Scientists were also called in to deal with an even more menacing pest which had spread an almost impenetrable mass of spiny arms that obliterated millions of acres of good land in southern Queensland and northern New South Wales. For years, attempts by landowners to keep prickly pear under control had failed. In the early days of settlement, various species of cactus had been introduced, either as decorative potplants or as garden plants, and later some of the larger types had been grown as hedges to protect homesteads. In southern Queensland such plants found a congenial setting and they established themselves freely. Hardy and drought resistant, they were soon invading adjoining areas. They spread rapidly by seeding and segmenting; soon their tough, fleshy and prickly arms were choking out all other plants and rendering the land they invaded unusable. More than 1,000,000 acres were being overrun each year, and graziers were giving up the unequal struggle. A special board set up in 1920 with funds from the Commonwealth and New South Wales and Queensland, supported the idea of control of the pest by insect and other natural enemies, and experts were sent to search for insects and fungi that attacked prickly pear in North and South America. Depots were set up where insects could be studied before being sent to Australia so that the danger of introducing any insects which might themselves become pests could be eliminated.

The early efforts to find a parasite that would attack the two most troublesome species of pear were under the direction of Dr Harvey Johnston. After he moved to other tasks, the work was taken over by others; in 1924 Alan Dodd, an entomologist, was in charge of the investigation. While travelling in Argentina at the end of 1924 Dodd noted the activity of a leaf-boring moth, whose caterpillars had a selective and voracious appetite for the plants, Dodd sent about 3000 eggs of this insect, *Cactoblastis cactorum*, from Buenos Aires in March 1925; the caterpillars hatched out on arrival in Brisbane, and scientists sent eggs to cactus-infected areas.

From that point it took just a few years for the battle to be won. The tough host was finally routed by the hungry insect, and by 1932, the bulk of the prickly pear infesting tens of millions of acres lay in shrivelled, blackened masses on the ground. With the two most difficult types of prickly pear eliminated it was possible to deal with the remaining types. Soon the wasteland, mainly unoccupied, was being reclaimed and settled, chiefly for pastoral purposes but also for dairying and general farming. When the scourge of King Pear was no more than a memory, a memorial hall was built at Boonarga, in the Chinchilla district, to mark the achievement. Significantly it was dedicated to *Cactoblastis* and not to the scientists who had discovered the insect's destructive ability.

By this time the Council for Scientific and Industrial Research, established under the Bruce-Page government in 1926 as an independent body, was undertaking programmes of research into some of the problems of primary and secondary industry. The organization was able to give valuable stimulus but most of the work in scientific research was still being done by state bodies.

When it came to the most basic industry of all—wool-growing—the studmaster was in no danger of being ousted by the scientist. From flock management to the processes of weaving cloth, the wool industry continued in its traditional ways, changing methods and objectives very little. If there were fears among some that wool was not holding its own, expressions of concern were mild and generally they were lost in the national preoccupation with finding means to diversify rural activity and settle more men on the land. The disposal of wartime accumulations of wool heartened even the pessimists, and by 1925 sheep numbers regained the early-1890s mark of

100,000,000 (after being as low as 80,000,000 in 1919). Average fleece weights were increasing slightly all the time, and there was some improvement in quality; but a counterforce was the trend to crossbred sheep, which were favoured by the smallholders on subdivisions who were seeking a dual purpose sheep for the production of mutton as well as wool, and for the fat lamb trade. This trend led to the introduction of several British breeds renowned for their mutton-producing qualities and early maturity. The merino was still unchallenged in the dry lands of the sheepman's choice, but in line with the trend towards smaller properties the proportion of merinos in the nation's flocks drifted below 90 per cent for the first time in 1924, and this trend was reflected in the character of the wool clip.

To meet changed needs, new breeds were being evolved. All were based on the merino with an admixture of one of the longwool British breeds. The Corriedale was developed at this time by Australian and New Zealand breeders; its merit was that it possessed the good points arising from a long-wool/merino cross, and the characteristics had been fixed through selective breeding of the crossbreds and careful culling over several generations. The Polwarth was evolved by Victorian breeders from crossbred-merino matings as the type reflecting greater merino content in its ancestry, while the "comeback" type gained just as wide acceptance (its name reflecting the fact that it was still closer to the merino in its breeding). The trend to smaller land holdings held down to some extent the rising trend in average fleece weights; but by 1929–30 average fleece weight exceeded 9 lb. Among dedicated merino men the drive for finer wool and heavier fleeces had not been blunted; in 1927 the Boonoke stud paid 5000 guineas for a ram, David of Dalkeith—a price that was to remain a record for almost thirty years.

To the chagrin of the elite among the merino studmasters (who had built up a significant export trade), the export of pure-bred merino stock was prohibited in 1929. The prevailing view of officials, reflecting concern among wool-growers in general, was that competitors in South Africa and Russia and South America would so improve their flocks by the introductions that Australia's pre-eminence as a producer of fine apparel wool would be lost; and although many challenged the contention and stressed the value of maintaining wool's integrity as a clothing fibre in world trade, successive governments were to hold firmly to the ban. Overseas buyers of Australian sheep henceforth had to content themselves with such part-merino breeds as Corriedales or Polwarths or comebacks.

Cattle breeds also had undergone change over the period. The merits of the shorter-leg, more compact and early-maturing type of Shorthorn were more widely appreciated. Anthony Hordern's Milton Park stud, near Bowral, was the early innovator, and as the influence of the improved Shorthorn strain spread, other breeders made importations, and gradually even some of the remoter stations began to replace the hardy but rangy stock of earlier days. Herefords were also being improved in quality by selective breeding and by the introduction of improved strains from abroad. In the heavier-rain-fall country the Aberdeen Angus were appearing in greater numbers, and a score of breeders began the job of developing stock for the graziers. The breed made marked progress after arrivals of stock direct from Scotland in 1927, and subsequent importations from Canada satisfied some hesitant cattlemen who had reservations about the hardiness of the cattle.

Although natural factors worked against the attainment of high milk yields, some improvement was recorded from the mid-1920s, particularly in New South Wales, as dairy farmers improved their feeding methods and general farm management, and introduced improved milk-producing strains. There was little change in the relative importance of the various breeds established thirty or forty years earlier, except that the Australian Illawarra, a milking Shorthorn, improved in uniformity and productive capacity, was beginning to spread over a wider area.

Nutritional factors were under closer study, and it was realized that, except under irrigation, natural or induced pastures could not provide adequate nutritive value for dairy cows on a year-round basis. Better pasture management was needed, and the complacency of many farmers was soon to be shattered by the admonishing voice of Professor Samuel MacMahon Wadham, and the declarations of other agricultural scientists, who drew attention to such issues as the drain on soil fertility exerted by a luxuriant pasture grazed by a dairy herd. Competition and an exchange of information among dairy farmers themselves were leading to a more progressive approach, and although the high yields of more favoured lands were unattainable, yields of milk and butter fat per cow were improving. The introduction of more nutritious strains of grasses and clovers, and of rotational grazing practices, helped. The most successful farmers were also giving greater attention to the addition of fertilizer and lime to the soil, and to cultivating and draining the land. Nevertheless, the cost structure within the industry was such that the dairy farmer remained in financial difficulty; and by 1934 voluntary stabilization of the butter price (introduced in 1926 under the "Paterson plan") no longer sufficed. The new support was in the form of a compulsory "price equalization" plan whereby the Australian consumer paid well above the world price for butter in order to subsidize export of the surplus.

The general trend towards wheat-and-sheep farms in southern areas of the continent brought into vogue a new grass found to be well suited to the farmers' need to maintain feed for their stock in the intervals between cereal crops. It was named Wimmera rye from the district in Victoria where it was first recorded officially in 1919. The variety flourished in warmer and drier climates, and in less fertile soil, than demanded by other varieties of rye grass, and it won a place on many smaller grazing properties as well as on farms.

By the mid-1920s subterranean clover was being grown on a far wider scale than ever before, and with the use of superphosphate it was establishing better carpets of pasture in many places. By 1929–30 the extent of land on which sown pastures were carried exceeded 5,000,000 acres. In addition, subterranean clover had been established on a less intensive basis in other pastures. Another significant addition to pastures was *Phalaris tuberosa*, which had been introduced in some districts a generation or so earlier and, having demonstrated its drought resistance, was now proving its ability to combine with clovers in mixed pastures. For more specialized conditions, Kikuyu grass, introduced from East Africa, was becoming a rival to paspalum in coastal districts of New South Wales, where it proved an effective counter to vigorous weeds like bracken and blackberry.

Expansion of the wheat acreage had gone on gradually in the 1920s as new farms were developed, some of them on land previously used for pasture and some on land cleared of scrub. Although production of wheat was notably high in terms of the manpower engaged in the industry, average yield per acre remained low by comparison with that of the other great wheat-producing lands. This low yield arose partly from extension of the wheat belt into lower rainfall areas.

Wheat was particularly vulnerable to the fluctuations of world supply and demand; of all the primary industries wheat-growing was hardest hit in the depression. The entry of Russian grain into world markets in 1929 had helped precipitate the commodity price collapse, and when the depression struck Australia, the federal government and the governments of all wheatgrowing states appealed to farmers to grow more wheat in an attempt to ensure a surplus which would help in meeting overseas commitments. The Scullin government formulated a plan for wheat marketing which involved the creation of a compulsory wheat pool and guaranteed a price of 4/– a bushel. The legislative measure, tied with Theodore's proposal for a fiduciary note issue, was killed in the Senate. The farmers, in anticipation of the higher price, had made a supreme effort to increase output, and the crop harvested was well in excess of 200,000,000 bushels. Wheat had meanwhile slumped to under 2/– a bushel at railheads, and the very large crop did little to alleviate the situation since the excess had come from extended acreage (a total of over 18,000,000) rather than improved yield. A general moratorium was enacted by Lang in New South Wales in 1930, and within a year a similar provision was in force in Victoria, South Australia, and Western Australia, thus covering the chief wheat-growing states. The measure proved inadequate, however, and even with further relief and debt adjustment the farmer remained in difficulty because of the low price. In terms of gold, wheat had dropped to its lowest price in four centuries; there was little that could be done to rescue the farmer even when the federal government stepped in and granted small bonuses in 1932 and 1933. An official inquiry in 1934 established the fact that the 60,000 wheat holdings involved a total indebtedness of about £150 million. It was further shown that about 40 per cent of farmers were in a sound financial position and about 26 per cent could become financially stable if they were given assistance that would adjust their indebtedness or interest cost, but that the remaining 34 per cent were faced with production costs that made it impossible for them to succeed at existing or prospective price levels. A shrinkage of wheat acreage began, and in 1935–36 less than 12,000,000 acres were sown.

Meanwhile, farm techniques were under closer scrutiny than ever before as hard times induced many farmers to think seriously about the problems of their individual farms. As technical knowledge was co-ordinated at the state agriculture department level, sounder methods were put into practice. Notable gains in the wheat industry were made with the introduction of improved grading methods and the adoption of bulk handling, which was introduced from the early 1930s. Farmers in the important Wimmera district of Victoria were among the hardest to convince of the need for change in handling methods, but in 1934 after many years of dispute a majority of wheatgrowers there agreed to move beyond the bags-and-grainsheds phase and the Victorian Grain Elevators Act was quickly passed, opening the way for country and terminal silos to be constructed.

Mining had run into hard times in the 1920s, but, as a result of adjustments to the economy that came with the depression, it was being revived.

The copper boom of the early years of the century that had taken thousands into western Queensland faded when the price of copper slumped in the immediate post-war years, and even though the Queensland government took over the Chillagoe smelters in an effort to assist the miners along the Cloncurry belt, by the late 1920s the mining fields were deserted by all but the hardiest and most resolute. Mount Morgan, the mine that had produced fantastic riches in gold before it became a great copper producer, had also run into difficulty; by 1924 the old company was in the hands of liquidators. Other coppermining areas deep in the bush—Cobar, in western New South Wales, and Moonta and Wallaroo, in South Australia—also were being abandoned. Only the Mount Lyell field, located on Tasmania's west coast and operated by a company able to draw upon profits earned by an investment portfolio, was able to struggle on; the operation was saved by adoption of a flotation process for copper extraction. Gold-mining had shared in the decline over the years; most mines in the main areas of Queensland (Charters Towers, Gympie, and Croydon) and in New South Wales and Tasmania had closed, and even mines along Kalgoorlie's unmatched Golden Mile were in decline by the mid-1920s. In a generation the number of men employed in gold-mining in Australia had dropped from well over 70,000 to only 6000 or so. Boards of the companies that operated the old and rich mines, aware that the extraction of gold was no longer profitable, invested in manufacturing and other types of industry. Mining engineers moved into other fields, some of them going to Malaya, where tin mining was expanding, and others taking jobs outside the industry. By 1929 the output in Western Australia, the main gold producing state, was well under 400,000 fine ounces—the lowest level in a continuous decline from the peak of 1903.

To old prospectors and miners—men with the glint of metal in their blood—the decline of mining was more than a threat to their livelihood; it was a personal tragedy, a final sign of defeat. Rather than abandon cherished hopes, such men were sometimes prepared to stake everything by pushing into the harshest, crudest parts of the continent in a search for the great lode of their dreams. One such prospector was John Campbell Miles, who had heard a cattle drover's tale of a great gold quartz reef deep in the Northern Territory; on his way to investigate, in March 1923 he camped in the dry valley of the Leichhardt River, in western Queensland, and along a low range he discovered large outcrops of ore which he felt had promise. On assay the ore proved to be very rich in lead and to contain much silver as well. Campbell, and a few of the miners from the Cloncurry copper fields who heard of the strike and pegged leases, were soon spinning wondrous stories of the riches of Mount Isa; by 1924 three mining companies had been floated. The Queensland government showed its support by undertaking to build a railway which would link Mount Isa with Townsville, 600 miles away; but investors were not prepared to put up the great sums needed to start a large-scale mining operation deep in the hinterland. Only when mining engineer William Courbould went to London was he able to secure support; there John Leslie Urquhart, a mining promoter who had made and lost fortunes in Russian enterprises, became interested and provided backing, and after that the American Smelting and Refining Company, with headquarters in New York, was induced to invest heavily. By the time the Mount Isa ore treatment plant opened in 1931 some £A.3,500,000 had been spent; but the yield of lead and silver was disappointing and for years the mine remained something of a white elephant. It was not until 1937, when technical difficulties had been overcome and metal prices were satisfactory that profits were earned. By then Mount Isa had been confirmed as one of the great ore bodies of the world, and the mine's future was assured.

Gold-mining revived quickly in the early 1930s when the price of gold rose sharply after Britain left the gold standard and Australia devalued. Many gold-mining companies were able to expand operations; old fields were re-explored and new methods of extraction developed, so that with the high price of gold low-yield ore became profitable again. The ranks of gold prospectors were suddenly swollen by thousands of men who left the cities in the hope of making a strike. In 1931 news that the largest nugget yet found in Western Australia—the Golden Eagle—had come to light at Coolgardie spurred new hope among the gold seekers. Western Australia's yield moved up steadily and in 1937 production exceeded 1,000,000 fine ounces for the first time in twenty years. Even in Victoria, where gold-mining had almost ceased, thousands of unemployed men took up the government's offer of a tent, mining tools, a prospector's guide, and a rail pass to any of the state's goldfields. At the same time, deep-reef mining at Bendigo was given a new lease of life.

Out in the never-never, lone prospectors searched constantly; some lost their lives in the process. The lucky ones turned up a little gold in remote places; but only Tennant Creek, in the Northern Territory, and Cracow, in central Queensland, proved to be valuable new fields. In 1930 "The Tennant" became the scene of a small but exciting gold rush; soon 500 to 600 men were on the sunbaked field, living in bough-and-hessian sheds.

In the rugged and inaccessible highlands forming New Guinea's backbone, where prospectors had struck gold in the early 1920s, new life was given to mining enterprises as aircraft filled the role of carry-alls. From the late 1920s aviators like Raymond John Paul Parer were pioneering the unknown valleys of New Guinea's central highlands, flying men and supplies across precipitous gorges and thick jungles barring the way by land. All through the 1930s passengers, cargo, mining equipment, and even livestock were involved in an airlift which was the biggest in the world, by far, to that time.

The "flying mailman" services of the inland were augmented when Edward John Connellan began a one-man airline in 1939 to link remote Northern Territory cattle stations with Alice Springs. His own pilot in the early days, Connellan was undeterred when he had to help in the clearing and levelling of bush runways—work which could be interrupted when a radio'd call for help meant an emergency flight with medico or patient of the Flying Doctor Service.

Hard times had brought to the surface many attitudes that had been submerged during the prosperous years. Out of the shock and dismay of adversity, a renewed search for a national identity was emerging along with an awareness of Australia as a distinctive land. At a time when new and unshakable faith was called for to replace the flaccid optimism of prosperous years, people were turning to listen not only to those who spoke out to urge a regimen of harder work but also those who called for a better appreciation of the Australian environment itself. Those few experts who had been struggling to catalogue its characteristics in terms of climate and geography, and to draw sound conclusions from comparisons with other lands, were now joined by a growing band ready to write about the inland for a new audience—an audience interested in hearing about the sprawling hinterland over which aircraft were flying and across which motor-cars were being driven in greater numbers.

The land had to come under closer and more critical scrutiny so that faith in its future might be more firmly based; and with the new determination to build Australia on sounder lines through scientific investigation and improvement of land industries on the one hand and more efficient industrial management and labour practices in industry on the other, came also a more penetrating interest in the nature of the difficult, roomy, unfilled land.

In the inland the advent of the motor vehicle in the 1920s had reduced the sense of remoteness and had eased general hardships. The telephone had been taken to more of the inland areas, and air services had been pushed deeper into the outback. Even as experts debated their views on what land in Australia was usable and what totally useless, and how the occupied areas might be better used, through improved transport and the introduction of modern communications, the great outback was losing its terror. Australians themselves had grown to a closer identity with their homeland through the efforts of naturalists and journalists interested in natural history, whom some newspaper editors had encouraged to conduct weekly columns dealing with wildlife and the countryside.

In the early 1930s an awakening curiosity among city people about the true nature of the hinterland was fed by books of personal narrative presenting graphic descriptions of little-known parts of Australia. Soon the trickle of stories, novels, and works of description had turned into a stream. For the most part the new writers who tackled the subject were earnest but uncomplicated men, and they contented themselves with recording and imparting information on a life they enjoyed without expounding their views on the shortcomings of the society in which they lived. They were not cast in the mould of Lawson with his self-pity or of Furphy with his preoccupation with improving the average man's lot.

Though there were now few who had heard of George or Bellamy, ideas they had put forth were still floating around among the shearers and other outdoorsmen. Those ideas had filtered through so many ears in the retelling that by now they had taken on a rather different identity from that of their originators—yet in the depression days of adversity they seemed valid again. Writing in the 1930s owed much to the early national movement which had taken shape half a century earlier in the days when Australians were struggling to reach the maturity of nationhood. Based as it was on the secluded distinctiveness of the outback, the early movement had lost its momentum under the pressure of mass media; now in the attempt to regain a national identity in the face of the standardizing influences, writers drew again upon the bush legend. The revival came as part of a resurgence; Australian writing began to move forward again as a new middle-class readership developed for local books.

The new generation of writers about the outdoors was made up of self-reliant men who had turned to writing as a relaxation and a means of earning a little extra money. Many of them had spent most of their lives on cattle stations as stockmen—practical, robust men who revelled in their spacious world of open skies and far horizons. They gave an air of reality mixed with romance and adventure to their stories based on the daily round in the outback. In their hands the rusticism of the 1890s was dispelled by a more substantial provincialism. In articles, novels, and short stories, these authors wrote about a challenging land with open, friendly people; to those facing the humdrum city round, such stories came as a breath of fresh air and inspiration. There were many parallels with America's romantic Old West, and in drawing upon the "frontier" atmosphere of the great untamed land Australian writers were doing much the same as those who had engaged in the glorification of America's "golden west" of gold seekers and cowboys.

In 1931, *Lasseter's Last Ride*, by Ion Idriess, and William Hatfield's *Sheepmates* appeared. They were the first widely-accepted books of the new style. Both were published in Australia—a turning point, since this was the first time in a generation that books were winning approval in Australia before finding acceptance overseas—and each was the forerunner of a dozen or so successful books by the same author.

Authentic backgrounds were also used effectively by Frank Dalby Davison, whose books were set mainly in the cattle country of southern Queensland. His *Manshy*—the story of a heifer—won the Australian Literary Society's award for 1931, and it was followed by a succession of finely written stories of enduring quality. Vance Palmer and Bernard Cronin, both professional writers who had been using Australian settings for short stories and historical re-creations, had no greater following than the newly discovered outback storytellers like Arthur William Upfield and Henry George Lamond—men who, without literary finesse, spun down-to-earth tales based on life as it was being lived in the inland.

Other new writers included Eleanor Dark (*Slow Dawning*) and Myrtle White, whose story about pioneering in the Outback, *No Roads Go By*, had an ingenuous charm; their work first appeared in 1932. Katherine Susannah Prichard's *Coonardoo* (1929), a story of Aborigines living as flotsam on the fringes of white settlement in the far north-west, and Miles Franklin's *Old Blastus of Bandicoot*, a story set in the sheeplands along the Molonglo River, carried a strong regional flavour; each was about a special and distinctive environment which the author knew well. Before long another woman, Henrietta Drake-Brockman, was to add her *Blue North* (1934) and *Sheba Lane* (1936)—both set on the north-west coast and drawing upon the pearling fleets for their colour. This emphasis on regionalism provided another strong parallel with the United States, where writers—again, many of them women—were weaving stories out of the way of life of various districts.

Appreciation was growing among perceptive writers of how the past had shaped the present, and how the nature of the land was having its effect on the Australian way of life. Among those who tackled the historical theme was Brian Penton. In two fine novels, *Landtakers* (1934) and *Inheritors* (1936) he reconstructed the rigours of the pioneering days and questioned many accepted attitudes about the "glorious pioneers" in general. In analysing and interpreting the attitudes of the early free settlers, Penton contended that many had been bent simply on making their fortunes and returning "home" yet finding themselves staying because they had to, "hating the place but unable to leave it."

Steadily the cult of the Inland was gaining a wider following. To the dedicated, identification with the continent's sprawling empty spaces—the "real Australia" to a growing circle—was becoming something of a test of patriotism. The sterility of John Walter Gregory's "dead heart" concept (put forward in 1906) was being superseded. Henceforth more Australians were prepared to participate—vicariously—in the new phase of pioneering in which the Outback was being opened up. Remote places and vast unoccupied lands, a region of spinifex and Aborigines, were coming to life. Ion Idriess's *Flynn of the Inland* (1932), recounting the life of the Reverend Dr John Flynn and telling of the work of the flying doctors, and Robert Bruce Plowman's *The Men from Oodnadatta* (1933) painted new and exciting pictures of the continent.

Throughout, *The Bulletin* had kept its columns open to Australian writers, but much of its material was now somewhat stereotyped. A new, more city-oriented approach came with the appearance in 1934 of the monthly magazine *Walkabout*, designed with the self-confessed aim of telling the story of "the romantic Australia that lies beyond the cities" and edited for the Australian

National Publicity Association by Charles Holmes, whose vision of Australia was shaped around an unswerving dedication to the Inland. Upfield and Lamond were among its early contributors. In a typical article, "Men, Sheep and Far Horizons," Upfield gave an unaffected dissertation on life on a 750,000 acre sheep station in western New South Wales, describing a world of "solitary, gnarled, and unlovely swamp gums—the favourite nesting trees of the galahs—box-trees, the yellow-flowering native tobacco bushes, and grand old men saltbush," in which the six station-hands spent their day. Lamond's first contribution, "A Bushman's Carnival," was set in "a bit of a township of Western Queensland" on the day of the annual camp draft, and it regaled anecdotes of tough-muscled stockmen and the carnival's assemblage of tawdry sideshows. In stories and photographs of a myriad-sided Australiana, *Walkabout* stayed close to the world of men and horses (and, now, the motor-car with water-bag-slung-in-front) in which the individual retained the personal freedom that seemed increasingly removed from the life of the city dweller.

At the same time, in demanding higher standards in local fiction, *The Australian Journal* was proving to be an expanding workshop for writers seeking to gain recognition and a livelihood while on their way to success in novel-writing. Many of the stories it ran were set in the Inland or in remote corners of the continent.

Even as stories with guileless cattle-and-blue-skies themes were finding wider reading audiences, novels of Australia's developing urban life also made their appearance. Eleanor Dark, the first novelist to make use of latter-day urban scenes reflecting the life of more sophisticated people, published *Prelude to Christopher* (1934), *Return to Coolami* (1936) and other novels interpreting behaviour psychologically while Kylie Tennant's first novel *Tiburon* (1935), with a country-town setting, moved the period up to the depression years themselves. Xavier Herbert's *Capricornia*—a bitter story built around the colour problem in the Northern Territory—was published in 1938; since the author was outspokenly critical in dealing with a subject on which Australians were extremely sensitive, the novel marked a new maturity in the Australian attitude.

In poetry, Slessor had by now assumed a leading place; he had outgrown the world of myth which had encompassed him in the 1920s. In poems dealing with character and adventure he related tales of sea-captain explorers which bore the stamp of realism and vigour. His "Five Visions of Captain Cook" and other poems published in *Cuckooz Contrey* (1932) marked the first wave of modernism; in them Slessor showed a mastery of technique both in producing effects and expressing attitudes. Sharing in the new spirit of adventure, Robert David Fitzgerald was developing as a fine and sensitive writer about nature. Mary Gilmore, her early socialism now tinged with a deeper appreciation of a broader Australia, was writing with a closer identification with the environment in which she lived. A transition from Australian to universal themes had been evident among some of the new writers, including John Alexander Ross McKellar, whose poetically-imaginative "Twenty Six" was published in 1932, the year of his death at the age of twenty-eight.

Some of the younger practitioners were moving towards a fresh appreciation of their homeland as a source of inspiration while seeking to enrich their work by use of uniquely Australian imagery. A trailblazer in this movement was a South Australian schoolteacher, Rex Ingamells, whose first volume, *Gumtops*, appeared in 1935. Imbued with a spirit of Australian life and landscapes, Ingamells found a special element of the national heritage in links that existed through Aboriginal tribes going back to a presettlement past. He was determined to spread the new gospel, and in 1937 he founded (in Adelaide) the Jindyworobak Club, dedicated to the renaissance of a national flavour in poetry. The *Jindyworobak Anthologies* provided a vehicle for the publication of the work of new poets, and the sponsorship of many books of verse was a factor in establishing Adelaide as a significant creative publishing centre.

The self-consciousness and exaggeration of earlier decades was no longer so evident, but the search for a sounder base was extending. Ingamells set out the problem of interpretation in this way:

> Inextricably interwoven with the transplanted European culture are our own experiences of Australian environment. How far we and this environment have changed and reacted through contact, we owe to self-honesty to understand, and such an understanding can arise properly only through cultural expression.

In art, a more robust Australia was coming to the fore in the work of landscapists. The rich colours of the great inland were at last being added to those of the soft-toned pallette traditionally used by the Australian school of impressionist landscape painters. Watercolourists, on field trips to the Centre, began to find new inspiration in the brilliant colours and unusual forms of the landscape. Australian art was breaking out of its old restraining mould, and soon use of richer colours absorbed from the inland landscapes were having an effect on painting in general.

More important for the future was the work of George Bell, an inspirational Melbourne art teacher who introduced the principles of the post-impressionist European painters to his students, a group of whom founded the Contemporary Art Society in Melbourne in 1938. In the following year the Melbourne *Herald* backed a project to bring to Australia a large and important collection of modern European paintings; it was a revelation and an inspiration to young painters.

The cultural base in Australia was still extremely narrow, however, and men or women capable of outstanding cultural achievement felt compelled to move out into the greater world. In cultural affairs, Australians as a people, as Brian Fitzpatrick noted at the time, were still "almost incredibly unsophisticated." The critic might have added that this was an inevitable result of living in a remote and still-raw land where pioneering in one shape or another had still to be done.

The old gulf between those thinking in terms of acceptance by Australians and those seeking acceptance in the world at large had scarcely narrowed. Most of the Australian achievement, in itself, could not yet be taken seriously; Australian history was barely recognized as a subject for academic study, and the bulk of Australian writing and painting could be dismissed as provincial or substandard. Yet, as Percy Reginald Stephensen noted at the time in *The Foundation of Culture in Australia*, it was "astonishing, but true" that Australians were among the foremost historical novelists and antiquarians in England. Stephensen noted that names in fiction—Henry Handel Richardson (whose *Fortunes of Richard Mahony* had been described in 1930 by the *Saturday Review of Literature*, in New York, as "the soundest accomplishment of English fiction in the twentieth century"), Helen Simpson, Jack Lindsay, Philip Lindsay, and Christina Stead, pianist Eileen Joyce, sculptors Sir Bertram Mackennal and Maurice Lambert, all with great reputations, were Australians, while other like Will Dyson and Henry Mayo Bateman (and adopted-Australian David Low) were household names in England for their work in pen and pencil. The number and variety of successful Australians abroad, Stephensen admitted, could be "welcomed as a gratifying sign that our country can produce genius and talent in many spheres"; but Australia had the reputation of being "the country that produces geniuses for export—and kills them slowly but surely if they stay here." By accepting this drain on brains, Australia was the loser, and Stephensen, himself a Rhodes scholar, made an anguished plea that "the creative intellectual worker" be given a better social and economic position in Australia.

Visitors were usually surprised to find that Australia's culture remained so firmly bound up in its English swaddling clothes. Isaac Kandel, Professor of Journalism at New York's Columbia University, observed this during a visit in 1938, and commented that Australians' unquestioned loyalty to Britain ("to which every Australian, even though he has never been nearer to it than through his grand-parents, refers to as 'home' ") was inhibiting creative thinking. Kandel found it regrettable that the successful Australian to win favour in his own country must first find success abroad—because, he said, "by that time he has frequently gone to London and stayed there."

As a more enlightened and widespread interest in the Australian environment developed, Australians became more deeply conscious of their responsibilities to people of primitive culture, and increasingly there was discussion on the status of the Aborigines.

Over much of the continent, the Aborigines had disappeared entirely; but a census taken in 1930 showed that there were more than 61,000 full-bloods and almost 18,000 half-castes. The tribal groups survived mainly in the remoter areas of the north and west; there, and in the desert areas, nearly 40,000 shy primitives were still living as nomads. Considerable numbers of the Aborigines were receiving some help from governments. At the same time, Aborigines were being accepted for employment on cattle stations over a wide area in greater numbers, and the census showed that almost 11,000 were in regular employment of some kind.

A few had made a transition to the white man's world—for example, the Aboriginal drover whom the author Arthur Upfield met in the early 1930s near the Darling River. As the man cantered over to the car, Upfield noticed that he was wearing polished elastic-side riding boots, white moleskin trousers, a khaki shirt and a wide-brimmed hat; on one finger was a diamond ring and between his teeth was clamped the stem of a silver-mounted pipe. Such examples of Aborigines who had successfully moved up from the primitive state were very few and far between; but at the same time, the Aborigines could no longer be shunned or ignored.

For many years—the dominant thought behind official policy had been that the Aborigines—both the remaining tribes and those of mixed blood—should be protected from contact with white civilization, since such contact in the past had been disastrous. Accordingly, as part of this benevolent protection, large reservations had been created in remoter parts of the continent, and only missionaries and officials were allowed to enter them. Aboriginal Protection Boards in each of the states and in the Northern Territory exercised general supervision over the reserves and over Aboriginal employment in general. One of the most important and persuasive advocates of this approach was the remarkable Irish-born writer and social worker Mrs Daisy Bates, who had been working among Aboriginal groups in both Western and South Australia from the turn of the century. Mrs Bates had fed and clothed the young and the old and the infirm in the groups with whom she had come in contact, and the tribal people felt a deep affection for the frail little woman whose counsel was accepted by the authorities in both states (where a large percentage of the tribal folk lived).

Comparatively little field work had been done and knowledge of the Aborigines remained meagre. Sir Baldwin Spencer and Francis James Gillen had shown in their books of a generation earlier that the Aborigines enjoyed a rich tribal life and that the tribe was really a dynamic social phenomenon; their writings had revealed the importance that could be attached to research by scientifically trained people among tribes whose way of life had not been seriously disturbed. Spencer, who spent 1912 as Chief Protector of the Aborigines in the Northern Territory, had recommended to the government a policy of strict segregation on reserves while this was still feasible. The Cambridge University expedition of 1910–11, which Mrs Bates accompanied, had done valuable work in the desert area east of Geraldton, but the lack of soundly-directed research on a continuing basis had held back a better appreciation of the general problem of the survival of the Aborigines as a people.

The Pan Pacific Science Congress of 1923 recommended that a systematic study should be made of the Aboriginal population without delay. Support for this proposal came from the National Research Council, and in 1925 a Department of Anthropology was initiated at Sydney University under Professor Adolphus Peter Elkin, whose crusading zeal had made him the best-known advocate of a better deal for the Aborigines. Both teaching and organized research began at the university in 1926. At the same time, a Board of Anthropological Research was set up in Adelaide. Funds to sustain field investigations were obtained from research foundations in the United States.

Conferences and commissions of inquiry were opening the Aboriginal question to public scrutiny, and throwing light on the problems arising out of the contact of white and black. As anthropologists returned from field trips and told of the humanity, courtesy, and intelligence of the Aborigines, the old attitude of scorn—or, at best, bland curiosity—began to be replaced. There was a quickening of interest among interested groups as debates in the League of Nations stressed the "sacred trust" held by civilized peoples in their care of primitives.

As the work being done in New Guinea mandated territory became better known, the merits of the old "reservation" policy for Aborigines was increasingly debated; it was argued that by now contact between the peoples had gone so far, the Aborigines' way of life had undergone such change, and the attraction drawing the Aborigines towards the European community had proved so strong, that such a policy could not be carried out successfully, even in remote areas. A succession of clashes between settlers and Aborigines in the Northern Territory, in which harsh judicial sentences were recorded against Aborigines, aroused public opinion. Gradually the idea of maintaining the Aborigine in isolation gave way to a policy of accepting (although not, as yet, actively encouraging) contact with the tribespeople as a first step towards their advancement and ultimate absorption within the community.

Two investigations into the conditions of Aborigines in the Northern Territory (where about one-third of the surviving Aborigines were to be found) had far-reaching effects on policy and administration. One was made by a man who had long experience of native administration, the other by an anthropologist. In 1929 John William Bleakley, Queensland's chief protector of Aborigines, surveyed the situation as it applied to half-caste and detribalized Aborigines in employment and in missions and government institutions; six years later Dr Donald Ferguson Thomson investigated the conditions of the tribal natives of Arnhem Land. Recommendations from both men for a more positive approach to the Aborigines' future were absorbed in official policy. In 1937 the Department of the Interior proclaimed new goals for Aborigines in the Northern Territory, based on the conviction that with appropriate health, housing, education, and employment measures they could ultimately be assimilated into the ordinary life of the community. From that time, federal and state administrators met regularly to exchange views and coordinate policies. Assimilation was accepted as the ultimate goal even for the tribal native, although there was no question of its immediate application to primitive tribespeople. In February 1939 Ernest William Pearson Chinnery, an administrator with long experience in New Guinea, was appointed Director of Native Affairs in the Northern Territory (the dropping of the word protector from his title was symbolic of the changed attitude) and the first district patrol officers soon began their duties.

By now, all those concerned with Aboriginal affairs in the various states were meeting much more frequently, the principle that assimilation was the goal had been accepted by all state governments, and the first steps had been taken in the direction of applying the principle in legislative and administrative action.

By 1933 it was apparent that fundamental changes had taken place in the economy. There had been a marked lowering in the standard of living. Currency depreciation had made it possible for the economy to stabilize at a lower level. The money market was more flexible, there was reduced and more carefully regulated public investment, and the burden of fixed interest charges had been lessened. Factory output had expanded, but the terms of international trade were still strongly against Australia. When a very favourable season in 1932–33 helped lift export production to a point some 30 per cent above the pre-depression level, it was clear that some progress was being made on the road to recovery. In order to improve the marketing of rural products overseas and at the same time secure a greater measure of co-ordination between the federal and state governments in plans for agricultural development, the Agricultural Council was set up in 1934; its members were the federal minister for commerce and the state ministers of agriculture. The council met each year to lay down and co-ordinate general policies in primary production—a function made more significant as boards were set up, under federal auspices, to control overseas marketing of various commodities.

For the three years of the first Lyons ministry the rift between the Country party and the United Australia party continued. The tariff issue now seemed less divisive than Lyons' insistence that in any ministry under his leadership policy questions would have to be decided at joint party meetings. The Country party was firmly committed to its traditional policy of a separate existence, and Page informed Lyons that he would not consider his offer of participation in a composite ministry without "clear understandings about policy and satisfactory safeguards" to this end. Nevertheless, by mid-1934, with an election in sight, Lyons was openly advocating "a complete union of the two Parties" as the only permanent and satisfactory solution. Page refused to entertain the merger suggestions, and although an electoral pact was concluded it was apparent that a wide divergence of opinion existed on many issues.

The Labor party meanwhile had been rebuilding its strength, and it had gone some of the way towards substantiating that in general the measures it had adopted in the dark days of the depression—and other proposals in which the party had been thwarted by a hostile Senate—had been, in fact, sound. Internal discord continued within the party, but the slowness of the recovery under the United Australia party had disappointed many who had rushed to vote for Lyons, and it was clear that Labor, in a chastened mood, was regaining support in the electorate. The theme of most political discussions turned on the obvious need to provide for the individual citizen—particularly the wage earner—some means of protection against the vagaries of economic collapse. Discussion hinged on two lines of approach —one related to the strengthening of the nation's economic fabric through improved regulatory techniques while the other related to the provision of basic personal protection for the individual through social security measures such as unemployment insurance. The same issues were being debated abroad, and both aspects of the problem had earnest and vocal advocates in the Australian community.

A surprising number of people were now listening to new and radical monetary theories spread by speakers and pamphleteers supporting the "social credit" concepts enunciated in Canada by Major Clifford Hugh Douglas, a Scottish engineer with his own recipe for social reform within the capitalist system. In the general election of December 1934, candidates supporting Douglas' "social credit" ideas polled an unexpected total of over 170,000 votes, and although they did not gain a single seat the strength of their electoral support indicated an aroused concern in the community at the inadequacy of measures to ensure at least one of the radical party's aims: "political liberty with economic security."

Labor campaigners also had emphasized banking and finance policy, and in the election Labor gained nine seats. The United Australia party was reduced to thirty-two members while the Country party (which lost only one seat) had fifteen members. Lyons no longer had an absolute majority, and a composite ministry seemed unavoidable, In the negotiations to form a coalition Lyons had to give in to Page on a number of issues, including the principle of representation of the two parties in cabinet in direct proportion to their parliamentary strength.

The demand for a system of national insurance as a protection against unemployment was becoming more insistent, and the Lyons government attempted to meet it. A fundamental cleavage on the issue existed within the ministry. In 1929 the Bruce-Page government had brought forward a national insurance bill but it had been shelved, and support for the proposal was still mixed. "Progressives" in the United Australia party favoured national insurance as a sound measure in step with the times, but Country party ministers opposed it since in their view it was more important to make things safe for the man on the land than it was to adopt policies that might pamper the wage-earner while placing extra burdens on the community in general. The clash within the cabinet on this and other issues became sharper.

The course of the second and third Lyons ministries was marked by growing tensions as ambitious men thrust their way forward. Three young Victorians who were to play significant roles in the country's affairs over the next thirty years or so had moved into the political arena—Robert Gordon Menzies, Richard Gardiner Casey, and Harold Edward Holt. Both Menzies and Casey had strong support within the political machine headquartered in Melbourne, and both were exerting pressure on their leader. Lyons found himself caught between them and other United Australia men on one side and, on the other, Country party ministers who showed equally great personal ambition but less ability. Lyons' response to a difficult situation was to undertake a series of cabinet reconstructions—a procedure which in 1937 was described by John Curtin, who had succeeded Scullin as Labor leader, as the Prime Minister's "most popular pastime ... the game of political musical chairs."

A brilliant advocate and debater, Menzies had already gained the eye of influential businessmen, and he was being freely spoken of as the next Prime Minister. Lyons, ailing and deeply concerned at the prospect of war, moved to set up a "senior group" within the cabinet to deal with government policy on major matters of national significance. The formation of an inner cabinet immediately touched off a new round of disagreement, and dissension was reported to be widespread. Cabinet meetings were being thrown into turmoil, the newspapers said, because Menzies took every opportunity to score off the Country party. In March 1939, with the ministry in a state of chronic chaos, Menzies resigned from the cabinet, giving as his reason the cabinet's final abandonment of the national insurance plan.

When Lyons died after a short illness a few weeks later, a period of confusion followed. Page, as Deputy Prime Minister, was sworn into succeed him, but it was generally agreed that Page would act only as a caretaker until the United Australia party elected a new leader to replace Lyons. Page fervently wanted Bruce to return from London, re-enter politics, and become Prime Minister; in this he was supported by Casey, who saw in Bruce the only individual "under whom the united and full effort of Australia can be achieved." Bruce, in reply to Page's urgent overtures, said he would become Prime Minister only if granted the widest powers in choosing his ministers; and in the light of the unworkable conditions he imposed, the idea of drawing Bruce back into politics faded completely. As Page had feared, Menzies was chosen as the new leader of the United Australia party, and he was then commissioned to form a new government.

Page launched an unprecedented personal attack on Menzies, and made it clear that because of the "change in relationship of the two Parties" that had occurred, the Country party would not participate in the new government. Menzies, he said, lacked the qualities of "courage, loyalty and judgment" needed in view of the danger of war. Curtin, speaking as leader of the Opposition, said that personal antagonisms had been one of the most important factors in making orderly government in Australia almost impossible over the preceding two years.

Out of the great debate on how to provide greater economic security without the sacrifice of personal liberty that had raged throughout the depression years, a new understanding was emerging of the role of a socially-conscious government in the orderly directing of economic affairs. At the same time, the mechanics of control were being studied. In all English-speaking countries, the end of *laissez-faire* as an economic doctrine had been accepted or was in sight, and a new understanding of the interaction of governments' money and credit policies was beginning to spread; and although the old conservatism was to live on in the corners of men's minds, measures to provide a greater degree of control over the economy (and over individuals' lives) were being accepted.

In Britain, the United States, and Canada, and elsewhere, sharp shrinkage of economic activity had left serious rents, and in the urgent study old policies were brought under serious scrutiny. The mystery element in monetary policy was greatly reduced with the publication in 1935 of John Maynard Keynes' *General Theory of Employment, Interest and Money*, which explained the interdependence of these factors. Keynes' analysis showed, in essence, that in a market economy the level of production and employment would always be determined by the level of spending: spending, that is, by households, by firms and businesses, and by public authorities and governments. This analysis of income and employment indicated ways in which effective control over economic activity might be exercised by governments. Keynes showed that if monetary credit and other financial policies were properly adjusted, a level of spending could be achieved which would be sufficient to employ the whole of the labour and other resources of the economy. The newly-acquired understanding led to a new appreciation of the importance of monetary policy, and it provided guidelines whereby policy-makers could produce certain general improvements or corrections in the economy. Although the Keynesian analysis came after the depression's effects were mitigated, it was the light on the hill by which economic policy-makers would chart their course in the future. It provided an appreciation of the constructive role that government might play in developing less depression-prone and more prosperous economies.

It was natural that the Australian Labor party should relish the evidence it found in the Keynesian theory for its own policies of social advancement. The party had nurtured a feeling that the banks' refusal to co-operate had spoiled the chances of the Scullin government's attempts to cope with the depression in Theodore's way. Over its period of travail the party had steadily been coming to realize the need for it to develop a more mature outlook on banking and finance and many related subjects. The party saw the role of the Commonwealth Bank as crucial; and although from time to time its proposals for the reorganization of banking changed quite considerably, the emphasis was on the reconstruction of the bank's management with the object of producing a more realistic co-ordination between the policies of the government and the bank. The party believed events had proved that the authority of the central bank over the private banks should be strengthened, and that the influence on the banks' policy exerted by representatives of private commercial and financial organizations should be removed. Some independent economists, and a few of the young men in banking, agreed that there was now a real need to distinguish between banking as a normal commercial function and the great social responsibilities that proper management of monetary and credit policy entailed.

Largely as a result of Labor's persistence in stressing banking policy as the key to reconstruction, a Royal Commission was set up in 1935 to study the subject. Its report, issued in 1937, indicated that the national interest would best be served by preserving the system of privately-owned banks, but it also proposed that the central bank should be strengthened. The report also stressed the need for closer identification of central banking policy with Treasury policy. In general, the report supported the contention that a more sophisticated banking system was needed and that the system should make it possible for the government's monetary and credit policies to prevail. The Lyons government, riven by discord and with many other issues before it, was content to put the report aside.

The final say in economic affairs was in the hands of four main agencies: the Loan Council and three largely-independent bodies, each operating under federal control—the Tariff Board, the Arbitration Court, and the Commonwealth Bank. The lessened role of the states and the accelerating process of centralization—arising, partly, from the conditions of the depression—were arousing new misgivings, especially on the part of the less populous states, South Australia, Western Australia, and Tasmania, where it was believed that the domination of the big states was acting against their interests. In financial relationships, the federal government had come to exercise undisputed dominance; its overriding power, first defined as a result of the financial agreement of 1928 and subsequently sustained by the High Court, had been strengthened further as a result of the Financial Agreements Act of 1932 under which it dealt with the recalcitrant premier of New South Wales. For many years the less populous states had chafed under protection—a policy which they believed favoured only the more industrialized states—and from the 1920s the position had been reviewed, first by the Tariff Board and then by a Royal Commission appointed by Bruce to inquire into the effects of federation on the finances of South Australia, Tasmania, and Western Australia. The depression aggravated the difficulties, and Western Australia in particular was vocal in claiming that its interests were being sacrificed. Its chief plaint was that high tariffs damaged its economy and benefited only the manufacturing states in the east.

The majority report of the 1924 Royal Commission had recommended that tariff autonomy be granted Western Australia for twenty-five years; but this proposal would have involved the State's virtual withdrawal from the Federation and it was as unacceptable as the minority report which favoured outright seccession. State political leaders continued to press for redress of Western Australia's difficulties, however, and in April 1933 a popular referendum was held in the state. The vote was nearly two-to-one in favour of secession from the Federation, and a deputation was sent to Westminster with a petition seeking legislation to enable Western Australia's withdrawal. The request was particularly embarrassing to Westminster since it had been recognized in 1926 that the Commonwealth of Australia held equal status with the United Kingdom; accordingly the petition was referred to a joint select committee of Lords and Commons for advice. Within a few weeks of the state referendum, the federal government created the Commonwealth Grants Commission, with power to aid states on the principle of need.

Two years later, when the Lords-Commons committee reported that no secession action could be taken (except at the Commonwealth's request), the matter of Western Australia's withdrawal from the Federation was shelved. Meanwhile the Grants Commission had been looking into the effect of tariffs on the smaller states and had concluded that there were valid grounds for complaint; increased grants from the federal Treasury were approved as a means of offsetting any disability they might suffer.

Defence—and war 22

William Morris Hughes' successful sallies into the international arena at the Paris peace conference were not emulated by his successors in office. In the 1920s Australians, snug in their vast cocoon, wanted nothing more than to see every nation minding its own business, and, although they welcomed the evidence of an enlarged American role in the Pacific, they took no special interest in foreign affairs. Far removed from tension areas—or so it seemed—and preoccupied with their own affairs, Australians remained unaware of the speed and violence of the changes that were taking place on the world stage.

Although the stiff peace terms imposed by the Allies at Versailles tended to mask the fact, World War I had hastened the relative decline in British power that had been taking place ever since the turn of the century. Henceforth membership in the British fraternity was, of necessity, to involve co-operation and interdependence rather than protection—but awareness of this significant change was to come slowly to Australians, to whom Britain's divine right of leadership still appeared axiomatic. Memories of the strength of British arms, the ever present evidence of British industry and British markets for exports, the prestige of British institutions, combined with the strong loyalty to the Crown and to British ideals in general, made it inevitable that most Australians would be happy to see the framing of foreign policy left in firm British hands.

The war had been the forcing-house for far-reaching changes in the conduct of the Empire's foreign policy. With its Dominions representation, the Imperial War Cabinet had provided a means of joint consultation in the creation of policy. The desirability of direct contact between Dominion prime ministers and the British government on a continuing basis had been urged by Hughes, and in July 1918 the Imperial War Cabinet had agreed that in important matters the various prime ministers should have the right to contact the British government directly, rather than through the medium of the Governor-General and the Colonial Office.

Thanks largely to the initiative of Sir Robert Borden, the Canadian Prime Minister, and the able backing of South Africa's Jan Smuts, as well as the forceful advocacy of Hughes, the Dominions had been accorded individual representation, within the British delegation, at the Versailles peace conference, and the same procedure had been followed in the Washington conference, where Senator George Pearce signed the naval treaties as chief Australian delegate.

The Dominions' new status in international affairs was acknowledged by their separate signing of the peace treaties and their separate membership of the League of Nations.

Problems of foreign policy were freely discussed at the Imperial conference of 1921, the first conference at which the Dominion Prime Ministers were invited to co-operate in formulating an Imperial foreign policy. Lloyd George dramatized the new state of affairs in a speech in the House of Commons, declaring that "the whole control of British foreign policy is now vested in the Empire as a whole," although at the same time he noted that

> ... the machinery [of foreign policy-making] must remain here [in Britain] ...
> The instrument of foreign policy of the Empire is the British Foreign Office.

Throughout, Hughes had been at pains to maintain the right of direct communication with the British Government, and when it seemed desirable to do so he had by-passed the Governor-General and the Dominions desk in London. At the 1921 conference—where he used his considerable influence to impress upon the British government Australia's special interests in regard to the future of Egypt and the Anglo-Japanese Alliance—he stressed the need for continuing consultation and discussion in the formulation of a joint common policy. The belief that the principle of consultation was fully established was rather disturbed by the Chanak incident of September 1922, when a cable asking whether the Dominions would be prepared to send contingents in the event of war with Turkey was the first intimation of foreign policy decisions that had led Britain to the brink of war.

Prime Minister Bruce, who said after this incident that if Australia were to take any responsibility for the Empire's foreign policy there must be a better system of consultation so that Australia's views would be taken into account, raised the matter of "improvement in the machinery and habit of consultation" at the Imperial Conference of 1923. He expressed the view that regular and more frequent Imperial conferences were necessary to lay down policy on major questions; from that point, decisions would be departed from by Britain only after consultation with the Dominions. He suggested to the conference that consultation might be assisted by the creation of an Imperial secretariat and by the appointment by each Dominion of a resident minister in London or of liaison officers to work within the British Foreign Office.

The proposal for resident ministers got nowhere, but in 1924 Bruce sent

Richard Gardiner Casey to London as liaison officer. Casey's task was simply to keep the Australian Government better informed of developments. The move did not represent any appreciable step towards the creation of a distinctive approach to foreign affairs. Rather, the innovation sought to fit Australia's interests more snugly into a niche in Britain's international relations.

Pressure for definition of Dominion rights had not come from Australia: rather the reverse. Bruce's main stress had been placed on aspects of Empire co-operation and integration—particularly dispersal of population from Britain to the Dominions and the development of stronger trading relations within the Empire.

The report of the 1923 conference recognized that it was "now established practice" for the Dominions and India to be separately represented as part of the British delegation to any international conference. It broke new ground by recognizing the right of the Dominions independently to negotiate and sign treaties with foreign powers, a right first exercised earlier in the year by Canada when it concluded a fishery treaty with the United States. A start was made towards solving the many problems involved in a joint foreign policy by passage of a resolution laying down principles to be followed in the negotiation, signature, and ratification of treaties. The resolution enjoined on each of the governments of the Empire the obligation to consider whether the interests of any other part of the Empire might be affected by its negotiation of a treaty, and to give the governments concerned the opportunity of expressing their views and possibly of participating in the negotiations.

Consultation within the Empire to resolve matters of concern was one thing; the provision of hard sinews of defence for a far-flung empire was another. The 1923 Imperial conference did its best to cope with the problems that had come with the ending of Britain's old dominance. Britain had emerged from the war too impoverished to maintain a capital-ship construction programme, leaving great issues within the framework of Imperial defence to be solved. The British government had announced in 1921 that it could no longer guarantee the naval protection of the Empire. Reflecting Westminster's mood of sober acceptance of Britain's shrunken role the Dominion prime ministers made the best of an unhappy situation by accepting the principle that henceforth each portion of the Empire would take primary responsibility for its own defence. At the same time, Britain undertook to make provision for safeguarding the Empire's communications, and promised that naval bases and facilities would be created for repair and fuelling of warships in order to maintain the mobility of the fleets.

The Washington naval treaty of 1922 and the accompanying Four-Power treaty had attested to the contraction of British power in the Pacific, ending hopes in Australia and New Zealand that a British fleet might again be established there. In their negotiations in Washington the Japanese had struck a hard bargain: in return for promised limitations on naval battle-strength, Britain had agreed, along with the United States, not to strengthen any existing defences in the western Pacific. The treaty parcelled out the oceans of the world into what were, in effect, spheres of maritime influence, with the United States controlling the north-eastern Pacific and the western Atlantic, Britain the eastern Atlantic and the Indian ocean, and Japan the the western Pacific. For Australia and New Zealand, poised uneasily in a kind of no-men's land between the Japanese and British spheres, the situation was far from satisfactory.

The Royal Navy was without a base in the Pacific area capable of maintaining a battle fleet. The Admiralty came to the conclusion that a major base must be constructed somewhere along the outer perimeter of its sphere of eastern influence. The choice was narrowed to Sydney and Singapore, and late in 1922 Singapore was chosen—on the grounds that it was closer to other strategic centres of Britain's line of defence. Early in 1923 plans for the construction of a major naval base at Singapore were debated in the British parliament, where opinion was divided on party lines, with Labor and Liberal members opposed. The wisdom of committing huge sums (£10,500,000 was the estimated cost) for construction of a base at a time of economic uncertainty was questioned, and latent feelings that such a move was a negation of the League convenant and of the disarmament treaties were aroused. In Australia, Prime Minister Bruce indicated that his government approved the proposal; but he did not offer—as some newspapers suggested he should—to contribute to the cost of creating the base.

At the Imperial Conference of 1923 Australia and New Zealand supported the Singapore concept; the report of the conference mentioned that the two southern Dominions, as well as India, had expressed "deep interest" in the project. Preliminary work on the base was begun; but almost immediately the whole undertaking suffered a setback when, in December 1923, Ramsay MacDonald's Labour administration took office at Westminster and decided to stop Singapore expenditures "for the time being." The dangers of the situation for Australia were increasingly apparent, and rather than await the final outcome Bruce approved a major move to build up Australia's own naval force. To replace the two old cruisers, *Sydney* and *Melbourne*, two new 10,000-ton cruisers were ordered (they were named *Australia* and *Canberra* when they joined the squadron in 1929) as well as two submarines, a seaplane carrier, and a floating dock.

Before the end of 1924 Labour was displaced at Westminster and the incoming government ordered resumption of work on the Singapore base. This decision was welcomed in Australia; one newspaper now hailed Singapore as "more than ever the keystone of the Empire's safety;" but the Bruce-Page government, adhering to the view that the base was Britain's responsibility, refused to contribute to the cost, as New Zealand was now doing.

The setting up of the Irish Free State in December 1921, with Dominion status, had brought to the fore the question of the precise constitutional position implied by such status. One anomaly seemed to be that Dominion affairs were still dealt with by a division of the Colonial Office. For some time the British press had urged that the new status of the Dominions should be acknowledged by the creation of a separate department to deal with dominion affairs as distinct from those of the colonies, and in 1925 a new Dominions Office was created. The first Dominions Secretary, Leopold Stennett Amery, noted the need to

> ... recognise the importance due to Dominion questions and to remove any lingering suspicion that the Dominions were still dealt with by officials accustomed to the bureaucratic control of subordinate dependencies.

The fact that the same minister held both the Colonial and the Dominions Secretaryships tended to reduce the effectiveness of the separation, but the Dominions Office was soon acting as a clearing-hourse for an increasing flow of communications on matters arising from the conduct of foreign affairs.

For most Australians interested in the matter, creation of the new office was more than enough evidence of the status and rights of the self-governing Dominions. There was no concerted pressure or informed opinion seeking any major revision of the views on foreign and defence policy expressed by the Prime Minister, who believed implicitly that Australia could best exert a desire for peace through Empire consultation; and, although he had earlier expressed some misgivings lest misguided foreign policy impose "unescapable obligations" on Australia, Bruce held to his formula of giving first priority to the maintaining of a united Empire. Greater activity in foreign affairs could be most effective, he believed, if it were directed towards the creation of an effective Empire voice; beyond that, he urged the closest possible relationships between the British nations and the United States, as well as support for the League of Nations.

All things considered, it seemed that in a world of growing tensions Australia might well make its most useful contribution to the cause of a strong Empire through the rapid development of its resources, and might assuage land-hungry nations by filling up its empty spaces, by now considered a standing invitation to aggressors. Similarly in matters of defence there was an emphasis on interdependence and a strong measure of reliance on Britain.

Meanwhile, in foreign affairs an increasing divergence of views among the Dominions was making it more difficult than ever to develop a cogent and coherent policy. The views of Canada and South Africa, in particular, were often found to differ quite widely from those held by Australia and New Zealand. There was already talk of preparation for war; Germany was rearming and Japan, by-passing the limitations of the Washington treaties, was engaged in a big naval construction programme. In the League of Nations, collective security was the paramount theme.

By 1925 the Dominions had largely detached themselves from responsibility for the creation of foreign policy; the generally-accepted formula was that the Dominions would leave the responsiblity for foreign policy with Britain, and would be free to decide for themselves what degree of support they would give if this policy led to war. An escape clause was inserted in the Locarno treaty of mutual guarantee, signed in October 1925; it took the form of a specific provision that no obligation was placed upon any of the Dominions or upon India "unless the government of such dominion, or of India, signifies its acceptance of the Locarno Treaty." Australia was not anxious to see the proviso included, and the notion of separate responsiblity was not taken far.

By this time, however, the Labor party was coming out with a plea that Australia should avoid commitments and rely on the League of Nations. The Opposition leader, Matthew Charlton, said in the Labor party's policy speech in 1925:

> The Labor party stands for an Australian policy, developed in Australia in the light of day; developed for a people and by a people who are determined to uphold the rights which properly belong to a nation and honest enough to admit that other nations have coequal rights. It will prize self-determination not merely for itself, but as the heritage of all men in all lands.

In August 1926, speaking on the agenda for the Imperial conference, Charlton took issue with the desire which Bruce's proposals expressed for a "change in policy whereby Australia will have a voice in foreign affairs." Charlton stressed that his view did not imply any lack of loyalty to Britain; if at any time a crisis made it necessary for Australia to play its part alongside the mother-country, as it had done in the past, he had no doubt what Australia's decision would be. Nevertheless, he saw no reason why Australia should become a party to agreements relating entirely to European affairs. "Australia," he declared, "cannot afford to become embroiled in the concerns of Europe." Similarly, he feared lest Australia should become involved in troubles arising from the business of British investors; disputes that could arise from commercial causes would be enough to threaten the disruption of the Empire.

The attitudes of the two parties towards defence were in line with their attitudes towards foreign policy. In 1926 Bruce, echoing the principles of a resolution passed by the Imperial Conference of 1923, summarized the government's views thus:

> On the question of Imperial defence, the attitude of Australia is that we believe that the local defence of each portion of the Empire is primarily a matter of local concern, but that this principle can and must be applied in conformity with a general plan of Imperial co-operation. We believe that the safeguarding of the routes and waterways along and through which the armed forces and trade of the Empire pass cannot be secured without the provision of adequate naval facilities in the Pacific and the construction of a first class naval base at Singapore. We regard such a base as vital to the preservation of Empire interests in this quarter of the globe.

Labor Party leaders on the other hand, usually protested against increased expenditure on defence; such expenditures were characterized as a waste of money, a repudiation of the covenant of the League and the obligation to disarm, and an act of preparation for war. In this, Labor spokesmen were following the same lines as British Labour and European social democratic parties, with emphasis on disarmament under the League of Nations as the best insurance against war.

In speaking of the possibility of creating a distinctive Australian policy, Charlton was striking at the very basis of the unity which his political opponents had been declaring to be the "vital principle of the Empire." Clinging to the Empire-first concept, the Nationalists and the Country party dramatized the issue by attacking Labor for "wanting to cut the painter with Britain," and their condemnation struck home. In the election of 1928 Labor adopted the tactic of soft-pedalling the issue of "self-determination," while Bruce played loudly the slogan of "Empire, and the maintenance of Law and Order."

The unexpected snap election that brought Labor to power in 1929 was confined to the arbitration issue, and the subject of foreign affairs was ignored in the campaign. Immediately after Labor's election to office the confusion caused by the economic collapse made any discussion of Australia's international relationships seem almost like a frivolous diversion from essential and pressing matters.

Solidarity with Britain and unity within the British Empire were still the guiding principles for most Australians, and belief in the invincible might of the British Commonwealth was strong. In 1929, Hughes the Imperialist, his voice far from stilled by the years, scathingly attacked the Australian Labor party for its earlier call for an independent policy. "Some people talk about the Empire as though its internal relations were those between a master and his slaves," Hughes wrote; but the plain truth was that Britain had gone on "stolidly tramping along its lonely beats, the policeman of the world, maintaining order and enabling peaceful nations to pursue their lawful occasions, a terror to evil-doers, a champion of the weak."

The impetus for formal recognition of the Dominions' new status which was achieved at the Imperial conference of 1926 came not from Australia but from Canada, South Africa, and the Irish Free State. A long history of bitterness and bloodshed had left in the Irish Free State a passionate insistence on its right to full constitutional equality with Britain. Canada, with its French-Canadian minority, and South Africa, with its population of non-British ancestry, felt the same. In Australia and New Zealand, where there was no minority or racial problem, there was no such demand, and the existing practice of partnership within the Empire was totally acceptable and unquestioned.

A special committee of the conference presided over by elder statesman Lord Balfour developed an important new formula defining the relations between Britain and the self-governing Dominions—Canada, Australia, New Zealand, South Africa, the Irish Free State, and Newfoundland. The committee's resolution, approved by the conference, became a declaration acknowledging that the Dominions and the United Kingdom were

> ... autonomous communities within the British Empire, equal in status, in no way subordinate one to another in any aspect of their domestic or external affairs, though united by common allegiance to the Crown and freely associated as members of the British Commonwealth of Nations.

Inevitably, the working out, in detail, of the abstract principle of equality of status and its "translation into the precise terms of positive law" was bound to be complicated—if only because the participating Dominions each had its own differing constitution. Inevitably many existing administrative, legislative, and judicial forms—survivals of colonial days—were not in harmony with the principle of equality. It was therefore recommended that an expert committee be set up to make detailed recommendations for giving legal definition to the changed Imperial relationships in a number of matters, the most important of which were the operation of the Colonial Laws Validity Act of 1865, the "reservation" of bills passed by Dominion legislatures, and the extra-territorial application of Dominion laws.

There was little reaction in Australia to the Balfour report, which seemed to editorial writers to represent no more than "an agreed and authoritative picture of the Empire as it is." A summary of the report was carried on the cable page of all newspapers, but only the Hobart *Mercury* published the text in full. This apparent lack of interest was noted by the Australian correspondent of *Round Table*, but he explained that the Australian attitude towards Imperial relations was neither frivolous nor indifferent. Rather, Australia was

> ... not interested in the dogmatic assertions of equality of status, for it has not been conscious of any inequality and considered that Australia was perfectly secure in whatever status it wanted.

Impatience over other Dominions' stress on the constitutional aspects of Empire development was widely held, and in newspapers the view was pressed on the government that it was both unnecessary and dangerous to try to give legal form to the constitutional standings on which Dominion status rested. Legal commentators emphasized the statements in the report that "the principles of equality and similarity, appropriate to status, do not universally extend to function," and that in the conduct of foreign policy and defence "the major share of responsibility rests now and must for some time continue to rest, with His Majesty's Government in Great Britain." This dominant viewpoint saw no contradiction in the Dominions being equal with Britain and yet leaving to London the chief responsibility for the conduct of foreign affairs and defence.

This interpretation was not shared by High Court judge Dr Herbert Vere Evatt, who denied that dissimilarity of function should be considered as a qualification upon equality of status. The distinction made in the report, Evatt said, could more properly be read as a distinction between the existence of Dominion power and the actual exercise of that power, the extent to which it might be exercised being a matter for determination by the Dominions themselves.

The prevailing Australian desire may have been nothing more than preservation of the status quo, but other Dominions were still less than satisfied with the situation. From a legal standpoint, Dominion legislatures did not in fact enjoy entire liberty of action, even in relation to their own internal affairs, since under the Colonial Laws Validity Act they were barred from repealing or amending any Imperial statutes extending to them, while certain types of bills were subject to "reservation" for the approval of the Crown. The Sovereign (acting on the advice of British ministers) retained the general power of disallowing any Dominion legislation, and the Dominions' power to legislate in the important matter of merchant shipping (including shipping in their own territorial waters) was narrowed by specific statues.

Recommendations on these matters were made by an expert legal-political committee representing Britain and all the Dominions which met in London late in 1929. The committee's report, issued in January 1930, gave a blueprint for enlargement of the powers of Dominion legislatures where present restrictions had proved to be practical grievances.

The recommendations, insofar as they required action by the British parliament, were carried into effect by the Statute of Westminster, passed in 1931. Under the statute, the Colonial Laws Validity Act no longer applied to "any law made after the commencement of this Act by the Parliament of a Dominion" (subject to the proviso that in Australia, New Zealand and Canada the existing law and pratice relating to constitutional amendment would be retained). Henceforth no Dominion legislation could be rendered inoperative because of conflict with enactments of the United Kingdom parliament, and substance was given to the established convention that Westminster would not legislate for any Dominion, except at its request and with its consent. The statute also provided that each Dominion's parliament had full power to make laws having extra-territorial operation.

Although not specifically dealt with in the statute, the position of Dominion governors also came under review at this time, and it was agreed that the appointment of a governor would henceforth be a matter for the Sovereign on the sole advice of the Dominion government concerned. Further, it was accepted that the governor was the representative of the Crown, and in no sense an agent of the United Kingdom government. Practical effect was given to this convention shortly afterwards when the Scullin Government pressed for and secured the appointment of Australian jurist Sir Isaac Isaacs as Governor-General.

The British parliament's enactment of the Statute of Westminster was if anything more regretted than welcomed in Australia. There were lingering fears that giving precise legal definition to the constitutional relations between Britain and the Dominion would be harmful; and so far as the government was concerned the whole matter was left in abeyance. It was not until 1936 that legislation was introduced into the federal parliament to adopt those sections of the Statute requiring specific approval; but the bill was not given a second reading, and again in 1937 a similar measure was allowed to lapse. It was not until 1942 that the Statute was adopted by the Australian parliament (with effect retroactive to September 3, 1939); and it was another five years before New Zealand accepted it.

However, one direct result of Australia's clearly-defined rights in extra-territorial matters was the move made in 1933 to accept responsibility for a vast tract of the ice-covered Antarctic continent. The borders of a territory covering almost 2,500,000 square miles were delineated and by an

Order of the King in Council made in London the territory was placed under Australia's control, the proclamation taking effect in August 1936.

In spite of the reluctance in Australia to do anything which might accelerate the new trend, the growing sense of separateness was also manifesting itself in the increasing number of treaties and trade agreements Canberra was making with foreign countries. In 1934 Sir Henry Gullett had been assigned the task of negotiating trade treaties and he had quickly discovered that European countries were convinced that measures taken by Australia under the Ottawa agreement had virtually closed Australia to their goods. Gullett reported in 1936 that the attitude and tendency throughout Europe was to exclude Australian products other than wool and to back scientific research aimed at finding wool substitutes. In order to reopen the channels of trade the government felt it essential to make concessions, and most-favoured-nation treatment was accorded, reciprocally, to Belgium, Czechoslovakia and France.

An independent foreign policy was still unthinkable in Canberra. Canada and the Irish Free State had appointed ministers to foreign countries, and received their ministers in return, but Australia had no inclination to follow their example. Not only were there obvious advantages in having the British voice strengthened to the greatest possible extent in days of challenge; equally important was the simple fact that the long period of tutelage had left Australian leaders and their advisers inexperienced in the handling of problems of foreign affairs. It was to be some years before the urge for a distinctive approach became imperative; and when, in the early 1940s, such a move became necessary Australia still had very limited resources in terms of skilled and knowledgeable people for the task.

Abroad, earlier hopes that law and justice would replace banditry and anarchy in international affairs were fading as the international situation worsened after the mid-1930s; but there was still little concern in Australia. Throughout, the initiative had remained with aggressor nations, and Australians felt powerless to affect the outcome. Britain's naval power had continued its relative decline; personnel in the Royal Navy in 1928 was far below the 1914 figure, and while the United States Navy's personnel had nearly doubled over the same period, the Japanese and Italian navies were growing fast and Germany's military power was being rebuilt quite rapidly.

Construction of the Singapore naval base had continued slowly. In 1928 a great floating dock capable of accommodating the largest of Britain's warships was completed on the Tyne and towed to Singapore, and in 1929 major contracts were let for engineering works and a graving dock, to be completed within seven years. Work was slowed when Labour was in office at Westminster in 1929 and there were world moves for naval limitation; Australia and New Zealand pressed for action but at the Imperial conference Prime Minister Scullin agreed that while construction of the base should not be abandoned it might be slowed down. Following a change of government in Britain in 1931 the construction rate was increased and the naval estimates for 1932 confirmed plans for the Singapore graving dock. In 1934 the Lyons Government embarked upon a developmental programme for the Australian squadron, purchasing the light cruiser *Sydney* from Britain and undertaking further construction of sloops and destroyers.

Japan's overrunning of Manchuria in 1931 was the opening round of a new phase of international terror-and-grab, but it resulted in nothing more than Japan's withdrawal from the League of Nations. Adopting new and frighteningly effective propaganda techniques, European dictators were meanwhile gaining wide acceptance in their own countries for villainous policies, and their wicked practices had been disguised to many people beyond their own borders by "the big lie." In 1935–36 Italy seized Abyssinia; and although the Commonwealth joined Britain in imposing economic sanctions against Italy the move was ineffective as a bar to aggression. By this time the Germans had gained air superiority. In March 1936 Hitler scrapped the Locarno treaties of 1925 by marching into the Rhineland; and failure of the Council of the League to take any action in rebuttal gave Hitler and others the green light to speed along the path of treaty-breaking and aggression. Civil war in Spain, beginning in 1936, provided opportunities for intervention by Germany, Italy and Russia. The following year Japan opened its attack on China proper.

It was becoming clear that Britain could not spare an adequate naval force for Australia's defence in the event of simultaneous trouble in Europe and the Pacific, and obviously the European situation was engaging practically all Whitehall's attention. Realization of the decay of British power in the Pacific created a sense of insecurity in Australia which was reinforced by the conclusion of the German-Japanese anti-Comintern pact of 1936. Soon afterwards, Frederic Eggleston, a respected commentator and correspondent, writing in *Pacific Affairs*, reflected a growing concern in Australia over possible involvement in military campaigns abroad when he stated that no issues except mere defence against invasion would ever be "clear enough to enable us to compel people to fight."

When Japan launched a major offensive against China in mid-1937 and Italy, the power most likely to threaten Britain's main sealane to the Pacific, joined the anti-Comintern pact a few months later, the situation became even more alarming. Yet throughout these years of crisis, events in Europe seemed to Australians to be more pressing than those of the western Pacific. This was due in part to the fact that practically all news came through London and therefore reflected priorities developed from a British standpoint. American news correspondents' reports from China appeared in some newspapers but little notice was taken either of them or of American commentators like Dorothy Parker (whose columns appeared in *Truth*) pressing for positive action to stem the tide of Japanese militarism.

Vacuous hopes that the threat from militant and expansion-minded nations could best be met by giving in to their demands were slowly replaced in Britain by a realization of the fact that Hitler's Germany constituted a greater menace than had the Germany of Wilhelm II or Napoleonic France. Divergent views within the British Commonwealth itself increased London's hesitancy; it was clear that bold action by Britain would be a double gamble: not only was it likely to fail because of lack of power, but it might have the further result of developing rifts and so disclosing a house divided. Britain found herself having to pocket her pride and tolerate "incidents" which at other times would almost surely have brought war.

At the conference of the prime ministers of all the British countries, held in London in 1937, the nature of the world threat was analysed, and Lyons returned to Canberra with a clear picture of the situation. In spite of pressure from Australia and New Zealand for the stationing of a British fleet in the Far East, the British government had reaffirmed its policy of maintaining its fleet in European waters, with a proviso that units would be sent to threatened areas as necessary. The main construction of the Singapore base had been completed, and naval manoeuvres had already been held for testing its defences; but there was growing concern among Australian military leaders that if Britain became involved in war in Europe the Admiralty would not be able to dispatch a significant naval force to the area. For the first time the Government saw a serious need to develop Australia's own sea defences against possible attack in order that the enemy might be "held at arm's length, and our shores maintained inviolate."

In August 1937, party attitudes to the defence issue were explained in parliament. Lyons indicated that the principal objective of the government's new defence policy was the protection of seaborne trade and the prevention of attack on Australia itself by raid or invasion. He added:

> It is an unavoidable geographical fact that [our] first line of defence . . . is naval, and if we expect a British fleet to be based on Singapore as a safeguard to Australia, we must be prepared to cooperate and provide for the squadron necessary in our own waters . . . Our defence rests on two pillars, one of which is our own maximum effort, and the other Empire co-operation.

The Labor party raised no objection to the substantial increase in defence expenditure. Its main criticism was directed against the policy of continued reliance on Britain—a policy line expressed earlier by Curtin when he declared that

> . . . the dependence of Australia upon the competence, let alone the readiness, of British statesmen to send forces to our aid is too dangerous a hazard upon which to found Australia's defence policy.

In the debate, and in the election campaign that followed in October 1937, Curtin (with the bulk of Labor opinion behind him) repudiated a declaration by the Australian Council of Trade Unions opposing the rearmament policy in favour of a policy of League-organized collective security. Curtin said he wanted to see Australia take the most effective steps possible to contribute to its capacity for effective defence; but at the same time he insisted that "in the final analysis" Australia should not be committed to warlike activities outside Australia without "the absolute and established consent" of the Australian people.

The Lyons government maintained the traditional policy of emphasizing that Australian defence would be chiefly naval and would dovetail with

Imperial policy. For its part the Labor party was questioning the value of increased expenditure on a navy which would range far and wide beyond Australia; instead, Labor maintained with increasing conviction, that more should be spent on air power capable of the direct defence of Australian territory in the event of an attempt being made to invade Australian soil.

To many voters it seemed as though Labor was suggesting a "go-it-alone" policy and in doing so was trying to shrug off real help without offering anything substantial in return. Labor's opponents were able to nurture the suspicion that such a policy might mean isolation from Britain. The electorate was sceptical, and although Labor made gains, the old government was returned to office.

As part of its active search for new or expanded markets for Australian commodities in the depression, the Lyons government had fostered closer trade relations with China, Japan, and other lands of the western Pacific region. Wool exports to Japan had grown consistently, China had been buying increased quantities of wheat, and the Netherlands East Indies had become a market for a wide range of goods. However, when the government came under pressure in 1936 to trim the flow of imports from Japan and other foreign countries, it adopted new tariff measures as part of a trade diversion policy to foster British commerce. The effect of this was to curb foreign imports. There was an immediate and hostile reaction in Japan, where retaliatory tariff and licensing measures were introduced and a boycott of Australian wool was imposed. About one-quarter of Australia's wool clip had been going to Japan, and wool-growers raised a loud cry against the government, increasing pressure (through the Country party) to have the policy modified. For months Japan was out of the wool market, and as other commodities were affected also, the volume of trade between the two countries fell away sharply. In the exchange Australia suffered most, for while imports from Japan were trimmed in a year from £A6,300,000 to £A5 million, exports to Japan dropped back from about £A18 million to under £A10 million.

Relations between Australia and Japan were affected by the fall in trade, but even more by a growing dislike of everything connected with Japan. Since the signature of the Japan-German anti-Comintern pact of 1936 and Japan's subsequent attack on China proper, Japan had been seen as an ever more threatening menace to Australia's security. The *Sydney Morning Herald*, reversing its earlier tolerant opinion, began to condemn Japanese policy in strong terms; in Melbourne the *Herald* denounced the bombing of Nanking as a war crime without precedent. Public demonstrations of protest against Japan's war actions were held, and there were demands for a boycott of all Japanese goods.

Generally, however, the succession of scare headlines and an absence of perceptive reporting had left Australians without a clear understanding of the situation. Jack Shepherd, writing of this period in *Australia's Interests and Policies in the Far East* (1940), noted the confused picture:

The nervousness, the indecision, the lack of continuity, the emotional sympathies, the conflicting hopes and fears, and even the incomplete knowledge of the facts which characterized popular reactions to the war in the Far East had their counterparts in the attitude of the Australian Government.

One of the proposals that emerged was that of a regional pact for the Pacific—some new collective system for maintaining order to replace that embodied in the defunct Washington treaties. At the Imperial conference of 1937 Lyons had put forward the idea, declaring that Australia would welcome "a regional understanding and a pact of non-aggression . . . conceived in the spirit and principles of the League." The proposal was left in the sketchiest form, however, and although some interest was expressed by the Soviet Union and Japan, as well as by British leaders, it fell out of view when the overt Japanese move was made against China.

A section of public opinion was now strong against trade with Japan, particularly insofar as it involved the export of materials such as scrap iron which might be used for the production of munitions. (One newspaper writer declared that it worried him to think of his old iron bedstead being transformed into a gun and used one day to shoot him.) The government refused to consider general sanctions against Japan—they had failed against Italy—since it believed they would be both futile and dangerous; but waterside workers who were handling the materials in question decided to take matters into their own hands.

A boycott on the loading of tin scrap began early in 1938 and dragged on for months. The govenment appealed to the waterside workers to "leave matters of foreign policy to the government," but those assigned to handle the scrap refused to work on it. Finally, in order to break the ban the government threatened to apply a licensing system to transport workers, and at last minute meetings the watersiders gave in on the issue.

A few months later a more serious difference arose over the loading of pig iron at Port Kembla, and this time the men decided to apply "working-class sanctions" against Japan. The government was determined to enforce its authority, as Attorney-General Menzies made clear:

> The question is not whether the waterside workers are right or wrong in their veiws on what the international policy of Australia should be: it is whether that policy is to be determined by the duly constituted Government of the country or by some individual section.

Menzies added that the government could not submit "to dictation by a section of its people;" but there was in fact widespread support among unions for the watersiders' stand, and although the government introduced the licensing system in the hope of breaking the boycott, no volunteers presented themselves for licences. Only when the union membership was convinced that the whole matter of export of raw materials to aggressor nations would be reviewed (as Menzies promised it would), was the pig iron shipment completed. Lyons and Menzies met union representatives for discussions; but when the matter went to the cabinet the union proposals were rejected because of the effect that "any interference with the ordinary flow of trade would have upon other industries and upon other Australian interests." The waterside workers could do nothing but load future shipments of pig iron "under protest."

At the same time, the government decided to impose an embargo on the export of iron ore. Japanese industrialists had been interested for some years in the extensive high-grade ore deposits at Yampi Sound, in Western Australia, and from 1937, when a worldwide steel shortage became apparent, their interest had quickened. The prospect of having Japan involved in the development of Yampi Sound aroused opposition in many quarters, especially when the newspaper reports spoke of Japan taking 1,000,000 tons or more of ore a year; and although the federal cabinet decided in March 1937 against any action to block iron ore exports, by mid-1938 this policy was reversed. In the meantime Japanese interests had provided money for investment in the project, and the Western Australian government had given its enthusiastic support. Defending the ban against sectional criticism (particularly from Western Australia), the government said that the embargo followed fresh surveys which had shown Australia's iron ore reserves to be less extensive than previously supposed and, further, that in view of the rapid expansion of Australian industry a conservation policy was now deemed necessary. In the event, it was to be a generation before the embargo ended.

Taken in conjunction with its insistence on the handling of pig iron shipments, the government's ban on iron ore exports seemed, as one newspaper noted, "blurred with inconsistencies." For its part the government relied on the explanation that its prohibition was necessary "to conserve our supplies of raw material for the use of Australian manufacturing industry and Australian workmen."

Lyons' expanded defence programme had been announced as a one-year effort in August 1937. With international tension mounting, there was a more urgent need to step up Australia's defence effort, and a month after the Singapore naval base was opened with elaborate ceremonies, a new three-year programme of considerably larger dimensions was announced by Lyons in March 1938. The fighting forces were to be enlarged, harbour facilities developed, and overland communications strengthened, while provision was to be made for the accumulation in Australia of food and fuel and other items as emergency reserves. The R.A.N. unobtrusively enrolled additional coastwatchers in northern areas to augment the growing numbers of men who, over some years, had been signed up to serve in an emergency.

In London, the United Kingdom government, in defining defence policy objectives, now ranked "protection of overseas territories" third in importance after the security of Britain itself and the preservation of essential sea routes. The Whitehall statement on the matter said that maintenance of naval bases at strategic points was no longer considered vital—and this admission was taken in Australia to indicate that the new Singapore base was not as significant from the British viewpoint as from the Australian. It was becoming clear that Britain gave a very low priority to the Pacific. Already the *Round Table* had noted that, until such time as Britain might be able to station a battle fleet permanently in Eastern waters, Australians would have "little reason for complacency" as a result of the Singapore base's establishment.

By now uneasiness over the defence situation was widespread among Australians, and there was growing criticism of the defence programme on the ground that it still placed too much reliance on the expectation of British naval support.

As headlines blackened and radio carried the news of Hitler's successive conquests, concern was intensified. After the Munich agreement (September 1938), Australians were coming to realize that a final showdown with Germany was inevitable.

An expanded and accelerated defence programme was announced in December, and three months later the government decided upon further extensions which were to lift the cost, over a three-year period, to £70 million. Special efforts were made to establish aircraft manufacture and to build munition factories so that in these fields Australia might become second only to Britain among the British countries. Rather than contribute to the cost of the Singapore base, the government decided to fortify Darwin as one of the series of naval bases running from South Africa through Trincomalee (in Ceylon) to the island of Penang, at the western entrance to the Straits of Malacca, and Singapore. A major effort was made in the strengthening of the Royal Australian Navy, and preliminary approval was given for the planning of a graving dock commodious enough to handle battleships; later, Sydney was chosen as the site. The military section of the new programme involved doubling the strength of the volunteer milita; before this objective was achieved (in March 1939) it was announced that recruiting would be continued until the militia strength reached 82,000. Air force recruiting was stepped up, and more aircraft ordered from Britain and the United States A compulsory national register of men between the ages of eighteen and sixty-four was instituted "in order to facilitate the organization of skilled labour in the event of an emergency and to avoid overlapping and misplacement of men."

The tense foreign situation did not bring any truce to the political struggles in Canberra. In both the United Australia party and the Country party, ambitious men were jockeying for position. In spite of the imminent danger of war at the time of Lyons' death in April 1939, Page had been unwilling to bring the Country party into Menzies' ministry. Menzies, who only a few months before had been calling for national leadership "as inspiring as that of the dictator countries," soon found that many parliamentarians on his own side were overtly or covertly questioning his ability to provide that leadership.

As part of their awakening to the realities of the world situation, Australians suddenly realized the need for closer association with friendly powers in the Pacific. Hurriedly the government in Canberra groped for some system of international co-operation in the region. In May 1939, increased diplomatic contact was foreshadowed with the United States, China, Japan, the Netherlands East Indies, and other countries fringing the Pacific.

Prime Minister Menzies said he could see no reason why Australia should not play "not only an adult but an effective part" in the affairs of the Pacific, and he went on to promise "a new Pacific policy" in the cultivation of friendship. However, in the thrust of the titanic forces gathering for a military decision, such a move was doomed to failure.

Throughout 1939, while the Nazi propaganda machine flooded the world with stories of German might, Hitler had begun dictating the trend and pace of political and military events, and exulting in the Nazis' conquest of neighbouring lands by subversion or invasion. After mid-year the question of Danzig was being made an excuse for tirades by Hitler against Poland. In a last-ditch effort to halt Hitler's march, Britain and France now pledged a guarantee of Poland's integrity, and opened negotiations for a military pact with Russia. In the midst of these negotiations the announcement on August 23 of the Hitler-Stalin pact startled the world. Hitler found a pretext for a massive attack on Poland which opened early on September 1; the British Prime Minister, Neville Chamberlain, at once informed the House of Commons that the British and French governments felt that the German action called for their assistance to Poland.

Early on September 3, London and Paris informed Germany that unless aggression in Poland was suspended immediately, a state of war would exist from 11 a.m. British summertime (8 p.m. Australian eastern time). As that hour approached, Prime Minister Menzies and senior officials gathered at the federal offices in Melbourne. At 8 p.m. on that Sunday evening shortwave listeners throughout Australia heard Chamberlain's announcement that Britain was at war with Germany. The Australian cabinet did not follow the course of the Canadian cabinet and submit the issue to parliament; instead it considered Australia automatically at war with Britain's enemy the moment war broke out, and at 9.15 p.m. Prime Minister Menzies spoke over every radio station in Australia, saying:

> It is my melancholy duty to inform you officially that, in consequence of a persistence by Germany in her invasion of Poland, Great Britain has declared war on her and that, as a result, Australia is also at war.

It was clear that much remained to be done to secure Australia's own defences, but the paramount thought was to send help to Britain. As in 1914 Australia's immediate duty was to protect its own coasts and the sealanes along which food and supplies passed. This time no enemy islands or hostile squadron called for immediate attention, and the war in Europe remained strangely dormant for some months after Poland had been battered into submission in a few weeks of devastating blitzkreig. By October two cruisers, *Perth* (in the West Indies from the eve of war) and *Hobart*, and five destroyers were serving with the Royal Navy on escort duties or in raider-hunting groups, while at home reserves were called up for the R.A.N., merchant ships were armed, and small ships converted into minesweepers. A second A.I.F. was formed under Lieutenant-General Sir Thomas Albert Blamey, who had served under Monash in France almost a generation before. In January 1940 his first brigade reached Palestine. It was intended that, after hardening-up in the Middle East, the Australian troops would go to France, as the first A.I.F. had done. Also expanding rapidly, the Royal Australian Air Force had more volunteers than it could train and use with its few aircraft.

The war effort was being shaped in other ways as the home front was geared for new tasks. The government moved urgently to gain parliament's sanction for authority to make wide and varying regulations to promote the security of Australia without the need to pass individual legislative items through parliament. The system set up in the National Security Bill (introduced within three days of war's outbreak) provided the executive with a greater degree of power than ever before, and it had the effect, for the duration of the war, of giving Australia government-under-parliament rather than government-by-parliament. The regulations which resulted were promulgated and administered by the relevant departments.

There was natural concern among many at the prospect that the individual's liberty and the rights of parliament would be curtailed; for some, there was a dangerous contradiction in the restrictions necessary for effective prosecution of the war and the prime objective for which the war was being fought, namely that of preserving a way of life in which the rights of individuals might still count. The preservation of traditional democratic rights and liberties was a matter that exercised the attention of the parliament from its earliest wartime sittings. On September 6, Prime Minister Menzies told the House of Representatives:

> However long this conflict may last I do not seek a muzzled Opposition. Our institutions of Parliament, and of liberal thought, free speech, and free criticism must go on.

The following day, Menzies told the House that whatever might be the extent of the powers taken to govern, direct, and control by regulation, "there must be as little interference with individual rights as is consistent with concerted national effort." He hoped that when the time came for him to cease to exercise the powers, he would be able to say that the powers had been exercised "firmly, definitely and promptly, but without intolerance and with a due respect for the interests of minorities."

The plain fact was that apart from excluding expressly the imposition by regulation of any form of compulsory naval, military, or air force service or any form of industrial conscription, the National Security Bill was designed to confer upon the executive powers that were as extensive as the prosecution of the war. Both within parliament and outside there were those who criticized the bill for its sweeping powers; their most significant line of criticism was that by combining the executive power with the legislative power the government was able to institute methods which smacked of totalitarian states. Some Labor members spoke out against "the abdication of power by parliament," and objected to the fact (as one member said) that parliament was being asked to authorize the government "to pass any laws that it liked and to disregard existing legislation." Memories of things done under the War Precautions Act during World War I caused some members to fear that serious abrogation of individual rights was involved. Attempts by long-time Labor parliamentarian Maurice Blackburn to have the "dragnet" power of the measure reduced and other Labor-sponsored efforts to put a time limit on the operation of the bill were unsuccessful; but at the same time the government met the criticism by an amendment in committee which provided that orders, rules, and by-laws "of legislative and not an executive character" should be tabled in Parliament in the same way as regulations, instead of merely being subject to approval or disallowance by a minister. This was a valuable safeguard against over-zealous action. The government also accepted the amendment by Blackburn which enlarged the limitation against compulsory service so that the government could not, by regulation, turn the Defence Act obligation for military service within Australia and its territories into a general obligation to serve elsewhere.

By September 9 the National Security Act had been passed, and four days later the first regulation promulgated under its provisions was issued. Before the war's end, a total of 190 regulations—many of them far-reaching in their effect—had been issued under the original or amended acts of 1940 or 1943. The regulations covered a wide range of subjects, and in some measure they reshaped the lives of all Australians.

It took some time for the nation to gear itself to war, and on the home front the feeling persisted that the war was being fought to preserve the good things of the democratic way of life. Accordingly the reshaping of the economy was relatively slow and somewhat hesitant; the philosophy of "business as usual" was deep-rooted, and it expressed the mood of hopeful optimism that "it can't happen here." A lack of administrative machinery and limited experience in the management of a modern economy combined to check any inclination the government might have had to strip the economy down to the essentials associated with war. Further, it was clear that under the prevailing circumstances the government's discretion in determining what was a necessary war measure was somewhat limited—a fact demonstrated by a series of High Court judgments establishing that there must be a "real connection" with the war effort to justify use of the defence power in fields otherwise beyond the federal parliament's legislative scope.

From the time he came to office Menzies—and those close to him—had been trying unsuccessfully to form a joint administration with the Country party. Negotiations for the formation of a composite ministry were reopened after the outbreak of war, but the rift between the parties was wider than either side cared to admit. It ran from discord between personalities all the way to a sharp divergence of views on some major issues. There was the further complication that the Country party believed it should be free to criticize publicly government decisions, even though jointly arrived at, where these differed from Country party dogma. The Country party still insisted on the right to select its own panel for cabinet rank, and nothing came of the new initiative to form a coalition, even though Page stood down from his party's leadership. Behind the impasse was the Prime Minister's unwillingness to accept the Country party's claim that it should be free to go its own way in a coalition, a sectional insistence strangely in conflict with the principle of cabinet responsibility.

From this time Menzies found himself under considerable political pressure. He was being widely criticized for lack of vigour in the handling of the war effort on the home front and even within his own party dissident voices were being heard. Early in 1940 the cabinet was reconstructed. Casey was appointed to Washington as first Australian Minister to the United States, and another minister resigned after it was disclosed that he had personal dealings with the businessman heading the company for which the government proposed to provide a bounty for the manufacture of motor-car engines.

The by-election to fill Casey's seat in Parliament resulted in a victory for Labor, and the call for a wider-based administration became louder. Menzies offered the new leader of the Country party, Archibald Galbraith Cameron, five cabinet posts, including the deputy-leadership of the government. Cameron bitterly opposed the government's motor vehicles agreement bill (designed to provide protection in the development of Australian automobile production), but nevertheless he was prepared to accept Menzies' offer, and the coalition ministry was formed in March 1940. An extraordinary situation then arose when Menzies announced that members of the government parties would be free to vote on the measure according to their opinion. During the debate, backbenchers of the Country party attacked the bill, and although the ministers remained silent they joined other members of the party (except one) in voting against it in divisions. The measure was passed only because Labor gave its support.

As Hitler's *blitzkrieg* raged through Belgium and Holland in May 1940, concern over the progress of the war was greatly intensified in Australia. The newspapers were calling for greater war effort. More shocks were in store in June. France asked for an armistice, and at Dunkirk the British Expeditionary Force narrowly escaped to a magnificently defiant but beleaguered Britain. Italy entered the war on June 10 and shortly afterward France signed an armistice, opening the way for Germany to control French ports. By mid-August the Battle of Britain—which commenced on July 10—was being fought with full intensity in the skies over the Channel and East Anglia and London, and the fate of the world hung in the balance as the resolute "few" in their Hurricanes and Spitfires denied victory to the endless waves of planes Hitler threw against the last citadel. Australian pilots (some with R.A.F. squadrons and others in Australian units) served with distinction in these most crucial of all air battles, in which less than 3000 pilots and aircrew of sixty-seven operational fighter squadrons were engaged over three and a half months.

Intrigues among government supporters in parliamentary lobbies in Canberra had been having their effect on the electorate, and in the general poll of September 1940 United Australia and Country party candidates gained less support. When returns were in the ministry found itself without a clear majority in the House, the balance of political power being held by two independents.

Within the Country party, support for Cameron quickly waned; a few weeks after the election he was eased out and Arthur William Fadden chosen to succeed him as leader. In his letter of resignation to the Prime Minister Cameron referred to his party's "internal state of simmering discontent, spiced by insatiable personal ambitions and incurable animosities," and said that in his view no party leader could face a situation where he had to watch every footfall lest he stumble on a mantrap or a mine. Cameron at once joined the ranks of those loudly criticizing wartime administration and cabinet's indecisiveness.

Menzies' unpopularity was widely held to be responsible for the steady disintegration within cabinet which followed. Public and party discontent with the war effort reached a point where a revolt against his leadership developed within the United Australia party itself. Matters came to a head in August 1941 when a protracted cabinet meeting in Melbourne ended in the withdrawal of Country party ministers. Fully aware that he was being cold-shouldered, Menzies told those remaining—his own party members—that he was prepared to resign if this was their wish. There was little support for a move by some ministers to dissuade him from this course.

Invective was being so freely exchanged by the principal figures in the drama that reconciliation was now impossible. At a joint United Australia-Country party meeting on August 28, Menzies formally announced his resignation as leader—an unusual course since normally ministers in disagreement with their Prime Minister might be expected to resign. Again there was no move to change his course. Fadden was at once elected, unopposed, as leader of the joint parties. Subsequently the Governor-General commissioned him to form a ministry.

Some newspapers dwelt on the theme that Menzies should have resigned earlier, the *Sydney Morning Herald* declaring that this would have been his "only sagacious course out of the impasse into which his manoeuvres had led the government." Generally, however, it was the political intrigue that commentators and editorial writers criticized most strongly. The Melbourne *Age* described the hostility to Menzies as being "no more than a species of personal vendetta." Arthur William Coles, one of the "independents" of 1940 who had attended United Australia party meetings, described the whole affair of Menzies' ousting as "a public lynching," and he at once resigned from the party.

Fadden's regime, obviously never more than a makeshift, was doomed to early failure. Coles and his fellow Independent were now convinced that Labor alone could provide a stable administration and a more vigorous war effort. The two voted against the new budget, and six weeks after the formation of his ministry Fadden found himself not only out of office but on the opposition side of the House. After ten years in the political wilderness, the Labor party had regained the government benches.

Under Curtin's leadership, the parliamentary Labor party had refused consistently to enter an all-party or "national" administration, even though it had been offered seats in cabinet several times. Menzies made his last appeal in July 1941, not long before his own resignation, when he proferred Labor equal representation in cabinet. Curtin had succeeded in healing the wounds of factional bitterness which had left Labor ineffectual in federal politics throughout the 1930s, but old suspicions and antagonisms still lingered and he was determined to avoid any course that might have laid himself open to his own party's charge that he was indifferent to "the interests of labour." He was deeply conscious of the disastrous split that had developed within Labor's ranks following Hughes's formation of a wartime national ministry in 1917, and he was determined to avoid repetition; but his attitudes sprang from even deeper convictions. He remained convinced of the rightness of views he had expressed six months before the outbreak of war when he had declared:

> However good a government may be, it will be all the better if it is composed of men who subscribe to one set of political principles, who are united in their outlook upon the problems of the country, and who may as a team translate into reality ideas that they have as to the way in which the country should be administered. That government would be a government of leadership and action. And any government, even if it has the best policies, would do far better service to the nation if there were arrayed against it in Parliament an opposition courageous, intelligent, and patriotic. It is not a good thing for democracies to have governments that are unchecked by criticism or honest opposition.

As the war went on, Curtin came to believe that if a national government were formed, the Communist element would come to constitute the *de facto* opposition, attracting all those who were dissatisfied with the government's efforts, and perhaps contributing to an increase in subversion or destructive acts.

While refusing to join an all-party administration, the parliamentary Labor party offered general support to the government in all major war issues as they arose, and there was never any lack of unity in parliament concerning Australia's participation. As an alternative to an all-party government, Labor pressed for the establishment of a national war council, to include Labor representatives, which would "advise the government in respect of the conduct of the war and in preparing for postwar reconstruction." Curtin had brought the matter to the Prime Minister's attention in June 1940, when the two had held discussions on the subject, after which the possibilities of a closer understanding between the principal parliamentary parties were explored by a ten-man meeting of leaders of the United Australia and Country parties and Labor; but cabinet had insisted that what was "most needed for a truly concerted national effort" was an all-party government.

When the general election of September 1940 produced an inconclusive result, there was more widespread clamour for a closer unity between the parties in the interests of the war effort. A thirteen-man meeting of "party managers" took place on October 16—Coles attended as an Independent, and there were three representatives of the Lang Labor faction—and as a result Curtin formally proposed to the Prime Minister "a complete overhaul of the war and home defence administration" virtually on the basis of the Labor party's election policy proposals. Menzies' reply reiterated the call for an all-party government, but also suggested a compromise, and almost at once a war council of an advisory, non-executive character, was created. The eight-man body, with membership equally divided between the government and the Opposition, was sworn in on October 29,1940. It continued to function when Labor replaced the coalition on the government benches.

The Advisory War Council enabled the best brains from both sides of parliament to make their contributions to the war effort, and probably suited Australian conditions better than the stricter discipline of an all-party government would have done. It avoided a split in the Labor party that could only have been harmful to the nation, and it gave Labor leaders nearly a year's intensive experience of the problems and developments of the war situation which proved invaluable when they came to power on October 7, 1941.

The Labor government carried the strong stamp of Curtin's personality. Curtin—a man of deep sincerity and integrity, dedicated, and a moderate in social reform—had built up and maintained a sense of unity within his party. Now, displaying great qualities of leadership, he set about invigorating the national effort on lines he had enunciated in the 1940 election campaign as Labor's blueprint for an intensified and, to some extent, redirected war effort. The programme he and his advisers now followed placed emphasis on the need to retain defence forces capable of resisting attacks on Australia itself and to provide the requisite staffing of industries vital to the war effort.

Australians had been fighting on many battlefronts, gaining distinction for their courage and ability. The empire air training scheme, begun in the early months of the war, had turned out thousands of flyers who were soon active in sea patrols against enemy submarines and in heavy-bomber squadrons, operating from Britain. Australian forces were active in the Mediterranean struggle, which quickly developed as a combined land-sea-air war of great complexity.

To match changed conditions, military plans underwent drastic revision. Italy's possession of Libya and other North African bases, and of Eritrea, combined with Germany's control of French ports after June 1940, threatened the British position in the Middle East and its important oil supplies. Malta and Egypt were vital as Allied strong points in the pivotal struggle. An early Axis attack (by Italian forces) on the headwaters of the Nile was beaten back, but British shipping operating between Gibraltar and Suez took heavy punishment from German dive-bombing attacks. British lines of communication ran east-west through the Mediterranean; the Italian (with German air support) extended north-south. Their main intersection was in the corrridor guarded by Malta, and in these narrow waters clashes were inevitable. In the first major engagement (July 9, 1940), the British forces—including the Australian vessels *Sydney*, *Stuart*, *Vampire* and *Voyager*—were heavily outnumbered but forced the Italian fleet to retire to within sight of the Italian coast. On July 19, in the first cruiser duel of the war, *Sydney*, with five British destroyers, exploited the all-seeing eye of radar in a successful action with two Italian cruisers off western Crete, destroying one, the *Bartolomeo Colleoni*, and forcing the other to use its superior speed to escape.

Swirling land battles were soon being fought along segments of the African Mediterranean littoral as the Axis powers sought to break out through the natural gateway of the eastern Mediterranean and Britain played a traditional role of containment. In September 1940 Italian land forces moved in North Africa, striking east from Libya and advancing to within 250 miles of Alexandria, main base of Britain's Mediterranean fleet; to meet the situation, the Australians were moved into Egypt. By this time the naval war in the Mediterranean had fallen into a pattern: the escorting of military convoys and naval reinforcements, the bombardment of Italian shore positions in Libya and Italian-held islands, and the conducting of sweeps north into the Aegean. In the Indian Ocean and Red Sea, the task was that of escorting ships, especially the large troop convoys from Australia and India and the British military convoys for the Middle East via the Cape. Australian ships undertaking these duties were frequently involved in clashes with the enemy. After the Italian attack on Greece, late in October, British forces were sent to garrison Crete, and in the escort work as well as in harrassment of enemy forces the Australian ships had no rest. British prestige was enhanced—and the strain in the eastern Mediterranean eased—when a successful raid was undertaken on the Italian fleet in Taranto harbour (after which Naples became Italy's main fleet base).

Australians were in the forefront of the desert fighting which now drove the Italians back from Egypt. Eight Italian divisions had been deployed between Bardia, a fortress area inside the Libyan border, and Sidi Barani, in Egypt; but they faced a strengthened army under General Sir Archibald Wavell, Commander-in-Chief, Middle East, and early in December an attack by Wavell's Western Desert Force broke the Italian springboard line. Australian units were engaged from December 9. As the Italians fell back in disorder towards Bardia they lost much equipment and nearly 40,000 men as prisoners. A fast moving offensive was mounted, with the Australian 6th Division its spearhead; before dawn on January 3, 1941 a carefully-planned attack began which carried the Australians into Bardia the following day. Another 40,000 Italians were taken prisoner. Less than three weeks later Tobruk, a coastal fortress 60 miles farther west, was captured, again with heavy losses to the enemy. The drive along the coast continued while Italian forces in the desert were pursued. Derna, and then Benghazi, fell to the Australians who then intercepted the retreating Italians to the south to complete the rout of ten divisions in two months. Believing that the British advance might reach Tripoli before it could be held, the German and Italian commands decided to move in reinforcements, including a German force (later to be known as the Afrika Korps) which was being gathered. By mid-February the first German units had arrived in Tripoli.

Before the desert drama could be concluded, attention turned to Greece, where Italian military efforts had also failed. Hitler, with preparations for a great attack on the Soviet Union well under way, had been anxious to avoid alarming the Russians prematurely by intervention in the Balkans; but the ultimate intention was clear. Early in February 1941 the Greek government requested British help and, with the threat to Egypt removed, Wavell set about organizing as large an expeditionary force as could be spared from the troops already successful in the Libyan campaign, including Australian and New Zealand troops. The 6th Australian Division was replaced in the desert by the 9th, which was not equipped for immediate action.

In March Australian cruisers and destroyers helped to win an important naval victory over the Italians off Cape Matapan; but German pressure on the Balkans was increasing. The first convoy of British forces reached Greece early in March; a month later German forces were thrown against Yugoslavia (which had been undermined by subversion) and the attack upon Greece followed. Greek heroism was no match for German armoured might, and although the onslaught was slowed it could not be held. The British force, including part of the 6th Australian Division and the New Zealand Division, was outnumbered on land and in the air by the Germans. The phrase, too little too late, echoed round the world. The Allied withdrawal was skilfully planned by Blamey, and each part of the force was able to withdraw in ordered sequence, so that 48,000 of the original 62,000 troops sent to Greece were embarked in late April; but much valuable equipment had to be abandoned at a time when British forces were still seriously short of weapons and vehicles.

The Greek administration retired to Crete, and there part of the Anzac force was landed as the ships shuttled back and forth to Greek withdrawal points. It was considered certain that the Germans would soon launch an airborne invasion. This fear was confirmed when relentless air attacks were launched on the island's three airfields, On May 20 the first parachute and glider-borne troops landed; a week later, after the onslaught had been stepped up and when the position had become hopeless, the decision to withdraw was taken. After desperate fighting most of the force on Crete was able to reach the embarkation point and, on three nights, be embarked; but an entire Australian battalion, forming the main rearguard, and about 5000 other troops, were left behind.

The German timetable had been upset, however, and the German paratroop losses had been so heavy that Hitler decided not to undertake a similar invasion of Cyprus, then only lightly defended by a small garrison including an Australian mechanized cavalry regiment. Nevertheless, the German threat to the Suez Canal had increased; German aircraft, staging through French airfields in Syria, were being used by dissident Iraqi forces to attack British positions. To block this Vichy-controlled by-pass, Wavell was ordered in June to invade Syria-Lebanon; his force consisted of the 7th Australian Division, an Indian Brigade and a Free French force, all under the command of General Lavarack. French resistance was however surprisingly strong. It was a few weeks before Damascus was taken, but by early July the Allied force, now reinforced by several Australian units, was able to overcome final resistance; Damour fell on July 9, an armistice was concluded, and Vichy control ended when the armistice was signed within the Australian lines.

The desert war had meanwhile taken a dramatic turn. On March 21, 1941 armoured units of the Afrika Korps under the command of General Erwin Rommel made their first contact with British patrols. Virtually only the Australian 9th Division and elements of an armoured division were holding the Italian territory; and the strength of the 9th was more nominal than real. Most of the fighting vehicles were back in Egypt for repair and reconditioning; communication lines were stretched to the limit, and the manning of a coherent front line of sufficient length was impossible in the absence of reinforcements (which had to move up in small numbers from far in the rear). The R.A.F. was greatly reduced in strength; the Luftwaffe, deployed in considerable numbers, operated from bases in Tripoli and Sicily and not only hit British shipping but provided direct support for Rommel's drive east. At first it was not recognized that a major offensive was developing, but when the Afrika Korps reached Benghazi (April 4) there could be no mistaking the gravity of the situation. The position became confused as small German units swept forward, cutting in behind British and Australian forces along the way. On April 6 the commanding general ordered the 9th Division and other units to retire by the coast route towards Tobruk, while the armour was to make for the old fort of Mechili, on the inland route across the desert. During the retirement several parties were ambushed and taken prisoner by the Germans.

Wavell had sent up reinforcements to Tobruk, where the old Italian defence perimeter was developed quickly and ingeniously, and on April 8 Wavell flew to Tobruk, taking with him Major-General John Dudley Lavarack, whom he placed in command of all forces in Cyrenaica. Tobruk was to be held, if possible, for two months, after which Wavell hoped to relieve the fortress by an advance from Egypt. Lavarack arranged with Major-General Leslie James Morshead, the Division commander, for the 9th to be withdrawn into the perimeter of Tobruk the following night. The defensive positions on the perimeter were no sooner manned than Rommel's advance units approached by the coast road from the west.

The garrison comprised about 35,700 men and included four Australian infantry brigades with their field engineers, four British artillery regiments, British and Australian anti-tank units, and various ancillary units. The German and Italian forces completed the investment of Tobruk on April 11; at night, on the 13th, the first infiltration of the defences began. Lavarack had appointed Morshead commander of Tobruk fortress and late on 14 April was himself withdrawn to Egypt to resume command of the 7th Division.

Rommel was determined to capitalize on his success and complete the sweep eastward into Egypt. On April 15 the onrushing German 21st Panzer division reached Tobruk but the attack was repulsed. Rommel decided to leave no more than a small holding force and then he continued eastward at full speed, regardless of his men's exhaustion. Tanks and dive-bombers pressed the attack; but not even the most rigorous training could equip the men to fulfil the German general's ruthless demands. The Allied forces defending the Egyptian border were faced by German attackers on the verge of collapse and insanity for lack of water, since water supplies had fallen behind ammunition columns. Many German prisoners were taken by the Allies, and the 21st Panzer Division came to a halt. Rommel turned back to assault Tobruk again, leaving only a screening detachment on the Egyptian border.

On May 1 Germans and Italians attacked the fortress in strength. Their drive pierced the perimeter in one section but was stopped after a slight advance. The Luftwaffe also maintained a steady attack, with one assault following another, but the defenders held their own.

The siege of Tobruk had begun. Each enemy attack was met with fierce counter-attacks, but the grip of the encircling forces tightened. Repeated attempts to relieve the garrison by land failed; but although the waterfront had been smashed and the harbour was strewn with wrecked vessels, on moonless nights British and Australian destroyers made risky runs with supplies and mail to sustain the "Tobruk rats" and to carry off the wounded. The men of Tobruk became a symbol of defiance; theirs was an epic example of how courageous and capable men might stand against the weight of mechanized and air attacks, and hold on. The siege was maintained month after month. In order to neutralize Tobruk as a roadblock, Rommel had a new road built to by-pass the fortress, but the thorn remained and the Germans found themselves unable to push eastward beyond the Egyptian border.

In July the Australian government began to urge the relief of the Australians in Tobruk, a demand that caused a controversy with the British government. In August an Australian brigade was replaced by a Polish group, and over the next two months the 9th Australian Division was relieved, unit by unit, by a British Division. By late October most of the Australians had been withdrawn.

As supplies and weapons poured in from the United States to build up British strength in Egypt, an offensive to relieve Tobruk was planned for November. As it turned out, the British move on November 18 preceded by only five days Rommel's intended major strike to subdue the outpost but the British held the initiative, and the Germans had the worst of the swirling battles that developed south and east of Tobruk. With no prospect of early reinforcement, the Axis command decided on December 7 to order a general retreat west of Tobruk. After 242 days, the gruelling siege ended; during that period, or in the fighting immediately preceding it, 3000 Australians were among those killed or wounded and nearly 1000 Australians had been taken prisoner.

War in the Pacific 23

In mid-1941 war burst out on a new and massive scale as Hitler hurled 250 divisions against the Soviet Union. Even as titanic battles of terrible ferocity flared across eastern Europe, the threat of Japanese intervention in the Pacific grew steadily more menacing, and the United States sensed the imminence of war in the Pacific; but in spite of the fact that Japan had signed a ten-year alliance with Germany and Italy in September 1940, Japan's grander intentions remained largely masked. In the English-speaking world it was widely held that the hands of Japan's militarists were already full as a result of the war in China and that consequently Japan's intervention as an active partner was unlikely. Prime Minister Churchill, overwhelmingly involved with the European conflict, refused to be sidetracked from concentration on defeating Hitler, and his views dominated British military planning. Australian defence authorities were anxious to assist in buttressing British strength in Singapore, linchpin of the British defence system of the whole region. However, British service chiefs on the scene, if they felt concern about the base's level of preparedness, failed to convey to London any sense of its inadequacy as a stronghold or as an active base for naval operations. Australian proposals were received without enthusiasm in London where —in the words of a military historian—Churchill was suffering "a blindness about the Far East." In conversations with the British military staff between January and March 1941, at which Japan's entry into the war was discussed as a likely eventuality, the American military authorities also came to accept the "beat-Hitler-first" view, and agreed that if the Japanese moved the strategy should be simply to contain and harass Japan; Germany would remain the prime enemy, and Washington and London would not be diverted from their main effort of forcing the unconditional surrender of the Third Reich.

Japan's grip on conquered Asian areas had been tightening, and plans for further conquests were being readied. An Asian Development Board had been set up in 1940 to exploit the resources of Japanese-dominated areas in a "co-prosperity sphere." At the same time, special groups in Tokyo devoted to total-war research and science mobilization studied ways of adopting the techniques of Hitler's Reich to Asia; censorship was imposed on the Japanese press and radio, and all political parties fused themselves into an Imperial Rule Assistance Association. The old and accepted social discipline of Japanese life was merged into a system of military dictatorship as Japanese leaders pursued their self-appointed destiny of overlordship of Asia and the Pacific. Government presses in Tokyo had begun printing military occupation money for the Philippines, Burma, and Malaya late in 1940, and by mid-1941 an imperial conference had secretly laid down Japan's "fundamental policy" of immediate southward expansion. By that time a Japanese mission in Batavia was demanding that the Netherlands East Indies (controlled by the free government of Holland) should be incorporated in the Japanese trading bloc.

Australia by this time had exchanged ministers with the United States, Japan, and China. In Washington, Richard Casey opened the legation in March 1940; the United States minister, Charles Gauss, reached Canberra four months later. Nevertheless, Australia had not quite achieved the status of an independent power in official Washington; it was seen still as a British associate, a role which Australia's emphasis on "diplomatic unity" tended to substantiate. In any case, Australia appeared far from the danger spot, north of the equator, where Japanese and American power might come into head-on collision.

Early in 1941, United States Naval Intelligence cracked the Japanese radio code, and thereafter dispatches from Tokyo were known to the American and British general staffs. It was learnt that Japanese commanders had in mind the seizure of military bases in Indochina and Thailand, and planned ultimately to attack Singapore. Warning alerts went to the Philippines (where General Douglas MacArthur was in charge of the American-Filipino defence forces), and Canadian reinforcements were sent to Hong Kong.

The Australian military authorities saw the need for a redeployment of forces. Small ground forces were needed to protect air bases located as far north as possible in the island screen, while ground strength in Malaya called for reinforcement and Australia's unprotected northern perimeter required some garrisoning. The War Cabinet accepted a recommendation that the 8th Division should not be sent to the Middle East but instead should be retained for use in Australia and the western Pacific. A battalion and a brigade group were established in the Darwin-Alice Springs area, and other garrison forces were sent to Port Moresby and to Rabaul (New Britain), largely to protect airfields. A major force—12,000 men of the 8th Division—was sent to Malaya; they arrived at Singapore on February 18, 1941. Small Australian detachments were also sent to Nauru and Ocean Island, and to the Solomons, New Ireland, and the Admiralties. Commitments were also entered into with the Dutch to send Australian battalion groups to augment garrisons on Ambon and Timor.

In July 1941, after negotiations with the Vichy government, the Japanese began a fateful military incursion into French Indochina. The objective was to force a way westward with the ultimate objective of moving into Burma and cutting the Burma Road lifeline (established to take American supplies to Chungking). Following the move into Indochina, economic restrictions upon Japan were imposed: but there was no means of stopping the deeper penetration of south-east Asia. In October, Dr Herbert Vere Evatt, speaking in Canberra as the new minister for external affairs, said he hoped Japan would "retrace her steps," adding that Australia had "supreme and special interest" in preventing forcible aggression in the Pacific.

Nevertheless, in spite of the mounting political tension, Japan's outright attack on any American or British possessions was considered in Washington and London to be a somewhat remote possibility; surely, the experts argued, it was unlikely that Japan's leaders would run the risks involved in open attack on the countries of the English-speaking world. Yet that was precisely what Tokyo was planning.

The thunderbolt struck on Sunday, December 7 (a day, President Roosevelt declared, which would "live in infamy") when soon after dawn the Japanese launched their sneak air attack on Pearl Harbour, inflicting crippling losses on United States ships and personnel. This raid was the opening gambit of a massive and carefully planned series of attacks against Allied positions far and wide around the Pacific designed to carry the Japanese to a position of impregnable strength. On December 8 a formal declaration of war against the Japanese empire was made by Australia.

Japan's dramatic entry into the conflict came only eight weeks after John Curtin's Labor administration had taken office in Canberra. It confronted Australia with a new and ruthless enemy and posed a far more direct and pressing threat than the nation had ever faced before. Curtin's long expressed fears on the question of the adequacy of Britain's naval screen in the Pacific became a grim reality; but, if the menace to Australia had suddenly been intensified to crisis point, the prospects for direct aid from a powerful ally, the United States, were simultaneously increased. Japanese intervention changed the entire nature of the world struggle by directly involving the erstwhile neutral United States. As war spattered across the Pacific, the United States Navy was fully conscious of the urgent need to rush support to Australia and protect communication lines.

Just a fortnight before Japan's entry, the naval war had been brought close to Australia's shores when the cruiser *Sydney* was lost with all hands in an engagement with the German raider *Kormoran* less than 150 miles off the West Australian coast. There had also been losses of merchant ships as a result of enemy mines laid in coastal waters. The country's naval defences were expanded as more coastal vessels were requisitioned as minesweepers and the shipbuilding programme was enlarged. The Naval Auxiliary Patrol of yachts and yachtsmen was formed to help in the protection of harbours. In August the first defensive minefield had been laid off Port Moresby; thereafter minefields were laid in the Torres Strait and in passages through the Great Barrier Reef. The coastwatching organization was further extended and its communications network improved in Australia's island territories.

The menace to Australia's security posed by the Japanese sweep southward was fully realized. Curtin spoke in a way that no Australian prime minister before him had ever spoken. He declared that Australia was faced by "a fanatically brave foe, armed with the very ultimate in machines and equipment," and it was no longer possible to wait upon debate; the Government, formed in freely elected Parliament, would accept responsibility "in total" for the conduct of the war in this time of great trial. He said:

> Never shall our enemy set foot upon the soil of this country without having arrayed against it the whole of the manhood of this nation, with such strength and quality that this nation will remain forever the home of sons of Britishers who came here in peace in order to establish in the South Seas an outpost of the British race . . . It must be recognized that we have not the forces to guard all our people from being bombed or shelled, but we have the courage and the determination and the capacity to beat off the invader in the end.

Curtin added that there could no longer be reliance on "appeals to the multitude"; the Government had to make the decisions, and "there must be no argument about the wisdom of those decisions; there must be a ready and immediate acceptance of them."

The electrifying news of the Pearl Harbour attack was followed by a succession of reports of Japan's tidal-wave onslaught. The Pacific seemed to be wide open to devastating attacks as Japanese forces struck in a colossal arc from Hawaii to the Gulf of Siam—at Hong Kong, at Siam, at Kota Bharu on the Siam-Malayan border; at Wake Island and at Guam. Land forces employed in the various drives were not large; but the war flaring so terrifyingly across tremendous distances was a different type of war from anything known before. It was a war carried by strong naval forces, including many aircraft-carriers, across vast stretches of the world's largest ocean. Japan's "battle wagons" cleared a path and the blows fell in quick succession; even the United States Navy reeled, temporarily caught off balance. Japan's immediate objective was to seize all territories within an area stretching from the Kurile Islands through Wake, the Marshalls, and New Guinea and around the southern and western limits of the Dutch East Indies to the western border of Burma. As the hammer blows fell it became starkly clear that Australia was dangerously close to the theatre of operations and inadequately equipped to meet the challenge. On December 11 the newspapers carried news of an almost incredible disaster—the sinking, off the east coast of Malaya, of the *Prince of Wales* and the *Repulse*, two battleships which were the vanguard of a fleet intended to bolster British naval strength in the western Pacific. Japan had gained naval superiority for some time to come.

The protective naval screen had been suddenly and terrifyingly removed. Militarily Australia was extremely exposed, and the fear was that help might be too meagre or too late. As the Prime Minister declared in a broadcast, the Australian nation was facing its "gravest hour,"

Concerned by the unchecked successes of the Japanese in Malaya, and fearing a repetition of the disasters suffered in Greece and Crete unless land reinforcements and more effective air cover were provided at once, Curtin appealed directly to President Roosevelt on December 26, urging immediate assistance in Malaya. He also indicated that Australia was ready, should the President desire it, to accept an American commander in the area. The following day the Prime Minister made a public statement setting down Australia's policy and role in the new and dangerous situation facing the nation. Curtin made it clear that he was unwilling to accept the view which relegated the Pacific war to the status of a side issue, and he said so in clear terms. In his widely-publicized message he spoke of the need for the United States and Australia to have "the fullest say" in the direction of the fighting plan to deal with the situation, and he added:

> Without any inhibitions of any kind I make it quite clear that Australia looks to America, free of any pangs as to our traditional links with the United Kingdom. We know the problems that the United Kingdom faces. We know the constant threat of invasion. We know the dangers of dispersal of strength. But we know, too, that Australia can go and Britain can still hold on. We are therefore determined that Australia shall not go.
>
> We shall exert our energies towards the shaping of a plan, with the United States as its keystone, which will give our country some confidence of being able to hold out until the tide of battle swings against the enemy.

The first American forces had already arrived. It had been decided in Washington that an advance American base—primarily an air base—should be established in Australia. On December 22 a convoy of four ships (with cruiser escort) arrived at Brisbane; it had been on its way to the Philippines when the Japanese attacked, and it had been diverted. As well as the ground echelon of a heavy bomber group, the ships carried over 4000 men of field artillery units, a variety of munitions, and sixty aircraft; they were followed closely by four other ships carrying over 200 fighter aircraft. By the end of the year there was no longer any doubt that the United States would be deeply involved and would make Australia an operational base for American forces. American troops, moved across from Brisbane to Darwin, found American aviators and navy units already established there.

As news from the war fronts worsened, the national pulse quickened. By Government direction, superfluous activities were stripped away to make way for greater concentration of the available manpower and technical skills on war production or direct military effort. Output of non-essential goods was curtailed and many sporting events were suspended.

The Japanese made their first attack against New Guinea on January 21, when 100 planes attacked Lae and Salamaua, but they did not attempt a landing. Here and elsewhere, Royal Australian Air Force pilots, outnumbered and flying obsolete planes, put up a hopeless but heroic defence. With the situation in Malaya deteriorating rapidly, Australian detachments were sent to Timor and Ambon in an effort to hold island strongpoints immediately north of Australia. At the same time, more men were sent to garrison northern Australian areas, while 114,000 militiamen were mobilized. The War Cabinet considered it advisable to arrange the transfer of an Australian division from the Middle East to Malaya; but the situation there was becoming so uncertain that instead the British Government suggested (and the Australian government agreed to) withdrawal of both the 6th and 7th Divisions plus corps staff and other units from the Middle East as reinforcements to bolster defences in the Netherlands Indies. General Archibald Wavell, newly-appointed as supreme commander in the south-east Asia-Indies area, planned that one division should be landed in southern Sumatra, the other in Java.

As the Japanese infiltrated rapidly through the Malayan jungle and plantation areas, pushing relentlessly south towards Singapore, there was no other course for the Indian and Australian defending forces but stage-by-stage withdrawal. Heavy fighting took place as the units fell back piecemeal to the south along the peninsula, always under heavy air attack; each new defence line was quickly outflanked by the Japanese, and by January 27 the decision was taken by Lieutenant-General Arthur Ernest Percival that a withdrawal back to Singapore Island must be made. Reinforcements (including some Australian units) were reaching Singapore; but the island lacked prepared defences and was thinly held, while the Japanese had been able to assemble three divisions for the attack. Although it had been built (and relied upon) as a great naval base, Singapore was in fact unfortified and could not be defended by land—posing a danger that was realized too late.

During the last week of January the main forces on the mainland withdrew to Singapore Island. The Australian 8th Division was assigned exceedingly long frontages to guard; they also faced the narrowest (and most threatened) part of the Straits. The attack on Singapore Island began on February 9. The Australian line was completely overwhelmed. On February 11 the naval base had to be abandoned. A black pall of smoke lay over the doomed city. Singapore's water supply was running out, and late on February 15 hostilities were brought to an end with a formal surrender.

Among Percival's force of 133,000 men who were taken prisoner were more than 15,000 Australians (almost one third of whom were to die during the three and a half years' captivity which was to follow). Major General Henry Gordon Bennett, 8th Division commander, with two officers of his staff, escaped to Australia. Other groups also got away. Official parties had been sent out before the capitulation—among them sixty-five Australian nurses, of whom twelve were lost at sea and twenty-one murdered by the Japanese on Banka island. Two Australian battalions from Singapore were transferred to Java, where the commander of 1st Australian Corps, General Lavarack, and his staff had arrived at the end of January.

Australians were engaging in other holding actions in the islands north of Australia. A large Japanese force landed round Rabaul (New Britain) late in January and quickly drove back the small Australian defending force; after a retreat during which many died of illness and more than 150 who surrendered were slaughtered by the Japanese, about 400 of the men were able to reach safety. On Ambon, the Australian force, heavily outnumbered, was forced to surrender, but some of the men escaped and later made their way to Australia by small craft, while a group making its escape from New Ireland by schooner managed to survive bombing attacks and regain Australian-held territory. On various islands, planters and lone settlers were involved in scores of remarkable escapes, many of them undertaken with the help of the islanders; as often as not the details went unrecorded. Many of these men returned to act as coastwatchers.

Meanwhile the small force sent to assist the Dutch to hold Timor had its hands full when a large Japanese invasion force landed. At first the defenders drew back into the mountain country. The troops divided into small parties, some of which reached isolated points on the coast, while others—Dutch as well as Australian—made their way into Portuguese Timor where they joined up with the Independent Company sent in December to defend the Portuguese territory. For two months from mid-February the 400 men of the force were out of communication with Australia; finally a radio transmitter was put together with scraps gathered from different parts of the island. Supplies were sent in from Darwin to the beleaguered guerrillas, who continued their harassing tactics against superior forces (numbering some 15,000 men in all) on whom they inflicted considerable losses, Because of Timor's proximity to northern Australia—less than 500 miles off the coast—the group was reinforced in September. Eventually, in January 1943, the Australians were withdrawn to Australia.

In February 1942 the threat to an exposed continent was emphasized to Americans in colourful news reports and commentaries. *Life*, describing Australia's development as being "at about the same stage as the United States was in 1850," went on to say that the continent was composed of the civilized east coast, the herdsmen's and miners' interior, and the scattered frontier towns of the west; and, the magazine added,

> Today the Australians are for the first time in their history fighting an invader on their own soil, as Japanese occupy Australia's outpost islands.

By mid-February their southern thrust had carried the Japanese as far south as Rabaul, while on February 19 a devastating bombing attack by more than 180 Japanese planes was launched against a virtually defenceless Darwin. The town's main buildings were extensively damaged; 243 people were killed and even more wounded, and eight ships were sunk in the harbour. A near panic developed; those who could fled, using any available vehicle or simply heading into the bush. News of the Darwin attack was kept tightly blanketed by censorship, but soon word-of-mouth stories of the destruction, and of incidents of desertion that followed the attack, were spreading. Meanwhile the authorities feared that an invasion might be launched against the Darwin area or at points along the exposed north and northwest coast.

In Canberra, crucial decisions were being taken, and Prime Minister Curtin adopted an even more forceful stand in order to impress upon the strategists in London and Washington the deadly danger of the situation.

During the brief life of the Fadden ministry which took office following Menzies' resignation as Prime Minister in August 1941, Dr Earle Page had been appointed special envoy to London with two specific tasks: one, to report to the British War Cabinet on matters affecting Australia before final decisions were made, and the other, to keep Canberra acquainted with British views as policy decisions were developing. Curtin considered that the existing machinery gave Australia an insufficient voice in decision-making affecting the Pacific, and he pressed his requests that Australia be given representation in an Imperial War Cabinet in London and also that a separate and distinct Pacific War Council be established in Washington. He was in no mood to accept an alternative which did not reach his acceptable minimum—that the direction of the war should be carried out in accordance with the undoubted fact that the Pacific war was primarily an American-Australian affair. There was no question of Curtin's personal access, as Prime Minister, to the War Cabinet, but this was insufficient for him. In the crisis he felt he had to remain in Australia, and he sought to establish a right to involvement in the day-to-day decision making. In London, Page was able to devise a plan to provide not only consultative machinery at a political level but also "continuous co-ordination on every vital plane of war activity" as well; and Curtin's constant pressure for full accreditation resulted in continuous representation. At the end of December the Dominions Secretary reported to the House of Lords that what Australia had asked for, and what Churchill had agreed to, was that

> . . . the accredited representative of the Commonwealth Government should have the right to be heard in the United Kingdom War Cabinet in the formation and direction of policy.

This was a step forward, but Curtin was not fully satisfied; he believed that it was also necessary for Australia's voice to be heard in the inner counsels of policy making in Washington. The threat to Australia itself had meanwhile grown more menacing.

General Wavell's appointment had placed him in control of commanders in Burma, Malaya, the Indies, and the Philippines; but by mid-March 1942, when Java fell, the entire defence position was in disarray. Australia's northern coast was in great jeopardy; Darwin had been badly mauled and was grievously threatened as Japanese strength was built up in the islands. In New Guinea the Japanese had strong footholds at Lae and Salamaua, and they were moving south in the Solomons, threatening communications with the United States. The ABDA (American, British, Dutch, Australian) strategic area had been dissolved, but responsibility for the strategic direction and control of Australia and New Zealand had not been settled. Curtin now pressed for an American commander for the south-west Pacific area. This was endorsed at a conference between members of the Australian and New Zealand governments, which also agreed on the need for the creation of a new strategic area to include both countries. On a visit to Washington Evatt, Curtin's minister for external affairs and a forceful advocate of the "Pacific" policy, appealed for approval of the proposal; it was accepted in principle, with the minor change that the area would be divided into two zones and each placed under separate United States commands. President Roosevelt was then asked to appoint General MacArthur supreme commander in the Australian zone.

At the same time the principal objective—first-hand contact with the United States in its war planning through a Pacific war council—was pursued by Evatt with the greatest possible vigour, causing some consternation and astonishment in Britain, and dismay even among some Australians. In spite of the threat, there were those (particularly older conservatives) who feared that the leaning towards the United States implied a loosening of the ties with Britain—but it was no more than an expression of the realities of a situation which could have spelled oblivion for Australia.

Eventually Australia's vigorous advocacy proved successful. Late in March a Pacific War Council bringing together the United States, Britain, Australia, New Zealand, Canada, China, and the Netherlands, was set up with headquarters in Washington. The *Sydney Morning Herald* welcomed the second Pacific War Council as a fruit of Canberra's "firm and justified insistence" on the principle that all the nations engaged in the Pacific war should have a direct voice in its management. However, neither the London nor the Washington council was seen by either Churchill or Roosevelt as much more than a fifth wheel; whatever courtesies might be extended to the lesser powers in the interests of Allied unity, the major direction of the war remained a joint American-British preserve even after Australia and other nations were consulted on developments and presented views. President Roosevelt, in a private letter made public later, described the Washington body as primarily serving "to disseminate information as to the progress of operations in the Pacific" and, secondly, providing a forum in which he could "keep everybody happy by telling stories and doing most of the talking."

With the threat to Australia's own security becoming daily more critical early in 1942, Curtin and his military advisers had insisted that Australia's own urgent defence needs must be given greater consideration in the overall war strategy. Churchill proposed the return of the 6th and 7th Australian Divisions from the Middle East for deployment in the Pacific theatre. However, the rapidity of the Japanese advance had made it unlikely that the Netherlands East Indies could hold out for long, and by mid-February the plan for landing the Australians at Java and Sumatra was no longer considered practical. On February 15 the chief of the Australian General Staff, Lieutenant-General Vernon Ashton Sturdee, advised the Prime Minister that the seasoned troops were needed in Australia to ensure the holding of a continental area from which to launch an eventual offensive. Curtin agreed wholeheartedly.

This touched off sharp behind-the-scenes exchanges with London over the use to be made of the Australian Middle East divisions, which were already steaming across the Indian Ocean. General Wavell urged that one division (or both) be diverted to Burma, in the hope that they might prevent the surrender of Rangoon and the closing of the Burma Road supply route to China. Members of the Pacific War Council in London (including Page) backed the Wavell plan, and on February 20 Churchill cabled Curtin, urging the diversion of part of the Australian force to Rangoon. His cable began:

> I suppose you realize that your leading division, the head of which is sailing south of Colombo to the Netherlands East Indies at this moment in our scanty British and American shipping, is the only force that can reach Rangoon in time to prevent its loss and the severance of communications with China. It can begin to disembark at Rangoon about the 26th or 27th. There is nothing else in the world that can fill the gap.

Churchill also stressed that the greatest military support for Australia in "this hour of peril" must be drawn from the United States; with this view President Roosevelt agreed and he cabled Curtin accordingly, pointing out that because of geographical factors the Americans could better handle the reinforcement of Australia than that of the other flank (that of Burma-India-China).

Curtin was unmoved. On February 22 Curtin cabled his reply to Churchill's appeal. The cable read, in part:

> In view of superior Japanese sea-power and air-power it would appear to be a matter of some doubt as to whether this division can be landed in Burma, and a matter for greater doubt whether it can be brought out as promised. . . . The Bay of Bengal is now vulnerable to what must be considered the superior sea- and air-power of Japan in that area.
>
> The involvement of our forces in this theatre therefore is not considered a reasonable hazard of war, having regard to what has gone before, and its adverse results would have the gravest consequences on the morale of the Australian people. The Government therefore must adhere to its decision.

Churchill, anticipating a favourable reply from Curtin, had meanwhile instructed that the convoy be headed northward towards Rangoon; on February 23 Curtin cabled again to reaffirm his government's decision, "which we made with the utmost care." Immediately the convoy was turned about.

Whether the Australian division could have saved the day in Burma remained a moot point. Those who opposed Curtin's stand held the view that the arrival of the Australians might have turned the tide; others were convinced that the force would have arrived too late to prevent the fall of Rangoon which came within a few weeks. Those who held to the latter view of the Burma situation could point to the fact that close to 300 Australians who landed in Batavia were taken prisoner when Java surrendered in March, and could argue that any Australians landed in Burma would have suffered the same fate.

Defence of the Australian mainland and of Australian territories, on land, turned out to be very much an Australian affair. Troops were needed to garrison the sprawling, empty north, where thousands of miles of coastline lay open and unguarded, and to hold New Guinea. Airfields had to be constructed in short order, and supply roads built, and these had to be protected. Unstinted participation in the general Allied effort had gravely compromised Australia's power for home defence. There was practically no effective air strength. Reliance on the plan of Pacific defence adopted by Britain, with its emphasis on Singapore as an impregnable bastion, had led Australia to take decisions which left the country denuded of strength in the face of direct attack.

The fall of Singapore had not only doomed the Indies and opened the door to the Indian Ocean: it had also given Japan dominance in the western Pacific, and sealed the fate of the Philippines. Admiral Isoroku Yamamoto's grandiose plan for a three-pronged sea offensive had been successful to an incredible degree: in the west, the invasion of Malaya and Borneo had gone like clockwork; in the centre the drive through the Macassar Straits already menaced Java; east of the Philippines, from island bases, the thrust was aimed at New Britain, whose splendid harbour of Rabaul could be a staging point for threats to Australia and the Pacific sealanes.

As Japanese domination expanded, potential Allied operation zones shrank. Allied flotillas—British, Dutch, and American—each with inadequate air protection, had been ineffectual in the separate actions they had undertaken in scattered areas, and even when all available ships were combined in one fleet, to operate in waters adjoining the Indies, the Japanese power was still dominant. The Allied force came under attack in the Macassar Straits and two United States vessels were severely damaged. There were running fights in a dozen minor battles; Japanese naval power seemed limitless, and many Allied vessels were sunk or severely damaged. The *Hobart* and *Perth* were in the thick of the fray, and on March 1 *Perth* went down in a night engagement.

Out in the broad Pacific the task of the United States Navy was to keep the sealanes open between America and Australia. Most of the heavy units of the United States Pacific fleet were still out of action, and as America was faced with the necessity of giving the fleet extended range to offset the superior numbers of Japanese craft, carrier task forces were organized, each of them built around a heavy aircraft carrier. Admiral Chester Nimitz, new commander-in-chief of the United States Pacific fleet, lost no time in arranging raids by the task forces on Japanese naval bases in the southern Marshalls and northern Gilbert islands—the first successful naval thrust against the enemy. When another strong task force was formed its first objective was Rabaul; but the Japanese were not be thwarted there, and they occupied all of New Britain and New Ireland, in a drive directed at the Solomons.

The position of the Philippines had become untenable. There were no United States bombers left in the islands, and by the end of February only three fighter planes remained.

On February 23, General MacArthur was directed from Washington to proceed to Australia and assume the new Southwest Pacific command. He and his party left Corregidor on March 12 in four torpedo boats which narrowly escaped interception by the Japanese as they skirted Mindoro on their way to Mindanao. MacArthur took off from Mindanao in a B–17 for Australia and landed at Batchelor Field while Darwin was under raid. When he reached Alice Springs his presence in Australia was reported, and at Melbourne thousands were on hand at the railway station to cheer his arrival. Australians felt a sense of relief, even in adversity; they were stimulated to greater efforts in the knowledge that they would not be alone in the desperate struggle. MacArthur then set up headquarters in Melbourne, issuing General Order No 1 on April 18.

American news correspondents using Australia as a base began to send back a flood of reports about the country and its war effort, while Australians made firsthand acquaintance with the thousands of Americans who were now arriving. To foster mutual understanding, individuals, community organizations, and governments made special efforts to help acquaint the two peoples with one another.

Ocean routes to Australia's west and east were still in jeopardy. Japanese submarines were ranging out across the Allied supply lines and around the Australian coast, playing havoc with coastal shipping. Meanwhile the Japanese invaders of many Pacific islands had established secure encampments close to the shore and worked on the construction of naval and air bases which soon became operational.

The first Japanese landings in eastern New Guinea were made early in March, when 3000 men landed at Lae. Before any effective opposition could be mounted to blunt the Japanese drive inland, supply routes had to be developed in a mountainous root-matted area where no wheeled traffic had ever been. The Australian army established camps in the Wau area and in the Bulolo valley late in March to block the infiltrators; but the Japanese had come to realize the this was not an effective route to Port Moresby.

The threat to Australia was growing on a more massive scale; but at the same time the significance of the Australian continent in the grand strategy of the Pacific was being more widely acknowledged. The distinguished American commentator, Major George Fielding Eliot, wrote at this time in *Foreign Affairs* that Allied operations in the southwestern Pacific now rested upon Australia as a house rests upon its foundations. "Possession of Australia is necessary if we are to have the mastery of the Pacific and Indian oceans," he added; "and in the mastery of those oceans are built our hopes of eventually smashing Japan."

In late March, the 1st Australian Corps (6th and 7th Divisions, less two brigades left in Ceylon) disembarked in Australia. These 46,000 veterans were the only seasoned troops in the country; another 63,000 men of the A.I.F. had not been out of Australia, and there were slightly over 250,000 militiamen. The 33,000 Americans included a contingent of air force men. MacArthur appointed General Blamey to command the Allied land forces, while American officers were placed in charge of the Allied air forces and Allied naval forces.

By April, Japanese ships, planes, and men were massed in the Indies and the Marshalls, and from these bases they were able to occupy harbours on the islands of Buka and Bougainville in the northern Solomons without opposition. Both sides realized that the war had entered a new and crucial stage. The Japanese believed they might now succeed in isolating Australia. The next phase of their plan remained contingent upon their securing Port Moresby, which would then become the pivot for further southwest Pacific conquests. They also needed air bases in the Solomons, and on May 1 they occupied Tulagi as a prelude to a move to Guadalcanal, increasing the threat to Allied supply lines. After Port Moresby, their next targets were to be New Caledonia, Fiji, and Samoa, which were now being strengthened as Allied naval bases.

Early in May the Japanese assembled a powerful force at Rabaul for the seaborne invasion of Port Moresby, while the Allies, anticipating the enemy's objective, mustered a fleet to stop this thrust. As it moved south the strongly guarded invasion fleet was to be shepherded by an attacking force from Truk whose task was to destroy Allied sea and air forces, raid Townsville (by this time a major defence base), and cover the landing at Port Moresby. By May 7 the invasion fleet was in the vicinity of the Louisiade Archipelago, off the eastern tip of New Guinea; as it moved into the Coral Sea an Allied force under Rear Admiral Frank Fletcher, consisting of two American carriers, eight cruisers (including H.M.A.S. *Australia* and *Hobart*) and eleven destroyers, deployed for interception. Not a shot was fired by opposing ships —they remained well out of gun range—but in a punishing two-day battle heavy air attacks inflicted big losses on both sides. Long-range planes operating from bases at Townsville, Cloncurry and Cairns were used for reconnaissance, but it was the carrier-borne planes of the opposing forces that engaged in the concentrated attacks. The Japanese lost an aircraft carrier, another was damaged, and most of the planes from a third were destroyed; one United States carrier was sunk, the other damaged, and there were other, minor losses. The Japanese assault had been stopped, however, and when the convoy turned back to Rabaul and the attacking force to Truk, Japan's first reverse was confirmed.

Within a month a great enemy force was on its way to attack Midway Island (which the Japanese had failed to take in the initial attack of December 1941) as a stepping-stone for an assault on Hawaii. On June 3, 1942, the fleet train including ten big transports was sighted 700 miles west of Midway by a United States Navy scout plane and was attacked by Flying Fortresses and torpedo-carrying Catalinas. Early the following day pilots reported powerful naval forces—actually Admiral Yamamoto's great battle fleet —converging on Midway, and a crucial battle began as Admiral Fletcher moved his carrier force between the Japanese units and began the attack with dive bombers and torpedo-carrying planes. The Japanese force consisted of five aircraft carriers, four battleships, nine cruisers, and thirty-four destroyers. From his flagship Yamamoto maintained radio silence. In the sky, the battle raged all day as planes swirled in attack and defence, and tremendous losses were inflicted as the American force steadily gained the upper hand. By nightfall Yamamoto's great force—the largest invasion fleet ever assembled—was in full retreat. The Japanese admiral's astonishing string of successes had ended, and with it his grand plan to eliminate America's aircraft carriers.

Although the extent of the victory was not fully appreciated at first, the Battle of Midway was a turning point in the great naval war. It helped to put an end to Japan's carrier supremacy and paved the way for United States superiority. The balance of power in the Pacific had been restored; from this moment the Japanese could be contained. With the situation stabilized, the outcome of the war at sea would henceforth depend on shipbuilding capacity. As Japanese naval power decreased and Japan faced a war of naval attrition, its hold on the island conquests was bound to shrink, since the number of land forces operating in island campaigns depended on the capacity to supply them.

The Japanese were firmly entrenched throughout the islands of the western Pacific, however, and for the time being General MacArthur was in no position to launch an offensive against them. The Japanese still had naval and air supremacy in his area, and the Allied ground forces in New Guinea were insufficient for more than guerrilla action against the Japanese who had established themselves at points along the northern coastline. In April, an Independent Company (the 5th) was sent from Australia to combine with the New Guinea Volunteer Rifles, a local militia unit, to step up ground action. By June, Kanga Force, composed mainly of these two units, was harassing the Japanese at Salamaua and along the Markham Valley (where they had established themselves following landings in March).

In July the United States Joint Chiefs of Staff, in a directive covering the strategy of the war in the Pacific, endorsed limited land offensives against the Japanese involving reconquest of the New Britain–New Ireland–New Guinea area. The first task—recapture of the Santa Cruz Islands, Tulagi, and adjacent positions—would be the responsibility of the South Pacific Area commander, Admiral William Frederick Halsey; the second—regaining the rest of the Solomons, and seizure of Lae and Salamaua—and the third, which involved recapture of Rabaul, were assigned to MacArthur. These Pacific operations were part of a plan approved at a conference between British and American representatives at which major strategic decisions, covering the entire field of the war, had been taken. The view of the United States Navy's commander-in-chief, Admiral Ernest King, stressing the danger of permitting Japan any further advance or consolidation, had been supported by President Roosevelt, and it was agreed to check Japan without further delay.

From their positions along the northern shore of eastern New Guinea the Japanese had begun to penetrate southward into the island, their aim being to converge on Port Moresby as a springboard for possible invasion of Australia. By mid-1942 they were ready to develop a two-pronged land drive to back up a planned naval movement. They decided to establish themselves at Milne Bay, easternmost point of the great island, for a drive along the south coast, while an assault was launched across the Owen Stanley range, the island's mountain barrier by following a little-used track that led from Buna-Gona south-west through the mountain village of Kokoda to Port Moresby. Accordingly on July 21 about 2500 troops went ashore on the north coast in the Buna-Gona area, in preparations for a drive through the Owen Stanleys, and shortly afterwards an amphibious attack on Milne Bay was initiated.

An Allied air base had been under construction at Milne Bay since early June. Early in August, scouts reported the Japanese preparations for the Milne Bay landing, and two Australian fighter squadrons and an Australian brigade were dispatched to the area. On August 25, Japanese transports, under the protection of bad weather, reached Milne Bay and a landing was effected after dark. Sharp fighting took place under the most difficult conditions of weather and terrain. Due to the effectiveness of Allied air opposition less than 2000 Japanese had reached the shore; but their tactics of attacking at night were well designed to exploit the terrain—a narrow muddy shore of thick jungle hemmed between mountains and sea. The struggle went on for some days. With Japanese vessels ranging the bay almost every night shelling shore positions to screen further landings, the situation remained perilous. The climax came just before dawn on August 31 when a determined Japanese attack on the main airstrip was repelled. After that, hard and skilful fighting finally carried the Australians into the main Japanese stronghold, which was destroyed on September 6. Stragglers who had evaded the Australians were being mopped up for months after the main campaign ended.

In repulsing the assault on Milne Bay, the Australians had scored the first land victory against the Japanese—or, as the Australian Army's official record put it, they had "knocked the first chip out of the Japanese war sword."

The overland drive from Buna-Gona had gathered pace, however. After the Australians were pressed back in a ferocious man-to-man struggle in the foothills, several thousand Japanese were shuttled across to New Guinea from Rabaul and thrown into the battle for the mountain trail leading through Kokoda (which had the only airfield in the rugged mountain country). Only a very small force of Australian troops had reached the Kokoda area to resist the Japanese when they fought their first engagement on July 23. As the build-up of Japanese forces continued—there were now 15,000 or more men involved—two Australian battalions began to push north across the mountains; soon the first of three brigades of Middle East veterans arrived in the area to help stem the Japanese advance.

The great problem was to maintain supplies to the frontline units. Lack of aircraft, and limited knowledge of supply-dropping techniques, meant that everything had to be carried over the mountains, and so the volume of supplies was limited by the capacity of the basic supply line of 2500 or so native carriers. Soon the Australians, fighting hard but heavily outnumbered, were forced back across the mountains. As the Army's official record noted, every man in the brigade of the original force, from commanders to cooks, played his part in the continuous delaying action. Nevertheless, by September 9 the Japanese, pouring through a 6,000-foot pass across the ridge of the Owen Stanleys, arrived in the region of the Myola lakes, 75 miles from their starting point. Seven days later the Australians lost Eoribaiwa, 30 miles from Port Moresby. As new Australian battalions were brought in, a firm base was established at Imita Ridge, where Major-General Sydney Fairbairn Rowell, the commander in New Guinea since mid-August, had ordered a stand. At this point the Japanese had outrun their supply lines and their stores were depleted. They could no longer find native supplies, and they were on the verge of starvation. Bombing and strafing, dysentery and malaria, had sapped their stamina.

Meanwhile MacArthur had been showing increasing concern over the Papuan fighting and in mid-September he urged Blamey to take command personally. Soon after his arrival in Port Moresby, Blamey removed Rowell from command of the New Guinea Force and appointed General Edmund Herring in his stead.

Infantrymen were already edging forward against the Japanese Eoribaiwa position, and the twenty-five pounders of the 14th Field Regiment, now brought into use for the first time in the mountain fighting, decimated the Japanese ranks. By September 28, when the Australians moved forward, the enemy had withdrawn. The advance, gathering pace, soon caught up with the enemy rearguard and enemy remnants. Back over the ridge the Japanese had constructed some strong well-sited defences, and heavy fighting produced considerable casualties. By November 2 the Kokoda Trail fighting ended and the stage was set for the coastal fighting in the Buna-Gona-Sanananda area.

In the gruelling jungle-mountain warfare, over 600 Australians had been killed, and 1,000 wounded. The terrain and climate had exacted a heavy toll, and several thousands of men had to be treated for illness. The only way for sick or wounded to be evacuated was on foot, or by stretcher-bearer. The help of the tribesmen had been an important factor in support of the Australians, and photographs, newsreels, and correspondents' stories that went out to the world recorded the courage and compassion of the Fuzzy-Wuzzies, as they came to be nicknamed.

While the Milne Bay and Kokoda Trail fighting was in progress, a great Allied campaign was being launched to clear the Solomon Islands, two parallel chains of volcanic ridges, separated by a 200-mile-long channel, the Slot. Many Japanese installations (and a 10,000 man garrison) had been established in the islands. On August 5, an Allied fleet of sixty-nine ships, including a battleship, three carriers, twelve cruisers of the United States Navy, and three Australian cruisers (H.M.A.S. *Australia, Canberra*, and *Hobart*) moved into the Coral Sea and, after dividing into two parts, on August 7 covered American Marines' landings on Tulagi (where the Japanese were constructing a base), Gavutu, and Tanambogo, and on the big island of Guadalcanal (where a Japanese airstrip was nearing completion). The assault on Guadalcanal involved 10,000 Marines, and it was successful in spite of repeated enemy air attacks lasting over two days. Thanks largely to the reports radioed by coastwatchers warning of the approach of bombers coming from Rabaul, it was possible to inflict severe losses on the Japanese; however during the night of August 8-9, a powerful Japanese cruiser force surprised patrolling Allied cruisers near Savo Island (between Guadalcanal and Tulagi) and during a swift action the *Canberra* was sunk with the loss of seventy-eight lives, along with three United States cruisers—all victims of gunfire or torpedoes.

By their actions, both the Japanese and the Americans indicated the importance they attached to the Solomons struggle in general and Guandalcanal in particular. It had become the chosen battleground for a major test, and both sides were prepared to commit large forces. The Japanese saw it as a key point in a great chain of island forts which they hoped would protect their stolen empire, and accordingly Admiral Yamamoto decided to fight to the death for its possession. The Americans believed it to be a suitable testing ground for tactics—land, sea, and air—which they could use against the Japanese in the new type of warfare dictated by conditions in the Pacific. Not surprisingly, the struggle for Guadalcanal continued for some months. Late in August, Henderson Field received its first planes; at about the same time a Japanese attempt to seize the airstrip was foiled.

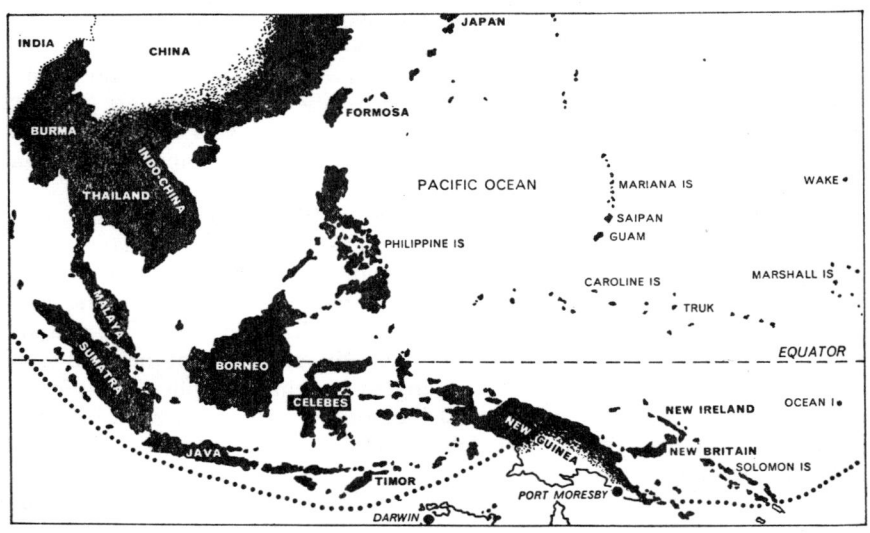

Sketch map, adapted from the Australian Army's *Five Fighting Years* (1944), showing the extent of Japanese conquests. The maximum penetration southward was reached about August 1942, and at that time the Japanese power extended almost six thousand miles along the Equator and in the region directly north of it.

Throughout, a key factor in the successful Allied plan to hold Guadalcanal and use the encounter there to vitiate Japanese strength was the foolproof warning system provided by Australian coastwatcher scouts on Bougainville, the 130-mile-long island lying directly along the path of Japanese aircraft on their long flight from Rabaul to attack the Guadalcanal area, and on adjacent islands. From their vantage points on Bougainville, coastwatchers Jack Read and Paul Edward Mason—Read at the island's northern tip, near Buka passage, and Mason at Kieta—were able to observe the Japanese attack flights and to radio details of the type and number of planes involved to the R.A.N's base at Townsville; from there the message was flashed to Melbourne and relayed to Pearl Harbor, so that within twenty minutes or so, United States ships and planes in the Solomons could be alerted with ample time to prepare for the attack. With this warning system in full operation, Allied airmen were able to inflict heavy losses on the Japanese.

As the struggle intensified, by day there was endless dog-fighting over the islands and ground patrols on Guadalcanal clashed in brief, close combat. Aircraft carriers, too valuable to risk in the narrow straits, exchanged punches at bomber range. The great Japanese counter-invasion attempt failed, and, although Japanese transports continued to land some troops and supplies, and while Japanese submarines lurked offshore, the Allied build up went on unchecked.

In November a Japanese attempt to reinforce the island garrison resulted in the severe mauling of the convoy, and no Japanese soldiers were landed. Japan never regained the initiative. Powerful reinforcements, including four aircraft carriers, were on their way to Admiral Halsey, and when the Japanese tried in January 1943 to rescue the remnants of their exhausted and beleagured garrison, the twenty destroyers failed to break through. A trickle of men got away; but by February the Japanese force on Guadalcanal had been sealed off.

The Japanese had suffered severely. Some of Japan's finest ground forces had been engaged, yet they had suffered losses in excess of 50,000 men, including naval and air personnel and troops aboard destroyed transports. Even more significantly, 500,000 tons of Japan's merchant shipping had been lost in the Solomons—a telling blow since back in the home islands strategic materials were fast being depleted, with stockpiles of fuel and iron ore already low; the absence of shipping to replenish supplies from Asian sources would soon be felt. Admiral Yamamoto's desperate gamble in the Solomons had failed. For his part, Admiral Halsey credited the coastwatchers with having saved Guadalcanal.

By the end of 1942 the Japanese land campaign in Papua had likewise failed. With the Kokoda airstrip again in Australian hands the problems of supplies was lessened, and as trails were cleared of Japanese infiltrators the drive against Japanse positions along the Buna-Gona coast accelerated. In coastal areas the Japanese had built a maze of earthworks and pillboxes to provide perimeter defences, and these strongposts were stoutly defended. Meeting stubborn opposition, Australian and American troops (who were involved in three separate drives) suffered heavy casualties. The Japanese worked desperately to reinforce their garrison from Rabaul, and they succeeded in landing some additional troops; however, punishing air strikes against barge convoys kept the reinforcements to a minimum. Using information relayed by coastwatchers, Allied planes were able to strike against the small craft which the Japanese were using to ferry men and supplies down the coast after they had been landed from submarines at secluded points. Nevertheless, the attrition suffered by the Allied forces in the land fighting remained great. Some Australian brigades lost three quarters of their original strength in the protracted, gruelling struggle; American units also suffered heavy losses from wounds and illness. More than 2000 Australian soldiers had been killed in New Guinea, with nearly twice as many wounded. American casualties in the New Guinea fighting were about half as great. Some of the most costly and difficult fighting was done by Australian militiamen; it included the bitterly contested Sanananda struggle, which resulted in 1400 Australian casualties.

Australia's high degree of concentration of settlement in the south and east of the continent aggravated the special problems of guarding the continent's 12,000 mile coastline. The northern areas, particularly in the Northern Territory and north-west Australia, had looked dangerously open to attack as the Japanese swept south early in 1942, but the return of the A.I.F. divisions which brought back equipment supplied in the Middle East helped strengthen the mainland defences. Although no landing was attempted by the Japanese, air attacks were launched on coastal areas of the north-west, including Broome and Wyndham in Western Australia. In all, ninety-six air raids were made against the Australian mainland. In addition, there were nuisance shellings of Sydney and Newcastle, and an ill-fated excursion by midget submarines into Sydney Harbour on the night of May 31—June 1 in which three two-man underwater craft were launched from larger submarines outside the harbour. One of the midget craft became entangled in nets forming a protective boom and was destroyed, but the other two managed to penetrate the harbour; although patrol craft quickly destroyed one with depth charges, the other launched its torpedoes against the United States cruiser *Chicago* and, in hitting a depot ship moored nearby, killed nineteen ratings.

When Japan entered the war, defence of the mainland was primarily the responsibility of militia troops. Support was available from the Volunteer Defence Corps, whose role was of necessity limited to that of watching isolated sections of the coast and static duty in the protection of vital industrial localities (which were thought to be in danger of enemy attack or sabotage). The composition of Australia's Home Army was described for Americans by Brian Penton, writing in the *Saturday Evening Post* in May 1942. He wrote:

> This army's beat extends from the hot, wet wastes of the north to Sydney and Melbourne—the largest white cities in the British Empire after London and Glasgow. It stretches from bomb blasted Darwin through the rocky and waterless salt plains of dead heat to the desert coast of the Great Australian Bight. It circles

through the lush jungles of Queensland to the dreary empty northwest, where the Japanese already have machine gunned the pearlers of the port of Broome and the cattle pens of Wyndham.

Today every man between eighteen and sixty is liable for service in this army, as a fighter or as a labourer, unless he is already working in a munitions factory or carrying on essential service.

To help in getting men and supplies to the northern garrison areas, new roads had been constructed. The main supply route, running north from Alice Springs (the railhead), was converted from dirt tracks to sealed highway able to carry trucks in all weather. Airfields were constructed at various points around the northern continental perimeter, and roads made to them. The army and civilian construction authorities shared the task. The road building authorities of the several states pooled their resources, and they were joined by the civilian army or civil construction corps, made up of men unfit or too old for active duty who were drafted compulsorily for this work. Eventually the empty areas were linked with the populous south and east by a network of roads, chief of which were an east-west highway (the Eyre) parallelling the transcontinental railway line, the Alice Springs-Darwin link, and a supply route to the Northern Territory from Queensland giving access to Darwin from Brisbane.

As men and arms were being rushed into threatened areas in the perilous days of early 1942, a great overlanding cattle drive was begun from the northern reaches of the continent so that any Japanese invasion force would be denied a ready source of food. Great herds were mustered and moved off the stations as rapidly as possible. With tens of thousands of cattle on the move the mobs were soon close to each other's heels as they were pushed southward along the main stock routes leading across the Northern Territory and into Queensland. Water supplies at some of the main bores were soon exhausted, and mobile engine-powered pumps had to be set up to supplement the normal wind-powered pumps. It was not long before some 80,000 head of cattle had been moved into safe areas. Some of them had walked well over 1000 miles across the continent.

Within twelve months of Japan's intervention in the war, enlistment in all Services had more than doubled; it then represented two-thirds of the male population aged between eighteen and forty years. Meanwhile, munitions production had been moving up steadily. Leading industrialist Essington Lewis, appointed as director-general of munitions in 1940, had expanded the organization, drawing support from civilian industry as well as from the established government production units.

Intensive organization of the home front for "total" war had become the prime task of the government. Control of the work force, as the key to mobilization of material resources as well as labour, was quickly found to be the most efficient means of restricting non-essential production. The reshaping of the industrial pattern went on apace. As economist Dr E. Ronald Walker, one of the architects of the diversion measures undertaken at this crucial time, noted subsequently in his review of Australia's wartime economy,

> ... many departments contributed to the execution of the Government's plans; but the strategy of the diversion of manpower and other resources was worked out in the Department of War Organization of Industry in the first weeks after Pearl Harbor, and the application of these plans by the various executive departments required continuous co-ordination through [the] Production Executive [created within Cabinet in November 1941].

The chairman of the executive was the Minister for War Organization of Industry, and its initial members included ministers responsible for munitions production, supply and manpower.

A manpower priorities board had been set up in mid-1941 to begin the task of resolving the competition for labour and to find more manpower, and under regulations issued in January 1942, Wallace Charles Wurth was given full authority as director-general of manpower. The directorate was empowered to take over all matters pertaining to manpower except wages and working conditions (which remained under the control of the Arbitration Courts). Essential undertakings were "protected" and movement of workers in and out of them, and call-up to the forces from them, were controlled. The production executive membership was by now extended to include ministers controlling finance, aircraft production, customs, trade, social services and health. In March 1942 registration with the directorate of all persons over sixteen years was made compulsory. "Identity" cards were issued to all civilians. Those who were unemployed were subject to direction to jobs.

New and enlarged government factories, and many annexes to civilian factories, were brought into operation, and large industrial organizations were assembling components made by groups of smaller manufacturers. Businessmen were appointed to various executive positions within the department of munitions and its various directorates. Increasingly large output was achieved, covering very great quantities of ammunition for small arms, medium and heavy artillery, and light and heavy anti-aircraft guns, and mines, aircraft bombs and mortar shells. Weapons of various types were produced, and the wide range of production was extended to include tanks, and radio, radar and signal units, as well as large quantities of barbed wire (for coastal defence, mainly), camouflage mesh, field cable, and an extraordinary multiplicity of other items. To help tap new sources of labour—and to avoid concentration in the coastal cities—"feeder" factories were set up in country centres, By 1943, a total of more than 150,000 men and women were engaged in munitions production and some 6000 in administration activities connected with it.

In course of time the department of war organization of industry became increasingly associated with many aspects of economic policy. Its minister, John Johnstone Dedman, a dour and doctrinaire planner, assiduously applied himself to the task at hand, and quickly he and his small group of newly-appointed experts devised the means of stripping the national economy down to wartime needs. Similarly the production executive of cabinet developed in the direction of economic planning and under Dedman became in effect a central planning authority rather than a body responsible for the execution of production programmes alone.

From early 1942 Australia was a nation virtually under siege. To meet the shortages and organize the civilian economy on a total-war footing, the national effort was intensified, concentrated, and made more effective. Many essential supplies were imported and there were serious shipping problems since supply routes were under attack and few ships were available. Items such as tinplate, aviation and motor spirit, kerosene, lubricating oils, cotton, rubber and aluminium were all in dangerously short supply. However, these, and materials needed for the manufacture of munitions, together with machine tools and other capital equipment, were secured from the United States. In February 1942 the government made its first move to prohibit a number of non-essential manufactures so that the output of essential goods could be maintained. At the same time, restrictions were placed on the use of certain materials which were needed for munitions production.

The diversion of resources and the prohibitions and other changes it involved could not be undertaken without cutting deeply into the life of the business community and of organized labour. The ever-present menace of invasion alone made acceptable the government's use of such sweeping powers over the individual. For its part, the government, deeply concerned with the need for the measures and for their acceptance, intensified its efforts to inform the public of the reasons behind them. At the same time, a permanent liaison was established by the department of war organization with manufacturers' and other businessmen's organizations and with the trade union movement in order to develop an interchange of ideas. One of the objectives was to eliminate unnecessary effort within each industry, and for this purpose labour-management committees were set up within various industries. Plans were developed for simplification of manufacturing processes and for the zoning of distribution and delivery systems so that by elimination of cross traffic strain on transport might be reduced.

In spite of the expert attention given the problem, the task of finding ways to devote the maximum resources to war while maintaining normal community life presented special problems for a nation of only 7,000,000 people with tremendous commitments, and a continent to defend. Basically, it came down to a matter of priorities; and civilian consumption had to be restricted. In announcing the introduction of clothes rationing, the Prime Minister made it plain that the easy days had gone when he said: "I say to you quite flatly that regard will be given only to the minimum requirements of the civilian population." There were wider issues than mere personal austerity, however. The government had come to realize, as an official explanation of the concept behind its win-the-war plan stated, that "a nation organized for total-war is itself an army." The need to maintain a delicate balance in the use of resources was explained this way:

> The fighting forces are only the first line of this [total] army. In the second line are the munitions workers, the men and women making war supplies of all kinds

which are necessary to keep our fighting forces in the field and to build up their striking power. Behind these is still another line—the transport and commercial workers who keep supplies moving, the farmers and the miners who produce the raw materials for war industries. But all these workers in turn have to be fed and clothed, to be kept warm and in good health. This is the last line of defence, and it includes the bread carter and the local doctor, the tram guard and the housewife.

The fundamental problem of organizing man-power in wartime is to ensure a proper balance in all these lines of defence. . . The war would be lost if we put too many men in the fighting services and left too few to maintain the necessary industrial basis of modern warfare; it could also be lost if we put too few men in the fighting services or war industries.

From January 1943 a special committee settled the rival claims for labour on a month-to-month basis. The committee took into account the effect on manpower of changes in general policy for the conduct of the war, and at the same time advised cabinet on matters related to the labour supply in order that various commitments might be kept in line with available man-power.

Imports were reduced further as shipping losses mounted. Australian industry faced a challenging task in producing more and more of the nation's fundamental needs, from machine tools such as lathes, drills, milking machines, precision grinders and presses to tradesmen's hand tools and a range of engines, locomotives, furnaces, and machinery of all kinds, as well as munitions ranging from rifles and machine guns to torpedoes, optical instruments, and a wide range of electronic commuxucations equipment.

To meet the challenge, a new reservoir of skills was created as thousands were trained by industry as fitters and turners, mechanics, metrologists, and in various other aspects of manufacturing. The "dilution scheme" was introduced to provide the numbers of operatives needed for the greatly expanded munitions industry. Concurrently with the development of technical training, facilities were developed for training in management. With the support of industry, classes were formed in connection with universities or senior technical schools in all states for the training of foremen. The Institute of Industrial Management, formed in Melbourne in 1941, provided for the further training of supervisors and managers from industry generally; branches were soon operating in Sydney, Brisbane, Adelaide, Newcastle, and Wollongong. A clear break was made with the older practice of many large firms under which reliance had been placed on managers or executives from overseas. To a very large extent management now became the responsibility of Australians. As new factories or additional annexes were opened, almost without exception the men in charge were Australians.

As a natural consequence of war, the federal government's power was greatly increased. Some state responsibilities were taken over by the Commonwealth, but generally the federal government had moved in to do, in war, what state governments would not wish to do in peace. There had been no successful challenge to the Commonwealth's right to peg prices and direct labour to specific employment as a wartime need; the High Court upheld this right. In March 1942 the Treasurer informed the states that the

Commonwealth intended to become the sole collector of income taxes, and in August a system of uniform tax replaced the old system. When the federal government's right to monopolize taxes was challenged, the High Court ruled that, in effect, under its normal tax power the Commonwealth was within its constitutional rights if it levied taxation at so high a rate that in practice the states could no longer levy taxes. Further it was held that the federal government has power to make grants to the states in return for their undertaking to refrain from taxing. The right to do these things was not limited to the Commonwealth's defence power during war.

As war costs rose, the Commonwealth tripled income tax, increased other taxes sharply, and imposed new taxes. The disbursement to the states was less than a quarter of the total income raised under the uniform tax system. Immediate programmes of federal aid were drawn up for such projects as state roads and duplication of rail tracks to cope with the transport of troops and munitions; other special help was given to such undertakings as the pipeline that carried water from the River Murray more than 200 miles to Whyalla, where the Broken Hill Proprietary Company built a shipyard. Although the state premiers met each year to discuss their state needs, defence requirements came first, and their old independence no longer meant very much.

By the beginning of 1943 the war of attrition was beginning to tell on Japan. The fighting in the Solomons had proved punishing to both sides; but whereas the Japanese Navy could not replace its tonnage, American shipyards were able to launch four units for each vessel lost. The Japanese were not yet being rolled back; but the tide had turned. In the South Pacific the shipping lanes were being cleared, and American tanks, planes and men were reaching Australia in greater numbers. Allied leaders met at Casablanca to set strategy for 1943, and the beat-Hitler-first policy was confirmed; but the United States Navy was already hammering at Japan's outer defences and Tokyo itself had been raided by Flying Fortresses.

It was clear that ultimately a major Allied military counter-offensive would be directed north from Australia to take advantage of island stepping-stones leading to the heart of the Japanese empire. It was necessary to break through Japan's outer ring of steel; and with this objective in mind MacArthur began the drive to neutralize Rabaul, less than 3000 miles from Tokyo, and to strike at Japanese-held positions within air range of New Britain. The Japanese, who had hacked fifty or more airfields out of the jungle to protect their New Guinea positions, were not passive; the Japanese commanders had six divisions based on Rabaul (with a total strength of about 90,000 men) which could be reinforced by 60,000 more within three weeks, and they still had the initiative locally.

If the over-all Allied plan for 1943 placed relatively little emphasis on the Pacific, the Australian forces were heavily committed. The Japanese still had to be cleared from large areas of the New Guinea mainland, particularly the Markham Valley-Huon Peninsula-Madang region—an objective for which Blamey had been developing plans for some months. It took prolonged and difficult fighting in jungles and over razorback mountains to eradicate the infiltrating Japanese, who were being steadily reinforced for a drive on Wau, which was to serve them as a mountain staging post from which a new push towards Port Moresby could be mounted. By mid-March, after constant patrolling and probing, Kanga Force had gained the upper hand. A major effort by the Japanese to revive their advance was to follow the dispatch of reinforcements from Rabaul, but this venture was thwarted when the Japanese convoy including eight transports was caught and virtually destroyed by land-based bombers in the Battle of the Bismarck Sea (May 1943).

There was a lull in the fighting as both sides reorganized. The Australian Army under General MacArthur still outnumbered the American. Of the four A.I.F. divisions, the 7th had been wholly committed to Papua together with two brigades of the 6th; another brigade of the 6th was the core of the Northern Territory garrison. Of the eighteen militia brigades, six had been committed to Papua, five were in Western Australia, and two in the Northern Territory; only five remained to meet commitments throughout eastern Australia. The Australian Army numbered some 466,000 men, of whom 280,000 were A.I.F. MacArthur had about 110,000 American troops, while in the South Pacific command Halsey had five divisions. Australian airmen, who had been heavily engaged throughout in helping to blunt the Japanese thrust, were in thirty-one operational squadrons, representing almost half of all the squadrons (sixty-nine) at the disposal of Major General George Kenney, commander of the United States Fifth Air Force. Twenty-four of the squadrons were under the operational control of Air Vice-Marshal William Dowling Bostock; they included six in the Darwin area. The remaining seven were under Kenney's direct control in a formation, No. 9 Group, deployed in the Port Moresby and Milne Bay areas. As pressure was increased against the Japanese in the Rabaul area in the opening moves of a concerted northward thrust by Admiral Halsey's Solomons forces and from General MacArthur's adjoining area, the R.A.A.F. No. 9 Group was called upon to help clear the way and protect the advance. The Japanese replied directly with strikes against the Solomons and, as a diversionary move with intensified air action against the Darwin area, where three Spitfire squadrons fought off the attackers.

Prime Minister Curtin, meanwhile, had come to the conclusion that voluntary enlistment for overseas service would not provide sufficient numbers of men to carry the war against Japan into the islands where it would have to be fought. He resolved to amend the law limiting the use of conscripts to Australian territory and—unlike Hughes a generation earlier—he decided to do this without resorting to a referendum. An active opponent of conscription in 1916, Curtin introduced the subject at a Labor party conference in 1942, pointing to the special reasons for extending the area for compulsory military service into a region adjacent to Australia and Australian territory. By his reasoned advocacy, he gained support for a reversal of the party's traditional policy. Legislation introduced and passed in February 1943 provided that the conscript militia could serve anywhere south of the equator between the 110th and 159th meridians of East longitude—an area which took in the Celebes in the west and most of the Solomons to the east.

In the general elections of September 1943 the Labor party gained a sweeping victory. In his election campaign Curtin had appealed for a mandate to continue the effort towards victory, while his opponents fell largely to mutual recriminations. In the House of Representatives Labor secured forty-nine seats to the Opposition's twenty-five, and in the Senate Labor held twenty-two seats out of thirty-six—the greatest Labor majority in a generation.

The Japanese initiative had been sapped, but Australian troops were still heavily committed to difficult and punishing engagements in New Guinea. Savage fighting went on for months as a major confrontation took place in the tangled ranges behind Huon Gulf. Ambushes, patrols, bombardments and assaults made up the daily round as attack and counter-attack met encirclement and stubborn resistance in difficult terrain and weather. After Lae was captured, the drive to secure the Vitiaz Straits met opposition from large Japanese forces as a deadly seek-and-destroy war was continued along ridge and valley.

By the beginning of October the Markham and Ramu valleys were in Australian hands, and soon the United States Fifth Air Force was at work on its great base at Gusap. A determined Japanese counter-attack in the Finschhafen area was finally defeated in a series of bitter exchanges involving considerable losses. The Japanese remained in strength in the high ground of the Sattelberg area, and there was heavy fighting as the Australian 26th Brigade inched its way forward, supported by daily air strikes, by tanks, and by artillery, mortars and small arms fire. On November 24 the drive reached the Sattelberg heights and, next day, Sattelberg was found abandoned. In the Finisterre Ranges, weeks of arduous, dangerous patrolling slowly cleared out the enemy. By now the Japanese strength was being severely reduced. Denied reinforcements and supplies, and under constant harassment, Japanese troops were dying by the thousand. By mid-1944 the remnants were incapable of offering effective opposition.

At that time, noting that the aggregate number of Australian troops employed in New Guinea had "approximated the equivalent of probably ten divisions," an army publication, *Five Fighting Years*, commented that

> ... in the South-West Pacific Area the Australian Army has fought as a unified command, and has been employed as required, irrespective of whether the uniformed have affixed the labels "A.I.F." or "Militia" to particular formations.

While the Australian offensive had been in progress, planning of operations had gone far ahead, and punishing attacks had been developed. A concentrated air offensive against Rabaul had been in progress since October 1943, and by the end of the year MacArthur's forces had begun operations to open the Vitiaz and Dampier Straits and a United States unit had been landed on the south-west coast of New Britain. In February 1944 New Zealand forces occupied Nissan Island, just over a hundred miles from Rabaul and within a month or so Rabaul had been effectively isolated.

The advance on the heart of the Japanese empire was by now moving rapidly as the leap-frog technique of by-passing Japanese island strongpoints had already carried General MacArthur's forces through the perimeter of Japanese power. Fleet Admiral Nimitz had gathered an immense naval force to support an advance into the Marshalls, and key islands there fell in the early months of 1944. By that time MacArthur's forces had moved far along the New Guinea coast—landing first at Aitape, and then at Hollandia, which was rapidly converted into an immense base. By mid-1944 Biak Island had been secured; even before the struggle there was concluded, Noemfoor Island was seized. Japanese efforts to dislodge the American force on Bougainville proved futile, and MacArthur's forces made their rapid advances. Nimitz unleashed an assault on the Marianas, where Saipan, Tinian, and Guam were taken after heavy fighting. Morotai was next on MacArthur's list, and from there he moved on to redeem his pledge to return to the Philippines. Anxious to have American forces freed for this task, he arranged that the 1st Australian Army (comprising four divisions) should relieve the six American divisions engaged in holding defensive lines around recently captured bases in the New Britain-New Guinea-Solomons area, and that the 1st Australian Corps (the 7th and 9th A.I.F. divisions) should take part in the northward advance.

In August 1944 MacArthur transferred his headquarters from Brisbane to Hollandia (his advance headquarters had been in Port Moresby since July 1942). By that time the American ground forces under his command (more than 500,000) outnumbered the Australian. Two months later the attack on the Philippines was launched with a landing on Leyte; at the same time American naval forces engaged the Japanese fleet in a series of battles in which it suffered losses that crippled it beyond hope of recovery. By early 1945 long-range bombers based in the Marianas were attacking targets in the Japanese home islands. From his headquarters at Pearl Harbor, Nimitz was in command of over 1000 ships and more than 2,000,000 men—the greatest accumulation of naval power ever assembled.

In the war against Hitler and Mussolini the Allies had suffered varying fortunes, but had finally moved from the defensive to the attack.

Immediately after Pearl Harbor, German prospects were enhanced as strategic considerations brought about a draining of Allied strength from the Middle East. Rommel, who had planned to pull all Axis forces out of the Tobruk area on the very day war broke out in the Pacific, suddenly found himself able to regain the initiative in the desert war. From early 1942 dangerous days were in store for the Allies. The Germans, strongly reinforced with tanks, armoured cars, and supplies, quickly gained the upper hand and, after local successes, swept eastward, capturing Tobruk from its South African, British, and Indian defending forces, and driving deep into Egypt.

The onrush was not stemmed until it reached El Alamein, only 60 miles from Alexandria, at the end of June 1942. Heavy air bombardment helped to halt Rommel's forces, and the British commander succeeded in applying infantry pressure against the quickly strengthening Axis forces. Early in June the 9th Australian Division arrived from Syria and the added strength made it possible for a British offensive to be mounted. In mid-July Rommel saw the situation as one of "crisis proportions"; he attacked the Australian and New Zealand positions inflicting heavy casualities but without making major gains. Further reinforcements arrived and a British attack was launched; it failed, and by the end of August Rommel had hopes of a breakthrough to the Nile delta, but General Bernard Montgomery, with strong forces at his command, planned diversionary raids and pinned Rommel's forces down. The great Battle of El Alamein, which opened at 10 o'clock on the evening of October 23, began the rout of the Axis forces; after ten days of bitter ar- moured and infantry fighting, in which the Australians played a key role, the breakthrough came, and on November 4 Rommel ordered a general withdrawal. Tobruk was retaken ten days later and Tripoli captured in January; in May 1943 all Axis forces in Africa surrendered at Tunis.

The titanic struggle in eastern Europe had not gone according to Hitler's plans. The Russians had fought desperately and had inflicted heavy losses in preventing the quick capture of vital objectives. By the spring of 1942 the Germans had found themselves committed to a long and punishing war as their drives were slowed or halted by Russian counter-attacks and scorched areas. By November 1942 a winter offensive by the Russians was inflicting tremendous casualties and losses of war materials; by mid-1943 Hitler's forces had been reduced to half their 1941 strength.

Following the collapse of the Axis forces in North Africa, Allied strength had been gathered for direct assaults on Europe. In July 1943 the attack on Sicily began as a prelude to the Mediterranean drive; the Allies landed in Italy in September in the face of German defenders, since Mussolini had been removed and the Italians were officially out of the war. History's greatest invasion was launched across the English Channel at daybreak on June 6, 1944, when the beaches of Normandy were stormed. Massive Allied bombings of German targets and the pressure of ground forces advancing from the west, combined with the inexorable advance of Soviet forces, doomed the Nazi stand as the Allied ring tightened. It was clear by the beginning of 1945 that the war in Europe was in its final phase.

In the western Pacific, as MacArthur's main thrust through the Philippines was being developed, far to the south Australian forces were engaged in three separate and isolated compaigns—on Bougainville and New Britain and in the Aitape-Wewak area of New Guinea. It had been the policy of the American commanders in these areas to defend a relatively small perimeter around the airfields but to leave the Japanese more or less unmolested beyond the defended lines. Deep patrolling was maintained, largely by Australians, with parties of armed natives, but little attempt was made to clean up these pockets of resistance. This might have been sound from a strictly military viewpoint, but Australian leaders were concerned about the implications of allowing large numbers of Japanese to become embedded in the islands, and they did not accept MacArthur's view that by-passed Japanese forces could be ignored because they were "strategically impotent." New Britain and the Solomons, as well as New Guinea, were too important in terms of Australia's long-term security for their occupation by the Japanese to be allowed to continue a day longer than necessary.

The fact was that Japanese garrisons on these islands were strong and well-organized, and those in them were busily cultivating crops. Nor could they be easily eradicated; they had formerly tied up six United States divisions and part of a seventh, and they were now pinning down three Australian divisions and part of a fourth. Blamey decided to order the destruction of the enemy where this could be done with relatively light casualties and, elsewhere, to aim at containing the enemy in a restricted area by use of a smaller force. As a result, on Bougainville the Australian force set out to drive the Japanese back to their main base; on New Britain its objective was to push the enemy back into the Gazelle peninsula and hold the neck of the peninsula, while in the Aitape-Wewak area the intention was to drive the enemy from his bases and gardens. These plans, Blamey determined, might be carried out by retaining a minimum of Australian troops in these areas and using native troops to wage guerrilla warfare until the Japanese had been annihilated. As this plan of attrition went into operation it was discovered that the numbers of Japanese involved were greater than suggested by earlier estimates; there were 40,000 or so on both Bougainville and New Britain, and about 25,000 in the Aitape-Wewak area.

As the main Allied thrust was now far to the north, there was comparatively little air or sea support for the Australians' mopping-up operations. In the difficult fighting on Bougainville and New Britain, commando and regular units carried out the main operations, while groups of native scouts and guerrillas led by officers and men of the Allied Intelligence Bureau harassed the Japanese and sent back information from points far behind the enemy's lines. In New Guinea, similar tactics, with Australian patrols led by officers of the Australian New Guinea Administrative Unit and Allied Intelligence Bureau, resulted in the clearing of the Torricelli Mountains and the capture of the main base at Wewak. In these operations many thousands of Japanese were killed, and thousands died of illness. Australian casualties were kept at a small fraction of the Japanese losses.

The Japanese war lords appeared determined to pursue the struggle, even though the pressure against Japan was growing almost daily. To help rebuild morale, the Japanese had stepped up the war in China with a new offensive directed towards Chungking; the attack had been blunted and finally stopped as more supplies reached China over the newly-constructed

Ledo Road (connecting the Indian railhead with the old Burma Road). The final stepping stones to Japan itself—Iwo Jima and Okinawa—had fallen to the Americans, and American bombers had stepped up their attacks on the home islands. In Asia, the great masses who were under Japan's domination were showing signs of restiveness; among them, millions were starving. Even though resistance among the conquered people was growing, defiance still came from Tokyo, and there was fear in many Allied quarters that the war might drag on for years. The mopping-up of bypassed Japanese garrisons and stragglers in the south-west Pacific went on throughout the areas of contact.

The Royal Australian Air Force shared in the assault on Morotai, in the Halmaheras, in September 1944, and Australian ships were prominent in the Allied task force which crippled the Japanese fleet off Leyte in October. In this battle an enemy plane crashed and exploded on the bridge of the flagship *Australia*, killing many officers and men; among those seriously wounded was Admiral John Augustine Collins, who six months earlier had been appointed Commodore, the first graduate of the Royal Australian Naval College to command the R.A.N. Throughout the various phases of the Allied offensive, ships of the R.A.N. squadron had been constantly engaged as a task force of the United States Seventh Fleet, while frigates, corvettes, and smaller craft had undertaken both routine patrolling and special assignments in the south-west Pacific and the Indian Ocean.

In Europe, the advance on Germany continued from both east and west. News of Hitler's suicide early on May 1, 1945 came almost as an anti-climax; for many months the paranoic Fuhrer had been hardly more than a fading symbol. The final German surrender was not long delayed; it became effective at midnight on May 8 as the Third Reich passed into history.

The final involvement of Australian land forces came when the Allied attack was made on Borneo in April 1945. Among the objects of the operations in British Borneo were the establishment of an advanced fleet base at Brunei Bay and the recapture of the oilfields. The task was allotted to the 9th Division, and involved a force totalling 29,000 men, including members of the R.A.A.F. A slightly stronger force (the 7th Division) attacked Balikpapan in July, seized its big refinery, and soon overcame resistance.

While the recapture of Borneo was being undertaken, weightier efforts were bringing the Pacific war to its final conclusion.

The colossal productive capacity of the United States was having its effect. Japan's strategy of building a great ring of steel on newly-won island bases as an impregnable protection for the inner empire had been thwarted, and as greater Allied strength was brought to bear in the Pacific, the Japanese found themselves strictly on the defensive.

Japan's fate was sealed early in July when a great flash lit the desert in New Mexico, briefly eclipsing the stars and raising mushroom-shaped incandescent cloud. President Truman warned Japan of "utter destruction" unless surrender came quickly; but the Japanese leaders failed to grasp the significance of that warning and the period of grace was allowed to pass. On August 6, destruction rained on Hiroshima from an atom bomb carried from Tinian and dropped on the city.

Three days later the Soviet Union announced its decision to declare war on Japan, and Russian armies at once overran Manchuria. On the same day, a second atom bomb fell—this one on Nagasaki shipyards. On August 14 the Emperor recorded a broadcast undertaking full surrender; thereupon more than fifty Japanese leaders chose suicide. Radio Tokyo conceded before closing down that Japan had lost the initial fight in her "hundred years' war" for domination.

On September 2 the U.S.S. *Missouri* standing in Tokyo harbour was the scene of the formal surrender as General MacArthur and Allied army, naval, and air force leaders watched a frockcoated Japanese delegation sign the documents drawn up for them.

Some eight weeks before, Australians had mourned the death of John Curtin, the man who had carried great burdens for nearly four years as Prime Minister.

In the six years of war Australian casualties exceeded 31,000 killed or died of wounds—one third of them members of the R.A.A.F.—and almost 2500 missing, presumed dead. Nearly 40,000 men had been wounded.

The horrors of war were not wholly over with the surrender. As the gates of the concentration camps of Europe were opened, the grisliest story of human bestiality was revealed. There were also shocks for those who shared in liberating prisoners of war, for the war years had been nightmares of sickness, hardship, and short rations for those behind the enemy lines. About 8000 Australian prisoners were released from Italy and Germany; about 250 had died during internment and some 700 had escaped.

Greater losses were suffered under Japanese hands; of the 22,000 Australian prisoners taken by the Japanese, nearly 8000 had died; of those liberated, some were in camps in Manchuria and Formosa, but most were in the Changi camp on Singapore Island. Thousands had been taken from Changi to work on the construction of the Siam-Burma railway; a fifth of these men did not survive the ordeal. Others, sent to Borneo camps, had suffered ruthless treatment, and hundreds had died in "death marches." Of all the prisoners of the Japanese, only a handful had escaped. Less than 14,000 members of the A.I.F., 400 of the R.A.A.F., and 231 of the R.A.N. were recovered from Japanese prison camps.

Although the Japanese had been brought finally to unconditional surrender, their nearly-four years' occupation of the islands of the western Pacific and of the lands of Southeast Asia had left an indelible mark on the conquered people. In their breakneck advance the Japanese had inflicted a tremendous defeat on the old colonial masters; they had taken hundreds of thousands of white men as prisoners, and they had studiously exploited this so as to leave in the minds of native peoples the certain knowledge that the white man was no longer invincible.

This legacy was to ferment slowly, and to cause a flare-up of nationalism after the Japanese themselves had surrendered and had been returned to their home islands.

Part
Seven

Part
Seven

New frontiers

THROUGHOUT WORLD WAR II the vision of a better world—a world of greater justice, of less poverty, and without enforced idleness—had been growing among people in all the English-speaking countries. Even as early as 1941 the question of general post-war reconstruction was assuming importance in the war aims of the Allies. In Australia, and in New Zealand, almost forgotten hopes and a reformist zeal were revived. This time a better world would be fashioned. The drive within the Labor party to achieve longtime goals gathered pace in concert with the determination evident among great nations to promote social justice through more positive government intervention in economic affairs. For the first time Labor leaders could feel that the English-speaking world was coming to accept many of the progressive objectives the party had long been advocating.

The dreams of the average citizen at home and the men at battle stations had been stimulated first by the high aims set down by President Roosevelt and Prime Minister Churchill in the Atlantic Charter, prepared during their historic shipboard conference of August 1941. In more specific terms, the Lend-Lease agreement signed by the United States and Britain provided for joint action by the two countries directed to "the expansion by appropriate international and domestic measures of production, employment and exchange and consumption of goods which are the material foundation of liberty and welfare of all peoples"; such action was open to all other countries participating in the Lend-Lease programme. The broad purposes and principles set down in the Atlantic Charter quickly won wide approval, and they were accepted by the twenty-six countries (including Australia) that signed the Declaration of the United Nations on January 1, 1942. As well as promising a peace that would offer all peoples security from aggression and freedom to choose their own government, the declaration supported the principles that all nations should have access on equal terms to the trade and raw materials of the world and that "all men in all the lands" should have freedom from fear and want; it also pledged collaboration between all signatory countries aimed at the attainment of improved labour standards and social security.

Faith was sustained by the inspiring words of great leadership, but as the war became more intense and involved greater sacrifices, men and women were less beguiled by abstractions and the eloquence of political leaders and instead sought positive programmes for social betterment. As a reaction to war waste and war-caused shortages, the Age of Longing dawned. It appeared first in the United States, then in all the British lands. It took the form of pressure from the ordinary citizen for policies which would produce the larger harvest and the greater productivity that science and nature and technology could now be made to yield. In practical terms it came down to a drive for more money and better working conditions, and the assurance of steady employment. Expectations submerged during the depression-ridden 1930s re-emerged as an active force in men's minds.

Seeing marvels of ingenuity beyond their dreams emerge from the workshops of war, men the world over were deeply stirred; they began to think of tomorrow; and from being tinged with fear and uncertainty their thoughts became enlivened with hopes for the future. Millions of men uprooted by war, their horizons broadened, formed a new force for change and improvement. Above all they, and the communities from which they came, supported a new spirit of determination that, this time, the opportunity to build a better world would not fade. In the desperation of war, seeming miracles were being wrought with machines and in laboratories, through a newly-developed capacity for co-operative effort which the common task had called into being. Money seemed to be less a limiting factor than in pre-war days; and, people asked, if money could be found for war, why could not even more be found for the constructive tasks of peace?

As never before, the world in the 1940s was looking to the United States for leadership in the search for that better world. The country had come out of the most catastrophic depression in its history, and Roosevelt, champion of the common man and architect of the New Deal, had become a universal symbol of progressive economic policies. By bringing together men of organizing skills in various fields and putting into practice the programmes they proposed, Roosevelt had demonstrated that positive and constructive effort could defeat many of the problems of economic stagnation, wasted resources, and poverty. The New Deal—a vast interlocked series of economic and social reforms introduced from the early 1930s—had by the war years transformed America's economic structure and given hope where there was previously despair. Its success had been a resounding victory for the Keynesian interpretation; and it was natural that the American experience should influence governments everywhere to experiment with more disciplined economies and greater governmental involvement in the affairs of the community. In Britain a new determination to give greater protection to the individual, and particularly the underdog, was steadily growing, and the same forces were even more strongly evident in Australia and New Zealand.

As the danger of Japanese invasion faded, the Curtin government began to look closely at the issues involved in building a stronger nation, and a nation of improved living standards, after the war. Its members generally admired the progressive policies Roosevelt had initiated, and they saw themselves as innovators in rather the same sense. Following the general election of 1943, when Labor gained control of the Senate, the way was cleared for reformist zeal to be channelled into the creation of positive plans for the better world on which the party had set its sights.

A new spirit of confidence was being created; it drew a good measure of its inspiration from the American "presence" in Australia. With an outlook shaped by the backing of a mighty economy and the urgent needs of war, the Americans showed by example that, in spite of apparent difficulties, great things could be achieved through planning and "know-how"; to Australians, used to intuitive and often makeshift methods, the more studied approach was something of a revelation. Close administrative contact with many high-ranking officers of the United States Services helped to raise the sights of Australian leaders and administrators, and businessmen as well. A close working partnership arising from the fact that Australia was the bread basket and supply base for the United States forces in the area brought as one of its important side effects a much bolder view of the way to tackle practical problems. A new respect for machine-power and studied management methods developed.

Not only was the stature of the United States immeasurably enhanced in the eyes of all freedom-loving peoples as a result of its tremendous war effort; it already afforded practical examples of constructive achievement in innumerable ways. On the broader canvas of national development undertakings, examples within the United States came under closer study. Occupying a continent beset by recurring drought over large areas and suffering from quite a low level of land productivity, Australians could draw inspiration and guidance from American achievements in the application of modern farming techniques, and in such reclamation enterprises as the Tennessee Valley Authority's great river-control and hydroelectric project, then a relatively new and glittering example to the world of constructive, co-ordinated large-scale planning. In *TVA: Democracy on the March*, published in 1943, David Lilienthal, the practical genius behind the T.V.A. project, recorded ten years of success in the great undertaking and gave it as an example of the things that men might do with imagination and faith. His book he declared to be "a book about tomorrow." Men with faith and imagination, he wrote, could move mountains; out of their skills they could create new jobs, relieve human drudgery, give new life to fruitless and worn-out lands, and transmute the minerals of the earth and the plants of the fields into machines of wizardry to spin out the stuff of a way of life new to this world.

Lilienthal's book was very much in the minds of the earnest men from the Murray Valley's many districts who gathered in Yarrawonga in 1944 to discuss water conservation and other ways of making their region more productive. Representing resource development on a comprehensive regional basis, and not in a piecemeal patchwork, T.V.A. was an inspiration to those seeking action to bring greater productivity to the Murray-Murrumbidgee region. Convinced that great and constructive projects must be started, they listened while federal ministers, including Dr Evatt (who had visited the Tennessee Valley), and engineers and technicians encouraged them to believe that a T.V.A.-type plan, supported by federal funds, might be developed for their area. It was not very long before a massive project for water storage and hydroelectric power development in the Snowy Mountains was on the engineers' drafting boards.

The chief emphasis in the Curtin government's post-war planning was on the need to assure full employment and social security. A determination to assure such policies at home was reinforced by an active desire to see similar policies adopted on a world-wide basis—a desire based, in the government's view, on "the enlightened self-interest and the practical idealism" not only of Australians but of other peoples as well. General acceptance by all nations of domestic policies of full employment was taken to be the indispensable basis of stable and fruitful peace. Above all, the government believed, it was essential to avoid the road that led to "depressed consumption and sluggish demand."

To government leaders, and to experts around them, the example of wide-ranging federal initiatives in conservation and resource development in the United States were particularly significant because of the parallel structure of federalism in the two countries. In Australia, it seemed, the limitations of federal powers and the failure to develop co-ordinated policies among the states in the past had sometimes led to stalemate and inertia. The bold role opened to the federal government in war and put into practice after 1942 through carefully integrated policy decisions, was held to demonstrate a new potential in nation-building efforts; and after the introduction of uniform taxation (confirmed by the High Court's decision that the federal parliament had full taxing powers) it was natural that the Labor administration should seek to enhance the federal Treasury's role as supreme arbiter in economic policy. Curtin and Chifley and members of their party were convinced that only through more direct federal action could some of the nation's emerging goals be achieved. Chifley gave special weight to the need initially for expansion of basic services; this could best be done by maintaining national taxation policies that would draw off spending power. "Our national productive capacity," he declared, "can be positively built up by public investment in developmental works—in hydroelectricity, afforestation, soil and water conservation, and transport development."

Even before he became Prime Minister, Chifley as Treasurer was creating a dynamic approach to the matter of post-war development by taking a leaf out of the book of wartime experience. He deplored the fact that in the inter-war years Australia had failed to behave, as a nation, "as though we were planning anything in particular"; as a consequence, progress had been all too slow and uneven. War, on the other hand, had brought into use resources, physical and human, which the nation had never thought to use in peace and as a result the nation had achieved remarkable success in meeting production goals—but, Chifley declared, only when set down and planned had things been achieved.

The reforming zeal of the hard-working Labor ministers found expression in various phases of national policy. Labor had its sights firmly set on the elimination of poverty and the creation of a society offering more for the average man. By this time the basic aspects of Keynes' theories had been absorbed into government thinking in the democratic countries since there was wider appreciation of his work in elucidating matters of basic concern and in identifying ways whereby governments might promote general welfare. Keynes' central theme was that the modern capitalist economy did not automatically work at top efficiency, but could be raised to that level by the intervention and influence of government. He demonstrated persuasively that governments had not only the ability but the responsibility to use their powers to increase production, incomes and jobs. Any government, he said, could achieve calculated prosperity by manipulating three main tools: tax policy, credit policy and budget planning; through their proper use, private spending, investment and production would be strengthened. Such enlightened measures would leave both competition and the profit-motive to operate within the economy, and could achieve the main objective of a prosperous and well-ordered society without imposing the central economic direction which characterized the Russian experiment and other totalitarian economic proposals.

The necessary machinery for international collaboration was steadily built up at landmark conferences attended by all the wartime partners from 1943—first the Hot Springs conference on food and agriculture, and then the Bretton Woods conference (1944) in which international financial agreements were arrived at; the Keynesian interpretation was enshrined in both these and other wide-ranging agreements that followed.

The notion that prosperity might be buttressed by carefully developed government policies could be only part of the answer. If Australia's national growth were to succeed in line with the obvious need, other ingredients were required and accordingly a large-scale population building programme was discussed and accepted and plans laid for resource development and industrial development at as rapid a rate as possible.

The case for augmenting Australia's population without delay had been reinforced by wartime dangers, and those who studied the problem believed that Australia might have no more than twenty years or so to create a greatly strengthened industrial base and to build up a sizeable population. The same basic arguments that Gullett had advanced a generation before in his plea for national growth were still valid—only now the danger of an empty land was even more obvious and the urgency greater. After investigation of many facets, a carefully planned immigration programme was developed; it went into operation two years after the war. It placed emphasis on the intake of British settlers, but it also made provision for a broader spectrum of European migration than Australia had known before.

Meanwhile, industrial development was taking place as men returned to civilian life, and companies began to put in new plant. Growth was still slow and fitful; but it had started. Confidence in the future was particularly strong among the Australian offshoots of overseas firms that had been active for some years and now saw the prospect of expansion. The Australian headquarters of an American automotive firm, reporting to its parent at this time and urging largescale expansion, noted that the outlook in Australia was for continued stable government and sound financial policies; it was convinced that private enterprise would prevail, but that it would be "subject to over-all controls designed for the purpose of curbing abuses, the protection of the public, and the orderly development of the country."

That was not only the observation of the company management; it happened also to be almost precisely Chifley's view. To the Prime Minister-Treasurer, the need to keep a tight rein on an economy still suffering serious shortages—which he did through strict price and rent control, rationing of many basic commodities, and heavy taxation—was vital for an orderly transition to peace and the expansion of utilities on which all depended.

In international affairs, Australia was occupying a new and unexpected position of prominence. The Australian voice was being heard as never before as the government pursued its objectives with a forthrightness unequalled in the national history. This loud and constant expression of the Australian view was undoubtedly making it possible for Australia to get its way on many issues; but to a large body of people at home it seemed as though the break with tradition was too sharp and that in its uninhibited expression the new Australian policy was being pushed too fast and too far.

Circumstances, beginning in 1942 with the American backing for Australia, had given the continent and nation a special significance in American eyes. The country's prominence in military considerations rested upon its location between the Pacific and Indian oceans and the fact that it was a land anchor large enough to be held and developed as a base from which the Japanese could be driven back from their strongholds in the western Pacific islands. Combined with these considerations were other factors: there was general admiration for the Australian fighting man, and Americans sensed in the Australian spirit something akin to their own, so that they felt a marked attachment for the country. President Roosevelt's response to Prime Minister Curtin's appeal, combined with the American presence in Australia, had drawn Australians closer to the United States; the belief was strong that in a world in which Britain's position had been weakened, Australia would be able to depend quite simply on a benign American protection. As things turned out, the intensity with which Australia's presence in the international arena was sustained, and the extent to which Australia veered from its traditional bland acceptance of British responsibility in policy-making, were matters highly shaped by the special abilities and propensities of Dr Evatt, who drove those around him to move forward with speed and a minimum of fuss and red tape.

An eminent scholar and jurist, Evatt had become Minister for External Affairs a year after stepping down from the High Court bench to move into politics, and he had been sent by Curtin to Washington to put Australia's case for increased attention to the Pacific theatre. On that visit and subsequently in Washington and London, and in special conferences, he made Australia's influence felt in the international preparations for peace. He also initiated a training programme so that the cadre of diplomats might be expanded to meet the needs of the new Australian foreign service which he was calling into being.

In the development of an Australian standpoint on international affairs, Evatt followed the precedent set up by William Morris Hughes in 1919, but with new overtones. In 1943 he was already setting down Australia's responsibilities in the post-war world. "The war and our successful war effort will have converted Australia into a great nation," he wrote. "We cannot escape such a destiny—we can only try to be worthy of it. In truth, we will be trustees, not only for British civilization, but also for a decent world order in the Pacific sphere of influence." In New Zealand, the Labor government led by Peter Fraser held generally similar views.

Whereas Hughes had played the role of an Australian nationalist within the British framework and had thought in terms of the Imperial power (which meant that Australia's voice was effective only when part of the British voice), Evatt was moving out to create a less dependent stance for Australia. From the early stages of World War II Australia had had full diplomatic representation in the United States and in China, with reciprocal representation in Canberra. It was on this foundation that Curtin and Evatt built as they sought to make Australia's voice heard.

The old passivity in foreign affairs was at an end. In the context of the time, Evatt and his party believed it appropriate to express views on issues which in other days would have seemed entirely beyond Australia's scope. As an internationalist, Evatt's broad aim was to bring Australia's voice and views to bear on broad issues of international concern with the object of building a better world in terms of co-operation among all nations to avoid war and to promote greater social justice within every country. He gave special weight to the importance of the south-west Pacific, in war and peace, emphasizing (as Hughes had done) the significance of the arc of islands to Australia's north, and he advanced proposals for the defence of the whole area on the basis of joint planning with all nations directly interested.

A positive step towards fulfilment of this concept was the conclusion of an agreement with New Zealand in January 1944 setting out joint aims for the peaceful development of the Pacific regions in which the two countries were vitally concerned. Known as the Anzac Agreement, a formal and hastily-prepared "treaty" provided specifically for a "fuller exchange of information regarding both the views of each government and the facts in the possession of either bearing on matters of common interest," set up a permanent secretariat to assure uninterrupted contact, and contained mutual declarations on the prosecution of the war, future security for both countries and the welfare of native peoples of the South Pacific. Such a treaty between two self-governing members of the British Commonwealth was without precedent. Whatever its limitations, the agreement was a significant stepping stone to a regional system of defence and security—something which Evatt saw as a valuable preliminary to the type of world-organization system of general security.

There were some loud critics of the Anzac Agreement, who claimed that Labor was moving the southern Dominions towards a policy of segregation within the British Commonwealth as part of a "regional isolation" and that in pursuing an independent path they were diminishing the strength which Britain, as spokesman for a united Commonwealth, might exercise. It was also contended that the old ties between Britain and Australia were being weakened, and that as an insignificant nation in the world scene, Australia could best exert influence through a strengthened Commonwealth. In rebuttal, Evatt said that instead of apologizing for what had been done, Australians should take pride in the Agreement, which had received "cordial and respectful" attention abroad. "Never again will the people of Australia and New Zealand leave their vital interests unprotected," he said, adding that the favourable reception of the Agreement by impartial observers overseas should act as a reminder that Australia "has emerged from a prolonged period of national adolescence." In answering the general criticism that old ties had been loosened, Evatt stressed the common interests that would continue to bind Australia to Britain—loyalty to the same political ideals, economic and military self-interest, and, above all, a sense of family. The emphasis within the British family of nations was not on equality of status so much as on better means of communication and less on autonomy than on partnership. "The real tie," he added, "is the tie of brotherhood and kinship, which transcends all national links."

At the Commonwealth Prime Ministers' Conference in May 1944, Prime Minister Curtin revived the proposal, first put forward by Deakin in 1907 and reiterated by Bruce, for a permanent secretariat in London which could develop a common policy on behalf of all British lands. Curtin firmly believed that the Commonwealth would be much strengthened in the international arena if it had means of co-ordinating the views of its component members on important issues; and he also felt a lingering concern that Whitehall often took decisions affecting the Commonwealth without prior consulation or even information. His formal proposal for a Commonwealth clearinghouse was put forward as a means of achieving his objective of creating an Imperial agency, so that the British Commonwealth might have, "if not an executive body, at least a standing consultative body with all the facilities for communication and meeting." New Zealand gave full support to Curtin's idea, but strong opposition came from Canada's Mackenzie King and the proposal was shelved.

The Prime Ministers' meeting discussed and approved the Four-Power Declaration of October 1943 in which China, the Soviet Union, the United Kingdom, and the United States had stated their intention of founding an international organization open to all peace-loving states, large and small, to carry out the functions and responsibilities foreshadowed earlier in the declaration of the United Nations. When the first concrete step towards creation of the organization was taken at the Dumbarton Oaks conference (August-

October 1944), the Commonwealth countries were not individually represented; the four major powers (Britain, China, the United States, and the
Soviet Union) approved a plan for organized security resembling the League
of Nations in its outlines and objectives, but with a Security Council made
up of the five great Powers (including France) as permanent members and
six other states elected to it by the all-nation General Assembly. The crucial
task of preventing war was to be reserved for the Security Council acting
on behalf of the powers as a whole and sitting continuously. Numerous
activities contributory to international friendship and wellbeing were to be
dealt with by an Economic and Social Council.

This general plan was approved at the Yalta meeting of Churchill,
Roosevelt, and Stalin early in February 1945, when it was resolved that
a conference of the United Nations should be convened at San Francisco
to prepare a charter.

At Dumbarton Oaks no agreement had been reached on the question of
veto rights of members of the proposed Security Council, and the matter
became a contentious issue when the fifty nations met in San Francisco in
April. The veto issue was bound up with the comparative influence of the
major powers as opposed to the small powers, and with the question of
whether the great powers were arrogating to themselves too dominant a
role. The foreign ministers of Britain, Russia, and the United States all
argued that authority for the council to act or refuse to act must rest with
those nations whose military power would be essential to prevent aggression.
Russia was particularly insistent upon the responsibility of the great powers
alone to preserve peace in the post-war world, while the United States took
the view that its government could not be placed in a position where other
governments, large or small, could dictate the course of action it was to
follow. Anthony Eden, British Foreign Secretary, also supported the position
that military action could be taken against an aggressor only on the unanimous vote of the five permanent members of the council and that each
member should have the right to withold his vote.

In the heated dispute that developed at San Francisco over the veto power,
Evatt became chief among the spokesmen for the smaller powers seeking its
modification, and he took the initiative in organizing them into groups to
counter the Big Power concept. His vigorous attack was ably supported by
the representatives of New Zealand, Canada, China, and some of the other
nations; but his attempts to secure an end to the right of the veto were finally
rejected, and the United Nations Charter (signed on June 26, 1945) provided
that any one permanent council member, whether or not a party to a dispute, had the power to block action by the council. However, a Russian
attempt to extend the right of veto to include the issue of whether or not
a given subject should be discussed by the council had been voted down.
Evatt could claim a good share of the credit for this and for general
clarification of the voting formula, which strengthened the place of the
General Assembly in the structure of the organization.

Australia was a member of the fourteen-member executive committee
at the ten-week San Francisco conference, and throughout the proceedings

Evatt was a tireless, driving, dynamic figure as he moved from committee to committee to take up the fight on each big issue that arose in forming and shaping the United Nations organization. In all, the Australian delegation proposed a total of thirty-eight amendments to the draft charter, and of these twenty-six were accepted in substance. Largely as a result of the Australian-New Zealand influence, the status of the Economic and Social Council was raised; but on the crucial issue of full employment the charter, as finally approved, provided no more than the pledge of each country to promote this objective and to co-operate with ECASOC towards this end. The Anzac view that the council should have power to enforce special directions to achieve full employment did not prevail.

The charter approved regional pacts or agencies for dealing with matters related to the maintenance of international peace and security within the United Nations framework.

A significant section of the charter dealt with the obligations of members with "dependent territories," and the provisions adopted by the conference cleared the way for the dismemberment of the great colonial empires. Support for the colonial provision came from many quarters, and among its strongest supporters were the Americans who were inclined (according to a delegate) to assume "that the possession of colonies, like the possession of wealth, was the mark of sin and that revolt by colonies was perhaps the noblest episode that history could ever record." Under the charter, countries administering colonial possessions not only recognized obligations for the political, social and educational advancement of the dependent peoples, but also undertook to develop self-government. Further, to take care of territories which had been mandates under the League of Nations, an international trusteeship system was set up; its provisions were much the same as those of the League. Among the objectives of the trusteeship which the administering power accepted were the general advancement of the inhabitants of the territory concerned and their "progressive development towards self-government or independence as may be appropriate to the particular circumstances of each territory and its people and the freely expressed will of the people concerned." Australia was granted trusteeship rights in the New Guinea territory and (with Britain and New Zealand) in Nauru, and continued as the administering power in both territories.

In the United States, Evatt had become a symbol of the new and better world which Americans yearned to see established. The United States had played a key role in the war, and the old isolationism was at an end; in their new enthusiasm for setting the world aright, many Americans saw in Evatt a dynamic force outspokenly in favour of the goal of greater social justice for all; they considered him an "honest broker" on behalf of small countries. He became an important and respected figure, and his views were widely quoted whenever he was in the United States. With his flair for publicity, Evatt was able to take the limelight at a time when a new style of open-door diplomacy had become the vogue. Combined with officially-sponsored publicity efforts, his projection of Australia as a progressive, enlightened, forward-looking country seeking nothing more than honest and democratic solutions to all problems brought Australia to notice as never before. Meanwhile, on most issues related to Asian-Pacific affairs, Evatt followed American rather than British lines of approach.

Evatt sought by his aggressive and somewhat unorthodox methods to gain recognition for Australia as a "middle" rather than a small power. He succeeded in this to the extent that Australia's views were usually given more attention than might have been expected in view of the country's small population and limited potential in terms of military power. His election as president of the United Nations General Assembly for 1948–49 was recognition of his personal status in the international sphere; it also appeared to substantiate the new status envisaged for Australia. If his notions of justice and equality between nations were too idealist for the hard world of power politics, the attention he attracted among enlightened and important audiences in the United States spread into many significant areas. His work in tying Australia into a select co-operative position in United States strategic plans set a pattern from which special direct and indirect Australian-American alliances and connections were later to evolve.

Japan remained in the forefront of Australian thought on the future of the western Pacific. From the earliest post-war period Australia assumed the chief role among the British Commonwealth nations taking part in the military occupation of Japan. The Australian voice was strengthened by the appointment of its representative as spokesman for all British countries in the Allied Council in Tokyo, and by having an Australian (first, Lieutenant-General John Northcott—in 1946 –and then Lieutenant-General Horace Robertson, to 1951) as commander-in-chief of BCOF, the Commonwealth's component of the occupying forces. From 1948 practically the whole of the Commonwealth's share of responsibility for the occupation, involving a considerable segment of Japan, devolved upon Australia and New Zealand.

From the start of the occupation the Australian government had stressed Australia's right to be a full party in any negotiations related to Japan's future, and in July 1947 Evatt discussed with General MacArthur, Supreme Commander-Allied Powers in Japan, Australia's principal concerns in an eventual peace treaty. The Australian view was harsher than that of the Americans; it refused to accept evidence of peaceful intent at face value, and while American policy-makers were moving steadily to regard Japan as a future American bastion in Asia, Australia remained gravely concerned about the possible resurgence of Japanese military power.

Important changes were already taking place in the world scene. Although Australia clearly had vital interests to preserve in the final settlement with Japan, new problems were being posed by the spread of Communist power in China, where Mao Tse-tung's theory of revolution-by-peasants was winning out over the crumbling armies of the Kuomintang.

During the high tide of its success Japan had treated its chosen Asian leaders as mere puppets, but as time went on larger drafts of autonomy had been granted and native administrators took over most of the functions in the areas where "national" governments were set up—Indochina, the East Indies, Burma, and the Philippines. By the end of the war, non-Japanese

Asians who staffed most of the governments had strong views against the return of European colonial powers. The Japanese occupation had brought disruption and starvation, but politically it had opened the doors to revolutionary change. The old submissiveness was at an end; the emergence of a new world in Asia had begun. In wartime discussions President Roosevelt had not concealed his sympathy with the aims of all colonial peoples; he had the backing of Stalin and, on occasion, of Chiang Kai-shek. Churchill alone held to his stout assertion against dissolution of the British Empire; but by mid-1945 he had given place to the far less imperialist Labour Prime Minister Clement Attlee. After the defeat of Japan, five years sufficed for the dismemberment of the colonial system and the establishment of new nations as Australia's northern neighbours. By the dawn of the 1950s power had been transferred by the old masters in all but a few special cases. Throughout, the Labor government in Canberra took a generally sympathetic view of the struggles for independence and quickly established cordial relations with each new nation in turn.

The first new nation to emerge was the Philippines Republic. Less than a year after VJ day (Victory in Japan), the United States granted full independence. There were some intermittent uprisings by small groups, but the country soon settled down to solid progress.

More confused and less constructive was the fervid brand of politics that brought independence to the teeming East Indies. Under the Dutch rule of prewar years, nationalism had been growing, and in 1940 the Indonesian National party had come into being (largely under the influence of Sukarno, whom the Dutch then outlawed). The Japanese had been widely hailed as liberators; Sukarno, recalled from exile, was set up as puppet president. As soon as the Japanese capitulated, Sukarno and Mohammed Hatta proclaimed Indonesian independence, and as there were no Allied troops in the archipelago the Indonesian nationalists accepted the surrender of Japanese arms. In September British troops, representing the Allies, moved in, but they were unable to quell the turmoil, and by the time Dutch forces replaced them (late in 1946) the revolution had moved into its most violent stage. The Dutch soon found that they were fighting a losing battle even though their superior weapons brought success in most of the clashes that occurred. Successive nationalist cabinets in Indonesia called for complete independence; but swirling struggles for power were taking place among the Indonesian *élite*, and under pressure of Dutch military superiority and international demands for compromise, the national leadership was prepared to negotiate.

There was quite widespread support in Australia for the Dutch position; the thought of removal of the European "screen" to Australia's north caused consternation to many, as indeed it posed a problem in Australian defence. Parliamentary debates were punctuated with references to the dangers; but the government was more anxious to see a peaceful transfer of power than to support overt action designed to perpetuate European domination against the will of the majority of the inhabitants. Evatt, spearheading the government's moves, regarded the emerging nationalism among Asian peoples as an inevitable development which Australians should accept without rancour. Attuned to American sentiments on the issue, he believed that, instead of resisting the freedom movements, Australia should work for a regional association and place greater confidence in the United Nations and enforcement of its precepts. He, like Chifley and other parliamentary Labor leaders, was anxious that Australia should not be aligned with the colonial powers. When wharf labourers refused to load ships carrying supplies to the Dutch the government made no move to coerce them. In all aspects of the conflict between the Dutch and Indonesian nationalists, the government was unwilling to come out in favour of the Dutch who, as Australia's wartime allies, expected support, at least for their view that the matter was an internal and not an international issue.

Instead, the Australian government took forthright action and joined newly-independent India in pressing for the matter to be brought before the United Nations Security Council. A conciliation group sent by the United Nations arrived in Java in October 1947, and within three months an agreement had been signed; it provided that there should be free elections within a year to measure the Indonesian desire for self-determination and that Dutch authority should be transferred to an independent union. The agreement was not ratified but when the Dutch resumed hostilities and imposed a sea blockade on Java the United States government threatened to cut off American financial aid. The Indies were yielding the Dutch no revenue, while commitments there were becoming an intolerable burden, and so in May 1949 another ceasefire was arranged. Six months later The Hague agreement provided for the transfer of power to a decentralized Netherlands-Indonesian union, with the republic as a member state, and retention (subject to later negotiation) of West New Guinea by the Dutch.

Within the British association, major changes were in the making, not only in the composition of the Commonwealth but also in its very nature. In the principal British lands on the rim of Asia, the granting of independence was carried out by planned stages after the advent to power of the Attlee government in mid-1945. In India, in spite of the continuing Hindu-Moslem impasse, the way had been cleared by the end of 1946 for a plan partitioning the country; and in July 1947 an Indian Independence Act was passed by the British parliament with little debate. On August 15 the British Indian Empire ceased to exist; in its place were the dominions of India and Pakistan. The following year self-government was granted to Ceylon. Later (in 1949) India was prepared to retain its association with other British lands only as a republic; this was agreed to at the Prime Ministers' meeting in London, even though it involved a change of style from British Commonwealth to Commonwealth of Nations. In Burma, where political groups formed to assist in defeating the Japanese were among those most actively pressing for rapid independence from Britain, London's offer of dominion status proved unacceptable; and when the Republic of Burma came into existence on January 14, 1948, the Burmese became the first people to sever their imperial ties with London since 1776.

Other British possessions overrun by the Japanese were regained. In Malaya, British administrators, freed from Japanese camps, quickly reinstated the British colonial system, but neither principal nor minor collaborators—who included virtually the whole Malay population—were punished, and the sultans regained their power. Responsible government in all but foreign affairs, defence and international security was granted to the federation, while Singapore Island, with its strongly Chinese population, remained a largely self-governing community. In Borneo, the former interests of the British North Borneo Company were taken over by the British government and the territory, with Labuan, became a Crown colony, while Sarawak and neighbouring Brunei, formerly protectorates, were placed directly under colonial administration. Although Hong Kong's future seemed uncertain, British forces reoccupied the colony in September 1945, and soon Hong Kong's important role in the trade of the area was being restored.

More confused was the picture of events in France's Indochina territories, which had remained nominally under Vichy officials until March 1945, when the Japanese had taken more direct control. The independence movement had gathered pace, and in the kingdoms of Laos and Cambodia the monarchy had assumed power. In Vietnam, occupying the coastal area, the Vietminh had grown to such proportions that both the French and the Japanese were being harassed. The Vietminh had been organized by General Nguyen Vo Giap, a follower of Ho Chi Minh, a legendary figure in the Communist world, who had been born near Hanoi but had spent much of his life in Europe. The Vietminh force grew quickly to number several thousand men, and Giap took over the countryside around Hanoi and other coastal areas before the Japanese surrender. With the Japanese collapse, Ho's provincial republican government asserted independence; the new regime received a setback, however, when the Potsdam conference gave the British control of all territory south of the sixteenth parallel and the Chinese control of the northern zone, with the object of concentrating, disarming, and repatriating the Japanese armies (still at large in the south). The British declared the Vietnam government a puppet of the Japanese, and to deal with the situation rearmed the Vichy French internees, placing them once more in control of Saigon. A terrible story of intrigue and massacre, treachery and murder had now begun; and although the French forces greatly outnumbered the Vietminh, the insurgents in December 1946 opened up an attack in Tonkin. The effort failed, and the French chased the Vietminh upcountry. In 1949, Laos, Cambodia, and Vietnam were recognized by the French as associated states of the French Union, with nominal independence; but Vietnam's French-oriented emperor was unable to win popular support. Meanwhile, deep in the mountains along the China border, Giap had regrouped his men while a network of agents was set up throughout Vietnam, and by 1949 Giap was again in a position to begin harassing the French military forces. His renewed drive and intensified subversion opened a new phase of a war of terrorism which was to convulse the area for years to come.

At the same time as affairs in southeast Asia and the western Pacific were being reshaped and the turbulence of emerging nationalism was sweeping closer to Australia's shores, a massive threat to world peace was developing out of the growing intransigence of the Soviet Union under Stalin's dictatorship and the basic challenge presented by communism in its aggressive march. In 1945, when an almost universal belief prevailed that differences between nations could be resolved by negotiation, there had been general demobilization in the democratic countries. In the relief at victory and peace, no great notice was taken in London or Washington of differences that had arisen between the Soviet Union and the North Atlantic allies, even though Stalin had protested against Washington's abrupt termination of lend-lease a week after Japan's surrender and the Americans' refusal to make loans to the Soviet Union such as they were making to London. However, it was not very long before Americans were showing deep concern at Stalin's failure to demobilize the Russian armies and at the consolidation of Russian power as far west as the Elbe. The Soviet had pushed its borders further west than the czars had ever thought to expand. In the last year of the European struggle, while France, Belgium and western Germany were being cleared, the Soviet armies had pushed across Poland and eastern Germany, and had taken possession of most of the Balkan peninsula. Soon Communist governments, backed by Russian arms, had been installed in Poland, East Germany, Rumania, Bulgaria and Hungary; Yugoslavia and Albania were close allies, completing the protective screen of satellite buffer-states along the Soviet's entire western borders.

The two super-powers produced by World War II were inexorably opposed on ideological grounds, and tension was to remain. The issue was dramatized by Winston Churchill in a speech at Fulton, Missouri, in March 1946, in which he delineated the Communist threat and in declaring that a shadow had fallen across the scene so lately lighted by Allied victory deplored the fact that "an iron curtain" had descended across Europe.

Non-Communist governments in countries bordering the Soviet bloc were being threatened by subversion, and in the face of this danger, the American attitude hardened. With the rapid spread of communism in China, concern over the world-wide threat intensified. In March 1947 President Truman initiated the Truman Doctrine, an aid programme aimed directly at preventing the spread of communism in Europe and Asia, and the Congress—although now under Republican control—readily approved the necessary appropriations. In effect, at this point the United States gave notice that no further encroachment of communism would be tolerated. Moscow's response, at a secret meeting of Communist leaders in Poland, was to create the Communist Information Bureau (Cominform); its first manifesto was levelled at "the imperialist camp and its directing force, the U.S.A." The limitation of geography prevented American intervention when Czechoslovakia was absorbed within the Communist orbit in 1948, but the differences between East and West had now hardened into the "cold war." The signing of the North Atlantic treaty in April 1949 committed the United States without reservation to the military support of Western Europe.

Australia's direct participation in an important aspect of the Western world's defence effort had begun earlier. Hardly had the war ended before Britain, made agonizingly aware of the dawning of the age of guided missiles by the wartime rain of V-2 rockets on London, began a major programme of research and development in the field of long-range missiles, and by 1946 discussions were in progress in Australia concerning locations where such weapons might be tested. Long stretches of uninhabited land and a suitable climate made Australia's desert lands an ideal test area, and in 1947 the Long Range Weapons Establishment was set up at Salisbury, South Australia, with a firing range planned to run northwest across the desert lands from Woomera, the rangehead site. The object was to create an experimental range and supporting establishment for the testing and development of guided weapons, pilotless aircraft, and air-launched equipment, including the necessary radio and radar control measures. Australia shared the cost with Britain, and in support of the commitment the Department of Supply set about creating a defence-science establishment.

By now, active programmes involving international co-operation through the United Nations and their agencies were being developed, and Australia participated wholeheartedly. Through other involvements Australia was also undertaking a variety of activities in the international field.

Australia had begun an active programme in the Antarctic, where its territorial claims extended to almost half of the 5,000,000 square mile Antarctic continent. In 1947 the first permanent research stations were established (on sub-Antarctic Heard and Macquarie Islands) by the Australian National Antarctic Research Expedition; in 1949 an Antarctic division was set up within the Department of External Affairs to administer subsequent yearly expeditions.

Civil administration had been restored throughout the New Guinea territories, and efforts were being made to advance the New Guineans' economic and social wellbeing. The old League mandate was replaced by a United Nations trusteeship for the territory of New Guinea, the new system differing in the sanction it gave to the administering authority to defend a trust territory. This meant that Australia could include New Guinea in its defence arrangements. The defence significance of the area came under discussion in 1948 when the government was widely criticized for failing to negotiate an agreement with the United States for continued occupation of the Seeadler Harbour base on Manus Island which United States forces had developed after recapture of the Admiralty Islands in 1944; however, the decision to pull out of Manus appeared to be taken by Washington as part of revised American strategy in the western Pacific.

In several trouble spots Australia had been helping the United Nations in its constructive and stabilizing task. In Kashmir, where fighting broke out between India and Pakistan in 1947 over the disputed "accession" of the territory to India, Australian army officers were with a United Nations group supervising the cease-fire line, and diplomat-jurist Sir Owen Dixon served as mediator for a time. Other Australians were attached to the United Nations truce supervision organizations in Greece and Palestine.

To some Australians the world of power politics still seemed somewhat remote, but the cold war steadily gained credibility as verbal clashes in the United Nations were reinforced by such Soviet actions as the interruption of Allied traffic into Berlin, which was met successfully by a massive twelve-month Berlin airlift. A new element of concern was added in 1949 when news of the first Russian atomic bomb test was released. From this time side effects of the cold war were increasingly evident in the Australian political scene as the growth of rampant nationalism and militant communism in the area to Australia's north caused increasing concern. Bertrand Russell, visiting Australia, detected "two nightmares haunting the imaginations of Australians": one, the possibility of synthetic wool, the other a dread of an invasion from Asia. Both the Liberal party (founded in 1943 under the aegis of Robert Gordon Menzies) and the Country party began to stress the dangers of communism and the need for more positive action against it, at home and abroad, than the Labor government had shown itself prepared to take. Both parties promised decisive action to curb communism in Australia, and although irritant issues like rationing and black-marketeering were of prime concern, this strong stand was a major influence in gaining the popular support which won office for the coalition in the elections of December 1949.

At the same time as their anxiety over direct encroachment was increased, many people were coming to equate their distaste for communism in all its forms with a determination to resist the future growth of government power in the citizen's everyday affairs. Unfortunately for Labor, the party was by 1949 clearly identified not only with the concept of enhancing the federal role in national planning but also with regulations and legislation of a restrictive nature. The policy of the Liberal and Country parties, on the other hand, was directed towards lessening controls and clearing the way for a less inhibited growth of private enterprise.

Even though there was a continuing emphasis on domestic issues, throughout the 1950s Australian politics were coloured by sparks from the abrasive international scene. Tensions produced by war in Korea (1950–51), in which Australia was directly involved, unresolved dangers of massive nuclear conflict, the expansion of Communist-backed subversion in countries of south-east Asia, and a Communist spy sensation in Australia, were sufficient to keep the issue of defence and security to the forefront, helping to assure successive election victories for the Liberal-Country party coalition. There was an increasing awareness of the long-range nature of Communist aims. Moscow and Peking, formally allied from February 1950, were busily engaged in efforts to win over to the Communist camp any of the new and uncommitted nations they could; as well as engaging in a war of words against the West they were making compacts with various countries by offering trade and technical and industrial aid as a forerunner to military aid and alliance. Against a background of unrelieved world tension, the Liberal-Country party's stand against communism at home and abroad—and even closer ties with the United States—won steady support from the electorate.

There was cause for justified national pride when the XVIth Olympic

Games were successfully staged in Melbourne in 1956. The granting of the Games in response to what many considered an audacious bid had been accepted as a signal honour. Pitfalls appeared along the way; but there was unstinted acclaim for the national achievement when, on November 22, all was in readiness for the grand opening. With more than 100,000 people in the stands and before 4250 competitors from sixty-seven nations, the Duke of Edinburgh declared the Games open as the torch—kindled from a flame lit at Olympia—reached the stadium in the hands of Ron Clarke, last of 2831 relay runners who had carried it across the continent, and the brilliant miler, John Landy, stepped forward to take the Olympic oath on behalf of all competitors.

Constructive work in nation-building was gathering pace, and the government still played a major role in it. The sustained immigration programme, supported by government assistance to new settlers and carried out through elaborate administrative machinery at home and abroad, made possible over-all annual population increases that usually exceeded 2.1 per cent, so that the population reached 10,000,000 in 1959. Prosperity was greater and more widely enjoyed than ever before. Money was pouring in from abroad for export commodities and for investment in industrial enterprises. Many important national undertakings of a developmental nature were being supported—most importantly, the Snowy Mountains hydro-electric and water conservation project which absorbed about one-fifth of the total public expenditure on all capital works (by 1959–60 amounting to £175 million a year). At the same time, industrial development was being encouraged as a result of the general prosperity and the soundness of the economy; much of the expansion was designed to meet burgeoning consumer demand. Farmers and graziers, supported by good seasons and a virtual end to the rabbit problem, spent liberally to improve their properties and lift output. Only about one per cent of the national income was spent on defence.

The view that prevailed in policy making throughout the early 1950s was that the most effective way of enhancing Australia's security, in the long run, was to devote a maximum of available resources to strengthening the country's economy; this meant adding to productive capacity throughout industry, and in public utilities, transport, and communications, and sustaining a bold immigration programme to accelerate population growth. Because of limited manpower and resources, any increase in formal defence would involve diversion of men and resources from the constructive tasks, or a lowered standard of living. In maintaining defence outlays at relatively low levels, the government considered that the nation's safety was not in jeopardy. The immediate danger to Australia's security from nationalist-Communist movements in south-east Asia seemed to have receded, and the danger of resurgence of Japanese power had been removed in the Japanese peace treaty and in the pact with the United States and New Zealand (both signed in 1951); and although the Communist regime in Peking loomed ever larger as a threat to peace, massive naval-air power assembled by the United States in the western Pacific and the Americans' active policy of containment of communism in Asia formed an effective shield.

The Menzies government continued to offer friendship and support to the governments and peoples of the newly-emerged nations, exchanging diplomatic representatives with them and arranging to send experts able to help with such basic matters as improving agricultural methods and health services. Through the Colombo Plan, considerable direct assistance was given in these and other fields, and in student training. Canberra became a major centre of diplomatic activity.

By the late 1950s Communist power had been consolidated in China with Soviet backing, while Indonesia was increasingly bellicose in its demands that the Dutch hand over western New Guinea. Subversion and terrorism were being fomented in many places as Peking challenged Moscow for leadership of the Communist world.

South-east Asia had become a powderkeg; for, although they had thrown out the Western colonial powers, its peoples had not acquired a real sense of loyalty to nation or to the idea of order, and the basic problems of poverty, disease and hunger had not been solved by the magic formula of independence. Communist cadres were busily exploiting the ferment. By the early 1960s, the government was finding it necessary to step up defence measures as the direct threat to Australia appeared to grow. A balance of atomic terror had largely nullified the threat of nuclear attack as a deterrent to war; limited or "brush" warfare was now a reality to be reckoned with, particularly in Asia.

The flare-up in the war in Vietnam (where the Americans found themselves taking over where the French left off after defeat in 1954) and Communist China's new atomic-weapons potential, spurred action to strengthen all three Australian armed services. Australia and New Zealand joined with the United Kingdom in action to suppress terrorism in Malaya. From early 1965 Australian forces were directly engaged in Vietnam, along with a New Zealand unit, and Australia was openly supporting the Malaysian government in its resistance to Indonesian attempts to break up the newly-formed federation.

Australia had meanwhile gained new strength and a new dimension from the influx of people, money and ideas from abroad. The country was being transformed and an affluent society was in the making. Links with the world were being strengthened by faster air travel and by electronic communication. The community was no longer limited in its objectives. A new tolerance was apparent. As well as a million people from Britain and another million from Europe, Australia had admitted some thousands from various Asian lands as permanent residents, as well as the thousands who came as students to spend three or four years at Australian schools or universities.

The exuberance of growth and nation-building was to be seen in the strengthened resolve to tackle the great tasks that remained a standing challenge to the community. The American influence was more noticeable in everyday affairs—in what people read, in habits and tastes—and in the economy and the over-all strategic scene. Australians were still firmly committed to British ties, but Australia in the 1960s was very much under

America's wing, and the American commitment was no longer on any indecisive basis. With British power east of Suez about to be replaced by growing American forces in the Indian Ocean, Australia moved into a pivotal position in the long and difficult process of containing communism on the Asian mainland.

Setting new goals 24

Fires of hope for social betterment, doused by the depression, had been rekindled quite early in the war. Escaping all but minor devastation on their own soil, Australians were resolved to do more with their heritage. In the community at large new objectives had come to the surface—and with them a new confidence born of expanded skills and steady earnings. As a result, the Australian political scene had gained a new sense of direction and purpose; and, although the quest for ways to assure the goal of greater social justice after the war was sometimes almost obliterated in the urgency of momentous events, at other times discussion of the subject came sharply to the fore as a constructive antidote to the depressing monotony of war. In the background were the bold aims of creating a better post-war world through policies of economic regulation and social reform, expressed in broad terms by Allied leaders, and these ideas were blended into discussions of ways and means whereby the economic well-being of individuals and the nation as a whole might be achieved.

Even as early as 1940 the need to consider ways of building a better world after the war had been recognized. The question of post-war reconstruction had been specifically mentioned in the resolution of the Australian Labor Party's annual conference of that year, and when the new Department of Labour and National Service was created by the Menzies cabinet late in 1940, a "reconstruction division" was included to prepare for the inevitable post-war labour problems. The division's activities were not limited to employment since such aspects as the re-establishment of servicemen and munition workers after the war could be handled only in association with other facets of post-war policy. The division's role was to stimulate an interest in reconstruction problems as a whole, and to undertake general research and investigation. Other federal departments were brought into discussion on various aspects and state governments were kept in touch.

The first serious consideration of the means whereby a better social order might be developed came in the wake of the momentous declaration of post-war aims by President Roosevelt and Prime Minister Churchill in August 1941, the Atlantic Charter. Australian attitudes were defined by Prime Minister Menzies when, in announcing the declaration to the House of Representatives, he declared that the Atlantic Charter set out in plain language "the fundamental aspirations" of all liberty-loving peoples. Menzies went on:

> It is a reminder to us that the new order for the world, of which we have from time to time spoken, is now in the making, and the war must be regarded not merely as a great struggle in which evil things will be overthrown, but as something from which positively good things for men and women must emerge.

Although much of the impetus was lost in the welter of pressing problems that came in the early months of the war with Japan, by the end of 1942 there was a wider appreciation of the need for constructive planning, at least to pave the way for the transition to peacetime conditions. It was already becoming evident that the scope of adequate national economic measures might be beyond the constitutional powers of the federal government; and, since in the Labor administration there was a considerable body of opinion favouring moves towards greater federal peacetime power, it seemed appropriate to attempt to secure the wider authority. The party had come to office when the circumstances of the war were impelling the federal government to assume an unprecedented degree of direction over the national life. The task was tackled by the members of cabinet with wide-ranging administrative zeal, and the success achieved quickly strengthened party confidence. The uncomplicated methods that were successfully bringing the nation to a pitch of efficiency for war seemed eminently suited to the tasks of building a better post-war world.

In November 1942 the government called a constitutional convention to consider the permanent expansion of the Commonwealth's legislative powers; however, the consensus of the convention was that an immediate referendum might prove a serious diversion from concentration on the war effort, and the government accepted the proposal that instead of seeking transfer-by-referendum, state parliaments be asked to refer additional powers to the Commonwealth (a move which ultimately proved futile).

At the same time, a new portfolio—that of Post-war Reconstruction—was created within the federal cabinet. Treasurer Chifley was selected to carry the added responsibility. As well as the department itself (which included a small group of economic planners), several commissions and committees of businessmen and civic leaders, charged with the responsibility of crystallizing thought on the major post-war problems in their special fields of competence, became Chifley's direct responsibility. The department undertook the research required by the special groups wherever this was necessary to supplement their own inquiries, and evaluated and commented upon their reports, while Chifley initiated an endless round of exploratory discussions taking in departmental officers, outside experts, and cabinet colleagues.

By 1943 the government had pinpointed "a high and stable level of employment" as the primary aim of post-war economic policy. At the same time as policies of full employment and economic-betterment-for-all were being advanced for universal acceptance by Australia's spokesmen in international councils, Chifley emphasized the need to undertake constructive economic and other measures to assure rising standards of living within the Australian community. The call was for "a really splendid vision." In 1943 he wrote:

> Before the war, too many lives were dominated by the fear of unemployment, and too little real effort was made by governments and administrators to banish it. During the war that fear has been absent. In winning the war we are learning ways of controlling our affairs by which we can put an end to enforced idleness. . . .
>
> We are determined to see that work, as well as being available to all, is adequately rewarded and directed toward worth-while ends . . . [This] means, above all, placing permanently within the reach of every one of us freedom from basic economic worries, the realization of some of our ambitions for personal development. and the opportunity of bringing up happy, healthy, well-educated families.

That, Chifley added, was what he understood by a policy of full employment. It was also the yardstick by which he measured plans for post-war reconstruction which came before him.

Chifley was also concerned with the need to improve Australia's social security programme, and stressed the view that, to be effective, "full employment and social security must go hand in hand." The government announced in 1943 the creation of a social welfare fund, drawing upon the proceeds of taxation, for the purpose of extending social services; the comprehensive plan was to include unemployment insurance, sickness, and maternity benefits, and contributions to the cost of medicines. A plan to pay part of patients' hospital fees was also approved, and a conference of federal and state ministers agreed to work together in the creation of a national health plan.

Fervently dedicated to the general objective of planning for a better peacetime world was John Johnstone Dedman, the minister in charge of war organization of industry. Dedman had recruited a number of economists, and they, like those around Chifley, convinced their minister of the efficacy of planning in the economic field. As Dedman moved among A.L.P. groups in all states, he pointed to the success of the wartime economic planning, spoke of what might be achieved in general social betterment when resources were available for the constructive tasks of peace, and campaigned for acceptance of a broader role for the planner in the post-war scene.

The A.L.P. conference of 1943 supported the post-war planning concept, recommending to the government that the portfolio should be given to a minister unencumbered by other tasks. The conference also recommended that planning be concentrated on five objectives, headed by that of achieving "proper use" of the nation's productive resources, techniques, skills, scientific discoveries and inventions in order to maintain a rising standard of living. These resources were to be used for the production and distribution of goods and services required to maintain sound nutrition, adequate clothing, housing, medical care, and education for all. Full employment must be achieved, and adequate social security provided; and as well as equality of educational and occupational opportunity for the whole community, there was to be "progressive reduction" of inequality of income, leisure, and working conditions.

In compiling their list, the sponsors were drawing upon the outline of objectives for the transition from a war to a peace economy put forward earlier in 1943 in the League of Nations Declaration on Economic Depressions and adopted by the United States National Resources Planning Board. Once the list was confirmed by the A.L.P. as its post-war blueprint, it was for the Curtin government to translate the ideals into practice.

However, if the federal government were to have competence to legislate in the areas necessary (as other national governments clearly had) then amendment of the Constitution would be required. Opposition to the objectives was aroused among conservatives when Curtin, Evatt, and other members of the government began to press for constitutional amendment to enlarge federal powers, and it grew quickly into political attack once departmental officials became active participants in public discussion on the need for wider constitutional powers for the Commonwealth. Very soon the press was backing the protests of Opposition politicians who saw the Labor move as a dangerous step towards an officially-controlled economy and a plot to destroy cherished and traditional ways. The government now faced sharp criticism from its political opponents and the press in general for the rapid build-up of personnel in the planning departments within the public service, and for its strong emphasis on planning in general.

Among the government leaders, the determination to press the issue remained undimmed. They were firm in their belief that the objective of building a bigger and better Australia, able to offer more to its citizens in terms of opportunity and security, could be achieved only through more direct government intervention and a larger federal role. As political scientist Professor Leslie Crisp, a wartime confidant of Chifley, pointed out, there was a strong and persistent belief in cabinet that economic administration and policy-making were "the central focus of government in a country like Australia."

Interim reports prepared by expert commissions on post-war housing needs, rural industries, and secondary industries gave strong support for this view. All three reports pointed up existing deficiencies and inadequacies, suggesting that these could be overcome only through federal initiative.

In October 1943, in an interim statement, the Housing Commission reported that its investigation had revealed "large areas of deplorable housing," with the unsatisfactory pre-war position accentuated by wartime restrictions on building. The commission recommended that the federal government should assume

> responsibility for eliminating the present appalling housing conditions and ensuring adequate, sound, effective, and hygienic housing of the people in cities, towns, and rural areas.

By 1945, it was estimated, there would be a deficiency of more than a quarter million dwelling units. Since the financial resources of the Commonwealth were greater than those of the states and since all building resources were under federal control during wartime, it was suggested that a federal authority should be set up to work in collaboration with state housing bodies. It was recommended also that the state housing authorities should build a large number of dwellings for rental, and that the federal government should subsidize approved projects. Subsequent reports elaborated the principles already laid down, and dealt also with matters related to control of land prices, with aspects of physical planning, and with the problems of providing adequate community facilities.

In January 1944 the Commonwealth proposed to the states that they should plan to borrow £30 million in the first post-war year in order to pay for the building of 30,000 houses for low-income families, while preparing also for private construction in the same year of 20,000 houses. The federal government agreed to underwrite part of any losses incurred under the plan and to give subsidies on the rent charged to families on "sub-economic" incomes. At the same time, the virtual prohibition on homebuilding (imposed when the war situation was most threatening) was to be lifted, and the scale of building operations steadily increased in preparation for the post-war building drive.

The Rural Reconstruction Commission, in presenting its recommendations on various phases of agricultural policy, stressed the unfortunate legacy from World War I soldier settlement schemes. Reviewing the accumulated losses, the commission found that the total stood at about £45 million—a result brought about to a large degree by the inexperience and unsuitability for farm work of many of the settlers, and the inflated value of land allotted to them. Assuming that in spite of past troubles there would be a post-war clamour to settle many returned men on the land, the commission urged that agreement be reached between the Commonwealth and the states on the essential principles to be adopted and on a division of responsibility which would leave the administrative aspects in the hands of the states but give the federal government an overriding financial say. In August 1944 the premiers' conference agreed to a plan (worked out and submitted by the Commission) stipulating that the number of settlers should be limited by the opportunities for settlement with reasonable economic prospects for success and not simply by the number of applicants for land. Further, it was accepted that suitability, qualifications, and experience (but not lack of capital) should be the determining factors for assistance, that allotments should be of an efficient size, and that adequate guidance and technical advice should be available to settlers, through agricultural extension services. South Australia, Western Australia, and Tasmania agreed to acquire land with federal funds, while New South Wales, Victoria, and Queensland decided to act as principals; a federal guarantee covering part of any losses was promised in both cases.

Other aspects of the Rural Reconstruction Commission's report covered proposals for dealing with a multitude of problems: soil erosion, the reconstruction of marginal areas, rural credit, debts adjustment, land tenure, and the general question of social amenities. The wool industry was given special attention in the light of the threat to wool posed by the steadily expanding production in consuming countries of the new synthetics which could be used in the production of clothing materials. The report underscored the need for a comprehensive programme of research into all aspects of the wool industry, and the government moved at once to initiate an investigation of processing and manufacturing practices as well as the rural side of the industry, and pledged major contributions to an expanded programme aimed at promoting the use of wool fabrics. Biological research (covering matters related to pastures, nutrition, genetics, and animal husbandry) and technical research into such aspects as the physical and chemical properties of wool and competitive fibres, and the processing of wool from the greasy state to the production of fabric, were placed under the control of the Council for Scientific and Industrial Research.

The need for a constructive and unified approach to matters related to rural industries appeared sufficiently pressing to make federal leadership acceptable to most people, and even in housing there was relatively little that could be said against federal initiative. There remained the matter of secondary industry, and particularly the question of what should be done with the government factories which had been established during the war, some of them in areas outside the main cities, to meet urgent needs in munitions and supplies. These subjects were under review by the Secondary Industries Commission, a body under the chairmanship of the secretary of the munitions department. By 1944 issues related to the future role of government in manufacturing had become a bone of contention between Labor and the Opposition.

A good case could be made for retention by the government of ownership of many of the wartime factories, since they were munitions plants pure and simple. Beyond that were other classes of plants. The Minister for Munitions, Norman John Makin, stated the case for retention of some of these in peacetime on the ground that the post-war demand for manufactured goods in Australia and adjacent countries would be beyond the capacity of commercial industry to supply. With memories of the Bruce-Page government's haste to dispose of wartime instrumentalities, Makin declared that it would be grossly inequitable for the public investment to be scrapped and the sole benefit arising from Australia's magnificent munitions effort bequeathed to private companies and individuals. At the same time, Prime Minister Curtin said that the government might decide to operate some of the plants for the production of civilian goods; but, he added,

. . . in such cases it is unlikely to enter into forms of production which are adequately catered for already. Its purpose will be to seek by this form of development to round out the Australian industrial structure by filling in those gaps which are known to exist, thereby making Australia progressively more capable of meeting her requirements in manufactured goods.

Curtin went on to say that the government's plans did not stop at finding profitable uses for government factories; while it recognized that there was a place for the expansion of public enterprise in industry, the government acknowledged that it must look primarily to private enterprise to provide for post-war industrial development in order to give employment.

The Prime Minister's statement was reasonably well received but business leaders and those who wished to maximize the role of private enterprise were not convinced that Labor would provide the type of economic environment they sought. They saw the proper role of government after the war as one of providing a healthy stimulating climate for the encouragement of business enterprise. Many were now willing to accept, though with some reluctance, the full employment objective; but they were not prepared to see a vast enlargement of the public sector of the economy and the relegation of the private sector to a position of secondary importance.

By early 1944 Labor leaders were convinced o the need for wider constitutional powers, especially in the light of the 1943 A.L.P. conference resolution on post-war planning. Members of the government believed that wartime experience had so conclusively demonstrated the value of concerted national direction over the whole economic activity of the country that a referendum would be carried and greatly extended power placed in federal hands. Evatt, as Attorney-General, took the lead in drafting the referendum proposals.

In the campaign leading to the referendum in August 1944, the government's emphasis was on the need for broad powers if the Commonwealth were to cope adequately with post-war problems. A series of fourteen amendments to the constitution was proposed; they would, among other things, have increased the power of the Commonwealth over employment and unemployment; production and distribution; profiteering and prices; trusts, combines, and monopolies; national works; national health, and family allowances. Though the list was somewhat more extensive than that which Hughes had submitted to the electorate in the World War I period, the fate of the referendum was the same; rejection—this time, of all fourteen points. While the war lasted (and in the immediate transition period) the federal government would retain its undisputed control; but it now had to plan with the knowledge that in peacetime the overriding federal power would not hold. In spite of the effectiveness of Canberra's direction of affairs, the community at large was by no means willing to sanction an aggregation of economic powers in the central government on a permanent basis; clearly, if carried, the proposed amendments would have destroyed the federal system, for they represented a major, if not a complete, step towards unification.

Beneath the surface ran a strong undercurrent of resistance to the growth of federal power. The referendum campaign sharpened political discussion of the broad issue of government involvement in economic affairs and in the every-day life of the community. For those who wished to confront Labor with positive alternatives rather than simple rejection, a notable development was the launching in 1943 of the Institute of Public Affairs, a Melbourne-based organization financed by business firms and individuals with the purpose of studying economic and industrial problems in order to advance the cause of free enterprise. The organization at once concerned itself with the kind of economic and industrial system Australia should strive to achieve after the war. In 1944 it published a comprehensive statement, representing the views of a dozen or so leading industrialists, under the title *Looking Forward*. In setting down ideas on "the new order" which was assuredly in the making, these business leaders in general accepted the view that in future the community would expect to see full employment maintained in conjunction with an acceptable minimum standard of living for all. *Looking Forward* became something of a rallying call. It was quite widely circulated, and its appearance was taken as a sign that important interests and influential individuals were no longer content merely to defend old citadels; instead, supporters of private enterprise were coming round to a position in which obligations were being emphasized equally with rights.

A great gulf, however, separated those holding the Labor view of centralized power and those who championed opposing causes. There were many people who were determined to do all they could to roll back the power being exercised by the Commonwealth; they were joined by others anxious to see the resurgence of a cohesive political force which might confront Labor with a more constructive economic and social programme than the United Australia and Country parties had been able to present. For all those who wished to challenge Labor with positive alternatives, resistance to the referendum proposals was a rallying point, and Menzies, once again leader of the opposition, took advantage of a floodtide of unanimity to press for the political reorganization which he considered necessary. After consultation with other U.A.P. members, Menzies arranged for a conference to discuss the establishment of a "nationwide political movement" which would have "a liberal policy and approach, and an effective popular organization." Menzies explained the situation in this way:

> The referendum campaign showed clearly that a great body of public opinion in this country is liberal and progressive, but distrusts and resists excessive government control and interference in the productive and business activities of citizens, and is not prepared to accept Socialism as the pathway to human happiness.

Responding to the call, representatives of fourteen political and semi-political organizations attended a "unity" conference in Canberra in October 1944, at which Menzies called for the creation of a new party. The objectives he set down as being those of an independent, constructive "liberalism"—to strive for

> . . . a true revival of liberal thought which will work for social justice and security,

for national power and national progress, and for the full development of the individual citizen.

In case some might think he was taking over much of the old Labor philosophy, Menzies attacked the "dull and deadening process of Socialism."

A second and larger conference, held at Albury in December, produced a new organization, which adopted the title Liberal Party. The new party presupposed the continuing and separate existence of the Country party (which was not invited to participate in the conference since it had its own Australia-wide organization) but Menzies hoped to draw into the Liberal party all the other non-Labor groups. As the United Australia party had never succeeded in building an Australia-wide organization, Menzies stressed the need for a uniform structure of local and state branches capped by a federal executive; although a completely unified organization could not be created, the Liberal party went on to erect a more effective federal structure than any of its predecessors had possessed. An elaborate party plan made provision for a federal council, with seven representatives from each state, to manage and control the federal affairs of the party; a federal executive of eleven to run the day-to-day affairs of the party secretariat; and various standing committees with specialized roles. The question of sources of financial support for the new organization was of special concern to the party's founders; Menzies had warned against leaning too heavily upon a few large donors. Since public opinion considered that the United Australia party had a close association with big-business interests, particularly in Melbourne, financial independence was considered essential to the success of the new party. To assure that the party's funds were untied, each of the state divisions was instructed not to accept "conditional" contributions from individual donors or from groups of donors such as trade or industrial associations. Many individuals contributed their membership fees, but before long substantial funds were being drawn from business and professional interests.

From early 1944 the new doctrine of full employment as a basic goal of national policy was being given greater emphasis in Canberra, while at the same time Australia's representatives at international conferences pressed for a full-employment provision in every economic or financial agreement which might operate in the post-war world. At the Bretton Woods conference on economic rehabilitation, the Australian delegation underscored the view that, in order to secure popular support for monetary and other proposals, it was first necessary to convince the man in the street that these proposals were a means to an end in which he had a vital interest; hence the Australian desire to see governments specifically accept the obligation to maintain employment. It was stressed that an agreement for such a purpose would be simple to draft and could be accepted more expeditiously than complex monetary plans and programmes of commercial policy. When the time came to present the Bretton Woods monetary agreement in parliament, Chifley emphasized the advantages it would bestow on all mankind, and he said he had been an ardent advocate of all international organizations because he believed

> ... that through them we are engaging in a great human experiment which is designed to prevent the catastrophes that result from wars and financial and economic depressions.

In its national application the doctrine of full employment was a reflection of the labour movement's bitter recollection of the mass unemployment of the depression; its international aspect sprang in part from a suspicion of overseas financial and trading interests, and in part from a realization that full employment abroad would provide an element of price stability for the country's exports of primary products.

Although not the only government prepared at this time to give credence to the notion that national economic policies might be shaped around the new concept, the Australian administration was the first to commit itself to the maintenance of full employment as the government's fundamental aim. In May 1945, just twelve months after the British government released its White Paper on employment policy, a largely similar but more definitive White Paper was tabled in the House of Representatives by John Dedman, who shortly before had taken over the portfolio of Post-war Reconstruction.

Here for the first time was set down in one wide-ranging document the outlines of a general plan for the Australian economy in time of peace. An active federal role was indicated. Dedman explained that the paper

> ... first sets forth boldly and unequivocally the Government's intention to secure full employment for the people of Australia after the war. Secondly, it outlines the method by which the Government proposes to achieve this aim. Thirdly, it examines the special problems which will face the Australian economy in the transition from war to peace.

Earlier, the director-general of the department, economist Dr Herbert Cole Coombs (by now the chief architect of the government's economic plans) had made it clear that while "high employment" did not simply mean "everybody in a job," the effect would be to have a few more jobs available than men and women to fill them, so that there would be "a slight but persistent shortage of labour." The method set out by Dr Coombs—and adopted in the White Paper—anticipated that advocated by British economist Sir William Beveridge in his *Full Employment in a Free Society* (published in November 1944), which owed much to the theories enunciated by Keynes. Its essential feature was maintenance of the community's total expenditure at a level equal to the maximum production that would be achieved "if our human resources are to be employed to the full." Economic thought was that the government had available to it two main ways of influencing the various types of outlays so as to maintain expenditure equal to the maximum production of which the economy was capable. These were by providing more stable incomes for primary producers and by determining public expenditure (particularly on investment goods) according to the need to maintain total expenditure at the desired level.

Pointing to Australia's special problems as an exporter of primary produce, the White Paper affirmed that the chief fluctuations in spending and employment in Australia arose from changes in export prices consequent upon the varying prosperity of foreign buyers. Because of this, Australia would seek to meet future threats to full employment by seeking agreement with other nations, so that each would do everything possible to maintain the level of employment while also collaborating in efforts to expand world trade and mitigate fluctuations in prices of raw materials and foodstuffs. Further, the government undertook

> ... to stabilize total expenditure and employment in Australia in the face of any expected reduction in spending from overseas on Australian goods and services by bringing about a compensating expansion in public capital expenditure and by other appropriate means.

Within the government it was already acknowledged that should the need arise, public works expenditure would be expanded to check unemployment. Australia was absorbing a lesson from the United States, where an act passed by the Congress at this time placed emphasis on a proposal that business firms should be asked the scope of their plans for expansion as a guide to public works policy. In Canberra it was now coming to be accepted that in the same context government expenditure might well be subject to adjustment according to the level of investment and the investment intentions of private enterprise.

In March 1945 a bill had been introduced to cover the demobilization and re-establishment in civilian life of those who had enlisted. The measure consolidated the provisions already made by National Security Regulations for the reinstatement of servicemen who wished to return to their former employment, and for the protection of apprentices. It also provided for preference in employment, for a period of seven years, to all servicemen. Provision was made for the formal establishment of the machinery for the reconstruction training programme, which had been in operation for more than a year. The training programme was primarily designed to assist ex-service personnel whose careers had been prejudiced by war, but it also opened the way for special industrial training of civilians where there was a strong need for extra personnel of particular skills. State technical education systems and the universities were to receive assistance for necessary building extensions. At the same time a nationwide employment service was established; through its operation, comprehensive and authoritative information on the labour market became available.

By VJ Day, demobilization and the initial transfers of labour to meet changing needs had already begun. Meanwhile, Chifley had become Prime Minister following John Curtin's death in May 1945. The demand for labour was such that there was no worry about jobs. Nevertheless it was some time before any dramatic growth could take place in manufacturing. Much of the factory equipment in use needed replacement. New plant had to be bought overseas and installed; this would take time and involve tremendous investment. With a community thirsting for consumer goods, factories did their best to lift output by absorbing whatever labour was available.

Sharply increased demand was felt as people who had been saving during the war years now wanted to turn their money into goods. The government called for continued austerity until the shortages could be relieved and a true Golden Age entered; meanwhile, to restrain excessive demand, the government kept taxation at a high level, resisted wage escalation, continued to ration petrol, clothing, and scarce food items, and maintained the machinery of price control, at the same time subsidizing various food costs in order to keep the consumer's outlays as low as possible. Of deep and fundamental concern was the sterling bloc's serious and persistent dollar shortage. Australia had a major stake in sterling's strength. Chifley maintained that the economic survival of Britain and the countries of Europe was of fundamental importance to Australia, and accordingly many of the government's policies were shaped by a scrupulous regard for keeping dollar expenditures to a minimum.

With Labour's victory at Westminster, governments of similar political complexion were in office in Britain, Australia, and New Zealand, and there was a strong sense of unity among the leaders of all three.

The end of the war had brought a revival of industrial unrest in Australia; there were demands for a forty-hour work week and reconsideration of the basic wage, and in the background there was dissatisfaction with the working of the arbitration system. Wage-earners generally believed that they were entitled to a greater share of the national income; but there was substantial disagreement among rank-and-file unionists and among union leaders on the question of how best to achieve reform. Broadly the division of opinion was between moderates who considered that reforms should be made by judicial process and the more militant who placed their faith in direct bargaining between unions and employers (with the strike as a weapon in such bargaining).

A series of strikes late in 1945 first brought to the fore the disruptive forces active within the trade unions. Steelworkers at Newcastle were the first to go on strike; they were joined by the coalminers and by the seamen's union, which in four states refused to man ships carrying coal or steel. Coal shortages quickly developed, and these were reflected in severe power, lighting, and transport restrictions in the big cities. There were other factors contributing to the unrest, but the strikes and the industrial disorder as a whole were generally attributed to the influence of Communist executives in some of the key unions. For the moment the issue was left unresolved; but the government's handling of the industrial issue was to become a matter of major concern to the electorate in the years ahead. The granting of the forty-hour work week by the federal Arbitration Court and the New South Wales parliament did not change the pattern of strikes so much as remove the question of hours from the leading causes; other and more trivial issues were substituted.

Meanwhile, at a time when the energy of union leaders and of the Labor party, nominally more unified and harmonious than it had been in decades, should have been directed to more constructive issues, it was dissipated in internecine struggles for power. Membership of the Australian Communist party had fallen from about 16,000 in 1945, but party followers were extremely active. Within the Labor party, there was an awareness of the disruptive tactics of Communist sympathizers, and at the annual conference of the New South Wales branch in June 1946 a resolution was passed emphatically condemning the Communist party as both a danger to Australian democracy and a permanent foe of the A.L.P.; all association with the party was rejected "without hesitation or qualification." Nevertheless the problem of guilt-by-association stayed with the Labor party and embarrassed the government simply because Communist officials remained in control of several of the unions from which the A.L.P. normally drew electoral and political support. At the same time, Labor's opponents naturally sought to make political capital out of the suggested link between communism and the Labor party, and denunciations of Labor's alleged Communist taint studded the 1946 election campaign.

In that election the two Opposition parties worked in close harmony. The unifying effect of the Liberal party in uniting earlier splinter groups was reflected in a sharp fall in the number of candidates nominated for the House of Representatives; the total was down by almost a third compared with the miscellany who had offered themselves at the previous election.

A referendum was held simultaneously with the 1946 election to seek approval for constitutional amendments proposed in three measures passed by parliament in March. The first proposal was designed to continue the existing federal social services (such as maternity allowances, widows' pensions, child endowment, and unemployment, sickness, hospital, and students' benefits) and to empower the federal parliament to set up a national health service. The second related to the marketing of primary products, and the third was designed to bring industrial disputes in a single state within the jurisdiction of the Commonwealth Arbitration Court. Only the first of the three proposals was accepted by the electorate; the other two, sharply criticized by the Opposition, were rejected. Once again the electorate had shown itself unwilling to approve constitutional amendments which would enlarge the federal power; there was an undiminished link between conservatism and states-rightism.

However, the High Court had decided that the defence power did not cease abruptly on the conclusion of hostilities but continued for a reasonable time into peace in order that the Commonwealth might unwind wartime organizations in an orderly fashion. For most purposes the transitional defence power was to run to December 1948.

During the election campaign there was comparatively little discussion on the referendum issues. Attention was turned to the Labor party's record and to the promises being made on behalf of the non-Labor parties. Strong fire from Menzies and Fadden was directed at the high rate of taxation maintained by Labor, and promises for reductions were made. Fadden said that he would invite David Lilienthal to visit Australia to discuss great developmental projects. Both Liberal and Country party candidates stressed the issue of Communists in trade unions—the Country party promised to outlaw the Communist party if returned—and condemned "government by union." Nevertheless, the election result was a clear-cut endorsement of the A.L.P.; even though the party strength in the House of Representatives was reduced by a tenth, it retained a sound majority there and overwhelming representation in the Senate.

Prosperity was general and expanding. Commodity prices remained at profitable levels. War-ravaged countries were in desperate need of food, and restrictions on wheatgrowing were quickly lifted so that Australia's wheat exports moved up sharply even with the first post-war harvest. Although the price of wheat rose in world markets from 1945, the Commonwealth (with the states' consent) bought in each harvest at fixed rates— building up a national profit overseas in the process—while controlling the cost of flour to local consumers. Concern about the disposal of huge wartime accumulations of wool was soon dispelled; as a result of war the world's wardrobes and clothes-racks were again empty, woolspinners were clamouring for fibre, and wool prices moved upward as stocks fell. Wool reverted to the auction system, but for most other exports wartime marketing authorities were retained. This applied not only to bodies like the dairy produce board and the meat board which existed before the war, but also to newer boards like those handling wheat and barley. These boards arranged contracts under which perishable foods continued to be sold to Britain under government-to-government agreements.

Steadily the returns from land industries mounted. Earnings from wool and wheat increased dramatically. Sheep numbers rose each year as wool prices leapt from 15 pence per pound in 1946 to more than 60 pence in 1949, while wheat production surpassed old records in 1948, when the overseas price exceeded £1 a bushel. Farmers' incomes rose more than 50 per cent a year, and these increases were reflected in the nation's export receipts, which increased from £196 million in 1945/46 to £611 million in 1949/50. Wool still was the main source of overseas earnings, representing an average of 43 per cent of export receipts.

Chifley was not prepared to see this swollen income squandered on imports; as Treasurer he believed that it could be better used to reduce Australia's indebtedness abroad. By maintaining tight wartime restrictions on imports he gave Australia a favourable balance of trade, and out of the proceeds of each year's exports returns the government paid off overseas loans as they fell due, at the same time building up reserves in London to unprecedented levels.

Import restrictions had helped materially in the expansion of Australia's industrial base. As early as 1945 the government, recognising the overriding importance of motor transportation to future prosperity and development, had declared an expanding automotive industry to be the "keystone that will consolidate the industrial structure built up during the war." The government had then announced that in response to its request, a specific proposal for building an "all-Australian" car had been submitted by General Motors-Holden and that as a result existing restrictions (in the form of a 1939 monopoly agreement with another company, which had not been acted upon) would be removed. The necessary legislation was passed, and work began on tooling up for production. Scores of small firms, some of them no more than one- or two-man enterprises a few years before, were brought into the programme as Australia became the eleventh nation to undertake complete automobile manufacture in volume. Newspapers proudly hailed it as a major achievement when the first all-Australian motor-car came off the assembly line in Melbourne on November 28, 1948; in the words of industrialist Laurence John Hartnett, the main architect of the project, automobile production filled what had been "a nasty void" in Australia's industrial capacity.

Meanwhile, the Labor view that private business could not best serve the public interest in sensitive fields, such as transport, had resulted in 1946 in the setting up of a national airlines commission, which was to establish a monopoly in air services. The effort to remove privately-owned airline companies was strongly criticized by champions of private enterprise. When the issue went to the High Court, the setting up of the government service, Trans Australian Airlines, was held to be valid, but the court upset those sections of the act which would have prevented other airlines from operating in competition.

Past experience had revealed problems inherent in the absorption of large numbers of people coming from abroad in a sustained influx; but expert studies in the 1940s were stressing the fact that the rate of natural increase had slowed to a point where the excess of births over deaths could not be expected to lift the population appreciably. During the 1930s there had been barely any growth—an increase of 500,000 or so in ten years, representing an annual rate of increase well under 1 per cent—and in the war years there had been little improvement. It seemed likely that the population would expand by less than 2,000,000 in a generation, and in the view of many, Australia might not have undisputed possession of the country for as long as that unless more was done to strengthen defence and fill the open spaces.

The shock of war close to Australia's shores had sharpened appreciation of the need to build up the population as rapidly as possible. Well before the war ended, problems associated with the revival of large-scale immigration were under study within the government. The initiative came from Arthur Augustus Calwell, who as Minister for Information (from 1944) became dedicated to the proposition that a rapid build-up in Australia's population was a crucial and urgent matter. When a department to operate exclusively in the field of immigration was created in 1945, it was placed under Calwell's ministerial direction.

A "target" of 70,000 new settlers a year (representing 1 per cent of the population) was decided upon as the optimum. Convinced that it would be sound and feasible to embark upon carefully planned immigration on this scale, Calwell initiated an extensive behind-the-scenes programme to gain public acceptance for this objective. Traditional opposition from within the Labor party and the trade union movement was met and countered, and opinion formers throughout the community were studiously converted so that they might become proselytes of the cause. The community was responsive; evidence of Australia's vulnerability was plain to see, and it was obvious that the nation would need more people if it were to attain its national aims. Calwell worked hard to see that immigration remained outside the realm of party politics and that everyone in the community realized the stake that he or she had in assuring its success. Calwell's slogan, "Populate or Perish," was soon absorbed into the national jargon; and before long an astonishing revolution in Australian opinion on immigration had taken place. Belief in large-scale immigration had become almost a test of patriotism.

Calwell boldly declared that immigration, far from harming the prospects of employment for Australians, would be a stimulant to demand and hence to employment opportunities. As reassurance on this aspect, he pointed to the fact that because of a decline in births caused by the depression, fewer young people would be entering the labour market in the years following the war. Above all, he laid stress on the urgency of population-building as a national safeguard. "The days of our isolation are over," he declared, adding:

> If we are to take our rightful place in world affairs, if we are to ensure the future security of our nation, our population must be greatly augmented, both by natural increase and by planned immigration.

The people were to be drawn principally from Britain, but provision was made for a European influx. In March 1946 an agreement was concluded with the United Kingdom government (to go into operation in March 1947) under which Canberra and London would share the cost of assistance to those nominated by Australian sponsors and to tradesmen chosen by selection teams (provided that the migrant paid £10 towards the cost of passage). Shipping shortages slowed the early stages of the programme, and only a few hundred had arrived by mid-1947. At that point an agreement was reached with the international refugee organization to bring in large numbers of European "displaced persons" who had been languishing in camps, some of them for years. Those who came under this plan agreed to work under official direction for two years; in return each was assured of a job at an Australian wage level. Calwell visited Europe in 1948 and found that the refugees had to be moved out in great numbers; obviously they would make first-rate settlers, and Calwell agreed to take more than originally planned. Even in the face of strains placed upon the economy by a mass of newcomers (whose presence seemed to be aggravating the housing shortage) there was ready support for continuation of a big migrant intake. Throughout 1949 and 1950 the Europeans were arriving in Australia at the rate of 6000 or so a month.

With the post-war baby boom the population was increasing at a rising rate. For the first time since the 1880s, an Australia-wide population increase of over 100,000 in a single year was recorded in 1947. By 1948 a net gain of over 30,000 was recorded in new arrivals and the total population growth rate exceeded 2 per cent. The following year, when the migrant intake was well over 100,000, the total population increase climbed to a rate of 3.3 per cent, and before the end of the year Australia had 8,000,000 people— an increase of 500,000 in three years. In January 1950 the first Citizenship Convention was held (in Canberra) to enlist community assistance in the assimilation of new arrivals from abroad. The convention was attended by representatives of the federal and state governments, the Churches, more than a hundred volunteer groups, trade unions, and employers' organizations; it brought into being the Good Neighbour movement, under whose co-ordinating efforts thousands of individuals throughout the country were able to join in activities designed to help the newcomers in various ways.

Meanwhile people were anxious to spend some of their wartime savings, and they were demanding goods of all types. In holding to tight economic controls and a pattern of federal dominance, the Chifley government ran into a succession of problems as the economy, readjusting rapidly in its efforts to catch up with many changes in demand, showed increasing strains; these strains in turn manifested themselves to the public as annoying shortages. During the war, expenditure on public works and public utilities, and on housing, had been kept to a minimum; now the deficiencies that had developed (sometimes dating back many years) had to be made good and facilities expanded to cope with greatly enlarged demand. Competition from the lighter industries, which were able to develop more rapidly, left many services with less than the required amount of labour, while the time needed to plan and initiate large public undertakings slowed down progress. Shortcomings rather than achievements were apparent as efforts were made to "catch up" in many directions at once. Impatience grew over the slow pace in clearing the road-blocks, and because of new federal-state financial relationships the national administration was usually identified as the offender.

The federal Treasury had become the main source of finance for state governments as a result of the 1942 uniform tax legislation, and after a High Court decision had in effect confirmed that the federal government had a monopoly of the most lucrative forms of taxation in peace as well as in wartime, Chifley informed the premiers in 1946 that the government had decided to continue indefinitely the system of a single income tax. Chifley proposed reimbursement to the states of a total base grant of £40 million a year, to be distributed (by decision of the premiers) according to a formula taking several factors into account, including changes in population and the average level of wages in the different states. In 1947 the states secured a higher grant, and year by year the reimbursement rose, while the formula itself was varied by compromise and improvisation to meet the states' special needs and pleading.

With the unrestricted taxing right, the Commonwealth had gained a position of pre-eminence quite new to the federal system, even though the electorate had refused to grant the Commonwealth the particular powers it had sought by referendum. Through its control of the purse strings of the nation as a whole, it could now form its own comprehensive view of the relative urgency and merit of the various tasks and obligations within the entire realm of public policy, whether within its own constitutional province or within the province of the states, and having passed judgment, could decide the order of national priorities. Where state governments' views differed from its own it could find ways to influence decisions in support of expenditures based on the priorities it favoured. Nor was the Treasury's influence limited to federal-state relationships; it extended also to a general oversight of business investment expenditures through direct Treasury control of capital raisings by companies as well as direction to all banks setting limits upon the overdrafts they might grant. Against the prevailing background of limited manpower and heavily-strained resources, the government's efforts were directed towards holding back the non-essential in order to get basic things done first.

Opposition to Labor was strengthening among various groups, and particularly among business and professional men. As part of its expansion of social services the government planned to expand programmes in the health and medical fields. Doctors were consistently opposed to all the proposals and to enacted law related to medical and health services, which they regarded as being a step towards "socialized medicine," and the profession moved from deep-rooted objection to active political opposition.

As part of its effort to secure more effective control over the economy, the government had acted in 1945 to remove "outside" influences from the Commonwealth Bank by abolishing the bank's board and placing full control in the hands of a governor responsible to the federal Treasurer alone. At the same time the bank's central banking functions were enlarged.

A separate but related Act gave legislative effect to a wartime provision requiring the trading banks to deposit their surplus investible funds with the Commonwealth Bank, whose governor would determine the level at which these funds would then be "frozen." At the same time the legislation introduced provisions to improve the bank's competitive position in ordinary banking business. With the latter objective in mind, Chifley, long-time supporter of the view that the banking system could be greatly strengthened by giving the Commonwealth Bank a dominant role, had included in the complementary Banking Act provisions under which the Treasurer could prevent a trading bank from handling the business of state or local government bodies.

Not all state authorities were prepared to accept direction on these lines, and the Melbourne City Council challenged the validity of the Act. When the High Court upheld the challenge and (in August 1947) ruled that this section of the legislation was invalid on the grounds that so long as private banks existed, states and state authorities could not be denied the use of their facilities, Chifley and those around him became convinced that the time was ripe to take over the entire banking system. In Chifley's view, the court's decision showed that full public control of banking (as sought under the 1945 legislation) could not be secured except through public ownership of banking. The idea of a monopoly of the banking function had long been in Chifley's mind; in a minority report as a member of the Royal Commission on banking in 1935 he had stated his conviction that the private banking system had frustrated Labor's efforts in the depression, declaring that private banks made the community "the victim of every wave of optimism and pessimism that surged through the minds of financial speculators."

Chifley's announcement of the government's intention to nationalize the banks came as a thunderbolt a few days after the High Court ruling. Outside the ranks of the labour movement there was immediate and widespread condemnation of the plan. Day-by-day newspaper editorials hammered on the theme that the measure marked the road to serfdom and represented a long step towards totalitarianism. In the chorus, the Melbourne *Age* branded the proposal a "revolutionary and extremely socialistic design," and the *Sydney Morning Herald*, which ran five leaders on banking in twelve days, castigated the legislation as "financial extremism which will establish in Australia a framework of a servile totalitarian State" and "the road to the economic enslavement of the Australian people." In the Premiers' conference, held immediately after Chifley's announcement, there was a straightout alignment of all states against the Commonwealth.

Formal opposition was quickly mobilized and while, behind the scenes, banking and business interests set in motion largescale efforts to build up political pressure against the measure, members of parliament were inundated with petitions, letters, and telegrams protesting the Labor initiative. The *Catholic Weekly*, of Sydney, declared its opposition in the form of an open letter to the Prime Minister saying that if the nationalization programme was based on a dedication to socialism as opposed to the system of private property, Catholics could not in conscience vote for the Labor party, Catholic ministers would be compelled to resign and Catholic members of the parliamentary Labor party, if they did the correct thing, would also resign. From many public forums men were saying that the nationalization move was the first step under which communism would be able to control all industry. Those who believed instinctively that such a measure, by removing freedom of choice in banking matters, would be putting the individual in a straitjacket, could point to the fact that no other democratic country tolerated a similar banking monopoly—but the government was unmoved.

Legislation to take over the banks was passed by parliament in October 1947 and received the Governor-General's assent the following month. It provided that the Commonwealth Bank could acquire shares of every Australian banking company, at an agreed price or at a price fixed by a federal claims court, and it was empowered to buy on a similar basis the Australian assets of banks incorporated in London and elsewhere. Its effect would be to confine all banking business to the Commonwealth Bank and the State banks.

A legal battle over the validity of the measure was begun before any action could be taken. An appeal was made to the High Court on behalf of the trading banks and the three non-Labor state governments—Victoria, South Australia, and Western Australia. After long legal argument the Court delivered a judgment in August 1948 which in effect made the act inoperative because, it was held, banking was a form of trade and commerce between the states (which under section 92 of the Constitution should be "absolutely free") and that a prohibition of all banking, including interstate banking, except government-managed banking, was an infringement.

In spite of the clear signs that the bank nationalization plan was unacceptable to a majority of voters—it had been thrust to the fore in the Victorian state election held late in 1947 and contributed to a resounding defeat for Labor in that state—Chifley was unwilling to let the matter die. He did not attempt to redraft the measure, but instead, as soon as the High Court judgment was handed down, he announced that the government would appeal the decision to the Privy Council. At this point Chifley's political judgment appeared to have been blinded by his determination to pursue a cherished doctrine. By keeping open the issue of bank nationalization, he seemed to be playing directly into the hands of his political opponents; the Privy Council hearing in London could not begin until well into 1949, and a federal election was due before the year was over.

Other important factors were now tarnishing Labor's image. There were signs that the economic master plan was not working out as successfully as its sponsors had hoped. A referendum (early in 1948) proposing that the Commonwealth have power over rents and prices had been rejected by the electorate, and the application of prices-rent controls now varied from state to state. Inflationary pressures were building up, and it seemed as though the granting of higher wages in industry was inevitably followed by price increases which nullified them. The Opposition was hammering the theme that the only source of greater material well-being was to be found in greater production and that the way to achieve greater production was through less controls, and there was much talk of the need to ease restraints. The average earnings of factory employees had gone up substantially, and by the end of 1948 they were close to double the pre-war levels. Rises in retail prices had been kept to about 40 per cent—yet the city dweller was beginning to feel that things were not what they should be. Meanwhile the prices of export commodities continued to rise, and in 1948 they were three times those of pre-war years.

Industrialists and other business leaders were stressing the need to improve relationships in industry and bring about a greater measure of trust and confidence between employers, management and employees. The most progressive of them were doing more to inform their employees about the organization in which they worked; some were also introducing bonus or profit sharing incentives and welfare and pension plans, as well as adopting higher standards of factory amenities and working conditions. Nevertheless, unrest remained in many industries, and the profit motive was frequently under attack; in spite of the general prosperity a feeling of tension was present in the community.

Industrial unrest had been working seriously against the Labor party, and as strikes spread, unattached voters became increasingly restive. State elections held during 1947—and there were five of them—had all indicated a definite weakening of Labor's hold on the electorate.

In an attempt to accelerate industrial arbitration, amendments to the Conciliation and Arbitration Act had been passed (in April 1947) assigning the settlement of industrial disputes to fifteen conciliation commissioners. The Arbitration Court's functions were reduced to those of making determinations related to basic wage rates, hours of work, and annual leave. The changes were consistent with the need to remedy difficulties that had arisen; the court's procedure was generally admitted to be slow, and legal delays were exasperating unionists. At this point the court had been considering the unions' application for reduction of the standard work week to forty hours; its judgment, delivered in September 1947 after almost two years' deliberation, was unanimous in favour of the shorter hours, which were to operate from the beginning of 1948. Close to 1,000,000 workers were affected by the decision. The court's ruling was based on evidence that industry was booming and that the economy was in a position to stand the added costs involved. The unions' request for the reduced hours had been based on the need for more leisure; but in most cases the net effect of the new award was simply that employers found themselves paying more in overtime, again pushing up the cost of labour.

In spite of the victory in the forty-hour week case, some union leaders were quick to find opportunities to foment unrest among members. In Melbourne, public transport was thrown into a chaotic state in January 1948 when the tram employees' union struck in protest against the rearrangement of hours by the Tramways Board; soon afterwards, railway maintenance men in Queensland, impatient at waiting for their application to be heard, went on strike; they were joined by the wharf labourers. By this time the stoppages were being generally linked with Communist-inspired moves, and in fact it was clear that they were the work of men who believed in waging "the class war" at all times and with all available means. The militants were exploiting the apathy that existed among unionists in general about union leadership, and strikes were now being called over the most trivial complaints.

Communist domination of the unions of wharfmen, coalminers, and steel workers became a more pressing issue as the worldwide spread of communism hardened into cold war. Within the Labor party there were men anxious to see a tougher line adopted against the Communist sympathizers within the unions and the trade union movement, but there were others—and Chifley was one of them—who held fast to the belief that the unions had the right to complete control of their own affairs. A long-time and dedicated unionist, Chifley maintained that every man had the right to his own political philosophy, and that in this regard communism, though misguided, was no different from other political philosophies. Chifley believed that the best way to combat communism was by offering secure employment and eliminating other grievance issues on which militancy could feed; the body of union membership would see the light and throw out their false leaders. However, the Prime Minister's appeals to the rank and file membership for an end to strikes were all in vain.

Coalminers were in a key position to hold the community to ransom, and the union leadership manoeuvred to embarrass the Labor government at this point. The Miners' Federation had submitted general claims to the arbitration tribunal, and as the government's attitude to industrial unrest stiffened, the union leadership decided to demonstrate its power by calling on the members for direct action to achieve its demands. The claims for a wage increase and a thirty-five-hour work week were suddenly withdrawn; instead in mid-June a strike ballot was conducted by the union leadership and the result was that before the end of the month the life of the community was disrupted as coalminers in all states except Western Australia left the pits.

The challenge could no longer be ignored by the government, and Chifley, now convinced that he faced a conspiracy, moved firmly to deal with the situation. The government contested the validity of the ballot by which the strike had been ordered, and then rushed emergency legislation through parliament to freeze the funds of the Miners' Federation and prevent their use in prolonging the strike. Troops were called in to work open-cut mines while the Commonwealth, acting in concert with state governments, moved against the miners' leadership. Several officials of the federation were prosecuted and imprisoned, and fines were imposed on the federation as a body and the supporting unions before the miners returned to work in mid-August.

Chifley had long acted as though the Communist issue was no more than a red herring used by his shrewd political opponents. By the time he realized that willingness to tolerate Communist-inspired strikes in key unions could spell electoral defeat for the A.L.P., his government had already strayed into politically dangerous territory in its initiatives on other issues. By doing too much rather than not enough at home, and by pursuing an active role in international affairs, the Labor government was causing consternation among people unprepared to move so rapidly.

At home and abroad the threat to security seemed to be growing menacingly. To those who sought to travel the middle of the road, Labor was driving perilously close to the edge. Evatt's activities in international affairs, especially in relation to the fighting which had been going on between Dutch and Indonesians in the Netherlands East Indies, had opened the way for sharp criticism. In discussions in the United Nations Security Council late in 1948, Australia had led the move to stiffen the terms against the Netherlands, and when this was followed by Australian participation in the Delhi conference of Asian-Pacific countries which criticized the

Dutch for a breach of the United Nations Charter, press and Opposition castigated a policy which, they said, could have only a dangerous result: removal of white friends who were a protective screen between Australia and the hordes of Asia. The government for its part saw the expulsion of the Dutch as inevitable and hoped to establish a friendly relationship with the new Indonesian administration from the start; but no matter how exaggerated the criticism or how outmoded the attitude of those opposed to such a view, the government's vehement stand in support of a rapid end to Dutch rule was sufficiently unorthodox to cause consternation at a time when the old system of European powers' domination of south-east Asia was disintegrating piecemeal. Why, the cautious asked, did not Australia resist, instead of aiding, this frightening process?

The menace from Asia seemed to be growing. By mid-year the continuing victories of the Communist regime in China had become a matter of pressing concern. In a review of the international scene Evatt explained the position being adopted by the government on questions related to diplomatic recognition of the regime; but his willingness to take a stand on emerging international issues without awaiting decisions made in London and Washington provided ammunition which political opponents and editorial writers could use against Labor.

On the domestic front, government under Labor appeared to be jostling the individual in minor but obtrusive ways. It seemed as though federal administration had grown arbitrary as well as bloated. Efforts by Immigration Minister Calwell to deport some Asian-born individuals who had come to Australia as wartime refugees were now creating bold headlines as deportation orders were challenged in the High Court. Price control had been taken over by the states—but now prices were rising sharply; petrol, butter, and tea were still rationed, and many other items were scarce and obtainable only on the black market.

In spite of a sound record in many fields, Labor was already facing a formidable barrage of criticism when in July, only a few months before the elections were due, the Privy Council's decision on the bank nationalization measures of 1947 was featured in banner headlines. The Privy Council's dismissal of the Commonwealth's appeal (actually, as stated later, on the grounds that it had no jurisdiction in the case) had the effect of confirming the High Court judgment in favour of the private banks—but even though Evatt declared (with a jurist's rather than a politician's logic) that bank nationalization was now dead and could not become an election issue, the whole subject of Labor's attitude to banking was back again in the spotlight.

The Opposition's attacks on Labor's socialist objectives, and increasingly bold claims by both Menzies and Fadden that their parties were the only bulwark against an onrushing communism, were now supported by a massive campaign backed by banking and business interests intent on ousting Labor. As polling day drew near, even the aging John Thomas Lang took his place on the New South Wales hustings to discredit "the Chifley Myth"; and though he might have been long discredited himself for all but destructive purposes, he was now widely reported as he added his voice to those out for

Chifley's defeat.

From the moment Menzies delivered his policy speech, the Liberal and Country parties held the offensive. Socialism was the focal point of the attack, and the bank nationalization measure was cited as evidence of Labor's intention to pursue its avowed objectives. Menzies said:

> This question of the Socialist objective cannot be avoided. In 1946 you could vote Labor, reasonably supposing that it was a party of reform and not socialization. In 1949 it is clear that the Labor vote is a vote for the Socialist objective and nothing else.

Fadden was on the platform when Menzies made his policy speech and in proposing a vote of thanks declared that Menzies had spoken "as the leader of a composite party with a composite platform and composite policy." The two men presented a united front throughout the campaign and both stressed that their two parties could successfully unite in a joint government. Prominent among the Liberal party's anti-Labor slogans, emblazoned in newspaper advertisements, was the line, "*Every* Candidate is a Socialist Candidate," while the Country party, attacking on the same lines, described the A.L.P. platform as a "Socialist blueprint."

The two parties joined in branding socialism as the policies of dependence and decay, and they promised to amend the Constitution so that it would be impossible for a future Labor government to introduce "socialist" legislation (except after a referendum vote). The Liberals had been won over to support a course of action long advocated by the Country party: the outlawing of the Communist party. They promised that this, plus the introduction of secret ballots in union elections, would "rid Australia of Communist wreckers." Other points put forward involved the launching of an extensive programme of national development and an expansion of production throughout the economy. At the same time promises were made to end shortages and rationing (with special emphasis on petrol) and to expand existing social benefits.

Labor's leaders evaded the issues advanced relentlessly by Menzies and Fadden relating to the question of how far and how fast Labor proposed to go in implementing its stated objectives. Chifley in his policy speech dismissed the issue of communism as one of the bogeys raised by Labor's opponents, and said the labour movement existed to promote social and economic security for the people, higher living standards, and the progressive expansion of Australia as a nation in a world community. He explained that his government had shaped all its financial and economic measures towards maintaining full employment, and would continue to do so. The voter was asked to accept Labor's past record as an assurance of a stable economy, full employment, and security for all in the future.

In their rejoinders, Labor's opponents made two telling points: that the private banks would continue to be in danger under a Labor government because the party was determined to achieve by indirect action what the courts had prevented it from doing openly, and that a party which had passed legislation to nationalize the banks without having mentioned such action in the previous election might well be harbouring more ambitious plans to spring on the country at the first opportunity.

Efforts to predict the outcome of the election were complicated because an increase in the House membership, lifting it to 121, had been approved earlier in 1949 and no one knew precisely what effect the consequent changes in electoral boundaries would have. Straw polls suggested a House majority for the Liberal-Country party coalition; but some nonpartisan observers were prepared to give the A.L.P. a fighting chance, and the sweeping success that was revealed for the Liberal-Country party candidates as ballots were counted on the night of December 10 was generally unexpected. The final figures showed that Labor's over-all vote had fallen from the 51 per cent in 1946 to under 47 per cent. Menzies, in a radio-telephone interview, told the London *Sunday Express* it was "a knockout blow; nationalization has taken it on the chin." At his first press conference after the victory, Menzies said that he believed part of the success could be attributed to the growing public resentment at bureaucratic controls, and a feeling that some ministers had enjoyed so much power that they were becoming high-handed and contemptuous of public rights.

The truth was that while Australians were prepared to acknowledge freely that Chifley's canniness as Treasurer had helped give the economy its sound post-war base, national horizons were expanding and the time had come to adopt a greater measure of economic freedom. Labor's defeat was a great personal triumph for Menzies; it also reflected the community's determination to move forward into a new world of bolder objectives.

Labor ministers had consistently encouraged administrative initiative in the shaping of projects of national significance, and in parliament they had withstood criticism and confounded the scepticism of political opponents who poured scorn on many of their proposals. In their final months in office Chifley and other members of cabinet were determined that, no matter what the outcome of the year-end elections—and no matter how great the criticism heaped on the party or its general policies—there would be indelible recognition of Labor's association with the planning of major undertakings of fundamental value to the community. Two of the most significant projects of a national character, sponsored and nurtured by the Chifley government, were inaugurated in October 1949. One was the Snowy Mountains hydroelectric and water storage undertaking, and the other the Australian National University.

The measure setting up the Snowy Mountains Hydroelectric Authority was passed early in 1949, when funds were voted for the initial phases of a bold and imaginative twenty-year construction project designed to double the nation's power-generating capacity and to expand significantly the water available for irrigation purposes. Attention had been focussed on the Snowy Mountains area because it contained the major snow source on the Australian continent. Investigations of the power-generating potential of the madcap Snowy River had revealed ways in which long-discussed plans to harness and direct alpine rivers might be developed. The idea of using the Snowy as a source of hydroelectric power (and at the same time ending its flood-producing rampages) had been supported by Victoria; in New South Wales, agitation had begun among land men in 1945 for action designed to cut off the Snowy's headwaters and direct extra water into the Murrumbidgee where they could be used to expand the area under irrigation The Murray Valley Development League, bringing together representative citizens from regions spread along the great valley, backed the idea of a large-scale water-conservation and diversion project. A special committee to investigate the resources of the Murray Valley on a regional basis was set up, under federal auspices, in 1946. At the same time, hydrographic studies began to substantiate the view that the snowlands of the main alpine knot were so significant to both irrigation and power-generation that only a complex and comprehensive combined-use plan would be appropriate for their development. The proposals set down by the committee of engineers and technical experts (representing the federal department of works and state water conservation bodies) and presented in 1949 as the basis for the national parliament's approval, provided such a balance.

The grandiose Snowy Mountains concept involved the creation of a series of storages designed to trap the maximum amount of water at high altitude, and to link the storages by tunnels driven through the mountains. Underground and other generating stations would draw power from the water as it was diverted into the Murray and Murrumbidgee Rivers, through turbogenerators with an installed capacity of close to 3,000,000 kilowatts. The merits of such a plan had been explained to the community, and for the first time the federal government accepted responsibility for an immense undertaking to yield electricity and augment water storages. When the Governor-General inaugurated the Snowy Mountains project on October 17, 1949, cabinet members and Labor parliamentarians were on hand—though all but two members of the Opposition boycotted the ceremony.

A week later the foundation stone was laid in Canberra of the Australian National University—the first institution in Australia designed solely to provide the special facilities required for postgraduate research. The large influx of ex-servicemen into the universities immediately after the war—a federally sponsored undertaking—had placed special strains on lecturers, demonstrators, and tutors, many of whom had little opportunity for research. Since the regular staff members were heavily involved in teaching, opportunities for research were severely reduced and the number of research-type papers fell. The need for a postgraduate institution was clear. Federal support for such a project reflected the views of Prime Minister Chifley and those around him; the drive to gain political acceptance of the proposal for a nationally-supported institution fell largely on Dedman, who took every opportunity to stress the value of facilities for scholarship in an expanding Australia. The Australian National University Act (passed in 1946) laid down that the new institution was, among other things,

> ... to encourage and provide facilities for postgraduate and research study, both generally and in relation to subjects of national importance to Australia.

It was also to give special attention to providing specialist training for members of the public service and public-authority staff members. By 1947 an interim council was in operation; it set up an academic advisory committee comprising four eminent scholars with interests within the ambit of the respective research schools. The committee's original members were Sir Howard Florey (adviser to the John Curtin School of Medical Research), Professor Marcus Laurence Oliphant (adviser to and later director of the Research School of Physical Sciences), Professor Raymond William Firth (adviser to the Research School of Pacific Studies), and Professor Sir Keith Hancock (adviser to the Research School of Social Sciences). The committee functioned until 1951, when the interim council was replaced by a permanent council.

Although education in general remained a matter for state administrations, by 1949 the federal government was already assisting to the extent of £15 million a year on grants for education and research, and 3000 selected students were receiving Commonwealth Scholarships each year.

Expansion   25
gathers pace

In ousting the Labor party and sweeping the progressive-conservative coalition into power at a time of widespread and sustained prosperity, the election showed that a majority of Australians still deemed politicians responsible for legislating to ensure the good life with a minimum of personal or business restrictions. The vote had been, in part at least, a vote for a loosening of federal control. It was soon apparent, however, that if either the voters in general or the successful politicians in particular believed it might be possible to regain old ways, they were to be disppointed.

Menzies and Fadden and their followers had been out of office for eight years, but judged from the changes in the Australia they inherited it might have been a generation. People were demanding far more of government than ever before, and no responsible administration could abandon its enlarged and more constructive role. The days of minimal taxes had gone forever. In the new situation, dismantling of the new federal structure could not, in fact, go very far. The incoming Prime Minister had been drawing political inspiration from the Republicans of the United States in their pressure for a reduction of the federal role there; but the American electorate had accepted the Democrats' Fair Deal in succession to President Roosevelt's New Deal, and in the process the United States had in fact moved towards "bigger" federal government. Once in office Menzies quickly found that there was little scope for carrying Australia back to a less complicated, less government-involved way of life. There was considerable opportunity, however, for the encouragement of industrial expansion by policies directed at creating a favourable environment for investment and enterprise; and the fact that a less regulation-minded government was in office in Canberra was enough in itself to spur action among businessmen towards creating new enterprises.

In fulfilment of its immediate promises, the new government abolished successively the rationing of butter and tea within a few months of coming to office. (Rationing of petrol had already been declared invalid.) When it came to honouring some of the more specific election points—such as the undertaking to reduce numbers within the federal public service by 10,000 —Menzies found it expedient to modify his position by more or less letting things ride. The promise to "put value back in the £" also proved unattainable; very soon prices were rising more rapidly than before under the pressure of pent up spending power. The issue of outlawing the Communist party—which had been specifically promised in Menzies' policy speech— remained to be fulfilled.

The Menzies government soon came to accept almost completely the forced-growth policy initiated under Chifley. Further, the new administration quickly came to the conclusion that there was little it could change in the over-all federal structure. Its more ambitious ministers in fact were espousing proposals, developed by departmental experts, which involved further expansion of what they had previously condemned as a dangerously bloated payroll. As inflationary pressures gathered force, those who had been loudest in their criticism of regulatory measures came grudgingly to accept that they were part of the new situation into which Australia and the world had moved.

The election had been a major victory for Menzies, who had successfully carried out the task on which he had embarked in 1945—to build a strong national party which would appeal to a broad following and reduce the splinter groups in opposition to Labor. The Liberals' vote-winning achievement (with 39.7 per cent of votes, compared with 33 per cent in 1946) had improved considerably on that of the old United Australia party of the 1930s. The Liberal party had strengthened its position in practically all states, with striking gains in Queensland, Western Australia, and Tasmania, while the Country party had held up well in Queensland (though down in Western Australia and merged with the Liberals in South Australia and Tasmania). Everywhere, Labor had failed to win its share of the new young voters; an unusually large proportion had gravitated to the Liberal party or to the Country party. In particular the Liberal party had made a successful appeal to women, who had borne the brunt of the inconveniences of rationing, shortages and lack of electricity.

In terms of popular vote, the A.L.P.'s percentage of total vote had fallen by a relatively narrow margin—from 51 to 46 per cent—but its percentage of seats had dropped from 60 per cent to less than 40 per cent in the new and enlarged House. Eleven Labor members were defeated, including four who had held cabinet posts. In contrast to this, all sitting members of both the Liberal and Country parties were returned. The Communists fared very badly; the total vote for Communist candidates was only half that polled eight years before.

In spite of success in the House of Representatives, the Liberal-Country party coalition faced a Senate still firmly controlled by Labor since only part of the Senate had been renewed. The A.L.P. was unwilling to concede that the resurgent non-Labor forces could not soon be rolled back. On the Liberal side it was a matter of making the final ramparts fall. The manoeuvring began. The struggle developed around three last-ditch issues; suppression of communism, banking policies, and industrial arbitration.

In its early months the Menzies-Fadden government did some administrative windowdressing by shuffling functions and staff in departmental reorganizations, but basic policies were little changed. In March 1950 a new department—that of national development—was set up soon after the Prime Minister announced the outlines of a policy for developing the country's resources; the department was to be under the ministerial guidance of Richard Gardiner Casey, who was also Minister for Works and Housing and Minister in charge of the Commonwealth Scientific and Industrial Organization. Work on the Snowy Mountains project went forward; and in August the Prime Minister returned from a tour overseas with a loan of $100 million from the International Bank of Reconstruction and Development intended to assist in expanding irrigation and power supply and in undertaking land clearance projects. A national health scheme based on a system of voluntary insurance with federal support was introduced, and payment of 5/- a week child endowment—which previously had excluded the first child in any family—was now extended to cover all children.

By mid-year the government found itself thwarted in the Senate on the three measures which contained the essence of its legislative intent. These bills comprised a measure to transfer control of the Commonwealth Bank from a single governor (responsible to the Treasurer) to a ten-man board and to make other changes in the banking laws, amendment of industrial arbitration intended to broaden the court's power to deal with those defying its awards, and—most controversial of all—the Communist Party Dissolution Bill.

This bill, which was designed to break the ring of power which Communists exerted over key unions, had far-reaching and unusual provisions. The Australian Communist party was declared an illegal association and was to be dissolved. Any affiliated organizations (other than trade unions) held to be under the domination of Communists, could also be dissolved. There were provisions for dealing with individual Communists: any person "declared" to be a Communist could be disqualified from employment in a government department, while "declared" persons were also debarred from holding office in a trade union in industries that were considered vital to defence and security. The provision relating to declared Communists was to be retroactive for two years. Appeals against a declaration of Communist status or affiliation could be made before a judge of the High Court, but the onus of proof rested with the individual, not the Crown.

The government made it clear that the bill was intended to deal with dangers arising from Communist power or influence in Australian unions involving the heavy industries, power, and transport, where Communist leadership was known to have played a disruptive role. The key groups led, controlled, or influenced by Communists included the seamen, coalminers, ironworkers, wharf-labourers, railwaymen, tram-men and engineers.

Newspaper opinion was virtually unanimous that something must be done about the Communist party and generally newspapers came out in favour of the measure in spite of its unpalatable infractions of British legal usage. The Melbourne *Age*, by now firmly conservative, considered the government had "a clear mandate" for such action; the rival *Argus* almost alone pointed to the dangers of the bill's illiberal provisions and asked whether it would result in the creation of "a vast secret police and spy system." Practically every other daily newspaper echoed the view that the measure was necessary.

Nevertheless, many responsible people in the community were concerned over the measure's dragnet powers. In its tone and provisions the measure seemed to be drawn on American rather than English lines, and it appeared to many to have been largely engendered by suspicion and fear. Labor still held firmly to the view expressed by Chifley that banning the Communist party "gets you nowhere: that has been proved in many countries," and charges that the legislation had been too hastily prepared gained added weight when early in the proceedings the Prime Minister confessed that five of the names he had listed as alleged Communist trade union leaders had been included in his statement in error. At some rowdy public gatherings, order was maintained only by the presence of large numbers of police; and the Prime Minister's speeches at public meetings in support of the case for the measure invariably produced demonstrations of protest. In its parliamentary opposition to the measure, the Labor party leadership concerned itself primarily with specific provisions. On the bill's second reading, in May 1950, Chifley attacked the onus-of-proof clause particularly. He said that the way was being opened for the liar and the perjurer "to make charges and damn men's reputations, and to do so in secret without having either to substantiate or prove any charges" that they might make. Some minor amendments were made by the government, but the general provisions remained; Opposition proposals for amendments to provide full onus of proof on the Crown, trial by jury for those who appealed, and compensation for any "declared" person found innocent, were rejected on the grounds that to fight communism the Government had to have exceptional powers.

The House quickly passed the bill, but the Labor party, although faced with a rising tide of criticism for its delaying tactics, continued to debate the measure in the Senate, attacking provisions which impinged on the individual's rights as a citizen and pressing for amendments designed to remove obnoxious provisions. Finally, under threat from the government of a double dissolution for obstructing the bill, Labor senators received a direction from the party's federal executive to allow the bill to pass in the form approved by the House. On October 19 the bill cleared the Senate when only eleven of the thirty-four Opposition senators were present in the chamber for the final vote. Three days later the act was proclaimed.

On October 24 ten trade unions under militant leadership and the

Australian Communist party sought an injunction by the High Court to restrain the Commonwealth from applying the act until its validity had been tested. Mr Justice Dixon granted interim injunctions to this effect. Dr Evatt accepted the brief to appear for the Waterside Workers' Federation and its general secretary, and led the attack on the act's legality.

The High Court hearing began in mid-November; the climax came on March 9, 1951, when by a six-to-one decision the High Court invalidated the act on the ground that it attempted to interfere directly with civil liberties and property rights which were properly matters under the control of the states. Federal intrusion into such matters was allowable solely under the defence power, which could be exercised only in time of open war; and, the court held, in spite of the conflict in Korea and extreme international tension, the present was in fact a time of peace. The court noted that parliament had not declared the act was passed for the prosecution of any war or that there was any danger of war; nor had it established that the Australian Communist party was a menace to the country. The lone dissentient, Chief Justice Latham, based his contrary argument on reasoning followed by some members of the United States Supreme Court, holding that the question of whether the defence of Australia required the suppression of the party was a question for parliament and not for the court.

Satisfied that it had been vindicated in its stand on the Communist party measure, the Labor party decided to continue its delaying tactics in the Senate over the hotly-disputed Commonwealth Bank bill (which had been passing back and forth between the Senate and the House for twelve months) by the device of referring it to a select committee. Also sidetracked in the Senate was the government's measure amending the arbitration act in order to strengthen the Arbitration Court's powers of dealing with disruptive tactics by militant union leaders.

At this point Menzies saw his chance to break the logjam by means of a dissolution of both Houses of Parliament. He considered that the Senate's sidetracking move on the banking bill constituted "failure to pass" as defined by the constitution, but fine legal points were involved. On March 15 the Prime Minister discussed the matter of Senate obstruction with Governor-General William McKell and, as he reported later, "made it clear to His Excellency that he was not bound" to follow the advice being tendered regarding conditions for a double dissolution under section 57 of the constitution. Advices on the subject were at once prepared by the government lawyers, and a strong case was made out for the view that the Senate's decision to remit the bill to "a Select Committee of some members of the Senate" was nothing more than a delaying procedure. The submission, made to the Governor-General, added:

> There is clear evidence that the design and intention of the Senate . . . has been to seek every opportunity for delay, upon the principle that protracted postponement may be in some political circumstances almost as efficacious, though not so dangerous, as straight-out rejection. Since failure to pass is, in Section 57, distinguished from rejection or unacceptable amendment, it must refer, among other things, to such a delay in passing the Bill or such a delaying intention as would amount to an expression of unwillingness to pass it.

The submission also referred to the "long conflict" with the Senate over the Communist Party Dissolution Bill and other measures, and said that as a consequence "the legislative machine, except in respect of relatively minor matters, has been materially slowed down and rendered extremely uncertain in its operation."

The Governor-General accepted the advice, and on March 16 handed the Prime Minister a letter agreeing to a simultaneous dissolution of the Senate and the House.

In the election campaign the A.L.P. emphasized the sharply rising inflation and the government's failure to take adequate corrective measures, but the government parties (and the press) kept the menace of communism before the voters, and promised that either a reference of powers from the states or a constitutional amendment would be sought to overcome the High Court's recent decision. At the same time, it was notable that the Liberals had come to the conclusion that although there was no intention to rush into controls—"we have," said Menzies, "an instinctive dislike of them"— some more effective counter-inflationary steps were needed. The Prime Minister promised that if emergency rendered them necessary, additional controls would be instituted to back up regulation of capital-raising by companies, recently reimposed.

The election, in April, showed that Labor had regained some ground; but though returned with a reduced margin in the House, the Liberal-Country party coalition now had a working majority in the Senate. Labor had lost its chance to regain power in what was to prove a crucial election, and after the sudden death of Chifley in June, the party was soon to find itself wandering again in a political wilderness. The issues of 1949 and 1951 had united the Liberal party and cemented its union with the Country party; they had sown the seeds of dissension within the A.L.P.

Strengthened in its resolve by the evidence of public support, the government next ordered a raid on the offices of Communist-led trade unions in Sydney and Melbourne. In July a bill was introduced for the holding of a referendum on a constitutional amendment which would give the Commonwealth power to ban the Communist party and prevent Communists from holding union office. Specifically the measure sought power for the federal parliament to legislate "with respect to Communists or communism as the Parliament considers to be necessary or expedient for the defence or security of the Commonwealth."

Success in two elections within eighteen months encouraged the government's hopes that the proposed amendment would be passed by the electors, but the A.L.P., now under Evatt's leadership, embarked upon a vigorous nationwide campaign to secure a negative vote in the referendum of September 1951. Support for the referendum proposal was strong at first, but it appeared to seep away steadily as the campaign progressed and the issue was more widely debated. By the time of the voting many people feared that a "yes" vote might eventually mean that any sharp critic of government could be denounced and punished as a Communist. In the referendum nearly 5,000,000 votes were cast. The proposal was rejected by an over-all margin of 52,000 votes, with "no" majorities in New South Wales, Victoria and South Australia.

While Australians were still debating the issue, a perceptive American economist writing in the businessman's monthly, *Fortune*, had noted underlying factors which were obscured in the fury of local discussions. He wrote:

> To attribute the nation's woes to the subversiveness of the Communists, as so many Australians do, is to miss the country's significant, underlying ailment. What can keep Australia from becoming great, what certainly keeps private enterprise in perennial jeopardy, is precisely the malaise that drives the worker to the less onerous jobs and makes him willing to be led by self-proclaimed Communists. This malaise is a factitious and absurd division into the camps of labour and capital (or management). . . .
>
> Workers regard one who joins the supervisory group as a pariah, seem to believe that all the talk of production is capitalist propaganda for increased profits, and tend to be against overtime and incentives. The manager, for his part, tends to regard all workers as shirkers, and has a hard time distinguishing between unionism and communism—a distinction he himself has done a lot to obliterate.

These factors had been important in the working man's willingness to tolerate militant leadership. As the *Fortune* writer went on to explain, the Australian actually did not "give a hoot" about Marxism or communism; what he wanted was what his union leaders might secure for him in terms of better award conditions—and of course the Communist leaders had done well for him in this regard.

In fact the membership of the Australian Communist party had been declining steadily, and it now stood at less than 8000. Likewise the heyday of Communist influence in the unions had already passed. Dedicated anti-Communists had launched a counter-offensive within the union organization which, thanks to the adoption of the secret ballot in union elections, brought about the defeat of Communist candidates for office in one union election after another throughout 1950 and 1951.

As a corollary, it was equally true that more and more unionists were splitting away from militant leaders when the issues were political rather than industrial.

In the debates on the Communist Dissolution measure and in the court action against it, Evatt had come into the public spotlight as never before, and although he won the legal battle his deep personal involvement was to have lasting effects within the Australian Labor party. The role in which he chose to cast himself was one that brought forth all his considerable talents and energy; but in becoming so totally devoted to the defeat of a measure which he deplored, Evatt emerged as an enigmatic and controversial figure. He not only damaged his—and Labor's—political reputation with the electorate at large but he also found himself cut off from a significant segment of his own party. The legal ethics according to which (as the Council of the Victorian Bar pointed out) a barrister might not refuse a brief merely because of the character of the cause or of the client, or because he did not share the ideas involved, meant nothing to the average voter. It was easy for Evatt's opponents to dramatize the issue and to foster a belief that he and his party were in fact "soft on communism"; and since among a great body of voters the Communist issue remained a matter of deep concern, Evatt's active and impassioned intervention could always be pointed to by Liberal and Country party members as an indication of political *naïveté* at best, or dangerous attitudes at worst.

Meanwhile, with the Senate obstruction cleared, the government had no difficulty in enacting its new banking law and the arbitration amendments which had been held up for so long.

While the·political issues were boiling over, a wave of prosperity had been sweeping through the land. Throughout 1950 Australia was engaged in an unprecedented spending spree. The pace of economic expansion had been growing for some time, and in 1950, as optimism floated higher on a tide of rising incomes, prices of everything from bread to real estate moved up sharply. Wage levels lagged behind the fast clip of the price increases, but overtime payments swelled many workers' pay envelopes. Money was being pumped into the economy at an unprecedented rate and it was turning over rapidly. Manufacturing industry was expanding to meet the clamour for goods of all kinds. People were arriving by the shipload —2000 and 3000 of them a week—and although the newcomers helped to meet the labour shortages they also had needs of their own which intensified demand.

The sharp increase in population accentuated an already-serious housing shortage and put direct strains on the public utilities. There was a shortage of electricity and gas in the cities; water supply systems lagged behind requirements to serve new areas; there were not enough schools or hospitals, and public transport was inadequate. While these matters were being attended to, private business was pressing to expand, and both government and farmers were pushing ahead with their own plans for rural development.

Basic to the situation was the accelerated migrant intake and the magnitude of government spending on public works in a time of tight labour supply; but the inflation was being fed from many streams as individuals, firms, and state and local governments, and the federal government, all rushed to fulfil long-held ambitions. With the job security of full and over-full employment, the average citizen not only spent more freely but he was prepared to borrow to do so. Consumer credit began to expand markedly. Wages were rising; in 1950 an amendment to the arbitration law enabled the Arbitration Court, in fixing the basic wage, to take into account economic disparity within industry as well as workers' "needs," and in exercise of this power the Court declared an increase of £1 a week in the basic rate for men and 15/- for women. Pacing all other inflationary factors was the tremendous rise in rural income. Graziers and farmers were receiving bigger cheques than they ever dreamed possible; and although some of the inflated earnings were drawn into tax coffers or into the banks to repay old loans, the result was the same: demand rose sharply as the new money elbowed its way into the economy, reaching out to command all kinds of goods and services and seeking investment opportunities.

The main engine of the boom was wool. Caught with minimum stocks at the outbreak of the Korean war in June 1950, American woolspinners began to buy heavily at the wool auctions. Late in 1950 a proposal that a portion of the clip might be pre-empted for the United States Army at a fixed price was considered; but since the wool was the property of the men and companies that produced it the question was put to a vote among wool-growers. After acrimonious debate the proposal was rejected by a four-to-one margin—64,000 votes to 16,000. One of the arguments used by the "no" proponents was that, in the light of the sterling area's chronic dollar gap, it would be unwise to make a move which would reduce dollar earnings from wool.

The volume of the Australian clip had now risen well above pre-war levels and, under the impetus of uninhibited buying for the United States, average wool prices had shot up to three times the average prices ruling in the immediate post-war years (and to eight times or so what they had been in the 1930s). The result was that the national returns from wool rose to £313 million in 1949–50 and £633 million in 1950–51 (compared with £43 million only twelve years earlier).

Other rural industries were sharing in the bonanza, though to a lesser extent. The total export figures moved up in 1950–51 to £982 million and although imports were far higher than in earlier years the net balance on current account in Australia's favour exceeded £101 million.

At the same time as a great flood of money was being released within the Australian economy by booming export industries, a record volume of money was being accumulated on Australia's behalf in London. At June 30, 1951 the reserves exceeded £821 million.

To help meet the expanded demand for goods within Australia the government adopted a more liberal policy in administering controls which had been constraining the volume of imports throughout the war and post-war years. These curbs, in the form of import-licensing regulations, had given the government direct administrative control over the total volume of imports and the volume of any type of goods or material that might be admitted. Import controls were acknowledged to be cumbersome and irksome, yet they served a dual purpose: they conserved overseas currency by holding down all imports (practically eliminating luxury goods and prohibiting most imports from the dollar area) and at the same time they provided a special form of shelter which was an effective encouragement for manufacturers.

In the second half of 1951, the unfavourable trade balance was £215 million; and the rundown in overseas reserves was proceeding at a tremendous rate. The dislocations to the economy that came as a result of the partial freeing of imports were sharper and more startling than anticipated by those who supported the "let's-try-it-and-see" approach.

At this point Britain was opening up a great export drive to regain old markets, and Australian importers suddenly found that instead of deferring orders suppliers could now make immediate shipments, and in full. No sooner had Canberra eased the import restrictions than a great mass of goods and equipment was on its way. For the first time in well over a decade Australian manufacturing industries were exposed to some of the cold winds of overseas competition—and at a time when the Australian economy was superheated under inflationary pressures.

Due largely to the time lag involved (arising from the distance over which the goods had to be shipped), conversion of the tremendous export earnings took some time. With the great wave of imports which began to arrive after mid-1951, the year's total imports by June 1952 exceeded £1000 million in cost. Exports had meanwhile fallen, so that the current account deficit for the year was a staggering £544 million; and although a strong inflow of money sent in for investment from overseas helped ease the situation, by mid-1952 international reserves had been drained to well under £400 million.

Not long after the main weight of imports began pouring on to Australian wharves and into the shops, shrinkages occurred in demand as a result of a sharp fall in wool prices and because of the effects of anti-inflationary measures which the government had taken. Soon the recession gathered pace.

With manufacturing languishing, unemployment rising, and an end in sight to the cushion of overseas reserves, the only sensible course open to the government was to return to stricter import controls. In March 1952 a change of policy was announced: quantitative import controls were back. Ostensibly the move was made in order to conserve Australia's overseas funds, but a factor of equal importance was the need to help revive the industrial economy.

It took some time for the adjustment to run its course. Businessmen felt more cautious now, and although behind the shield of import curbs manufacturing began to move forward again, this time it was on a more subdued basis.

The gyrations of the economy had taken a toll. Practically all wage increases had been swallowed up in price increases. In money terms, the gross national income had risen 35 per cent in one year—from £2307 million (in 1949–50) to £3130 million in 1950–51—while the population had increased by more than 250,000, or slightly over 3 per cent, as a result of natural increase and expanded migration. Over-all, however, prices were climbing so steeply in the same period that the gain in "real" national income per head was only 13 per cent (an increase from £263 to £299 a head). In the sharp recession which followed, all this gain in "real" income was lost, for although people had more money to spend it was buying them less in 1951–52. The gross national income for the year showed a slight gain in money terms; but this was an illusion of inflation since income per head in real terms was down to £253, and it was to decline further in 1952–53 to £248 before it began a slow improvement in the late 1950s.

The table on the following page shows how the gross national income and "real" income levels moved:

National Income Related to "Real" National Income, 1948–49 to 1953–54, with 1938–39 Comparisons.

	Gross National Income £'000,000	Mean Population (Millions)	"Real" National Income, per head £
1938–39	780	6.9	171
1948–49	1961	7.8	251
1949–50	2307	8.0	263
1950–51	3130	8.3	299
1951–52	3293	8.5	253
1952–53	3610	8.7	248
1953–54	3867	8.9	253

Part of the explanation for the decline in real income was to be found in the policy of building for the future. As private investment fell sharply in 1952–53, the federal and state governments moved forward with greatly expanded programmes of public works. The easing of the pressure on the labour market in industry thus cleared the way for added effort in the public sector of the economy. The government adopted the policy of increasing the proportion of public works expenditure drawn from current income (through taxation) and held back on local loan-raising, while at the same time it drew additional funds from the International Bank for Reconstruction and Development to support the major undertakings such as the Snowy Mountains project. With the sharp decline in private investment, this meant that the government authorities were pushing ahead with essential works in place of normal business and private outlays. The pattern of private-business and public investment was as follows:

Composition of Gross Investment, 1948–49 to 1954–55

	Investment in business undertakings and other private outlays of a capital nature (including all motor vehicles)	Government investment, federal and state, in public works and undertakings	Total Investment as a percentage of gross national product
	£'000,000		%
1948–49	380	142	22.9
1949–50	580	198	28.5
1950–51	803	288	30.0
1951–52	1112	393	38.9
1952–53	517	385	21.4
1953–54	823	397	26.7
1954–55	1047	418	29.8

The easing of credit in 1953, together with reductions in taxation, increased government expenditure, and an active programme of public works helped keep the economy at a high pitch; but the rate of real expansion had fallen to about 2 per cent a year, barely exceeding a lowered rate of increase in the population. Immigration, which the previous year had dropped to less than half its previous rate, began to pick up again in 1954. By that time the community's total expenditure on goods and services was showing about a 7 per cent annual increase, in money terms; after allowing for spiralling prices, the real gain, from effort, productivity, and other factors, probably remained under 3 per cent. There was, in addition, an uncounted gain in a significant improvement in quality of goods and services produced.

An improved level of investment, sustained from 1953, was devoted to expanding production and improving technical facilities in all phases of activity. The introduction of new products helped change the pattern of consumer expenditure. People were now spending less of their income on clothing, footwear, and drapery; and as consumer credit became more readily available, more household appliances were bought. The work force had grown to 3,700,000 and there had been significant changes in its composition. A national census revealed that those employed in rural industries represented only 15 per cent of the total work force (compared with 18 per cent in 1947); those engaged in manufacturing had remained at slightly over 27 per cent, while, with new commercial buildings now changing city skylines for the first time in decades, the percentage of male labour engaged in the building and construction industry had moved up in seven years from 9.7 to 11.3 per cent. Commerce and associated activities had also expanded, employing almost one-seventh of the male work force and 22 per cent of the women and girls in employment.

A low point for prices of rural products was reached early in 1955, but thereafter increased output of wool, grains, and other commodities counterbalanced the effect of the price decline so that total returns from exports (£760 million in 1954–55) were holding up well. The drive for greater efficiency in manufacturing was also producing results, and manufactured goods were contributing 10 per cent or more to export earnings. Australia was moving toward fulfilment of its aim of becoming the workshop of the South Pacific. Imports still exceeded exports but the trade gap was narrowing; the over-all deficit on trading operations (including freight and insurance outlays) was down to £142 million in 1954–55, with a £100 million offset from capital invested from abroad. From this point the tide flowed more rapidly in Australia's favour; imports slackened and export earnings rose, so that by 1956 there was a favourable trade balance and international reserves were again at a safe level.

The government's economic policy, applied principally through the annual budget but buttressed by the increasingly significant day-to-day regulatory role played by the central bank's monetary and credit policies, was designed to provide a background for sustained and sound growth. The role of the economic planner remained important, even though he had to work indirectly and with less-than-sufficient tools. Both within the official policy-making groups and in the community at large there was an endless dialogue on the question of whether the country was trying to do too much too fast; but the victory went to those who believed that Australia's only safe course was to continue its expansion of resources as rapidly as possible, even though this might involve alternating between stop and go policies at fairly frequent intervals.

Federal policies were frequently criticized by commentators, economists, and businessmen as being inconsistent or wavering; but a solid pattern of expansion was emerging, in spite of the severe growing pains. Fundamentally the problems were those of a nation with a large land area and a limited population undertaking a massive range of development processes at the same time as the community was demanding—and receiving—more of the good things of life. For the world's most sparsely populated country (the population gave an over-all density in relation to area of less than three people to the square mile) it was nation-building under special difficulties. Above all, the development had to be financed, in the end, basically from the sale of rural products abroad, with some assistance from minerals and a lesser contribution from manufactured goods. The commitments were great, while the available resources in terms of people to do the job were extremely limited.

By the late 1950s the pattern of a modern economy had emerged: wages and salaries made up about 60 per cent of the national income, company income 15 per cent, professional and small business some 12 per cent, with primary producers' incomes fluctuating (according to world demands and prices) around 10 per cent or so.

Government spending had assumed a more important role. Over-all the public-sector outlays, including contributions to state governments' loans, debt redemption, and other items, represented 28 per cent of the national income (and were equivalent to £137 a head a year). At this point, annual outlays on defence were equivalent to £20 a head while £25 a head was spent on pensions, medical, and other welfare benefits and £28 a head on payments to the states, most of it for road construction and as university grants. Federal capital works amounted to £12 a head a year, and the cost of running the Post Office with all its services £10 a head.

In the national programme of public works the federal government was allocating large sums from current revenue. Public works expenditure, federal and state, during the ten years to 1958 was about £3600 million and all but between 20 and 25 per cent or so of this money came from revenue without increasing the national debt. In this important aspect of national policy, the pattern set by Prime Minister-Treasurer Chifley in the late 1940s had survived. Thus, the future was being underwritten at minimum cost, while in an economy of full employment the pay-as-you-build was the safest way (in economic terms) to undertake essential public works without adding dangerously to inflationary pressures. Great outlays were made to increase power, water, and irrigation projects, to build new schools and other educational facilities, and to improve and extend roads, harbours, and hospitals. The railway systems were being rehabilitated; apart from track improvements railways had made major gains following steady conversion from steam to diesel traction. Diesel locomotives, introduced in 1951 for freight, and later extended to passenger trains, made possible steady gains in reliability, ease, and economy of operation. Other aspects of railway operation were updated as the various systems embarked upon rehabilitation programmes. These included the introduction of mechanical operations for track maintenance, new construction, and improvement in the load-bearing capacity of older lines.

The rewards from the heavy investment of public money in developmental projects would be years in coming; the official plan therefore amounted to taxing the present to provide for the future. Annual interest liability on the national debt remained at little over £14 a head, negligible compared with pre-war levels, and the total debt of £4000 million meant that the permanent national debt load was only slightly more than £400 a head—equivalent to well under a year's national income by the late 1950s. For a young and growing country, this low level of debt was a significantly advantageous factor.

Rural industries were employing a steadily declining proportion of the labour force, but spectacular gains were nevertheless being scored by the man on the land. Problems and disabilities that had long plagued farmer and pastoralist were steadily resolved as incomes rose and the long-awaited rehabilitation of the rural sector of the economy became a reality. At the same time, two extremely important scientific achievements were beginning to take effect. One was the new method of controlling the rabbit scourge, the other the unlocking of the mystery of impoverished soils; together these discoveries enhanced immeasurably the nation's long-range prospects for agricultural and pastoral development. All the technical and scientific gains, taken together, represented a breakthrough of major significance in terms of the national future.

A long run of good seasons from the late 1940s and a generally favourable price level for the various rural commodities made it possible for men and companies engaged in land industries to invest quite heavily in improvements. This investment steadily lifted efficiency on farms and stations and in so doing enhanced the output of practically all types of rural products. The wool industry made the most striking gains. Year by year sheep numbers rose, while by selective breeding and the continued culling of flocks average wool yield, per sheep, was raised to 10 lb annually. In 1953 the nation's sheep numbers surpassed the earlier (1942) record of 125,000,000 head, and by the late 1950s the total had passed 150,000,000. Over the same period the annual wool clip moved up from about 1,000,000,000 lbs a year in the 1940s to more than 1,500,000,000 lbs by the late 1950s. Wheat, with a basic price of about 14/– per bushel, and other grain crops, were also profitable, and in many areas it became a matter for individual farmers to strike a balance between the gains to be made from cropping their land and running sheep on it. Wheat acreages moved up steadily after the mid-

1950s (when wool prices were at lower levels than for some time) while plantings of barley and oats also expanded steadily. In the drier country, and in the northern areas, beef cattle were being grazed in greater numbers as meat prices rose.

Increases in wages paid to all rural workers tended to accelerate the trend to smaller holdings (since farmer-owners could work these properties without outside help for most of the year) and to force the use of more mechanized methods everywhere. The drive to settle returned servicemen on the land was having effect as governments took over larger properties, subdivided them into living-area blocks, and assisted in setting up new settlers on them. In the early 1950s, when the land settlement programme was fully under way, a few thousand new farms were coming into production each year. By 1953, about 7,000,000 acres had been allotted (averaging about 1500 acres per farm). There were still many vast sheep-grazing properties, and the great merino studs run as large-scale enterprises remained the most vital factor in assuring a pre-eminent place for wool-growing in the national economy; yet the rise of the small farmer-grazier (whether an "old" or a new settler) was a significant development in the sheep-raising industry. By the late 1950s more than half the nation's sheep holdings carried a flock of 1000 sheep or less. Other changes were being reflected in the patterns of employment in the pastoral industry. Fewer of the big shearing teams were needed as a larger proportion of the nation's sheep were shorn by their owners or local contractors, and the droving team was rapidly giving way to the livestock-transport operator able to move sheep or cattle over long distances in quick time.

The higher returns from land use were largely devoted to improving the efficiency of farms and stations, and so to enhancing production. At the same time, the amenities of life in the country were greatly improved, and the rural housewife was not far behind her city counterpart in the number and variety of appliances she had at her fingertips.

As steady advances were made in farming and general land management techniques, gains of outstanding significance were made by scientific investigators. The more spectacular of these successes was scored by the use of the rabbit-killing virus, myxomatosis; this quickly lifted a bane which had long weighed heavily on the individual landholder and for more than half a century had stifled rural progress. The search for a means of dealing on a grand scale with the continent's hordes of rabbits had gone on for years. As early as 1919 there had been talk of introducing myxomatosis (a virus endemic to the tapiti of South America), but it was not until the late 1930s that the matter was thoroughly investigated. At that time tests undertaken in dry areas of South Australia brought only partial success; the disease killed off rabbits in the experimental enclosure area but failed to spread, and myxomatosis was not used again for some years beyond small-scale experiments related to its spread by mosquitoes and other insects. After the rabbit scourge had increased during the years of rural labour shortages in the 1940s, the Commonwealth Scientific and Industrial Research Organization undertook further trials, this time in areas of better rainfall. Between

May and November 1950 the virus was liberated in several localities, and during the summer of 1950–51, the disease "caught on" and hordes of rabbits in areas of the Murray-Darling basin were killed by it. In succeeding years the spread of the virus into new areas was accelerated through further releases of infected rabbits and through its transmission by a variety of carriers. The disease flared up in epidemic form over wide tracts of the main pastoral and agricultural areas across the south-eastern crescent of the continent. By 1953 myxomatosis had spread to rabbits from southern Queenland through New South Wales and Victoria to South Australia. Some degree of natural immunity to the disease developed; from the late 1950s it was clear that the build-up of this resistance among survivors to less virulent attacks had reached such proportions that conventional methods—trapping, hunting, digging-out, and poisoning—would have to be reintroduced; but rabbit numbers had been reduced to manageable proportions. Over-all, the nation's livestock-carrying capacity had been increased by tens of millions of sheep as a result of the wholesale reduction of rabbits that had taken place.

The second great landmark was the discovery that by addition of very small quantities of certain mineral elements, great tracts of otherwise useless land could be made fertile and productive. Systematic analysis and mapping of soils, begun nearly twenty years before, paid its first major dividends by the early 1950s. A soil-study division had been created within the CSIRO in 1929, with headquarters in the Waite Institute, and over the years investigations were undertaken into specialized phases of the subject, including the physical characteristics and mineral composition of soils, and soil microbiology (dealing with matters such as nitrogen fixation and the availability of plant nutrients in soil). State agricultural departments participated in the work. Studies were made of soil erosion and related matters; but the most notable work was done in revealing the basic mineral deficiencies affecting soils of large tracts of the continent's better-rainfall areas. From the late 1940s research showed that land previously believed worthless could be made fertile by the addition of small quantities of certain mineral elements which were found to be lacking. By putting these chemicals into the soil with superphosphate, once "desert" or useless scrubland could be transformed so that it would carry fine pastures and grow good crops. In different areas, different chemicals were needed in addition to the phosphorus which superphosphate supplied. Sometimes, copper, zinc, molybdenum and cobalt were found to be missing, while in other cases sulphur or calcium might be absent. Field experiments showed that once land was cleared and the correct chemicals added, plants could be grown and normal soil fertility soon established. In southern Australia the main types of suitable plants were found to be subterranean clover, white clover, lucerne, and red clover, while in other areas lupins and other plants could be grown to help build up soil nitrogen.

A new "desert conquest" began. Each of the mainland states had large areas capable of development as a result of the unlocking of the mystery of impoverished soils. The state that gained most in the early years was

Western Australia where, from the late 1940s, an average of over 700,000 acres of "new" land was brought into production each year by use of trace elements. By the late 1950s some large pockets of wasteland in South Australia, Victoria and New South Wales were undergoing conversion to rich pasture (for dairying or fat lamb raising) or cropland. The success achieved in "reclaiming" much of the Ninety Mile Desert area of South Australia and in an adjoining region of Victoria drew attention to a regenerative process that would continue to change the face of Australia over many years.

Less spectacular but no less important was the improvement in farming techniques in established areas. In the 1950s the countryman came to appreciate more fully the value of the help and advice that was now at hand from state agricultural experts. No longer was the farmer sceptical about the guidance or knowledge he might gain from the scientists; instead he realized that he could learn more about his own problems from attendance at special "field" days organized by state departments of agriculture and from the experts who called at his farm from time to time. As farmers saw tangible results from better farming practices they became converts to the new agriculture. Meanwhile, more agricultural scientists were being trained—by the late 1950s a hundred or so were graduating each year—and this made possible a much wider diffusion of expert knowledge than ever before. Regular sessions on radio devoted to rural matters, some broadcast on a national or state basis and others of a regional nature, helped keep the countryman more closely in touch with developments in his increasingly complex world. In their various ways, the inventor, the engineer, the transportation expert, the banker and the publicist all had a hand in the work of farm improvement.

Favourable seasonal conditions, greater use of machinery and fertilizers, and improved varieties continued to lift crop yields. From an average of about 14 bushels an acre over the 1940s wheat yield went up to an average of 17 bushels in the 1950s, though with wide fluctuations due to seasonal conditions. Notable improvements in yield were also recorded for oats, barley and sugarcane. Gains in yield came partly as a result of research by agronomists and partly as a result of investment by individual farmers of larger amounts of capital to improve facilities and methods. The main source of funds for investment was the landman's own income; taxation policy strongly favoured the ploughing-back of income for farm and station improvement purposes.

Special agricultural equipment was gaining in use; new types of machines were now available for clearing, cultivation, harvesting, fencing, transport of crops and pasture treatment, and mechanical planters and pickers were coming into use for small crops. The number of tractors rose from 100,000 in 1950 to 250,000 by 1958—and in many cases tractors were fitted with various attachments so that they might perform a wide range of tasks. The area of sown pastures was being steadily expanded, and improved types of grasses were being introduced. By the late 1950s, superphosphate fertilizer was being spread on more than 4,000,000 acres, while the area under irrigation reached 2,000,000 acres.

New strains of cattle were being introduced to tropical and subtropical areas so that beef production could be increased in the hotter and drier parts of the country. By use of better management practices on the larger stations in the north, average herd quality was steadily improved, while the drilling of more bores in the grazing areas and the introduction of long-distance road transports meant that cattle were being turned off in better condition than in the old days of long overland treks.

With the defeat of the constitutional referendum in September 1951, it seemed as though the menace of communism might recede as a political issue. The strike wave had ended, and industrial conditions showed marked improvement. Wage-earners in general were taking home more pay than ever before, and they had money with which to improve their homes. Attempts by employers to secure court approval for lower wages and longer hours failed, and average earnings moved up. With increased credit available, the ordinary citizen could borrow more freely than ever before to buy a motor-car or household appliances or for other forms of home improvement. A new stability had come from the gains stemming from a more productive society, and industrial discord had died away as a result.

The right-wing element in the unions had strengthened its position, recapturing control of some of the key unions. Within the Labor party uneasiness on ideological issues had been growing behind Evatt's back, as right-wing elements pushed for a more positive line against remaining Communist influence which they considered was still "white-anting" the party, but no open split had occurred. By 1954 the A.L.P. leadership had reason to expect that the sapping of the effective power of militants in the unions and the greater industrial harmony would put an end to attempts to attach any Communist stigma to the labour movement in general and the Labor party in particular. State elections in 1952 and 1953 showed growing support for the A.L.P., and this had been confirmed in the Senate poll of May 1953. Suddenly, however, the drama surrounding the defection of a minor Soviet official in Canberra brought the whole issue of communism and national security into the fiercest spotlight of attention.

Before the complex overtones of this episode died away, the course of Australian politics had undergone a major change.

On the night of April 14, 1954, Prime Minister Menzies rose in the House of Representatives and in an atmosphere of solemn urgency announced the defection of Vladimir Petrov, a Ministry of State Security official at the Soviet embassy. As well as seeking political asylum, the Prime Minister said, Petrov had admitted the existence in Australia of a Soviet espionage system. The case seemed to parallel spy dramas that had been reported from Canada and the United States as, a few days later, the Soviet Union broke off diplomatic relations with Australia. The House of Representatives was already close to its triennial election, and legislation approving a Royal Commission of three state judges to investigate Petrov's disclosures was hurriedly passed; it had the full support of the Labor party.

The House election of May 1954 was fought in the shadow of the smouldering Petrov case. The Prime Minister refrained from making political capital out of the affair, but inevitably public sensitiveness to communism was revived and many members of the government parties, including Fadden, spoke pointedly of dangers inherent in Labor's attitude to communism and Communists. An atmosphere of tension was created by highly dramatic events that occurred when two Soviet agents escorted Mrs Petrov from Sydney, and Australian officials intervened when the group reached Darwin. Mrs Petrov was induced to remain and seek political asylum after her gun-carrying Russian escorts were forcibly dealt with by Commonwealth police at the Darwin airport. Political commentators noted that the women's vote might well have been influenced by "the inference that the Prime Minister and his government were protecting a helpless woman." At the same time there were many who felt that the whole Petrov affair had been overplayed. The government was returned to office; but its majority was reduced by four seats, and Labor, with fifty-seven seats, came within four seats of victory.

At this crucial point, with almost half the electorate supporting Labor, Evatt blundered into a series of political indiscretions which were to rob him of his cherished ambition to lead Labor to victory. In August 1954 Evatt appeared before the Royal Commission in order to defend two members of his own staff—who were, in fact, on the federal payroll—named as possible sources of information contained in one of the documents handed over by Petrov to the Australian Security Service. In an impassioned outburst, Evatt objected to the commission's giving special prominence to his staff members when other persons were similarly mentioned in the document. In September Evatt was again in the spotlight as he championed the cause of Madame Ollier, a French diplomat in Canberra, who, Petrov asserted, had promised to supply him with information on arms shipments to Indochina. The French embassy sent Madame Ollier to Noumea, where she was arrested and taken to Paris for trial, whereupon Evatt denounced the Petrov correspondence as deliberately falsified and fabricated. Further, Evatt said, the whole of the Royal Commission's proceedings smacked of the "McCarthyism" that had gripped the United States. The commission asked Evatt to withdraw from the inquiry and after deliberating upon his charges of political conspiracy found them to be "fantastic and wholly unsupported by any credible evidence."

Evatt was by now widely considered to be motivated in his attacks by political pique, and public confidence in him was weakened. His undoubtedly erratic behaviour had undermined his earnest attempts to keep the Labor party united in its traditional policies. While he held the personal loyalty of many, considerable forces within the A.L.P. were now thoroughly antagonistic to him.

The two-month visit of Queen Elizabeth and Prince Philip in February-

April 1954—the first visit to Australia ever made by a reigning sovereign—was an occasion for deep and widespread expressions of loyalty. Political antagonisms could be temporarily forgotten, but nevertheless the smouldering issues remained, and they were soon fanned into flame.

Differences within Labor arising out of issues related to the Communist menace in Asia had grown to be a major source of friction and discord. The French defeats and withdrawals in Indochina, following long and exhausting struggles (in which Australian forces had participated) undertaken against Communist forces in Korea and in Malaya had sharpened appreciation of Australia's exposed position; yet the Labor party continued to oppose most of the government's efforts to cope with the situation. Labor had thrown cold water on the government's support of collective defence arrangements for the southeast Asian area, and had urged instead that greater emphasis should be given to negotiating settlements with insurgent forces there. Evatt's reckless attacks on the Petrov commission now produced rumblings of dissension among right-wing A.L.P. members. The division of power within the Labor party, combined with Evatt's unwillingness to condone compromise, meant that the efforts of Evatt and his supporters to enforce party discipline on the right-wingers ended in a sharp and irreparable cleavage.

The rupture within the A.L.P. burst into the open in October 1954 when Evatt issued a statement denouncing "a small minority of Labor members located particularly in the state of Victoria," whom he accused of being disloyal to the labour movement and the party leadership, and helping the Menzies government to win the last election. Evatt went on to say that their activities were directed largely from outside Labor, and he named the Catholic *News Weekly*, of Melbourne, as their organ.

As the newspapers pointed out, the reference was to the industrial-political organization known as the Industrial Group movement. It had been begun in Melbourne in the early 1940s as a Catholic counter-offensive against Communist infiltration and activity in the trade unions; it spread throughout the unions and into other states. The A.L.P. gave its sponsorship in 1947 but the hard core of the movement remained Catholic. In Melbourne, the Movement drew inspiration and direction from a group close to Archbishop Mannix who, with advancing years, had shown increasing concern over Labor's more socialistic policies; the key figure was Bartholomew Augustine Santamaria, a young lawyer and official of Catholic Action, a worldwide organization of Catholic laymen.

From the earliest days of the A.L.P., Catholics had tended to vote and work for Labor; and while there was some inconsistency between Labor's avowed socialist objective and the Catholic church's views on socialism, this was normally dormant, and did not become a serious divisive force until the late 1940s. Chifley's attempt to nationalize the banks lost the party the support of the Catholic hierarchy and a considerable body of Catholic voters; Evatt's attitude to communism added fuel to the fire.

From 1950 the Industrial Group movement, taking advantage of the introduction of secret balloting for union elections, had a remarkable run of success in capturing the unions from Communist control. As a result, since Labor remained essentially a trade union party, with union nominees dominating the party's state conferences, at which executives and delegates to federal conferences were elected, control of the unions meant that the groupers won representation at A.L.P. conferences, and with that the opportunity to work for the rewriting of Labor policies they considered dangerous.

The industrial groupers found among newly-arrived Europeans an important source of inspiration and support for their political aim of attacking any and every manifestation of support for Communist-backed ideas in trade unions. Objections to the groupers' methods were a complicating factor, as were personal struggles for the power and perquisites of union office; but basically the struggle was ideological. The labour movement had been divided into two worlds, politically as well as industrially. Yet the dangers of a split—and especially one with sectarian overtones—were realized and the divergencies smoothed over until Evatt's dramatic denunciation tore apart the fabric of Labor unity.

It was the federal executive rather than Evatt which organized the attacks on the groupers, and it did so with masterly use of procedural tactics. Since the groupers dominated the Victorian state executive, the federal executive withdrew recognition from this body and summoned a special state conference (elected under altered rules) for the purpose of choosing a new state executive. The existing executive boycotted the special conference (February 1955) which proceeded to elect a new executive and new delegates to the coming federal conference; all the successful candidates belonged to the pro-Evatt ticket. Both the "new" and the "old" delegates from Victoria were in Hobart for the federal conference which opened on March 15. Seventeen accredited delegates, from New South Wales, Queensland, Tasmania and Western Australia, demanded that it should be left to the five undisputed delegations to decide whether Victoria should be represented by the old or the new delegation, but since the groupers would have held a majority in a thirty-man conference the federal executive insisted that any appeal from the old Victorian delegates should be heard by the thirty-six man body, including the new Victorian representatives. The seventeen rebels there upon boycotted the conference which, in their absence, confirmed the appointment of the new executive in Victoria, ordered state branches to withdraw recognition of industrial groups, rewrote the party's foreign policy, and passed a vote of confidence in Evatt's leadership.

Three weeks later the new Victorian executive expelled 140 Labor party members, including seven members of the House of Representatives and four members of the Victorian cabinet and running all the way through the party ranks down to municipal councillors, who refused to pledge support. The Cain government—the first Labor majority government in Victoria's history—went to the polls in May; the dissident group campaigned independently and although it won only one of the forty-four seats it contested, its influence in marginal seats was clearly an important factor in the government's defeat.

Before this, Evatt had resigned his leadership and been overwhelmingly re-elected in a secret ballot of the Labor caucus; he polled fifty-two of seventy-nine votes.

The warning of the Labor disarray in Victoria was plain, and it was heeded by the Labor and Catholic leaders in other states; there were recriminations and expulsions, but not on the scale of the mass upset in Victoria. The groupers had a clear majority in the New South Wales state Labor conference, but they accepted the decisions of the Hobart federal conference without demur. At this stage few of the dissidents wanted to take the final step of setting up a separate party.

Apart from the windfall of discord within Labor's ranks, the Liberal-Country party coalition's position had been strengthened by economic prosperity that persisted in spite of somewhat lowered export earnings. There was full employment with rising wages and practically no industrial unrest; consumer spending and private investment were increasing steadily. Major industrial developments were under way. The first of the powerhouses in the Snowy Mountains complex had been brought into use. The gains from the immigration programme were now apparent; labour shortages were less severe, and the economy appeared to be in excellent balance.

In October 1955 the report of the Royal Commission on espionage was tabled in parliament. It affirmed that the documents Petrov had handed over were genuine, and concluded that espionage had occurred before 1949 when the Australian Security Intelligence Organization had been established; it found no evidence to suggest successful espionage after that year.

Evatt leapt to the attack, repeating his allegations that some of the documents had been trumped up in order to discredit both himself and the Labor party, and offering in support of his contention a letter from the Soviet Foreign Minister, from whom he had inquired about the authenticity of the documents. Evatt's action in making such an approach to Moscow, though perfectly logical to him, was the height of political folly under the circumstances, and his reputation with the public suffered grievously as a result of the disclosure.

The government as well as independent commentators had been expressing concern about inflationary trends and it seemed likely that before long some unpopular restrictive measures would be necessary. Labor's disarray presented an extraordinary opportunity to clear the decks for three years. The triennial elections for the Senate were due in December; the Prime Minister decided to call House elections at the same time. The campaign was short. This time Evatt was a direct target of Menzies' attack, although it was former members of the A.L.P. (campaigning in four states as the Anti-Communist Labor party) who "threw the punches" at Evatt while Menzies had to do no more than keep the ball rolling. Labor promised increases in social services to be financed from a tax on excessive company profits and by reductions in defence expenditures, but these proposals were taken as being extraordinarily extravagant. The Liberal-Country party coalition went back with a House majority increased from seven to twenty-six; and, although it failed narrowly to win a clear majority in the Senate, the two Labor rebels who gained seats there supported it on practically all issues.

Enhanced prospects for the sale of Australian products, including wheat and flour, were opened up by a new trade agreement concluded in 1958 with the United Kingdom, which took into account changes in trade patterns since the last revision of the Ottawa agreement in 1938. Britain's trade with Australia had become very lopsided; the new five year arrangement with Britain provided not only for Australia to have a bigger share of the British market to help redress the balance but it also reduced tariff preferences on many British goods imported into Australia, thus clearing the way for Canberra to negotiate trade agreements with other countries (including Japan) which were growing in importance as trading partners.

By the time the next general election came around—in November 1958— all attempts to bridge the schism within the Labor ranks had broken down completely. Internal struggles for power had worked right through the party structure, bringing to light sharp discords existing within its various layers and segments as party members revelled in factional battles.

In the election, the A.L.P. had three national parties against it—Liberal, Country, and Democratic Labor. The last-named party had been formally set up by breakaway groups in Victoria, New South Wales and Tasmania in March 1957. Soon afterwards, Queensland Labor split, the premier and most of his colleagues forming the Queensland Labor party (affiliated with but independent of the D.L.P.); at the state election in August, the split led to Queensland's first non-Labor government in twenty-five years. In the federal election campaign the Democratic Labor party excoriated the A.L.P. leadership, and stressed the urgent need for combating communism at home and abroad; its principal purpose appeared to be to keep the A.L.P. out of office. When the election returns were in, the Labor party's strength was found to have been cut considerably. The Democratic Labor party had drawn sufficient support away from A.L.P. candidates in closely contested electorates to assure Liberal or Country party candidates of success. In the House, the non-Labor coalition gained two seats.

To Evatt, who had set himself a gruelling pace in the election campaign, the failure was a severe blow. In February 1960 his political career ended when he accepted the post of Chief Justice of the New South Wales Supreme Court. His successor as leader of parliamentary Labor was Arthur Calwell, a party stalwart. With Edward Gough Whitlam, a Sydney lawyer, as his deputy, Calwell had strong hopes that he could heal many of Labor's wounds and rebuild support for the A.L.P.

Meanwhile, changes within the national economy were steadily robbing the Labor platform of its old appeal in the electorate. A new way of life was opening up for the average citizen; the community was moving on towards new objectives, but the Labor party, showing a conservatism that now seemed incongruous, lagged behind in the reframing of policies.

The benefits of increased output from factory, farm and mine were being widely shared, and the government was managing affairs with the object of maintaining a high level of economic activity. There was closer contact than ever before between the various interests within the community—rural producers, manufacturers, transport operators, trade union groups, and so on—and government in all its phases. The businessman was taking a more intelligent and informed interest in economic trends and was exerting greater influence through trade associations and similar groups. Newspapers and commentators had come increasingly to acknowledge the overwhelming importance of federal policies on the economy in general. Stability combined with a continuation of economic expansion had become the major objective of the government, and it was widely accepted that policies should be shaped around this goal.

Australians could now boast that in terms of widespread possession of such amentities as telephones, refrigerators, radios, motorcars, vacuum cleaners, washing machines and television sets, they ranked third or fourth among the world's peoples—and that to purchase these once-luxuries, now enjoyed by average families, Australians had a shorter working week than people in most other lands. The long-awaited promise of a better world for all had been fulfilled for many.

By the end of 1959 the Australian work force numbered 4,000,000 or about two-in-five of the entire population. Manufacturing was now providing employment for three out of every ten male workers and about one in four of the women workers. Growing even faster were the service activities—banking, insurance, advertising, retailing, real estate handling and so on. The breakup of the labour force between the various sectors was now very similar in pattern to that in the United States. In occupational groups, employment followed this pattern:

Distribution of Employment by Major Industry Groups, 1959

Type of Industry	Percentage of total	
Primary:		
Farm and pastoral	12.2	
Mining	1.4	13.6
Manufacturing		30.3
Building and power:		
Building/construction	8.2	
Power and water	1.6	9.8
Commerce, including finance & property		18.1
Transport and communications		9.1
Public authorities*		3.6
Professions		8.8
Other:		
Amusements and services	5.5	
Miscellaneous	1.2	6.7
		100.0

*Excluding public authority employees in other groups mentioned.

As a contribution to gross national product, the return from primary production (pastoral and agricultural) and mining was somewhat lower after 1956–57, reflecting slightly shrunken returns from rural products and minerals, while the relative contribution of manufacturing and professional and business services moved up slightly. These were the only significant changes over the five-year period during which the lineaments of a modern economy were being shaped. The share of the national wealth contributed by each segment is shown in this table:

Contributions Made to Gross National Product by Various Sectors.

	1954–55 %	1959–60 %
Manufacturing	28.2	29.2
Farm and station production	16.4	13.5
Commerce	15.8	15.3
Transport and communications	7.8	7.8
Building and construction	7.6	7.6
Professional and business services	5.5	6.5
Public administration and defence	4.1	4.0
Finance and property	2.4	3.2
Electricity, gas and water supply	2.3	3.0
Mining and quarrying	2.2	1.7
All other industries	4.3	4.3
Dwelling ownership	3.4	3.9
	100.0	100.0

The A.L.P.'s poor showing in the 1958 general election meant that the government at last had a clear majority in the Senate and could pass new legislation to overhaul the banking system and clarify the powers of the central bank. A series of measures provided for the separation of the specialized functions of central banking from routine banking business carried out by the Commonwealth Bank. The Reserve Bank Act preserved and continued in existence the original corporate body known as the Commonwealth Bank of Australia under the new name, the Reserve Bank of Australia, and retained in it the departments dealing with the note issue and rural credits. The Commonwealth Banking Corporation, an organization entirely separate from the Reserve Bank, took over all the trading and savings bank activities. The Commonwealth Development Bank was set up to provide backing for the creation and expansion of enterprise in rural and general industries which would otherwise be unable to secure the necessary finance on reasonable terms.

Control of the Commonwealth Banking Corporation was vested in an eleven-man board, including the corporation's managing director and the secretary of the Treasury; the board's function, as stated in the Act, was to see that the policy of its three divisions (trading, savings, and development) was directed to the greatest advantage of the people of Australia, with due regard to the stability and balanced development of the nation's economy.

The Reserve Bank was given responsibility for issuing paper currency, acting as fiscal agent for the Treasury and custodian of government funds, carrying the gold reserves, and serving as a depository for other banks; it was also, in effect, placed in control of the supply of credit. The Reserve Bank was to operate with a nine-man board under the chairmanship of the bank's governor. The Secretary to the Treasury and the bank's deputy governor were ex-officio members of the board, while the six other seats were for businessmen representing various phases of the national economy, or experts on finance. The legislation specifically declared it to be the duty of the Reserve Bank board to advance—within the limits of its power—a monetary and banking policy directed towards maintaining full employment and the economic prosperity and well-being of Australians, as well as maintaining the stability of the currency.

As a result of the new banking measures, the Reserve Bank was able to enforce a system of statutory ratios as a substitute for the former "special accounts" which the trading banks were obliged to maintain with the central bank.

The new legislation was strenuously opposed by Labor. Nor was it quite what the private banks and many members of the Liberal party had been seeking since 1949, for it did nothing to lessen the Commonwealth Bank's strong competitive position. Yet a sound and logical banking structure had been constructed, that was due largely to unremitting pressure from the Country party, exercised effectively through Fadden, as Treasurer.

The growing sophistication of the economy was already reducing the effectiveness of the control that might be exercised over the volume of money as a means of regulating the economy. There was increasing concern over the inability of monetary policy to exert any real influence over non-banking financial activities. Other sources of credit and borrowings had been adding to inflation, and they were soon to create a dangerous situation of spiralling prices, endangering the stability of the economy.

Australia in   26
the world

In the immediate post-war years, with so many tasks at hand, Australians had shown little inclination to dwell on world problems. To people who clung tenaciously to the belief that, with the defeat of the Axis powers, problems of international concern could be solved through discussion and peaceful settlement, the hardening of the international situation came as an unpleasant shock. By the time the Liberal-Country party assumed office in December 1949, the co-operative spirit that had existed between the great powers as allies in war had been replaced by mutual distrust as the rift between the Soviet Union and the Western powers widened. The cold war had come to divide the world into two clearly defined and opposing camps, Communist and non-Communist. Finding themselves in a condition of stalemate, the two great power blocs had sought in regional defence pacts a means of providing multi-nation security and of overcoming stultification born of the great deadlock in the United Nations. The North Atlantic Treaty Organization (NATO) had been formed, under United States aegis, to shore up the defences of western Europe, and the Communist bloc had created a counter force. In 1949 Russia's development of the atomic bomb, coupled with Mao Tse-tung's success in China, added new dimensions to Communist power and introduced dangerous new factors into the world power struggle. The changed circumstances of the world situation were to influence the Menzies government, strengthening the determination already expressed by its leaders to give different priorities from those followed by Dr Evatt as Minister for External Affairs.

The new administration, acting in concert with the newly-elected Nationalist party government in New Zealand, looked first to strengthening the role of British nations in world affairs. Menzies and Fadden and their followers were more concerned with re-emphasising Australia's role in the partnership of British lands than with maintaining the studied policies for projection of an "Australian" viewpoint in world councils which Evatt had initiated and the Chifley government had pursued. Immediately his electoral success was known, Menzies said that the new government's first task would be "to re-establish complete co-operation in British Empire countries."

In opposition, the Liberal-Country party members had frequently criticized policies in which they saw a tendency to minimize the association with the British Commonwealth and to give an undue weight to Australia's "independent" role within the United Nations. Similar criticism had been raised in Britain and New Zealand against Labour governments there. Growing concern had been expressed over the shrunken role of Britain and the Commonwealth. In the belief that traditional trading patterns and London's role as sterling banker would maintain effective commercial ties and that a less encumbered Britain would be better able to plan a new course in its own affairs, the Attlee government (in office from mid-1945) had been prepared to accept and even hasten the transfer of political power in former dependent territories. For his part Chifley had accepted such a development without qualms; for, although he had constantly placed great emphasis on Australia's links with Britain, particularly in economic affairs, he had accepted as inevitable the political transformation taking place within the association as members of the old dependent empire became self-governing and showed determination to shape their own destinies. However, if the trends could be accepted without undue concern by Labour policy-makers in London, Canberra, and Wellington, evidence that old bonds were loosening was enough to stir sharp reaction from conservatives. As the cold war intensified there were louder calls for revival of British strength through unified Commonwealth action. Once in power, Menzies was determined to contribute to the rebuilding of British influence in world affairs.

The proposed regeneration was not an easy task. Deep and important changes had been taking place within the British countries and these had affected relationships within the British association (now officially the Commonwealth of Nations). When matched against the two super-powers, the United States and Soviet Russia, Britain had relatively little strength and had to rely heavily on the alliance with the United States. At the same time the fragile nature of Commonwealth ties had been demonstrated in 1948 when Burma, on being granted self-government, decided not to join the Commonwealth but strike out on a separate path, and Eire exercised its prerogative and withdrew.

The Imperially-minded hoped that a solution to the Commonwealth's problems of division and diffusion might be found in the creation of a secretariat through which closer consultation might be established as a means to forming a common policy.

The British government (which by 1949 had replaced the Dominions office with the Office of Commonwealth Relations) was still not willing to move in the direction of a more formal and unified association. When, in 1950, Prime Minister Menzies called for the creation of an "Imperial foreign policy committee" to sit regularly and for the setting-up of flexible localized machinery or a small secretariat in each Commonwealth capital, Britain's Minister for Commonwealth Relations, Patrick Gordon-Walker, said in reply that the Commonwealth must be careful not to have too much formalism in its machinery for discussion. The nations would be driven apart and not unified by the creation of permanent machinery, Gordon-Walker said.

Rejection of this idea still left unanswered the question of how best to achieve close and effective association within the Commonwealth, and the Menzies government continued to support the principle that some more formalized contact point for the formulation of Commonwealth policy in foreign relationships was needed. As one of Australia's chief spokesmen said later, with the members of the Commonwealth scattered all over the world, no one of them might now be able to maintain itself by the strength of its own right arm—but there was the probability "that if we all stick together, we will at least have a greater chance of surviving."

In one of the practical moves to maintain Britain's military potential in the new age of missiles, Australia had already been accorded a key role, as a testing ground for long-range and atomic weapons. The important work undertaken by British and Australian defence equipment for the nuclear age was not solely for Australia's defence needs but was essentially a contribution to the armed capacity of all British lands and Britain's allies.

Basic changes had come also to Asia. With the breakdown of the Kuomintang and the withdrawal from the Chinese mainland to Formosa of Chiang Kai-shek and the Nationalists, all of China proper had come under Communist control. The possibility of a strengthened partnership between Peking and Moscow and the initiation of an active programme of Communist expansion in south Asia now began to cause deep concern in Australia, as it did throughout the Western world.

The Chifley government had not been altogether opposed to establishing some commercial relationship with Peking when, in October 1949, the Communists constituted their government as the People's Republic of China. At this point it was believed in Canberra that the most logical policy might be to accord *de facto* recognition; but Evatt delayed action in sympathy with the American view that in the absence of specific assurances that the new Peking government would respect the territorial integrity of neighbouring countries and discharge all its international obligations, all diplomatic recognition should be withheld. The issue of recognition was still in abeyance when the Liberal-Country party government took office.

In terms of practical diplomacy, the new government's efforts were directed largely to using personal contact and diplomatic channels to minimize any difference of viewpoint that might exist between countries of the Commonwealth and Britain or between Britain and the United States. At the same time, intensive work was begun towards the development of increasingly close links with Australia's non-Communist northern neighbours with the object of raising standards of living there and maintaining security both by alliances and by arrangements for regional co-operation. Active pursuit of these objectives, and positive strengthening of Australian-Asian ties, were the chief aims of policies followed by Percy Claude Spender, the coalition ministry's first Minister for External Affairs. New impetus was given to the quest when, in February 1950, a formal Sino-Soviet alliance was signed in Moscow.

In March 1950, Spender gave the new parliament a comprehensive statement on foreign policy in which he emphasized that Australia's "first and constant interest must be the security of our homeland and the maintenance of peace in the area in which our country is geographically located." He went on to say that the country's security had become an immediate and vital issue

> ... because changes since the war have resulted in a shifting of potential aggression from the European to the Asian area, and our traditional British Commonwealth and United States friends have not yet completed their adjustments to the new situation.
>
> A very great burden of responsibility rests especially on us, but also upon the other British Commonwealth countries of this area. The birth of new members of the Commonewalth, Pakistan and Ceylon and the Republic of India, the creation of new international entities in the form of the Republic of Indonesia, and the States of Vietnam, Laos, and Cambodia in what was previously known as French Indo-China, are developments which have helped to shift the centre of gravity of world affairs more and more to this area.
>
> Our policy must be to ensure, to the fullest extent we can, that these new States co-operate with each other and with us in meeting positively and actively the new problems created in the area by the emergence of a Communist China, and by the ever-increasing thrust of communism, which endeavours to ally itself, in pursuit of its ends, with the national aspirations of the millions of people of south-east Asia.

Spender urged consideration of the possibility of a regional defence pact for south-east Asia, and stressed the need to work with the new nations "economically, commercially, in the technical as well as the practical fields," in order to maintain their newly-won independence.

The first expression of Australia's practical interest in the under-developed lands was the strong support accorded the concept of the Colombo Plan, devised early in 1950 as a practical means of furthering development in south and south-east Asia through economic and technical assistance, on a co-operative bilateral basis, between the Asian nations themselves and between the countries constructively interested in the region. A year or so after the plan was approved at the meeting of ministerial representatives of Commonwealth governments, the sponsoring group was joined by the United States. Believing strongly that economic advance was the soundest antidote to unrest, Australia supported the entire concept and contributed actively to the technical co-operation phase, covering academic and technical training, and also played an important role in the programme of more direct aid to economic development.

Communist pressures had been building up for some time over the future of Korea, and this erupted into war only a few months after the new government took office in Canberra. The promise to establish a free and independent Korea after the war had been given by Britain, China, and the United States in the Cairo Declaration of 1943, but after Russia's entry into the war against Japan the 38th parallel of latitude became the demarcation line between the American and Russian occupation forces. In September 1947 the United States referred the problem of Korea's future to the United Nations, whereupon the General Assembly voted to hold Korea-wide elections under United Nations supervision; but the Soviet authorities in the north refused to co-operate. After the Republic of Korea was formally proclaimed in August 1948, the Russian occupation authorities pushed plans to set up a separate North Korean government, and soon both North and South Korea were strengthening their armies. On June 25, 1950, the North Korean army launched a full-scale invasion of the south. The attack was immediately called to the attention of the Security Council and in the absence of the Russian delegate (who had boycotted the meeting) the Council took its historic decision to initiate military measures in support of South Korea. The Council recommended that United Nations members furnish such assistance as might be required to repel the North Koreans' attack and to restore international peace and security in the area. Australians were the first to join the United States forces in answering the call; a R.A.A.F. unit (the 77th Squadron) and an army contingent—the last of the British Commonwealth occupation forces—were still in Japan, and when General MacArthur asked if the squadron could participate approval was given immediately, thus signalizing that it was United Nations action. Australia quickly committed naval vessels and ground forces. Soon an international army under United Nations auspices had come into being; in all, the forces of sixteen member states combined to drive the North Koreans back.

Late in 1950, when United Nations forces in their drive north of the 38th parallel were moving close to the Manchurian border, Chinese forces moved into Korea on a large scale. Any chance of an easing of tension now vanished; the United States became more determined than ever to contain Asian communism and allow it no further gains on any front. Britain had by now established formal relations with Peking, but Australia did not take a similar step, adopting instead the stand taken by the United States, which insisted that the conditions for recognition had not been met by the Peking regime.

Communist aggression in Korea had brought a sharp realization of the new forces at work in Asia. Richard Casey, who succeeded Spender as Minister for External Affairs early in 1951, later described the United Nations Korea stand as "decisive action to cope with aggression," and added that "Korea" had become a symbol in the minds of many peoples who lived anxiously on the borders of the Communist world.

Communist countries were totally opposed to the completion of a peace treaty with Japan, but by now Washington was anxious to end the occupation. The United States and Britain were the main architects of the treaty, which they believed should be one of reconciliation rather than retribution. Neither country was anxious to extract heavy reparations or to place restrictions on Japan's capacity for armament or industrial and economic expansion—omissions which greatly concerned both Australia and New Zealand. Australia succeeded in having a clause inserted in the treaty making provision for compensation for former prisoners-of-war, but on the major issues of rehabilitating Japan American views prevailed. Australians might still harbour fears that in allowing the rebuilding of Japan's industrial strength and foreign trade, the way was being opened for Japan to re-establish industrial and economic supremacy in eastern Asia which future leaders could exploit for political purposes; but in American and British eyes Japan was an important bulwark against Communist expansion; as Professor William MacMahon Ball phrased it, the Americans had already begun to move into the shadow of a third World War while Australians were lingering in the shadow of the second.

In the year-long negotiations over the formulation of the peace treaty which began in October 1950 the question of assuring Japan's defence was a foremost consideration. The treaty (signed in San Francisco in September 1951) recognised Japan's inherent right of individual or collective self-defence as provided in the United Nations Charter, while a separate defence treaty between the United States and Japan which came into force at the same time gave the United States the right to maintain land, sea and air forces in and around Japan. The United States held, as "strategic trustee," the former Japanese-mandated islands of Micronesia—the Marianas, Carolines, and Marshalls—which had been occupied by United States forces after the surrender of Japan and held by them as a United Nations Trust Territory since 1947, and retained control of the Bonin and Ruyuku Islands, including use of Okinawa. The continuing presence of the United States in the area was the real guarantee against any resurgence of Japanese militarism. At the same time Japan's new constitution limited the national standing army to a purely defensive force of 250,000 men.

In speaking in the House of Representatives in support of the treaty, Casey pointed out that the Communist threat had brought with it a need to consider "not only security *against* Japan but also the security *of* Japan"; Australia's policy, he added, would be to endeavour to avoid twin dangers: revived Japanese imperialism or a Japan under Communist control. The Labor party maintained its resistance to having Japan restored so readily to the comity of nations, and attacked the treaty as a precipitate development. Evatt pointed out that war criminals were still powerful in Japan, and he roundly condemned the treaty as "an open, unashamed abandonment of all the standards of international justice."

During the negotiations leading to the Japanese peace treaty, the Anzac pact partners made it clear that in their view south-west Pacific security would continue to be precarious without a formal defence pact involving the United States. The matter of mutual regional defensive arrangements in the Pacific came to the fore when the chief United States negotiator, John Foster Dulles, was in Canberra early in 1951 for discussions with the representatives of the Australian, New Zealand and British governments on the Japanese settlement. A subsequent United States Senate committee report noted that Australia and New Zealand "could agree to a generous treaty, imposing no restrictions upon Japanese rearmament, only if the United States would formally express concern for their security and agree to stand with them in the event of an attack." In fact, however, the pact which was negotiated between Australia, New Zealand and the United States—the ANZUS Treaty—was an alliance of mutual assistance, making no attempt to define the quarter from which the security of the parties to it might be threatened.

In the treaty emphasis was placed on "continuous and effective self-help and mutual aid" as a means of maintaining and developing the individual and collective capacity of the three participating nations. Shortly after the signing, which took place in San Francisco on September 1, 1951, Prime Minister Menzies noted this aspect when he wrote in *Foreign Affairs*:

> After the treaty has come into effect, our Australian defence preparations are not merely our own business; we owe them also to our friends, without whose help we cannot hope to maintain our freedom against a major challenge. In other words, our defence effort ceases to be of merely local significance, but becomes part of the concerted efforts of the free world.

Within the new regional-defence framework, Australia and New Zealand were assuming a new role involving responsibilities of a rather special character.

Effective machinery of consultation was soon in operation in the ANZUS Council, bringing together the foreign ministers of the three member countries. The treaty itself placed no time limits on its duration; and even if the machinery of the Council itself were dissolved, the over-all "Monroe Doctrine" concept developed in the treaty would still remain in force.

ANZUS was the first such collective agreement signed with the United States and involving British nations in which the United Kingdom government was not a participant, and the omission was sharply criticized in some quarters. However, the pact was no more than a tacit acknowledgment by the southern British lands of the hard facts of shrunken British power east of Suez. Significantly, it was the result of pressure from a Liberal government in Australia and a National party government in New Zealand, both traditionally more concerned than Labor with retaining close ties with Britain. Through the treaty Australia and New Zealand secured a special defence relationship with the United States, and its completion marked a most significant stage in the development of Australia's foreign policy.

Shortly before the pact was concluded, Casey made a goodwill visit to Djakarta, Singapore, Saigon, Bangkok, Hong Kong, Manila, Tokyo and Seoul—a visit which came to be regarded later as something of a watershed in the Australian government's attitudes to the south-east Asia region. On his return Casey emphasized the need for Australia to show "a sympathetic interest" in all the problems confronting countries of the area—cultural, economic, and political problems as well as military aspects. His observations set in train a plan for greatly strengthening Australian diplomatic representation in the region. Within a comparatively short time Australia had set up posts able to report quickly and directly to Canberra, and over the coming years an Australian "presence" was established in south-east Asia.

Australia's own defence effort was necessarily limited. It had proved difficult to keep the regular forces up to their planned strength at a time of abounding prosperity. Compulsory military training for all young men over the age of eighteen years had been introduced in March 1951; but by late 1953 the training period had been cut to a point (twenty-two weeks in all, spread over three years) where the value of the compulsory training effort was very much in doubt. The concentration of the national effort on population-building, through immigration, and on large-scale development of resources, was seen as more important than diversion of greater effort for formal defence. The annual defence budget of about £190 million was sufficient only to maintain the lineaments of a defence programme.

Meanwhile, in New York, Australian representatives played a leading part in the protracted negotiations which began in June 1951 and led to an armistice in Korea in mid-1953. During the protracted ground fighting in Korea, the Australian Army had suffered over 1500 casualties.

The under-developed world stretching from the Atlantic coast of Africa across the Middle East to south-east Asia, holding some of the oldest civilizations, the most backward economies, the greatest poverty, and the most massive populations, was being swept as never before by revolutionary zeal and by aspirations to build a new life—and these national aspirations were being aligned in many cases with the Communist world. By 1954 fears were mounting that communism would spill into all the unstable countries to Australia's north. The suppression of terrorism in Malaya, conducted primarily by British forces, was approaching its seventh year, and the French were fighting a losing battle in Vietnam. At annual meetings of the ANZUS Council considerable attention was given to the main danger spots; this involved, in Casey's words, "a particularly close study of the designs and intentions of Communist China." At the time the pact was concluded it had been envisaged that wider security arrangements would be necessary; and as concern grew over an expansionist China, interest quickened in setting up a broad mutual defence organization for the neglected area of south-east Asia, where a gap existed in the security screen. The difficulty of dealing with the spread of communism in a region where general standards of living remained so lamentably low was being more thoroughly appreciated. Australia stressed the view that security must be furthered not only by the creation of a mutual defence pact in which the countries and territories of the region and the United States could join, but also by giving a new emphasis to international efforts to improve economic and social conditions in the countries concerned.

The deteriorating French position in Vietnam brought a new assessment of the Asian danger-spots. By early 1954 the dedicated and often fanatic anti-Western guerrilla forces led by Nguyen No Giap held the French almost powerless. In the north, where the terrain favoured their activities, Giap's Vietminh were able to draw encouragement and supplies from Communist China, while in the south their punishing terrorist attacks and ambushes were maintained against wearying forces. A military solution favourable to the French was now seen as impossible; the political nature of the problem had become clear. An international conference met in April 1954 at Geneva in an effort to restore peace; the great powers were all represented, as well as the direct participants in the struggle. While the conference was still going on, Giap's forces finally overwhelmed the French at the "fortress" of Dienbienphu. Up to this point the United States had avoided direct commitments on the mainland of Asia, except in the special case of Korea, but the French collapse brought a sharp change in American policy. On May 7, the very day of Dienbienphu, Dulles, who had become United States Secretary of State, said that America and other countries immediately concerned were considering a collective defence arrangement for south-east Asia.

Australian parliamentarians, newspaper editorial writers, and commentators had been calling loudly for a military pact to shore up the crumbling defences of Asia's south-eastern rim against a feared Chinese-backed Communist attack, covert or overt, in south-east Asia. In August Prime Minister Menzies announced that, as Australia's security problem had become more acute, his government would accept the necessary military commitments as a member of any security system that might be devised. A basic change in Australian policy was involved, as the Prime Minister explained when he told parliament:

> In the past it has been one of the traditions of Australian government that commitments are not accepted in advance, that such matters are for determination by the government and parliament if and when the event of war occurs. There are sound reasons to explain why this should have been the tradition. In the two great world wars, Australia has had an opportunity to decide what she was going to do and enough time to assemble, train, equip and dispatch armed forces.
>
> We cannot gamble on this being our position any longer. If there is one thing that seems clear, it is that there will be no pause, no period of stalemate, should the Communists determine to attack. . . It is for these reasons that we have decided that in any great defensive organization of the kind envisaged, we must accept military commitments.

The resulting South-East Asia Collective Defence Treaty was signed in September at Manila by Britain, France, Pakistan, the Philippines, Thailand and the United States, as well as Australia and New Zealand. Laos, Cambodia and South Vietnam were named as "designated states" to bring them under the protection of the treaty although they were not signatories. The treaty brought into being the South-East Asia Treaty Organization

(SEATO). It was less specific in its military terms than the Australian government would have wished; no provision was made for a unified command, and it had obvious limitations as an effective instrument of military cooperation. The parties undertook to develop their own individual capacities to resist armed aggression and also to counter subversive activities directed from outside their borders, and further stated that they would render assistance to one another towards these ends. In addition to covering military security, the treaty also had provisions for the promotion of economic well-being and advancement of all the peoples of the area. Provision was made for a permanent secretariat. An accompanying document, the Pacific Charter, declared support for the principle of self-determination of peoples, and the signatories undertook to strive for the promotion of independence and self-government of those peoples who desired it and could undertake its responsibilities.

Casey freely admitted that SEATO's primary purpose was to combat communism, and the United States believed this to be virtually its only purpose. The treaty itself did not make specific reference to Communist aggression, but in signing the treaty, Secretary of State Dulles added an "understanding" to the effect that the American commitment to resist armed attack applied only to Communist aggression. For his part, Casey, in presenting the treaty to parliament, added a special rider, saying that the Australian government would never regard itself as being committed, contractually or morally, to military action against any other member of the Commonwealth.

In spite of its shortcomings, the treaty (which came into force in February 1955) signified the concentration of Australia's foreign policy on problems of the region. The signing of the treaty was soon followed by the dispatch of Australian troops to join the Commonwealth's Strategic Reserve force stationed in Malaya, which had been formed to counter Malayan terrorist-guerrillas. Singapore and Malaya had assumed greater importance in regional defence, and the decision to station troops in Malaya, announced in Canberra in April 1955, marked a significant new phase in Australia's commitment to arrangements for collective defence. As the Prime Minister said, Australia considered it of immense importance that the free countries of south-east Asia should not fall one by one, and participation in regional arrangements for collective defence provided the best means of co-ordinating defence policy and planning with that of Australia's allies.

The Labor party did not agree with the government's basic reliance on military pacts; instead, it believed that Australia should give "greater practical support" to the United Nations in order to enhance its prestige, and that all questions likely to breed international tension should be handled through United Nations machinery. In what Opposition Leader Evatt hoped might be a new look foreign policy for Australia, the party's federal conference of 1955 set down its own propositions. The statement supported Australia's membership in the Commonwealth and co-operation with the United States, but went on to say that the use of armed forces in Malaya would "gravely injure Australia's relations with Asian neighbours while in no way contributing to the prevention of aggression." Drawing a distinction between genuine nationalist anti-colonial movements in Asia and communism, the statement claimed that lack of United Nations intervention and neglect of United Nations principles led to Communists taking over nationalist movements, as had happened in Indochina. Closer links with Asian countries were advocated, and it was proposed that "in particular, the Australian Labor movement itself should seek direct contact with Asian countries."

In Australia's other area of special interest, the South Pacific, there had been constructive change and steady development without any of the disruptive influences so painfully apparent in the Asian area. However, by the mid-1950s the interplay of forces had focused Australia's interest on the future of the territories in the island of New Guinea and adjacent island chains.

Advancement of the welfare of the island peoples of the South Pacific had been a central theme of discussions between Australia and New Zealand leading to and following the completion of the Anzac Agreement in 1944, and provision was made in the agreement for the creation of an advisory Commission to work to this end with the various governments concerned. The South Pacific Commission, formed in 1947, with headquarters in Noumea, brought together representatives of all governments in the region for discussion of common problems and exchange of information on such matters as health, transport, economic development and the islanders' general welfare.

Australia's interest in the area was in part that of a good neighbour prepared to help in furthering general welfare; but it was also more specifically that of an administering authority with direct responsibility for a total of more than 180,000 square miles of island territories (eastern New Guinea and associated islands including New Britain, New Ireland, Lavongai and the Admiralties, Buka and Bougainville).

In the island of New Guinea which Australia shared with the Dutch, Australia had a major task to undertake in the territories of Papua and New Guinea, where wild-eyed tribesmen in feathers and paint still roamed the jungles and mountains. In pre-war years, strategic considerations rather than native welfare had been the driving force behind Australia's interest in New Guinea, and little was done to accelerate the extension of authority and control over the primitive peoples of the great island, although rudimentary services in such fields as education, health, and village councils were developed. The division of Australian administration between Papua, a Crown possession, and the old mandated territory of New Guinea, tended to complicate matters. In some areas missions had been active; but the nature of much of the terrain and the fragmentation of tribal groups limited the speed with which the interior could be opened up. The administration, scrupulous in its protection of native rights, was unwilling to sell any land and few Europeans were prepared to move in and invest without security of land tenure. In the mandated area practically nothing was done; there

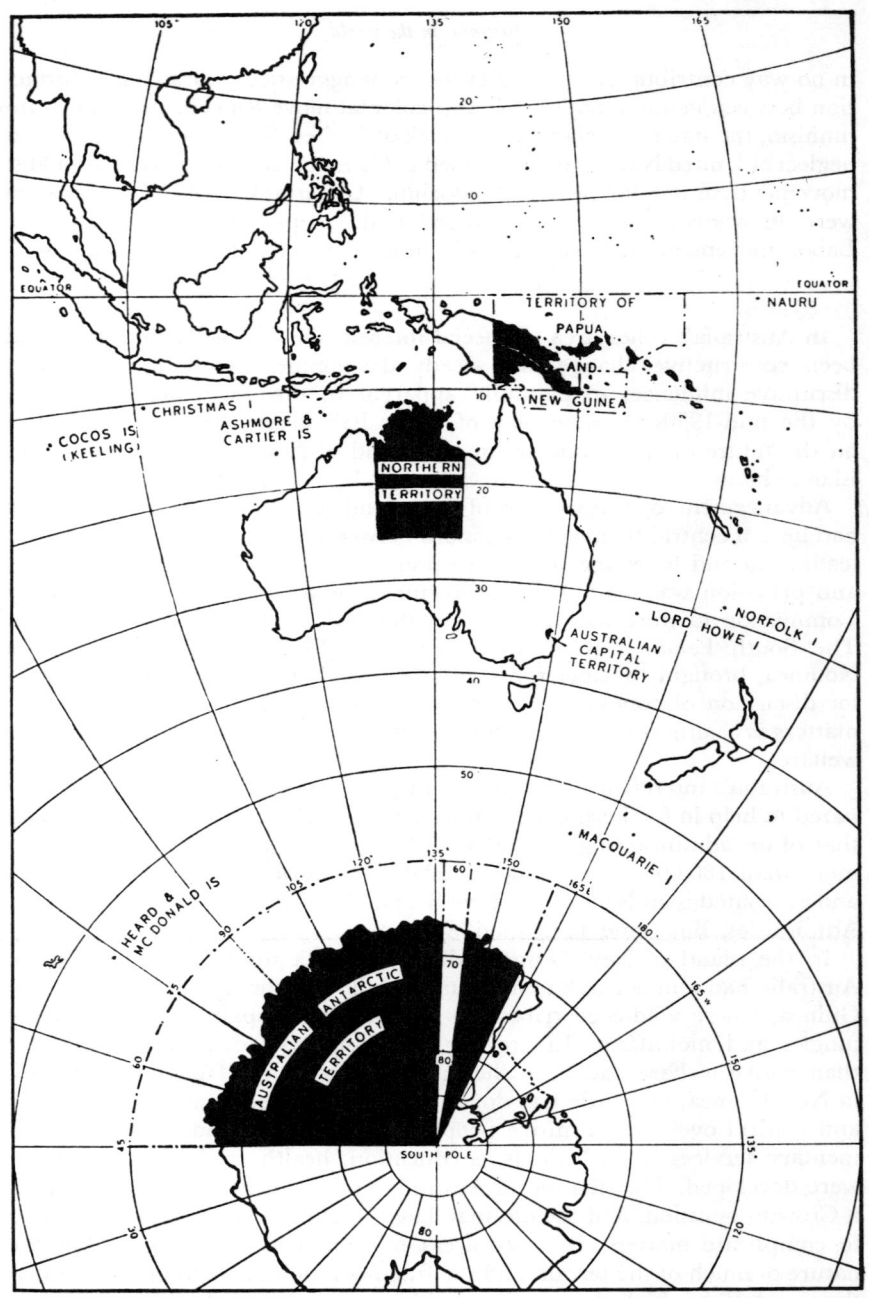

Department of Territories

Territories administered by the Commonwealth of Australia spread from the Equator to the South Pole; they include almost half the Antarctic continent as well as approximately half the island of New Guinea, and various individual islands in the Indian and Pacific oceans.

was little inclination to interfere with tribal ways, and with unrelieved parsimony in the budgets Canberra provided for New Guinea's administration, progress remained slow.

The scene was changed drastically by the war which early in 1942 moved south to New Guinea and deep into the interior. As part of the military operations, roads and bridges were built and these, along with new airfields, provided access to many districts that might otherwise have remained isolated. As early as March 1942 the Australian New Guinea Administrative Unit (ANGAU), staffed partly by former civil administrators in the territories, was set up within the Australian Army. New problems were posed by the disruptive effects of military operations. At first ANGAU's main function was the organization of native labour to help the war effort, but as successive victories re-established more territory under Allied control, preparations were made for the return of civil administration.

The Curtin government's policies in New Guinea were largely shaped by Edward John Ward, who as Minister for External Territories took an active interest in policies for native welfare; but while Ward quickly moved the administration out of its old ways, some of his measures were backed by too little planning and research to be fully effective. Nevertheless, the special circumstances of the war in New Guinea made change inevitable, and there was definite progress in government attitudes to the welfare of the native peoples. Early in 1944 two anthropologists were appointed to ANGAU's directorate of research and civil affairs so that anthropological knowledge might be available to those planning the rehabilitation of invaded areas and the framing of post-war policy. A special school set up in Canberra to train administrative officers for ANGAU, which remained the administering body in New Guinea until after the end of the war, was later expanded into the peacetime Australian School of Pacific Administration, based in Sydney.

Practical measures for raising employment standards came as soon as civil administration was restored to the territories. In introducing a measure foreshadowing the return to civil administration, Ward announced to the federal parliament in July 1945 that henceforth there would be a combined administration for Papua and New Guinea. He also announced that the common method of an indenture system of labour in the territories would be abolished within five years and the professional recruiting of indentured labour eliminated. Henceforth, Ward said, natives were to be engaged by employers under licence for not more than twelve months, and no man would be eligible for re-employment until he had spent three months in his native village. The work week was to be cut from fifty-five hours in the New Guinea territory and fifty-hours in Papua to forty-four throughout; sixteen years was set as the minimum age for employment, and the old minimum wage rates of 5/- a month in New Guinea and 10/- in Papua were to be raised to a uniform 15/- plus rations, housing and medical care. In June 1946 Colonel Jack Keith Murray took up office as administrator.

In August 1946 Prime Minister Chifley announced the terms of an agreement whereby the old mandated territory of New Guinea would become a United Nations trusteeship territory administered by Australia. The

United Nations General Assembly approved the arrangement before the end of the year, at the same time confirming Australia's right to join the trust territory with the territory of Papua in an administrative union. A measure to give effect to this agreement was passed by the Australian parliament and came into operation on July 1, 1949. Unlike the old League mandate, the trusteeship agreement permitted Australia to take measures for the defence of the territory.

The welfare and advancement of native peoples of Papua-New Guinea was already a guiding principle of policy; now a sense of active partnership could grow with the close-to-2,000,000 inhabitants of the combined territory. A great deal had already been accomplished during the three-year provisional administration: war damage had been repaired, all the pre-war administrative centres had been reopened, and a uniform public service (with new departments dealing with education, agriculture, and labour) had been established. An educational plan had been initiated in co-operation with the missions; its purpose was to achieve "universal literacy and the development of the native peoples within their own environment." Agricultural extension services had been set up with the aim of improving both native and plantation agriculture, and the indentured labour system had been largely replaced.

As well as an executive council consisting of at least nine officers of the territory, a twenty-eight member advisory legislative council presided over by the administrator, was created. At least sixteen of the twenty-eight members of the advisory body were to be official members from the administrative departments; of the remainder, three were to represent the interests of the Christian missions, three were to be natives and three were to be elected by the voters of the territory. The large official majority made it certain that only those ordinances supported by the administration would be passed, and an overriding power of disallowance still remained in Canberra with the Department of Territories. Nevertheless, for the native peoples the new legislative body represented a start on the road to political advancement and when the new council convened late in 1951, its three nominated native representatives were the first indigenes ever to sit in an Australian legislature.

A primary aim of the administration was to achieve mass literacy as quickly as possible. Although there were over 100,000 native pupils at school in the combined territories by the beginning of 1950, very few New Guineans could read and write and only a small proportion of the population had reached a level where local government councils could be instituted. At least 65,000 square miles of the island's interior remained to be brought under control, and the administration was anxious to push its efforts among the more backward tribespeople. Patrolling was accelerated, so that the area not under full control was halved to 32,000 square miles in five years. At the same time, local government councils, with responsibility for maintaining law and order, raising local taxes, and setting up small-scale enterprises for the community welfare, were established in many more villages.

Under the United Nations Charter the advancement of all dependent

peoples towards participation in political affairs had become a direct responsibility of the administering power, and the rate of progress towards this
goal in New Guinea was questioned from time to time in the United Nations
Trusteeship Council. Much of the comment came from representatives of
countries notorious for the shortcomings of their political life. The government considered that criticism of its efforts in New Guinea was often misinformed and prejudiced; but it was not long before the pressure of comment
in the United Nations was suggesting that Australia must do more than
maintain a slow-and-steady pace of advancement there.

After allowing for the fact that some of the censure was undoubtedly
exaggerated and ignored both the difficulties involved and the real gains
made in the improvement of the native people's welfare, it became increasingly apparent that Canberra's views on the issue were lagging behind the
prevailing mood as expressed in a United Nations whose membership was
steadily being enlarged with the addition of many newly-independent and
strongly anti-colonialist nations. In a report issued by the United Nations
Trusteeship Mission which visited New Guinea in 1953, attention was
drawn to shortcomings and positive action proposed. Specifically the report
suggested that, even though it had been used in some parts of the territory
for generations as the only common tongue, the corrupted form of English
known as "pidgin" should be discarded as a language for instruction. In the
territory, pidgin had long been regarded as an indispensable minimum
linguistic basis for understanding where hundreds of local languages or
dialects were spoken; but the mission report characterized use of pidgin
as reflecting "outmoded concepts of the relationship between indigenous
inhabitants and immigrant groups." The government itself was not happy
about the continuing spread of pidgin as a *lingua franca* and had plans to
introduce standard English as soon as practical; nevertheless the mission
proposal was received unfavourably in Port Moresby and Canberra, where
it was considered "unrealistic." The mission praised the administration's
land policy (dating back to the 1920s) which respected the native ownership
of land and the strengthening of native co-operative commercial enterprise
taking place with the administration's encouragement.

Year by year the federal parliament was voting more money for the
administration of New Guinea; over-all expenditure in the territory moved
up to £7 million in 1951–52; six years later outlays were over £16 million.
About two-thirds of the revenue came from a special annual grant made to
supplement revenue from customs and other charges. Increasing numbers
of New Guineans were being drawn into the economic system—giving up
the old subsistence horticulture of growing crops simply to meet their own
needs—and, largely through steadily expanding ownership and development
of coconut, cocoa and coffee plantations, the economic fabric was being
strengthened, with more of the native people earning wages.

The report of the Trusteeship mission of 1956 noted "with approval"
that the administration now accepted the principle of placing added emphasis on the teaching of standard English, and proposed that more should
be done to expand secondary education. The mission also suggested that

if Australia's resources were not adequate for the rapid development of the territory in accordance with trusteeship principles, Australia should not hesitate to invoke international assistance, particularly in matters such as the recruitment of staff in the professional and technical fields.

As the worldwide move for the grant of self-government to dependent peoples gathered pace, the Trusteeship Council's resolutions on New Guinea became more forceful, and Australia was asked to set a date for the grant of self-government. Because this most primitive and fragmented area faced an immense span of development before hopes for self-government and a viable economy might be realized, Canberra believed strongly that political self-determination must await advancement in more practical aspects of government and community life.

Increasingly, however, New Guinea was a touchstone by which Australia's international policies were judged.

The situation was complicated by defence considerations, since along the western border of the Australian-held sector was Australia's only land contact with a foreign power. West New Guinea had not been included in the territories released by the Dutch in 1949 when the issue had appeared certain to deadlock the Round Table negotiations. At the suggestion of an Australian member of the United Nations Commission for Indonesia, West New Guinea's future had been left open to negotiation between the Netherlands and Indonesia.

The change of government in Canberra which occurred soon afterwards brought a change of attitude in Australia's relations with Indonesia, since the Liberal-Country party administration tended to favour the Dutch rather than the Indonesian position on West New Guinea. In August 1950 the government indicated that it did not consider Djakarta had any valid claim, and the Dutch were encouraged by this support. Canberra's hope was that the issue of West New Guinea might be kept dormant until Australia had built closer ties of friendship with Indonesia. The hope was vain; very soon President Sukarno and his nationalist followers were clamouring for the transfer of West New Guinea, claiming that Indonesia, as the heir to the former Netherlands East Indies, should possess all the former Dutch territories in the area.

There was general recognition of New Guinea's vital role in Australia's security and fears that Indonesia might be a quarrelsome and unstable neighbour with whom to share a common land border. At first, arguments advanced in resistance to the transfer rested heavily on purely legal aspects, with Australia supporting the Dutch interpretation of The Hague agreement. As time went on, more emphasis was placed on the right of self-determination of the affected people; it was emphasized by Dutch and Australian spokesmen that undeniable differences in ethnic origin, language, and culture, separated the people of West New Guinea from the peoples of the Indonesian islands, and (as Casey said) "if West New Guinea passed to Indonesia, the native inhabitants would lose, once and for all, any opportunity of determining their own future." It was pointed out that complicated and intractable political and economic problems facing Indonesia in its extensive territories must limit its ability to provide for proper administration and development of the New Guinea territory. In the background was a growing fear that at any time Indonesia might fall under Communist domination.

Following the visit to Canberra in mid-1953 of two members of the Netherlands cabinet directly concerned with West New Guinea affairs, plans were made for a working partnership between Australian and Dutch officials at the administrative level.

A new urgency came to the issue as President Sukarno's calls for Dutch withdrawal became more insistent. In 1954 Indonesia took the matter to the United Nations—a move which Australia regretted since, in Casey's words, the United Nations appeared to be "quite inappropriate forum for discussion of a demand for the handing over of territory from one country to another." Nevertheless, since a legal-political impasse existed, the move was inevitable. Fundamental to the problem was the fact that the claims of the Netherlands and of Indonesia on legal and political grounds were balanced so evenly that they offered no basis for solution. As Gavin Souter wrote later in *New Guinea, the Last Unknown,* with both cases valid in their different ways "outsiders were free to support whichever of the two they regarded as being in accordance with their own national interest."

Although it was widely supported among Australians at the time, Canberra's policy on the West New Guinea dispute had many weaknesses. There was a lack of cohesion within the policy itself; for, if Australia was unwilling to give military backing to the Dutch stand, there was little point in building up resistance to Indonesian demands; and, since the Dutch alone could not be expected to stay indefinitely, Asian nations meanwhile would interpret Australia's stand as backing for a colonial power thwarting the natural aims of an independent nation.

In fact, however, matters were moving to a crisis in which Australia's views were irrelevant. In the chronic instability affecting Indonesia's political affairs, the centre of gravity was slipping gradually leftward. By April 1955, when a conference of twenty-nine Asian and African nations was held at Bandung (Java), and Indonesia was given an opportunity to show prideful leadership among the under-privileged, there had been a sharp swing away from the cautiously pro-Western policy followed by early Indonesian cabinets. It was now evident that the influence of the Chinese Communists was a growing factor in Indonesian affairs.

The principal binding force between the Bandung conferees was a common antipathy to colonialism. The Bandung conference showed the likelihood of the new nationalism falling under concerted direction; there appeared to be evidence that Communist influence had become dominant in many of the governments. From this time a stiffening of attitude to Indonesia and other associated "neutralist" nations was apparent in Canberra as the weight of Prime Minister Menzies' hardening views on foreign affairs was more strongly felt.

The dream which hopefully projected Australia as a leader among and a friend to the Asian nations seemed to fade. With rampant nationalism sweeping through many lands previously under the control of European powers, Menzies, reflecting a growing public mood of disenchantment with examples of direct action undertaken to satisfy national emotions by newly-established governments in disregard of international conventions, was already leading Australia back into the British East-of-Suez strategy.

Concern over international affairs boiled up in Australia in July 1956 when President Abdul Nasser of Egypt suddenly proclaimed the nationalization of the Suez Canal Company twelve years before the Suez Canal convention was due to expire. The Middle East had long been a trouble spot, with Arab and Moslem nationalism violent, Arab-Israeli border incidents frequent, and British influence greatly diminished, especially after Nasser's assumption of power in Egypt in 1954. Forsaking a policy of non-alignment, Egypt signed an arms pact with Czechoslovakia and in May 1956 recognized Communist China, at the same time stepping up widespread propaganda attacks against Britain and France. In the hope of forestalling further moves towards the Communist bloc, the United States withdrew its offer to assist in the building of the projected High Dam on the Nile. Nasser's counter-move was to take over the canal.

In Australia, as in Britain, the immediate reaction was indignation. Casey expressed the government's concern at "any move that might restrict the free use of the Canal to world shipping", while Menzies, on a visit to Washington, described the seizure of the canal as "quite illegal, high-handed and perhaps dangerous." Almost all the newspapers condemned Nasser's action in such terms of "international robbery" and "an indefensible act of appropriation," and reported with approval the British government's economic and precautionary military measures. Labor, however, drew a distinction between Egypt's right to nationalize the company and "the entirely different question of ensuring the right of the ships of all nations to use the canal," and urged that the dispute be brought before the United Nations at once.

Instead of following this line of approach twenty-two nations attended a conference of canal-users in London in mid-August; eighteen of the nations supported a proposal that President Nasser be asked to negotiate a new convention on the basis of their views. A five-man mission, led by Menzies, went to Cairo to present the proposals and early in September met Nasser on several occasions. Menzies presented a submission designed to preserve the status of the Suez Canal as an international waterway, conducted by an impartial international organization. The move proved fruitless; the mission was tartly rebuffed by Nasser. The dispute was now referred to the United Nations, but attempts to reconcile differences met with no success in or outside that body.

When the crisis was debated in the Australian parliament for the first time late in September, the debate revealed the fundamental differences in outlook between Government and Opposition. Menzies, back in Australia after nearly four months abroad, reiterated his conviction that Nasser's repudiation of the Suez Canal convention was a breach of international law, and went on to state what he considered the alternative courses of action if—as seemed likely—the Security Council was deadlocked. One of these alternatives was to use force against Nasser; he argued that the use of force must never be the first resort, but that "the right to employ it cannot be completely abandoned, or made subject to impossible conditions"; if the Soviet use of the veto prevented any positive United Nations action, it might be necessary to organize economic sanctions against Egypt, or even to use force to restore economic control of the canal. Evatt denounced the Prime Minister's speech as provocative, a relic of nineteenth-century "gunboat diplomacy" and tantamount to a suggestion of war.

With the main tensions apparently lessened, Egypt's raids into Israel were resumed, and border friction increased. On October 23 a joint military command between Egypt, Jordan and Syria was announced. Six days later Israeli forces invaded Sinai. The British and French governments at once sent an ultimatum demanding that the Israeli and Egyptian armies each withdraw ten miles back from the canal. When the Egyptians rejected the ultimatum, British-French military action began, and the canal was blocked.

Evatt was caustic in denouncing the ultimatum, which he saw as a "transparent device" for attacking Egypt and occupying the canal zone. He blamed the British and French governments for not consulting with the Commonwealth and the United States—"they were not informed because Britain and France did not want them to know of it until action had been taken"—and declared that Labor would oppose any attempt by the Menzies government to involve Australia in a war for the Suez Canal.

Menzies still had no doubt of the wisdom and probity of British policy. A few months earlier the Prime Minister had been emphasizing the importance of improved consultation within the Commonwealth—"everything will turn upon our means and spirit of contact and consultation," he had written in *The Times* in June—but now he declared that Britain was correct in proceeding upon her own judgment without waiting for the approval of the Commonwealth countries, since

> . . . there was literally no time to be lost if any action was to be taken to keep the combatants out of the Canal Zone, and afford it proper protection. Effective consultation (and I say "effective" because a mere "form of consultation" would have been quite useless) would plainly have occupied considerable time and the urgent position might have fallen into irretrievable disaster.

Military action against Eqypt by Britain and France continued. The Australian newspapers, previously in support of British policy, were now confused and critical; most regretted that military force had been used, or at least deplored the rift between Britain and the United States, and Britain's failure to consult her Commonwealth partners. By now Britain and France were almost completely isolated from the current of world opinion, and even within Britain criticism was widespread. The United States completely dissociated itself from the use of force, the Arab countries cut Britain off from oil supplies, while the Soviet Union threatened inter-vention. India and the Afro-Asian bloc regarded the British-French action as "naked aggression," while Canada redoubled its efforts to work out a solution within the United Nations.

The British-French assault had been swift and unexpected, but under the pressure of United Nations opinion it had to be as precipitately ended. On November 2, when the United Nations Assembly voted for an immediate cease fire, Australia and New Zealand were the sole supporters of Britain, France, and Israel. On November 6 Egypt severed diplomatic relations with Australia because of the endorsement of the British-French-Israeli action. On November 7 the cease fire took effect, and shortly afterwards a United Nations emergency force began its peace-keeping task. President Nasser was eventually left in possession of the Canal, for which he agreed to pay compensation to the proprietary company.

Australian newspapers had meanwhile pointed to a need to repair what one of them described as "the ugly damage of the crisis." Under the heading, "We need our own Foreign Policy," the Melbourne *Herald* ran a dispatch from its Canberra observer dealing with the crucial nature of the issue before Australia. He wrote:

> The basic tradition of Australian foreign policy—the doctrine that Australia goes where Britain goes and fights where Britain fights—has been changed by this week's developments in the Middle East. When the Prime Minister announced that Cabinet had endorsed Britain's advance into Egypt he followed a road Australia has trodden since Federation. But that Cabinet decision which made Australia one of the few odd men out among her friends of west and east, may well be the last of these orthodox decisions.

In his personal sally into the international arena, Menzies had found that the new nationalism transforming once-subservient lands was a potent and determined force. After the well-ordered ways of a stable and conservative Australia in which he was personally such a dominant figure, his experience in the new post-Bandung world of diplomacy had come as a shock to the Prime Minister. He had little patience with visionary and quixotic leaders of countries of newly-acquired independence (though of proud and quite ancient cultures), and he was more anxious than ever to uphold the world of known and traditional values which he saw in full flower around the British edifice. It was clear that Menzies now considered the United Nations in its new form to be doing no more than affording legitimacy to the flouting of old international obligations. The Egyptian fiasco he saw as the worst of all these defections; and he declared the exclusion of British and French troops from the United Nations emergency force for Egypt to be "sheer bedlam nonsense." To Menzies—as to many other Australians—the com-pliance of Britain and France with the United Nations' cease-fire directive made a bitter contrast with the Soviet's almost simultaneous refusal to act on United Nations directives on Hungary and showed the weakness of the United Nations peace-keeping machinery. The Prime Minister was highly critical of the developments which had given the small countries such a powerful voice, and he saw cause for alarm in the shift in emphasis within the United Nations from the Security Council to the General Assembly (where, he noted, "there are eighty-one nations, each with one vote"). The Assembly, he said, had now, rightly or wrongly, legally or illegally, become the centre of the world's interests; yet the world's peace could not be maintained by resolutions or the ardent views of smaller countries: the great powers alone could keep it.

Menzies' stand on the Suez issue was not universally accepted as prudent, even among his followers, and it divided his cabinet, where Casey was among those who considered it unwise for Australia to become so directly involved in such a sensitive issue. From the beginning, Menzies' role as leader of the mission to Cairo surprised some, and while many Australians felt flattered that their Prime Minister had been chosen, the task was one that would have been more appropriately left to the British to handle. The move may have seemed sound in the light of the close rapport that existed between Eden and Menzies, but the consequences were incalculable. When the Prime Minister went on to justify use of force by unilaterial decision and to disparage the United Nations and the part played in it by smaller nations, he was alienating many of the new nations and swinging away from the United States position.

Yet Menzies' reaffirmation of old ties was generally well received among Australians and appeared to have widespread public support; emotional links were strong and the Suez life-line was an issue of direct significance to Australians. There was an uneasy feeling that Dulles had been manoeuvred into an anti-British-French stand by astute Soviet diplomacy, and many newspapers expressed irritation at American policy.

It was now recognized in Canberra that Nasser's action was having its effect among other "new" nations anxious to take revenge on former overlords As one commentator noted, the Suez take-over gave young nations fresh courage, for they thought the old European giants were at last falling. While the crisis was still at its height, Indonesia, which had begun to rank as one of the greatest of the new nations because of its vast population (close to 100 million) and natural resources, took a leaf from Nasser's book and cancelled most of the external debts it had taken over from the Netherlands East Indies as part of the independence agreement.

Behind the scenes, Communist China was building up strength, supported by assistance from Moscow in the form of huge credits and technical assistance for industrial development. In 1957 an agreement was signed under which Soviet Russia undertook to help China manufacture its own atomic bombs. In international affairs, Moscow and Peking maintained close co-operation, and their missions were gaining influence in the affairs of many of the new nations.

Australian doubts about the stability of the regime in Djakarta were intensified early in 1957 by mounting evidence of its economic difficulties and news of the inclusion of Communists in the new all-party administration. Dutch as well as Australian attitudes on the New Guinea issue were hardening; a determination was growing to maintain West New Guinea under Dutch rule until such time as it could be granted self-government. Links between the Australian and Dutch authorities in New Guinea were further strengthened with an announcement in November 1957 of Dutch-Australian administrative co-operation, while in diplomatic contacts Canberra stressed the need for restraint on the part of both the Indonesians and the Dutch. In the United Nations General Assembly, Indonesia failed for the third time in three years to secure the two-thirds majority required for acceptance of a resolution supporting its aims in West New Guinea—a refusal which sparked Indonesia's confiscation of Dutch property and in turn the exodus of Dutch families from Indonesia.

President Sukarno was using the West New Guinea issue for direct political ends. He now assumed greater power, promising meanwhile to continue the struggle against "economic and political imperialism," and spoke of "liberating" West Irian, the Indonesian title for West New Guinea, as part of this struggle. As the Dutch made greater efforts to improve administration and accelerate development, Indonesian pressure grew. Indonesian fears that Australian-Dutch administrative collaboration might be a preliminary step to a military alliance appeared to deepen with Casey's visit to Holland in September 1958. On his return home Casey invited Indonesia's Foreign Minister, Dr Subandrio, to visit Australia. A joint announcement at the end of the talks in Canberra acknowledged the different views held on West New Guinea but said Australian ministers had explained that if any agreement were arrived at between the Netherlands and Indonesia "by peaceful processes and in accordance with internationally accepted principles," Australia would not oppose such an agreement. The statement appeared to many to be a backdown by Australia and there was a storm in press and parliament. However, following. Subandrio's return to Djakarta there was a lull which lasted more than a year. Meanwhile, Indonesia was showing more definite leanings towards the Communist bloc; within the country, Communist party membership was extensive, and close ties had been developed with Communist capitals.

In August 1960 Indonesia severed diplomatic relations with the Netherlands, and before the end of the year had negotiated large-scale arms purchases from the Soviet—linking them to an alleged Dutch military build-up in West New Guinea. By 1961, the Americans and British—neither of whom had shared Australia's extremely deep concern over the West New Guinea issue—were coming to the conclusion that the prospect of gaining Indonesian goodwill held more significance than the retention of the Dutch in West New Guinea.

By early 1962 it was clear to Canberra that there was no inclination in Washington or London to stand firm on Dutch New Guinea, and Menzies, who held the additional portfolio of External Affairs for two years after Casey's elevation to the peerage in 1960, could not secure a statement of outright support for Australia's position. The Australian cabinet had no alternative but to accept the inevitable when the war of words took on a grimmer aspect as Dutch forces were increased and Sukarno began to "confront" the Dutch by sending patrol vessels into Dutch-held waters and dropping armed parachutists into West New Guinea. In Canberra,

Sir Garfield Barwick, now External Affairs Minister, urging moderation, spoke of the dangers of armed conflict when he said that to introduce war and its abiding animosities "could create intolerable burdens for all peoples of the area and for their descendants for generations to come." Labor's voice was raised loudly against Sukarno; Calwell, now leader of the Opposition, described Sukarno's speeches as reminiscent of Hitler's, and he accused the government of failing to stand firm against Sukarno's threats.

On August 15, 1962, after several months of negotiations in which the United States used its good offices, the Netherlands and Indonesia signed a formal agreement at United Nations headquarters transferring the 150,000 square mile territory from the Dutch to Indonesia after a brief period of United Nations supervision. American willingness to acquiesce in the transfer of the territory to Indonesian hands came as a shock to Australia. It had become evident that with slender military resources and a scattering of forces on the ground in south-east Asia, Australia's military commitment in the region was too slight to support representations of national interest that might be made to London, Washington—or, for that matter, Djakarta.

The pace of development in Australian-held New Guinea had already been greatly accelerated under the prod of world opinion. With the virtual end of colonial administration throughout Black Africa as well as in south-east Asia, and with international interest focusing on a dwindling number of colonial and trust territories, it was clear that scrupulous concern for the welfare of wards was no longer enough. Demands for a target date for the granting of self-government to Australian-held New Guinea were becoming more insistent each year, especially from 1960, when seventeen new countries in Africa achieved independent status and the "African bloc" in the United Nations became a considerable political force. No matter how severe the practical difficulties posed by rugged terrain and the primitiveness of New Guinea's peoples, a laggard administration was now certain to attract increasingly severe criticism.

A sharper appreciation of the need for accelerating development had come to Canberra largely as a result of discussions held during the meeting of Commonwealth Prime Ministers in May 1960. Paul Meerna Hasluck, who had held the Territories portfolio since 1951, accompanied Prime Minister Menzies to London for the meeting, and both men returned to Australia accepting the view that to be premature in granting self-government to such areas was preferable to risking the bitterness that could arise from delays, no matter how soundly motivated they might be. Prime Minister MacMillan had explained Britain's views on the "winds of change" sweeping Africa, and Menzies, while admitting that he had previously believed it wiser to move slowly towards independence, said he accepted the new school of thought that it was "better to go sooner than later." There was still no inclination to set a timetable for political advancement in New Guinea, but from hints in official statements it appeared that the government foresaw the possibility of self-government in a generation or so.

A further degree of representative government was granted under legislation introduced in September 1960 which expanded the Territory's legislative council to thirty-seven and eliminated the administration's former official majority in the council. The number of officials (including the administrator, the council's chairman) was reduced to fifteen, while the nominated component was increased to ten, including five indigenes, and the elected component to twelve, including six representatives elected directly by the native voters. The reconstructed legislative council, although subordinate to the Commonwealth, possessed wide legislative powers as well as the complete structure of a parliament, even if still only with a one-third elective membership.

The practical aspects were being given greater attention, and there was increasing public expenditure to back the work being done by missions and through commercial investment, including airline, mining and plantation enterprises. Hospitals and medical facilities and more and better schools were being set up, the quality and supply of food was being improved, and increased numbers of native peoples were being trained to earn sufficient to maintain higher living standards. The value of the territory's exports, which had trebled during the 1950s, continued to move up sharply. In 1959, export duties had been abolished and import duties reduced; at the same time an income tax (at about half the Australian mainland rate) was introduced which helped to lift local revenue and stimulate activity. The rudiments of industrial activity were in evidence. Meanwhile, greater spending power in urban centres was helping to provide more scope for the sale of locally-grown products, as plantings of new crops marked a change-over from subsistence gardening to a cash-crop economy for greater numbers of the indigenous population.

Nevertheless, the fifth United Nations Trusteeship Mission to the Territory (in 1962) took issue with the gradualist policies and urged that progress should be at a faster pace, saying in effect that the rate of progress should not be at the whim of circumstance but should be determined by policy. It rejected the administration's philosophy of uniform development, and disagreed with its unwillingness to create an educational *élite*. On political aspects, the mission made sweeping recommendations; the existing legislative council, it said, should be replaced after its first three-year term by a hundred-member house of representatives, elected on a universal franchise.

The legislative council in Port Moresby had already appointed a select committee to study constitutional changes, and its report (presented in October 1962) proposed increasing the membership of the legislative body to sixty-five, including up to forty-four elected native members. The government accepted the proposals, and legislation to give effect to them was introduced to parliament in May 1963.

The first general election for Papua-New Guinea's newly-constituted House of Assembly took place in February 1964 after nine months of preparation in which the electoral staff undertook the extremely difficult task of preparing a common roll of voters. Genuinely political issues had not arisen, nor had political parties; campaign speeches were usually about the need for more roads and bridges. The franchise was open to all men and women over twenty-one years, and slightly over 1,000,000 voters were finally enrolled. Preparation for the election involved patrols ploughing through mountain and rain forest to reach primitive villages, and after the roll was prepared the vote collectors moved out to cover the nearly 3000 polling places, using motor vehicles, small aircraft, helicopters and canoes, but for the most part walking, so that there would be a ballot box within eight hours' walk of every village right up to the West Irian border. Illiterate voters were helped to fill in their ballot papers, but no advice or "lead" of any kind could be given to influence a voter's choice of candidate.

The whole exercise was something new in ready-made democracy. A reporter for the Melbourne *Herald* who followed the voting preparations, wrote:

> Never before has an adolescent nation received a build-it-yourself kit for political development like the one Australia is throwing in the laps of a million first-time voters in Papua and New Guinea. . .
> As the last hectic days of half-understood electioneering draw to a close, sanity is rubbing shoulders with sorcery, showmanship with shyness, and foresight with foolishness. On the one hand are election promises to obtain a magic serum which will turn the black man's skin white, and on the other are reasoned plans for a long and friendly co-existence with Australia.

The election resulted in thirty-eight native members being returned.

Whatever its shortcomings, the new legislature was clearly destined to become an effective school of learning for future leaders—an "apprentice" body, representing the people, where the art and science of self-government might be studied and practised. A nucleus of leaders had emerged; and behind them, in the secondary schools and colleges, in the public service and in private industry young men and women were preparing themselves for citizenship in a country moving towards full responsibility for the conduct of its affairs. The seed of hope had been planted.

Political changes, however, could not be an answer to other basic problems. It was evident that in spite of Canberra's increasing cash contributions, and rising local revenue, any dramatic lift in New Guineans' basic living standards from the little-better-than-subsistence level would involve a re-evaluation of some of the basic policies being followed. Further, the failure to call in international aid to assist in the development of New Guinea had reached a stage where it was conspicuous, and the lack of clear aims in New Guinea policy began to draw increasing fire. Following the report of the 1962 United Nations Mission, the International Bank for Reconstruction and Development was invited to formulate a plan to stimulate economic growth and raise living standards, and a ten-member Bank mission investigated all aspects. The group's findings, released late in 1964, assessed the progress already made, in economic terms, and provided pointers for the future. In effect the report urged concentration of effort in areas and on activities where the prospective return would be highest. It foretold development of the country closely identified with expansion of agriculture and forestry, and suggested that such new crops as tea, pyrethrum, peanuts, and bananas should be added to the established crops—copra, coffee, cocoa and rubber. Cattle raising and the milling of timber were also considered to be capable of rapid expansion. The place of business investment, as distinct from government outlays, in stimulating growth was stressed.

The report proposed that a development-finance corporation should be set up to provide funds and steps taken to encourage Europeans to remain in the territory. Over a five-year period, at least £250 million would be required to meet New Guinea's needs, and Australia might reasonably provide 70 per cent of this money, with the remainder coming from the territory's own resources. In planning governmental expenditure, priority should be given to roads, coastal shipping and the improvement of ports, and available funds should be spent primarily on the development of agriculture, forestry, transport, visitor facilities and on technical and secondary education, rather than extending primary education. The clear implication was that the Bank mission saw a need to concentrate men and money in certain areas in order to undertake selected tasks and so create sound economic development, rather than a mere continuation of the administration's admirable but generalized social programme. It was, in effect, reinforcing the views of the United Nations Trusteeship Mission.

Soon after its formation, the new national assembly set up a select committee, with a majority of New Guineans, to study constitutional development. It was anticipated that by the time of the next general elections (1968) all seats might be freely contested, and a limited form of ministerial government might follow. By 1965 each administrative department had an Assembly-member indigene (with the title of under-secretary) as an understudy to its director; these posts were expected to change to full portfolios when a ministerial government came into being. Other aspects under discussion were the need for a name to replace Papua-New Guinea—and Paradisea led in popularity among initial proposals—and the need for a national anthem and a national flag.

Late in 1965 the committee on constitutional development tabled in the legislature an interim report on its discussions, in which it asked Canberra for a definition of the constitutional alternatives that were in fact open. One suggestion that had emerged in earlier discussions concerned the possibility of the territory's becoming a seventh Australian state—but this prospect seemed remote, since such a move would open up at least as many problems as it might solve. There were also the alternatives of absolute independence, with no political attachment to Australia, and a self-governing status combined with some political dependence on Australia. In the event that New Guineans sought full independence, there was always the possibility that they might become the beneficiaries of some international agency for backward peoples; but most commentators—including Australian writer Osmar White in his *Parliament of a Thousand Tribes*—considered it more likely that they would attach themselves to their Indonesian neighbours. Early in 1966, a member of the New Guinea legislature said that talk of early independence worried him; if Australia left, the country would go back to tribal warfare. In reply, the Minister for Territories made it clear that Australia would remain "as long as the people of the territory want this."

Meanwhile, secondary education was making progress and training facilities were being expanded. In 1964 a twenty-four-year-old Yule islander became the first New Guinean to graduate when he passed his final year in agricultural science at Sydney University. In 1965 an agricultural college was opened, and plans were completed for an institute of higher technical education. Plans were also completed for the new university at Port Moresby to enrol its first students in 1967.

From the late 1950s, when Australia's attention was largely concentrated on Indonesia's intentions, mutual suspicion between the West and the Communist world remained as great as ever. A balance of atomic terror had cancelled out military superiority, but the "cold war" continued unabated, with intensified political propaganda and an enlargement of scientific and military competition and additional commitments for aid to underdeveloped nations.

New and terrible weapons, including intercontinental ballistic missiles and nuclear-powered submarines carrying atomic weapons, were being added to the super-powers' armouries, ushering in new concepts of defence and attack. As the over-all threat from militant communism grew, the dangers of pressure from China's vast manpower reserves were more apparent and there was greater concern in Washington over the south-east Asia situation. A unified command was established for all American forces in the Pacific in January 1959 as a prelude to their build-up to a point where the two great United States fleets and large air and ground forces had a total fire-power unmatched in the Pacific or in any other ocean during peacetime. In United States policy-making, south-east Asia was being accorded a higher priority than ever before in the strategic concept for the containment of communism. This new priority was confirmed by President John Kennedy when he was elected at the end of 1960. Henceforth, with the European situation more or less stabilized, American interest would be concentrated on Asia to an unprecedented degree.

The situation in Vietnam had worsened. General elections envisaged for all Vietnam in the Geneva arrangements had not been held in 1956; the plan was not heeded by Ngo Dinh Diem's regime in Saigon on the ground that there was no assurance against Communist rigging of the voting in North Vietnam; and the Hanoi regime was too busy with peasant revolts against introduction of the commune system on the farms to complain about the lack of elections. Instead, by 1960 Hanoi was giving new support to the insurgent forces in the South. The International Control Committee set up under the Geneva accords found its position untenable and reported this fact to the United Nations. The ability of the West to keep South Vietnam from falling under Communist control was now a crucial issue in the face of unrelieved internal discord and increasing Communist pressure. Washington was prepared to back Diem, arguing that introduction of United States arms and also military personnel as "advisers" was justified because the Geneva accords had been violated through infiltration of men and weapons into South Vietnam. An appeal for backing was made by the United States to other SEATO countries.

The Australian government supported the American stand—not merely because of standing friendship and treaty arrangements but because the commitment of American power and resources appeared vital to the balance of power in south-east Asia. The fall of South Vietnam, it was held, would imperil the whole area since it could open the way for all other countries successively to come under greater Communist pressure with the clear danger of great instability and destructive conflict. Among Australians there was a widespread feeling of doubt about the situation in south-east Asia and a bewildered concern which clearly buttressed the pro-Menzies vote in the general elections of December 1961.

Moscow and Peking were now vying with each other for leadership of the Communist world, and as each stepped up the use of trade, aid, and military supplies under agreements with smaller countries as bargaining weapons in the struggle, the threat of growing Communist pressure in Asia was intensified.

Trouble spots were reviewed at the meeting of the ANZUS Council of Foreign Ministers at Canberra in May 1962 to which the American Secretary of State, Dean Rusk, brought a penetrating and sobering analysis of the strategic issues involved. The outcome was a new awareness of the blacker side of the picture in south-east Asia and of the harsher problems thrown up in the maelstrom of conflict there. Newspaper editorials suggested that as a result of Rusk's visit and the sense of solidarity with the United States which it fostered, Australia would assuredly be undertaking new commitments, even if (as the *Age* felt) essential elements in the decision remained vague. It was evident that the discussions had brought to policy-makers in Canberra a sharper appreciation of the dangers to be faced; and from this time Prime Minister Menzies made it clear that Australia must give more weight to its role in sharing the American determination to see that Asian communism made no further territorial gains. Australia's defence programme had been framed against the strategic background that any outbreak of war was likely to be of the limited "brush-fire" type, and events were proving the correctness of this concept.

The government now decided to move in beside the Americans by sending a small group of "military advisers" to the South Vietnam army. It was generally considered that the Australian forces were being committed to meet a long-term threat and not because the situation in south-east Asia had suddenly or seriously worsened. There was widespread approval of the move as one which would clearly demonstrate the collective will to resist communism. Commentator Denis Warner put it succinctly when he wrote that Australia was taking out "a sort of life assurance cover." He added:

> The chances are that it's going to be increasingly lonely in this part of the world, and we are going to need Washington's support in future.

In Canberra, the growing complexity of Australia's strategic position was recognized by the creation of a standing committee of cabinet, the Defence and Foreign Affairs Committee, to co-ordinate policies in these spheres.

Clinging to the hope that Australia might remain beyond the fringe of areas of active strategic concern, the A.L.P. remained strongly opposed to military involvement in Asia. While the general lines of foreign policy formulated at the A.L.P. federal conference of March 1955 were still un-challenged, some members of the party were conscious of a need to adapt Labor's policies to the new situation in which Australia could no longer ignore the encroachment of the world. Opposition Leader Calwell worked hard to bring the Labor party to a sounder appreciation of the issues; as yet, however, Labor was unable to put forward any clearly defined policy beyond holding to the basic view that military intervention was no solution to south-east Asia's problems, and seeking parliamentary action to secure the creation of a nuclear-free zone in the Southern Hemisphere.

The concept of the Australian continent as the stable reserve platform off Asia had gained acceptance in Washington; now it was time for Aus-tralia to become more intimately involved in the increasingly complex defence structure which the United States was erecting as a bulwark for the western Pacific-Indian Ocean region. The new strategic plan called for the deployment of nuclear-powered Polaris submarines in the Indian ocean as well as the Pacific and, in order to provide the essential radio communi-cation (by Very-Low-Frequency transmission) essential for their guidance, the United States government sought a secure site for a radio communi-cations base on the Indian Ocean shore. After investigation, the north-western tip of the continent—North-West Cape, bordering Exmouth Gulf—was chosen as the best location, and the Australian government gave its approval for the United States Navy to establish the base there.

The government's announcement in May 1962 that an agreement on the base had been signed opened the way for many serious policy aspects to come into open debate, with the division between those attaching prime importance to the American relationship as the basis of Australian security and those primarily concerned with avoiding deep, binding and potentially dangerous commitments. Many people felt that the North-West Cape base agreement, which was about to be ratified, would open the way for serious infringement of Australian sovereignty, and those who believed that Australia should be moving closer to Asian countries were concerned that it might impair relations and prevent Australia reaching a regional under-standing with them. There were also fears that the radio base itself would make Australia "a prime target in the event of nuclear war." A special federal conference on foreign policy held by the A.L.P. in March 1963 accepted the need for the construction of the base, but added a rider that the treaty agreement with Washington should be renegotiated to provide for joint American-Australian control and operation of the facilities. Labor also wanted the renegotiated treaty to include an undertaking for prior consultation with Australia for any use of the base which might involve Australia in war. The party was still unwilling to modify its policy, formulated in 1962, of calling for a conference of all interested powers to discuss the possibility of creating a nuclear-free zone for the whole South Pacific-Indian Ocean region.

As the public discussion on these and other aspects of the nation's responsibilities and commitments intensified, Australians were drawn closer than ever before to an understanding of the extent to which independent policies on specific issues would have to become subordinate to the realities of the world power struggle and, specifically, to the larger purposes of the alliance with the United States and commitments under SEATO. With a tightening Canberra-Washington partnership, and with dangers in south-east Asia more pressing than ever, Australia's options were, of necessity, limited.

The A.L.P. decisions calling for qualification of Australia's commitments were roundly condemned by practically all newspapers and many journals of opinion. When the North-West Cape radio base agreement was presented to parliament for ratification in May 1963 the Opposition pressed its proposal for joint control of the base, but this was rejected and the Bill was passed without amendment.

Events took on a new urgency for Australia as Indonesia's rampant nationalism showed signs of erupting into open war against a country Australia was committed to defend. The immediate cause of Sukarno's hostility was the creation of a new multi-racial federation comprising the Malayan states, Singapore, and the colonies of North Borneo (renamed Sabah) and Sarawak, as the independent Commonwealth nation of Malaysia.

Moves for the creation of the Federation of Malaysia had been consistently opposed by Sukarno, who condemned it as an example of "British neo-colonialism" when the final steps were confirmed in July 1963 and it was agreed that defence arrangements between Britain and Malaya (in effect since 1957) would be continued and that Britain's right to maintain existing bases would not be affected. Opposition to Malaysia's formation had been stirred up in many directions, and Sukarno was able to secure the support of the Philippines to propose a union of Malaya, the Philippines, and Indonesia ("Maphilindo") instead of the proposed federation. The British government quickly rejected Maphilindo as "a tawdry subterfuge" advanced to disguise Indonesia's animus towards Malaysia; but Sukarno was already committed to a "confrontation" policy, and soon casualties were multiplying as Indonesian units infiltrated across the border into Sarawak and Indonesian naval units moved challengingly in the Straits of Malacca. The declaration of Malaysia's founding was delayed, but after a United Nations inquiry team confirmed that the majority of people in Britain's Borneo territories favoured joining Malaysia, the new nation of 10,000,000 people was proclaimed on September 16, 1963—a move which Australia welcomed as "a progressive development in the history of south-east Asia."

Djakarta's reaction was violent; Indonesia's diplomatic relations with

Kuala Lumpur were severed, while in Djakarta mobs burned and sacked the British embassy. As pressure on Malaysia built up, Canberra promised "unlimited support" to Britain in the crisis, confirming that the ANZAM arrangement providing Australian forces in Malaya (as part of the Strategic Reserve) would now be extended to the whole of Malaysia. At the same time, Australia's diplomatic efforts were directed to lessening tension, and· although relations at times seemed to be under great strain, there were no anti-Australian demonstrations in Djakarta at any time.

The United States government was meanwhile using its influence to dissuade Sukarno from precipitate action. Nevertheless, Indonesia continued to move detachments to the Sarawak border to give effect to its "confrontation" policy. In reply, additional British troops were landed in British Borneo, while Royal Navy vessels patrolled the coast.

In October 1963 Prime Minister Menzies decided to take his government's policies to the electorate by cutting short the life of the House of Representatives and calling an election a full year before the normal expiry date. The Prime Minister's prestige was at its height: in February, the Queen had conferred the Order of the Thistle upon him, and on July 4, during a four-week tour in which he had discussions with British and American leaders, he had delivered the Thomas Jefferson Memorial Oration at Monticello, Virginia—an honour never previously accorded a non-American.

The immediate economic outlook in Australia was encouraging, with prices and costs stable, and official stimulus to the economy combined with a recovery in world prices for practically all export commodities, including wool, had brought a return of buoyant conditions throughout the community. Nevertheless, the government decided to concentrate attention on international issues and defence, seeking electoral support largely on the issue of preserving a "hard line" in foreign policy and for its newly-announced defence expansion.

While parliament was still in session, Sir Robert Menzies indicated the foreign policy questions upon which Government and Opposition differed. Labor, he said, had decided that it would seek to renegotiate the treaty establishing the United States Navy's communications base; since the station was about to be constructed it was important that Australia's intentions be clarified. Second, Labor wanted Australia's military assistance to Malaysia to be formalized by a definite mutual defence treaty, to which Malaysia, as a non-aligned nation, was unwilling to accede; the countries concerned should know whether the Australian people backed the government's unilateral declaration of military assistance to Malaysia. Third, he said, Labor's proposal that Australia should participate in a nuclear-free zone south of the equator must be resolved, since the government regarded the proposal as "suicidal" because it would leave Australia without the protection of the nuclear deterrent. As the election campaign proceeded, the attack on the A.L.P. ranged wider: the Prime Minister said it was obvious that the Labor party machine, and not Calwell, would formulate policy if Labor won the election, and that this machine was under left-wing influence.

The Labor party conducted a vigorous campaign. Calwell accepted the challenge on foreign policy and assured the electorate of his party's concern in maintaining a policy based on membership in the Commonwealth of Nations, the Australia-United States alliance, and loyalty to the United Nations; however, Labor would follow Britain's example in recognising the Peking government. He made a number of promises covering education, home financing, and social services, and attempted to force more interest on domestic issues.

Labor took the government to task for earlier inaction in defence matters, and sought to make electoral capital out of the newly-announced decision to purchase for the Royal Australian Air Force two squadrons of the American TFX two-man strike bombers instead of the British TSR-2s. Both aircraft appeared to satisfy basic requirements; and although the TFX was still no more than a project on the designers' tables, the government maintained that the plane would be more suitable for Australian conditions. Labor's case against the TFX was weakened when the authoritative London *Economist* said the TSR-2 project was a failure because of bungling by the Air Ministry; nevertheless, Labor remained critical of the government's decision, promising to reconsider the TFX transaction if it won the election.

During the election campaign, the Democratic Labor party launched a bitter campaign against the A.L.P., which, it claimed, was still under the domination of trade unions manipulated by Communists. In Victoria and New South Wales, at least, the D.L.P.'s influence was considerable since its preferences went almost wholly to support the government parties' candidates.

The electorate's endorsement of the policy of closer ties with the United States and an enlarged role in regional defence was overwhelming; the Liberal-Country party coalition won its seventh successive electoral victory, and in the new House held seventy-two seats to the Labor party's fifty.

Although Indonesia had failed to achieve the disintegration of Malaysia, guerrilla activities by Indonesian infiltrators continued in Malaysian Borneo. Early in 1964 External Affairs Minister Barwick said that Indonesia's line of action merited international disapproval, and he suggested that Indonesia "pause in its present course and review the position in which it has placed itself." In April, the Indonesian ambassador, returning to Canberra after a visit to Djakarta, said that the question of Malaysia was one "to be solved by Asians in an Asian atmosphere and an Asian way," and that Australia should not "interfere." Soon afterwards, a SEATO Council meeting was held in Manila, and at its conclusion Barwick said that Australia might become more involved in the Malaysian crisis. A small contingent of Australian troops left for Malaysian Borneo shortly afterwards.

Meanwhile the fighting in Vietnam had escalated sharply. Communist activity in South Vietnam had been intensified; earlier, the Hanoi-backed

People's Revolutionary Party had taken over the National Liberation Front and, using the tactics of subversion, had come close to success with widespread disorders and violence; when this failed, early in 1964 a new emphasis was placed on revolutionary guerrilla warfare, speeded and reinforced by the arrival of northern Communists whose experience went back to the Vietminh war against the French. From this time greater American forces were committed in an effort to block the Communist expansion. For Australia, with military advisers in South Vietnam since 1962, deeper military involvement was now in prospect.

In June came the announcement from Canberra that additional defence expenditure would be undertaken. It was explained that Australia must now be in a position to commit forces at short notice in a variety of situations; the immediate need was for well-trained regular forces to deal with subversion and insurgency, but Australia also had to be ready to make "an immediate and effective contribution should hostilities on a large scale develop." It was planned to have fifty Mirage fighter aircraft, equipped with radar-guided missiles, in commission by November 1965.

In June Sir Robert Menzies left for discussions in Washington and London. On his return he said that the United States had agreed with Australia that ANZUS contained "an acceptance of responsibility on Malaysia, and that the United States fully supported Australia's general policy in Asia." As though to back the Washington pledge, in September the United States Navy's nuclear-powered aircraft carrier *Enterprise*, the largest warship afloat, and an accompanying guided-missile cruiser visited Sydney, where they were accorded a tremendous welcome by the public.

In November 1964 the government again stepped up defence plans in what newspapers hailed as a "historic defence review." Declaring that there was a real risk of war with Indonesia, and stressing also the dangers of the Vietnam situation, the Prime Minister announced sweeping changes in the defence programme to increase expenditure over the following three years to more than £1220 million, or almost 50 per cent more than outlays that had been planned earlier. The plan was to provide a regular army of 37,500 men, and provision was made for the creation of a national register of all young men as they turned twenty as the basis for the introduction of selective national service training. The Navy and Air Force were also to be expanded, with emphasis on guided-missile anti-submarine patrol craft, and a submarine base was to be developed at Sydney. The R.A.A.F. was to develop a major airfield near Wewak, New Guinea, and other airfields were to be established at Learmouth (North-West Cape), Cocos-Keeling Island in the Indian ocean, and in New Guinea. Manus Island was to be restored as a base.

The Labor party opposed the government's plan for conscription with service overseas in peacetime, but the necessary measure was passed in November.

In February 1965 the government announced that the Australian infantry battalion located in Malaya would in future serve in Malaysian Borneo in rotation with British and Malaysian units, and in addition a paratroop group would be made available for periodic service there. As an American journalist sensed the atmosphere, Australians were bending over backwards to give Sukarno "a fair go," but they were oiling up their rifles while they talked. Before long, the firm resistance to Sukarno's Peking-backed belligerency had a cooling effect. Although Sukarno continued to proclaim his intention of fighting and destroying the Malaysian union, his forces were unable to make much headway and "confrontation" subsided from an active to a dormant political volcano. The subsequent splitting of Singapore from Malaysia as a result of racial differences between the Malays and the Chinese majority in Singapore, aggravated by personal differences between the Malaysian Prime Minister, Tunku Abdul Rahman, and Singapore's Lee Kwan Yew, caused concern in Canberra temporarily; but pressure from Djakarta fell away once pro-Communist members of Sukarno's government were ousted late in 1965. Antagonism to Malaysia subsided; soon "confrontation" was at an end.

By 1965 the Chinese Communists, having tested their first atomic device, were openly attacking Russia's policy of peaceful co-existence with the West; but Peking was suffering severe diplomatic reverses as the pro-Chinese group among Communist countries was sharply reduced. The swing-to-the-West in Indonesia was one of the most significant of these reverses. One side effect of the easing of Indonesian-Malaysian confrontation in 1966 was that the Philippines accorded diplomatic recognition to Malaysia, while Indonesia recognized Singapore, apparently accepting the continuing presence there of the British naval base.

In the other south-east Asian trouble spot, South Vietnam, the conflict had grown more bitter and the fighting had reached substantial proportions. Australia's increasing involvement was in step with that of the United States, moving up from the involvement of a few "military advisers" to the commitment of combat troops. The conflict had entered a new phase following the so-called Gulf of Tonkin incident of August 1964 involving United States destroyers, as a result of which a resolution of the United States Congress gave President Johnson virtually unlimited power to pursue the still undeclared war.

The Australian determination to support the intensified war was expressed by External Affairs Minister Hasluck when he said that Australia's presence in South Vietnam stemmed from a double necessity:

> One is to defeat the aggressor and to halt the southward move of Mainland China. The other is to demonstrate plainly and victoriously to the other small nations of southern Asia, whether they are neutralist or committed, that aggression will fail.

In April 1965 direct military aid, provided under SEATO, was stepped up when an Australian infantry battalion, totalling some 1,500 men, was dispatched to Saigon. New Zealand responded to the same call, and the Anzac unit was soon involved in heavy fighting beside American forces. It was the first occasion on which Australian-New Zealand forces had ever been engaged when Britain was not directly involved, but this was accepted without reservation.

Explaining the commitment of Australian ground forces in April 1965 the Prime Minister said that a Communist take-over of South Vietnam would be a direct military threat to Australia and to all countries of southern Asia, since "it must be seen as part of a thrust by Communist China between the Indian and Pacific oceans." He went on to say:

> We do not and must not overlook the point that our alliances, as well as providing guarantees and assurances for our security, make demands upon us.

Newspaper opinion generally supported the government's action as inevitable in the circumstances. Those who applauded the decision justified it primarily as a gesture of support for the United States. A typical comment was that of *The Bulletin*, which said that while the commitment of the Australian force would obviously not turn the tide of war, "it will help South Vietnam, it will help the Americans, but above all it shows that Australia recognizes its obligations as a Pacific power." Hasluck stated the government's concern that in south-east Asia no less than in any other region, aggression should be resisted and the established conventions of international conduct observed; for here, as elsewhere, he said, any unwillingness to resist, or failure in resistance, would dissipate the only climate in which Australia's independence, freedom and safety could endure.

However, there was sharp difference of opinion among Australians on the wisdom of involvement in a land war on the Asian mainland—particularly in a country with the political, social, and religious complexities of Vietnam —even though the United States administration had made it clear that, by design, the scale of the war would be held down. A large body of religious leaders, many academics, and the Labor party all continued to stress the need for a negotiated ceasefire and remained outspokenly critical of Australia's involvement in the war. At a "teach-in" at the Australian National University, the professor of Far Eastern History, Charles Patrick Fitzgerald, deplored the way in which

> ... we are being led step by step, and without realizing where we are going, into a war which will be seen throughout Asia and the world at large as a war of white men against yellow men, of Western imperialism reimposing its rule on Asian people.

Opposition was strongest in Labor ranks, but as in other Western countries, the Vietnam issue cut across party alignments. There was a widespread realization that the Australian involvement was "perhaps the most momentous government decision in the country's recent history." The announcement, made in March 1966, that Australian national servicemen would be sent to Vietnam as part of the expanded ground force (trebled to 4500 men) provided a focus for stronger and more vehement criticism. General misgivings were reinforced, and public opinion polls indicated that conscription for service in Vietnam was opposed by many supporters of each of the political parties. The government stood firm in its conviction that South

Vietnam had become "the testing point of the determination to prevent Communist aggression."

By 1966 the R.A.N. had twenty-eight ships under construction or on order; most were being built in Australia but key units were being bought from the United States and Britain. The R.A.A.F's order for Mirage III fighters had been increased to a hundred.

Australia's stature had been growing consistently during the 1960s. Expansion of the nation's industrial base (with all that implied in terms of accompanying technology) had steadily enhanced Australia's significance, but the new stature sprang in large measure from the special association Australia had been able to develop with the United States as a partner in ANZUS, as well as from its important role within the Commonwealth of Nations. Other important underlying reasons for the new prestige related simply to Australia's location; the continent's geographical position meant that Australia had special significance in the Space Age, and a series of stations established to track orbital flights and deep-space probes made Australia a complementary partner in the immense space effort undertaken by the Americans.

Among the intangible factors enhancing the nation's standing was the eminence acquired over the years by Sir Robert Menzies as a senior figure in British and American counsels. In London, by common consent, Sir Robert had become an honorary member of the Establishment, and in Washington he was held in high regard. Through him, and through those around him, the association with the United States, given formal recognition in ANZUS, came to be a real and meaningful partnership. The good impression created by the Prime Minister when, on his annual trips to the Commonwealth Prime Ministers' meetings in London he stopped in Washington for discussions, was backed up by the warmth of feeling that Americans—whether publicists, businessmen, administrators, or legislators—felt for the Australian nation; and this close identity gave added meaning to the formal pacts which bound the two nations.

The majority of Australians backed Menzies' strongly pro-American policies; but by the time of his retirement in January 1966 uneasiness was being expressed in some quarters that Australia had failed to maintain its essential identity in foreign policy. There was a persistent feeling that all too little had been done to foster the policy of Asian accord begun with such high hopes. The *Australian Financial Review* early in 1966 said that Australia, which in many ways was a young "developing" nation itself, should have a unique and useful contribution to make to "preventive diplomacy" in the Pacific, but insufficient had been done to develop this. Other comments were echoing the view that Australia's role should be more positive and more truly that of a bridge between the West and Asian lands. The importance of practical and constructive policies to further Asian development was stressed.

In fifteen years Australia had spent some £55 million on Colombo Plan programmes, and another £10 million on other aid projects to countries in the Asian region; but this was still less than 1 per cent of the total contributions of over £7000 million that had been made under the Colombo Plan by other countries. Questions were being raised both regarding the limited extent of Australia's contribution and the merits of the assistance provided. Meanwhile there was unanimous support for Australia's strong financial backing for the Asian Development Bank, set up in 1966.

After Menzies' retirement, the call was strengthened for a search to build better relationships with countries of the Asian continent and the western Pacific. Declaring that ANZUS was not enough in itself, the *Sydney Morning Herald* said the pact should be balanced by "a closer relationship and better understanding with our neighbours"; the time had come when Australia must treat the Asian and African nations as "equals, as friends, and possibly as allies." Menzies' successor, Harold Edward Holt, quickly made clear his personal interest in Asia, and confirmed this by making his first visit abroad as Prime Minister to countries of south-east Asia, including Vietnam and Malaysia, within a few months of his taking over the prime ministership in January, 1966.

Among journalists, academics, and others, a great debate was under way regarding Australia's military role in the years ahead. Political commentator Bruce Grant, writing in *The Times*, summed up the differing viewpoints this way:

> The opposing positions are taken by advocates of forward defence, on the one hand, some urging even greater Australian military intervention, and, on the other, proponents of what is called "armed neutrality." who argue that if Australia were able to defend itself it would not need to adopt a military position in the region.
>
> The debate cut across party lines, for although the Labor party has isolationist tendencies it is formally on record in support of ANZUS and, with qualifications, SEATO, and its disapproval of the presence of Australian forces in Malaysia has been lately concentrated not on the commitment itself but that it has been done without a public treaty. It does not follow that effective Australian self-defence would be cheaper or strategically more simple than the present piecemeal integration with Britain or America . . . [but] what is involved in the debate is that, whether or not Australian policies can be independent, they can be related more directly to national interest.

The prospects for creation of military policies on the basis of narrower national interest appeared remote. At the same time, Britain's declared intention to phase out defence forces in the Asian area brought to the surface a need to reassess defence and foreign policy and ways whereby collective security arrangements in the area might be developed. Prime Minister Holt made clear the government's long-range desire to develop a distinctive stewardship for Australia in south-east Asia rather than simply become heir to Britain's role. Australia was a foundation member, along with New Zealand, in the nine-nation Asian and Pacific Council, which met for the first time in June 1966; the body also had as members Japan, South Korea, Malaysia, the Philippines, Thailand and South Vietnam. Creation of the

Council enhanced prospects for regional cooperation.

Overshadowing all other considerations was the involvement Australia now had in the world power struggle, and External Affairs Minister Hasluck had brought this aspect into focus when he said that Australians could no longer read their national future except in the language of world politics. The Indian Ocean had become of as great strategic and diplomatic importance to Australia as the Pacific, underscoring the need to have a two-ocean policy in both foreign affairs and defence.

It was clear that new responsibilities lay ahead. Inevitably, as the United States assumed greater defence commitments in the Indian Ocean, taking over a growing share of Britain's role east of Suez, Australia's strategic significance would be further enhanced. Plans for an interdependent American-British defence system involving the Indian Ocean islands had been under development since 1964. By 1966 it was evident that, as the pivotal land mass in the integrated defence alliance stretching from Tokyo to Zanzibar, Australia would have an increasingly substantial role to play, in conjunction with American, British, and New Zealand partners, in a cohesive defence plan covering the entire hemisphere.

"Faster, wider, greater"   27

In Australia's economic life, the year 1960 was ushered in as a glittering and expansive climax to the 1950s. Steady growth in population of around 250,000 a year—half of the increases from immigration—was having its effect. The work force was rising by about 75,000 a year—twice the number of a few years previously. With improved training arrangements, workers were becoming progressively more skilled. More scientists and engineers were being trained, the graduation list running close to 900 in science and over 1000 in engineering in 1960. Gross national product rose 10 per cent in the twelve months to mid-year and was running at the rate of £7000 million a year. Export industries were prospering. Everyone who could work had a job. Salaries and wages were at record levels, business firms were reporting good profits, and money was circulating freely. Industry had been expanding with the encouragement of policies directed at creating a favourable environment for investment and enterprise, and capital had been flowing in from abroad at the rate of about £200 million a year. The nation's industrial achievement was impressive, and a new industrial maturity was being demonstrated. Output of coal, constantly lagging behind requirements in earlier years, had increased in the late 1950s as mechanization was extended; mine-owners had spent huge sums on mechanical equipment, and although the number of miners had declined, individual productivity and wages in the industry had moved up and a resumption of large-scale coal exporting was in sight. Meanwhile, the range of industrial production extended not only to ships and diesel locomotives but to such sophisticated products of modern technology as guided missiles, machine tools, transistor radios, and radio isotopes. With a new blast furnace at Port Kembla, the Broken Hill Proprietary company was producing 3,000,000 tons of steel a year, while great automobile plants were turning out a total of 20,000 cars and trucks a month.

Australia held an assured place among the great trading nations, and commercial links with the rest of the world were stronger than ever. There were more than forty international flights a week into Sydney as businessmen and other travellers were flying in from a score of countries. Representatives of Australian business and government were going out to sell the products of the factories, to initiate discussions on the sale of products, or to study industrial processes and factory management in leading manufacturing countries. The Jet Age had opened on the Pacific, slicing flight time on the San Francisco-Sydney route to less than seventeen hours. As part of the export drive in manufactured goods, Australian-built motor cars were being sold in sixty countries. Australia was putting a greater range of minerals into world trade than any other nation, and the volume of exports was growing steadily as new mineral wealth was being developed and vast new deposits uncovered. As a base for the expansion of new export strength, markets for food and fibre had remained sound. The Prime Minister declared with pride that no other country of comparable size or population was so busy building its future. At the same time, private firms were supplementing the work of official agencies in telling investors and businessmen abroad that Australia was the land of opportunity.

Australia was receiving attention in more quarters than ever before—and practically all the assessments were flattering. As part of the federal government's drive to expand export markets, efforts to promote Australia's products had been intensified wherever there appeared to be prospects for expansion of existing markets or the creation of new outlets. At the same time as an intensified publicity drive was being made in the countries bordering the Pacific and Indian oceans, a new dimension was added to efforts in Britain, Europe, the United States, and Canada by expanding from the promotion of products to a broader programme designed to interest manufacturing firms in setting up plants in Australia. The state governments, each anxious to attract new industries in order to augment activities and expand prospects in its area, had pressed Canberra to include the attraction of investment in its continuing publicity efforts abroad, and the Commonwealth agreed since it saw benefits, both in extending the range of local manufactures to replace imports and in attracting capital which would help produce a favourable balance of international payments.

Widely-circulated newspapers and magazines in world centres were giving their readers striking impressions of the "new" Australia seen to be emerging —a land of almost unalloyed prosperity and boundless growth potential. Australia was thrust into prominence for a large body of readers in the United States and other English-speaking lands when, in April 1960, *Time* magazine devoted twelve pages to a review of the country's progress and a portrait of Prime Minister Menzies appeared on its cover. In distinctive *Time* style, the report captured something of the excitement of a booming continent which was "no longer a backwater, but confident of its dynamism and independence," when it said:

Amidst the dry, gum-tree scrub of Rum Jungle, 60 miles inland from the Timor

Sea, miners clad only in boots and shorts drilled uranium out of soft shale. At Woomera, where the waterless South Australian plain stretches endlessly off the horizon, romantically named drones and missiles—Jindiviks, Blue Streaks, and Black Knights—soared over the free world's largest land rocket range. In beach-girt Sydney, schoolteachers and tram conductors exchanged stock market tips, and in stately Adelaide, where Australia's first major Festival of the Arts was in full swing, T.S. Eliot's *Murder in the Cathedral* played to capacity.

These—and the industrious bustle of a hundred once-sleepy towns—were tangible evidence last week of the biggest news to come out of the South Pacific vastness since the end of the war. The news: Australia, rawest and least favored by nature of the English-speaking countries, is savoring a real prosperity and discovering a national maturity.

Time went on to record the industrial growth that had taken place over the previous decade, noting that factory production had trebled and output of electricity had risen to two and a half times the level of ten years before, and that the population was increasing 2.5 per cent a year. Other leading publications struck much the same optimistic note, pointing out that a growing population and greatly expanded investment were reshaping the nation and its people just as surely as external forces were changing Australia's strategic environment.

Official agencies engaged in publicizing Australia abroad had stepped up their activities. Special supplements dealing with Australia were appearing in newspapers in world centres; Australia was participating in exhibitions and trade fairs, and publications dealing with Australian affairs were being distributed to businessmen and financiers.

Australian Profile, the government's handsomely-produced trilingual publication marking Australia's participation in the Lausanne exposition of 1960—a book designed for distribution to businessmen in Europe, Britain, and North America—documented the evidence supporting the expansionist view. After proclaiming that Australia was "on its way to becoming the United States of the Southern Hemisphere," the book went on to say that Australia was unique in its mixture of attraction for "both the adventurer looking for his fortune and the traditional investor looking for a sure and stable enterprise."

The motto the book carried was Faster, Wider, Greater: and in spite of vicissitudes and occasional setbacks, this bold objective was to be a pace-setter in economic affairs over the coming years.

The adventure of nation-building had come to hold a special meaning for Australians. There were growing pains, however. From 1959 there had been signs of a superheated economy; Australia was sharing in an inflation gripping all the English-speaking nations, and the special circumstances of accelerated development were intensifying the phenomenon locally. In many ways "development" was being turned into sheer speculative enterprise, for with soaring prices in the property market and on the stock exchanges there was an eagerness to invest and to speculate as local people and overseas groups outbid each other to buy property and shares. The fever was contagious.

Turnover of real estate and securities moved up to record levels. There was a surplus of funds available for lending at high interest rates for speculative enterprises, and this overwhelmed efforts by the Reserve Bank to keep down the investment rates charged for normal loans. Company raisings of loan money and share capital, and the expansion of consumer credit—both matters outside the banking system and beyond the control of the monetary authorities—had together created a new engine of inflation.

Consumer outlays were rising at a phenomenal rate—10 per cent or more a year. As the speculative boom and the unabated importing spree began to overshadow all other factors in the economic scene, the government found it necessary to change signals in order to dampen demand and put an end to spiralling speculation. It had been hoped that the upsurge in imports which followed the relaxation early in 1960 of all import curbs would soon subside in the face of mild monetary restraints imposed within the banking system. However, the volume had not eased after eight or nine months of importing freedom, and by that time a sharp rundown in overseas funds had occurred. There was the further worry that the inevitable break in the property-share boom would produce a major economic disturbance when it eventually came.

In an attempt to restrain the general inflationary pressures, the Reserve Bank issued a series of directives to the trading banks in May and again in August. The banks were specifically instructed to achieve a considerable reduction in their total advances; but the boom gathered pace.

In November 1960 the government moved to correct the situation; but instead of reimposing import controls, as many had suggested and even more expected, its counteraction was a series of hammer-blows under which bank lending was restrained, bank interest rates and bond rates were raised and company borrowings made unattractive, and the sales tax on motor-cars was raised to 40 per cent. Advances made by all trading banks were, by Reserve Bank direction, to be reduced—and virtually eliminated where the purpose was for "land and share speculation, for consumer credit, and for purely financial dealings." The reaction was sharp and the effect of the measures was quickly felt throughout the entire economy. Almost overnight, it seemed, the domestic boom was at an end.

The government was widely criticized for having waited so long to take corrective action, and for then applying such severe measures—described by one influential body as "a savage mauling of the money market." It was widely held that the import problem should have been handled as a separate matter and corrected by direct curbs. Further, it was almost universally claimed that the government's hand had been far too heavy, and that in moving to stop speculative features in the economy it had disrupted sound and desirable activities. Manufacturers, who had been making heavy investment in line with the government's earlier expressions of an expansionist philosophy for Australian industry, were loudest in their condemnation, pointing out that unless tariff levels were raised their competitive position would be destroyed against unrestrained importing.

The decision of February 1960 to open the Australian economy to imports had marked a major turning point, however, and the government took the view that it was up to Australian industry to meet the competition by becoming more efficient—and that those who failed to measure up to this could not expect to have special assistance. Provision was made for immediate tariff protection where any worthwhile industry was threatened, but generally some weeding-out was accepted as inevitable.

Part of the sharp downturn in industrial activity came as a consequence of cyclical factors. Sales in several fields had been running in excess of underlying demand, and an easing had been apparent in economic indicators even before the November measures were introduced. In the United States and elsewhere, a long cycle of business growth and inflationary expansion had similarly run its course, and inevitable readjustments were being made in all English-speaking lands at about the same time. Reaction in Australia was sharper because the preceding boom had been greater.

The ebullient mood that had gripped businessmen and politicians evaporated quickly as stocks piled up in warehouses and shops, production of goods fell sharply, share prices tumbled, and real estate became hard to sell. Building activity was severely affected, sales of motor vehicles were clipped, and the electronic and textile industries struck hard times. It was to be some time before the full magnitude of company failures arising from the speculative spree and unsound credit practices was revealed, but meanwhile many investors found their incomes curtailed and their assets sharply reduced. The over-full employment position had been replaced by a new situation in which the jobs available were well below the total applicants. The unemployment rate rose in April 1961 to 2.1 per cent of the work force. The Reserve Bank recorded the dilemma obliquely in its report which said: "The problem of reconciling external balance with internal full employment and high rates of economic growth remains a challenging one."

The government took the opportunity of an easier labour market to increase expenditure on public works. Some stimulus was applied to the economy in general by an easing of credit before mid-1961. With a large wool clip and a high level of agricultural production, the main export industries were recording solid growth (although manufactured products, apart from iron and steel, added little to the total). There was also a slight gain in Australia's terms of trade. By late 1961 the volume of imports was at more reasonable levels. However, the economy remained sluggish and conditions in the business world were highly competitive, so that even though volume picked up many businessmen complained of "profitless activity" and the unemployment problem remained. Recovery was slower than might have been anticipated—in part, because in many instances funds which might have been available for expansion, based on long-term prospects, were being employed to reduce indebtedness.

At the same time, concern was developing about both the short-term and long-term effects to Australia if Britain joined the European Economic Community. The Common Market issue grew rapidly to be a dominant factor in discussions related to the economic outlook; coupled with it, reduced rates of growth reported in the leading industrial countries of Europe, brought more sober assessments of prospects for Australian development.

Faced with unfavourable public reaction to the deflation measures, the government was fortunate to survive the vigorous Labor Party challenge in the election at the end of 1961. The state of the economy was inevitably the central issue; in its campaign the government pointed to its record over the years and claimed it could best look after Australia's cause in negotiations relating to the Common Market issue, while the Labor Party put forward a detailed programme for reducing unemployment and reinvigorating business and industry activity. Although it scarcely seemed likely that the A.L.P. could make up the leeway needed to win the election, sentiment showed a surprisingly strong swing against the government. In the voting Labor made marked gains in New South Wales (where the *Sydney Morning Herald* had come out strongly in favour of a change of government, unexpectedly supporting Labor's programme as "more in accordance with the country's immediate needs") and in Queensland, where unemployment was most severe. The Liberal-Country party coalition found its majority of thirty-two in the House down to only two, which was reduced to one after the election of a Speaker. Among those defeated were three members of the cabinet. In the Senate, the government had to rely upon the support of an Independent (who was a former Labor member in Tasmania), and the sole parliamentary representative of the Democratic Labor party. The government had underestimated the electorate's solid support for policies of expansion and growth, combined with full employment, and had failed to realize how firmly Australians in general were committed to a sound and prosperous manufacturing activity.

There could be no denying the implications of the vote. The government, determined not to allow Labor to regain the initiative, accepted the close result as being as much a warning as a rebuke, and at once set about the task of getting the economy out of the trough. Previously there had been close contact between representatives of government and business at various levels as part of the normal dialogue between businessmen and officials, but this contact had generally been limited to explaining government policies. In January 1962, the cabinet held a series of meetings with business and industrial leaders in order to strengthen its appreciation of the situation as seen by businessmen and experts outside government. A few weeks later, new steps to stimulate the economy were announced; they included a rebate in income tax, reduced sales tax on motor vehicles, and special grants to the states for public works to relieve unemployment. Monetary measures were directed towards reducing the retarding effect on expenditures arising from the heavy remaining indebtedness of firms and individuals. Banking policy was directed to making access to bank loans easier. The budget presented in August provided for deficit-financing to the extent of £118 million as a further stimulus to the economy.

In Australia's drive for industrial expansion, investment undertaken by British and American firms had long been of basic significance. From the mid-1950s the inflow of overseas capital and attendant technology had begun to gather pace, becoming progresively of greater importance. British investment continued to outrank all other, but the influence of American companies in the industrial complex was growing, while Canadian and European firms were adding to the lengthening list of enterprises directed from abroad or established jointly by overseas and Australian capital.

The government held out no blandishments to the incoming firms; instead it explained that firms from oversea suffered no disability since they were on an identical footing with Australian enterprises. For the overseas businessman, Australia's climate of political stability and fair treatment of business, coupled with a appreciation of the opportunities that go with an expanding economy, were sufficient attraction. Able to take the long-term view, large enterprises saw the advantage of establishing themselves in Austtralia and using the new plants to produce for the local market and sometimes for exports as well. In many cases the firms setting up production units in Australia already had a market for their products, so that the local manufacture became an "import replacement."

Overseas capital tended to find its way into the large undertakings demanding heavy investment and advanced or specialized knowledge. The new petrochemical plants, like the large refineries with which they were associated, were in many instances financed by international firms. Products included carbon black, synthetic rubber, polyethylene, and detergent alkylate, making possible a whole new range of products of wholly Australian manufacture. In automobile production, another field dominated by overseas firms, great sums were invested in setting up plants based on the latest mass-production techniques, and the total capacity of automobile plants was lifted sharply to more than 30,000 a month by 1963. An outgrowth of the technological advance arising from large-scale automotive production, the GM-H technical centre was opened in 1964 and its 800 engineers, designers, and technicians—who had at their disposal some of the world's latest equipment—began a continuing programme of technology and research.

Even in cases where there was no direct investment from abroad in an industrial enterprise, technical know-how was frequently secured under licence agreements with overseas organizations. The list of firms operating in Australia with some form of affiliation with one or more firms abroad grew steadily as the exchange of information was constantly expanded. Visits to the United States, Britain and Europe by Australian businessmen and industrial specialists, and leaders in scientific and technical fields, in order to study latest developments in their particular spheres, matched the visits of experts from abroad who came in as advisers to international concerns or at the behest of Australian affiliates.

Under the impact of this continuing two-pronged drive, Australian industry and business, all the way from minerals processing and machine-tool designing to advertising, was able to draw upon the most advanced technological developments. In the shortest possible time, Australia absorbed directly many of the gains that intensified research in applied science was bringing to the world's leading industrial nations. Australians were giving up their resistance to the introduction of more advanced production tech-niques even where mechanization might mean an immediate shrinkage in jobs, and job-change was being accepted as part of the price to be paid for a higher standard of living.

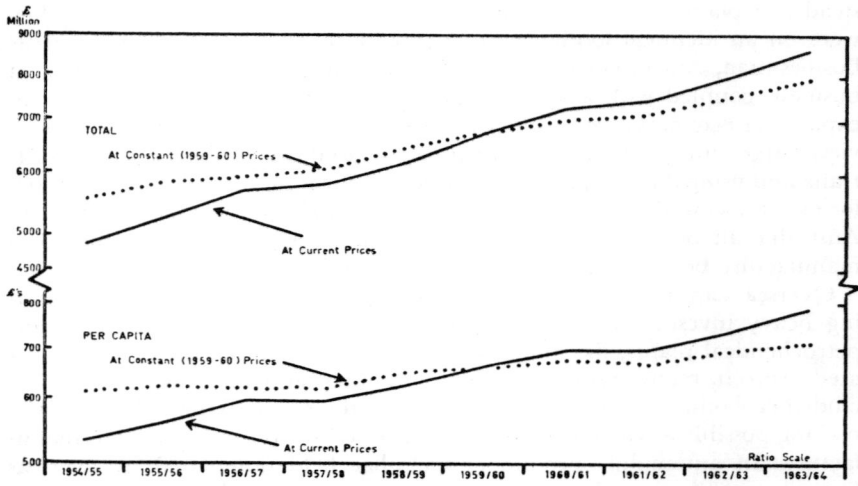

Rural Bank of New South Wales

Australia's Gross National Product, 1954–55 to 1963–64. When the effects of inflation are allowed for (by conversion of the "current prices" graph to "constant prices"), the rate of growth is seen to have averaged about 1.7 per cent a year, on a per capita basis, over the period.

In broader context, the community's attitudes had changed. The impact of an unprecedented advance of the frontiers of scientific knowledge was being felt. No longer was science being shrugged off; instead it was now accepted that Australia's special circumstances demanded that the best methods be adopted so that the nation might pursue its objective of pressing forward with the utmost speed on every front. Progress in science and tech-nology was assisted to a marked degree by active programmes under the control of the federal government. As well as scoring notable gains in applied research related to the rural industries, the Commonwealth Scientific and Industrial Research Organization was now giving greater technical support to activities in industrial fields; at the same time the brilliant and original work CSIRO scientists were undertaking (in conjunction with the University of New South Wales) in the field of radio astronomy was helping to gain a new stature for Australian scientific achievement. In 1964 the University of Sydney and Cornell University (of Ithica, New York) announced a plan for the pooling of equipment and research-technical staff in a joint venture in radio astronomy and cosmic ray research, providing for the largest concentration of astronomers and associated scientists ever assembled in an organization; staffs of both universities and postgraduate research students were interchangeable under this imaginative concept.

Perhaps most significant of all, under the Department of Supply scientific teams of the highest order had been built up; their work was in specialized fields, some related directly to sophisticated weaponry and others concerned with developments in satellite-tracking and the space probe as well as the conventional ordnance fields. The Weapons Research Establishment's activities, pivoted on Salisbury and Woomera, had grown and had become part of a great scientific complex for defence research and development with many international ramifications. The "back-room" work behind the more spectacular efforts in guided missile research and associated activities now involved activities in the fields of aerodynamics, kinetics, electronics and ballistics as well as relevant complexities within the wide ambit of chemistry and physics. Research and investigation, analysis and testing were being undertaken on an increasing scale and into an ever-widening range of subject matter. At the same time, skilled staffs, working with precision engineering equipment, were producing specialized equipments needed in such diverse fields as mining and metallurgical operations, telecommunications and electronics and transportation. In the strictly defence field, by 1965 government-owned aircraft factories alone had nearly 6000 employees, most of them engaged on the manufacture of the French-designed Mirage supersonic aircraft (which Australia decided in 1960 to adopt as its frontline fighter), the Ikara anti-submarine "homing" weapon system, developed for the R.A.N. and later adopted by the Royal Navy, and the Australian-devised Jindivik pilotless target aircraft (which was also being exported for use as a missile target in the United Kingdom, the United States and Sweden).

Active co-operation between Australia and the United States in the field of space research had begun in 1957 with the installation of satellite-tracking facilities at Woomera as part of the International Geophysical Year programme. Three years later the co-operative effort was extended; the object was to facilitate space-flight operations contributing to the mutual advancement of scientific knowledge "of man's spatial environment and its effects." As the United States space effort accelerated, a world-wide network of tracking-communication stations was created by the National Aeronautics and Space Administration (NASA) for the control of orbital flights; the Australian continent's geographical location "opposite" the United States gave it special significance in the tracking of globe-circling spacecraft. The installation at Muchea, near Perth, came into the news with Colonel John Glenn's historic three-orbit flight of February 1962; it was also involved in subsequent Mercury flights before being closed. A new location, nearer the Equator, was needed for the next phase of NASA's effort, the Gemini programme, and Carnarvon was chosen as the site; the new station became one in the chain set up around the world by NASA as part of the ambitious and complex project aimed at eventually landing a man on the moon. The first tracking was done from Carnarvon early in 1964, and the station was important in the Gemini rendezvous the following year.

As part of NASA's deep-space probe, involving ground stations for two-way communication with unmanned spacecraft travelling millions of miles on interplanetary missions, a special communication station was built in the Tidbinbilla Valley, about 25 miles from Canberra (to supplement a similar instrumentation facility at Woomera). Construction began in mid-1963, and soon the great disc-type antenna, 85 feet in diameter, was being tuned to spacecraft speeding through outer space. With Goldstone (California) and three other key stations around the world, Tinbinbilla and Woomera became significant elements of the communications system specifically designed to give continuous surveillance of space vehicles on interplanetary probes. A second station in the Canberra area (at Orroral Valley) was opened in 1966. At Honeysuckle Creek a further satellite communications unit, this one part of Project Apollo, was completed in the same year. From the beginning the stations were staffed and operated by Australians, with the assistance initially of American support personnel on special missions.

Australia was also involved in the European Launcher Development Organization (ELDO), established by Britain and five western European countries in order that collectively they might join the space club. ELDO decided to make use of facilities at Woomera for its experiments and for launching the communications satellites which it expected to have operating commercially by 1970. The first experimental launching was made from Woomera in 1965.

A changing pattern had become evident in Australia's trade in the late 1950s as Britain's prominence among buyers of Australian commodities was steadily reduced and other trading partners grew in importance. From being unimportant in the Australian trading picture, Japan acquired a greater significance after the 1957 agreements and Japan's purchases moved up 25 per cent or so a year thereafter.

Nevertheless, Britain remained the most important single importer of Australian products (taking about 30 per cent of all exports, by value), and questions relating to the national trading future came sharply to the fore in 1961 when Britain's decision to seek membership in the European Economic Community was announced. Unless Britain obtained suitable terms for entry into the Common Market Australia faced the danger of a substantial loss in export earnings. McEwen outlined the government's approach in a parliamentary statement in May 1962, when he said:

> No one could validly challenge Britain's right to join. Our attitude is to accept her application as real, to take in good faith her assurances that she would not join if the price was serious damage to Commonwealth trade, and, with these pointers constantly as the background of our thoughts, to proceed to propose constructively the kind of solution which would protect our trade.

Although Canberra accepted Britain's unquestionable right to join, the elimination of the system of British preferences was seen as a danger not only to Australia but to other temperate-zone lands associated with Britain as trading partners; in this context it was clear that damage to the economy of New Zealand would adversely affect Australia's prospects for sale of manufactured goods there. By mid-1962 Australia was voicing the deepest concern over the influence then being exerted by the United States Administration and some members of the European Economic Community to hasten an end to the system of British preferences. In London for discussion on the Common Market issue, Prime Minister Menzies said he believed that those in Europe and America who pressed too hard for the "doctrinaire" view that preferences must disappear before 1970, would have to accept great responsibility before history.

Concern over the economic consequences of Britain's action was most acute among those directly involved in the export industries, and within the federal government the Country party managed to dominate the coalition's policy on the Common Market issue, pressing for Australia to insist on the right of direct intervention in the negotiations related to the commodities involved. Some Liberal party members took a different view of the matter, believing that the seriousness of the likely effects on Australia was being exaggerated; but when he expressed such views publicly, one Liberal member of cabinet was forced (by Country party pressure) to resign. Those who gave emphasis in their assessment to broader implications of Britain's move admitted that the Australian economy might have to undergo quite marked change, but they believed that by accelerating its development and moving into new forms of production the country would still be able to prosper. However, few could deny the seriousness of possible short-term consequences; for, although Australia's economy was no longer a colonial one highly dependent on Britain as an outlet for its products, Australia's whole economic structure continued to rest on its ability to sell large quantities of raw materials or semi-processed products abroad at satisfactory prices and in rising volume. Under these circumstances, economic troubles arising from trade disruption could imperil the nation's stability and its over-all development.

Success already achieved in spreading the pattern of Australia's export trade encouraged hopes that new markets could be developed, particularly among countries bordering the Pacific and Indian oceans, with special emphasis on New Zealand (as a market for manufactured goods) and Japan (as a buyer of wool, foodstuffs and minerals). An unremitting trade expansion drive had been under way for some years, with the federal government, through its trade commissioner serivce, commissioning market surveys in all likely areas as backing for more intensive promotional efforts. As the export drive intensified, existing offices were expanded and additional offices opened Exporters were urged to step up their efforts and export incentives in the form of special taxation concessions were added to the more basic protection provided to Australian exporters through the government-sponsored Export Payments Insurance Corporation. Trade groups of various types, from book publishers to manufacturers of medical equipment, were encouraged to pool their efforts in promotion, advertising and representation abroad.

Early in 1963, France's action in blocking Britain's bid for admission settled the Common Market issue for the moment at least. By this time, the likelihood of Britain's eventual inclusion in the European trading bloc was accepted; but this prospect could now be viewed as a far less threatening prospect as far Australia's trading future was concerned. Japan, where outstanding gains in economic development had been made in the 1950s, had meanwhile moved up to a position of virtual equality with Britain as a purchaser of Australian products; furthermore, the volume of Japan's buying was growing strongly while Britain's purchases were barely steady. In 1963 the Australia-Japan commercial agreement was revised. In the year to June 1964 exports to Japan rose 40 per cent to a total value of £244 million and—to the surprise of many—Japan moved up to become Australia's best customer for wool as well as for sugar, hides and skins, coal and copper ore and concentrates, and number two customer for other important export items. In this record export year Britain's purchases also rose; but over-all they barely topped Japan's, and their value was below that in some earlier trading years, while Communist China displaced New Zealand as Australia's fourth-best customer (mainly as a result of big wheat sales). At this point, one third of all Australia's exports went to Asian lands.

Optimistic forecasts on still further expansion of trade with the Asian area, and particularly with Japan, were being voiced in many quarters. By now the Japanese government was showing concern about the persistent deficit in trade with Australia—imports from Japan had risen but still remained comparatively low compared with imports from Britain and the United States, which had been rising steadily—and special efforts were made to lift Japans' exports to Australia. In the year to June 1965, Australia's sales to Japan eased, while purchases from Japan rose sharply, but a considerable trade gap remained in Australia's favour. Suggestions that a closer balance should be struck were countered by fears that a considerable segment of Australia's manufacturing industry would be endangered. As it was, a three-way trade between the United States, Japan, and Australia was providing its own balance, since the United States ran a deficit in its trade with Japan but had a surplus in its trade with Australia; this meant that Japan's surplus in dollar trade could be used to help pay for imports from Australia, whose trade with the dollar area seemed to be in permanent imbalance. Australia's deficit on trade with the United States had risen from about £40 million in 1958 to over £130 million by 1964; as Britain's share in Australia's exports dropped from 27 per cent to 20 per cent and the proportion of imports bought from Britain declined from 35 per cent of the total to 27 per cent, the significance of Pacific trade became more marked. Over the years, the shift in Australia's trade pattern had been quite striking,

Special factors had prompted the growth of exports to Japan and China, and pessimists could say that in the highly-competitive markets represented by other trading partners in Asia, Australia had only "a tenuous foothold."

Australia's External Trade Showing the Share of Australia's Exports Taken by Various Countries and the Origin of Australia's Imports.

Country to which exports sent	1949–50		1956–57		1964–65	
	Value	Percentage	Value	Percentage	Value	Percentage
	(£000)		(£000)		(£000)	
United Kingdom	237,526	38.7	277,550	27.9	258,113	19.5
Other Sterling Area	129,346	21.1	191,812	19.3	276,984	20.9
United States	49,644	8.1	66,111	6.7	134,220	10.1
Canada	9 048	1.4	10,681	1.1	19,957	1.5
Common Market "Six"	114,015	18.6	232,583	23.4	192,869	14.6
E.F.T.A. (exc. Britain)	11,606	1.9	10,103	1.0	16,136	1.2
Japan	23,974	3.9	139,010	14.0	220,370	16.6
All Other	38,538	6.3	65,455	6.6	207.076*	15.6*
Total	613,697	100.0	993,305	100.0	1,325,725	100.0

*Mainly wheat to Mainland China

Country from which imports originated						
United Kingdom	278,748	51.8	296,251	41.2	380,706	26.2
Other Sterling Area	81,534	15.1	126,623	17.6	174,128	12.0
United States	52,232	9.7	95,544	13.3	346,178	23.8
Canada	13,276	2.5	22,157	3.1	58,503	4.0
Common Market "Six"	33,079	6.2	67,505	9.4	172,618	11.9
E.F.T.A. (exc. Britain)	14,650	2.7	29,472	4.1	66,792	4.6
Japan	6,999	1.3	12,884	1.8	129,287	8.9
All Other	57,551	10.7	68,555	9.5	124,140	8.6
Total	538,069	100.0	718,991	100.0	1,452,352	100.0

In spite of limited population—at least forty nations could claim larger populations—Australia ranked twelfth among the world's trading nations; and by this time there were few countries to which Australian products did not go. Export income showed solid rises, aided by slightly higher exports of manufactured products and steadily expanding minerals shipments. Exports were equivalent to about 14 per cent of gross national product each year, imports about the same. Cyclic movements in the balance of trade were still a troublesome factor; but after the long slide in commodity prices was halted in 1962, good seasonal conditions in Australia's pastoral and agricultural areas combined with increasing efficiency in rural industries to bring about bumper crops which were sold at satisfactory prices. Sheep numbers were still moving up and the annual wool clip was almost 1,700,000,000 lbs; but the wool clip's proportion of Australia's total export earnings was now less than the 50 per cent or more maintained over the 1950s—a reflection of the trend to greater diversity apparent in Australia's exports.

In 1965 Trade and Industry Minister McEwen, reviewing what he called the exciting progress of Australian efforts to move into world markets, acknowledged the "vigour and enterprise" applying to exporting by manufacturing industries. Australian manufacturers, he said, had been the "new boys" in many world markets but they were now moving fast towards maturity as worldwide traders. Although accounting for less than one-eighth of total exports, manufactures were important not only because they contributed £150 million a year to overseas earnings but because they were "secure exports not subject to the sharp fluctuations and gradual decline in price with which many primary products have had to contend."

In international trade relations, important negotiations had been started. In the "Kennedy round" of tariff discussions a concerted attempt was being made to break down the long-standing barriers to world trade in agricultural products. Australia was anxious to see "realistic and equitable solutions" to these problems, and supported the setting up of special groups to consider grains, meat and dairy products. In stressing the need for "meaningful negotiations" on these matters, the government was aware that satisfactory solutions could go a long way towards improving the prospects for Australian trade far into the future.

After prolonged negotiation, an agreement was reached for the formation of a free trade area between Australia and New Zealand; this came into operation in January 1966. Items making up about 60 per cent of the total trade between the two countries were covered by the arrangement, which made it possible for the goods to be traded duty free, while at the same time each country continued to maintain separate tariffs on imports from countries

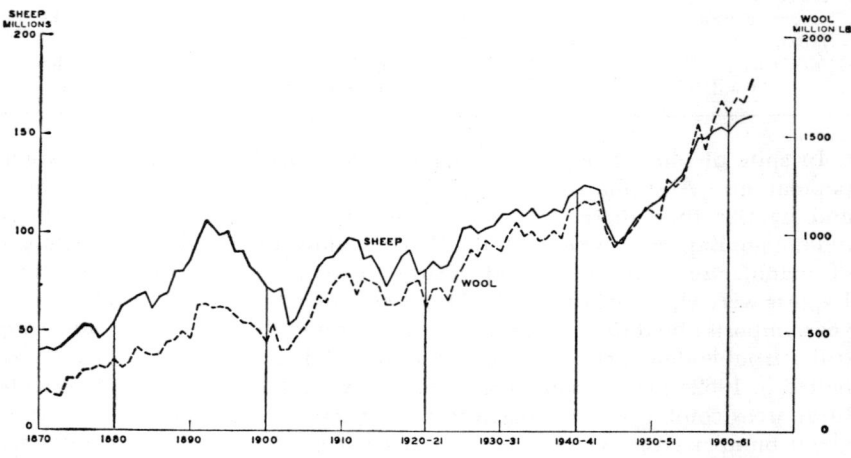

Commonwealth Bureau of Census and Statistics

Sheep numbers and wool production in Australia, since 1870. Over the period there has been an almost uninterrupted improvement in average fleece weight. Drought has been the major cause of the occasional shrinkages in sheep numbers.

outside the agreement. Creation of the two-nation free trade area was seen as a forward move which would help promote a sustained and mutually beneficial expansion of trade.

Meanwhile Australia was doing its best to assist the less-developed countries of the world—the countries of Africa, Asia and Latin America, many of them still struggling to create viable economies above the subsistence level. In 1965 Australia took a significant lead in positive and practical steps towards assisting these lands by offering preferential import duties for a wide range of their rural products. McEwen, sponsoring this action, said that Australia was only too familiar with the problem of earning enough from exports of primary products to pay for the imports needed for development; everything done to assist the trade of the developing countries would not only help these countries on to their feet, but would benefit developed countries by expanding markets for their manufactured goods.

Riding the commodity boom which was in evidence from 1963, Australia was moving to new levels of prosperity. Once again there was virtually full employment, and family incomes were higher than ever before. Consumer prices were steady, personal savings had reached a new high, and large-scale developmental undertakings (including road-building and power projects) continued. Immigration had been stepped up, and there was an upturn in private investment. The index of factory output was showing improvement. Throughout 1964 rising export earnings accelerated the expansion induced by earlier measures designed to overcome businessmen's hesitancy; and a buoyant situation quickly developed. Stock exchanges reflected quickened business activity and general optimism. With the announcement by the Arbitration Court of a rise of about 7 per cent in the standard minimum wage content of all award wages (equal to about a 4 per cent over-all rise in all wages) the economy had reached a point where the government became concerned that some braking measures were necessary. Monetary measures, including a rise in interest rates, were introduced to hold the economy on a steady course. Backed by record export earnings of £1,400 million, gross national product for the year to mid-1964 showed a rise of almost 10 per cent; and although this growth quickly slackened, the economy remained in high gear.

American firms and the American public were now showing deeper interest in Australia than ever before. Magazines and news media again turned the spotlight on Australia, seeing in the great open spaces of the country a vision which seemed to re-create the limitless opportunity that the United States had itself represented in earlier days. The message of the laudatory reports and articles splashed through many American publications was that Australia was at last breaking out of its cocoon, and that it had an entirely new dimension as a result of the discovery of unsuspected natural resources in incredible abundance. An article in the *Readers's Digest* declared that the curtain was just rising on "the Cinderella story of the century": the sudden emergence of Australia into a position of dramatic wealth and a shining

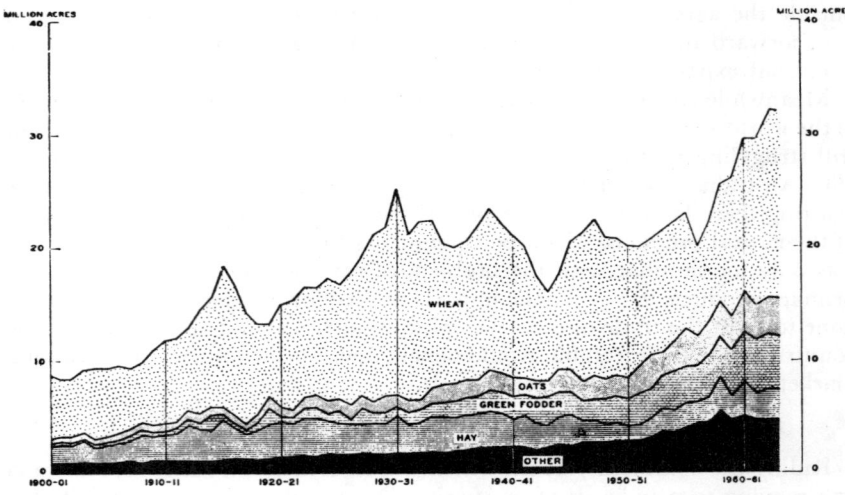

Rural Bank of New South Wales

Graph showing area of crops planted in Australia since 1900–01. Wheat has held its position throughout as the most important grain crop, but since the early 1950s its dominance has steadily lessened.

future. The island-continent had recently unearthed "what seem to be limitless storehouses of some of the most valuable resources on earth," the magazine reported, and it would take a great influx of people to cope with upcoming developments. Other leading magazines and newspapers told a similar story, one offering a warning in the bold headline, "Don't Dig a Hole in Australia Unless you Want to Get Rich." The trickle of new settlers from the United States, growing steadily over the years, was increasing noticeably; close to 2000 Americans arrived in 1964. An officially-sponsored United States trade mission visiting Australia that year found that the economy was buoyant and the Americans were being invited to share in a market that was "rich, prosperous, growing, up-to-date, modern," and with tastes and preferences often following American patterns. The mission's report added that Australians were asking for United States products and participation in industrial and other activities.

Interest in Australia had also strengthened in Britain; reports that flooded British news media during and after the six-week visit of Queen Elizabeth and Prince Philip early in 1963 spoke of Australia in glowing terms, and inundated Australia House with applications from prospective migrants. The waiting list for berths to Australia reached 100,000. The buoyant economy was also attracting British trade interests, and the following year a spectacular exhibition was staged in Sydney as a showcase for British wares and developments. Some 400 companies, either British or Australian-with-British-interests, were represented in the grand display—the most elaborate ever presented to promote British trade. Coinciding with the exhibition, an "action council" for Australian-British trade was formed with the object of preventing a further decline in trade relations between the two countries, and to strengthen and improve mutual understanding.

By 1965 there were signs that the discipline being exercised over the economy by various government-inspired measures (fiscal and monetary) was reaching new levels of effectiveness. Transition from recovery to stability had been accomplished. Some commentators considered that the "management" of Australia had been so effective that the economic state of the nation was almost ideal.

However, some established ideas on national development were being seriously challenged by the impact of events beyond Australia's control. First, out of a basic re-evaluation arising from the situation in the south-east Asian powderkeg came a new realization that development of resources could not be a simple substitute for formal defence preparedness. For twenty years or so, the belief had prevailed that Australia's security could best be served by building up population and industrial strength and (over a shorter period) by forcing development in the continent's empty northern reaches, and Australia had slipped through on minimum defence budgets; but in the face of new and tangible dangers, greater emphasis had to be given to the defence establishment. As part of the adjustment, there was now less official support for widely held hopes of accelerating the establishment of rural undertakings in the tropical regions and establishing centres of population there; in fact, the Prime Minister made it clear that any large-scale federal support for "northern development" was out of the question for the time being.

Early in 1965 a more fundamental engine of expansion seemed likely to falter when a slackening in overseas funds for investment was threatened. Private overseas investment had reached a point where it represented about one-quarter of all private investment in industries; and it was important not only in providing the spur to large-scale developmental projects but also as a significant contribution to Australia's international liquidity.

The danger that this inflow of capital might be staunched arose as a result of official curbs placed on company outlays abroad (and calls for increased repatriation of profits) by both the American and British governments; and although there had been a tendency for some Australians to complain that overseas money might one day "take over" Australian industry, the prospect of withered investment from the two main sources of overseas capital quickly brought a new appreciation of how important this capital (and attendant technology or "know-how") had been in the nation's accelerated growth.

Restraints on overseas investment by American and British firms were being imposed because of the international payments deficits which both Washington and London faced. The British balance-of-payments problem had reached a point where only an emergency loan prevented a sharp devaluation of the £ sterling, while Washington was grappling with an equally disquieting dollar drain. There was little Australia could do to seek modification of the British decision to curb investment; as the largest single holder of sterling funds, Australia of necessity had to support measures essential to maintain sterling's strength. The same factor did not apply in Australia's relationships with Washington, however, and the government decided to make a special plea to the United States administration for less rigid application of the new American rules so far as Australia was concerned. In a letter to President Johnson, the Prime Minister pointed to the heavy commitments Australia had undertaken and the basic need to maintain a strong capital inflow if development and defence requirements were to be met. In reply President Johnson promised to review any particular case that might cause difficulty.

A seminar dealing with Australian development and trade, bringing together Australian and American trade and business-investment leaders, was held in New York at this time. The consensus among the American participants was that while there might be some temporary easing in the United States capital inflow to Australia, American interests would be awaiting the opportunity to resume a strong flow of investment capital.

Even as some consumer-supplying industries were finding times more difficult, an important new phase of mineral development for Australia was beginning in two of the states that had been largely passed over in earlier phases of industrial growth—Queensland and Western Australia—as ore deposits of extraordinary size were surveyed, and plans completed for their development. The search for oil in these States had also produced tangible results. One commercial oilfield in southern Queensland had been brought into production and another was on the point of commercial production, while at Barrow Island, off Western Australia's coast, reserves of commercial proportions had been proved, dispelling an old myth that Australia was without petroliferous deposits capable of commercial development. Natural-gas fields, some of them associated with oil deposits, had also been discovered at many points on the continent and in Bass Strait, off the Gippsland coast.

The lifting in 1961 of the blanket law prohibiting export of iron ore had brought a rush of American firms to stake out and develop newly revealed deposits. Experts had verified iron-ore deposits of staggering proportions (at least 15,000,000,000 tons) in the Pilbara region of Western Australia. The existence of iron ore in the remote hinterland had been discovered by accident in the late 1950s when stationowner-cum-prospector Lang Hancock chanced upon the great deposit in the Hamersley Ranges; but Hancock had kept the discovery to himself. In 1956 another prospector, Stan Hilditch, working quite independently, found some rich outcrops of hematite in the east Pilbara, but he too kept his secret. Talk of mineral deposits was in the air in Western Australia before long—a great bauxite deposit had been surveyed in the Darling Ranges—and reports of iron ore deposits in the Pilbara district drifted into the Mines Department in Perth. In 1961 the Western Australian government called tenders for the development of a deposit at Mount Goldsworthy, north of Hamersley Range, and after that the discoveries made by Hancock and Hilditch came to light as a rush began for iron-ore leases. As American mining companies joined with Australian firms to survey the area, one of the centres of greatest activity was Mount Tom Price—the richest of all the deposits uncovered in the investigation of Hancock's original find.

The great minerals search had also revealed the existence of some of the world's greatest bauxite deposits. These were located around the northern coastline (on Cape York Peninsula and in Arnhem Land) and in the west, and were about to be brought under active development. Copper from the great copper-ore body at Mount Isa, in western Queensland, was now being refined in Townsville, while bauxite from Weipa was to be treated at Gladstone, where a huge refinery was being built to produce 600,000 tons of alumina a year for export. On the remote Arnhem Land coast, over 400 miles east of Darwin, an alumina plant to process bauxite from the Gove deposits was planned; the operation would ultimately support a local population of at least 3000. Discoveries of extensive deposits of base metals in western Queensland and the McArthur River area of the Northern Territory, and of manganese on Groote Eylandt, suggested that the region around the Gulf of Carpentaria would eventually prove to be a great mineral treasure-house. There were also many significant mineral discoveries in other areas of the continent and in Tasmania.

Contracts were completed between mining companies (all at least partly American-owned) and Japanese steel interests for the export of 300,000,000 tons of raw or pelletized iron ore from the Western Australia deposits over a twenty-year period, and work began in 1964 on installations necessary to handle the ore—a task made more difficult because of the lack of facilities in the remote Pilbara district.

Great investment outlays were needed to develop the various iron-ore mines; it would be necessary to construct complete townships, to lay a number of short range-to-coast rail lines, and to install handling and port-side equipment. The funds were being drawn largely from abroad, but returns from the sale of ores would help underwrite a steady growth of Australia's export income for decades to come. By early 1966 thousands of men were working on the iron-ore projects, and exports of ore to Japan were beginning. Eventually, it was aniticipated, this phase of development would settle at least 15,000 people in the area; and beyond that, their contracts provided that, after twenty years the companies must submit to the Western Australian government proposals for the establishment of local iron and steel industries.

In all more than 100 major mining enterprises, many of them involving large-scale investment from abroad, were opening unsuspected riches.

While minerals development would add significantly to the future of both Western Australia and Queensland—together covering more than half the continental area—extensive land development projects in the same states were already providing new strength. A steady expansion of agricultural output in Western Australia had been achieved largely through the conversion of vast sand-plain and other areas with the use of soil additives, while in central Queensland a start had been made on the spectacular "brigalow lands" development for the reclamation of a huge scrub zone in the Fitzroy River basin (covering in all 20,000,000 acres) into rich pasture and crop land.

Throughout the community, the need to sustain economic development at the highest possible level had become a widely accepted objective; but the question remained of how this might best be achieved in the light of the resources available and the limitations that applied. Discussions, investigations and reports related to the issue showered the scene throughout the early 1960s, but the great debate remained unresolved at the time of Sir Robert Menzies' retirement early in 1966.

Underlying most of the discussions was a feeling that opportunities were being missed, that some of the zest had gone out of the drive, and that the country should be tackling its developmental tasks to greater effect.

Throughout, there were two divergent views on the developmental process held within government. Backed by an expansionist philosophy in his department, Trade Minister McEwen pressed the viewpoint that where a choice must be made between policies of economic stability and growth, it was wiser for Australia to choose expansion; but this approach was countered by the Treasury, where the risks inherent in overstretching Australia's resources were stressed and inflation arising from expansionary policies was seen as certain to cause grave problems in the long run.

However, there were more fundamental reasons for a national stocktaking on matters related to expansion and ways of meeting the increasing claims on resources. Economist Sir Douglas Copland outlined these in *The Adventure of Growth* (1960) when he said that development

> . . . may yield its full fruits with less error if it operates within the framework of a well co-ordinated plan on a national basis, a plan to which the community as a whole is pledged, and of which it is conscious. It is true that the idea of a plan in a free community is at a discount, but the course ahead for Australia is now clear, and many of the facts that will determine the rate of development can be clearly stated. We have to reconcile the supposedly conflicting interests of the Commonwealth and State governments, of primary and secondary industries, of the public and private sectors of the economy.

The same point was made later by economist Sir John Crawford when he said that it was the prime task of management in private enterprise and of government to establish "permanent machinery for closer working relations in the effort to find those solutions which seem best to fit with the national interests of Australia."

In 1963, when the economy had almost fully recovered from a two-year recession, the expansionist gusto of the late 1950s was still absent and there was a widespread feeling that something must be done to avoid the need for a "stop-go" approach in national policies. Questions were being asked in many quarters about the relative value of various types of "developmental" undertakings; where a balance might best be struck between expansion of public and private undertakings; whether greater investment should be made in rural as opposed to urban activities; the level at which consumer demand might be held; whether government-sponsored development was as economically sound as it was claimed to be, and scores of other aspects.

The Australian Development Research Foundation, set up by a Sydney businessman, commissioned the Stanford Research Institute, of California, to undertake a study of the possibilities of attracting settlement to undeveloped areas and to suggest a programme of action appropriate to this problem. Late in 1963 the report, written by the distinguished Australian-born economist, Dr John Bell Condliffe, was released; it covered a broad canvas—the development problem of Australia as a whole—and it brought to light many unresolved issues. The report pieced together and analyzed facts, opinions and ideas; it went on to diagnose difficulties facing Australia in its efforts. It stressed that underlying issues must be studied, and that "situations should not be dealt with piecemeal on a year to year basis"; rather, they should be approached as "integral parts of a national programme looking to the future rather than the past." The report recommended that a national development council drawn from leaders of industry and commerce be established as a fact-finding body able to sift plans and recommend priorities to the states as well as the federal government.

Canberra had already set in train a major inquiry into the economy which, in the Prime Minister's words, was intended to "provide a chart or prospectus of Australia's economic potential to show the extent, capabilities, and limitations of Australia's resources." Three leading businessmen and two distinguished economists formed the committee, which met under the chairmansip of industrialist Sir James Vernon. Terms of reference required the committee to keep in mind that the objective of the government's economic policy was a high rate of economic and population growth, with full employment, increasing productivity, rising standards of living and stability of costs and prices. The committee was invited to survey practically the whole economy, including matters relating to the work force, basic physical resources, investment (both local and overseas), import-replacement production and the effects of the tariff.

After two and a half years of investigation the Vernon committee completed its report. The committee considered a 5 per cent annual growth in the gross national product a "reasonable goal," and proposed this should be a planned objective; it was predicated on an average yearly gain in national productivity of 2.3 per cent and on a projected annual increase in the work force of 2.7 per cent. It suggested that the net intake of immigrants should be limited to 100,000 a year, at least up to 1970, and it held that overseas investment should be on a more selective basis and that capital inflow should not exceed £150 million a year. Decisions taken by the Commonwealth Conciliation and Arbitration Commission should fully take into account the economic and industrial consequences, the committee considered; price stability was central to the commission's work, and "capacity to pay" should be interpreted as capacity to pay higher wages without inflationary consequences. The committee also concerned itself with the matter of co-ordination of economic policy. In this field it considered that a "special projects commision" should be set up to advise the government on urgent developmental works, and that a permanent Economic Advisory Council was needed to review growth and long-term prospects annually.

By the time the Vernon committee's report was completed, the cold economic winds that had influenced the government to initiate the inquiry had long since abated and Canberra was no longer admitting any institutional weakness in the management of economic affairs. Accordingly, at the very moment of its release in September 1965, Sir Robert Menzies launched a strong parliamentary attack on some of its major proposals. His attitude came as a surprise, since the committee had been careful to reject the idea of far-reaching economic planning and "target-setting" (which it clearly considered concepts inapplicable to the rugged and untidy Australian environment), and had stated categorically that the complete elimination of "stop-go" in the economy was an impossibility. Nevertheless, the Prime Minister made it clear that he considered the committee had exceeded its charter by offering opinions or sugestions on matters of policy, and he said flatly that no government could abdicate its authority and responsibility for framing national policies. Dismissing the proposal for a permanent economic advisory council, Sir Robert said that no Australian government could hand over to bodies outside the government "the choice of objectives and the means of obtaining them in important fields of policy, particularly when such bodies would, through the power of publication, come to exercise ... a coercive influence upon government." As some commentators pointed out, the Prime Minister did not go on to explain how he reconciled these objections to an advisory council on economic growth with the advisory role of the Tariff Board, or what it was about Australian democracy that made it incapable of accommodating institutions that worked effectively in the United States, Canada and Britain. However, spokesmen for groups close to the Liberal party soon made it clear that the concept of a council of economic advice was unacceptable because such a body would tend to introduce a rigidity in economic thinking and a doctrinaire approach.

Even though the report was destined to be pigeonholed in Canberra, its release and initial airing set in train a new round of discussion of the general problem of economic development. There were many points at which the report might be criticized, but the consensus among commentators suggested that, no matter what the report's fate, in the world of post-Keynesian doctrine it was in fact up the to government to set and make known clearer guidelines to future economic policy.

Broadening   28
horizons

Economic objectives had come in large measure to cluster around the central purpose of achieving accelerated growth—a concept springing from the premise that Australia could establish a firmer basis for future security and make a proper contibution to defence alliances only if the national economy continued to expand and new wealth continued to be created. A whole range of subsidiary objectives stemmed from the pursuit of the central theme. Maintenance of a high growth rate involved a steadily increasing population; this implied a continuing high immigration rate, which in turn depended basically upon job opportunity for immigrants. In a world of expanding prosperity, desirable immigrants were attracted not by jobs alone but by high living standards, so that steady improvement of living standards had become not only something to be desired for its own sake but also a national objective.

Broad acceptance of the aims of maintaining an expanding economy and a rising standard of living did not mean that there was political unanimity upon the measures best calculated to achieve them. Nevertheless, acceptance by the Liberal-Country party coalition of the policy of full employment and accelerated growth—which had been the basis for the programme of national expansion initiated by the Labor government in the 1940s—had helped to narrow the gap between the two main political groups on domestic issues. There was, in fact, a greater divergence on matters related to the rate and nature of "national growth" between extreme viewpoints held within both Labor and Liberal-Country party groups than between the main body of opinion existing in the two opposed political groupings. The Liberal party, adopting views closely related to those held by Treasury officials and the rest of the financial establishment, had come increasingly to follow cautious economic policies which gave great weight to the need to hold inflationary tendencies in check and so maintain economic stability. By contrast the Country party pressed for a more adventurous line of policy, proposing that in cases where a choice between "growth" and "stability" was involved the need for expansion should take priority, particularly if the project would contribute to growth in an area away from the main cities. The A.L.P. was also in favour of rapid and vigorous development, but generally the party wanted to see projects of a basic developmental character given even greater emphasis; the party believed that water conservation, road building, school construction, and other public undertakings deserved attention ahead of some types of commercial expansion.

In his wide-ranging review of the current political and social scene, *Labor's Role in Modern Society*, A.L.P. Parliamentary Leader Arthur Calwell declared that for a "young" country Australia's economic growth was not fast enough, and accordingly he called for more consistent policies of development, based on a greater degree of planning "on the national level." He proposed preparation of a four or five year plan for economic development of resources after consultation and discussion with representatives of private industry, so that definite growth-rate objectives could be worked out in the basic sectors of the economy and specific targets laid down for particular areas.

In its disciplining of the economy, the Liberal-Country government in the 1950s and 1960s held consistently to the policy of drawing off, through taxation, sufficient money to maintain a high level of public investment in the expansion of great public utilities without creating a heavy load of debt to be met in the future. In all, the outlay on public works ran to about half that undertaken by private business enterprise on fixed capital investment; the public sector covered such important and basic aspects as water supply, irrigation, railways, roads, power, housing, and provision for education and health services.

In the same way that most companies and businessmen prudently retained a good proportion of their profits for investment in expansion, the bulk of the capital expenditure (75 per cent) on public works was met from current revenue—that is, through taxation or by ploughing back for expansion part of the revenue received for services rendered. In the twenty years to 1965, the total public authority expenditure on public works was £8,589 million but the net increase in the public indebtedness of all public authorities over the period was kept down to £2,180 million.

The federal government had been steadily increasing its role in matters related to education. The first formal body had been created in 1943, when the Universities Commission was set up under National Security regulations to organize post-war education and training for ex-service men and women.

The Education Act of 1945 gave permanent form to the commission and also established the Commonwealth Office of Education, which became the central co-ordinating body for Australia's contact with the world educational body, the United Nations Educational, Scientific, and Cultural Organization. Subsequently, the stimulus provided by UNESCO's broad plans combined with developments within Australia to bring new influences to bear on the entire educational scene. As its commitments under the rehabilitation programme tapered off, the federal government established a general scholarship system. Grants to universities and to scientific bodies and awards of thousands of scholarships annually to enable selected students to undertake higher studies, were important features of the growing federal involvement.

Education in general remained a responsibility of the state governments and more than one-quarter of all state expenditure was devoted to education in some form. The school system had to develop rapidly to meet the needs of an expanding population and the special demands of an education-seeking generation. Reflecting the high birthrate of the war and post-war years, the total number of students rose steadily by about 100,000 a year in the late 1950s to reach 2,000,000 in 1959, and there was considerable pressure on the various school systems.

Government schools, for their part, took care of 76 per cent of all school-goers, and outlays by the public authorities responsible for education more than doubled in seven years. By 1960–61, overall expenditure by public authorities was approximately £150 million. With outlays for education in nongovernment schools added in, the total cost of schooling was about £200 million a year, equal to 3.4 per cent of the gross national product (compared with less than 2 per cent in 1948–49). However, this percentage was still relatively low.

Owing to the consolidation of a number of small schools (often with one teacher only and sometimes with less than twenty pupils) into a single central school of perhaps 200 to 400 pupils with seven to fourteen teachers in many country districts, and the establishment of an extensive bus system provided at the public expense, the total number of primary schools increased only slightly, despite the large number of additional primary schools that were established in all metropolitan areas and in the larger country towns. The number of secondary schools however rose sharply as aggregate enrolments increased explosively—often from 10 per cent to 15 per cent annually for several years in succession. These heavy increases in secondary enrolments were due in all states not only to the much larger numbers entering the first year of secondary courses but also to the striking increases in the proportion of students who remained at school beyond the age required by law. In spite of considerably larger numbers of enrolments, the ratio of students to teachers in government schools remained substantially unaltered. However, in the case of non-government schools there was a significant increase in the student / teacher ratio from 26:1 in 1953 to 29:1 in 1958; in large degree the ratio change reflected the strain placed upon the Catholic school system by immigration from Europe.

Australia still held tenaciously to the principle of equality in educational opportunity. It had been accepted as a cardinal rule that children living in the sparsely-populated areas should receive educational facilities as nearly as possible equal to those of children in the cities. Since the early 1950s a unique system of instruction by two-way radio—the School of the Air—had supplemented the comprehensive system of education by correspondence, providing means whereby children living far from the main centres might gain knowledge and develop intellectual capacity in the same way as those living close to well-equipped city schools. In 1966, ten schools-of-the-air operated in conjunction with the two-way radio facilities of the Flying Doctor service reached children spread over 1,000,000 square miles of the Outback. In spite of special problems, illiteracy had been reduced to vanishing point.

Since World War II, the concept of equal educational opportunity had been extended to mean that some years of free secondary education should be available to all children. With advancing prosperity and wider appreciation of the benefits to be derived from additional schooling, the percentage of pupils who remained to complete a full secondary school course moved up sharply. This was in line with a trend apparent in all advanced countries; but the percentage of those who stayed to complete the course was still well below that in the United States and Canada (though greater than the proportion in Britain).

Another aspect of the modern interpretation of the concept of equal educational oportunity was that all types of school, and all school subjects, should be regarded as equal, without implied bias in favour of university-oriented schools and university-oriented subjects. In sympathy with this concept there was a trend in some states towards re-organizing secondary education by developing what came to be called comprehensive schools—a singularly inept title—in which students could follow any one of several different paths or tracks instead of requiring all to follow the courses which were designed to lead to matriculation and entry upon university studies.

In some states, however, and notably in South Australia an extensive alternative system of schools was developed from 1945 onwards. These schools were intended to cater for boys and girls who had no intention of proceeding to university studies and provided a wide range of alternative courses in craft subjects of all kinds as well as such basic subjects as English, History, Geography, Mathematics, and Science. Moreover, the courses in these subjects were constructed quite differently from the corresponding subjects prescribed for the public examinations and were designed to meet the educational needs of non-academically inclined students.

It was generally conceded that the Australian emphasis on "fair average quality" in education had disadvantages to balance its advantages. The continuing centralized form of administration, in which education in all its details was managed from a state's capital city, combined with the fact that three out of four of all teachers were trained in state-run teachers' colleges, resulted in uniform standards and an acknolwledged thoroughness in education; but by the second half of the twentieth century there was little evidence that educational authorities were seeking to strike out along new paths. If experts reviewing the over-all effect of the system were inclined to stress this aspect, they conceded a considerable achievement in the lifting of primary and secondary education standards; the general system had been fashioned around the needs of the community and so far had grown more or less in conformity with those needs—even if a more enterprising approach might be called for in coming years.

Technical education was still far behind the best offering in overseas countries; the apprenticeship system of on-the-job training could no longer be regarded as adequate, and there were few colleges of note. The state governments acknowledged that there was a shortage of qualified teachers, that some accommodation was makeshift, substandard, or obsolete, that there were shortages of equipment, and that there was a need for rationalization of technical institutions.

Throughout the post-war years the demand for university education was far higher than ever before. Returned servicemen had been encouraged to take university courses and those who qualified were offered financial assistance in order that they might do so: the influx sharply increased the numbers attending university. Thereafter high enrolment levels were maintained as a result of a number of factors, including the higher post-war birth rate, the immigration programme, an influx of students from Asian lands and, above all, the wider appreciation of the value of tertiary education in a time of ever-higher living standards. With advancing prosperity, from the mid-1950s enrolments of new student moved up about 10 per cent a year, so that the total number attending universities rose from 30,000 in 1955 to more than 50,000 five years later. By 1964 total enrolments exceeded 76,000 of whom about 30 per cent were women. Expenditures increased even more sharply, moving from £12 million in 1955 to £53 million in 1963.

The increased demand for university education in the 1950s had posed a challenge to governments and university administrators. Pressure on accommodation and staff had increased, classes were overcrowded, library facilities were inadequate, and laboratory equipment was obsolete. The emphasis in most of the universities remained on the preparation of students for a particular profession, and the fundamental interests of those students remained that of passing the necessary qualifying examination. A dearth of honours students and a lack of postgraduate study remained to be overcome. A committee under the chairmanship of distinguished scholar Sir Keith Murray was set up by the Prime Minister in 1957 to investigate the situation and recommend remedies; the committee's report was to become the charter for future university development. Emergency federal grants over a three-year period were proposed by the committee, and in November 1957 the Prime Minister announced acceptance of this plan and of the committee's further recommendation that a permanent advisory body be established.

In 1959 the Australian Universities Commission was created; its function was that of advising the Prime Minister on the financial requirements and the balanced development of tertiary education. Its forecasts of university enrolments into the late 1960s were well in advance of the Murray Committee's projections, reflecting the newly enhanced demand by industry for graduates in science and technology and by the teaching profession and governmental and managerial services for graduates in arts. By the mid-1960s the proportion of higher-degree students had risen sharply; there were ten times the number of the early 1950s.

All aspects of tertiary education were investigated by a committee set up in 1961 under the chairmanship of physicist Sir Leslie Martin. The committee's report, containing recommendations to the Universities Commission, was presented in August 1964. The committee found that the total enrolment in Australian tertiary establishments (in 1963, 60,000 in universities, 15,000 in teacher-training colleges and 34,000 in technical and other institutions) was likely to increase to about 250,000 by 1975. It recommended changes in the training of teachers and proposed that the standards in teacher-training colleges be raised. In engineering and technological education, Australia was found to rank very low in terms of university graduates, and in an attempt to bring better order into technical and other non-university education the committee recommended the creation of an Institute of Colleges in each state; such an organization would be a means of bringing together various existing institutions, whose scope could be expanded, it also proposed that the Australian Universities Commission should be moulded into a body with responsibilities in all aspects of tertiary education.

In commenting on the Martin Committee report, Prime Minister Menzies left it up to the states, if they wished, to act on the proposals for teacher training and creation of boards of technical education, and he rejected outright the idea of an expansion of the role of the Australian Universities Commission. Later he undertook to find £24 million over a three-year period to help develop the colleges, provided the amounts were matched by the states. The view of most educationists was that the absence of a federal initiative put an end to any hope that Australia might be on the threshold of a transformation of higher education in terms of quality, variety, and flexibility.

By the 1960s it was clear that the revolution in secondary education—arising from the greatly increased number of young people wanting a secondary education—had created a financial crisis, which was complicated by the financial relationship between the Commonwealth (holding the purse strings) and the state governments (responsible for administering their education systems). In 1961 the first combined call for federal assistance in general education was made by the state education ministers. It took the form of a special report calling upon Canberra to provide special grants to tide them over until a committee of inquiry assessed future needs. At the federal-states meeting of 1962 the premier of New South Wales, speaking on behalf of all premiers, said that it was realized that the task of providing adequately for the expanding needs of education was beyond the financial capacity of the states, and he declared that the stage had been reached where the problem had to be looked on as a national one. In reply the Prime Minister outlined the extensive assistance given to the states in education matters through tax reimbursement grants, provision of loan funds and other ways, as well as through indirect assistance provided to parents in allowing education costs as deductions under tax laws, and he turned down the states' request for assistance, saying that he could not accept financial commitments in primary, secondary and technical education. However, late in 1963, after a further submission from the states, a change came about, and in anticipation of the year-end election Sir Robert Menzies promised £10 million in federal funds as an aid to the teaching of science in secondary and technical schools, and said that up to £2,500,000 would be made available for secondary school scholarships. The A.L.P., not to be outdone, also promised federal assistance to the states for educational purposes and undertook to create a federal ministry of education and science. The Liberal Country party proposals—duly implemented after electoral victory—were far below the amounts asked for by the states to overcome their main problems, but they represented a new type of federal commitment.

They also represented a significant change in political attitudes towards the hoary issue of government grants-in-aid to independent or denominational schools, since these schools were eligible for the science-aid grants. Opposition to any form of government aid for such purposes had been a feature of the political life of the country since the passage of the "free, compulsory and secular" education acts of the 1870s and 1880s; although from time to time Catholic leaders had urged upon state political groups the merits of a revision, the issue remained in the background. The post-war crisis in state-run educational systems was felt with no less severity by the Catholic school system, where the development of secondary schools had closely followed that of the state secondary schools; between 1945 and 1956 enrolments in Catholic schools rose by over 60 per cent.

The broad issue of state aid for denominational schools was a pressing one for Catholic voters. In 1951 the A.L.P. federal conference adopted an ambiguously-worded declaration proposing "assistance to all forms of education." Traditionalists within the party insisted on giving the clause its narrowest possible interpretation and they resisted pressure to expand it; nevertheless the federal executive in 1952 ruled that the assistance was meant to apply to denominational schools. "State aid" remained a contentious issue which helped widen the split within the party; members of the group which subsequently became the D.L.P. strongly advocated the strengthening of A.L.P. policy to embrace the principle of providing federal funds for the expansion of non-government schools, while the majority of the party adamantly maintained opposition. After the D.L.P. breakaway of 1955, the A.L.P. rescinded the 1951 "assistance" clause. As a separate party, the D.L.P. consistently pressed the issue, particularly at the federal level, intensifying its campaign in the early 1960s. With more than 500,000 pupils (more than one fifth of the school population), Catholic schools had truly attained the stature of "a seventh system of education," rivalling in scope the states' systems. In twenty years the number of pupils had more than doubled; in some places the overflow from Catholic primary schools had to be accommodated in state schools.

The break on state aid came when Sir Robert Menzies in his policy speech before the 1963 election made it clear that private as well as government secondary schools would be eligible for their share of the annual federal grant to establish school science laboratories. Although during the election campaign Labor invoked the traditional rejection of any form of "state aid," many who had formerly upheld that view felt constrained from opposing such a limited and nationally desirable proposal as a science-study subsidy. After the government's electoral success, however, it was apparent that a new principle had been established. The *Sydney Morning Herald* was among the newspapers that stressed the significance of the move; in an editorial it conceded that if the Menzies government had benefited from "a change in the allegiance of Roman Catholic voters" as a result of its new policy, it was equally clear that the old battle against state aid had been lost since the undertaking had been "approved or condoned" by the mass of the government's regular supporters. The newpaper warned of the possible quicksands into which the political parties might be led, and added:

> Now that direct aid is an accomplished fact it can only be kept within bounds by public insistence that any proposals by a Government or a political party must, as a first requirement, be specific enough in relation to their effect upon the proper care of the established system of secular education.

The A.L.P. was still opposed to government assistance for denominational schools at either federal or state level, and the issue remained a thorny and electorally-dangerous one for the Party. In 1965, when the issue came up during the Party's federal conference, only the New South Wales branch delegates were in support of reversing the policy. The first suggestion of science grants for all schools had come from the party in New South Wales in 1963, and the state branch was inclined to attribute A.L.P. losses within the state at the 1963 federal election, as well as its reversal in the 1965 state election—in which it lost office for the first time in twenty years—to the inflexible stand on state aid. Subsequently a crisis was precipitated in the party's federal parliamentary leadership when Deputy Leader Whitlam came into collision with the thirty-six man federal executive, still firmly opposed to the party's involvement in support of state aid. By 1966 it appeared that in deference to the trends of public opinion (as expressed in Gallup poll results) the Labor party also was moving towards adoption of some forms of state aid. Already most state governments were giving substantial indirect aid to denominational schools, usually in the form of free transport for country pupils, scholarships, the training of their teachers, and subsidies for interest payable on building loans. The Queensland Government had been making financial grants on a student per capita basis to church secondary schools for a number of years.

The leisure-time energy and interests of most Australians were still given over largely to sports activities; but as well as maintaining a predilection for the outdoors and the competitive challenge on the playing field, increasingly

Australians were balancing this with an interest in serious subjects and offering greater encouragement to the arts. Cultural activities were still limited to widely separated capital cities, retarding the advance; but writers who came from abroad in the 1960s to report on the Australian way of life expecting to find only the old hedonistic attitude usually felt compelled to record that Australians had built up a lively culture in which creative activities were no longer being ignored or sublimated and there was wider appreciation of literature and the performing arts. Adelaide's biennial Festival of Arts, first held in 1960, provided a challenge to larger cities; in 1962 a writer in a national magazine declared that Adelaide's successful effort had "dealt another blow to that national image of the Australian as the amiable yahoo."

In the search for a homogeneous culture, the Australian effort, with roots going back over three generations or so, appeared to have come of age by the 1960s. Basic to the achievement was an enlargement of horizon. The inspiration of the great outdoors and man's struggle to win a living from an often unwilling land was still discernible, but broader and more sophisticated themes were being added, and the cultural effort in general was no longer dependent for its inspiration upon the secluded distinctiveness of the Australian bush. The old reliance on caricature rather than competent delineation of character was being replaced. Australian literature was now acknowledged to possess qualities which set it apart from the mainstream of English writing, and it was substantial and important enough to be studied in universities in Europe as well as in Australia, while the new affluence and the community's wider appreciation of art supported a growing circle of painters and sculptors whose work reflected a vigorous new approach. Young artists of promise might expect to sell paintings at first showing, and banks and insurance companies, which previously put store in the solidity of marble, were commissioning murals and groups of statuary.

In literature, the range and volume of talented and perceptive work increased steadily. The crop of war-theme stories dealing with campaigns in which Australians had been engaged was practically exhausted by the mid-1950s, and the blue-skies-and-cattle phase had also run its course. Popular taste was being conditioned to more substantial themes and more penetrating writing; an Australian background was no longer considered sufficient, and, as one observer wrote, Australians were "no longer so bemused by the miracle of their rapid emergence from a colonial cradle."

The enlargement of horizon was prompted in many quarters and shaped by various factors; the outsider's view of the local scene was having its effect and Australians who had spent time abroad were seeing their land in a new light. After settling in Australia, English-born writer Nevil Shute (Nevil Shute Norway) introduced local settings for some of his popular novels, but he was writing more for American and English readers than for Australians. Sydney novelist Patrick White, who had spent some years abroad, was the first to show a modern intellectuality. His *Tree of Man* (1955) and *Voss* (1957), both set in Australia but using universal themes—the mysterious hidden poetry of humdrum lives in the *Tree of Man*, the heroic tragedy of an uncommon man in *Voss*—won high praise from the critics abroad, particularly in the United States, and his reputation was sustained by *Riders in the Chariot* (1961). On his return to Australia, Morris West ignored Australian subjects in *The Devil's Advocate* and other best-sellers which he wrote for a universal readership in the early 1960s. John O'Grady, writing under the pseudonym Nino Culotta, won outstanding success in Australia with *They're A Weird Mob*, an impish story of a young Italian-born journalist-cum-builder's labourer and his struggles to resolve bewildering contrasts between textbook English and Australian slang. Other novelists, while often showing far greater technical skill than earlier writers, usually appeared to be working with one eye on the prospect of adaptation of their stories for film-making, and they failed to produce books of more than passing interest; but the quality of the "average novel" had improved. Excellent short stories were also being written—among them were many outstanding examples by Hal Porter; the extensive collection, *A Bachelor's Children*, revealed the fine polish of Porter's writing technique.

Interest in non-fiction was reflected in an improved quality of writing and a greater diversity of books dealing with various aspects of the Australian scene. Writers were assisted by the Commonwealth Literary Fund (which by the mid-1960s had £33,000 a year to disburse). Serious but lively biographies, books of reminiscences and essays, well-constructed economic and social studies, and penetrating books on numerous phases of Australia's history and development were appearing in profusion. The awakening of interest in things Australian was reflected also in the prices being paid for Australiana and in such ways as the formation of National Trust societies and local historical associations, the publication by the South Australian Public Libraries Board of facsimile editions of important historical works long out of print, and the appearance of facsimile editions, reproduced with great care and fidelity, of early newspapers of Sydney and Hobart Town.

The merit of Australian writing was now being appreciated as never before in both the United States and Britain, where its appeal was in part a reflection of the increasing attention being accorded Australia as a land of surpassing interest. The most widely read of the non-fiction writers was Melbourne-born Alan Moorehead, who had lived abroad since the 1930s; in *Cooper's Creek* (1963), based on the tragedy of the Burke and Wills expedition, he maintained the standard of excellence which had established him in the front rank of non-fiction writers in the English language.

In poetry, the range and quality as well as the vitality of the Australian effort had been arousing interest. In the academic revaluation and revival, Alec Derwent Hope had been a leading figure. A realist frequently holding humanity up to ridicule and contempt, Hope contributed a considerable volume of poetry to the literary magazines before it was collected in book form; his first book of verse, *The Wandering Islands*, appeared in 1955. Also prominent in the academic group—each of whom struck out on distinctive lines—were James McAuley, whose poems ranged from subjects drawn from Greek mythology, and some satirical writing, to the epic poem *Captain Quiros* on the Spanish navigator's search for Terra Australis, and Vincent Buckley, whose *New Land for My Family* linked the quest for the earthly paradise with the dreams of Australian immigrants in general. Other notable poets of the post-war period included Max Harris, Douglas Stewart (whose *Fire on the Snow*, 1944, had first revealed his consummate skill), and Nancy Keesing. Lyrist Judith Wright won acclaim for her mastery of technique combined with richness of imagery; in *The Bullocky* she showed a depth of feeling for the country which sprang from her family's experiences as pioneer pastoralists and at the same time created an aura around a legendary Australian figure. The work of Kenneth Slessor and Robert FitzGerald continued to reveal the rare gift each possessed for imparting colour and creating imagery. Some of the young writers were establishing reputations for first-class poetry.

Literary magazines, including the quarterlies *Meanjin* and *Southerly*, had been important influences on taste, and their encouragement of original writing and penetrating criticism had been especially significant at a time when mass circulation media ignored such work. From its inception in 1940 as *Meanjin Papers*, *Meanjin* helped to give direction to the quickening of national imagination; its editor, Clem Christensen, made the magazine a crucible from which an important phase of the nation's cultural development might be cast. The magazine struggled through its early years, and relied largely on indirect support from the University of Melbourne and, later, from the federal government. Setting literary excellence as the only criterion, Christensen followed the rule of publishing the best available literary work, irrespective of the locale of its subject matter. Over the years the magazine was able to exercise an influence comparable with that of *The Bulletin* two generations earlier. From the late 1950s, the paucity of serious newspapers and journals was alleviated by the appearance of two fortnightly journals devoted to subjects of political and cultural interest: *Nation*, which remained vigorous and independent, and the *Observer*, later amalgamated with *The Bulletin*—which, after the merger, developed a more penetrating approach to the arts in general. At the same time, the literary magazines were widening their scope, and new publications were appearing.

In painting, values had undergone quite sharp change. For long Australia had lagged far behind the rest of the world, pundits and public alike persisting in glorification of the painting of gum-tree landscapes, when in Europe and America modern art had outgrown the impressionist style and outlook. In Australian art circles, the slow and belated transition to modern techniques, which gathered pace in the 1940s, was strongly resisted; yet steadily, artists who had returned after study abroad, and others who had absorbed evidence of more advanced art trends, set new standards and, painting in the modern manner, were able to express their own distinctively Australian personalities and produce something at once subjective, Australian, and of high quality.

The great clash between Australian art traditionalists and newer forces came in a startling manner in 1944 with a legal challenge to an art award. The case arose when two artists took court action to upset the judging panel's award of the Archibald prize for portraiture to William Dobell (who had returned to Sydney in 1939 after ten years spent abroad). The challenger claimed that

Dobell's winning entry showed a degree of distortion which made it a caricature rather than a true portrait, and that it was therefore ineligible; but the court upheld the art judges and Dobell retained the prize. Dobell was by no means a "modernist"; yet at the heart of the controversy was the new subjective approach to painting which he personified. Supporting Dobell were all the younger painters who were groping for new means of expression and in opposition were the exponents of established but dying tradition. The controversy and widespread publicity that the court case aroused did much to enhance public interest in art matters; newspapers not only carried regular columns of serious criticism but also devoted considerable attention to art as news. Dobell, appalled by the publicity, for a time gave up painting altogether, and his later work lacked something of the exuberant satire of his early canvasses. He had little direct influence on his contemporaries, yet his reputation continued to grow and his paintings were eagerly sought at increasingly high prices. He continued to attract attention and win acclaim not only for portraiture but for landscapes and for paintings capturing the strangeness of New Guinea and Asia.

A greater freedom had come to the Australian art world from the 1940s; the way was opening for originality and a new insight among Australian painters. At a time when Australians were concerned with self-definition it was natural that painters should share in the search for national self-expression, and that those of them whose work most strikingly interpreted the national character and the environment that shaped it should attract great attention. What was perhaps surprising was that these artists should win equal acclaim overseas. In opening a comprehensive exhibition of Australian paintings exhibited at Whitechapel gallery in London, art historian Sir Kenneth Clark said in 1961 that the sudden appearence of an Australian school of painting was "one of those blessed events which help to free the arts from the iron grip of historical determinism." In 1965 art reviewer William Gaunt, writing in a supplement on the arts in the Commonwealth published by *The Times*, declared:

> There can be no doubt that Australian artists have made a brilliant and even a unique contribution to modern painting. Substantially, it is the product of the past twenty-five years. During that time there has been a great surge of artistic energy and many gifted individuals have come to the fore. Those who have followed their work have experienced the exciting feeling of witnessing the birth of a national school.

Gaunt acknowledged Sidney Nolan as "the great exemplar" of the post-war artists who were opening new art horizons by capturing the spirit of the Australian environment in "a style responsive to the fascinating strangeness of the scene." Nolan, who began painting outback landscapes and Melbourne urban scenes in the early 1940s, first attracted attention for his series of twenty-five pictures developed around Ned Kelly as a bushranger; he moved to Sydney, where he painted more landscapes and extended the series on colonial legends and history before moving to London in 1953. He concentrated on extreme simplification of expression and, in his own words, "dug into Australia's past to find myths that explained the present." His later work included series on Gallipoli and Antarctica.

Others who gained international acclaim for the sharpness of vision and energy of execution of their work included Russell Drysdale, whose attenuated figures added drama to the astringent ochre-red inland scenes, Arthur Boyd, painter of mysterious allegories in a dark and tangled bushscape, and Albert Tucker, whose recurrent symbol was the "antipodean head," a hatchet profile, rocky and scarred and eroded. In their own ways both Drysdale and Tucker expressed the pioneer's struggle for survival in the harsh environment of a new land. Drysdale was considered by most of his contemporaries to be the most genuinely Australian of all; he saw the harsher Australia of drought and erosion. Drawing upon the myth of the Great Australian Loneliness, Drysdale in the 1940s captured the spirit of the back country in "Man Feeding His Dogs" and "Man Reading a Newspaper," with isolated figures set in a vast bare landscape, and he followed these with three other widely known pictures: "The Countrywoman," "The Drover's Wife," and "Woman in a Landscape." In his later work the Aborigines of the extreme north became symbolic figures, barely distinguishable from the totems and trees and fire-red rocks of their tribal land. Donald Friend, Charles Blackman, Ian Fairweather, Leonard French, Clifton Pugh, and Godfrey Miller were prominent among the three score or more new artists whose work maintained vitality and quality.

There was a "lingering kind of colonial patronism" in some overseas critics' evaluation of Nolan, Boyd, and Tucker as the national exemplar, in the view of Chris Wallace-Crabbe, writing in the *Observer* in 1960. Wallace-Crabbe was not surprised that these artists had received such acclaim overseas; their myth-making Australianism made them more acceptable than other equally valuable and original artists because they had come to be accepted as "the guaranteed National product." He considered that Australians should resist the European—and particularly the London—account of what Australian art *ought* to be like; in all the arts, he wrote, English commentators loudly demanded that the Australian product should be crude, vital, stark, sardonic, and nationalistic, but this was in fact a demand that "the (probably surburban) backwoods artist should concern himself with cattle-duffers, overlanders, kangaroos, gibbers etc., which typify the pioneering society from which (by definition) he comes."

As popular interest grew in art in many different forms, additional commercial galleries were opened and exhibitions of painting, prints, sculpture, and ceramics were held more frequently. By the mid-1960s about a hundred commercial galleries were catering to the demand; most were in Sydney and Melbourne, but they were also to be found in other capitals and in provincial centres. Their rise accelerated the decline of the old exhibiting societies. The art dealer was now a more active force in the art world, giving direct support to artists in a way new to Australia. Close to £1 million a year was being spent in art purchases, the great bulk on new work and most of that Australian in origin. Meanwhile, new art contests had been added to the great Sydney trio, the Archibald, Wynne, and Sulman prizes, judged simultaneously, and Ballarat's Crouch prize; other cities and many smaller centres established regular competitions and an increasing list of business firms introduced handsome awards. The expansion of awards, while not always pleasing to established artists, was an effective means of encouraging young artists; at the same time the widespread publicity attending the contests helped in awakening public interest.

In the performing arts, Australia continued to produce people of outstanding talent, but the old tendency for such people to seek greater opportunity abroad had barely weakened. In the 1950s and 1960s, Australians thrilled to the scintillating success won in the world's great opera houses by Joan Sutherland, and in 1965 opera-goers accorded the prima donna a tumultuous welcome when she returned home, after fourteen years abroad, as the star of her own touring company. There was also acclaim for the achievements of other Australians whose names studded operatic programmes at London's Covent Garden and Sadler's Wells and at European opera houses. The success won in London in 1957 by Ray Lawler's *Summer of the Seventeenth Doll*, followed by Richard Benyon's *The Shifting Heart*, awakened hope that Australia was about to produce distinctive drama. However, the initiative abroad was barely sustained. Alan Seymour's *The One Day of the Year*—with its universal theme, the conflict between the generations, set against a specifically Australian situation, the celebration of Anzac Day—did well in several European capitals, but had a mixed reception in London.

In the main cities drama was being kept alive in professional repertory or "little" theatres. The success of Lawler's play had broken down local audience prejudice against Australian plays, and from the time of its first startling success such theatres as the Union and St Martin's, in Melbourne, and the Independent, in Sydney, had provided a stage for Australian plays as well as for experimental or controversial work from abroad. The drive and enthusiasm of Doris Fitton (the Independent), Brett Randall (St Martin's), and Alan Sumner kept intellectual theatre alive. Adelaide's Festival of Arts encouraged Australian playwriting; the Adelaide University Theatre Guild staged Patrick White's *The Ham Funeral* (1960), *Season at Sarsaparilla* (1962), and *Night on Bald Mountain* (1964). In commercial theatre there was little support for any productions but the established successes of London or New York; and although the Elizabethan Theatre Trust offered some encouragement, the tendency was increasingly towards support of the performing arts as such rather than the creation of a non-imitative national theatre.

Ballet had gained a considerable following. Colonel De Basil's ballet companies in the 1920s and 1930s had first awakened interest; this was extended when ballet companies were formed by Edouard Borovansky and Helene Kirsova (touring artists who had remained in Australia) in the 1940s. During the 1950s interest was heightened by the visits of leading figures of the ballet world as guest artists, and although many of the most promising of local performers joined companies abroad the standard of performance improved consistently. The Borovansky professional company won an enthusiastic following in all state capitals and in New Zealand; after Boro-vansky's death in 1959 its direction was taken over by English dancer, Peggy van Praagh, who in 1962 became the first artistic director of the Australian Ballet Company, a national company and advanced ballet school formed with government support. Van Praagh was joined in 1965 as co-director by dancer-choreographer Robert Helpmann (who had returned after thirty years or so in London). In 1965 the company's performance of Helpmann's *The Display* at the Baalbek festival was hailed as brilliant. The company made its London debut in the Commonwealth Festival, appearing at Covent Garden opera house, and went on to appear in Europe and the United States.

In its British appearances, the ballet company was accompanied by the Sydney Symphony Orchestra, the oldest of the symphony orchestras which had been developed by the Australian Broadcasting Commission, with state, government, and municipal support, in each of the state capitals. These orchestras had developed from studio broadcasting groups of the 1930s, and by the 1960s they together provided hundreds of concerts a year. Resident and visiting conductors of world standing helped build up the quality of the orchestras, whose performances attracted large and discriminating audiences. Sponsorship of a youth orchestra, music scholarships, and special concerts for children and young people were other ways in which the A.B.C. helped develop music talents and appreciation. Concerts were also sponsored on a large scale, and tours by eminent soloists from Europe and the Americas arranged; throughout the year an average of three recitals a week was given by A.B.C.-sponsored artists.

Hopes that television might offer scope for Australian-produced entertainment were dashed from the very moment of the introduction of television in 1956. By that time the world, and particularly the United States, knew a great deal about the medium, and expensively produced programmes were available to Australian stations at low cost. The temptation to use imported material was so great that Australia did less than any other country to present programmes reflecting its own way of life, and although government spokesmen declared that the importation of American productions could not be allowed to continue to the detriment of Australian productions, the American content steadily increased. Early in 1960 the government directed all stations to devote at least 40 per cent of transmission time to Australian programmes; however, the prescribed quota meant very little since there was no stipulation about the type of programme that could be used to fill the quota; sports coverage and trivial or routine programmes from afternoon quiz shows to late night folk concerts qualified in the same way as serious or creative material. Subsequently a writer in *The Times* declared that prime viewing hours on Australian television were still choked with "refuse from America's cultural wasteland" and unrelieved by "some pretty beastly British comedies"; all the commercial channels seemed to ignore the potential of Australian drama, and the Australian Broadcasting Commission managed only about two locally written plays a month and two serials a year. The writer went on to deplore a situation in which children were getting to know more about the topography of Manchester or the history of the Wild West than the folklore of Australia.

A searching inquiry into ways of encouraging Australian productions for television was conducted by a Senate select committee in 1963. The committee found that although almost 40 per cent of the transmission time of the ten commercial stations in the main cities was taken up with material of Australian origin, drama represented less than 1 per cent of the locally produced programmes. In its report the committee pointed out that the A.B.C., although doing much more for drama than the commercial stations, spent about six times as much on music as it did on drama, and it urged that "a more balanced proportion" be struck between the two, adding that a great many more of the productions from the professional theatre could be converted to television. The committee expressed concern tht the A.B.C. and the Broadcasting Control Board (the body exercising over-all authority in all matters of programme content) appeared to accept a situation in which the proportion of Australian drama in relation to imported drama was so low and "the even more inadequate" proportion of telecast drama written by Australian authors. The committee said that until drama was made the subject of a special quota within the over-all quota the industry would continue to ignore "its most significant deficiency" in programming. In 1965 more than three hundred people with an interest in the industry attended a congress in Sydney, held to discuss television in the light of the Senate committee's report. The meeting considered that some form of protection should be given local television producers so that they might compete against programmes available from the United States at minimum cost.

In film-making the record was only little better than in televison, since after early initiatives Australia had fallen back to a position of almost total dependence on imported films. As part of an effort to capitalize on the distinctive Australian landscape and outdoors tradition, there were various attempts in earlier years to set up a local film producing centre as an offshoot of British or American productions, and though memorable films based on Australian subjects like *The Overlanders* (1946), *On the Beach* (1959), and the *Sundowners* (1960)— as well as many less memorable—were made under these conditions, no real Australian cinema emerged.

Even in documentary film production, the story was disappointing. Stimulated by a rapid build-up of interest in documentary films in the early 1950s, some distinguished work was done in the days before television by both privately sponsored units and by the federal government's film division. The Shell Oil Company's production, *Back of Beyond*, was awarded the first prize for documentaries and also the grand prize for all categories at the Venice film festival in 1954. After this, documentary film-making declined; to a large degree the difficulty was that the greater rewards to be earned in television had drawn away most of the competent men or occupied existing facilities. Even though the national film unit expanded, the National Film Board (created in 1945) in drawing up the official film production programme found it necessary to give increasing weight to a wide range of limited-purpose films for specialized departmental uses, with the emphasis on utility, and obviously this further cramped the outlook of official film makers.

By 1966 well over 2,000,000 people from abroad had settled in Australia during the preceding twenty years. About half of all the new settlers were British (including Maltese, who numbered some 50,000); next in order were the Italians (about 12½ per cent of the total), Greek and Dutch (each about 6 per cent), German (4 per cent), and Polish (3 per cent). Others included Yugoslavs, Russians and Ukrainians, Hungarians, Austrians, and Spaniards, and minor groups from Lithuania, Estonia, and Latvia and from Czechoslovakia. A small percentage had come in from Asian lands, including some thousands of Chinese. The numbers coming in from the United States, although small, grew steadily.

Figures prepared by the Immigration department listed 50.9 per cent of arrivals as "workers," with the remainder dependants. A preponderance of males (about 55 per cent over-all) was maintained throughout. Of all the new arrivals, slightly less than half came with some form of government assistance. Separate agreements operated with the United Kingdom, Malta, Germany, the Netherlands, Italy, Greece, Spain, and Belgium; the refugee settlement programme (initiated in 1947) merged into the "general assisted passage scheme" of 1954.

Throughout, assimilation of the newcomers was a matter of prime concern, and government agencies, federal and state, had elaborate machinery to provide language and other general instruction to the foreign-born in order that impediments to their absorption within the community might be removed. It was hoped that enclaves of the foreign-born would be avoided. Naturalization of foreign-born was at an annual rate of about 50,000 a year, and it included a few hundred a year from Asian lands.

Careful integration of immigration with the requirements of the labour market was a basic feature of the over-all plan; official selection teams combing Europe and Britian were kept up to date on what types of new settlers were needed, where, and in what numbers. In the various aspects of its programme the government had the benefit of advice from special groups, who were able not only to bring a wealth of expert knowledge to the task but also to undertake much of the detailed work of settling the newcomer in the community. Of prime importance in assessing the nation's labour-absorbing capacity was the sixteen-man Immigration Planning Council, made up of leaders in the fields of industry, economics, and public adminis-tration; the council played a special role in developing long-range plans in which immigration was related to the development of the national economy in general. A larger body, the twenty-eight-man Advisory Council, dealt mainly with sociological, legislative, and administrative aspects, while the widely represenative Citizenship Convention placed its main emphasis on the practical problems of assimilation, and the nationwide Good Neighbour movement had some 10,000 volunteers to assist the newcomer at a personal level.

Generally the assimilation effort succeeded, although inevitably there were cases where the system failed or where the established ways and habits of a lifetime so shaped the individual that acceptance of the new environment was difficult, if not impossible. Even though the newcomer faced little animosity—and few outward signs of goodwill—he still had serious hurdles to overcome. Sometimes people from the British Isles felt out of place in Australia and unhappy even though they admitted that they had done well and could name only intangible factors as the basis of their discontent. It was the same with those foreign-born who pined for their homeland. Foreign-language newspapers—which proliferated and flourished as a result of the steady stream of settlers from European lands—were quick to seize upon evidence of the slightest discrimination, real or imagined; but at the same time, they mingled their protests with censure where it was found that any arrival failed to adjust and overcome the frustrations that might be expected in any foreign country.

Such difficulties did exist, day by day and year by year, for the uprooted; and it was to the credit of the great body of new settlers that they accepted them in good part. In 1959 English writer Kingsley Martin described in the *New Statesman* how effectively integration of the new settlers had been proceeding, and he went on to set down his impressions of people typical of those who were building a new life in Australia. Detailing three conversations he had with such people, Martin wrote

> The first was with an English north country couple who had found working in a Western Australian pub intolerably arduous; the main reason was the terrific heat. But they had settled down on a well-run sheep station, the one as cook, the other as handyman in the house and garden, and had no intention of returning to the old country. The second was a central European musician with a good university job who had no complaint of his treatment. He, I thought, was unlikely to stay long in Australia, simply because he made few friends. He belonged to a cultural life which was not expressed in Australia.
>
> The third conversation was with a Ukrainian woman who also found herself quite unable to 'mix' in Australia. She couldn't bear her children to forget their own language; she told me when they came home from school, she pretended that she couldn't understand English. But she readily admitted that they were wonderfully happy, healthy, and ready themselves to be real Australians. That, I think, is a general rule. Second and third generation immigrants will become fully and happily a part of Australian life.

The community was no longer opposed to non-British settlers; it saw in them a source of strength for the building of a greater Australia. Australian-born author Alan Moorehead, revisiting his homeland in 1964, considered that the "original Anglo-Saxon core" was still completely dominant in politics and banking, and added that "at their tables you are not yet likely to meet a 'New Australian'." Yet the average newcomer's goals—a good job or a successful business, a car, a university education for his children—were more likely to be realized here than in his own country.

There were other, less material, aspects of the good life, as successful book publisher Dr Andrew Fabinyi, who came to Australia from Hungary just before World War II, told Jeanne Heal in *A Thousand and One Australians:*

> When I eat my lunch here, I know that everyone else in Melbourne has lunch
> to eat, too. All the things that most of the world works for to have in thirty years,
> we have here, now, yet there is no terrible strain; there is time for the good life.
> All that Christianity means is here. No one who has not lived in Europe can know
> just what it means to take it for granted that one lives in the future. . . . There is
> no longing for the past, no worrying about the present, no fear of the future.

By the 1960s less rigid attitudes were discernible in discussions of possible
modification of the traditional policy of limiting permanent immigration to
people of European origin. At that time there were more than 30,000 people of non-European ancestry, apart from Aborigines and part-Aborigines
living permanently in Australia; they included 20,000 of Chinese ancestry
and 4,000 Indians. Fear of "opening the floodgates" to Asian migration
still remained, and suggestions that a quota system (then used by the
United States) might be introduced to admit specified numbers from
countries of Asia were rejected by the main political parties, whose attitudes
to the issue varied only in detail; however, the legal provisions for the admission to permanent residence in Australia of individuals, no matter what their
origin, were eased in 1958 with the introduction of a system of entry permits.
By doing away with the old dictation test, obnoxious because it was obviously no more than a device to be used in a one-sided way, the government
showed that it was prepared to admit individuals on a fairer and less legalistic
basis. Although no responsible political leader foresaw any likelihood of
drastic change in terms of actual numbers of people of Asian origin who
might be admitted, the new policy provided flexibility in administering
the immigration law. It was acknowledged to be a step in the right direction,
and by the early 1960s public discussion on the issue of restrictive immigration laws showed stronger support than ever before for less rigid policies.

For a decade or so Australians had been welcoming thousands of young
people from Asian lands who came to study at Australian schools, technical
colleges, or universities—some under the Colombo Plan, many others at their
own expense. In 1965 the Australian Labor party rewrote its immigration
"plank" in milder terms which conceded the merit of a less rigid approach,
thus helping to rob the issue of any dangerous political overtones. In 1966
Prime Minister Holt announced that following a review which arose in part
from Australia's increasing involvement in Asian developments, the rapid
growth of trade with Asian countries, and the increasing numbers of Asian
students receiving education in Australia, the government had decided upon
"some modification and a degree of liberalization" of its policy affecting non-
European people. The existing fifteen-year term Asians needed to qualify for
resident status for Australian citizenship was reduced to five-years (in line
with conditions for Europeans); and while it remained the "primary aim"
to maintain "a generally integrated and predominantly homogeneous
population," the minister for immigration was given greater freedom to
admit non-Europeans who were considered "capable of becoming Australian

and joining in the national development".

The relaxation gave the immigration authorities more latitude, and it was expected that the severest forms of discrimination would disappear, with benefit to Australia's relations with Asian lands and without impairment of the basic principles of national immigration policy.

The complex and difficult problem of how best to assist the Aboriginal population had been given increasing attention by governments, federal and state, and had aroused more widespread interest in the community, where the Aborigines' slow progress towards attainment of full and equal status seemed to many to be a standing rebuke to the Australian concept of fair play. As one observer wrote: that the Aborigines were so grossly neglected had come to be regarded by many Australians as a national disgrace.

Efforts towards assimilation, pursued more or less actively from the late 1930s, had carried many Aborigines closer to absorption within the general community, but of the 47,000 full-blood Aborigines (most of whom lived in the remote and undeveloped northern and western sectors of the continent) there were relatively few who had made a successful transition from the tribal life of their ancestors. Many of the full-bloods—and many of the equally numerous part-Aborigines—were to be found living in squalor on the outskirts of towns. Some were able to make good money; but those who did usually gambled it away as freely as a sheep crops grass. The evidence of over-all success in assimilation remained meagre.

The analytical approach of anthropologists had thrown light on the Aborigines as a people, and the work of missions spread through the remote areas was laying a foundation for their advancement; but it remained for a few especially talented Aborigines to dramatize the capabilities of their race. In the late 1940s the artistic ability of Arunta tribesman Albert Namatjira, a camel driver, first came to notice, and in the 1950s his watercolours of striking central Australian landscapes were sold in ever greater volume and at mounting prices both within Australia and abroad. A dozen other members of the Arunta tribe were soon demonstrating similar talents and their pictures also sold readily. Twenty-two-year-old tenor Harold Blair, from the canefields of Queensland, gained the spotlight of attention when he won a nationwide radio contest in 1946 and went to New York to further his training. These were isolated examples, however, and they were exceptions to the rule that the Aborigines were an almost forgotten people, tens of thousands of whom remained separated from the community in general in spite of the efforts of missions and governments over the years. Throughout, the greatest number remained close to the settlements, where they spent lethargic lives.

The appointment in 1951 of Paul Hasluck to the post of federal minister for Territories marked the beginning of the crusade for assimilation; he set up a division of native welfare with responsibility for preparing Aborigines in the Northern Territory for full citizenship. A meeting of Commonwealth and state ministers the same year agreed that full citizenship for Aborigines was the eventual goal. An important step in this direction was the 1953 Welfare ordinance passed by the legislative council in the Northern Territory to replace the Aborginals ordinance. Under the new ordinance, which came into operation in 1957, half-castes automatically became citizens and full-bloods could apply for citizenship, which was granted if they were considered fully able to look after themselves and their families. (Most of the states already had similar provisions.) The welfare ordinances were not to apply to Aborigines as a race, but merely to individuals—called "wards of the State"—who needed special care and protection. A complementary Wards' Employment ordinance made provision for job training and other assistance.

By the late 1950s there were definite signs that the gulf was being narrowed. The federal government was not only setting the pace in assimilation but was also encouraging Queensland and Western Australia, where the bulk of Aborigines lived, to hasten development. The first Aborigine to matriculate did so in 1957, in Western Australia, and in both Queensland and Western Australia a university scholarship was awarded that year to an Aborigine for the first time.

Co-ordination between various non-government bodies interested in Aboriginal welfare was brought about in 1958 when the federal Council for Aboriginal Advancement was formed by eight organizations, based within the five mainland states. Three Aborigines were among the twenty-five people who formulated a charter which called for acceptance of five basic principles: equal rights with other citizens, a standard of living "adequate for health and well-being, including food, clothing, housing, and medical care," equal pay for equal work, with industrial protection, free and compulsory education for detribalized Aborigines, and the absolute retention of all remaining Aboriginal reserves. At subsequent meetings of the council (held each February), these objectives were pressed.

In 1959 the social welfare provision restricting pensions and maternity allowances to the comparatively few Aborigines who had been granted citizenship was removed. In 1960 a conference of federal and state ministers resolved that the practice of isolating Aborigines in reservations should be abandoned as soon as possible, and measures taken to assist Aborigines in their assimilation into the mainstream of contemporary Australian life. A survey conducted in 1961 by a federal parliamentary committee disclosed that fewer than 2000 bush primitives remained; these nomads of the desert areas bordering Western Australia and the Northern Territory were the only Aborigines who remained completely out of touch with civilization, and even they were stepping out of their isolation a few at a time.

Almost half of all full-blood Aborigines lived in the Northern Territory, and the federal government was by now spending over £1 million year on their welfare. In the settlements, both mission stations and government-run settlements, vocational and other training was being given not only to children but also adults who could benefit from it. In the Northern Territory Aborigines and part-Aborigines numbered almost 20,000. Stationowners had been encouraged to employ them, and many were working as stockmen, mechanics, or handymen, while many young women had homestead jobs.

To improve standards of employment, the administration issued new regulations in May 1960; under them, employers of Aboriginal labour were required to hold a licence, and this could be revoked if correct conditions of work were not observed. The regulations set out minimum standards of housing, and laid down that Aborigines were to receive regular wages (in effect, a cash wage of about £2/10/- a week) with two weeks' annual holiday on full pay and the right to notice of dismissal. Meanwhile, the number of Aborigines in some form of gainful employment was growing steadily. Some had taken jobs as mechanics in towns; others were active in mining or fishing ventures, and there were those who had gone back to hunting—but with rifles; the objective: crocodiles, whose skins were bringing £1 or so an inch.

In its report, the federal parliamentary committee of 1961 recommended that the right to vote in federal elections should be conferred on all adult Aborigines. Those in New South Wales, Victoria, and South Australia already possessed the right to vote in state elections, and therefore in federal elections; but those living in Queensland, Western Australia, and the Northern Territory—in fact, the vast majority—were still denied the franchise. In 1962 a measure giving effect to the committee's recommendation of political equality was passed by the federal parliament; it left the matter of enrolment by any Aborigine a matter of choice, but made those who enrolled subject to the normal penalty for failure to vote.

Clearly the way was being opened for Aborigines eventually to attain the same manner of living as other Australians, with the same rights, privileges and responsibilities; but some experts were questioning the validity of this objective. The National Missionary Council was one of the first to raise the issue; in 1963 it issued a statement declaring that the assimilation of Aborigines into the life of the community must be subject to their consent, and calling for recognition of the principle that continuation of the existence of distinctively Aboriginal groups, at the request of the Aborigines themselves, "need not be detrimental to national well-being." Concurrently, sociological and demographic studies demonstrated that assimilation was in fact still proceeding slowly, and there was increasing evidence that a strong desire existed among Aborigines for some separate community existence of their own. Some anthropologists, and other informed critics, were suggesting that instead of the government's maintaining policies which emphasized paternalism, it should encourage Aborigines to form self-acting communities able to achieve economic integration with the general community; at the same time some Aboriginal spokesmen were expressing concern over what they feared to be the threatened extinction of their people's cultural and social identity.

Aborigines were becoming more vocal. In 1963, when the federal government granted mining leases for bauxite in the Northern Territory, involving the cession of 140 square miles of tribal hunting grounds, a group of Aborigines at the Methodist mission at Yirrakala signed a petition which was sent to Canberra; and when parliament rejected the petition on the grounds that it had not been attested by the tribal elders, Wandjuh, one of the mission-trained Aborigines, typed out another petition, on which a hundred witnessed thumbprints of the tribal elders were impressed, asking for an inquiry. An all-party committee was then set up; by recommending that no land should be alienated from reserves without just compensation, the committee's report recognized the Aborigines' moral if not legal right to tribal lands. The government undertook to see that a royalty was paid into a general fund for the benefit of Northern Territory Aborigines for the forty-three-year period of the mining lease. Later, the same principle of compensation was adopted in arrangements for the working of manganese deposits on Groote Eylandt.

People prominent in Northern Territory affairs had been showing more active interest in the welfare of the Aborigines. In 1964 a select committee of the legislative council, reporting on proposed social welfare legislation for the Aborigines, took evidence from nearly three hundred witnesses, including more than a hundred Aborigines. The committee came out strongly for ending all discriminatory measures and proposed legislation, backed by administrative action, to correct the situation. The report was adopted and the council went on to pass a measure under which Aborigines in the Northern Territory were granted full citizenship rights. The Welfare Ordinance of 1953 was repealed and replaced by a Social Welfare Act which conferred on Aborigines the same rights, privileges, and responsibilities as those applying to other Australians, while at the same time continuing the educational and vocational programme of special assistance which was already established.

Throughout the northern cattle country most stations had a floating population of Aborigines still addicted to "going walk-about"—a relic of Stone Age nomadism in which they vanished into the bush for months at a time—and they would have to be trained in a new sort of responsibility. The transformation of such people into literate, time-conscious, industrially skilled, and domesticated home-owners would of necessity take a long time, and the question of when they might vanish into Australia's general population remained an open one.

One major obstacle in the way of any real social equality was the differing wages rates for Aborigines and whites. The application of separate rates to Aborigines was challenged in 1965 when the North Australian Workers Union asked the Arbitration Court to delete a clause excluding Aborigines from wage awards; the judgment delivered early in 1966 accepted the principle of equal wages but delayed operation of the new scale until the end of 1968. The move for equal wages touched off comment from the stationowners that on a competitive basis they would be compelled to employ white stockmen and dispense with Aborigines; but it seemed unlikely that there would be dismissals on any substantial scale.

In states or in areas where Aborigines made up only a small segment of the population and the massive problems did not exist, the emphasis was on education as the only sound road to true emancipation from the "fringe living" that was the inheritance of most Aboriginal families. In most states Aboriginal children living in settled areas were able to attend ordinary schools on the same basis as white children—indeed they were required to do so. In some sparsely settled areas special schools for Aboriginal children were set up, while in some states specialized agencies were operating; for example, in Sydney, Tranby Co-operative College, operating since the late 1950s under a scholarship fund supported by trade unions, co-operative societies, and the Australian Board of Missions, offered specialized training for Aboriginal men and women from far afield who wished to work in their own co-operative societies. Most of the students stayed twelve to fifteen months and attended technical or business college as well as working in co-operatives to gain practical experience. Also in Sydney, a committee on Aboriginal education was formed in 1963 to help equalize educational opportunities and to support endeavours towards social acceptance of Aborigines, and it brought together many organizations striving to help Aboriginal families living in the state.

With the ending of Australia's days of isolation, complacency had been dispelled in a national effort devoted to making Australia a serious political and economic force. As part of the awakening, a compelling goal had come to the fore: it was the urge to develop the vast and largely empty continent at the same time as prosperity was increased.

During all the years of economic expansion, the bulk of the growth had been concentrated in the already developed areas, and the large cities in particular. Fast as the growth rate of employment in manufacturing might be, it was outpaced by far by the growth rate of employment in tertiary and service industries, such as banking, insurance, retailing, finance and advertising—activites which were almost wholly city-based. By 1961 Sydney and Melbourne each had about 2,000,000 people. Almost 6,000,000 were living in the six state capitals, representing 55.5 per cent of the nation's population. With the inclusion of additional industrial centres also located along the coast, the proportion of the population living in large seaboard concentrations exceeded 60 per cent. This highly-urbanized, heavy aggregation alarmed many Australians.

Politicians and other community leaders continued to deplore the unbridled growth of the big cities, and spoke of the need to secure a more balanced spread of population; but geography and special problems of the Australian environment were not easily overcome. Australians were still prisoners of distance and of climate. Ways had to be found to offset the peculiar shortcomings of the continent—soil deficiencies, dryness, and a high degree of variability in rainfall—if the rural sector of the economy were to absorb more people; and the cost of such development had to be reckoned. Rural expansion and decentralization involved heavy public investment in such undertakings as water conservation and improvement of transport facilities, and it also called for intensified research and the application of scientific knowledge gained as a result.

Significant increases in national yields of agricultural products had come in the wake of such innovations as greater mechanization, improved ploughing and fertilizing methods as part of better farming techniques in general, higher yielding strains or more suitable types of plant or animals. Over the fifteen-year period beginning in 1950, the total area under crop rose from 20,000,000 acres to over 32,000,000 acres; this, with studied efforts to improve soil fertility, introduce better grasses and crop strains, and extend knowledge of animal husbandry and conservation methods—measures applied on both established farms and the newly-opened land of large-scale reclamation projects—resulted in total agricultural output being raised by two thirds. Nevertheless, the nation's achievement did not stand up so well when compared with the gains in output per man in the United States, Britain, and many European countries over the same period of increasingly mechanized and scientific agriculture. In many cases Australian farmers still resisted change, ignoring the experts' exhortations about the need to improve efficiency in farm management. Keith Campbell, Professor of Agricultural Economics in the University of Sydney, writing on this theme in 1965, said that it was of prime importance that Australians should realize that improvement in rural efficiency and progress generally was not necessarily or solely achieved by extending agricultural areas or undertaking research designed to raise crop and livestock yields. "Advances in output avail little if they are secured at great cost," Professor Campbell wrote, adding:

> Eye-catching schemes for irrigation development or dry-land development, often in the most out-of-the-way places, may lift aggregate production a little, but too frequently they do so at a tremendous cost in terms of wasted opportunities to use the resources employed more productively elsewhere.

Meanwhile, banks and other lending institutions, wool brokers, and livestock agents had been encouraging rural property owners to adopt more advanced business practices. Some farmers, seeing the need to supplement the help available from state-appointed agricultural advisers, were beginning to band together so that they might employ their own advisers. Farm management clubs, which originated in Europe and operated also in New Zealand, began to spread after Australia's first such club was formed at Bombala, New South Wales, in 1956: within a decade sixty or so were operating, half of them in Western Australia. Each club, made up of forty or so farmers, employed an adviser—usually a graduate in agricultural, rural, or veterinary science who had completed a comprehensive course covering management, agricultural economics, and animal husbandry. It was the adviser's responsibility to keep abreast of all new agricultural trends and techniques by visiting research establishments, attending conferences, and meeting his fellow extension officers. Spending some time with each member-farmer every two or three months, the adviser could review all aspects of the property and its management. Club meetings such as field days were held from time to time and provided an opportunity for illustrating the practical application of the professional advice that was offered.

Not only farms were involved in the change: the big stations were no longer simply vast expanses of pasture land; instead they had become great enterprises, many with their own scientists and their own accountants. The age of the shepherd king had passed and the age of the shepherd business-man had come. Even shearing methods were still undergoing refinement, now with active support from the Wool Board, whose field officers demon-strated improved techniques for faster shearing. One expert broke his own world record in 1965 with a tally of 346 sheep shorn in an eight-hour day.

Even as rural output rose, employment in rural industries declined slowly but inexorably; between 1950 and 1965 the number employed went down by about 10 per cent. This meant that the imbalance between country popula-tion and city population became even greater than before, while the concen-tration in a few major industrial areas intensified. Just as climatic factors and the nature of the land had dictated relatively large holdings and had thwarted attempts to produce a more intensive settlement pattern in early days, so in industrial development the drive for efficiency and the dictates of competition placed the emphasis in plant location upon accessibility to seaboard facilities. Against the concentrating forces, little headway could be made in the effort to spread population. Some "decentralized" manufacturing enterprises were operating in factories set up in provincial centres during the war years, but most were suffering because of heavy freight costs. Even long-established processing operations (such as flour milling) in rural centres were struggling to survive. Only the largest provincial cities showed themselves capable of consolidating their position as commercial and communication centres; in most cases smaller towns near larger centres were tending to lose population. An awareness of the problem began to spread in the late 1950s; discussion was encouraged by some small dedicated groups who pinpointed factors pertinent to the issue of maintaining a reasonable spread of population.

By the mid-1960s there was less talk of general "decentralization" of in-dustry as a simple formula and an answer to the problem. More emphasis was being placed by experienced planners on the need for local communities to survey the resources of the area, and its potential, with an eye to develop-ing actitivites closely integrated with the rural industries or special features of the district. In a few cases the drive was to build up a thriving tourist in-dustry; in others new enterprises for the processing of rural products came in the wake of expanded or changed production patterns. Constructive local efforts were found to be effective in attracting small-scale and specialized industry, but the examples of success were all too rare, and the problem remained a challenging one.

Australia's population pattern had unique and disturbing features. The nation as a whole had the extremely low average density of four people to the square mile, and if the population of the few large centres were deducted an extraordinary sparsity of population over the great bulk of the land was revealed. Major mining enterprises held a few relatively large groups at isolated inland centres, and sugar production on the north-east coast helped to produce some substantial pockets of settlement beyond the main fertile crescent in the southeast of the continent; but over the entire nation there remained in the mid-1960s only 125 centres with populations of 2000 to 4000 and 127 with populations of 4000 to 40,000; there were no more than ten cities apart from the capitals with populations exceeding 40,000. In twenty years the number of centres of substantial population had shown some improvement; yet the over-all balance in population distribution between the few big cities and the rest of the country remained disappointing; and even worse, signs of a more promising trend apparent in the decade after the war's end seemed to have faded with the declining rate of growth in most provincial centres.

Of even deeper concern was the settlement picture of the "empty North," and newspapers and politicians and groups devoted to public issues all urged greater attention to developing the drier and more challenging "problem lands" of the north and north-west. For half a century or so the lack of population across the 1,000,000 square miles of the continent's tropical zone had created gnawing fears; the stark fact was that in the third of the nation's area lying north of the Tropic of Capricorn lived only about 1 per cent of the nation's white population. In a world facing the pressures of rapidly expanding population—with the greatest growth of all centered mainly in the lands to the north of Australia—the significance of this vast underpopulated area could not be overlooked.

The only developed sector in the tropics remained the narrow, intensely cultivated, high-rainfall strip along the north-east coast given over to sugar cane; elsewhere, only piecemeal development had been possible. Inland, the sparseness of population arose from the pervading aridity. Over most of the northern belt and other large areas in the "centre" and the west, little if anything could be done with land except leave it in vast holdings on which cattle might run; shortage of water, transportation costs, and the general nature of the terrain ruled out the possibility of any marked change. There were pockets of better land, however, and areas where rainfall was adequate, and an intensive scientific effort was directed towards learning more about the northern region and its potential. In the important Queensland cattle areas, research in the 1960s opened the way for the introduction of improved pastures in a wide variety of environments, as several plants new to Australia (and some never before used in world agriculture) were tested; one of the legumes found to be of special value was Townsville lucerne. which in trials made possible a threefold increase in carrying capacity. The possibilities of agricultural crops were being investigated, and some pilot operations started, such as the Ord River development.

The discovery of oil or natural gas in some of the remoter areas also opened new prospects, and pockets of settlement developed as a result of important mineral discoveries. The £27,500,000 rebuilding and strengthening of the railway line running 600 miles inland from Townsville to Mount Isa, completed in 1965, made it possible to expand the mining operation, and the line also brightened prospects for development of other resources along the route. Along the continent's northern coast, extraction of ore from huge bauxite deposits took people into new areas, while the building of a great new refinery quickly lifted population at Gladstone. In the tropical zone of Western Australia, exploitation of great iron-ore deposits began to create new settlements both at the points of shipment and at mine sites. The commercial operation of the Barrow Island oilfield suggested the possibility of establishing an oil refinery somewhere in the coastal region serving the great iron-ore enterprises. There were long-range plans under discussion for the harnessing of tremendous tidal forces along the northwest coast in order to produce cheap and abundant power; such a development, and use of atomic energy in remote locations, might make possible a new settlement pattern in the north.

Mining experts spoke of the probability that the vast dry heartland contained great mineral deposits which might be uncovered with better access roads and a large-scale search. The deposits uncovered or surveyed in the 1950s and early 1960s consistently gave support to the theory that Australia's remoter areas might well be a tremendous treasure-house of minerals. In addition to the growth and potential of mining, there was also the prospect that cattle raising might be developed further; it appeared certain to remain the significant factor in settlement of the north, at least while the future of agricultural settlements on the Ord pattern remained uncertain. The cattle industry continued to move forward, in spite of recurring droughts over large areas. Its progress was closely linked with the extension and improvement of inland roads; transport of cattle by "road train" meant that the long overland treks were becoming a thing of the past. The rapid transport helped particularly in the marketing of smaller groups of prime cattle. The federal government supported a road building programme in the cattle areas of western Queensland and the Northern Territory and by the mid-1960s road transports were moving the bulk of the cattle being turned off from these areas.

Evidence that some scattered development was taking place in the tropical zone was insufficient to slake the thirst of many citizens for bolder and more comprehensive action. Experts in different fields put forward ideas on how the north might be opened up on a large scale, or conversely why the concept of accelerated northern development was unsound; in debate, discussion, and symposium a patchwork of views emerged which were still being weighed and considered by the mid-1960s. It was clear that sooner or later the nation would have to tackle the problem in a more conscientious way, but meanwhile the proposition that something must be done and done quickly was canvassed widely. Melbourne journalist, Frank Devine, sent on a special assignment in 1964 to report on the scene, wrote a series of forceful articles on the theme, We Must People the Empty North—Fast. In the articles, featured in the Melbourne *Herald* and other newspapers, Devine urged that Australia be made "a real country instead of a jumble of camping sites tucked away in odd corners of a huge empty continent." Australians, he wrote, were custodians of a land of unrivalled opportunity, but Australia must establish at least the framework of total development; the question of the "vacant North" could not be left.

In spite of all the discussion, however, development of the northern reaches clearly had to shape itself around specific projects, and each of these had to be evaluated in relation to many other projects awaiting action.

Even in the main areas of economic development much remained to be done to improve transport efficiency. One such project was that of co-ordinating the rail system to correct the classic original mistake of different gauges. An important step in this task was the completion in 1962 of a standard-gauge track across Victoria, after which through trains could operate between Melbourne and Sydney and the costly time-wasting change-over of goods and passengers at Albury could be avoided. The opening of the standard-gauge line meant that for the first time rail traffic could run uninterrupted from Melbourne 1100 miles north to Brisbane. Before 1970, it was hoped, every mainland capital from Perth to Brisbane would be linked by standard-gauge track. In the mid-1960s Australian railway authorities were engaged in a major building programme: some 1200 miles of track were under construction.

In large degree, radicalism had given way to research and slogans to statistics in the Australian political lexicon. Much of the burning zeal had been drained from political arguments, but in its stead had come more reasoned discussion. Labor party leaders increasingly quoted business indicators, consumption levels, and gross national product figures to substantiate points of criticism, and the government made the most of the record of economic progress that had marked its years in office. The issues between parties had generally been narrowed considerably. As in Europe and the United States, the immediate post-war era of experiment, and intellectual and political ferment, appeared to have run its course by the mid-1960s. Social change at the measured pace set by progressive-conservative parties was acceptable; adjustment to technological change was absorbed, anything riskier was refused. Sound administration rather than overbold policies had become the watchword of the Liberal Party. Inevitably from their support of the policies of full employment and sustained large-scale immigration, the Liberals had come to accept the concept of a tightly disciplined economy, so that there was no longer any major division on this issue. The Country party was content to secure a maximum of rural-oriented concessions, while frequently showing more expansionist ideas than those current among the Liberal leadership and seeking to loosen the rein on the economy.

Unrestricted power over taxation, combined with control or influence over the money supply and credit sources, meant that the federal government could virtually decide the shape and form of development throughout the economy as well as exercising a strong influence on the level of aggregate demand. It could greatly influence, if not decide, what the states might borrow each year, and determine the scale and pattern of their spending. Because of the uniform tax provision, the people living in the wealthiest states were left with no alternative but to help some of the less advanced states. On the credit side, the exercise of federal power had the effect of creating more systematic planning of the nation's resources than ever before, and much of the success of difficult and complicated developmental undertakings could be traced to the co-ordination thus achieved. At the same time, federal monopoly of income tax policy had taken much of the sting of financial responsibility out of the competitive proposals of the state political groups. The old balance in federal-state relationships had been overturned, and by the mid-1960s it was increasingly apparent that the federal tax monopoly had diminished the tone of political life in the states and reduced the dignity of state leaders by making them persistent supplicants.

The working of the federal system in Australia had been deeply affected particularly by the preponderance of power (in terms of popular vote and of economic strength) represented in New South Wales and Victoria. As individual states, each represented a substantial portion—more than a third—of the national strength. By comparison, in the United States, where a broadly similar constitutional division operated, no single state could exert any really significant influence, in relation to the whole, in the way that was possible for either of the two major Australian states.

Yet, paradoxically, the Commonwealth's power over important issues remained unimpaired. In fact the expansion of federal influence and federal activities in the postwar years had not come about as a result of any reshaping of the constitution (apart from that achieved by the successful social services referendum of 1946). The federal initiatives in such matters as resource development, employment, and economic and financial matters had paralleled the trend in other democratic countries, including both the federal United States and the unitary United Kingdom. This wider role of the central government was the inevitable consequence of the new concepts which had been ushered in with Keynesian and post-Keynesian economic policies. The Australian constitution, as interpreted in a number of judicial decisions climaxing in the Uniform Tax decision of 1942, had proved flexible enough to adapt to the new concepts.

There was room for concern about the degree of integration in economic affairs between the federal government and the states, and doubts remained about the lack of definition of respective roles within the federal system. Experience showed that even with the scales heavily weighted in favour of the Commonwealth, the states had an enduring role. The central constitutional issue concerned the fixing of responsiblity for decisions which belonged to the states but which the states could no longer make freely with their diminished financial independence. Writing on this subject in the 1950s, Sir Douglas Copland emphasized the need for closer and sustained consultation at the official level and for much greater integration of administration in agriculture, health, social services, industrial relations, development, and migration than had been produced in the federation's first half-century. Such consultation, he maintained, was essential if the continuing division of power were to be made workable; and, he added: "As in other federations the structure itself is a product of both history and geography, and short cuts to central control will not efface the influence of either."

A changing role of parliament was also seen. It was conceded that there had been erosion of parliamentary control over the executive and its administrators. The role of government had become complex; and, as a commentator noted in the *Sydney Morning Herald* in 1965, public demands upon individual members for representation and redress of grievances had increased to a point where most parliamentarians were engaged mainly in services for their constituents. Governments had refined their techniques of administration and public servants had gained a greater say in the formulation of the proposals submitted. In some areas of policy-making, outside opinion influenced decisions very frequently through discussions in which powerful interests like employers' organizations or the major unions found it expedient to discuss questions direct with ministers, boards, or departments. Cabinets had consolidated an effective monopoly in putting forward legislation, and parliaments were expected merely to register approval or disapproval of legislative proposals made by a smaller, more expert group. From the point of view of the average citizen there was the further fact that regulations over which parliaments exercised little effective control formed a large part of the rules under which the community and the individual lived.

There was a considerable body of opinion which held that Australia might do better with fewer parliaments and stronger local and regional government. The existence of seven parliaments, with close to a thousand members in all, was held by some commentators to spread too thinly the available supply of political leadership, while there was obvious duplication in the work of various departments. Partly as a result of the proliferation, one in four of all Australians in employment was on a public payroll when all the employees of government-sponsored services as well as those of federal and state departments were taken into account.

The federal parliament's Joint Committee on Constitutional Review, which sat in 1958 and 1959, decided in favour of constitutional amendment which would allow the Commonwealth to perform the wider range of activities called for by the public in a modern society; but the government did not act on the committee's recommendations. Proposals for limited constitutional amendment were finally approved by the parliament in 1965 but the referendum was delayed until 1967; the proposals had the objectives of including Aborigines in the census, bringing matters related to Aboriginal affairs into the federal sphere and of breaking the two-to-one nexus in the ratio of members in the House of Representatives and the Senate. On broader aspects of constitutional reform, political leaders showed no sign of agreement.

Meanwhile the city of Canberra had become a symbol of national identity. The "bush capital" of an earlier generation had outgrown its old isolation and had become a city of unique character. With its twenty-nine Embassies and Legations and seven High Commissions, it ranked as a major diplomatic centre.

The continuing transfer to Canberra of central functions of federal departments together with the growth of other official activities and the attraction of headquarters of various non-government organizations all contributed to the city's physical expansion as well as to its growing stature. No longer was it a city of public servants and a way station for reporters. It had become the centre for an active exchange of ideas and information between academics, politicians, administrators, and informed groups in various fields. By the mid-1960s Canberra's population was close to 100,000 and more than 500,000 Australians (as well as, many people from overseas) were visiting the city each year. The prospect was that by 1990 Canberra's population would be in excess of 250,000.

Canberra had become a national showcase, and planning and design of buildings and facilities were of a standard higher than might be possible elsewhere. The National Capital Development Commission, guardian and mentor of Canberra's development since 1957, had been careful to see that expansion of the suburbs did not interfere with functions related to Canberra's role as the seat of government. The central area, the Parliamentary Triangle, was reserved for the permanent Parliament House and other buildings which would be erected over decades and endure for centuries.

Today—and   29
tomorrow

In the Space-and-Computer Age, Australia remained divided into two separate worlds: one characterized by the great cities with their deepening chasms of metal-and-glass and their sprawling ˙suburbs, and the other by a largely empty land where a declining proportion of the population lived. In the interplay between the two worlds, countrymen had fought hard to maintain the old values of rural life—independence and individuality —but for the most part it had been a losing battle. Only the relatively few who occupied the latter-day frontier land of the Outback were able to sustain their predilection and stem the inroads of the new sophistication and standardization.

The dwellers in the main cities and those in the towns and countryside of the well-watered southern and eastern coastal regions, far outnumbering the rugged individualists of the inland, had come overwhelmingly to accept an all-pervading degree of regulation in economic life. The great bulk of Australians—whether businessmen, professional men, or employees—belonged to some organization created for the express purpose of protecting its members' special interests. Through the regulatory process of tariffs and the marketing arrangements of producer-dominated commodity control boards, manufacturers and farmers gained protection, while the Arbitration Commission determined wage levels not only for all manual workers but also for professional groups such as engineers, scientists, architects, designers, surveyors, draftsmen and other "white collar" workers. Orderliness and control had come to replace the old hit-and-miss way of life of earlier days. Resentment against wealth, which had once seemed an inevitable part of the Australian scene, had declined.

In terms of general economic expansion, Australia had been maintaining a growth rate exceeded by only six or seven nations, and very few countries, other than the United States and Canada, could claim as high a standard of living.

Part of the price of the new affluence might be the loss of free and easy ways, but the prosperity of city dweller and rural producer alike had been translated into the possibility of a fuller life for the ordinary citizen. Many more young people were continuing their education beyond the age for compulsory school attendance; older universities had expanded and new universities were being founded so that a more comprehensive system had emerged. As part of the revolution of rising educational aspirations, the proportion of the seventeen-to-twenty-two age group receiving a tertiary education increased sixfold in a generation. Young people travelled overseas in greater numbers than ever before, some spending a year or more abroad, absorbing ideas and attitudes (as well as technical and academic knowledge, in many cases) which made them active proponents of progress on their return. An equally fundamental influence in helping to reshape the community's ways and outlook was to be found in the effect of the large-scale immigration. Twenty years after World War II the cumulative effect of the influx of a great mass of people of varying cultures was apparent; the newcomers had added a leavening of new ideas. The interchange was also stimulated increasingly by the growing number of visitors from abroad—nearly 200,000 a year by 1965.

Other striking changes in habits and outlook had come as a result of new influences and the new prosperity. The immediacy of the television screen combined with the more penetrating coverage of local and overseas events on radio, in newspapers and in magazines to bring world leaders and world events to notice, and there was an awakened interest in national affairs. People were becoming more knowledgeable and more eager to acquire knowledge, more curious about many things—and above all more conscious of the Australian community's place in the world picture.

A new sense of national destiny was being forged as Australians, encouraged by their friends and allies and heartened by the success of their own nation-building efforts, became convinced that a great future lay ahead if opportunities were firmly grasped. By the late 1960s there was a new determination among individuals as well as Government leaders that they should pursue the aim of building a stronger Australia and do more to assist in the creation of a more stable and better fed world.

At the root of Australia's traditional relationships with Britain and within the Commonwealth the emphasis had been on interdependence rather than independence; now, with new ties forming, the question was whether Australians would happily accept the inevitable new relationships and responsibilities.

Australia was in fact moving out of the backwater and into the mainstream. What remained was insulation rather than isolation from the world at large.

Australians, by and large, were still somewhat unsure about the direction of the path ahead. There were many voices questioning where Australia's national future lay: how soon the old British ties might loosen further, whether Australia could sustain a binding relationship with the United States without losing its own identity, whether more might not be done to bring the nation closer to the peoples of Asia and the western Pacific, and whether Australia's future role should not be that of a bridge between the peoples of Western culture and those in countries struggling to make independence a viable way of life.

The hope was that relationships between the United States and Britain might become closer—a possibility being speculated upon in Washington and London—thus reducing the danger that Australia would have to choose between American and British policies in relation to Asia. The idea of a loose federation involving Britain and the United States, with such countries as Canada, Australia, and New Zealand joining, would clearly be to the advantage of the two southern outposts of the North Atlantic bloc. On the specific issue of the defence effort in the area east of Suez, with Whitehall placing special emphasis on interdependence but not always seeing eye to eye with Washington, Canberra was clearly anxious to foster long-range decisions based on a co-ordinated plan for regional defence.

Australians had found it difficult to adjust to major changes that had come within the Commonwealth. In less than twenty years the British government had withdrawn its rule from 700,000,000 people spread through two hemispheres, creating more than twenty new nations in the process; and relationships within the Commonwealth had changed drastically, particularly in the 1960s. At the Commonwealth Prime Ministers' conference of 1965, the bulk of the seventeen heads of government and four senior ministers were non-white; nine of them were Africans. As an international-relations writer noted in *The Bulletin*, the majority represented republics for whom the British monarchy was almost, if not quite, irrelevant; several were one-party states, in name or in fact, which had eschewed many of the basic principles of the rule of law and of parliamentary democracy.

These factors, coupled with divisive issues increasingly in evidence within the Commonwealth, created concern in Canberra and throughout the country. The Commonwealth Prime Ministers' conferences were no longer small meetings of "like minded men." South Africa's withdrawal from the Commonwealth in 1961, followed in 1965 by Rhodesia's unilateral "declaration of independence," shocked and saddened many; these moves obviously marked the end of an era. The parliamentary debate that took place in Canberra late in 1965 on the Rhodesian issue showed how nonplussed the Commonwealth-minded were over signs of sharpening divisions within the old British family. In 1966 Prime Minister Holt indicated that he doubted the value of the annual London meetings, which had deteriorated into divisive rather than cohesive gatherings.

Increasingly Australia was being called upon to define its attitude and chart a course in foreign policy and defence in conformity with its position. No longer was it merely a continent in a no-man's land. With adjustments in defence and foreign policies under discussion, the wisdom of scattering Australian land forces to meet threats at various pressure points seemed likely to come under serious review. In supporting the British forces in Malaysia and joining the American effort in Vietnam, the Australian Army's contribution in men and material was splintered. The belief was growing that in less than a decade the concept of Fortress Australia might develop to a point where an effective land force, complete with top-class transport and supporting requirements, ready for instant deployment, would be brought into being.

At the same time as the government faced expanding strategic commitments, thoughtful Australians were asking whether Australia should not also seek to play a profoundly constructive role. Such a proposal brought into sharper focus the need to broaden cultural exchanges as well as the benefits to be gained by expanding study courses within Australia devoted to Asian languages, culture, histories and socio-economics.

It was widely held that a more positive attitude should be adopted and that an understanding of Asian lands, as well as a reciprocal Asian understanding of Australia, needed to be cultivated. In spite of the stationing of some correspondents in Singapore, reporting of Asian affairs in Australian newspapers still fell short of a penetrating coverage, and the growing number of people interested in south-east Asian affairs usually had to turn to American or British newspapers and magazines. Except in the few places where Australian correspondents were stationed, reports were practically confined to coverage by newsgathering agencies or reprints from overseas publications. Crises and big events in Asian lands made headlines but little was published about less spectacular though fundamental developments or about significant trends. The Australian Broadcasting Commission attempted to overcome the leeway with special reports and in its regular session, "This Week in Asia," but like most of the newspapers it had very limited representation anywhere in the south-east Asian region.

In reviewing its role, Australia was looking forward to the day when the threat of subversion and violence in south-east Asia would pass and more attention might be given to the constructive tasks awaiting attention. There was no inclination to minimize the great political problems of the region—problems far beyond Australia's capacity to cope with alone—but Canberra felt confident that with the continuing American-British presence in the area practical solutions would be found. At the same time, Australian interest in the broader issues of world affairs remained, even though the involvement with the special problems of the region seemed certain to bring more and more responsibilities to Australia as a regional power.

A new element, national self-criticism, which had first appeared in the late 1950s, was being more widely voiced.

Many complacent notions were under attack as the updating of Australians' views of affairs gathered pace. For the first time the old attitude of whatever was "Australian" must be right (and best) was under severe challenge; Australians were beginning to find such a tenet a foolish sign of national immaturity, and increasingly they were inclined to listen to those voices which told them so. The old bush idiom was dying. Typical of its critics was social commentator Clive Turnbull, who spoke out against writers harping on themes from "the country of the jumbucks" which he considered to be now about as remote as the Wild West; it was ridiculous to maintain that the Australian character still sprang "fresh-cooked from the billy-can and the damper ashes." Soon after his return to Australia from a sojourn in the United States, architect Robin Boyd castigated Australians for their lack of taste in clothing styles, interior decorating, and other everyday aspects of their surroundings. In *The Australian Ugliness*, published in 1960, Boyd called upon Australians to halt the march of the "non-pattern of unrelated snippets of blight" which marred the countryside. Geoffrey Dutton, adopting the role of an angry young man, contrasted the widely-held illusion of "Australia young and free" with the actual fact that youth in Australia controlled nothing; instead, Dutton wrote in *Nation*, "institutionalized old men" dominated Australian politics, law, business and sport; and, because the way to achieve respectability was to become aged as soon as possible, "there are probably more old men of thirty in Australia than in any other country." A broader sweep of criticism was that of journalist Donald Horne, who did his best to shatter the Australian Dream ("Innocent happiness; Nation without a mind") and poured scorn on the complacent theories behind such Australianisms as "fair go, mate," "having a good time," and "give it a go." In *The Lucky Country*, published in 1964, Horne "discovered" his own country and drew a caricature of it and its people. He considered that Australians could no longer trust to luck that events in Asia would pass Australia by, and that the country would have to change its life pattern profoundly if it were to maintain its prosperity in the new technological age.

Instead of *The Lucky Country* being placed on an unofficial black list it became a national best-seller. Its success, quickly followed by a phenomenal response to *Let Stalk Strine*, a collection based on the peculiarities of Australian idiom and the Australian accent, indicated that many Australians had reached the point where they could poke fun at some of their national foibles.

At the same time as Australia and its people were being placed under the examining glass by Australian commentators and critics, the country was being scrutinized by observers from abroad. In reaching conclusions about Australia and the Australian of the 1960s, commentators from America, Britain, or Europe were usually reflecting their own predilections; the characteristics the visiting writer found most significant were often determined by what he or she expected to find but perhaps more importantly, by comparison with the national aspirations of the writer's homeland. In this context, Americans tended consistently to stress the similarities with the American saga which they detected, and they applauded the progress of a "young" country; to Englishmen and Europeans, on the other hand, the most vivid impression was one of cultural aridity set against wholly material progress—a harsh land, producing an astringent people.

The American commentator was usually quick to seize on the fact that Australia had the exciting qualities of a latter-day frontier land. Here, roving reporters and serious business writers now found, was a country in the midst of a national expansion such as the United States had experienced in its halcyon days before being burdened with the responsibilities of greatness. The American could not only look nostalgically at a young nation; he could also detect signs of boundless ambition. Typical of this approach was the view expressed in *Argosy* magazine in 1965:

> Australia is a rugged country, such as our own west was a hundred years ago. But Australia is more. A man seeking a world to conquer can expect to find in the vast, largely untouched continent fabulous natural resources, limitless in variety and amount; towns by the score where important booms are just getting under way; and jobs, jobs, jobs, in almost every category . . . If you intend to work hard in a new land, Australia offers you a glittering chance to strike it happy and—who knows?—even very rich.

Newsweek, declaring that the Great Australian Boom had just begun, considered that most Australians no longer had patience for anything but progress. Even the less exultant found engaging similarities between Australia and the United States. Peggy Durdin wrote in *Saturday Review* that Australia should not be considered a "blurred replica or uninspired imitation" of Britain or America, but she had to admit that in no other foreign land could the American feel closer to home, and she added:

> He quickly concludes he is among a people as friendly, open, casually kind, informal, and gregarious as he. They seem to think and feel and act pretty much like Americans, go to the same movies, watch the same bevy of gangsters, cowboys, and doctors—and endure the same commercials on television.

The British or European reporter, on the other hand, was tempted to compare a country so ostensibly British in traditions and sentiment with his homeland—and by concentrating on those aspects which were commonplace in an older land but of necessity undeveloped in a new land, he tended to stress Australia's shortcomings. To visitors from lands of ancient culture and orderly farmlands, it usually seemed that the all-pervading emptiness of the Australian landscape was matched by barrenness of the intellectual climate.

Italian journalist Mario Cervi, after visiting all states in 1961, reported to readers of his Milan newspaper that the average Australian was not cultured and was sometimes "incredibly ingenuous and ignorant" even though he possessed an inborn curiosity. Peter Michaels, in a French-language paperback, *Australie*, divided Australians into two opposed groups, typified by "le larrikin" and "le wowser"; he saw "les wowsers" as the country's moral guardians, dictating (among other things) its Spartan Sundays. Other Europeans stressed the sense of boredom they detected. Hungarian author Tibor Meray, in *L'Australie* (1964) declared Australia to be the country in which "dullness has reached a paradox that makes it startling" and "boredom has been elevated to the status of an institution." Meray found that the monotony in Australian life arose from the general simplification of European culture suffered by its being transplanted, but he went on to stress Australians' sense of exile as being of paramount importance. "Australians feel themselves a little on the outside, exiled, the poor relations of the great family," he wrote. In 1966 Professor Mario Praz took up the same point in an article in Rome's *Il Tempo* and went on to say that a general lack of contact with the Western world's great artistic tradition had affected Australians' taste and sentiments.

To the Japanese, Australians were rather an amalgam. Newspaper editor Kimpei Shibu, visiting Australia in 1960, was reminded at times of Britain and at times of the United States. He saw the likeness to Britain in the affection for the Queen and the pomp and circumstance on special occasions, like the departure of the Governor-General, and the American influence in Sydney's advertising signs, ultra-modern office buildings and the advertising layout of the newspapers. Four years later a Japanese TV team was intrigued by the comparative calm of Australia's political life and the easygoing ways of Australians. The team's director commented that "it's all so smooth, so placid I am left wondering whether this is a good or a bad thing for the country's own future." In 1966 a Tokyo newspaper correspondent considered that since the war Australia had become less of a British dependency and more authentically the southernmost part of Asia.

One writer who found some things to admire and much to fault was journalist James Morris, who set down his impressions on the Australian way of life in a series of articles in the *Manchester Guardian Weekly* in 1962. He asked why "some more vivid stimulants" were not being extracted from Australia's position in the world instead of an unemotional acceptance of British and European standards. He wrote searchingly about the loneliness he found in Australia, how tentative was man's toehold on the continent, how tenacious the wild emptiness of the country. The dominant note was that of rawness—and Morris found this not only in the inland. He admitted Sydney's size, but added:

> Sydney does not yet feel a great city—not a generous, confident serene city, nor a city of any warmth or splendour. Turn your back on the bridge, and you will travel through a wilderness of ugly suburbs, a labyrinth of unlovely boulevards, a humdrum desolation, until at last you reach the outskirts of the place: and there before you, if you persevere, stretches the emptiness of Australia, which is inescapable, which runs like some chill virus through the bloodstream of the country.

There were times, Morris wrote, when to the visitor Australia felt terribly old for so young a country, and "terribly resigned to empty mediocrity." He found that Australians often failed to appreciate the glamour of things indigenous—the great cattle stations, the splendid graziers, the fun of the prospectors and the swagmen, but at the same time "pitifully overestimated" the excitement of their urban societies. Even though the links between Britain and Australia were still intricately meshed—links which Morris defined as those "of instinct as well as economics, of thought as well as strategy"—Morris considered it incongruous that Prime Minister Menzies should be so concerned to emphasize that Australians "are British to our boot heels." He went on to say that

> ... even now after more than half a century as a sovereign federation Australia does not feel an absolutely independent State, not absolutely on her own, not absolutely adult.

Morris's articles produced less violent rebuttal than similar views expressed in earlier years would have done. Nevertheless, those who defended Australian ways against Morris's criticism tended to follow old lines. It was said that his impressions were surface impressions only, that he had not spent enough time in the country to understand it and its problems, and that he had been unduly harsh in his judgment since he had failed to give proper weight to the factors that had produced the effects he deplored. This reaction was typical of that of people believing fervently in the goodness of their land, their objectives, and the national way of life.

The Australian of the 1960s was still firmly tied by traditional and continuing influences and by circumstance to the English-speaking communities of the North Atlantic. From these the country continued to draw its inspiration, its technology, most of its new settlers and much of the capital that helped make its good life possible; and although Australians had not hardened to match their more sophisticated, more standardized counterparts of the United States or Britain, the trend was unmistakable as a growing emphasis was placed on material gain and the easier, well-ordered life. Nevertheless, the critic might still stress the makeshift nature of much that was Australian, an absence of goals of excellence, acceptance of the mediocre, a cloying conformity in Australian life, a continuing concentration on "the bank balance and the bungalow."

The change in the Australian scene in twenty years or so was both unmistakable and exciting: in the big cities—Sydney, particularly—there were traces of a European influence to be picked up in shop signs, in scraps of conversation overheard on buses and at street-corners, in the German watch-repairer and the Viennese hairdresser, and in eating habits. Yet the travelled Australian had ruefully to admit that the stimulating and eccentric influences of the Old World appeared to have been rejected or beaten back—or perhaps, as one returnee wrote, not to have penetrated to Australia as yet.

Even as the percentage of the population located in the big cities continued to grow, urban society became even more imitative, with many superficial manifestations of the American scene overlaying vestiges of the older British influence. Based on any measurement of urbanization, Australia ranked among the most urbanized of all countries. Yet, as Professor Thomas Brennan pointed out in his review of urban communities in *Australian Society* (1965), for the resident of the sprawling suburbs it was difficult to see what exactly was the city-like quality in their style of living except access to a variety of employment opportunities. By far the greatest slice of the suburban dweller's non-work time was being spent in doing jobs around the house; this, together with shopping and up to ninety minutes' daily travel to work left little time for other leisure pursuits. To possess a suburban house, however cut off from the land, however inconveniently far from the central city, and however banal and monotonous in appearance, still appeared part of the Australian dream. An accelerating trend to the urban way of life was being backed by industrialization and mechanization, linking it to the quest for a higher standard of living and closer contact with standardized equipment and tastes.

Young people—those who knew only the postwar world—wanted the good life from the beginning. The electric blanket had joined the motor car as virtually a necessity of life. The up-and-coming generation had cut loose from the old identification with pioneering and the open spaces. The typical young man wanted to make his way in the city environment, and his sister was even more determined to avoid the "bush." No one under the age of twenty-five years could subscribe to the idea that the greatest success was that achieved against the almost impossible odds of the back country, and secretly they wondered why their elders held as their ideal the venturesome pioneer who carved out a fortune alone in such a setting; for, outside the field of sport, the young person's hero worship was reserved for the talented scientist or the highly trained executive moving closer, step by step, to the boardroom of a big organization.

Only in the remoter hinterland was the individual still reasonably free from standardizing influences and only there could the old-time individualist survive—a man strong in himself, of tougher fibre and more resilient than those who lived in more crowded places. In such an environment the call for individual fortitude and hardihood and common-sense would scarcely diminish. There could be no lessening of the need for the individual to possess courage and the special qualities called for in tackling everyday problems without outside help. It was in such a setting, in the Northern Territory, that James Morris found "the Australian as we have always thought of him." Whoever he might be, Morris wrote,

> ... he is magnificent to meet: as free a spirit as you can find in the world today, shackled by no inhibition of class or disadvantage, with little sense of thrift and still less of decorum, no agonizing reserve, no envy, no contempt, no meanness. He is like some splendid English workingman relieved of the burden of the centuries, strengthened and cleansed by the southern sun, and allowed to begin history all over again.

In a strange and nostalgic way, the man of the Outback—statistically outnumbered and something of an oddity in the highly industrialized nation —still appeared to many as a genuine archetype. He was still held to possess admirable qualities; as a rugged individualist, he lived a life of his own, untrammelled by the day-to-day round, still involved in the struggle between man and nature. In remoter areas life could go on with little change, and there in small towns people clung to accustomed ways. One young man, Sydney-based journalist John Stubbs, who was brought up in the far west of New South Wales, returned to his home town in 1966 to find that the great social changes which had taken place in the fertile crescent of the continent in the previous fifteen years had not penetrated west of Bourke. The old streak of sentimental tenderness that, with physical toughness, had been so much part of the make-up of the western people, remained, Stubbs found. In *The Australian* he wrote:

> They're still showing B-grade westerns in galvanized-iron picture theatres with dirt floors, and the Aborigines sit on forms down the front. The kids still go to the pictures in their pyjamas with blankets, and sit on the edge of the footpath, and they're mostly thin and tanned.

Stubbs also found that each of the western towns still had a man or two who could reminisce about the old days, talk about the mulga or the spinifex as geographical rather than botanical entities, and tell tales of his own or his mates' adventures as they broke in hundreds of horses a year on northern cattle stations, or faced stampedes in cattle camps.

The sprawling red backland, with its mere sprinkling of settlements, station homesteads or sparse towns might seem far removed from the everyday life of the bustling cities which looked out on the sea; yet the inland and its people remained an ever-present force even if year by year the figure of the lone horseman and his dog was becoming an ever-tinier unit in the mosaic of Australian life. In fact the foreboding inland could never be quite forgotten; it lurked like some evil djinn insecurely corked in a transparent vessel. From time to time drought set the djinn free and more of the marginal land was engulfed as the raw blazing Never-Never pushed closer to the fertile fringe of the continent. The battle was a ceaseless one, with victory going sometimes to the more benign forces, then to the gloating desert, in an unending see-saw. Hardly a summer went by without the cars on the streets of Melbourne and Sydney being spattered with rain reddened by dust scoured from the back country. When inland pastures were seared and wheat crops withered, city businesses felt the side effects which were soon reflected in trimmed balance sheets, while the housewife found that meat and other foodstuffs were costing more so that drought in the hinterland still came as a jolting reminder that the nation as a whole lived closer to the land than its population distribution might suggest. The big swings in the fortunes of political parties since federation had all followed serious droughts; and even as the adding machine was being replaced by the computer and space vehicles were tracked overhead, the great Australian outdoors retained much of its old influence on the nation as a whole. Beyond the paved streets of the cities the Great Outback was no myth but a living force.

Not only did the back-country continue to colour the folklore and form an important element in shaping national attitudes; it also played its part in adumbrating national values. The Australian working in shop or factory still tended to make the man of the outback, the individualist, his archetype of true success, rather than the postal messenger who rose to be departmental head or the migrant who turned the sixpence in his pocket into a business empire—or even the country boy who became Prime Minister. The qualities of resourcefulness and hardihood called for in the pioneer and the back-country man were still held in special esteem; and somewhere in his heart the older citizen cherished the hope that in the vast open spaces of the continent, on sandplain and in the brigalow, the pioneer might still be able to carve out a future for himself and that in the land of mulga and spinifex the lone prospector might stumble upon wealth to match his dreams. Because of a steady downward age shift, a shrinking proportion of the community held to this conviction; yet those for whom it had a meaning—they were mainly in the over-forty age group—saw little reason to relinquish what, to the dedicated, still appeared as a valid if not a strongly-motivating force.

There was still a need for men prepared to pioneer the land in the face of adversity—men prepared to face trials and inconvenience in the tough job of converting raw land or opening remote mines, men content to think in terms of building something for the future. In the brigalow lands of central Queensland, in 1962, reporter Frank Devine met such a latter-day pioneer, "tough, straight-spoken J.W. ('Jock') Anderson," and drew this penpicture in the Melbourne *Herald*:

> His situation is that he is hard up (despite £24,000 worth of government loan credit and a few thousand of his own above the £12,000 in liquid assets an applicant must possess before being considered for a brigalow block), living like a Sicilian peasant, and likely to remain that way for four or five years.
>
> I found Anderson cooking himself a billy of tea in the one-room, dirt-floored shack which he and his 17-year-old son 'Rusty' had built of corrugated iron and tree trunks chopped down on their own property. The shanty had no glass in its windows, no doors in its doorways. The furniture consisted principally of a battered old table and some chairs, an ancient kerosene refrigerator, three neatly-made-up, but so far as I could see, sheetless camp stretchers, and a huge cardboard carton of canned food. Outside, a bucket-shower, screened with sacking, comprised the ablution facilities. . . .
>
> By the time he has paid off his land (8,500 acres at £2 an acre over 25 years) plus interest on money borrowed, bought the 800 head of cattle his property is expected to carry, paid off plant and improvements, he estimates he will have committed himself for about £70,000. . . But he is not on a sure thing. A couple of bad seasons in an area of rich soil but no guaranteed rainfall could finish him, wipe out two or three years of ferocious work, and also his life savings. . . Is the game worth the candle?
>
> "The other day," Anderson said, "Rusty and I worked right through the day. We didn't stop for lunch or tea. We went on with the lights on the tractor. We were both absolutely filthy, bedraggled specimens. I stopped beside the tractor and looked at Rusty sitting up on the tractor. The poor little beggar was just about asleep over the wheel. I must have a perverted sense of humor. I started laughing. I said to Rusty 'It's plain ridiculous. One day we—us two wrecks—may be worth thousands'."

While pioneering remained to be done, there would still be a need for such men. "The genius of this country resides in its individuals," the *Sydney Morning Herald* wrote in an editorial. "We are living in a country crying still for development and offering rich rewards to those who will dare its hardships. From youth today we need a new generation of pioneers."

Old ways could not be quickly swept out of the national consciousness in a land that remained over so much of its expanse fundamentally unchanged and in a national setting in which sheep and cattle still provided the bulk of export earnings and the money coming from rural activities remained a key to national solvency. The nation was still in transition. Twentieth century progress and an ancient landscape remained side by side; the untamed bush remained to defy the comfortable, artificial conformity that moved in the wake of bulldozer and concrete mixer. Australians were absorbing new ideas while clinging tenaciously in many cases to old values. It was the task of the future to blend the old qualities—strength of character and purpose—of the outdoorsman with the new technology of the scientist and the expert. In the community at large, new values were certainly taking hold, and there was a willingness to adopt new ideas; yet the old intangibles, the emphasis on the individual, remained.

Hardihood was no longer enough, however. Nor were old hopes; and for many young people the old sense of reliance on mateship and the supreme value of the individual were features of Australian life to be read about rather than felt. The "average citizen"—the city-dweller—was living in a community which seemed ever more closely linked with the outside world than with the Australian hinterland.

The world had moved on; new frontiers continued to open up through technical advances in great industrial undertakings and in the laboratories and through the new technology which made it possible to design and build radio telescopes capable of picking up emanations from star clusters believed to be close to the absolute limits of space.

A new respect for the world of the computer and advanced technology was evident; this reverence came as an overlay to the revival of a strong national spirit which developed when Australians came to realize that the future of their country was very much in their own hands. By the year 2000, or within the lifetime of most Australians now living, the country might have a population of 25,000,000 or so—enough people, with enough talent, to make everything possible. Meanwhile, in an age when man began to rocket into space in his yearning for new worlds to explore, the vast hinterland still held its surpassing mysteries and offered an incomparable challenge.

Australian scientific achievement was already winning acclaim. In the early 1960s Nobel prizes were awarded to two Australian leaders in medical research—Sir Frank Macfarlane Burnet, director of the Walter and Eliza Hall Institute, in Melbourne, for his work in immunology, and Sir John Eccles, professor of physiology at the Australian National University's John Curtin School of Medical Research, for his lifetime studies in neurophysiology. Other scientists who had outstanding records of achievement included nuclear physicist Sir Marcus Oliphant, and Dr Edward George Bowen, chief of the radio-physics division of CSIRO, and Dr Bernard Yarnton Mills, both of whom had contributed to man's knowledge of the universe through work of major significance in the new science of radio astronomy.

Such men were achieving goals of excellence and enhancing Australia's reputation abroad. Nevertheless, Australians were still reluctant to acknowledge genius among their countrymen.

Nor were they willing to bestow the accolade of greatness upon their leaders, past or present; and they still did not have a genuine folk hero. The reputation of many of those who had done most for their land was still blemished, their true role obscured by partisan assessments. There had been no epoch-making event to sharpen issues; Australia had not had to fight for independence and had not undergone any traumatic test of nationhood. Consequently no truly heroic figure, no leader of great quality and stature, had emerged. A tendency among Australians to be derogatory of their leaders, to stress weaknesses rather than acknowledge capabilities, remained; but this old characteristic was already on the wane and doubtless it would diminish further.

Traditions of sportsmanship continued to shape the outlook and actions of citizens young and old. There was scarcely an Australian who was not involved, as either active participant in some sport or avid follower of many. The Australian was also expected to join in community projects and a broad spectrum of citizens offered their time and support to worthwhile efforts undertaken without thought of personal gain. In personal relationships the emphasis was on basic human values, and the average citizen stood ready to label cant or self-seeking wherever it might be found.

Throughout, the electorate had held to its underlying liberalism in spite of the tensions and challenges, and it had continued to show itself ready to protect democratic procedures against those who would impose illiberal restraints.

The task ahead of Australians was to draw together the threads so that a country of tremendous variety and infinite potential might move forward to greater things—and a future which might confound all the critics and fulfil the grandest prophesies of the visionaries. More than ever before in the nation's history, the future in terms of economic development seemed boundless. Newly-charted deposits of mineral ores were so vast that the national blueprints could be re-drawn; the wealth represented by the massive deposits, added to that of great stores of natural gas and oil which were tapped offshore close to the Victorian coast in 1966, assured a more buoyant national future than had seemed possible even a decade earlier.

Opportunites—still barely grasped—had also come Australia's way as a result of the national participation in special projects. In the space tracking stations developed with NASA, Australia had the right to use the highly-sophisticated equipment; and if by 1966 little had been done with this for any purpose except in direct support of American efforts, nevertheless the experience gained by scientists and technicians in the handling of the equipment was having its effect in Australian science and industry. Under the programme put forward by the United Nations World Meteorological Organization, Melbourne was one of three centres (and the only one in the

Southern Hemisphere) for observing, collating and distributing information for the World Weather Watch, and again use of latest innovations in communications, data-processing, instrumentation and space technology provided experience which could be turned to advantage in wider fields. Similarly, participation with Britain in the joint project in long-range weaponry, while in essence one for the British Government, had already provided the basis for a scientific organization which would not otherwise have been available. The stimulation provided by such projects, as well as their direct spin-off in technical gains, helped to keep Australia abreast of world developments, and, although the general level of the research effort in the industrial field remained disappointingly low, the need for Australian industry to expand its research and development activities had come to the fore.

In the second half of the twentieth century Australia was trying to plot a course in a world of violent paradoxes. It was a time of conflict and co-operation, of affluence and misery, of untidy crises and orderly progress. Grave food shortages haunted the world's most populous lands, while economic forecasts for the advanced nations were a continuance of the record levels of growth and prosperity. Australians faced the future with a growing awareness of the world in which they lived and of their own place in it. Perceptive leadership could help them continue and expand the constructive tasks at hand and help shape new goals.

In seeking to improve its own standard of living and that of other lands where hunger remained, the nation showed its determination to devote resolution and effort, thrift and enterprise to tackling practical common-sense tasks. By the mid-1960s, various organizations as well as the government were working for closer cultural links with countries to Australia's north and also with island neighbours. A technical assistance programme for the South Pacific was set up by the Government in 1965, and Australia joined with Britain and New Zealand in a three-nation mission to investigate the higher educational needs of the island territories and nations of the area. Early in 1966 the Returned Servicemen's League announced a plan—hailed by newspapers as "an imaginative, humanitarian concept"—to bring children from Asia, the Pacific islands, and Africa to Australia to study. These were signs of new and spontaneous efforts to move into new spheres.

More remained to be done. There appeared to be special opportunities for Australia as a nation to expand its constructive role in the countries of south-east Asia, where the Colombo Plan had been an initial effort to grapple with the tremendous problems of raising living standards. It was generally conceded that the next phase of the development commitment would involve greater understanding of the basic problem of finding ways to help the peoples of the region to help themselves. Australia's geographical position, and particularly the country's experience of elevation from colonial status to nationhood in recent times, provided a background from which Australians might communicate more readily with Asian peoples. It was considered by some that the nation's most effective role might be in training more men in the practical tasks of modern farming and improved agriculture, in order that they in turn might help their homelands in the urgent search for ways to increase food production.

Within the Australian scene itself, the setting of national priorities was still a contentious issue; but for themselves and their children Australians seemed to be fashioning a nation in which constructive planning might enlarge and not circumscribe the individual's opportunity for initiative and enterprise. No one could yet delineate the new kind of civilization that would emerge from the great fusion of ideas already begun.

FURTHER READING

GENERAL

The following listing covers mainly general histories and specialist studies dealing with long periods of Australian history; included are works with subject matter dealt with in two or more sections of this book.

Austin, A.G., *Australian Education 1788–1900: Church, State and Public Education in Colonial Australia* (Melbourne 1951)

The Australian Encyclopaedia, general editor, A.H. Chisholm (Sydney 1958)

Barnard, M., *A History of Australia* (Sydney 1962)

Blainey, G., *The Rush that Never Ended* (Melbourne 1963)

Bolton, G.C., *A Thousand Miles Away: A History of North Queensland to 1920* (Brisbane 1963)

Border, J.T.R., *Church and State in Australia 1788–1872: A Constitutional Study of the Church of England in Australia* (London 1962)

Bryce, J. (Viscount Bryce), *Modern Democracies*, Vol. II (New York 1921)

Butlin, N.G., *Australian Domestic Product: Investment and Foreign Borrowing 1861–1938/39* (Cambridge 1962)

  id., *Investment in Australian Economic Development, 1861–1900* (Cambridge 1964)

Butlin, S.J., *Foundations of the Australian Monetary System 1788–1851* (Melbourne 1953)

Cambridge History of the British Empire, Vol. VII, Part 1, *Australia* (Cambridge 1933)

Churchill, W.S., *A History of the English-Speaking Peoples*, Vol. IV, *The Great Democracies* (New York 1956)

Cilento, R., and Lack, C., *Triumph in the Tropics: An Historical Sketch of Queensland* (Brisbane 1959)

Clark, C.M.H., ed., *Select Documents in Australian History, 1788–1900*, 2 vols. (Sydney 1950–55)

  id., ed., *Sources of Australian History* (Sydney 1962)

  id., *A Short History of Australia* (London 1964)

Cox, E.W., *The Evolution of the Australian Merino* (Sydney 1936)

Crawford, R.M., *Australia*, 2nd ed. (London 1964)

Crisp, L.F., *The Australian Federal Labor Party 1901–51* (London 1955)

Crowley, F.K., *Australia's Western Third: A History of Western Australia from the First Settlement to Modern Times* (London 1960)

Davis, S.R., ed., *The Government of the Australian States* (Melbourne 1960)
Dow, G.M., *George Higinbotham: Church and State* (Melbourne 1964)
Downing, R.L., *National Income and Social Accounts,* 9th ed. (Melbourne 1965)
Doyle, E., ed., *The Story of the Century 1851–1951* (Melbourne 1951)
Durack, M., *Kings in Grass Castles* (Melbourne 1959)
Ebbels, R.N. *The Australian Labor Movement 1850–1907* (Melbourne 1965)
Ellis, M.H., *John Macarthur* (Sydney 1955)
Favenc, E., *History of Australian Exploration* (Sydney 1888)
  id., *Explorers of Australia and Their Life Work* (Christchurch 1908)
Fitzhardinge, L.F., *Nation Building in Australia: The Life and Work of Sir Littleton Ernest Groom* (Sydney 1941)
Fitzpatrick, B., *The British Empire in Australia: An Economic History, 1834–1939,* 2nd ed. (Melbourne 1949)
Fitzpatrick, K.E., ed., *Australian Explorers: A Selection of Their Writings* (London 1958)
Foenander, O. de R., *Industrial Regulation in Australia* (Melbourne 1947)
Fogarty, R., *Catholic Education in Australia 1806–1950* (Melbourne 1959)
Ford P., *Cardinal Moran and the A.L.P.: A Study in the Encounter between Moran and Socialism 1890–1907; Its Effects upon the Australian Labor Party; the Foundation of Catholic Social Thought and Action in Modern Australia* (Melbourne 1966)
Gollan, R., *Radical and Working Class Politics: A Study of Eastern Australia 1850–1910* (Melbourne 1960)
Gordon, M., *Sir Isaac Isaacs* (London 1963)
Grattan, C.H., *The South West Pacific to 1900,* and *The South West Pacific Since 1900* (Ann Arbor, Mich., 1963)
Greenwood, G., ed., *Australia: A Social and Political History,* 3rd. ed. (Sydney 1964)
Hancock, W.K., *Australia,* 3rd ed. (Brisbane 1961)
Hetherington, J., *Blamey: The Biography of Field Marshal Sir Thomas Blamey* (Melbourne 1954)
Heydon, P.R., *Quiet Decision: A Study of George Foster Pearce* (Melbourne 1965)
Historical Records of Australia; edited by J.F. Watson; 34 vols. (Sydney 1914–25)
Historical Records of New South Wales 1762–1811; edited by E.M. Bladen (Sydney 1893–1901)
Hussey, W.D., *The British Empire and Commonwealth, 1500 to 1961* (Cambridge 1963)
Kiddle, M., *Men of Yesterday: A Social History of the Western District of Victoria 1834–1890* (Melbourne 1963)
Knaplund, P., *The British Empire 1815–1939* (London 1941)
Lawson, W., *When Cobb and Co. was King* (Sydney 1959)
Macarthur-Onslow, S., ed., *Some Early Records of the Macarthurs of Camden* (Sydney 1914)
Madgwick, R.B., *Immigration into Eastern Australia 1788–1851* (London 1937)
Melbourne, A.C.V., *Early Constitutional Development in Australia: New South Wales 1788–1856* (Brisbane 1963)
Mills, R.C., *The Colonization of Australia: The Wakefield Experiment in Empire Building* (London 1915)
Murtagh, J.G., *Australia: The Catholic Chapter,* 2nd ed. (Sydney 1959)
Overacker, L., *The Australian Party System* (New York 1952)
Palmer, V., *National Portraits,* 3rd ed. (Melbourne 1962)
Pike, D.H., *Australia: The Quiet Continent* (Cambridge 1962)
Reese, T.R., *Australia in the Twentieth Century: A Short Political History* (Melbourne 1964)
Rivett, R., *Australian Citizen, Herbert Brookes, 1867–1963* (Melbourne 1965)
Roberts, S.H., *History of Australian Land Settlement 1788–1902* (Melbourne 1924)

Rusden, G.W., *History of Australia,* 3 vols. (London 1897)

Scholes, W.A., *Seventh Continent: Saga of Exploration in Antarctica 1895–1950* (London 1953)

Scott, E., *A Short History of Australia,* 8th ed. (Melbourne 1961)

  id., *Australian Discovery by Sea* and *Australian Discovery by Land* (London 1929)

Serle, P., *Dictionary of Australian Biography,* 2 vols. (Sydney 1949)

Shann, E., *An Economic History of Australia,* rev. ed. (Melbourne 1963)

Shaw, A.G.L., *Economic Development of Australia,* 4th ed. (Melbourne 1964)

Smith, A.N., *Thirty Years: The Commonwealth of Australia, 1901–31* (Melbourne 1933)

Smith, B., *Place, Taste and Tradition* (Sydney 1945)

Suttor, T.L., *Hierarchy and Democracy in Australia, 1788–1870: The Formation of Australian Catholicism* (Melbourne 1965)

Swann, R.A., *Australia in the Antarctic: Interest, Activity and Endeavour* (Melbourne 1961)

Sweetman, E., *Australian Constitutional Development* (Melbourne 1925)

Taylor, T.G., *Australia: A Study of Warm Environments on British Settlement,* 7th ed. (London 1961)

Wadham, S.M., and Wood, G.L., *Land Utilization in Australia* (Melbourne 1950)

Ward, J.M., *British Policy in the South Pacific 1786–1893* (Sydney 1948)

Ward, R., *The Australian Legend* (Melbourne 1958)

White, H.L., *Source Material for Australian Studies* (Melbourne 1957)

Whyte, W.F., *William Morris Hughes: His Life and Times* (Sydney 1957)

Wigmore, L., *The Long View: A History of Canberra* (Melbourne 1963)

Yarwood, A.T., *Asian Migration to Australia: The Background to Exclusion, 1896–1923* (Melbourne 1964)

Books dealing with a limited period or a specific topic covered in a single section of the book are listed below. For convenience, the titles are grouped under the particular section of the book to which they apply.

I: DISCOVERY

Amherst of Hackney and Thomson, B., eds., *The Discovery of the Solomon Islands by Alvaro de Mendana,* 2 vols. (London 1901)

Beaglehole, J.C., *The Exploration of the Pacific* (London 1934)

  id., ed., *The Journals of Captain James Cook on His Voyages of Discovery;* Vol. I, *The Voyage of the Endeavour, 1768–71* (London 1955)

  id., ed., *The Endeavour Journal of Joseph Banks, 1768–71* (Sydney 1962)

Callander, J., *Terra Australis Cognita: or Voyages to the Terra Australis, or Southern Hemisphere, during the Sixteenth, Seventeenth and Eighteenth Centuries,* 3 vols (Edinburgh 1766–68)

Calvert, A.F., *The Discovery of Australia* (London 1893)

Cipolla, C.M. *Guns, Sails, and Empires: Technological Innovation and the Early Phases of European Expansion (1400–1700)* (New York 1966)

Giblin, R.W., *The Early History of Tasmania,* Vol. I *The Geographical Era 1642–1804* (London 1928)

Harris, J., *Navigantium atque itinerantium bibliotheca; or, A Complete Collection of Voyages and Travels,* 2 vols. (London 1744–48)

Heeres, J.E., *The Part Borne by the Dutch in the Discovery of Australia, 1606–1765* (London 1899)

id., ed., *Abel Janszoon Tasman: Journal of His Discovery of Van Diemen's Land and New Zealand in 1642, with Documents relating to His Exploration of Australia in 1644* (Amsterdam 1898)

Mahan, A.T., *The Influence of Sea Power Upon History, 1600–1783,* 12th ed. (Boston 1964)

Major, A.J., ed., *Early Voyages to Terra Australis to the Time of Captain Cook, as Told in Original Documents* (Adelaide 1963)

Markham, C., ed., *The Voyages of Pedro Fernandez de Quiros 1595–1606,* 2 vols. (London 1904)

Parkinson, S., *A Journal of a Voyage to the South Seas in His Majesty's Ship The Endeavour* (London 1773)

Steven, H.N., ed., *New Light on the Discovery of Australia as Revealed by the Journal of Captain Don Diego de Prado y Tovar* (London 1930)

Wood, G.A., *The Discovery of Australia* (London 1922)

II: SETTLEMENT

Bateson, C., *The Convict Ships, 1787–1868* (Glasgow 1959)

Bigge, J.T., *Report of the Commissioner of Inquiry into the State of the Colony of New South Wales* (London 1823)

Cobley, J., *Sydney Cove, 1788* (London 1962)

id., *Sydney Cove, 1789–90* (Sydney 1963)

id., *Sydney Cove, 1791–92* (Sydney 1965)

Collins, D., *An Account of the English Colony in New South Wales,* 2 vols. (London 1798–1802)

Eldershaw, M. Barnard, *Phillip of Australia; An Account of the Settlement at Sydney Cove, 1788–1792* (London 1938)

Ellis, M.H., *Lachlan Macquarie, His Life, Adventures and Times* (Sydney 1947)

Evatt, H.V., *Rum Rebellion* (Sydney 1955)

Fitzpatrick, B., *British Imperialism and Australia, 1783–1833* (London 1939)

Flower, W.H., *The Aborigines of Tasmania, An Extinct Race* (London 1878)

Forsyth, W.D., *Governor Arthur's Convict System* (London 1878)

Giblin, R.W., *The Early History of Tasmania,* Vol. II, *The Penal Settlement Era 1804–28* (Melbourne 1939)

Harlow, V.T., *The Founding of the Second British Empire 1763–93* (London 1852)

Hasham, J., *Convict Ships: A Narrative of a Voyage to New South Wales in the Year 1816* (London 1819)

Hasluck, A., *Thomas Peel of Swan River* (Melbourne 1965)

Lang, J.D., *A Historical and Statistical Account of New South Wales from the Founding of the Colony,* Vol I. (London 1875)

Mackaness, G., *Admiral Arthur Phillip, Founder of New South Wales, 1738–1814* (Sydney 1937)

id., *The Life of Vice Admiral William Bligh,* 2nd. ed. (Sydney 1951)

O'Brien, E.M., *The Foundation of Australia 1786–1800* 2nd. ed. (Sydney 1950)

Oxley, J., *Journals of Two Expeditions into the Interior of New South Wales, 1817–18* (London 1820)

Perry, T.M., *Australia's First Frontier: The Spread of Settlement in New South Wales 1788–1829* (Melbourne 1963)

Pike, D., *Paradise of Dissent: South Australia 1829–57* (Melbourne 1957)

Ramsden, E., *Marsden and the Missions* (Sydney 1936)

Robson, L., *Convict Settlers in Australia* (Melbourne 1965)

Scott, E., *Terre Napoléon: A History of French Exploration and Projects in Australia* (London 1910)

Steven, M., *Merchant Campbell 1796–1846: A Study of Colonial Trade* (Melbourne 1965)

Tench, W.W., *Sydney's First Four Years;* being a Reprint of "*A Narrative of the Expedition to Botany Bay*" and "*A Complete Account of the Settlement at Port Jackson*" (Sydney 1961)

Turnbull, C., *Black War* (Melbourne 1948)

Wakefield, E.G., *A Letter from Sydney* (London 1829)

id., *A View of the Art of Colonization* (London 1841)

Walker, J.B., *Early Tasmania* (Hobart 1914)

Wentworth, W.C., *A Statistical Account of the Colony of New South Wales and its Dependent Settlements,* 2 vols, (London 1819–24)

White, J., *Journal of a Voyage to New South Wales, by John White, Surgeon-General to the First Fleet and the Settlement at Port Jackson;* edited by A.H. Chisholm (Sydney 1962)

Whitington, D.T., *William Grant Broughton* (Sydney 1936)

Woolls, W., *A Short Account of the Character and Labours of the Reverend Samuel Marsden* (Parramatta 1844)

III: THE FRONTIER PHASE

Backhouse, J., *Narrative of a Visit to the Australian Colonies* (London 1843)

Barrett, J., *That Better Country: The Religious Aspect of Life in Eastern Australia, 1835–50* (Melbourne 1966)

Bassett, M., *The Hentys: An Australian Colonial Tapestry* (Melbourne 1962)

Bonwick, J., *Discovery and Settlement of Port Phillip* (London 1856)

Boxall, G.E., *The Story of Australian Bushranging* (London 1899)

Cumpston, J.H.L., *Charles Sturt, His Life and Journeys of Exploration* (Melbourne 1951)

id., *Thomas Mitchell, Surveyor-General and Explorer* (London 1954)

id., *The Inland Sea and the Great River: the Story of Australian Exploration* (Sydney 1964)

Curr, E.M., *Recollections of Squatting in Victoria,* rev. ed. (Melbourne 1965)

Doyle, E., ed., *Golden Years* (Melbourne 1951)

Eyre, J., *Journals of Expeditions of Discovery* (London 1845)

Dauchery, A., *Letters from a Miner in Australia,* translated from the French by A.R. Chisholm (Melbourne 1965)

Fitzpatrick, K., *Sir John Franklin in Tasmania 1837–43* (Melbourne 1949)

Grey, G., *Two Expeditions of Discovery in North-west and Western Australia in 1837-8-9* (London 1841)

Grey, H.G. (Earl Grey), *The Colonial Policy of Lord John Russell's Administration* (London 1853)

Harris, A., *Settlers and Convicts; or Recollections of Sixteen Years in the Australian Backwoods, by an Emigrant Mechanic*—first published London 1847 (Melbourne 1964)

Irwin, F.C., *State and Position of Western Australia* (London 1835)

Kiddle, M., *Caroline Chisholm* (Melbourne 1950)

Leichhardt, L., *Journal of an Overland Expedition* (London 1847)

Macarthur, J., *New South Wales: Its Present and Future Prospects* (London 1837)

Mitchell, T., *Three Expeditions into the Interior of Eastern Australia* (London 1838)

id., *Journal of an Expedition into the Interior of Tropical Australia* (London 1848)

Nadel, G., *Australia's Colonial Culture: Ideas, Men and Institiutions in Mid-Nineteenth-Century Eastern Australia* (Cambridge, Mass. 1957)

Price, A.G., *Founders and Pioneers of South Australia* (Adelaide 1929)

Roe, M., *Quest for Authority in Eastern Australia 1835-51* (Melbourne 1965)

Sturt, C., *Two Expeditions into the Interior of Southern Australia* (London 1833)

Townsley, W.A., *The Struggle for Self Government in Tasmania, 1842-56* (Hobart 1951)

IV: COLONIAL SEPARATISM

Alexander, J.A., *The Life of George Chaffey* (Melbourne 1928)

Bell, A., *Melbourne: John Batman's Village* (Melbourne 1965)

Blainey, G., *Gold and Paper* (Melbourne 1962)

Bowen, G., *Thirty Years of Colonial Government* (London 1889)

Casey, M., *An Australian Story 1837-1907* (London 1962)

Forrest, J. (Lord Forrest), *Explorations of Australia* (London 1875)

Giles, E., *Australia Twice Traversed: The Romance of Exploration, being a Narrative compiled from the Journals of Five Exploring into and through Central South Australia, and Western Australia, from 1872 to 1876* (London 1889)

Hill, E., *Water into Gold*, rev. ed. (Sydney 1965)

Hodder, E., *History of South Australia* (London 1893)

Hogan, J.F., *The Gladstone Colony* (London 1898)

Landsborough, W., *Explorations of Australia* (Melbourne 1867)

Loveday, P., and Martin, A.W., *Parliament, Factions and Parties: The First Thirty Years of Responsible Government in New South Wales, 1856-89* (Melbourne 1966)

Macgillivray, J., *Narrative of the Voyage of HMS Rattlesnake* (London 1852)

Moorehead, A., *Cooper's Creek* (London 1963)

Moresby, J., *New Guinea and Polynesia: Discoveries and Surveys in New Guinea and the D'Entrecasteaux Islands* (London 1876)

Priestley, S., *Echuca: A Centenary History* (Brisbane 1965)

Raffaello, C., *The Eureka Stockade* (Melbourne 1947)

Serle, A.G., *The Golden Age: A History of the Colony of Victoria 1851-61* (Melbourne 1963)

Stuart, J. McD., *Exploration across the Continent of Australia* (London 1862)

   id., *Explorations in Australia* (London 1865)

Turnbull, C., *Bluestone: The Story of James Stephens, Leader of the Eight Hours Movement* (Melbourne 1945)

   id., *Eureka: The Story of Peter Lalor* (Melbourne 1956)

Turner, G., *History of the Colony of Victoria* (Melbourne 1904)

Ward, J.M., *Earl Grey and the Australian Colonies 1846-57: A Study of Self-Government and Self-Interest* (Melbourne 1958)

V: CREATING A NATION

Bean, C.W.E., ed., *The Official History of Australia in the War of 1914-1918,* 12 vols. (Sydney 1921-42)

   id., *On the Wool Track*, rev. ed. (Sydney 1963)

Bellamy, E., *Looking Backward, 2000-1887* (New York 1887)

Bowman, S.E., ed., et al., *Edward Bellamy Abroad: An American Prophet's Influence* (New York 1962)

Brennan, N., *Dr. Mannix* (Adelaide 1964)

Cannon, M., *The Land Boomers* (Melbourne 1966)
Coghlan T.A., *Labour and Industry in Australia,* 4 vols. (Oxford 1918)
Deakin, A., *The Federal Story: The Inner History of the Federal Cause;* edited by J.A. La Nauze (Melbourne 1963)
Evatt, H.V., *Australian Labour Leader: The Story of W.A. Holman and the Labour Movement* (Sydney 1954)
Fitzhardinge, L.D., *William Morris Hughes:* I: *That Fiery Particle, 1862–1914* (Sydney 1964)
George, H., *Progress and Poverty: An Inquiry into the Cause of Industrial Depressions and of Increase of Want with Increase of Wealth; The Remedy* (New York 1880)
    id., *The Science of Political Economy* (New York 1898)
Gordon, D.C., *The Australian Frontier in New Guinea, 1870–85* (New York 1951)
Green, H.M., *A History of Australian Literature,* vol. I, *1788–1922* (Sydney 1962)
Hamilton, I., *Gallipoli Diaries* (London 1920)
James, R.H., *Gallipoli* (Sydney 1965)
La Nauze, J.A., *Alfred Deakin: A Biography* (Melbourne 1965)
Lindsay, N., *Bohemians of The Bulletin* (Sydney 1965)
Macgregor, W., *British New Guinea* (London 1897)
Mansfield, B., *Australian Democrat: The Career of Edward William O'Sullivan, 1846–1901* (Sydney 1965)
Monash, J., *The Australian Victories in France* (Melbourne 1920)
Palmer, N., *Henry Bournes Higgins: A Memoir* (London 1931)
Palmer, V., *The Legend of the Nineties* (Melbourne 1963)
Parkes, H., *Fifty Years in the Making of Australian History* (London 1892)
Pollard, A.F., *The Commonwealth at War* (London 1917)
Quick, J., *Sir John Quick's Notebook;* edited by L.E. Freedman (Newcastle 1965)
Reeves, W.P., *State Experiments in Australia and New Zealand* (London 1902)
Ross, L., *William Lane and the Australian Labor Movement* (Sydney 1938)
Rowley, C.D., *The Australians in German New Guinea from 1914 to 1921* (Melbourne 1958)
Roydhouse, T.R., and Taperall, H.J., *The Labor Party in New South Wales; a History of Its Formation* (London 1892)
Spence, W.G., *Australia's Awakening: Thirty Years in the Life of an Australian Agitator* (Melbourne 1919)
Spencer, W.B., *Native Tribes of the Northern Territory of Australia* (London 1914)
    id., and Gillen, F.J., *The Northern Tribes of Central Australia* (London 1904)
Sutcliffe, J.T., *A History of Trade Unionism in Australia* (Melbourne 1921)
Turner, I., *Industrial Labor and Politics: The Dynamics of the Labor Movement in Eastern Australia, 1900–21* (Canberra 1965)

VI: GROWING UP

Australia, *Report of the Royal Commission on Monetary and Banking Systems in Australia* (Canberra 1937)
Bates, D., *The Passing of the Aborigines,* new ed., (Melbourne 1966)
Blainey, G., *Mines in the Spinifex: The Story of Mount Isa Mines* (Sydney 1960)
Brigden J.B., and Copland, D.B., et al., *The Australian Tariff: An Economic Inquiry* (Melbourne 1929)
Campbell, E., *The Rallying Point: My Story of the New Guard* (Melbourne 1965)
Churchill, W.S., *While England Slept: A Survey of World Affairs, 1932–38* (New York 1938)
    id., *The Second World War,* 6 vols. (Boston 1948–53)

Clark, C., *The National Income of Australia* (Sydney 1938)

Copland, D.B., *Australia in the World Crisis, 1929–33* (Cambridge 1934)

    id., *The Australian Economy* (Sydney 1941)

Denning, W., *Caucus Crisis: The Rise and Fall of the Scullin Government* (Parramatta 1937)

Edmonds, W.D., *They Fought with What They Had: The Story of the U.S. Army Air Forces in the Southwest Pacific 1941–42* (Boston 1951)

Edwards, C., *Viscount Bruce of Melbourne* (London 1965)

Eichelberger, R.L., *Our Jungle Road to Tokyo* (New York 1950)

Ellis, U.R., *A History of the Australian Country Party* (Melbourne 1963)

Feldt, E.A., *The Coastwatchers* (Melbourne 1946)

Forsyth, W.D., *The Myth of the Open Spaces* (Melbourne 1942)

Foxcroft, E.J.B., *Australian Native Policy* (Melbourne 1941)

Fuchida, M., *Midway, the Battle that Doomed Japan; the Japanese Navy's Story,* edited by C.H. Kawakami and R. Pineau (Annapolis 1955)

Fysh, W.H., *Qantas Rising: The Autobiography of the Flying Fysh* (Sydney 1965)

Giblin, L.F., *The Growth of a Central Bank: The Development of the Commonwealth Bank of Australia 1924–45* (Melbourne 1951)

Green, H.M., *A History of Australian Literature,* vol. II, *1923–50* (Sydney 1962)

Gullett, H., *Unguarded Australia* (Melbourne 1919)

Gunn, H., ed., *The British Empire: A Survey;* vol. I, *The Dominions and Dependencies;* IV, *The Resources of the Empire and Their Development;* XII, *Migration within the Empire* (London 1924)

Hasluck, P.M.C., *Black Australians* (Melbourne 1942)

Heaton, H., *The British Way to Recovery: Plans and Policies in Australia, Canada and Great Britain* (Minneapolis 1934)

Hughes, W.M., *The Splendid Adventure: A Review of Empire within and without the Commonwealth of Britannic Nations* (London 1929)

Hides, J.G., *Through Wildest Papua* (London 1935)

    id., *Savages in Serge* (Sydney 1938)

Ho, M., *The End of the Japanese Imperial Navy* (New York 1956)

Hodson, H.V., ed., for the Royal Institute of International Affairs, *The British Empire: A Report on Its Structure and Problems* (London 1937)

Johnston, G. H., *My Brother Jack* (Sydney 1964)

Latham, J.G., *Australia and the British Commonwealth* (Melbourne 1928)

Leacock, S.B., *The British Empire: Its Structure, Its Unity, Its Strength* (New York 1940)

Leckie, R., *Challenge for the Pacific: Guadalcanal—Turning Point of the War* (New York 1965)

Legg, F., *The Gordon Bennett Story* (Sydney 1965)

Lockwood, D., *Australia's Pearl Harbor: Darwin 1942* (Melbourne 1966)

Long, G.M., ed., *Australia in the War of 1939–1945,* Series I to V. 19 vols, (Canberra 1952 to date)

Lyons, E., *So We Take Comfort* (Melbourne 1965)

MacArthur, D., *Reminiscences* (New York 1964)

McPheat, W.S., *John Flynn, Apostle of the Inland* (London 1963)

Moorehead, A., *The Desert War, 1940–43* (London 1965)

Morison, S.E., *History of United States Naval Operations in World War II,* 15 vols, (Boston 1947–62)

Murray, J.H.P., *Papua Today* (London 1925)

Page E., *Truant Surgeon: The Inside Story of Forty Years of Australian Political Life* (Sydney 1963)

Phillips, P.D., and Wood, G.L., ed., *The Peopling of Australia* (Melbourne 1930)

Reed, S.W., *The Making of Modern New Guinea* (Philadelphia 1943)
Shann, E.O.G., and Copland, D.B., compilers, *The Crisis in Australian Finance 1929–31* (Sydney 1932)
Smith, N. S., *Structure and Working of the Australian Tariff: with Special Reference to Empire Trading* (Melbourne 1929)
Walker, E.R., *The Australian Economy in War and Reconstruction* (London 1947)
Willoughby, C.A., and Chamberlain, J., *MacArthur 1941–51* (New York 1954)
Wright, M., *If I Die: Coast Watching and Guerrilla Warfare Behind Japanese Lines* (Melbourne 1965)

VII: NEW FRONTIERS

Arndt, H. W., *Australian Foreign Policy* (Adelaide 1964)
Australia, Ministry of Post-War Reconstruction, *Full Employment in Australia* (Canberra 1945)
　　id., Departments of Works & Housing and Post-War Reconstruction, *Report on Proposals to Divert the Snowy River into the Murrumbidgee and the Murray Rivers* (Canberra 1947)
　　id., Department of Trade and Industry, *Australian Manufacturing Industry,* 3rd ed. (Melbourne 1963)
　　id., Comittee of Economic Enquiry, *Report* (Canberra 1965)
Australian Industries Development Association, *Development in Australia 1965* (Melbourne 1965)
Borrie, W.D., *Immigration: Australia's Problems and Prospects* (Sydney 1949)
　　id., and Spencer, G., *Australia's Population Structure and Growth* (Melbourne 1965)
Boyd, R., *The Australian Ugliness* (Melbourne 1963)
Calwell, A.A., *How Many Australians Tomorrow?* (Melbourne 1945)
　　id., *Labor's Role in Modern Society* (Melbourne 1965)
Campbell, L., *Moonie and Oil Search: the Story of the Discovery of Oil in Australia* (Sydney 1964)
Casey, R.G., (Baron Casey of Berwick), *Friends and Neighbours: Australia and the World* (East Lansing, Mich. 1962)
Condliffe, J.B., *The Development of Australia* (Sydney 1964)
Copland, D.B., and Barback, R.H., ed., *The Conflict of Expansion and Stability: Documents Relating to Australian Economic Policy 1945–52* (Melbourne 1957)
Cowan, Z., *Federal Jurisdiction in Australia* (Melbourne 1959)
Crisp, L.F., *Ben Chifley: A Biography* (Melbourne 1961)
Davidson, B.R., *The Northern Myth* (Melbourne 1965)
Davidson, F.G., *The Industrialization of Australia,* 3rd ed. (Melbourne 1962)
Davies, A.F., and Encel, S., eds., *Australian Society: A Sociological Introduction* (Melbourne 1965)
Davis, S.R., ed., *The Australian Political Party System* (Sydney 1954)
Doyle, B., *Catholics and Labor's Socialist Objective* (Haberfield, N.S.W. 1949)
Eayers, J.G., ed., *The Commonwealth and Suez: A Documentary Survey* (London 1964)
Eggleston, F. W., *Reflections on Australian Foreign Policy* (Melbourne 1957)
Elkin, A. P., *The Aborigines: How to Understand Them* (Sydney 1964)
Evatt, H.V., *Foreign Policy of Australia* (Sydney 1945)
Fenner, F., and Ratcliffe, F.N., *Myxomatosis* (Cambridge 1965)
Greenwood, G., ed. with Harper, N., *Australia in World Affairs* (Melbourne 1957)
Harper, N., and Sissons, D., *Australia and the United Nations* (New York 1959)
Hetherington, J.A., *Australian Painters: Forty Profiles* (Melbourne 1963)
Harrod, R., *The Life of John Maynard Keynes* (London 1951)
Holt, H.E., Calwell, A.A., et al., *Australia and the Migrant* (Sydney 1953)

Horne, D., *The Lucky Country: Australia in the Sixties* (Sydney 1965)

Hughes, H., *The Australian Iron and Steel Industry 1948–62* (Melbourne 1964)

Hunter, A., ed., *The Economics of Australian Industry: Studies in Environment and Structure* (Melbourne 1963)

Jupp, J., *Australian Labour and the World* (London 1965)

Lett, L., *Sir Hubert Murray of Papua* (London 1949)

Lockwood, D., *I, The Aboriginal* (Adelaide 1962)

McLeod, A.L., ed., *The Pattern of Australian Culture* (New York 1963)

Mair, L.P., *Australia in New Guinea* (London 1948)

Mayer, H., ed., *Australian Politics: A Reader* (Melbourne 1966)

Menzies, R.G., *The Forgotten People, and Other Studies in Democracy* (Sydney 1943)

    id., *Speech is of Time* (Melbourne 1958)

Millar, T.B., *Australia's Defence* (Melbourne 1965)

Miller, J.D.B., *Australia and Foreign Policy* (Sydney 1963)

Neutze, G.M., *Economic Policy and the Size of Cities* (Canberra 1965)

Perkins, J.O.N., *Anti-Cyclical Policy in Australia 1960–64* (Melbourne 1965)

Price, C.A., *A Study of Immigrants in Australia* (Canberra 1960)

Pringle, J.D., *Australian Accent* (London 1958)

    id., *Australian Painting Today* (London 1963)

Rawson, D.W., *Labor in Vain? A Survey of the Australian Labor Party* (Melbourne 1966)

Ross, I. Clunies, *Memoirs and Papers: Some Fragments of Autobiography,* edited by F. Eyre (Melbourne 1961)

Ruhen, O., *Mountains in the Clouds* (Adelaide 1963)

Royal Institute of International Affairs, *The British Commonwealth and World Society: Proceedings of the Third Unofficial Conference* (London 1947)

Santamaria, B.A., *The Price of Freedom* (Melbourne 1964)

Sawer, G., *Australian Government Today* (Sydney 1957)

Simpson, C., *Adam in Ochre: Inside Aboriginal Australia,* 5th ed. (Sydney 1962)

Souter, G., *New Guinea, the Last Unknown* (Sydney 1963)

Spratt, E.D., *Eddie Ward, Firebrand of East Sydney* (Adelaide 1965)

Starke, J.G., *The ANZUS Treaty Alliance* (Melbourne 1965)

Thompson, J.J.M., ed., *On the Lips of Living Men* (Melbourne 1962)

United Nations: Trusteeship Council; Visiting Mission to the Trust Territories of Nauru and New Guinea, *The People Speaking;* texts of daily progress reports covering work of the 1965 visiting Mission (Canberra 1965)

Victorian Chamber of Manufactures, *The Australian Economy Today and Tomorrow: An Economic Forum* (Melbourne 1965)

West, K., *Power in the Liberal Party: A Study in Australian Politics* (Melbourne 1965)

Wheelwright, E.C, ed., *Higher Education in Australia* (Melbourne 1965)

Whitington, D., *The Rulers—Fifteen Years of the Liberals,* 2nd ed. (Melbourne 1965)

Hansard, the official record of proceedings of the parliament of the Commonwealth, contains verbatim reports of all parliamentary debates. Each of the state parliaments issues its own *Hansard* record.

Material of basic importance is to be found also in the British Parliamentary Papers. Official reports of the Colonial, Imperial and Commonwealth conferences and the record of the debates in the House of Lords and the House of Commons provide valuable material on changing relations.

The record of the League of Nations and its agencies covers the period between World War I and World War II. Since 1945 documents recording the deliberations of various United Nations bodies have been issued by the United Nations, and wide-ranging United Nations statistical reports compiled on a world-wide basis are released regularly.

The following official publications issued in Canberra are among those which deal with current trends in various fields, in most cases providing statistical information:

Australia, Bureau of Census and Statistics: *Official Year Book of the Commonwealth of Australia* (annually)
  id., *Quarterly Summary of Australian Statistics*
Commonwealth Scientific and Industrial Research Organization: *Annual Reports;* together with technical bulletins relating to subjects under study by the various Divisions of the organization
Department of External Affairs: *Current Notes on International Affairs* (monthly)
Department of the Interior News and Information Bureau: *Australia in Facts and Figures* (quarterly)
Department of Territories: *Annual Reports on the Northern Territory and Papua-New Guinea*
Department of the Treasury: *Treasury Information Bulletin* and White Papers dealing with the economy in general

In addition, various departments and statutory bodies of the Commonwealth also issue reports and summaries.

Separate Year Books are published for each of the states.

AUSTRALIAN COLONIES: SETTLEMENT AND GOVERNMENT

	New South Wales	Victoria	Queensland	South Australia	Western Australia	Tasmania	Northern Territory
Date of first permanent settlement	1788	1834	1824	1836	1829	1803	1864
Date of establishment as separate colony (or Territory)	1786	1851	1859	1834	1829	1825	1911
Date of Acts of Parliament (or orders-in-Council) authorising establishment of a legislative body representing the people of the colony	1823	1850	1859	1842	1830	1825	1947
Dates of Acts of Parliament under which responsible government was authorised, and as a result of which legislative bodies were established in the various colonies in forms which have lasted (with various amendments) up to the present day. The Acts in question were drafted in the colonies concerned, and became law after being passed by the Imperial Parliament and receiving the Royal assent	1855	1855	1859	1856	1890	1855	—

UPPER HOUSE

	New South Wales	Victoria	Queensland	South Australia	Western Australia	Tasmania	Northern Territory
Name	Legislative Council	Legislative Council	Legislative Council	Legislative Council	Legislative Council	Legislative Council	Legislative Council
How appointed	1856 nominated by Governor on advice of Executive Council 1933 Nominee Council replaced by Electoral College consisting of members of Legislative Assembly and non-retiring members of Legislative Council voting together on proportional representation system.	1856 elected; substantial property qualification for voters 1950 elected by adult suffrage	1859 nominated 1922 Legislative Council abolished	1856 one-third nominated; two-thirds elected. 1857 elected on restricted franchise (virtually householder franchise) *	1890 nominated, but to be elected after 6 years, or when population reached 60,000. 1893 elected; virtually householder franchise *	1856 elected on restricted franchise (owner or occupier of dwelling; graduate; naval or military officer or retired officer). 1903 adult suffrage *	1947 part elective, part nominated

* Franchises in South Australia, Western Australia and Tasmania are based on property qualifications and some other qualifications, such as possession of a University degree or a Returned-from-active-service badge. Because of reductions in the requisite value of land to be owned or occupied, combined with enhanced property values, virtually every occupier of a home has become qualified to vote. The practical result has been to produce a head-of-household franchise, with a total Upper House electorate about one third, in number, that of the Lower House.

LOWER HOUSE

Name	Legislative Assembly	Legislative Assembly	Legislative Assembly	House of Assembly	Legislative Assembly	House of Assembly
How appointed	1856 elected on slightly restricted franchise 1858 manhood suffrage 1902 adult suffrage	1856 elected; small property qualification for voters 1857 manhood suffrage 1908 adult suffrage	1895 manhood suffrage 1905 adult suffrage	1856 elected; manhood suffrage (1st colony) 1895 adult suffrage (first Australian colony female suffrage)	1890 elected restricted franchise 1893 manhood suffrage 1899 adult suffrage	1856 elected restricted franchise 1900 manhood suffrage 1903 adult suffrage

CHANGES IN COMPOSITION OF AUSTRALIAN PARLIAMENTS

The following tables show the dates on which changes have been made in the numbers of members forming the upper and lower houses of the various parliaments since the introduction of Responsible government.

NEW SOUTH WALES

Date of Act	Legislative Assembly	Legislative Council
1856	54	No definite number (but not less than 21) was set down in the Constitution; accordingly the numbers varied widely. Appointment, by nomination, for life, after first 5 years. Some sample numbers: 1856, 48; 1885, 58; 1911, 51; 1917, 71; 1926, 97; and 1932, 124.
1860	72	
1880*	108	
1885	122	
1891	141	
1894	125	
1933		Number fixed at 60 members elected for 12 years; not to be altered without referendum.
1939	90	
1949	95	

*Provision made for automatic increases according to population.

VICTORIA

Date of Act	Legislative Assembly	Legislative Council
1855	60	30
1858	78	
1876	86	
1881		42
1888	95	48
1903	68	35
1906	65	34
1953	66	
1965	73 (effective 1968)	36

SOUTH AUSTRALIA

Date of Act	House of Assembly	Legislative Council
1855/56	36	18
1872	46	
1881		24
1882	52	
1889	54	
1901	42	18
1910	40	
1913	46	20
1936	39	

QUEENSLAND

Date of Act	Legislative Assembly	Legislative Council
1860	26	15 (but variable; not less than 5, with no upper limit).
1863	32	
1872	42	
1875	43	
1878	55	
1885	59	
1887	72	36
1921		59
1922		Legislative Council abolished.
1931	62	—
1949	75	—
1958	78	—

WESTERN AUSTRALIA

Date of Act	Legislative Assembly	Legislative Council
1890	30	15
1893	33	21
1893	33	21
1896	44	24
1899	50	30
1965	51 (effective 1968)	

TASMANIA

Date of Act	House of Assembly	Legislative Council
1870	32	
1890		18
1870	32	
1885	36	
1890		18
1893	37	
1898	38	
1901	35	
1907*	30	
1946		19
1958	35	

*Hare-Clark System of Proportional Representation Introduced.

COMMONWEALTH

Date	House of Representatives	Senate
1901	75	36
1949	121	60
1954	122*	

Note: House of Representatives figures exclude members for the Australian Capital Territory and the Northern Territory, who may take part in debates but vote only on legislation relating solely to the territory they represent.
* Increase occasioned by population changes (as disclosed by census) and undertaken to adjust representation as between states.
In the Northern Territory, a Legislative Council of 14 (including the Administrator with six members elected and eight appointed) was set up in 1947.

COMMONWEALTH OF AUSTRALIA

UPPER HOUSE: The Senate

How appointed: Elected: An equal number of Senators is returned from each State, irrespective of the population of the State. The people of the State vote as one electorate. Adult suffrage.

LOWER HOUSE: House of Representatives

How Appointed: Elected: Adult suffrage.

Section 24 of the Commonwealth of Australia Constitution Act reads:

The House of Representatives shall be composed of members directly chosen by the people of the Commonwealth and the number of such members shall be, as nearly as practicable, twice the number of Senators. The number of the members of the House of Representatives of the several States shall be in proportion to the respective numbers of their people and shall, until the Parliament otherwise provides, be determined whenever necessary, in the following manner:

(I)   a quota shall be ascertained by dividing the number of the people of the Commonwealth as shown by the latest statistics of the Commonwealth by twice the number of senators;

(II) the number of members to be chosen in each State shall be determined by dividing the number of the people of the State, as shown by the latest statistics of the Commonwealth by the quota; and if on such division there is a remainder greater than one half of the quota one more member shall be chosen in that State.

But notwithstanding anything in this section, five members at least shall be chosen in each original State.

On the franchise, the Constitution (Sections 30, 8 and 41) states;
Until the Parliament otherwise provides, the qualification of the electors is as in the respective States; (but each elector to have one vote only). [At that time South Australia was the only State with female suffrage.] Proviso that no adult who is entitled to vote for a State Parliament shall be disenfranchised for Commonwealth.

Under the Franchise Act (1902) qualifications for electors for the House are the same as for the election of Senators, viz. adult male and female suffrage.

Index

575